LITERATURE

Other books by X. J. Kennedy

Nude Descending a Staircase, poems
Mark Twain's Frontier (with JAMES CAMP), text-anthology
Growing into Love, poems
Bulsh, a poem
Breaking and Entering, poems
Pegasus Descending, A Book of the Best Bad Verse
    (with JAMES CAMP and KEITH WALDROP), anthology
An Introduction to Poetry, Sixth Edition
Messages: A Thematic Anthology of Poetry
Emily Dickinson in Southern California, poems
Celebrations after the Death of John Brennan, a poem
One Winter Night in August, poems for children
The Phantom Ice Cream Man, poems for children
Three Tenors, One Vehicle
    (with JAMES CAMP and KEITH WALDROP), song lyrics
An Introduction to Fiction, Fourth Edition
Tygers of Wrath: Poems of Hate, Anger, and Invective, anthology
The Bedford Reader, Second Edition
    (with DOROTHY M. KENNEDY)
Did Adam Name the Vinegarroon? poems for children
Knock at a Star: A Child's Introduction to Poetry
    (with DOROTHY M. KENNEDY)
The Owlstone Crown, a novel for children
Hangover Mass, poems
French Leave: Translations
Cross Ties: Selected Poems
The Forgetful Wishing Well: Poems for Young People
Brats, poems for children
The Bedford Guide for College Writers
    (with DOROTHY M. KENNEDY)

LITERATURE
An Introduction to Fiction, Poetry, and Drama

Fourth Edition

X. J. KENNEDY

LITTLE, BROWN AND COMPANY
Boston · Toronto

Library of Congress Cataloging-in-Publication Data

Literature : an introduction to fiction, poetry, and
  drama.

  Includes indexes.
  1. Literature—Collections.   I. Kennedy, X. J.
PN6014.L58 1987   808   86–21036
ISBN 0–316–48880–1

Library of Congress Catalog Card No. 86–21036

ISBN 0-673-39225-2

9 8 7 6 5 4 3

KPF

Printed in the United States of America

Acknowledgments

   Cover art: Detail from "Enchanted Wood, 1983" by Thomas McKnight. From the collection of Mr. and Mrs. Morton J.
Stark, Baltimore. Photograph © 1985 Thomas McKnight.

FICTION

   Toni Cade Bambara. "My Man Bovanne." Copyright © 1971 by Toni Cade Bambara. Reprinted from *Gorilla, My Love*,
by Toni Cade Bambara, by permission of Random House, Inc.
   T. Coraghessan Boyle. "Greasy Lake" from *Greasy Lake & Other Stories* by T. Coraghessan Boyle. Copyright © 1982 by T.
Coraghessan Boyle. Reprinted by permission of Viking Penguin Inc.
   Willa Cather. "Paul's Case" from *Youth and the Bright Medusa* by Willa Cather (Alfred A. Knopf, 1920).
   Walter Van Tilburg Clark. "The Portable Phonograph." Reprinted by permission of International Creative Management,
Inc. Copyright 1941, 1969 by Walter Van Tilburg Clark.
   Isak Dinesen. "A Sailor Boy's Tale" from *Winter's Tales* by Isak Dinesen. Copyright 1942 by Random House, Inc., and
renewed 1970 by Johan Philip Thomas Ingerslev c/o The Rungstedlund Foundation. Reprinted by permission of the
publisher, Random House, Inc., and The Rungstedlund Foundation of Denmark.
   William Faulkner. "A Rose for Emily." Copyright 1930 and renewed 1958 by William Faulkner. "Barn Burning," copyright
1939 and renewed 1967 by Estelle Faulkner and Jill Faulkner Summers. Reprinted from *Collected Stories of William Faulkner*, by
permission of Random House, Inc.
   Stanley Fish. Excerpt from *Is There a Text in This Class?* Reprinted by permission of the publishers from *Is There a Text in
This Class?* by Stanley Fish, Cambridge, Mass.: Harvard University Press, Copyright © 1980 by the President and Fellows
of Harvard College.
   Gustave Flaubert. Excerpt from *Madame Bovary* by Gustave Flaubert, translated by Francis Steegmuller, Copyright © 1957
by Francis Steegmuller. Reprinted by permission of Random House, Inc.
   E. M. Forster. Excerpt from *Aspects of the Novel* by E. M. Forster. Copyright 1927 Harcourt Brace Jovanovich, Inc.; renewed
1955 by E. M. Forster. Reprinted by permission of Harcourt Brace Jovanovich, Inc., and Edward Arnold, London.
   Jakob and Wilhelm Grimm. "Godfather Death" from *The Juniper Tree and Other Tales from the Brothers Grimm*, translated by
Lore Segal and Randall Jarrell. Copyright © 1973 by Lore Segal. Reprinted by permission of Farrar, Straus & Giroux,
Inc.
   Dashiell Hammett. Excerpt from *The Maltese Falcon* by Dashiell Hammett. Copyright 1929, 1930 by Alfred A. Knopf, Inc.,
and renewed 1957, 1958 by Dashiell Hammett. Reprinted by permission of the publisher.
   Ernest Hemingway. "A Clean, Well-Lighted Place" from *The Short Stories of Ernest Hemingway*. Copyright 1933 Charles
Scribner's Sons; copyright © 1961 Mary Hemingway. Reprinted with the permission of Charles Scribner's Sons.
   Shirley Jackson. "The Lottery" from *The Lottery* by Shirley Jackson. Copyright 1948, 1949 by Shirley Jackson. Copyright
renewed © 1976, 1977 by Laurence Hyman, Barry Hyman, Mrs. Sarah Webster, and Mrs. Joanne Schnurer. Reprinted by
permission of Farrar, Straus & Giroux, Inc. "The Lottery" originally appeared in *The New Yorker*.

(continued on page 1421)

PREFACE

Literature, in the widest sense, is just about anything written. It is even what you receive in the mail if you send for free information about a weight-reducing plan or a motorcycle. In the sense that matters to us in this book, literature is a kind of art, usually written, which offers pleasure and illumination. We say it is *usually* written, for we have an oral literature, too. Few would deny the name of literature to "Bonny Barbara Allan" and other immortal folk ballads, though they were not set down in writing until centuries after they were originated.

Literature—the book in your hands—is really three books between one cover. Its opening third contains the whole of the text-anthology *An Introduction to Fiction, Fourth Edition;* its middle third, the whole of *An Introduction to Poetry, Sixth Edition;* and its closing third is a text-anthology of drama that includes twelve plays. All together, the book is an attempt to provide the college student with a reasonably compact introduction to the study and appreciation of stories, poems, and plays.

I assume that appreciation begins in loving attention to words on a page. Speed reading has its uses; but at times, as Robert Frost said, the reader who reads for speed "misses the best part of what a good writer puts into it." Close reading, then, is essential. Still, I do not believe that close reading tells us everything, that it is wrong to read a literary work by any light except that of the work itself. At times I suggest different approaches: referring to facts of an author's life; comparing an early draft with a finished version; looking for myth; seeing the conventions (or usual elements) of a kind of writing—seeing, for instance, that an old mansion, cobwebbed and creaking, is the setting for a Gothic horror story.

Although I cannot help having a few convictions about the meanings of stories, poems, and plays, I have tried to step back and give you room to make up your own mind. Here and there, in the wording of a question, a conviction may stick out. If you should notice any, please ignore them. Be assured that no one interpretation, laid down by authority, is the only right one, for any work of literature. Trust your own interpretation—provided that, in making it, you have looked clearly and carefully at the evidence.

Reading literature often will provide you with reason to write. At the back of the book, the large supplement has for the student writer some practical advice. It will guide you, step by step, in finding a topic, planning an essay, writing, revising, and putting your paper into finished form. Further, you will find there specific help in writing about fiction, poetry, and drama, and even sections with pointers for writing stories, poems, and plays of your own. (Even if you don't venture into creative writing, you will find these sections full of glimpses into the processes of literary composition.)

To help you express yourself easily and accurately, both in writing papers and in class discussion, this book supplies critical terms that may be of use to you. These words and phrases appear in **boldface** when they are first defined. If anywhere in this book you meet a critical term you don't know or don't recall—what is a *carpe diem* poem? a *dramatic question?* —just look it up in the Index of Terms on the inside back cover.

A Word about Careers

Most students agree that to read celebrated writers such as Faulkner and Tolstoi is probably good for the spirit, and most even take some pleasure in the experience. But many, not planning to teach English and impatient to begin some other career, wonder if the study of literature, however enjoyable, isn't a waste of time—or at least, an annoying obstacle.

This objection, reasonable though it may seem, rests on a shaky assumption. On the contrary, it can be argued, success in a career is not merely a matter of learning the information and skills required to join a profession. In most careers, according to one senior business executive, people often fail not because they don't understand their jobs, but because they don't understand the people they work with, or their clients or customers. They don't ever see the world from another person's point of view. Their problem is a failure of imagination.

To leap over the wall of self, to look through another's eyes—this is valuable experience, which literature offers. If you are lucky, you may never meet (or have to do business with) anyone *exactly* like Mrs. Turpin in the story "Revelation," and yet you will learn much about the kind of person she is from Flannery O'Connor's fictional portrait of her. In reading Tolstoi's "The Death of Ivan Ilych," you will enter the mind and heart of another human being. He is someone unlike you: a Russian petty bureaucrat of the nineteenth century. Still, you may find him amazingly similar to many people now living in America.

What is it like to be black, a white may wonder? Gwendolyn Brooks, Langston Hughes, James C. Kilgore, Etheridge Knight, Dudley Randall, Alice Walker, Toni Cade Bambara, and others have knowledge to impart. What is it like to be a woman? If a man would learn, let him read (for a start) Kate Chopin, Susan Glaspell, Sylvia Plath, Katherine Anne Porter,

Flannery O'Connor, Tillie Olsen, Adrienne Rich, Edith Wharton—perhaps, too, John Steinbeck's story "The Chrysanthemums."

Plodding singlemindedly toward careers, some people are like horses wearing blinders. For many, the goals look fixed and predictable. Competent nurses, accountants, and dental technicians seem always in demand. Others may find that in our society some careers, like waves in the sea, will rise or fall unexpectedly. Think how many professions we now take for granted, which only a few years ago didn't even exist: computer programming, energy conservation, tofu manufacture, videotape rental. Others that once looked like lifetime meal tickets have been cut back and nearly ruined: shoe repairing, commercial fishing, railroading.

In a society perpetually in change, it may be risky to lock yourself on one track to a career, refusing to consider any other. "We are moving," writes John Naisbitt in *Megatrends,* a study of our changing society, "from the specialist, soon obsolete, to the generalist who can adapt." Perhaps the greatest opportunity in your whole life lies in a career that has yet to be invented. If you do change your career as you go along, you will be like most people. According to U.S. Department of Labor statistics, the average person in a working life changes occupations three times. When for some unforeseen reason you have to make such a change, basic skills may be your most valuable credentials—and a knowledge of humanity.

Literature has much practical knowledge to offer you. An art of words, it can help you become more sensitive to language, both your own and other people's. It can make you aware of the difference between the word that is exactly right and the word that is merely good enough—Mark Twain calls it "the difference between the lightning and the lightning-bug." Read a fine work of literature alertly, and some of its writer's sensitivity to words may grow on you. A Supreme Court justice, John Paul Stevens, gave his opinion (informally) that the best preparation for law school is to study poetry. Why? George D. Gopen, an English professor with a law degree, says it may be because "no other discipline so closely replicates the central question asked in the study of legal thinking: Here is a text; in how many ways can it have meaning?" (By the way, if a career you plan has anything to do with advertising, whether writing it or buying it or resisting it, be sure to read Chapter 16, "Saying and Suggesting," on the hints inherent in words.)

Many careers today, besides law, call for close reading and for clear thinking expressed on paper. Lately, college placement directors have reported more demand for graduates who are good readers and writers. The reason is evident: employers need people who can handle words. In a recent survey conducted by Cornell University, business executives were asked to rank in importance the traits they look for when hiring. Leadership was first, but skill in writing and speaking came in fourth, ahead of managerial skill, ahead of skill in analysis. Times change, but to think cogently and to express yourself well are abilities the world still needs.

That is why most colleges, however thorough the career training they may provide, still insist on general training as well, including basic courses in the humanities. No one can promise that your study of literature will result in cash profit, but at least the kind of wealth that literature provides is immune to fluctuations of the Dow Jones average. A highly paid tool and die maker, asked by his community college English instructor why he had enrolled in an evening literature course, said, "Oh, I just decided there has to be more to life than work, a few beers, and the bowling alley." If you should discover in yourself a fondness for great reading, then in no season of your life are you likely to become incurably bored or feel totally alone —even after you make good in your career, even when there is nothing on television.

Changes in This Edition

Those instructors, 180 strong, who made comments and suggestions, have profoundly influenced this revision. Although I wished for a book-spine-widener to accommodate everything each of them wanted, a consensus grew clear. Now you have two Shakespeare plays to use or choose from, *Othello* and *The Tempest* (neither of them commonly taught in high school), and two plays of Sophocles: both *Antigone* and *Oedipus Rex*. Other changes were called for besides.

In the Fiction section, two chapters have been added: "Setting," including Joyce's familiar "Araby" but otherwise new in content; and "Irony," promoted from a mere note in "Tone and Style." Of the forty-one stories included, eighteen are new to this edition. Nine women fiction writers who were not in the book last time are now represented: Toni Cade Bambara, Willa Cather, Kate Chopin, Isak Dinesen, Ursula K. LeGuin, Katherine Mansfield, Alice Munro, Alice Walker, and Virginia Woolf. In all, the number of stories by women writers, both classic and contemporary, has been increased from nine to seventeen.

The Poetry third has been repacked more efficiently. Three chapters less often taught ("Poems for the Eye," "Myth," "Alternatives") have been slightly curtailed, and three have been slightly enlarged: "Listening to a Voice," "Imagery, and "Figures of Speech"—chapters that most instructors find more useful. "Telling Good from Bad" and "Knowing Excellence" are now one chapter: "Evaluating a Poem." Seventy-two poems are new to this edition, including a few first printed in 1985. Sixty poems by women are included now, reflecting the growing importance of women in contemporary American poetry and reevaluation of such earlier poets as Emily Brontë, Christina Rossetti, Elizabeth Barrett Browning, Charlotte Mew, and I hope, Maria Lowell. The poet Bob Dylan has yielded his space to later lyricist Bruce Springsteen. The times, they are achangin'.

In Drama, six plays are new selections. Besides *The Tempest* and *Antigone*, we have short plays by Molière, Yeats, Woody Allen, and Susan

Glaspell—whose *Trifles* is now up front, to illustrate the elements of a play.

Instructors who feel that their students need more background information will be pleased to see that every story and play is now accompanied by a biographical note—110 notes in all. For Poetry, a biography is provided for each of sixty poets represented by more than one poem. Instead of being strewn throughout the book, these notes are collected in "Lives of the Poets," pages 793–817, for easier reference. In the text, each poet receiving a biography is identified by an asterisk (*) after his or her name.

Using This Book to Teach Writing

Deep changes have occurred, too, in the "Supplement: Writing," especially in "Writing about Literature." In the past, advice on writing here has been conventional, quite uninformed by recent advances in composition theory. In earlier editions, I used to see the writing of a paper as a lockstep trip through stages, with an always-foreseeable product at the end. This advice has now been recast, more accurately to describe real life. Strategies for discovering material are given priority. Students are still told they may find it helpful to state a thesis, but this advice is offered as only one possible way to write. Editing and mechanics, though given careful attention, take a back seat to more vital matters, such as the tendency of fresh ideas to arrive when it's time to revise. The directions for documenting sources now follow the latest *MLA Handbook for Writers of Research Papers.*

Recently, many instructors have been using this book in a combined literature-and-writing course. To serve their needs, I have tried to improve the guidance offered to student writers—improve, but not lengthen it. This book keeps its essential focus on literature; I have sought not to let apparatus intrude or dominate. The editor's words, I believe, matter less in the study of literature than William Faulkner's or Emily Dickinson's.

The suggestions for writing, at the end of each main chapter, have been freshened and rethought. Some instructors prefer to let students discover their own writing topics, and these suggestions may merely be helpful to start them thinking on their own. The well-received sections "Criticism: On Fiction," "Criticism: On Poetry," and "Criticism: On Drama" remain. The instructor need not do anything about them, but they can provide not only ideas for class discussion but also further writing possibilities. (For these, please see the Instructor's Manual to Accompany Literature, Fourth Edition.)

Texts and Dates

Every effort has been made to provide the best available texts and (when necessary) translations. A date appears to the right of each title: generally it is the date of first publication in book form or, for a play, of first performance. Parentheses around a date indicate a date of composition, given when a work, such as a poem by Emily Dickinson, was composed much earlier than its first printing. Brackets around a date indicate that the work was written much earlier, but that its exact date of composition is not known. Spelling has been modernized (*rose-lipped* for *ros-lip'd*) and rendered American, unless to do so would alter meter or sound. But I have left the *y* in Blake's strange "Tyger" and let Walt Whitman keep his characteristic *bloom'd*. Untitled poems are identified by first lines, unless customarily assigned titles ("Western Wind").

Thanks

Besides the many debts this book has contracted for me over the past eleven years, it has now been reshaped with the aid of instructors who taught from its last edition and gave advice. Among those who made specific comments and suggestions for book or manual (or for the book's components *An Introduction to Fiction,* Fourth Edition, and *An Introduction to Poetry,* Sixth Edition) are DeAnne Adams, S. K. Ahern, Jaquita Albin, Timothy R. Austin, Carol Bachman, M. LeRoy Badger, Sheila C. Bailey, R. L. Barth, Peter Berek, Harvey Birenbaum, Peter Blair, William H. Blanchard, Victor Bobb, Wilson C. Boynton, Peggy L. Brayfield, Margaret Broderick, Laurel Brodsley, Lurene Brooks, Duane Bruce, John J. Brugaletta, Ed Buban, Jerrold E. Buchholz, Terre Burton, George F. Butler, Michael Calvello, Kit Carlson, Ellen Miller Casey, Vivian Casper, Helen Caudill, Alma Chan, Rob Ciapetta, Deborah L. Clarke, Carol Cloos, Archibald C. Coolidge, Jr., William Collins, Lynda Corbin, Peter Cousins, Charles E. Cowdrick, Virginia P. Critchlow, Robert Con Davis, Diane Day, Virginia de Araujo, Robert M. De Graaff, Brian J. Delaney, Linda Donahue, Charles Clay Doyle, Natalie Dunn, William C. Edinger, William D. Eisenberg, Ed Eleazer, Julie Fay, Marilyn Fisher, Stephen Fix, Rosemary E. Franklin, J. L. Funston, Jerome Garger, Silas H. Garrison, David Frederick George, Nancy Gish, John M. Gissendanner, Sue Grady, Edward Guiliano, R. S. Gwynn, Donna Graham, Jane Guerin, Bruce Guernsey, John Z. Guzlowski, Robert Halkeboer, Jon Harned, Helen E. Harris, Louise E. Harris, Mark Hawkins, He Gong-jie (of Anhwei University, China), Terry Heller, Donald J. Herzog, Steven Hind, Ruth Hoberman, James Hoogenakker, Frederick W. Hopkins, Dorothy G. Horwitz, R. A. Hughes, Darrell W. Hurst, Anne Johnson, Beth Kalikoff, Sandra Katz, Terrance B. Kearns, David Kerner, Enno Klammer, Joan Smolin Korenman, Arlene E. Kuhner, Juliann Lange, Ingrid Lansford, Walter Lazenby, Richard Leveroni, Carolyn S. Lightsey, Nancy G. Little, Marcus López, Clarinda Lott, Celeste Loughman, Nancy Adams Malone, Lawrence W. Manglitz, Thomas Mauch, Randall R. Mawer, Charles E. May, Eleanor Hope McCarthy, Jack McDermott, Nayan McNeil, Gunhild T. Miller, Michael Miller, Sylvia T. Miner, John S. Mizner, Laura Moffet, Peggy A. Moore, Edward F. Murphy, Alan F. Nagel,

Gilman Norton, M. G. O'Hara, Louis Oldani, S.J., Ghita Orth, Richard H. Osberg, Janice J. Osterholm, Judith S. Palmer, Joe Parks, Gary Pittenger, Charles Plymell, Margie Presley, Richard Publow, Jim Quinn, Jo Radner, R. S. Rainbow, Cleatus Rattan, David Raybin, Robin Reagler, John and Muriel Ridland, Judith Root, Robert Ross, Fred Roux, Gibbons Ruark, Jules Ryckebusch, Julie Launhardt Ryden, B. Sandlin, Epifanio San Juan, Jr., Gerald J. Schiffhorst, Nicola Seed, Cynthia L. Selfe, Jim Shepard, Theresa Showalter, Robert Slaughter, Barbara Sloan, Helen M. Sloan, Donald M. Smith, Frank P. Steele, Carol D. Stevens, R. E. Stratton, Dabney Stuart, Sheldon Stump, Stan Sulkes, Patrick Sullivan, Shirley D. Sykes, Debra Tenney, Thomas J. Trout, Lee Upton, B. Verwiel, Robert C. Vetrick, William O. Walker, Timothy F. Walsh, Robert Watson, Theodore A. Wiebe, Louis A. Willand, Gary Williams, Trudy Williams, Tom Windt, Florence Winston, Neal Woodruff, Sister Rita Yeasted, Clemewell Young, and Bernice Zeldith. I remain grateful to that host of instructors named in the prefaces to earlier editions, much of whose advice is still evident.

On the publisher's staff, Carolyn Potts has continued to give firm but kindly guidance. David W. Lynch, Janice Friedman, Sally Stickney, Adrienne Weiss, Amy Johnson, and Carolyn Woznick have made generous contributions as well. Dorothy M. Kennedy (coauthor of the *Instructor's Manual*) supplied questions, and immeasurably more.

Scores of students, some of them using the questionnaire at the back of the book, wrote reactions and suggestions. I wish there were space to name them all, and to thank properly all the students at Tufts, Michigan, North Carolina (Greensboro), California (Irvine), and Leeds who let me read stories, poems, and plays in their instructive company.

TOPICAL CONTENTS

CONTENTS

12   Criticism: On Fiction

POETRY

Contents   xxix

28 What Is Poetry?   674

29 Poems for Further Reading   679

30   Lives of the Poets

> While the menfolk try to solve a domestic murder, two women in the kitchen turn up revealing clues.

> "This is the king who solved the famous riddle / And towered up, most powerful of men. / No mortal eyes but looked on him with envy, / Yet in the end ruin swept over him."

Contents xxxix

Writing a Poem

Writing about a Play

Writing a Play

INDEX TO FIRST LINES OF POETRY

INDEX TO AUTHORS AND TITLES

INDEX TO TERMS

LITERATURE

FICTION

Here is a story, perhaps one of the shortest ever written, and one of the most difficult to forget:

> A woman is sitting in her old, shuttered house. She knows that she is alone in the whole world; every other thing is dead.
> The doorbell rings.

This small tale of terror, credited to Thomas Bailey Aldrich, has much to be said for it despite its brevity. It sets a scene, it places a character in a situation that awakens our interest. Although we don't really have time to come to know the character well, for a moment we enter her thoughts and begin to share her feelings. Then something happens. The story ends with impact, and leaves us with cause to wonder — who or what rang the doorbell? Like a good many richer, longer, and more complicated stories, this one — in just a few words — engages our imagination.

Evidently, what a story contains (and suggests) doesn't depend on its size. Our discussion of fiction will begin with stories that happen to be brief. We will look first at two ancient kinds of story — the fable and the tale — then at a modern short story. Because not all stories are short, later on you will find a chapter giving a terse history of the novel and some advice on reading novels and studying them. Chapter by chapter, the elements of fiction will be considered in the hope that by being able to break up a story into its parts, you will come to a keener appreciation of how a story is put together. All in all, here are forty-one stories. Among them, may you meet at least a few that you will enjoy and care to remember.

1 Reading a Story

After the shipwreck that marooned him on his desert island, Robinson Crusoe, in the story by Daniel Defoe, stood gazing over the water where pieces of cargo from his ship were floating by. Along came "two shoes, not mates." It is the qualification *not mates* that makes the detail memorable. We could well believe that a thing so striking and odd must have been seen, and not invented. But in truth Defoe, like other masters of the art of fiction, had the power to make us believe his imaginings. Borne along by the art of the storyteller, we trust what we are told, even though the story may be sheer fantasy.

Fiction (from the Latin *fictio,* "a shaping, a counterfeiting") is a name for stories not entirely factual, but at least partially shaped, made up, imagined. It is true that in some fiction, such as a historical novel, a writer draws upon factual information in presenting scenes, events, and characters. But the factual information in a historical novel, unlike that in a history book, is of secondary importance. Many firsthand accounts of the American Civil War were written by men who had fought in it, but few eyewitnesses give us so keen a sense of actual life on the battlefront as the author of *The Red Badge of Courage,* Stephen Crane, born after the war was over. In fiction, the "facts" may or may not be true, and a story is none the worse for their being entirely imaginary. We expect from fiction a sense of how people act, not an authentic chronicle of how, at some past time, a few people acted.

As children, we used to read (if we were lucky and formed the habit) to steep ourselves in romance, mystery, and adventure. As adults, we still do: at an airport, perhaps, while waiting for a flight, we pass the time with some newsstand paperback full of fast action and brisk dialogue. Certain fiction, of course, calls for closer attention. To read a novel by the Russian master Dostoevsky instead of a thriller about secret agent James Bond is somewhat like playing chess instead of a game of tic-tac-toe. Not that a great novel does not provide entertainment. In fact, it may offer more deeply satisfying entertainment than a novel of violence and soft-core pornography, in which stick figures connive, go to bed, and kill one another in accord with some market-tested formula. Reading **literary fiction** (as distinguished from fiction as a commercial product — the formula kind of spy, detective, Western, love, jungle, or other adventure story), we are not necessarily led on by the promise of thrills; we do not keep reading mainly to find out what happens next. Indeed, a literary story might even disclose in its opening lines everything that happened, then spend the rest of its length revealing what that happening meant. Reading literary fiction is no merely passive activity, but one that demands both attention and insight-lending participation. In return, it offers rewards. In some works of literary fiction, in Stephen Crane's "The Open Boat" and Leo Tolstoi's "The Death of Ivan Ilych," we see more deeply into the minds and hearts of the characters than we ever see into those of our family, our close friends, our lovers — or even ourselves.

FABLE AND TALE

Modern literary fiction in English has been dominated by two forms: the novel and the short story. The two have many elements in common (and in this book a further discussion of the novel as a special form will be given in Chapter Ten). Perhaps we will be able to define the short story more meaningfully — for it has traits more essential than just a particular length — if first, for comparison, we consider some related varieties of fiction: the fable and the tale. Ancient forms whose origins date back to the time of word-of-mouth storytelling, the fable and the tale are relatively simple in structure; in them we can plainly see elements also found in the short story (and in the novel). To begin, here is a **fable:** a brief story that sets forth some pointed statement of truth. The writer, W. Somerset Maugham, an English novelist and playwright (1874 – 1965), is retelling an Arabian folk story. (Samarra, by the way, is a city sixty miles from Bagdad.)

W. Somerset Maugham
THE APPOINTMENT IN SAMARRA   1933

Death speaks: There was a merchant in Bagdad who sent his servant to market to buy provisions and in a little while the servant came back, white and trembling, and said, Master, just now when I was in the market-place I was jostled by a woman in the crowd and when I turned I saw it was Death that jostled me. She looked at me and made a threatening gesture; now, lend me your horse, and I will ride away from this city and avoid my fate. I will go to Samarra and there Death will not find me. The merchant lent him his horse, and the servant mounted it, and he dug his spurs in its flanks and as fast as the horse could gallop he went. Then the merchant went down to the market-place and he saw me standing in the crowd and he came to me and said, Why did you make a threatening gesture to my servant when you saw him this morning? That was not a threatening gesture, I said, it was only a start of surprise. I was astonished to see him in Bagdad, for I had an appointment with him tonight in Samarra.

This brief story seems practically all skin and bones; that is, it contains little decoration. For in a fable everything leads directly to the **moral,** or message, sometimes stated at the end ("Moral: Haste makes waste"). In "The Appointment in Samarra" the moral isn't stated outright, it is merely implied. How would you state it in your own words?

You are probably acquainted with some of the fables credited to the Greek slave Aesop (about 620 – 560 B.C.), whose stories seem designed to teach lessons about human life. Such is the fable of "The Fox and the Grapes," in which a fox, unable to reach a bunch of grapes that hangs too high, decides that they were sour anyway. (Implied moral: It is easy to spurn what we cannot attain.) Another is the fable of "The Tortoise and the Hare" (implied moral: "Slow, steady plodding wins the race"). The characters in a fable may be talking animals (as in many of Aesop's fables), inanimate objects, or people and supernatural beings (as in "The Appointment in Samarra"). Whoever they may be, these characters are merely sketched, not greatly developed. Evidently, it would not have helped Maugham's fable to put across its point if he had portrayed the merchant, the servant, and Death in fuller detail. A more elaborate description of the market-place would not have improved the story. Probably, such a description would strike us as unnecessary and distracting. By its very bareness and simplicity, a fable fixes itself — and its message — in memory.

The name *tale* (from the Old English *talu,* "speech") is sometimes applied to any story, whether short or long, true or fictitious. *Tale* being a more evocative name than *story,* writers sometimes call their stories "tales" as if to imply something handed down from the past (as Nathaniel Hawthorne did in naming his *Twice-Told Tales*). But defined in a more limited sense, a **tale** is a story, usually short, that sets forth strange and wonderful events in more or less bare summary, without detailed character-drawing. "Tale" is pretty much synonymous with "yarn," for it implies a story in which the goal is revelation of the marvelous rather than revelation of character. In the English folk tale "Jack and the Beanstalk," we take away a more vivid impression of the miraculous beanstalk and the giant who dwells at its top than of Jack's mind or personality. Because such venerable stories were told aloud before someone set them down in writing, the storytellers had to limit themselves to brief descriptions. Probably spoken around a fire or hearth, such a tale tends to be less complicated and less closely detailed than a story written for the printed page, whose reader can linger over it. Still, such tales *can* be complicated. It is not merely greater length that makes a short story different from a tale or a fable: a mark of a short story is a fully delineated character.

Even modern tales favor supernatural or fantastic events: for instance, the **tall tale,** that variety of folk story which recounts the deeds of a superhero (Paul Bunyan, John Henry, Mike Fink) or of the storyteller. If the storyteller is telling about his own imaginary experience, his bragging yarn is usually told with a straight face to listeners who take pleasure in scoffing at it. Although the **fairy tale,** set in a world of magic and enchantment, is sometimes the work of a modern author (notably Hans Christian Andersen), well-known examples are those German folktales probably originated in the Middle Ages, collected by the brothers Grimm. The label *fairy tale* is something of an English misnomer, for in the Grimm stories, though witches and goblins abound, fairies are a minority.

Jakob and Wilhelm Grimm

GODFATHER DEATH   1812 (from oral tradition)

Translated by Lore Segal

Jakob Grimm (1785 – 1863) and Wilhelm Grimm (1786 – 1859), brothers and scholars, were born near Frankfurt-am-Main, Germany. For most of their lives they worked together — lived together, too, even when in 1825 Wilhelm married. In 1838, as librarians, they began toiling on their Deutsch Wörterbuch, *or German dictionary, a vast project that was to outlive them by a century. (It was completed only in 1960.) In 1840 King Friedrich Wilhelm IV appointed both brothers to the Royal Academy of Sciences, and both taught at the University of Berlin for the rest of their days. Although Jakob had a side-career as a diplomat, wrote a great* Deutsche Grammatik, *or German grammar (1819 – 37), and propounded Grimm's Law (an explanation of shifts in consonant sounds, of interest to students of linguistics), the name Grimm is best known to us for that splendid collection of ancient German folk stories we call* Grimm's Fairy Tales — *in German,* Kinder- und Hausmärchen *("Childhood and Household Tales," 1812 – 15). This classic work spread German children's stories around the world. Many tales we hear early in life were collected by the Grimms: "Hansel and Gretel," "Snow White and the Seven Dwarfs," "Rapunzel," "Puss-in-Boots," "Little Red Riding Hood," "Rumpelstiltskin." Versions of some of these tales had been written down as early as the sixteenth century, but mainly the brothers relied on the memories of Hessian peasants who recited the stories aloud for them.*

A poor man had twelve children and worked night and day just to get enough bread for them to eat. Now when the thirteenth came into the world, he did not know what to do and in his misery ran out onto the great highway to ask the first person he met to be godfather. The first to come along was God, and he already knew what it was that weighed on the man's mind and said, "Poor man, I pity you. I will hold your child at the font and I will look after it and make it happy upon earth." "Who are you?" asked the man. "I am God." "Then I don't want you for a godfather," the man said. "You give to the rich and let the poor go hungry." That was how the man talked because he did not understand how wisely God shares out wealth and poverty, and thus he turned from the Lord and walked on. Next came the Devil and said, "What is it you want? If you let me be godfather to your child, I will give him gold as much as he can use, and all the pleasures of the world besides." "Who are you?" asked the man. "I am the Devil." "Then I don't want you for a godfather," said the man. "You deceive and mislead mankind." He walked on and along came spindle-legged Death striding toward him and said, "Take me as godfather." The man asked, "Who are you?" "I am Death who makes all men equal." Said the man, "Then you're the one for me; you take rich and poor without distinction. You shall be godfather." Answered Death, "I will make your child rich and famous, because the one who has me for a friend shall want for nothing." The man said, "Next Sunday is the baptism. Be there in good time." Death appeared as he had promised and made a perfectly fine godfather.

When the boy was of age, the godfather walked in one day, told him to come along, and led him out into the woods. He showed him an herb which grew there and said, "This is your christening gift. I shall make you into a famous doctor. When you are called to a patient's bedside I will appear and if I stand at the sick man's head you can boldly say that you will cure him and if you give him some of this herb he will recover. But if I stand at the sick man's feet, then he is mine, and you must say there is no help for him and no doctor on this earth could save him. But take care not to use the herb against my will or it could be the worse for you."

It wasn't long before the young man had become the most famous doctor in the whole world. "He looks at a patient and right away he knows how things stand, whether he will get better or if he's going to die." That is what they said about him, and from near and far the people came, took him to see the sick, and gave him so much money he became a rich man. Now it happened that the king fell ill. The doctor was summoned to say if he was going to get well. When he came to the bed, there stood Death at the feet of the sick man, so that no herb on earth could have done him any good. If I could only just this once outwit Death! thought the doctor. He'll be annoyed, I know, but I am his godchild and he's sure to turn a blind eye. I'll take my chance. And so he lifted the sick man and laid him the other way around so that Death was standing at his head. Then he gave him some of the herb and the king began to feel better and was soon in perfect health. But Death came toward the doctor, his face dark and angry, threatened him with raised forefinger, and said, "You have tricked me. This time I will let it pass because you are my godchild, but if you ever dare do such a thing again, you put your own head in the noose and it is you I shall carry away with me."

Soon after that, the king's daughter lapsed into a deep illness. She was his only child, he wept day and night until his eyes failed him and he let it be known that whoever saved the princess from death should become her husband and inherit the crown. When the doctor came to the sick girl's bed, he saw Death at her feet. He ought to have remembered his godfather's warning, but the great beauty of the princess and the happiness of becoming her husband so bedazzled him that he threw caution to the winds, nor did he see Death's angry glances and how he lifted his hand in the air and threatened him with his bony fist. He picked the sick girl up and laid her head where her feet had lain, then he gave her some of the herb and at once her cheeks reddened and life stirred anew.

When Death saw himself cheated of his property the second time, he 5 strode toward the doctor on his long legs and said, "It is all up with you, and now it is your turn," grasped him harshly with his ice-cold hand so that the doctor could not resist, and led him to an underground cave, and here he saw thousands upon thousands of lights burning in rows without end, some big, some middle-sized, others small. Every moment some went out and others lit up so that the little flames seemed to be jumping here and there in perpetual exchange. "Look," said Death, "these are the life lights of mankind. The big ones belong to children, the middle-sized ones to married couples in their best years, the little ones belong to very old people. Yet children and the young often have only little lights." "Show me my life light," said the doctor, imagining that it must be one of the big ones. Death pointed to a little stub threatening to go out and said, "Here it is." "Ah, dear godfather," said the terrified doctor, "light me a new one, do it, for my sake, so that I may enjoy my life and become king and marry the beautiful princess." "I cannot," answered Death. "A light must go out before a new one lights up." "Then set the old on top of a new one so it can go on burning when the first is finished," begged the doctor. Death made as if to grant his wish, reached for a tall new taper, but because he wanted revenge he purposely fumbled and the little stub fell over and went out. Thereupon the doctor sank to the ground and had himself fallen into the hands of death.

PLOT

Like a fable, the Grimm brothers' tale seems stark in its lack of detail and in the swiftness of its telling. Compared with the fully portrayed characters of many modern stories, the characters of father, son, king, princess, and even Death himself seem hardly more than stick figures. It may have been that to draw ample characters would not have contributed to the storytellers' design; that, indeed, to have done so would have been inartistic. Yet "Godfather Death" is a compelling story. By what methods does it arouse and sustain our interest?

From the opening sentence of the tale, we watch the unfolding of a **dramatic situation:** a person is involved in some conflict. First, this character is a poor man with children to feed, in conflict with the world; very soon, we find him in conflict with God and with the Devil besides. Drama in fiction occurs in any clash of wills, desires, or powers — whether it be a conflict of character against character, character against society, character against some natural force, or, as in "Godfather Death," character against some supernatural entity.

Like any shapely tale, "Godfather Death" has a beginning, a middle, and an end. In fact, it is unusual to find a story so clearly displaying the elements of structure that critics have found in many classic works of fiction and drama. The tale begins with an **exposition:** the opening portion that sets the scene (if any), introduces the main characters, tells us what happened before the story opened, and provides any other background information that we need in order to understand and care about the events to follow. In "Godfather Death," the exposition is brief — all in the opening paragraph. The middle section of the story begins with Death's giving the herb to the boy, and his warning not to defy him. This moment introduces a new conflict (a **complication**), and by this time it is clear that the son and not the father is to be the central human character of the story. Death's godson is the principal person who strives: the **protagonist** (a better term than **hero,** for it may apply equally well to a central character who is not especially brave or virtuous).

The **suspense,** the pleasurable anxiety we feel that heightens our attention to the story, inheres in our wondering how it will all turn out. Will the doctor triumph over Death? Even though we suspect, early in the story, that the doctor stands no chance against such a superhuman **antagonist,** we want to see for ourselves the outcome of his defiance. A storyteller can try to incite our anticipation by giving us some **foreshadowing** or indication of events to come. In "Godfather Death" the foreshadowings are apparent in Death's warnings ("but if you ever dare do such a thing again, you put your own head in the noose"). When the doctor defies his godfather for the first time — when he saves the king — we have a **crisis,** a moment of high tension. The tension is momentarily resolved when Death lets him off. Then an even greater crisis — the turning point in the action — occurs with the doctor's second defiance in restoring the princess to life. In the last section of the story, with the doctor in the underworld, events come to a **climax,** the moment of greatest tension at which the outcome is to be decided, when the terrified doctor begs for a new candle. Will Death grant him one? Will he live, become king, and marry the princess? The outcome or **conclusion** — also called the **resolution** or **denouement** ("the untying of the knot") — quickly follows as Death allows the little candle to go out.

Such a structure of events arising out of a conflict may be called the plot of the story. Like many terms used in literary discussion, *plot* is blessed with several meanings. Sometimes it refers simply to the events in a story. In this book, **plot** will mean the artistic arrangement of those events. Different arrangements of the same material are possible. A writer might decide to tell of the events in chronological order, beginning with the earliest; or he might open his story with the last event, then tell what led up to it. Sometimes a writer chooses to skip rapidly over the exposition and begin **in medias res** (Latin, "in the midst of things"), first presenting some exciting or significant moment, then filling in what happened earlier. This method is by no means a modern invention: Homer begins the *Odyssey* with his hero mysteriously late in returning from war and his son searching for him; John Milton's *Paradise Lost* opens with Satan already defeated in his revolt against the Lord. A device useful to writers for filling in what happened earlier is the **flashback** (or **retrospect**), a scene relived in a character's memory.

To have a plot, a story does not need an intense, sustained conflict such as we find in "Godfather Death," a tale especially economical in its structure of crisis, climax, and conclusion. Although a highly dramatic story may tend to assume such a clearly recognizable structure, many contemporary writers avoid it, considering it too contrived and arbitrary. In commercial fiction, in which exciting conflict is everything and in which the writer has to manufacture all possible suspense, such a structure is often obvious. In popular detective, Western, and adventure novels; in juvenile fiction (the perennial Hardy Boys and Nancy Drew books); and in popular series on television (soap operas, police and hospital thrillers, mysteries, and cowboy stories), it is often easy to recognize crisis, climax, and conclusion. The presence of these elements does not necessarily indicate inferior literature (as "Godfather Death" shows); yet when reduced to parts of a formula, the result may seem stale and contrived.[1] Such plots may be (as contemporary French novelist Alain Robbe-Grillet describes them) mere anecdotes, providing trumped-up surprises for "the panting reader."

THE SHORT STORY

The teller of a tale relies heavily upon the method of **summary:** terse, general narration as in "Godfather Death" ("It wasn't long before the young man had become the most famous doctor in the whole world"). But in a **short story,** a form more realistic than the tale and of modern origin, the writer usually presents the main events in greater fullness. Fine writers of short stories, although they may use summary at times (often to give some portion of a story less emphasis), are skilled in rendering a **scene:** a vivid or dramatic moment described in enough detail to create the illusion that the reader is practically there. Avoiding long summary, they try to *show* rather than simply to *tell;* as if following Mark Twain's advice to authors: "Don't say, 'The old lady screamed.' Bring her on and let her scream."

A short story is more than just a sequence of happenings. A finely wrought short story has the richness and conciseness of an excellent lyric poem. Spontaneous and natural as the finished story may seem, the writer

---

[1] In the heyday of the **pulp magazines** (so called for their cheap paper), some professional writers even relied on a mechanical device called Plotto: a tin arrow-spinner pointed to numbers and the writer looked them up in a book that listed necessary ingredients — type of hero, type of villain, sort of conflict, crisis, climax, conclusion.

has written it so artfully that there is meaning in even seemingly casual speeches and apparently trivial details. If we skim it hastily, skipping the descriptive passages, we miss significant parts. Some literary short stories, unlike commercial fiction in which the main interest is in physical action or conflict, tell of an **epiphany:** some moment of insight, discovery, or revelation by which a character's life, or view of life, is greatly altered.[2] (For such moments in fiction, see the stories in this book by James Joyce, Leo Tolstoi, John Steinbeck, Edith Wharton, and Joyce Carol Oates.) Other short stories tell of a character initiated into experience or maturity: one such **story of initiation** is William Faulkner's "Barn Burning" (Chapter Five), in which a boy finds it necessary to defy his father and suddenly to grow into manhood. Less obviously dramatic, perhaps, than "Godfather Death," such a story may be no less powerful.

The fable and the tale are ancient forms; the short story is of more recent origin. In the nineteenth century, writers of fiction were encouraged by a large, literate audience of middle-class readers who wanted to see their lives reflected in faithful mirrors. Skillfully representing ordinary life, many writers perfected the art of the short story: in Russia, Anton Chekhov; in France, Honoré de Balzac, Gustave Flaubert, and Guy de Maupassant; and in America, Nathaniel Hawthorne and Edgar Allan Poe (although the Americans seem less fond of everyday life than of dream and fantasy). It would be false to claim that, in passing from the fable and the tale to the short story, fiction has made a triumphant progress; or to claim that, because short stories are modern, they are superior to fables and tales. Fable, tale, and short story are distinct forms, each achieving its own effects. (Incidentally, fable and tale are far from being extinct today: you can find many recent examples.) Lately, in the hands of Donald Barthelme, Joyce Carol Oates, John Barth, and other innovative writers, the conventions of the short story have been changing; and at the moment, stories of epiphany and initiation have become scarcer.

But let us begin with a contemporary short story whose protagonist *does* undergo an initiation into maturity. To notice the difference between a short story and a tale, you may find it helpful to compare John Updike's "A & P" with "Godfather Death." Although Updike's short story is centuries distant from the Grimm tale in its method of telling and in its setting, you may be reminded of "Godfather Death" in the main character's dramatic situation. To defend a young woman, a young man has to defy his mentor — here, the boss of a supermarket! So doing, he places himself in jeopardy. Updike has the protagonist tell his own story, amply and with humor. How does it differ from a tale?

---

[2]From the Greek *epiphainein,* "to show forth." In Christian tradition, the Feast of the Epiphany commemorates the revelation to the Magi of the birth of Christ. For James Joyce's description of epiphanies in everyday life, see page 400.

John Updike
A & P

John Updike, born in Shillingford, Pennsylvania in 1932, received his B.A. from Harvard, then studied drawing and fine art at Oxford. But writing soon became his main interest. From 1955 to 1957 he worked on the staff of The New Yorker, *sometimes doing errands for the aged James Thurber. Though he quit to be a full-time writer, he has continued to supply the magazine with bright stories and searching book reviews. Author of more than two dozen books, including both clever light verse and serious poetry, Updike is best known as a hardworking, versatile, highly productive novelist. (Hardly a fall goes by without a new Updike novel.) For* The Centaur *(1963) he received a National Book Award, and for* Rabbit Is Rich *(1982), a Pulitzer prize and an American Book Award.*

In walks these three girls in nothing but bathing suits. I'm in the third check-out slot, with my back to the door, so I don't see them until they're over by the bread. The one that caught my eye first was the one in the plaid green two-piece. She was a chunky kid, with a good tan and a sweet broad soft-looking can with those two crescents of white just under it, where the sun never seems to hit, at the top of the backs of her legs. I stood there with my hand on a box of HiHo crackers trying to remember if I rang it up or not. I ring it up again and the customer starts giving me hell. She's one of these cash-register-watchers, a witch about fifty with rouge on her cheekbones and no eyebrows, and I know it made her day to trip me up. She'd been watching cash registers for fifty years and probably never seen a mistake before.

By the time I got her feathers smoothed and her goodies into a bag — she gives me a little snort in passing, if she'd been born at the right time they would have burned her over in Salem — by the time I get her on her way the girls had circled around the bread and were coming back, without a push-cart, back my way along the counters, in the aisle between the check-outs and the Special bins. They didn't even have shoes on. There was this chunky one, with the two-piece — it was bright green and the seams on the bra were still sharp and her belly was still pretty pale so I guessed she just got it (the suit) — there was this one, with one of those chubby berry-faces, the lips all bunched together under her nose, this one, and a tall one, with black hair that hadn't quite frizzed right, and one of these sunburns right across under the eyes, and a chin that was too long — you know, the kind of girl other girls think is very "striking" and "attractive" but never quite makes it, as they very well know, which is why they like her so much — and then the third one, that wasn't quite so tall. She was the queen. She kind of led them, the other two peeking around and making their shoulders round. She didn't look around, not this queen, she just walked straight on slowly, on these long white prima-donna legs. She came down a little hard on her heels, as if she didn't walk in her bare feet that much, putting down her heels and then letting the weight move along to her toes as if she was testing the floor with every step, putting a little deliberate extra action into it. You never know for sure how girls' minds work (do you really think it's a mind in there or just a little buzz like a bee in a glass jar?) but you got the idea she had talked the other two into coming in here with her, and now she was showing them how to do it, walk slow and hold yourself straight.

She had on a kind of dirty-pink — beige maybe, I don't know — bathing suit with a little nubble all over it and, what got me, the straps were down. They were off her shoulders looped loose around the cool tops of her arms, and I guess as a result the suit had slipped a little on her, so all around the top of the cloth there was this shining rim. If it hadn't been there you wouldn't have known there could have been anything whiter than those shoulders. With the straps pushed off, there was nothing between the top of the suit and the top of her head except just *her,* this clean bare plane of the top of her chest down from the shoulder bones like a dented sheet of metal tilted in the light. I mean, it was more than pretty.

She had sort of oaky hair that the sun and salt had bleached, done up in a bun that was unravelling, and a kind of prim face. Walking into the A & P with your straps down, I suppose it's the only kind of face you *can* have. She held her head so high her neck, coming up out of those white shoulders, looked kind of stretched, but I didn't mind. The longer her neck was, the more of her there was.

She must have felt in the corner of her eye me and over my shoulder Stokesie in the second slot watching, but she didn't tip. Not this queen. She kept her eyes moving across the racks, and stopped, and turned so slow it made my stomach rub the inside of my apron, and buzzed to the other two, who kind of huddled against her for relief, and they all three of them went up the cat-and-dog-food-breakfast-cereal-macaroni-rice-raisins-seasonings-spreads-spaghetti-soft-drinks-crackers-and-cookies aisle. From the third slot I look straight up this aisle to the meat counter, and I watched them all the way. The fat one with the tan sort of fumbled with the cookies, but on second thought she put the packages back. The sheep pushing their carts down the aisle — the girls were walking against the usual traffic (not that we have one-way signs or anything) — were pretty hilarious. You could see them, when Queenie's white shoulders dawned on them, kind of jerk, or hop, or hiccup, but their eyes snapped back to their own baskets and on they pushed. I bet you could set off dynamite in an A & P and the people would by and large keep reaching and checking oatmeal off their lists and muttering "Let me see, there was a third thing, began with A, asparagus, no, ah, yes, applesauce!" or whatever it is they do mutter. But there was no doubt, this jiggled them. A few houseslaves in pin curlers even looked around after pushing their carts past to make sure what they had seen was correct.

You know, it's one thing to have a girl in a bathing suit down on the beach, where what with the glare nobody can look at each other much anyway, and another thing in the cool of the A & P, under the fluorescent lights, against all those stacked packages, with her feet paddling along naked over our checkerboard green-and-cream rubber-tile floor.

"Oh Daddy," Stokesie said beside me. "I feel so faint."

"Darling," I said. "Hold me tight." Stokesie's married, with two babies chalked up on his fuselage already, but as far as I can tell that's the only difference. He's twenty-two, and I was nineteen this April.

"Is it done?" he asks, the responsible married man finding his voice. I forgot to say he thinks he's going to be manager some sunny day, maybe in 1990 when it's called the Great Alexandrov and Petrooshki Tea Company or something.

What he meant was, our town is five miles from a beach, with a big summer colony out on the Point, but we're right in the middle of town, and the women generally put on a shirt or shorts or something before they get out of the car into the street. And anyway these are usually women with six children and varicose veins mapping their legs and nobody, including them, could care less. As I say, we're right in the middle of town, and if you stand at our front doors you can see two banks and the Congregational church and the newspaper store and three real-estate offices and about twenty-seven old freeloaders tearing up Central Street because the sewer broke again. It's not as if we're on the Cape; we're north of Boston and there's people in this town haven't seen the ocean for twenty years.

The girls had reached the meat counter and were asking McMahon something. He pointed, they pointed, and they shuffled out of sight behind a pyramid of Diet Delight peaches. All that was left for us to see was old McMahon patting his mouth and looking after them sizing up their joints. Poor kids, I began to feel sorry for them, they couldn't help it.

Now here comes the sad part of the story, at least my family says it's sad but I don't think it's sad myself. The store's pretty empty, it being Thursday afternoon, so there was nothing much to do except lean on the register and wait for the girls to show up again. The whole store was like a pinball machine and I didn't know which tunnel they'd come out of. After a while they come around out of the far aisle, around the light bulbs, records at discount of the Caribbean Six or Tony Martin Sings or some such gunk you wonder they waste the wax on, sixpacks of candy bars, and plastic toys done up in cellophane that fall apart when a kid looks at them anyway. Around they come, Queenie still leading the way, and holding a little gray jar in her hand. Slots Three through Seven are unmanned and I could see her wondering between Stokes and me, but Stokesie with his usual luck draws an old party in baggy gray pants who stumbles up with four giant cans of pineapple juice (what do these bums *do* with all that pineapple juice? I've often asked myself) so the girls come to me. Queenie puts down the jar and I take it into my fingers icy cold. Kingfish Fancy Herring Snacks in Pure Sour Cream: 49¢. Now her hands are empty, not a ring or a bracelet, bare as God made them, and I wonder where the money's coming from. Still with that prim look she lifts a folded dollar bill out of the hollow at the center of her nubbled pink top. The jar went heavy in my hand. Really, I thought that was so cute.

Then everybody's luck begins to run out. Lengel comes in from haggling with a truck full of cabbages on the lot and is about to scuttle into that door marked MANAGER behind which he hides all day when the girls touch his eye. Lengel's pretty dreary, teaches Sunday school and the rest, but he doesn't miss that much. He comes over and says, "Girls, this isn't the beach."

Queenie blushes, though maybe it's just a brush of sunburn I was noticing for the first time, now that she was so close. "My mother asked me to pick up a jar of herring snacks." Her voice kind of startled me, the way voices do when you see the people first, coming out so flat and dumb yet kind of tony, too, the way it ticked over "pick up" and "snacks." All of a sudden I slid right down her voice into her living room. Her father and the other men were standing around in ice-cream coats and bow ties and the women were in sandals picking up herring snacks on toothpicks off a big plate and they were all holding drinks the color of water with olives and sprigs of mint in them. When my parents have somebody over they get lemonade and if it's a real racy affair Schlitz in tall glasses with "They'll Do It Every Time" cartoons stencilled on.

"That's all right," Lengel said. "But this isn't the beach." His repeating this struck me as funny, as if it had just occurred to him, and he had been thinking all these years the A & P was a great big dune and he was the head lifeguard. He didn't like my smiling — as I say he doesn't miss much — but he concentrates on giving the girls that sad Sunday-school-superintendent stare.

Queenie's blush is no sunburn now, and the plump one in plaid, that I liked better from the back — a really sweet can — pipes up, "We weren't doing any shopping. We just came in for the one thing."

"That makes no difference," Lengel tells her, and I could see from the way his eyes went that he hadn't noticed she was wearing a two-piece before. "We want you decently dressed when you come in here."

"We *are* decent," Queenie says suddenly, her lower lip pushing, getting sore now that she remembers her place, a place from which the crowd that runs the A & P must look pretty crummy. Fancy Herring Snacks flashed in her very blue eyes.

"Girls, I don't want to argue with you. After this come in here with your shoulders covered. It's our policy." He turns his back. That's policy for you. Policy is what the kingpins want. What the others want is juvenile delinquency.

All this while, the customers had been showing up with their carts but, you know, sheep, seeing a scene, they had all bunched up on Stokesie, who shook open a paper bag as gently as peeling a peach, not wanting to miss a word. I could feel in the silence everybody getting nervous, most of all Lengel, who asks me, "Sammy, have you rung up this purchase?"

I thought and said "No" but it wasn't about that I was thinking. I go through the punches, 4, 9, GROC, TOT — it's more complicated than you think, and after you do it often enough, it begins to make a little song, that you hear words to, in my case "Hello *(bing)* there, you *(gung)* hap-py *pee-*pul *(splat)!*" — the *splat* being the drawer flying out. I uncrease the bill, tenderly as you may imagine, it just having come from between the two smoothest scoops of vanilla I had ever known were there, and pass a half and a penny into her narrow pink palm, and nestle the herrings in a bag and twist its neck and hand it over, all the time thinking.

The girls, and who'd blame them, are in a hurry to get out, so I say "I quit" to Lengel quick enough for them to hear, hoping they'll stop and watch me, their unsuspected hero. They keep right on going, into the electric eye; the door flies open and they flicker across the lot to their car, Queenie and Plaid and Big Tall Goony-Goony (not that as raw material she was so bad), leaving me with Lengel and a kink in his eyebrow.

"Did you say something, Sammy?"

"I said I quit."

"I thought you did."

"You didn't have to embarrass them."

"It was they who were embarrassing us."

I started to say something that came out "Fiddle-de-doo." It's a saying of my grandmother's, and I know she would have been pleased.

"I don't think you know what you're saying," Lengel said.

"I know you don't," I said. "But I do." I pull the bow at the back of my 30 apron and start shrugging it off my shoulders. A couple customers that had been heading for my slot begin to knock against each other, like scared pigs in a chute.

Lengel sighs and begins to look very patient and old and gray. He's been a friend of my parents for years. "Sammy, you don't want to do this to your Mom and Dad," he tells me. It's true, I don't. But it seems to me that once you begin a gesture it's fatal not to go through with it. I fold the apron, "Sammy" stitched in red on the pocket, and put it on the counter, and drop the bow tie on top of it. The bow tie is theirs, if you've ever wondered. "You'll feel this for the rest of your life," Lengel says, and I know that's true, too, but remembering how he made that pretty girl blush makes me so scrunchy inside I punch the No Sale tab and the machine whirs "pee-pul" and the drawer splats out. One advantage to this scene taking place in summer, I can follow this up with a clean exit, there's no fumbling around getting your coat and galoshes, I just saunter into the electric eye in my white shirt that my mother ironed the night before, and the door heaves itself open, and outside the sunshine is skating around on the asphalt.

I look around for my girls, but they're gone, of course. There wasn't anybody but some young married screaming with her children about some candy they didn't get by the door of a powder-blue Falcon station wagon. Looking back in the big windows, over the bags of peat moss and aluminum lawn furniture stacked on the pavement, I could see Lengel in my place in the slot, checking the sheep through. His face was dark gray and his back stiff, as if he'd just had an injection of iron, and my stomach kind of fell as I felt how hard the world was going to be to me hereafter.

QUESTIONS

1. Notice how artfully Updike arranges details to set the story in a perfectly ordinary supermarket. What details stand out for you as particularly true to life? What does this close attention to detail contribute to the story?
2. How fully does Updike draw the character of Sammy? What traits (admirable or otherwise) does Sammy show? Is he any less a hero for wanting the girls to notice his heroism? To what extent is he more thoroughly and fully portrayed than the doctor in "Godfather Death"?
3. What part of the story seems exposition? (See the definition of *exposition* on page 9.) Of what value to the story is the carefully detailed portrait of Queenie, the leader of the three girls?
4. As the story develops, do you detect any change in Sammy's feelings toward the girls?
5. Where in "A & P" does the dramatic conflict become apparent? What moment in the story brings the crisis? What is the climax of the story?

6. Why, exactly, does Sammy quit his job?
7. Does anything lead you to *expect* Sammy to make some gesture of sympathy for the three girls? What incident earlier in the story (before Sammy quits) seems a foreshadowing?
8. What do you understand from the conclusion of the story? What does Sammy mean when he acknowledges "how hard the world was going to be . . . hereafter"?
9. What comment does Updike — through Sammy — make on supermarket society?

Suggestions for Writing

1. In a paragraph or two, referring to John Updike's "A & P," consider this remark: "Sammy is a sexist pig who suddenly sees the light." What evidence supporting (or refuting) this comment do you find in the story?
2. Imagining you are Sammy, write a brief letter to a friend explaining why you quit your job.
3. Look up Anne Sexton's retelling of the Grimm tale "Godfather Death" in her book of poems *Transformations* (1971); also included in *The Complete Poems of Anne Sexton* (1981). In a short essay of three to five paragraphs, discuss the differences you find between the Grimm and Sexton versions. What is the effect of Sexton's retelling? What does she retain from the original? Which version of the story do you prefer? Why?
4. If you have had any experience in telling stories aloud (to children or to others), write a brief but detailed account of your experience, giving tips to adults who wish to become storytellers.
5. Write a brief fable of your own invention, perhaps illustrating some familiar proverb ("Too many cooks spoil the broth," "A rolling stone gathers no moss"). Your fable might be inspired by "The Appointment in Samarra" or by a fable of Aesop. You can state a moral at the end, or, if you prefer, let the moral be unstated but obvious.
6. After you have written such a fable, write a short account of your writing process. Tell of the problems you encountered in thinking up your fable and in writing it, and how you surmounted them.

2 Point of View

In the opening lines of *The Adventures of Huckleberry Finn,* Mark Twain takes care to separate himself from the leading character, who is to tell his own story:

> You don't know about me, without you have read a book by the name of *The Adventures of Tom Sawyer,* but that ain't no matter. That book was made by Mr. Mark Twain, and he told the truth, mainly.

Twain wrote the novel, but the **narrator** or speaker is Huck Finn, the one from whose perspective the story is told. Obviously, in *Huckleberry Finn,* the narrator of a story is not the same person as the "real-life" author, the one given the by-line. In employing Huck as his narrator, Twain selects a special angle of vision: not his own, exactly, but that of a resourceful boy moving through the thick of events, with a mind at times shrewd, at other times innocent. Through Huck's eyes, Twain takes in certain scenes, actions, and characters and — as only Huck's angle of vision could have enabled Twain to do so well — records them memorably.

Not every narrator in fiction is, like Huck Finn, a main character, one in the thick of events. Some narrators play only minor parts in the stories they tell; others take no active part at all. In the tale of "Godfather Death," we have a narrator who does not participate in the events he recounts. He is not a character in the story but is someone not even named, who stands at some distance from the action recording what the main characters say and do; recording also, at times, what they think, feel, or desire. He seems to have unlimited knowledge: he even knows the mind of Death, who "because he wanted revenge" let the doctor's candle go out. More humanly restricted in their knowledge, other narrators can see into the mind of only one character. They may be less willing to express opinions than the narrator of "Godfather Death" ("He ought to have remembered his godfather's warning"). A story may even be told by a narrator who seems so impartial and aloof that he limits himself to reporting only overheard conversation and to describing, without comment or opinion, the appearances of things. Evidently, narrators greatly differ in kind; however, because stories usually are told by someone, almost every story has some kind of narrator.[1] It is rare in modern fiction for the "real-life" author to try to step out from behind the typewriter and tell the story. Real persons can tell stories, but when such a story is *written,* the result is usually *non*fiction: a memoir, an account of travels, an autobiography.[2]

To identify the narrator of a story, describing any part he or she plays in the events and any limits placed upon his knowledge, is to identify the story's **point of view.** In a short story, it is usual for the writer to maintain one point of view from beginning to end, but there is nothing to stop him from introducing other points of view as well. In his long, panoramic novel *War and Peace,* Leo Tolstoi, encompassing the vast drama of Napoleon's invasion of Russia, freely shifts the point of view in and out of the minds of many characters, among them Napoleon himself.

Theoretically, a great many points of view are possible. A narrator who says "I" might conceivably be involved in events to a much greater or a much lesser degree: as the protagonist, as some other major character, as some minor character, as a mere passive spectator, or even as a character who arrives late upon the scene and then tries to piece together what happened. Evidently, too, a narrator's knowledge might vary in gradations from total omniscience to almost total ignorance. But in reading fiction, again and again we encounter familiar and recognizable points of view. Here is a list of them — admittedly just a rough abstraction — that may provide a few terms with which to discuss the stories that you read and to describe their points of view:

Narrator a participant (writing in the first person):
  1. a major character
  2. a minor character

Narrator a nonparticipant (writing in the third person):
  3. all-knowing (seeing into any of the characters)
  4. seeing into one major character
  5. seeing into one minor character
  6. objective (not seeing into any characters)

When the narrator is cast as a **participant** in the events of the story, he or she is a dramatized character who says "I." Such a narrator may be

---

[1]Some theorists reserve the term *narrator* for a character who tells a story in the first person. We use it in a wider sense: to mean a recording consciousness that an author creates, who may or may not be a participant in the events of the story. In the view of Wayne C. Booth, the term *narrator* can be dispensed with in dealing with a rigorously impersonal "fly-on-the-wall" story, containing no editorializing and confined to the presentation of surfaces: "In Hemingway's 'The Killers,' for example, there is no narrator other than the implicit second self that Hemingway creates as he writes" *(The Rhetoric of Fiction* [Chicago: U of Chicago P, 1961] 151).

[2]Another relationship between the author and the story will be discussed in Chapter Five, "Tone and Style."

the protagonist (Huck Finn) or may be an **observer,** a minor character standing a little to one side, watching a story unfold that mainly involves someone else.

A narrator who remains a **nonparticipant** does not appear in the story as a character. Viewing the characters, perhaps seeing into the minds of one or more of them, such a narrator refers to them as "he," "she," or "they." When **all-knowing** (or **omniscient**), the narrator sees into the minds of all (or some) characters, moving when necessary from one to another. This is the point of view in "Godfather Death," whose narrator knows the feelings and motives of the father, of the doctor, and even of Death himself. In that he adds an occasional comment or opinion, this narrator may be said also to show **editorial omniscience** (as we can tell from his disapproving remark that the doctor "ought to have remembered" and his observation that the father did not understand "how wisely God shares out wealth and poverty"). A narrator who shows **impartial omniscience** presents the thoughts and actions of the characters, but does not judge them or comment on them.

When a nonparticipating narrator sees events through the eyes of a single character, whether a major character or a minor one, the resulting point of view is sometimes called **limited omniscience** or **selective omniscience.** The author, of course, selects which character to see through; the omniscience is his and not the narrator's. In William Faulkner's "Barn Burning" (Chapter Five), the narrator is almost entirely confined to knowing the thoughts and perceptions of a boy, the central character. Here is another example. Early in his novel *Madame Bovary,* Gustave Flaubert tells of the first time a young country doctor, Charles Bovary, meets Emma, the woman later to become his wife. The doctor has been summoned late at night to set the broken leg of a farmer, Emma's father.

A young woman wearing a blue merino dress with three flounces came to the door of the house to greet Monsieur Bovary, and she ushered him into the kitchen, where a big open fire was blazing. Around its edges the farm hands' breakfast was bubbling in small pots of assorted sizes. Damp clothes were drying inside the vast chimney-opening. The fire shovel, the tongs, and the nose of the bellows, all of colossal proportions, shone like polished steel; and along the walls hung a lavish array of kitchen utensils, glimmering in the bright light of the fire and in the first rays of the sun that were now beginning to come in through the window-panes.

Charles went upstairs to see the patient. He found him in bed, sweating under blankets, his nightcap lying where he had flung it. He was a stocky little man of fifty, fair-skinned, blue-eyed, bald in front and wearing earrings. On a chair beside him was a big decanter of brandy: he had been pouring himself drinks to keep up his courage. But as soon as he saw the doctor he dropped his bluster, and instead of cursing as he had been doing for the past twelve hours he began to groan weakly.

The fracture was a simple one, without complications of any kind.

Charles couldn't have wished for anything easier. Then he recalled his teachers' bedside manner in accident cases, and proceeded to cheer up his patient with all kinds of facetious remarks — a truly surgical attention, like the oiling of a scalpel. For splints, they sent someone to bring a bundle of laths from the carriage shed. Charles selected one, cut it into lengths and smoothed it down with a piece of broken window glass, while the maidservant tore sheets for bandages and Mademoiselle Emma tried to sew some pads. She was a long time finding her workbox, and her father showed his impatience. She made no reply; but as she sewed she kept pricking her fingers and raising them to her mouth to suck.

Charles was surprised by the whiteness of her fingernails. They were almond-shaped, tapering, as polished and shining as Dieppe ivories. Her hands, however, were not pretty — not pale enough, perhaps, a little rough at the knuckles; and they were too long, without softness of line. The finest thing about her was her eyes. They were brown, but seemed black under the long eyelashes; and she had an open gaze that met yours with fearless candor.[3]

In this famous scene, Charles Bovary is beholding people and objects in a natural sequence. On first meeting Emma, he notices only her dress, as though less interested in the woman who opens the door than in passing through to the warm fire. Needing pads for his patient's splint, the doctor observes just the hands of the woman sewing them. Obliged to wait for the splints, he then has the leisure to notice her face, her remarkable eyes. (By the way, notice the effect of the word *yours* in the last sentence of the passage. It is as if the reader, seeing through the doctor's eyes, suddenly became one with him.) Who is the narrator? Not Charles Bovary, nor Gustave Flaubert, but someone able to enter the minds of others — here limited to knowing the thoughts and perceptions of one character.

In the **objective** point of view, the narrator does not enter the mind of any character but describes events from the outside. Telling us what people say and how their faces look, he leaves us to infer their thoughts and feelings. So inconspicuous is the narrator that this point of view has been called "the fly on the wall." This metaphor assumes the existence of a fly with a highly discriminating gaze, who knows which details to look for to communicate the deepest meaning. Some critics would say that in the objective point of view, the narrator disappears altogether. Consider this passage by a writer famous for remaining objective, Dashiell Hammett, in his mystery novel *The Maltese Falcon*, describing his private detective Sam Spade:

Spade's thick fingers made a cigarette with deliberate care, sifting a measured quantity of tan flakes down into curved paper, spreading the flakes so that they lay equal at the ends with a slight depression in the middle, thumbs rolling the paper's inner edge down and up under the outer edge as forefingers pressed it over, thumb and fingers sliding

[3]*Madame Bovary*, translated by Francis Steegmuller (New York: Random, 1957) 16 – 17.

to the paper cylinder's ends to hold it even while tongue licked the flap, left forefinger and thumb pinching their ends while right forefinger and thumb smoothed the damp seam, right forefinger and thumb twisting their end and lifting the other to Spade's mouth.[4]

In Hammett's novel, this sentence comes at a moment of crisis: just after Spade has been roused from bed in the middle of the night by a phone call telling him that his partner has been murdered. Even in time of stress (we infer) Spade is deliberate, cool, efficient, and painstaking. Hammett refrains from applying all those adjectives to Spade; to do so would be to exercise editorial omniscience and to destroy the objective point of view.

Besides the common points of view just listed, uncommon points of view are possible. In *Flush,* a fictional biography of Elizabeth Barrett Browning, Virginia Woolf employs an unusual observer as narrator: the poet's pet cocker spaniel. In "The Circular Valley," a short story by Paul Bowles, a man and a woman are watched by a sinister spirit trying to take possession of them, and we see the human characters through the spirit's vague consciousness. The narrator, however, is human and a nonparticipant. Possible also, but unusual, is a story written in the second person, *you.* This point of view results in an attention-getting directness, as in Jay McInerney's novel *Bright Lights, Big City* (1985), which begins:

> You are not the kind of guy who would be at a place like this at this time of the morning. But here you are, and you cannot say that the terrain is entirely unfamiliar, although the details are fuzzy. You are at a nightclub talking to a girl with a shaved head.

This arresting way to tell a story is effective, too, in a novel by Carlos Fuentes, *Aura* (1962), in some startling stories by Lorrie Moore in *Self-Help* (1985), and (apparently with great popular success) in a recent line of juvenile paperbound books, "The Adventures of You Series."[5]

The attitudes and opinions of a narrator aren't necessarily those of the author; in fact, we may notice a lively conflict between what we are told and what, apparently, we are meant to believe. A story may be told by an **innocent narrator** or a **naive narrator,** a character who fails to understand all the implications of the story. One such innocent narrator (despite his sometimes shrewd perceptions) is Huckleberry Finn. Because Huck accepts without question the morality and lawfulness of slavery, he feels guilty about helping Jim, a runaway slave. But, far from condemning Huck for his defiance of the law — "All right, then, I'll *go* to hell," Huck

[4]Chapter Two, "Death in the Fog," *The Maltese Falcon* (New York: Knopf, 1929).
[5]Each book starts out with you, the main character, facing some challenge or danger. Then you are offered a choice: "Will you leap forward and struggle with the vampire? Turn to page 20. Will you flee? Turn to page 22." If you choose badly, you may be told, "Suddenly you feel the searing pain of a spear in your back. You sink to the ground — finished for good" (from Edward Packard, *Sugarcane Island* [New York: Pocket, 1978] 60).

tells himself, deciding against returning Jim to captivity — the author, and the reader along with him, silently applaud. Naive in the extreme is the narrator of one part of William Faulkner's novel *The Sound and the Fury,* the idiot Benjy, a grown man with the intellect of a child. In a story told by an **unreliable narrator,** the point of view is that of a person who, we perceive, is deceptive, self-deceptive, deluded, or deranged. As though seeking ways to be faithful to uncertainty, contemporary writers have been particularly fond of unreliable narrators.

Virginia Woolf compared life to "a luminous halo, a semi-transparent envelope surrounding us from the beginning of consciousness to the end."[6] To capture such a reality, modern writers of fiction have employed many strategies. One is the method of writing called **stream of consciousness,** from a phrase coined by psychologist William James to describe the procession of thoughts passing through the mind. In fiction, stream of consciousness is a kind of selective omniscience: the presentation of thoughts and sense impressions in a lifelike fashion — not in a sequence arranged by logic, but mingled randomly. When in his novel *Ulysses* James Joyce takes us into the mind of Leopold Bloom, an ordinary Dublin mind well-stocked with trivia and fragments of odd learning, the reader may have an impression not of a smoothly flowing stream but of an ocean of miscellaneous things, all crowded and jostling.

> As he set foot on O'Connell bridge a puffball of smoke plumed up from the parapet. Brewery barge with export stout. England. Sea air sours it, I heard. Be interesting some day to get a pass through Hancock to see the brewery. Regular world in itself. Vats of porter, wonderful. Rats get in too. Drink themselves bloated as big as a collie floating.[7]

Perceptions — such as the smoke from the brewery barge — trigger Bloom's reflections. A moment later, as he casts a crumpled paper ball off the bridge, he recalls a bit of science he learned in school, the rate of speed of a falling body: "thirty-two feet per sec."

Stream-of-consciousness writing usually occurs in relatively short passages, but in *Ulysses* Joyce employs it extensively. Similar in method, an **interior monologue** is an extended presentation of a character's thoughts, not in the seemingly helter-skelter order of a stream of consciousness, but in an arrangement as if the character were speaking out loud to himself, for us to overhear. A famous interior monologue comes at the end of *Ulysses* when Joyce gives us the rambling memories and reflections of earth-mother Molly Bloom.

Every point of view has limitations. Even **total omniscience,** a knowledge of the minds of all the characters, has its disadvantages. Such

[6]"Modern Fiction," in *Collected Essays* (New York: Harcourt, 1967). For the entire statement, see page 401.
[7]*Ulysses* (New York: Random, 1934) 150.

a point of view requires high skill to manage, without the storyteller's losing his way in a multitude of perspectives. In fact, there are evident advantages in having a narrator not know everything. We are accustomed to seeing the world through one pair of eyes, to having truths gradually occur to us. Henry James, whose theory and practice of fiction have been influential, held that an excellent way to tell a story was through the fine but bewildered mind of an observer. "It seems probable," James wrote, "that if we were never bewildered there would never be a story to tell about us; we should partake of the superior nature of the all-knowing immortals whose annals are dreadfully dull so long as flurried humans are not, for the positive relief of bored Olympians, mixed up with them."[8]

By using a particular point of view, an author may artfully withhold information, if need be, rather than immediately present it to us. If, for instance, the suspense in a story depends upon our not knowing until the end that the protagonist is a secret agent, the author would be ill advised to tell the story from the protagonist's point of view. If a character acts as the narrator, the author must make sure that the character possesses (or can obtain) enough information to tell the story adequately. Clearly, the author makes a fundamental decision in selecting, from many possibilities, a story's point of view. What we readers admire, if the story is effective, is not only skill in execution, but also powers of choice.

Here is a short story memorable for many reasons, among them for its point of view.

William Faulkner

A ROSE FOR EMILY   1931

William Faulkner (1897 – 1962) spent most of his days in Oxford, Missis-sippi, where he attended the University of Mississippi and where he served as postmaster until angry townspeople ejected him after they had long failed to receive mail. During World War I he served with the Royal Canadian Air Force, and afterward worked as a feature writer for the New Orleans Times-Picayune. *Faulkner's private life was a long struggle to stay solvent: even after fame came to him, he had to write Hollywood scripts and teach at the University of Virginia. The violent comic novel* Sanctuary *(1931) caused a stir and turned a profit, but critics tend most to admire* The Sound and the Fury *(1929), a tale partially told through the eyes of an idiot;* As I Lay Dying *(1930);* Light in August *(1932);* Absalom, Absalom *(1936); and* The Hamlet *(1940). Beginning with* Sartoris *(1929), Faulkner in his fiction imagines a Mississippi county named Yoknapatawpha*

---

[8]Preface to *The Princess Casamassima,* reprinted in *The Art of the Novel,* ed. R. P. Blackmur (New York: Scribner's, 1934).

and traces the fortunes of several of its families, including the aristocratic Compsons and Sartorises and the white-trash, dollar-grubbing Snopeses, from the Civil War to modern times. His influence on his fellow southern writers (and others) has been profound. In 1950 he received the Nobel prize for literature with a stirring speech (quoted on page 403). Although we think of Faulkner primarily as a novelist, he wrote nearly a hundred short stories. Forty-two of the best are available in his Collected Stories *(1950).*

I

When Miss Emily Grierson died, our whole town went to her funeral: the men through a sort of respectful affection for a fallen monument, the women mostly out of curiosity to see the inside of her house, which no one save an old manservant — a combined gardener and cook — had seen in at least ten years.

It was a big, squarish frame house that had once been white, decorated with cupolas and spires and scrolled balconies in the heavily lightsome style of the seventies, set on what had once been our most select street. But garages and cotton gins had encroached and obliterated even the august names of that neighborhood; only Miss Emily's house was left, lifting its stubborn and coquettish decay above the cotton wagons and the gasoline pumps — an eyesore among eyesores. And now Miss Emily had gone to join the representatives of those august names where they lay in the cedar-bemused cemetery among the ranked and anonymous graves of Union and Confederate soldiers who fell at the battle of Jefferson.

Alive, Miss Emily had been a tradition, a duty, and a care; a sort of hereditary obligation upon the town, dating from that day in 1894 when Colonel Sartoris, the mayor — he who fathered the edict that no Negro woman should appear on the streets without an apron — remitted her taxes, the dispensation dating from the death of her father on into perpetuity. Not that Miss Emily would have accepted charity. Colonel Sartoris invented an involved tale to the effect that Miss Emily's father had loaned money to the town, which the town, as a matter of business, preferred this way of repaying. Only a man of Colonel Sartoris' generation and thought could have invented it, and only a woman could have believed it.

When the next generation, with its more modern ideas, became mayors and aldermen, this arrangement created some little dissatisfaction. On the first of the year they mailed her a tax notice. February came, and there was no reply. They wrote her a formal letter, asking her to call at the sheriff's office at her convenience. A week later the mayor wrote her himself, offering to call or to send his car for her, and received in reply a note on paper of an archaic shape, in a thin, flowing calligraphy in faded ink, to the effect that she no longer went out at all. The tax notice was also enclosed, without comment.

They called a special meeting of the Board of Aldermen. A deputation ⁵ waited upon her, knocked at the door through which no visitor had passed since she ceased giving china-painting lessons eight or ten years earlier. They were admitted by the old Negro into a dim hall from which a stairway mounted into still more shadow. It smelled of dust and disuse — a close, dank smell. The Negro led them into the parlor. It was furnished in heavy, leather-covered furniture. When the Negro opened the blinds of one window, they could see that the leather was cracked; and when they sat down, a faint dust rose sluggishly about their thighs, spinning with slow motes in the single sun-ray. On a tarnished gilt easel before the fireplace stood a crayon portrait of Miss Emily's father.

They rose when she entered — a small, fat woman in black, with a thin gold chain descending to her waist and vanishing into her belt, leaning on an ebony cane with a tarnished gold head. Her skeleton was small and spare; perhaps that was why what would have been merely plumpness in another was obesity in her. She looked bloated, like a body long submerged in motionless water, and of that pallid hue. Her eyes, lost in the fatty ridges of her face, looked like two small pieces of coal pressed into a lump of dough as they moved from one face to another while the visitors stated their errand.

She did not ask them to sit. She just stood in the door and listened quietly until the spokesman came to a stumbling halt. Then they could hear the invisible watch ticking at the end of the gold chain.

Her voice was dry and cold. "I have no taxes in Jefferson. Colonel Sartoris explained it to me. Perhaps one of you can gain access to the city records and satisfy yourselves."

"But we have. We are the city authorities, Miss Emily. Didn't you get a notice from the sheriff, signed by him?"

"I received a paper, yes," Miss Emily said. "Perhaps he considers himself the sheriff . . . I have no taxes in Jefferson."   10

"But there is nothing on the books to show that, you see. We must go by the — "

"See Colonel Sartoris. I have no taxes in Jefferson."

"But, Miss Emily — "

"See Colonel Sartoris." (Colonel Sartoris had been dead almost ten years.) "I have no taxes in Jefferson. Tobe!" The Negro appeared. "Show these gentlemen out."

II

So she vanquished them, horse and foot, just as she had vanquished their   15
fathers thirty years before about the smell. That was two years after her father's death and a short time after her sweetheart — the one we believed would marry her — had deserted her. After her father's death she went out very little; after her sweetheart went away, people hardly saw her at all. A few of the ladies had the temerity to call, but were not received, and the only sign of life about the place was the Negro man — a young man then — going in and out with a market basket.

"Just as if a man — any man — could keep a kitchen properly," the ladies said; so they were not surprised when the smell developed. It was another link between the gross, teeming world and the high and mighty Griersons.

A neighbor, a woman, complained to the mayor, Judge Stevens, eighty years old.

"But what will you have me do about it, madam?" he said.

"Why, send her word to stop it," the woman said. "Isn't there a law?"

"I'm sure that won't be necessary," Judge Stevens said. "It's probably just a snake or a rat that nigger of hers killed in the yard. I'll speak to him about it."

The next day he received two more complaints, one from a man who came in diffident deprecation. "We really must do something about it, Judge. I'd be the last one in the world to bother Miss Emily, but we've got to do something." That night the Board of Aldermen met — three graybeards and one younger man, a member of the rising generation.

"It's simple enough," he said. "Send her word to have her place cleaned up. Give her a certain time to do it in, and if she don't . . ."

"Dammit, sir," Judge Stevens said, "will you accuse a lady to her face of smelling bad?"

So the next night, after midnight, four men crossed Miss Emily's lawn and slunk about the house like burglars, sniffing along the base of the brickwork and at the cellar openings while one of them performed a regular sowing motion with his hand out of a sack slung from his shoulder. They broke open the cellar door and sprinkled lime there, and in all the outbuildings. As they recrossed the lawn, a window that had been dark was lighted and Miss Emily sat in it, the light behind her, and her upright torso motionless as that of an idol. They crept quietly across the lawn and into the shadow of the locusts that lined the street. After a week or two the smell went away.

That was when people had begun to feel really sorry for her. People in our town, remembering how old lady Wyatt, her great-aunt, had gone completely crazy at last, believed that the Griersons held themselves a little too high for what they really were. None of the young men were quite good enough for Miss Emily and such. We had long thought of them as a tableau, Miss Emily a slender figure in white in the background, her father a spraddled silhouette in the foreground, his back to her and clutching a horsewhip, the two of them framed by the back-flung front door. So when she got to be thirty and was still single, we were not pleased exactly, but vindicated; even with insanity in the family she wouldn't have turned down all of her chances if they had really materialized.

When her father died, it got about that the house was all that was left to her; and in a way, people were glad. At last they could pity Miss Emily. Being left alone, and a pauper, she had become humanized. Now she too would know the old thrill and the old despair of a penny more or less.

The day after his death all the ladies prepared to call at the house and offer condolence and aid, as is our custom. Miss Emily met them at the door, dressed as usual and with no trace of grief on her face. She told them that her father was not dead. She did that for three days, with the ministers calling on her, and the doctors, trying to persuade her to let them dispose of the body. Just as they were about to resort to law and force, she broke down, and they buried her father quickly.

We did not say she was crazy then. We believed she had to do that. We remembered all the young men her father had driven away, and we knew that with nothing left, she would have to cling to that which had robbed her, as people will.

III

She was sick for a long time. When we saw her again, her hair was cut short, making her look like a girl, with a vague resemblance to those angels in colored church windows — sort of tragic and serene.

The town had just let the contracts for paving the sidewalks, and in the summer after her father's death they began the work. The construction company came with niggers and mules and machinery, and a foreman named Homer Barron, a Yankee — a big, dark, ready man, with a big voice and eyes lighter than his face. The little boys would follow in groups to hear him cuss the niggers, and the niggers singing in time to the rise and fall of picks. Pretty soon he knew everybody in town. Whenever you heard a lot of laughing anywhere about the square, Homer Barron would be in the center of the group. Presently we began to see him and Miss Emily on Sunday afternoons driving in the yellow-wheeled buggy and the matched team of bays from the livery stable.

At first we were glad that Miss Emily would have an interest, because the ladies all said, "Of course a Grierson would not think seriously of a Northerner, a day laborer." But there were still others, older people, who said that even grief could not cause a real lady to forget *noblesse oblige*° — without calling it *noblesse oblige.* They just said, "Poor Emily. Her kinsfolk should come to her." She had some kin in Alabama; but years ago her father had fallen out with them over the estate of old lady Wyatt, the crazy woman, and there was no communication between the two families. They had not even been represented at the funeral.

And as soon as the old people said, "Poor Emily," the whispering began. "Do you suppose it's really so?" they said to one another. "Of course it is. What else could . . ." This behind their hands; rustling of craned silk and satin behind jalousies closed upon the sun of Sunday afternoon as the thin, swift clop-clop-clop of the matched team passed: "Poor Emily."

She carried her head high enough — even when we believed that she was fallen. It was as if she demanded more than ever the recognition of her dignity as the last Grierson; as if it had wanted that touch of earthiness to reaffirm her imperviousness. Like when she bought the rat poison, the arsenic. That was over a year after they had begun to say "Poor Emily," and while the two female cousins were visiting her.

"I want some poison," she said to the druggist. She was over thirty then, still a slight woman, though thinner than usual, with cold, haughty black eyes in a face the flesh of which was strained across the temples and about the eye-sockets as you imagine a lighthouse-keeper's face ought to look. "I want some poison," she said.

"Yes, Miss Emily. What kind? For rats and such? I'd recom — "

"I want the best you have. I don't care what kind."

The druggist named several. "They'll kill anything up to an elephant. But what you want is — "

"Arsenic," Miss Emily said. "Is that a good one?"

"Is . . . arsenic? Yes, ma'am. But what you want — "

---

noblesse oblige: the obligation of a member of the nobility to behave with honor and dignity.

"I want arsenic."

The druggist looked down at her. She looked back at him, erect, her face like a strained flag. "Why, of course," the druggist said. "If that's what you want. But the law requires you to tell what you are going to use it for."

Miss Emily just stared at him, her head tilted back in order to look him eye for eye, until he looked away and went and got the arsenic and wrapped it up. The Negro delivery boy brought her the package; the druggist didn't come back. When she opened the package at home there was written on the box, under the skull and bones: "For rats."

IV

So the next day we all said, "She will kill herself"; and we said it would be the best thing. When she had first begun to be seen with Homer Barron, we had said, "She will marry him." Then we said, "She will persuade him yet," because Homer himself had remarked — he liked men, and it was known that he drank with the younger men in the Elks' Club — that he was not a marrying man. Later we said, "Poor Emily" behind the jalousies as they passed on Sunday afternoon in the glittering buggy, Miss Emily with her head high and Homer Barron with his hat cocked and a cigar in his teeth, reins and whip in a yellow glove.

Then some of the ladies began to say that it was a disgrace to the town and a bad example to the young people. The men did not want to interfere, but at last the ladies forced the Baptist minister — Miss Emily's people were Episcopal — to call upon her. He would never divulge what happened during that interview, but he refused to go back again. The next Sunday they again drove about the streets, and the following day the minister's wife wrote to Miss Emily's relations in Alabama.

So she had blood-kin under her roof again and we sat back to watch developments. At first nothing happened. Then we were sure that they were to be married. We learned that Miss Emily had been to the jeweler's and ordered a man's toilet set in silver, with the letters H. B. on each piece. Two days later we learned that she had bought a complete outfit of men's clothing, including a nightshirt, and we said, "They are married." We were really glad. We were glad because the two female cousins were even more Grierson than Miss Emily had ever been.

So we were not surprised when Homer Barron — the streets had been finished some time since — was gone. We were a little disappointed that there was not a public blowing-off, but we believed that he had gone on to prepare for Miss Emily's coming, or to give her a chance to get rid of the cousins. (By that time it was a cabal, and we were all Miss Emily's allies to help circumvent the cousins.) Sure enough, after another week they departed. And, as we had expected all along, within three days Homer Barron was back in town. A neighbor saw the Negro man admit him at the kitchen door at dusk one evening.

And that was the last we saw of Homer Barron. And of Miss Emily for some time. The Negro man went in and out with the market basket, but the front door remained closed. Now and then we would see her at a window for a moment, as the men did that night when they sprinkled the lime, but for almost six months she did not appear on the streets. Then we knew that this was to be expected too; as if that quality of her father which had thwarted her woman's life so many times had been too virulent and too furious to die.

When we next saw Miss Emily, she had grown fat and her hair was turning gray. During the next few years it grew grayer and grayer until it attained an even pepper-and-salt iron-gray, when it ceased turning. Up to the day of her death at seventy-four it was still that vigorous iron-gray, like the hair of an active man.

From that time on her front door remained closed, save for a period of six or seven years, when she was about forty, during which she gave lessons in china-painting. She fitted up a studio in one of the downstairs rooms, where the daughters and granddaughters of Colonel Sartoris' contemporaries were sent to her with the same regularity and in the same spirit that they were sent to church on Sundays with a twenty-five-cent piece for the collection plate. Meanwhile her taxes had been remitted.

Then the newer generation became the backbone and the spirit of the town, and the painting pupils grew up and fell away and did not send their children to her with boxes of color and tedious brushes and pictures cut from the ladies' magazines. The front door closed upon the last one and remained closed for good. When the town got free postal delivery, Miss Emily alone refused to let them fasten the metal numbers above her door and attach a mailbox to it. She would not listen to them.

Daily, monthly, yearly we watched the Negro grow grayer and more stooped, going in and out with the market basket. Each December we sent her a tax notice, which would be returned by the post office a week later, unclaimed. Now and then we would see her in one of the downstairs windows — she had evidently shut up the top floor of the house — like the carven torso of an idol in a niche, looking or not looking at us, we could never tell which. Thus she passed from generation to generation — dear, inescapable, impervious, tranquil, and perverse.

And so she died. Fell ill in the house filled with dust and shadows, with only a doddering Negro man to wait on her. We did not even know she was sick; we had long since given up trying to get any information from the Negro. He talked to no one, probably not even to her, for his voice had grown harsh and rusty, as if from disuse.

She died in one of the downstairs rooms, in a heavy walnut bed with a curtain, her gray head propped on a pillow yellow and moldy with age and lack of sunlight.

V

The Negro met the first of the ladies at the front door and let them in, with their hushed, sibilant voices and their quick, curious glances, and then he disappeared. He walked right through the house and out the back and was not seen again.

The two female cousins came at once. They held the funeral on the second day, with the town coming to look at Miss Emily beneath a mass of bought flowers, with the crayon face of her father musing profoundly above the bier and the ladies sibilant and macabre; and the very old men — some in their brushed Confederate uniforms — on the porch and the lawn, talking of

Miss Emily as if she had been a contemporary of theirs, believing that they had danced with her and courted her perhaps, confusing time with its mathematical progression, as the old do, to whom all the past is not a diminishing road but, instead, a huge meadow which no winter ever quite touches, divided from them now by the narrow bottle-neck of the most recent decade of years.

Already we knew that there was one room in that region above stairs which no one had seen in forty years, and which would have to be forced. They waited until Miss Emily was decently in the ground before they opened it.

The violence of breaking down the door seemed to fill this room with pervading dust. A thin, acrid pall as of the tomb seemed to lie everywhere upon this room decked and furnished as for a bridal: upon the valance curtains of faded rose color, upon the rose-shaded lights, upon the dressing table, upon the delicate array of crystal and the man's toilet things backed with tarnished silver, silver so tarnished that the monogram was obscured. Among them lay collar and tie, as if they had just been removed, which, lifted, left upon the surface a pale crescent in the dust. Upon a chair hung the suit, carefully folded; beneath it the two mute shoes and the discarded socks.

The man himself lay in the bed.

For a long while we just stood there, looking down at the profound and fleshless grin. The body had apparently once lain in the attitude of an embrace, but now the long sleep that outlasts love, that conquers even the grimace of love, had cuckolded him. What was left of him, rotted beneath what was left of the nightshirt, had become inextricable from the bed in which he lay; and upon him and upon the pillow beside him lay that even coating of the patient and biding dust.

Then we noticed that in the second pillow was the indentation of a head. 60 One of us lifted something from it, and leaning forward, that faint and invisible dust dry and acrid in the nostrils, we saw a long strand of iron-gray hair.

QUESTIONS

1. What is meaningful in the final detail that the strand of hair on the second pillow is *iron-gray?*
2. Who is the unnamed narrator? For whom does he profess to be speaking?
3. Why does "A Rose for Emily" seem better told from his point of view than if it were told (like John Updike's "A & P") from the point of view of the main character?
4. What foreshadowings of the discovery of the body of Homer Barron are we given earlier in the story? Share your experience in reading "A Rose for Emily": did the foreshadowings give away the ending for you? Did they heighten your interest?
5. What contrasts does the narrator draw between changing reality and Emily's refusal or inability to recognize change?
6. How do the character and background of Emily Grierson differ from those of Homer Barron? What general observations about the society that Faulkner depicts can be made from his portraits of these two characters and from his account of life in this one Mississippi town?
7. Does the story seem to you totally grim, or do you find any humor in it?
8. What do you infer to be the author's attitude toward Emily Grierson? Is she simply a murderous madwoman? Why do you suppose Faulkner calls his story "A Rose . . ."?

Frank O'Connor

FIRST CONFESSION

1952

Frank O'Connor was the pen name that Michael O'Donovan (1903 – 1966) adopted when he feared that to be known as a writer would hurt his career in civil service. He was born in Cork, Ireland's second city. Desperate poverty forced his parents to take him out of school after he had completed only fourth grade. During the troubles of 1918 – 21 that led to the new Irish Free State, he served in the Republican Army. After peace came, he worked as a librarian and for several years served as a director of Dublin's influential Abbey Theatre. America offered O'Connor-O'Donovan early hospitality: in 1931 The Atlantic *printed his first story. In the 1950s he lived in America, teaching at Northwestern and Harvard. For a time he regularly appeared on CBS television on Sunday mornings, just sitting and telling stories. A fine literary critic, besides, he wrote* The Mirror in the Roadway *(1956), a study of the novel, and* The Lonely Voice *(1963), a study of the short story. In* Kings, Lords & Commons *(1959), he proved himself a master translator of Gaelic poetry. O'Connor toiled hard over his stories, trying to polish each to the perfection of a good lyric. "First Confession" appeared in print in three versions because he kept rewriting it. The story is based upon his boyhood memories.*

All the trouble began when my grandfather died and my grandmother — my father's mother — came to live with us. Relations in the one house are a strain at the best of times, but, to make matters worse, my grandmother was a real old countrywoman and quite unsuited to the life in town. She had a fat, wrinkled old face, and, to Mother's great indignation, went round the house in bare feet — the boots had her crippled, she said. For dinner she had a jug of porter and a pot of potatoes with — sometimes — a bit of salt fish, and she poured out the potatoes on the table and ate them slowly, with great relish, using her fingers by way of a fork.

Now, girls are supposed to be fastidious, but I was the one who suffered most from this. Nora, my sister, just sucked up to the old woman for the penny she got every Friday out of the old-age pension, a thing I could not do. I was too honest, that was my trouble; and when I was playing with Bill Connell, the sergeant-major's son, and saw my grandmother steering up the path with the jug of porter sticking out from beneath her shawl I was mortified. I made excuses not to let him come into the house, because I could never be sure what she would be up to when we went in.

When Mother was at work and my grandmother made the dinner I wouldn't touch it. Nora once tried to make me, but I hid under the table from her and took the bread-knife with me for protection. Nora let on to be very indignant (she wasn't, of course, but she knew Mother saw through her, so she sided with Gran) and came after me. I lashed out at her with the bread-knife, and after that she left me alone. I stayed there till Mother came in from work and made my dinner, but when Father came in later Nora said in a shocked voice: "Oh, Dadda, do you know what Jackie did at dinnertime?" Then, of course, it all came out; Father gave me a flaking; Mother interfered, and for days after that he didn't speak to me and Mother barely spoke to Nora. And all because of that old woman! God knows, I was heart-scalded.

Then, to crown my misfortunes, I had to make my first confession and communion. It was an old woman called Ryan who prepared us for these. She was about the one age with Gran; she was well-to-do, lived in a big house on Montenotte, wore a black cloak and bonnet, and came every day to school at three o'clock when we should have been going home, and talked to us of hell. She may have mentioned the other place as well, but that could only have been by accident, for hell had the first place in her heart.

She lit a candle, took out a new half-crown, and offered it to the first boy   5
who would hold one finger — only one finger! — in the flame for five minutes by the school clock. Being always very ambitious I was tempted to volunteer, but I thought it might look greedy. Then she asked were we afraid of holding one finger — only one finger! — in a little candle flame for five minutes and not afraid of burning all over in roasting hot furnaces for all eternity. "All eternity! Just think of that! A whole lifetime goes by and it's nothing, not even a drop in the ocean of your sufferings." The woman was really interesting about hell, but my attention was all fixed on the half-crown. At the end of the lesson she put it back in her purse. It was a great disappointment; a religious woman like that, you wouldn't think she'd bother about a thing like a half-crown.

Another day she said she knew a priest who woke one night to find a fellow he didn't recognize leaning over the end of his bed. The priest was a bit frightened — naturally enough — but he asked the fellow what he wanted, and the fellow said in a deep, husky voice that he wanted to go to confession. The priest said it was an awkward time and wouldn't it do in the morning, but the fellow said that last time he went to confession, there was one sin he kept back, being ashamed to mention it, and now it was always on his mind. Then the priest knew it was a bad case, because the fellow was after making a bad confession and committing a mortal sin. He got up to dress, and just then the cock crew in the yard outside, and — lo and behold! — when the priest looked round there was no sign of the fellow, only a smell of burning timber, and when the priest looked at his bed didn't he see the print of two hands burned in it? That was because the fellow had made a bad confession. This story made a shocking impression on me.

But the worst of all was when she showed us how to examine our conscience. Did we take the name of the Lord, our God, in vain? Did we honor our father and our mother? (I asked her did this include grandmothers and she said it did.) Did we love our neighbors as ourselves? Did we covet our neighbor's goods? (I thought of the way I felt about the penny that Nora got every Friday.) I decided that, between one thing and another, I must have broken the whole ten commandments, all on account of that old woman, and so far as I could see, so long as she remained in the house I had no hope of ever doing anything else.

I was scared to death of confession. The day the whole class went I let on to have a toothache, hoping my absence wouldn't be noticed; but at three o'clock, just as I was feeling safe, along comes a chap with a message from Mrs. Ryan that I was to go to confession myself on Saturday and be at the chapel for communion with the rest. To make it worse, Mother couldn't come with me and sent Nora instead.

Now, that girl had ways of tormenting me that Mother never knew of. She held my hand as we went down the hill, smiling sadly and saying how sorry she was for me, as if she were bringing me to the hospital for an operation.

"Oh, God help us!" she moaned. "Isn't it a terrible pity you weren't a good boy? Oh, Jackie, my heart bleeds for you! How will you ever think of all your sins? Don't forget you have to tell him about the time you kicked Gran on the shin." 10

"Lemme go!" I said, trying to drag myself free of her. "I don't want to go to confession at all."

"But sure, you'll have to go to confession, Jackie," she replied in the same regretful tone. "Sure, if you didn't, the parish priest would be up to the house, looking for you. 'Tisn't, God knows, that I'm not sorry for you. Do you remember the time you tried to kill me with the bread-knife under the table? And the language you used to me? I don't know what he'll do with you at all, Jackie. He might have to send you up to the bishop."

I remember thinking bitterly that she didn't know the half of what I had to tell — if I told it. I knew I couldn't tell it, and understood perfectly why the fellow in Mrs. Ryan's story made a bad confession; it seemed to me a great shame that people wouldn't stop criticizing him. I remember that steep hill down to the church, and the sunlit hillsides beyond the valley of the river, which I saw in the gaps between the houses like Adam's last glimpse of Paradise.

Then, when she had maneuvered me down the long flight of steps to the chapel yard, Nora suddenly changed her tone. She became the raging malicious devil she really was.

"There you are!" she said with a yelp of triumph, hurling me through the church door. "And I hope he'll give you the penitential psalms, you dirty little caffler." 15

I knew then I was lost, given up to eternal justice. The door with the colored-glass panels swung shut behind me, the sunlight went out and gave place to deep shadow, and the wind whistled outside so that the silence within seemed to crackle like ice under my feet. Nora sat in front of me by the confession box. There were a couple of old women ahead of her, and then a miserable-looking poor devil came and wedged me in at the other side, so that I couldn't escape even if I had the courage. He joined his hands and rolled his eyes in the direction of the roof, muttering aspirations in an anguished tone, and I wondered had he a grandmother too. Only a grandmother could account for a fellow behaving in that heartbroken way, but he was better off than I, for he at least could go and confess his sins; while I would make a bad confession and then die in the night and be continually coming back and burning people's furniture.

Nora's turn came, and I heard the sound of something slamming, and then her voice as if butter wouldn't melt in her mouth, and then another slam, and out she came. God, the hypocrisy of women! Her eyes were lowered, her head was bowed, and her hands were joined very low down on her stomach, and she walked up the aisle to the side altar looking like a saint. You never saw such an exhibition of devotion; and I remembered the devilish malice with which she had tormented me all the way from our door, and wondered were all religious people like that, really. It was my turn now. With the fear of damnation in my soul I went in, and the confessional door closed of itself behind me.

It was pitch-dark and I couldn't see priest or anything else. Then I really began to be frightened. In the darkness it was a matter between God and me, and He had all the odds. He knew what my intentions were before I even started; I had no chance. All I had ever been told about confession got mixed up in my mind, and I knelt to one wall and said: "Bless me, father, for I have sinned; this is my first confession." I waited for a few minutes, but nothing happened, so I tried it on the other wall. Nothing happened there either. He had me spotted all right.

It must have been then that I noticed the shelf at about one height with my head. It was really a place for grown-up people to rest their elbows, but in my distracted state I thought it was probably the place you were supposed to kneel. Of course, it was on the high side and not very deep, but I was always good at climbing and managed to get up all right. Staying up was the trouble. There was room only for my knees, and nothing you could get a grip on but a sort of wooden moulding a bit above it. I held on to the moulding and repeated the words a little louder, and this time something happened all right. A slide was slammed back; a little light entered the box, and a man's voice said: "Who's there?"

" 'Tis me, father," I said for fear he mightn't see me and go away again. 20 I couldn't see him at all. The place the voice came from was under the moulding, about level with my knees, so I took a good grip of the moulding and swung myself down till I saw the astonished face of a young priest looking up at me. He had to put his head on one side to see me, and I had to put mine on one side to see him, so we were more or less talking to one another upside-down. It struck me as a queer way of hearing confessions, but I didn't feel it my place to criticize.

"Bless me, father, for I have sinned; this is my first confession," I rattled off all in one breath, and swung myself down the least shade more to make it easier for him.

"What are you doing up there?" he shouted in an angry voice, and the strain the politeness was putting on my hold of the moulding, and the shock of being addressed in such an uncivil tone, were too much for me. I lost my grip, tumbled, and hit the door an unmerciful wallop before I found myself flat on my back in the middle of the aisle. The people who had been waiting stood up with their mouths open. The priest opened the door of the middle box and came out, pushing his biretta back from his forehead; he looked something terrible. Then Nora came scampering down the aisle.

"Oh, you dirty little caffler!" she said. "I might have known you'd do it. I might have known you'd disgrace me. I can't leave you out of my sight for one minute."

Before I could even get to my feet to defend myself she bent down and gave me a clip across the ear. This reminded me that I was so stunned I had even forgotten to cry, so that people might think I wasn't hurt at all, when in fact I was probably maimed for life. I gave a roar out of me.

"What's all this about?" the priest hissed, getting angrier than ever and ²⁵ pushing Nora off me. "How dare you hit the child like that, you little vixen?"

"But I can't do my penance with him, father," Nora cried, cocking an outraged eye up at him.

"Well, go and do it, or I'll give you some more to do," he said, giving me a hand up. "Was it coming to confession you were, my poor man?" he asked me.

" 'Twas, father," said I with a sob.

"Oh," he said respectfully, "a big hefty fellow like you must have terrible sins. Is this your first?"

" 'Tis, father," said I. ³⁰

"Worse and worse," he said gloomily. "The crimes of a life-time. I don't know will I get rid of you at all today. You'd better wait now till I'm finished with these old ones. You can see by the looks of them they haven't much to tell."

"I will, father," I said with something approaching joy.

The relief of it was really enormous. Nora stuck out her tongue at me from behind his back, but I couldn't even be bothered retorting. I knew from the very moment that man opened his mouth that he was intelligent above the ordinary. When I had time to think, I saw how right I was. It only stood to reason that a fellow confessing after seven years would have more to tell than people that went every week. The crimes of a lifetime, exactly as he said. It was only what he expected, and the rest was the cackle of old women and girls with their talk of hell, the bishop, and the penitential psalms. That was all they knew. I started to make my examination of conscience, and barring the one bad business of my grandmother it didn't seem so bad.

The next time, the priest steered me into the confession box himself and left the shutter back the way I could see him get in and sit down at the further side of the grille from me.

"Well, now," he said, "what do they call you?" ³⁵

"Jackie, father," said I.

"And what's a-trouble to you, Jackie?"

"Father," I said, feeling I might as well get it over while I had him in good humor, "I had it all arranged to kill my grandmother."

He seemed a bit shaken by that, all right, because he said nothing for quite a while.

"My goodness," he said at last, "that'd be a shocking thing to do. What ⁴⁰ put that into your head?"

"Father," I said, feeling very sorry for myself, "she's an awful woman."

"Is she?" he asked. "What way is she awful?"

"She takes porter, father," I said, knowing well from the way Mother talked of it that this was a mortal sin, and hoping it would make the priest take a more favorable view of my case.

"Oh, my!" he said, and I could see he was impressed.

"And snuff, father," said I. ⁴⁵

"That's a bad case, sure enough, Jackie," he said.

"And she goes round in her bare feet, father," I went on in a rush of self-pity, "and she knows I don't like her, and she gives pennies to Nora and none to me, and my da sides with her and flakes me, and one night I was so heart-scalded I made up my mind I'd have to kill her."

"And what would you do with the body?" he asked with great interest.

"I was thinking I could chop that up and carry it away in a barrow I have," I said.

"Begor, Jackie," he said, "do you know you're a terrible child?"

"I know, father," I said, for I was just thinking the same thing myself. "I tried to kill Nora too with a bread-knife under the table, only I missed her."

"Is that the little girl that was beating you just now?" he asked.

" 'Tis, father."

"Someone will go for her with a bread-knife one day, and he won't miss her," he said rather cryptically. "You must have great courage. Between ourselves, there's a lot of people I'd like to do the same to but I'd never have the nerve. Hanging is an awful death."

"Is it, father?" I asked with the deepest interest — I was always very keen on hanging. "Did you ever see a fellow hanged?"

"Dozens of them," he said solemnly. "And they all died roaring."

"Jay!" I said.

"Oh, a horrible death!" he said with great satisfaction. "Lots of the fellows I saw killed their grandmothers too, but they all said 'twas never worth it."

He had me there for a full ten minutes talking, and then walked out the chapel yard with me. I was genuinely sorry to part with him, because he was the most entertaining character I'd ever met in the religious line. Outside, after the shadow of the church, the sunlight was like the roaring of waves on a beach; it dazzled me; and when the frozen silence melted and I heard the screech of trams on the road my heart soared. I knew now I wouldn't die in the night and come back, leaving marks on my mother's furniture. It would be a great worry to her, and the poor soul had enough.

Nora was sitting on the railing, waiting for me, and she put on a very sour puss when she saw the priest with me. She was mad jealous because a priest had never come out of the church with her.

"Well," she asked coldly, after he left me, "what did he give you?"

"Three Hail Marys," I said.

"Three Hail Marys," she repeated incredulously. "You mustn't have told him anything."

"I told him everything," I said confidently.

"About Gran and all?"

"About Gran and all."

(All she wanted was to be able to go home and say I'd made a bad confession.)

"Did you tell him you went for me with the bread-knife?" she asked with a frown.

"I did to be sure."

"And he only gave you three Hail Marys?"

"That's all."

She slowly got down from the railing with a baffled air. Clearly, this was beyond her. As we mounted the steps back to the main road she looked at me suspiciously.

"What are you sucking?" she asked.

"Bullseyes."

"Was it the priest gave them to you?"

" 'Twas."

"Lord God," she wailed bitterly, "some people have all the luck! 'Tis no advantage to anybody trying to be good. I might just as well be a sinner like you."

QUESTIONS

1. Does the narrator of "First Confession" seem a boy — an innocent or naive narrator — or a grown-up looking back through seven-year-old eyes?
2. At what moments in the story did you sense a discrepancy between the boy's view of things and Frank O'Connor's? What is *funny* in the following moments (or in any others you care to point out)?

   Jackie's attitude toward his grandmother and her terrible vices.

   His reaction to Mrs. Ryan's yarn about the spirit with burning hands.

   His explanation for the long silence that follows his confessing his plot to kill his grandmother.

   (Why do *you* suppose the priest was silent for such a long time?)

   His plan for disposing of the body ("I could chop that up and carry it away in a barrow I have").

3. Imagine "First Confession" retold from a *different* point of view: that of the priest, say, or that of an objective narrator (the "fly on the wall"). What would be lost?
4. In what ways is Jackie not entirely naive, but sometimes shrewd and perceptive? (Suggestion: Take a close look at what he says about Mrs. Ryan and about his sister Nora.)
5. What traits of character do you find in the priest? How does he differ from Mrs. Ryan as a teacher of the young?
6. Do you believe Frank O'Connor to be saying — as Nora says at the end — that there is no use in trying to live a virtuous life?

Edgar Allan Poe

THE TELL-TALE HEART   1850

Edgar Allan Poe (1809 – 1849), orphaned child of traveling actors, was raised by well-off foster parents, John and Frances Allan, in Richmond, Virginia. At eighteen he published his first book of poems. When Poe ran up heavy gambling debts as a student at the University of Virginia, Allan called him home and eventually disowned him. After two years in the army and a brief stay at West Point, Poe became a successful editor in Richmond, Philadelphia, and New York and an industrious contributor to newspapers and magazines. Marriage in 1836 to his thirteen-year-old cousin Virginia Clemm increased his happiness but also his burdens; mercilessly, he drove his pen to support wife, self, and mother-in-law. Virginia, five years an invalid, died of tuberculosis in 1847. Poe, whose tolerance for alcohol was low, increased his drinking. He was found dead in a street in Baltimore. As a writer, Poe was a true innovator. His bizarre, macabre tales have held generations spellbound, as have some of his highly musical poems ("The

Raven," "Annabel Lee"). His tales of private sleuth C. Auguste Dupin ("The Murders in the Rue Morgue," "The Purloined Letter") have earned him the title of father of the modern detective story. Other tales and his one novel, The Narrative of Arthur Gordon Pym, figure in the history of science fiction. A trail-blazing critic, Poe laid down laws for the short story (see page 397). His work has profoundly influenced not only American literature but European literature through French translations by Charles Baudelaire.

True! — nervous — very, very dreadfully nervous I had been and am; but why *will* you say that I am mad? The disease had sharpened my senses — not destroyed — not dulled them. Above all was the sense of hearing acute. I heard all things in the heaven and in the earth. I heard many things in hell. How, then, am I mad? Hearken! and observe how healthily — how calmly I can tell you the whole story.

It is impossible to say how first the idea entered my brain; but once conceived, it haunted me day and night. Object there was none. Passion there was none. I loved the old man. He had never wronged me. He had never given me insult. For his gold I had no desire. I think it was his eye! yes, it was this! One of his eyes resembled that of a vulture — a pale blue eye, with a film over it. Whenever it fell upon me, my blood ran cold; and so by degrees — very gradually — I made up my mind to take the life of the old man, and thus rid myself of the eye for ever.

Now this is the point. You fancy me mad. Madmen know nothing. But you should have seen *me.* You should have seen how wisely I proceeded — with what caution — with what foresight — with what dissimulation I went to work! I was never kinder to the old man than during the whole week before I killed him. And every night, about midnight, I turned the latch of his door and opened it — oh, so gently! And then, when I had made an opening sufficient for my head, I put in a dark lantern, all closed, closed, so that no light shone out, and then I thrust in my head. Oh, you would have laughed to see how cunningly I thrust it in! I moved it slowly — very, very slowly, so that I might not disturb the old man's sleep. It took me an hour to place my whole head within the opening so far that I could see him as he lay upon his bed. Ha! — would a madman have been so wise as this? And then, when my head was well in the room, I undid the lantern cautiously — oh, so cautiously — cautiously (for the hinges creaked) — I undid it just so much that a single thin ray fell upon the vulture eye. And this I did for seven long nights — every night just at midnight — but I found the eye always closed; and so it was impossible to do the work; for it was not the old man who vexed me, but his Evil Eye. And every morning, when the day broke, I went boldly into the chamber, and spoke courageously to him, calling him by name in a hearty tone, and inquiring how he had passed the night. So you see he would have been a very profound old man, indeed, to suspect that every night, just at twelve, I looked in upon him while he slept.

Upon the eighth night I was more than usually cautious in opening the door. A watch's minute hand moves more quickly than did mine. Never before that night had I *felt* the extent of my own powers — of my sagacity. I could scarcely contain my feelings of triumph. To think that there I was, opening the door, little by little, and he not even to dream of my secret deeds or thoughts. I fairly chuckled at the idea; and perhaps he heard me; for he moved on the bed suddenly, as if startled. Now you may think that I drew back — but no. His room was as black as pitch with the thick darkness (for the shutters were close fastened, through fear of robbers), and so I knew that he could not see the opening of the door, and I kept pushing it on steadily, steadily.

I had my head in, and was about to open the lantern, when my thumb 5 slipped upon the tin fastening, and the old man sprang up in the bed, crying out — "Who's there?"

I kept quite still and said nothing. For a whole hour I did not move a muscle, and in the meantime I did not hear him lie down. He was still sitting up in the bed listening; — just as I have done, night after night, hearkening to the death watches° in the wall.

Presently I heard a slight groan, and I knew it was the groan of mortal terror. It was not a groan of pain or of grief — oh, no! — it was the low stifled sound that arises from the bottom of the soul when overcharged with awe. I knew the sound well. Many a night, just at midnight, when all the world slept, it has welled up from my own bosom, deepening, with its dreadful echo, the terrors that distracted me. I say I knew it well. I knew what the old man felt, and pitied him, although I chuckled at heart. I knew that he had been lying awake ever since the first slight noise, when he had turned in the bed. His fears had been ever since growing upon him. He had been trying to fancy them causeless, but could not. He had been saying to himself — "It is nothing but the wind in the chimney — it is only a mouse crossing the floor," or "it is merely a cricket which has made a single chirp." Yes, he had been trying to comfort himself with these suppositions; but he had found all in vain. *All in vain;* because Death, in approaching him, had stalked with his black shadow before him, and enveloped the victim. And it was the mournful influence of the unperceived shadow that caused him to feel — although he neither saw nor heard — to *feel* the presence of my head within the room.

When I had waited a long time, very patiently, without hearing him lie down, I resolved to open a little — a very, very little crevice in the lantern. So I opened it — you cannot imagine how stealthily, stealthily — until, at length, a single dim ray, like the thread of the spider, shot from out the crevice and full upon the vulture eye.

It was open — wide, wide open — and I grew furious as I gazed upon it. I saw it with perfect distinctness — all a dull blue, with a hideous veil over it that chilled the very marrow in my bones; but I could see nothing else of the old man's face or person: for I had directed the ray as if by instinct, precisely upon the damned spot.

And now have I not told you that what you mistake for madness is but 10 over-acuteness of the senses? — now, I say, there came to my ears a low, dull, quick sound, such as a watch makes when enveloped in cotton. I knew *that* sound well too. It was the beating of the old man's heart. It increased my fury, as the beating of a drum stimulates the soldier into courage.

death watches: beetles that infest timbers. Their clicking sound was thought to be an omen of death.

But even yet I refrained and kept still. I scarcely breathed. I held the lantern motionless. I tried how steadily I could maintain the ray upon the eye. Meantime the hellish tattoo of the heart increased. It grew quicker and quicker, and louder and louder every instant. The old man's terror *must* have been extreme! It grew louder, I say, louder every moment! — do you mark me well? I have told you that I am nervous: so I am. And now at the dead hour of the night, amid the dreadful silence of that old house, so strange a noise as this excited me to uncontrollable terror. Yet, for some minutes longer I refrained and stood still. But the beating grew louder, louder! I thought the heart must burst. And now a new anxiety seized me — the sound would be heard by a neighbor! The old man's hour had come! With a loud yell, I threw open the lantern and leaped into the room. He shrieked once — once only. In an instant I dragged him to the floor, and pulled the heavy bed over him. I then smiled gaily, to find the deed so far done. But, for many minutes, the heart beat on with a muffled sound. This, however, did not vex me; it would not be heard through the wall. At length it ceased. The old man was dead. I removed the bed and examined the corpse. Yes, he was stone, stone dead. I placed my hand upon the heart and held it there many minutes. There was no pulsation. He was stone dead. His eye would trouble me no more.

If still you think me mad, you will think so no longer when I describe the wise precautions I took for the concealment of the body. The night waned, and I worked hastily, but in silence. First of all I dismembered the corpse. I cut off the head and the arms and the legs.

I then took up three planks from the flooring of the chamber, and deposited all between the scantlings. I then replaced the boards so cleverly, so cunningly, that no human eye — not even *his* — could have detected anything wrong. There was nothing to wash out — no stain of any kind — no blood-spot whatever. I had been too wary for that. A tub had caught all — ha! ha!

When I had made an end of these labors, it was four o'clock — still dark as midnight. As the bell sounded the hour, there came a knocking at the street door. I went down to open it with a light heart, — for what had I *now* to fear? There entered three men, who introduced themselves, with perfect suavity, as officers of the police. A shriek had been heard by a neighbor during the night; suspicion of foul play had been aroused; information had been lodged at the police office, and they (the officers) had been deputed to search the premises.

I smiled, — for *what* had I to fear? I bade the gentlemen welcome. The shriek, I said, was my own in a dream. The old man, I mentioned, was absent in the country. I took my visitors all over the house. I bade them search — search *well*. I led them, at length, to *his* chamber. I showed them his treasures, secure, undisturbed. In the enthusiasm of my confidence, I brought chairs into the room, and desired them *here* to rest from their fatigues, while I myself, in the wild audacity of my perfect triumph, placed my own seat upon the very spot beneath which reposed the corpse of the victim.

The officers were satisfied. My *manner* had convinced them. I was singularly at ease. They sat, and while I answered cheerily, they chatted familiar things. But, ere long, I felt myself getting pale and wished them gone. My head ached, and I fancied a ringing in my ears: but still they sat and still they chatted. The ringing became more distinct: — it continued and became more distinct: I talked more freely to get rid of the feeling: but it continued and gained

15

definitiveness — until, at length, I found that the noise was *not* within my ears.

No doubt I now grew *very* pale: — but I talked more fluently, and with a heightened voice. Yet the sound increased — and what could I do? It was *a low, dull, quick sound — much such a sound as a watch makes when enveloped in cotton.* I gasped for breath — and yet the officers heard it not. I talked more quickly — more vehemently; but the noise steadily increased. I arose and argued about trifles, in a high key and with violent gesticulations, but the noise steadily increased. Why *would* they not be gone? I paced the floor to and fro with heavy strides, as if excited to fury by the observation of the men — but the noise steadily increased. Oh God! what *could* I do? I foamed — I raved — I swore! I swung the chair upon which I had been sitting, and grated it upon the boards, but the noise arose over all and continually increased. It grew louder — louder — *louder!* And still the men chatted pleasantly, and smiled. Was it possible they heard not? Almighty God! — no, no! They heard! — they suspected! — they *knew!* — they were making a mockery of my horror! — this I thought, and this I think. But any thing was better than this agony! Any thing was more tolerable than this derision! I could bear those hypocritical smiles no longer! I felt that I must scream or die! — and now — again! — hark! louder! louder! louder! *louder!* —

"Villains!" I shrieked, "dissemble no more! I admit the deed! — tear up the planks! — here, here! — it is the beating of his hideous heart!"

QUESTIONS

1. From what point of view is Poe's story told? Why is this point of view particularly effective for "The Tell-Tale Heart"?
2. Point to details in the story that identify its speaker as an unreliable narrator.
3. What do we know about the old man in the story? What motivates the narrator to kill him?
4. In spite of all his precautions, the narrator does not commit the perfect crime. What trips him up?
5. How do you account for the police officers' chatting calmly with the murderer instead of reacting to the sound that stirs the murderer into a frenzy?
6. See the students' comments on this story on pages 1350 and 1354. What do they point out that enlarges your own appreciation of Poe's art?

Doris Lessing

A WOMAN ON A ROOF   1963

Doris Lessing was born Doris Taylor in Iran in 1919. At five she moved with her family to a remote farm in the white-controlled British colony of Rhodesia (today Zimbabwe). She attended a convent school in Salisbury, the capital city. Like Isak Dinesen, Lessing found that her African experience nurtured her early writing: her experience led to her first novel, The Grass Is Singing *(1950), and two collections of short stories. In her teens she quit school, an act of defiance against her mother's plans to give her a proper, ladylike British education. In 1949, with her third child, she settled in*

London to earn her living as a writer. For a short time she belonged to the British Communist party, working as an organizer. Soon Lessing attracted a following in Britain and America for her five-novel series, Children of Violence *(1950 – 69), based on her own varied experiences, and* The Golden Notebook *(1962), exploring the lives of intelligent women who struggle for independence. Though Lessing became a heroine to feminists, she has declared herself mainly interested in larger social and cultural issues. Lately these questions have led her to write a five-volume series of science-fiction novels,* Canopus in Argus: Archives *(1979 – 83). With* The Good Terrorist *(1985), Lessing returned to the realistic vein of fiction that made her famous.*

It was during the week of hot sun, that June.

Three men were at work on the roof, where the leads got so hot they had the idea of throwing water on to cool them. But the water steamed, then sizzled; and they made jokes about getting an egg from some woman in the flats under them, to poach it for their dinner. By two it was not possible to touch the guttering they were replacing, and they speculated about what workmen did in regularly hot countries. Perhaps they should borrow kitchen gloves with the egg? They were all a bit dizzy, not used to the heat; and they shed their coats and stood side by side squeezing themselves into a foot-wide patch of shade against a chimney, careful to keep their feet in the thick socks and boots out of the sun. There was a fine view across several acres of roofs. Not far off a man sat in a deck chair reading the newspapers. Then they saw her, between chimneys, about fifty yards away. She lay face down on a brown blanket. They could see the top part of her: black hair, a flushed solid back, arms spread out.

"She's stark naked," said Stanley, sounding annoyed.

Harry, the oldest, a man of about forty-five, said: "Looks like it."

Young Tom, seventeen, said nothing, but he was excited and grinning. 5

Stanley said: "Someone'll report her if she doesn't watch out."

"She thinks no one can see," said Tom, craning his head all ways to see more.

At this point the woman, still lying prone, brought her two hands up behind her shoulders with the ends of a scarf in them, tied it behind her back, and sat up. She wore a red scarf tied around her breasts and brief red bikini pants. This being the first day of the sun she was white, flushing red. She sat smoking, and did not look up when Stanley let out a wolf whistle. Harry said: "Small things amuse small minds," leading the way back to their part of the roof, but it was scorching. Harry said: "Wait, I'm going to rig up some shade," and disappeared down the skylight into the building. Now that he'd gone, Stanley and Tom went to the farthest point they could to peer at the woman. She had moved, and all they could see were two pink legs stretched on the blanket. They whistled and shouted but the legs did not move. Harry came back with a blanket and shouted: "Come on, then." He sounded irritated with them. They clambered back to him and he said to Stanley: "What about your missus?" Stanley was newly married, about three months. Stanley said, jeering: "What about my missus?" — preserving his independence. Tom said nothing, but his mind was full of the nearly naked woman. Harry slung the blanket, which he had borrowed from a friendly woman downstairs, from the stem of a television aerial to a row of chimney-pots. This shade fell across the piece of gutter they had to replace. But the shade kept moving, they had to adjust the blanket, and not much progress was made. At last some of the heat left the roof, and they worked fast, making up for lost time. First Stanley, then Tom, made a trip to the end of the roof to see the woman. "She's on her back," Stanley said, adding a jest which made Tom snicker, and the older man smile tolerantly. Tom's report was that she hadn't moved, but it was a lie. He wanted to keep what he had seen to himself: he had caught her in the act of rolling down the little red pants over her hips, till they were no more than a small triangle. She was on her back, fully visible, glistening with oil.

Next morning, as soon as they came up, they went to look. She was already there, face down, arms spread out, naked except for the little red pants. She had turned brown in the night. Yesterday she was a scarlet-and-white woman, today she was a brown woman. Stanley let out a whistle. She lifted her head, startled, as if she'd been asleep, and looked straight over at them. The sun was in her eyes, she blinked and stared, then she dropped her head again. At this gesture of indifference, they all three, Stanley, Tom and old Harry, let out whistles and yells. Harry was doing it in parody of the younger men, making fun of them, but he was also angry. They were all angry because of her utter indifference to the three men watching her.

"Bitch," said Stanley.   10

"She should ask us over," said Tom, snickering.

Harry recovered himself and reminded Stanley: "If she's married, her old man wouldn't like that."

"Christ," said Stanley virtuously, "if my wife lay about like that, for everyone to see, I'd soon stop her."

Harry said, smiling: "How do you know, perhaps she's sunning herself at this very moment?"

"Not a chance, not on our roof." The safety of his wife put Stanley into   15 a good humor, and they went to work. But today it was hotter than yesterday; and several times one or the other suggested they should tell Matthew, the foreman, and ask to leave the roof until the heat wave was over. But they didn't. There was work to be done in the basement of the big block of flats, but up here they felt free, on a different level from ordinary humanity shut in the streets or the buildings. A lot more people came out on to the roofs that day, for an hour at midday. Some married couples sat side by side in deck chairs, the women's legs stockingless and scarlet, the men in vests with reddening shoulders.

The woman stayed on her blanket, turning herself over and over. She ignored them, no matter what they did. When Harry went off to fetch more screws, Stanley said: "Come on." Her roof belonged to a different system of roofs, separated from theirs at one point by about twenty feet. It meant a scrambling climb from one level to another, edging along parapets, clinging to chimneys, while their big boots slipped and slithered, but at last they stood on a small square projecting roof looking straight down at her, close. She sat smoking, reading a book. Tom thought she looked like a poster, or a magazine cover, with the blue sky behind her and her legs stretched out. Behind her a great crane at work on a new building in Oxford Street° swung its black arm across roofs in a great arc. Tom imagined himself at work on the crane, adjusting the arm to swing over and pick her up and swing her back across the sky to drop her near him.

They whistled. She looked up at them, cool and remote, then went on reading. Again, they were furious. Or, rather, Stanley was. His sun-heated face was screwed into a rage as he whistled again and again, trying to make her look up. Young Tom stopped whistling. He stood beside Stanley, excited, grinning; but he felt as if he were saying to the woman: Don't associate me with *him*, for his grin was apologetic. Last night he had thought of the unknown woman before he slept, and she had been tender with him. This tenderness he was remembering as he shifted his feet by the jeering, whistling Stanley, and watched the indifferent, healthy brown woman a few feet off, with the gap that plunged to the street between them. Tom thought it was romantic, it was like being high on two hilltops. But there was a shout from Harry, and they clambered back. Stanley's face was hard, really angry. The boy kept looking at him and wondered why he hated the woman so much, for by now he loved her.

They played their little games with the blanket, trying to trap shade to work under; but again it was not until nearly four that they could work seriously, and they were exhausted, all three of them. They were grumbling about the weather by now. Stanley was in a thoroughly bad humor. When they made their routine trip to see the woman before they packed up for the day, she was apparently asleep, face down, her back all naked save for the scarlet triangle on her buttocks. "I've got a good mind to report her to the police," said Stanley, and Harry said: "What's eating you? What harm's she doing?"

"I tell you, if she was my wife!"

"But she isn't, is she?" Tom knew that Harry, like himself, was uneasy   20 at Stanley's reaction. He was normally a sharp young man, quick at his work, making a lot of jokes, good company.

"Perhaps it will be cooler tomorrow," said Harry.

But it wasn't; it was hotter, if anything, and the weather forecast said the good weather would last. As soon as they were on the roof, Harry went over to see if the woman was there, and Tom knew it was to prevent Stanley going, to put off his bad humor. Harry had grownup children, a boy the same age as Tom, and the youth trusted and looked up to him.

Harry came back and said: "She's not there."

"I bet her old man has put his foot down," said Stanley, and Harry and Tom caught each other's eyes and smiled behind the young married man's back.

Harry suggested they should get permission to work in the basement,   25 and they did, that day. But before packing up Stanley said: "Let's have a breath of fresh air." Again Harry and Tom smiled at each other as they followed Stanley up to the roof. Tom in the devout conviction that he was there to protect the woman from Stanley. It was about five-thirty, and a calm, full

Oxford Street: busy shopping street in central London.

sunlight lay over the roofs. The great crane still swung its black arm from Oxford Street to above their heads. She was not there. Then there was a flutter of white from behind a parapet, and she stood up, in a belted, white dressing-gown. She had been there all day, probably, but on a different patch of roof, to hide from them. Stanley did not whistle; he said nothing, but watched the woman bend to collect papers, books, cigarettes, then fold the blanket over her arm. Tom was thinking: If they weren't here, I'd go over and say . . . what? But he knew from his nightly dreams of her that she was kind and friendly. Perhaps she would ask him down to her flat? Perhaps . . . He stood watching her disappear down the skylight. As she went, Stanley let out a shrill derisive yell; she started, and it seemed as if she nearly fell. She clutched to save herself, they could hear things falling. She looked straight at them, angry. Harry said, facetiously: "Better be careful on those slippery ladders, love." Tom knew he said it to save her from Stanley, but she could not know it. She vanished, frowning. Tom was full of a secret delight, because he knew her anger was for the others, not for him.

"Roll on some rain," said Stanley, bitter, looking at the blue evening sky.

Next day was cloudless, and they decided to finish the work in the basement. They felt excluded, shut in the grey cement basement fitting pipes, from the holiday atmosphere of London in a heat wave. At lunchtime they came up for some air, but while the married couples, and the men in shirt-sleeves or vests, were there, she was not there, either on her usual patch of roof or where she had been yesterday. They all, even Harry, clambered about, between chimney-pots, over parapets, the hot leads stinging their fingers. There was not a sign of her. They took off their shirts and vests and exposed their chests, feeling their feet sweaty and hot. They did not mention the woman. But Tom felt alone again. Last night she had him into her flat: it was big and had fitted white carpets and a bed with a padded white leather head-board. She wore a black filmy negligée and her kindness to Tom thickened his throat as he remembered it. He felt she had betrayed him by not being there.

And again after work they climbed up, but still there was nothing to be seen of her. Stanley kept repeating that if it was as hot as this tomorrow he wasn't going to work and that's all there was to it. But they were all there next day. By ten the temperature was in the middle seventies, and it was eighty long before noon. Harry went to the foreman to say it was impossible to work on the leads in that heat; but the foreman said there was nothing else he could put them on, and they'd have to. At midday they stood, silent, watching the skylight on her roof open, and then she slowly emerged in her white gown, holding a bundle of blanket. She looked at them, gravely, then went to the part of the roof where she was hidden from them. Tom was pleased. He felt she was more his when the other men couldn't see her. They had taken off their shirts and vests, but now they put them back again, for they felt the sun bruising their flesh. "She must have the hide of a rhino," said Stanley, tugging at guttering and swearing. They stopped work, and sat in the shade, moving around behind chimney stacks. A woman came to water a yellow window box opposite them. She was middleaged, wearing a flowered summer dress. Stanley said to her: "We need a drink more than them." She smiled and said: "Better drop down to the pub quick, it'll be closing in a minute." They exchanged pleasantries, and she left them with a smile and a wave.

"Not like Lady Godiva°," said Stanley. "She can give us a bit of a chat and a smile."

"You didn't whistle at *her,* " said Tom, reproving.

"Listen to him," said Stanley, "you didn't whistle, then?"

But the boy felt as if he hadn't whistled, as if only Harry and Stanley had. He was making plans, when it was time to knock off work, to get left behind and somehow make his way over to the woman. The weather report said the hot spell was due to break, so he had to move quickly. But there was no chance of being left. The other two decided to knock off work at four, because they were exhausted. As they went down, Tom quickly climbed a parapet and hoisted himself higher by pulling his weight up a chimney. He caught a glimpse of her lying on her back, her knees up, eyes closed, a brown woman lolling in the sun. He slipped and clattered down, as Stanley looked for information: "She's gone down," he said. He felt as if he had protected her from Stanley, and that she must be grateful to him. He could feel the bond between the woman and himself.

Next day, they stood around on the landing below the roof, reluctant to climb up into the heat. The woman who had lent Harry the blanket came out and offered them a cup of tea. They accepted gratefully, and sat around Mrs. Pritchett's kitchen an hour or so, chatting. She was married to an airline pilot. A smart blonde, of about thirty, she had an eye for the handsome sharp-faced Stanley; and the two teased each other while Harry sat in a corner, watching, indulgent, though his expression reminded Stanley that he was married. And young Tom felt envious of Stanley's ease in badinage°; felt, too, that Stanley's getting off with Mrs. Pritchett left his romance with the woman on the roof safe and intact.

"I thought they said the heat wave'd break," said Stanley, sullen, as the time approached when they really would have to climb up into the sunlight.

"You don't like it, then?" asked Mrs. Pritchett.

"All right for some," said Stanley. "Nothing to do but lie about as if it was a beach up there. Do you ever go up?"

"Went up once," said Mrs. Pritchett. "But it's a dirty place up there, and it's too hot."

"Quite right too," said Stanley.

Then they went up, leaving the cool neat little flat and the friendly Mrs. Pritchett.

As soon as they were up they saw her. The three men looked at her, resentful at her ease in this punishing sun. Then Harry said, because of the expression on Stanley's face: "Come on, we've got to pretend to work, at least."

They had to wrench another length of guttering that ran beside a parapet out of its bed, so that they could replace it. Stanley took it in his two hands, tugged, swore, stood up. "Fuck it," he said, and sat down under a chimney.

Lady Godiva: Stanley compares the woman on the roof to the heroine of a medieval English legend. On a bet with her husband, to make him abolish a heavy tax on the people of Coventry, Godiva rode naked through the streets. No one was supposed to look at her. (Peeping Tom looked, and was struck blind.)

badinage: (French), teasing, playful conversation.

He lit a cigarette. "Fuck them," he said. "What do they think we are, lizards? I've got blisters all over my hands." Then he jumped up and climbed over the roofs and stood with his back to them. He put his fingers either side of his mouth and let out a shrill whistle. Tom and Harry squatted, not looking at each other, watching him. They could just see the woman's head, the beginnings of her brown shoulders. Stanley whistled again. Then he began stamping with his feet, and whistled and yelled and screamed at the woman, his face getting scarlet. He seemed quite mad, as he stamped and whistled, while the woman did not move, she did not move a muscle.

"Barmy," said Tom.

"Yes," said Harry, disapproving.

Suddenly the older man came to a decision. It was, Tom knew, to save some sort of scandal or real trouble over the woman. Harry stood up and began packing tools into a length of oily cloth. "Stanley," he said, commanding. At first Stanley took no notice, but Harry said: "Stanley, we're packing it in, I'll tell Matthew."

Stanley came back, cheeks mottled, eyes glaring.   45

"Can't go on like this," said Harry. "It'll break in a day or so. I'm going to tell Matthew we've got sunstroke, and if he doesn't like it, it's too bad." Even Harry sounded aggrieved, Tom noted. The small, competent man, the family man with his grey hair, who was never at a loss, sounded really off balance. "Come on," he said, angry. He fitted himself into the open square in the roof, and went down, watching his feet on the ladder. Then Stanley went, with not a glance at the woman. Then Tom, who, his throat beating with excitement, silently promised her on a backward glance: Wait for me, wait, I'm coming.

On the pavement Stanley said: "I'm going home." He looked white now, so perhaps he really did have sunstroke. Harry went off to find the foreman, who was at work on the plumbing of some flats down the street. Tom slipped back, not into the building they had been working on, but the building on whose roof the woman lay. He went straight up, no one stopping him. The skylight stood open, with an iron ladder leading up. He emerged on to the roof a couple of yards from her. She sat up, pushing back her black hair with both hands. The scarf across her breasts bound them tight, and brown flesh bulged around it. Her legs were brown and smooth. She stared at him in silence. The boy stood grinning, foolish, claiming the tenderness he expected from her.

"What do you want?" she asked.

"I . . . I came to . . . make your acquaintance," he stammered, grinning, pleading with her.

They looked at each other, the slight, scarlet-faced excited boy, and the   50
serious, nearly naked woman. Then, without a word, she lay down on her brown blanket, ignoring him.

"You like the sun, do you?" he enquired of her glistening back.

Not a word. He felt panic, thinking of how she had held him in her arms, stroked his hair, brought him where he sat, lordly, in her bed, a glass of some exhilarating liquor he had never tasted in life. He felt that if he knelt down, stroked her shoulders, her hair, she would turn and clasp him in her arms.

He said: "The sun's all right for you, isn't it?"

She raised her head, set her chin on two small fists. "Go away," she said.

He did not move. "Listen," she said, in a slow reasonable voice, where anger was kept in check, though with difficulty; looking at him, her face weary with anger, "if you get a kick out of seeing women in bikinis, why don't you take a sixpenny bus ride to the Lido°? You'd see dozens of them, without all this mountaineering."

She hadn't understood him. He felt her unfairness pale him. He stammered: "But I like you, I've been watching you and . . ." 55

"Thanks," she said, and dropped her face again, turned away from him.

She lay there. He stood there. She said nothing. She had simply shut him out. He stood, saying nothing at all, for some minutes. He thought: She'll have to say something if I stay. But the minutes went past, with no sign of them in her, except in the tension of her back, her thighs, her arms — the tension of waiting for him to go.

He looked up at the sky, where the sun seemed to spin in heat; and over the roofs where he and his mates had been earlier. He could see the heat quivering where they had worked. And they expect us to work in these conditions! he thought, filled with righteous indignation. The woman hadn't moved. A bit of hot wind blew her black hair softly; it shone, and was iridescent. He remembered how he had stroked it last night.

Resentment of her at last moved him off and away down the ladder, through the building, into the street. He got drunk then, in hatred of her.

Next day when he woke the sky was grey. He looked at the wet grey 60 and thought, vicious: Well, that's fixed you, hasn't it now? That's fixed you good and proper.

The three men were at work early on the cool leads, surrounded by damp drizzling roofs where no one came to sun themselves, black roofs, slimy with rain. Because it was cool now, they would finish the job that day, if they hurried.

QUESTIONS

1. What do you understand from the story's last line?
2. What is a *protagonist*? (See the definition on page 9, if necessary.) Who is the protagonist in this story?
3. Who tells the story? Does this narrator take us into the mind of each character? Of specific characters? Of one?
4. Suppose "A Woman on a Roof" were told in the first person, from the point of view of the sunbather herself. What do you think the story would lose, or gain?
5. Pay special notice to the setting in this story. How does weather help account for the behavior of the characters? Comment on the effectiveness of the descriptions of the heat wave; of the final rain.
6. Recall Stanley's calling the sunbather Lady Godiva. What is meaningful in Tom's name? How accurate is a critic's remark that this is "a recent rooftop version of the Godiva story"?
7. What do you think Doris Lessing is saying? Do you find her story a comment on any familiar attitudes of men toward women? Does she show any sympathy for the three men?

Lido: a section of London's Hyde Park.

Suggestions for Writing

1. Here is a writing exercise to help you sense what a difference a point of view makes. Write a short statement from the point of view of one of these characters:

    William Faulkner's Homer Barron (on "My Affair with Miss Emily").

    Frank O'Connor's Nora (on "Why My Brother Jackie Deserves Damnation").

    Doris Lessing's woman on the roof (on "The Difficulties of Sunbathing").

2. Write a brief narrative account of a decisive moment in your life — one that changed your outlook or your future — from two quite different, contrasting points of view. One instance: a memory of buying a first car, told in two ways: from the first-person point of view of the buyer and from the third-person point of view of a worried parent or a gloating car dealer. Another example: An account of meeting a person who profoundly affected your life, from (1) your point of view and then (2) from the point of view of that other person.

3. Topic for an essay of two or three paragraphs: How William Faulkner Sees North and South in "A Rose for Emily."

4. Taking examples from short stories you have read, point out some differences between male and female ways of looking at things. Some stories especially to consider: "A & P" and "First Confession"; also "The Jilting of Granny Weatherall" (in Chapter Four) and "I Stand Here Ironing" (in "Stories for Further Reading"). (Note: Because a character holds a certain attitude in a specific situation doesn't oblige you to argue that such an attitude is universally held by women and men.)

5. Adopt the point of view of a naive, innocent commentator — either a younger, less-knowing version of yourself, or some imagined character. From this point of view, discuss the proposed ban of nuclear weapons, the case for legislation against the sale of pornography, or another issue in the news. Sound off like a true ignoramus. An effective paper will make clear to your reader that your speaker is full of malarkey. (This task means that you, the knowing writer, and not the uninformed speaker who is your mask, will need to know something about your subject.)

6. Choosing one of the "Stories for Further Reading" (pages 233 – 393), briefly describe whatever point of view you find in it. Then, in a paragraph or two, explain why this angle of vision seems right and fitting to the telling of this story. If you like, you may argue that the story might be told more effectively from some other point of view.

7. Write a one-paragraph story in the first person. Some recent small event in your life is a possible subject. Then rewrite your story from the *objective*, or "fly-on-the-wall," point of view. (See the passage by Dashiell Hammett on page 21 for an illustration.) Following your two terse stories, make a comment summing up what this exercise told you about point of view.

3 Setting

By the **setting** of a story, we mean its time and place. The word might remind you of the metal that holds a diamond in a ring, or of a *set* used in a play — perhaps a bare chair in front of a slab of painted canvas. But often, in an effective short story, setting may figure as more than mere background or underpinning. It can make things happen. It can prompt characters to act, bring them to realizations, or cause them to reveal their inmost natures.

To be sure, the idea of setting includes the physical environment of a story: a house, a street, a city, a landscape, a region. (*Where* a story takes place is sometimes called its **locale**.) Physical places mattered so greatly to French novelist Honoré de Balzac that sometimes, before writing a story set in a town, he would visit that town, select a few houses, and describe them in detail, down to their very smells. "The place in which an event occurred," Henry James admiringly said of him, "was in his view of equal moment with the event itself . . . it had a part to play; it needed to be made as definite as anything else."

But besides place, setting may crucially involve the *time* of the story — hour, year, or century. It might matter greatly that a story takes place at dawn, or on the day of the first moon landing. When we begin to read a historical novel, we are soon made aware that we aren't reading about life in the 1980s. In *The Scarlet Letter,* nineteenth-century author Nathaniel Hawthorne, by a long introduction and a vivid opening scene at a prison door, prepares us to witness events in the Puritan community of Boston in the earlier seventeenth century. This setting, together with scenes of Puritan times we recall from high school history, helps us understand what happens in the novel. We can appreciate the shocked agitation in town when a woman is accused of adultery: she has given illegitimate birth. Such an event might seem more nearly common today, but in the stern, God-fearing New England Puritan community, it was a flagrant defiance of church and state, which are all-powerful (and are all one). That reader will make no sense of *The Scarlet Letter* who ignores its setting — if to ignore the setting is possible, so much attention does Hawthorne pay to it.

That Hawthorne's novel takes place in a time remote from our own leads us to expect different customs, different attitudes. Some critics and teachers regard the setting of a story as its whole society, including the beliefs and assumptions of its characters, which might well be a helpful way of looking at *The Scarlet Letter*. From this view, the setting of Frank O'Connor's "First Confession" might be said to include not just a church and a confessional, but turn-of-the-century Irish Catholicism and the ritual of going to confession. Still, we suggest that for now you keep your working definition of *setting* simple. Call it time and place. If later you should feel that your definition needs widening and deepening, you can always widen and deepen it.

Besides time and place, setting may also include the weather — which indeed, in some stories, may be crucial. Climate seems as substantial as any character in William Faulkner's "Dry September." After sixty-two rainless days, a long-unbroken spell of late-summer heat has frayed every nerve in a small town and caused the main character, a hotheaded white supremacist, to feel more and more irritation. The weather, someone remarks, is "enough to make a man do anything." When a false report circulates that a woman has been raped by a black man, the rumor, like a match flung into a dry field, ignites rage and provokes a lynching. Evidently, to understand the story we have to recognize its locale, a small town in Mississippi. The action (the 1930s) and that infernal heat wave matter, too. Fully to take in the meaning of Faulkner's story, we have to take in the setting in its entirety.

Physical place, by the way, is especially vital to a **regional writer,** who usually sets stories (or other work) in one geographic area. Such a writer, often a native of the place, tries to bring it alive to readers who live no matter where. William Faulkner, a distinguished regional writer, almost always sets his novels and stories in his native Mississippi. Though born in St. Louis, Kate Chopin became known as a regional writer for writing about Louisiana in many of her short stories and in her novel *The Awakening.* Willa Cather, for her novels of frontier Nebraska, often is regarded as another outstanding regionalist (though she also set fiction in Quebec, the Southwest, and in "Paul's Case," in Pittsburgh and New York). The expression is generally heard only in discussions of American and Canadian writing. (In a sense, we might think of James Joyce as a regional writer, in that all his fiction takes place in the city of Dublin, but instead we usually call him an Irish one.)

As such writers show, a place can profoundly affect the character who grew up in it. Willa Cather is fond of portraying strong-minded, independent women, such as the heroine of her novel *My Ántonia,* strengthened in part by years of coping with the hardships of life on the wind-lashed prairie. Not that every writer of stories in which a place matters greatly will draw the characters as helpless puppets of their environment. Few writers do so, although that may be what you find in novels of **naturalism** — fiction of grim realism, in which the writer observes human characters like a scientist observing ants, seeing them as the products and victims of environment and heredity.[1] Theodore Dreiser carries on the tradition of naturalism in novels such as *The Financier* (1912). It begins in a city setting. A young lad (who will grow up to be a ruthless industrialist) is watching a battle to death between a lobster and a squid in a fish-market tank. Dented for the rest of his life by this grim scene, he decides that's exactly the way to live in human society.

Setting may operate more subtly than that fish tank. Often, setting and character will reveal each other. Recall how Faulkner, at the start of "A Rose for Emily," depicts Emily Grierson's house, once handsome but now "an eyesore among eyesores" surrounded by gas stations. Still standing, refusing to yield its old-time horse-and-buggy splendor to the age of the automobile, the house in "its stubborn and coquettish decay" embodies the character of its owner. In some fiction, setting is closely bound with theme (what the story is saying) — as you will find in John Steinbeck's "The Chrysanthemums" (Chapter 8), a story beginning with a fog that has sealed off a valley from the rest of the world — a fog like the lid on a pot. In *The Scarlet Letter,* even small details contain powerful hints. At the beginning of his story, Hawthorne remarks of a colonial jailhouse:

> Before this ugly edifice, and between it and the wheel-track of the street, was a grass-plot, much overgrown with burdock, pigweed, apple-peru, and such unsightly vegetation, which evidently found something congenial in the soil that had so early borne the black flower of civilized society, a prison. But, on one side of the portal, and rooted almost at the threshold, was a wild rose-bush, covered, in this month of June, with its delicate gems, which might be imagined to offer their fragrance and fragile beauty to the prisoner as he went in, and to the condemned criminal as he came forth to his doom, in token that the deep heart of Nature could pity and be kind to him.

Apparently, Hawthorne wishes to show us that Puritan Boston, a town of rutted streets and an ugly jail with a tangled grass-plot, may be rough but has beauty in it. As the story unfolds, he will further suggest (among other things) that secret sin and a beautiful child may go together like pigweed and wild roses. In his artfully crafted novel, setting is one with — not separate from — characters, theme, and symbols.

In some stories, a writer will seem to draw a setting mainly to evoke atmosphere. In such a story, setting starts us feeling whatever the storyteller would have us feel. In "The Tell-Tale Heart," Poe's setting the action in an old, dark, lantern-lit house greatly contributes to our sense of unease — and so helps the story's effectiveness. (Old, dark mansions are favorite

[1]The founder of naturalism in fiction was French novelist Émile Zola (1840 – 1902), who in a vast series of twenty novels about the family Rougon-Macquart traced a case of syphilis through several generations. In America, Stephen Crane wrote an early naturalist novel, *Maggie: A Girl of the Streets* (1893), and showed the way for later novelists such as Dreiser, Frank Norris, Upton Sinclair, and James T. Farrell.

settings for the Gothic story, a long-popular kind of fiction mentioned again on page 223.)

But be warned: you'll meet stories in which setting appears hardly to matter. In W. Somerset Maugham's fable, "The Appointment in Samarra," all we need be told about the setting is that it is a marketplace in Bagdad. In that brief fable, the inevitability of death is the point, not an exotic setting. In this chapter, though, you will meet three fine stories in which setting, for one reason or another, counts greatly. Without it, none of these stories could happen.

James Joyce
ARABY   1905

James Joyce (1884 – 1941) quit Ireland at twenty to spend his mature life in voluntary exile on the continent, writing of nothing but Dublin, where he was born. In Trieste, Zurich, and Paris, he supported his family with difficulty, sometimes teaching in Berlitz language schools, until his writing won him fame and wealthy patrons. At first Joyce met difficulty in getting his work printed and circulated. Publication of Dubliners *(1914), the collection of stories that includes "Araby," was delayed seven years because its prospective Irish publisher feared libel suits. (The book depicts local citizens, some of them recognizable, and views Dubliners mostly as a thwarted, self-deceived lot.)* Portrait of the Artist as a Young Man *(1916), a novel of thinly veiled autobiography, recounts a young intellectual's breaking away from country, church, and home. Joyce's immense comic novel,* Ulysses *(1922), a parody of the Odyssey, spans eighteen hours in the life of a wandering Jew, a Dublin seller of advertising. Frank about sex but untitillating, the book was banned at one time by the U.S. Post Office. Joyce's later work stepped up its demands on readers. The challenging* Finnegans Wake *(1939), if read aloud, sounds as though a learned comic poet were sleep-talking, jumbling several languages. Joyce was an innovator whose bold experiments showed many other writers possibilities in fiction that had not earlier been imagined.*

North Richmond Street, being blind°, was a quiet street except at the hour when the Christian Brothers' School set the boys free. An uninhabited house of two stories stood at the blind end, detached from its neighbors in a square ground. The other houses of the street, conscious of decent lives within them, gazed at one another with brown imperturbable faces.

The former tenant of our house, a priest, had died in the back drawing-room. Air, musty from having long been enclosed, hung in all the rooms, and the waste room behind the kitchen was littered with old useless papers.

being blind: being a dead-end street.

Among these I found a few paper-covered books, the pages of which were curled and damp: *The Abbot,* by Walter Scott, *The Devout Communicant* and *The Memoirs of Vidocq°.* I liked the last best because its leaves were yellow. The wild garden behind the house contained a central apple-tree and a few straggling bushes under one of which I found the late tenant's rusty bicycle-pump. He had been a very charitable priest; in his will he had left all his money to institutions and the furniture of his house to his sister.

When the short days of winter came dusk fell before we had well eaten our dinners. When we met in the street the houses had grown somber. The space of sky above us was the color of ever-changing violet and towards it the lamps of the street lifted their feeble lanterns. The cold air stung us and we played till our bodies glowed. Our shouts echoed in the silent street. The career of our play brought us through the dark muddy lanes behind the houses where we ran the gantlet of the rough tribes from the cottages, to the back doors of the dark dripping gardens where odors arose from the ashpits, to the dark odorous stables where a coachman smoothed and combed the horse or shook music from the buckled harness. When we returned to the street light from the kitchen windows had filled the areas. If my uncle was seen turning the corner we hid in the shadow until we had seen him safely housed. Or if Mangan's sister° came out on the doorstep to call her brother in to his tea we watched her from our shadow peer up and down the street. We waited to see whether she would remain or go in and, if she remained, we left our shadow and walked up to Mangan's steps resignedly. She was waiting for us, her figure defined by the light from the half-opened door. Her brother always teased her before he obeyed and I stood by the railings looking at her. Her dress swung as she moved her body and the soft rope of her hair tossed from side to side.

Every morning I lay on the floor in the front parlor watching her door. The blind was pulled down within an inch of the sash so that I could not be seen. When she came out on the doorstep my heart leaped. I ran to the hall, seized my books and followed her. I kept her brown figure always in my eye and, when we came near the point at which our ways diverged, I quickened my pace and passed her. This happened morning after morning. I had never spoken to her, except for a few casual words, and yet her name was like a summons to all my foolish blood.

Her image accompanied me even in places the most hostile to romance. 5 On Saturday evenings when my aunt went marketing I had to go to carry some of the parcels. We walked through the flaring streets, jostled by drunken men and bargaining women, amid the curses of laborers, the shrill litanies of shop-boys who stood on guard by the barrels of pigs' cheeks, the nasal chanting of street singers, who sang a *come-all-you* about O'Donovan Rossa°, or a ballad

The Abbot . . . Vidocq: a popular historical romance (1820); a book of pious meditations by an eighteenth-century English Franciscan, Pacificus Baker; and the autobiography of François-Jules Vidocq (1775 – 1857), a criminal who later turned detective.

Mangan's sister: an actual young woman in this story, but the phrase recalls Irish poet James Clarence Mangan (1803 – 1849) and his best-known poem, "Dark Rosaleen," which personifies Ireland as a beautiful woman for whom the poet yearns.

come-all-you about O'Donovan Rossa: the street singers earned their living by singing timely songs that usually began, "Come all you gallant Irishmen / And listen to my song." Their subject, about the troubles in our native land. These noises converged in a single sensation of life for me: I imagined that I bore my chalice safely through the throng of foes. Her name sprang to my lips at moments in strange prayers and praises which I myself did not understand. My eyes were often full of tears (I could not tell why) and at times a flood from my heart seemed to pour itself out into my bosom. I thought little of the future. I did not know whether I would ever speak to her or not or, if I spoke to her, how I could tell her of my confused adoration. But my body was like a harp and her words and gestures were like fingers running upon the wires.

One evening I went into the back drawing-room in which the priest had died. It was a dark rainy evening and there was no sound in the house. Through one of the broken panes I heard the rain impinge upon the earth, the fine incessant needles of water playing in the sodden beds. Some distant lamp or lighted window gleamed below me. I was thankful that I could see so little. All my senses seemed to desire to veil themselves and, feeling that I was about to slip from them, I pressed the palms of my hands together until they trembled, murmuring: *O love! O love!* many times.

At last she spoke to me. When she addressed the first words to me I was so confused that I did not know what to answer. She asked me was I going to *Araby.* I forget whether I answered yes or no. It would be a splendid bazaar, she said; she would love to go.

— And why can't you? I asked.

While she spoke she turned a silver bracelet round and round her wrist. She could not go, she said, because there would be a retreat that week in her convent°. Her brother and two other boys were fighting for their caps and I was alone at the railings. She held one of the spikes, bowing her head towards me. The light from the lamp opposite our door caught the white curve of her neck, lit up her hair that rested there and, falling, lit up the hand upon the railing. It fell over one side of her dress and caught the white border of a petticoat, just visible as she stood at ease.

— It's well for you, she said.   10

— If I go, I said, I will bring you something.

What innumerable follies laid waste my waking and sleeping thoughts after that evening! I wished to annihilate the tedious intervening days. I chafed against the work of school. At night in my bedroom and by day in the classroom her image came between me and the page I strove to read. The syllables of the word *Araby* were called to me through the silence in which my soul luxuriated and cast an Eastern enchantment over me. I asked for leave to go to the bazaar on Saturday night. My aunt was surprised and hoped it was not some Freemason° affair. I answered few questions in class. I watched my master's face pass from amiability to sternness; he hoped I was

---

also called Dynamite Rossa, was a popular hero jailed by the British for advocating violent rebellion.

a retreat . . . in her convent: a week devoted to religious observances more intense than usual, at the convent school Miss Mangan attends; probably she will have to listen to a number of Hellfire sermons.

Freemason: Catholics in Ireland viewed the masonic order as a Protestant conspiracy against them.

not beginning to idle. I could not call my wandering thoughts together. I had hardly any patience with the serious work of life which, now that it stood between me and my desire, seemed to me child's play, ugly monotonous child's play.

On Saturday morning I reminded my uncle that I wished to go to the bazaar in the evening. He was fussing at the hall-stand, looking for the hat-brush, and answered me curtly:

— Yes, boy, I know.

As he was in the hall I could not go into the front parlor and lie at the window. I left the house in bad humor and walked slowly towards the school. The air was pitilessly raw and already my heart misgave me.

When I came home to dinner my uncle had not yet been home. Still it was early. I sat staring at the clock for some time and, when its ticking began to irritate me, I left the room. I mounted the staircase and gained the upper part of the house. The high cold empty gloomy rooms liberated me and I went from room to room singing. From the front window I saw my companions playing below in the street. Their cries reached me weakened and indistinct and, leaning my forehead against the cool glass, I looked over at the dark house where she lived. I may have stood there for an hour, seeing nothing but the brown-clad figure cast by my imagination, touched discreetly by the lamplight at the curved neck, at the hand upon the railings and at the border below the dress.

When I came downstairs again I found Mrs. Mercer sitting at the fire. She was an old garrulous woman, a pawnbroker's widow, who collected used stamps for some pious purpose. I had to endure the gossip of the tea-table. The meal was prolonged beyond an hour and still my uncle did not come. Mrs. Mercer stood up to go: she was sorry she couldn't wait any longer, but it was after eight o'clock and she did not like to be out late, as the night air was bad for her. When she had gone I began to walk up and down the room, clenching my fists. My aunt said:

— I'm afraid you may put off your bazaar for this night of Our Lord.

At nine o'clock I heard my uncle's latchkey in the halldoor. I heard him talking to himself and heard the hall-stand rocking when it had received the weight of his overcoat. I could interpret these signs. When he was midway through his dinner I asked him to give me the money to go to the bazaar. He had forgotten.

— The people are in bed and after their first sleep now, he said.

I did not smile. My aunt said to him energetically:

— Can't you give him the money and let him go? You've kept him late enough as it is.

My uncle said he was very sorry he had forgotten. He said he believed in the old saying: *All work and no play makes Jack a dull boy.* He asked me where I was going and, when I had told him a second time he asked me did I know *The Arab's Farewell to His Steed°*. When I left the kitchen he was about to recite the opening lines of the piece to my aunt.

The Arab's Farewell to His Steed: This sentimental ballad by a popular poet, Caroline Norton (1808 – 1877), tells the story of a nomad of the desert who, in a fit of greed, sells his beloved horse, then regrets the loss and flings away the gold he has received. Notice the echo of "Araby" in the song title.

I held a florin tightly in my hand as I strode down Buckingham Street towards the station. The sight of the streets thronged with buyers and glaring with gas recalled to me the purpose of my journey. I took my seat in a third-class carriage of a deserted train. After an intolerable delay the train moved out of the station slowly. It crept onward among ruinous houses and over the twinkling river. At Westland Row Station a crowd of people pressed to the carriage doors; but the porters moved them back, saying that it was a special train for the bazaar. I remained alone in the bare carriage. In a few minutes the train drew up beside an improvised wooden platform. I passed out on to the road and saw by the lighted dial of a clock that it was ten minutes to ten. In front of me was a large building which displayed the magical name.

I could not find any sixpenny entrance and, fearing that the bazaar would 25 be closed, I passed in quickly through a turnstile, handing a shilling to a weary-looking man. I found myself in a big hall girdled at half its height by a gallery. Nearly all the stalls were closed and the greater part of the hall was in darkness. I recognized a silence like that which pervades a church after a service. I walked into the center of the bazaar timidly. A few people were gathered about the stalls which were still open. Before a curtain, over which the words *Café Chantant*° were written in colored lamps, two men were counting money on a salver°. I listened to the fall of the coins.

Remembering with difficulty why I had come I went over to one of the stalls and examined porcelain vases and flowered tea-sets. At the door of the stall a young lady was talking and laughing with two young gentlemen. I remarked their English accents and listened vaguely to their conversation.

— O, I never said such a thing!

— O, but you did!

— O, but I didn't!

— Didn't she say that? 30

— Yes. I heard her.

— O, there's a . . . fib!

Observing me the young lady came over and asked me did I wish to buy anything. The tone of her voice was not encouraging; she seemed to have spoken to me out of a sense of duty. I looked humbly at the great jars that stood like eastern guards at either side of the dark entrance to the stall and murmured:

— No, thank you.

The young lady changed the position of one of the vases and went back 35 to the two young men. They began to talk of the same subject. Once or twice the young lady glanced at me over her shoulder.

I lingered before her stall, though I knew my stay was useless, to make my interest in her wares seem the more real. Then I turned away slowly and walked down the middle of the bazaar. I allowed the two pennies to fall against the sixpence in my pocket. I heard a voice call from one end of the gallery that the light was out. The upper part of the hall was now completely dark.

Gazing up into the darkness I saw myself as a creature driven and derided by vanity; and my eyes burned with anguish and anger.

Café Chantant: name for a Paris nightspot featuring topical songs.
salver: a tray like that used in serving Holy Communion.

1. In general, how would you describe the physical setting of "Araby" as Joyce details it in the opening five paragraphs? Does he make Dublin strike you as a beautiful place, a merry place, an ugly place, or what? What do you make of the detail, in the opening sentence, that the boy's street has a dead-end?
2. What images are conjured up by the name of the bazaar?
3. At what other moments in the story does the boy romanticize, or project an air of enchantment upon the commonplace?
4. Exactly what, in his visit to the bazaar, does the boy find so bitterly disillusioning? Does his confrontation with reality take place only at the end? At what moments in the story — and in what details — does he confront the actual?
5. From what point of view does James Joyce tell this story? Does the narrator of "Araby" seem a boy — a naive or innocent narrator — or a mature man looking back through a boy's eyes?
6. Imagine "Araby" told from some other point of view. Why would the story probably be less moving and less effective?
7. Who besides the boy is a major character in the story? How do we know that the boy's view of this character is not the author's view? (It may help to look closely at some of the narrator's descriptions of the other major character, and of his own feelings.)
8. How does the time of day matter to this story? What is meaningful or suggestive, in the end, about the fall of night?

Kate Chopin

THE STORM   1898

Kate Chopin (1851 – 1904) was born Katherine O'Flaherty in St. Louis, daughter of an Irish immigrant grown wealthy in retailing. On his death, young Kate was raised by her mother's family: aristocratic Creoles, descendants of the French and Spaniards who had colonized Louisiana. Young Kate received a convent schooling, and at nineteen married Oscar Chopin, a Creole cotton broker from New Orleans. Later, the Chopins lived on a plantation near Cloutierville, Louisiana, a region whose varied people — Creoles, Cajuns, blacks — Kate Chopin was later to write about with loving care in Bayou Folk *(1894) and* A Night in Arcadie *(1897). The shock of her husband's sudden death in 1883, which left her with the raising of six children, seems to have plunged Kate Chopin into writing. She read and admired fine woman writers of her day, such as the Maine realist Sarah Orne Jewett. She also read Maupassant, Zola, and other new (and scandalous) French naturalist writers. She began to bring into American fiction some of their hard-eyed observation and their passion for telling unpleasant truths. Determined, in defiance of her times, frankly to show the sexual feelings of her characters, Chopin suffered from neglect and censorship. When her major novel,* The Awakening, *appeared in 1899, critics were outraged by her candid portrait of a woman who seeks sexual and professional independence. After causing such a literary scandal, Chopin was unable to get her later work published, and wrote little more before she died.* The Awakening *and many of her stories had to wait seven decades for a sympathetic audience.*

I

The leaves were so still that even Bibi thought it was going to rain. Bobinôt, who was accustomed to converse on terms of perfect equality with his little son, called the child's attention to certain somber clouds that were rolling with sinister intention from the west, accompanied by a sullen, threatening roar. They were at Friedheimer's store and decided to remain there till the storm had passed. They sat within the door on two empty kegs. Bibi was four years old and looked very wise.

"Mama'll be 'fraid, yes," he suggested with blinking eyes.

"She'll shut the house. Maybe she got Sylvie helpin' her this evenin'," Bobinôt responded reassuringly.

"No; she ent got Sylvie. Sylvie was helpin' her yistiday," piped Bibi.

Bobinôt arose and going across to the counter purchased a can of shrimps, of which Calixta was very fond. Then he returned to his perch on the keg and sat stolidly holding the can of shrimps while the storm burst. It shook the wooden store and seemed to be ripping great furrows in the distant field. Bibi laid his little hand on his father's knee and was not afraid.

II

Calixta, at home, felt no uneasiness for their safety. She sat at a side window sewing furiously on a sewing machine. She was greatly occupied and did not notice the approaching storm. But she felt very warm and often stopped to mop her face on which the perspiration gathered in beads. She unfastened her white sacque at the throat. It began to grow dark, and suddenly realizing the situation she got up hurriedly and went about closing windows and doors.

Out on the small front gallery she had hung Bobinôt's Sunday clothes to air and she hastened out to gather them before the rain fell. As she stepped outside, Alcée Laballière rode in at the gate. She had not seen him very often since her marriage, and never alone. She stood there with Bobinôt's coat in her hands, and the big rain drops began to fall. Alcée rode his horse under the shelter of a side projection where the chickens had huddled and there were plows and a harrow piled up in the corner.

"May I come and wait on your gallery till the storm is over, Calixta?" he asked.

"Come 'long in, M'sieur Alcée."

His voice and her own startled her as if from a trance, and she seized Bobinôt's vest. Alcée, mounting to the porch, grabbed the trousers and snatched Bibi's braided jacket that was about to be carried away by a sudden gust of wind. He expressed an intention to remain outside, but it was soon apparent that he might as well have been out in the open: the water beat in upon the boards in driving sheets, and he went inside, closing the door after him. It was even necessary to put something beneath the door to keep the water out.

"My! what a rain! It's good two years sence it rain' like that," exclaimed Calixta as she rolled up a piece of bagging and Alcée helped her to thrust it beneath the crack.

She was a little fuller of figure than five years before when she married; but she had lost nothing of her vivacity. Her blue eyes still retained their melting quality; and her yellow hair, dishevelled by the wind and rain, kinked more stubbornly than ever about her ears and temples.

The rain beat upon the low, shingled roof with a force and clatter that threatened to break an entrance and deluge them there. They were in the dining room — the sitting room — the general utility room. Adjoining was her bed room, with Bibi's couch along side her own. The door stood open, and the room with its white, monumental bed, its closed shutters, looked dim and mysterious.

Alcée flung himself into a rocker and Calixta nervously began to gather up from the floor the lengths of a cotton sheet which she had been sewing.

"If this keeps up, *Dieu sait*° if the levees goin' to stan' it!" she exclaimed.   15

"What have you got to do with the levees?"

"I got enough to do! An' there's Bobinôt with Bibi out in that storm — if he only didn' left Friedheimer's!"

"Let us hope, Calixta, that Bobinôt's got sense enough to come in out of a cyclone."

She went and stood at the window with a greatly disturbed look on her face. She wiped the frame that was clouded with moisture. It was stiflingly hot. Alcée got up and joined her at the window, looking over her shoulder. The rain was coming down in sheets obscuring the view of far-off cabins and enveloping the distant wood in a gray mist. The playing of the lightning was incessant. A bolt struck a tall chinaberry tree at the edge of the field. It filled all visible space with a blinding glare and the crash seemed to invade the very boards they stood upon.

Calixta put her hands to her eyes, and with a cry, staggered backward.   20
Alcée's arm encircled her, and for an instant he drew her close and spasmodically to him.

"*Bonte!*°" she cried, releasing herself from his encircling arm and retreating from the window, "the house'll go next! If I only knew w'ere Bibi was!" She would not compose herself; she would not be seated. Alcée clasped her shoulders and looked into her face. The contact of her warm, palpitating body when he had unthinkingly drawn her into his arms, had aroused all the old-time infatuation and desire for her flesh.

"Calixta," he said, "don't be frightened. Nothing can happen. The house is too low to be struck, with so many tall trees standing about. There! aren't you going to be quiet? say, aren't you?" He pushed her hair back from her face that was warm and steaming. Her lips were as red and moist as pomegranate seed. Her white neck and a glimpse of her full, firm bosom disturbed him

Dieu sait: God only knows.
Bonte!: Heavens!

powerfully. As she glanced up at him the fear in her liquid blue eyes had given place to a drowsy gleam that unconsciously betrayed a sensuous desire. He looked down into her eyes and there was nothing for him to do but to gather her lips in a kiss. It reminded him of Assumption°.

"Do you remember — in Assumption, Calixta?" he asked in a low voice broken by passion. Oh! she remembered; for in Assumption he had kissed her and kissed and kissed her; until his senses would well nigh fail, and to save her he would resort to a desperate flight. If she was not an immaculate dove in those days, she was still inviolate; a passionate creature whose very defenselessness had made her defense, against which his honor forbade him to prevail. Now — well, now — her lips seemed in a manner free to be tasted, as well as her round, white throat and her whiter breasts.

They did not heed the crashing torrents, and the roar of the elements made her laugh as she lay in his arms. She was a revelation in that dim, mysterious chamber; as white as the couch she lay upon. Her firm, elastic flesh that was knowing for the first time its birthright, was like a creamy lily that the sun invites to contribute its breath and perfume to the undying life of the world.

The generous abundance of her passion, without guile or trickery, was like a white flame which penetrated and found response in depths of his own sensuous nature that had never yet been reached.

When he touched her breasts they gave themselves up in quivering ecstasy, inviting his lips. Her mouth was a fountain of delight. And when he possessed her, they seemed to swoon together at the very borderland of life's mystery.

He stayed cushioned upon her, breathless, dazed, enervated, with his heart beating like a hammer upon her. With one hand she clasped his head, her lips lightly touching his forehead. The other hand stroked with a soothing rhythm his muscular shoulders.

The growl of the thunder was distant and passing away. The rain beat softly upon the shingles, inviting them to drowsiness and sleep. But they dared not yield.

The rain was over; and the sun was turning the glistening green world into a palace of gems. Calixta, on the gallery, watched Alcée ride away. He turned and smiled at her with a beaming face; and she lifted her pretty chin in the air and laughed aloud.

III

Bobinôt and Bibi, trudging home, stopped without at the cistern to make themselves presentable.

"My! Bibi, w'at will yo' mama say! You ought to be ashame'. You oughtn' put on those good pants. Look at 'em! An' that mud on yo' collar! How you got that mud on yo' collar, Bibi? I never saw such a boy!" Bibi was the picture of pathetic resignation. Bobinôt was the embodiment of serious solicitude as he strove to remove from his own person and his son's the signs of their tramp over heavy roads and through wet fields. He scraped the mud off Bibi's

Assumption: Feast day, August 15, to celebrate Mary's bodily rising to Heaven.

bare legs and feet with a stick and carefully removed all traces from his heavy brogans. Then, prepared for the worst — the meeting with an over-scrupulous housewife, they entered cautiously at the back door.

Calixta was preparing supper. She had set the table and was dripping coffee at the hearth. She sprang up as they came in.

"Oh, Bobinôt! You back! My! but I was uneasy. W'ere you been during the rain? An' Bibi? he ain't wet? he ain't hurt?" She had clasped Bibi and was kissing him effusively. Bobinôt's explanations and apologies which he had been composing all along the way, died on his lips as Calixta felt him to see if he were dry, and seemed to express nothing but satisfaction at their safe return.

"I brought you some shrimps, Calixta," offered Bobinôt, hauling the can from his ample side pocket and laying it on the table.

"Shrimps! Oh, Bobinôt! you too good fo' anything!" and she gave him a smacking kiss on the cheek that resounded. *"J'vous reponds°*, we'll have a feas' to night! umph-umph!" 35

Bobinôt and Bibi began to relax and enjoy themselves, and when the three seated themselves at table they laughed much and so loud that anyone might have heard them as far away as Laballière's.

IV

Alcée Laballière wrote to his wife, Clarisse, that night. It was a loving letter, full of tender solicitude. He told her not to hurry back, but if she and the babies liked it at Biloxi, to stay a month longer. He was getting on nicely; and though he missed them, he was willing to bear the separation a while longer — realizing that their health and pleasure were the first things to be considered.

V

As for Clarisse, she was charmed upon receiving her husband's letter. She and the babies were doing well. The society was agreeable; many of her old friends and acquaintances were at the bay. And the first free breath since her marriage seemed to restore the pleasant liberty of her maiden days. Devoted as she was to her husband, their intimate conjugal life was something which she was more than willing to forego for a while.

So the storm passed and everyone was happy.

QUESTIONS

1. Exactly where does Chopin's story take place? How can you tell?
2. What circumstances introduced in Part I turn out to have a profound effect on events in the story?
3. What details in "The Storm" emphasize the fact that Bobinôt loves his wife? What details reveal how imperfectly he comprehends her nature?
4. What general attitudes toward sex, love, and marriage does Chopin imply? Cite evidence to support your answer.

J'vous reponds: Let me tell you.

5. What meanings do you find in the title "The Storm"?
6. In the story as a whole, how do setting and plot reinforce each other?

T. Coraghessan Boyle
GREASY LAKE
1985

T. Coraghessan Boyle (the "T" stands for Tom) was born in 1948 in Peekskill, New York, in the Hudson River Valley, a region about which he has been writing a novel that involves the lives of three families and spans three hundred years. A graduate of the University of Iowa Writers' Workshop, he now lives in Woodland Hills, California, and teaches creative writing at the University of Southern California. Winner of the St. Lawrence Award for Short Fiction and an Aga Khan Award from The Paris Review, *he contributes stories to* Antaeus, Esquire, The Atlantic, Iowa Review, Paris Review, TriQuarterly, *and other leading magazines. Boyle has published two novels: a ribald historical saga,* Water Music *(1982), which makes fiction out of an actual expedition to Africa led by Scottish explorer Mungo Park, and* Budding Prospects *(1984), a picaresque (or scoundrel-adventure) novel of life among marijuana growers. Boyle has also written two remarkable volumes of short stories:* The Descent of Man *(1979) and* Greasy Lake and Other Stories *(1985). His work has quickly won attention for its macabre humor, verve, and inventiveness — or, as critics have said, "tumbling exuberance" and "a raw ability to make one laugh." Another recent story imagines a love affair between Mrs. Nina Khrushchev and Dwight D. Eisenhower.*

It's about a mile down on the dark side of Route 88.
           — Bruce Springsteen

    There was a time when courtesy and winning ways went out of style, when it was good to be bad, when you cultivated decadence like a taste. We were all dangerous characters then. We wore torn-up leather jackets, slouched around with toothpicks in our mouths, sniffed glue and ether and what somebody claimed was cocaine. When we wheeled our parents' whining station wagons out into the street we left a patch of rubber half a block long. We drank gin and grape juice, Tango, Thunderbird, and Bali Hai. We were nineteen. We were bad. We read André Gide° and struck elaborate poses to show that we didn't give a shit about anything. At night, we went up to Greasy Lake.

    Through the center of town, up the strip, past the housing developments and shopping malls, street lights giving way to the thin streaming illumination of the headlights, trees crowding the asphalt in a black unbroken wall: that was the way out to Greasy Lake. The Indians had called it Wakan, a reference to

André Gide: controversial French writer (1869 – 1951) whose novels, including *The Counterfeiters* and *Lafcadio's Adventures,* often show individuals in conflict with accepted morality.

the clarity of its waters. Now it was fetid and murky, the mud banks glittering with broken glass and strewn with beer cans and the charred remains of bonfires. There was a single ravaged island a hundred yards from shore, so stripped of vegetation it looked as if the air force had strafed it. We went up to the lake because everyone went there, because we wanted to snuff the rich scent of possibility on the breeze, watch a girl take off her clothes and plunge into the festering murk, drink beer, smoke pot, howl at the stars, savor the incongruous full-throated roar of rock and roll against the primeval susurrus of frogs and crickets. This was nature.

I was there one night, late, in the company of two dangerous characters. Digby wore a gold star in his right ear and allowed his father to pay his tuition at Cornell; Jeff was thinking of quitting school to become a painter/musician/head-shop proprietor. They were both expert in the social graces, quick with a sneer, able to manage a Ford with lousy shocks over a rutted and gutted blacktop road at eighty-five while rolling a joint as compact as a Tootsie Roll Pop stick. They could lounge against a bank of booming speakers and trade "man"s with the best of them or roll out across the dance floor as if their joints worked on bearings. They were slick and quick and they wore their mirror shades at breakfast and dinner, in the shower, in closets and caves. In short, they were bad.

I drove. Digby pounded the dashboard and shouted along with Toots & the Maytals while Jeff hung his head out the window and streaked the side of my mother's Bel Air with vomit. It was early June, the air soft as a hand on your cheek, the third night of summer vacation. The first two nights we'd been out till dawn, looking for something we never found. On this, the third night, we'd cruised the strip sixty-seven times, been in and out of every bar and club we could think of in a twenty-mile radius, stopped twice for bucket chicken and forty-cent hamburgers, debated going to a party at the house of a girl Jeff's sister knew, and chucked two dozen raw eggs at mailboxes and hitchhikers. It was 2:00 A.M.; the bars were closing. There was nothing to do but take a bottle of lemon-flavored gin up to Greasy Lake.

The taillights of a single car winked at us as we swung into the dirt lot with its tufts of weed and washboard corrugations; '57 Chevy, mint, metallic blue. On the far side of the lot, like the exoskeleton of some gaunt chrome insect, a chopper leaned against its kickstand. And that was it for excitement: some junkie half-wit biker and a car freak pumping his girlfriend. Whatever it was we were looking for, we weren't about to find it at Greasy Lake. Not that night.

But then all of a sudden Digby was fighting for the wheel. "Hey, that's Tony Lovett's car! Hey!" he shouted, while I stabbed at the brake pedal and the Bel Air nosed up to the gleaming bumper of the parked Chevy. Digby leaned on the horn, laughing, and instructed me to put my brights on. I flicked on the brights. This was hilarious. A joke. Tony would experience premature withdrawal and expect to be confronted by grim-looking state troopers with flashlights. We hit the horn, strobed the lights, and then jumped out of the car to press our witty faces to Tony's windows; for all we knew we might even catch a glimpse of some little fox's tit, and then we could slap backs with red-faced Tony, roughhouse a little, and go on to new heights of adventure and daring.

The first mistake, the one that opened the whole floodgate, was losing my grip on the keys. In the excitement, leaping from the car with the gin in one hand and a roach clip in the other, I spilled them in the grass — in the dark, rank, mysterious nighttime grass of Greasy Lake. This was a tactical error, as damaging and irreversible in its way as Westmoreland's decision to dig in at Khe Sanh°. I felt it like a jab of intuition, and I stopped there by the open door, peering vaguely into the night that puddled up round my feet.

The second mistake — and this was inextricably bound up with the first — was identifying the car as Tony Lovett's. Even before the very bad character in greasy jeans and engineer boots ripped out of the driver's door, I began to realize that this chrome blue was much lighter than the robin's-egg of Tony's car, and that Tony's car didn't have rear-mounted speakers. Judging from their expressions, Digby and Jeff were privately groping toward the same inevitable and unsettling conclusion as I was.

In any case, there was no reasoning with this bad greasy character — clearly he was a man of action. The first lusty Rockette° kick of his steel-toed boot caught me under the chin, chipped my favorite tooth, and left me sprawled in the dirt. Like a fool, I'd gone down on one knee to comb the stiff hacked grass for the keys, my mind making connections in the most dragged-out, testudineous way, knowing that things had gone wrong, that I was in a lot of trouble, and that the lost ignition key was my grail and my salvation. The three or four succeeding blows were mainly absorbed by my right buttock and the tough piece of bone at the base of my spine.

Meanwhile, Digby vaulted the kissing bumpers and delivered a savage   10 kung-fu blow to the greasy character's collarbone. Digby had just finished a course in martial arts for phys-ed credit and had spent the better part of the past two nights telling us apocryphal tales of Bruce Lee types and of the raw power invested in lightning blows shot from coiled wrists, ankles, and elbows. The greasy character was unimpressed. He merely backed off a step, his face like a Toltec mask, and laid Digby out with a single whistling roundhouse blow . . . but by now Jeff had got into the act, and I was beginning to extricate myself from the dirt, a tinny compound of shock, rage, and impotence wadded in my throat.

Jeff was on the guy's back, biting at his ear. Digby was on the ground, cursing. I went for the tire iron I kept under the driver's seat. I kept it there because bad characters always keep tire irons under the driver's seat, for just such an occasion as this. Never mind that I hadn't been involved in a fight since sixth grade, when a kid with a sleepy eye and two streams of mucus depending from his nostrils hit me in the knee with a Louisville slugger°, never mind that I'd touched the tire iron exactly twice before, to change tires: it was there. And I went for it.

Westmoreland's decision . . . Khe Sanh: General William C. Westmoreland commanded United States troops in Vietnam (1964 – 68). In late 1967 the North Vietnamese and Viet Cong forces attacked Khe Sanh (or Khesanh) with a show of strength, causing Westmoreland to expend great effort to defend a plateau of relatively little tactical importance.

Rockette: member of a dancing troupe in the stage show at Radio City Music Hall, New York, famous for ability to kick fast and high with wonderful coordination.

Louisville slugger: a brand of baseball bat.

I was terrified. Blood was beating in my ears, my hands were shaking, my heart turning over like a dirtbike in the wrong gear. My antagonist was shirtless, and a single cord of muscle flashed across his chest as he bent forward to peel Jeff from his back like a wet overcoat. "Motherfucker," he spat, over and over, and I was aware in that instant that all four of us — Digby, Jeff, and myself included — were chanting "motherfucker, motherfucker," as if it were a battle cry. (What happened next? the detective asks the murderer from beneath the turned-down brim of his porkpie hat. I don't know, the murderer says, something came over me. Exactly.)

Digby poked the flat of his hand in the bad character's face and I came at him like a kamikaze, mindless, raging, stung with humiliation — the whole thing, from the initial boot in the chin to this murderous primal instant involving no more than sixty hyperventilating, gland-flooding seconds — I came at him and brought the tire iron down across his ear. The effect was instantaneous, astonishing. He was a stunt man and this was Hollywood, he was a big grimacing toothy balloon and I was a man with a straight pin. He collapsed. Wet his pants. Went loose in his boots.

A single second, big as a zeppelin, floated by. We were standing over him in a circle, gritting our teeth, jerking our necks, our limbs and hands and feet twitching with glandular discharges. No one said anything. We just stared down at the guy, the car freak, the lover, the bad greasy character laid low. Digby looked at me; so did Jeff. I was still holding the tire iron, a tuft of hair clinging to the crook like dandelion fluff, like down. Rattled, I dropped it in the dirt, already envisioning the headlines, the pitted faces of the police inquisitors, the gleam of handcuffs, clank of bars, the big black shadows rising from the back of the cell . . . when suddenly a raw torn shriek cut through me like all the juice in all the electric chairs in the country.

It was the fox. She was short, barefoot, dressed in panties and a man's shirt. "Animals!" she screamed, running at us with her fists clenched and wisps of blow-dried hair in her face. There was a silver chain round her ankle, and her toenails flashed in the glare of the headlights. I think it was the toenails that did it. Sure, the gin and the cannabis and even the Kentucky Fried may have had a hand in it, but it was the sight of those flaming toes that set us off — the toad emerging from the loaf in *Virgin Spring*°, lipstick smeared on a child: she was already tainted. We were on her like Bergman's deranged brothers — see no evil, hear none, speak none — panting, wheezing, tearing at her clothes, grabbing for flesh. We were bad characters, and we were scared and hot and three steps over the line — anything could have happened.

It didn't.

Before we could pin her to the hood of the car, our eyes masked with lust and greed and the purest primal badness, a pair of headlights swung into the lot. There we were, dirty, bloody, guilty, dissociated from humanity and civilization, the first of the Ur-crimes behind us, the second in progress, shreds of nylon panty and spandex brassiere dangling from our fingers, our flies open, lips licked — there we were, caught in the spotlight. Nailed.

We bolted. First for the car, and then, realizing we had no way of starting

Virgin Spring: film by Swedish director Ingmar Bergman.

it, for the woods. I thought nothing. I thought escape. The headlights came at me like accusing fingers. I was gone.

Ram-bam-bam, across the parking lot, past the chopper and into the feculent undergrowth at the lake's edge, insects flying up in my face, weeds whipping, frogs and snakes and red-eyed turtles splashing off into the night: I was already ankle-deep in muck and tepid water and still going strong. Behind me, the girl's screams rose in intensity, disconsolate, incriminating, the screams of the Sabine women°, the Christian martyrs, Anne Frank° dragged from the garret. I kept going, pursued by those cries, imagining cops and bloodhounds. The water was up to my knees when I realized what I was doing: I was going to swim for it. Swim the breadth of Greasy Lake and hide myself in the thick clot of woods on the far side. They'd never find me there.

I was breathing in sobs, in gasps. The water lapped at my waist as I looked out over the moon-burnished ripples, the mats of algae that clung to the surface like scabs. Digby and Jeff had vanished. I paused. Listened. The girl was quieter now, screams tapering to sobs, but there were male voices, angry, excited, and the high-pitched ticking of the second car's engine. I waded deeper, stealthy, hunted, the ooze sucking at my sneakers. As I was about to take the plunge — at the very instant I dropped my shoulder for the first slashing stroke — I blundered into something. Something unspeakable, obscene, something soft, wet, moss-grown. A patch of weed? A log? When I reached out to touch it, it gave like a rubber duck, it gave like flesh.

In one of those nasty little epiphanies for which we are prepared by films and TV and childhood visits to the funeral home to ponder the shrunken painted forms of dead grandparents, I understood what it was that bobbed there so inadmissibly in the dark. Understood, and stumbled back in horror and revulsion, my mind yanked in six different directions (I was nineteen, a mere child, an infant, and here in the space of five minutes I'd struck down one greasy character and blundered into the waterlogged carcass of a second), thinking, The keys, the keys, why did I have to go and lose the keys? I stumbled back, but the muck took hold of my feet — a sneaker snagged, balance lost — and suddenly I was pitching face forward into the buoyant black mass, throwing out my hands in desperation while simultaneously conjuring the image of reeking frogs and muskrats revolving in slicks of their own deliquescing juices. AAAAArrrgh! I shot from the water like a torpedo, the dead man rotating to expose a mossy beard and eyes cold as the moon. I must have shouted out, thrashing around in the weeds, because the voices behind me suddenly became animated.

"What was that?"

"It's them, it's them: they tried to, tried to . . . *rape* me!" Sobs.

A man's voice, flat Midwestern accent. "You sons a bitches, we'll kill you!"

20

Sabine women: members of an ancient tribe in Italy, according to legend, forcibly carried off by the early Romans under Romulus to be their wives. The incident is depicted in a famous painting, "The Rape of the Sabine Women," by seventeenth-century French artist Nicolas Poussin.

Anne Frank: German Jewish girl (1929 – 1945) whose diary written during the Nazi occupation of the Netherlands later became world famous. She hid with her family in a secret attic in Amsterdam, but was caught by storm troopers and sent to the concentration camp at Belsen, where she died.

Frogs, crickets.

Then another voice, harsh, r-less, Lower East Side: "Motherfucker!" I recognized the verbal virtuosity of the bad greasy character in the engineer boots. Tooth chipped, sneakers gone, coated in mud and slime and worse, crouching breathless in the weeds waiting to have my ass thoroughly and definitively kicked and fresh from the hideous stinking embrace of a three-days-dead-corpse, I suddenly felt a rush of joy and vindication: the son of a bitch was alive! Just as quickly, my bowels turned to ice. "Come on out of there, you pansy mothers!" the bad greasy character was screaming. He shouted curses till he was out of breath.

The crickets started up again, then the frogs. I held my breath. All at once there was a sound in the reeds, a swishing, a splash: thunk-a-thunk. They were throwing rocks. The frogs fell silent. I cradled my head. Swish, swish, thunk-a-thunk. A wedge of feldspar the size of a cue ball glanced off my knee. I bit my finger.

It was then that they turned to the car. I heard a door slam, a curse, and then the sound of the headlights shattering — almost a good-natured sound, celebratory, like corks popping from the necks of bottles. This was succeeded by the dull booming of the fenders, metal on metal, and then the icy crash of the windshield. I inched forward, elbows and knees, my belly pressed to the muck, thinking of guerrillas and commandos and *The Naked and the Dead*°. I parted the weeds and squinted the length of the parking lot.

The second car — it was a Trans-Am — was still running, its high beams washing the scene in a lurid stagy light. Tire iron flailing, the greasy bad character was laying into the side of my mother's Bel Air like an avenging demon, his shadow riding up the trunks of the trees. Whomp. Whomp. Whomp-whomp. The other two guys — blond types, in fraternity jackets — were helping out with tree branches and skull-sized boulders. One of them was gathering up bottles, rocks, muck, candy wrappers, used condoms, pop-tops, and other refuse and pitching it through the window on the driver's side. I could see the fox, a white bulb behind the windshield of the '57 Chevy. "Bobbie," she whined over the thumping, "come *on.*" The greasy character paused a moment, took one good swipe at the left taillight, and then heaved the tire iron halfway across the lake. Then he fired up the '57 and was gone.

Blond head nodded at blond head. One said something to the other, too low for me to catch. They were no doubt thinking that in helping to annihilate my mother's car they'd committed a fairly rash act, and thinking too that there were three bad characters connected with that very car watching them from the woods. Perhaps other possibilities occurred to them as well — police, jail cells, justices of the peace, reparations, lawyers, irate parents, fraternal censure. Whatever they were thinking, they suddenly dropped branches, bottles, and rocks and sprang for their car in unison, as if they'd choreographed it. Five seconds. That's all it took. The engine shrieked, the tires squealed, a cloud of dust rose from the rutted lot and then settled back on darkness.

I don't know how long I lay there, the bad breath of decay all around me, my jacket heavy as a bear, the primordial ooze subtly reconstituting itself to accommodate my upper thighs and testicles. My jaws ached, my knee throbbed, my coccyx was on fire. I contemplated suicide, wondered if I'd need

The Naked and the Dead: novel (1948) by Norman Mailer, of U.S. Army life in World War II.

bridgework, scraped the recesses of my brain for some sort of excuse to give my parents — a tree had fallen on the car, I was blindsided by a bread truck, hit and run, vandals had got to it while we were playing chess at Digby's. Then I thought of the dead man. He was probably the only person on the planet worse off than I was. I thought about him, fog on the lake, insects chirring eerily, and felt the tug of fear, felt the darkness opening up inside me like a set of jaws. Who was he, I wondered, this victim of time and circumstance bobbing sorrowfully in the lake at my back. The owner of the chopper, no doubt, a bad older character come to this. Shot during a murky drug deal, drowned while drunkenly frolicking in the lake. Another headline. My car was wrecked; he was dead.

When the eastern half of the sky went from black to cobalt and the trees began to separate themselves from the shadows, I pushed myself up from the mud and stepped out into the open. By now the birds had begun to take over for the crickets, and dew lay slick on the leaves. There was a smell in the air, raw and sweet at the same time, the smell of the sun firing buds and opening blossoms. I contemplated the car. It lay there like a wreck along the highway, like a steel sculpture left over from a vanished civilization. Everything was still. This was nature.

I was circling the car, as dazed and bedraggled as the sole survivor of an air blitz, when Digby and Jeff emerged from the trees behind me. Digby's face was crosshatched with smears of dirt; Jeff's jacket was gone and his shirt was torn across the shoulder. They slouched across the lot, looking sheepish, and silently came up beside me to gape at the ravaged automobile. No one said a word. After a while Jeff swung open the driver's door and began to scoop the broken glass and garbage off the seat. I looked at Digby. He shrugged. "At least they didn't slash the tires," he said.

It was true: the tires were intact. There was no windshield, the headlights were staved in, and the body looked as if it had been sledge-hammered for a quarter a shot at the county fair, but the tires were inflated to regulation pressure. The car was drivable. In silence, all three of us bent to scrape the mud and shattered glass from the interior. I said nothing about the biker. When we were finished, I reached in my pocket for the keys, experienced a nasty stab of recollection, cursed myself, and turned to search the grass. I spotted them almost immediately, no more than five feet from the open door, glinting like jewels in the first tapering shaft of sunlight. There was no reason to get philosophical about it: I eased into the seat and turned the engine over.

It was at that precise moment that the silver Mustang with the flame decals rumbled into the lot. All three of us froze; then Digby and Jeff slid into the car and slammed the door. We watched as the Mustang rocked and bobbed across the ruts and finally jerked to a halt beside the forlorn chopper at the far end of the lot. "Let's go," Digby said. I hesitated, the Bel Air wheezing beneath me.

Two girls emerged from the Mustang. Tight jeans, stiletto heels, hair like frozen fur. They bent over the motorcycle, paced back and forth aimlessly, glanced once or twice at us, and then ambled over to where the reeds sprang up in a green fence round the perimeter of the lake. One of them cupped her hands to her mouth. "Al," she called. "Hey, Al!"

"Come on," Digby hissed. "Let's get out of here."

But it was too late. The second girl was picking her way across the lot, unsteady on her heels, looking up at us and then away. She was older — twenty-five or -six — and as she came closer we could see there was something wrong with her: she was stoned or drunk, lurching now and waving her arms for balance. I gripped the steering wheel as if it were the ejection lever of a flaming jet, and Digby spat out my name, twice, terse and impatient.

"Hi," the girl said.

We looked at her like zombies, like war veterans, like deaf-and-dumb pencil peddlers.   40

She smiled, her lips cracked and dry. "Listen," she said, bending from the waist to look in the window, "you guys seen Al?" Her pupils were pinpoints, her eyes glass. She jerked her neck. "That's his bike over there — Al's. You seen him?"

Al. I didn't know what to say. I wanted to get out of the car and retch, I wanted to go home to my parents' house and crawl into bed. Digby poked me in the ribs. "We haven't seen anybody," I said.

The girl seemed to consider this, reaching out a slim veiny arm to brace herself against the car. "No matter," she said, slurring the *t*'s, "he'll turn up." And then, as if she'd just taken stock of the whole scene — the ravaged car and our battered faces, the desolation of the place — she said: "Hey, you guys look like some pretty bad characters — been fightin', huh?" We stared straight ahead, rigid as catatonics. She was fumbling in her pocket and muttering something. Finally she held out a handful of tablets in glassine wrappers: "Hey, you want to party, you want to do some of these with me and Sarah?"

I just looked at her. I thought I was going to cry. Digby broke the silence. "No, thanks," he said, leaning over me. "Some other time."

I put the car in gear and it inched forward with a groan, shaking off   45 pellets of glass like an old dog shedding water after a bath, heaving over the ruts on its worn springs, creeping toward the highway. There was a sheen of sun on the lake. I looked back. The girl was still standing there, watching us, her shoulders slumped, hand outstretched.

QUESTIONS

1. Around what year, would you say, was it that "courtesy and winning ways went out of style, when it was good to be bad, when you cultivated decadence like a taste"?
2. What is it about Digby and Jeff that inspires the narrator to call them "bad"?
3. Twice in "Greasy Lake" — in paragraphs 2 and 32 — appear the words, "This was nature." What contrasts do you find between the "nature" of the narrator's earlier and later views?
4. What makes the narrator and his friends run off into the woods?
5. How does the heroes' encounter with the two girls at the end of the story differ from their earlier encounter with the girl from the blue Chevy? How do you account for the difference? When at the end of the story the girl offers to party with the three friends, what makes the narrator say, "I thought I was going to cry"?
6. How important to what happens in this story is Greasy Lake itself? What details about the lake and its shores strike you as particularly memorable (whether funny, disgusting, or both)?

7. The setting of Boyle's story is very different from that of James Joyce's "Araby." But in what ways do the two stories resemble each other?

SUGGESTIONS FOR WRITING

1. In a few paragraphs, not necessarily a complete essay or story, recreate a time and place you know intimately. Write about it like a fiction writer, giving reality to a setting in which a story is about to unfold. Imagine this setting in detail — or, if you can, go take a fresh look at it. Ensure that your reader can virtually see, hear, smell, and taste your chosen time and place.

   You might find it revealing to choose for your subject some nearby, present-day place that your audience will recognize, then read your paper aloud in class. If, without your dropping place names or giving them other obvious clues, your listeners can identify your subject, then you have written well.

2. From a different chapter of this book, or from the Stories for Further Reading, choose a story that particularly interests you. Start out by defining for your reader its exact time and place. Then, in two or three more paragraphs, go on to show how this setting functions in the story. Does the setting supply atmosphere? Make things happen? Reveal the natures of certain people? Prompt a character to a realization? Suggested stories to work on (but your instructor may be saving some stories for other purposes and may wish to narrow or add to this list): "Gimpel the Fool" (Chapter 4); "A Clean, Well-Lighted Place," "Barn Burning" (Chapter 5); "Revelation," "The Open Boat" (Chapter 7); "The Chrysanthemums," "Wild Swans" (Chapter 8); "The Death of Ivan Ilych," "The Birthmark," "A Haunted House," "The Garden-Party," "Roman Fever," "A Worn Path," "The Portable Phonograph" (Stories for Further Reading).

3. Rewrite the first page or two of a story you have read, picking up the characters and putting them down in an entirely different setting. This new time and place might be the setting of another story, or it might be some actual place your readers will recognize. As you write, you might find yourself deciding to seek laughs, or you might decide to make the rewrite serious. You might try, for instance, a satire in the vein of *Monty Python*, shifting Hawthorne's "The Birthmark" to the setting of Updike's "A & P." Or, without trying to be funny, you might rewrite the opening of Joyce's "Araby," setting the story in the neighborhood where you grew up.

   End with a short comment in answer to the question, "What did this exercise prove to you?" If your attempt should seem to you a failure, try to explain why the original story proved so reluctant to give up its time and place. (The purpose of this exercise is not to produce a new masterpiece, but to experience at first hand how the setting of a story works.)

4 Character

From popular fiction and drama, both classic and contemporary, we are acquainted with many stereotyped characters. Called **stock characters,** they are often known by some outstanding trait or traits: the *bragging* soldier of Greek and Roman comedy, the prince *charming* of fairy tales, the *mad* scientist of horror movies, the *loyal* sidekick of Westerns, the *greedy* explorer of Tarzan films, the *brilliant but alcoholic* brain surgeon of medical thrillers on television. Stock characters are especially convenient for writers of commercial fiction: they require little detailed portraiture, for we already know them well. Most writers of the literary story, however, attempt to create characters who strike us not as stereotypes but as unique individuals. Although stock characters tend to have single dominant virtues and vices, characters in the finest contemporary short stories tend to have many facets, like people we meet.

A **character,** then, is presumably an imagined person who inhabits a story — although that simple definition may admit to a few exceptions. In George Stewart's novel *Storm,* the protagonist is the wind; in Richard Adams's *Watership Down,* the main characters are rabbits. But usually we recognize, in the main characters of a story, human personalities that become familiar to us. If the story seems "true to life," we generally find that its characters act in a reasonably consistent manner, and that the author has provided them with **motivation:** sufficient reason to behave as they do. Should a character behave in a sudden and unexpected way, seeming to deny what we have been told about his nature or personality, we trust that he had a reason, and that sooner or later we will discover it. This is not to claim that *all* authors insist that their characters behave with absolute consistency, for (as we shall see later in this chapter) some contemporary stories feature characters who sometimes act without apparent reason. Nor can we say that, in good fiction, characters never change or develop. In "A Christmas Carol," Charles Dickens tells how Ebeneezer Scrooge, a tightfisted miser, reforms overnight, suddenly gives to the poor, and endeavors to assist his clerk's struggling family. But Dickens amply demonstrates why Scrooge had such a change of heart: four ghostly visitors, stirring kind memories the old miser had forgotten and also warning him of the probable consequences of his habits, provide the character (and hence the story) with adequate motivation.

To borrow the useful terms of the English novelist E. M. Forster, characters may seem **flat** or **round,** depending on whether a writer sketches or sculptures them. A flat character usually has only one outstanding trait or feature, or at most a few distinguishing marks: for example, the familiar stock character of the mad scientist, with his lust for absolute power and his crazily gleaming eyes. Flat characters, however, need not be stock characters: in all of literature there is probably only one Tiny Tim, though his functions in "A Christmas Carol" are mainly to invoke blessings and to remind others of their Christian duties. Some writers, notably Balzac, who peopled his many novels with hosts of characters, try to distinguish the flat ones by giving each a single odd physical feature or mannerism — a nervous twitch, a piercing gaze, an obsessive fondness for oysters. Round characters, however, present us with more facets — that is, their authors portray them in greater depth and in more generous detail. Such a round character may appear to us only as he appears to the other characters in the story. If their views of him differ, we will see him from more than one side. In other stories, we enter a character's mind and come to know him through his own thoughts, feelings, and perceptions. By the time we finish reading James Joyce's "Araby" (page 54), we are well acquainted with the boy who tells his story and probably find him amply three-dimensional.

Flat characters tend to stay the same throughout a story, but round characters often change — learn or become enlightened, grow or deteriorate. In William Faulkner's "Barn Burning" (Chapter Five), the boy Sarty Snopes, driven to defy his proud and violent father, becomes at the story's end more knowing and more mature. (Some critics call a fixed character **static;** a changing one, **dynamic.**) This is not to damn a flat character as an inferior work of art. In most fiction — even the greatest — minor characters tend to be flat instead of round. Why? Rounding them would cost time and space; and so enlarged, they might only distract us from the main characters.

"A character, first of all, is the noise of his name," according to novelist William Gass.[1] Names, chosen artfully, can indicate natures. A simple illustration is the completely virtuous Squire Allworthy, the foster father in *Tom Jones* by Henry Fielding. Subtler, perhaps, is the custom of giving a character a name that makes an **allusion:** a reference to some famous person, place, or thing in history, in other fiction, or in actuality. For his central characters in *Moby-Dick,* Herman Melville chose names from the Old Testament, calling his tragic and domineering Ahab after a biblical tyrant who came to a bad end, and his wandering narrator Ishmael after a biblical outcast. Whether or not it includes an allusion, a good name often

---

[1]"The Concept of Character in Fiction," in *Fiction and the Figures of Life* (New York: Knopf, 1970).

reveals the character of the character. Charles Dickens, a vigorous and richly suggestive christener, named a charming confidence man Mr. Jingle (suggesting something jingly, light, and superficially pleasant), named a couple of shyster lawyers Dodgson and Fogg (suggesting dodging evasiveness and foglike obfuscation), and named two heartless educators, who grimly drill their schoolchildren in "hard facts," Gradgrind and M'Choakumchild. Henry James, who so loved names that he kept lists of them for characters he might someday conceive, chose for a sensitive, cultured gentleman the name of Lambert Strether; for a down-to-earth, benevolent individual, the name of Mrs. Bread. (But James may have wished to indicate that names cannot be identified with people absolutely, in giving the fragile, considerate heroine of *The Spoils of Poynton* the harsh-sounding name of Fleda Vetch.)

Instead of a hero, many a recent novel has featured an **antihero:** an ordinary, unglorious twentieth-century citizen, usually drawn (according to Sean O'Faolain) as someone "groping, puzzled, cross, mocking, frustrated, and isolated.[2] (Evidently, there are antiheroines too.) If epic poets once drew their heroes as decisive leaders of their people, embodying their people's highest ideals, antiheroes tend to be loners, without perfections, just barely able to survive. Antiheroes lack "character," as defined by psychologist Anthony Quinton to mean a person's conduct or "persistence and consistency in seeking to realize his long-term aims."[3] A gulf separates Leopold Bloom, antihero of James Joyce's novel *Ulysses,* from the hero of the Greek *Odyssey.* In Homer's epic, Ulysses wanders the Mediterranean, battling monsters and overcoming enchantments. In Joyce's novel, Bloom wanders the littered streets of Dublin, peddling advertising space. In recent fiction, by the way, female antiheroes abound.

Evidently, not only fashions in heroes but also attitudes toward human nature have undergone change. In the eighteenth century, Scottish philosopher David Hume argued that the nature of an individual is relatively fixed and unalterable. Hume mentioned, however, a few exceptions: "A person of an obliging disposition gives a peevish answer; but he has the toothache or has not dined. A stupid fellow discovers an obvious alacrity in his carriage; but he has met with a sudden piece of good fortune." For a long time after Hume, novelists and short-story writers seem to have assumed that characters behave nearly always in a predictable fashion and that their actions ought to be consistent with their personalities. Now and again, a writer differed: Jane Austen in *Pride and Prejudice* has her protagonist Elizabeth Bennet remark to the citified Mr. Darcy, who fears that life in the country cannot be amusing, "But people themselves alter so much, that there is something to be observed in them forever."

[2] *The Vanishing Hero* (Boston: Little, 1957).
[3] "The Continuity of Persons," *Times Literary Supplement* issue on "The Nature of Character," 27 July 1973.

Many contemporary writers of fiction would deny even that people have definite selves to alter. Following Sigmund Freud and other modern psychologists, they assume that a large part of human behavior is shaped in the unconscious — that, for instance, a person might fear horses not because of a basically timid nature, but because of unconscious memories of having been nearly trampled by a horse when a child. To some writers it now appears that what Hume called a "disposition" (now called a "personality") is more vulnerable to change from such causes as age, disease, neurosis, psychic shock, or brainwashing than was once believed. Hence, some characters in twentieth-century fiction appear to be shifting bundles of impulses. "You mustn't look in my novel for the old stable ego of character," wrote D. H. Lawrence to a friend about *The Rainbow;* and in that novel and other novels Lawrence demonstrated his view of individuals as bits of one vast Life Force, spurred to act by incomprehensible passions and urges — the "dark gods" in them. The idea of the **gratuitous act,** a deed without cause or motive, is explored in André Gide's novel *Lafcadio's Adventures,* in which an ordinary young man without homicidal tendencies abruptly and for no reason pushes a stranger from a speeding train. The usual limits of character are playfully violated by Virginia Woolf in *Orlando,* a novel whose protagonist, defying time, lives right on from Elizabethan days into the present, changing in midstory from a man into a woman. Characterization, as practiced by nineteenth-century novelists, almost entirely disappears in Franz Kafka's *The Castle,* whose protagonist has no home, no family, no definite appearance — not even a name, just the initial *K.* Characters are things of the past, insists the contemporary French novelist Alain Robbe-Grillet. Still, many writers of fiction go on portraying them.

James Thurber
THE CATBIRD SEAT   1945

James Thurber (1894 – 1961), a humorist sometimes mentioned in the same breath with Mark Twain, was born in Columbus, Ohio and took a degree from Ohio State University. As a young man he gravitated to New York, where he became a prolific contributor to The New Yorker *along with E. B. White, his collaborator on a book-length spoof of popular psychology,* Is Sex Necessary? *(1929). Despite weak eyesight, Thurber gained fame as a cartoonist known for his childlike drawings of timid little men and hound dogs with floppy ears. As blindness descended in his last years, Thurber drew less and less, wrote more and more. Besides essays and stories, his works include a fable for children,* The Thirteen Clocks *(1950); a memoir of working on the* New Yorker *staff,* The Years with Ross *(1959); and with Elliott Nugent, a comedy,* The Male Animal, *produced on Broadway in 1940.*

Mr. Martin bought the pack of Camels on Monday night in the most crowded cigar store on Broadway. It was theater time and seven or eight men were buying cigarettes. The clerk didn't even glance at Mr. Martin, who put the pack in his overcoat pocket and went out. If any of the staff at F & S had seen him buy the cigarettes, they would have been astonished, for it was generally known that Mr. Martin did not smoke, and never had. No one saw him.

It was just a week to the day since Mr. Martin had decided to rub out Mrs. Ulgine Barrows. The term "rub out" pleased him because it suggested nothing more than the correction of an error — in this case an error of Mr. Fitweiler. Mr. Martin had spent each night of the past week working out his plan and examining it. As he walked home now he went over it again. For the hundredth time he resented the element of imprecision, the margin of guesswork that entered into the business. The project as he had worked it out was casual and bold, the risks were considerable. Something might go wrong anywhere along the line. And therein lay the cunning of his scheme. No one would ever see in it the cautious, painstaking hand of Erwin Martin, head of the filing department at F & S, of whom Mr. Fitweiler had once said, "Man is fallible but Martin isn't." No one would see his hand, that is, unless it were caught in the act.

Sitting in his apartment, drinking a glass of milk, Mr. Martin reviewed his case against Mrs. Ulgine Barrows, as he had every night for seven nights. He began at the beginning. Her quacking voice and braying laugh had first profaned the halls of F & S on March 7, 1941 (Mr. Martin had a head for dates). Old Roberts, the personnel chief, had introduced her as the newly appointed special adviser to the president of the firm, Mr. Fitweiler. The woman had appalled Mr. Martin instantly, but he hadn't shown it. He had given her his dry hand, a look of studious concentration, and a faint smile. "Well," she had said, looking at the papers on his desk, "are you lifting the oxcart out of the ditch?" As Mr. Martin recalled that moment, over his milk, he squirmed slightly. He must keep his mind on her crimes as a special adviser, not on her peccadillos as a personality. This he found difficult to do, in spite of entering an objection and sustaining it. The faults of the woman as a woman kept chattering on in his mind like an unruly witness. She had, for almost two years now, baited him. In the halls, in the elevator, even in his own office, into which she romped now and then like a circus horse, she was constantly shouting out these silly questions at him. "Are you lifting the oxcart out of the ditch? Are you tearing up the pea patch? Are you hollering down the rain barrel? Are you scraping around the bottom of the pickle barrel? Are you sitting in the catbird seat?"

It was Joey Hart, one of Mr. Martin's two assistants, who had explained what the gibberish meant. "She must be a Dodger fan°," he had said. "Red

Dodger fan: At the time of this story, the Dodgers were the Brooklyn Dodgers.

Barber announces the Dodger games over the radio and he uses those expressions — picked 'em up down South." Joey had gone on to explain one or two. "Tearing up the pea patch" meant going on a rampage; "sitting in the catbird seat" meant sitting pretty, like a batter with three balls and no strikes on him. Mr. Martin dismissed all this with an effort. It had been annoying, it had driven him near to distraction, but he was too solid a man to be moved to murder by anything so childish. It was fortunate, he reflected as he passed on to the important charges against Mrs. Barrows, that he had stood up under it so well. He had maintained always an outward appearance of polite tolerance. "Why, I even believe you like the woman," Miss Paird, his other assistant, had once said to him. He had simply smiled.

A gavel rapped in Mr. Martin's mind and the case proper was resumed. 5
Mrs. Ulgine Barrows stood charged with willful, blatant, and persistent attempts to destroy the efficiency and system of F & S. It was competent, material, and relevant to review her advent and rise to power. Mr. Martin had got the story from Miss Paird, who seemed always able to find things out. According to her, Mrs. Barrows had met Mr. Fitweiler at a party, where she had rescued him from the embraces of a powerfully built drunken man who had mistaken the president of F & S for a famous retired Middle Western football coach. She had led him to a sofa and somehow worked upon him a monstrous magic. The aging gentleman had jumped to the conclusion there and then that this was a woman of singular attainments, equipped to bring out the best in him and in the firm. A week later he had introduced her into F & S as his special adviser. On that day confusion got its foot in the door. After Miss Tyson, Mr. Brundage, and Mr. Bartlett had been fired and Mr. Munson had taken his hat and stalked out, mailing in his resignation later, old Roberts had been emboldened to speak to Mr. Fitweiler. He mentioned that Mr. Munson's department had been "a little disrupted" and hadn't they perhaps better resume the old system there? Mr. Fitweiler had said certainly not. He had the greatest faith in Mrs. Barrows' ideas. "They require a little seasoning, a little seasoning, is all," he had added. Mr. Roberts had given it up. Mr. Martin reviewed in detail all the changes wrought by Mrs. Barrows. She had begun chipping at the cornices of the firm's edifice and now she was swinging at the foundation stones with a pickaxe.

Mr. Martin came now, in his summing up, to the afternoon of Monday, November 2, 1942 — just one week ago. On that day, at 3 P.M., Mrs. Barrows had bounced into his office. "Boo!" she had yelled. "Are you scraping around the bottom of the pickle barrel?" Mr. Martin had looked at her from under his green eyeshade, saying nothing. She had begun to wander about the office, taking it in with her great, popping eyes. "Do you really need *all* these filing cabinets?" she had demanded suddenly. Mr. Martin's heart had jumped. "Each of these files," he had said, keeping his voice even, "plays an indispensable part in the system of F & S." She had brayed at him, "Well, don't tear up the pea patch!" and gone to the door. From there she had bawled, "But you sure have got a lot of fine scrap in here!" Mr. Martin could no longer doubt that the finger was on his beloved department. Her pickaxe was on the upswing, poised for the first blow. It had not come yet; he had received no blue memo from the enchanted Mr. Fitweiler bearing nonsensical instructions deriving from the obscene woman. But there was no doubt in Mr. Martin's mind that one would be forthcoming. He must act quickly. Already a precious week had gone by. Mr. Martin stood up in his living room, still holding his milk glass. "Gentlemen of the jury," he said to himself, "I demand the death penalty for this horrible person."

The next day Mr. Martin followed his routine, as usual. He polished his glasses more often and once sharpened an already sharp pencil, but not even Miss Paird noticed. Only once did he catch sight of his victim; she swept past him in the hall with a patronizing "Hi!" At five-thirty he walked home, as usual, and had a glass of milk, as usual. He had never drunk anything stronger in his life — unless you could count ginger ale. The late Sam Schlosser, the S of F & S, had praised Mr. Martin at a staff meeting several years before for his temperate habits. "Our most efficient worker neither drinks nor smokes," he had said. "The results speak for themselves." Mr. Fitweiler had sat by, nodding approval.

Mr. Martin was still thinking about that red-letter day as he walked over to the Schrafft's on Fifth Avenue near Forty-sixth Street. He got there, as he always did, at eight o'clock. He finished his dinner and the financial page of the *Sun* at a quarter to nine, as he always did. It was his custom after dinner to take a walk. This time he walked down Fifth Avenue at a casual pace. His gloved hands felt moist and warm, his forehead cold. He transferred the Camels from his overcoat to a jacket pocket. He wondered, as he did so, if they did not represent an unnecessary note of strain. Mrs. Barrows smoked only Luckies. It was his idea to puff a few puffs on a Camel (after the rubbing-out), stub it out in the ashtray holding her lipstick-stained Luckies, and thus drag a small red herring across the trail. Perhaps it was not a good idea. It would take time. He might even choke, too loudly.

Mr. Martin had never seen the house on West Twelfth Street where Mrs. Barrows lived, but he had a clear enough picture of it. Fortunately, she had bragged to everybody about her ducky first-floor apartment in the perfectly darling three-story redbrick. There would be no doorman or other attendants; just the tenants of the second and third floors. As he walked along, Mr. Martin realized that he would get there before nine-thirty. He had considered walking north on Fifth Avenue from Schrafft's to a point from which it would take him until ten o'clock to reach the house. At that hour people were less likely to be coming in or going out. But the procedure would have made an awkward loop in the straight thread of his casualness, and he had abandoned it. It was impossible to figure when people would be entering or leaving the house, anyway. There was a great risk at any hour. If he ran into anybody, he would simply have to place the rubbing-out of Ulgine Barrows in the inactive file forever. The same thing would hold true if there were someone in her apartment. In that case he would just say that he had been passing by, recognized her charming house and thought to drop in.

It was eighteen minutes after nine when Mr. Martin turned into Twelfth Street. A man passed him, and a man and a woman talking. There was no one within fifty paces when he came to the house, halfway down the block. He was up the steps and in the small vestibule in no time, pressing the bell under the card that said "Mrs. Ulgine Barrows." When the clicking in the lock started, he jumped forward against the door. He got inside fast, closing the door behind him. A bulb in a lantern hung from the hall ceiling on a chain seemed to give a monstrously bright light. There was nobody on the stair, which went up ahead of him along the left wall. A door opened down the hall in the wall on the right. He went toward it swiftly, on tiptoe.

"Well, for God's sake, look who's here!" bawled Mrs. Barrows, and her braying laugh rang out like the report of a shotgun. He rushed past her like a football tackle, bumping her. "Hey, quit shoving!" she said, closing the door behind them. They were in her living room, which seemed to Mr. Martin to be lighted by a hundred lamps. "What's after you?" she said. "You're as jumpy as a goat." He found he was unable to speak. His heart was wheezing in his throat. "I — yes," he finally brought out. She was jabbering and laughing as she started to help him off with his coat. "No, no," he said. "I'll put it there." He took it off and put it on a chair near the door. "Your hat and gloves, too," she said. "You're in a lady's house." He put his hat on top of the coat. Mrs. Barrows seemed larger than he had thought. He kept his gloves on. "I was passing by," he said. "I recognized — is there anyone here?" She laughed louder than ever. "No," she said, "we're all alone. You're as white as a sheet, you funny man. Whatever *has* come over you? I'll mix you a toddy." She started toward a door across the room. "Scotch-and-soda be all right? But say, you don't drink, do you?" She turned and gave him her amused look. Mr. Martin pulled himself together. "Scotch-and-soda will be all right," he heard himself say. He could hear her laughing in the kitchen.

Mr. Martin looked quickly around the living room for the weapon. He had counted on finding one there. There were andirons and a poker and something in a corner that looked like an Indian club. None of them would do. It couldn't be that way. He began to pace around. He came to a desk. On it lay a metal paper knife with an ornate handle. Would it be sharp enough? He reached for it and knocked over a small brass jar. Stamps spilled out of it and it fell to the floor with a clatter. "Hey," Mrs. Barrows yelled from the kitchen, "are you tearing up the pea patch?" Mr. Martin gave a strange laugh. Picking up the knife, he tried its point against his left wrist. It was blunt. It wouldn't do.

When Mrs. Barrows reappeared, carrying two highballs, Mr. Martin, standing there with his gloves on, became acutely conscious of the fantasy he had wrought. Cigarettes in his pocket, a drink prepared for him — it was all too grossly improbable. It was more than that; it was impossible. Somewhere in the back of his mind a vague idea stirred, sprouted. "For heaven's sake, take off those gloves," said Mrs. Barrows. "I always wear them in the house," said Mr. Martin. The idea began to bloom, strange and wonderful. She put the glasses on a coffee table in front of a sofa and sat on the sofa. "Come over here, you odd little man," she said. Mr. Martin went over and sat beside her. It was difficult getting a cigarette out of the pack of Camels, but he managed it. She held a match for him, laughing. "Well," she said, handing him his drink, "this is perfectly marvelous. You with a drink and a cigarette."

Mr. Martin puffed, not too awkwardly, and took a gulp of the highball. "I drink and smoke all the time," he said. He clinked his glass against hers. "Here's nuts to that old windbag, Fitweiler," he said, and gulped again. The stuff tasted awful, but he made no grimace. "Really, Mr. Martin," she said, her voice and posture changing, "you are insulting our employer." Mrs. Barrows was now all special adviser to the president. "I am preparing a bomb," said Mr. Martin, "which will blow the old goat higher than hell." He had only had a little of the drink, which was not strong. It couldn't be that. "Do you take dope or something?" Mrs. Barrows asked coldly. "Heroin," said Mr. Martin. "I'll be coked to the gills when I bump that old buzzard off." "Mr. Martin!" she shouted, getting to her feet. "That will be all of that. You must go at once." Mr. Martin took another swallow of his drink. He tapped his cigarette out in the ashtray and put the pack of Camels on the coffee table. Then he got up. She stood glaring at him. He walked over and put on his hat and coat. "Not a word about this," he said, and laid an index finger against his lips. All Mrs. Barrows could bring out was "Really!" Mr. Martin put his hand on the doorknob. "I'm sitting in the catbird seat," he said. He stuck his tongue out at her and left. Nobody saw him go.

Mr. Martin got to his apartment, walking, well before eleven. No one 15 saw him go in. He had two glasses of milk after brushing his teeth, and he felt elated. It wasn't tipsiness, because he hadn't been tipsy. Anyway, the walk had worn off all effects of the whisky. He got in bed and read a magazine for a while. He was asleep before midnight.

Mr. Martin got to the office at eight-thirty the next morning, as usual. At a quarter to nine, Ulgine Barrows, who had never before arrived at work before ten, swept into his office. "I'm reporting to Mr. Fitweiler now!" she shouted. "If he turns you over to the police, it's no more than you deserve!" Mr. Martin gave her a look of shocked surprise. "I beg your pardon?" he said. Mrs. Barrows snorted and bounced out of the room, leaving Miss Paird and Joey Hart staring after her. "What's the matter with that old devil now?" asked Miss Paird. "I have no idea," said Mr. Martin, resuming his work. The other two looked at him and then at each other. Miss Paird got up and went out. She walked slowly past the closed door of Mr. Fitweiler's office. Mrs. Barrows was yelling inside, but she was not braying. Miss Paird could not hear what the woman was saying. She went back to her desk.

Forty-five minutes later, Mrs. Barrows left the president's office and went into her own, shutting the door. It wasn't until half an hour later that Mr. Fitweiler sent for Mr. Martin. The head of the filing department, neat, quiet, attentive, stood in front of the old man's desk. Mr. Fitweiler was pale and nervous. He took his glasses off and twiddled them. He made a small, bruffing sound in his throat. "Martin," he said, "you have been with us more than twenty years." "Twenty-two, sir," said Mr. Martin. "In that time," pursued the president, "your work and your — uh — manner have been exemplary." "I trust so, sir," said Mr. Martin. "I have understood, Martin," said Mr. Fitweiler, "that you have never taken a drink or smoked." "That is correct, sir," said Mr. Martin. "Ah, yes." Mr. Fitweiler polished his glasses. "You may describe what you did after leaving the office yesterday, Martin," he said. Mr. Martin allowed less than a second for his bewildered pause. "Certainly, sir," he said. "I walked home. Then I went to Schrafft's for dinner. Afterward I walked home again. I went to bed early, sir, and read a magazine for a while. I was asleep before eleven." "Ah, yes," said Mr. Fitweiler again. He was silent for a moment, searching for the proper words to say to the head of the filing department. "Mrs. Barrows," he said finally, "Mrs. Barrows has worked hard,

Martin, very hard. It grieves me to report that she has suffered a severe breakdown. It has taken the form of a persecution complex accompanied by distressing hallucinations." "I am very sorry, sir," said Mr. Martin. "Mrs. Barrows is under the delusion," continued Mr. Fitweiler, "that you visited her last evening and behaved yourself in an — uh — unseemly manner." He raised his hand to silence Mr. Martin's little pained outcry. "It is the nature of these psychological diseases," Mr. Fitweiler said, "to fix upon the least likely and most innocent party as the — uh — source of persecution. These matters are not for the lay mind to grasp, Martin. I've just had my psychiatrist, Dr. Fitch, on the phone. He would not, of course, commit himself, but he made enough generalizations to substantiate my suspicions. I suggested to Mrs. Barrows when she had completed her — uh — story to me this morning, that she visit Dr. Fitch, for I suspected a condition at once. She flew, I regret to say, into a rage, and demanded — uh — requested that I call you on the carpet. You may not know, Martin, but Mrs. Barrows had planned a reorganization of your department — subject to my approval, of course, subject to my approval. This brought you, rather than anyone else, to her mind — but again that is a phenomenon for Dr. Fitch and not for us. So, Martin, I am afraid Mrs. Barrows' usefulness here is at an end." "I am dreadfully sorry, sir," said Mr. Martin.

It was at this point that the door to the office blew open with the suddenness of a gas-main explosion and Mrs. Barrows catapulted through it. "Is the little rat denying it?" she screamed. "He can't get away with that!" Mr. Martin got up and moved discreetly to a point beside Mr. Fitweiler's chair. "You drank and smoked at my apartment," she bawled at Mr. Martin, "and you know it! You called Mr. Fitweiler an old windbag and said you were going to blow him up when you got coked to the gills on your heroin!" She stopped yelling to catch her breath and a new glint came into her popping eyes. "If you weren't such a drab, ordinary little man," she said, "I'd think you'd planned it all. Sticking your tongue out, saying you were sitting in the catbird seat, because you thought no one would believe me when I told it! My God, it's really too perfect!" She brayed loudly and hysterically, and the fury was on her again. She glared at Mr. Fitweiler. "Can't you see how he has tricked us, you old fool? Can't you see his little game?" But Mr. Fitweiler had been surreptitiously pressing all the buttons under the top of his desk and employees of F & S began pouring into the room. "Stockton," said Mr. Fitweiler, "you and Fishbein will take Mrs. Barrows to her home. Mrs. Powell, you will go with them." Stockton, who had played a little football in high school, blocked Mrs. Barrows as she made for Mr. Martin. It took him and Fishbein together to force her out of the door into the hall, crowded with stenographers and office boys. She was still screaming imprecations at Mr. Martin, tangled and contradictory imprecations. The hubbub finally died out down the corridor.

"I regret that this has happened," said Mr. Fitweiler. "I shall ask you to dismiss it from your mind, Martin." "Yes, sir," said Mr. Martin, anticipating his chief's "That will be all" by moving to the door. "I will dismiss it." He went out and shut the door, and his step was light and quick in the hall. When he entered his department he had slowed down to his customary gait, and he walked quietly across the room to the W20 file, wearing a look of studious concentration.

QUESTIONS

1. What are the outstanding traits of Mr. Martin's character, as others in the story see him? What false impressions of himself does he leave with Mrs. Barrows after he visits her apartment?
2. What do we know about Mr. Martin's inner self that is unknown to the other characters in the story? Why *isn't* he a stock character — merely the fussy, colorless, mild-mannered little man familiar from comic strips and television comedy?
3. Sum up your impressions of Mrs. Ulgine Barrows. What peculiarities does Thurber give her? What elements of her character lead her into conflict with Mr. Martin?
4. How convincing is the motivation that the author gives Mr. Martin? For what reasons does Martin go to Mrs. Barrows's apartment with the notion of killing her? Why does he then pretend to vices he doesn't have, insult his employer, and stick out his tongue at Mrs. Barrows?
5. What is the point of view, and how is it appropriate to this story? Why could not the story be told equally well from the point of view of Mrs. Barrows, or from that of a totally objective narrator, who could not see into the mind of any character?
6. Recall the definition of an *antihero* (page 75). Would you call Mr. Martin an antihero? What do you take to be James Thurber's attitude toward him? How can you tell?

Katherine Anne Porter

THE JILTING OF GRANNY WEATHERALL   1930

Katherine Anne Porter (1890 – 1980) was born in Indian Creek, Texas. Her mother died when she was two, and Porter was raised by a grandmother who surrounded the growing girl with books. At sixteen, apparently bored with her studies at an Ursuline convent, Porter ran away from home. Three years later, she began supporting herself as a news reporter in Chicago, Denver, and Forth Worth, and sometimes as an actress and ballad singer traveling through the South. Sojourns in Europe and in Mexico supplied her with matter for some of her finest stories. Her brilliant, sensitive short fiction, first collected in Flowering Judas *(1930), won her a high reputation. Her one novel,* Ship of Fools *(1962), with which she had struggled for twenty years, received harsh critical notices, but proved a commercial success. Made into a movie, it ended Porter's lifelong struggle to earn a living. In 1965 her* Collected Stories *received a Pulitzer prize and a National Book Award.*

She flicked her wrist neatly out of Doctor Harry's pudgy careful fingers and pulled the sheet up to her chin. The brat ought to be in knee breeches. Doctoring around the country with spectacles on his nose! "Get along now, take your schoolbooks and go. There's nothing wrong with me."

Doctor Harry spread a warm paw like a cushion on her forehead where the forked green vein danced and made her eyelids twitch. "Now, now, be a good girl, and we'll have you up in no time."

"That's no way to speak to a woman nearly eighty years old just because she's down. I'd have you respect your elders, young man."

"Well, Missy, excuse me." Doctor Harry patted her cheek. "But I've got to warn you, haven't I? You're a marvel, but you must be careful or you're going to be good and sorry."

"Don't tell me what I'm going to be. I'm on my feet now, morally speaking. It's Cornelia. I had to go to bed to get rid of her."

Her bones felt loose, and floated around in her skin, and Doctor Harry floated like a balloon around the foot of the bed. He floated and pulled down his waistcoat and swung his glasses on a cord. "Well, stay where you are, it certainly can't hurt you."

"Get along and doctor your sick," said Granny Weatherall. "Leave a well woman alone. I'll call for you when I want you. . . . Where were you forty years ago when I pulled through milk-leg and double pneumonia? You weren't even born. Don't let Cornelia lead you on," she shouted, because Doctor Harry appeared to float up to the ceiling and out. "I pay my own bills, and I don't throw my money away on nonsense!"

She meant to wave good-by, but it was too much trouble. Her eyes closed of themselves, it was like a dark curtain drawn around the bed. The pillow rose and floated under her, pleasant as a hammock in a light wind. She listened to the leaves rustling outside the window. No, somebody was swishing newspapers: no, Cornelia and Doctor Harry were whispering together. She leaped broad awake, thinking they whispered in her ear.

"She was never like this, *never* like this!" "Well, what can we expect?" "Yes, eighty years old. . . ."

Well, and what if she was? She still had ears. It was like Cornelia to whisper around doors. She always kept things secret in such a public way. She was always being tactful and kind. Cornelia was dutiful; that was the trouble with her. Dutiful and good: "So good and dutiful," said Granny, "that I'd like to spank her." She saw herself spanking Cornelia and making a fine job of it.

"What'd you say, Mother?"

Granny felt her face tying up in hard knots.

"Can't a body think, I'd like to know?"

"I thought you might want something."

"I do. I want a lot of things. First off, go away and don't whisper."

She lay and drowsed, hoping in her sleep that the children would keep out and let her rest a minute. It had been a long day. Not that she was tired. It was always pleasant to snatch a minute now and then. There was always so much to be done, let me see: tomorrow.

Tomorrow was far away and there was nothing to trouble about. Things were finished somehow when the time came; thank God there was always a little margin over for peace: then a person could spread out the plan of life and tuck in the edges orderly. It was good to have everything clean and folded away, with the hair brushes and tonic bottles sitting straight on the white embroidered linen: the day started without fuss and the pantry shelves laid out with rows of jelly glasses and brown jugs and white stone-china jars with blue whirligigs and words painted on them: coffee, tea, sugar, ginger, cinnamon, allspice: and the bronze clock with the lion on top nicely dusted off. The dust that lion could collect in twenty-four hours! The box in the attic with all those letters tied up, well, she'd have to go through that tomorrow. All those letters — George's letters and John's letters and her letters to them both — lying around for the children to find afterwards made her uneasy. Yes, that would be tomorrow's business. No use to let them know how silly she had been once.

While she was rummaging around she found death in her mind and it felt clammy and unfamiliar. She had spent so much time preparing for death there was no need for bringing it up again. Let it take care of itself now. When she was sixty she had felt very old, finished, and went around making farewell trips to see her children and grandchildren, with a secret in her mind: This is the very last of your mother, children! Then she made her will and came down with a long fever. That was all just a notion like a lot of other things, but it was lucky too, for she had once for all got over the idea of dying for a long time. Now she couldn't be worried. She hoped she had better sense now. Her father had lived to be one hundred and two years old and had drunk a noggin of strong hot toddy on his last birthday. He told the reporters it was his daily habit, and he owed his long life to that. He had made quite a scandal and was very pleased about it. She believed she'd just plague Cornelia a little.

"Cornelia! Cornelia!" No footsteps, but a sudden hand on her cheek. "Bless you, where have you been?"

"Here, Mother."

"Well, Cornelia, I want a noggin of hot toddy."

"Are you cold, darling?"

"I'm chilly, Cornelia. Lying in bed stops the circulation. I must have told you that a thousand times."

Well, she could just hear Cornelia telling her husband that Mother was getting a little childish and they'd have to humor her. The thing that most annoyed her was that Cornelia thought she was deaf, dumb, and blind. Little hasty glances and tiny gestures tossed around her and over her head saying, "Don't cross her, let her have her way, she's eighty years old," and she sitting there as if she lived in a thin glass cage. Sometimes Granny almost made up her mind to pack up and move back to her own house where nobody could remind her every minute that she was old. Wait, wait, Cornelia, till your own children whisper behind your back!

In her day she had kept a better house and had got more work done. She wasn't too old yet for Lydia to be driving eighty miles for advice when one of the children jumped the track, and Jimmy still dropped in and talked things over: "Now, Mammy, you've a good business head, I want to know what you think of this? . . ." Old. Cornelia couldn't change the furniture around without asking. Little things, little things! They had been so sweet when they were little. Granny wished the old days were back again with the children young and everything to be done over. It had been a hard pull, but not too much for her. When she thought of all the food she had cooked, and all the clothes she had cut and sewed, and all the gardens she had made — well, the children showed it. There they were, made out of her, and they couldn't get away from that. Sometimes she wanted to see John again and point to them and say, Well, I didn't do so badly, did I? But that would have to wait. That was for tomorrow. She used to think of him as a man, but now all the children were older than their father, and he would be a child beside her if she saw him now. It seemed strange and there was something wrong in the idea. Why, he couldn't

20

25

possibly recognize her. She had fenced in a hundred acres once, digging the post holes herself and clamping the wires with just a negro boy to help. That changed a woman. John would be looking for a young woman with the peaked Spanish comb in her hair and the painted fan. Digging post holes changed a woman. Riding country roads in the winter when women had their babies was another thing: sitting up nights with sick horses and sick negroes and sick children and hardly ever losing one. John, I hardly ever lost one of them! John would see that in a minute, that would be something he could understand, she wouldn't have to explain anything!

It made her feel like rolling up her sleeves and putting the whole place to rights again. No matter if Cornelia was determined to be everywhere at once, there were a great many things left undone on this place. She would start tomorrow and do them. It was good to be strong enough for everything, even if all you made melted and changed and slipped under your hands, so that by the time you finished you almost forgot what you were working for. What was it I set out to do? she asked herself intently, but she could not remember. A fog rose over the valley, she saw it marching across the creek swallowing the trees and moving up the hill like an army of ghosts. Soon it would be at the near edge of the orchard, and then it was time to go in and light the lamps. Come in, children, don't stay out in the night air.

Lighting the lamps had been beautiful. The children huddled up to her and breathed like little calves waiting at the bars in the twilight. Their eyes followed the match and watched the flame rise and settle in a blue curve, then they moved away from her. The lamp was lit, they didn't have to be scared and hang on to mother any more. Never, never, never more. God, for all my life I thank Thee. Without Thee, my God, I could never have done it. Hail, Mary, full of grace.

I want you to pick all the fruit this year and see that nothing is wasted. There's always someone who can use it. Don't let good things rot for want of using. You waste life when you waste good food. Don't let things get lost. It's bitter to lose things. Now, don't let me get to thinking, not when I am tired and taking a little nap before supper. . . .

The pillow rose about her shoulders and pressed against her heart and the memory was being squeezed out of it: oh, push down the pillow, somebody: it would smother her if she tried to hold it. Such a fresh breeze blowing and such a green day with no threats in it. But he had not come, just the same. What does a woman do when she has put on the white veil and set out the white cake for a man and he doesn't come? She tried to remember. No, I swear he never harmed me but in that. He never harmed me but in that . . . and what if he did? There was the day, the day, but a whirl of dark smoke rose and covered it, crept up and over into the bright field where everything was planted so carefully in orderly rows. That was hell, she knew hell when she saw it. For sixty years she had prayed against remembering him and against losing her soul in the deep pit of hell, and now the two things were mingled in one and the thought of him was a smoky cloud from hell that moved and crept in her head when she had just got rid of Doctor Harry and was trying to rest a minute. Wounded vanity, Ellen, said a sharp voice in the top of her mind. Don't let your wounded vanity get the upper hand of you. Plenty of girls get jilted. You were jilted, weren't you? Then stand up to it. Her eyelids wavered and let in

streamers of blue-gray light like tissue paper over her eyes. She must get up
and pull the shades down or she'd never sleep. She was in bed again and the
shades were not down. How could that happen? Better turn over, hide from
the light, sleeping in the light gave you nightmares. "Mother, how do you feel
now?" and a stinging wetness on her forehead. But I don't like having my face
washed in cold water!

Hapsy? George? Lydia? Jimmy? No, Cornelia, and her features were   30
swollen and full of little puddles. "They're coming, darling, they'll all be here
soon." Go wash your face, child, you look funny.

Instead of obeying, Cornelia knelt down and put her head on the pillow.
She seemed to be talking but there was no sound. "Well, are you tongue-tied?
Whose birthday is it? Are you going to give a party?"

Cornelia's mouth moved urgently in strange shapes. "Don't do that, you
bother me, daughter."

"O, no, Mother. Oh, no. . . ."

Nonsense. It was strange about children. They disputed your every
word. "No what, Cornelia?"

"Here's Doctor Harry."   35

"I won't see that boy again. He just left five minutes ago."

"That was this morning, Mother. It's night now. Here's the nurse."

"This is Doctor Harry, Mrs. Weatherall. I never saw you look so young
and happy!"

"Ah, I'll never be young again — but I'd be happy if they'd let me lie in
peace and get rested."

She thought she spoke up loudly, but no one answered. A warm weight   40
on her forehead, a warm bracelet on her wrist, and a breeze went on whispering, trying to tell her something. A shuffle of leaves in the everlasting hand
of God. He blew on them and they danced and rattled. "Mother, don't mind,
we're going to give you a little hypodermic." "Look here, daughter, how do
ants get in this bed? I saw sugar ants yesterday." Did you send for Hapsy too?

It was Hapsy she really wanted. She had to go a long way back through
a great many rooms to find Hapsy standing with a baby on her arm. She
seemed to herself to be Hapsy also, and the baby on Hapsy's arm was Hapsy
and himself and herself, all at once, and there was no surprise in the meeting.
Then Hapsy melted from within and turned flimsy as gray gauze and the baby
was a gauzy shadow, and Hapsy came up close and said, "I thought you'd
never come," and looked at her very searchingly and said, "You haven't
changed a bit!" They leaned forward to kiss, when Cornelia began whispering
from a long way off, "Oh, is there anything you want to tell me? Is there
anything I can do for you?"

Yes, she had changed her mind after sixty years and she would like to
see George. I want you to find George. Find him and be sure to tell him I forgot
him. I want him to know I had my husband just the same and my children
and my house like any other woman. A good house too and a good husband
that I loved and fine children out of him. Better than I hoped for even. Tell
him I was given back everything he took away and more. Oh, no, oh, God,
no, there was something else besides the house and the man and the children.
Oh, surely they were not all? What was it? Something not given back. . . . Her
breath crowded down under her ribs and grew into a monstrous frightening

shape with cutting edges; it bored up into her head, and the agony was unbelievable: Yes, John, get the Doctor now, no more talk, my time has come.

When this one was born it should be the last. The last. It should have been born first, for it was the one she had truly wanted. Everything came in good time. Nothing left out, left over. She was strong, in three days she would be as well as ever. Better. A woman needed milk in her to have her full health.

"Mother, do you hear me?"

"I've been telling you — " 45

"Mother, Father Connolly's here."

"I went to Holy Communion only last week. Tell him I'm not so sinful as all that."

"Father just wants to speak to you."

He could speak as much as he pleased. It was like him to drop in and inquire about her soul as if it were a teething baby, and then stay on for a cup of tea and a round of cards and gossip. He always had a funny story of some sort, usually about an Irishman who made his little mistakes and confessed them, and the point lay in some absurd thing he would blurt out in the confessional showing his struggles between native piety and original sin. Granny felt easy about her soul. Cornelia, where are your manners? Give Father Connolly a chair. She had her secret comfortable understanding with a few favorite saints who cleared a straight road to God for her. All as surely signed and sealed as the papers for the new Forty Acres. Forever . . . heirs and assigns forever. Since the day the wedding cake was not cut, but thrown out and wasted. The whole bottom dropped out of the world, and there she was blind and sweating with nothing under her feet and the walls falling away. His hand had caught her under the breast, she had not fallen, there was the freshly polished floor with the green rug on it, just as before. He had cursed like a sailor's parrot and said, "I'll kill him for you." Don't lay a hand on him, for my sake leave something to God. "Now, Ellen, you must believe what I tell you. . . ."

So there was nothing, nothing to worry about any more, except some- 50 times in the night one of the children screamed in a nightmare, and they both hustled out shaking and hunting for the matches and calling, "There, wait a minute, here we are!" John, get the doctor now, Hapsy's time has come. But there was Hapsy standing by the bed in a white cap. "Cornelia, tell Hapsy to take off her cap. I can't see her plain."

Her eyes opened very wide and the room stood out like a picture she had seen somewhere. Dark colors with the shadows rising towards the ceiling in long angles. The tall black dresser gleamed with nothing on it but John's picture, enlarged from a little one, with John's eyes very black when they should have been blue. You never saw him, so how do you know how he looked? But the man insisted the copy was perfect, it was very rich and handsome. For a picture, yes, but it's not my husband. The table by the bed had a linen cover and a candle and a crucifix. The light was blue from Cornelia's silk lampshades. No sort of light at all, just frippery. You had to live forty years with kerosene lamps to appreciate honest electricity. She felt very strong and she saw Doctor Harry with a rosy nimbus around him.

"You look like a saint, Doctor Harry, and I vow that's as near as you'll ever come to it."

"She's saying something."

"I heard you, Cornelia. What's all this carrying-on?"

"Father Connolly's saying — " 55

Cornelia's voice staggered and bumped like a cart in a bad road. It rounded corners and turned back again and arrived nowhere. Granny stepped up in the cart very lightly and reached for the reins, but a man sat beside her and she knew him by his hands, driving the cart. She did not look in his face, for she knew without seeing, but looked instead down the road where the trees leaned over and bowed to each other and a thousand birds were singing a Mass. She felt like singing too, but she put her hand in the bosom of her dress and pulled out a rosary, and Father Connolly murmured Latin in a very solemn voice and tickled her feet. My God, will you stop that nonsense? I'm a married woman. What if he did run away and leave me to face the priest by myself? I found another a whole world better. I wouldn't have exchanged my husband for anybody except St. Michael himself, and you may tell him that for me with a thank you in the bargain.

Light flashed on her closed eyelids, and a deep roaring shook her. Cornelia, is that lightning? I hear thunder. There's going to be a storm. Close all the windows. Call the children in. . . . "Mother, here we are, all of us." "Is that you, Hapsy?" "Oh, no, I'm Lydia. We drove as fast as we could." Their faces drifted above her, drifted away. The rosary fell out of her hands and Lydia put it back. Jimmy tried to help, their hands fumbled together, and Granny closed two fingers around Jimmy's thumb. Beads wouldn't do, it must be something alive. She was so amazed her thoughts ran round and round. So, my dear Lord, this is my death and I wasn't even thinking about it. My children have come to see me die. But I can't, it's not time. Oh, I always hated surprises. I wanted to give Cornelia the amethyst set — Cornelia, you're to have the amethyst set, but Hapsy's to wear it when she wants, and, Doctor Harry, do shut up. Nobody sent for you. Oh, my dear Lord, do wait a minute. I meant to do something about the Forty Acres, Jimmy doesn't need it and Lydia will later on, with that worthless husband of hers. I meant to finish the altar cloth and send six bottles of wine to Sister Borgia for her dyspepsia. I want to send six bottles of wine to Sister Borgia, Father Connolly, now don't let me forget.

Cornelia's voice made short turns and tilted over and crashed. "Oh, Mother, oh, Mother, oh, Mother. . . ."

"I'm not going, Cornelia. I'm taken by surprise. I can't go."

You'll see Hapsy again. What about her? "I thought you'd never come." 60 Granny made a long journey outward, looking for Hapsy. What if I don't find her? What then? Her heart sank down and down, there was no bottom to death, she couldn't come to the end of it. The blue light from Cornelia's lampshade drew into a tiny point in the center of her brain, it flickered and winked like an eye, quietly it fluttered and dwindled. Granny lay curled down within herself, amazed and watchful, staring at the point of light that was herself; her body was now only a deeper mass of shadow in an endless darkness and this darkness would curl around the light and swallow it up. God, give a sign!

For the second time there was no sign. Again no bridegroom and the priest in the house. She could not remember any other sorrow because this grief wiped them all away. Oh, no, there's nothing more cruel than this —

Katherine Anne Porter 89

I'll never forgive it. She stretched herself with a deep breath and blew out the light.

QUESTIONS

1. In the very first paragraph, what does the writer tell us about Ellen (Granny) Weatherall?
2. What does the name of Weatherall have to do with Granny's nature (or her life story)? What other traits or qualities do you find in her?
3. "Her bones felt loose, and floated around in her skin, and Doctor Harry floated like a balloon" (paragraph 6). What do you understand from this statement? By what other remarks does the writer indicate Granny's condition? In paragraph 56, why does Father Connolly tickle Granny's feet? At what other moments in the story does she fail to understand what is happening, or confuse the present with the past?
4. Exactly what happened to Ellen Weatherall sixty years earlier? What effects did this event have on her?
5. In paragraph 49, who do you guess to be the man who "cursed like a sailor's parrot"? In paragraph 56, who do you assume to be the man driving the cart? Is the fact that these persons are not clearly labeled and identified a failure on the author's part?
6. What is stream of consciousness? (The term is discussed on page 23.) Would you call "The Jilting of Granny Weatherall" a stream of consciousness story? Refer to the story in your reply.
7. Sum up the character of the daughter Cornelia.
8. Why doesn't Granny's last child Hapsy come to her mother's deathbed?
9. Would you call the character of Doctor Harry "flat" or "round"? Why is his flatness (or roundness) appropriate to the story?
10. How is this the story of another "jilting"? What is similar between that fateful day of sixty years ago (described in paragraphs 29, 49, and 61) and the moment when Granny is dying? This time, who is the "bridegroom" not in the house?
11. "This is the story of an eighty-year-old woman lying in bed, getting groggy, and dying; I can't see why it should interest anybody." How would you answer this critic?

Willa Cather

PAUL'S CASE   1905

Willa Cather (1876 – 1947) was born in Gore, Virginia, but at nine moved to Webster County, Nebraska, where pioneer sod houses still clung to the windswept plains. There, mainly in the town of Red Cloud, she grew up among Scandinavians, Czechs, Bohemians, and other immigrant settlers, for whom she felt a quick kinship: they too had been displaced from their childhood homes. After graduation from the University of Nebraska, Cather went east to spend ten years in Pittsburgh, where the story "Paul's Case" opens. (When she wrote the story, she was a high school teacher of Latin and English and music critic for a newspaper.) Then, because her early stories had attracted notice, New York beckoned. A job on the staff of McClure's led to her becoming managing editor of the popular magazine. Her early

novels of Nebraska won immense popularity: O Pioneers! *(1913),* My
Ántonia *(1918), and* A Lost Lady *(1923). In her later novels Cather
explores other regions of the North American past: in* Death Comes to the
Archbishop *(1927), frontier New Mexico; in* Shadows on the Rock
*(1931), seventeenth-century Quebec. She does not romanticize the rugged
lives of farm people on the plains, or glamorize village life. Often, as in*
The Song of the Lark *(1915), the story of a Colorado girl who becomes
an opera singer, she depicts a small town as stifling. With remarkable skill,
she may tell a story from a man's point of view, but her favorite characters
are likely to be women of strong will who triumph over obstacles.*

It was Paul's afternoon to appear before the faculty of the Pittsburgh
High School to account for his various misdemeanors. He had been suspended
a week ago, and his father had called at the Principal's office and confessed his
perplexity about his son. Paul entered the faculty room suave and smiling. His
clothes were a trifle outgrown and the tan velvet on the collar of his open
overcoat was frayed and worn; but for all that there was something of the
dandy about him, and he wore an opal pin in his neatly knotted black four-in-
hand, and a red carnation in his buttonhole. This latter adornment the faculty
somehow felt was not properly significant of the contrite spirit befitting a boy
under the ban of suspension.

Paul was tall for his age and very thin, with high, cramped shoulders and
a narrow chest. His eyes were remarkable for a certain hysterical brilliancy and
he continually used them in a conscious, theatrical sort of way, peculiarly
offensive in a boy. The pupils were abnormally large, as though he were
addicted to belladonna, but there was a glassy glitter about them which that
drug does not produce.

When questioned by the Principal as to why he was there, Paul stated,
politely enough, that he wanted to come back to school. This was a lie, but
Paul was quite accustomed to lying; found it, indeed, indispensable for overcoming friction. His teachers were asked to state their respective charges
against him, which they did with such a rancor and aggrievedness as evinced
that this was not a usual case. Disorder and impertinence were among the
offenses named, yet each of his instructors felt that it was scarcely possible to
put into words the real cause of the trouble, which lay in a sort of hysterically
defiant manner of the boy's; in the contempt which they all knew he felt for
them, and which he seemingly made not the least effort to conceal. Once, when
he had been making a synopsis of a paragraph at the blackboard, his English
teacher had stepped to his side and attempted to guide his hand. Paul had
started back with a shudder and thrust his hands violently behind him. The
astonished woman could scarcely have been more hurt and embarrassed had
he struck at her. The insult was so involuntary and definitely personal as to
be unforgettable. In one way and another, he had made all his teachers, men
and women alike, conscious of the same feeling of physical aversion. In one
class he habitually sat with his hand shading his eyes; in another he always
looked out of the window during the recitation; in another he made a running
commentary on the lecture, with humorous intention.

His teachers felt this afternoon that his whole attitude was symbolized by his shrug and his flippantly red carnation flower, and they fell upon him without mercy, his English teacher leading the pack. He stood through it smiling, his pale lips parted over his white teeth. (His lips were continually twitching, and he had a habit of raising his eyebrows that was contemptuous and irritating to the last degree.) Older boys than Paul had broken down and shed tears under that baptism of fire, but his set smile did not once desert him, and his only sign of discomfort was the nervous trembling of the fingers that toyed with the buttons of his overcoat, and an occasional jerking of the other hand that held his hat. Paul was always smiling, always glancing about him, seeming to feel that people might be watching him and trying to detect something. This conscious expression, since it was as far as possible from boyish mirthfulness, was usually attributed to insolence or "smartness."

As the inquisition proceeded, one of his instructors repeated an impertinent remark of the boy's, and the Principal asked him whether he thought that a courteous speech to have made a woman. Paul shrugged his shoulders slightly and his eyebrows twitched.

"I don't know," he replied. "I didn't mean to be polite or impolite, either. I guess it's a sort of way I have of saying things regardless."

The Principal, who was a sympathetic man, asked him whether he didn't think that a way it would be well to get rid of. Paul grinned and said he guessed so. When he was told that he could go, he bowed gracefully and went out. His bow was but a repetition of the scandalous red carnation.

His teachers were in despair, and his drawing master voiced the feeling of them all when he declared there was something about the boy which none of them understood. He added: "I don't really believe that smile of his comes altogether from insolence; there's something sort of haunted about it. The boy is not strong, for one thing. I happen to know that he was born in Colorado, only a few months before his mother died out there of a long illness. There is something wrong about the fellow."

The drawing master had come to realize that, in looking at Paul, one saw only his white teeth and the forced animation of his eyes. One warm afternoon the boy had gone to sleep at his drawing-board, and his master had noted with amazement what a white, blue-veined face it was; drawn and wrinkled like an old man's about the eyes, the lips twitching even in his sleep, and stiff with a nervous tension that drew them back from his teeth.

His teachers left the building dissatisfied and unhappy; humiliated to have felt so vindictive toward a mere boy, to have uttered this feeling in cutting terms, and to have set each other on, as it were, in the gruesome game of intemperate reproach. Some of them remembered having seen a miserable street cat set at bay by a ring of tormentors.

As for Paul, he ran down the hill whistling the Soldiers' Chorus from *Faust*° looking wildly behind him now and then to see whether some of his teachers were not there to writhe under this light-heartedness. As it was now late in the afternoon and Paul was on duty that evening as usher at Carnegie Hall°, he decided that he would not go home to supper. When he reached the

Faust: tragic grand opera (1859) by French composer Charles Gounod.
Carnegie Hall: concert hall endowed by Pittsburgh steel manufacturer Andrew Carnegie, not to be confused with the better-known Carnegie Hall in New York City.

concert hall the doors were not yet open and, as it was chilly outside, he decided to go up into the picture gallery — always deserted at this hour — where there were some of Raffaelli's° gay studies of Paris streets and an airy blue Venetian scene or two that always exhilarated him. He was delighted to find no one in the gallery but the old guard, who sat in one corner, a newspaper on his knee, a black patch over one eye and the other closed. Paul possessed himself of the place and walked confidently up and down, whistling under his breath. After a while he sat down before a blue Rico° and lost himself. When he bethought him to look at his watch, it was after seven o'clock, and he rose with a start and ran downstairs, making a face at Augustus, peering out from the cast-room°, and an evil gesture at the Venus of Milo as he passed her on the stairway.

When Paul reached the ushers' dressing-room half-a-dozen boys were there already, and he began excitedly to tumble into his uniform. It was one of the few that at all approached fitting, and Paul thought it very becoming — though he knew that the tight, straight coat accentuated his narrow chest, about which he was exceedingly sensitive. He was always considerably excited while he dressed, twanging all over to the tuning of the strings and the preliminary flourishes of the horns in the music-room; but to-night he seemed quite beside himself, and he teased and plagued the boys until, telling him that he was crazy, they put him down on the floor and sat on him.

Somewhat calmed by his suppression, Paul dashed out to the front of the house to seat the early comers. He was a model usher; gracious and smiling he ran up and down the aisles; nothing was too much trouble for him; he carried messages and brought programmes as though it were his greatest pleasure in life, and all the people in his section thought him a charming boy, feeling that he remembered and admired them. As the house filled, he grew more and more vivacious and animated, and the color came to his cheeks and lips. It was very much as though this were a great reception and Paul were the host. Just as the musicians came out to take their places, his English teacher arrived with checks for the seats which a prominent manufacturer had taken for the season. She betrayed some embarrassment when she handed Paul the tickets, and a hauteur° which subsequently made her feel very foolish. Paul was startled for a moment, and had the feeling of wanting to put her out; what business had she here among all these fine people and gay colors? He looked her over and decided that she was not appropriately dressed and must be a fool to sit downstairs in such togs. The tickets had probably been sent her out of kindness, he reflected as he put down a seat for her, and she had about as much right to sit there as he had.

When the symphony began Paul sank into one of the rear seats with a long sigh of relief, and lost himself as he had done before the Rico. It was not that symphonies, as such, meant anything in particular to Paul, but the

Raffaelli: Jean-François Raffaelli (1850 – 1921), painter and graphic artist, native and lifelong resident of Paris, attained great popularity for his paintings and drawings of that city.

Rico: Andreas Rico (flourished 1500 – 1550), painter of the Byzantine school, a native of Crete.

Augustus . . . cast-room: Paul mocks a plaster cast of the Vatican Museum's famous statue of the first Roman emperor (63 B.C. – A.D. 14), whom an unknown sculptor posed sternly pointing an index finger at his beholders.

hauteur: haughtiness.

first sigh of the instruments seemed to free some hilarious and potent spirit within him; something that struggled there like the Genius in the bottle found by the Arab fisherman°. He felt a sudden zest of life; the lights danced before his eyes and the concert hall blazed into unimaginable splendor. When the soprano soloist came on, Paul forgot even the nastiness of his teacher's being there and gave himself up to the peculiar stimulus such personages always had for him. The soloist chanced to be a German woman, by no means in her first youth, and the mother of many children; but she wore an elaborate gown and a tiara, and above all she had that indefinable air of achievement, that world-shine upon her, which, in Paul's eyes, made her a veritable queen of Romance.

After a concert was over Paul was always irritable and wretched until he got to sleep, and tonight he was even more than usually restless. He had the feeling of not being able to let down, of its being impossible to give up this delicious excitement which was the only thing that could be called living at all. During the last number he withdrew and, after hastily changing his clothes in the dressing-room, slipped out to the side door where the soprano's carriage stood. Here he began pacing rapidly up and down the walk, waiting to see her come out.

Over yonder the Schenley, in its vacant stretch, loomed big and square through the fine rain, the windows of its twelve stories glowing like those of a lighted cardboard house under a Christmas tree. All the actors and singers of the better class stayed there when they were in the city, and a number of the big manufacturers of the place lived there in the winter. Paul had often hung about the hotel, watching the people go in and out, longing to enter and leave school-masters and dull care behind him forever.

At last the singer came out, accompanied by the conductor, who helped her into her carriage and closed the door with a cordial *auf wiedersehen*° which set Paul to wondering whether she were not an old sweetheart of his. Paul followed the carriage over to the hotel, walking so rapidly as not to be far from the entrance when the singer alighted and disappeared behind the swinging glass doors that were opened by a negro in a tall hat and a long coat. In the moment that the door was ajar it seemed to Paul that he, too, entered. He seemed to feel himself go after her up the steps, into the warm, lighted building, into an exotic, a tropical world of shiny, glistening surfaces and basking ease. He reflected upon the mysterious dishes that were brought into the dining-room, the green bottles in buckets of ice, as he had seen them in the supper party pictures of the *Sunday World* supplement. A quick gust of wind brought the rain down with sudden vehemence, and Paul was startled to find that he was still outside in the slush of the gravel driveway; that his boots were letting in the water and his scanty overcoat was clinging wet about him; that the lights in front of the concert hall were out, and that the rain was driving in sheets between him and the orange glow of the windows above him. There it was, what he wanted — tangibly before him, like the fairy world of a Christmas pantomime, but mocking spirits stood guard at the doors, and, as

Genius: genie in a tale from *The Arabian Nights.*
auf wiedersehen: German equivalent of *au revoir*, or, "here's to seeing you again."

the rain beat in his face, Paul wondered whether he were destined always to shiver in the black night outside, looking up at it.

He turned and walked reluctantly toward the car tracks. The end had to come sometime; his father in his night-clothes at the top of the stairs, explanations that did not explain, hastily improvised fictions that were forever tripping him up, his upstairs room and its horrible yellow wall-paper, the creaking bureau with the greasy plush collar-box, and over his painted wooden bed the pictures of George Washington and John Calvin°, and the framed motto, "Feed my Lambs," which had been worked in red worsted by his mother.

Half an hour later, Paul alighted from his car and went slowly down one of the side streets off the main thoroughfare. It was a highly respectable street, where all the houses were exactly alike, and where businessmen of moderate means begot and reared large families of children, all of whom went to Sabbath-school and learned the shorter catechism, and were interested in arithmetic; all of whom were as exactly alike as their homes, and of a piece with the monotony in which they lived. Paul never went up Cordelia Street without a shudder of loathing. His home was next to the house of the Cumberland° minister. He approached it tonight with the nerveless sense of defeat, the hopeless feeling of sinking back forever into ugliness and commonness that he had always had when he came home. The moment he turned into Cordelia Street he felt the waters close above his head. After each of these orgies of living, he experienced all the physical depression which follows a debauch; the loathing of respectable beds, of common food, of a house penetrated by kitchen odors; a shuddering repulsion for the flavorless, colorless mass of every-day existence; a morbid desire for cool things and soft lights and fresh flowers.

The nearer he approached the house, the more absolutely unequal Paul felt to the sight of it all; his ugly sleeping chamber; the cold bathroom with the grimy zinc tub, the cracked mirror, the dripping spiggots; his father, at the top of the stairs, his hairy legs sticking out from his night-shirt, his feet thrust into carpet slippers. He was so much later than usual that there would certainly be inquiries and reproaches. Paul stopped short before the door. He felt that he could not be accosted by his father tonight; that he could not toss again on that miserable bed. He would not go in. He would tell his father that he had no car fare, and it was raining so hard he had gone home with one of the boys and stayed all night.

Meanwhile, he was wet and cold. He went around to the back of the house and tried one of the basement windows, found it open, raised it cautiously, and scrambled down the cellar wall to the floor. There he stood, holding his breath, terrified by the noise he had made, but the floor above him was silent, and there was no creak on the stairs. He found a soap-box, and carried it over to the soft ring of light that streamed from the furnace door, and sat down. He was horribly afraid of rats, so he did not try to sleep, but sat looking distrustfully at the dark, still terrified lest he might have awakened his father. In such reactions, after one of the experiences which made days and

John Calvin: French Protestant theologian of the Reformation (1509 – 1564) whose teachings are the basis of Presbyterianism.
Cumberland: industrial city in western Maryland.

nights out of the dreary blanks of the calendar, when his senses were deadened, Paul's head was always singularly clear. Suppose his father had heard him getting in at the window and had come down and shot him for a burglar? Then, again, suppose his father had come down, pistol in hand, and he had cried out in time to save himself, and his father had been horrified to think how nearly he had killed him? Then, again, suppose a day should come when his father would remember that night, and wish there had been no warning cry to stay his hand? With this last supposition Paul entertained himself until daybreak.

The following Sunday was fine; the sodden November chill was broken by the last flash of autumnal summer. In the morning Paul had to go to church and Sabbath-school, as always. On seasonable Sunday afternoons the burghers of Cordelia Street always sat out on their front "stoops," and talked to their neighbors on the next stoop, or called to those across the street in neighborly fashion. The men usually sat on gay cushions placed upon the steps that led down to the sidewalk, while the women, in their Sunday "waists," sat in rockers on the cramped porches, pretending to be greatly at their ease. The children played in the streets; there were so many of them that the place resembled the recreation grounds of a kindergarten. The men on the steps — all in their shirt sleeves, their vests unbuttoned — sat with their legs well apart, their stomachs comfortably protruding, and talked of the prices of things, or told anecdotes of the sagacity of their various chiefs and overlords. They occasionally looked over the multitude of squabbling children, listened affectionately to their high-pitched, nasal voices, smiling to see their own proclivities reproduced in their offspring, and interspersed their legends of the iron kings with remarks about their sons' progress at school, their grades in arithmetic, and the amounts they had saved in their toy banks.

On this last Sunday of November, Paul sat all the afternoon on the lowest step of his "stoop," staring into the street, while his sisters, in their rockers, were talking to the minister's daughters next door about how many shirt-waists they had made in the last week, and how many waffles some one had eaten at the last church supper. When the weather was warm, and his father was in a particularly jovial frame of mind, the girls made lemonade, which was always brought out in a red-glass pitcher, ornamented with forget-me-nots in blue enamel. This the girls thought very fine, and the neighbors always joked about the suspicious color of the pitcher.

Today Paul's father sat on the top step, talking to a young man who shifted a restless baby from knee to knee. He happened to be the young man who was daily held up to Paul as a model, and after whom it was his father's dearest hope that he would pattern. This young man was of a ruddy complexion, with a compressed, red mouth, and faded, near-sighted eyes, over which he wore thick spectacles, with gold bows that curved about his ears. He was clerk to one of the magnates of a great steel corporation, and was looked upon in Cordelia Street as a young man with a future. There was a story that, some five years ago — he was now barely twenty-six — he had been a trifle dissipated but in order to curb his appetites and save the loss of time and strength that a sowing of wild oats might have entailed, he had taken his chief's advice, oft reiterated to his employees, and at twenty-one had married the first woman whom he could persuade to share his fortunes. She happened to be an angular school-mistress, much older than he, who also wore thick glasses, and who had now borne him four children, all near-sighted, like herself.

The young man was relating how his chief, now cruising in the Mediterranean, kept in touch with all the details of the business, arranging his office hours on his yacht just as though he were at home, and "knocking off work enough to keep two stenographers busy." His father told, in turn, the plan his corporation was considering, of putting in an electric railway plant at Cairo. Paul snapped his teeth; he had an awful apprehension that they might spoil it all before he got there. Yet he rather liked to hear these legends of the iron kings, that were told and retold on Sundays and holidays; these stories of palaces in Venice, yachts on the Mediterranean, and high play at Monte Carlo appealed to his fancy, and he was interested in the triumphs of these cash boys who had become famous, though he had no mind for the cash-boy stage.

After supper was over, and he had helped to dry the dishes, Paul nervously asked his father whether he could go to George's to get some help in his geometry, and still more nervously asked for car fare. This latter request he had to repeat, as his father, on principle, did not like to hear requests for money, whether much or little. He asked Paul whether he could not go to some boy who lived nearer, and told him that he ought not to leave his school work until Sunday; but he gave him the dime. He was not a poor man, but he had a worthy ambition to come up in the world. His only reason for allowing Paul to usher was, that he thought a boy ought to be earning a little.

Paul bounded upstairs, scrubbed the greasy odor of the dish-water from his hands with the ill-smelling soap he hated, and then shook over his fingers a few drops of violet water from the bottle he kept hidden in his drawer. He left the house with his geometry conspicuously under his arm, and the moment he got out of Cordelia Street and boarded a downtown car, he shook off the lethargy of two deadening days, and began to live again.

The leading juvenile of the permanent stock company which played at one of the downtown theatres was an acquaintance of Paul's, and the boy had been invited to drop in at the Sunday-night rehearsals whenever he could. For more than a year Paul had spent every available moment loitering about Charley Edwards's dressing-room. He had won a place among Edwards's following not only because the young actor, who could not afford to employ a dresser, often found him useful, but because he recognized in Paul something akin to what churchmen term "vocation."

It was at the theatre and at Carnegie Hall that Paul really lived; the rest was but a sleep and a forgetting. This was Paul's fairy tale, and it had for him all the allurement of a secret love. The moment he inhaled the gassy, painty, dusty odor behind the scenes, he breathed like a prisoner set free, and felt within him the possibility of doing or saying splendid, brilliant, poetic things. The moment the cracked orchestra beat out the overture from *Martha*°, or jerked at the serenade from *Rigoletto*°, all stupid and ugly things slid from him, and his senses were deliciously, yet delicately fired.

Perhaps it was because, in Paul's world, the natural nearly always wore

Martha: grand opera about romance among English aristocrats (1847) by German composer Friedrich von Flotow.

Rigoletto: tragic grand opera (1851) by Italian composer Giuseppe Verdi.

the guise of ugliness, that a certain element of artificiality seemed to him necessary in beauty. Perhaps it was because his experience of life elsewhere was so full of Sabbath-school picnics, petty economies, wholesome advice as to how to succeed in life, and the unescapable odors of cooking, that he found this existence so alluring, these smartly-clad men and women so attractive, that he was so moved by these starry apple orchards that bloomed perennially under the lime-light.

It would be difficult to put it strongly enough how convincingly the stage entrance of that theatre was for Paul the actual portal of Romance. Certainly none of the company ever suspected it, least of all Charley Edwards. It was very like the old stories that used to float about London of fabulously rich Jews, who had subterranean halls there, with palms, and fountains, and soft lamps and richly apparelled women who never saw the disenchanting light of London day. So, in the midst of that smoke-palled city, enamored of figures and grimy toil, Paul had his secret temple, his wishing carpet, his bit of blue-and-white Mediterranean shore bathed in perpetual sunshine.

Several of Paul's teachers had a theory that his imagination had been perverted by garish fiction, but the truth was that he scarcely ever read at all. The books at home were not such as would either tempt or corrupt a youthful mind, and as for reading the novels that some of his friends urged upon him — well, he got what he wanted much more quickly from music; any sort of music, from an orchestra to a barrel organ. He needed only the spark, the indescribable thrill that made his imagination master of his senses, and he could make plots and pictures enough of his own. It was equally true that he was not stage struck — not, at any rate, in the usual acceptation of that expression. He had no desire to become an actor, any more than he had to become a musician. He felt no necessity to do any of these things; what he wanted was to see, to be in the atmosphere, float on the wave of it, to be carried out, blue league after blue league, away from everything.

After a night behind the scenes, Paul found the school-room more than ever repulsive; the bare floors and naked walls; the prosy men who never wore frock coats, or violets in their buttonholes; the women with their dull gowns, shrill voices, and pitiful seriousness about prepositions that govern the dative. He could not bear to have the other pupils think, for a moment, that he took these people seriously; he must convey to them that he considered it all trivial, and was there only by way of a jest, anyway. He had autographed pictures of all the members of the stock company which he showed his classmates, telling them the most incredible stories of his familiarity with these people, of his acquaintance with the soloists who came to Carnegie Hall, his suppers with them and the flowers he sent them. When these stories lost their effect, and his audience grew listless, he became desperate and would bid all the boys good-bye, announcing that he was going to travel for a while; going to Naples, to Venice, to Egypt. Then, next Monday, he would slip back, conscious and nervously smiling; his sister was ill, and he should have to defer his voyage until spring.

Matters went steadily worse with Paul at school. In the itch to let his instructors know how heartily he despised them and their homilies, and how thoroughly he was appreciated elsewhere, he mentioned once or twice that he had no time to fool with theorems; adding — with a twitch of the eyebrows and a touch of that nervous bravado which so perplexed them — that he was helping the people down at the stock company; they were old friends of his.

The upshot of the matter was that the Principal went to Paul's father, and Paul was taken out of school and put to work. The manager at Carnegie Hall was told to get another usher in his stead; the door-keeper at the theatre was warned not to admit him to the house; and Charley Edwards remorsefully promised the boy's father not to see him again.

The members of the stock company were vastly amused when some of Paul's stories reached them — especially the women. They were hardworking women, most of them supporting indigent husbands or brothers, and they laughed rather bitterly at having stirred the boy to such fervid and florid inventions. They agreed with the faculty and with his father that Paul's was a bad case.

The east-bound train was ploughing through a January snow-storm; the dull dawn was beginning to show grey when the engine whistled a mile out of Newark. Paul started up from the seat where he had lain curled in uneasy slumber, rubbed the breath-misted window glass with his hand, and peered out. The snow was whirling in curling eddies above the white bottom lands, and the drifts lay already deep in the fields and along the fences, while here and there the long dead grass and dried weed stalks protruded black above it. Lights shone from the scattered houses, and a gang of laborers who stood beside the track waved their lanterns.

Paul had slept very little, and he felt grimy and uncomfortable. He had made the all-night journey in a day coach, partly because he was ashamed, dressed as he was, to go into a Pullman, and partly because he was afraid of being seen there by some Pittsburgh businessmen, who might have noticed him in Denny & Carson's office. When the whistle awoke him, he clutched quickly at his breast pocket, glancing about him with an uncertain smile. But the little, clay-bespattered Italians were still sleeping, the slatternly women across the aisle were in open-mouthed oblivion, and even the crumby, crying babies were for the nonce stilled. Paul settled back to struggle with his impatience as best he could.

When he arrived at the Jersey City station, he hurried through his breakfast, manifestly ill at ease and keeping a sharp eye about him. After he reached the Twenty-third Street station°, he consulted a cabman, and had himself driven to a men's furnishing establishment that was just opening for the day. He spent upward of two hours there, buying with endless reconsidering and great care. His new street suit he put on in the fitting-room; the frock coat and dress clothes he had bundled into the cab with his linen. Then he drove to a hatter's and a shoe house. His next errand was at Tiffany's, where he selected his silver and a new scarf-pin. He would not wait to have his silver marked, he said. Lastly, he stopped at a trunk shop on Broadway, and had his purchases packed into various travelling bags.

It was a little after one o'clock when he drove up to the Waldorf, and after settling with the cabman, went into the office. He registered from Washington; said his mother and father had been abroad, and that he had come

Twenty-third Street station: The scene is now New York City.

down to await the arrival of their steamer. He told his story plausibly and had no trouble, since he volunteered to pay for them in advance, in engaging his rooms; a sleeping-room, sitting-room and bath.

Not once, but a hundred times Paul had planned this entry into New York. He had gone over every detail of it with Charley Edwards, and in his scrap book at home there were pages of description about New York hotels, cut from the Sunday papers. When he was shown to his sitting-room on the eighth floor, he saw at a glance that everything was as it should be; there was but one detail in his mental picture that the place did not realize, so he rang for the bell boy and sent him down for flowers. He moved about nervously until the boy returned, putting away his new linen and fingering it delightedly as he did so. When the flowers came, he put them hastily into water, and then tumbled into a hot bath. Presently he came out of his white bath-room, resplendent in his new silk underwear, and playing with the tassels of his red robe. The snow was whirling so fiercely outside his windows that he could scarcely see across the street, but within the air was deliciously soft and fragrant. He put the violets and jonquils on the taboret beside the couch, and threw himself down, with a long sigh, covering himself with a Roman blanket. He was thoroughly tired; he had been in such haste, he had stood up to such a strain, covered so much ground in the last twenty-four hours, that he wanted to think how it had all come about. Lulled by the sound of the wind, the warm air, and the cool fragrance of the flowers, he sank into deep, drowsy retrospection.

It had been wonderfully simple; when they had shut him out of the theatre and concert hall, when they had taken away his bone, the whole thing was virtually determined. The rest was a mere matter of opportunity. The only thing that at all surprised him was his own courage — for he realized well enough that he had always been tormented by fear, a sort of apprehensive dread that, of late years, as the meshes of the lies he had told closed about him, had been pulling the muscles of his body tighter and tighter. Until now, he could not remember the time when he had not been dreading something. Even when he was a little boy, it was always there — behind him, or before, or on either side. There had always been the shadowed corner, the dark place into which he dared not look, but from which something seemed always to be watching him — and Paul had done things that were not pretty to watch, he knew.

But now he had a curious sense of relief, as though he had at last thrown down the gauntlet to the thing in the corner.

Yet it was but a day since he had been sulking in the traces; but yesterday afternoon that he had been sent to the bank with Denny & Carson's deposit, as usual — but this time he was instructed to leave the book to be balanced. There was above two thousand dollars in checks, and nearly a thousand in the bank notes which he had taken from the book and quietly transferred to his pocket. At the bank he had made out a new deposit slip. His nerves had been steady enough to permit of his returning to the office, where he had finished his work and asked for a full day's holiday tomorrow, Saturday, giving a perfectly reasonable pretext. The bank book, he knew, would not be returned before Monday or Tuesday, and his father would be out of town for the next week. From the time he slipped the bank notes into his pocket until he boarded the night train for New York, he had not known a moment's hesitation. It was not the first time Paul had steered through treacherous waters.

How astonishingly easy it had all been; here he was, the thing done; and this time there would be no awakening, no figure at the top of the stairs. He watched the snow flakes whirling by his window until he fell asleep. 45

When he awoke, it was three o'clock in the afternoon. He bounded up with a start; half of one of his precious days gone already! He spent more than an hour in dressing, watching every stage of his toilet carefully in the mirror. Everything was quite perfect; he was exactly the kind of boy he had always wanted to be.

When he went downstairs, Paul took a carriage and drove up Fifth Avenue toward the Park. The snow had somewhat abated; carriages and tradesmen's wagons were hurrying soundlessly to and fro in the winter twilight; boys in woollen mufflers were shovelling off the doorsteps; the avenue stages made fine spots of color against the white street. Here and there on the corners were stands, with whole flower gardens blooming under glass cases, against the sides of which the snow flakes stuck and melted; violets, roses, carnations, lilies of the valley — somewhat vastly more lovely and alluring that they blossomed thus unnaturally in the snow. The Park itself was a wonderful stage winterpiece.

When he returned, the pause of the twilight had ceased, and the tune of the streets had changed. The snow was falling faster, lights streamed from the hotels that reared their dozen stories fearlessly up into the storm, defying the raging Atlantic winds. A long, black stream of carriages poured down the avenue, intersected here and there by other streams, tending horizontally. There were a score of cabs about the entrance of his hotel, and his driver had to wait. Boys in livery were running in and out of the awning stretched across the sidewalk, up and down the red velvet carpet laid from the door to the street. Above, about, within it all was the rumble and roar, the hurry and toss of thousands of human beings as hot for pleasure as himself, and on every side of him towered the glaring affirmation of the omnipotence of wealth.

The boy set his teeth and drew his shoulders together in a spasm of realization: the plot of all dramas, the text of all romances, the nerve-stuff of all sensations was whirling about him like the snow flakes. He burnt like a faggot in a tempest.

When Paul went down to dinner, the music of the orchestra came floating up the elevator shaft to greet him. His head whirled as he stepped into the thronged corridor, and he sank back into one of the chairs against the wall to get his breath. The lights, the chatter, the perfumes, the bewildering medley of color — he had, for a moment, the feeling of not being able to stand it. But only for a moment; these were his own people, he told himself. He went slowly about the corridors, through the writing-rooms, smoking-rooms, reception-rooms, as though he were exploring the chambers of an enchanted palace, built and peopled for him alone. 50

When he reached the dining-room he sat down at a table near a window. The flowers, the white linen, the many-colored wine glasses, the gay toilettes of the women, the low popping of corks, the undulating repetitions of the *Blue Danube* from the orchestra, all flooded Paul's dream with bewildering radiance. When the roseate tinge of his champagne was added — that cold, precious, bubbling stuff that creamed and foamed in his glass — Paul wondered that there were honest men in the world at all. This was what all the world was fighting for, he reflected; this was what all the struggle was about. He doubted the reality of his past. Had he ever known a place called Cordelia Street, a place where fagged-looking businessmen got on the early car; mere rivets in a machine they seemed to Paul — sickening men, with combings of children's hair always hanging to their coats, and the smell of cooking in their clothes. Cordelia Street — Ah! that belonged to another time and country; had he not always been thus, had he not sat here night after night, from as far back as he could remember, looking pensively over just such shimmering textures, and slowly twirling the stem of a glass like this one between his thumb and middle finger? He rather thought he had.

He was not in the least abashed or lonely. He had no especial desire to meet or to know any of these people; all he demanded was the right to look on and conjecture, to watch the pageant. The mere stage properties were all he contended for. Nor was he lonely later in the evening, in his loge at the Metropolitan. He was now entirely rid of his nervous misgivings, of his forced aggressiveness, of the imperative desire to show himself different from his surroundings. He felt now that his surroundings explained him. Nobody questioned the purple; he had only to wear it passively. He had only to glance down at his attire to reassure himself that here it would be impossible for anyone to humiliate him.

He found it hard to leave his beautiful sitting-room to go to bed that night, and sat long watching the raging storm from his turret window. When he went to sleep it was with the lights turned on in his bedroom; partly because of his old timidity, and partly so that, if he should wake in the night, there would be no wretched moment of doubt, no horrible suspicion of yellow wall-paper, or of Washington and Calvin above his bed.

Sunday morning the city was practically snow-bound. Paul breakfasted late, and in the afternoon he fell in with a wild San Francisco boy, a freshman at Yale, who said he had run down for a "little flyer" over Sunday. The young man offered to show Paul the night side of the town, and the two boys went out together after dinner, not returning to the hotel until seven o'clock the next morning. They had started out in the confiding warmth of a champagne friendship, but their parting in the elevator was singularly cool. The freshman pulled himself together to make his train, and Paul went to bed. He awoke at two o'clock in the afternoon, very thirsty and dizzy, and rang for ice-water, coffee, and the Pittsburgh papers.

On the part of the hotel management, Paul excited no suspicion. There was this to be said for him, that he wore his spoils with dignity and in no way made himself conspicuous. Even under the glow of his wine he was never boisterous, though he found the stuff like a magician's wand for wonder-building. His chief greediness lay in his ears and eyes, and his excesses were not offensive ones. His dearest pleasures were the grey winter twilights in his sitting-room; his quiet enjoyment of his flowers, his clothes, his wide divan, his cigarette, and his sense of power. He could not remember a time when he had felt so at peace with himself. The mere release from the necessity of petty lying, lying every day and every day, restored his self-respect. He had never lied for pleasure, even at school; but to be noticed and admired, to assert his difference from other Cordelia Street boys; and he felt a good deal more manly, more honest, even, now that he had no need for boastful pretensions, now that he could, as his actor friends used to say, "dress the part." It was characteristic that remorse did not occur to him. His golden days went by without a shadow, and he made each as perfect as he could.

On the eighth day after his arrival in New York, he found the whole affair exploited in the Pittsburgh papers, exploited with a wealth of detail which indicated that local news of a sensational nature was at a low ebb. The firm of Denny & Carson announced that the boy's father had refunded the full amount of the theft, and that they had no intention of prosecuting. The Cumberland minister had been interviewed, and expressed his hope of yet reclaiming the motherless lad, and his Sabbath-school teacher declared that she would spare no effort to that end. The rumor had reached Pittsburgh that the boy had been seen in a New York hotel, and his father had gone East to find him and bring him home.

Paul had just come in to dress for dinner; he sank into a chair, weak to the knees, and clasped his head in his hands. It was to be worse than jail, even; the tepid waters of Cordelia Street were to close over him finally and forever. The grey monotony stretched before him in hopeless, unrelieved years; Sabbath-school, Young People's Meeting, the yellow-papered room, the damp dish-towels; it all rushed back upon him with a sickening vividness. He had the old feeling that the orchestra had suddenly stopped, the sinking sensation that the play was over. The sweat broke out on his face, and he sprang to his feet, looked about him with his white, conscious smile, and winked at himself in the mirror. With something of the old childish belief in miracles with which he had so often gone to class, all his lessons unlearned, Paul dressed and dashed whistling down the corridor to the elevator.

He had no sooner entered the dining-room and caught the measure of the music than his remembrance was lightened by his old elastic power of claiming the moment, mounting with it, and finding it all sufficient. The glare and glitter about him, the mere scenic accessories had again, and for the last time, their old potency. He would show himself that he was game, he would finish the thing splendidly. He doubted, more than ever, the existence of Cordelia Street, and for the first time he drank his wine recklessly. Was he not, after all, one of those fortunate beings born to the purple, was he not still himself and in his own place? He drummed a nervous accompaniment to the Pagliacci music and looked about him, telling himself over and over that it had paid.

He reflected drowsily, to the swell of the music and the chill sweetness of his wine, that he might have done it more wisely. He might have caught an outboard steamer and been well out of their clutches before now. But the other side of the world had seemed too far away and too uncertain then; he could not have waited for it; his need had been too sharp. If he had to choose over again, he would do the same thing tomorrow. He looked affectionately about the dining-room, now gilded with a soft mist. Ah, it had paid indeed!

Paul was awakened next morning by a painful throbbing in his head and feet. He had thrown himself across the bed without undressing, and had slept with his shoes on. His limbs and hands were lead heavy, and his tongue and throat were parched and burnt. There came upon him one of those fateful

60

attacks of clear-headedness that never occurred except when he was physically exhausted and his nerves hung loose. He lay still and closed his eyes and let the tide of things wash over him.

His father was in New York; "stopping at some joint or other," he told himself. The memory of successive summers on the front stoop fell upon him like a weight of black water. He had not a hundred dollars left; and he knew now, more than ever, that money was everything, the wall that stood between all he loathed and all he wanted. The thing was winding itself up; he had thought of that on his first glorious day in New York, and had even provided a way to snap the thread. It lay on his dressing-table now; he had got it out last night when he came blindly up from dinner, but the shiny metal hurt his eyes, and he disliked the looks of it.

He rose and moved about with a painful effort, succumbing now and again to attacks of nausea. It was the old depression exaggerated; all the world had become Cordelia Street. Yet somehow he was not afraid of anything, was absolutely calm; perhaps because he had looked into the dark corner at last and knew. It was bad enough, what he saw there, but somehow not so bad as his long fear of it had been. He saw everything clearly now. He had a feeling that he had made the best of it, that he had lived the sort of life he was meant to live, and for half an hour he sat staring at the revolver. But he told himself that was not the way, so he went downstairs and took a cab to the ferry.

When Paul arrived at Newark, he got off the train and took another cab, directing the driver to follow the Pennsylvania tracks out of the town. The snow lay heavy on the roadways and had drifted deep in the open fields. Only here and there the dead grass or dried weed stalks projected, singularly black, above it. Once well into the country, Paul dismissed the carriage and walked, floundering along the tracks, his mind a medley of irrelevant things. He seemed to hold in his brain an actual picture of everything he had seen that morning. He remembered every feature of both his drivers, of the toothless old woman from whom he had bought the red flowers in his coat, the agent from whom he had got his ticket, and all of his fellow-passengers on the ferry. His mind, unable to cope with vital matters near at hand, worked feverishly and deftly at sorting and grouping these images. They made for him a part of the ugliness of the world, of the ache in his head, and the bitter burning on his tongue. He stooped and put a handful of snow into his mouth as he walked, but that, too, seemed hot. When he reached a little hillside, where the tracks ran through a cut some twenty feet below him, he stopped and sat down.

The carnations in his coat were drooping with the cold, he noticed; their red glory all over. It occurred to him that all the flowers he had seen in the glass cases that first night must have gone the same way, long before this. It was only one splendid breath they had, in spite of their brave mockery at the winter outside the glass; and it was a losing game in the end, it seemed, this revolt against the homilies by which the world is run. Paul took one of the blossoms carefully from his coat and scooped a little hole in the snow, where he covered it up. Then he dozed a while, from his weak condition, seemingly insensible to the cold.

The sound of an approaching train awoke him, and he started to his feet, 65 remembering only his resolution, and afraid lest he should be too late. He stood watching the approaching locomotive, his teeth chattering, his lips drawn away from them in a frightened smile; once or twice he glanced nervously sidewise, as though he were being watched. When the right moment came, he jumped. As he fell, the folly of his haste occurred to him with merciless clearness, the vastness of what he had left undone. There flashed through his brain, clearer than ever before, the blue of Adriatic water, the yellow of Algerian sands.

He felt something strike his chest, and that his body was being thrown swiftly through the air, on and on, immeasurably far and fast, while his limbs were gently relaxed. Then, because the picture making mechanism was crushed, the disturbing visions flashed into black, and Paul dropped back into the immense design of things.

Questions

1. What is it about Paul that so disturbs his teachers? Recall any of his traits that they find irritating, any actions that trouble them. Do they irritate or trouble *you?*
2. How does Paul relate to his father, his neighbors, and his fellow students?
3. What do the arts — music, painting, theater — mean to Paul? How does he react when exposed to them? Is he himself an artist?
4. In what different places do we follow Paul throughout the story? How do these settings (and the boy's reactions to them) help us understand him, his attitudes, his personality?
5. What, exactly, does Paul want out of life? Cite evidence for your answer, paying attention to what most pleases him in New York.
6. What is the point of view in "Paul's Case"? Does it ever change, or does it remain the same throughout the story? Imagine the story told in the first person. Why wouldn't that point of view have been so effective?
7. Does Cather's brief introduction into the story of the wild Yale freshman from San Francisco (in paragraph 54) serve any purpose? If you had been writing this story, would you have given this minor character more importance? Why do you suppose he and Paul have such a "singularly cool" parting? What is Cather's point?
8. Is Paul a static character or a dynamic one? (If you find him changing and developing in the story, can you indicate what changes him?)
9. Comment on some of the concrete details Cather dwells on. What, for instance, do you make of the portraits of Washington and Calvin and the motto placed over Paul's bed (paragraph 18)? Of the carnation Paul buries in the snow (paragraph 64)?
10. What implications, if any, does the title "Paul's Case" have for this story? Is Paul mentally ill, or does Cather place the roots of his malaise elsewhere?
11. What motivates Paul to commit suicide? To what extent does his decision to kill himself seem to grow from his character? (Suggestion: Consider what Paul reveals about himself by his earlier behavior: his lies to his father and teachers, the exaggerated tales he tells his schoolmates about his acquaintance with theater people, his frequent attendance at the stock theater productions, his runaway trip to New York.)
12. Does this story contain any message, stated or implied? Do you get any sense of how the author feels toward Paul? How far does she appear to sympathize with him? Point to any passages in the story that seem to reveal her attitude.
13. When Cather first published "Paul's Case" in 1905, she subtitled it "A Study in Temperament." Three of the possible meanings of temperament (according

to *Webster's New Collegiate Dictionary*) are "peculiar or distinguishing mental or physical character," "characteristic or habitual inclination or mode of emotional response ['he is of a nervous temperament']," and "extremely high sensibility, especially excessive sensitiveness." Which of these definitions seems to you best to fit the story? How do you describe Paul's temperament?

14. What circumstances of Paul's boyhood environment make his temperament a particularly dangerous and unfortunate one for him?

Isaac Bashevis Singer

GIMPEL THE FOOL   1953

Translated by Saul Bellow

Isaac Bashevis Singer, born in Poland in 1904, the son of a rabbi, grew up in the Jewish ghetto in Warsaw in a family where money was scarce, but intellectual stimuli plentiful. "My father's house," he recalls, "was a study house, a court of justice, a house of prayer, of storytelling." For a time he pursued rabbinical studies. In 1935, when the Nazi invasion of Poland was imminent, he came to New York and became a journalist for the Jewish Daily Forward, *a Yiddish-language newspaper for which, ever since, he has continued to write. For years he contributed a daily serial story to the* Forward *and for a time wrote scripts for a Yiddish soap opera on radio station WEVD. He became a naturalized United States citizen in 1943. Only in 1950 when* The Family Moskat, *a novel of three generations of Warsaw Jews, appeared in English translation, did a larger audience become aware of him. (Singer, whose command of English is excellent, has always worked closely with his translators.) In 1978 he was awarded the Nobel prize for literature. Singer's work often (as in "Gimpel the Fool") recreates the vanished world of the* shtetl, *or Jewish village of Eastern Europe. Traditional Jewish legends inform many of his novels, including* Satan in Goray *(1955),* The Magician of Lublin *(1960), and* The Golem *(1982). Singer has also written many volumes of short fiction (see* Collected Stories, *1982), children's books, the play* Yentl *(1975), and three volumes of autobiography.*

I

I am Gimpel the fool. I don't think myself a fool. On the contrary. But that's what folks call me. They gave me the name while I was still in school. I had seven names in all: imbecile, donkey, flax-head, dope, glump, ninny, and fool. The last name stuck. What did my foolishness consist of? I was easy to take in. They said, "Gimpel, you know the rabbi's wife has been brought to childbed?" So I skipped school. Well, it turned out to be a lie. How was I supposed to know? She hadn't had a big belly. But I never looked at her belly. Was that really so foolish? The gang laughed and hee-hawed, stomped and danced and chanted a good-night prayer. And instead of the raisins they give when a woman's lying in, they stuffed my hand full of goat turds. I was no weakling. If I slapped someone he'd see all the way to Cracow. But I'm really not a slugger by nature. I think to myself, Let it pass. So they take advantage of me.

I was coming home from school and heard a dog barking. I'm not afraid of dogs, but of course I never want to start up with them. One of them may be mad, and if he bites there's not a Tartar in the world who can help you. So I made tracks. Then I looked around and saw the whole market place wild with laughter. It was no dog at all but Wolf-Leib the thief. How was I supposed to know it was he? It sounded like a howling bitch.

When the pranksters and leg-pullers found that I was easy to fool, every one of them tried his luck with me. "Gimpel, the Czar is coming to Frampol; Gimpel, the moon fell down in Turbeen; Gimpel, little Hodel Furpiece found a treasure behind the bathhouse." And I like a *golem*° believed everyone. In the first place, everything is possible, as it is written in the Wisdom of the Fathers, I've forgotten just how. Second, I had to believe when the whole town came down on me! If I ever dared to say, "Ah, you're kidding!" there was trouble. People got angry. "What do you mean! You want to call everyone a liar?" What was I to do? I believed them, and I hope at least that did them some good.

I was an orphan. My grandfather who brought me up was already bent toward the grave. So they turned me over to a baker, and what a time they gave me there! Every woman or girl who came to bake a pan of cookies or dry a batch of noodles had to fool me at least once. "Gimpel, there's a fair in heaven; Gimpel, the rabbi gave birth to a calf in the seventh month; Gimpel, a cow flew over the roof and laid brass eggs." A student from the *yeshiva*° came once to buy a roll, and he said, "You, Gimpel, while you stand here scraping with your baker's shovel the Messiah has come. The dead have arisen." "What do you mean?" I said. "I heard no one blowing the ram's horn!" He said, "Are you deaf?" And all began to cry, "We heard it, we heard!" Then in came Reitze the candle-dipper and called out in her hoarse voice, "Gimpel, your father and mother have stood up from the grave. They're looking for you."

To tell the truth, I knew very well that nothing of the sort had happened, but all the same, as folks were talking, I threw on my wool vest and went out. Maybe something had happened. What did I stand to lose by looking? Well, what a cat music went up! And then I took a vow to believe nothing more. But that was no go either. They confused me so that I didn't know the big end from the small.

I went to the rabbi to get some advice. He said, "It is written, better to be a fool all your days than for one hour to be evil. You are not a fool. They are the fools. For he who causes his neighbor to feel shame loses Paradise himself." Nevertheless the rabbi's daughter took me in. As I left the rabbinical court she said, "Have you kissed the wall yet?" I said, "No; what for?" She answered, "It's a law; you've got to do it after every visit." Well, there didn't

5

golem: simpleton. From the Hebrew: "a yet-unformed thing" (*Psalms* 139:16); a mere robot, a shapeless mass.
yeshiva: school of theology.

seem to be any harm in it. And she burst out laughing. It was a fine trick. She put one over on me, all right.

I wanted to go off to another town, but then everyone got busy matchmaking, and they were after me so they nearly tore my coat tails off. They talked at me and talked until I got water on the ear. She was no chaste maiden, but they told me she was virgin pure. She had a limp, and they said it was deliberate, from coyness. She had a bastard, and they told me the child was her little brother. I cried, "You're wasting your time. I'll never marry that whore." But they said indignantly, "What a way to talk! Aren't you ashamed of yourself? We can take you to the rabbi and have you fined for giving her a bad name." I saw then that I wouldn't escape them so easily and I thought, They're set on making me their butt. But when you're married the husband's the master, and if that's all right with her it's agreeable to me too. Besides, you can't pass through life unscathed, nor expect to.

I went to her clay house, which was built on the sand, and the whole gang, hollering and chorusing, came after me. They acted like bearbaiters. When we came to the well they stopped all the same. They were afraid to start anything with Elka. Her mouth would open as if it were on a hinge, and she had a fierce tongue. I entered the house. Lines were strung from wall to wall and clothes were drying. Barefoot she stood by the tub, doing the wash. She was dressed in a worn hand-me-down gown of plush. She had her hair put up in braids and pinned across her head. It took my breath away, almost, the reek of it all.

Evidently she knew who I was. She took a look at me and said, "Look who's here! He's come, the drip. Grab a seat."

I told her all; I denied nothing. "Tell me the truth," I said, "are you really a virgin, and is that mischievous Yechiel actually your little brother? Don't be deceitful with me, for I'm an orphan."

"I'm an orphan myself," she answered, "and whoever tries to twist you up, may the end of his nose take a twist. But don't let them think they can take advantage of me. I want a dowry of fifty guilders, and let them take up a collection besides. Otherwise they can kiss my you-know-what." She was very plain-spoken. I said, "It's the bride and not the groom who gives a dowry." Then she said, "Don't bargain with me. Either a flat 'yes' or a flat 'no' — go back where you came from."

I thought, No bread will ever be baked from *this* dough. But ours is not a poor town. They consented to everything and proceeded with the wedding. It so happened that there was a dysentery epidemic at the time. The ceremony was held at the cemetery gates, near the little corpse-washing hut. The fellows got drunk. While the marriage contract was being drawn up I heard the most pious high rabbi ask, "Is the bride a widow or a divorced woman?" And the sexton's wife answered for her, "Both a widow and divorced." It was a black moment for me. But what was I to do, run away from under the marriage canopy?

There was singing and dancing. An old granny danced opposite me, hugging a braided white *chalah*°. The master of revels made a "God 'a mercy" in memory of the bride's parents. The schoolboys threw burrs, as on *Tishe b'*

chalah: loaf of bread glazed with egg white, a Sabbath and holiday delicacy.

Av fast day°. There were a lot of gifts after the sermon: a noodle board, a kneading trough, a bucket, brooms, ladles, household articles galore. Then I took a look and saw two strapping young men carrying a crib. "What do we need this for?" I asked. So they said, "Don't rack your brains about it. It's all right, it'll come in handy." I realized I was going to be rooked. Take it another way though, what did I stand to lose? I reflected, I'll see what comes of it. A whole town can't go altogether crazy.

II

At night I came where my wife lay, but she wouldn't let me in. "Say, look here, is this what they married us for?" I said. And she said, "My monthly has come." "But yesterday they took you to the ritual bath, and that's afterward, isn't it supposed to be?" "Today isn't yesterday," said she, "and yesterday's not today. You can beat it if you don't like it." In short, I waited.

Not four months later she was in childbed. The townsfolk hid their   15
laughter with their knuckles. But what could I do? She suffered intolerable pains and clawed at the walls. "Gimpel," she cried, "I'm going. Forgive me!" The house filled with women. They were boiling pans of water. The screams rose to the welkin.

The thing to do was to go to the House of Prayer to repeat Psalms, and that was what I did.

The townsfolk liked that, all right. I stood in a corner saying Psalms and prayers, and they shook their heads at me. "Pray, pray!" they told me. "Prayer never made any woman pregnant." One of the congregation put a straw to my mouth and said, "Hay for the cows." There was something to that too, by God!

She gave birth to a boy. Friday at the synagogue the sexton stood up before the Ark, pounded on the reading table, and announced, "The wealthy Reb Gimpel invites the congregation to a feast in honor of the birth of a son." The whole House of Prayer rang with laughter. My face was flaming. But there was nothing I could do. After all, I *was* the one responsible for the circumcision honors and rituals.

Half the town came running. You couldn't wedge another soul in. Women brought peppered chick-peas, and there was a keg of beer from the tavern. I ate and drank as much as anyone, and they all congratulated me. Then there was a circumcision, and I named the boy after my father, may he rest in peace. When all were gone and I was left with my wife alone, she thrust her head through the bed-curtain and called me to her.

"Gimpel," said she, "why are you silent? Has your ship gone and sunk?"   20

"What shall I say?" I answered. "A fine thing you've done to me! If my mother had known of it she'd have died a second time."

She said, "Are you crazy, or what?"

"How can you make such a fool," I said, "of one who should be the lord and master?"

"What's the matter with you?" she said. "What have you taken it into your head to imagine?"

Tishe b' Av: day of mourning that commemorates disasters and persecutions.

I saw that I must speak bluntly and openly. "Do you think this is the ₂₅
way to use an orphan?" I said. "You have borne a bastard."

She answered, "Drive this foolishness out of your head. The child is
yours."

"How can he be mine?" I argued. "He was born seventeen weeks after
the wedding."

She told me then that he was premature. I said, "Isn't he a little too
premature?" She said she had had a grandmother who carried just as short a
time and she resembled this grandmother of hers as one drop of water does
another. She swore to it with such oaths that you would have believed a
peasant at the fair if he had used them. To tell the plain truth, I didn't believe
her; but when I talked it over next day with the schoolmaster he told me that
the very same thing had happened to Adam and Eve. Two they went up to
bed, and four they descended.

"There isn't a woman in the world who is not the granddaughter of Eve,"
he said.

That was how it was — they argued me dumb. But then, who really ₃₀
knows how such things are?

I began to forget my sorrow. I loved the child madly, and he loved me
too. As soon as he saw me he'd wave his little hands and want me to pick him
up, and when he was colicky I was the only one who could pacify him. I
bought him a little bone teething ring and a little gilded cap. He was forever
catching the evil eye from someone, and then I had to run to get one of those
abracadabras for him that would get him out of it. I worked like an ox. You
know how expenses go up when there's an infant in the house. I don't want
to lie about it; I didn't dislike Elka either, for that matter. She swore at me and
cursed, and I couldn't get enough of her. What strength she had! One of her
looks could rob you of the power of speech. And her orations! Pitch and
sulphur, that's what they were full of, and yet somehow also full of charm.
I adored her every word. She gave me bloody wounds though.

In the evening I brought her a white loaf as well as a dark one, and also
poppyseed rolls I baked myself. I thieved because of her and swiped everything I could lay hands on, macaroons, raisins, almonds, cakes. I hope I may
be forgiven for stealing from the Saturday pots the women left to warm in the
baker's oven. I would take out scraps of meat, a chunk of pudding, a chicken
leg or head, a piece of tripe, whatever I could nip quickly. She ate and became
fat and handsome.

I had to sleep away from home all during the week, at the bakery. On
Friday nights when I got home she always made an excuse of some sort. Either
she had heartburn, or a stitch in the side, or hiccups, or headaches. You know
what women's excuses are. I had a bitter time of it. It was rough. To add to
it, this little brother of hers, the bastard, was growing bigger. He'd put lumps
on me, and when I wanted to hit back she'd open her mouth and curse so
powerfully I saw a green haze floating before my eyes. Ten times a day she
threatened to divorce me. Another man in my place would have taken French
leave and disappeared. But I'm the type that bears it and says nothing. What's
one to do? Shoulders are from God, and burdens too.

One night there was a calamity in the bakery; the oven burst, and we
almost had a fire. There was nothing to do but go home, so I went home. Let

me, I thought, also taste the joy of sleeping in bed in midweek. I didn't want to wake the sleeping mite and tiptoed into the house. Coming in, it seemed to me that I heard not the snoring of one but, as it were, a double snore, one a thin enough snore and the other like the snoring of a slaughtered ox. Oh, I didn't like that! I didn't like it at all. I went up to the bed, and things suddenly turned black. Next to Elka lay a man's form. Another in my place would have made an uproar, and enough noise to rouse the whole town, but the thought occurred to me that I might wake the child. A little thing like that — why frighten a little swallow like that, I thought. All right then, I went back to the bakery and stretched out on a sack of flour, and till morning I never shut an eye. I shivered as if I had had malaria. "Enough of being a donkey," I said to myself. "Gimpel isn't going to be a sucker all his life. There's a limit even to the foolishness of a fool like Gimpel."

In the morning I went to the rabbi to get advice, and it made a great commotion in the town. They sent the beadle for Elka right away. She came, carrying the child. And what do you think she did? She denied it, denied everything, bone and stone! "He's out of his head," she said. "I know nothing of dreams or divinations." They yelled at her, warned her, hammered on the table, but she stuck to her guns: it was a false accusation, she said.

The butchers and the horse-traders took her part. One of the lads from the slaughterhouse came by and said to me, "We've got our eye on you, you're a marked man." Meanwhile the child started to bear down and soiled itself. In the rabbinical court there was an Ark of the Covenant, and they couldn't allow that, so they sent Elka away.

I said to the rabbi, "What shall I do?"

"You must divorce her at once," said he.

"And what if she refuses?" I asked.

He said, "You must serve the divorce, that's all you'll have to do."

I said, "Well, all right, Rabbi. Let me think about it."

"There's nothing to think about," said he. "You mustn't remain under the same roof with her."

"And if I want to see the child?" I asked.

"Let her go, the harlot," said he, "and her brood of bastards with her."

The verdict he gave was that I mustn't even cross her threshold — never again, as long as I should live.

During the day it didn't bother me so much. I thought, It was bound to happen, the abscess had to burst. But at night when I stretched out upon the sacks I felt it all very bitterly. A longing took me, for her and for the child. I wanted to be angry, but that's my misfortune exactly, I don't have it in me to be really angry. In the first place — this was how my thoughts went — there's bound to be a slip sometimes. You can't live without errors. Probably that lad who was with her led her on and gave her presents and what not, and women are often long on hair and short on sense, and so he got around her. And then since she denies it so, maybe I was only seeing things? Hallucinations do happen. You see a figure or a mannikin or something, but when you come up closer it's nothing, there's not a thing there. And if that's so, I'm doing her an injustice. And when I got so far in my thoughts I started to weep. I sobbed so that I wet the flour where I lay. In the morning I went to the rabbi and told him that I had made a mistake. The rabbi wrote on with his quill, and he said that if that were so he would have to reconsider the whole case. Until he had finished I wasn't to go near my wife, but I might send her bread and money by messenger.

III

Nine months passed before all the rabbis could come to an agreement. Letters went back and forth. I hadn't realized that there could be so much erudition about a matter like this.

Meantime Elka gave birth to still another child, a girl this time. On the Sabbath I went to the synagogue and invoked a blessing on her. They called me up to the Torah, and I named the child for my mother-in-law, may she rest in peace. The louts and loudmouths of the town who came into the bakery gave me a going over. All Frampol refreshed its spirits because of my trouble and grief. However, I resolved that I would always believe what I was told. What's the good of *not* believing? Today it's your wife you don't believe; tomorrow it's God Himself you won't take stock in.

By an apprentice who was her neighbor I sent her daily a corn or a wheat loaf, or a piece of pastry, rolls or bagels, or, when I got the chance, a slab of pudding, a slice of honeycake, or wedding strudel — whatever came my way. The apprentice was a goodhearted lad, and more than once he added something on his own. He had formerly annoyed me a lot, plucking my nose and digging me in the ribs, but when he started to be a visitor to my house he became kind and friendly. "Hey, you, Gimpel," he said to me, "you have a very decent little wife and two fine kids. You don't deserve them."

"But the things people say about her," I said.   50

"Well, they have long tongues," he said, "and nothing to do with them but babble. Ignore it as you ignore the cold of last winter."

One day the rabbi sent for me and said, "Are you certain, Gimpel, that you were wrong about your wife?"

I said, "I'm certain."

"Why, but look here! You yourself saw it."

"It must have been a shadow," I said.   55

"The shadow of what?"

"Just of one of the beams, I think."

"You can go home then. You owe thanks to the Yanover rabbi. He found an obscure reference in Maimonides that favored you."

I seized the rabbi's hand and kissed it.

I wanted to run home immediately. It's no small thing to be separated   60
for so long a time from wife and child. Then I reflected, I'd better go back to work now, and go home in the evening. I said nothing to anyone, although as far as my heart was concerned it was like one of the Holy Days. The women teased and twitted me as they did every day, but my thought was, Go on, with your loose talk. The truth is out, like the oil upon the water. Maimonides says it's right, and therefore it is right!

At night, when I had covered the dough to let it rise, I took my share of bread and a little sack of flour and started homeward. The moon was full and the stars were glistening, something to terrify the soul. I hurried onward, and before me darted a long shadow. It was winter, and a fresh snow had fallen. I had a mind to sing, but it was growing late and I didn't want to wake the householders. Then I felt like whistling, but remembered that you don't whistle at night because it brings the demons out. So I was silent and walked as fast as I could.

Dogs in the Christian yards barked at me when I passed, but I thought, Bark your teeth out! What are you but mere dogs? Whereas I am a man, the husband of a fine wife, the father of promising children.

As I approached the house my heart started to pound as though it were the heart of a criminal. I felt no fear, but my heart went thump! thump! Well, no drawing back. I quietly lifted the latch and went in. Elka was asleep. I looked at the infant's cradle. The shutter was closed, but the moon forced its way through the cracks. I saw the newborn child's face and loved it as soon as I saw it — immediately — each tiny bone.

Then I came nearer to the bed. And what did I see but the apprentice lying there beside Elka. The moon went out all at once. It was utterly black, and I trembled. My teeth chattered. The bread fell from my hands and my wife waked and said, "Who is that, ah?"

I muttered, "It's me." 65

"Gimpel?" she asked. "How come you're here? I thought it was forbidden."

"The rabbi said," I answered and shook as with a fever.

"Listen to me, Gimpel," she said, "go out to the shed and see if the goat's all right. It seems she's been sick." I have forgotten to say that we had a goat. When I heard she was unwell I went into the yard. The nannygoat was a good little creature. I had a nearly human feeling for her.

With hesitant steps I went up to the shed and opened the door. The goat stood there on her four feet. I felt her everywhere, drew her by the horns, examined her udders, and found nothing wrong. She had probably eaten too much bark. "Good night, little goat," I said. "Keep well." And the little beast answered with a "Maa" as though to thank me for the good will.

I went back. The apprentice had vanished. 70

"Where," I asked, "is the lad?"

"What lad?" my wife answered.

"What do you mean?" I said. "The apprentice. You were sleeping with him."

"The things I have dreamed this night and the night before," she said, "may they come true and lay you low, body and soul! An evil spirit has taken root in you and dazzles your sight." She screamed out, "You hateful creature! You moon calf! You spook! You uncouth man! Get out, or I'll scream all Frampol out of bed!"

Before I could move, her brother sprang out from behind the oven and 75 struck me a blow on the back of the head. I thought he had broken my neck. I felt that something about me was deeply wrong, and I said, "Don't make a scandal. All that's needed now is that people should accuse me of raising spooks and *dybbuks*°." For that was what she had meant. "No one will touch bread of my baking."

In short, I somehow calmed her.

dybbuks: demons, or souls of the dead, who take possession of people.

"Well," she said, "that's enough. Lie down, and be shattered by wheels."

Next morning I called the apprentice aside. "Listen here, brother!" I said. And so on and so forth. "What do you say?" He stared at me as though I had dropped from the roof or something.

"I swear," he said, "you'd better go to an herb doctor or some healer. I'm afraid you have a screw loose, but I'll hush it up for you." And that's how the thing stood.

To make a long story short, I lived twenty years with my wife. She bore me six children, four daughters and two sons. All kinds of things happened, but I neither saw nor heard. I believed, and that's all. The rabbi recently said to me, "Belief in itself is beneficial. It is written that a good man lives by his faith."

Suddenly my wife took sick. It began with a trifle, a little growth upon the breast. But she evidently was not destined to live long; she had no years. I spent a fortune on her. I have forgotten to say that by this time I had a bakery of my own and in Frampol was considered to be something of a rich man. Daily the healer came, and every witch doctor in the neighborhood was brought. They decided to use leeches, and after that to try cupping. They even called a doctor from Lublin, but it was too late. Before she died she called me to her bed and said, "Forgive me, Gimpel."

I said, "What is there to forgive? You have been a good and faithful wife."

"Woe, Gimpel!" she said. "It was ugly how I deceived you all these years. I want to go clean to my Maker, and so I have to tell you that the children are not yours."

If I had been clouted on the head with a piece of wood it couldn't have bewildered me more.

"Whose are they?" I asked.

"I don't know," she said, "there were a lot. . . . But they're not yours." And as she spoke she tossed her head to the side, her eyes turned glassy, and it was all up with Elka. On her whitened lips there remained a smile.

I imagined that, dead as she was, she was saying, "I deceived Gimpel. That was the meaning of my brief life."

IV

One night, when the period of mourning was done, as I lay dreaming on the flour sacks, there came the Spirit of Evil himself and said to me, "Gimpel, why do you sleep?"

I said, "What should I be doing? Eating *kreplach*°?"

"The whole world deceives you," he said, "and you ought to deceive the world in your turn."

"How can I deceive all the world?" I asked him.

He answered, "You might accumulate a bucket of urine every day and at night pour it into the dough. Let the sages of Frampol eat filth."

"What about judgment in the world to come?" I said.

kreplach: a kind of dumpling containing meat, cheese, or other filling.

"There is no world to come," he said. "They've sold you a bill of goods and talked you into believing you carried a cat in your belly. What nonsense!"

"Well then," I said, "and is there a God?" 95

He answered, "There is no God either."

"What," I said, "*is* there, then?"

"A thick mire."

He stood before my eyes with a goatish beard and horns, longtoothed, and with a tail. Hearing such words, I wanted to snatch him by the tail, but I tumbled from the flour sacks and nearly broke a rib. Then it happened that I had to answer the call of nature, and, passing, I saw the risen dough, which seemed to say to me, "Do it!" In brief, I let myself be persuaded.

At dawn the apprentice came. We kneaded the bread, scattered caraway 100 seeds on it, and set it to bake. Then the apprentice went away, and I was left sitting in the little trench by the oven, on a pile of rags. Well, Gimpel, I thought, you've revenged yourself on them for all the shame they've put on you. Outside the frost glittered, but it was warm beside the oven. The flames heated my face. I bent my head and fell into a doze.

I saw in a dream, at once, Elka in her shroud. She called to me, "What have you done, Gimpel?"

I said to her, "It's all your fault," and started to cry.

"You fool!" she said. "You fool! Because I was false is everything false too? I never deceived anyone but myself. I'm paying for it all, Gimpel. They spare you nothing here."

I looked at her face. It was black. I was startled and waked, and remained sitting dumb. I sensed that everything hung in the balance. A false step now and I'd lose Eternal Life. But God gave me His help. I seized the long shovel and took out the loaves, carried them into the yard, and started to dig a hole in the frozen earth.

My apprentice came back as I was doing it. "What are you doing, boss?" 105 he said, and grew pale as a corpse.

"I know what I'm doing," I said, and I buried it all before his very eyes.

Then I went home, took my hoard from its hiding place, and divided it among the children. "I saw your mother tonight," I said. "She's turning black, poor thing."

They were so astounded they couldn't speak a word.

"Be well," I said, "and forget that such a one as Gimpel ever existed." I put on my short coat, a pair of boots, took the bag that held my prayer shawl in one hand, my stick in the other, and kissed the *mezzuzah*°. When people saw me in the street they were greatly surprised.

"Where are you going?" they said. 110

I answered, "Into the world." And so I departed from Frampol.

I wandered over the land, and good people did not neglect me. After many years I became old and white; I heard a great deal, many lies and falsehoods, but the longer I lived the more I understood that there were really

---

mezzuzah: a small oblong container, affixed near the front door of the house, which holds copies of Biblical verses (including a reminder to obey God's laws when traveling away from home).

no lies. Whatever doesn't really happen is dreamed at night. It happens to one if it doesn't happen to another, tomorrow if not today, or a century hence if not next year. What difference can it make? Often I heard tales of which I said, "Now this is a thing that cannot happen." But before a year had elapsed I heard that it actually had come to pass somewhere.

Going from place to place, eating at strange tables, it often happens that I spin yarns — improbable things that could never have happened — about devils, magicians, windmills, and the like. The children run after me, calling, "Grandfather, tell us a story." Sometimes they ask for particular stories, and I try to please them. A fat young boy once said to me, "Grandfather, it's the same story you told us before." The little rogue, he was right.

So it is with dreams too. It is many years since I left Frampol, but as soon as I shut my eyes I am there again. And whom do you think I see? Elka. She is standing by the washtub, as at our first encounter, but her face is shining and her eyes are radiant as the eyes of a saint, and she speaks outlandish words to me, strange things. When I wake I have forgotten it all. But while the dream lasts I am comforted. She answers all my queries, and what comes out is that all is right. I weep and implore, "Let me be with you." And she consoles me and tells me to be patient. The time is nearer than it is far. Sometimes she strokes and kisses me and weeps upon my face. When I awaken I feel her lips and taste the salt of her tears.

No doubt the world is entirely an imaginary world, but it is only once removed from the true world. At the door of the hovel where I lie, there stands the plank on which the dead are taken away. The gravedigger Jew has his spade ready. The grave waits and the worms are hungry; the shrouds are prepared — I carry them in my beggar's sack. Another *shnorrer*° is waiting to inherit my bed of straw. When the time comes I will go joyfully. Whatever may be there, it will be real, without complication, without ridicule, without deception. God be praised: there even Gimpel cannot be deceived.

Questions

1. In what ways does Gimpel appear to deserve his nickname *the fool?* In what other ways is Gimpel not foolish at all?
2. What does Gimpel find to love in the character of Elka? Consider in particular the scene of her deathbed confession and her later appearance in Gimpel's dreams.
3. Why does Gimpel momentarily listen to the Devil? How is he delivered from temptation? For what reasons does he finally divide his wealth and become a poor wanderer? Would you call him a dynamic character, or a static character — one who grows and develops in the course of the story, or one who remains unchanged?
4. "No doubt the world is entirely an imaginary world, but it is only once removed from the true world." Comment on this statement in the closing paragraph. What do you think it means?
5. What elements of the supernatural do you find in "Gimpel the Fool"? What details of down-to-earth realism?
6. In what respects does the story resemble a fable? Is it possible to draw any moral from it?

shnorrer: a beggar, a traveling panhandler.

Suggestions for Writing

1. Here is a topic for a lively essay if you are familiar with some variety of popular fiction — detective stories, science fiction, Gothic novels, romances, "adolescent agony" novels written for teenagers, or other kinds of paperback storytelling. Portray some of the stock characters you find prevalent in it. Suggestion: It might be simplistic to condemn stock characters as bad. They have long been valuable ingredients in much excellent literature. (For a discussion of stock characters, see page 73).

2. Alternate topic: Portray a few stock characters we meet in current television programs. It might focus your essay to confine it to just one variety of stock character (for instance, the little man who peddles information to the police, the glamorous Russian spy), or to just one kind of program (situation comedies, say, or soap operas, or police thrillers).

3. In a brief essay, study a dynamic character in a story, showing exactly how that character changed, or grew and developed. Possible subjects: Granny Weatherall, Gimpel, Sammy in John Updike's "A & P," Paul in "Paul's Case," the boy Sarty Snopes in William Faulkner's "Barn Burning" (in Chapter 5). (For a discussion of dynamic characters, see page 74.)

4. Alternate topic: Have you ever in your life known anyone whose character, over months or years, has altered deeply? If so, try to explain what may have caused that person to be a "dynamic character."

5. Topics for brief papers:

    The motivation of Gimpel in leaving Frampol to wander the world.

    The motivation of Sammy in quitting his job (in "A & P").

    The motivation of someone (whether in your reading or in your experience) who made a similar gesture of throwing over everything and taking off.

6. Here are topics for an essay you can write by the method of comparison and contrast (explained in "Writing about a Story," page 1358).

    Compare the characters of two forceful women: Granny Weatherall and Mrs. Ulgine Barrows (in "The Catbird Seat").

    Compare two sly deceivers: Mr. Martin (in "The Catbird Seat") and Elka (in "Gimpel the Fool").

    Compare two black mothers in their attitudes toward young people: Mama (in "Everyday Use") and Miss Hazel (in "My Man Bovanne").

    Look up Emily Dickinson's poem "I heard a Fly buzz – when I died" and compare it with "The Jilting of Granny Weatherall" in its account of a woman's deathbed experience.

5 Tone and Style

In many Victorian novels it was customary for some commentator, presumably the author, to interrupt the story from time to time, remarking upon the action, offering philosophic asides, or explaining the procedures to be followed in telling the story.

> Two hours later, Dorothea was seated in an inner room or boudoir of a handsome apartment in the Via Sistina. I am sorry to add that she was sobbing bitterly. . . .
> — George Eliot in *Middlemarch* (1873)

> But let the gentle-hearted reader be under no apprehension whatsoever. It is not destined that Eleanor shall marry Mr. Slope or Bertie Stanhope.
> — Anthony Trollope in *Barchester Towers* (1857)

> And, as we bring our characters forward, I will ask leave, as a man and a brother, not only to introduce, but occasionally to step down from the platform, and talk about them: if they are good and kindly, to love them and shake them by the hand; if they are silly, to laugh at them confidentially in the reader's sleeve; if they are wicked and heartless, to abuse them in the strongest terms which politeness admits of.
> — William Makepeace Thackeray in *Vanity Fair* (1847 – 1848)

Of course, the voice of this commentator was not identical with that of the "real life" author — the one toiling over an inkpot, worrying about publication deadlines and whether the rent would be paid. At times the living author might have been far different in personality from that usually wise and cheerful intruder who kept addressing the reader of the book. Much of the time, to be sure, the author probably agreed with whatever attitudes his alter ego expressed. But, in effect, the author created the character of a commentator to speak for him and throughout the novel artfully sustained that character's voice.

Such intrusions, although sometimes useful to the "real" author and enjoyable to the reader, are today rare. Modern storytellers, carefully keeping out of sight, seldom comment on their plots and characters. Apparently they agree with Anton Chekhov that a writer should not judge the characters but should serve as their "impartial witness." And yet, no less definitely than Victorian novelists who introduced commentators, writers of effective stories no doubt have feelings toward their characters and events. The authors presumably care about these imaginary people and, in order for the story to grasp and sustain our interest, have to make us see these people in such a way that we, too, will care about them. When at the beginning of the short story "In Exile" Chekhov introduces us to a character, he does so with a description that arouses sympathy:

> The Tartar was worn out and ill, and, wrapping himself in his rags, he talked about how good it was in the province of Simbirsk, and what a beautiful and clever wife he had left at home. He was not more than twenty-five, and in the firelight his pale, sickly face and woebegone expression made him seem like a boy.

Other than the comparison of the Tartar to a child, the details in this passage seem mostly factual: the young man's illness, ragged clothes, facial expression, and topics of conversation. But these details form a portrait that stirs pity. By his selection of these imaginary details out of countless others that he might have included, Chekhov firmly directs our feelings about the Tartar, so miserable and pathetic in his sickness and his homesickness. We cannot know, of course, exactly what the living Chekhov felt; but at least we can be sure that we are supposed to share the compassion and tenderness of the narrator — Chekhov's impartial (but human) witness.

Not only the author's choice of details may lead us to infer his attitude, but also his choice of characters, events, and situations, and his choice of words. When the narrator of Joseph Conrad's *Heart of Darkness* comes upon an African outpost littered with abandoned machines and notices "a boiler wallowing in the grass," the exact word *wallowing* conveys an attitude: that there is something swinish about this scene of careless waste. Whatever leads us to infer the author's attitude is commonly called **tone.** Like a tone of voice, the tone of a story may communicate amusement, anger, affection, sorrow, contempt. It implies the feelings of the author, so far as we can sense them. Those feelings may be similar to feelings expressed by the narrator of the story (or by any character), but sometimes they may be dissimilar, even sharply opposed. The characters in a story may regard an event as sad, but we sense that the author regards it as funny. To understand the tone of a story, then, is to understand some attitude more fundamental to the story than whatever attitude the characters explicitly declare.

The tone of a story, like a tone of voice, may convey not simply one attitude, but a medley. Reading "Gimpel the Fool" (Chapter Four), we have mingled feelings toward Gimpel and his "foolishness": amusement that Gimpel is so easily deceived; sympathy, perhaps, for his excessive innocence; admiration for his unwavering faith in God and fellow man. Often the tone of a literary story will be too rich and complicated to sum up in one or two words. But to try to describe the tone of such a story may be a useful way to penetrate to its center and to grasp the whole of it.

One of the clearest indications of the tone of a story is the **style** in which it is written. In general, style refers to the individual traits or characteristics of a piece of writing; to a writer's particular ways of managing words that we come to recognize as habitual or customary. A distinctive style marks the work of a fine writer: we can tell his or her work from that of anyone else. From one story to another, however, the writer may fittingly change style; and in some stories, style may be altered meaningfully as the story goes along. In his novel *As I Lay Dying,* William Faulkner changes narrators with every chapter, and he distinguishes the narrators one from another by giving each an individual style or manner of speaking. Though each narrator has his own style, the book as a whole demonstrates Faulkner's style as well. For instance, one chapter is written from the point of view of a small boy, Vardaman Bundren, member of a family of poor Mississippi tenant farmers, whose view of a horse in a barn reads like this:

> It is as though the dark were resolving him out of his integrity, into an unrelated scattering of components — snuffings and stampings; smells of cooling flesh and ammoniac hair; an illusion of a coordinated whole of splotched hide and strong bones within which, detached and secret and familiar, an *is* different from my is.[1]

How can a small boy unaccustomed to libraries use words like *integrity, components, illusion,* and *coordinated?* Elsewhere in the story, Vardaman says aloud, with no trace of literacy, "Hit was a-laying right there on the ground." Apparently, in the passage it is not the voice of the boy that we are hearing, but something resembling the voice of William Faulkner, elevated and passionate, expressing the boy's thoughts in a style that admits Faulknerian words.

Usually, *style* indicates a mode of expression: the language a writer uses. In this sense, the notion of style includes such traits as the length and complexity of sentences, and **diction,** or choice of words: abstract or concrete, bookish ("unrelated scattering of components") or close to speech ("Hit was a-laying right there on the ground"). Involved in the idea of style, too, is any habitual use of imagery, patterns of sound, figures of speech, or other devices.

To see what style means, compare the stories in this chapter by William Faulkner ("Barn Burning") and by Ernest Hemingway ("A Clean, Well-Lighted Place"). Faulkner frequently falls into a style in which a statement, as soon as uttered, is followed by another statement expressing

[1]Modern Library edition (New York: Random, 1930) 379.

the idea in a more emphatic way. Sentences are interrupted with paren-thetical elements (asides, like this) thrust into them unexpectedly. At times, Faulkner writes of seemingly ordinary matters as if giving a speech in a towering passion. Here, from "Barn Burning," is a description of how a boy's father delivers a rug:

> "Don't you want me to help?" he whispered. His father did not answer and now he heard again that stiff foot striking the hollow portico with that wooden and clocklike deliberation, that outrageous overstatement of the weight it carried. The rug, hunched, not flung (the boy could tell that even in the darkness) from his father's shoulder struck the angle of wall and floor with a sound unbelievably loud, thunderous, then the foot again, unhurried and enormous; a light came on in the house and the boy sat, tense, breathing steadily and quietly and just a little fast, though the foot itself did not increase its beat at all, descending the steps now; now the boy could see him.

Faulkner is not merely indulging in language for its own sake. As you will find when you read the whole story, this rug delivery is vital to the story, and so too is the father's profound defiance — indicated by his walk. By devices of style — by *metaphor* and *simile* ("wooden and clocklike"), by exact qualification ("not flung"), by emphatic adjectives ("loud, thunder-ous") — Faulkner is carefully placing his emphases. By the words he se-lects to describe the father's stride, Faulkner directs how we feel toward the man and perhaps also indicates his own wondering but skeptical atti-tude toward a character whose very footfall is "outrageous" and "enor-mous." (Fond of long sentences like the last one in the quoted passage, Faulkner remarked that there are sentences that need to be written in the way a circus acrobat pedals a bicycle on a high wire: rapidly, so as not to fall off.)

Hemingway's famous style includes both short sentences and long, but when the sentences are long they tend to be relatively simple in construction. Hemingway likes long compound sentences (clause plus clause plus clause), sometimes joined with "and's." He interrupts such a sentence with a dependent clause or a parenthetical element much less frequently than Faulkner does. The effect is like listening to speech:

> In the day time the street was dusty, but at night the dew settled the dust and the old man liked to sit late because he was deaf and now at night it was quiet and he felt the difference.

Hemingway is a master of swift, terse dialogue, and often casts whole scenes in the form of conversation. As if he were a closemouthed speaker unwilling to let his feelings loose, the narrator of a Hemingway story often addresses us in understatement, implying greater depths of feeling than he puts into words. Read the following story and you will see that its style and tone cannot be separated.

Ernest Hemingway

A CLEAN, WELL-LIGHTED PLACE

1933

Ernest Hemingway (1898 – 1961), born in Oak Park, Illinois, bypassed college to be a cub reporter. In World War I, as an eighteen-year-old volunteer ambulance driver in Italy, he was wounded in action. In 1922 he settled in Paris, then aswarm with writers: days he later recalled in A Moveable Feast *(1964). Hemingway won swift acclaim for his early stories,* In Our Time *(1925), and for his first, perhaps finest novel,* The Sun Also Rises *(1926), portraying a "lost generation" of postwar American drifters in France and Spain.* For Whom the Bell Tolls *(1940) depicts life during the Spanish Civil War. Hemingway became a celebrity, often photographed as a marlin fisherman or a lion hunter. A fan of bullfighting, he wrote two nonfiction books on the subject:* Death in the Afternoon *(1932) and* The Dangerous Summer *(1985). After World War II, with his fourth wife, journalist Mary Welsh, he made his home in Cuba, where he wrote* The Old Man and the Sea *(1952). The Nobel prize for literature came to him in 1954. In 1961, mentally distressed and physically ailing, he shot himself. Hemingway brought a hard-bitten realism into American fiction. His heroes live dangerously, by personal codes of honor, courage, and endurance. Hemingway's distinctively crisp, unadorned style left American literature permanently changed.*

It was late and every one had left the café except an old man who sat in the shadow the leaves of the tree made against the electric light. In the day time the street was dusty, but at night the dew settled the dust and the old man liked to sit late because he was deaf and now at night it was quiet and he felt the difference. The two waiters inside the café knew that the old man was a little drunk, and while he was a good client they knew that if he became too drunk he would leave without paying, so they kept watch on him.

"Last week he tried to commit suicide," one waiter said.

"Why?"

"He was in despair."

"What about?"

"Nothing." 5

"How do you know it was nothing?"

"He has plenty of money."

They sat together at a table that was close against the wall near the door of the café and looked at the terrace where the tables were all empty except where the old man sat in the shadow of the leaves of the tree that moved slightly in the wind. A girl and a soldier went by in the street. The street light shone on the brass number on his collar. The girl wore no head covering and hurried beside him.

"The guard will pick him up," one waiter said. 10

"What does it matter if he gets what he's after?"

"He had better get off the street now. The guard will get him. They went by five minutes ago."

The old man sitting in the shadow rapped on his saucer with his glass. The younger waiter went over to him.

"What do you want?"

The old man looked at him. "Another brandy," he said.   15

"You'll be drunk," the waiter said. The old man looked at him. The waiter went away.

"He'll stay all night," he said to his colleague. "I'm sleepy now. I never get into bed before three o'clock. He should have killed himself last week."

The waiter took the brandy bottle and another saucer from the counter inside the café and marched out to the old man's table. He put down the saucer and poured the glass full of brandy.

"You should have killed yourself last week," he said to the deaf man. The old man motioned with his finger. "A little more," he said. The waiter poured on into the glass so that the brandy slopped over and ran down the stem into the top saucer of the pile. "Thank you," the old man said. The waiter took the bottle back inside the café. He sat down at the table with his colleague again.

"He's drunk now," he said.   20

"He's drunk every night."°

"What did he want to kill himself for?"

"How should I know."

"How did he do it?"

"He hung himself with a rope."   25

"Who cut him down?"

"His niece."

"Why did they do it?"

"Fear for his soul."

"How much money has he got?"   30

"He's got plenty."

"He must be eighty years old."

"Anyway I should say he was eighty."°

"I wish he would go home. I never get to bed before three o'clock. What kind of hour is that to go to bed?"

"He stays up because he likes it."   35

"He's lonely. I'm not lonely. I have a wife waiting in bed for me."

"He had a wife once too."

"A wife would be no good to him now."

"You can't tell. He might be better with a wife."

"His niece looks after him."   40

"I know. You said she cut him down."

"I wouldn't want to be that old. An old man is a nasty thing."

"Not always. This old man is clean. He drinks without spilling. Even now, drunk. Look at him."

"I don't want to look at him. I wish he would go home. He has no regard for those who must work."

"He's drunk now," he said. "He's drunk every night": The younger waiter says both these lines. A device of Hemingway's style is sometimes to have a character pause, then speak again — as often happens in actual speech.

"He must be eighty years old." "Anyway I should say he was eighty": Is this another instance of the same character's speaking twice? Clearly, it is the younger waiter who says the next line, "I wish he would go home."

The old man looked from his glass across the square, then over at the waiters.

"Another brandy," he said, pointing to his glass. The waiter who was in a hurry came over.

"Finished," he said, speaking with that omission of syntax stupid people employ when talking to drunken people or foreigners. "No more tonight. Close now."

"Another," said the old man.

"No. Finished." The waiter wiped the edge of the table with a towel and shook his head.

The old man stood up, slowly counted the saucers, took a leather coin purse from his pocket and paid for the drinks, leaving half a peseta tip.

The waiter watched him go down the street, a very old man walking unsteadily but with dignity.

"Why didn't you let him stay and drink?" the unhurried waiter asked. They were putting up the shutters. "It is not half-past two."

"I want to go home to bed."

"What is an hour?"

"More to me than to him."

"An hour is the same."

"You talk like an old man yourself. He can buy a bottle and drink at home."

"It's not the same."

"No, it is not," agreed the waiter with a wife. He did not wish to be unjust. He was only in a hurry.

"And you? You have no fear of going home before your usual hour?"

"Are you trying to insult me?"

"No, hombre, only to make a joke."

"No," the waiter who was in a hurry said, rising from pulling down the metal shutters. "I have confidence. I am all confidence."

"You have youth, confidence, and a job," the older waiter said. "You have everything."

"And what do you lack?"

"Everything but work."

"You have everything I have."

"No. I have never had confidence and I am not young."

"Come on. Stop talking nonsense and lock up."

"I am of those who like to stay late at the café," the older waiter said. "With all those who do not want to go to bed. With all those who need a light for the night."

"I want to go home and into bed."

"We are of two different kinds," the older waiter said. He was now dressed to go home. "It is not only a question of youth and confidence although those things are very beautiful. Each night I am reluctant to close up because there may be some one who needs the café."

"Hombre, there are bodegas° open all night long."

"You do not understand. This is a clean and pleasant café. It is well

---

bodegas: wineshops.

lighted. The light is very good and also, now, there are shadows of the leaves."

"Good night," said the younger waiter.

"Good night," the other said. Turning off the electric light he continued the conversation with himself. It is the light of course but it is necessary that the place be clean and pleasant. You do not want music. Certainly you do not want music. Nor can you stand before a bar with dignity although that is all that is provided for these hours. What did he fear? It was not fear or dread. It was a nothing that he knew too well. It was all a nothing and a man was nothing too. It was only that and light was all it needed and a certain cleanness and order. Some lived in it and never felt it but he knew it all was nada y pues nada y nada y pues nada°. Our nada who art in nada, nada be thy name thy kingdom nada thy will be nada in nada as it is in nada. Give us this nada our daily nada and nada us our nada as we nada our nadas and nada us not into nada but deliver us from nada; pues nada. Hail nothing full of nothing, nothing is with thee. He smiled and stood before a bar with a shining steam pressure coffee machine.

"What's yours?" asked the barman.

"Nada."

"Otro loco más°," said the barman and turned away.

"A little cup," said the waiter.

The barman poured it for him.

"The light is very bright and pleasant but the bar is unpolished," the waiter said.

The barman looked at him but did not answer. It was too late at night for conversation.

"You want another copita°?" the barman asked.

"No, thank you," said the waiter and went out. He disliked bars and bodegas. A clean, well-lighted café was a very different thing. Now, without thinking further, he would go home to his room. He would lie in the bed and finally, with daylight, he would go to sleep. After all, he said to himself, it is probably only insomnia. Many must have it.

QUESTIONS

1. What besides insomnia makes the older waiter reluctant to go to bed? Comment especially on his meditation with its *nada* refrain. Why does he so well understand the old man's need for a café? What does the café represent for the two of them?
2. Compare the younger waiter and the older waiter in their attitudes toward the old man. Whose attitude do you take to be closer to that of the author? Even though Hemingway does not editorially state his own feelings, how does he make them clear to us?
3. Point to sentences that establish the style of the story. What is distinctive in them? What repetitions of words or phrases seem particularly effective? Does Hemingway seem to favor a simple or an erudite vocabulary?
4. What is the story's point of view? Discuss its appropriateness.

nada y pues . . . nada: nothing and then nothing and nothing and then nothing.
Otro loco más: another lunatic.
copita: little cup.

William Faulkner

BARN BURNING

William Faulkner (1897 – 1962) receives a capsule biography on page 24, along with his story "A Rose for Emily." His "Barn Burning" is among his many contributions to the history of Yoknapatawpha, an imaginary Mississippi county in which the Sartorises and the de Spains are landed aristocrats living by a code of honor and the Snopeses — most of them — shiftless ne'er-do-wells.

The store in which the Justice of the Peace's court was sitting smelled of cheese. The boy, crouched on his nail keg at the back of the crowded room, knew he smelled cheese, and more: from where he sat he could see the ranked shelves close-packed with the solid, squat, dynamic shapes of tin cans whose labels his stomach read, not from the lettering which meant nothing to his mind but from the scarlet devils and the silver curve of fish — this, the cheese which he knew he smelled and the hermetic meat which his intestines believed he smelled coming in intermittent gusts momentary and brief between the other constant one, the smell and sense just a little of fear because mostly of despair and grief, the old fierce pull of blood. He could not see the table where the Justice sat and before which his father and his father's enemy *(our enemy he thought in that despair; ourn! mine and hisn both! He's my father!)* stood, but he could hear them, the two of them that is, because his father had said no word yet:

"But what proof have you, Mr. Harris?"

"I told you. The hog got into my corn. I caught it up and sent it back to him. He had no fence that would hold it. I told him so, warned him. The next time I put the hog in my pen. When he came to get it I gave him enough wire to patch up his pen. The next time I put the hog up and kept it. I rode down to his house and saw the wire I gave him still rolled on to the spool in his yard. I told him he could have the hog when he paid me a dollar pound fee. That evening a nigger came with the dollar and got the hog. He was a strange nigger. He said, 'He say to tell you wood and hay kin burn.' I said, 'What?' 'That whut he say to tell you,' the nigger said. 'Wood and hay kin burn.' That night my barn burned. I got the stock out but I lost the barn."

"Where is the nigger? Have you got him?"

"He was a strange nigger, I tell you. I don't know what became of him."   5

"But that's not proof. Don't you see that's not proof?"

"Get that boy up here. He knows." For a moment the boy thought too that the man meant his older brother until Harris said, "Not him. The little one. The boy," and, crouching, small for his age, small and wiry like his father, in patched and faded jeans even too small for him, with straight, uncombed, brown hair and eyes gray and wild as storm scud, he saw the men between himself and the table part and become a lane of grim faces, at the end of which he saw the Justice, a shabby, collarless, graying man in spectacles, beckoning him. He felt no floor under his bare feet; he seemed to walk beneath the palpable weight of the grim turning faces. His father, still in his black Sunday coat donned not for the trial but for the moving, did not even look at him. *He aims for me to lie,* he thought, again with that frantic grief and despair. *And I will have to do hit.*

"What's your name, boy?" the Justice said.

"Colonel Sartoris Snopes," the boy whispered.

"Hey?" the Justice said. "Talk louder. Colonel Sartoris? I reckon any- 10 body named for Colonel Sartoris in this country can't help but tell the truth, can they?" The boy said nothing. *Enemy! Enemy!* he thought; for a moment he could not even see, could not see that the Justice's face was kindly nor discern that his voice was troubled when he spoke to the man named Harris: "Do you want me to question this boy?" But he could hear, and during those subsequent long seconds while there was absolutely no sound in the crowded little room save that of quiet and intent breathing it was as if he had swung outward at the end of a grape vine, over a ravine, and at the top of the swing had been caught in a prolonged instant of mesmerized gravity, weightless in time.

"No!" Harris said violently, explosively. "Damnation! Send him out of here!" Now time, the fluid world, rushed beneath him again, the voices coming to him again through the smell of cheese and sealed meat, the fear and despair and the old grief of blood:

"This case is closed. I can't find against you, Snopes, but I can give you advice. Leave this country and don't come back to it."

His father spoke for the first time, his voice cold and harsh, level, without emphasis: "I aim to. I don't figure to stay in a country among people who . . ." he said something unprintable and vile, addressed to no one.

"That'll do," the Justice said. "Take your wagon and get out of this country before dark. Case dismissed."

His father turned, and he followed the stiff black coat, the wiry figure 15 walking a little stiffly from where a Confederate provost's man's musket ball had taken him in the heel on a stolen horse thirty years ago, followed the two backs now, since his older brother had appeared from somewhere in the crowd, no taller than the father but thicker, chewing tobacco steadily, between the two lines of grim-faced men and out of the store and across the worn gallery and down the sagging steps and among the dogs and half-grown boys in the mild May dust, where as he passed a voice hissed:

"Barn burner!"

Again he could not see, whirling; there was a face in a red haze, moonlike, bigger than the full moon, the owner of it half again his size, he leaping in the red haze toward the face, feeling no blow, feeling no shock when his head struck the earth, scrabbling up and leaping again, feeling no blow this time either and tasting no blood, scrabbling up to see the other boy in full flight and himself already leaping into pursuit as his father's hand jerked him back, the harsh, cold voice speaking above him: "Go get in the wagon."

It stood in a grove of locusts and mulberries across the road. His two hulking sisters in their Sunday dresses and his mother and her sister in calico and sunbonnets were already in it, sitting on and among the sorry residue of the dozen and more movings which even the boy could remember — the battered stove, the broken beds and chairs, the clock inlaid with mother-of-pearl, which would not run, stopped at some fourteen minutes past two o'clock of a dead and forgotten day and time, which had been his mother's dowry. She was crying, though when she saw him she drew her sleeve across her face and began to descend from the wagon. "Get back," the father said.

"He's hurt. I got to get some water and wash his . . ."

"Get back in the wagon," his father said. He got in too, over the tail-gate. His father mounted to the seat where the older brother already sat and struck the gaunt mules two savage blows with the peeled willow, but without heat. It was not even sadistic; it was exactly that same quality which in later years would cause his descendants to over-run the engine before putting a motor car into motion, striking and reining back in the same movement. The wagon went on, the store with its quiet crowd of grimly watching men dropped behind; a curve in the road hid it. *Forever* he thought. *Maybe he's done satisfied now, now that he has . . .* stopping himself, not to say it aloud even to himself. His mother's hand touched his shoulder.

"Does hit hurt?" she said.

"Naw," he said. "Hit don't hurt. Lemme be."

"Can't you wipe some of the blood off before hit dries?"

"I'll wash to-night," he said. "Lemme be, I tell you."

The wagon went on. He did not know where they were going. None of them ever did or ever asked, because it was always somewhere, always a house of sorts waiting for them a day or two days or even three days away. Likely his father had already arranged to make a crop on another farm before he . . . Again he had to stop himself. He (the father) always did. There was something about his wolflike independence and even courage when the advantage was at least neutral which impressed strangers, as if they got from his latent ravening ferocity not so much a sense of dependability as a feeling that his ferocious conviction in the rightness of his own actions would be of advantage to all whose interest lay with his.

That night they camped, in a grove of oaks and beeches where a spring ran. The nights were still cool and they had a fire against it, of a rail lifted from a nearby fence and cut into lengths — a small fire, neat, niggard almost, a shrewd fire; such fires were his father's habit and custom always, even in freezing weather. Older, the boy might have remarked this and wondered why not a big one; why should not a man who had not only seen the waste and extravagance of war, but who had in his blood an inherent voracious prodigality with material not his own, have burned everything in sight? Then he might have gone a step farther and thought that that was the reason: that niggard blaze was the living fruit of nights passed during those four years in the woods hiding from all men, blue or gray, with his strings of horses (captured horses, he called them). And older still, he might have divined the true reason: that the element of fire spoke to some deep mainspring of his father's being, as the element of steel or of powder spoke to other men, as the one weapon for the preservation of integrity, else breath were not worth the breathing, and hence to be regarded with respect and used with discretion.

But he did not think this now and he had seen those same niggard blazes all his life. He merely ate his supper beside it and was already half asleep over his iron plate when his father called him, and once more he followed the stiff back, the stiff and ruthless limp, up the slope and on to the starlit road where, turning, he could see his father against the stars but without face or depth — a shape black, flat, and bloodless as though cut from tin in the iron folds of the frockcoat which had not been made for him, the voice harsh like tin and without heat like tin:

"You were fixing to tell them. You would have told him."

He didn't answer. His father struck him with the flat of his hand on the side of the head, hard but without heat, exactly as he had struck the two mules at the store, exactly as he would strike either of them with any stick in order to kill a horse fly, his voice still without heat or anger: "You're getting to be a man. You got to learn. You got to learn to stick to your own blood or you ain't going to have any blood to stick to you. Do you think either of them, any man there this morning, would? Don't you know all they wanted was a chance to get at me because they knew I had them beat? Eh?" Later, twenty years later, he was to tell himself, "If I had said they wanted only truth, justice, he would have hit me again." But now he said nothing. He was not crying. He just stood there. "Answer me," his father said.

"Yes," he whispered. His father turned. 30

"Get on to bed. We'll be there tomorrow."

Tomorrow they were there. In the early afternoon the wagon stopped before a paintless two-room house identical almost with the dozen others it had stopped before even in the boy's ten years, and again, as on the other dozen occasions, his mother and aunt got down and began to unload the wagon, although his two sisters and his father and brother had not moved.

"Likely hit ain't fitten for hawgs," one of the sisters said.

"Nevertheless, fit it will and you'll hog it and like it," his father said. "Get out of them chairs and help your Ma unload."

The two sisters got down, big, bovine, in a flutter of cheap ribbons; one 35 of them drew from the jumbled wagon bed a battered lantern, the other a worn broom. His father handed the reins to the older son and began to climb stiffly over the wheel. "When they get unloaded, take the team to the barn and feed them." Then he said, and at first the boy thought he was still speaking to his brother: "Come with me."

"Me?" he said.

"Yes," his father said. "You."

"Abner," his mother said. His father paused and looked back — the harsh level stare beneath the shaggy, graying, irascible brows.

"I reckon I'll have a word with the man that aims to begin tomorrow owning me body and soul for the next eight months."

They went back up the road. A week ago — or before last night, that is 40 — he would have asked where they were going, but not now. His father had struck him before last night but never before had he paused afterward to explain why; it was as if the blow and the following calm, outrageous voice still rang, repercussed, divulging nothing to him save the terrible handicap of being young, the light weight of his few years, just heavy enough to prevent his soaring free of the world as it seemed to be ordered but not heavy enough to keep him footed solid in it, to resist it and try to change the course of its events.

Presently he could see the grove of oaks and cedars and the other flowering trees and shrubs where the house would be, though not the house yet. They walked beside a fence massed with honeysuckle and Cherokee roses and came to a gate swinging open between two brick pillars, and now, beyond a sweep of drive, he saw the house for the first time and at that instant he forgot his father and the terror and despair both, and even when he remembered his father again (who had not stopped) the terror and despair did not return. Because, for all the twelve movings, they had sojourned until now in a poor country, a land of small farms and fields and houses, and he had never seen a house like this before. *Hit's big as a courthouse* he thought quietly, with a surge of peace and joy whose reason he could not have thought into words, being too young for that: *They are safe from him. People whose lives are a part of this peace and dignity are beyond his touch, he no more to them than a buzzing wasp: capable of stinging for a little moment but that's all; the spell of this peace and dignity rendering even the barns and stable and cribs which belong to it impervious to the puny flames he might contrive . . .* this, the peace and joy, ebbing for an instant as he looked again at the stiff black back, the stiff and implacable limp of the figure which was not dwarfed by the house, for the reason that it had never looked big anywhere and which now, against the serene columned backdrop, had more than ever that impervious quality of something cut ruthlessly from tin, depthless, as though, sidewise to the sun, it would cast no shadow. Watching him, the boy remarked the absolutely undeviating course which his father held and saw the stiff foot come squarely down in a pile of fresh droppings where a horse had stood in the drive and which his father could have avoided by a simple change of stride. But it ebbed only for a moment, though he could not have thought this into words either, walking on in the spell of the house, which he could even want but without envy, without sorrow, certainly never with that ravening and jealous rage which unknown to him walked in the ironlike black coat before him: *Maybe he will feel it too. Maybe it will even change him now from what maybe he couldn't help but be.*

They crossed the portico. Now he could hear his father's stiff foot as it came down on the boards with clocklike finality, a sound out of all proportion to the displacement of the body it bore and which was not dwarfed either by the white door before it, as though it had attained to a sort of vicious and ravening minimum not to be dwarfed by anything — the flat, wide, black hat, the formal coat of broadcloth which had once been black but which had now that friction-glazed greenish cast of the bodies of old house flies, the lifted sleeve which was too large, the lifted hand like a curled claw. The door opened so promptly that the boy knew the Negro must have been watching them all the time, an old man with neat grizzled hair, in a linen jacket, who stood barring the door with his body, saying, "Wipe yo foots, white man, fo you come in here. Major ain't home nohow."

"Get out of my way, nigger," his father said, without heat too, flinging the door back and the Negro also and entering, his hat still on his head. And now the boy saw the prints of the stiff foot on the doorjamb and saw them appear on the pale rug behind the machinelike deliberation of the foot which seemed to bear (or transmit) twice the weight which the body compassed. The Negro was shouting "Miss Lula! Miss Lula!" somewhere behind them, then the boy, deluged as though by a warm wave by a suave turn of the carpeted stair and a pendant glitter of chandeliers and a mute gleam of gold frames, heard the swift feet and saw her too, a lady — perhaps he had never seen her like before either — in a gray, smooth gown with lace at the throat and an apron tied at the waist and the sleeves turned back, wiping cake or biscuit dough from her hands with a towel as she came up the hall, looking not at his father at all but at the tracks on the blond rug with an expression of incredulous amazement.

"I tried," the Negro cried. "I tole him to . . ."

"Will you please go away?" she said in a shaking voice. "Major de Spain is not at home. Will you please go away?" 45

His father had not spoken again. He did not speak again. He did not even look at her. He just stood stiff in the center of the rug, in his hat, the shaggy iron-gray brows twitching slightly above the pebble-colored eyes as he appeared to examine the house with brief deliberation. Then with the same deliberation he turned; the boy watched him pivot on the good leg and saw the stiff foot drag around the arc of the turning, leaving a final long and fading smear. His father never looked at it, he never once looked down at the rug. The Negro held the door. It closed behind them, upon the hysteric and indistinguishable woman-wail. His father stopped at the top of the steps and scraped his boot clean on the edge of it. At the gate he stopped again. He stood for a moment, planted stiffly on the stiff foot, looking back at the house. "Pretty and white, ain't it?" he said. "That's sweat. Nigger sweat. Maybe it ain't white enough yet to suit him. Maybe he wants to mix some white sweat with it."

Two hours later the boy was chopping wood behind the house within which his mother and aunt and the two sisters (the mother and aunt, not the two girls, he knew that; even at this distance and muffled by walls the flat loud voices of the two girls emanated an incorrigible idle inertia) were setting up the stove to prepare a meal, when he heard the hooves and saw the linen-clad man on a fine sorrel mare, whom he recognized even before he saw the rolled rug in front of the Negro youth following on a fat bay carriage horse — a suffused, angry face vanishing, still at full gallop, beyond the corner of the house where his father and brother were sitting in the two tilted chairs; and a moment later, almost before he could have put the axe down, he heard the hooves again and watched the sorrel mare go back out of the yard, already galloping again. Then his father began to shout one of the sisters' names, who presently emerged backward from the kitchen door dragging the rolled rug along the ground by one end while the other sister walked behind it.

"If you ain't going to tote, go on and set up the wash pot," the first said.

"You, Sarty!" the second shouted. "Set up the wash pot!" His father appeared at the door, framed against that shabbiness, as he had been against that other bland perfection, impervious to either, the mother's anxious face at his shoulder.

"Go on," the father said. "Pick it up." The two sisters stooped, broad, 50 lethargic; stooping, they presented an incredible expanse of pale cloth and a flutter of tawdry ribbons.

"If I thought enough of a rug to have to git hit all the way from France I wouldn't keep hit where folks coming in would have to tromp on hit," the first said. They raised the rug.

"Abner," the mother said. "Let me do it."

"You go back and git dinner," his father said. "I'll tend to this."

From the woodpile through the rest of the afternoon the boy watched them, the rug spread flat in the dust beside the bubbling wash pot, the two sisters stooping over it with that profound and lethargic reluctance, while the father stood over them in turn, implacable and grim, driving them though never raising his voice again. He could smell the harsh homemade lye they were using; he saw his mother come to the door once and look toward them with an expression not anxious now but very like despair; he saw his father turn, and he fell to with the axe and saw from the corner of his eye his father raise from the ground a flattish fragment of field stone and examine it and return to the pot, and this time his mother actually spoke: "Abner. Abner. Please don't. Please, Abner."

Then he was done too. It was dusk; the whippoorwills had already begun. He could smell coffee from the room where they would presently eat the cold food remaining from the mid-afternoon meal, though when he entered the house he realized they were having coffee again probably because there was a fire on the hearth, before which the rug now lay spread over the backs of the two chairs. The tracks of his father's foot were gone. Where they had been were now long, water-cloudy scoriations resembling the sporadic course of a lilliputian mowing machine. 55

It still hung there while they ate the cold food and then went to bed, scattered without order or claim up and down the two rooms, his mother in one bed, where his father would later lie, the older brother in the other, himself, the aunt, and the two sisters on pallets on the floor. But his father was not in bed yet. The last thing the boy remembered was the depthless, harsh silhouette of the hat and coat bending over the rug and it seemed to him that he had not even closed his eyes when the silhouette was standing over him, the fire almost dead behind it, the stiff foot prodding him awake. "Catch up the mule," his father said.

When he returned with the mule his father was standing in the black door, the rolled rug over his shoulder. "Ain't you going to ride?" he said.

"No. Give me your foot."

He bent his knee into his father's hand, the wiry, surprising power flowed smoothly, rising, he rising with it, on to the mule's bare back (they had owned a saddle once; the boy could remember it though not when or where) and with the same effortlessness his father swung the rug up in front of him. Now in the starlight they retraced the afternoon's path, up the dusty road rife with honeysuckle, through the gate and up the black tunnel of the drive to the lightless house, where he sat on the mule and felt the rough warp of the rug drag across his thighs and vanish.

"Don't you want me to help?" he whispered. His father did not answer 60 and now he heard again that stiff foot striking the hollow portico with that wooden and clocklike deliberation, that outrageous overstatement of the weight it carried. The rug, hunched, not flung (the boy could tell that even in the darkness) from his father's shoulder struck the angle of wall and floor with a sound unbelievably loud, thunderous, then the foot again, unhurried and enormous; a light came on in the house and the boy sat, tense, breathing steadily and quietly and just a little fast, though the foot itself did not increase its beat at all, descending the steps now; now the boy could see him.

"Don't you want to ride now?" he whispered. "We kin both ride now," the light within the house altering now, flaring up and sinking. *He's coming down the stairs now,* he thought. He had already ridden the mule up beside the horse block; presently his father was up behind him and he doubled the reins over and slashed the mule across the neck, but before the animal could begin to trot the hard, thin arm came around him, the hard, knotted hand jerking the mule back to a walk.

In the first red rays of the sun they were in the lot, putting plow gear on the mules. This time the sorrel mare was in the lot before he heard it at all, the rider collarless and even bareheaded, trembling, speaking in a shaking voice as the woman in the house had done, his father merely looking up once before stooping again to the hame he was buckling, so that the man on the mare spoke to his stooping back:

"You must realize you have ruined that rug. Wasn't there anybody here, any of your women . . ." he ceased, shaking, the boy watching him, the older brother leaning now in the stable door, chewing, blinking slowly and steadily at nothing apparently. "It cost a hundred dollars. But you never had a hundred dollars. You never will. So I'm going to charge you twenty bushels of corn against your crop. I'll add it in your contract and when you come to the commissary you can sign it. That won't keep Mrs. de Spain quiet but maybe it will teach you to wipe your feet off before you enter her house again."

Then he was gone. The boy looked at his father, who still had not spoken or even looked up again, who was now adjusting the logger-head in the hame.

"Pap," he said. His father looked at him — the inscrutable face, the shaggy brows beneath which the gray eyes glinted coldly. Suddenly the boy went toward him, fast, stopping as suddenly. "You done the best you could!" he cried. "If he wanted hit done different why didn't he wait and tell you how? He won't git no twenty bushels! He won't git none! We'll gether hit and hide hit! I kin watch . . ."

"Did you put the cutter back in that straight stock like I told you?"

"No, sir," he said.

"Then go do it."

That was Wednesday. During the rest of that week he worked steadily, at what was within his scope and some which was beyond it, with an industry that did not need to be driven nor even commanded twice; he had this from his mother, with the difference that some at least of what he did he liked to do, such as splitting wood with the half-size axe which his mother and aunt had earned, or saved money somehow, to present him with at Christmas. In company with the two older women (and on one afternoon, even one of the sisters), he built pens for the shoat and the cow which were a part of his father's contract with the landlord, and one afternoon, his father being absent, gone somewhere on one of the mules, he went to the field.

They were running a middle buster now, his brother holding the plow straight while he handled the reins, and walking beside the straining mule, the rich black soil shearing cool and damp against his bare ankles, he thought *Maybe this is the end of it. Maybe even that twenty bushels that seems hard to have to pay for just a rug will be a cheap price for him to stop forever and always from being what he used to be;* thinking, dreaming now, so that his brother had to speak sharply to him to mind the mule: *Maybe he even won't collect the twenty bushels. Maybe it will all add up and balance and vanish — corn, rug, fire; the terror and grief; the being pulled two ways like between two teams of horses — gone, done with for ever and ever.*

Then it was Saturday; he looked up from beneath the mule he was harnessing and saw his father in the black coat and hat. "Not that," his father said. "The wagon gear." And then, two hours later, sitting in the wagon bed behind his father and brother on the seat, the wagon accomplished a final curve, and he saw the weathered paintless store with its tattered tobacco- and patent-medicine posters and the tethered wagons and saddle animals below the gallery. He mounted the gnawed steps behind his father and brother, and there again was the lane of quiet, watching faces for the three of them to walk through. He saw the man in spectacles sitting at the plank table and he did not need to be told this was a Justice of the Peace; he sent one glare of fierce, exultant, partisan defiance at the man in collar and cravat now, whom he had seen but twice before in his life, and that on a galloping horse, who now wore on his face an expression not of rage but of amazed unbelief which the boy could not have known was at the incredible circumstance of being sued by one of his own tenants, and came and stood against his father and cried at the Justice: "He ain't done it! He ain't burnt . . ."

"Go back to the wagon," his father said.

"Burnt?" the Justice said. "Do I understand this rug was burned too?"

"Does anybody here claim it was?" his father said. "Go back to the wagon." But he did not, he merely retreated to the rear of the room, crowded as that other had been, but not to sit down this time, instead, to stand pressing among the motionless bodies, listening to the voices:

"And you claim twenty bushels of corn is too high for the damage you did to the rug?"

"He brought the rug to me and said he wanted the tracks washed out of it. I washed the tracks out and took the rug back to him."

"But you didn't carry the rug back to him in the same condition it was in before you made the tracks on it."

His father did not answer, and now for perhaps half a minute there was no sound at all save that of breathing, the faint, steady suspiration of complete and intent listening.

"You decline to answer that, Mr. Snopes?" Again his father did not answer. "I'm going to find against you, Mr. Snopes. I'm going to find that you were responsible for the injury to Major de Spain's rug and hold you liable for it. But twenty bushels of corn seems a little high for a man in your circumstances to have to pay. Major de Spain claims it cost a hundred dollars. October corn will be worth about fifty cents. I figure that if Major de Spain can stand a ninety-five dollar loss on something he paid cash for, you can stand a five-dollar loss you haven't earned yet. I hold you in damages to Major de Spain to the amount of ten bushels of corn over and above your contract with him, to be paid to him out of your crop at gathering time. Court adjourned."

It had taken no time hardly, the morning was but half begun. He thought they would return home and perhaps back to the field, since they were late, far behind all other farmers. But instead his father passed on behind the wagon, merely indicating with his hand for the older brother to follow with it, and crossed the road toward the blacksmith shop opposite, pressing on after his father, overtaking him, speaking, whispering up at the harsh, calm face beneath the weathered hat: "He won't git no ten bushels neither. He won't git one. We'll . . ." until his father glanced for an instant down at him, the face absolutely calm, the grizzled eyebrows tangled above the cold eyes, the voice almost pleasant, almost gentle:

"You think so? Well, we'll wait till October anyway."

The matter of the wagon — the setting of a spoke or two and the tightening of the tires — did not take long either, the business of the tires accomplished by driving the wagon into the spring branch behind the shop and letting it stand there, the mules nuzzling into the water from time to time, and the boy on the seat with the idle reins, looking up the slope and through the sooty tunnel of the shed where the slow hammer rang and where his father sat on an upended cypress bolt, easily, either talking or listening, still sitting there when the boy brought the dripping wagon up out of the branch and halted it before the door.

"Take them on to the shade and hitch," his father said. He did so and returned. His father and the smith and a third man squatting on his heels inside the door were talking, about crops and animals; the boy, squatting too in the ammoniac dust and hoof-parings and scales of rust, heard his father tell a long and unhurried story out of the time before the birth of the older brother even when he had been a professional horsetrader. And then his father came up beside him where he stood before a tattered last year's circus poster on the other side of the store, gazing rapt and quiet at the scarlet horses, the incredible poisings and convolutions of tulle and tights and the painted leers of comedians, and said, "It's time to eat."

But not at home. Squatting beside his brother against the front wall, he watched his father emerge from the store and produce from a paper sack a segment of cheese and divide it carefully and deliberately into three with his pocket knife and produce crackers from the same sack. They all three squatted on the gallery and ate, slowly, without talking; then in the store again, they drank from a tin dipper tepid water smelling of the cedar bucket and of living beech trees. And still they did not go home. It was a horse lot this time, a tall rail fence upon and along which men stood and sat and out of which one by one horses were led, to be walked and trotted and then cantered back and forth along the road while the slow swapping and buying went on and the sun began to slant westward, they — the three of them — watching and listening, the older brother with his muddy eyes and his steady, inevitable tobacco, the father commenting now and then on certain of the animals, to no one in particular.

It was after sundown when they reached home. They ate supper by lamplight, then, sitting on the doorstep, the boy watched the night fully accomplish, listening to the whippoorwills and the frogs, when he heard his mother's voice: "Abner! No! No! Oh, God. Oh, God. Abner!" and he rose, whirled, and saw the altered light through the door where a candle stub now burned in a bottle neck on the table and his father, still in the hat and coat, at once formal and burlesque as though dressed carefully for some shabby and ceremonial violence, emptying the reservoir of the lamp back into the five-gallon kerosene can from which it had been filled, while the mother tugged at his arm until he shifted the lamp to the other hand and flung her back, not savagely or viciously, just hard, into the wall, her hands flung out against the wall for balance, her mouth open and in her face the same quality of hopeless despair as had been in her voice. Then his father saw him standing in the door.

"Go to the barn and get that can of oil we were oiling the wagon with," he said. The boy did not move. Then he could speak.

"What . . ." he cried. "What are you . . ."

"Go get that oil," his father said. "Go."

Then he was moving, running, outside the house, toward the stable: this the old habit, the old blood which he had not been permitted to choose for himself, which had been bequeathed him willy nilly and which had run for so long (and who knew where, battening on what of outrage and savagery and lust) before it came to him. *I could keep on,* he thought. *I could run on and on and never look back, never need to see his face again. Only I can't. I can't,* the rusted can in his hand now, the liquid sploshing in it as he ran back to the house and into it, into the sound of his mother's weeping in the next room, and handed the can to his father.

"Ain't you going to even send a nigger?" he cried. "At least you sent a nigger before!"   90

This time his father didn't strike him. The hand came even faster than the blow had, the same hand which had set the can on the table with almost excruciating care flashing from the can toward him too quick for him to follow it, gripping him by the back of his shirt and on to tiptoe before he had seen it quit the can, the face stooping at him in breathless and frozen ferocity, the cold, dead voice speaking over him to the older brother who leaned against the table, chewing with that steady, curious, sidewise motion of cows:

"Empty the can into the big one and go on. I'll catch up with you."

"Better tie him up to the bedpost," the brother said.

"Do like I told you," the father said. Then the boy was moving, his bunched shirt and the hard, bony hand between his shoulder-blades, his toes just touching the floor, across the room and into the other one, past the sisters sitting with spread heavy thighs in the two chairs over the cold hearth, and to where his mother and aunt sat side by side on the bed, the aunt's arms about his mother's shoulders.

"Hold him," the father said. The aunt made a startled movement. "Not   95
you," the father said. "Lennie. Take hold of him. I want to see you do it." His mother took him by the wrist. "You'll hold him better than that. If he gets loose don't you know what he is going to do? He will go up yonder." He jerked his head toward the road. "Maybe I'd better tie him."

"I'll hold him," his mother whispered.

"See you do then." Then his father was gone, the stiff foot heavy and measured upon the boards, ceasing at last.

Then he began to struggle. His mother caught him in both arms, he jerking and wrenching at them. He would be stronger in the end, he knew that. But he had no time to wait for it. "Lemme go!" he cried. "I don't want to have to hit you!"

"Let him go!" the aunt said. "If he don't go, before God, I am going up there myself!"

"Don't you see I can't?" his mother cried. "Sarty! Sarty! No! No! Help   100
me, Lizzie!"

Then he was free. His aunt grasped at him but it was too late. He whirled, running, his mother stumbled forward on to her knees behind him, crying to the nearer sister: "Catch him, Net! Catch him!" But that was too late too, the sister (the sisters were twins, born at the same time, yet either of them now gave the impression of being, encompassing as much living meat and volume and weight as any other two of the family) not yet having begun to rise from the chair, her head, face, alone merely turned, presenting to him in the flying instant an astonishing expanse of young female features untroubled by any surprise even, wearing only an expression of bovine interest. Then he was out of the room, out of the house, in the mild dust of the starlit road and the heavy rifeness of honeysuckle, the pale ribbon unspooling with terrific slowness under his running feet, reaching the gate at last and turning in, running, his heart and lungs drumming, on up the drive toward the lighted house, the lighted door. He did not knock, he burst in, sobbing for breath, incapable for the moment of speech; he saw the astonished face of the Negro in the linen jacket without knowing when the Negro had appeared.

"De Spain!" he cried, panted. "Where's . . ." then he saw the white man too emerging from a white door down the hall. "Barn!" he cried. "Barn!"

"What?" the white man said. "Barn?"

"Yes!" the boy cried. "Barn!"

"Catch him!" the white man shouted.

But it was too late this time too. The Negro grasped his shirt, but the entire sleeve, rotten with washing, carried away, and he was out that door too and in the drive again, and had actually never ceased to run even while he was screaming into the white man's face.

Behind him the white man was shouting, "My horse! Fetch my horse!" and he thought for an instant of cutting across the park and climbing the fence into the road, but he did not know the park nor how high the vine-massed fence might be and he dared not risk it. So he ran on down the drive, blood and breath roaring; presently he was in the road again though he could not see it. He could not hear either: the galloping mare was almost upon him before he heard her, and even then he held his course, as if the very urgency of his wild grief and need must in a moment more find him wings, waiting until the ultimate instant to hurl himself aside and into the weed-choked roadside ditch as the horse thundered past and on, for an instant in furious silhouette against the stars, the tranquil early summer night sky which, even before the shape of the horse and rider vanished, stained abruptly and violently upward: a long, swirling roar incredible and soundless, blotting the stars, and he springing up and into the road again, running again, knowing it was too late yet still running even after he heard the shot and an instant later, two shots, pausing now without knowing he had ceased to run, crying "Pap! Pap!", running again before he knew he had begun to run, stumbling, tripping over something and scrabbling up again without ceasing to run, looking backward over his shoulder at the glare as he got up, running on among the invisible trees, panting, sobbing, "Father! Father!"

At midnight he was sitting on the crest of a hill. He did not know it was midnight and he did not know how far he had come. But there was no glare behind him now and he sat now, his back toward what he had called home for four days anyhow, his face toward the dark woods which he would enter when breath was strong again, small, shaking steadily in the chill darkness, hugging himself into the remainder of his thin, rotten shirt, the grief and despair now no longer terror and fear but just grief and despair. *Father. My father*, he thought.

105

William Faulkner   137

"He was brave!" he cried suddenly, aloud but not loud, no more than a whisper. "He was! He was in the war! He was in Colonel Sartoris' cav'ry!" not knowing that his father had gone to that war a private in the fine old European sense, wearing no uniform, admitting the authority of and giving fidelity to no man or army or flag, going to war as Malbrouck himself did: for booty — it meant nothing and less than nothing to him if it were enemy booty or his own.

The slow constellations wheeled on. It would be dawn and then sun-up after a while and he would be hungry. But that would be tomorrow and now he was only cold, and walking would cure that. His breathing was easier now and he decided to get up and go on, and then he found that he had been asleep because he knew it was almost dawn, the night almost over. He could tell that from the whippoorwills. They were everywhere now among the dark trees below him, constant and inflectioned and ceaseless, so that, as the instant for giving over to the day birds drew nearer and nearer, there was no interval at all between them. He got up. He was a little stiff, but walking would cure that too as it would the cold, and soon there would be the sun. He went on down the hill, toward the dark woods within which the liquid silver voices of the birds called unceasing — the rapid and urgent beating of the urgent and quiring heart of the late spring night. He did not look back.

Questions

1. After delivering his warning to Major de Spain, the boy Snopes does not actually witness what happens to his father and brother, nor what happens to the Major's barn. But what do you assume does happen? What evidence is given in the story?
2. What do you understand to be Faulkner's opinion of Abner Snopes? Make a guess, indicating details in the story that convey attitudes.
3. Which adjectives best describe the general tone of the story: calm, amused, disinterested, scornful, marveling, excited, impassioned? Point out passages that may be so described. What do you notice about the style in which these passages are written?
4. In tone and style, how does "Barn Burning" compare with Faulkner's story "A Rose for Emily" (Chapter Two)? To what do you attribute any differences?
5. Suppose that, instead of "Barn Burning," Faulkner had written another story told by Abner Snopes in the first person. Why would such a story need a style different from that of "Barn Burning"? (Suggestion: Notice Faulkner's descriptions of Abner Snopes's voice.)
6. Although "Barn Burning" takes place some thirty years after the Civil War, how does the war figure in it?

Alice Walker

Everyday Use

1973

Alice Walker, a leading black writer and social activist, was born in 1944 in Eatonton, Georgia, the youngest of eight children. Her father, a sharecropper and dairy farmer, usually earned about $300 a year; her mother helped by working as a maid. Both entertained their children by telling stories.

When Alice Walker was eight, accidentally struck by a pellet from a brother's BB gun, she lost the sight of one eye because the Walkers had no car to rush her to the hospital. Later she attended Spelman College in Atlanta and finished college at Sarah Lawrence on a scholarship. While working for the civil rights movement in Mississippi, she met a young lawyer, Melvyn Leventhal; and in 1967 they settled in Jackson, Mississippi, the first legally married interracial couple in town. They returned to New York in 1974, and were later divorced. First known as a poet, Walker has published four books of her verse. She also has edited a collection of the work of neglected black woman author Zora Neale Hurston, and has written a study of Langston Hughes. She has collected her essays as In Search of Our Mothers' Gardens: Womanist Prose *(1983), in which she recalls her mother and addresses her own daughter. (By* womanist *she means "black feminist.") But the largest part of Walker's reading audience knows her fiction: two story collections,* In Love and Trouble *(1973), from which "Everyday Use" is taken, and* You Can't Keep a Good Woman Down *(1981); and her novels,* The Third Life of Grange Copeland *(1970);* Meridian *(1976); and, best known,* The Color Purple *(1982), which won a Pulitzer prize. In 1985 Steven Spielberg made it into a film.*

for your grandmama

I will wait for her in the yard that Maggie and I made so clean and wavy yesterday afternoon. A yard like this is more comfortable than most people know. It is not just a yard. It is like an extended living room. When the hard clay is swept clean as a floor and the fine sand around the edges lined with tiny, irregular grooves, anyone can come and sit and look up into the elm tree and wait for the breezes that never come inside the house.

Maggie will be nervous until after her sister goes: she will stand hopelessly in corners, homely and ashamed of the burn scars down her arms and legs, eying her sister with a mixture of envy and awe. She thinks her sister has held life always in the palm of one hand, that "no" is a word the world never learned to say to her.

You've no doubt seen those TV shows where the child who has "made it" is confronted, as a surprise, by her own mother and father, tottering in weakly from backstage. (A pleasant surprise, of course: What would they do if parent and child came on the show only to curse out and insult each other?) On TV mother and child embrace and smile into each other's faces. Sometimes the mother and father weep, the child wraps them in her arms and leans across the table to tell how she would not have made it without their help. I have seen these programs°.

Sometimes I dream a dream in which Dee and I are suddenly brought

these programs: The NBC television show "This Is Your Life," with Ralph Edwards as producer and master of ceremonies, publicly and often tearfully reunited people with friends, relatives, and teachers they had not seen in years. It was aired 1952 – 61 and 1970 – 73.

together on a TV program of this sort. Out of a dark and soft-seated limousine I am ushered into a bright room filled with many people. There I meet a smiling, gray, sporty man like Johnny Carson who shakes my hand and tells me what a fine girl I have. Then we are on the stage and Dee is embracing me with tears in her eyes. She pins on my dress a large orchid, even though she has told me once that she thinks orchids are tacky flowers.

In real life I am a large, big-boned woman with rough, man-working 5
hands. In the winter I wear flannel nightgowns to bed and overalls during the day. I can kill and clean a hog as mercilessly as a man. My fat keeps me hot in zero weather. I can work outside all day, breaking ice to get water for washing; I can eat pork liver cooked over the open fire minutes after it comes steaming from the hog. One winter I knocked a bull calf straight in the brain between the eyes with a sledge hammer and had the meat hung up to chill before nightfall. But of course all this does not show on television. I am the way my daughter would want me to be: a hundred pounds lighter, my skin like an uncooked barley pancake. My hair glistens in the hot bright lights. Johnny Carson has much to do to keep up with my quick and witty tongue.

But that is a mistake. I know even before I wake up. Who ever knew a Johnson with a quick tongue? Who can even imagine me looking a strange white man in the eye? It seems to me I have talked to them always with one foot raised in flight, with my head turned in whichever way is farthest from them. Dee, though. She would always look anyone in the eye. Hesitation was no part of her nature.

"How do I look, Mama?" Maggie says, showing just enough of her thin body enveloped in pink skirt and red blouse for me to know she's there, almost hidden by the door.

"Come out into the yard," I say.

Have you ever seen a lame animal, perhaps a dog run over by some careless person rich enough to own a car, sidle up to someone who is ignorant enough to be kind to him? That is the way my Maggie walks. She has been like this, chin on chest, eyes on ground, feet in shuffle, ever since the fire that burned the other house to the ground.

Dee is lighter than Maggie, with nicer hair and a fuller figure. She's a 10
woman now, though sometimes I forget. How long ago was it that the other house burned? Ten, twelve years? Sometimes I can still hear the flames and feel Maggie's arms sticking to me, her hair smoking and her dress falling off her in little black papery flakes. Her eyes seemed stretched open, blazed open by the flames reflected in them. And Dee. I see her standing off under the sweet gum tree she used to dig gum out of; a look of concentration on her face as she watched the last dingy gray board of the house fall in toward the red-hot brick chimney. Why don't you do a dance around the ashes? I'd wanted to ask her. She had hated the house that much.

I used to think she hated Maggie, too. But that was before we raised the money, the church and me, to send her to Augusta to school. She used to read to us without pity; forcing words, lies, other folks' habits, whole lives upon us two, sitting trapped and ignorant underneath her voice. She washed us in a river of make-believe, burned us with a lot of knowledge we didn't necessarily need to know. Pressed us to her with the serious way she read, to shove us away at just the moment, like dimwits, we seemed about to understand.

Dee wanted nice things. A yellow organdy dress to wear to her graduation from high school; black pumps to match a green suit she'd made from an old suit somebody gave me. She was determined to stare down any disaster in her efforts. Her eyelids would not flicker for minutes at a time. Often I fought off the temptation to shake her. At sixteen she had a style of her own, and knew what style was.

I never had an education myself. After second grade the school was closed down. Don't ask me why: in 1927 colored asked fewer questions than they do now. Sometimes Maggie reads to me. She stumbles along good-naturedly but can't see well. She knows she is not bright. Like good looks and money, quickness passed her by. She will marry John Thomas (who has mossy teeth in an earnest face) and then I'll be free to sit here and I guess just sing church songs to myself. Although I never was a good singer. Never could carry a tune. I was always better at a man's job. I used to love to milk till I was hooked in the side in '49. Cows are soothing and slow and don't bother you, unless you try to milk them the wrong way.

I have deliberately turned my back on the house. It is three rooms, just like the one that burned, except the roof is tin; they don't make shingle roofs any more. There are no real windows, just some holes cut in the sides, like the portholes in a ship, but not round and not square, with rawhide holding the shutters up on the outside. This house is in a pasture, too, like the other one. No doubt when Dee sees it she will want to tear it down. She wrote me once that no matter where we "choose" to live, she will manage to come see us. But she will never bring her friends. Maggie and I thought about this and Maggie asked me, "Mama, when did Dee ever *have* any friends?"

She had a few. Furtive boys in pink shirts hanging about on washday ₁₅ after school. Nervous girls who never laughed. Impressed with her they worshiped the well-turned phrase, the cute shape, the scalding humor that erupted like bubbles in lye. She read to them.

When she was courting Jimmy T she didn't have much time to pay to us, but turned all her faultfinding power on him. He *flew* to marry a cheap city girl from a family of ignorant flashy people. She hardly had time to recompose herself.

When she comes I will meet — but there they are!

Maggie attempts to make a dash for the house, in her shuffling way, but I stay her with my hand. "Come back here," I say. And she stops and tries to dig a well in the sand with her toe.

It is hard to see them clearly through the strong sun. But even the first glimpse of leg out of the car tells me it is Dee. Her feet were always neat-looking, as if God himself had shaped them with a certain style. From the other side of the car comes a short, stocky man. Hair is all over his head a foot long and hanging from his chin like a kinky mule tail. I hear Maggie suck in her breath. "Uhnnnh," is what it sounds like. Like when you see the wriggling end of a snake just in front of your foot on the road. "Uhnnnh."

Dee next. A dress down to the ground, in this hot weather. A dress so loud ₂₀ it hurts my eyes. There are yellows and oranges enough to throw back the light of the sun. I feel my whole face warming from the heat waves it throws out. Earrings gold, too, and hanging down to her shoulders. Bracelets dangling and making noises when she moves her arm up to shake the folds of the dress out of her armpits. The dress is loose and flows, and as she walks closer, I like it. I hear Maggie go "Uhnnnh" again. It is her sister's hair. It stands straight up like the wool on a sheep. It is black as night and around the edges are two long pigtails that rope about like small lizards disappearing behind her ears.

"Wa-su-zo-Tean-o!"° she says, coming on in that gliding way the dress makes her move. The short stocky fellow with the hair to his navel is all grinning and he follows up with "Asalamalakim°, my mother and sister!" He moves to hug Maggie but she falls back, right up against the back of my chair. I feel her trembling there and when I look up I see the perspiration falling off her chin.

"Don't get up," says Dee. Since I am stout it takes something of a push. You can see me trying to move a second or two before I make it. She turns, showing white heels through her sandals, and goes back to the car. Out she peeks next with a Polaroid. She stoops down quickly and lines up picture after picture of me sitting there in front of the house with Maggie cowering behind me. She never takes a shot without making sure the house is included. When a cow comes nibbling around the edge of the yard she snaps it and me and Maggie *and* the house. Then she puts the Polaroid in the back seat of the car, and comes up and kisses me on the forehead.

Meanwhile Asalamalakim is going through motions with Maggie's hand. Maggie's hand is as limp as a fish, and probably as cold, despite the sweat, and she keeps trying to pull it back. It looks like Asalamalakim wants to shake hands but wants to do it fancy. Or maybe he don't know how people shake hands. Anyhow, he soon gives up on Maggie.

"Well," I say. "Dee."

"No, Mama," she says. "Not 'Dee,' Wangero Leewanika Kemanjo!"   25

"What happened to 'Dee'?" I wanted to know.

"She's dead," Wangero said. "I couldn't bear it any longer, being named after the people who oppress me."

"You know as well as me you was named after your aunt Dicie," I said. Dicie is my sister. She named Dee. We called her "Big Dee" after Dee was born.

"But who was *she* named after?" asked Wangero.

"I guess after Grandma Dee," I said.   30

"And who was she named after?" asked Wangero.

"Her mother," I said, and saw Wangero was getting tired. "That's about as far back as I can trace it," I said. Though, in fact, I probably could have carried it back beyond the Civil War through the branches.

"Well," said Asalamalakim, "there you are."

"Uhnnnh," I heard Maggie say.

"There I was not," I said, "before 'Dicie' cropped up in our family, so   35
why should I try to trace it that far back?"

Wa-su-zo-Tean-o!: Salutation in Swahili, an African language. Notice that Dee has to sound it out, syllable by syllable.
Asalamalakim: Salutation in Arabic: "Peace be upon you."

He just stood there grinning, looking down on me like somebody inspecting a Model A car°. Every once in a while he and Wangero sent eye signals over my head.

"How do you pronounce this name?" I asked.

"You don't have to call me by it if you don't want to," said Wangero.

"Why shouldn't I?" I asked. "If that's what you want us to call you, we'll call you."

"I know it might sound awkward at first," said Wangero. 40

"I'll get used to it," I said. "Ream it out again."

Well, soon we got the name out of the way. Asalamalakim had a name twice as long and three times as hard. After I tripped over it two or three times he told me to just call him Hakim-a-barber. I wanted to ask him was he a barber, but I didn't really think he was, so I didn't ask.

"You must belong to those beef-cattle peoples down the road," I said. They said "Asalamalakim" when they met you, too, but they didn't shake hands. Always too busy: feeding the cattle, fixing the fences, putting up salt-lick shelters, throwing down hay. When the white folks poisoned some of the herd the men stayed up all night with rifles in their hands. I walked a mile and a half just to see the sight.

Hakim-a-barber said, "I accept some of their doctrines, but farming and raising cattle is not my style." (They didn't tell me, and I didn't ask, whether Wangero (Dee) had really gone and married him.)

We sat down to eat and right away he said he didn't eat collards and pork 45 was unclean. Wangero, though, went on through the chitlins and corn bread, the greens and everything else. She talked a blue streak over the sweet potatoes. Everything delighted her. Even the fact that we still used the benches her daddy made for the table when we couldn't afford to buy chairs.

"Oh, Mama!" she cried. Then turned to Hakim-a-barber. "I never knew how lovely these benches are. You can feel the rump prints," she said, running her hands underneath her and along the bench. Then she gave a sigh and her hand closed over Grandma Dee's butter dish. "That's it!" she said. "I knew there was something I wanted to ask you if I could have." She jumped up from the table and went over in the corner where the churn stood, the milk in it clabber° by now. She looked at the churn and looked at it.

"This churn top is what I need," she said. "Didn't Uncle Buddy whittle it out of a tree you all used to have?"

"Yes," I said.

"Uh huh," she said happily. "And I want the dasher, too."

"Uncle Buddy whittle that, too?" asked the barber. 50

Dee (Wangero) looked up at me.

"Aunt Dee's first husband whittled the dash," said Maggie so low you almost couldn't hear her. "His name was Henry, but they called him Stash."

"Maggie's brain is like an elephant's," Wangero said, laughing. "I can use the churn top as a centerpiece for the alcove table," she said, sliding a plate over the churn, "and I'll think of something artistic to do with the dasher."

When she finished wrapping the dasher the handle stuck out. I took it

Model A car: popular low-priced automobile introduced by the Ford Motor Company in 1927.
clabber: sour milk or buttermilk.

for a moment in my hands. You didn't even have to look close to see where hands pushing the dasher up and down to make butter had left a kind of sink in the wood. In fact, there were a lot of small sinks; you could see where thumbs and fingers had sunk into the wood. It was beautiful light yellow wood, from a tree that grew in the yard where Big Dee and Stash had lived.

After dinner Dee (Wangero) went to the trunk at the foot of my bed and started rifling through it. Maggie hung back in the kitchen over the dishpan. Out came Wangero with two quilts. They had been pieced by Grandma Dee and then Big Dee and me had hung them on the quilt frames on the front porch and quilted them. One was in the Lone Star pattern. The other was Walk Around the Mountain. In both of them were scraps of dresses Grandma Dee had worn fifty and more years ago. Bits and pieces of Grandpa Jarrell's Paisley shirts. And one teeny faded blue piece, about the size of a penny matchbox, that was from Great Grandpa Ezra's uniform that he wore in the Civil War.

"Mama," Wangero said sweet as a bird. "Can I have these old quilts?"

I heard something fall in the kitchen, and a minute later the kitchen door slammed.

"Why don't you take one or two of the others?" I asked. "These old things was just done by me and Big Dee from some tops your grandma pieced before she died."

"No," said Wangero. "I don't want those. They are stitched around the borders by machine."

"That'll make them last better," I said.

"That's not the point," said Wangero. "These are all pieces of dresses Grandma used to wear. She did all this stitching by hand. Imagine!" She held the quilts securely in her arms, stroking them.

"Some of the pieces, like those lavender ones, come from old clothes her mother handed down to her," I said, moving up to touch the quilts. Dee (Wangero) moved back just enough so that I couldn't reach the quilts. They already belonged to her.

"Imagine!" she breathed again, clutching them closely to her bosom.

"The truth is," I said, "I promised to give them quilts to Maggie, for when she marries John Thomas."

She gasped like a bee had stung her.

"Maggie can't appreciate these quilts!" she said. "She'd probably be backward enough to put them to everyday use."

"I reckon she would," I said. "God knows I been saving 'em for long enough with nobody using 'em. I hope she will!" I didn't want to bring up how I had offered Dee (Wangero) a quilt when she went away to college. Then she had told me they were old-fashioned, out of style.

"But they're *priceless!*" she was saying now, furiously; for she has a temper. "Maggie would put them on the bed and in five years they'd be in rags. Less than that!"

"She can always make some more," I said. "Maggie knows how to quilt."

Dee (Wangero) looked at me with hatred. "You just will not understand. The point is these quilts, *these* quilts!"

"Well," I said, stumped. "What would *you* do with them?"

"Hang them," she said. As if that was the only thing you *could* do with quilts.

Maggie by now was standing in the door. I could almost hear the sound her feet made as they scraped over each other.

"She can have them, Mama," she said, like somebody used to never winning anything, or having anything reserved for her. "I can 'member Grandma Dee without the quilts."

I looked at her hard. She had filled her bottom lip with checkerberry snuff and it gave her face a kind of dopey, hangdog look. It was Grandma Dee and Big Dee who taught her how to quilt herself. She stood there with her scarred hands hidden in the folds of her skirt. She looked at her sister with something like fear but she wasn't mad at her. This was Maggie's portion. This was the way she knew God to work. 75

When I looked at her like that something hit me in the top of my head and ran down to the soles of my feet. Just like when I'm in church and the spirit of God touches me and I get happy and shout. I did something I never had done before: hugged Maggie to me, then dragged her on into the room, snatched the quilts out of Miss Wangero's hands and dumped them into Maggie's lap. Maggie just sat there on my bed with her mouth open.

"Take one or two of the others," I said to Dee.

But she turned without a word and went out to Hakim-a-barber.

"You just don't understand," she said, as Maggie and I came out to the car.

"What don't I understand?" I wanted to know. 80

"Your heritage," she said. And then she turned to Maggie, kissed her, and said, "You ought to try to make something of yourself, too, Maggie. It's really a new day for us. But from the way you and Mama still live you'd never know it."

She put on some sunglasses that hid everything above the tip of her nose and her chin.

Maggie smiled; maybe at the sunglasses. But a real smile, not scared. After we watched the car dust settle I asked Maggie to bring me a dip of snuff. And then the two of us sat there just enjoying, until it was time to go in the house and go to bed.

QUESTIONS

1. What is the basic conflict in "Everyday Use"?
2. What is the tone of Walker's story? By what means does the author communicate it?
3. From whose point of view is "Everyday Use" told? What does the story gain from this point of view — instead of, say, from the point of view of Dee (Wangero)?
4. How does the narrator of the story feel toward Dee? What seems to be Dee's present attitude toward her mother and sister?
5. What do you take to be the author's attitude toward each of her characters? How does she convey it?
6. What levels of meaning do you find in the story's title?
7. Contrast Dee's attitude toward her heritage with the attitudes of her mother and sister. How much truth is there in Dee's accusation that her mother and sister don't understand their heritage?
8. Does the knowledge that "Everyday Use" was written by a black writer in any way influence your reactions to it? Explain.

SUGGESTIONS FOR WRITING

1. This is an exercise in communicating your feelings. Choose a subject you greatly admire — some person, place, film, sports team, or work of fiction — and in a paragraph, describe it so that you forcefully indicate your admiration. Then rewrite the paragraph from the point of view of someone who *detests* your subject. Try not to declare "I love this" or "I hate this," but choose details and characteristics of your subject that make the tone of each paragraph clear.

2. Consider a short story in which the narrator is the central character (perhaps "A & P," "First Confession," "Araby," "I Stand Here Ironing," "My Man Bovanne," or "The Wife's Story." In a brief essay, show how the character of the narrator determines the language of the story. What words or phrases, slang expressions, figures of speech, local or regional speech do you find the narrator using? In general, how would you describe the style of the story?

3. Take a short story or novel not included in this book: one by a writer of high reputation and distinctive style, such as William Faulkner, Ernest Hemingway, Flannery O'Connor, Joyce Carol Oates, or another writer suggested by your instructor. Write a passage of your own, and insert it somewhere in the story. Imitate the writer's style as closely as possible, paying attention to vocabulary, length and variety of sentences, amount of description, and tone. Then type out two or three pages of the story, including your forgery, and make copies for the other members of the class. See if anyone can tell where the writer's prose stops and yours begins.

6 Irony

If a friend declares, "Oh, sure, I just *love* to have four papers fall due on the same day," you detect that the statement contains **irony.** This is **verbal irony,** the most familiar kind, in which we understand the speaker's meaning to be far from the usual meaning of the words — in this case, quite the opposite. (When the irony is, as here, a somewhat sour statement tinged with mockery, it is usually called **sarcasm.**)

Irony, of course, occurs in writing as well as in conversation. When in a comic moment in Isaac Bashevis Singer's "Gimpel the Fool" (Chapter Four) the sexton announces, "The wealthy Reb Gimpel invites the congregation to a feast in honor of the birth of a son," the people at the synagogue burst into laughter. They know that Gimpel, in contrast to the sexton's words, is not a wealthy man but a humble baker; that the son is not his own but his wife's lover's; and that the birth brings no honor to anybody. Verbal irony, then, implies a contrast or discrepancy between what is *said* and what is *meant.* But stories often contain other kinds of irony besides such verbal irony. A situation, for example, can be ironic if it contains some wry contrast or incongruity. In James Thurber's "The Catbird Seat" (Chapter Four), it is an **ironic situation** that the mildest, most apparently harmless man in an office should plot murder, claim to be a heroin addict, and cause the firing of the office tyrant.

An entire story may be told from an **ironic point of view.** Whenever we sense a sharp distinction between the narrator of a story and the author, irony is likely to occur — especially when the narrator is telling us something that we are clearly expected to doubt or to interpret very differently. In "Gimpel the Fool," Gimpel (who tells his own story) keeps insisting on trusting people; but the author, a shrewder observer, makes it clear to us that the people Gimpel trusts are only tricking him. (This irony, by the way, does not prevent Gimpel from expressing a few things that Isaac Bashevis Singer believes, and perhaps expects us to believe.) And when we read Hemingway's "A Clean, Well-Lighted Place," surely we feel that most of the time the older waiter speaks for the author. Though the waiter gives us a respectful, compassionate view of a lonely old man, and we don't doubt that the view is Hemingway's, still, in the closing lines of the story we are reminded that author and waiter are not identical. Musing on the sleepless night ahead of him, the waiter tries to shrug off his problem — "After all, it is probably only insomnia" — but the reader, who recalls the waiter's bleak view of *nada,* nothingness, knows that it certainly isn't mere insomnia that keeps him awake, but a dread of solitude and death. At that crucial moment, Hemingway and the older waiter part company, and we perceive an ironic point of view, and also a verbal irony, "After all, it is probably only insomnia."

Storytellers are sometimes fond of ironic twists of fate — developments that reveal a terrible distance between what people deserve and what they get, between what is and what ought to be. In the novels of Thomas Hardy, some hostile fate keeps playing tricks to thwart the main characters. In *Tess of the D'Urbervilles,* an all-important letter, thrust under a door, by chance slides beneath a carpet and is not received. An obvious prank of fate occurs in O. Henry's short story "The Gift of the Magi," in which a young wife sells her beautiful hair to buy her poor young husband a watch chain for Christmas, not knowing that, to buy combs for her hair, he has sold his watch. Such an irony is sometimes called an **irony of fate** or a **cosmic irony,** for it suggests that some malicious fate (or other spirit in the universe) is deliberately frustrating human efforts. (In O. Henry's story, however, the twist of fate leads to a happy ending; for the author suggests that, by their futile sacrifices, the lovers are drawn closer together.) Evidently, there is an irony of fate in the servant's futile attempt to escape Death in the fable "The Appointment in Samarra."

To notice an irony gives pleasure. It may move us to laughter, make us feel wonder, or arouse our sympathy. By so involving us, irony — whether in a statement, a situation, an unexpected event, or a point of view — can render a story more likely to strike us, to affect us, and to be remembered.

Shirley Jackson
THE LOTTERY   1948

Shirley Jackson (1919 – 1965), a native of San Francisco, moved in her teens to Rochester, New York. She started college at the University of Rochester, but had to drop out, stricken by severe depression, a problem that was to recur at intervals throughout her life. Later she was graduated from Syracuse University. With her husband Stanley Edgar Hyman, a literary critic, she settled in Bennington, Vermont, in a sprawling house built in the nineteenth century. There Jackson conscientiously set herself to produce a fixed number of words each day. She wrote novels: The Road Through the Wall *(1948), and three psychological thrillers —* Hangsaman *(1951),* The Haunting of Hill House *(1959), and* We Have Always Lived in the

Castle *(1962). She wrote light, witty articles for* Good Housekeeping *and other popular magazines about the horrors of housekeeping and rearing four children, collected in* Life among the Savages *(1953) and* Raising Demons *(1957); but she claimed to have written these only for money. When in 1948 "The Lottery" appeared in* The New Yorker, *that issue of the magazine quickly sold out. Her purpose in writing the story, Jackson declared, had been "to shock the story's readers with a graphic demonstration of the pointless violence and general inhumanity in their own lives."*

The morning of June 27th was clear and sunny, with the fresh warmth of a full-summer day; the flowers were blossoming profusely and the grass was richly green. The people of the village began to gather in the square, between the post office and the bank, around ten o'clock; in some towns there were so many people that the lottery took two days and had to be started on June 26th, but in this village, where there were only about three hundred people, the whole lottery took less than two hours, so it could begin at ten o'clock in the morning and still be through in time to allow the villagers to get home for noon dinner.

The children assembled first, of course. School was recently over for the summer, and the feeling of liberty sat uneasily on most of them; they tended to gather together quietly for a while before they broke into boisterous play, and their talk was still of the classroom and the teacher, of books and reprimands. Bobby Martin had already stuffed his pockets full of stones, and the other boys soon followed his example, selecting the smoothest and roundest stones; Bobby and Harry Jones and Dickie Delacroix — the villagers pronounced this name "Dellacroy" — eventually made a great pile of stones in one corner of the square and guarded it against the raids of the other boys. The girls stood aside, talking among themselves, looking over their shoulders at the boys, and the very small children rolled in the dust or clung to the hands of their older brothers or sisters.

Soon the men began to gather, surveying their own children, speaking of planting and rain, tractors and taxes. They stood together, away from the pile of stones in the corner, and their jokes were quiet and they smiled rather than laughed. The women, wearing faded house dresses and sweaters, came shortly after their menfolk. They greeted one another and exchanged bits of gossip as they went to join their husbands. Soon the women, standing by their husbands, began to call to their children, and the children came reluctantly, having to be called four or five times. Bobby Martin ducked under his mother's grasping hand and ran, laughing, back to the pile of stones. His father spoke up sharply, and Bobby came quickly and took his place between his father and his oldest brother.

The lottery was conducted — as were the square dances, the teenage club, the Halloween program — by Mr. Summers, who had time and energy to devote to civic activities. He was a roundfaced, jovial man and he ran the coal business, and people were sorry for him, because he had no children and his wife was a scold. When he arrived in the square, carrying the black wooden box, there was a murmur of conversation among the villagers and he waved and called, "Little late today, folks." The postmaster, Mr. Graves, followed him, carrying a three-legged stool, and the stool was put in the center of the square and Mr. Summers set the black box down on it. The villagers kept their distance, leaving a space between themselves and the stool, and when Mr. Summers said, "Some of you fellows want to give me a hand?" there was a hesitation before two men, Mr. Martin and his oldest son, Baxter, came forward to hold the box steady on the stool while Mr. Summers stirred up the papers inside it.

The original paraphernalia for the lottery had been lost long ago, and the 5 black box now resting on the stool had been put into use even before Old Man Warner, the oldest man in town, was born. Mr. Summers spoke frequently to the villagers about making a new box, but no one liked to upset even as much tradition as was represented by the black box. There was a story that the present box had been made with some pieces of the box that had preceded it, the one that had been constructed when the first people settled down to make a village here. Every year, after the lottery, Mr. Summers began talking again about a new box, but every year the subject was allowed to fade off without anything's being done. The black box grew shabbier each year; by now it was no longer completely black but splintered badly along one side to show the original wood color, and in some places faded or stained.

Mr. Martin and his oldest son, Baxter, held the black box securely on the stool until Mr. Summers had stirred the papers thoroughly with his hand. Because so much of the ritual had been forgotten or discarded, Mr. Summers had been successful in having slips of paper substituted for the chips of wood that had been used for generations. Chips of wood, Mr. Summers had argued, had been all very well when the village was tiny, but now that the population was more than three hundred and likely to keep on growing, it was necessary to use something that would fit more easily into the black box. The night before the lottery, Mr. Summers and Mr. Graves made up the slips of paper and put them in the box, and it was then taken to the safe of Mr. Summers's coal company and locked up until Mr. Summers was ready to take it to the square next morning. The rest of the year, the box was put away, sometimes one place, sometimes another; it had spent one year in Mr. Graves's barn and another year underfoot in the post office, and sometimes it was set on a shelf in the Martin grocery and left there.

There was a great deal of fussing to be done before Mr. Summers declared the lottery open. There were lists to make up — of heads of families, heads of households in each family, members of each household in each family. There was the proper swearing-in of Mr. Summers by the postmaster, as the official of the lottery; at one time, some people remembered, there had been a recital of some sort, performed by the official of the lottery, a perfunctory, tuneless chant that had been rattled off duly each year; some people believed that the official of the lottery used to stand just so when he said or sang it, others believed that he was supposed to walk among the people, but years and years ago this part of the ritual had been allowed to lapse. There had been, also, a ritual salute, which the official of the lottery had had to use in addressing each person who came up to draw from the box, but this also had changed with time, until now it was felt necessary only for the official to speak to each person approaching. Mr. Summers was very good at all this; in his clean white shirt and blue jeans, with one hand resting carelessly on the black box, he seemed very proper and important as he talked interminably to Mr. Graves and the Martins.

Just as Mr. Summers finally left off talking and turned to the assembled villagers, Mrs. Hutchinson came hurriedly along the path to the square, her sweater thrown over her shoulders, and slid into place in the back of the crowd. "Clean forgot what day it was," she said to Mrs. Delacroix, who stood next to her, and they both laughed softly. "Thought my old man was out back stacking wood," Mrs. Hutchinson went on, "and then I looked out the window and the kids were gone, and then I remembered it was the twenty-seventh and came a-running." She dried her hands on her apron, and Mrs. Delacroix said, "You're in time, though. They're still talking away up there."

Mrs. Hutchinson craned her neck to see through the crowd and found her husband and children standing near the front. She tapped Mrs. Delacroix on the arm as a farewell and began to make her way through the crowd. The people separated good-humoredly to let her through; two or three people said, in voices just loud enough to be heard across the crowd, "Here comes your Missus, Hutchinson," and "Bill, she made it after all." Mrs. Hutchinson reached her husband, and Mr. Summers, who had been waiting, said cheerfully, "Thought we were going to have to get on without you, Tessie." Mrs. Hutchinson said, grinning, "Wouldn't have me leave m'dishes in the sink, now would you, Joe?" and soft laughter ran through the crowd as the people stirred back into position after Mrs. Hutchinson's arrival.

"Well, now," Mr. Summers said soberly, "guess we better get started, get 10 this over with, so's we can go back to work. Anybody ain't here?"

"Dunbar," several people said. "Dunbar, Dunbar."

Mr. Summers consulted his list. "Clyde Dunbar," he said. "That's right. He's broke his leg, hasn't he? Who's drawing for him?"

"Me, I guess," a woman said, and Mr. Summers turned to look at her. "Wife draws for her husband," Mr. Summers said. "Don't you have a grown boy to do it for you, Janey?" Although Mr. Summers and everyone else in the village knew the answer perfectly well, it was the business of the official of the lottery to ask such questions formally. Mr. Summers waited with an expression of polite interest while Mrs. Dunbar answered.

"Horace's not but sixteen yet," Mrs. Dunbar said regretfully. "Guess I gotta fill in for the old man this year."

"Right," Mr. Summers said. He made a note on the list he was holding. 15 Then he asked, "Watson boy drawing this year?"

A tall boy in the crowd raised his hand. "Here," he said. "I'm drawing for m'mother and me." He blinked his eyes nervously and ducked his head as several voices in the crowd said things like "Good fellow, Jack," and "Glad to see your mother's got a man to do it."

"Well," Mr. Summers said, "guess that's everyone. Old Man Warner make it?"

"Here," a voice said, and Mr. Summers nodded.

A sudden hush fell on the crowd as Mr. Summers cleared his throat and looked at the list. "All ready?" he called. "Now, I'll read the names — heads of families first — and the men come up and take a paper out of the box. Keep the paper folded in your hand without looking at it until everyone has had a turn. Everything clear?"

The people had done it so many times that they only half listened to the   20
directions; most of them were quiet, wetting their lips, not looking around.
Then Mr. Summers raised one hand high and said, "Adams." A man disen-
gaged himself from the crowd and came forward. "Hi, Steve," Mr. Summers
said, and Mr. Adams said, "Hi, Joe." They grinned at one another humorlessly
and nervously. Then Mr. Adams reached into the black box and took out a
folded paper. He held it firmly by one corner as he turned and went hastily
back to his place in the crowd, where he stood a little apart from his family,
not looking down at his hand.

"Allen," Mr. Summers said. "Anderson. . . . Bentham."

"Seems like there's no time at all between lotteries any more," Mrs.
Delacroix said to Mrs. Graves in the back row. "Seems like we got through
with the last one only last week."

"Time sure goes fast," Mrs. Graves said.

"Clark. . . . Delacroix."

"There goes my old man," Mrs. Delacroix said. She held her breath while   25
her husband went forward.

"Dunbar," Mr. Summers said, and Mrs. Dunbar went steadily to the box
while one of the women said, "Go on, Janey," and another said, "There she
goes."

"We're next," Mrs. Graves said. She watched while Mr. Graves came
around from the side of the box, greeted Mr. Summers gravely, and selected
a slip of paper from the box. By now, all through the crowd there were men
holding the small folded papers in their large hands, turning them over and
over nervously. Mrs. Dunbar and her two sons stood together, Mrs. Dunbar
holding the slip of paper.

"Harburt. . . . Hutchinson."

"Get up there, Bill," Mrs. Hutchinson said, and the people near her
laughed.

"Jones."   30

"They do say," Mr. Adams said to Old Man Warner, who stood next to
him, "that over in the north village they're talking of giving up the lottery."

Old Man Warner snorted, "Pack of crazy fools," he said. "Listening to
the young folks, nothing's good enough for *them*. Next thing you know, they'll
be wanting to go back to living in caves, nobody work any more, live *that* way
for a while. Used to be a saying about 'Lottery in June, corn be heavy soon.'
First thing you know, we'd all be eating stewed chickweed and acorns. There's
always been a lottery," he added petulantly. "Bad enough to see young Joe
Summers up there joking with everybody."

"Some places have already quit lotteries," Mrs. Adams said.

"Nothing but trouble in *that*," Old Man Warner said stoutly. "Pack of
young fools."

"Martin." And Bobby Martin watched his father go forward. "Over-   35
dyke. . . . Percy."

"I wish they'd hurry," Mrs. Dunbar said to her older son. "I wish they'd
hurry."

"They're almost through," her son said.

"You get ready to run tell Dad," Mrs. Dunbar said.

Mr. Summers called his own name and then stepped forward precisely
and selected a slip from the box. Then he called, "Warner."

"Seventy-seventh year I been in the lottery," Old Man Warner said as he went through the crowd. "Seventy-seventh time."

"Watson." The tall boy came awkwardly through the crowd. Someone said, "Don't be nervous, Jack," and Mr. Summers said, "Take your time, son."

"Zanini."

After that, there was a long pause, a breathless pause, until Mr. Summers, holding his slip of paper in the air, said, "All right, fellows." For a minute, no one moved, and then all the slips of paper were opened. Suddenly, all women began to speak at once, saying, "Who is it?" "Who's got it?" "Is it the Dunbars?" "Is it the Watsons?" Then the voices began to say, "It's Hutchinson. It's Bill." "Bill Hutchinson's got it."

"Go tell your father," Mrs. Dunbar said to her older son.

People began to look around to see the Hutchinsons. Bill Hutchinson was standing quiet, staring down at the paper in his hand. Suddenly, Tessie Hutchinson shouted to Mr. Summers, "You didn't give him time enough to take any paper he wanted. I saw you. It wasn't fair!"

"Be a good sport, Tessie," Mrs. Delacroix called, and Mrs. Graves said, "All of us took the same chance."

"Shut up, Tessie," Bill Hutchinson said.

"Well, everyone," Mr. Summers said, "that was done pretty fast, and now we've got to be hurrying a little more to get done in time." He consulted his next list. "Bill," he said, "you draw for the Hutchinson family. You got any other households in the Hutchinsons?"

"There's Don and Eva," Mrs. Hutchinson yelled. "Make *them* take their chance!"

"Daughters draw with their husbands' families, Tessie," Mr. Summers said gently. "You know that as well as anyone else."

"It wasn't fair," Tessie said.

"I guess not, Joe," Bill Hutchinson said regretfully. "My daughter draws with her husband's family, that's only fair. And I've got no other family except the kids."

"Then, as far as drawing for families is concerned, it's you," Mr. Summers said in explanation, "and as far as drawing for households is concerned, that's you, too. Right?"

"Right," Bill Hutchinson said.

"How many kids, Bill?" Mr. Summers asked formally.

"Three," Bill Hutchinson said. "There's Bill, Jr., and Nancy, and little Dave. And Tessie and me."

"All right, then," Mr. Summers said. "Harry, you got their tickets back?"

Mr. Graves nodded and held up the slips of paper. "Put them in the box, then," Mr. Summers directed. "Take Bill's and put it in."

"I think we ought to start over," Mrs. Hutchinson said, as quietly as she could. "I tell you it wasn't *fair*. You didn't give him time enough to choose. *Every* body saw that."

Mr. Graves had selected the five slips and put them in the box, and he dropped all the papers but those onto the ground, where the breeze caught them and lifted them off.

"Listen, everybody," Mrs. Hutchinson was saying to the people around her.

"Ready, Bill?" Mr. Summers asked, and Bill Hutchinson, with one quick glance around at his wife and children, nodded.

"Remember," Mr. Summers said, "take the slips and keep them folded until each person has taken one. Harry, you help little Dave." Mr. Graves took the hand of the little boy, who came willingly with him up to the box. "Take a paper out of the box, Davy," Mr. Summers said. Davy put his hand into the box and laughed. "Take just *one* paper," Mr. Summers said. "Harry, you hold it for him." Mr. Graves took the child's hand and removed the folded paper from the tight fist and held it while little Dave stood next to him and looked up at him wonderingly.

"Nancy next," Mr. Summers said. Nancy was twelve, and her school friends breathed heavily as she went forward, switching her skirt, and took a slip daintily from the box. "Bill, Jr.," Mr. Summers said, and Billy, his face red and his feet over-large, nearly knocked the box over as he got a paper out. "Tessie," Mr. Summers said. She hesitated for a minute, looking around defiantly, and then set her lips and went up to the box. She snatched a paper out and held it behind her.

"Bill," Mr. Summers said, and Bill Hutchinson reached into the box and   65
felt around, bringing his hand out at last with the slip of paper in it.

The crowd was quiet. A girl whispered, "I hope it's not Nancy," and the sound of the whisper reached the edges of the crowd.

"It's not the way it used to be," Old Man Warner said clearly. "People ain't the way they used to be."

"All right," Mr. Summers said. "Open the papers. Harry, you open little Dave's."

Mr. Graves opened the slip of paper and there was a general sigh through the crowd as he held it up and everyone could see that it was blank. Nancy and Bill, Jr., opened theirs at the same time, and both beamed and laughed, turning around to the crowd and holding their slips of paper above their heads.

"Tessie," Mr. Summers said. There was a pause, and then Mr. Summers   70
looked at Bill Hutchinson, and Bill unfolded his paper and showed it. It was blank.

"It's Tessie," Mr. Summers said, and his voice was hushed. "Show us her paper, Bill."

Bill Hutchinson went over to his wife and forced the slip of paper out of her hand. It had a black spot on it, the black spot Mr. Summers had made the night before with the heavy pencil in the coal-company office. Bill Hutchinson held it up, and there was a stir in the crowd.

"All right, folks," Mr. Summers said, "let's finish quickly."

Although the villagers had forgotten the ritual and lost the original black box, they still remembered to use stones. The pile of stones the boys had made earlier was ready; there were stones on the ground with the blowing scraps of paper that had come out of the box. Mrs. Delacroix selected a stone so large she had to pick it up with both hands and turned to Mrs. Dunbar. "Come on," she said. "Hurry up."

Mrs. Dunbar had small stones in both hands, and she said, gasping for   75
breath, "I can't run at all. You'll have to go ahead and I'll catch up with you."

The children had stones already, and someone gave little Davy Hutchinson a few pebbles.

Tessie Hutchinson was in the center of a cleared space by now, and she held her hands out desperately as the villagers moved in on her. "It isn't fair," she said. A stone hit her on the side of the head.

Old Man Warner was saying, "Come on, come on, everyone." Steve Adams was in the front of the crowd of villagers, with Mrs. Graves beside him.

"It isn't fair, it isn't right," Mrs. Hutchinson screamed, and then they were upon her.

QUESTIONS

1. Where do you think "The Lottery" takes place? What purpose do you suppose the writer has in making this setting appear so familiar and ordinary?
2. In paragraphs 2 and 3, what details foreshadow the ending of the story?
3. What is ironic in this statement (in paragraph 76): "The children had stones already, and someone gave little Davy Hutchinson a few pebbles"?
4. What else did you notice in the story that strikes you as an irony?
5. What particular details lend vividness to the story? Take a close look at Jackson's description of the black wooden box (paragraph 5) and of the black spot on the fatal slip of paper (paragraph 72).
6. From what point of view is the story told? Why does Jackson's choice of this point of view seem effective?
7. What do you understand to be the writer's own attitude toward the lottery and the stoning? Exactly what in the story makes her attitude clear to us?
8. What do you make of Old Man Warner's saying, "Lottery in June, corn be heavy soon"?
9. What do you think Shirley Jackson is driving at? Consider each of the following interpretations and, looking at the story, see if you can find any evidence for it.

Jackson takes a primitive fertility rite and playfully transfers it to a small town in North America.

Jackson, writing her story soon after World War II, indirectly expresses her horror at the Holocaust. She assumes that the massacre of the Jews was carried out by unwitting, obedient people, like these villagers. (This suggestion has been advanced by critic Richard Moore.)

Jackson is satirizing our own society, in which men are selected for the army by lottery.

Jackson is just writing a memorable, entertaining story that signifies nothing at all.

Flann O'Brien
TWO IN ONE
1978

Flann O'Brien (1911 – 1966), whose real name was Brian O'Nolan, was born in County Tyrone, Ireland. After his graduation from University College, Dublin (where he edited a magazine called Blather*), he spent eighteen years as a civil servant. As a writer, so prolific was O'Nolan that he needed more than one pen name. Under the byline of Miles na Gopaleen,* *for twenty-five years he contributed a much-beloved column to* The Irish Times, *which James Thurber considered the funniest newspaper feature he knew. O'Nolan's masterpiece (as Flann O'Brien) was the wildly inventive comic novel,* At Swim-Two-Birds *(1939)* — *"just the book to give to your sister," said poet Dylan Thomas, "if she is a wild, dirty, boozy girl." The novel at first escaped notice, having appeared on the day Hitler invaded Poland, precipitating World War II. O'Brien also produced stories, essays, plays, and four other novels:* The Hard Life *(1962);* The Dalkey Archive *(1964);* The Third Policeman *(1967); and one novel written in Irish,* An Beál Bocht *(1941), translated as* The Poor Mouth *(1973). Characteristically, the author died on April Fool's Day. Flann O'Brien has long been cherished by his countrymen, and by an international audience that keeps growing.* A Flann O'Brien Reader, *edited by Stephen Jonas (1978), affords an overall glimpse of him.*

The story I have to tell is a strange one, perhaps unbelievable. I will try to set it down as simply as I can. I do not expect to be disturbed in my literary labors, for I am writing this in the condemned cell.

Let us say my name is Murphy. The unusual occurrence which led me here concerns my relations with another man whom we shall call Kelly. Both of us were taxidermists.

I will not attempt a treatise on what a taxidermist is. The word is ugly and inadequate. Certainly it does not convey to the layman that such an operator must combine the qualities of zoologist, naturalist, chemist, sculptor, artist and carpenter. Who would blame such a person for showing some temperament now and again, as I did?

It is necessary, however, to say a brief word about this science. First, there is no such thing in modern practice as "stuffing" an animal. There is a record of stuffed gorillas having been in Carthage in the 5th century, and it is a fact that an Austrian prince, Siegmund Herberstein, had stuffed bison in the great hall of his castle in the 16th century — it was then the practice to draw the entrails of animals and to substitute spices and various preservative substances. There is a variety of methods in use today but, except in particular cases — snakes, for example, where preserving the translucency of the skin is a problem calling for special measures — the basis of all modern methods is simply this: you skin the animal very carefully according to a certain pattern, and you encase the skinless body in plaster of Paris. You bisect the plaster when cast providing yourself with two complementary moulds from which you can make a casting of the animal's body — there are several substances, all very light, from which such castings can be made. The next step, calling for infinite skill and patience, is to mount the skin on the casting of the body. That is all I need explain here, I think.

Kelly carried on a taxidermy business and I was his assistant. He was the boss — a swinish, overbearing mean boss, a bully, a sadist. He hated me, but enjoyed his hatred too much to sack me. He knew I had a real interest in the work, and a desire to broaden my experience. For that reason, he threw me all the commonplace jobs that came in. If some old lady sent her favorite terrier to be done, that was me; foxes and cats and Shetland ponies and white rabbits — they were all strictly *my* department. I could do a perfect job on such animals in my sleep, and got to hate them. But if a crocodile came in, or a Great Borneo spider, or (as once happened) a giraffe — Kelly kept them all for himself. In the meantime he would treat my own painstaking work with sourness and sneers and complaints.

One day the atmosphere in the workshop had been even fouler than usual, with Kelly in a filthier temper than usual. I had spent the forenoon finishing a cat, and at about lunch-time put it on the shelf where he left completed orders.

I could nearly *hear* him glaring at it. Where was the tail? I told him there was no tail, that it was a Manx cat. How did I know it was a Manx cat, how did I know it was not an ordinary cat which had lost its tail in a motor accident or something? I got so mad that I permitted myself a disquisition on cats in general, mentioning the distinctions as between *felis manul, felis silvestris* and *felis lybica,* and on the unique structure of the Manx cat. His reply to that? He called me a slob. That was the sort of life *I* was having.

On this occasion something within me snapped. I was sure I could hear the snap. I had moved up to where he was to answer his last insult. The loathsome creature had his back to me, bending down to put on his bicycle clips. Just to my hand on the bench was one of the long, flat steel instruments we use for certain operations with plaster. I picked it up and hit him a blow with it on the back of the head. He gave a cry and slumped forward. I hit him again. I rained blow after blow on him. Then I threw the tool away. I was upset. I went out into the yard and looked around. I remembered he had a weak heart. Was he dead? I remember adjusting the position of a barrel we had in the yard to catch rainwater, the only sort of water suitable for some of the mixtures we used. I found I was in a cold sweat but strangely calm. I went back into the workshop.

Kelly was just as I had left him. I could find no pulse. I rolled him over on his back and examined his eyes, for I have seen more lifeless eyes in my day than most people. Yes, there was no doubt: Kelly was dead. I had killed him. I was a murderer. I put on my coat and hat and left the place. I walked the streets for a while, trying to avoid panic, trying to think rationally. Inevitably, I was soon in a public house. I drank a lot of whiskey and finally went home to my digs. The next morning I was very sick indeed from this terrible mixture of drink and worry. Was the Kelly affair merely a fancy, a drunken fancy? No, there was no consolation in that sort of hope. He was dead all right.

It was as I lay in bed there, shaking, thinking and smoking, that the mad idea came into my head. No doubt this sounds incredible, grotesque, even disgusting, but I decided I would treat Kelly the same as any other dead creature that found its way to the workshop.

Once one enters a climate of horror, distinction of degree as between one infamy and another seems slight, sometimes undetectable. That evening I went to the workshop and made my preparations. I worked steadily all next day. I will not appall the reader with gruesome detail. I need only say that I applied the general technique and flaying pattern appropriate to apes. The job took me four days at the end of which I had a perfect skin, face and all. I made the usual castings before committing the remains of, so to speak, the remains, to the furnace. My plan was to have Kelly on view asleep on a chair, for the benefit

10

of anybody who might call. Reflection convinced me that this would be far too dangerous. I had to think again.

A further idea began to form. It was so macabre that it shocked even myself. For days I had been treating the inside of the skin with the usual preservatives — cellulose acetate and the like — thinking all the time. The new illumination came upon me like a thunderbolt. *I would don his skin and, when the need arose, BECOME Kelly!* His clothes fitted me. So would his skin. Why not?

Another day's agonized work went on various alterations and adjustments but that night I was able to look into a glass and see Kelly looking back at me, perfect in every detail except for the teeth and eyes, which had to be my own but which I knew other people would never notice.

Naturally I wore Kelly's clothes, and had no trouble in imitating his unpleasant voice and mannerisms. On the second day, having "dressed," so to speak, I went for a walk, receiving salutes from newsboys and other people who had known Kelly. And on the day after, I was foolhardy enough to visit Kelly's lodgings. Where on earth had I been, his landlady wanted to know. (She had noticed nothing.) What, I asked — had that fool Murphy not told her that I had to go to the country for a few days? No? I had told the good-for-nothing to convey the message.

I slept that night in Kelly's bed. I was a little worried about what the other landlady would think of my own absence. I decided not to remove Kelly's skin the first night I spent in his bed but to try to get the rest of my plan of campaign perfected and into sharper focus. I eventually decided that Kelly should announce to various people that he was going to a very good job in Canada, and that he had sold his business to his assistant Murphy. I would then burn the skin, I would own a business and — what is more stupid than vanity! — I could secretly flatter myself that I had committed the perfect crime.

Need I say that I had overlooked something?

The mummifying preparation with which I had dressed the inside of the skin was, of course, quite stable for the ordinary purposes of taxidermy. It had not occurred to me that a night in a warm bed would make it behave differently. The horrible truth dawned on me the next day when I reached the workshop and tried to take the skin off. *It wouldn't come off!* It had literally fused with my own! And in the days that followed, this process kept rapidly advancing. Kelly's skin got to live again, to breathe, to perspire.

Then followed more days of terrible tension. My own landlady called one day, inquiring about me of "Kelly." I told her I had been on the point of calling on *her* to find out where I was. She was disturbed about my disappearance — it was so unlike me — and said she thought she should inform the police. I thought it wise not to try to dissuade her. My disappearance would eventually come to be accepted, I thought. My Kelliness, so to speak, was permanent. It was horrible, but it was a choice of that or the scaffold.

I kept drinking a lot. One night, after many drinks, I went to the club for a game of snooker°. This club was in fact one of the causes of Kelly's bitterness towards me. I had joined it without having been aware that Kelly was a member. His resentment was boundless. He thought I was watching him, and taking note of the attentions he paid the lady members.

snooker: billiard game played with fifteen red balls and six balls of other colors.

On this occasion I nearly made a catastrophic mistake. It is a simple fact 20
that I am a very good snooker player, easily the best in that club. As I was
standing watching another game in progress awaiting my turn for the table,
I suddenly realised that Kelly did not play snooker at all! For some moments, a cold sweat
stood out on Kelly's brow at the narrowness of this escape. I went to the bar.
There, a garrulous lady (who thinks her unsolicited conversation is a fair
exchange for a drink) began talking to me. She remarked the long absence of
my nice Mr. Murphy. She said he was missed a lot in the snooker room. I was
hot and embarrassed and soon went home. To Kelly's place, of course.

Not embarrassment, but a real sense of danger, was to be my next portion
in this adventure. One afternoon, two very casual strangers strolled into the
workshop, saying they would like a little chat with me. Cigarettes were produced. Yes indeed, they were plain-clothesmen making a few routine inquiries. This man Murphy had been reported missing by several people. Any idea
where he was? None at all. When had I last seen him? Did he seem upset or
disturbed? No, but he was an impetuous type. I had recently reprimanded him
for bad work. On similar other occasions he had threatened to leave and seek
work in England. Had I been away for a few days myself? Yes, down in Cork
for a few days. On business. Yes . . . yes . . . some people thinking of starting
a natural museum down there, technical school people — that sort of thing.

The casual manner of these men worried me, but I was sure they did not
suspect the truth and that they were genuinely interested in tracing Murphy.
Still, I knew I was in danger, without knowing the exact nature of the threat
I had to counter. Whiskey cheered me somewhat.

Then it happened. The two detectives came back accompanied by two
other men in uniform. They showed me a search warrant. It was purely a
formality; it had to be done in the case of all missing persons. They had already
searched Murphy's digs and had found nothing of interest. They were very
sorry for upsetting the place during my working hours.

A few days later the casual gentlemen called and put me under arrest for
the willful murder of Murphy, of myself. They proved the charge in due course
with all sorts of painfully amassed evidence, including the remains of human
bones in the furnace. I was sentenced to be hanged. Even if I could now prove
that Murphy still lived by shedding the accursed skin, what help would that
be? Where, they would ask, is Kelly?

That is my strange and tragic story. And I end it with the thought that 25
if Kelly and I must each be either murderer or murdered, it is perhaps better
to accept my present fate as philosophically as I can and be cherished in the
public mind as the victim of this murderous monster, Kelly. He *was* a murderer,
anyway.

QUESTIONS

1. With what details does O'Brien establish the verisimilitude of his narrator
   — show us that, indeed, Murphy would be entirely capable of pulling off this
   perfect-seeming crime?
2. What is the narrator's motivation for killing his employer? For deciding to "treat
   Kelly the same as any other dead creature that found its way to the workshop"?
   For donning the dead man's skin?
3. At what moment — and for what reason — does Murphy's neat plan go askew?

4. In the end, the narrator says of Kelly, "He *was* a murderer, anyway." In what sense is this remark to be taken?
5. When does it begin to dawn on you that the whole story just might be a preposterous lot of cock and bull and that O'Brien may be pulling your leg? Do you resent the absurdity of the story — that it couldn't possibly happen? (There is, of course, no one right answer to this last question.)
6. What sorts of irony do you find in "Two in One"? What is ironic about the "macabre idea" that Murphy determines to try out (paragraphs 12 – 15)? What is ironic in the narrator's situation at the end? Is the story told from an ironic point of view? Explain.
7. What similarities do you find between "Two in One" and Edgar Allan Poe's "The Telltale Heart" (page 38)? Did you find any irony in Poe's story? In what important ways do the two stories differ?
8. Would you care to read any more of Flann O'Brien's work, or have you had enough? (If you care to pursue him further, see any of the books listed in the biographical note at the start of the story.)

Suggestions for Writing

1. Freewrite for fifteen or twenty minutes, rapidly jotting down any thoughts you may have in answer to this question: From your daily contacts with people, what ironies do you at times become aware of? Consider ironies of language (in deliberately misleading or sarcastic remarks), ironies of situation (here you are, a trained computer programmer unable to convince a counterperson in a fast-food joint that you can correctly add up a check). Then, using any good perceptions you have generated, write and polish a short answer to the question, illustrating your remarks by reference to your own recalled experience and recent observations. You might find it useful too, of course, to cite some ironies in any stories about everyday life you know.
2. Inspired by Flann O'Brien's "Two in One," write a brief tall tale, keeping an absolutely straight poker face. Make your tale as convincing as possible, by including plenty of convincing detail and perhaps openly recognizing that your readers are likely to be skeptical. Then, following your tale, write a comment recalling the problems you had in telling the story and how you coped with them.
3. Write an answer to the last question on "The Lottery." Try to show, by referring to particulars in the story, what if anything you think Shirley Jackson is driving at.
4. Here are some other topics: "Irony in 'A Rose for Emily.'" "Irony in 'Greasy Lake.'" "Irony in 'The Jilting of Granny Weatherall.'" (Or what other story have you read that more keenly interests you?) What sorts of irony make the story more effective? In dealing with any of them, you may find the method of analysis a help to you. Before you write, read about this useful method in "Writing about a Story" (page 1353).

7 Theme

The **theme** of a story is whatever general idea or insight the entire story reveals. In some stories the theme is unmistakable. At the end of Aesop's fable about the council of the mice that can't decide who will bell the cat, the theme is stated in the moral: *It is easier to propose a thing than to carry it out.* In a work of commercial fiction, too, the theme (if any) is usually obvious. Consider a typical detective thriller in which, say, a rookie policeman trained in scientific methods of crime detection sets out to solve a mystery sooner than his rival, a veteran sleuth whose only laboratory is carried under his hat. Perhaps the veteran solves the case, leading to the conclusion (and the theme), "The old ways are the best ways after all." Another story by the same writer might dramatize the same rivalry but reverse the outcome, having the rookie win, thereby reversing the theme: "The times are changing! Let's shake loose from old-fashioned ways." In such commercial entertainments, a theme is like a length of rope with which the writer, patently and mechanically, trusses the story neatly (usually too neatly) into meaningful shape.

In literary fiction, a theme is seldom so obvious. That is, a theme need not be a moral or a message; it may be what the happenings add up to, what the story is about. When we come to the end of a finely wrought short story such as Ernest Hemingway's "A Clean, Well-Lighted Place" (Chapter Five), it may be easy to sum up the plot — to say what happens — but it is more difficult to sum up the story's main idea. Evidently, Hemingway relates events — how a younger waiter gets rid of an old man and how an older waiter then goes to a coffee bar — but in themselves these events seem relatively slight, though the story as a whole seems large (for its size) and full of meaning. For the meaning, we must look to other elements in the story besides what happens in it. And it is clear that Hemingway is most deeply interested in the thoughts and feelings of the older waiter, the character who has more and more to say as the story progresses, until at the end the story is entirely confined to his thoughts and perceptions. What is meaningful in these thoughts and perceptions? The older waiter understands the old man and sympathizes with his need for a clean, well-lighted place. If we say that, we are still talking about what happens in the story, though we have gone beyond merely recording its external events. But a theme is usually stated in *general* words. Another try: "Solitary people who cannot sleep need a cheerful, orderly place where they can drink with dignity." That's a little better. We have indicated, at least, that Hemingway's story is about more than just an old man and a couple of waiters. But what about the older waiter's meditation on *nada,* nothingness? Coming near the end of the story, it takes great emphasis; and probably no good statement of Hemingway's theme can leave it out. Still another try at a statement: "Solitary people need a place of refuge from their terrible awareness that their lives (or perhaps, human lives) are essentially meaningless." Neither this nor any other statement of the story's theme is unarguably right, but at least the sentence helps the reader to bring into focus one primary idea that Hemingway seems to be driving at. When we finish reading "A Clean, Well-Lighted Place," we feel that there *is* such a theme, a unifying vision, even though we cannot reduce it absolutely to a tag. Like some freshwater lake alive with creatures, Hemingway's story is a broad expanse, reflecting in many directions. No wonder that many readers will view it differently.

Moral inferences may be drawn from the story, no doubt — for Hemingway is indirectly giving us advice for properly regarding and sympathizing with the lonely, the uncertain, and the old. But the story doesn't set forth a lesson that we are supposed to put into practice. One could argue that "A Clean, Well-Lighted Place" contains *several* themes — and other statements could be made to take in Hemingway's views of love, of communication between people, of dignity. Great short stories, like great symphonies, frequently have more than one theme.

In many a fine short story, theme is the center, the moving force, the principle of unity. Clearly, such a theme is something other than the characters and events of its story. To say of James Joyce's "Araby" (page 54) that it is about a boy who goes to a bazaar to buy a gift for a young woman, only to arrive too late, is to summarize plot, not theme. (The theme *might* be put, "The illusions of a romantic child are vulnerable," or it might be put in any of a few hundred other ways.) Although the title of Isaac Bashevis Singer's "Gimpel the Fool" (Chapter Four) indicates the main character and suggests the subject (his "foolishness"), the theme — the larger realization that the story leaves us with — has to do not with foolishness, but with how to be wise.

Sometimes you will hear it said that the theme of a story (say, Faulkner's "Barn Burning") is "loss of innocence" or "initiation into maturity"; or that the theme of some other story (Thurber's "The Catbird Seat," for instance) is "the revolt of the downtrodden." This is to use *theme* in a larger and more abstract sense than we use it here. Although such general descriptions of theme can be useful — as in sorting a large number of stories into rough categories — we suggest that, in the beginning, you look for whatever truth or insight you think the writer of a story reveals. Try to sum it up *in a sentence.* By doing so, you will find yourself looking closely at the story, trying to define its principal meaning. You may find it helpful, in making your sentence-statement of theme, to consider these points:

1. Look back once more at the title of the story. From what you have read, what does it indicate?

2. Does the main character in any way change in the story? Does this character arrive at any eventual realization or understanding? Are you left with any realization or understanding you did not have before?

3. Does the author make any general observations about life or human nature? Do the characters make any? (Caution: Characters now and again will utter opinions with which the reader is not necessarily supposed to agree.)

4. Does the story contain any especially curious objects, mysterious flat characters, significant animals, repeated names, song titles, or whatever, that hint toward meanings larger than such things ordinarily have? In literary stories, such symbols may point to central themes. (For a short discussion of symbolism and a few illustrations, see Chapter Eight.)

5. When you have worded your statement of theme, have you cast your statement into general language, not just given a plot summary?

6. Does your statement hold true for the story as a whole, not for just part of it?

In distilling a statement of theme from a rich and complicated story, we have, of course, no more encompassed the whole story than a paleontologist taking a plaster mold of a petrified footprint has captured a living brontosaurus. A writer (other than a fabulist) does not usually set out with theme in hand, determined to make every detail in the story work to demonstrate it. Well then, the skeptical reader may ask, if only *some* stories have themes, if those themes may be hard to sum up, and if readers will probably disagree in their summations, why bother to state themes? Isn't it too much trouble? Surely it is, unless the effort to state a theme ends in pleasure and profit. Trying to sum up the point of a story in our own words is merely one way to make ourselves better aware of whatever we may have understood vaguely and tentatively. Attempted with loving care, such statements may bring into focus our scattered impressions of a rewarding story, may help to clarify and hold fast whatever wisdom the storyteller has offered us.

Flannery O'Connor

Revelation   1965

Mary Flannery O'Connor (she dropped the first name from her byline) spent most of her life (1925 – 1964) in Milledgeville, Georgia. While she was a student at Georgia State College for Women, in her home town, her fledgling stories won her local fame. She went on to study at the Writers

Workshop of the University of Iowa, from which in 1946 she obtained her M.F.A. degree. On discovering that she was afflicted with lupus erythematosus, the progressive and incurable blood disease that had killed her father, O'Connor returned to Milledgeville to live with her mother, undergo treatment, raise peacocks, and write. The bulk of her work consists of two novels, Wise Blood *(1952) and* The Violent Bear It Away *(1960);* Complete Stories of Flannery O'Connor *(1971); a book of essays and talks,* Mystery and Manners *(1961); her brilliant, modest, cheerful letters, collected in* The Habit of Being *(1979); and terse book reviews written for Catholic newspapers in Georgia, collected in* The Presence of Grace *(1983). Since O'Connor's early death, her fiction, once blamed as gratuitously violent and jarringly grotesque, has enjoyed a steady and triumphant rise in critical favor. Its themes derive from her devoutly Christian faith, but its dark and often hilarious humor derives from her own view — perhaps also from a native Georgian tradition of tall-taletelling.*

The doctor's waiting room, which was very small, was almost full when the Turpins entered and Mrs. Turpin, who was very large, made it look even smaller by her presence. She stood looming at the head of the magazine table set in the center of it, a living demonstration that the room was inadequate and ridiculous. Her little bright black eyes took in all the patients as she sized up the seating situation. There was one vacant chair and a place on the sofa occupied by a blond child in a dirty blue romper who should have been told to move over and make room for the lady. He was five or six, but Mrs. Turpin saw at once that no one was going to tell him to move over. He was slumped down in the seat, his arms idle at his sides and his eyes idle in his head; his nose ran unchecked.

Mrs. Turpin put a firm hand on Claud's shoulder and said in a voice that included anyone who wanted to listen, "Claud, you sit in that chair there," and gave him a push down into the vacant one. Claud was florid and bald and sturdy, somewhat shorter than Mrs. Turpin, but he sat down as if he were accustomed to doing what she told him to.

Mrs. Turpin remained standing. The only man in the room besides Claud was a lean stringy old fellow with a rusty hand spread out on each knee, whose eyes were closed as if he were asleep or dead or pretending to be so as not to get up and offer her his seat. Her gaze settled agreeably on a well-dressed grey-haired lady whose eyes met hers and whose expression said: if that child belonged to me, he would have some manners and move over — there's plenty of room there for you and him too.

Claud looked up with a sigh and made as if to rise.

"Sit down," Mrs. Turpin said. "You know you're not supposed to stand on that leg. He has an ulcer on his leg," she explained.

Claud lifted his foot onto the magazine table and rolled his trouser leg up to reveal a purple swelling on a plump marble-white calf.

"My!" the pleasant lady said. "How did you do that?"

"A cow kicked him," Mrs. Turpin said.

"Goodness!" said the lady.

5

Claud rolled his trouser leg down.

"Maybe the little boy would move over," the lady suggested, but the child did not stir.

"Somebody will be leaving in a minute," Mrs. Turpin said. She could not understand why a doctor — with as much money as they made charging five dollars a day to just stick their head in the hospital door and look at you — couldn't afford a decent-sized waiting room. This one was hardly bigger than a garage. The table was cluttered with limp-looking magazines and at one end of it there was a big green glass ash tray full of cigaret butts and cotton wads with little blood spots on them. If she had had anything to do with the running of the place, that would have been emptied every so often. There were no chairs against the wall at the head of the room. It had a rectangular-shaped panel in it that permitted a view of the office where the nurse came and went and the secretary listened to the radio. A plastic fern in a gold pot sat in the opening and trailed its fronds down almost to the floor. The radio was softly playing gospel music.

Just then the inner door opened and a nurse with the highest stack of yellow hair Mrs. Turpin had ever seen put her face in the crack and called for the next patient. The woman sitting beside Claud grasped the two arms of her chair and hoisted herself up; she pulled her dress free from her legs and lumbered through the door where the nurse had disappeared.

Mrs. Turpin eased into the vacant chair, which held her tight as a corset. "I wish I could reduce," she said, and rolled her eyes and gave a comic sigh.

"Oh, *you* aren't fat," the stylish lady said.

"Ooooo I am too," Mrs. Turpin said. "Claud he eats all he wants to and never weighs over one hundred and seventy-five pounds, but me I just look at something good to eat and I gain some weight," and her stomach and shoulders shook with laughter. "You can eat all you want to, can't you, Claud?" she asked, turning to him.

Claud only grinned.

"Well, as long as you have such a good disposition," the stylish lady said, "I don't think it makes a bit of difference what size you are. You just can't beat a good disposition."

Next to her was a fat girl of eighteen or nineteen, scowling into a thick blue book which Mrs. Turpin saw was entitled *Human Development.* The girl raised her head and directed her scowl at Mrs. Turpin as if she did not like her looks. She appeared annoyed that anyone should speak while she tried to read. The poor girl's face was blue with acne and Mrs. Turpin thought how pitiful it was to have a face like that at that age. She gave the girl a friendly smile but the girl only scowled the harder. Mrs. Turpin herself was fat but she had always had good skin, and, though she was forty-seven years old, there was not a wrinkle in her face except around her eyes from laughing too much.

Next to the ugly girl was the child, still in exactly the same position, and next to him was a thin leathery old woman in a cotton print dress. She and Claud had three sacks of chicken feed in their pump house that was in the same print. She had seen from the first that the child belonged with the old woman. She could tell by the way they sat — kind of vacant and white-trashy, as if they would sit there until Doomsday if nobody called and told them to get up. And at right angles but next to the well-dressed pleasant lady was a lank-faced woman who was certainly the child's mother. She had on a yellow sweat shirt and wine-colored slacks, both gritty-looking, and the rims of her lips were stained with snuff. Her dirty yellow hair was tied behind with a little piece of red paper ribbon. Worse than niggers any day, Mrs. Turpin thought.

The gospel hymn playing was, "When I looked up and He looked down," and Mrs. Turpin, who knew it, supplied the last line mentally, "And wona these days I know I'll we-eara crown."

Without appearing to, Mrs. Turpin always noticed people's feet. The well-dressed lady had on red and grey suede shoes to match her dress. Mrs. Turpin had on her good black patent leather pumps. The ugly girl had on Girl Scout shoes and heavy socks. The old woman had on tennis shoes and the white-trashy mother had on what appeared to be bedroom slippers, black straw with gold braid threaded through them — exactly what you would have expected her to have on.

Sometimes at night when she couldn't go to sleep, Mrs. Turpin would occupy herself with the question of who she would have chosen to be if she couldn't have been herself. If Jesus had said to her before he made her, "There's only two places available for you. You can either be a nigger or white-trash," what would she have said? "Please, Jesus, please," she would have said, "just let me wait until there's another place available," and he would have said, "No, you have to go right now and I have only those two places so make up your mind." She would have wiggled and squirmed and begged and pleaded but it would have been no use and finally she would have said, "All right, make me a nigger then — but that don't mean a trashy one." And he would have made her a neat clean respectable Negro-woman, herself but black.

Next to the child's mother was a red-headed youngish woman, reading one of the magazines and working a piece of chewing gum, hell for leather, as Claud would say. Mrs. Turpin could not see the woman's feet. She was not white-trash, just common. Sometimes Mrs. Turpin occupied herself at night naming the classes of people. On the bottom of the heap were most colored people, not the kind she would have been if she had been one, but most of them; then next to them — not above, just away from — were the white-trash; then above them were the home-owners, and above them the home-and-land owners, to which she and Claud belonged. Above she and Claud° were people with a lot of money and much bigger houses and much more land. But here the complexity of it would begin to bear in on her, for some of the people with a lot of money were common and ought to be below she and Claud and some of the people who had good blood had lost their money and had to rent and then there were colored people who owned their homes and land as well. There was a colored dentist in town who had two red Lincolns and a swimming pool and a farm with registered white-face cattle on it. Usually by the time she had fallen asleep all the classes of people were moiling and roiling around in her head, and she would dream they were all crammed in together in a box car, being ridden off to be put in a gas oven.

"That's a beautiful clock," she said and nodded to her right. It was a big   25
wall clock, the face encased in a brass sunburst.

Above she and Claud: ungrammatical construction. Putting herself first, Mrs. Turpin presumably would say (if she were speaking aloud), "Above I and Claud . . ."

"Yes, it's very pretty," the stylish lady said agreeably. "And right on the dot too," she added, glancing at her watch.

The ugly girl beside her cast an eye upward at the clock, smirked, then looked directly at Mrs. Turpin and smirked again. Then she returned her eyes to her book. She was obviously the lady's daughter because, although they didn't look anything alike as to disposition, they both had the same shape of face and the same blue eyes. On the lady they sparkled pleasantly but in the girl's seared face they appeared alternately to smolder and to blaze.

What if Jesus had said, "All right, you can be white-trash or a nigger or ugly"!

Mrs. Turpin felt an awful pity for the girl, though she thought it was one thing to be ugly and another to act ugly.

The woman with the snuff-stained lips turned around in her chair and looked up at the clock. Then she turned back and appeared to look a little to the side of Mrs. Turpin. There was a cast in one of her eyes. "You want to know wher you can get you one of themther clocks?" she asked in a loud voice.

"No, I already have a nice clock," Mrs. Turpin said. Once somebody like her got a leg in the conversation, she would be all over it.

"You can get you one with green stamps," the woman said. "That's most likely wher he got hisn. Save you up enough, you can get you most anythang. I got me some joo'ry."

Ought to have got you a wash rag and some soap, Mrs. Turpin thought.

"I get contour sheets with mine," the pleasant lady said.

The daughter slammed her book shut. She looked straight in front of her, directly through Mrs. Turpin and on through the yellow curtain and the plate glass window which made the wall behind her. The girl's eyes seemed lit all of a sudden with a peculiar light, an unnatural light like night road signs give. Mrs. Turpin turned her head to see if there was anything going on outside that she should see, but she could not see anything. Figures passing cast only a pale shadow through the curtain. There was no reason the girl should single her out for her ugly looks.

"Miss Finley," the nurse said, cracking the door. The gum-chewing woman got up and passed in front of her and Claud and went into the office. She had on red high-heeled shoes.

Directly across the table, the ugly girl's eyes were fixed on Mrs. Turpin as if she had some very special reason for disliking her.

"This is wonderful weather, isn't it?" the girl's mother said.

"It's good weather for cotton if you can get the niggers to pick it," Mrs. Turpin said, "but niggers don't want to pick cotton any more. You can't get the white folks to pick it and now you can't get the niggers — because they got to be right up there with the white folks."

"They gonna *try* anyways," the white-trash woman said, leaning forward.

"Do you have one of those cotton-picking machines?" the pleasant lady asked.

"No," Mrs. Turpin said, "they leave half the cotton in the field. We don't have much cotton anyway. If you want to make it farming now, you have to have a little of everything. We got a couple of acres of cotton and a few hogs and chickens and just enough white-face that Claud can look after them himself."

"One thang I don't want," the white-trash woman said, wiping her mouth with the back of her hands. "Hogs. Nasty stinking things, a-gruntin and a-rootin all over the place."

Mrs. Turpin gave her the merest edge of her attention. "Our hogs are not dirty and they don't stink," she said. "They're cleaner than some children I've seen. Their feet never touch the ground. We have a pig-parlor — that's where you raise them on concrete," she explained to the pleasant lady, "and Claud scoots them down with the hose every afternoon and washes off the floor." Cleaner by far than that child right there, she thought. Poor nasty little thing. He had not moved except to put the thumb of his dirty hand into his mouth.

The woman turned her face away from Mrs. Turpin. "I know I wouldn't 45 scoot down no hog with no hose," she said to the wall.

You wouldn't have no hog to scoot down, Mrs. Turpin said to herself.

"A-gruntin and a-rootin and a-groanin," the woman muttered.

"We got a little of everything," Mrs. Turpin said to the pleasant lady. "It's no use in having more than you can handle yourself with help like it is. We found enough niggers to pick our cotton this year but Claud he has to go after them and take them home again in the evening. They can't walk that half a mile. No they can't. I tell you," she said and laughed merrily, "I sure am tired of buttering up niggers, but you got to love em if you want em to work for you. When they come in the morning, I run out and I say, 'Hi yawl this morning?' and when Claud drives them off to the field I just wave to beat the band and they just wave back." And she waved her hand rapidly to illustrate.

"Like you read out of the same book," the lady said, showing she understood perfectly.

"Child, yes," Mrs. Turpin said. "And when they come in from the field, 50 I run out with a bucket of icewater. That's the way it's going to be from now on," she said. "You may as well face it."

"One thang I know," the white-trash woman said. "Two thangs I ain't going to do: love no niggers or scoot down no hog with no hose." And she let out a bark of contempt.

The look that Mrs. Turpin and the pleasant lady exchanged indicated they both understood that you had to *have* certain things before you could *know* certain things. But every time Mrs. Turpin exchanged a look with the lady, she was aware that the ugly girl's peculiar eyes were still on her, and she had trouble bringing her attention back to the conversation.

"When you got something," she said, "you got to look after it." And when you ain't got a thing but breath and britches, she added to herself, you can afford to come to town every morning and just sit on the Court House coping and spit.

A grotesque revolving shadow passed across the curtain behind her and was thrown palely on the opposite wall. Then a bicycle clattered down against the outside of the building. The door opened and a colored boy glided in with a tray from the drug store. It had two large red and white paper cups on it with tops on them. He was a tall, very black boy in discolored white pants and a green nylon shirt. He was chewing gum slowly, as if to music. He set the tray down in the office opening next to the fern and stuck his head through to look for the secretary. She was not in there. He rested his arms on the ledge and waited, his narrow bottom stuck out, swaying slowly to the left and right. He raised a hand over his head and scratched the base of his skull.

"You see that button there, boy?" Mrs. Turpin said. "You can punch that ⁵⁵ and she'll come. She's probably in the back somewhere."

"Is thas right?" the boy said agreeably, as if he had never seen the button before. He leaned to the right and put his finger on it. "She sometime out," he said and twisted around to face his audience, his elbows behind him on the counter. The nurse appeared and he twisted back again. She handed him a dollar and he rooted in his pocket and made the change and counted it out to her. She gave him fifteen cents for a tip and he went out with the empty tray. The heavy door swung to slowly and closed at length with the sound of suction. For a moment no one spoke.

"They ought to send all them niggers back to Africa," the white-trash woman said. "That's wher they come from in the first place."

"Oh, I couldn't do without my good colored friends," the pleasant lady said.

"There's a heap of things worse than a nigger," Mrs. Turpin agreed. "It's all kinds of them just like it's all kinds of us."

"Yes, and it takes all kinds to make the world go round," the lady said ⁶⁰ in her musical voice.

As she said it, the raw-complexioned girl snapped her teeth together. Her lower lip turned downwards and inside out, revealing the pale pink inside of her mouth. After a second it rolled back up. It was the ugliest face Mrs. Turpin had ever seen anyone make and for a moment she was certain that the girl had made it at her. She was looking at her as if she had known and disliked her all her life — all of Mrs. Turpin's life, it seemed too, not just all the girl's life. Why, girl, I don't even know you, Mrs. Turpin said silently.

She forced her attention back to the discussion. "It wouldn't be practical to send them back to Africa," she said. "They wouldn't want to go. They got it too good here."

"Wouldn't be what they wanted — if I had anythang to do with it," the woman said.

"It wouldn't be a way in the world you could get all the niggers back over there," Mrs. Turpin said. "They'd be hiding out and lying down and turning sick on you and wailing and hollering and raring and pitching. It wouldn't be a way in the world to get them over there."

"They got over here," the trashy woman said. "Get back like they got ⁶⁵ over."

"It wasn't so many of them then," Mrs. Turpin explained.

The woman looked at Mrs. Turpin as if here was an idiot indeed but Mrs. Turpin was not bothered by the look, considering where it came from.

"Nooo," she said, "they're going to stay here where they can go to New York and marry white folks and improve their color. That's what they all want to do, every one of them, improve their color."

"You know what comes of that, don't you?" Claud asked.

"No, Claud, what?" Mrs. Turpin said. ⁷⁰

Claud's eyes twinkled. "White-faced niggers," he said with never a smile.

Everybody in the office laughed except the white-trash and the ugly girl. The girl gripped the book in her lap with white fingers. The trashy woman looked around her from face to face as if she thought they were all idiots. The old woman in the feed sack dress continued to gaze expressionless across the floor at the high-top shoes of the man opposite her, the one who had been pretending to be asleep when the Turpins came in. He was laughing heartily, his hands still spread out on his knees. The child had fallen to the side and was lying now almost face down in the old woman's lap.

While they recovered from their laughter, the nasal chorus on the radio kept the room from silence.

"You go to blank blank
And I'll go to mine
But we'll all blank along
To-geth-ther,
And all along the blank
We'll hep each other out
Smile-ling in any kind of
Weath-ther!"

Mrs. Turpin didn't catch every word but she caught enough to agree with the spirit of the song and it turned her thoughts sober. To help anybody out that needed it was her philosophy of life. She never spared herself when she found somebody in need, whether they were white or black, trash or decent. And of all she had to be thankful for, she was most thankful that this was so. If Jesus had said, "You can be high society and have all the money you want and be thin and svelte-like, but you can't be a good woman with it," she would have had to say, "Well don't make me that then. Make me a good woman and it don't matter what else, how fat or how ugly or how poor!" Her heart rose. He had not made her a nigger or white-trash or ugly! He had made her herself and given her a little of everything. Jesus, thank you! she said. Thank you thank you thank you! Whenever she counted her blessings she felt as buoyant as if she weighed one hundred and twenty-five pounds instead of one hundred and eighty.

"What's wrong with your little boy?" the pleasant lady asked the white-trashy woman.

"He has a ulcer," the woman said proudly. "He ain't give me a minute's peace since he was born. Him and her are just alike," she said, nodding at the old woman, who was running her leathery fingers through the child's pale hair. "Look like I can't get nothing down them two but Co' Cola and candy."

That's all you try to get down em, Mrs. Turpin said to herself. Too lazy to light the fire. There was nothing you could tell her about people like them that she didn't know already. And it was not just that they didn't have anything. Because if you gave them everything, in two weeks it would all be broken or filthy or they would have chopped it up for lightwood. She knew all this from her own experience. Help them you must, but help them you couldn't.

All at once the ugly girl turned her lips inside out again. Her eyes were fixed like two drills on Mrs. Turpin. This time there was no mistaking that there was something urgent behind them.

Girl, Mrs. Turpin exclaimed silently, I haven't done a thing to you! The ⁸⁰ girl might be confusing her with somebody else. There was no need to sit by and let herself be intimidated. "You must be in college," she said boldly, looking directly at the girl. "I see you reading a book there."

The girl continued to stare and pointedly did not answer.

Her mother blushed at this rudeness. "The lady asked you a question, Mary Grace," she said under her breath.

"I have ears," Mary Grace said.

The poor mother blushed again. "Mary Grace goes to Wellesley College," she explained. She twisted one of the buttons on her dress. "In Massachusetts," she added with a grimace. "And in the summer she just keeps right on studying. Just reads all the time, a real book worm. She's done real well at Wellesley; she's taking English and Math and History and Psychology and Social Studies," she rattled on, "and I think it's too much. I think she ought to get out and have fun."

The girl looked as if she would like to hurl them all through the plate ⁸⁵ glass window.

"Way up north," Mrs. Turpin murmured and thought, well, it hasn't done much for her manners.

"I'd almost rather to have him sick," the white-trash woman said, wrenching the attention back to herself. "He's so mean when he ain't. Look like some children just take natural to meanness. It's some gets bad when they get sick but he was the opposite. Took sick and turned good. He don't give me no trouble now. It's me waitin to see the doctor," she said.

If I was going to send anybody back to Africa, Mrs. Turpin thought, it would be your kind, woman. "Yes, indeed," she said aloud, but looking up at the ceiling, "it's a heap of things worse than a nigger." And dirtier than a hog, she added to herself.

"I think people with bad dispositions are more to be pitied than anyone on earth," the pleasant lady said in a voice that was decidedly thin.

"I thank the Lord he has blessed me with a good one," Mrs. Turpin said. ⁹⁰ "The day has never dawned that I couldn't find something to laugh at."

"Not since she married me anyways," Claud said with a comical straight face.

Everybody laughed except the girl and the white-trash.

Mrs. Turpin's stomach shook. "He's such a caution," she said, "that I can't help but laugh at him."

The girl made a loud ugly noise through her teeth.

Her mother's mouth grew thin and tight. "I think the worst thing in the ⁹⁵ world," she said, "is an ungrateful person. To have everything and not appreciate it. I know a girl," she said, "who has parents who would give her anything, a little brother who loves her dearly, who is getting a good education, who wears the best clothes, but who can never say a kind word to anyone, who never smiles, who just criticizes and complains all day long."

"Is she too old to paddle?" Claud asked.

The girl's face was almost purple.

"Yes," the lady said, "I'm afraid there's nothing to do but leave her to her folly. Some day she'll wake up and it'll be too late."

"It never hurt anyone to smile," Mrs. Turpin said. "It just makes you feel better all over."

"Of course," the lady said sadly, "but there are just some people you can't tell anything to. They can't take criticism."

"If it's one thing I am," Mrs. Turpin said with feeling, "it's grateful. When I think who all I could have been besides myself and what all I got, a little of everything, and a good disposition besides, I just feel like shouting, 'Thank you, Jesus, for making everything the way it is!' It could have been different!" For one thing, somebody else could have got Claud. At the thought of this, she was flooded with gratitude and a terrible pang of joy ran through her. "Oh thank you, Jesus, Jesus, thank you!" she cried aloud.

The book struck her directly over her left eye. It struck almost at the same instant that she realized the girl was about to hurl it. Before she could utter a sound, the raw face came crashing across the table toward her, howling. The girl's fingers sank like clamps into the soft flesh of her neck. She heard the mother cry out and Claud shout, "Whoa!" There was an instant when she was certain that she was about to be in an earthquake.

All at once her vision narrowed and she saw everything as if it were happening in a small room far away, or as if she were looking at it through the wrong end of a telescope. Claud's face crumpled and fell out of sight. The nurse ran in, then out, then in again. Then the gangling figure of the doctor rushed out of the inner door. Magazines flew this way and that as the table turned over. The girl fell with a thud and Mrs. Turpin's vision suddenly reversed itself and she saw everything large instead of small. The eyes of the white-trashy woman were staring hugely at the floor. There the girl, held down on one side by the nurse and on the other by her mother, was wrenching and turning in their grasp. The doctor was kneeling astride her, trying to hold her arm down. He managed after a second to sink a long needle into it.

Mrs. Turpin felt entirely hollow except for her heart which swung from side to side as if it were agitated in a great empty drum of flesh.

"Somebody that's not busy call for the ambulance," the doctor said in the off-hand voice young doctors adopt for terrible occasions. 105

Mrs. Turpin could not have moved a finger. The old man who had been sitting next to her skipped nimbly into the office and made the call, for the secretary still seemed to be gone.

"Claud!" Mrs. Turpin called.

He was not in his chair. She knew she must jump up and find him but she felt like some one trying to catch a train in a dream, when everything moves in slow motion and the faster you try to run the slower you go.

"Here I am," a suffocated voice, very unlike Claud's, said.

He was doubled up in the corner on the floor, pale as paper, holding his 110 leg. She wanted to get up and go to him but she could not move. Instead, her gaze was drawn slowly downward to the churning face on the floor, which she could see over the doctor's shoulder.

The girl's eyes stopped rolling and focused on her. They seemed a much lighter blue than before, as if a door that had been tightly closed behind them was now open to admit light and air.

Mrs. Turpin's head cleared and her power of motion returned. She leaned forward until she was looking directly into the fierce brilliant eyes. There was no doubt in her mind that the girl did know her, knew her in some intense and personal way, beyond time and place and condition. "What you got to say

Theme

to me?" she asked hoarsely and held her breath, waiting, as for a revelation.

The girl raised her head. Her gaze locked with Mrs. Turpin's. "Go back to hell where you came from, you old wart hog," she whispered. Her voice was low but clear. Her eyes burned for a moment as if she saw with pleasure that her message had struck its target.

Mrs. Turpin sank back in her chair.

After a moment the girl's eyes closed and she turned her head wearily to the side. 115

The doctor rose and handed the nurse the empty syringe. He leaned over and put both hands for a moment on the mother's shoulders, which were shaking. She was sitting on the floor, her lips pressed together, holding Mary Grace's hand in her lap. The girl's fingers were gripped like a baby's around her thumb. "Go on to the hospital," he said. "I'll call and make the arrangements."

"Now let's see that neck," he said in a jovial voice to Mrs. Turpin. He began to inspect her neck with his first two fingers. Two little moon-shaped lines like pink fish bones were indented over her windpipe. There was the beginning of an angry red swelling above her eye. His fingers passed over this also.

"Lea' me be," she said thickly and shook him off. "See about Claud. She kicked him."

"I'll see about him in a minute," he said and felt her pulse. He was a thin grey-haired man, given to pleasantries. "Go home and have yourself a vacation the rest of the day," he said and patted her on the shoulder.

Quit your pattin me, Mrs. Turpin growled to herself. 120

"And put an ice pack over that eye," he said. Then he went and squatted down beside Claud and looked at his leg. After a moment he pulled him up and Claud limped after him into the office.

Until the ambulance came, the only sounds in the room were the tremulous moans of the girl's mother, who continued to sit on the floor. The white-trash woman did not take her eyes off the girl. Mrs. Turpin looked straight ahead at nothing. Presently the ambulance drew up, a long dark shadow, behind the curtain. The attendants came in and set the stretcher down beside the girl and lifted her expertly onto it and carried her out. The nurse helped the mother gather up her things. The shadow of the ambulance moved silently away and the nurse came back in the office.

"That ther girl is going to be a lunatic, ain't she?" the white-trash woman asked the nurse, but the nurse kept on to the back and never answered her.

"Yes, she's going to be a lunatic," the white-trash woman said to the rest of them.

"Po' critter," the old woman murmured. The child's face was still in her 125 lap. His eyes looked idly out over her knees. He had not moved during the disturbance except to draw one leg up under him.

"I thank Gawd," the white-trash woman said fervently, "I ain't a lunatic."

Claud came limping out and the Turpins went home.

As their pick-up truck turned into their own dirt road and made the crest of the hill, Mrs. Turpin gripped the window ledge and looked out suspiciously. The land sloped gracefully down through a field dotted with lavender weeds and at the start of the rise their small yellow frame house, with its little flower beds spread out around it like a fancy apron, sat primly in its accustomed place between two giant hickory trees. She would not have been startled to see a burnt wound between two blackened chimneys.

Neither of them felt like eating so they put on their house clothes and lowered the shade in the bedroom and lay down, Claud with his leg on a pillow and herself with a damp washcloth over her eye. The instant she was flat on her back, the image of a razor-backed hog with warts on its face and horns coming out behind its ears snorted into her head. She moaned, a low quiet moan.

"I am not," she said tearfully, "a wart hog. From hell." But the denial had no force. The girl's eyes and her words, even the tone of her voice, low but clear, directed only to her, brooked no repudiation. She had been singled out for the message, though there was trash in the room to whom it might justly have been applied. The full force of this fact struck her only now. There was a woman there who was neglecting her own child but she had been overlooked. The message had been given to Ruby Turpin, a respectable, hard-working, church-going woman. The tears dried. Her eyes began to burn instead with wrath.

She rose on her elbow and the washcloth fell into her hand. Claud was lying on his back, snoring. She wanted to tell him what the girl had said. At the same time, she did not wish to put the image of herself as a wart hog from hell into his mind.

"Hey, Claud," she muttered and pushed his shoulder.

Claud opened one pale baby blue eye.

She looked into it warily. He did not think about anything. He just went his way.

"Wha, whasit?" he said and closed the eye again.

"Nothing," she said. "Does your leg pain you?"

"Hurts like hell," Claud said.

"It'll quit terreckly," she said and lay back down. In a moment Claud was snoring again. For the rest of the afternoon they lay there. Claud slept. She scowled at the ceiling. Occasionally she raised her fist and made a small stabbing motion over her chest as if she was defending her innocence to invisible guests who were like the comforters of Job, reasonable-seeming but wrong.

About five-thirty Claud stirred. "Got to go after those niggers," he sighed, not moving.

She was looking straight up as if there were unintelligible handwriting on the ceiling. The protuberance over her eye had turned a greenish-blue. "Listen here," she said.

"What?"

"Kiss me."

Claud leaned over and kissed her loudly on the mouth. He pinched her side and their hands interlocked. Her expression of ferocious concentration did not change. Claud got up, groaning and growling, and limped off. She continued to study the ceiling.

She did not get up until she heard the pick-up truck coming back with the Negroes. Then she rose and thrust her feet in her brown oxfords, which she did not bother to lace, and stumped out onto the back porch and got her red plastic bucket. She emptied a tray of ice cubes into it and filled it half full of water and went out into the back yard. Every afternoon after Claud brought the hands in, one of the boys helped him put out hay and the rest waited in the back of the truck until he was ready to take them home. The truck was parked in the shade under one of the hickory trees.

"Hi yawl this evening?" Mrs. Turpin asked grimly, appearing with the bucket and the dipper. There were three women and a boy in the truck.

"Us doin nicely," the oldest woman said. "Hi you doin?" and her gaze stuck immediately on the dark lump on Mrs. Turpin's forehead. "You done fell down, ain't you?" she asked in a solicitous voice. The old woman was dark and almost toothless. She had on an old felt hat of Claud's set back on her head. The other two women were younger and lighter and they both had new bright green sun hats. One of them had hers on her head; the other had taken hers off and the boy was grinning beneath it.

Mrs. Turpin set the bucket down on the floor of the truck. "Yawl hep yourselves," she said. She looked around to make sure Claud had gone. "No. I didn't fall down," she said, folding her arms. "It was something worse than that."

"Ain't nothing bad happen to you!" the old woman said. She said it as if they all knew that Mrs. Turpin was protected in some special way by Divine Providence. "You just had you a little fall."

"We were in town at the doctor's office for where the cow kicked Mr. Turpin," Mrs. Turpin said in a flat tone that indicated they could leave off their foolishness. "And there was this girl there. A big fat girl with her face all broke out. I could look at that girl and tell she was peculiar but I couldn't tell how. And me and her mama were just talking and going along and all of a sudden WHAM! She throws this big book she was reading at me and . . ."

"Naw!" the old woman cried out.

"And then she jumps over the table and commences to choke me."

"Naw!" they all exclaimed, "naw!"

"Hi come she do that?" the old woman asked. "What ail her?"

Mrs. Turpin only glared in front of her.

"Something ail her," the old woman said.

"They carried her off in an ambulance," Mrs. Turpin continued, "but before she went she was rolling on the floor and they were trying to hold her down to give her a shot and she said something to me." She paused. "You know what she said to me?"

"What she say?" they asked.

"She said," Mrs. Turpin began, and stopped, her face very dark and heavy. The sun was getting whiter and whiter, blanching the sky overhead so that the leaves of the hickory tree were black in the face of it. She could not bring forth the words. "Something real ugly," she muttered.

"She sho shouldn't said nothin ugly to you," the old woman said. "You so sweet. You the sweetest lady I know."

"She pretty too," the one with the hat on said.

"And stout," the other one said. "I never knowed no sweeter white lady."

"That's the truth befo' Jesus," the old woman said. "Amen! You des as sweet and pretty as you can be."

Mrs. Turpin knew just exactly how much Negro flattery was worth and it added to her rage. "She said," she began again and finished this time with a fierce rush of breath, "that I was an old wart hog from hell."

There was an astounded silence.

"Where she at?" the youngest woman cried in a piercing voice. 165

"Lemme see her. I'll kill her!"

"I'll kill her with you!" the other one cried.

"She b'long in the sylum," the old woman said emphatically. "You the sweetest white lady I know."

"She pretty too," the other two said. "Stout as she can be and sweet. Jesus satisfied with her!"

"Deed he is," the old woman declared. 170

Idiots! Mrs. Turpin growled to herself. You could never say anything intelligent to a nigger. You could talk at them but not with them. "Yawl ain't drunk your water," she said shortly. "Leave the bucket in the truck when you're finished with it. I got more to do than just stand around and pass the time of day," and she moved off and into the house.

She stood for a moment in the middle of the kitchen. The dark protuberance over her eye looked like a miniature tornado cloud which might any moment sweep across the horizon of her brow. Her lower lip protruded dangerously. She squared her massive shoulders. Then she marched into the front of the house and out the side door and started down the road to the pig parlor. She had the look of a woman going single-handed, weaponless, into battle.

The sun was a deep yellow now like a harvest moon and was riding westward very fast over the far tree line as if it meant to reach the hogs before she did. The road was rutted and she kicked several good-sized stones out of her path as she strode along. The pig parlor was on a little knoll at the end of a lane that ran off from the side of the barn. It was a square of concrete as large as a small room, with a board fence about four feet high around it. The concrete floor sloped slightly so that the hog wash could drain off into a trench where it was carried to the field for fertilizer. Claud was standing on the outside, on the edge of the concrete, hanging onto the top board, hosing down the floor inside. The hose was connected to the faucet of a water trough nearby.

Mrs. Turpin climbed up beside him and glowered down at the hogs inside. There were seven long-snouted bristly shoats in it — tan with liver-colored spots — and an old sow a few weeks off from farrowing. She was lying on her side grunting. The shoats were running about shaking themselves like idiot children, their little slit pig eyes searching the floor for anything left. She had read that pigs were the most intelligent animal. She doubted it. They were supposed to be smarter than dogs. There had even been a pig astronaut. He had performed his assignment perfectly but died of a heart attack afterwards because they left him in his electric suit, sitting upright throughout his examination when naturally a hog should be on all fours.

A-gruntin and a-rootin and a-groanin. 175

"Gimme that hose," she said, yanking it away from Claud. "Go on and carry them niggers home and then get off that leg."

"You look like you might have swallowed a mad dog," Claud observed, but he got down and limped off. He paid no attention to her humors.

Until he was out of earshot, Mrs. Turpin stood on the side of the pen, holding the hose and pointing the stream of water at the hind quarters of any shoat that looked as if it might try to lie down. When he had had time to get over the hill, she turned her head slightly and her wrathful eyes scanned the path. He was nowhere in sight. She turned back again and seemed to gather herself up. Her shoulders rose and she drew in her breath.

"What do you send me a message like that for?" she said in a low fierce voice, barely above a whisper but with the force of a shout in its concentrated fury. "How am I a hog and me both? How am I saved and from hell too?" Her free fist was knotted and with the other she gripped the hose, blindly pointing the stream of water in and out of the eye of the old sow whose outraged squeal she did not hear.

The pig parlor commanded a view of the back pasture where their 180 twenty beef cows were gathered around the hay-bales Claud and the boy had put out. The freshly cut pasture sloped down to the highway. Across it was their cotton field and beyond that a dark green dusty wood which they owned as well. The sun was behind the wood, very red, looking over the paling of trees like a farmer inspecting his own hogs.

"Why me?" she rumbled. "It's no trash around here, black or white, that I haven't given to. And break my back to the bone every day working. And do for the church."

She appeared to be the right size woman to command the arena before her. "How am I a hog?" she demanded. "Exactly how am I like them?" and she jabbed the stream of water at the shoats. "There was plenty of trash there. It didn't have to be me.

"If you like trash better, go get yourself some trash then," she railed. "You could have made me trash. Or a nigger. If trash is what you wanted why didn't you make me trash?" She shook her fist with the hose in it and a watery snake appeared momentarily in the air. "I could quit working and take it easy and be filthy," she growled. "Lounge about the sidewalks all day drinking root beer. Dip snuff and spit in every puddle and have it all over my face. I could be nasty.

"Or you could have made me a nigger. It's too late for me to be a nigger," she said with deep sarcasm, "but I could act like one. Lay down in the middle of the road and stop traffic. Roll on the ground."

In the deepening light everything was taking on a mysterious hue. The 185 pasture was growing a peculiar glassy green and the streak of highway had turned lavender. She braced herself for a final assault and this time her voice rolled out over the pasture. "Go on," she yelled, "call me a hog! Call me a hog again. From hell. Call me a wart hog from hell. Put that bottom rail on top. There'll still be a top and bottom!"

A garbled echo returned to her.

A final surge of fury shook her and she roared, "Who do you think you are?"

The color of everything, field and crimson sky, burned for a moment with a transparent intensity. The question carried over the pasture and across the highway and the cotton field and returned to her clearly like an answer from beyond the wood.

She opened her mouth but no sound came out of it.

A tiny truck, Claud's, appeared on the highway, heading rapidly out of 190 sight. Its gears scraped thinly. It looked like a child's toy. At any moment a bigger truck might smash into it and scatter Claud's and the niggers' brains all over the road.

Mrs. Turpin stood there, her gaze fixed on the highway, all her muscles rigid, until in five or six minutes the truck reappeared, returning. She waited until it had had time to turn into their own road. Then like a monumental statue coming to life, she bent her head slowly and gazed, as if through the very heart of mystery, down into the pig parlor at the hogs. They had settled all in one corner around the old sow who was grunting softly. A red glow suffused them. They appeared to pant with a secret life.

Until the sun slipped finally behind the tree line, Mrs. Turpin remained there with her gaze bent to them as if she were absorbing some abysmal life-giving knowledge. At last she lifted her head. There was only a purple streak in the sky, cutting through a field of crimson and leading, like an extension of the highway, into the descending dusk. She raised her hands from the side of the pen in a gesture hieratic and profound. A visionary light settled in her eyes. She saw the streak as a vast swinging bridge extending upward from the earth through a field of living fire. Upon it a vast horde of souls were rumbling toward heaven. There were whole companies of white-trash, clean for the first time in their lives, and bands of black niggers in white robes, and battalions of freaks and lunatics shouting and clapping and leaping like frogs. And bringing up the end of the procession was a tribe of people whom she recognized at once as those who, like herself and Claud, had always had a little of everything and the God-given wit to use it right. She leaned forward to observe them closer. They were marching behind the others with great dignity, accountable as they had always been for good order and common sense and respectable behavior. They alone were on key. Yet she could see by their shocked and altered faces that even their virtues were being burned away. She lowered her hands and gripped the rail of the hog pen, her eyes small but fixed unblinkingly on what lay ahead. In a moment the vision faded but she remained where she was, immobile.

At length she got down and turned off the faucet and made her slow way on the darkening path to the house. In the woods around her the invisible cricket choruses had struck up, but what she heard were the voices of the souls climbing upward into the starry field and shouting hallelujah.

QUESTIONS

1. How does Mrs. Turpin see herself before Mary Grace calls her a wart hog?
2. What is the narrator's attitude toward Mrs. Turpin in the beginning of the story? How can you tell? Does this attitude change, or stay the same, at the end?
3. Describe the relationship between Mary Grace and her mother. What annoying platitudes does the mother mouth? Which of Mrs. Turpin's opinions seem especially to anger Mary Grace?
4. Sketch the plot of the story. What moment or event do you take to be the crisis, or turning point? What is the climax? What is the conclusion?
5. What do you infer from Mrs. Turpin's conversation with the black farm workers? Is she their friend? Why does she now find their flattery unacceptable ("Jesus satisfied with her")?

6. When, near the end of the story, Mrs. Turpin roars, "Who do you think you are?" an echo "returned to her clearly like an answer from beyond the wood" (paragraph 188). Explain.
7. What is the final revelation given to Mrs. Turpin? (To state it is to state the theme of the story.) What new attitude does the revelation impart? (How is Mrs. Turpin left with a new vision of humanity?)
8. Other stories in this book contain revelations: "Gimpel the Fool," "The Death of Ivan Ilych." If you have read them, try to sum up the supernatural revelation made to the central character in each story. In each, is the revelation the same as a statement of the story's main theme?

E. B. White
THE DOOR

Elwyn Brooks White (1899 – 1985) was one of America's most widely admired craftsmen of the English language, and indeed, so he remains. For a half-century beginning in 1926, White steadily contributed to The New Yorker, *turning out essays, stories, editorials, verse, and unsigned fillers, and reporting for a weekly feature, "The Talk of the Town." His work helped the magazine erect a reputation for trenchant wit and lively writing. Besides, White wrote the lastingly popular children's stories* Stuart Little *(1945),* Charlotte's Web *(1952), and* The Trumpet of the Swan *(1970), and he successfully revised a textbook of grammar and usage he had used as a college student at Cornell:* The Elements of Style *by William Strunk, Jr. (republished as by Strunk and White in 1959). In 1976 White's* Letters *were collected, in 1977 his* Essays, *and in 1981 his* Poems and Sketches. *In later life, White quit Manhattan for a farm in North Brooklin, Maine.*

Everything (he kept saying) is something it isn't. And everybody is always somewhere else. Maybe it was the city, being in the city, that made him feel how queer everything was and that it was something else. Maybe (he kept thinking) it was the names of the things. The names were tex and frequently koid. Or they were flex and oid or they were duroid (sani) or flexsan (duro), but everything was glass (but not quite glass) and the thing that you touched (the surface, washable, crease-resistant) was rubber, only it wasn't quite rubber and you didn't quite touch it but almost. The wall, which was glass but thrutex, turned out on being approached not to be a wall, it was something else, it was an opening or doorway — and the doorway (through which he saw himself approaching) turned out to be something else, it was a wall. And what he had eaten not having agreed with him.

He was in a washable house, but he wasn't sure. Now about those rats, he kept saying to himself. He meant the rats that the Professor had driven crazy by forcing them to deal with problems which were beyond the scope of rats, the insoluble problems. He meant the rats that had been trained to jump at the square card with the circle in the middle, and the card (because it was something it wasn't) would give way and let the rat into a place where the food was, but then one day it would be a trick played on the rat, and the card would be changed, and the rat would jump but the card wouldn't give way, and it was an impossible situation (for a rat) and the rat would go insane and into its eyes would come the unspeakably bright imploring look of the frustrated, and after the convulsions were over and the frantic racing around, then the passive stage would set in and the willingness to let anything be done to it, even if it was something else.

He didn't know which door (or wall) or opening in the house to jump at, to get through, because one was an opening that wasn't a door (it was a void, or koid) and the other was a wall that wasn't an opening, it was a sanitary cupboard of the same color. He caught a glimpse of his eyes staring into his eyes, in the thrutex, and in them was the expression he had seen in the picture of the rats — weary after convulsions and the frantic racing around, when they were willing and did not mind having anything done to them. More and more (he kept saying) I am confronted by a problem which is incapable of solution (for this time even if he chose the right door, there would be no food behind it) and that is what madness is, and things seeming different from what they are. He heard, in the house where he was, in the city to which he had gone (as toward a door which might, or might not, give way), a noise — not a loud noise but more of a low prefabricated humming. It came from a place in the base of the wall (or stat) where the flue carrying the filterable air was, and not far from the Minipiano, which was made of the same material nailbrushes are made of, and which was under the stairs. "This, too, has been tested," she said, pointing, but not at it, "and found viable." It wasn't a loud noise, he kept thinking, sorry that he had seen his eyes, even though it was through his own eyes that he had seen them.

First will come the convulsions (he said), then the exhaustion, then the willingness to let anything be done. "And you better believe it *will* be."

All his life he had been confronted by situations which were incapable of being solved, and there was a deliberateness behind all this, behind this changing of the card (or door), because they would always wait till you had learned to jump at the certain card (or door) — the one with the circle — and then they would change it on you. There have been so many doors changed on me, he said, in the last twenty years, but it is now becoming clear that it is an impossible situation, and the question is whether to jump again, even though they ruffle you in the rump with a blast of air — to make you jump. He wished he wasn't standing by the Minipiano. First they would teach you the prayers and the Psalms, and that would be the right door (the one with the circle), and the long sweet words with the holy sound, and that would be the one to jump at to get where the food was. Then one day you jumped and it didn't give way, so that all you got was the bump on the nose, and the first bewilderment, the first young bewilderment.

I don't know whether to tell her about the door they substituted or not, he said, the one with the equation on it and the picture of the amoeba reproducing itself by division. Or the one with the photostatic copy of the check for thirty-two dollars and fifty cents. But the jumping was so long ago, although the bump is . . . how those old wounds hurt! Being crazy this way wouldn't be so bad if only, if only. If only when you put your foot forward to take a step, the ground wouldn't come up to meet your foot the way it does. And the same way in the street (only I may never get back to the street unless I jump at the right door), the curb coming up to meet your foot, anticipating ever so delicately the weight of the body, which is somewhere else. "We could take your name," she said, "and send it to you." And it wouldn't be so bad if only you could read a sentence all the way through without jumping (your eye) to something else on the same page; and then (he kept thinking) there was that man out in Jersey, the one who started to chop his trees down, one by one, the man who began talking about how he would take his house to pieces, brick by brick, because he faced a problem incapable of solution, probably, so he began to hack at the trees in the yard, began to pluck with trembling fingers at the bricks in the house. Even if a house is not washable, it is worth taking down. It is not till later that the exhaustion sets in.

But it is inevitable that they will keep changing the doors on you, he said, because that is what they are for; and the thing is to get used to it and not let it unsettle the mind. But that would mean not jumping, and you can't. Nobody can not jump. There will be no not-jumping. Among rats, perhaps, but among people never. Everybody has to keep jumping at a door (the one with the circle on it) because that is the way everybody is, specially some people. You wouldn't want me, standing here, to tell you, would you, about my friend the poet (deceased) who said, "My heart has followed all my days something I cannot name"? (It had the circle on it.) And like many poets, although few so beloved, he is gone. It killed him, the jumping. First, of course, there were the preliminary bouts, the convulsions, and the calm and the willingness.

I remember the door with the picture of the girl on it (only it was spring), her arms outstretched in loveliness, her dress (it was the one with the circle on it) uncaught, beginning the slow, clear, blinding cascade — and I guess we would all like to try that door again, for it seemed like the way and for a while it was the way, the door would open and you would go through winged and exalted (like any rat) and the food would be there, the way the Professor had it arranged, everything O.K., and you had chosen the right door for the world was young. The time they changed that door on me, my nose bled for a hundred hours — how do you like that, Madam? Or would you prefer to show me further through this so strange house, or you could take my name and send it to me, for although my heart has followed all my days something I cannot name, I am tired of the jumping and I do not know which way to go, Madam, and I am not even sure that I am not tried beyond the endurance of man (rat, if you will) and have taken leave of sanity. What are you following these days, old friend, after your recovery from the last bump? What is the name, or is it something you cannot name? The rats have a name for it by this time, perhaps, but I don't know what they call it. I call it plexikoid and it comes in sheets, something like insulating board, unattainable and ugli-proof.

And there was the man out in Jersey, because I keep thinking about his terrible necessity and the passion and trouble he had gone to all those years in the indescribable abundance of a householder's detail, building the estate and the planting of the trees and in spring the lawn dressing and in fall the bulbs for the spring burgeoning, and the watering of the grass on the long light evenings in summer and the gravel for the driveway (all had to be thought out, planned) and the decorative borders, probably, the perennials and the bug spray, and the building of the house from plans of the architect, first the sills, then the studs, then the full corn in the ear, the floors laid on the floor timbers, smoothed, and then the carpets upon the smooth floors and the curtains and the rods therefor. And then, almost without warning, he would be jumping at the same old door and it wouldn't give: they had changed it on him, making life no longer supportable under the elms in the elm shade, under the maples in the maple shade.

"Here you have the maximum of openness in a small room."

It was impossible to say (maybe it was the city) what made him feel the way he did, and I am not the only one either, he kept thinking — ask any doctor if I am. The doctors, they know how many there are, they even know where the trouble is only they don't like to tell you about the prefrontal lobe because that means making a hole in your skull and removing the work of centuries. It took so long coming, this lobe, so many, many years. (Is it something you read in the paper, perhaps?) And now, the strain being so great, the door having been changed by the Professor once too often . . . but it only means a whiff of ether, a few deft strokes, and the higher animal becomes a little easier in his mind and more like the lower one. From now on, you see, that's the way it will be, the ones with the small prefrontal lobes will win because the other ones are hurt too much by this incessant bumping. They can stand just so much, eh, Doctor? (And what is that, pray, that you have in your hand?) Still, you never can tell, eh, Madam?

He crossed (carefully) the room, the thick carpet under him softly, and went toward the door carefully, which was glass and he could see himself in it, and which, at his approach, opened to allow him to pass through; and beyond he half expected to find one of the old doors that he had known, perhaps the one with the circle, the one with the girl her arms outstretched in loveliness and beauty before him. But he saw instead a moving stairway, and descended in light (he kept thinking) to the street below and to the other people. As he stepped off, the ground came up slightly, to meet his foot.

QUESTIONS

1. Who is the "I" in "The Door"?
2. Where does this story take place?
3. In the opening paragraphs, what is suggested by the odd un-English-sounding language — *tex, koid, duroid (sani), flexsan (duro), thrutex, stat,* and *Minipiano?* Where have you heard words (or parts of words) like those before? Would you expect a lover of the English language, like White, to be fond of such words? Why or why not?
4. In paragraph 2, White refers to "the rats that the Professor had driven crazy." Where else in his story does he refer to these rats? What do rats and the Professor have to do with you and me?
5. What does the main character mean when he suggests that at first the door with the prayers, Psalms, and "long sweet words with the holy sound" was "the one to jump at" (paragraph 5)? What do you understand him to mean by "the first young bewilderment"?
6. What does the author suggest by the doors bearing the equation and picture of the amoeba, the photostatic copy of the check (paragraph 6), and the picture of the girl (paragraph 8)? Who are "they," the ones who keep changing these doors on you?

7. What does the man in New Jersey who set out to destroy his trees and house have to do with the rest of the story?
8. What does the main character mean by "There will be no not-jumping" (paragraph 7)?
9. ". . . But it only means a whiff of ether, a few deft strokes, and the higher animal becomes a little easier in his mind and more like the lower one" (paragraph 11). Explain what you understand by this remark.
10. How would you sum up the story's theme or themes?

Stephen Crane

The Open Boat   1897

Stephen Crane (1871 – 1900) was born in Newark, New Jersey, a Methodist minister's last and fourteenth child. After flunking out of both Lafayette College and Syracuse University, he became a journalist in New York, specializing in grim life among the down-and-out who people his early self-published novel Maggie: A Girl of the Streets *(1893). Restlessly generating material for stories, Crane trekked to the Southwest, New Orleans, and Mexico. "The Open Boat" is based on experience. En route to Havana to report the Cuban revolution for the New York* Press, *Crane was shipwrecked when the S.S.* Commodore *sank in heavy seas east of New Smyrna, Florida, on January 2, 1897. He escaped in a ten-foot lifeboat with the captain and two members of the crew. Later that year, Crane moved into a stately home in England with Cora Taylor, former Madam of a Florida brothel, hobnobbed with literary greats, and lived beyond his means. Hounded by creditors, afflicted by tuberculosis, he died in Germany at twenty-eight. Crane has been called the first writer of American realism. His famed novel* The Red Badge of Courage *(1895) gives an imagined but convincing account of a young Union soldier's initiation into battle. A handful of his short stories appear immortal. He was an original poet, too, writing terse, sardonic poems in open forms, at the time considered radical. In his short life, Crane greatly helped American literature to come of age.*

A Tale Intended to be after the Fact:
Being the Experience of Four Men from the Sunk Steamer Commodore

I

None of them knew the color of the sky. Their eyes glanced level, and were fastened upon the waves that swept toward them. These waves were of the hue of slate, save for the tops, which were of foaming white, and all of the men knew the colors of the sea. The horizon narrowed and widened, and dipped and rose, and at all times its edge was jagged with waves that seemed thrust up in points like rocks.

Many a man ought to have a bathtub larger than the boat which here rode upon the sea. These waves were most wrongfully and barbarously abrupt and tall, and each frothtop was a problem in small-boat navigation.

The cook squatted in the bottom, and looked with both eyes at the six inches of gunwale which separated him from the ocean. His sleeves were rolled over his fat forearms, and the two flaps of his unbuttoned vest dangled as he bent to bail out the boat. Often he said, "Gawd! that was a narrow clip." As he remarked it he invariably gazed eastward over the broken sea.

The oiler, steering with one of the two oars in the boat, sometimes raised himself suddenly to keep clear of water that swirled in over the stern. It was a thin little oar, and it seemed often ready to snap.

The correspondent°, pulling at the other oar, watched the waves and   5
wondered why he was there.

The injured captain, lying in the bow, was at this time buried in that profound dejection and indifference which comes, temporarily at least, to even the bravest and most enduring when, willy-nilly, the firm fails, the army loses, the ship goes down. The mind of the master of a vessel is rooted deep in the timbers of her, though he command for a day or a decade; and this captain had on him the stern impression of a scene in the grays of dawn of seven turned faces, and later a stump of a topmast with a white ball on it, that slashed to and fro at the waves, went low and lower, and down. Thereafter there was something strange in his voice. Although steady, it was deep with mourning, and of a quality beyond oration or tears.

"Keep 'er a little more south, Billie," said he.

"A little more south, sir," said the oiler in the stern.

A seat in this boat was not unlike a seat upon a bucking broncho, and by the same token a broncho is not much smaller. The craft pranced and reared and plunged like an animal. As each wave came, and she rose for it, she seemed like a horse making at a fence outrageously high. The manner of her scramble over these walls of water is a mystic thing, and, moreover, at the top of them were ordinarily these problems in white water, the foam racing down from the summit of each wave requiring a new leap, and a leap from the air. Then, after scornfully bumping a crest, she would slide and race and splash down a long incline, and arrive bobbing and nodding in front of the next menace.

A singular disadvantage of the sea lies in the fact that after successfully   10
surmounting one wave you discover that there is another behind it just as important and just as nervously anxious to do something effective in the way of swamping boats. In a ten-foot dinghy one can get an idea of the resources of the sea in the line of waves that is not probable to the average experience which is never at sea in a dinghy. As each slaty wall of water approached, it shut all else from the view of the men in the boat, and it was not difficult to imagine that this particular wave was the final outburst of the ocean, the last effort of the grim water. There was a terrible grace in the move of the waves, and they came in silence, save for the snarling of the crests.

In the wan light the faces of the men must have been gray. Their eyes must have glinted in strange ways as they gazed steadily astern. Viewed from a balcony, the whole thing would doubtless have been weirdly picturesque.

correspondent: foreign correspondent, newspaper reporter.

But the men in the boat had no time to see it, and if they had had leisure, there were other things to occupy their minds. The sun swung steadily up the sky, and they knew it was broad day because the color of the sea changed from slate to emerald green streaked with amber lights, and the foam was like tumbling snow. The process of the breaking day was unknown to them. They were aware only of this effect upon the color of the waves that rolled toward them.

In disjointed sentences the cook and the correspondent argued as to the difference between a life-saving station and a house of refuge. The cook had said: "There's a house of refuge just north of the Mosquito Inlet Light, and as soon as they see us they'll come off in their boat and pick us up."

"As soon as who see us?" said the correspondent.

"The crew," said the cook.

"Houses of refuge don't have crews," said the correspondent. "As I understand them, they are only places where clothes and grub are stored for the benefit of shipwrecked people. They don't carry crews."

"Oh, yes, they do," said the cook.

"No, they don't," said the correspondent.

"Well, we're not there yet, anyhow," said the oiler, in the stern.

"Well," said the cook, "perhaps it's not a house of refuge that I'm thinking of as being near Mosquito Inlet Light; perhaps it's a life-saving station."

"We're not there yet," said the oiler in the stern.

II

As the boat bounced from the top of each wave the wind tore through the hair of the hatless men, and as the craft plopped her stern down again the spray slashed past them. The crest of each of these waves was a hill, from the top of which the men surveyed for a moment a broad tumultuous expanse, shining and wind-riven. It was probably splendid, it was probably glorious, this play of the free sea, wild with lights of emerald and white and amber.

"Bully good thing it's an on-shore wind," said the cook. "If not, where would we be? Wouldn't have a show."

"That's right," said the correspondent.

The busy oiler nodded his assent.

Then the captain, in the bow, chuckled in a way that expressed humor, contempt, tragedy, all in one. "Do you think we've got much of a show now, boys?" said he.

Whereupon the three were silent, save for a trifle of hemming and hawing. To express any particular optimism at this time they felt to be childish and stupid, but they all doubtless possessed this sense of the situation in their minds. A young man thinks doggedly at such times. On the other hand, the ethics of their condition was decidedly against any open suggestion of hopelessness. So they were silent.

"Oh, well," said the captain, soothing his children, "we'll get ashore all right."

But there was that in his tone which made them think; so the oiler quoth, "Yes! if this wind holds."

The cook was bailing. "Yes! if we don't catch hell in the surf."

Canton-flannel gulls flew near and far. Sometimes they sat down on the sea, near patches of brown seaweed that rolled over the waves with a movement like carpets on a line in a gale. The birds sat comfortably in groups, and they were envied by some in the dinghy, for the wrath of the sea was no more to them than it was to a covey of prairie chickens a thousand miles inland. Often they came very close and stared at the men with black bead-like eyes. At these times they were uncanny and sinister in their unblinking scrutiny, and the men hooted angrily at them, telling them to be gone. One came, and evidently decided to alight on the top of the captain's head. The bird flew parallel to the boat and did not circle, but made short sidelong jumps in the air in chicken-fashion. His black eyes were wistfully fixed upon the captain's head. "Ugly brute," said the oiler to the bird. "You look as if you were made with a jackknife." The cook and the correspondent swore darkly at the creature. The captain naturally wished to knock it away with the end of the heavy painter, but he did not dare do it, because anything resembling an emphatic gesture would have capsized this freighted boat; and so, with his open hand, the captain gently and carefully waved the gull away. After it had been discouraged from the pursuit the captain breathed easier on account of his hair, and others breathed easier because the bird struck their minds at this time as being somehow gruesome and ominous.

In the meantime the oiler and the correspondent rowed. And also they rowed. They sat together in the same seat, and each rowed an oar. Then the oiler took both oars; then the correspondent took both oars; then the oiler; then the correspondent. They rowed and they rowed. The very ticklish part of the business was when the time came for the reclining one in the stern to take his turn at the oars. By the very last star of truth, it is easier to steal eggs from under a hen than it was to change seats in the dinghy. First the man in the stern slid his hand along the thwart and moved with care, as if he were of Sèvres°. Then the man in the rowing-seat slid his hand along the other thwart. It was all done with the most extraordinary care. As the two sidled past each other, the whole party kept watchful eyes on the coming wave, and the captain cried: "Look out, now! Steady, there!"

The brown mats of seaweed that appeared from time to time were like islands, bits of earth. They were travelling, apparently, neither one way nor the other. They were, to all intents, stationary. They informed the men in the boat that it was making progress slowly toward the land.

The captain, rearing cautiously in the bow after the dinghy soared on a great swell, said that he had seen the lighthouse at Mosquito Inlet. Presently the cook remarked that he had seen it. The correspondent was at the oars then, and for some reason he too wished to look at the lighthouse; but his back was toward the far shore, and the waves were important, and for some time he could not seize an opportunity to turn his head. But at last there came a wave more gentle than the others, and when at the crest of it he swiftly scoured the western horizon.

"See it?" said the captain.

"No," said the correspondent, slowly; "I didn't see anything."

Sèvres: chinaware made in this French town.

"Look again," said the captain. He pointed. "It's exactly in that direction."

At the top of another wave the correspondent did as he was bid, and this time his eyes chanced on a small, still thing on the edge of the swaying horizon. It was precisely like the point of a pin. It took an anxious eye to find a lighthouse so tiny.

"Think we'll make it, Captain?"

"If this wind holds and the boat don't swamp, we can't do much else," said the captain.

The little boat, lifted by each towering sea and splashed viciously by the crests, made progress that in the absence of seaweed was not apparent to those in her. She seemed just a wee thing wallowing, miraculously top up, at the mercy of five oceans. Occasionally a great spread of water, like white flames, swarmed into her.

"Bail her, cook," said the captain, serenely.

"All right, Captain," said the cheerful cook.

III

It would be difficult to describe the subtle brotherhood of men that was here established on the seas. No one said that it was so. No one mentioned it. But it dwelt in the boat, and each man felt it warm him. They were a captain, an oiler, a cook, and a correspondent, and they were friends — friends in a more curiously iron-bound degree than may be common. The hurt captain, lying against the water-jar in the bow, spoke always in a low voice and calmly; but he could never command a more ready and swiftly obedient crew than the motley three of the dinghy. It was more than a mere recognition of what was best for the common safety. There was surely in it a quality that was personal and heart-felt. And after this devotion to the commander of the boat, there was this comradeship, that the correspondent, for instance, who had been taught to be cynical of men, knew even at the time was the best experience of his life. But no one said that it was so. No one mentioned it.

"I wish we had a sail," remarked the captain. "We might try my overcoat on the end of an oar, and give you two boys a chance to rest." So the cook and the correspondent held the mast and spread wide the overcoat; the oiler steered; and the little boat made good way with her new rig. Sometimes the oiler had to scull sharply to keep a sea from breaking into the boat, but otherwise sailing was a success.

Meanwhile the lighthouse had been growing slowly larger. It had now almost assumed color, and appeared like a little gray shadow on the sky. The man at the oars could not be prevented from turning his head rather often to try for a glimpse of this little gray shadow.

At last, from the top of each wave, the men in the tossing boat could see land. Even as the lighthouse was an upright shadow on the sky, this land seemed but a long black shadow on the sea. It certainly was thinner than paper. "We must be about opposite New Smyrna," said the cook, who had coasted this shore often in schooners. "Captain, by the way, I believe they abandoned that life-saving station there about a year ago."

"Did they?" said the captain.

The wind slowly died away. The cook and the correspondent were not now obliged to slave in order to hold high the oar. But the waves continued their old impetuous swooping at the dinghy, and the little craft, no longer under way, struggled woundily over them. The oiler or the correspondent took the oars again.

Shipwrecks are apropos of nothing. If men could only train for them and have them occur when the men had reached pink condition, there would be less drowning at sea. Of the four in the dinghy none had slept any time worth mentioning for two days and two nights previous to embarking in the dinghy, and in the excitement of clambering about the deck of a foundering ship they had also forgotten to eat heartily.

For these reasons, and for others, neither the oiler nor the correspondent was fond of rowing at this time. The correspondent wondered ingenuously how in the name of all that was sane could there be people who thought it amusing to row a boat. It was not an amusement; it was a diabolical punishment, and even a genius of mental aberrations could never conclude that it was anything but a horror to the muscles and a crime against the back. He mentioned to the boat in general how the amusement of rowing struck him, and the weary-faced oiler smiled in full sympathy. Previously to the foundering, by the way, the oiler had worked double watch in the engine-room of the ship.

"Take her easy now, boys," said the captain. "Don't spend yourselves. If we have to run a surf you'll need all your strength, because we'll sure have to swim for it. Take your time."

Slowly the land arose from the sea. From a black line it became a line of black and a line of white — trees and sand. Finally the captain said that he could make out a house on the shore. "That's the house of refuge, sure," said the cook. "They'll see us before long, and come out after us."

The distant lighthouse reared high. "The keeper ought to be able to make us out now, if he's looking through a glass," said the captain. "He'll notify the life-saving people."

"None of those other boats could have got ashore to give word of the wreck," said the oiler, in a low voice, "else the life-boat would be out hunting us."

Slowly and beautifully the land loomed out of the sea. The wind came again. It had veered from the north-east to the south-east. Finally a new sound struck the ears of the men in the boat. It was the low thunder of the surf on the shore. "We'll never be able to make the lighthouse now," said the captain. "Swing her head a little more north, Billie."

"A little more north, sir," said the oiler.

Whereupon the little boat turned her nose once more down the wind, and all but the oarsman watched the shore grow. Under the influence of this expansion doubt and direful apprehension were leaving the minds of the men. The management of the boat was still most absorbing, but it could not prevent a quiet cheerfulness. In an hour, perhaps, they would be ashore.

Their backbones had become thoroughly used to balancing in the boat, and they now rode this wild colt of a dinghy like circus men. The correspondent thought that he had been drenched to the skin, but happening to feel in the top pocket of his coat, he found therein eight cigars. Four of them were soaked with sea-water; four were perfectly scatheless. After a search, some-body produced three dry matches; and thereupon the four waifs rode impudently in their little boat and, with an assurance of an impending rescue shining in their eyes, puffed at the big cigars, and judged well and ill of all men. Everybody took a drink of water.

IV

"Cook," remarked the captain, "there don't seem to be any signs of life about your house of refuge."

"No," replied the cook. "Funny they don't see us!"

A broad stretch of lowly coast lay before the eyes of the men. It was of low dunes topped with dark vegetation. The roar of the surf was plain, and sometimes they could see the white lip of a wave as it spun up the beach. A tiny house was blocked out black upon the sky. Southward, the slim lighthouse lifted its little gray length.

Tide, wind, and waves were swinging the dinghy northward. "Funny they don't see us," said the men.

The surf's roar was here dulled, but its tone was nevertheless thunderous and mighty. As the boat swam over the great rollers the men sat listening to this roar. "We'll swamp sure," said everybody.

It is fair to say here that there was not a life-saving station within twenty miles in either direction; but the men did not know this fact, and in consequence they made dark and opprobrious remarks concerning the eyesight of the nation's life-savers. Four scowling men sat in the dinghy and surpassed records in the invention of epithets.

"Funny they don't see us."

The light-heartedness of a former time had completely faded. To their sharpened minds it was easy to conjure pictures of all kinds of incompetency and blindness and, indeed, cowardice. There was the shore of the populous land, and it was bitter and bitter to them that from it came no sign.

"Well," said the captain, ultimately, "I suppose we'll have to make a try for ourselves. If we stay out here too long, we'll none of us have strength left to swim after the boat swamps."

And so the oiler, who was at the oars, turned the boat straight for the shore. There was a sudden tightening of muscles. There was some thinking.

"If we don't all get ashore," said the captain — "if we don't all get ashore, I suppose you fellows know where to send news of my finish?"

They then briefly exchanged some addresses and admonitions. As for the reflections of the men, there was a great deal of rage in them. Perchance they might be formulated thus: "If I am going to be drowned — if I am going to be drowned — if I am going to be drowned, why, in the name of the seven mad gods who rule the sea, was I allowed to come thus far and contemplate sand and trees? Was I brought here merely to have my nose dragged away as I was about to nibble the sacred cheese of life? It is preposterous. If this old ninny-woman, Fate, cannot do better than this, she should be deprived of the management of men's fortunes. She is an old hen who knows not her intention. If she has decided to drown me, why did she not do it in the beginning and save me all this trouble? The whole affair is absurd. — But no; she cannot mean to drown me. She dare not drown me. She cannot drown me. Not after all this work." Afterward the man might have had an impulse to shake his fist at the clouds. "Just you drown me, now, and then hear what I call you!"

The billows that came at this time were more formidable. They seemed always just about to break and roll over the little boat in a turmoil of foam. There was a preparatory and long growl in the speech of them. No mind unused to the sea would have concluded that the dinghy could ascend these sheer heights in time. The shore was still afar. The oiler was a wily surfman. "Boys," he said swiftly, "she won't live three minutes more, and we're too far out to swim. Shall I take her to sea again, Captain?"

"Yes; go ahead!" said the captain.

This oiler, by a series of quick miracles and fast and steady oarsmanship, turned the boat in the middle of the surf and took her safely to sea again.

There was a considerable silence as the boat bumped over the furrowed sea to deeper water. Then somebody in gloom spoke: "Well, anyhow, they must have seen us from the shore by now."

The gulls went in slanting flight up the wind toward the gray, desolate 75 east. A squall, marked by dingy clouds and clouds brick-red like smoke from a burning building, appeared from the south-east.

"What do you think of those life-saving people? Ain't they peaches?"

"Funny they haven't seen us."

"Maybe they think we're out here for sport! Maybe they think we're fishin'. Maybe they think we're damned fools."

It was a long afternoon. A changed tide tried to force them southward, but wind and wave said northward. Far ahead, where coast-line, sea, and sky formed their mighty angle, there were little dots which seemed to indicate a city on the shore.

"St. Augustine?" 80

The captain shook his head. "Too near Mosquito Inlet."

And the oiler rowed, and then the correspondent rowed; then the oiler rowed. It was a weary business. The human back can become the seat of more aches and pains than are registered in books for the composite anatomy of a regiment. It is a limited area, but it can become the theatre of innumerable muscular conflicts, tangles, wrenches, knots, and other comforts.

"Did you ever like to row, Billie?" asked the correspondent.

"No," said the oiler; "hang it!"

When one exchanged the rowing-seat for a place in the bottom of the 85 boat, he suffered a bodily depression that caused him to be careless of everything save an obligation to wiggle one finger. There was cold sea-water swashing to and fro in the boat, and he lay in it. His head, pillowed on a thwart, was within an inch of the swirl of a wave-crest, and sometimes a particularly obstreperous sea came inboard and drenched him once more. But these matters did not annoy him. It is almost certain that if the boat had capsized he would have tumbled comfortably upon the ocean as if he felt sure that it was a great soft mattress.

"Look! There's a man on the shore!"

"Where?"

"There! See 'im?"

"Yes, sure! He's walking along."

"Now he's stopped. Look! He's facing us!"

"He's waving at us!"

"So he is! By thunder!"

"Ah, now we're all right! Now we're all right! There'll be a boat out here for us in half an hour."

"He's going on. He's running. He's going up to that house there."

The remote beach seemed lower than the sea, and it required a searching glance to discern the little black figure. The captain saw a floating stick, and they rowed to it. A bath towel was by some weird chance in the boat, and, tying this on the stick, the captain waved it. The oarsman did not dare turn his head, so he was obliged to ask questions.

"What's he doing now?"

"He's standing still again. He's looking, I think. — There he goes again — toward the house. — Now he's stopped again."

"Is he waving at us?"

"No, not now; he was, though."

"Look! There comes another man!"

"He's running."

"Look at him go, would you!"

"Why, he's on a bicycle. Now he's met the other man. They're both waving at us. Look!"

"There comes something up the beach."

"What the devil is that thing?"

"Why, it looks like a boat."

"Why, certainly, it's a boat."

"No; it's on wheels."

"Yes, so it is. Well, that must be the life-boat. They drag them along shore on a wagon."

"That's the life-boat, sure."

"No, by God, it's — it's an omnibus."

"I tell you it's a life-boat."

"It is not! It's an omnibus. I can see it plain. See? One of these big hotel omnibuses."

"By thunder, you're right. It's an omnibus, sure as fate. What do you suppose they are doing with an omnibus? Maybe they are going around collecting the life-crew, hey?"

"That's it, likely. Look! There's a fellow waving a little black flag. He's standing on the steps of the omnibus. There come those other two fellows. Now they're all talking together. Look at the fellow with the flag. Maybe he ain't waving it!"

"That ain't a flag, is it? That's his coat. Why, certainly, that's his coat."

"So it is; it's his coat. He's taken it off and is waving it around his head. But would you look at him swing it!"

"Oh, say, there isn't any life-saving station there. That's just a winter-resort hotel omnibus that has brought over some of the boarders to see us drown."

"What's that idiot with the coat mean? What's he signalling, anyhow?"

"It looks as if he were trying to tell us to go north. There must be a life-saving station up there."

"No; he thinks we're fishing. Just giving us a merry hand. See? Ah, there, Willie!"

"Well, I wish I could make something out of those signals. What do you suppose he means?"

"He don't mean anything; he's just playing."

"Well, if he'd just signal us to try the surf again, or to go to sea and wait, or go north, or go south, or go to hell, there would be some reason in it. But look at him! He just stands there and keeps his coat revolving like a wheel. The ass!"

"There come more people." 125

"Now there's quite a mob. Look! Isn't that a boat?"

"Where? Oh, I see where you mean. No, that's no boat."

"That fellow is still waving his coat."

"He must think we like to see him do that. Why don't he quit it? It don't mean anything."

"I don't know. I think he is trying to make us go north. It must be that 130 there's a life-saving station there somewhere."

"Say, he ain't tired yet. Look at 'im wave!"

"Wonder how long he can keep that up. He's been revolving his coat ever since he caught sight of us. He's an idiot. Why aren't they getting men to bring a boat out? A fishingboat — one of those big yawls — could come out here all right. Why don't he do something?"

"Oh, it's all right now."

"They'll have a boat out here for us in less than no time, now that they've seen us."

A faint yellow tone came into the sky over the low land. The shadows 135 on the sea slowly deepened. The wind bore coldness with it, and the men began to shiver.

"Holy smoke!" said one, allowing his voice to express his impious mood, "If we keep on monkeying out here! If we've got to flounder out here all night!"

"Oh, we'll never have to stay here all night! Don't you worry. They've seen us now, and it won't be long before they'll come chasing out after us."

The shore grew dusky. The man waving a coat blended gradually into this gloom, and it swallowed in the same manner the omnibus and the group of people. The spray, when it dashed uproariously over the side, made the voyagers shrink and swear like men who were being branded.

"I'd like to catch the chump who waved the coat. I feel like socking him one, just for luck."

"Why? What did he do?" 140

"Oh, nothing, but then he seemed so damned cheerful."

In the meantime the oiler rowed, and then the correspondent rowed, and then the oiler rowed. Gray-faced and bowed forward, they mechanically, turn by turn, plied the leaden oars. The form of the lighthouse had vanished from the southern horizon, but finally a pale star appeared, just lifting from the sea. The streaked saffron in the west passed before the all-merging darkness, and the sea to the east was black. The land had vanished, and was expressed only by the low and drear thunder of the surf.

"If I am going to be drowned — if I am going to be drowned — if I am going to be drowned, why, in the name of the seven gods who rule the sea, was I allowed to come thus far and contemplate sand and trees? Was I brought here merely to have my nose dragged away as I was about to nibble the sacred cheese of life?"

The patient captain, drooped over the water-jar, was sometimes obliged to speak to the oarsman.

"Keep her head up! Keep her head up!"

"Keep her head up, sir." The voices were weary and low. 145

This was surely a quiet evening. All save the oarsman lay heavily and listlessly in the boat's bottom. As for him, his eyes were just capable of noting the tall black waves that swept forward in a most sinister silence, save for an occasional subdued growl of a crest.

The cook's head was on a thwart, and he looked without interest at the water under his nose. He was deep in other scenes. Finally he spoke. "Billie," he murmured, dreamfully, "what kind of pie do you like best?"

V

"Pie!" said the oiler and the correspondent, agitatedly. "Don't talk about those things, blast you!"

"Well," said the cook, "I was just thinking about ham sandwiches, 150 and —"

A night on the sea in an open boat is a long night. As darkness settled finally, the shine of the light, lifting from the sea in the south, changed to full gold. On the northern horizon a new light appeared, a small bluish gleam on the edge of the waters. These two lights were the furniture of the world. Otherwise there was nothing but waves.

Two men huddled in the stern, and distances were so magnificent in the dinghy that the rower was enabled to keep his feet partly warm by thrusting them under his companions. Their legs indeed extended far under the rowing-seat until they touched the feet of the captain forward. Sometimes, despite the efforts of the tired oarsman, a wave came piling into the boat, an icy wave of the night, and the chilling water soaked them anew. They would twist their bodies for a moment and groan, and sleep the dead sleep once more, while the water in the boat gurgled about them as the craft rocked.

The plan of the oiler and the correspondent was for one to row until he lost the ability, and then arouse the other from his sea-water couch in the bottom of the boat.

The oiler plied the oars until his head drooped forward and the overpowering sleep blinded him; and he rowed yet afterward. Then he touched a man in the bottom of the boat, and called his name. "Will you spell me for a little while?" he said meekly.

"Sure, Billie," said the correspondent, awaking and dragging himself to 155 a sitting position. They exchanged places carefully, and the oiler, cuddling down in the sea-water at the cook's side, seemed to go to sleep instantly.

The particular violence of the sea had ceased. The waves came without snarling. The obligation of the man at the oars was to keep the boat headed so that the tilt of the rollers would not capsize her, and to preserve her from filling when the crests rushed past. The black waves were silent and hard to be seen in the darkness. Often one was almost upon the boat before the oarsman was aware.

In a low voice the correspondent addressed the captain. He was not sure that the captain was awake, although this iron man seemed to be always awake. "Captain, shall I keep her making for that light north, sir?"

The same steady voice answered him. "Yes. Keep it about two points off the port bow."

The cook had tied a life-belt around himself in order to get even the warmth which this clumsy cork contrivance could donate, and he seemed almost stove-like when a rower, whose teeth invariably chattered wildly as soon as he ceased his labor, dropped down to sleep.

The correspondent, as he rowed, looked down at the two men sleeping 160
underfoot. The cook's arm was around the oiler's shoulders, and, with their fragmentary clothing and haggard faces, they were the babes of the sea — a grotesque rendering of the old babes in the wood.

Later he must have grown stupid at his work, for suddenly there was a growling of water, and a crest came with a roar and a swash into the boat, and it was a wonder that it did not set the cook afloat in his life-belt. The cook continued to sleep, but the oiler sat up, blinking his eyes and shaking with the new cold.

"Oh, I'm awful sorry, Billie," said the correspondent, contritely.

"That's all right, old boy," said the oiler, and lay down again and was asleep.

Presently it seemed that even the captain dozed, and the correspondent thought that he was the one man afloat on all the oceans. The wind had a voice as it came over the waves, and it was sadder than the end.

There was a long, loud swishing astern of the boat, and a gleaming trail 165
of phosphorescence, like blue flame, was furrowed on the black waters. It might have been made by a monstrous knife.

Then there came a stillness, while the correspondent breathed with open mouth and looked at the sea.

Suddenly there was another swish and another long flash of bluish light, and this time it was alongside the boat, and might almost have been reached with an oar. The correspondent saw an enormous fin speed like a shadow through the water, hurling the crystalline spray and leaving the long glowing trail.

The correspondent looked over his shoulder at the captain. His face was hidden, and he seemed to be asleep. He looked at the babes of the sea. They certainly were asleep. So, being bereft of sympathy, he leaned a little way to one side and swore softly into the sea.

But the thing did not then leave the vicinity of the boat. Ahead or astern, on one side or the other, at intervals long or short, fled the long sparkling streak, and there was to be heard the *whirroo* of the dark fin. The speed and power of the thing was greatly to be admired. It cut the water like a gigantic and keen projectile.

The presence of this biding thing did not affect the man with the same 170
horror that it would if he had been a picnicker. He simply looked at the sea dully and swore in an undertone.

Nevertheless, it is true that he did not wish to be alone with the thing. He wished one of his companions to awake by chance and keep him company with it. But the captain hung motionless over the water-jar, and the oiler and the cook in the bottom of the boat were plunged in slumber.

VI

"If I am going to be drowned — if I am going to be drowned — if I am going to be drowned, why, in the name of the seven mad gods who rule the sea, was I allowed to come thus far and contemplate sand and trees?"

During this dismal night, it may be remarked that a man would conclude that it was really the intention of the seven mad gods to drown him, despite the abominable injustice of it. For it was certainly an abominable injustice to drown a man who had worked so hard, so hard. The man felt it would be a crime most unnatural. Other people had drowned at sea since galleys swarmed with painted sails, but still ——

When it occurs to a man that nature does not regard him as important, and that she feels she would not maim the universe by disposing of him, he at first wishes to throw bricks at the temple, and he hates deeply the fact that there are no bricks and no temples. Any visible expression of nature would surely be pelleted with his jeers.

Then, if there be no tangible thing to hoot, he feels, perhaps, the desire to confront a personification and indulge in pleas, bowed to one knee, and with hands supplicant, saying, "Yes, but I love myself."

A high cold star on a winter's night is the word he feels that she says to him. Thereafter he knows the pathos of his situation.

The men in the dinghy had not discussed these matters, but each had, no doubt, reflected upon them in silence and according to his mind. There was seldom any expression upon their faces save the general one of complete weariness. Speech was devoted to the business of the boat.

To chime the notes of his emotion, a verse mysteriously entered the correspondent's head. He had even forgotten that he had forgotten this verse, but it suddenly was in his mind.

A soldier of the Legion lay dying in Algiers;
There was lack of woman's nursing, there was dearth of woman's
    tears;
But a comrade stood beside him, and he took that comrade's hand,
And he said, "I never more shall see my own, my native land°."

In his childhood the correspondent had been made acquainted with the fact that a soldier of the Legion lay dying in Algiers, but he had never regarded the fact as important. Myriads of his school-fellows had informed him of the soldier's plight, but the dinning had naturally ended by making him perfectly indifferent. He had never considered it his affair that a soldier of the Legion lay dying in Algiers, nor had it appeared to him as a matter for sorrow. It was less to him than the breaking of a pencil's point.

A soldier of the Legion . . . native land: The correspondent remembers a Victorian ballad about a German dying in the French Foreign Legion, "Bingen on the Rhine" by Caroline Norton.

Now, however, it quaintly came to him as a human, living thing. It was no longer merely a picture of a few throes in the breast of a poet, meanwhile drinking tea and warming his feet at the grate; it was an actuality — stern, mournful, and fine.

The correspondent plainly saw the soldier. He lay on the sand with his feet out straight and still. While his pale left hand was upon his chest in an attempt to thwart the going of his life, the blood came between his fingers. In the far Algerian distance, a city of low square forms was set against a sky that was faint with the last sunset hues. The correspondent, plying the oars and dreaming of the slow and slower movements of the lips of the soldier, was moved by a profound and perfectly impersonal comprehension. He was sorry for the soldier of the Legion who lay dying in Algiers.

The thing which had followed the boat and waited had evidently grown bored at the delay. There was no longer to be heard the slash of the cutwater, and there was no longer the flame of the long trail. The light in the north still glimmered, but it was apparently no nearer to the boat. Sometimes the boom of the surf rang in the correspondent's ears, and he turned the craft seaward then and rowed harder. Southward, some one had evidently built a watch-fire on the beach. It was too low and too far to be seen, but it made a shimmering, roseate reflection upon the bluff in back of it, and this could be discerned from the boat. The wind came stronger, and sometimes a wave suddenly raged out like a mountain cat, and there was to be seen the sheen and sparkle of a broken crest.

The captain, in the bow, moved on his water-jar and sat erect. "Pretty long night," he observed to the correspondent. He looked at the shore. "Those life-saving people take their time."

"Did you see that shark playing around?"   185

"Yes, I saw him. He was a big fellow, all right."

"Wish I had known you were awake."

Later the correspondent spoke into the bottom of the boat.

"Billie!" There was a slow and gradual disentanglement.

"Billie, will you spell me?"   190

"Sure," said the oiler.

As soon as the correspondent touched the cold, comfortable sea-water in the bottom of the boat and had huddled close to the cook's life-belt he was deep in sleep, despite the fact that his teeth played all the popular airs. This sleep was so good to him that it was but a moment before he heard a voice call his name in a tone that demonstrated the last stages of exhaustion. "Will you spell me?"

"Sure, Billie."

The light in the north had mysteriously vanished, but the correspondent took his course from the wide-awake captain.

Later in the night they took the boat farther out to sea, and the captain   195
directed the cook to take one oar at the stern and keep the boat facing the seas. He was to call out if he should hear the thunder of the surf. This plan enabled the oiler and the correspondent to get respite together. "We'll give those boys a chance to get into shape again," said the captain. They curled down and, after a few preliminary chatterings and trembles, slept once more the dead sleep. Neither knew they had bequeathed to the cook the company of another shark, or perhaps the same shark.

As the boat caroused on the waves, spray occasionally bumped over the side and gave them a fresh soaking, but this had no power to break their repose. The ominous slash of the wind and the water affected them as it would have affected mummies.

"Boys," said the cook, with the notes of every reluctance in his voice, "she's drifted in pretty close. I guess one of you had better take her to sea again." The correspondent, aroused, heard the crash of the toppled crests.

As he was rowing, the captain gave him some whisky-and-water, and this steadied the chills out of him. "If I ever get ashore and anybody shows me even a photograph of an oar ——"

At last there was a short conversation.

"Billie! — Billie, will you spell me?"

"Sure," said the oiler. 200

VII

When the correspondent again opened his eyes, the sea and the sky were each of the gray hue of the dawning. Later, carmine and gold was painted upon the waters. The morning appeared finally, in its splendor, with a sky of pure blue, and the sunlight flamed on the tips of the waves.

On the distant dunes were set many little black cottages, and a tall white windmill reared above them. No man, nor dog, nor bicycle appeared on the beach. The cottages might have formed a deserted village.

The voyagers scanned the shore. A conference was held in the boat. "Well," said the captain, "if no help is coming, we might better try a run through the surf right away. If we stay out here much longer we will be too weak to do anything for ourselves at all." The others silently acquiesced in this reasoning. The boat was headed for the beach. The correspondent wondered if none ever ascended the tall wind-tower, and if then they never looked seaward. This tower was a giant, standing with its back to the plight of the ants. It represented in a degree, to the correspondent, the serenity of nature amid the struggles of the individual — nature in the wind, and nature in the vision of men. She did not seem cruel to him then, nor beneficent, nor treacherous, nor wise. But she was indifferent, flatly indifferent. It is, perhaps, plausible that a man in this situation, impressed with the unconcern of the universe, should see the innumerable flaws of his life, and have them taste wickedly in his mind, and wish for another chance. A distinction between right and wrong seems absurdly clear to him, then, in this new ignorance of the grave-edge, and he understands that if he were given another opportunity he would mend his conduct and his words, and be better and brighter during an introduction or at a tea.

"Now, boys," said the captain, "she is going to swamp sure. All we can 205 do is to work her in as far as possible, and then when she swamps, pile out and scramble for the beach. Keep cool now, and don't jump until she swamps sure."

The oiler took the oars. Over his shoulders he scanned the surf. "Captain," he said, "I think I'd better bring her about and keep her head-on to the seas and back her in."

"All right, Billie," said the captain. "Back her in." The oiler swung the boat then, and, seated in the stern, the cook and the correspondent were obliged to look over their shoulders to contemplate the lonely and indifferent shore.

The monstrous inshore rollers heaved the boat high until the men were again enabled to see the white sheets of water scudding up the slanted beach. "We won't get in very close," said the captain. Each time a man could wrest his attention from the rollers, he turned his glance toward the shore, and in the expression of the eyes during this contemplation there was a singular quality. The correspondent, observing the others, knew that they were not afraid, but the full meaning of their glances was shrouded.

As for himself, he was too tired to grapple fundamentally with the fact. He tried to coerce his mind into thinking of it, but the mind was dominated at this time by the muscles, and the muscles said they did not care. It merely occurred to him that if he should drown it would be a shame.

There were no hurried words, no pallor, no plain agitation. The men simply looked at the shore. "Now, remember to get well clear of the boat when you jump," said the captain. $\quad$ 210

Seaward the crest of a roller suddenly fell with a thunderous crash, and the long white comber came roaring down upon the boat.

"Steady now," said the captain. The men were silent. They turned their eyes from the shore to the comber and waited. The boat slid up the incline, leaped at the furious top, bounced over it, and swung down the long back of the wave. Some water had been shipped, and the cook bailed it out.

But the next crest crashed also. The tumbling, boiling flood of white water caught the boat and whirled it almost perpendicular. Water swarmed in from all sides. The correspondent had his hands on the gunwale at this time, and when the water entered at that place he swiftly withdrew his fingers, as if he objected to wetting them.

The little boat, drunken with this weight of water, reeled and snuggled deeper into the sea.

"Bail her out, cook! Bail her out!" said the captain. $\quad$ 215

"All right, Captain," said the cook.

"Now, boys, the next one will do for us sure," said the oiler. "Mind to jump clear of the boat."

The third wave moved forward, huge, furious, implacable. It fairly swallowed the dinghy, and almost simultaneously the men tumbled into the sea. A piece of life-belt had lain in the bottom of the boat, and as the correspondent went overboard he held this to his chest with his left hand.

The January water was icy, and he reflected immediately that it was colder than he had expected to find it off the coast of Florida. This appeared to his dazed mind as a fact important enough to be noted at the time. The coldness of the water was sad; it was tragic. This fact was somehow mixed and confused with his opinion of his own situation, so that it seemed almost a proper reason for tears. The water was cold.

When he came to the surface he was conscious of little but the noisy $\quad$ 220 water. Afterward he saw his companions in the sea. The oiler was ahead in the race. He was swimming strongly and rapidly. Off to the correspondent's left, the cook's great white and corked back bulged out of the water; and in the rear the captain was hanging with his one good hand to the keel of the overturned dinghy.

There is a certain immovable quality to a shore, and the correspondent wondered at it amid the confusion of the sea.

It seemed also very attractive; but the correspondent knew that it was a long journey, and he paddled leisurely. The piece of life-preserver lay under him, and sometimes he whirled down the incline of a wave as if he were on a hand-sled.

But finally he arrived at a place in the sea where travel was beset with difficulty. He did not pause swimming to inquire what manner of current had caught him, but there his progress ceased. The shore was set before him like a bit of scenery on a stage, and he looked at it and understood with his eyes each detail of it.

As the cook passed, much farther to the left, the captain was calling to him, "Turn over on your back, cook! Turn over on your back and use the oar."

"All right, sir." The cook turned on his back, and, paddling with an oar, 225 went ahead as if he were a canoe.

Presently the boat also passed to the left of the correspondent, with the captain clinging with one hand to the keel. He would have appeared like a man raising himself to look over a board fence if it were not for the extraordinary gymnastics of the boat. The correspondent marvelled that the captain could still hold to it.

They passed on nearer to shore—the oiler, the cook, the captain — and following them went the water-jar, bouncing gaily over the seas.

The correspondent remained in the grip of this strange new enemy — a current. The shore, with its white slope of sand and its green bluff topped with little silent cottages, was spread like a picture before him. It was very near to him then, but he was impressed as one who, in a gallery, looks at a scene from Brittany or Algiers.

He thought: "I am going to drown? Can it be possible? Can it be possible? Can it be possible?" Perhaps an individual must consider his own death to be the final phenomenon of nature.

But later a wave perhaps whirled him out of this small deadly current, 230 for he found suddenly that he could again make progress toward the shore. Later still he was aware that the captain, clinging with one hand to the keel of the dinghy, had his face turned away from the shore and toward him, and was calling his name. "Come to the boat! Come to the boat!"

In his struggle to reach the captain and the boat, he reflected that when one gets properly wearied drowning must really be a comfortable arrangement — a cessation of hostilities accompanied by a large degree of relief; and he was glad of it, for the main thing in his mind for some moments had been horror of the temporary agony. He did not wish to be hurt.

Presently he saw a man running along the shore. He was undressing with most remarkable speed. Coat, trousers, shirt, everything flew magically off him.

"Come to the boat!" called the captain.

"All right, Captain." As the correspondent paddled, he saw the captain let himself down to bottom and leave the boat. Then the correspondent performed his one little marvel of the voyage. A large wave caught him and flung him with ease and supreme speed completely over the boat and far beyond it. It struck him even then as an event in gymnastics and a true miracle of the sea. An overturned boat in the surf is not a plaything to a swimming man.

The correspondent arrived in water that reached only to his waist, but his condition did not enable him to stand for more than a moment. Each wave knocked him into a heap, and the undertow pulled at him. 235

Then he saw the man who had been running and undressing, and undressing and running, come bounding into the water. He dragged ashore the cook, and then waded toward the captain; but the captain waved him away and sent him to the correspondent. He was naked — naked as a tree in winter; but a halo was about his head, and he shone like a saint. He gave a strong pull, and a long drag, and a bully heave at the correspondent's hand. The correspondent, schooled in the minor formulae, said, "Thanks, old man." But suddenly the man cried, "What's that?" He pointed a swift finger. The correspondent said, "Go."

In the shallows, face downward, lay the oiler. His forehead touched sand that was periodically, between each wave, clear of the sea.

The correspondent did not know all that transpired afterward. When he achieved safe ground he fell, striking the sand with each particular part of his body. It was as if he had dropped from a roof, but the thud was grateful to him.

It seems that instantly the beach was populated with men with blankets, clothes, and flasks, and women with coffee-pots and all the remedies sacred to their minds. The welcome of the land to the men from the sea was warm and generous; but a still and dripping shape was carried slowly up the beach, and the land's welcome for it could only be the different and sinister hospitality of the grave.

When it came night, the white waves paced to and fro in the moonlight, and the wind brought the sound of the great sea's voice to the men on the shore, and they felt that they could then be interpreters. 240

Questions

1. In actuality, Crane, the captain of the *Commodore,* and the two crew members spent nearly thirty hours in the open boat. William Higgins, the oiler, was drowned as Crane describes. Does a knowledge of these facts in any way affect your response to the story? Would you admire the story less if you believed it to be pure fiction?
2. Sum up the personalities of each of the four men in the boat: captain, cook, oiler, and correspondent.
3. What is the point of view of the story?
4. In paragraph 9, we are told that as each wave came, the boat "seemed like a horse making for a fence outrageously high." Point to other vivid similes or figures of speech. What do they contribute to the story's effectiveness?
5. Notice some of the ways in which Crane, as a storyteller conscious of plot, builds suspense. What enemies or obstacles do the men in the boat confront? What is the effect of the scene of the men who wave from the beach (paragraphs 86 – 141)? What is the climax of the story? (If you need to be refreshed on the meaning of *climax,* see page 9.)

6. In paragraph 70 (and again in paragraph 143), the men wonder, "Was I brought here merely to have my nose dragged away as I was about to nibble the sacred cheese of life?" What variety of irony do you find in this quotation?

7. Why does the scrap of verse about the soldier dying in Algiers (paragraph 179) suddenly come to mean so much to the correspondent?

8. What theme in "The Open Boat" seems most important to you? Where is it stated?

9. What secondary themes also enrich the story? See for instance paragraph 43 (the thoughts on comradeship).

10. How do you define *heroism*? Who is a hero in "The Open Boat"?

SUGGESTIONS FOR WRITING

1. In "The Door" E. B. White expresses a theme or two worth thinking on. Once you feel sure you know what point or points White is making (and if you aren't yet sure, discuss the story further with your instructor or your peers), write a letter to White. Take him to task for failing to get with modern high-tech civilization, or thank him for making you aware of things you have noticed but which haven't quite landed home. Tell him your own recollections or observations of city life.

2. Have you, like the narrator of "The Open Boat," ever been in physical danger? Not that your life needs to be as thrilling as an episode of *Miami Vice;* but think and see what you can recall. What have you learned from your experience? Tell of it, comparing your memory with what Crane observes of people in danger, with what Crane's reporter notices within himself.

   Note: In a sense, you are often in real danger from forces sometimes beyond your control (storms, rapists and other criminals, crazed souls who tamper with capsules in drugstores, disease carriers). In a way, passively to face such ordinary perils may seem less heroic than rowing an open boat in a heaving sea. In another way — well, if you're looking for a danger to recall, you might think about this comparison. Reading Crane's story, do you feel that, in any sense, you and the news correspondent are in the same boat?

3. In "The Open Boat," recall the poem that comes to matter greatly to the correspondent (paragraphs 179 – 182). Have you ever been in a situation when a story, an Aesop fable, a saying, a line of poetry, or a song lyric took on fresh and immediate meaning for you? If so, relate your experience. (If no such experience has befallen you, don't make one up.)

4. Compare Mrs. Turpin's defiance of God in "Revelation" ("Who do you think you are?" — paragraph 187) with the urge of a shipwrecked man in "The Open Boat" to shake his fist at the clouds ("Just you drown me, now, and then hear what I call you!" — paragraph 70). Do Flannery O'Connor and Stephen Crane express similar or different concepts of Whoever runs the universe?

5. Pick a story not included in this chapter and, in your own words, sum up its main theme. Then indicate what you find in the story that makes this theme clear. Among stories whose themes stand out are "Gimpel the Fool," "Barn Burning," "Paul's Case," "Everyday Use," "The Chrysanthemums," "I Stand Here Ironing," "The Death of Ivan Ilych," and "The Birthmark." Is the author making any statement you can agree or disagree with? Why do you feel the way you do? Suggestion: Before you write, refresh your memory of the method of analysis (in "Writing about a Story," page 1353). This useful method might come in handy.

6. Compare two stories similar in theme. Both Joyce in "Araby" and Singer in "Gimpel the Fool" set forth a conflict between illusion and reality. Poe in "The Tell-Tale Heart" and O'Brien in "Two in One" show us that murder, even

ingeniously clever murder, will out. Browse in other chapters and in "Stories for Further Reading" and see what other pairs of stories go together in theme. Then set them side by side and point out their similarities and differences. This topic will lead you to use the method of comparison and contrast, discussed in "Writing about a Story" on page 1358.

7. Here is a topic for science fiction fans: Trace a general theme in two or more science fiction novels or stories you know. Choose works that express similar views. Suggestion: If you know two science fiction writers who distrust the benefits of technology, or who take a keen interest in the future of women, look closely at their work and you will probably find an intriguing theme.

8 Symbol

In F. Scott Fitzgerald's novel *The Great Gatsby,* a huge pair of bespectacled eyes stares across a wilderness of ash heaps, from a billboard advertising the services of an oculist. Repeatedly entering into the story, the advertisement comes to mean more than simply the availability of eye examinations. Fitzgerald has a character liken it to the eyes of God; he hints that some sad, compassionate spirit is brooding as it watches the passing procession of mankind. Such an object is a **symbol:** in literature, a thing that suggests more than its literal meaning. Symbols generally do not "stand for" any one meaning, nor for anything absolutely definite; they point, they hint, or, as Henry James put it, they cast long shadows. To take a large example: in Herman Melville's *Moby-Dick,* the great white whale of the book's title apparently means more than the literal dictionary-definition meaning of an aquatic mammal. He also suggests more than the devil, to whom some of the characters liken him. The great whale, as the story unfolds, comes to imply an amplitude of meanings: among them the forces of nature and the whole created universe. This indefinite multiplicity of meanings is characteristic of a symbolic story and distinguishes it from an **allegory,** a story in which persons, places, and things form a system of clearly labeled equivalents.

In a simple allegory, characters and other ingredients often stand for other definite meanings, which are often abstractions. Supreme allegories are found in some biblical parables ("The kingdom of Heaven is like a man who sowed good seed in his field . . . ," Matthew 13:24 – 30).[1] A classic allegory is the medieval play *Everyman,* whose hero represents us all, and who, deserted by false friends called Kindred and Goods, faces the judgment of God accompanied only by a faithful friend called Good Deeds. In John Bunyan's seventeenth-century *Pilgrim's Progress,* the protagonist, Christian, struggles along the difficult road toward salvation, meeting along the way persons such as Mr. Worldly Wiseman, who directs him into a more comfortable path (a wrong turn), and the residents of a town called Fair Speech, among them a hypocrite named Mr. Facing-both-ways. Not

---

[1] A **parable** is a brief story that teaches a lesson. Some (but not all) parables are allegories.

all allegories are simple: Dante's *Divine Comedy*, written in the Middle Ages, continues to reveal new meanings to careful readers. Allegory was much beloved in the Middle Ages, but in contemporary fiction it is rare. One modern instance is George Orwell's long fable *Animal Farm*, in which (among its double meanings) barnyard animals stand for human victims and totalitarian oppressors.

Symbols in fiction are not generally abstract terms like *love* or *truth*, but are likely to be perceptible objects (or worded descriptions that cause us to imagine them). In William Faulkner's "A Rose for Emily" (Chapter Two), Miss Emily's invisible watch ticking at the end of a golden chain not only indicates the passage of time, but suggests that time passes without even being noticed by the watch's owner, and the golden chain carries suggestions of wealth and authority. Often the symbols we meet in fiction are inanimate objects, but other things also may function symbolically. In James Joyce's "Araby" (page 54), the very name of the bazaar, Araby — the poetic name for Arabia — suggests magic, romance, and *The Arabian Nights;* its syllables (the narrator tells us) "cast an Eastern enchantment over me." Even a locale, or a feature of physical topography, can provide rich suggestions. Recall Ernest Hemingway's "A Clean, Well-Lighted Place" (Chapter Five), in which the café is not merely a café, but an island of refuge from night, chaos, loneliness, old age, and impending death.

In some novels and stories, symbolic characters make brief cameo appearances. Such characters often are not well-rounded and fully known, but are seen fleetingly and remain slightly mysterious. In *Heart of Darkness,* a short novel by Joseph Conrad, a steamship company that hires men to work in the Congo maintains in its waiting room two women who knit black wool — like the classical Fates. Usually such a symbolic character is more a portrait than a person — or somewhat portraitlike, as Faulkner's Miss Emily, who twice appears at a window of her house "like the carven torso of an idol in a niche." Though Faulkner invests Miss Emily with life and vigor, he also clothes her in symbolic hints: she seems almost to personify the vanishing aristocracy of the antebellum south, still maintaining a black servant and being ruthlessly betrayed by a moneymaking Yankee. Sometimes a part of a character's body or an attribute may convey symbolic meaning: a baleful eye, as in Edgar Allan Poe's "The Tell-Tale Heart" (page 38).

Much as a symbolic whale holds more meaning than an ordinary whale, a **symbolic act** is a gesture with larger significance than usual. For the boy's father in Faulkner's "Barn Burning" (Chapter Five), the act of destroying a barn is no mere act of spite, but an expression of his profound hatred for anything not belonging to him. Faulkner adds that burning a barn reflects the father's memories of the "waste and extravagance of war"; and further adds that "the element of fire spoke to some deep mainspring" in his being. A symbolic act, however, doesn't have to be a gesture as large as starting a conflagration. Before setting out in pursuit of the great white whale, Melville's Captain Ahab in *Moby-Dick* deliberately snaps his to-bacco pipe and throws it away, as if to suggest (among other things) that he will let no pleasure or pastime distract him from his vengeance.

Why do writers have to symbolize — why don't they tell us outright? One advantage of a symbol is that it is so compact, and yet so fully laden. Both starkly concrete and slightly mysterious, like Miss Emily's invisibly ticking watch, it may impress us with all the force of something beheld in a dream or in a nightmare. The watch suggests, among other things, the slow and invisible passage of time. What this symbol says, it says more fully and more memorably than could be said, perhaps, in a long essay on the subject.

To some extent (it may be claimed), all stories are symbolic. Merely by holding up for our inspection these characters and their actions, the writer lends them *some* special significance. But this is to think of *symbol* in an extremely broad and inclusive way. For the usual purposes of reading a story and understanding it, there is probably little point in looking for symbolism in every word, in every stick or stone, in every striking of a match, in every minor character. Still, to be on the alert for symbols when reading fiction is perhaps wiser than to ignore them. Not to admit that symbolic meanings may be present, or to refuse to think about them, would be another way to misread a story — or to read no further than its outer edges.

How, then, do you recognize a symbol in fiction when you meet it? Fortunately, the storyteller often gives the symbol particular emphasis. It may be mentioned repeatedly throughout the story; it may even supply the story with a title ("Araby," "Barn Burning," "A Clean, Well-Lighted Place"). At times, a crucial symbol will open a story or end it. Unless an object, act, or character is given some such special emphasis and impor-tance, we may generally feel safe in taking it at face value. Probably it isn't a symbol if it points clearly and unmistakably toward some one meaning, like a whistle in a factory, whose blast at noon means lunch. But an object, an act, or a character is surely symbolic (and almost as surely displays high literary art) if, when we finish the story, we realize that it was that item — those gigantic eyes; that clean, well-lighted café; that burning of a barn — which led us to the author's theme, the essential meaning.

John Steinbeck
THE CHRYSANTHEMUMS   1938

John Steinbeck (1902 – 1968), was born in Salinas, California, in the fertile valley he remembers in "The Chrysanthemums." Off and on, he attended Stanford University, then sojourned in New York as a reporter and a bricklayer. After years of struggle to earn his bread from fiction, Steinbeck reached a large audience with Tortilla Flat *(1935), a loosely woven novel portraying Mexican-Americans in Monterey with fondness and sympathy. Great acclaim greeted* The Grapes of Wrath *(1939), the story of a family of Oklahoma farmers who, ruined by dust storms in the 1930s, join a mass migration to California. Like Ernest Hemingway and Stephen Crane, Steinbeck prided himself on his journalism: in World War II, he filed dispatches from battlefronts in Italy and Africa, and in 1966 he wrote a column from South Vietnam. Known widely behind the Iron Curtain, Steinbeck accepted an invitation to visit the Soviet Union, and reported his trip in* A Russian Journal *(1948). In 1962 he became the seventh American to win the Nobel prize for literature, but critics have never placed Steinbeck on the same high shelf with Faulkner and Hemingway. He wrote much, not all good, and yet his best work adds to an impressive total. Besides* The Grapes of Wrath, *it includes* In Dubious Battle *(1936) a novel of an apple-pickers' strike;* Of Mice and Men, *a powerful short novel (also a play) of comradeship between a hobo and a moron;* The Log from the Sea of Cortez, *a nonfiction account of a marine biological expedition; and the short stories in* The Long Valley *(1938). Through the fiction he wrote in his prime, Steinbeck maintains an appealing sympathy for the poor and downtrodden, the lonely and dispossessed.*

The high grey-flannel fog of winter closed off the Salinas Valley° from the sky and from all the rest of the world. On every side it sat like a lid on the mountains and made of the great valley a closed pot. On the broad, level land floor the gang plows bit deep and left the black earth shining like metal where the shares had cut. On the foothill ranches across the Salinas River, the yellow stubble fields seemed to be bathed in pale cold sunshine, but there was no sunshine in the valley now in December. The thick willow scrub along the river flamed with sharp and positive yellow leaves.

It was a time of quiet and of waiting. The air was cold and tender. A light wind blew up from the southwest so that the farmers were mildly hopeful of a good rain before long; but fog and rain do not go together.

Across the river, on Henry Allen's foothill ranch there was little work to be done, for the hay was cut and stored and the orchards were plowed up to receive the rain deeply when it should come. The cattle on the higher slopes were becoming shaggy and rough-coated.

Elisa Allen, working in her flower garden, looked down across the yard and saw Henry, her husband, talking to two men in business suits. The three of them stood by the tractor shed, each man with one foot on the side of the little Fordson. They smoked cigarettes and studied the machine as they talked.

Elisa watched them for a moment and then went back to her work. She ⁵ was thirty-five. Her face was lean and strong and her eyes were as clear as water. Her figure looked blocked and heavy in her gardening costume, a man's black hat pulled low down over her eyes, clod-hopper shoes, a figured print dress almost completely covered by a big corduroy apron with four big pockets

Salinas Valley: south of San Francisco in the Coast Ranges region of California.

to hold the snips, the trowel and scratcher, the seeds and the knife she worked with. She wore heavy leather gloves to protect her hands while she worked.

She was cutting down the old year's chrysanthemum stalks with a pair of short and powerful scissors. She looked down toward the men by the tractor shed now and then. Her face was eager and mature and handsome; even her work with the scissors was over-eager, over-powerful. The chrysanthemum stems seemed too small and easy for her energy.

She brushed a cloud of hair out of her eyes with the back of her glove, and left a smudge of earth on her cheek in doing it. Behind her stood the neat white farm house with red geraniums close-banked around it as high as the windows. It was a hard-swept looking little house with hard-polished windows, and a clean mud-mat on the front steps.

Elisa cast another glance toward the tractor shed. The strangers were getting into their Ford coupe. She took off a glove and put her strong fingers down into the forest of new green chrysanthemum sprouts that were growing around the old roots. She spread the leaves and looked down among the close-growing stems. No aphids were there, no sowbugs or snails or cutworms. Her terrier fingers destroyed such pests before they could get started.

Elisa started at the sound of her husband's voice. He had come near quietly, and he leaned over the wire fence that protected her flower garden from cattle and dogs and chickens.

"At it again," he said. "You've got a strong new crop coming." 10

Elisa straightened her back and pulled on the gardening glove again. "Yes. They'll be strong this coming year." In her tone and on her face there was a little smugness.

"You've got a gift with things," Henry observed. "Some of those yellow chrysanthemums you had this year were ten inches across. I wish you'd work out in the orchard and raise some apples that big."

Her eyes sharpened. "Maybe I could do it, too. I've a gift with things, all right. My mother had it. She could stick anything in the ground and make it grow. She said it was having planters' hands that knew how to do it."

"Well, it sure works with flowers," he said.

"Henry, who were those men you were talking to?" 15

"Why, sure, that's what I came to tell you. They were from the Western Meat Company. I sold those thirty head of three-year-old steers. Got nearly my own price, too."

"Good," she said. "Good for you."

"And I thought," he continued, "I thought how it's Saturday afternoon, and we might go into Salinas for dinner at a restaurant, and then to a picture show — to celebrate, you see."

"Good," she repeated. "Oh, yes. That will be good."

Henry put on his joking tone. "There's fights tonight. How'd you like 20 to go to the fights?"

"Oh, no," she said breathlessly. "No, I wouldn't like fights."

"Just fooling, Elisa. We'll go to a movie. Let's see. It's two now. I'm going to take Scotty and bring down those steers from the hill. It'll take us maybe two hours. We'll go in town about five and have dinner at the Cominos Hotel. Like that?"

"Of course I'll like it. It's good to eat away from home."

"All right, then. I'll go get up a couple of horses."

She said, "I'll have plenty of time to transplant some of these sets, I guess." 25

She heard her husband calling Scotty down by the barn. And a little later she saw the two men ride up the pale yellow hillside in search of the steers.

There was a little square sandy bed kept for rooting the chrysanthemums. With her trowel she turned the soil over and over, and smoothed it and patted it firm. Then she dug ten parallel trenches to receive the sets. Back at the chrysanthemum bed she pulled out the little crisp shoots, trimmed off the leaves of each one with her scissors and laid it on a small orderly pile.

A squeak of wheels and plod of hoofs came from the road. Elisa looked up. The country road ran along the dense bank of willows and cottonwoods that bordered the river, and up this road came a curious vehicle, curiously drawn. It was an old spring-wagon, with a round canvas top on it like the cover of a prairie schooner. It was drawn by an old bay horse and a little grey-and-white burro. A big stubble-bearded man sat between the cover flaps and drove the crawling team. Underneath the wagon, between the hind wheels, a lean and rangy mongrel dog walked sedately. Words were painted on the canvas, in clumsy, crooked letters. "Pots, pans, knives, sisors, lawn mores, Fixed." Two rows of articles, and the triumphantly definitive "Fixed" below. The black paint had run down in little sharp points beneath each letter.

Elisa, squatting on the ground, watched to see the crazy, loose-jointed wagon pass by. But it didn't pass. It turned into the farm road in front of her house, crooked old wheels skirling and squeaking. The rangy dog darted from between the wheels and ran ahead. Instantly the two ranch shepherds flew out at him. Then all three stopped, and with stiff and quivering tails, with taut straight legs, with ambassadorial dignity, they slowly circled, sniffing daintily. The caravan pulled up to Elisa's wire fence and stopped. Now the newcomer dog, feeling out-numbered, lowered his tail and retired under the wagon with raised hackles and bared teeth.

The man on the wagon seat called out, "That's a bad dog in a fight when he gets started." 30

Elisa laughed. "I see he is. How soon does he generally get started?"

The man caught up her laughter and echoed it heartily. "Sometimes not for weeks and weeks," he said. He climbed stiffly down, over the wheel. The horse and the donkey drooped like unwatered flowers.

Elisa saw that he was a very big man. Although his hair and beard were greying, he did not look old. His worn black suit was wrinkled and spotted with grease. The laughter had disappeared from his face and eyes the moment his laughing voice ceased. His eyes were dark, and they were full of the brooding that gets in the eyes of teamsters and of sailors. The calloused hands he rested on the wire fence were cracked, and every crack was a black line. He took off his battered hat.

"I'm off my general road, ma'am," he said. "Does this dirt road cut over across the river to the Los Angeles highway?"

Elisa stood up and shoved the thick scissors in her apron pocket. "Well, yes, it does, but it winds around and then fords the river. I don't think your team could pull through the sand." 35

He replied with some asperity. "It might surprise you what them beasts can pull through."

"When they get started?" she asked.

He smiled for a second. "Yes. When they get started."

"Well," said Elisa, "I think you'll save time if you go back to the Salinas road and pick up the highway there."

He drew a big finger down the chicken wire and made it sing. "I ain't in any hurry, ma'am. I go from Seattle to San Diego and back every year. Takes all my time. About six months each way. I aim to follow nice weather." 40

Elisa took off her gloves and stuffed them in the apron pocket with the scissors. She touched the under edge of her man's hat, searching for fugitive hairs. "That sounds like a nice kind of a way to live," she said.

He leaned confidentially over the fence. "Maybe you noticed the writing on my wagon. I mend pots and sharpen knives and scissors. You got any of them things to do?"

"Oh, no," she said quickly. "Nothing like that." Her eyes hardened with resistance.

"Scissors is the worst thing," he explained. "Most people just ruin scissors trying to sharpen 'em, but I know how. I got a special tool. It's a little bobbit kind of thing, and patented. But it sure does the trick."

"No. My scissors are all sharp." 45

"All right, then. Take a pot," he continued earnestly, "a bent pot, or a pot with a hole. I can make it like new so you don't have to buy no new ones. That's a saving for you."

"No," she said shortly. "I tell you I have nothing like that for you to do."

His face fell to an exaggerated sadness. His voice took on a whining undertone. "I ain't had a thing to do today. Maybe I won't have no supper tonight. You see I'm off my regular road. I know folks on the highway clear from Seattle to San Diego. They save their things for me to sharpen up because they know I do it so good and save them money."

"I'm sorry," Elisa said irritably. "I haven't anything for you to do."

His eyes left her face and fell to searching the ground. They roamed about until they came to the chrysanthemum bed where she had been working. "What's them plants, ma'am?" 50

The irritation and resistance melted from Elisa's face. "Oh, those are chrysanthemums, giant whites and yellows. I raise them every year, bigger than anybody around here."

"Kind of a long-stemmed flower? Looks like a quick puff of colored smoke?" he asked.

"That's it. What a nice way to describe them."

"They smell kind of nasty till you get used to them," he said.

"It's a good bitter smell," she retorted, "not nasty at all." 55

He changed his tone quickly. "I like the smell myself."

"I had ten-inch blooms this year," she said.

The man leaned farther over the fence. "Look. I know a lady down the road a piece, has got the nicest garden you ever seen. Got nearly every kind of flower but no chrysanthemums. Last time I was mending a copper-bottom washtub for her (that's a hard job but I do it good), she said to me, 'If you ever run acrost some nice chrysanthemums I wish you'd try to get me a few seeds.' That's what she told me."

Elisa's eyes grew alert and eager. "She couldn't have known much about chrysanthemums. You *can* raise them from seed, but it's much easier to root the little sprouts you see there."

"Oh," he said. "I s'pose I can't take none to her, then." 60

"Why yes you can," Elisa cried. "I can put some in damp sand, and you can carry them right along with you. They'll take root in the pot if you keep them damp. And then she can transplant them."

"She'd sure like to have some, ma'am. You say they're nice ones?"

"Beautiful," she said. "Oh, beautiful." Her eyes shone. She tore off the battered hat and shook out her dark pretty hair. "I'll put them in a flower pot, and you can take them right with you. Come into the yard."

While the man came through the picket gate Elisa ran excitedly along the geranium-bordered path to the back of the house. And she returned carrying a big red flower pot. The gloves were forgotten now. She kneeled on the ground by the starting bed and dug the sandy soil with her fingers and scooped it into the bright new flower pot. Then she picked up the little pile of shoots she had prepared. With her strong fingers she pressed them into the sand and tamped around them with her knuckles. The man stood over her. "I'll tell you what to do," she said. "You remember so you can tell the lady."

"Yes, I'll try to remember." 65

"Well, look. These will take root in about a month. Then she must set them out, about a foot apart in good rich earth like this, see?" She lifted a handful of dark soil for him to look at. "They'll grow fast and tall. Now remember this: In July tell her to cut them down, about eight inches from the ground."

"Before they bloom?" he asked.

"Yes, before they bloom." Her face was tight with eagerness. "They'll grow right up again. About the last of September the buds will start."

She stopped and seemed perplexed. "It's the budding that takes the most care," she said hesitantly. "I don't know how to tell you." She looked deep into his eyes, searchingly. Her mouth opened a little, and she seemed to be listening. "I'll try to tell you," she said. "Did you ever hear of planting hands?"

"Can't say I have, ma'am." 70

"Well, I can only tell you what it feels like. It's when you're picking off the buds you don't want. Everything goes right down into your fingertips. You watch your fingers work. They do it themselves. You can feel how it is. They pick and pick the buds. They never make a mistake. They're with the plant. Do you see? Your fingers and the plant. You can feel that, right up your arm. They know. They never make a mistake. You can feel it. When you're like that you can't do anything wrong. Do you see that? Can you understand that?"

She was kneeling on the ground looking up at him. Her breast swelled passionately.

The man's eyes narrowed. He looked away self-consciously. "Maybe I know," he said. "Sometimes in the night in the wagon there — "

Elisa's voice grew husky. She broke in on him, "I've never lived as you do, but I know what you mean. When the night is dark — why, the stars are sharp-pointed, and there's quiet. Why, you rise up and up! Every pointed star gets driven into your body. It's like that. Hot and sharp and — lovely." 75

Kneeling there, her hand went out toward his legs in the greasy black trousers. Her hesitant fingers almost touched the cloth. Then her hand dropped to the ground. She crouched low like a fawning dog.

He said, "It's nice, just like you say. Only when you don't have no dinner, it ain't."

She stood up then, very straight, and her face was ashamed. She held the flower pot out to him and placed it gently in his arms. "Here. Put it in your wagon, on the seat, where you can watch it. Maybe I can find something for you to do."

At the back of the house she dug in the can pile and found two old and battered aluminum saucepans. She carried them back and gave them to him. "Here, maybe you can fix these."

His manner changed. He became professional. "Good as new I can fix them." At the back of his wagon he set a little anvil, and out of an oily tool box dug a small machine hammer. Elisa came through the gate to watch him while he pounded out the dents in the kettles. His mouth grew sure and knowing. At a difficult part of the work he sucked his under-lip.

"You sleep right in the wagon?" Elisa asked. 80

"Right in the wagon, ma'am. Rain or shine I'm dry as a cow in there."

"It must be nice," she said. "It must be very nice. I wish women could do such things."

"It ain't the right kind of a life for a woman."

Her upper lip raised a little, showing her teeth. "How do you know? How can you tell?" she said.

"I don't know, ma'am," he protested. "Of course I don't know. Now 85 here's your kettles, done. You don't have to buy no new ones."

"How much?"

"Oh, fifty cents'll do. I keep my prices down and my work good. That's why I have all them satisfied customers up and down the highway."

Elisa brought him a fifty-cent piece from the house and dropped it in his hand. "You might be surprised to have a rival some time. I can sharpen scissors, too. And I can beat the dents out of little pots. I could show you what a woman might do."

He put his hammer back in the oily box and shoved the little anvil out of sight. "It would be a lonely life for a woman, ma'am, and a scarey life, too, with animals creeping under the wagon all night." He climbed over the single-tree, steadying himself with a hand on the burro's white rump. He settled himself in the seat, picked up the lines. "Thank you kindly, ma'am," he said. "I'll do like you told me; I'll go back and catch the Salinas road."

"Mind," she called, "if you're long in getting there, keep the sand damp." 90

"Sand, ma'am? . . . Sand? Oh, sure. You mean around the chrysanthemums. Sure I will." He clucked his tongue. The beasts leaned luxuriously into their collars. The mongrel dog took his place between the back wheels. The wagon turned and crawled out the entrance road and back the way it had come, along the river.

Elisa stood in front of her wire fence watching the slow progress of the caravan. Her shoulders were straight, her head thrown back, her eyes half-closed, so that the scene came vaguely into them. Her lips moved silently, forming the words "Good-bye — good-bye." Then she whispered, "That's a bright direction. There's a glowing there." The sound of her whisper startled her. She shook herself free and looked about to see whether anyone had been listening. Only the dogs had heard. They lifted their heads toward her from their sleeping in the dust, and then stretched out their chins and settled asleep again. Elisa turned and ran hurriedly into the house.

In the kitchen she reached behind the stove and felt the water tank. It was full of hot water from the noonday cooking. In the bathroom she tore off her soiled clothes and flung them into the corner. And then she scrubbed herself with a little block of pumice, legs and thighs, loins and chest and arms, until her skin was scratched and red. When she had dried herself she stood in front of a mirror in her bedroom and looked at her body. She tightened her stomach and threw out her chest. She turned and looked over her shoulder at her back.

After a while she began to dress, slowly. She put on her newest under-clothing and her nicest stockings and the dress which was the symbol of her prettiness. She worked carefully on her hair, penciled her eyebrows and rouged her lips.

Before she was finished she heard the little thunder of hoofs and the shouts of Henry and his helper as they drove the red steers into the corral. She heard the gate bang shut and set herself for Henry's arrival. 95

His step sounded on the porch. He entered the house calling, "Elisa, where are you?"

"In my room, dressing. I'm not ready. There's hot water for your bath. Hurry up. It's getting late."

When she heard him splashing in the tub, Elisa laid his dark suit on the bed, and shirt and socks and tie beside it. She stood his polished shoes on the floor beside the bed. Then she went to the porch and sat primly and stiffly down. She looked toward the river road where the willow-line was still yellow with frosted leaves so that under the high grey fog they seemed a thin band of sunshine. This was the only color in the grey afternoon. She sat unmoving for a long time. Her eyes blinked rarely.

Henry came banging out of the door, shoving his tie inside his vest as he came. Elisa stiffened and her face grew tight. Henry stopped short and looked at her. "Why — why, Elisa. You look so nice!"

"Nice? You think I look nice? What do you mean by 'nice'?" 100

Henry blundered on. "I don't know. I mean you look different, strong and happy."

"I am strong? Yes, strong. What do you mean 'strong'?"

He looked bewildered. "You're playing some kind of a game," he said helplessly. "It's a kind of a play. You look strong enough to break a calf over your knee, happy enough to eat it like a watermelon."

For a second she lost her rigidity. "Henry! Don't talk like that. You didn't know what you said." She grew complete again. "I'm strong," she boasted. "I never knew before how strong."

Henry looked down toward the tractor shed, and when he brought his eyes back to her, they were his own again. "I'll get out the car. You can put on your coat while I'm starting." 105

Elisa went into the house. She heard him drive to the gate and idle down his motor, and then she took a long time to put on her hat. She pulled it here and pressed it there. When Henry turned the motor off she slipped into her coat and went out.

The little roadster bounced along on the dirt road by the river, raising the birds and driving the rabbits into the brush. Two cranes flapped heavily over the willow-line and dropped into the river-bed.

Far ahead on the road Elisa saw a dark speck. She knew.

She tried not to look as they passed it, but her eyes would not obey. She whispered to herself sadly, "He might have thrown them off the road. That wouldn't have been much trouble, not very much. But he kept the pot," she explained. "He had to keep the pot. That's why he couldn't get them off the road."

The roadster turned a bend and she saw the caravan ahead. She swung   110
full around toward her husband so she could not see the little covered wagon and the mismatched team as the car passed them.

In a moment it was over. The thing was done. She did not look back.

She said loudly, to be heard above the motor, "It will be good, tonight, a good dinner."

"Now you're changed again," Henry complained. He took one hand from the wheel and patted her knee. "I ought to take you in to dinner oftener. It would be good for both of us. We get so heavy out on the ranch."

"Henry," she asked, "could we have wine at dinner?"

"Sure we could. Say! That will be fine."   115

She was silent for a while; then she said, "Henry, at those prize fights, do the men hurt each other very much?"

"Sometimes a little, not often. Why?"

"Well, I've read how they break noses, and blood runs down their chests. I've read how the fighting gloves get heavy and soggy with blood."

He looked around at her. "What's the matter, Elisa? I didn't know you read things like that." He brought the car to a stop, then turned to the right over the Salinas River bridge.

"Do any women ever go to the fights?" she asked.   120

"Oh, sure, some. What's the matter, Elisa? Do you want to go? I don't think you'd like it, but I'll take you if you really want to go."

She relaxed limply in the seat. "Oh, no. No. I don't want to go. I'm sure I don't." Her face was turned away from him. "It will be enough if we can have wine. It will be plenty." She turned up her coat collar so he could not see that she was crying weakly — like an old woman.

QUESTIONS

1. When we first meet Elisa in her garden, with what details does Steinbeck delineate her character for us?
2. Elisa works inside a "wire fence that protected her flower garden from cattle and dogs and chickens" (paragraph 9). What does this wire fence suggest?
3. How would you describe Henry and Elisa's marriage? Cite details from the story to support your description.
4. For what motive does the traveling salesman take an interest in Elisa's chrysanthemums? What immediate effect does his interest have on Elisa?

John Steinbeck 213

5. For what possible purpose does Steinbeck give us such a detailed account of Elisa's preparations for her evening out? Notice her tearing off her soiled clothes, her scrubbing her body with pumice (paragraphs 93 – 94).
6. Of what significance to Elisa is the sight of the contents of the flower pot discarded in the road? Notice that, as her husband's car overtakes the covered wagon, Elisa averts her eyes; and then Steinbeck adds, "In a moment it was over. The thing was done. She did not look back" (paragraph 111). Explain this passage.
7. How do you interpret Elisa's asking for wine with dinner? How do you account for her new interest in prize fights?
8. In a sentence, try to state this short story's theme.
9. Why are Elisa Allen's chrysanthemums so important to this story? Sum up what you understand them to mean.

Alice Munro
WILD SWANS   1978

Alice Munro, one of the bright new comets of Canadian fiction, was born of farm parents in 1931 in Wingham in southwestern Ontario, an area whose small-town characters figure in her stories. She attended the University of Western Ontario and now lives in Clinton, Ontario. She is the mother of three daughters. Her books, all fiction, include Dance of the Happy Shades *(1968);* Lives of Girls and Women *(1971);* Something I've Been Meaning to Tell You *(1974);* The Beggar Maid: Stories of Flo and Rose *(1982), first published in Canada as* Who Do You Think You Are? *(1978); and* The Moons of Jupiter *(1983). "The Wild Swans" comes from* The Beggar Maid, *a related collection of sensitive short stories about a stepmother and her daughter.*

Flo said to watch for White Slavers. She said this was how they operated: an old woman, a motherly or grandmotherly sort, made friends while riding beside you on a bus or train. She offered you candy, which was drugged. Pretty soon you began to droop and mumble, were in no condition to speak for yourself. Oh, help, the woman said, my daughter (granddaughter) is sick, please somebody help me get her off so that she can recover in the fresh air. Up stepped a polite gentleman, pretending to be a stranger, offering assistance. Together, at the next stop, they hustled you off the train or bus, and that was the last the ordinary world ever saw of you. They kept you a prisoner in the White Slave place (to which you had been transported drugged and bound so you wouldn't even know where you were), until such time as you were thoroughly degraded and in despair, your insides torn up by drunken men and invested with vile disease, your mind destroyed by drugs, your hair and teeth fallen out. It took about three years, for you to get to this state. You wouldn't want to go home, then, maybe couldn't remember home, or find your way if you did. So they let you out on the streets.

Flo took ten dollars and put it in a little cloth bag which she sewed to the strap of Rose's slip. Another thing likely to happen was that Rose would get her purse stolen.

Watch out, Flo said as well, for people dressed up as ministers. They were the worst. That disguise was commonly adopted by White Slavers, as well as those after your money.

Rose said she didn't see how she could tell which ones were disguised.

Flo had worked in Toronto once. She had worked as a waitress in a coffee shop in Union Station. That was how she knew all she knew. She never saw sunlight, in those days, except on her days off. But she saw plenty else. She saw a man cut another man's stomach with a knife, just pull out his shirt and do a tidy cut, as if it was a watermelon not a stomach. The stomach's owner just sat looking down surprised, with no time to protest. Flo implied that that was nothing, in Toronto. She saw two bad women (that was what Flo called whores, running the two words together, like badminton) get into a fight, and a man laughed at them, other men stopped and laughed and egged them on, and they had their fists full of each other's hair. At last the police came and took them away, still howling and yelping.

She saw a child die of a fit, too. Its face was black as ink.

"Well I'm not scared," said Rose provokingly. "There's the police, anyway."

"Oh, them! They'd be the first ones to diddle you!"

She did not believe anything Flo said on the subject of sex. Consider the undertaker.

A little bald man, very neatly dressed, would come into the store sometimes and speak to Flo with a placating expression.

"I only wanted a bag of candy. And maybe a few packages of gum. And one or two chocolate bars. Could you go to the trouble of wrapping them?"

Flo in her mock-deferential tone would assure him that she could. She wrapped them in heavy-duty white paper, so they were something like presents. He took his time with the selection, humming and chatting, then dawdled for a while. He might ask how Flo was feeling. And how Rose was, if she was there.

"You look pale. Young girls need fresh air." To Flo he would say, "You work too hard. You've worked hard all your life."

"No rest for the wicked," Flo would say agreeably.

When he went out she hurried to the window. There it was—the old black hearse with its purple curtains.

"He'll be after them today!" Flo would say as the hearse rolled away at a gentle pace, almost a funeral pace. The little man had been an undertaker, but he was retired now. The hearse was retired too. His sons had taken over the undertaking and bought a new one. He drove the old hearse all over the country, looking for women. So Flo said. Rose could not believe it. Flo said he gave them the gum and the candy. Rose said he probably ate them himself. Flo said he had been seen, he had been heard. In mild weather he drove with the windows down, singing, to himself or to somebody out of sight in the back.

Her brow is like the snowdrift
Her throat is like the swan

Flo imitated him singing. Gently overtaking some woman walking on a back road, or resting at a country crossroads. All compliments and courtesy and chocolate bars, offering a ride. Of course every woman who reported being asked said she had turned him down. He never pestered anybody, drove politely on. He called in at houses, and if the husband was home he seemed to like just as well as anything to sit and chat. Wives said that was all he ever did anyway but Flo did not believe it.

"Some women are taken in," she said. "A number." She liked to speculate on what the hearse was like inside. Plush. Plush on the walls and the roof and the floor. Soft purple, the color of the curtains, the color of dark lilacs.

All nonsense, Rose thought. Who could believe it, of a man that age?

Rose was going to Toronto on the train for the first time by herself. She had been once before, but that was with Flo, long before her father died. They took along their own sandwiches and bought milk from the vendor on the train. It was sour. Sour chocolate milk. Rose kept taking tiny sips, unwilling to admit that something so much desired could fail her. Flo sniffed it, then hunted up and down the train until she found the old man in his red jacket, with no teeth and the tray hanging around his neck. She invited him to sample the chocolate milk. She invited people nearby to smell it. He let her have some ginger ale for nothing. It was slightly warm.

"I let him know," Flo said looking around after he had left. "You have to let them know." 20

A woman agreed with her but most people looked out the window. Rose drank the warm ginger ale. Either that, or the scene with the vendor, or the conversation Flo and the agreeing woman now got into about where they came from, why they were going to Toronto, and Rose's morning constipation which was why she was lacking color, or the small amount of chocolate milk she had got inside her, caused her to throw up in the train toilet. All day long she was afraid people in Toronto could smell vomit on her coat.

This time Flo started the trip off by saying, "Keep an eye on her, she's never been away from home before!" to the conductor, then looking around and laughing, to show that was jokingly meant. Then she had to get off. It seemed the conductor had no more need for jokes than Rose had, and no intention of keeping an eye on anybody. He never spoke to Rose except to ask for her ticket. She had a window seat, and was soon extraordinarily happy. She felt Flo receding, West Hanratty flying away from her, her own wearying self discarded as easily as everything else. She loved the towns less and less known. A woman was standing at her back door in her nightgown, not caring if everybody on the train saw her. They were traveling south, out of the snow belt, into an earlier spring, a tenderer sort of landscape. People could grow peach trees in their backyards.

Rose collected in her mind the things she had to look for in Toronto. First, things for Flo. Special stockings for her varicose veins. A special kind of cement for sticking handles on pots. And a full set of dominoes.

For herself Rose wanted to buy hair-remover to put on her arms and legs, and if possible an arrangement of inflatable cushions, supposed to reduce your hips and thighs. She thought they probably had hair-remover in the drugstore in Hanratty, but the woman in there was a friend of Flo's and told everything.

She told Flo who bought hair dye and slimming medicine and French safes. As for the cushion business, you could send away for it but there was sure to be a comment at the Post Office, and Flo knew people there as well. She also planned to buy some bangles, and an angora sweater. She had great hopes of silver bangles and powder-blue angora. She thought they could transform her, make her calm and slender and take the frizz out of her hair, dry her underarms and turn her complexion to pearl.

The money for these things, as well as the money for the trip, came from a prize Rose had won, for writing an essay called "Art and Science in the World of Tomorrow." To her surprise, Flo asked if she could read it, and while she was reading it, she remarked that they must have thought they had to give Rose the prize for swallowing the dictionary. Then she said shyly, "It's very interesting."

She would have to spend the night at Cela McKinney's. Cela McKinney was her father's cousin. She had married a hotel manager and thought she had gone up in the world. But the hotel manager came home one day and sat down on the dining room floor between two chairs and said, "I am never going to leave this house again." Nothing unusual had happened, he had just decided not to go out of the house again, and he didn't, until he died. That had made Cela McKinney odd and nervous. She locked her doors at eight o'clock. She was also very stingy. Supper was usually oatmeal porridge, with raisins. Her house was dark and narrow and smelled like a bank.

The train was filling up. At Brantford a man asked if she would mind if he sat down beside her.

"It's cooler out than you'd think," he said. He offered her part of his newspaper. She said no thanks.

Then lest he think her rude she said it really was cooler. She went on looking out the window at the spring morning. There was no snow left, down here. The trees and bushes seemed to have a paler bark than they did at home. Even the sunlight looked different. It was as different from home, here, as the coast of the Mediterranean would be, or the valleys of California.

"Filthy windows, you'd think they'd take more care," the man said. "Do you travel much by train?"

She said no.

Water was lying in the fields. He nodded at it and said there was a lot this year.

"Heavy snows."

She noticed his saying *snows,* a poetic-sounding word. Anyone at home would have said *snow.*

"I had an unusual experience the other day. I was driving out in the country. In fact I was on my way to see one of my parishioners, a lady with a heart condition — "

She looked quickly at his collar. He was wearing an ordinary shirt and tie and a dark blue suit.

"Oh, yes," he said. "I'm a United Church minister. But I don't always wear my uniform. I wear it for preaching in. I'm off duty today.

"Well as I said I was driving through the country and I saw some Canada geese down on a pond, and I took another look, and there were some swans down with them. A whole great flock of swans. What a lovely sight they were.

They would be on their spring migration, I expect, heading up north. What a spectacle. I never saw anything like it."

Rose was unable to think appreciatively of the wild swans because she was afraid he was going to lead the conversation from them to Nature in general and then to God, the way a minister would feel obliged to do. But he did not, he stopped with the swans.

"A very fine sight. You would have enjoyed them."   40

He was between fifty and sixty years old, Rose thought. He was short, and energetic-looking, with a square ruddy face and bright waves of gray hair combed straight up from his forehead. When she realized he was not going to mention God she felt she ought to show her gratitude.

She said they must have been lovely.

"It wasn't even a regular pond, it was only some water lying in a field. It was just luck the water was lying there and they came down and I came driving by at the right time. Just luck. They come in at the east end of Lake Erie, I think. But I never was lucky enough to see them before."

She turned by degrees to the window, and he returned to his paper. She remained slightly smiling, so as not to seem rude, not to seem to be rejecting conversation altogether. The morning really was cool, and she had taken down her coat off the hook where she put it when she first got on the train, she had spread it over herself, like a lap robe. She had set her purse on the floor when the minister sat down, to give him room. He took the sections of the paper apart, shaking and rustling them in a leisurely, rather showy, way. He seemed to her the sort of person who does everything in a showy way. A ministerial way. He brushed aside the sections he didn't want at the moment. A corner of newspaper touched her leg, just at the edge of her coat.

She thought for some time that it was the paper. Then she said to herself,   45
what if it is a hand? That was the kind of thing she could imagine. She would sometimes look at men's hands, at the fuzz on their forearms, their concentrating profiles. She would think about everything they could do. Even the stupid ones. For instance the driver-salesman who brought the bread to Flo's store. The ripeness and confidence of manner, the settled mixture of ease and alertness with which he handled the bread truck. A fold of mature belly over the belt did not displease her. Another time she had her eye on the French teacher at school. Not a Frenchman at all, really, his name was McLaren, but Rose thought teaching French had rubbed off on him, made him look like one. Quick and sallow; sharp shoulders; hooked nose and sad eyes. She saw him lapping and coiling his way through slow pleasures, a perfect autocrat of indulgences. She had a considerable longing to be somebody's object. Pounded, pleasured, reduced, exhausted.

But what if it was a hand? What if it really was a hand? She shifted slightly, moved as much as she could toward the window. Her imagination seemed to have created this reality, a reality she was not prepared for at all. She found it alarming. She was concentrating on that leg, that bit of skin with the stocking over it. She could not bring herself to look. Was there a pressure, or was there not? She shifted again. Her legs had been, and remained, tightly closed. It was. It was a hand. It was a hand's pressure.

Please don't. That was what she tried to say. She shaped the words in her mind, tried them out, then couldn't get them past her lips. Why was that? The embarrassment, was it, the fear that people might hear? People were all around them, the seats were full.

It was not only that.

She did manage to look at him, not raising her head but turning it cautiously. He had tilted his seat back and closed his eyes. There was his dark blue suit sleeve, disappearing under the newspaper. He had arranged the paper so that it overlapped Rose's coat. His hand was underneath, simply resting, as if flung out in sleep.

Now, Rose could have shifted the newspaper and removed her coat. If he was not asleep, he would have been obliged to draw back his hand. If he was asleep, if he did not draw it back, she could have whispered, *Excuse me,* and set his hand firmly on his own knee. This solution, so obvious and foolproof, did not occur to her. And she would have to wonder, why not? The minister's hand was not, or not yet, at all welcome to her. It made her feel uncomfortable, resentful, slightly disgusted, trapped and wary. But she could not take charge of it, to reject it. She could not insist that it was there, when he seemed to be insisting that it was not. How could she declare him responsible, when he lay there so harmless and trusting, resting himself before his busy day, with such a pleased and healthy face? A man older than her father would be, if he were living, a man used to deference, an appreciator of Nature, delighter in wild swans. If she did say *Please don't* she was sure he would ignore her, as if overlooking some silliness or impoliteness on her part. She knew that as soon as she said it she would hope he had not heard.

But there was more to it than that. Curiosity. More constant, more imperious, than any lust. A lust in itself, that will make you draw back and wait, wait too long, risk almost anything, just to see what will happen. *To see what will happen.*

The hand began, over the next several miles, the most delicate, the most timid, pressures and investigations. Not asleep. Or if he was, his hand wasn't. She did feel disgust. She felt a faint, wandering nausea. She thought of flesh: lumps of flesh, pink snouts, fat tongues, blunt fingers, all on their way trotting and creeping and lolling and rubbing, looking for their comfort. She thought of cats in heat rubbing themselves along the top of board fences, yowling with their miserable complaint. It was pitiful, infantile, this itching and shoving and squeezing. Spongy tissues, inflamed membranes, tormented nerve-ends, shameful smells; humiliation.

All that was starting. His hand, that she wouldn't ever have wanted to hold, that she wouldn't have squeezed back, his stubborn patient hand was able, after all, to get the ferns to rustle and the streams to flow, to waken a sly luxuriance.

Nevertheless, she would rather not. She would still rather not. Please remove this, she said out the window. Stop it, please, she said to the stumps and barns. The hand moved up her leg past the top of her stocking to her bare skin, had moved higher, under her suspender, reached her underpants and the lower part of her belly. Her legs were still crossed, pinched together. While her legs stayed crossed she could lay claim to innocence, she had not admitted anything. She could still believe that she would stop this in a minute. Nothing was going to happen, nothing more. Her legs were never going to open.

But they were. They were. As the train crossed the Niagara Escarpment

Alice Munro   219

above Dundas, as they looked down at the preglacial valley, the silver-wooded rubble of little hills, as they came sliding down to the shores of Lake Ontario, she would make this slow, and silent, and definite, declaration, perhaps disappointing as much as satisfying the hand's owner. He would not lift his eyelids, his face would not alter, his fingers would not hesitate, but would go powerfully and discreetly to work. Invasion, and welcome, and sunlight flashing far and wide on the lake water; miles of bare orchards stirring round Burlington.

This was disgrace, this was beggary. But what harm in that, we say to ourselves at such moments, what harm in anything, the worse the better, as we ride the cold wave of greed, of greedy assent. A stranger's hand, or root vegetables or humble kitchen tools that people tell jokes about; the world is tumbling with innocent-seeming objects ready to declare themselves, slippery and obliging. She was careful of her breathing. She could not believe this. Victim and accomplice she was borne past Glassco's Jams and Marmalades, past the big pulsating pipes of oil refineries. They glided into suburbs where bedsheets, and towels used to wipe up intimate stains, flapped leeringly on the clotheslines, where even the children seemed to be frolicking lewdly in the school-yards, and the very truckdrivers stopped at the railway crossings must be thrusting their thumbs gleefully into curled hands. Such cunning antics now, such popular visions. The gates and towers of the Exhibition Grounds came into view, the painted domes and pillars floated marvelously against her eyelids' rosy sky. Then flew apart in celebration. You could have had such a flock of birds, wild swans, even, wakened under one big dome together, exploding from it, taking to the sky.

She bit the edge of her tongue. Very soon the conductor passed through the train, to stir the travelers, warn them back to life.

In the darkness under the station the United Church minister, refreshed, opened his eyes and got his paper folded together, then asked if she would like some help with her coat. His gallantry was self-satisfied, dismissive. No, said Rose, with a sore tongue. He hurried out of the train ahead of her. She did not see him in the station. She never saw him again in her life. But he remained on call, so to speak, for years and years, ready to slip into place at a critical moment, without even any regard, later on, for husband or lovers. What recommended him? She could never understand it. His simplicity, his arrogance, his perversely appealing lack of handsomeness, even of ordinary grown-up masculinity? When he stood up she saw that he was shorter even than she had thought, that his face was pink and shiny, that there was something crude and pushy and childish about him.

Was he a minister, really, or was that only what he said? Flo had mentioned people who were not ministers, dressed up as if they were. Not real ministers dressed as if they were not. Or, stranger still, men who were not real ministers pretending to be real but dressed as if they were not. But that she had come as close as she had, to what could happen, was an unwelcome thing. Rose walked through Union Station feeling the little bag with the ten dollars rubbing at her, knew she would feel it all day long, rubbing its reminder against her skin.

She couldn't stop getting Flo's messages, even with that. She remembered, because she was in Union Station, that there was a girl named Mavis working here, in the Gift Shop, when Flo was working in the coffee shop.

Mavis had warts on her eyelids that looked like they were going to turn into sties but they didn't, they went away. Maybe she had them removed, Flo didn't ask. She was very good-looking, without them. There was a movie star in those days she looked a lot like. The movie star's name was Frances Farmer.

Frances Farmer. Rose had never heard of her.

That was the name. And Mavis went and bought herself a big hat that dipped over one eye and a dress entirely made of lace. She went off for the weekend to Georgian Bay, to a resort up there. She booked herself in under the name of Florence Farmer. To give everybody the idea she was really the other one, Frances Farmer, but calling herself Florence because she was on holiday and didn't want to be recognized. She had a little cigarette holder that was black and mother-of-pearl. She could have been arrested, Flo said. For the *nerve.*

Rose almost went over to the Gift Shop, to see if Mavis was still there and if she could recognize her. She thought it would be an especially fine thing, to manage a transformation like that. To dare it; to get away with it, to enter on preposterous adventures in your own, but newly named, skin.

QUESTIONS

1. By what hints does Munro indicate Rose's age and her level of sophistication?
2. What sort of person is Flo? Cite passages that reveal her attitude toward sex. What effect on Rose do her warnings seem to have?
3. Where in the early part of the story do you find *foreshadowing?* (The word is defined on page 9.)
4. What, if anything, does the minister's mention of the wild swans contribute to our understanding of his character? What part does his appreciation of the swans play in Rose's behavior toward him?
5. What forces conspire to prevent Rose from asking her seatmate to take his hand off her leg? How would you explain her apparent lack of resistance to his advances?
6. Where in "Wild Swans" does the point of view shift? What do these shifts contribute to the story's effect?
7. How are the references to the retired undertaker and his old hearse, Cela McKinney and her hotel manager husband, and the shopgirl named Mavis more than entertaining digressions?
8. What is the tone of Munro's story? What passages make it clear to you?
9. Reread the passages that refer to wild swans. What do the swans suggest?
10. What other details in the story are suggestive enough to be called symbolic?
11. What similarities do you find between this story and "Where Are You Going, Where Have You Been?" by Joyce Carol Oates (in Stories for Further Reading)? In what vital ways are the two stories *not* alike?

SUGGESTIONS FOR WRITING

1. Reexamine one of these stories you have already read: "A Rose for Emily," "The Tell-Tale Heart," "Araby," "Greasy Lake," "Barn Burning," "A Clean, Well-Lighted Place," "The Lottery," "Revelation," "The Open Boat." Reread carefully, looking for rich hints. In writing, indicate what actions and objects now seem to you symbolic in their suggestions. Do these actions or objects point toward any central theme in the story? (Note: Watch out for Poe. He eschews messages, and his stories keep away from central themes.)

2. For an alternate topic, look for symbols in a story you have not read before. In the Stories for Further Reading, you might take a look at "The Birthmark," "The Garden-Party," "A Hunger Artist," "The Portable Phonograph," "The Night of the Curlews," and "Where Are You Going, Where Have You Been?"
3. Write a short comment inspired by the title "Absolutely Nothing Is Symbolic" or "There Isn't a Thing You Can't Make a Symbol of." Draw upon your experiences in reading the stories in this chapter, or any other literature. Give concrete examples.
4. Pick a tangible *thing* that intrigues you — an animal, a plant, or another part of nature; a house or another man-made object. Recall it, observe it, meditate on it. Then write an opening paragraph for a story that will make a symbol of that object, doing your best to fill the passage with hints. For inspiration, look back over John Steinbeck's "The Chrysanthemums" and Alice Munro's "Wild Swans."

9 Evaluating a Story

When we **evaluate** a story, we consider it and place a value on it. Perhaps we decide that it is a masterpiece, or a bit of trash, or (like most fiction we read) a work of some value in between. No cut-and-dried method of judgment will work on every story, and so in this chapter I have none to propose. Still, there are things we can look for in a story — usually clear indications of its author's competence.

In judging the quality of a baseball glove, we first have to be aware that a catcher's mitt differs — for good reasons — from a first baseman's glove. It is no less true that, before evaluating a story, we need to recognize its nature. To see, for instance, that a story is a fable (or perhaps a tale) may save us from condemning it as a failed short story.

Good critics of literature have at least a working knowledge of some of its conventions. By **conventions** we mean usual devices and features of a literary work, by which we can recognize its kind. When in movies or on television we watch a yarn about a sinister old mansion full of horrors, we recognize the conventions of that long-lived species of fiction, the **Gothic story.** *The Castle of Otranto, A Gothic Story* (1764), by English author Horace Walpole, started the genre, supplied its name, and established its favorite trappings. In Walpole's short novel, Otranto is a cobwebbed ruin full of underground passages and massive doors that slam unexpectedly. There are awful objects: a statue that bleeds, a portrait that steps from its frame, a giant helmet that falls and leaves its victim "dashed to pieces." Atmosphere is essential to a Gothic story: dusty halls, shadowy landscapes, whispering servants "seen at a distance imperfectly through the dusk" (I quote from Anne Radcliffe's novel *The Mysteries of Udolpho,* 1794). In Charlotte Brontë's *Jane Eyre* (1847), we find the model for a legion of heroines in the Gothic fiction of our own day. In the best-selling Gothic romances of Victoria Holt, Phyllis A. Whitney, and others, young women similarly find love while working as governesses in ominous mansions. Lacking for English castles, American authors of Gothic fiction have had to make do with dark old houses — like those in Nathaniel Hawthorne's novel *The House of the Seven Gables* and in the short stories of Edgar Allan Poe, such as "The Tell-Tale Heart" (page 38). William Faulkner, who brought the tradition to Mississippi, gives "A Rose for Emily" some familiar conventions: a rundown mansion, a mysterious servant, a madwoman, a hideous secret. But Faulkner's story, in its portrait of an aristocrat who refuses to admit that her world has vanished, goes far beyond Gothic conventions. Evidently, when you set up court as a judge of stories, to recognize such conventions will be an advantage. Knowing a Gothic story for what it is, you won't condemn it for lacking "realism." And to be aware of the Gothic elements in "A Rose for Emily" may help you see how original Faulkner manages to be, though employing some handed-down conventions.

Is the story a piece of commercial fiction tailored to a formula, or is it unique in its design? You can't demand the subtlety of a Katherine Anne Porter of a writer of hard-boiled detective stories. Neither can you put down "The Jilting of Granny Weatherall" for lacking slam-bang action. Some stories are no more than light, entertaining bits of fluff — no point in damning them, unless you dislike fluff or find them written badly. Of course, you are within your rights to prefer solidity to fluff, or to prefer a Porter story to a typical paperback romance by a hack writer. James Thurber's "The Catbird Seat," though a simpler and briefer story than Leo Tolstoi's "The Death of Ivan Ilych," is no less finished, complete, and satisfactory a work of art. Yet, considered in another light, Tolstoi's short novel may well seem a greater work than Thurber's. It reveals greater meaning and enfolds more life.

Masterpieces often have flaws; and so, whenever we can, we need to consider a story in its entirety. Some novels by Thomas Hardy and by Theodore Dreiser impress (on the whole), despite passages of stilted dialogue and other clumsy writing. If a story totally fails to enlist our sympathies, probably it suffers from some basic ineptitude: choice of an inappropriate point of view, a style ill suited to its theme, or possibly insufficient knowledge of human beings. In some ineffectual stories, things important to the writer (and to the story) remain private and unmentioned. In other stories, the writer's interests may be perfectly clear but they may not interest the reader, for they are not presented with sufficient art.

Some stories fail from **sentimentality,** a defect in a work whose writer seems to feel tremendous emotion and implies that we too should feel it, but does not provide us enough reason to share such feelings. Sentimentality is rampant in televised weekday afternoon soap operas, whose characters usually palpitate with passion for reasons not quite known, and who speak in melodramatic tones as if heralding the end of the world. In some fiction, conventional objects (locks of baby hair, posthumously awarded medals, pressed roses) frequently signal, "Let's have a good cry!" Revisiting home after her marriage, the character Amelia in William Makepeace Thackeray's *Vanity Fair* effuses about the bed she slept in when a virgin: "Dear little bed! how many a long night had she wept on its pillow."[1] Teary sentimentality is more common in nineteenth-

[1]Sentimentality in fiction is older than the Victorians. Popular in eighteenth-century England, the **sentimental novel** (or **novel of sensibility**) specialized in characters whose ability to shed

century fiction than in ours. We have gone to the other extreme, some critics think, into a sentimentality of the violent and the hard-boiled. But in a grossly sentimental work of any kind, failure inheres in our refusal to go along with the author's implied attitudes. We laugh when we are expected to cry, feel delight when we are supposed to be horrified.

In evaluating a story, we may usefully ask a few questions:

1. What is the tone of the story? By what means and how effectively is it communicated?
2. What is the point of view? Does it seem appropriate and effective in this story? Imagine the story told from a different point of view; would such a change be for the worse or for the better?
3. Does the story show us unique and individual scenes, events, and characters — or weary stereotypes?
4. Are any symbols evident? If so, do they direct us to the story's central theme, or do they distract us from it?
5. How appropriate to the theme of the story, and to its subject matter, are its tone and style? Is it ever difficult or impossible to sympathize with the attitudes of the author (insofar as we can tell what they are)?
6. Does our interest in the story mainly depend on following its plot, on finding out what will happen next? Or does the author go beyond the events to show us what they mean? Are the events (however fantastic) credible, or are they incredibly melodramatic? Does the plot greatly depend upon farfetched coincidence?
7. Has the writer caused characters, events, and settings to come alive? Are they full of breath and motion, or simply told about in the abstract ("She was a lovable girl whose life had been highly exciting")? Unless the story is a fable or a tale, which need no detailed description or deep portrayal of character, then we may well expect the story to contain enough vividly imagined detail to make us believe in it.

Suggestions for Writing

1. In a short essay, take two stories that you find differing markedly in quality and evaluate them, giving evidence to support your judgments. Stories similar enough to compare might include two character studies of women, as in "Revelation" and "The Chrysanthemums."
2. Write a blast against a story in this book that you dislike intensely. Stick to the text of the story in making your criticisms and support your charges with plenty of evidence.
3. By comparing two stories that strike you as similar (" 'The Lottery' and 'The Hunger Artist': Two Stories of Human Sacrifice"), evaluate them.

---

quick and copious tears signified their virtuous hearts. Oliver Goldsmith's *The Vicar of Wakefield* (1766) and Henry Mackenzie's *The Man of Feeling* (1771) are classics of the genre. An abundance of tears does not prevent such novels from having merit.

10 Reading a Novel

Among the forms of imaginative literature in our language, the novel has been the favorite of both writers and readers for more than two hundred years. Broadly defined, a **novel** is a book-length story in prose, whose author tries to create the sense that while we read, we experience actual life.

This sense of actuality, also found in artful short stories, may be the quality that sets the novel apart from other long prose narratives. Why do we not apply the name *novel* to, for instance, *Gulliver's Travels*? In his marvel-filled account of Lemuel Gulliver's voyages among pygmies, giants, civilized horses, and noxious humanoid swine, Jonathan Swift does not seem primarily to care if we find his story credible. Though he arrays the adventures of Gulliver in painstaking detail (and, ironically, has Gulliver swear to the truth of them), Swift neither attempts nor achieves a convincing illusion of life. For his book is a fantastic satire that finds resemblances between noble horses and man's reasoning faculties, between debased apes and man's kinship with the beasts.

Unlike other major literary forms — drama, lyric, ballad, and epic — the novel is a relative newcomer. Originally, the drama in ancient Greece came alive only when actors performed it; the epic or heroic poem (from the classic *Iliad* through the Old English *Beowulf*), only when a bard sang or chanted it. But the English novel came to maturity in literate times, in the eighteenth century, and by its nature was something different: a story to be communicated silently, at whatever moment and at whatever pace (whether quickly or slowly and meditatively) the reader desired.

Some definitions of the novel would more strictly limit its province. "The Novel is a picture of real life and manners, and of the time in which it was written," declared Clara Reeve in 1785, thus distinguishing the novel from the romance, which "describes what never happened nor is likely to happen." By so specifying that the novel depicts life in the present day, the critic was probably observing the derivation of the word *novel*. Akin to the French word for "news" *(nouvelles)*, it comes from the Italian *novella* ("something new and small"), a term applied to a newly made story taking place in recent times, and not a traditional story taking place long ago.

Also drawing a line between novel and romance, Nathaniel Hawthorne, in his preface to *The House of the Seven Gables* (1851), restricted the novel "not merely to the possible, but to the probable and ordinary course of man's experience." A **romance** had no such limitations. Such a definition would deny the name of *novel* to any fantastic or speculative story — to, say, the gothic novel and the science fiction novel. Carefully bestowed, the labels *novel* and *romance* may be useful to distinguish between the true-to-life story of usual people in ordinary places (such as George Eliot's *Silas Marner* or John Updike's *Couples*) and the larger-than-life story of daring deeds and high adventure, set in the past or future or in some timeless land (such as Walter Scott's *Ivanhoe* or J. R. R. Tolkien's *Lord of the Rings*). But the labels are difficult to apply to much modern fiction, in which ordinary life is sometimes mingled with outlandishness. Who can say that James Joyce's *Ulysses* is not a novel, though it contains moments of dream and drunken hallucination? (At one moment, a cake of soap rises where the moon ought to be.) And yet the total effect, as in any successful novel, is a sense of the actual.

This sense of the actual is, perhaps, the hallmark of a novel, whether or not the events it relates are literally possible. To achieve this sense, novelists have employed many devices, and frequently have tried to pass off their storytelling as reporting. Nathaniel Hawthorne, in his introduction to *The Scarlet Letter*, gives a minute account of his finding documents on which he claims to base his novel, tied with a faded red ribbon and gathering dust in a customshouse. More recently, Vladimir Nabokov's *Pale Fire* (1962) tells its story in the form of a scholarly edition of a 999-line poem, complete with a biographical commentary by a friend of the late poet. Samuel Richardson's casting *Pamela* (1740) into the form of personal letters helped lend the story an appearance of being not invented, but discovered. Another method favored by early novelists was to write as though setting down a memoir or an autobiography. Daniel Defoe, whose skill in feigning such memoirs was phenomenal, even succeeded in writing the supposedly true confessions of a woman retired from a life of crime, *Moll Flanders* (1722), and in maintaining a vivid truthfulness:

> Going through Aldersgate Street, there was a pretty little child who had been at a dancing-school, and was going home all alone; and my prompter, like a true devil, set me upon this innocent creature. I talked to it, and it prattled to me again, and I took it by the hand and led it along till I came to a paved alley that goes into Bartholomew Close, and I led it in there. The child said that was not its way home. I said, "Yes, my dear, it is; I'll show you the way home." The child had a little necklace on of gold beads, and I had my eye upon that, and in the dark of the alley I stooped, pretending to mend the child's clog that was loose, and took off her necklace, and the child never felt it, and so led the child on again.

Here, I say, the devil put me upon killing the child in the dark alley, that it might not cry, but the very thought frighted me so that I was ready to drop down; but I turned the child about and bade it go back again. . . . The last affair left no great concern upon me, for as I did the poor child no harm, I only said to myself, I had given the parents a just reproof for their negligence in leaving the poor little lamb to come home by itself, and it would teach them to take more care of it another time.

What could sound more like the voice of an experienced child-robber than this manner of excusing her crime, and even justifying it?

Informed that a student had given up the study of mathematics to become a novelist, the logician David Hilbert drily remarked, "It was just as well: he did not have enough imagination to become a first-rate mathematician."[1] It is true that some novelists place great emphasis on research and notetaking. Arthur Halley, author of bestsellers such as *Wheels* (about the Detroit car industry) and *Airport,* reportedly starts work on a novel by interviewing people in whatever glamorous profession he plans to expose, gathering stacks of note cards to make sure that his slightest detail is accurate. Clearly, however, any novel can grow to completion only through a procedure of creation, selection, and arrangement. Raw facts cannot leap into a novel by themselves — whether the novel is a paperback shocker about a famous crime, or Theodore Dreiser's impressive study of a murder case, inspired by newspaper accounts, *An American Tragedy.*

In "The Open Boat," Stephen Crane brings high literary art to bear upon his own experience. The result is a short story based on fact. More recently, we have heard much about the **nonfiction novel,** in which the author presents actual people and events in story form. Norman Mailer, in *The Executioner's Song* (1979), chronicles the life and death of Gary Gilmore, the Utah murderer who demanded his own execution. Truman Capote's *In Cold Blood* (1966) sets forth an account of crime and punishment in Kansas, based on interviews with the accused and other principals. Perhaps the name "nonfiction novel" (Capote's name for it) or "true life novel" (as Mailer calls his Gilmore story) is newer than the form. In the past, writers of autobiography have cast their memoirs into what looks like novel form: Richard Wright in *Black Boy* (1945), William Burroughs in *Junkie* (1953). Derived not from the author's memory but from his reporting, John Hersey's *Hiroshima* (1946) reconstructs the lives of six survivors of the atom bomb as if they were fictional. In reading such works we may nearly forget we are reading literal truth, so well do the techniques of the novel lend remembered facts an air of immediacy.

A familiar kind of fiction that claims a basis in fact is the **historical novel,** a detailed reconstruction of life in another time, perhaps in another place. In some historical novels the author attempts a faithful picture of daily life in another era, as does Robert Graves in *I, Claudius* (1934), a novel

[1]Quoted by William H. Gass, *Fiction and the Figures of Life* (New York: Knopf, 1970).

of patrician Rome. More often, history is a backdrop for an exciting story of love and heroic adventure. Nathaniel Hawthorne's *The Scarlet Letter* (set in Puritan Boston), Herman Melville's *Moby-Dick* (set in the heyday of Yankee whalers), and Stephen Crane's *The Red Badge of Courage* (set in the battlefields of the Civil War) are historical novels in that their authors lived considerably later than the scenes and events that they depicted — and strove for truthfulness, by imaginative means.

Other varieties of novel will be familiar to anyone who scans the racks of paperback books in any drugstore: the mystery or detective novel, the Western novel, the science fiction novel, and other enduring types. Classified according to less well-known species, novels are sometimes said to belong to a category if they contain some recognizable kind of structure or theme. Such a category is the **bildungsroman** (German for a "novel of growth or development"), sometimes called the **apprenticeship novel** after its classic example, *Wilhelm Meister's Apprenticeship* (1796) by Johann Wolfgang von Goethe. This is the kind of novel in which a youth struggles toward maturity, seeking, perhaps, some consistent world view or philosophy of life. Sometimes the apprenticeship novel is evidently the author's recollection of his own early life: James Joyce's *Portrait of the Artist as a Young Man* and Mark Twain's *Tom Sawyer.*

In a **picaresque novel** (another famous category), a likable scoundrel wanders through adventures, living by his wits, duping the straight citizenry. The name comes from Spanish: *Pícaro,* "rascal" or "rogue." The classic picaresque novel is the anonymous Spanish *Life of Lazarillo de Tormes* (1554), imitated by many English writers, among them Henry Fielding in his story of a London thief and racketeer, *Jonathan Wild* (1743). Mark Twain's *Huckleberry Finn* owes something to the tradition; like early picaresque novels, it is told in episodes rather than in one all-unifying plot and is narrated in the first person by a hero at odds with respectable society ("dismal regular and decent," Huck Finn calls it). In Twain's novel, however, the traveling swindlers who claim to be a duke and a dauphin are much more typical rogues of picaresque fiction than Huck himself, an honest innocent. Modern novels worthy of the name include J. P. Donleavy's *The Ginger Man* (1965), Saul Bellow's *The Adventures of Augie March* (1953), and Erica Jong's *Fanny* (1981).

Mainly (but not merely) a description of size, the term **short novel** refers to a narrative midway in length between a short story and a novel (the latter, according to E. M. Forster, has to have at least 50,000 words). Generally a short novel, like a short story, is focused on just one or two characters but, unlike a short story, has room to reveal them in greater fullness and depth, sometimes taking in a longer span of time. A short novel is included in this book: Leo Tolstoi's *The Death of Ivan Ilych.* Sometimes a short novel is also called a **novelette** (a name formerly much used by magazines that featured long fiction), or a **nouvelle,** or a **novella;** but these names are out of fashion.

Trying to perceive a novel as a whole, we may find it helpful to look for the same elements that we have noticed in reading short stories. By asking ourselves leading questions, we may be drawn more deeply into the novel's world, and may come to recognize and appreciate the techniques of the novelist. Does the novel have themes, or an overall theme? Who is its main character? What is the author's kind of narrative voice? What do we know about the tone, style, and use of irony? Why is this novel written from one point of view rather than from another? If the novel in question is large and thickly populated, it may help to read it with a pencil, taking brief notes. Forced to put the novel aside and later return to it, the reader may find that the notes refresh the memory. Notetaking habits differ, but perhaps these might be no more than, say, "Theme introduced, p. 27," or, "Old clothes dealer, p. 109 — walking symbol?" Some readers find it useful to list briefly whatever each chapter accomplishes. Others make lists of a novel's characters, especially when reading classic Russian novels in which the reader has to recall that Alexey Karamazov is also identified by his pet name Aloysha, or that, in Leo Tolstoi's *Anna Karenina,* Princess Catherine Alexándrovna Shcherbátskaya and "Kitty" are one and the same.

Once our reading of a novel is finished and we prepare to discuss it or write about it, it may be a good idea to browse through it again, rereading brief portions. This method of overall browsing may also help when first approaching a bulky and difficult novel. Just as an explorer mapping unfamiliar territory may find it best to begin by taking an aerial view of it, so too the reader approaching an exceptionally thick and demanding novel may wish, at the start, to look for its general shape. This is the method of some professional book reviewers, who size up a novel (even an easy-to-read spy story, because they are not reading for pleasure) by skimming the first chapter, a middle chapter or two, and the last chapter; then going back and browsing at top speed through the rest. Reading a novel in this grim fashion, of course, the reviewer does not really know it thoroughly, any more than a tourist knows the mind and heart of a foreign people after just strolling in a capital city and riding a tour bus to a few monuments. The reviewer's method will, however, provide a general notion of what the author is doing, and at the very least will tell something of her tone, style, point of view, and competence. We suggest this method only as a way to *approach* a book that, otherwise, the reader might not want to approach at all. It may be a comfort in studying some obdurate-looking or highly experimental novel, such as James Joyce's *Ulysses* or Henry James's *The Sacred Fount.* But the reader will find it necessary to return to the book, in order to know it, and to read it honestly, in detail. There is, of course, no short cut to novel reading, and probably the best method is to settle in comfort and read the book through: with your own eyes, not with the borrowed glasses of literary criticism.

The death of the novel is continually being predicted. The competition of television drama is too much for it, some believe; indeed, some evidence says that such competition is taking hold. In Brittany, France, when antigovernment protesters blew up the only television transmitter in the province, booksellers the very next day reported their business increased by as much as twenty percent. But recently in England and North America, television dramas have been sending people in vast numbers back to the books dramatized: Tolstoi's *War and Peace,* Evelyn Waugh's *Brideshead Revisited.* Meanwhile, each year new novels by the hundreds continue to appear, their authors wistfully looking for a public. A chosen few reach tens of thousands of readers through book clubs, and, through paperback reprint editions, occasionally millions more. To forecast the end of the novel seems risky. For the novel exercises the imagination of the beholder. At any hour, at a touch of the hand, it opens and (with no warm-up) begins to speak. Once printed, it consumes no further energy. Often so small it may be carried in a pocket, it may yet survive by its ability to contain multitudes (a "capacious vessel," Henry James called it): a thing both a work of art and an amazingly compact system for the storage and retrieval of imagined life.

Suggestions for Writing

1. In one carefully thought-out paragraph, try to sum up what you believe Tolstoi is saying in his short novel, *The Death of Ivan Ilych* (in Stories for Further Reading).
2. Compare Tolstoi's short novel with another story of spiritual awakening: Flannery O'Connor's "Revelation," or Isaac Bashevis Singer's "Gimpel the Fool." In each, what brings about the enlightenment of the central character?
3. Compare the last thoughts of Ivan Ilych with the last thoughts of Katherine Anne Porter's Granny Weatherall.
4. Topic for a long term paper: Read either *War and Peace* or *Anna Karenina* and show how some theme present in *Ivan Ilych* is essential to it as well.
5. Read a novel chosen from a list provided by your instructor, or chosen with your instructor's approval. Selecting some element in it that interests you, write an essay in which you demonstrate the importance to the book of that one element. You might write, for instance, on "The Character of the Monster in Mary Shelley's *Frankenstein"*; for an essay on theme, "A Plea for Paganism in D. H. Lawrence's *The Plumed Serpent"*; "Violence in John Irving's *The Hotel New Hampshire"*; or "Symbolism in *The Scarlet Letter"* (or in *The Great Gatsby*). (Suggestion: You might find it helpful to read the discussion of the method of analysis in "Writing about a Story," page 1353.)

11 Stories for Further Reading

For human intercourse, as soon as we look at it for its own sake and not as a social adjunct, is seen to be haunted by a specter. We cannot understand each other, except in a rough-and-ready way; we cannot reveal ourselves, even when we want to; what we call intimacy is only a makeshift; perfect knowledge is an illusion. But in the novel we can know people perfectly, and, apart from the general pleasure of reading, we can find here a compensation for their dimness in life. In this direction fiction is truer than history, because it goes beyond the evidence, and each of us knows from his own experience that there is something beyond the evidence, and even if the novelist has not got it correctly, well — he has tried.

— E. M. Forster, *Aspects of the Novel*

Leo Tolstoi

THE DEATH OF IVAN ILYCH   1886

Translated by Louise and Aylmer Maude

Leo Tolstoi (1828 – 1910), who inherited the title of Count, was born into a family who owned vast lands in Tula province, Russia. As a young man disgruntled with self and schooling, he left Kazan University without taking a degree. After a period of fast living in Moscow and St. Petersburg, he became an army officer and took part in the siege of Sevastopol in the Crimean War. Returning to his estate, Tolstoi opened a school for the children of serfs, based on the ideas (then radical) that learning should be a joy and that individuals should be taught according to their needs. In 1862 he married young, well-educated Sophia Bers. Thirteen children followed, and Tolstoi's years of tremendous achievement as a novelist. About 1876, after a religious illumination, Tolstoi became convinced that one should do good, eschew alcohol, tobacco, meat, and violence, and stop owning things. These tenets brought him into conflict with his wife and family, the Russian Orthodox Church, and the Czarist government. Tolstoi renounced his lands and his book royalties. He dressed like a peasant, made his own boots, and dug potatoes. From his driven pen poured books, tracts, and articles expounding his radically Christian moral and social ideas. In What Is Art? *(1898) he held that artists have a God-given duty to produce only what most people can understand and appreciate. In his seventh decade Tolstoi returned to the novel, seeing in fiction a means to preach. Yet, impressive though they are,* The Kreutzer Sonata *(1891) and* Resurrection *(1899) have never won readers' love as have his earlier masterpieces* War and Peace *(1863 – 69), that immense saga of Russian society before, during, and after Napoleon's invasion, and* Anna Karenina *(1875 – 77), a compassionate history of the decline and fall of a woman who defies convention.*

I

During an interval in the Melvinski trial in the large building of the Law Courts, the members and public prosecutor met in Ivan Egorovich Shebek's private room, where the conversation turned on the celebrated Krasovski case. Fëdor Vasilievich warmly maintained that it was not subject to their jurisdiction, Ivan Egorovich maintained the contrary, while Peter Ivanovich, not having entered into the discussion at the start, took no part in it but looked through the *Gazette* which had just been handed in.

"Gentlemen," he said, "Ivan Ilych has died!"

"You don't say so!"

"Here, read it yourself," replied Peter Ivanovich, handing Fëdor Vasilievich the paper still damp from the press. Surrounded by a black border were the words: "Praskovya Fëdorovna Golviná, with profound sorrow, informs relatives and friends of the demise of her beloved husband Ivan Ilych Golovin,

Member of the Court of Justice, which occurred on February the 4th of this year 1882. The funeral will take place on Friday at one o'clock in the afternoon."

Ivan Ilych had been a colleague of the gentlemen present and was liked 5 by them all. He had been ill for some weeks with an illness said to be incurable. His post had been kept open for him, but there had been conjectures that in case of his death Alexeev might receive his appointment, and that either Vinnikov or Shtabel would succeed Alexeev. So on receiving the news of Ivan Ilych's death the first thought of each of the gentlemen in that private room was of the changes and promotions it might occasion among themselves or their acquaintances.

"I shall be sure to get Shtabel's place or Vinnikov's," thought Fëdor Vasilievich. "I was promised that long ago, and the promotion means an extra eight hundred rubles a year for me besides the allowance."

"Now I must apply for my brother-in-law's transfer from Kaluga," thought Peter Ivanovich. "My wife will be very glad, and then she won't be able to say that I never do anything for her relations."

"I thought he would never leave his bed again," said Peter Ivanovich aloud. "It's very sad."

"But what really was the matter with him?"

"The doctors couldn't say — at least they could, but each of them said 10 something different. When last I saw him I thought he was getting better."

"And I haven't been to see him since the holidays. I always meant to go."

"Had he any property?"

"I think his wife had a little — but something quite trifling."

"We shall have to go to see her, but they live so terribly far away."

"Far away from you, you mean. Everything's far away from your place." 15

"You see, he never can forgive my living on the other side of the river," said Peter Ivanovich, smiling at Shebek. Then, still talking of the distances between different parts of the city, they returned to the Court.

Besides considerations as to the possible transfers and promotions likely to result from Ivan Ilych's death, the mere fact of the death of a near acquaintance aroused, as usual, in all who heard of it the complacent feeling that "it is he who is dead and not I."

Each one thought or felt, "Well, he's dead but I'm alive!" But the more intimate of Ivan Ilych's acquaintances, his so-called friends, could not help thinking also that they would now have to fulfil the very tiresome demands of propriety by attending the funeral service and paying a visit of condolence to the widow.

Fëdor Vasilievich and Peter Ivanovich had been his nearest acquaintances. Peter Ivanovich had studied law with Ivan Ilych and had considered himself to be under obligations to him.

Having told his wife at dinner-time of Ivan Ilych's death and of his 20 conjecture that it might be possible to get her brother transferred to their circuit, Peter Ivanovich sacrificed his usual nap, put on his evening clothes, and drove to Ivan Ilych's house.

At the entrance stood a carriage and two cabs. Leaning against the wall in the hall downstairs near the cloak-stand was a coffin-lid covered with cloth of gold, ornamented with gold cord and tassels, that had been polished up with metal powder. Two ladies in black were taking off their fur cloaks. Peter Ivanovich recognized one of them as Ivan Ilych's sister, but the other was a stranger to him. His colleague Schwartz was just coming downstairs, but on seeing Peter Ivanovich enter he stopped and winked at him, as if to say: "Ivan Ilych has made a mess of things — not like you and me."

Schwartz's face with his Piccadilly whiskers and his slim figure in evening dress had as usual an air of elegant solemnity which contrasted with the playfulness of his character and had a special piquancy here, or so it seemed to Peter Ivanovich.

Peter Ivanovich allowed the ladies to precede him and slowly followed them upstairs. Schwartz did not come down but remained where he was, and Peter Ivanovich understood that he wanted to arrange where they should play bridge that evening. The ladies went upstairs to the widow's room, and Schwartz with seriously compressed lips but a playful look in his eyes, indicated by a twist of his eyebrows the room to the right where the body lay.

Peter Ivanovich, like everyone else on such occasions, entered feeling uncertain what he would have to do. All he knew was that at such times it is always safe to cross oneself. But he was not quite sure whether one should make obeisances while doing so. He therefore adopted a middle course. On entering the room he began crossing himself and made a slight movement resembling a bow. At the same time, as far as the motion of his head and arm allowed, he surveyed the room. Two young men — apparently nephews, one of whom was a high-school pupil — were leaving the room, crossing themselves as they did so. An old woman was standing motionless, and a lady with strangely arched eyebrows was saying something to her in a whisper. A vigorous, resolute Church Reader, in a frock-coat, was reading something in a loud voice with an expression that precluded any contradiction. The butler's assistant, Gerasim, stepping lightly in front of Peter Ivanovich, was strewing something on the floor. Noticing this, Peter Ivanovich was immediately aware of a faint odor of a decomposing body.

The last time he had called on Ivan Ilych, Peter Ivanovich had seen 25 Gerasim in the study. Ivan Ilych had been particularly fond of him and he was performing the duty of a sick nurse.

Peter Ivanovich continued to make the sign of the cross, slightly inclining his head in an intermediate direction between the coffin, the Reader, and the icons on the table in a corner of the room. Afterwards, when it seemed to him that this movement of his arm in crossing himself had gone on too long, he stopped and began to look at the corpse.

The dead man lay, as dead men always lie, in a specially heavy way, his rigid limbs sunk in the soft cushions of the coffin, with the head forever bowed on the pillow. His yellow waxen brow with bald patches over his sunken temples was thrust up in the way peculiar to the dead, the protruding nose seeming to press on the upper lip. He was much changed and had grown even thinner since Peter Ivanovich had last seen him, but, as is always the case with the dead, his face was handsomer and above all more dignified than when he was alive. The expression on the face said that what was necessary had been accomplished, and accomplished rightly. Besides this there was in that expression a reproach and a warning to the living. This warning seemed to Peter Ivanovich out of place, or at least not applicable to him. He felt a certain discomfort and so he hurriedly crossed himself once more and turned and went out of the door — too hurriedly and too regardless of propriety, as he himself was aware.

Schwartz was waiting for him in the adjoining room with legs spread wide apart and both hands toying with his top-hat behind his back. The mere sight of that playful, well-groomed, and elegant figure refreshed Peter Ivanovich. He felt that Schwartz was above all these happenings and would not surrender to any depressing influences. His very look said that this incident of a church service for Ivan Ilych could not be a sufficient reason for infringing the order of the session — in other words, that it would certainly not prevent his unwrapping a new pack of cards and shuffling them that evening while a footman placed four fresh candles on the table: in fact, that there was no reason for supposing that this incident would hinder their spending the evening agreeably. Indeed he said this in a whisper as Peter Ivanovich passed him, proposing that they should meet for a game at Fëdor Vasilievich's. But apparently Peter Ivanovich was not destined to play bridge that evening. Praskovya Fëdorovna (a short, fat woman who despite all efforts to the contrary had continued to broaden steadily from her shoulders downwards and who had the same extraordinarily arched eyebrows as the lady who had been standing by the coffin), dressed all in black, her head covered with lace, came out of her own room with some other ladies, conducted them to the room where the dead body lay, and said: "The service will begin immediately. Please go in."

Schwartz, making an indefinite bow, stood still, evidently neither accepting nor declining this invitation. Praskovya Fëdorovna, recognizing Peter Ivanovich, sighed, went close up to him, took his hand, and said: "I know you were a true friend of Ivan Ilych . . ." and looked at him awaiting some suitable response. And Peter Ivanovich knew that, just as it had been the right thing to cross himself in that room, so what he had to do here was to press her hand, sigh, and say, "Believe me. . . ." So he did all this and as he did it felt that the desired result had been achieved: that both he and she were touched.

"Come with me. I want to speak to you before it begins," said the widow. "Give me your arm." 30

Peter Ivanovich gave her his arm and they went to the inner rooms, passing Schwartz, who winked at Peter Ivanovich compassionately.

"That does for our bridge! Don't object if we find another player. Perhaps you can cut in when you do escape," said his playful look.

Peter Ivanovich sighed still more deeply and despondently, and Praskovya Fëdorovna pressed his arm gratefully. When they reached the drawing-room, upholstered in pink cretonne and lighted by a dim lamp, they sat down at the table — she on a sofa and Peter Ivanovich on a low pouffe, the springs of which yielded spasmodically under his weight. Praskovya Fëdorovna had been on the point of warning him to take another seat, but felt that such a warning was out of keeping with her present condition and so changed her mind. As he sat down on the pouffe Peter Ivanovich recalled how Ivan Ilych had arranged this room and had consulted him regarding this pink cretonne with green leaves. The whole room was full of furniture and knick-knacks, and on her way to the sofa the lace of the widow's black shawl caught on the carved edge of the table. Peter Ivanovich rose to detach it, and the springs of the pouffe, relieved of his weight, rose also and gave him a push. The widow began detaching her shawl herself, and Peter Ivanovich again sat down, suppressing the rebellious springs of the pouffe under him. But the widow had not quite freed herself and Peter Ivanovich got up again, and again the pouffe rebelled and even creaked. When this was all over she took out a clean cambric handkerchief and began to weep. The episode with the shawl and the struggle with the pouffe had cooled Peter Ivanovich's emotions and he sat there with a sullen look on his face. This awkward situation was interrupted by Sokolov, Ivan Ilych's butler, who came to report that the plot in the cemetery that Praskovya Fëdorovna had chosen would cost two hundred rubles. She stopped weeping and, looking at Peter Ivanovich with the air of a victim, remarked in French that it was very hard for her. Peter Ivanovich made a silent gesture signifying his full conviction that it must indeed be so.

"Please smoke," she said in a magnanimous yet crushed voice, and turned to discuss with Sokolov the price of the plot for the grave.

Peter Ivanovich while lighting his cigarette heard her inquiring very 35
circumstantially into the prices of different plots in the cemetery and finally decide which she would take. When that was done she gave instructions about engaging the choir. Sokolov then left the room.

"I look after everything myself," she told Peter Ivanovich, shifting the albums that lay on the table; and noticing that the table was endangered by his cigarette-ash, she immediately passed him an ashtray, saying as she did so: "I consider it an affectation to say that my grief prevents my attending to practical affairs. On the contrary, if anything can — I won't say console me, but — distract me, it is seeing to everything concerning him." She again took out her handkerchief as if preparing to cry, but suddenly, as if mastering her feeling, she shook herself and began to speak calmly. "But there is something I want to talk to you about."

Peter Ivanovich bowed, keeping control of the springs of the pouffe, which immediately began quivering under him.

"He suffered terribly the last few days."

"Did he?" said Peter Ivanovich.

"Oh, terribly! He screamed unceasingly, not for minutes but for hours. 40
For the last three days he screamed incessantly. It was unendurable. I cannot understand how I bore it; you could hear him three rooms off. Oh, what I have suffered!"

"Is it possible that he was conscious all that time?" asked Peter Ivanovich.

"Yes," she whispered. "To the last moment. He took leave of us a quarter of an hour before he died, and asked us to take Volodya away."

The thought of the sufferings of this man he had known so intimately, first as a merry little boy, then as a school-mate, and later as a grown-up colleague, suddenly struck Peter Ivanovich with horror, despite an unpleasant consciousness of his own and this woman's dissimulation. He again saw that brow, and that nose pressing down on the lip, and felt afraid for himself.

"Three days of frightful suffering and then death! Why, that might suddenly, at any time, happen to me," he thought, and for a moment felt terrified. But — he did not himself know how — the customary reflection at once occurred to him that this had happened to Ivan Ilych and not to him, and that it should not and could not happen to him, and that to think that it could would be yielding to depression which he ought not to do, as Schwartz's expression plainly showed. After which reflection Peter Ivanovich felt reassured, and began to ask with interest about the details of Ivan Ilych's death, as though death was an accident natural to Ivan Ilych but certainly not to himself.

After many details of the really dreadful physical sufferings Ivan Ilych had endured (which details he learnt only from the effect those sufferings had produced on Praskovya Fëdorovna's nerves) the widow apparently found it necessary to get to business. 45

"Oh, Peter Ivanovich, how hard it is! How terribly, terribly hard!" and she again began to weep.

Peter Ivanovich sighed and waited for her to finish blowing her nose. When she had done so he said, "Believe me . . . ." and she again began talking and brought out what was evidently her chief concern with him — namely, to question him as to how she could obtain a grant of money from the government on the occasion of her husband's death. She made it appear that she was asking Peter Ivanovich's advice about her pension, but he soon saw that she already knew about that to the minutest detail, more even than he did himself. She knew how much could be got out of the government in consequence of her husband's death, but wanted to find out whether she could not possibly extract something more. Peter Ivanovich tried to think of some means of doing so, but after reflecting for a while and, out of propriety, condemning the government for its niggardliness, he said he thought that nothing more could be got. Then she sighed and evidently began to devise means of getting rid of her visitor. Noticing this, he put out his cigarette, rose, pressed her hand, and went out into the anteroom.

In the dining-room where the clock stood that Ivan Ilych had liked so much and had bought at an antique shop, Peter Ivanovich met a priest and a few acquaintances who had come to attend the service, and he recognized Ivan Ilych's daughter, a handsome young woman. She was in black and her slim figure appeared slimmer than ever. She had a gloomy, determined, almost angry expression, and bowed to Peter Ivanovich as though he were in some way to blame. Behind her, with the same offended look, stood a wealthy young man, an examining magistrate, whom Peter Ivanovich also knew and who was her fiancé, as he had heard. He bowed mournfully to them and was about to pass into the death-chamber, when from under the stairs appeared the figure of Ivan Ilych's schoolboy son, who was extremely like his father. He seemed a little Ivan Ilych, such as Peter Ivanovich remembered when they studied law together. His tear-stained eyes had in them the look that is seen in the eyes of boys of thirteen or fourteen who are not pure-minded. When he saw Peter Ivanovich he scowled morosely and shamefacedly. Peter Ivanovich nodded to him and entered the death-chamber. The service began: candles, groans, incense, tears, and sobs. Peter Ivanovich stood looking gloomily down at his feet. He did not look once at the dead man, did not yield to any depressing influence, and was one of the first to leave the room. There was no one in the anteroom, but Gerasim darted out of the dead man's room, rummaged with his strong hands among the fur coats to find Peter Ivanovich's, and helped him on with it.

"Well, friend Gerasim," said Peter Ivanovich, so as to say something. "It's a sad affair, isn't it?"

"It's God's will. We shall all come to it some day," said Gerasim, display- ₅₀ ing his teeth — the even, white teeth of a healthy peasant — and, like a man in the thick of urgent work, he briskly opened the front door, called the coachman, helped Peter Ivanovich into the sledge, and sprang back to the porch as if in readiness for what he had to do next.

Peter Ivanovich found the fresh air particularly pleasant after the smell of incense, the dead body, and carbolic acid.

"Where to, sir?" asked the coachman.

"It's not too late even now. . . . I'll call round on Fëdor Vasilievich."

He accordingly drove there and found them just finishing the first rubber, so that it was quite convenient for him to cut in.

II

Ivan Ilych's life had been most simple and most ordinary and therefore ₅₅ most terrible.

He had been a member of the Court of Justice, and died at the age of forty-five. His father had been an official who after serving in various ministries and departments in Petersburg had made the sort of career which brings men to positions from which by reason of their long service they cannot be dismissed, though they are obviously unfit to hold any responsible position, and for whom therefore posts are specially created, which though fictitious carry salaries of from six to ten thousand rubles that are not fictitious, and in receipt of which they live on to a great age.

Such was the Privy Councillor and superfluous member of various superfluous institutions, Ilya Epimovich Golovin.

He had three sons, of whom Ivan Ilych was the second. The eldest son was following in his father's footsteps only in another department, and was already approaching that stage in the service at which a similar sinecure would be reached. The third son was a failure. He had ruined his prospects in a number of positions and was now serving in the railway department. His father and brothers, and still more their wives, not merely disliked meeting him, but avoided remembering his existence unless compelled to do so. His sister had married Baron Greff, a Petersburg official of her father's type. Ivan Ilych was *le phénix de la famille*° as people said. He was neither as cold and formal as his elder brother nor as wild as the younger, but was a happy mean between them — an intelligent, polished, lively, and agreeable man. He had studied with his younger brother at the School of Law, but the latter had failed to complete the course and was expelled when he was in the fifth class. Ivan Ilych finished the course well. Even when he was at the School of Law he was just what he remained for the rest of his life: a capable, cheerful, good-natured, and sociable man, though strict in the fulfillment of what he considered to be his duty: and he considered his duty to be what was so considered by those in authority. Neither as a boy nor as a man was he a toady, but from early youth was by nature attracted to people of high station as a fly is drawn to the light, assimilating their ways and views of life and establishing friendly relations with them. All the enthusiasms of childhood and youth passed without leav-

le phénix de la famille: "the prize of the family."

ing much trace on him; he succumbed to sensuality, to vanity, and latterly among the highest classes to liberalism, but always within limits which his instinct unfailingly indicated to him as correct.

At school he had done things which had formerly seemed to him very horrid and made him feel disgusted with himself when he did them; but when later on he saw that such actions were done by people of good position and that they did not regard them as wrong, he was able not exactly to regard them as right, but to forget about them entirely or not be at all troubled at remembering them.

Having graduated from the School of Law and qualified for the tenth rank of the civil service, and having received money from his father for his equipment, Ivan Ilych ordered himself clothes at Scharmer's, the fashionable tailor, hung a medallion inscribed *respice finem*° on his watch-chain, took leave of his professor and the prince who was patron of the school, had a farewell dinner with his comrades at Donon's first-class restaurant, and with his new and fashionable portmanteau, linen, clothes, shaving and other toilet appliances, and a travelling rug all purchased at the best shops, he set off for one of the provinces where, through his father's influence, he had been attached to the Governor as an official for special service.

In the province Ivan Ilych soon arranged as easy and agreeable a position for himself as he had had at the School of Law. He performed his official tasks, made his career, and at the same time amused himself pleasantly and decorously. Occasionally he paid official visits to country districts, where he behaved with dignity both to his superiors and inferiors, and performed the duties entrusted to him, which related chiefly to the sectarians°, with an exactness and incorruptible honesty of which he could not but feel proud.

In official matters, despite his youth and taste for frivolous gaiety, he was exceedingly reserved, punctilious, and even severe; but in society he was often amusing and witty, and always good-natured, correct in his manner, and *bon enfant*°, as the Governor and his wife — with whom he was like one of the family — used to say of him.

In the province he had an affair with a lady who made advances to the elegant young lawyer, and there was also a milliner; and there were carousals with aides-de-camp who visited the district, and after-supper visits to a certain outlying street of doubtful reputation; and there was too some obsequiousness to his chief and even to his chief's wife, but all this was done with such a tone of good breeding that no hard names could be applied to it. It all came under the heading of the French saying: *"Il faut que jeunesse se passe."*° It was all done with clean hands, in clean linen, with French phrases, and above all among people of the best society and consequently with the approval of people of rank.

So Ivan Ilych served for five years and then came a change in his official life. The new and reformed judicial institutions were introduced, and new men were needed. Ivan Ilych became such a new man. He was offered the post of examining magistrate, and he accepted it though the post was in another province and obliged him to give up the connections he had formed and to

60

respice finem: "Think of the end (of your life)."
sectarians: dissenters from the Orthodox Church.
bon enfant: like a well-behaved child.
"Il faut que jeunesse se passe": "Youth doesn't last."

make new ones. His friends met to give him a send-off; they had a group-photograph taken and presented him with a silver cigarette-case, and he set off to his new post.

As examining magistrate Ivan Ilych was just as *comme il faut*° and decorous a man, inspiring general respect and capable of separating his official duties from his private life, as he had been when acting as an official on special service. His duties now as examining magistrate were far more interesting and attractive than before. In his former position it had been pleasant to wear an undress uniform made by Scharmer, and to pass through the crowd of petitioners and officials who were timorously awaiting an audience with the Governor, and who envied him as with free and easy gait he went straight into his chief's private room to have a cup of tea and a cigarette with him. But not many people had been directly dependent on him — only police officials and the sectarians when he went on special missions — and he liked to treat them politely, almost as comrades, as if he were letting them feel that he who had the power to crush them was treating them in this simple, friendly way. There were then but few such people. But now, as an examining magistrate, Ivan Ilych felt that everyone without exception, even the most important and self-satisfied, was in his power, and that he need only write a few words on a sheet of paper with a certain heading, and this or that important, self-satisfied person would be brought before him in the role of an accused person or a witness, and if he did not choose to allow him to sit down, would have to stand before him and answer his questions. Ivan Ilych never abused his power; he tried on the contrary to soften its expression, but the consciousness of it and of the possibility of softening its effect, supplied the chief interest and attraction of his office. In his work itself, especially in his examinations, he very soon acquired a method of eliminating all considerations irrelevant to the legal aspect of the case, and reducing even the most complicated case to a form in which it would be presented on paper only in its externals, completely excluding his personal opinion of the matter, while above all observing every prescribed formality. The work was new and Ivan Ilych was one of the first men to apply the new Code of 1864°.

On taking up the post of examining magistrate in a new town, he made new acquaintances and connections, placed himself on a new footing, and assumed a somewhat different tone. He took up an attitude of rather dignified aloofness towards the provincial authorities, but picked out the best circle of legal gentlemen and wealthy gentry living in the town and assumed a tone of slight dissatisfaction with the government, of moderate liberalism, and of enlightened citizenship. At the same time, without at all altering the elegance of his toilet, he ceased shaving his chin and allowed his beard to grow as it pleased.

Ivan Ilych settled down very pleasantly in this new town. The society there, which inclined towards opposition to the Governor, was friendly, his salary was larger, and he began to play *vint*°, which he found added not a little to the pleasure of life, for he had a capacity for cards, played good-humoredly, and calculated rapidly and astutely, so that he usually won.

comme il faut: "as required," rule-abiding.
Code of 1864: The emancipation of the serfs in 1861 was followed by a thorough all-round reform of judicial proceedings. [Translators' note.]
vint: a form of bridge. [Translators' note.]

After living there for two years he met his future wife, Praskovya Fëdo-rovna Mikhel, who was the most attractive, clever, and brilliant girl of the set in which he moved, and among other amusements and relaxations from his labors as examining magistrate, Ivan Ilych established light and playful rela-tions with her.

While he had been an official on special service he had been accustomed to dance, but now as an examining magistrate it was exceptional for him to do so. If he danced now, he did it as if to show that though he served under the reformed order of things, and had reached the fifth official rank, yet when it came to dancing he could do it better than most people. So at the end of an evening he sometimes danced with Praskovya Fëdorovna, and it was chiefly during these dances that he captivated her. She fell in love with him. Ivan Ilych had at first no definite intention of marrying, but when the girl fell in love with him he said to himself: "Really, why shouldn't I marry?"

Praskovya Fëdorovna came of a good family, was not bad-looking, and had some little property. Ivan Ilych might have aspired to a more brilliant match, but even this was good. He had his salary, and she, he hoped, would have an equal income. She was well connected, and was a sweet, pretty, and thoroughly correct young woman. To say that Ivan Ilych married because he fell in love with Praskovya Fëdorovna and found that she sympathized with his views of life would be as incorrect as to say that he married because his social circle approved of the match. He was swayed by both these considera-tions: the marriage gave him personal satisfaction, and at the same time it was considered the right thing by the most highly placed of his associates.

So Ivan Ilych got married.

The preparations for marriage and the beginning of married life, with its conjugal caresses, the new furniture, new crockery, and new linen, were very pleasant until his wife became pregnant — so that Ivan Ilych had begun to think that marriage would not impair the easy, agreeable, gay, and always decorous character of his life, approved of by society and regarded by himself as natural, but would even improve it. But from the first months of his wife's pregnancy, something new, unpleasant, depressing, and unseemly, and from which there was no way of escape, unexpectedly showed itself.

His wife, without any reason — *de gaieté de cœur*° as Ivan Ilych expressed it to himself — began to disturb the pleasure and propriety of their life. She began to be jealous without any cause, expected him to devote his whole attention to her, found fault with everything, and made coarse and ill-mannered scenes.

At first Ivan Ilych hoped to escape from the unpleasantness of this state of affairs by the same easy and decorous relation to life that had served him heretofore: he tried to ignore his wife's disagreeable moods, continued to live in his usual easy and pleasant way, invited friends to his house for a game of cards, and also tried going out to his club or spending his evenings with friends. But one day his wife began upbraiding him so vigorously, using such coarse words, and continued to abuse him every time he did not fulfil her demands, so resolutely and with such evident determination not to give way till he submitted — that is, till he stayed at home and was bored just as she was

de gaieté de cœur: "from pure whim."

— that he became alarmed. He now realized that matrimony — at any rate with Praskovya Fëdorovna — was not always conducive to the pleasures and amenities of life, but on the contrary often infringed both comfort and propriety, and that he must therefore entrench himself against such infringement. And Ivan Ilych began to seek for means of doing so. His official duties were the one thing that imposed upon Praskovya Fëdorovna, and by means of his official work and the duties attached to it he began struggling with his wife to secure his own independence.

With the birth of their child, the attempts to feed it and the various $_{75}$ failures in doing so, and with the real and imaginary illnesses of mother and child, in which Ivan Ilych's sympathy was demanded but about which he understood nothing, the need of securing for himself an existence outside his family life became still more imperative.

As his wife grew more irritable and exacting and Ivan Ilych transferred the center of gravity of his life more and more to his official work, so did he grow to like his work better and become more ambitious than before.

Very soon, within a year of his wedding, Ivan Ilych had realized that marriage, though it may add some comforts to life, is in fact a very intricate and difficult affair towards which in order to perform one's duty, that is, to lead a decorous life approved of by society, one must adopt a definite attitude just as towards one's official duties.

And Ivan Ilych evolved such an attitude towards married life. He only required of it those conveniences — dinner at home, housewife, and bed — which it could give him, and above all that propriety of external forms required by public opinion. For the rest he looked for light-hearted pleasure and propriety, and was very thankful when he found them, but if he met with antagonism and querulousness he at once retired into his separate fenced-off world of official duties, where he found satisfaction.

Ivan Ilych was esteemed a good official, and after three years was made Assistant Public Prosecutor. His new duties, their importance, the possibility of indicting and imprisoning anyone he chose, the publicity his speeches received, and the success he had in all these things, made his work still more attractive.

More children came. His wife became more and more querulous and $_{80}$ ill-tempered, but the attitude Ivan Ilych had adopted towards his home life rendered him almost impervious to her grumbling.

After seven years' service in that town he was transferred to another province as Public Prosecutor. They moved, but were short of money and his wife did not like the place they moved to. Though the salary was higher the cost of living was greater, besides which two of their children died and family life became still more unpleasant for him.

Praskovya Fëdorovna blamed her husband for every inconvenience they encountered in their new home. Most of the conversations between husband and wife, especially as to the children's education, led to topics which recalled former disputes, and those disputes were apt to flare up again at any moment. There remained only those rare periods of amorousness which still came to them at times but did not last long. These were islets at which they anchored for a while and then again set out upon that ocean of veiled hostility which showed itself in their aloofness from one another. This aloofness might have grieved Ivan Ilych had he considered that it ought not to exist, but he now regarded the position as normal, and even made it the goal at which he aimed in family life. His aim was to free himself more and more from those unpleasantnesses and to give them a semblance of harmlessness and propriety. He attained this by spending less and less time with his family, and when obliged to be at home he tried to safeguard his position by the presence of outsiders. The chief thing, however, was that he had his official duties. The whole interest of his life now centered in the official world and that interest absorbed him. The consciousness of his power, being able to ruin anybody he wished to ruin, the importance, even the external dignity of his entry into court, or meetings with his subordinates, his success with superiors and inferiors, and above all his masterly handling of cases, of which he was conscious — all this gave him pleasure and filled his life, together with chats with his colleagues, dinners, and bridge. So that on the whole Ivan Ilych's life continued to flow as he considered it should do — pleasantly and properly.

So things continued for another seven years. His eldest daughter was already sixteen, another child had died, and only one son was left, a schoolboy and a subject of dissension. Ivan Ilych wanted to put him in the School of Law, but to spite him Praskovya Fëdorovna entered him at the High School. The daughter had been educated at home and had turned out well: the boy did not learn badly either.

III

So Ivan Ilych lived for seventeen years after his marriage. He was already a Public Prosecutor of long standing, and had declined several proposed transfers while awaiting a more desirable post, when an unanticipated and unpleasant occurrence quite upset the peaceful course of his life. He was expecting to be offered the post of presiding judge in a University town, but Happe somehow came to the front and obtained the appointment instead. Ivan Ilych became irritable, reproached Happe, and quarrelled both with him and with his immediate superiors — who became colder to him and again passed him over when other appointments were made.

This was in 1880, the hardest year of Ivan Ilych's life. It was then that it became evident on the one hand that his salary was insufficient for them to live on, and on the other that he had been forgotten, and not only this, but that what was for him the greatest and most cruel injustice appeared to others a quite ordinary occurrence. Even his father did not consider it his duty to help him. Ivan Ilych felt himself abandoned by everyone, and that they regarded his position with a salary of 3,500 rubles as quite normal and even fortunate. He alone knew that with the consciousness of the injustices done him, with his wife's incessant nagging, and with the debts he had contracted by living beyond his means, his position was far from normal.

In order to save money that summer he obtained leave of absence and went with his wife to live in the country at her brother's place.

In the country, without his work, he experienced *ennui* for the first time in his life, and not only *ennui* but intolerable depression, and he decided that it was impossible to go on living like that, and that it was necessary to take energetic measures.

Having passed a sleepless night pacing up and down the veranda, he decided to go to Petersburg and bestir himself, in order to punish those who had failed to appreciate him and to get transferred to another ministry.

Next day, despite many protests from his wife and her brother, he started for Petersburg with the sole object of obtaining a post with a salary of five thousand rubles a year. He was no longer bent on any particular department, or tendency, or kind of activity. All he now wanted was an appointment to another post with a salary of five thousand rubles, either in the administration, in the banks, with the railways, in one of the Empress Marya's Institutions°, or even in the customs — but it had to carry with it a salary of five thousand rubles and be in a ministry other than that in which they had failed to appreciate him.

And this quest of Ivan Ilych's was crowned with remarkable and unexpected success. At Kursk an acquaintance of his, F. I. Ilyin, got into the first-class carriage, sat down beside Ivan Ilych, and told him of a telegram just received by the Governor of Kursk announcing that a change was about to take place in the ministry: Peter Ivanovich was to be superseded by Ivan Semënovich. 90

The proposed change, apart from its significance for Russia, had a special significance for Ivan Ilych, because by bringing forward a new man, Peter Petrovich, and consequently his friend Zachar Ivanovich, it was highly favorable for Ivan Ilych, since Zachar Ivanovich was a friend and colleague of his.

In Moscow this news was confirmed, and on reaching Petersburg Ivan Ilych found Zachar Ivanovich and received a definite promise of an appointment in his former department of Justice.

A week later he telegraphed to his wife: "Zachar in Miller's place. I shall receive appointment on presentation of report."

Thanks to this change of personnel, Ivan Ilych had unexpectedly obtained an appointment in his former ministry which placed him two stages above his former colleagues besides giving him five thousand rubles salary and three thousand five hundred rubles for expenses connected with his removal. All his ill humor towards his former enemies and the whole department vanished, and Ivan Ilych was completely happy.

He returned to the country more cheerful and contented than he had been for a long time. Praskovya Fëdorovna also cheered up and a truce was arranged between them. Ivan Ilych told of how he had been fêted by everybody in Petersburg, how all those who had been his enemies were put to shame and now fawned on him, how envious they were of his appointment, and how much everybody in Petersburg had liked him. 95

Praskovya Fëdorovna listened to all this and appeared to believe it. She did not contradict anything, but only made plans for their life in the town to which they were going. Ivan Ilych saw with delight that these plans were his plans, that he and his wife agreed, and that, after a stumble, his life was regaining its due and natural character of pleasant lightheartedness and decorum.

Ivan Ilych had come back for a short time only, for he had to take up his new duties on the 10th of September. Moreover, he needed time to settle

Empress Marya's Institutions: orphanages.

into the new place, to move all his belongings from the province, and to buy and order many additional things: in a word, to make such arrangements as he had resolved on, which were almost exactly what Praskovya Fëdorovna too had decided on.

Now that everything had happened so fortunately, and that he and his wife were at one in their aims and moreover saw so little of one another, they got on together better than they had done since the first years of marriage. Ivan Ilych had thought of taking his family away with him at once, but the insistence of his wife's brother and her sister-in-law, who had suddenly become particularly amiable and friendly to him and his family, induced him to depart alone.

So he departed, and the cheerful state of mind induced by his success and by the harmony between his wife and himself, the one intensifying the other, did not leave him. He found a delightful house, just the thing both he and his wife had dreamt of. Spacious, lofty reception rooms in the old style, a convenient and dignified study, rooms for his wife and daughter, a study for his son — it might have been specially built for them. Ivan Ilych himself superintended the arrangements, chose the wallpapers, supplemented the furniture (preferably with antiques which he considered particularly *comme il faut*), and supervised the upholstering. Everything progressed and progressed and approached the ideal he had set himself: even when things were only half completed they exceeded his expectations. He saw what a refined and elegant character, free from vulgarity, it would all have when it was ready. On falling asleep he pictured to himself how the reception-room would look. Looking at the yet unfinished drawing-room he could see the fireplace, the screen, the what-not, the little chairs dotted here and there, the dishes and plates on the walls, and the bronzes, as they would be when everything was in place. He was pleased by the thought of how his wife and daughter, who shared his taste in this matter, would be impressed by it. They were certainly not expecting as much. He had been particularly successful in finding, and buying cheaply, antiques which gave a particularly aristocratic character to the whole place. But in his letters he intentionally understated everything in order to be able to surprise them. All this so absorbed him that his new duties — though he liked his official work — interested him less than he had expected. Sometimes he even had moments of absentmindedness during the Court Sessions, and would consider whether he should have straight or curved cornices for his curtains. He was so interested in it all that he often did things himself, rearranging the furniture, or rehanging the curtains. Once when mounting a stepladder to show the upholsterer, who did not understand, how he wanted the hangings draped, he made a false step and slipped, but being a strong and agile man he clung on and only knocked his side against the knob of the window frame. The bruised place was painful but the pain soon passed, and he felt particularly bright and well just then. He wrote: "I feel fifteen years younger." He thought he would have everything ready by September, but it dragged on till mid-October. But the result was charming not only in his eyes but to everyone who saw it.

In reality it was just what is usually seen in the houses of people of moderate means who want to appear rich, and therefore succeed only in resembling others like themselves: there were damasks, dark wood, plants,

100

rugs, and dull and polished bronzes — all the things people of a certain class have in order to resemble other people of that class. His house was so like the others that it would never have been noticed, but to him it all seemed to be quite exceptional. He was very happy when he met his family at the station and brought them to the newly furnished house all lit up, where a footman in a white tie opened the door into the hall decorated with plants, and when they went on into the drawing-room and the study uttering exclamations of delight. He conducted them everywhere, drank in their praises eagerly, and beamed with pleasure. At tea that evening, when Praskovya Fëdorovna among other things asked him about his fall, he laughed and showed them how he had gone flying and had frightened the upholsterer.

"It's a good thing I'm a bit of an athlete. Another man might have been killed, but I merely knocked myself, just here; it hurts when it's touched, but it's passing off already — it's only a bruise."

So they began living in their new home — in which, as always happens, when they got thoroughly settled in they found they were just one room short — and with the increased income, which as always was just a little (some five hundred rubles) too little, but it was all very nice.

Things went particularly well at first, before everything was finally arranged and while something had still to be done: this thing bought, that thing ordered, another thing moved, and something else adjusted. Though there were some disputes between husband and wife, they were both so well satisfied and had so much to do that it all passed off without any serious quarrels. When nothing was left to arrange it became rather dull and something seemed to be lacking, but they were then making acquaintances, forming habits, and life was growing fuller.

Ivan Ilych spent his mornings at the law courts and came home to dinner, and at first he was generally in a good humor, though he occasionally became irritable just on account of his house. (Every spot on the tablecloth or the upholstery, and every broken window-blind string, irritated him. He had devoted so much trouble to arranging it all that every disturbance of it distressed him.) But on the whole his life ran its course as he believed life should do: easily, pleasantly, and decorously.

He got up at nine, drank his coffee, read the paper, and then put on his undress uniform and went to the law courts. There the harness in which he worked had already been stretched to fit him and he donned it without a hitch: petitioners, inquiries at the chancery, the chancery itself, and the sittings public and administrative. In all this the thing was to exclude everything fresh and vital, which always disturbs the regular course of official business, and to admit only official relations with people, and then only on official grounds. A man would come, for instance, wanting some information. Ivan Ilych, as one in whose sphere the matter did not lie, would have nothing to do with him: but if the man had some business with him in his official capacity, something that could be expressed on officially stamped paper, he would do everything, positively everything he could within the limits of such relations, and in doing so would maintain the semblance of friendly human relations, that is, would observe the courtesies of life. As soon as the official relations ended, so did everything else. Ivan Ilych possessed this capacity to separate his real life from the official side of affairs and not mix the two, in the highest degree, and by

105

long practice and natural aptitude had brought it to such a pitch that sometimes, in the manner of a virtuoso, he would even allow himself to let the human and official relations mingle. He let himself do this just because he felt that he could at any time he chose resume the strictly official attitude again and drop the human relation. And he did it all easily, pleasantly, correctly, and even artistically. In the intervals between the sessions he smoked, drank tea, chatted a little about politics, a little about general topics, a little about cards, but most of all about official appointments. Tired, but with the feelings of a virtuoso — one of the first violins who has played his part in an orchestra with precision — he would return home to find that his wife and daughter had been out paying calls, or had a visitor, and that his son had been to school, had done his homework with his tutor, and was duly learning what is taught at High Schools. Everything was as it should be. After dinner, if they had no visitors, Ivan Ilych sometimes read a book that was being much discussed at the time, and in the evening settled down to work, that is, read official papers, compared the depositions of witnesses, and noted paragraphs of the Code applying to them. This was neither dull nor amusing. It was dull when he might have been playing bridge, but if no bridge was available it was at any rate better than doing nothing or sitting with his wife. Ivan Ilych's chief pleasure was giving little dinners to which he invited men and women of good social position, and just as his drawing-room resembled all other drawing-rooms so did his enjoyable little parties resemble all other such parties.

Once they even gave a dance. Ivan Ilych enjoyed it and everything went off well, except that it led to a violent quarrel with his wife about the cakes and sweets. Praskovya Fëdorovna had made her own plans, but Ivan Ilych insisted on getting everything from an expensive confectioner and ordered too many cakes, and the quarrel occurred because some of those cakes were left over and the confectioner's bill came to forty-five rubles. It was a great and disagreeable quarrel. Praskovya Fëdorovna called him "a fool and an imbecile," and he clutched at his head and made angry allusions to divorce.

But the dance itself had been enjoyable. The best people were there, and Ivan Ilych had danced with Princess Trufonova, a sister of the distinguished founder of the Society "Bear my Burden."

The pleasures connected with his work were pleasures of ambition; his social pleasures were those of vanity; but Ivan Ilych's greatest pleasure was playing bridge. He acknowledged that whatever disagreeable incident happened in his life, the pleasure that beamed like a ray of light above everything else was to sit down to bridge with good players, not noisy partners, and of course to four-handed bridge (with five players it was annoying to have to stand out, though one pretended not to mind), to play a clever and serious game (when the cards allowed it), and then to have supper and drink a glass of wine. After a game of bridge, especially if he had won a little (to win a large sum was unpleasant), Ivan Ilych went to bed in specially good humor.

So they lived. They formed a circle of acquaintances among the best people and were visited by people of importance and by young folk. In their views as to their acquaintances, husband, wife, and daughter were entirely agreed, and tacitly and unanimously kept at arm's length and shook off the various shabby friends and relations who, with much show of affection, gushed into the drawing-room with its Japanese plates on the walls. Soon these shabby friends ceased to obtrude themselves and only the best people remained in the Golovins' set.

Young men made up to Lisa, and Petrishchev, an examining magistrate and Dmitri Ivanovich Petrischev's son and sole heir, began to be so attentive to her that Ivan Ilych had already spoken to Praskovya Fëdorovna about it, and considered whether they should not arrange a party for them, or get up some private theatricals.

So they lived, and all went well, without change, and life followed pleasantly.

IV

They were all in good health. It could not be called ill health if Ivan Ilych sometimes said that he had a queer taste in his mouth and felt some discomfort in his left side.

But this discomfort increased and, though not exactly painful, grew into a sense of pressure in his side accompanied by ill humor. And his irritability became worse and worse and began to mar the agreeable, easy, and correct life that had established itself in the Golovin family. Quarrels between husband and wife became more and more frequent, and soon the ease and amenity disappeared and even the decorum was barely maintained. Scenes again became frequent, and very few of those islets remained on which husband and wife could meet without an explosion. Praskovya Fëdorovna now had good reason to say that her husband's temper was trying. With characteristic exaggeration she said he had always had a dreadful temper, and that it had needed all her good nature to put up with it for twenty years. It was true that now the quarrels were started by him. His bursts of temper always came just before dinner, often just as he began to eat his soup. Sometimes he noticed that a plate or dish was chipped, or the food was not right, or his son put his elbow on the table, or his daughter's hair was not done as he liked it, and for all this he blamed Praskovya Fëdorovna. At first she retorted and said disagreeable things to him, but once or twice he fell into such a rage at the beginning of dinner that she realized it was due to some physical derangement brought on by taking food, and so she restrained herself and did not answer, but only hurried to get the dinner over. She regarded this self-restraint as highly praiseworthy. Having come to the conclusion that her husband had a dreadful temper and made her life miserable, she began to feel sorry for herself, and the more she pitied herself the more she hated her husband. She began to wish he would die; yet she did not want him to die because then his salary would cease. And this irritated her against him still more. She considered herself dreadfully unhappy just because not even his death could save her, and though she concealed her exasperation, that hidden exasperation of hers increased his irritation also.

After one scene in which Ivan Ilych had been particularly unfair and after which he had said in explanation that he certainly was irritable but that it was due to his not being well, she said that if he was ill it should be attended to, and insisted on his going to see a celebrated doctor.

He went. Everything took place as he had expected and as it always does. There was the usual waiting and the important air assumed by the doctor, with which he was so familiar (resembling that which he himself assumed in court), and the sounding and listening, and the questions which called for answers that were foregone conclusions and were evidently unnecessary, and the look of importance which implied that "if only you put yourself in our hands we will arrange everything — we know indubitably how it has to be done, always in the same way for everybody alike." It was all just as it was in the law courts. The doctor put on just the same air towards him as he himself put on towards an accused person.

The doctor said that so-and-so indicated that there was so-and-so inside the patient, but if the investigation of so-and-so did not confirm this, then he must assume that and that. If he assumed that and that, then . . . and so on. To Ivan Ilych only one question was important: was his case serious or not? But the doctor ignored that inappropriate question. From his point of view it was not the one under consideration, the real question was to decide between a floating kidney, chronic catarrh, or appendicitis. It was not a question of Ivan Ilych's life or death, but one between a floating kidney and appendicitis. And that question the doctor solved brilliantly, as it seemed to Ivan Ilych, in favor of the appendix, with the reservation that should an examination of the urine give fresh indications the matter would be reconsidered. All this was just what Ivan Ilych had himself brilliantly accomplished a thousand times in dealing with men on trial. The doctor summed up just as brilliantly, looking over his spectacles triumphantly and even gaily at the accused. From the doctor's summing up Ivan Ilych concluded that things were bad, but that for the doctor, and perhaps for everybody else, it was a matter of indifference, though for him it was bad. And this conclusion struck him painfully, arousing in him a great feeling of pity for himself and of bitterness towards the doctor's indifference to a matter of such importance.

He said nothing of this, but rose, placed the doctor's fee on the table, and remarked with a sigh: "We sick people probably often put inappropriate questions. But tell me, in general, is this complaint dangerous, or not? . . ."

The doctor looked at him sternly over his spectacles with one eye, as if to say: "Prisoner, if you will not keep to the questions put to you, I shall be obliged to have you removed from the court."

"I have already told you what I consider necessary and proper. The analysis may show something more." And the doctor bowed.

Ivan Ilych went out slowly, seated himself disconsolately in his sledge, and drove home. All the way home he was going over what the doctor had said, trying to translate those complicated, obscure, scientific phrases into plain language and find in them an answer to the question: "Is my condition bad? Is it very bad? Or is there as yet nothing much wrong?" And it seemed to him that the meaning of what the doctor had said was that it was very bad. Everything in the streets seemed depressing. The cabmen, the houses, the passers-by, and the shops, were dismal. His ache, this dull gnawing ache that never ceased for a moment, seemed to have acquired a new and more serious significance from the doctor's dubious remarks. Ivan Ilych now watched it with a new and oppressive feeling.

He reached home and began to tell his wife about it. She listened, but in the middle of his account his daughter came in with her hat on, ready to go out with her mother. She sat down reluctantly to listen to this tedious story, but could not stand it long, and her mother too did not hear him to the end.

"Well, I am very glad," she said. "Mind now to take your medicine regularly. Give me the prescription and I'll send Gerasim to the chemist's." And she went to get ready to go out.

While she was in the room Ivan Ilych had hardly taken time to breathe, but he sighed deeply when she left it.

"Well," he thought, "perhaps it isn't so bad after all."

He began taking his medicine and following the doctor's directions, which had been altered after the examination of the urine. But then it happened that there was a contradiction between the indications drawn from the examination of the urine and the symptoms that showed themselves. It turned out that what was happening differed from what the doctor had told him, and that he had either forgotten, or blundered, or hidden something from him. He could not, however, be blamed for that, and Ivan Ilych still obeyed his orders implicitly and at first derived some comfort from doing so.

From the time of his visit to the doctor, Ivan Ilych's chief occupation was the exact fulfilment of the doctor's instructions regarding hygiene and the taking of medicine, and the observation of his pain and his excretions. His chief interests came to be people's ailments and people's health. When sickness, deaths, or recoveries were mentioned in his presence, especially when the illness resembled his own, he listened with agitation which he tried to hide, asked questions, and applied what he heard to his own case.

The pain did not grow less, but Ivan Ilych made efforts to force himself to think that he was better. And he could do this so long as nothing agitated him. But as soon as he had any unpleasantness with his wife, any lack of success in his official work, or held bad cards at bridge, he was at once acutely sensible of his disease. He had formerly borne such mischances, hoping soon to adjust what was wrong, to master it and attain success, or make a grand slam. But now every mischance upset him and plunged him into despair. He would say to himself: "There now, just as I was beginning to get better and the medicine had begun to take effect, comes this accursed misfortune, or unpleasantness. . . ." And he was furious with the mishap, or with the people who were causing the unpleasantness and killing him, for he felt that this fury was killing him but could not restrain it. One would have thought that it should have been clear to him that this exasperation with circumstances and people aggravated his illness, and that he ought therefore to ignore unpleasant occurrences. But he drew the very opposite conclusion: he said that he needed peace, and he watched for everything that might disturb it and became irritable at the slightest infringement of it. His condition was rendered worse by the fact that he read medical books and consulted doctors. The progress of his disease was so gradual that he could deceive himself when comparing one day with another — the difference was so slight. But when he consulted the doctors it seemed to him that he was getting worse, and even very rapidly. Yet despite this he was continually consulting them.

That month he went to see another celebrity, who told him almost the same as the first had done but put his questions rather differently, and the interview with this celebrity only increased Ivan Ilych's doubts and fears. A friend of a friend of his, a very good doctor, diagnosed his illness again quite differently from the others, and though he predicted recovery, his questions and suppositions bewildered Ivan Ilych still more and increased his doubts. A homœopathist diagnosed the disease in yet another way, and prescribed medicine which Ivan Ilych took secretly for a week. But after a week, not feeling any improvement and having lost confidence both in the former doctor's treatment and in this one's, he became still more despondent. One day a lady acquaintance mentioned a cure effected by a wonder-working icon. Ivan Ilych caught himself listening attentively and beginning to believe that it had occurred. This incident alarmed him. "Has my mind really weakened to such an extent?" he asked himself. "Nonsense! It's all rubbish. I mustn't give way to nervous fears but having chosen a doctor must keep strictly to his treatment. That is what I will do. Now it's all settled. I won't think about it, but will follow the treatment seriously till summer, and then we shall see. From now there must be no more of this wavering!" This was easy to say but impossible to carry out. The pain in his side oppressed him and seemed to grow worse and more incessant, while the taste in his mouth grew stranger and stranger. It seemed to him that his breath had a disgusting smell, and he was conscious of a loss of appetite and strength. There was no deceiving himself: something terrible, new, and more important than anything before in his life, was taking place within him of which he alone was aware. Those about him did not understand or would not understand it, but thought everything in the world was going on as usual. That tormented Ivan Ilych more than anything. He saw that his household, especially his wife and daughter who were in a perfect whirl of visiting, did not understand anything of it and were annoyed that he was so depressed and so exacting, as if he were to blame for it. Though they tried to disguise it he saw that he was an obstacle in their path, and that his wife had adopted a definite line in regard to his illness and kept to it regardless of anything he said or did. Her attitude was this: "You know," she would say to her friends, "Ivan Ilych can't do as other people do, and keep to the treatment prescribed for him. One day he'll take his drops and keep strictly to his diet and go to bed in good time, but the next day unless I watch him he'll suddenly forget his medicine, eat sturgeon — which is forbidden — and sit up playing cards till one o'clock in the morning."

"Oh, come, when was that?" Ivan Ilych would ask in vexation. "Only once at Peter Ivanovich's."

"And yesterday with Shebek."

130

"Well, even if I hadn't stayed up, this pain would have kept me awake."

"Be that as it may you'll never get well like that, but will always make us wretched."

Praskovya Fëdorovna's attitude to Ivan Ilych's illness, as she expressed it both to others and to him, was that it was his own fault and was another of the annoyances he caused her. Ivan Ilych felt that this opinion escaped her involuntarily — but that did not make it easier for him.

At the law courts too, Ivan Ilych noticed, or thought he noticed, a strange attitude towards himself. It sometimes seemed to him that people were watching him inquisitively as a man whose place might soon be vacant. Then again, his friends would suddenly begin to chaff him in a friendly way about his low spirits, as if the awful, horrible, and unheard-of thing that was going on within him, incessantly gnawing at him and irresistibly drawing him away, was a very agreeable subject for jests. Schwartz in particular irritated him by his jocularity, vivacity, and *savoir-faire*, which reminded him of what he himself had been ten years ago.

Friends came to make up a set and they sat down to cards. They dealt, bending the new cards to soften them, and he sorted the diamonds in his hand and found he had seven. His partner said "No trumps" and supported him with two diamonds. What more could be wished for? It ought to be jolly and lively. They would make a grand slam. But suddenly Ivan Ilych was conscious of that gnawing pain, that taste in his mouth, and it seemed ridiculous that in such circumstances he should be pleased to make a grand slam.

He looked at his partner Mikhail Mikhaylovich, who rapped the table with his strong hand and instead of snatching up the tricks pushed the cards courteously and indulgently towards Ivan Ilych that he might have the pleasure of gathering them up without the trouble of stretching out his hand for them. "Does he think I am too weak to stretch out my arm?" thought Ivan Ilych, and forgetting what he was doing he over-trumped his partner, missing the grand slam by three tricks. And what was most awful of all was that he saw how upset Mikhail Mikhaylovich was about it but did not himself care. And it was dreadful to realize why he did not care.

They all saw that he was suffering, and said: "We can stop if you are tired. Take a rest." Lie down? No, he was not at all tired, and he finished the rubber. All were gloomy and silent. Ivan Ilych felt that he had diffused this gloom over them and could not dispel it. They had supper and went away, and Ivan Ilych was left alone with the consciousness that his life was poisoned and was poisoning the lives of others, and that this poison did not weaken but penetrated more and more deeply into his whole being.

With this consciousness, and with physical pain besides the terror, he must go to bed, often to lie awake the greater part of the night. Next morning he had to get up again, dress, go to the law courts, speak, and write; or if he did not go out, spend at home those twenty-four hours a day each of which was a torture. And he had to live thus all alone on the brink of an abyss, with no one who understood or pitied him.

V

So one month passed and then another. Just before the New Year his brother-in-law came to town and stayed at their house. Ivan Ilych was at the law courts and Praskovya Fëdorovna had gone shopping. When Ivan Ilych came home and entered his study he found his brother-in-law there — a healthy, florid man — unpacking his portmanteau himself. He raised his head on hearing Ivan Ilych's footsteps and looked up at him for a moment without a word. That stare told Ivan Ilych everything. His brother-in-law opened his mouth to utter an exclamation of surprise but checked himself, and that action confirmed it all.

"I have changed, eh?"

"Yes, there is a change."

And after that, try as he would to get his brother-in-law to return to the subject of his looks, the latter would say nothing about it. Praskovya Fëdorovna came home and her brother went out to her. Ivan Ilych locked the door and began to examine himself in the glass, first full face, then in profile. He took up a portrait of himself taken with his wife, and compared it with what he saw in the glass. The change in him was immense. Then he bared his arms to the elbow, looked at them, drew the sleeves down again, sat down on an ottoman, and grew blacker than night.

"No, no, this won't do!" he said to himself, and jumped up, went to the table, took up some law papers, and began to read them, but could not continue. He unlocked the door and went into the reception-room. The door leading to the drawing-room was shut. He approached it on tiptoe and listened.

"No, you are exaggerating!" Praskovya Fëdorovna was saying.

"Exaggerating! Don't you see it? Why, he's a dead man! Look at his eyes 145 — there's no light in them. But what is it that is wrong with him?"

"No one knows. Nikolaevich said something, but I don't know what. And Leshchetitsky° said quite the contrary. . . ."

Ivan Ilych walked away, went to his own room, lay down, and began musing: "The kidney, a floating kidney." He recalled all the doctors had told him of how it detached itself and swayed about. And by an effort of imagination he tried to catch that kidney and arrest it and support it. So little was needed for this, it seemed to him. "No, I'll go to see Peter Ivanovich° again." He rang, ordered the carriage, and got ready to go.

"Where are you going, Jean?" asked his wife, with a specially sad and exceptionally kind look.

This exceptionally kind look irritated him. He looked morosely at her.

"I must go to see Peter Ivanovich." 150

He went to see Peter Ivanovich, and together they went to see his friend, the doctor. He was in, and Ivan Ilych had a long talk with him.

Reviewing the anatomical and physiological details of what in the doctor's opinion was going on inside him, he understood it all.

There was something, a small thing, in the vermiform appendix. It might all come right. Only stimulate the energy of one organ and check the activity of another, then absorption would take place and everything would come right. He got home rather late for dinner, ate his dinner, and conversed cheerfully, but could not for a long time bring himself to go back to work in his room. At last, however, he went to his study and did what was necessary, but the consciousness that he had put something aside — an important, intimate matter which he would revert to when his work was done — never left him. When he had finished his work he remembered that this intimate matter was the thought of his vermiform appendix. But he did not give himself up to it, and went to the drawing-room for tea. There were callers there, including the examining magistrate who was a desirable match for his daughter, and they were conversing, playing the piano, and singing. Ivan Ilych, as Praskovya Fëdorovna remarked, spent that evening more cheerfully than usual, but he never for a moment forgot that he had postponed the important matter of the appendix. At eleven o'clock he said good-night and went to his bedroom. Since his illness he had slept alone in a small room next to his study. He undressed and took up a novel by Zola, but instead of reading it he fell into thought, and

Nikolaevich, Leshchetitsky: two doctors, the latter a celebrated specialist. [Translators' note.]
Peter Ivanovich: That was the friend whose friend was a doctor. [Translators' note.]

in his imagination that desired improvement in the vermiform appendix occurred. There was the absorption and evacuation and the re-establishment of normal activity. "Yes, that's it!" he said to himself. "One need only assist nature, that's all." He remembered his medicine, rose, took it, and lay down on his back watching for the beneficent action of the medicine and for it to lessen the pain. "I need only take it regularly and avoid all injurious influences. I am already feeling better, much better." He began touching his side: it was not painful to the touch. "There, I really don't feel it. It's much better already." He put out the light and turned on his side.... "The appendix is getting better, absorption is occurring." Suddenly he felt the old, familiar, dull, gnawing pain, stubborn and serious. There was the same familiar loathsome taste in his mouth. His heart sank and he felt dazed. "My God! My God!" he muttered. "Again, again! and it will never cease." And suddenly the matter presented itself in a quite different aspect. "Vermiform appendix! Kidney!" he said to himself. "It's not a question of appendix or kidney, but of life and . . . death. Yes, life was there and now it is going, going and I cannot stop it. Yes. Why deceive myself? Isn't it obvious to everyone but me that I'm dying, and that it's only a question of weeks, days . . . it may happen this moment. There was light and now there is darkness. I was here and now I'm going there! Where?" A chill came over him, his breathing ceased, and he felt only the throbbing of his heart.

"When I am not, what will there be? There will be nothing. Then where shall I be when I am no more? Can this be dying? No, I don't want to!" He jumped up and tried to light the candle, felt for it with trembling hands, dropped candle and candlestick on the floor, and fell back on his pillow.

"What's the use? It makes no difference," he said to himself, staring with wide-open eyes into the darkness. "Death. Yes, death. And none of them know or wish to know it, and they have no pity for me. Now they are playing." (He heard through the door the distant sound of a song and its accompaniment.) "It's all the same to them, but they will die too! Fools! I first, and they later, but it will be the same for them. And now they are merry . . . the beasts!"

Anger choked him and he was agonizingly, unbearably miserable. "It is impossible that all men have been doomed to suffer this awful horror!" He raised himself.

"Something must be wrong. I must calm myself — must think it all over from the beginning." And he again began thinking. "Yes, the beginning of my illness: I knocked my side, but I was still quite well that day and the next. It hurt a little, then rather more. I saw the doctors, then followed despondency and anguish, more doctors, and I drew nearer to the abyss. My strength grew less and I kept coming nearer and nearer, and now I have wasted away and there is no light in my eyes. I think of the appendix — but this is death! I think of mending the appendix, and all the while here is death! Can it really be death?" Again terror seized him and he gasped for breath. He leant down and began feeling for the matches, pressing with his elbow on the stand beside the bed. It was in his way and hurt him, he grew furious with it, pressed on it still harder, and upset it. Breathless and in despair he fell on his back, expecting death to come immediately.

Meanwhile the visitors were leaving. Praskovya Fëdorovna was seeing them off. She heard something fall and came in.

155

"What has happened?"

"Nothing. I knocked it over accidentally." 160

She went out and returned with a candle. He lay there panting heavily, like a man who has run a thousand yards, and stared upwards at her with a fixed look.

"What is it, Jean?"

"No . . . o . . . thing. I upset it." ("Why speak of it? She won't understand," he thought.)

And in truth she did not understand. She picked up the stand, lit his candle, and hurried away to see another visitor off. When she came back he still lay on his back, looking upwards.

"What is it? Do you feel worse?" 165

"Yes."

She shook her head and sat down.

"Do you know, Jean, I think we must ask Leshchetitsky to come and see you here."

This meant calling in the famous specialist, regardless of expense. He smiled malignantly and said "No." She remained a little longer and then went up to him and kissed his forehead.

While she was kissing him he hated her from the bottom of his soul and 170 with difficulty refrained from pushing her away.

"Good-night. Please God you'll sleep."

"Yes."

VI

Ivan Ilych saw that he was dying, and he was in continual despair.

In the depth of his heart he knew he was dying, but not only was he not accustomed to the thought, he simply did not and could not grasp it.

The syllogism he had learnt from Kiezewetter's Logic: "Caius is a man, 175 men are mortal, therefore Caius is mortal," had always seemed to him correct as applied to Caius, but certainly not as applied to himself. That Caius — man in the abstract — was mortal, was perfectly correct, but he was not Caius, not an abstract man, but a creature quite, quite separate from all others. He had been little Vanya, with a mamma and a papa, with Mitya and Volodya, with the toys, a coachman and a nurse, afterwards with Katenka and with all the joys, griefs, and delights of childhood, boyhood, and youth. What did Caius know of the smell of that striped leather ball Vanya had been so fond of? Had Caius kissed his mother's hand like that, and did the silk of her dress rustle so for Caius? Had he rioted like that at school when the pastry was bad? Had Caius been in love like that? Could Caius preside at a session as he did? "Caius really was mortal, and it was right for him to die; but for me, little Vanya, Ivan Ilych, with all my thoughts and emotions, it's altogether a different matter. It cannot be that I ought to die. That would be too terrible."

Such was his feeling.

"If I had to die like Caius I should have known it was so. An inner voice would have told me so, but there was nothing of the sort in me and I and all my friends felt that our case was quite different from that of Caius. And now here it is!" he said to himself. "It can't be. It's impossible! But here it is. How is this? How is one to understand it?"

He could not understand it, and tried to drive this false, incorrect, morbid thought away and to replace it by other proper and healthy thoughts. But that thought, and not the thought only but the reality itself, seemed to come and confront him.

And to replace that thought he called up a succession of others, hoping to find in them some support. He tried to get back into the former current of thoughts that had once screened the thought of death from him. But strange to say, all that had formerly shut off, hidden, and destroyed his consciousness of death, no longer had that effect. Ivan Ilych now spent most of his time in attempting to re-establish that old current. He would say to himself: "I will take up my duties again — after all I used to live by them." And banishing all doubts he would go to the law courts, enter into conversation with his colleagues, and sit carelessly as was his wont, scanning the crowd with a thoughtful look and leaning both his emaciated arms on the arms of his oak chair; bending over as usual to a colleague and drawing his papers nearer he would interchange whispers with him, and then suddenly raising his eyes and sitting erect would pronounce certain words and open the proceedings. But suddenly in the midst of those proceedings the pain in his side, regardless of the stage the proceedings had reached, would begin its own gnawing work. Ivan Ilych would turn his attention to it and try to drive the thought of it away, but without success. *It* would come and stand before him and look at him, and he would be petrified and the light would die out of his eyes, and he would again begin asking himself whether *It* alone was true. And his colleagues and subordinates would see with surprise and distress that he, the brilliant and subtle judge, was becoming confused and making mistakes. He would shake himself, try to pull himself together, manage somehow to bring the sitting to a close, and return home with the sorrowful consciousness that his judicial labors could not as formerly hide from him what he wanted them to hide, and could not deliver him from *It*. And what was worst of all was that *It* drew his attention to itself not in order to make him take some action but only that he should look at *It*, look it straight in the face: look at it and, without doing anything, suffer inexpressibly.

And to save himself from this condition Ivan Ilych looked for consolations — new screens — and new screens were found and for a while seemed to save him, but then they immediately fell to pieces or rather became transparent, as if *It* penetrated them and nothing could veil *It*. 180

In these latter days he would go into the drawing-room he had arranged — that drawing-room where he had fallen and for the sake of which (how bitterly ridiculous it seemed) he had sacrificed his life — for he knew that his illness originated with that knock. He would enter and see that something had scratched the polished table. He would look for the cause of this and find that it was the bronze ornamentation of an album, that had got bent. He would take up the expensive album which he had lovingly arranged, and feel vexed with his daughter and her friends for their untidiness — for the album was torn here and there and some of the photographs turned upside down. He would put it carefully in order and bend the ornamentation back into position. Then it would occur to him to place all those things in another corner of the room, near the plants. He could call the footman, but his daughter or wife would come to help him. They would not agree, and his wife would contradict him, and he would dispute and grow angry. But that was all right, for then he did not think about *It. It* was invisible.

But then, when he was moving something himself, his wife would say: "Let the servants do it. You will hurt yourself again." And suddenly *It* would flash through the screen and he would see it. It was just a flash, and he hoped it would disappear, but he would involuntarily pay attention to his side. "It sits there as before, gnawing just the same!" And he could no longer forget *It*, but could distinctly see it looking at him from behind the flowers. "What is it all for?"

"It really is so! I lost my life over that curtain as I might have done when storming a fort. Is that possible? How terrible and how stupid. It can't be true! It can't, but it is."

He would go to his study, lie down, and again be alone with *It:* face to face with *It*. And nothing could be done with *It* except to look at it and shudder.

VII

How it happened it is impossible to say because it came about step by step, unnoticed, but in the third month of Ivan Ilych's illness, his wife, his daughter, his son, his acquaintances, the doctors, the servants, and above all he himself, were aware that the whole interest he had for other people was whether he would soon vacate his place, and at last release the living from the discomfort caused by his presence and be himself released from his sufferings.

He slept less and less. He was given opium and hypodermic injections of morphine, but this did not relieve him. The dull depression he experienced in a somnolent condition at first gave him a little relief, but only as something new, afterwards it became as distressing as the pain itself or even more so.

Special foods were prepared for him by the doctors' orders, but all those foods became increasingly distasteful and disgusting to him.

For his excretions also special arrangements had to be made, and this was a torment to him every time — a torment from the uncleanliness, the unseemliness, and the smell, and from knowing that another person had to take part in it.

But just through this most unpleasant matter, Ivan Ilych obtained comfort. Gerasim, the butler's young assistant, always came in to carry the things out. Gerasim was a clean, fresh peasant lad, grown stout on town food and always cheerful and bright. At first the sight of him, in his clean Russian peasant costume, engaged on that disgusting task embarrassed Ivan Ilych.

Once when he got up from the commode too weak to draw up his trousers, he dropped into a soft armchair and looked with horror at his bare, enfeebled thighs with the muscles so sharply marked on them.

Gerasim with a firm light tread, his heavy boots emitting a pleasant smell of tar and fresh winter air, came in wearing a clean Hessian apron, the sleeves of his print shirt tucked up over his strong, bare young arms; and refraining from looking at his sick master out of consideration for his feelings, and restraining the joy of life that beamed from his face, he went up to the commode.

"Gerasim!" said Ivan Ilych in a weak voice.

Gerasim started, evidently afraid he might have committed some blunder, and with a rapid movement turned his fresh, kind, simple young face which just showed the first downy signs of a beard.

"Yes, sir?"

"That must be very unpleasant for you. You must forgive me. I am helpless."

"Oh, why, sir," and Gerasim's eyes beamed and he showed his glistening white teeth, "what's a little trouble? It's a case of illness with you, sir."

And his deft strong hands did their accustomed task, and he went out of the room stepping lightly. Five minutes later he as lightly returned.

Ivan Ilych was still sitting in the same position in the armchair.

"Gerasim," he said when the latter had replaced the freshly-washed utensil. "Please come here and help me." Gerasim went up to him. "Lift me up. It is hard for me to get up, and I have sent Dmitri away."

Gerasim went up to him, grasped his master with his strong arms deftly but gently, in the same way that he stepped — lifted him, supported him with one hand, and with the other drew up his trousers and would have set him down again, but Ivan Ilych asked to be led to the sofa. Gerasim, without an effort and without apparent pressure, led him, almost lifting him, to the sofa and placed him on it.

"Thank you. How easily and well you do it all!"

Gerasim smiled again and turned to leave the room. But Ivan Ilych felt his presence such a comfort that he did not want to let him go.

"One thing more, please move up that chair. No, the other one — under my feet. It is easier for me when my feet are raised."

Gerasim brought the chair, set it down gently in place, and raised Ivan Ilych's legs on to it. It seemed to Ivan Ilych that he felt better while Gerasim was holding up his legs.

"It's better when my legs are higher," he said. "Place that cushion under them."

Gerasim did so. He again lifted the legs and placed them, and again Ivan Ilych felt better while Gerasim held his legs. When he set them down Ivan Ilych fancied he felt worse.

"Gerasim," he said. "Are you busy now?"

"Not at all, sir," said Gerasim, who had learnt from the townsfolk how to speak to gentlefolk.

"What have you still to do?"

"What have I to do? I've done everything except chopping the logs for tomorrow."

"Then hold my legs up a bit higher, can you?"

"Of course I can. Why not?" And Gerasim raised his master's legs higher and Ivan Ilych thought that in that position he did not feel any pain at all.

"And how about the logs?"

"Don't trouble about that, sir. There's plenty of time."

Ivan Ilych told Gerasim to sit down and hold his legs, and began to talk to him. And strange to say it seemed to him that he felt better while Gerasim held his legs up.

After that Ivan Ilych would sometimes call Gerasim and get him to hold his legs on his shoulders, and he liked talking to him. Gerasim did it all easily, willingly, simply, and with a good nature that touched Ivan Ilych. Health, strength, and vitality in other people were offensive to him, but Gerasim's strength and vitality did not mortify but soothed him.

What tormented Ivan Ilych most was the deception, the lie, which for some reason they all accepted, that he was not dying but was simply ill, and that he only need keep quiet and undergo a treatment and then something very good would result. He, however, knew that do what they would nothing would come of it, only still more agonizing suffering and death. This deception tortured him — their not wishing to admit what they all knew and what he knew, but wanting to lie to him concerning his terrible condition, and wishing and forcing him to participate in that lie. Those lies — lies enacted over him on the eve of his death and destined to degrade this awful, solemn act to the level of their visitings, their curtains, their sturgeon for dinner — were a terrible agony for Ivan Ilych. And strangely enough, many times when they were going through their antics over him he had been within a hairbreadth of calling out to them: "Stop lying! You know and I know that I am dying. Then at least stop lying about it!" But he had never had the spirit to do it. The awful, terrible act of his dying was, he could see, reduced by those about him to the level of a casual, unpleasant, and almost indecorous incident (as if someone entered a drawing-room diffusing an unpleasant odor) and this was done by that very decorum which he had served all his life long. He saw that no one felt for him, because no one even wished to grasp his position. Only Gerasim recognized it and pitied him. And so Ivan Ilych felt at ease only with him. He felt comforted when Gerasim supported his legs (sometimes all night long) and refused to go to bed, saying: "Don't you worry, Ivan Ilych. I'll get sleep enough later on," or when he suddenly became familiar and exclaimed: "If you weren't sick it would be another matter, but as it is, why should I grudge a little trouble?" Gerasim alone did not lie; everything showed that he alone understood the facts of the case and did not consider it necessary to disguise them, but simply felt sorry for his emaciated and enfeebled master. Once when Ivan Ilych was sending him away he even said straight out: "We shall all of us die, so why should I grudge a little trouble?" — expressing the fact that he did not think his work burdensome, because he was doing it for a dying man and hoped someone would do the same for him when his time came.

Apart from this lying, or because of it, what most tormented Ivan Ilych was that no one pitied him as he wished to be pitied. At certain moments after prolonged suffering he wished most of all (though he would have been ashamed to confess it) for someone to pity him as a sick child is pitied. He longed to be petted and comforted. He knew he was an important functionary, that he had a beard turning grey, and that therefore what he longed for was impossible, but still he longed for it. And in Gerasim's attitude towards him there was something akin to what he wished for, and so that attitude comforted him. Ivan Ilych wanted to weep, wanted to be petted and cried over, and then his colleague Shebek would come, and instead of weeping and being petted, Ivan Ilych would assume a serious, severe, and profound air, and by force of habit would express his opinion on a decision of the Court of Cassation and would stubbornly insist on that view. This falsity around him and within him did more than anything else to poison his last days.

VIII

It was morning. He knew it was morning because Gerasim had gone, and Peter the footman had come and put out the candles, drawn back one of the curtains, and begun quietly to tidy up. Whether it was morning or evening, Friday or Sunday, made no difference, it was all just the same: the gnawing, unmitigated, agonizing pain, never ceasing for an instant, the consciousness of life inexorably waning but not yet extinguished, the approach of that ever dreaded and hateful Death which was the only reality, and always the same falsity. What were days, weeks, hours, in such a case?

"Will you have some tea, sir?"   220

"He wants things to be regular, and wishes the gentlefolk to drink tea in the morning," thought Ivan Ilych, and only said "No."

"Wouldn't you like to move onto the sofa, sir?"

"He wants to tidy up the room, and I'm in the way. I am uncleanliness and disorder," he thought, and said only:

"No, leave me alone."

The man went on bustling about. Ivan Ilych stretched out his hand. Peter   225
came up, ready to help.

"What is it, sir?"

"My watch."

Peter took the watch which was close at hand and gave it to his master.

"Half-past eight. Are they up?"

"No, sir, except Vladimir Ivanovich" (the son) "who has gone to school.   230
Praskovya Fëdorovna ordered me to wake her if you asked for her. Shall I do so?"

"No, there's no need to." "Perhaps I'd better have some tea," he thought, and added aloud: "Yes, bring me some tea."

Peter went to the door, but Ivan Ilych dreaded being left alone. "How can I keep him here? Oh yes, my medicine." "Peter, give me my medicine." "Why not? Perhaps it may still do me some good." He took a spoonful and swallowed it. "No, it won't help. It's all tomfoolery, all deception," he decided as soon as he became aware of the familiar, sickly, hopeless taste. "No, I can't believe in it any longer. But the pain, why this pain? If it would only cease just for a moment!" And he moaned. Peter turned towards him. "It's all right. Go and fetch me some tea."

Peter went out. Left alone Ivan Ilych groaned not so much with pain, terrible though that was, as from mental anguish. Always and forever the same, always these endless days and nights. If only it would come quicker! If only *what* would come quicker? Death, darkness? . . . No, no! Anything rather than death!

When Peter returned with the tea on a tray, Ivan Ilych stared at him for a time in perplexity, not realizing who and what he was. Peter was disconcerted by that look and his embarrassment brought Ivan Ilych to himself.

"Oh, tea! All right, put it down. Only help me to wash and put on a clean   235
shirt."

And Ivan Ilych began to wash. With pauses for rest, he washed his hands and then his face, cleaned his teeth, brushed his hair, and looked in the glass. He was terrified by what he saw, especially by the limp way in which his hair clung to his pallid forehead.

While his shirt was being changed he knew that he would be still more frightened at the sight of his body, so he avoided looking at it. Finally he was ready. He drew on a dressing-gown, wrapped himself in a plaid, and sat down in the armchair to take his tea. For a moment he felt refreshed, but soon as he began to drink the tea he was again aware of the same taste, and the pain also returned. He finished it with an effort, and then lay down stretching out his legs, and dismissed Peter.

Always the same. Now a spark of hope flashes up, then a sea of despair rages, and always pain; always pain, always despair, and always the same. When alone he had a dreadful and distressing desire to call someone, but he knew beforehand that with others present it would be still worse. "Another dose of morphine — to lose consciousness. I will tell him, the doctor, that he must think of something else. It's impossible, impossible, to go on like this."

An hour and another pass like that. But now there is a ring at the door bell. Perhaps it's the doctor? It is. He comes in fresh, hearty, plump, and cheerful, with that look on his face that seems to say: "There now, you're in a panic about something, but we'll arrange it all for you directly!" The doctor knows this expression is out of place here, but he has put it on once for all and can't take it off — like a man who has put on a frock-coat in the morning to pay a round of calls.

The doctor rubs his hands vigorously and reassuringly.   240

"Brr! How cold it is! There's such a sharp frost; just let me warm myself!" he says, as if it were only a matter of waiting till he was warm, and then he would put everything right.

"Well now, how are you?"

Ivan Ilych feels that the doctor would like to say: "Well, how are our affairs?" but that even he feels that this would not do, and says instead: "What sort of a night have you had?"

Ivan Ilych looks at him as much as to say: "Are you really never ashamed of lying?" But the doctor does not wish to understand this question, and Ivan Ilych says: "Just as terrible as ever. The pain never leaves me and never subsides. If only something . . ."

"Yes, you sick people are always like that. . . . There, now I think I am   245
warm enough. Even Praskovya Fëdorovna, who is so particular, could find no fault with my temperature. Well, now I can say good-morning," and the doctor presses his patient's hand.

Then, dropping his former playfulness, he begins with a most serious face to examine the patient, feeling his pulse and taking his temperature, and then begins the sounding and auscultation.

Ivan Ilych knows quite well and definitely that all this is nonsense and pure deception, but when the doctor, getting down on his knee, leans over him, putting his ear first higher then lower, and performs various gymnastic movements over him with a significant expression on his face, Ivan Ilych submits to it all as he used to submit to the speeches of the lawyers, though he knew very well that they were all lying and why they were lying.

The doctor, kneeling on the sofa, is still sounding him when Praskovya Fëdorovna's silk dress rustles at the door and she is heard scolding Peter for not having let her know of the doctor's arrival.

She comes in, kisses her husband, and at once proceeds to prove that she has been up a long time already, and only owing to a misunderstanding failed to be there when the doctor arrived.

Ivan Ilych looks at her, scans her all over, sets against her the whiteness and plumpness and cleanness of her hands and neck, the gloss of her hair, and the sparkle of her vivacious eyes. He hates her with his whole soul. And the thrill of hatred he feels for her makes him suffer from her touch.

Her attitude towards him and his disease is still the same. Just as the doctor had adopted a certain relation to his patient which he could not abandon, so had she formed one towards him — that he was not doing something he ought to do and was himself to blame, and that she reproached him lovingly for this — and she could not now change that attitude.

"You see he doesn't listen to me and doesn't take his medicine at the proper time. And above all he lies in a position that is no doubt bad for him — with his legs up."

She described how he made Gerasim hold his legs up.

The doctor smiled with a contemptuous affability that said: "What's to be done? These sick people do have foolish fancies of that kind, but we must forgive them."

When the examination was over the doctor looked at his watch, and then Praskovya Fëdorovna announced to Ivan Ilych that it was of course as he pleased, but she had sent today for a celebrated specialist who would examine him and have a consultation with Michael Danilovich (their regular doctor).

"Please don't raise any objections. I am doing this for my own sake," she said ironically, letting it be felt that she was doing it all for his sake and only said this to leave him no right to refuse. He remained silent, knitting his brows. He felt that he was so surrounded and involved in a mesh of falsity that it was hard to unravel anything.

Everything she did for him was entirely for her own sake, and she told him she was doing for herself what she actually was doing for herself, as if that was so incredible that he must understand the opposite.

At half-past eleven the celebrated specialist arrived. Again the sounding began and the significant conversations in his presence and in another room, about the kidneys and the appendix, and the questions and answers, with such an air of importance that again, instead of the real question of life and death which now alone confronted him, the question arose of the kidney and appendix which were not behaving as they ought to and would now be attacked by Michael Danilovich and the specialist and forced to amend their ways.

The celebrated specialist took leave of him with a serious though not hopeless look, and in reply to the timid question Ivan Ilych, with eyes glistening with fear and hope, put to him as to whether there was a chance of recovery, said that he could not vouch for it but there was a possibility. The look of hope with which Ivan Ilych watched the doctor out was so pathetic that Praskovya Fëdorovna, seeing it, even wept as she left the room to hand the doctor his fee.

The gleam of hope kindled by the doctor's encouragement did not last long. The same room, the same pictures, curtains, wallpaper, medicine bottles, were all there, and the same aching suffering body, and Ivan Ilych began to moan. They gave him a subcutaneous injection and he sank into oblivion.

It was twilight when he came to. They brought him his dinner and he swallowed some beef tea with difficulty, and then everything was the same again and night was coming on.

After dinner, at seven o'clock, Praskovya Fëdorovna came into the room in evening dress, her full bosom pushed up by her corset, and with traces of powder on her face. She had reminded him in the morning that they were going to the theatre. Sarah Bernhardt was visiting the town and they had a box, which he had insisted on their taking. Now he had forgotten about it and her toilet offended him, but he concealed his vexation when he remembered that he had himself insisted on their securing a box and going because it would be an instructive and aesthetic pleasure for the children.

Praskovya Fëdorovna came in, self-satisfied but yet with a rather guilty air. She sat down and asked how he was, but, as he saw, only for the sake of asking and not in order to learn about it, knowing that there was nothing to learn — and then went on to what she really wanted to say: that she would not on any account have gone but that the box had been taken and Helen and their daughter were going, as well as Petrishchev (the examining magistrate, their daughter's fiancé), and that it was out of the question to let them go alone; but that she would have much preferred to sit with him for a while; and he must be sure to follow the doctor's orders while she was away.

"Oh, and Fëdor Petrovich" (the fiancé) "would like to come in. May he? And Lisa?"

"All right."

Their daughter came in in full evening dress, her fresh young flesh exposed (making a show of that very flesh which in his own case caused so much suffering), strong, healthy, evidently in love, and impatient with illness, suffering, and death, because they interfered with her happiness.

Fëdor Petrovich came in too, in evening dress, his hair curled *à la Capoul*°, a tight stiff collar round his long sinewy neck, an enormous white shirt-front, and narrow black trousers tightly stretched over his strong thighs. He had one white glove tightly drawn on, and was holding his opera hat in his hand.

Following him the schoolboy crept in unnoticed, in a uniform, poor little fellow, and wearing gloves. Terribly dark shadows showed under his eyes, the meaning of which Ivan Ilych knew well.

His son had always seemed pathetic to him, and now it was dreadful to see the boy's frightened look of pity. It seemed to Ivan Ilych that Vasya was the only one besides Gerasim who understood and pitied him.

They all sat down and again asked how he was. A silence followed. Lisa asked her mother about the opera-glasses, and there was an altercation between mother and daughter as to who had taken them and where they had been put. This occasioned some unpleasantness.

Fëdor Petrovich inquired of Ivan Ilych whether he had ever seen Sarah Bernhardt. Ivan Ilych did not at first catch the question, but then replied: "No, have you seen her before?"

"Yes, in *Adrienne Lecouvreur*."

Praskovya Fëdorovna mentioned some rôles in which Sarah Bernhardt

à la Capoul: imitating the hair-do of Victor Capoul, a contemporary French singer.

was particularly good. Her daughter disagreed. Conversation sprang up as to the elegance and realism of her acting — the sort of conversation that is always repeated and is always the same.

In the midst of the conversation Fëdor Petrovich glanced at Ivan Ilych and became silent. The others also looked at him and grew silent. Ivan Ilych was staring with glittering eyes straight before him, evidently indignant with them. This had to be rectified, but it was impossible to do so. The silence had to be broken, but for a time no one dared to break it and they all became afraid that the conventional deception would suddenly become obvious and the truth become plain to all. Lisa was the first to pluck up courage and break that silence, but by trying to hide what everybody was feeling, she betrayed it.

"Well, if we are going it's time to start," she said, looking at her watch, a present from her father, and with a faint and significant smile at Fëdor Petrovich relating to something known only to them. She got up with a rustle of her dress.

They all rose, said good-night, and went away.

When they had gone it seemed to Ivan Ilych that he felt better; the falsity had gone with them. But the pain remained — that same pain and that same fear that made everything monotonously alike, nothing harder and nothing easier. Everything was worse.

Again minute followed minute and hour followed hour. Everything remained the same and there was no cessation. And the inevitable end of it all became more and more terrible.

"Yes, send Gerasim here," he replied to a question Peter asked.

IX

His wife returned late at night. She came in on tiptoe, but he heard her, opened his eyes, and made haste to close them again. She wished to send Gerasim away and to sit with him herself, but he opened his eyes and said: "No, go away."

"Are you in great pain?"

"Always the same."

"Take some opium."

He agreed and took some. She went away.

Till about three in the morning he was in a state of stupefied misery. It seemed to him that he and his pain were being thrust into a narrow, deep black sack, but though they were pushed further and further in they could not be pushed to the bottom. And this, terrible enough in itself, was accompanied by suffering. He was frightened yet wanted to fall through the sack, he struggled but yet cooperated. And suddenly he broke through, fell, and regained consciousness. Gerasim was sitting at the foot of the bed dozing quietly and patiently, while he himself lay with his emaciated stockinged legs resting on Gerasim's shoulders; the same shaded candle was there and the same unceasing pain.

"Go away, Gerasim," he whispered.

"It's all right, sir. I'll stay a while."

"No. Go away."

He removed his legs from Gerasim's shoulders, turned sideways onto his arm, and felt sorry for himself. He only waited till Gerasim had gone into the next room and then restrained himself no longer but wept like a child. He wept on account of his helplessness, his terrible loneliness, the cruelty of man, the cruelty of God, and the absence of God.

"Why hast Thou done all this? Why hast Thou brought me here? Why, why dost Thou torment me so terribly?" 290

He did not expect an answer and yet wept because there was no answer and could be none. The pain again grew more acute, but he did not stir and did not call. He said to himself: "Go on! Strike me! But what is it for? What have I done to Thee? What is it for?"

Then he grew quiet and not only ceased weeping but even held his breath and became all attention. It was as though he were listening not to an audible voice but to the voice of his soul, to the current of thoughts arising within him.

"What is it you want?" was the first clear conception capable of expression in words, that he heard.

"What do you want? What do you want?" he repeated to himself.

"What do I want? To live and not to suffer," he answered. 295

And again he listened with such concentrated attention that even his pain did not distract him.

"To live? How?" asked his inner voice.

"Why, to live as I used to — well and pleasantly."

"As you lived before, well and pleasantly?" the voice repeated.

And in imagination he began to recall the best moments of his pleasant 300
life. But strange to say none of those best moments of his pleasant life now seemed at all what they had then seemed — none of them except the first recollections of childhood. There, in childhood, there had been something really pleasant with which it would be possible to live if it could return. But the child who had experienced that happiness existed no longer, it was like a reminiscence of somebody else.

As soon as the period began which had produced the present Ivan Ilych, all that had then seemed joys now melted before his sight and turned into something trivial and often nasty.

And the further he departed from childhood and the nearer he came to the present the more worthless and doubtful were the joys. This began with the School of Law. A little that was really good was still found there — there was lightheartedness, friendship, and hope. But in the upper classes there had already been fewer of such good moments. Then during the first years of his official career, when he was in the service of the Governor, some pleasant moments again occurred; they were the memories of love for a woman. Then all became confused and there was still less of what was good; later on again there was still less that was good, and the further he went the less there was. His marriage, a mere accident, then the disenchantment that followed it, his wife's bad breath and the sensuality and hypocrisy: then that deadly official life and those preoccupations about money, a year of it, and two, and ten, and twenty, and always the same thing. And the longer it lasted the more deadly it became. "It is as if I had been going downhill while I imagined I was going up. And that is really what it was. I was going up in public opinion, but to the same extent life was ebbing away from me. And now it is all done and there is only death."

"Then what does it mean? Why? It can't be that life is so senseless and horrible. But if it really has been so horrible and senseless, why must I die and die in agony? There is something wrong!"

"Maybe I did not live as I ought to have done," it suddenly occurred to him. "But how could that be, when I did everything properly?" he replied, and immediately dismissed from his mind this, the sole solution of all the riddles of life and death, as something quite impossible.

"Then what do you want now? To live? Live how? Live as you lived in the law courts when the usher proclaimed 'The judge is coming!' The judge is coming, the judge!" he repeated to himself. "Here he is, the judge. But I am not guilty!" he exclaimed angrily. "What is it for?" And he ceased crying, but turning his face to the wall continued to ponder on the same question: Why, and for what purpose, is there all this horror? But however much he pondered he found no answer. And whenever the thought occurred to him, as it often did, that it all resulted from his not having lived as he ought to have done, he at once recalled the correctness of his whole life and dismissed so strange an idea.

X

Another fortnight passed. Ivan Ilych now no longer left his sofa. He would not lie in bed but lay on the sofa, facing the wall nearly all the time. He suffered ever the same unceasing agonies and in his loneliness pondered always on the same insoluble question: "What is this? Can it be that it is Death?" And the inner voice answered: "Yes, it is Death."

"Why these sufferings?" And the voice answered, "For no reason — they just are so." Beyond and besides this there was nothing.

From the very beginning of his illness, ever since he had first been to see the doctor, Ivan Ilych's life had been divided between two contrary and alternating moods: now it was despair and the expectation of this uncomprehended and terrible death, and now hope and an intently interested observation of the functioning of his organs. Now before his eyes there was only a kidney or an intestine that temporarily evaded its duty, and now only that incomprehensible and dreadful death from which it was impossible to escape.

These two states of mind had alternated from the very beginning of his illness, but the further it progressed the more doubtful and fantastic became the conception of the kidney, and the more real the sense of impending death.

He had but to call to mind what he had been three months before and what he was now, to call to mind with what regularity he had been going downhill, for every possibility of hope to be shattered.

Latterly during that loneliness in which he found himself as he lay facing the back of the sofa, a loneliness in the midst of a populous town and surrounded by numerous acquaintances and relations but that yet could not have been more complete anywhere — either at the bottom of the sea or under the earth — during that terrible loneliness Ivan Ilych had lived only in memories of the past. Pictures of his past rose before him one after another. They always began with what was nearest in time and then went back to what was most remote — to his childhood — and rested there. If he thought of the stewed prunes that had been offered him that day, his mind went back to the raw shrivelled French plums of his childhood, their peculiar flavor and the flow of saliva when he sucked their stones, and along with the memory of that taste came a whole series of memories of those days: his nurse, his brother, and their toys. "No, I mustn't think of that. . . . It is too painful," Ivan Ilych said to himself, and brought himself back to the present — to the button on the back of the sofa and the creases in its morocco. "Morocco is expensive, but it does not wear well: there had been a quarrel about it. It was a different kind of quarrel and a different kind of morocco that time when we tore father's portfolio and were punished, and mamma brought us some tarts. . . ." And again his thoughts dwelt on his childhood, and again it was painful and he tried to banish them and fix his mind on something else.

Then again together with that chain of memories another series passed through his mind — of how his illness had progressed and grown worse. There also the further back he looked the more life there had been. There had been more of what was good in life and more of life itself. The two merged together. "Just as the pain went on getting worse and worse, so my life grew worse and worse," he thought. "There is one bright spot there at the back, at the beginning of life, and afterwards all becomes blacker and blacker and proceeds more and more rapidly — in inverse ratio to the square of the distance from death," thought Ivan Ilych. And the example of a stone falling downwards with increasing velocity entered his mind. Life, a series of increasing sufferings, flies further and further towards its end — the most terrible suffering. "I am flying. . . ." He shuddered, shifted himself, and tried to resist, but was already aware that resistance was impossible, and again, with eyes weary of gazing but unable to cease seeing what was before them, he stared at the back of the sofa and waited — awaiting that dreadful fall and shock and destruction.

"Resistance is impossible!" he said to himself. "If I could only understand what it is all for! But that too is impossible. An explanation would be possible if it could be said that I have not lived as I ought to. But it is impossible to say that," and he remembered all the legality, correctitude, and propriety of his life. "That at any rate can certainly not be admitted," he thought, and his lips smiled ironically as if someone could see that smile and be taken in by it. "There is no explanation! Agony, death. . . . What for?"

XI

Another two weeks went by in this way and during that fortnight an event occurred that Ivan Ilych and his wife had desired. Petrishchev formally proposed. It happened in the evening. The next day Praskovya Fëdorovna came into her husband's room considering how best to inform him of it, but that very night there had been a fresh change for the worse in his condition. She found him still lying on the sofa but in a different position. He lay on his back, groaning and staring fixedly straight in front of him.

She began to remind him of his medicines, but he turned his eyes towards her with such a look that she did not finish what she was saying; so great an animosity, to her in particular, did that look express.

"For Christ's sake let me die in peace!" he said.

She would have gone away, but just then their daughter came in and went up to say good morning. He looked at her as he had done at his wife, and in reply to her inquiry about his health said dryly that he would soon free them all of himself. They were both silent and after sitting with him for a while went away.

"Is it our fault?" Lisa said to her mother. "It's as if we were to blame! I am sorry for papa, but why should we be tortured?"

The doctor came at his usual time. Ivan Ilych answered "Yes" and "No," never taking his angry eyes from him, and at last said: "You know you can do nothing for me, so leave me alone."

"We can ease your sufferings."   320

"You can't even do that. Let me be."

The doctor went into the drawing-room and told Praskovya Fëdorovna that the case was very serious and that the only resource left was opium to allay her husband's sufferings, which must be terrible.

It was true, as the doctor said, that Ivan Ilych's physical sufferings were terrible, but worse than the physical sufferings were his mental sufferings, which were his chief torture.

His mental sufferings were due to the fact that one night, as he looked at Gerasim's sleepy, good-natured face with its prominent cheekbones, the question suddenly occurred to him: "What if my whole life has really been wrong?"

It occurred to him that what had appeared perfectly impossible before,   325
namely that he had not spent his life as he should have done, might after all be true. It occurred to him that his scarcely perceptible attempts to struggle against what was considered good by the most highly placed people, those scarcely noticeable impulses which he had immediately suppressed, might have been the real thing, and all the rest false. And his professional duties and the whole arrangement of his life and of his family, and all his social and official interests, might all have been false. He tried to defend all those things to himself and suddenly felt the weakness of what he was defending. There was nothing to defend.

"But if that is so," he said to himself, "and I am leaving this life with the consciousness that I have lost all that was given me and it is impossible to rectify it — what then?"

He lay on his back and began to pass his life in review in quite a new way. In the morning when he saw first his footman, then his wife, then his daughter, and then the doctor, their every word and movement confirmed to him the awful truth that had been revealed to him during the night. In them he saw himself — all that for which he had lived — and saw clearly that it was not real at all, but a terrible and huge deception which had hidden both life and death. This consciousness intensified his physical suffering tenfold. He groaned and tossed about, and pulled at his clothing which choked and stifled him. And he hated them on that account.

He was given a large dose of opium and became unconscious, but at noon his sufferings began again. He drove everybody away and tossed from side to side.

His wife came to him and said:

"Jean, my dear, do this for me. It can't do any harm and often helps.   330
Healthy people often do it."

He opened his eyes wide.

"What? Take communion? Why? It's unnecessary! However . . ."

She began to cry.

"Yes, do, my dear. I'll send for our priest. He is such a nice man."

"All right. Very well," he muttered.

When the priest came and heard his confession, Ivan Ilych was softened and seemed to feel a relief from his doubts and consequently from his sufferings, and for a moment there came a ray of hope. He again began to think of the vermiform appendix and the possibility of correcting it. He received the sacrament with tears in his eyes.

When they laid him down again afterwards he felt a moment's ease, and the hope that he might live awoke in him again. He began to think of the operation that had been suggested to him. "To live! I want to live!" he said to himself.

His wife came in to congratulate him after his communion, and when uttering the usual conventional words she added:

"You feel better, don't you?"

Without looking at her he said "Yes."

Her dress, her figure, the expression of her face, the tone of her voice, all revealed the same thing. "This is wrong, it is not as it should be. All you have lived for and still live for is falsehood and deception, hiding life and death from you." And as soon as he admitted that thought, his hatred and his agonizing physical suffering again sprang up, and with that suffering a consciousness of the unavoidable, approaching end. And to this was added a new sensation of grinding shooting pain and a feeling of suffocation.

The expression of his face when he uttered that "yes" was dreadful. Having uttered it, he looked her straight in the eyes, turned on his face with a rapidity extraordinary in his weak state and shouted:

"Go away! Go away and leave me alone!"

XII

From that moment the screaming began that continued for three days, and was so terrible that one could not hear it through two closed doors without horror. At the moment he answered his wife he realized that he was lost, that there was no return, that the end had come, the very end, and his doubts were still unsolved and remained doubts.

"Oh! Oh! Oh!" he cried in various intonations. He had begun by screaming "I won't!" and continued screaming on the letter *O*.

For three whole days, during which time did not exist for him, he struggled in that black sack into which he was being thrust by an invisible, resistless force. He struggled as a man condemned to death struggles in the hands of the executioner, knowing that he cannot save himself. And every moment he felt that despite all his efforts he was drawing nearer and nearer to what terrified him. He felt that his agony was due to his being thrust into that black hole and still more to his not being able to get right into it. He was hindered from getting into it by his conviction that his life had been a good one. That very justification of his life held him fast and prevented his moving forward, and it caused him most torment of all.

Suddenly some force struck him in the chest and side, making it still harder to breathe, and he fell through the hole and there at the bottom was a light. What had happened to him was like the sensation one sometimes experiences in a railway carriage when one thinks one is going backwards while one is really going forwards and suddenly becomes aware of the real direction.

"Yes, it was all not the right thing," he said to himself, "but that's no matter. It can be done. But what *is* the right thing?" he asked himself, and suddenly grew quiet.

This occurred at the end of the third day, two hours before his death. Just then his schoolboy son had crept softly in and gone up to the bedside. The dying man was still screaming desperately and waving his arms. His hand fell on the boy's head, and the boy caught it, pressed it to his lips, and began to cry.

At that very moment Ivan Ilych fell through and caught sight of the light, and it was revealed to him that though his life had not been what it should have been, this could still be rectified. He asked himself, "What *is* the right thing?" and grew still, listening. Then he felt that someone was kissing his hand. He opened his eyes, looked at his son, and felt sorry for him. His wife came up to him and he glanced at her. She was gazing at him open-mouthed, with undried tears on her nose and cheek and a despairing look on her face. He felt sorry for her too.

"Yes, I am making them wretched," he thought. "They are sorry, but it will be better for them when I die." He wished to say this but had not the strength to utter it. "Besides, why speak? I must act," he thought. With a look at his wife he indicated his son and said: "Take him away . . . sorry for him . . . sorry for you too. . . ." He tried to add, "Forgive me," but said "forgo" and waved his hand, knowing that He whose understanding mattered would understand.

And suddenly it grew clear to him that what had been oppressing him and would not leave him was all dropping away at once from two sides, from ten sides, and from all sides. He was sorry for them, he must act so as not to hurt them: release them and free himself from these sufferings. "How good and how simple!" he thought. "And the pain?" he asked himself. "What has become of it? Where are you, pain?"

He turned his attention to it.

"Yes, here it is. Well, what of it? Let the pain be."

"And death . . . where is it?"

He sought his former accustomed fear of death and did not find it. "Where is it? What death?" There was no fear because there was no death.

In place of death there was light.

"So that's what it is!" he suddenly exclaimed aloud. "What joy!"

To him all this happened in a single instant, and the meaning of that instant did not change. For those present his agony continued for another two hours. Something rattled in his throat, his emaciated body twitched, then the gasping and rattle became less and less frequent.

"It is finished!" said someone near him.

He heard these words and repeated them in his soul.

"Death is finished," he said to himself. "It is no more!"

He drew in a breath, stopped in the midst of a sigh, stretched out, and died.

350

355

360

Nathaniel Hawthorne

THE BIRTHMARK   1846

Nathaniel Hawthorne (1804 – 1864) was born in the clipper-ship seaport of Salem, Massachusetts, son of a merchant captain and grandson of a judge at the notorious Salem witchcraft trials. Hawthorne takes a keen interest in New England's sin-and-brimstone Puritan past in many of his stories and in The Scarlet Letter *(1848), that enduring novel of a woman taken in adultery. After college, Hawthorne lived at home and trained to be a writer. Only when his first collection,* Twice-Told Tales *(1837), made money did he feel secure enough to marry Sophia Peabody and settle in the Old Manse in Concord, Massachusetts. Three more novels followed* The Scarlet Letter: The House of the Seven Gables *(1851, a story tinged with nightmarish humor),* The Blithedale Romance *(1852, drawn from his short, disgruntled stay at a Utopian commune, Brook Farm), and* The Marble Faun *(1860, inspired by a stay in Italy). Hawthorne wrote for children, too, retelling classic legends in* The Wonder Book *(1852) and* Tanglewood Tales *(1853). At Bowdoin College, he had been a classmate of Franklin Pierce; later, when Pierce ran for President of the United States, Hawthorne wrote him a campaign biography. The victorious Pierce appointed his old friend American counsel at Liverpool, England. With his contemporary Edgar Allan Poe, Hawthorne sped the transformation of the American short story from popular magazine filler into a form of art.*

In the latter part of the last century there lived a man of science, an eminent proficient in every branch of natural philosophy, who not long before our story opens had made experience of a spiritual affinity more attractive than any chemical one. He had left his laboratory to the care of an assistant, cleared his fine countenance from the furnace smoke, washed the stain of acids from his fingers, and persuaded a beautiful woman to become his wife. In those days when the comparatively recent discovery of electricity and other kindred mysteries of Nature seemed to open paths into the region of miracle, it was not unusual for the love of science to rival the love of woman in its depth and absorbing energy. The higher intellect, the imagination, the spirit, and even the heart might all find their congenial aliment in pursuits which, as some of their ardent votaries believed, would ascend from one step of powerful intelligence to another, until the philosopher should lay his hand on the secret of creative force and perhaps make new worlds for himself. We know not whether Aylmer possessed this degree of faith in man's ultimate control over Nature. He had devoted himself, however, too unreservedly to scientific studies ever to be weaned from them by any second passion. His love for his young wife might prove the stronger of the two; but it could only be by intertwining itself with his love of science, and uniting the strength of the latter to his own.

Such a union accordingly took place, and was attended with truly remarkable consequences and a deeply impressive moral. One day, very soon after their marriage, Aylmer sat gazing at his wife with a trouble in his countenance that grew stronger until he spoke.

"Georgiana," said he, "has it never occurred to you that the mark upon your cheek might be removed?"

"No, indeed," said she, smiling; but perceiving the seriousness of his manner, she blushed deeply. "To tell you the truth it has been so often called a charm that I was simple enough to imagine it might be so."

"Ah, upon another face perhaps it might," replied her husband; "but never on yours. No, dearest Georgiana, you came so nearly perfect from the hand of Nature that this slightest possible defect, which we hesitate whether to term a defect or a beauty, shocks me, as being the visible mark of earthly imperfection."

"Shocks you, my husband!" cried Georgiana, deeply hurt; at first reddening with momentary anger, but then bursting into tears. "Then why did you take me from my mother's side? You cannot love what shocks you!"

To explain this conversation it must be mentioned that in the center of Georgiana's left cheek there was a singular mark, deeply interwoven, as it were, with the texture and substance of her face. In the usual state of her complexion — a healthy though delicate bloom — the mark wore a tint of deeper crimson, which imperfectly defined its shape amid the surrounding rosiness. When she blushed it gradually became more indistinct, and finally vanished amid the triumphant rush of blood that bathed the whole cheek with its brilliant glow. But if any shifting motion caused her to turn pale there was the mark again, a crimson stain upon the snow, in what Aylmer sometimes deemed an almost fearful distinctness. Its shape bore not a little similarity to the human hand, though of the smallest pygmy size. Georgiana's lovers were wont to say that some fairy at her birth hour had laid her tiny hand upon the infant's cheek, and left this impress there in token of the magic endowments that were to give her such sway over all hearts. Many a desperate swain would have risked life for the privilege of pressing his lips to the mysterious hand. It must not be concealed, however, that the impression wrought by this fairy sign manual varied exceedingly, according to the difference of temperament in the beholders. Some fastidious persons — but they were exclusively of her own sex — affirmed that the bloody hand, as they chose to call it, quite destroyed the effect of Georgiana's beauty, and rendered her countenance even hideous. But it would be as reasonable to say that one of those small blue stains which sometimes occur in the purest statuary marble would convert the Eve of Powers to a monster. Masculine observers, if the birthmark did not heighten their admiration, contented themselves with wishing it away, that the world might possess one living specimen of ideal loveliness without the semblance of a flaw. After his marriage — for he thought little or nothing of the matter before — Aylmer discovered that this was the case with himself.

Had she been less beautiful — if Envy's self could have found aught else to sneer at — he might have felt his affection heightened by the prettiness of this mimic hand, now vaguely portrayed, now lost, now stealing forth again and glimmering to and fro with every pulse of emotion that throbbed within her heart; but seeing her otherwise so perfect, he found this one defect grow more and more intolerable with every moment of their united lives. It was the fatal flaw of humanity which Nature, in one shape or another, stamps ineffaceably on all her productions, either to imply that they are temporary and finite, or that their perfection must be wrought by toil and pain. The crimson hand expressed the ineludible grip in which mortality clutches the highest and purest of earthly mould, degrading them into kindred with the lowest, and even with the very brutes, like whom their visible frames return to dust. In this manner, selecting it as the symbol of his wife's liability to sin, sorrow, decay, and death, Aylmer's somber imagination was not long in rendering the birthmark a frightful object, causing him more trouble and horror than ever Georgiana's beauty, whether of soul or sense, had given him delight.

At all the seasons which should have been their happiest, he invariably and without intending it, nay, in spite of a purpose to the contrary, reverted to this one disastrous topic. Trifling as it at first appeared, it so connected itself with innumerable trains of thought and modes of feeling that it became the central point of all. With the morning twilight Aylmer opened his eyes upon his wife's face and recognized the symbol of imperfection; and when they sat together at the evening hearth his eyes wandered stealthily to her cheek, and beheld, flickering with the blaze of the wood fire, the spectral hand that wrote mortality where he would fain have worshipped. Georgiana soon learned to shudder at his gaze. It needed but a glance with the peculiar expression that his face often wore to change the roses of her cheek into a deathlike paleness, amid which the crimson hand was brought strongly out, like a bas-relief of ruby on the whitest marble.

Late one night when the lights were growing dim, so as hardly to betray   10
the stain on the poor wife's cheek, she herself, for the first time, voluntarily took up the subject.

"Do you remember, my dear Aylmer," said she, with a feeble attempt at a smile, "have you any recollection of a dream last night about this odious hand?"

"None! none whatever!" replied Aylmer, starting; but then he added, in a dry, cold tone, affected for the sake of concealing the real depth of his emotion, "I might well dream of it; for before I fell asleep it had taken a pretty firm hold of my fancy."

"And you did dream of it?" continued Georgiana, hastily; for she dreaded lest a gush of tears should interrupt what she had to say. "A terrible dream! I wonder that you can forget it. Is it possible to forget this one expression? — 'It is in her heart now; we must have it out!' Reflect, my husband; for by all means I would have you recall that dream."

The mind is in a sad state when Sleep, the all-involving, cannot confine her specters within the dim region of her sway, but suffers them to break forth, affrighting this actual life with secrets that perchance belong to a deeper one. Aylmer now remembered his dream. He had fancied himself with his servant Aminadab° attempting an operation for the removal of the birthmark; but the deeper went the knife, the deeper sank the hand, until at length its tiny grasp appeared to have caught hold of Georgiana's heart; whence, however, her husband was inexorably resolved to cut or wrench it away.

When the dream had shaped itself perfectly in his memory, Aylmer sat   15

Aminadab: Spelled backward, the name becomes _bad anima_ — "bad soul" or "evil spirit."

in his wife's presence with a guilty feeling. Truth often finds its way to the mind close muffled in robes of sleep, and then speaks with uncompromising directness of matters in regard to which we practice an unconscious self-deception during our waking moments. Until now he had not been aware of the tyrannizing influence acquired by one idea over his mind, and of the lengths which he might find in his heart to go for the sake of giving himself peace.

"Aylmer," resumed Georgiana, solemnly. "I know not what may be the cost to both of us to rid me of this fatal birthmark. Perhaps its removal may cause cureless deformity; or it may be the stain goes as deep as life itself. Again: do we know that there is a possibility, on any terms, of unclasping the firm grip of this little hand which was laid upon me before I came into the world?"

"Dearest Georgiana, I have spent much thought upon the subject," hastily interrupted Aylmer. "I am convinced of the perfect practicability of its removal."

"If there be the remotest possibility of it," continued Georgiana, "let the attempt be made at whatever risk. Danger is nothing to me; for life, while this hateful mark makes me the object of your horror and disgust — life is a burden which I would fling down with joy. Either remove this dreadful hand, or take my wretched life! You have deep science. All the world bears witness of it. You have achieved great wonders. Cannot you remove this little, little mark, which I cover with the tips of two small fingers? Is this beyond your power, for the sake of your own peace, and to save your poor wife from madness?"

"Noblest, dearest, tenderest wife," cried Aylmer, rapturously, "doubt not my power. I have already given this matter the deepest thought — thought which might almost have enlightened me to create a being less perfect than yourself. Georgiana, you have led me deeper than ever into the heart of science. I feel myself fully competent to render this dear cheek as faultless as its fellow; and then, most beloved, what will be my triumph when I shall have corrected what Nature left imperfect in her fairest work! Even Pygmalion, when his sculptured woman assumed life, felt not greater ecstasy than mine will be."

"It is resolved, then," said Georgiana, faintly smiling. "And, Aylmer, spare me not, though you should find the birthmark take refuge in my heart at last." 20

Her husband tenderly kissed her cheek — her right cheek — not that which bore the impress of the crimson hand.

The next day Aylmer apprised his wife of a plan that he had formed whereby he might have opportunity for the intense thought and constant watchfulness which the proposed operation would require; while Georgiana, likewise, would enjoy the perfect repose essential to its success. They were to seclude themselves in the extensive apartments occupied by Aylmer as a laboratory, and where, during his toilsome youth, he had made discoveries in the elemental powers of Nature that had roused the admiration of all the learned societies in Europe. Seated calmly in this laboratory, the pale philosopher had investigated the secrets of the highest cloud region and of the profoundest mines; he had satisfied himself of the causes that kindled and kept alive the fires of the volcano; and had explained the mystery of fountains, and how it is that they gush forth, some so bright and pure, and others with such rich medicinal virtues, from the dark bosom of the earth. Here, too, at an earlier period, he had studied the wonders of the human frame, and attempted to fathom the very process by which Nature assimilates all her precious influences from earth and air, and from the spiritual world, to create and foster man, her masterpiece. The latter pursuit, however, Aylmer had long laid aside in unwilling recognition of the truth — against which all seekers sooner or later stumble — that our great creative Mother, while she amuses us with apparently working in the broadest sunshine, is yet severely careful to keep her own secrets, and, in spite of her pretended openness, shows us nothing but results. She permits us, indeed, to mar, but seldom to mend, and, like a jealous patentee, on no account to make. Now, however, Aylmer resumed these half-forgotten investigations; not, of course, with such hopes or wishes as first suggested them; but because they involved much physiological truth and lay in the path of his proposed scheme for the treatment of Georgiana.

As he led her over the threshold of the laboratory, Georgiana was cold and tremulous. Aylmer looked cheerfully into her face, with intent to reassure her, but was so startled with the intense glow of the birthmark upon the whiteness of her cheek that he could not restrain a strong convulsive shudder. His wife fainted.

"Aminadab! Aminadab!" shouted Aylmer, stamping violently on the floor.

Forthwith there issued from an inner apartment a man of low stature, but bulky frame, with shaggy hair hanging about his visage, which was grimed with the vapors of the furnace. This personage had been Aylmer's underworker during his whole scientific career, and was admirably fitted for that office by his great mechanical readiness, and the skill with which, while incapable of comprehending a single principle, he executed all the details of his master's experiments. With his vast strength, his shaggy hair, his smoky aspect, and the indescribable earthiness that incrusted him, he seemed to represent man's physical nature; while Aylmer's slender figure, and pale, intellectual face, were no less apt a type of the spiritual element.

"Throw open the door of the boudoir, Aminadab," said Aylmer, "and burn a pastil°."

"Yes, master," answered Aminadab, looking intently at the lifeless form of Georgiana; and then he muttered to himself, "If she were my wife, I'd never part with that birthmark."

When Georgiana recovered consciousness she found herself breathing an atmosphere of penetrating fragrance, the gentle potency of which had recalled her from her deathlike faintness. The scene around her looked like enchantment. Aylmer had converted those smoky, dingy, somber rooms, where he had spent his brightest years in recondite pursuits, into a series of beautiful apartments not unfit to be the secluded abode of a lovely woman. The walls were hung with gorgeous curtains, which imparted the combination of grandeur and grace that no other species of adornment can achieve; and as they fell from the ceiling to the floor, their rich and ponderous folds, concealing all angles and straight lines, appeared to shut in the scene from infinite space. For aught

pastil: a pellet of aromatic paste, burned to deodorize the air.

278   Stories for Further Reading

Georgiana knew, it might be a pavilion among the clouds. And Aylmer, excluding the sunshine, which would have interfered with his chemical processes, had supplied its place with perfumed lamps, emitting flames of various hue, but all uniting in a soft, impurpled radiance. He now knelt by his wife's side, watching her earnestly, but without alarm; for he was confident in his science, and felt that he could draw a magic circle round her within which no evil might intrude.

"Where am I? Ah, I remember," said Georgiana, faintly; and she placed her hand over her cheek to hide the terrible mark from her husband's eyes.

"Fear not, dearest!" exclaimed he. "Do not shrink from me! Believe me, 30 Georgiana, I even rejoice in this single imperfection, since it will be such a rapture to remove it."

"Oh, spare me!" sadly replied his wife. "Pray do not look at it again. I never can forget that convulsive shudder."

In order to soothe Georgiana, and, as it were, to release her mind from the burden of actual things, Aylmer now put in practice some of the light and playful secrets which science had taught him among its profounder lore. Airy figures, absolutely bodiless ideas, and forms of unsubstantial beauty came and danced before her, imprinting their momentary footsteps on beams of light. Though she had some indistinct idea of the method of these optical phenomena, still the illusion was almost perfect enough to warrant the belief that her husband possessed sway over the spiritual world. Then again, when she felt a wish to look forth from her seclusion, immediately, as if her thoughts were answered, the procession of external existence flitted across a screen. The scenery and the figures of actual life were perfectly represented, but with that bewitching, yet indescribable difference which always makes a picture, an image, or a shadow so much more attractive than the original. When wearied of this, Aylmer bade her cast her eyes upon a vessel containing a quantity of earth. She did so, with little interest at first; but was soon startled to perceive the germ of a plant shooting upward from the soil. Then came the slender stalk; the leaves gradually unfolded themselves; and amid them was a perfect and lovely flower.

"It is magical!" cried Georgiana. "I dare not touch it."

"Nay, pluck it," answered Aylmer — "pluck it, and inhale its brief perfume while you may. The flower will wither in a few moments and leave nothing save its brown seed vessels; but thence may be perpetuated a race as ephemeral as itself."

But Georgiana had no sooner touched the flower than the whole plant 35 suffered a blight, its leaves turning coal-black as if by the agency of fire.

"There was too powerful a stimulus," said Aylmer, thoughtfully.

To make up for this abortive experiment, he proposed to take her portrait by a scientific process of his own invention. It was to be effected by rays of light striking upon a polished plate of metal. Georgiana assented; but, on looking at the result, was affrighted to find the features of the portrait blurred and indefinable; while the minute figure of a hand appeared where the cheek should have been. Aylmer snatched the metallic plate and threw it into a jar of corrosive acid.

Soon, however, he forgot these mortifying failures. In the intervals of study and chemical experiment he came to her flushed and exhausted, but seemed invigorated by her presence, and spoke in glowing language of the resources of his art. He gave a history of the long dynasty of the alchemists, who spent so many ages in quest of the universal solvent by which the golden principle might be elicited from all things vile and base. Aylmer appeared to believe that, by the plainest scientific logic, it was altogether within the limits of possibility to discover this long-sought medium; "but," he added, "a philosopher who should go deep enough to acquire the power would attain too lofty a wisdom to stoop to the exercise of it." Not less singular were his opinions in regard to the elixir vitæ. He more than intimated that it was at his option to concoct a liquid that should prolong life for years, perhaps interminably; but that it would produce a discord in Nature which all the world, and chiefly the quaffer of the immortal nostrum, would find cause to curse.

"Aylmer, are you in earnest?" asked Georgiana, looking at him with amazement and fear. "It is terrible to possess such power, or even to dream of possessing it."

"Oh, do not tremble, my love," said her husband. "I would not wrong   40 either you or myself by working such inharmonious effects upon our lives; but I would have you consider how trifling, in comparison, is the skill requisite to remove this little hand."

At the mention of the birthmark, Georgiana, as usual, shrank as if a redhot iron had touched her cheek.

Again Aylmer applied himself to his labors. She could hear his voice in the distant furnace room giving directions to Aminadab, whose harsh, uncouth, misshapen tones were audible in response, more like the grunt or growl of a brute than human speech. After hours of absence, Aylmer reappeared and proposed that she should now examine his cabinet of chemical products and natural treasures of the earth. Among the former he showed her a small vial, in which, he remarked, was contained a gentle yet most powerful fragrance, capable of impregnating all the breezes that blow across a kingdom. They were of inestimable value, the contents of that little vial; and, as he said so, he threw some of the perfume into the air and filled the room with piercing and invigorating delight.

"And what is this?" asked Georgiana, pointing to a small crystal globe containing a gold-colored liquid. "It is so beautiful to the eye that I could imagine it the elixir of life."

"In one sense it is," replied Aylmer; "or, rather, the elixir of immortality. It is the most precious poison that ever was concocted in this world. By its aid I could apportion the lifetime of any mortal at whom you might point your finger. The strength of the dose would determine whether he were to linger out years, or drop dead in the midst of a breath. No king on his guarded throne could keep his life if I, in my private station, should deem that the welfare of millions justified me in depriving him of it."

"Why do you keep such a terrific drug?" inquired Georgiana in horror.   45

"Do not mistrust me, dearest," said her husband, smiling; "its virtuous potency is yet greater than its harmful one. But see! here is a powerful cosmetic. With a few drops of this in a vase of water, freckles may be washed away as easily as the hands are cleansed. A stronger infusion would take the blood out of the cheek, and leave the rosiest beauty a pale ghost."

"Is it with this lotion that you intend to bathe my cheek?" asked Georgiana, anxiously.

"Oh, no," hastily replied her husband; "this is merely superficial. Your case demands a remedy that shall go deeper."

In his interviews with Georgiana, Aylmer generally made minute inquiries as to her sensations and whether the confinement of the rooms and the temperature of the atmosphere agreed with her. These questions had such a particular drift that Georgiana began to conjecture that she was already subjected to certain physical influences, either breathed in with the fragrant air or taken with her food. She fancied likewise, but it might be altogether fancy, that there was a stirring up of her system — a strange, indefinite sensation creeping through her veins, and tingling, half painfully, half pleasurably, at her heart. Still, whenever she dared to look into the mirror, there she beheld herself pale as a white rose and with the crimson birthmark stamped upon her cheek. Not even Aylmer now hated it so much as she.

To dispel the tedium of the hours which her husband found it necessary 50
to devote to the processes of combination and analysis, Georgiana turned over the volumes of his scientific library. In many dark old tomes she met with chapters full of romance and poetry. They were the works of philosophers of the middle ages, such as Albertus Magnus, Cornelius Agrippa, Paracelsus, and the famous friar who created the prophetic Brazen Head°. All these antique naturalists stood in advance of their centuries, yet were imbued with some of their credulity, and therefore were believed, and perhaps imagined themselves to have acquired from the investigation of Nature a power above Nature, and from physics a sway over the spiritual world. Hardly less curious and imaginative were the early volumes of the Transactions of the Royal Society, in which the members, knowing little of the limits of natural possibility, were continually recording wonders or proposing methods whereby wonders might be wrought.

But to Georgiana the most engrossing volume was a large folio from her husband's own hand, in which he had recorded every experiment of his scientific career, its original aim, the methods adopted for its development, and its final success or failure, with the circumstances to which either event was attributable. The book, in truth, was both the history and emblem of his ardent, ambitious, imaginative, yet practical and laborious life. He handled physical details as if there were nothing beyond them; yet spiritualized them all, and redeemed himself from materialism by his strong and eager aspiration

---

Albertus Magnus . . . Brazen Head: medieval experimental scientists popularly supposed to be magicians. Albertus Magnus, or Saint Albert the Great (1206 – 1280), was a learned German scholar, teacher, and philosopher. He made contributions to botany, zoology, and astronomy, and succeeded in producing arsenic in his laboratory. Heinrich Cornelius Agrippa (1486 – 1535), German physician and theologian, wrote a treatise on the occult. He figures in early legends of Faust, who traded his soul in exchange for knowledge and power. Paracelsus (born Theophrastus Bombastus von Hohenheim, 1493? – 1541), Swiss physician and alchemist, introduced several drugs to medicine and proved that goiter in a parent can cause cretinism in a child. According to one story, he tried to grow babies in bottles. The "famous friar" was Roger Bacon, English Franciscan (c. 1220 – 1284?), author of an encyclopedia of scientific knowledge. In a popular story, the basis of Robert Greene's play *Friar Bacon and Friar Bungay* (1594), Bacon with the help of the Devil constructs a talking head of brass. It utters the words "Time is," "Time was," and "Time is past," then smashes to bits.

towards the infinite. In his grasp the veriest clod of earth assumed a soul. Georgiana, as she read, reverenced Aylmer and loved him more profoundly than ever, but with a less entire dependence on his judgment than heretofore. Much as he had accomplished, she could not but observe that his most splendid successes were almost invariably failures, if compared with the ideal at which he aimed. His brightest diamonds were the merest pebbles, and felt to be so by himself, in comparison with the inestimable gems which lay hidden beyond his reach. The volume, rich with achievements that had won renown for its author, was yet as melancholy a record as ever mortal hand had penned. It was the sad confession and continual exemplification of the shortcomings of the composite man, the spirit burdened with clay and working in matter, and of the despair that assails the higher nature at finding itself so miserably thwarted by the earthly part. Perhaps every man of genius in whatever sphere might recognize the image of his own experience in Aylmer's journal.

So deeply did these reflections affect Georgiana that she laid her face upon the open volume and burst into tears. In this situation she was found by her husband.

"It is dangerous to read in a sorcerer's books," said he with a smile, though his countenance was uneasy and displeased. "Georgiana, there are pages in that volume which I can scarcely glance over and keep my senses. Take heed lest it prove as detrimental to you."

"It has made me worship you more than ever," said she.

"Ah, wait for this one success," rejoined he, "then worship me if you will. I shall deem myself hardly unworthy of it. But come, I have sought you for the luxury of your voice. Sing to me, dearest." ⁵⁵

So she poured out the liquid music of her voice to quench the thirst of his spirit. He then took his leave with a boyish exuberance of gayety, assuring her that her seclusion would endure but a little longer, and that the result was already certain. Scarcely had he departed when Georgiana felt irresistibly impelled to follow him. She had forgotten to inform Aylmer of a symptom which for two or three hours past had begun to excite her attention. It was a sensation in the fatal birthmark, not painful, but which induced a restlessness throughout her system. Hastening after her husband, she intruded for the first time into the laboratory.

The first thing that struck her eye was the furnace, that hot and feverish worker, with the intense glow of its fire, which by the quantities of soot clustered above it seemed to have been burning for ages. There was a distilling apparatus in full operation. Around the room were retorts, tubes, cylinders, crucibles, and other apparatus of chemical research. An electrical machine stood ready for immediate use. The atmosphere felt oppressively close, and was tainted with gaseous odors which had been tormented forth by the processes of science. The severe and homely simplicity of the apartment, with its naked walls and brick pavement, looked strange, accustomed as Georgiana had become to the fantastic elegance of her boudoir. But what chiefly, indeed almost solely, drew her attention, was the aspect of Aylmer himself.

He was pale as death, anxious and absorbed, and hung over the furnace as if it depended upon his utmost watchfulness whether the liquid which it was distilling should be the draught of immortal happiness or misery. How different from the sanguine and joyous mien that he had assumed for Georgiana's encouragement!

"Carefully now, Aminadab; carefully, thou human machine; carefully, thou man of clay!" muttered Aylmer, more to himself than his assistant. "Now, if there be a thought too much or too little, it is all over."

"Ho! ho!" mumbled Aminadab. "Look, master! Look!"

Aylmer raised his eyes hastily, and at first reddened, then grew paler than ever, on beholding Georgiana. He rushed towards her and seized her arm with a grip that left the print of his fingers upon it.

"Why do you come hither? Have you no trust in your husband?" cried he, impetuously. "Would you throw the blight of that fatal birthmark over my labors? It is not well done. Go, prying woman, go!"

"Nay, Aylmer," said Georgiana with the firmness of which she possessed no stinted endowment, "it is not you that have a right to complain. You mistrust your wife; you have concealed the anxiety with which you watch the development of this experiment. Think not so unworthily of me, my husband. Tell me all the risk we run, and fear not that I shall shrink; for my share in it is far less than your own."

"No, no, Georgiana!" said Aylmer, impatiently; "it must not be."

"I submit," replied she calmly. "And, Aylmer, I shall quaff whatever draught you bring me; but it will be on the same principle that would induce me to take a dose of poison if offered by your hand."

"My noble wife," said Aylmer, deeply moved, "I knew not the height and depth of your nature until now. Nothing shall be concealed. Know, then, that this crimson hand, superficial as it seems, has clutched its grasp into your being with a strength of which I had no previous conception. I have already administered agents powerful enough to do aught except to change your entire physical system. Only one thing remains to be tried. If that fail us we are ruined."

"Why did you hesitate to tell me this?" asked she.

"Because, Georgiana," said Aylmer, in a low voice, "there is danger."

"Danger? There is but one danger — that this horrible stigma shall be left upon my cheek!" cried Georgiana. "Remove it, remove it, whatever be the cost, or we shall both go mad!"

"Heaven knows your words are too true," said Aylmer, sadly. "And now, dearest, return to your boudoir. In a little while all will be tested."

He conducted her back and took leave of her with a solemn tenderness which spoke far more than his words how much was now at stake. After his departure Georgiana became rapt in musings. She considered the character of Aylmer, and did it completer justice than at any previous moment. Her heart exulted, while it trembled, at his honorable love — so pure and lofty that it would accept nothing less than perfection nor miserably make itself contented with an earthlier nature than he had dreamed of. She felt how much more precious was such a sentiment than that meaner kind which would have borne with the imperfection for her sake, and have been guilty of treason to holy love by degrading its perfect idea to the level of the actual; and with her whole spirit she prayed that, for a single moment, she might satisfy his highest and deepest conception. Longer than one moment she well knew it could not be; for his

spirit was ever on the march, ever ascending, and each instant required something that was beyond the scope of the instant before.

The sound of her husband's footsteps aroused her. He bore a crystal
goblet containing a liquor colorless as water, but bright enough to be the
draught of immortality. Aylmer was pale; but it seemed rather the consequence
of a highly-wrought state of mind and tension of spirit than of fear or doubt.

"The concoction of the draught has been perfect," said he, in answer to
Georgiana's look. "Unless all my science have deceived me, it cannot fail."

"Save on your account, my dearest Aylmer," observed his wife, "I might
wish to put off this birthmark of mortality by relinquishing mortality itself in
preference to any other mode. Life is but a sad possession to those who have
attained precisely the degree of moral advancement at which I stand. Were I
weaker and blinder it might be happiness. Were I stronger, it might be endured
hopefully. But, being what I find myself, methinks I am of all mortals the most
fit to die."

"You are fit for heaven without tasting death!" replied her husband. "But   75
why do we speak of dying? The draught cannot fail. Behold its effect upon
this plant."

On the window seat there stood a geranium diseased with yellow blotches, which had overspread all its leaves. Aylmer poured a small quantity of
the liquid upon the soil in which it grew. In a little time, when the roots of
the plant had taken up the moisture, the unsightly blotches began to be
extinguished in a living verdure.

"There needed no proof," said Georgiana, quietly. "Give me the goblet,
I joyfully stake all upon your word."

"Drink, then, thou lofty creature!" exclaimed Aylmer, with fervid admiration. "There is no taint of imperfection on thy spirit. Thy sensible frame, too,
shall soon be all perfect."

She quaffed the liquid and returned the goblet to his hand.

"It is grateful," said she with a placid smile. "Methinks it is like water   80
from a heavenly fountain; for it contains I know not what of unobtrusive
fragrance and deliciousness. It allays a feverish thirst that had parched me for
many days. Now, dearest, let me sleep. My earthly senses are closing over my
spirit like the leaves around the heart of a rose at sunset."

She spoke the last words with a gentle reluctance, as if it required almost
more energy than she could command to pronounce the faint and lingering
syllables. Scarcely had they loitered through her lips ere she was lost in slumber. Aylmer sat by her side, watching her aspect with the emotions proper to
a man the whole value of whose existence was involved in the process now
to be tested. Mingled with this mood, however, was the philosophic investigation characteristic of the man of science. Not the minutest symptom escaped
him. A heightened flush of the cheek, a slight irregularity of breath, a quiver
of the eyelid, a hardly perceptible tremor through the frame — such were the
details which, as the moments passed, he wrote down in his folio volume.
Intense thought had set its stamp upon every previous page of that volume,
but the thoughts of years were all concentrated upon the last.

While thus employed, he failed not to gaze often at the fatal hand, and
not without a shudder. Yet once, by a strange and unaccountable impulse, he
pressed it with his lips. His spirit recoiled, however, in the very act; and

Georgiana, out of the midst of her deep sleep, moved uneasily and murmured as if in remonstrance. Again Aylmer resumed his watch. Nor was it without avail. The crimson hand, which at first had been strongly visible upon the marble paleness of Georgiana's cheek, now grew more faintly outlined. She remained not less pale than ever; but the birthmark, with every breath that came and went, lost somewhat of its former distinctness. Its presence had been awful; its departure was more awful still. Watch the stain of the rainbow fading out the sky, and you will know how that mysterious symbol passed away.

"By Heaven! it is well-nigh gone!" said Aylmer to himself, in almost irrepressible ecstasy. "I can scarcely trace it now. Success! success! And now it is like the faintest rose color. The lightest flush of blood across her cheek would overcome it. But she is so pale!"

He drew aside the window curtain and suffered the light of natural day to fall into the room and rest upon her cheek. At the same time he heard a gross, hoarse chuckle, which he had long known as his servant Aminadab's expression of delight.

"Ah, clod! ah, earthly mass!" cried Aylmer, laughing in a sort of frenzy, 85 "you have served me well! Matter and spirit — earth and heaven — have both done their part in this! Laugh, thing of the senses! You have earned the right to laugh."

These exclamations broke Georgiana's sleep. She slowly unclosed her eyes and gazed into the mirror which her husband had arranged for that purpose. A faint smile flitted over her lips when she recognized how barely perceptible was now that crimson hand which had once blazed forth with such disastrous brilliancy as to scare away all their happiness. But then her eyes sought Aylmer's face with a trouble and anxiety that he could by no means account for.

"My poor Aylmer!" murmured she.

"Poor? Nay, richest, happiest, most favored!" exclaimed he. "My peerless bride, it is successful! You are perfect!"

"My poor Aylmer," she repeated, with a more than human tenderness, "you have aimed loftily; you have done nobly. Do not repent that with so high and pure a feeling, you have rejected the best the earth could offer. Aylmer, dearest Aylmer, I am dying!"

Alas! it was too true! The fatal hand had grappled with the mystery of 90 life, and was the bond by which an angelic spirit kept itself in union with a mortal frame. As the last crimson tint of the birthmark — that sole token of human imperfection — faded from her cheek, the parting breath of the now perfect woman passed into the atmosphere, and her soul, lingering a moment near her husband, took its heavenward flight. Then a hoarse, chuckling laugh was heard again! Thus ever does the gross fatality of earth exult in its invariable triumph over the immortal essence which, in this dim sphere of half development, demands the completeness of a higher state. Yet, had Aylmer reached a profounder wisdom, he need not thus have flung away the happiness which would have woven his mortal life of the selfsame texture with the celestial. The momentary circumstance was too strong for him; he failed to look beyond the shadowy scope of time, and, living once for all in eternity, to find the perfect future in the present.

Virginia Woolf

A HAUNTED HOUSE

Virginia Woolf (1882 – 1941), born in London, was educated mostly at home, where she read widely and deeply in the large personal library of her father, Sir Leslie Stephen, a prominent critic and editor. In 1904 she moved to London's Bloomsbury district, taking a dominant place in the Bloomsbury Group, a lively circle of young highbrows including biographer Lytton Strachey and economist John Maynard Keynes. With her husband Leonard Woolf, she established the influential Hogarth Press, publishing her own novels, the stories of her friend Katherine Mansfield, and the first English translations of Sigmund Freud's works. Woolf's fiction displays her keen interest in psychology. Mrs. Dalloway *(1920) reveals the minds of its characters as flowing streams of consciousness;* To the Lighthouse *(1927) abounds in dream symbols, sexual and otherwise. During World War II, saddened by bombing raids and by her long struggle with recurrent mental illness, Woolf took her life. A brilliant critic and essayist, she has seemed a writer of heightened importance to recent feminists, who especially admire* A Room of One's Own *(1929) and* Three Guineas *(1938).*

Whatever hour you woke there was a door shutting. From room to room they went, hand in hand, lifting here, opening there, making sure — a ghostly couple.

"Here we left it," she said. And he added, "Oh, but here too!" "It's upstairs," she murmured. "And in the garden," he whispered. "Quietly," they said, "or we shall wake them."

But it wasn't that you woke us. Oh, no. "They're looking for it; they're drawing the curtain," one might say, and so read on a page or two. "Now they've found it," one would be certain, stopping the pencil on the margin. And then, tired of reading, one might rise and see for oneself, the house all empty, the doors standing open, only the wood pigeons bubbling with content and the hum of the threshing machine sounding from the farm. "What did I come in here for? What did I want to find?" My hands were empty. "Perhaps it's upstairs then?" The apples were in the loft. And so down again, the garden still as ever, only the book had slipped into the grass.

But they had found it in the drawing-room. Not that one could ever see them. The window panes reflected apples, reflected roses; all the leaves were green in the glass. If they moved in the drawing-room, the apple only turned its yellow side. Yet, the moment after, if the door was opened, spread about the floor, hung upon the walls, pendant from the ceiling — what? My hands were empty. The shadow of a thrush crossed the carpet; from the deepest wells of silence the wood pigeon drew its bubble of sound. "Safe, safe, safe," the pulse of the house beat softly. "The treasure buried; the room . . ." the pulse stopped short. Oh, was that the buried treasure?

A moment later the light had faded. Out in the garden then? But the trees spun darkness for a wandering beam of sun. So fine, so rare, coolly sunk

5

beneath the surface the beam I sought always burnt behind the glass. Death was the glass; death was between us; coming to the woman first, hundreds of years ago, leaving the house, sealing all the windows; the rooms were darkened. He left it, left her, went North, went East, saw the stars turned in the Southern sky; sought the house, found it dropped beneath the Downs. "Safe, safe, safe," the pulse of the house beat gladly. "The Treasure yours."

The wind roars up the avenue. Trees stoop and bend this way and that. Moonbeams splash and spill wildly in the rain. But the beam of the lamp falls straight from the window. The candle burns stiff and still. Wandering through the house, opening the windows, whispering not to wake us, the ghostly couple seek their joy.

"Here we slept," she says. And he adds, "Kisses without number." "Waking in the morning — " "Silver between the trees — " "Upstairs — " "In the garden — " "When summer came — " "In winter snowtime — " The doors go shutting far in the distance, gently knocking like the pulse of a heart.

Nearer they come; cease at the doorway. The wind falls, the rain slides silver down the glass. Our eyes darken; we hear no steps beside us; we see no lady spread her ghostly cloak. His hands shield the lantern. "Look," he breathes. "Sound asleep. Love upon their lips."

Stooping, holding their silver lamp above us, long they look and deeply. Long they pause. The wind drives straightly; the flame stoops slightly. Wild beams of moonlight cross both floor and wall, and, meeting, stain the faces bent; the faces pondering; the faces that search the sleepers and seek their hidden joy.

"Safe, safe, safe," the heart of the house beats proudly. "Long 10 years — " he sighs. "Again you found me." "Here," she murmurs, "sleeping; in the garden reading; laughing, rolling apples in the loft. Here we left our treasure — " Stooping, their light lifts the lids upon my eyes. "Safe! safe! safe!" the pulse of the house beats wildly. Waking, I cry "Oh, is this *your* buried treasure? The light in the heart."

Katherine Mansfield

THE GARDEN-PARTY   1922

Katherine Mansfield Beauchamp (1888 – 1923), who shortened her byline, was born into a sedate Victorian family in New Zealand, daughter of a successful businessman. At fifteen she emigrated to England to attend school and did not ever permanently return Down Under. In 1918, after a time of wild-oat sowing in bohemian London, she married the journalist and critic John Middleton Murray. All at once, Mansfield found herself struggling to define her sexual identity, to earn a living by her pen, to endure World War I (in which her brother was killed in action), and to survive the ravages of tuberculosis. She died at thirty-four, in France, at a spiritualist commune where she had sought to regain her health. Mansfield wrote no novels, but during her brief career concentrated on the short story, in which form of art she has few peers. Bliss (1920) and The Garden-Party and Other

*Stories (1922) were greeted with an acclaim that has continued; her
Short Stories were collected in 1937. Some celebrate life, others wryly poke
fun at it. Many reveal, in ordinary lives, small incidents that open like
doorways into significances.*

And after all the weather was ideal. They could not have had a more
perfect day for a garden-party if they had ordered it. Windless, warm, the sky
without a cloud. Only the blue was veiled with a haze of light gold, as it is
sometimes in early summer. The gardener had been up since dawn, mowing
the lawns and sweeping them, until the grass and the dark flat rosettes where
the daisy plants had been seemed to shine. As for the roses, you could not help
feeling they understood that roses are the only flowers that impress people at
garden-parties; the only flowers that everybody is certain of knowing. Hundreds, yes, literally hundreds, had come out in a single night; the green bushes
bowed down as though they had been visited by archangels.

Breakfast was not yet over before the men came to put up the mar-
quee°.

"Where do you want the marquee put, mother?"

"My dear child, it's no use asking me. I'm determined to leave everything
to you children this year. Forget I am your mother. Treat me as an honored
guest."

But Meg could not possibly go and supervise the men. She had washed   5
her hair before breakfast, and she sat drinking her coffee in a green turban,
with a dark wet curl stamped on each cheek. Jose, the butterfly, always came
down in a silk petticoat and a kimono jacket.

"You'll have to go, Laura; you're the artistic one."

Away Laura flew, still holding her piece of bread-and-butter. It's so
delicious to have an excuse for eating out of doors, and besides, she loved
having to arrange things; she always felt she could do it so much better than
anybody else.

Four men in their shirt-sleeves stood grouped together on the garden
path. They carried staves covered with rolls of canvas, and they had big
tool-bats slung on their backs. They looked impressive. Laura wished now that
she had not got the bread-and-butter, but there was nowhere to put it, and
she couldn't possibly throw it away. She blushed and tried to look severe and
even a little bit short-sighted as she came up to them.

"Good morning," she said, copying her mother's voice. But that sounded
so fearfully affected that she was ashamed, and stammered like a little girl,
"Oh — er — have you come — is it about the marquee?"

"That's right, miss," said the tallest of the men, a lanky, freckled fellow,   10
and he shifted his tool-bag, knocked back his straw hat and smiled down at
her. "That's about it."

His smile was so easy, so friendly that Laura recovered. What nice eyes
he had, small, but such a dark blue! And now she looked at the others, they
were smiling too. "Cheer up, we won't bite," their smile seemed to say. How

marquee: a large, showy tent or canopy supported by poles, to be set up for the party.

very nice workmen were! And what a beautiful morning! She mustn't mention the morning; she must be businesslike. The marquee.

"Well, what about the lily-lawn? Would that do?"

And she pointed to the lily-lawn with the hand that didn't hold the bread-and-butter. They turned, they stared in the direction. A little fat chap thrust out his under-lip, and the tall fellow frowned.

"I don't fancy it," said he. "Not conspicuous enough. You see, with a thing like a marquee," and he turned to Laura in his easy way, "you want to put it somewhere where it'll give you a bang slap in the eye, if you follow me."

Laura's upbringing made her wonder for a moment whether it was quite respectful of a workman to talk to her of bangs slap in the eye. But she did quite follow him.

"A corner of the tennis-court," she suggested. "But the band's going to be in one corner."

"H'm, going to have a band, are you?" said another of the workmen. He was pale. He had a haggard look as his dark eyes scanned the tennis-court. What was he thinking?

"Only a very small band," said Laura gently. Perhaps he wouldn't mind so much if the band was quite small. But the tall fellow interrupted.

"Look here, miss, that's the place. Against those trees. Over there. That'll do fine."

Against the karakas. Then the karaka-trees would be hidden. And they were so lovely, with their broad, gleaming leaves, and their clusters of yellow fruit. They were like trees you imagined growing on a desert island, proud, solitary, lifting their leaves and fruits to the sun in a kind of silent splendor. Must they be hidden by a marquee?

They must. Already the men had shouldered their staves and were making for the place. Only the tall fellow was left. He bent down, pinched a sprig of lavender, put his thumb and forefinger to his nose and snuffed up the smell. When Laura saw that gesture she forgot all about the karakas in her wonder at him caring for things like that — caring for the smell of lavender. How many men that she knew would have done such a thing? Oh, how extraordinarily nice workmen were, she thought. Why couldn't she have workmen for friends rather than the silly boys she danced with and who came to Sunday night supper? She would get on much better with men like these.

It's all the fault, she decided, as the tall fellow drew something on the back of an envelope, something that was to be looped up or left to hang, of these absurd class distinctions. Well, for her part, she didn't feel them. Not a bit, not an atom. . . . And now there came the chock-chock of wooden hammers. Some one whistled, some one sang out, "Are you right there, matey?" "Matey!" The friendliness of it, the — the — Just to prove how happy she was, just to show the tall fellow how at home she felt, and how she despised stupid conventions, Laura took a big bite of her bread-and-butter as she stared at the little drawing. She felt just like a work-girl.

"Laura, Laura, where are you? Telephone, Laura!" a voice cried from the house.

"Coming!" Away she skimmed, over the lawn, up the path, up the steps, across the veranda, and into the porch. In the hall her father and Laurie were brushing their hats ready to go to the office.

"I say, Laura," said Laurie very fast, "you might just give a squiz at my coat before this afternoon. See if it wants pressing." 25

"I will," said she. Suddenly she couldn't stop herself. She ran at Laurie and gave him a small, quick squeeze. "Oh, I do love parties, don't you?" gasped Laura.

"Ra-ther," said Laurie's warm, boyish voice, and he squeezed his sister too, and gave her a gentle push. "Dash off to the telephone, old girl."

The telephone. "Yes, yes; oh yes. Kitty? Good morning, dear. Come to lunch? Do, dear. Delighted of course. It will only be a very scratch meal — just the sandwich crusts and broken meringue-shells and what's left over. Yes, isn't it a perfect morning? Your white? Oh, I certainly should. One moment — hold the line. Mother's calling." And Laura sat back. "What, mother? Can't hear."

Mrs. Sheridan's voice floated down the stairs. "Tell her to wear that sweet hat she had on last Sunday."

"Mother says you're to wear that *sweet* hat you had on last Sunday. Good. One o'clock. Bye-bye." 30

Laura put back the receiver, flung her arms over her head, took a deep breath, stretched and let them fall. "Huh," she sighed, and the moment after the sigh she sat up quickly. She was still, listening. All the doors in the house seemed to be open. The house was alive with soft, quick steps and running voices. The green baize door that led to the kitchen regions swung open and shut with a muffled thud. And now there came a long, chuckling absurd sound. It was the heavy piano being moved on its stiff castors. But the air! If you stopped to notice, was the air always like this? Little faint winds were playing chase, in at the tops of the windows, out at the doors. And there were two tiny spots of sun, one on the inkpot, one on a silver photograph frame, playing too. Darling little spots. Especially the one on the inkpot lid. It was quite warm. A warm little silver star. She could have kissed it.

The front door bell pealed, and there sounded the rustle of Sadie's print skirt on the stairs. A man's voice murmured; Sadie answered, careless, "I'm sure I don't know. Wait. I'll ask Mrs. Sheridan."

"What is it, Sadie?" Laura came into the hall.

"It's the florist, Miss Laura."

It was, indeed. There, just inside the door, stood a wide, shallow tray full of pots of pink lilies. No other kind. Nothing but lilies — canna lilies, big pink flowers, wide open, radiant, almost frighteningly alive on bright crimson stems. 35

"O-oh, Sadie!" said Laura, and the sound was like a little moan. She crouched down as if to warm herself at that blaze of lilies; she felt they were in her fingers, on her lips, growing in her breast.

"It's some mistake," she said faintly. "Nobody ever ordered so many. Sadie, go and find mother."

But at that moment Mrs. Sheridan joined them.

"It's quite right," she said calmly. "Yes, I ordered them. Aren't they lovely?" She pressed Laura's arm. "I was passing the shop yesterday, and I saw them in the window. And I suddenly thought for once in my life I shall have enough canna lilies. The garden-party will be a good excuse."

"But I thought you said you didn't mean to interfere," said Laura. Sadie   40
had gone. The florist's man was still outside at his van. She put her arm round
her mother's neck and gently, very gently, she bit her mother's ear.

"My darling child, you wouldn't like a logical mother, would you? Don't
do that. Here's the man."

He carried more lilies still, another whole tray.

"Bank them up, just inside the door, on both sides of the porch, please,"
said Mrs. Sheridan. "Don't you agree, Laura?"

"Oh, I *do*, mother."

In the drawing-room Meg, Jose and good little Hans had at last succeeded   45
in moving the piano.

"Now, if we put this chesterfield against the wall and move everything
out of the room except the chairs, don't you think?"

"Quite."

"Hans, move these tables into the smoking-room, and bring a sweeper
to take these marks off the carpet and — one moment, Hans — " Jose loved
giving orders to the servants, and they loved obeying her. She always made
them feel they were taking part in some drama. "Tell mother and Miss Laura
to come here at once."

"Very good, Miss Jose."

She turned to Meg. "I want to hear what the piano sounds like, just in   50
case I'm asked to sing this afternoon. Let's try over 'This Life is Weary.'"

Pom! Ta-ta-ta *Tee*-ta! The piano burst out so passionately that Jose's face
changed. She clasped her hands. She looked mournfully and enigmatically at
her mother and Laura as they came in.

This Life is *Wee*-ary,
A Tear — a Sigh.
A Love that *Chan*-ges,
    This Life is *Wee*-ary,
A Tear — a Sigh.
A Love that *Chan*-ges,
And then . . . Goodbye!

But at the word "Goodbye," and although the piano sounded more
desperate than ever, her face broke into a brilliant, dreadfully unsympathetic
smile.

"Aren't I in good voice, mummy?" she beamed.

This Life is *Wee*-ary,
Hope comes to Die.
A Dream — a *Wa*-kening.

But now Sadie interrupted them. "What is it, Sadie?"

"If you please, m'm, cook says have you got the flags for the sand-   55
wiches?"

"The flags for the sandwiches, Sadie?" echoed Mrs. Sheridan dreamily.
And the children knew by her face that she hadn't got them. "Let me see." And
she said to Sadie firmly, "Tell cook I'll let her have them in ten minutes."

Sadie went.

"Now, Laura," said her mother quickly. "Come with me into the smoking-room. I've got the names somewhere on the back of an envelope. You'll have to write them out for me. Meg, go upstairs this minute and take that wet thing off your head. Jose, run and finish dressing this instant. Do you hear me, children, or shall I have to tell your father when he comes home to-night? And — and, Jose, pacify cook if you do go into the kitchen, will you? I'm terrified of her this morning."

The envelope was found at last behind the dining-room clock, though how it had got there Mrs. Sheridan could not imagine.

"One of you children must have stolen it out of my bag, because I remember vividly — cream cheese and lemon-curd. Have you done that?" 60

"Yes."

"Egg and — " Mrs. Sheridan held the envelope away from her. "It looks like mice. It can't be mice, can it?"

"Olive, pet," said Laura, looking over her shoulder.

"Yes, of course, olive. What a horrible combination it sounds. Egg and olive."

They were finished at last, and Laura took them off to the kitchen. She 65 found Jose there pacifying the cook, who did not look at all terrifying.

"I have never seen such exquisite sandwiches," said Jose's rapturous voice. "How many kinds did you say there were, cook? Fifteen?"

"Fifteen, Miss Jose."

"Well, cook, I congratulate you."

Cook swept up crusts with the long sandwich knife, and smiled broadly.

"Godber's has come," announced Sadie, issuing out of the pantry. She 70 had seen the man pass the window.

That meant the cream puffs had come. Godber's were famous for their cream puffs. Nobody ever thought of making them at home.

"Bring them in and put them on the table, my girl," ordered cook.

Sadie brought them in and went back to the door. Of course Laura and Jose were far too grown-up to really care about such things. All the same, they couldn't help agreeing that the puffs looked very attractive. Very. Cook began arranging them, shaking off the extra icing sugar.

"Don't they carry one back to all one's parties?" said Laura.

"I suppose they do," said practical Jose, who never liked to be carried 75 back. "They look beautifully light and feathery, I must say."

"Have one each, my dears," said cook in her comfortable voice. "Yer ma won't know."

Oh, impossible. Fancy cream puffs so soon after breakfast. The very idea made one shudder. All the same, two minutes later Jose and Laura were licking their fingers with that absorbed inward look that only comes from whipped cream.

"Let's go into the garden, out by the back way," suggested Laura. "I want to see how the men are getting on with the marquee. They're such awfully nice men."

But the back door was blocked by cook, Sadie, Godber's man and Hans. Something had happened. 80

"Tuk-tuk-tuk," clucked cook like an agitated hen. Sadie had her hand clapped to her cheek as though she had toothache. Hans's face was screwed up in the effort to understand. Only Godber's man seemed to be enjoying himself; it was his story.

"What's the matter? What's happened?"

"There's been a horrible accident," said Cook. "A man killed."

"A man killed! Where? How? When?"

But Godber's man wasn't going to have his story snatched from under his very nose.

"Know those little cottages just below here, miss?" Know them? Of course, she knew them. "Well, there's a young chap living there, name of Scott, a carter. His horse shied at a traction-engine, corner of Hawke Street this morning, and he was thrown out on the back of his head. Killed."

"Dead!" Laura stared at Godber's man.

"Dead when they picked him up," said Godber's man with relish. "They were taking the body home as I come up here." And he said to the cook, "He's left a wife and five little ones."

"Jose, come here." Laura caught hold of her sister's sleeve and dragged her through the kitchen to the other side of the green baize door. There she paused and leaned against it. "Jose!" she said, horrified, "however are we going to stop everything?"

"Stop everything, Laura!" cried Jose in astonishment. "What do you mean?"

"Stop the garden-party, of course." Why did Jose pretend?

But Jose was still more amazed. "Stop the garden-party? My dear Laura, don't be so absurd. Of course we can't do anything of the kind. Nobody expects us to. Don't be so extravagant."

"But we can't possibly have a garden-party with a man dead just outside the front gate."

That really was extravagant, for the little cottages were in a lane to themselves at the very bottom of a steep rise that led up to the house. A broad road ran between. True, they were far too near. They were the greatest possible eyesore, and they had no right to be in that neighborhood at all. They were little mean dwellings painted a chocolate brown. In the garden patches there was nothing but cabbage stalks, sick hens and tomato cans. The very smoke coming out of their chimneys was poverty-stricken. Little rags and shreds of smoke, so unlike the great silvery plumes that uncurled from the Sheridans' chimneys. Washerwomen lived in the lane and sweeps and a cobbler, and a man whose house-front was studded all over with minute bird-cages. Children swarmed. When the Sheridans were little they were forbidden to set foot there because of the revolting language and of what they might catch. But since they were grown up, Laura and Laurie on their prowls sometimes walked through. It was disgusting and sordid. They came out with a shudder. But still one must go everywhere; one must see everything. So through they went.

"And just think of what the band would sound like to that poor woman," said Laura.

"Oh, Laura!" Jose began to be seriously annoyed. "If you're going to stop a band playing every time some one has an accident, you'll lead a very strenuous life. I'm every bit as sorry about it as you. I feel just as sympathetic." Her eyes hardened. She looked at her sister just as she used to when they were little and fighting together. "You won't bring a drunken workman back to life by being sentimental," she said softly.

"Drunk! Who said he was drunk?" Laura turned furiously on Jose. She said, just as they had used to say on those occasions, "I'm going straight up to tell mother."

"Do, dear," cooed Jose.

"Mother, can I come into your room?" Laura turned the big glass door-knob.

"Of course, child. Why, what's the matter? What's given you such a color?" And Mrs. Sheridan turned round from her dressing-table. She was trying on a new hat. 100

"Mother, a man's been killed," began Laura.

"*Not* in the garden?" interrupted her mother.

"No, no!"

"Oh, what a fright you gave me!" Mrs. Sheridan sighed with relief, and took off the big hat and held it on her knees.

"But listen, mother," said Laura. Breathless, half-choking, she told the 105 dreadful story. "Of course, we can't have our party, can we?" she pleaded. "The band and everybody arriving. They'd hear us, mother; they're nearly neighbors!"

To Laura's astonishment her mother behaved just like Jose; it was harder to bear because she seemed amused. She refused to take Laura seriously.

"But, my dear child, use your common sense. It's only by accident we've heard of it. If some one had died there normally — and I can't understand how they keep alive in those poky little holes — we should still be having our party, shouldn't we?"

Laura had to say "yes" to that, but she felt it was all wrong. She sat down on her mother's sofa and pinched the cushion frill.

"Mother, isn't it really terribly heartless of us?" she asked.

"Darling!" Mrs. Sheridan got up and came over to her, carrying the hat. 110 Before Laura could stop her she had popped it on. "My child!" said her mother, "the hat is yours. It's made for you. It's much too young for me. I have never seen you look such a picture. Look at yourself!" And she held up her hand-mirror.

"But, mother," Laura began again. She couldn't look at herself; she turned aside.

This time Mrs. Sheridan lost patience just as Jose had done.

"You are being very absurd, Laura," she said coldly. "People like that don't expect sacrifices from us. And it's not very sympathetic to spoil every-body's enjoyment as you're doing now."

"I don't understand," said Laura, and she walked quickly out of the room into her own bedroom. There, quite by chance, the first thing she saw was this charming girl in the mirror, in her black hat trimmed with gold daisies, and a long black velvet ribbon. Never had she imagined she could look like that. Is mother right? she thought. And now she hoped her mother was right. Am I being extravagant? Perhaps it was extravagant. Just for a moment she had another glimpse of that poor woman and those little children, and the body being carried into the house. But it all seemed blurred, unreal, like a picture in the newspaper. I'll remember it again after the party's over, she decided. And somehow that seemed quite the best plan. . . .

Lunch was over by half-past one. By half-past two they were all ready for the fray. The green-coated band had arrived and was established in a corner of the tennis-court.

"My dear!" trilled Kitty Maitland, "aren't they too like frogs for words? You ought to have arranged them round the pond with the conductor in the middle on a leaf."

Laurie arrived and hailed them on his way to dress. At the sight of him Laura remembered the accident again. She wanted to tell him. If Laurie agreed with the others, then it was bound to be all right. And she followed him into the hall.

"Laurie!"

"Hallo!" He was half-way upstairs, but when he turned round and saw Laura he suddenly puffed out his cheeks and goggled his eyes at her. "My word, Laura! You do look stunning," said Laurie, "What an absolutely topping hat!"

Laura said faintly "Is it?" and smiled up at Laurie, and didn't tell him after all.

Soon after that people began coming in streams. The band struck up; the hired waiters ran from the house to the marquee. Wherever you looked there were couples strolling, bending to the flowers, greeting, moving on over the lawn. They were like bright birds that had alighted in the Sheridans' garden for this one afternoon, on their way to — where? Ah, what happiness it is to be with people who all are happy, to press hands, press cheeks, smile into eyes.

"Darling Laura, how well you look!"

"What a becoming hat, child!"

"Laura, you look quite Spanish. I've never seen you look so striking."

And Laura, glowing, answered softly, "Have you had tea? Won't you have an ice? The passion-fruit ices really are rather special." She ran to her father and begged him. "Daddy darling, can't the band have something to drink?"

And the perfect afternoon slowly ripened, slowly faded, slowly its petals closed.

"Never a more delightful garden-party . . ." "The greatest success . . ." "Quite the most . . ."

Laura helped her mother with the good-byes. They stood side by side in the porch till it was all over.

"All over, all over, thank heaven," said Mr. Sheridan. "Round up the others, Laura. Let's go and have some fresh coffee. I'm exhausted. Yes, it's been very successful. But oh, these parties, these parties! Why will you children insist on giving parties!" And they all of them sat down in the deserted marquee.

"Have a sandwich, daddy dear. I wrote the flag."

"Thanks." Mr. Sheridan took a bite and the sandwich was gone. He took another. "I suppose you didn't hear of a beastly accident that happened to-day?" he said.

"My dear," said Mrs. Sheridan, holding up her hand, "we did. It nearly ruined the party. Laura insisted we should put it off."

"Oh, mother!" Laura didn't want to be teased about it.

"It was a horrible affair all the same," said Mr. Sheridan. "The chap was married too. Lived just below in the lane, and leaves a wife and half a dozen kiddies, so they say."

An awkward little silence fell. Mrs. Sheridan fidgeted with her cup. 135 Really, it was very tactless of father . . .

Suddenly she looked up. There on the table were all those sandwiches, cakes, puffs, all uneaten, all going to be wasted. She had one of her brilliant ideas.

"I know," she said. "Let's make up a basket. Let's send that poor creature some of this perfectly good food. At any rate, it will be the greatest treat for the children. Don't you agree? And she's sure to have neighbors calling in and so on. What a point to have it all ready prepared. Laura!" She jumped up. "Get me the big basket out of the stairs cupboard."

"But, mother, do you really think it's a good idea?" said Laura.

Again, how curious, she seemed to be different from them all. To take scraps from their party. Would the poor woman really like that?

"Of course! What's the matter with you today? An hour or two ago you 140 were insisting on us being sympathetic, and now — "

Oh, well! Laura ran for the basket. It was filled, it was heaped by her mother.

"Take it yourself, darling," said she. "Run down just as you are. No, wait, take the arum lilies too. People of that class are so impressed by arum lilies."

"The stems will ruin her lace frock," said practical Jose.

So they would. Just in time. "Only the basket, then. And, Laura!" — her mother followed her out of the marquee — "don't on any account — "

"What, mother?" 145

No, better not put such ideas into the child's head! "Nothing! Run along."

It was just growing dusky as Laura shut their garden gates. A big dog ran by like a shadow. The road gleamed white, and down below in the hollow the little cottages were in deep shade. How quiet it seemed after the afternoon. Here she was going down the hill to somewhere where a man lay dead, and she couldn't realize it. Why couldn't she? She stopped a minute. And it seemed to her that kisses, voices, tinkling spoons, laughter, the smell of crushed grass were somehow inside her. She had no room for anything else. How strange! She looked up at the pale sky, and all she thought was, "Yes, it was the most successful party."

Now the broad road was crossed. The lane began, smoky and dark. Women in shawls and men's tweed caps hurried by. Men hung over the palings; the children played in the doorways. A low hum came from the mean little cottages. In some of them there was a flicker of light, and a shadow, crab-like, moved across the window. Laura bent her head and hurried on. She wished now she had put on a coat. How her frock shone! And the big hat with the velvet streamer — if only it was another hat! Were the people looking at her? They must be. It was a mistake to have come; she knew all along it was a mistake. Should she go back even now?

No, too late. This was the house. It must be. A dark knot of people stood outside. Beside the gate an old, old woman with a crutch sat in a chair, watching. She had her feet on a newspaper. The voices stopped as Laura drew near. The group parted. It was as though she was expected, as though they had known she was coming here.

Laura was terribly nervous. Tossing the velvet ribbon over her shoulder, she said to a woman standing by, "Is this Mrs. Scott's house?" and the woman, smiling queerly, said, "It is, my lass." ₁₅₀

Oh, to be away from this! She actually said, "Help me, God," as she walked up the tiny path and knocked. To be away from those staring eyes, or to be covered up in anything, one of those women's shawls even. I'll just leave the basket and go, she decided. I shan't even wait for it to be emptied.

Then the door opened. A little woman in black showed in the gloom.

Laura said, "Are you Mrs. Scott?" But to her horror the woman answered, "Walk in please, miss," and she was shut in the passage.

"No," said Laura, "I don't want to come in. I only want to leave this basket. Mother sent — "

The little woman in the gloomy passage seemed not to have heard her. "Step this way, please, miss," she said in an oily voice, and Laura followed her. ₁₅₅

She found herself in a wretched little low kitchen, lighted by a smoky lamp. There was a woman sitting before the fire.

"Em," said the little creature who had let her in. "Em! It's a young lady." She turned to Laura. She said meaningly, "I'm 'er sister, Miss. You'll excuse 'er, won't you?"

"Oh, but of course!" said Laura. "Please, please don't disturb her. I — I only want to leave — "

But at that moment the woman at the fire turned round. Her face, puffed up, red, with swollen eyes and swollen lips, looked terrible. She seemed as though she couldn't understand why Laura was there. What did it mean? Why was this stranger standing in the kitchen with a basket? What was it all about? And the poor face puckered up again.

"All right, my dear," said the other. "I'll thank the young lady." ₁₆₀

And again she began, "You'll excuse her, miss, I'm sure," and her face, swollen too, tried an oily smile.

Laura only wanted to get out, to get away. She was back in the passage. The door opened. She walked straight through into the bedroom, where the dead man was lying.

"You'd like a look at 'im, wouldn't you?" said Em's sister, and she brushed past Laura over to the bed. "Don't be afraid, my lass — " and now her voice sounded fond and sly, and fondly she drew down the sheet — " 'e looks a picture. There's nothing to show. Come along, my dear."

Laura came.

There lay a young man, fast asleep — sleeping so soundly, so deeply, that he was far, far away from them both. Oh, so remote, so peaceful. He was dreaming. Never wake him up again. His head was sunk in the pillow, his eyes were closed; they were blind under the closed eyelids. He was given up to his dream. What did garden-parties and baskets and lace frocks matter to him? He was far from all those things. He was wonderful, beautiful. While they were laughing and while the band was playing, this marvel had come to the lane. Happy . . . happy. . . . All is well, said that sleeping face. This is just as it should be. I am content. ₁₆₅

But all the same you had to cry, and she couldn't go out of the room without saying something to him. Laura gave a loud childish sob.

"Forgive my hat," she said.

And this time she didn't wait for Em's sister. She found her way out of the door, down the path, past all those dark people. At the corner of the lane she met Laurie.

He stepped out of the shadow. "Is that you, Laura?"

"Yes." 170

"Mother was getting anxious. Was it all right?"

"Yes, quite. Oh, Laurie!" She took his arm, she pressed up against him.

"I say, you're not crying, are you?" asked her brother.

Laura shook her head. She was.

Laurie put his arm round her shoulder. "Don't cry," he said in his warm, 175 loving voice. "Was it awful?"

"No," sobbed Laura. "It was simply marvelous. But, Laurie — " She stopped, she looked at her brother. "Isn't life," she stammered, "isn't life — " But what life was she couldn't explain. No matter. He quite understood.

"Isn't it, darling?" said Laurie.

Franz Kafka

A HUNGER ARTIST 1924

Translated by Willa and Edwin Muir

Franz Kafka (1883 – 1924) was born into a German-speaking Jewish family in Prague, Czechoslovakia (then part of Austria). After taking a doctor's degree in law, he settled into the routine of a government claims investigator. By night when he couldn't sleep he toiled on stories. Kafka's work is rich in macabre humor and unforgettable nightmares: the long story The Metamorphosis *(1915), for instance, begins with the great line, "As Gregor Samsa awoke one morning from uneasy dreams he found himself transformed in his bed into a gigantic insect." Kafka was a writer of such impeccably high standards that he could bring himself to publish little in his lifetime; he never finished his major novels* The Trial *and* The Castle. *Both depict huge, remote, bumbling, irresponsible bureaucracies in whose power an individual feels helplessly isolated. Before he died, Kafka left his friend Max Brod orders to burn his incomplete manuscripts; Brod pondered, but didn't obey. Kafka, who succumbed to tuberculosis, did not live to see his stories appear startlingly prophetic to readers looking back on them by the later light of the Holocaust. Only after World War II did his work achieve international fame.*

During these last decades the interest in professional fasting has markedly diminished. It used to pay very well to stage such great performances under one's own management, but today that is quite impossible. We live in a different world now. At one time the whole town took a lively interest in the hunger artist; from day to day of his fast the excitement mounted; everybody wanted to see him at least once a day; there were people who bought season tickets for the last few days and sat from morning till night in front of his small barred cage; even in the nighttime there were visiting hours, when the whole effect was heightened by torch flares; on fine days the cage was set out in the open air, and then it was the children's special treat to see the hunger artist; for their elders he was often just a joke that happened to be in fashion, but the children stood open-mouthed, holding each other's hands for greater security, marveling at him as he sat there pallid in black tights, with his ribs sticking out so prominently, not even on a seat but down among straw on the ground, sometimes giving a courteous nod, answering questions with a constrained smile, or perhaps stretching an arm through the bars so that one might feel how thin it was, and then again withdrawing deep into himself, paying no attention to anyone or anything, not even to the all-important striking of the clock that was the only piece of furniture in his cage, but merely staring into vacancy with half-shut eyes, now and then taking a sip from a tiny glass of water to moisten his lips.

Besides casual onlookers there were also relays of permanent watchers selected by the public, usually butchers, strangely enough, and it was their task to watch the hunger artist day and night, three of them at a time, in case he should have some secret recourse to nourishment. This was nothing but a formality, instituted to reassure the masses, for the initiates knew well enough that during his fast the artist would never in any circumstances, not even under forcible compulsion, swallow the smallest morsel of food; the honor of his profession forbade it. Not every watcher, of course, was capable of understanding this, there were often groups of night watchers who were very lax in carrying out their duties and deliberately huddled together in a retired corner to play cards with great absorption, obviously intending to give the hunger artist the chance of a little refreshment, which they supposed he could draw from some private hoard. Nothing annoyed the artist more than such watchers; they made him miserable; they made his fast seem unendurable; sometimes he mastered his feebleness sufficiently to sing during their watch for as long as he could keep going, to show them how unjust their suspicions were. But that was of little use; they only wondered at his cleverness in being able to fill his mouth even while singing. Much more to his taste were the watchers who sat close up to the bars, who were not content with the dim night lighting of the hall but focused him in the full glare of the electric pocket torch given them by the impresario. The harsh light did not trouble him at all. In any case he could never sleep properly, and he could always drowse a little, whatever the light, at any hour, even when the hall was thronged with noisy onlookers. He was quite happy at the prospect of spending a sleepless night with such watchers; he was ready to exchange jokes with them, to tell them stories out of his nomadic life, anything at all to keep them awake and demonstrate to them again that he had no eatables in his cage and that he was fasting as not one of them could fast. But his happiest moment was when the morning came and an enormous breakfast was brought them, at his expense, on which they flung themselves with the keen appetite of healthy men after a weary night of wakefulness. Of course there were people who argued that this breakfast was an unfair attempt to bribe the watchers, but that was going rather too far, and when they were invited to take on a night's vigil without a breakfast, merely for the sake of the cause, they made themselves scarce, although they stuck stubbornly to their suspicions.

Such suspicions, anyhow, were a necessary accompaniment to the profession of fasting. No one could possibly watch the hunger artist continuously, day and night, and so no one could produce first-hand evidence that the fast had really been rigorous and continuous; only the artist himself could know that; he was therefore bound to be the sole completely satisfied spectator of his own fast. Yet for other reasons he was never satisfied; it was not perhaps mere fasting that had brought him to such skeleton thinness that many people had regretfully to keep away from his exhibitions, because the sight of him was too much for them, perhaps it was dissatisfaction with himself that had worn him down. For he alone knew, what no other initiate knew, how easy it was to fast. It was the easiest thing in the world. He made no secret of this, yet people did not believe him; at the best they set him down as modest, most of them, however, thought he was out for publicity or else was some kind of cheat who found it easy to fast because he had discovered a way of making it easy, and then had the impudence to admit the fact, more or less. He had to put up with all that, and in the course of time had got used to it, but his inner dissatisfaction always rankled, and never yet, after any term of fasting — this must be granted to his credit — had he left the cage of his own free will. The longest period of fasting was fixed by his impresario at forty days, beyond that term he was not allowed to go, not even in great cities, and there was good reason for it, too. Experience had proved that for about forty days the interest of the public could be stimulated by a steadily increasing pressure of advertisement, but after that the town began to lose interest, sympathetic support began notably to fall off; there were of course local variations as between one town and another or one country and another, but as a general rule forty days marked the limit. So on the fortieth day the flower-bedecked cage was opened, enthusiastic spectators filled the hall, a military band played, two doctors entered the cage to measure the results of the fast, which were announced through a megaphone, and finally two young ladies appeared, blissful at having been selected for the honor, to help the hunger artist down the few steps leading to a small table on which was spread a carefully chosen invalid repast. And at this very moment the artist always turned stubborn. True, he would entrust his bony arms to the outstretched helping hands of the ladies bending over him, but stand up he would not. Why stop fasting at this particular moment, after forty days of it? He had held out for a long time, an illimitably long time; why stop now, when he was in his best fasting form, or rather, not yet quite in his best fasting form? Why should he be cheated of the fame he would get for fasting longer, for being not only the record hunger artist of all time, which presumably he was already, but for beating his own record by a performance beyond human imagination, since he felt that there were no limits to his capacity for fasting? His public pretended to admire him so much, why should it have so little patience with him; if he could endure fasting longer, why shouldn't the public endure it? Besides, he was tired, he was comfortable sitting in the straw, and now he was supposed to lift himself to his full height and go down to a meal the very thought of which gave him a nausea that only the presence of the ladies kept him from betraying, and even that with an effort. And he looked up into the eyes of the ladies who were apparently so friendly and in reality so cruel, and shook his head, which felt too heavy on its strengthless neck. But then there happened yet again what always happened. The impresario came forward, without a word — for the band made speech impossible — lifted his arms in the air above the artist, as if inviting Heaven to look down upon its creature here in the straw, this suffering martyr, which indeed he was, although in quite another sense; grasped him around the emaciated waist, with exaggerated caution, so that the frail condition he was in might be appreciated; and committed him to the care of the blenching ladies, not without secretly giving him a shaking so that his legs and body tottered and swayed. The artist now submitted completely; his head rolled on his breast as if it had landed there by chance; his body was hollowed out; his legs in a spasm of self-preservation clung close to each other at the knees, yet scraped on the ground as if it were not really solid ground, as if they were only trying to find solid ground; and the whole weight of his body, a featherweight after all, relapsed onto one of the ladies, who, looking round for help and panting a little — this post of honor was not at all what she had expected it to be — first stretched her neck as far as she could to keep her face at least free from contact with the artist, then finding this impossible, and her more fortunate companion not coming to her aid but merely holding extended on her own trembling hand the little bunch of knucklebones that was the artist's, to the great delight of the spectators burst into tears and had to be replaced by an attendant who had long been stationed in readiness. Then came the food, a little of which the impresario managed to get between the artist's lips, while he sat in a kind of half-fainting trance, to the accompaniment of cheerful patter designed to distract the public's attention from the artist's condition; after that, a toast was drunk to the public, supposedly prompted by a whisper from the artist in the impresario's ear; the band confirmed it with a mighty flourish, the spectators melted away, and no one had any cause to be dissatisfied with the proceedings, no one except the hunger artist himself, he only, as always.

So he lived for many years, with small regular intervals of recuperation, in visible glory, honored by the world, yet in spite of that troubled in spirit, and all the more troubled because no one would take his trouble seriously. What comfort could he possibly need? What more could he possibly wish for? And if some good-natured person, feeling sorry for him, tried to console him by pointing out that his melancholy was probably caused by fasting, it could happen, especially when he had been fasting for some time, that he reacted with an outburst of fury and to the general alarm began to shake the bars of his cage like a wild animal. Yet the impresario had a way of punishing these outbreaks which he rather enjoyed putting into operation. He would apologize publicly for the artist's behavior, which was only to be excused, he admitted, because of the irritability caused by fasting; a condition hardly to be understood by well-fed people; then by natural transition he went on to mention the artist's equally incomprehensible boast that he could fast for much longer than he was doing; he praised the high ambition, the good will, the great self-denial undoubtedly implicit in such a statement; and then quite simply countered it by bringing out photographs, which were also on sale to the public, showing the artist on the fortieth day of a fast lying in bed almost dead from exhaustion. This perversion of the truth, familiar to the artist though it was, always unnerved him afresh and proved too much for him. What was a consequence of the premature ending of his fast was here presented as the cause of it! To fight against this lack of understanding, against a whole world of non-understanding, was impossible. Time and again in good faith he stood by the bars listening to the impresario, but as soon as the photographs appeared he always let go and sank with a groan back on to his straw, and the reassured public could once more come close and gaze at him.

A few years later when the witnesses of such scenes called them to mind, they often failed to understand themselves at all. For meanwhile the aforementioned change in public interest had set in; it seemed to happen almost overnight; there may have been profound causes for it, but who was going to bother about that; at any rate the pampered hunger artist suddenly found himself deserted one fine day by the amusement seekers, who went streaming past him to other more favored attractions. For the last time the impresario hurried him over half Europe to discover whether the old interest might still survive here and there; all in vain; everywhere, as if by secret agreement, a positive revulsion from professional fasting was in evidence. Of course it could not really have sprung up so suddenly as all that, and many premonitory symptoms which had not been sufficiently remarked or suppressed during the rush and glitter of success now came retrospectively to mind, but it was now too late to take any countermeasures. Fasting would surely come into fashion again at some future date, yet that was no comfort for those living in the present. What, then, was the hunger artist to do? He had been applauded by thousands in his time and could hardly come down to showing himself in a street booth at village fairs, and as for adopting another profession, he was not only too old for that but too fanatically devoted to fasting. So he took leave of the impresario, his partner in an unparalleled career, and hired himself to a large circus; in order to spare his own feelings he avoided reading the conditions of his contract.

A large circus with its enormous traffic in replacing and recruiting men, animals and apparatus can always find a use for people at any time, even for a hunger artist, provided of course that he does not ask too much, and in this particular case anyhow it was not only the artist who was taken on but his famous and long-known name as well; indeed considering the peculiar nature of his performance, which was not impaired by advancing age, it could not be objected that here was an artist past his prime, no longer at the height of his professional skill, seeking a refuge in some quiet corner of a circus; on the contrary, the hunger artist averred that he could fast as well as ever, which was entirely credible; he even alleged that if he were allowed to fast as he liked, and this was at once promised him without more ado, he could astound the world by establishing a record never yet achieved, a statement which certainly provoked a smile among the other professionals, since it left out of account the change in public opinion, which the hunger artist in his zeal conveniently forgot.

He had not, however, actually lost his sense of the real situation and took it as a matter of course that he and his cage should be stationed, not in the middle of the ring as a main attraction, but outside, near the animal cages, on a site that was after all easily accessible. Large and gaily painted placards made a frame for the cage and announced what was to be seen inside it. When the public came thronging out in the intervals to see the animals, they could hardly avoid passing the hunger artist's cage and stopping there for a moment; perhaps they might even have stayed longer had not those pressing behind them in the narrow gangway, who did not understand why they should be held up on their way towards the excitements of the menagerie, made it impossible for anyone to stand gazing quietly for any length of time. And that was the reason why the hunger artist, who had of course been looking forward to these visiting hours as the main achievement of his life, began instead to shrink from them. At first he could hardly wait for the intervals; it was exhilarating to watch the crowds come streaming his way, until only too soon — not even the most obstinate self-deception, clung to almost consciously, could hold out against the fact — the conviction was borne in upon him that these people, most of them, to judge from their actions, again and again, without exception, were all on their way to the menagerie. And the first sight of them from the distance remained the best. For when they reached his cage he was at once deafened by the storm of shouting and abuse that arose from the two contending factions, which renewed themselves continuously, of those who wanted to stop and stare at him — he soon began to dislike them more than the others — not out of real interest but only out of obstinate self-assertiveness, and those who wanted to go straight on to the animals. When the first great rush was past, the stragglers came along, and these, whom nothing could have prevented from stopping to look at him as long as they had breath, raced past with long strides, hardly even glancing at him, in their haste to get to the menagerie in time. And all too rarely did it happen that he had a stroke of luck, when some father of a family fetched up before him with his children, pointed a finger at the hunger artist and explained at length what the phenomenon meant, telling stories of earlier years when he himself had watched similar but much more thrilling performances, and the children, still rather uncomprehending, since neither inside nor outside school had they been sufficiently prepared for this lesson — what did they care about fasting? — yet showed by the brightness of their intent eyes that new and better times might be coming. Perhaps, said the hunger artist to himself many a time, things would be a little better if his cage were set not quite so near the menagerie. That made it too easy for people to make their choice, to say nothing of what he suffered from the stench of the menagerie, the animals' restlessness by night, the carrying past of raw lumps of flesh for the beasts of prey, the roaring at feeding times, which depressed him continually. But he did not dare to lodge a complaint with the management; after all, he had the animals to thank for the troops of people who passed his cage, among whom there might always be one here and there to take an interest in him, and who could tell where they might seclude him if he called attention to his existence and thereby to the fact that, strictly speaking, he was only an impediment on the way to the menagerie.

A small impediment, to be sure, one that grew steadily less. People grew familiar with the strange idea that they could be expected, in times like these, to take an interest in a hunger artist, and with this familiarity the verdict went out against him. He might fast as much as he could, and he did so; but nothing could save him now, people passed him by. Just try to explain to anyone the art of fasting! Anyone who has no feeling for it cannot be made to understand it. The fine placards grew dirty and illegible, they were torn down; the little notice board telling the number of fast days achieved, which at first was changed carefully every day, had long stayed at the same figure, for after the first few weeks even this small task seemed pointless to the staff; and so the artist simply fasted on and on, as he had once dreamed of doing, and it was no trouble to him, just as he had always foretold, but no one counted the days, no one, not even the artist himself, knew what records he was already breaking, and his heart grew heavy. And when once in a time some leisurely passer-by stopped, made merry over the old figure on the board and spoke of swindling, that was in its way the stupidest lie ever invented by indifference and inborn malice, since it was not the hunger artist who was cheating; he was working honestly, but the world was cheating him of his reward.

Many more days went by, however, and that too came to an end. An overseer's eye fell on the cage one day and he asked the attendants why this perfectly good cage should be left standing there unused with dirty straw inside it; nobody knew, until one man, helped out by the notice board, remembered about the hunger artist. They poked into the straw with sticks and found him in it. "Are you still fasting?" asked the overseer. "When on earth do you mean to stop?" "Forgive me, everybody," whispered the hunger artist; only the overseer, who had his ear to the bars, understood him. "Of course," said the overseer, and tapped his forehead with a finger to let the attendants know what state the man was in, "we forgive you." "I always wanted you to admire my fasting," said the hunger artist. "We do admire it," said the overseer, affably. "But you shouldn't admire it," said the hunger artist. "Well, then we don't admire it," said the overseer, "but why shouldn't we admire it?" "Because I have to fast, I can't help it," said the hunger artist. "What a fellow you are," said the overseer; "and why can't you help it?" "Because," said the hunger artist, lifting his head a little and speaking, with his lips pursed, as if for a kiss, right into the overseer's ear, so that no syllable might be lost, "because I couldn't find the food I liked. If I had found it, believe me, I should have made no fuss and stuffed myself like you or anyone else." These were his last words, but in his dimming eyes remained the firm though no longer proud persuasion that he was still continuing to fast.

"Well, clear this out now!" said the overseer, and they buried the hunger artist, straw and all. Into the cage they put a young panther. Even the most insensitive felt it refreshing to see this wild creature leaping around the cage that had so long been dreary. The panther was all right. The food he liked was brought him without hesitation by the attendants; he seemed not even to miss his freedom; his noble body, furnished almost to the bursting point with all that it needed, seemed to carry freedom around with it too; somewhere in his jaws it seemed to lurk; and the joy of life streamed with such ardent passion from his throat that for the onlookers it was not easy to stand the shock of it. But they braced themselves, crowded round the cage, and did not want ever to move away.

10

D. H. Lawrence

THE ROCKING-HORSE WINNER

1933

David Herbert Lawrence (1885 – 1930) was born in Nottinghamshire, England, child of a coalminer and a schoolteacher who hated her husband's toil and vowed that her son should escape it. He took up fiction writing, attaining early success. During World War I, Lawrence and his wife were unjustly suspected of treason (he because of his pacifism, she because of her aristocratic German birth). After the armistice they left England and, seeking a climate healthier for Lawrence, who suffered from tuberculosis, wandered in Italy, France, Australia, Mexico, and the American Southwest. Lawrence is an impassioned spokesman for our unconscious, instinctive natures, which we moderns (he argues) have neglected in favor of our overweening intellects. In Lady Chatterley's Lover *(1928), he strove to restore explicit sexuality to English fiction. The book, which today seems tame and repetitious, was long banned in Britain and the United States. Deeper Lawrence novels include* Sons and Lovers *(1913), a veiled account of his breaking away from his fiercely possessive mother;* The Rainbow *(1915);* Women in Love *(1921); and* The Plumed Serpent *(1926), about a revival of pagan religion in Mexico. Besides fiction, Lawrence left a rich legacy of poetry, essays, criticism (*Studies in Classic American Literature, *1923, is especially shrewd and funny), and travel writing. Lawrence exerted deep influence on others, both by the message in his work and by his personal magnetism.*

There was a woman who was beautiful, who started with all the advantages, yet she had no luck. She married for love, and the love turned to dust. She had bonny children, yet she felt they had been thrust upon her, and she could not love them. They looked at her coldly, as if they were finding fault with her. And hurriedly she felt she must cover up some fault in herself. Yet what it was that she must cover up she never knew. Nevertheless, when her children were present, she always felt the center of her heart go hard. This troubled her, and in her manner she was all the more gentle and anxious for her children, as if she loved them very much. Only she herself knew that at the center of her heart was a hard little place that could not feel love, no, not for anybody. Everybody else said of her: "She is such a good mother. She adores her children." Only she herself, and her children themselves, knew it was not so. They read it in each other's eyes.

There were a boy and two little girls. They lived in a pleasant house, with a garden, and they had discreet servants, and felt themselves superior to anyone in the neighborhood.

Although they lived in style, they felt always an anxiety in the house. There was never enough money. The mother had a small income, and the father had a small income, but not nearly enough for the social position which they had to keep up. The father went in to town to some office. But though he had good prospects, these prospects never materialized. There was always the grinding sense of the shortage of money, though the style was always kept up.

At last the mother said: "I will see if *I* can't make something." But she did not know where to begin. She racked her brains, and tried this thing and the other, but could not find anything successful. The failure made deep lines come into her face. Her children were growing up, they would have to go to school. There must be more money, there must be more money. The father, who was always very handsome and expensive in his tastes, seemed as if he never *would* be able to do anything worth doing. And the mother, who had a great belief in herself, did not succeed any better, and her tastes were just as expensive.

And so the house came to be haunted by the unspoken phrase: *There* 5 *must be more money! There must be more money!* The children could hear it all the time, though nobody said it aloud. They heard it at Christmas, when the expensive and splendid toys filled the nursery. Behind the shining modern rocking-horse, behind the smart doll's house, a voice would start whispering: "There *must* be more money! There *must* be more money!" And the children would stop playing, to listen for a moment. They would look into each other's eyes, to see if they had all heard. And each one saw in the eyes of the other two that they too had heard. "There *must* be more money! There *must* be more money!"

It came whispering from the springs of the still-swaying rocking-horse, and even the horse, bending his wooden, champing head, heard it. The big doll, sitting so pink and smirking in her new pram, could hear it quite plainly, and seemed to be smirking all the more self-consciously because of it. The foolish puppy, too, that took the place of the teddy-bear, he was looking so extraordinarily foolish for no other reason but that he heard the secret whisper all over the house: "There *must* be more money!"

Yet nobody ever said it aloud. The whisper was everywhere, and therefore no one spoke it. Just as no one ever says: "We are breathing!" in spite of the fact that breath is coming and going all the time.

"Mother," said the boy Paul one day, "why don't we keep a car of our own? Why do we always use uncle's, or else a taxi?"

"Because we're the poor members of the family," said the mother.

"But why *are* we, mother?" 10

"Well — I suppose," she said slowly and bitterly, "it's because your father has no luck."

The boy was silent for some time.

"Is luck money, mother?" he asked rather timidly.

"No, Paul. Not quite. It's what causes you to have money."

"Oh!" said Paul vaguely. "I thought when Uncle Oscar said *filthy lucker,* 15 it meant money."

"*Filthy lucre* does mean money," said the mother. "But it's lucre, not luck."

"Oh!" said the boy. "Then what *is* luck, mother?"

"It's what causes you to have money. If you're lucky you have money. That's why it's better to be born lucky than rich. If you're rich, you may lose your money. But if you're lucky, you will always get more money."

"Oh! Will you? And is father not lucky?"

"Very unlucky, I should say," she said bitterly. 20

The boy watched her with unsure eyes.

"Why?" he asked.

"I don't know. Nobody ever knows why one person is lucky and another unlucky."

"Don't they? Nobody at all? Does *nobody* know?"

"Perhaps God. But He never tells."

"He ought to, then. And aren't you lucky either, mother?"

"I can't be, if I married an unlucky husband."

"But by yourself, aren't you?"

"I used to think I was, before I married. Now I think I am very unlucky indeed."

"Why?"

"Well — never mind! Perhaps I'm not really," she said.

The child looked at her, to see if she meant it. But he saw, by the lines of her mouth, that she was only trying to hide something from him.

"Well, anyhow," he said stoutly, "I'm a lucky person."

"Why?" said his mother, with a sudden laugh.

He stared at her. He didn't even know why he had said it.

"God told me," he asserted, brazening it out.

"I hope He did, dear!" she said, again with a laugh, but rather bitter.

"He did, mother!"

"Excellent!" said the mother, using one of her husband's exclamations.

The boy saw she did not believe him; or, rather, that she paid no attention to his assertion. This angered him somewhat, and made him want to compel her attention.

He went off by himself, vaguely, in a childish way, seeking for the clue to "luck." Absorbed, taking no heed of other people, he went about with a sort of stealth, seeking inwardly for luck. He wanted luck, he wanted it, he wanted it. When the two girls were playing dolls in the nursery, he would sit on his big rocking-horse, charging madly into space, with a frenzy that made the little girls peer at him uneasily. Wildly the horse careered, the waving dark hair of the boy tossed, his eyes had a strange glare in them. The little girls dared not speak to him.

When he had ridden to the end of his mad little journey, he climbed down and stood in front of his rocking-horse, staring fixedly into its lowered face. Its red mouth was slightly open, its big eye was wide and glassy-bright.

"Now!" he would silently command the snorting steed. "Now, take me to where there is luck! Now take me!"

And he would slash the horse on the neck with the little whip he had asked Uncle Oscar for. He *knew* the horse could take him to where there was luck, if only he forced it. So he would mount again, and start on his furious ride, hoping at last to get there. He knew he could get there.

"You'll break your horse, Paul!" said the nurse.

"He's always riding like that! I wish he'd leave off!" said his elder sister Joan.

But he only glared down on them in silence. Nurse gave him up. She could make nothing of him. Anyhow he was growing beyond her.

One day his mother and his Uncle Oscar came in when he was on one of his furious rides. He did not speak to them.

"Hallo, you young jockey! Riding a winner?" said his uncle.

"Aren't you growing too big for a rocking-horse? You're not a very little   50
boy any longer, you know," said his mother.

But Paul only gave a blue glare from his big, rather close-set eyes. He
would speak to nobody when he was in full tilt. His mother watched him with
an anxious expression on her face.

At last he suddenly stopped forcing his horse into the mechanical gallop,
and slid down.

"Well, I got there!" he announced fiercely, his blue eyes still flaring, and
his sturdy long legs straddling apart.

"Where did you get to?" asked his mother.

"Where I wanted to go," he flared back at her.   55

"That's right, son!" said Uncle Oscar. "Don't you stop till you get there.
What's the horse's name?"

"He doesn't have a name," said the boy.

"Gets on without all right?" asked the uncle.

"Well, he has different names. He was called Sansovino last week."

"Sansovino, eh? Won the Ascot. How did you know his name?"   60

"He always talks about horse-races with Bassett," said Joan.

The uncle was delighted to find that his small nephew was posted with
all the racing news. Bassett, the young gardener, who had been wounded in
the left foot in the war and had got his present job through Oscar Cresswell,
whose batman he had been, was a perfect blade of the "turf." He lived in the
racing events, and the small boy lived with him.

Oscar Cresswell got it all from Bassett.

"Master Paul comes and asks me, so I can't do more than tell him, sir,"
said Bassett, his face terribly serious, as if he were speaking of religious matters.

"And does he ever put anything on a horse he fancies?"   65

"Well — I don't want to give him away — he's a young sport, a fine
sport, sir. Would you mind asking him himself? He sort of takes a pleasure in
it, and perhaps he'd feel I was giving him away, sir, if you don't mind."

Bassett was serious as a church.

The uncle went back to his nephew and took him off for a ride in the
car.

"Say, Paul, old man, do you ever put anything on a horse?" the uncle
asked.

The boy watched the handsome man closely.   70

"Why, do you think I oughtn't to?" he parried.

"Not a bit of it. I thought perhaps you might give me a tip for the
Lincoln."

The car sped on into the country, going down to Uncle Oscar's place in
Hampshire.

"Honor bright?" said the nephew.

"Honor bright, son!" said the uncle.   75

"Well, then, Daffodil."

"Daffodil! I doubt it, sonny. What about Mirza?"

"I only know the winner," said the boy. "That's Daffodil."

"Daffodil, eh?"

There was a pause. Daffodil was an obscure horse comparatively.   80

"Uncle!"

"Yes, son?"

"You won't let it go any further, will you? I promised Bassett."

"Bassett be damned, old man! What's he got to do with it?"

"We're partners. We've been partners from the first. Uncle, he lent me my first five shillings, which I lost. I promised him, honor bright, it was only between me and him; only you gave me that ten-shilling note I started winning with, so I thought you were lucky. You won't let it go any further, will you?"

The boy gazed at his uncle from those big, hot, blue eyes, set rather close together. The uncle stirred and laughed uneasily.

"Right you are, son! I'll keep your tip private. Daffodil, eh? How much are you putting on him?"

"All except twenty pounds," said the boy. "I keep that in reserve."

The uncle thought it a good joke.

"You keep twenty pounds in reserve, do you, you young romancer? What are you betting, then?"

"I'm betting three hundred," said the boy gravely. "But it's between you and me, Uncle Oscar! Honor bright?"

The uncle burst into a roar of laughter.

"It's between you and me all right, you young Nat Gould," he said, laughing. "But where's your three hundred?"

"Bassett keeps it for me. We're partners."

"You are, are you! And what is Bassett putting on Daffodil?"

"He won't go quite as high as I do, I expect. Perhaps he'll go a hundred and fifty."

"What, pennies?" laughed the uncle.

"Pounds," said the child, with a surprised look at his uncle. "Basset keeps a bigger reserve than I do."

Between wonder and amusement Uncle Oscar was silent. He pursued the matter no further, but he determined to take his nephew with him to the Lincoln races.

"Now, son," he said, "I'm putting twenty on Mirza, and I'll put five for you on any horse you fancy. What's your pick?"

"Daffodil, uncle."

"No, not the fiver on Daffodil!"

"I should if it was my own fiver," said the child.

"Good! Good! Right you are! A fiver for me and a fiver for you on Daffodil."

The child had never been to a race-meeting before, and his eyes were blue fire. He pursed his mouth tight, and watched. A Frenchman just in front had put his money on Lancelot. Wild with excitement, he flayed his arms up and down, yelling, *"Lancelot! Lancelot!"* in his French accent.

Daffodil came in first, Lancelot second, Mirza third. The child, flushed and with eyes blazing, was curiously serene. His uncle brought him four five-pound notes, four to one.

"What am I to do with these?" he cried, waving them before the boy's eyes.

"I suppose we'll talk to Bassett," said the boy. "I expect I have fifteen hundred now; and twenty in reserve; and this twenty."

His uncle studied him for some moments.

"Look here, son!" he said. "You're not serious about Bassett and that fifteen hundred, are you?"

"Yes, I am. But it's between you and me, uncle. Honor bright!"

"Honor bright all right, son! But I must talk to Bassett."

"If you'd like to be a partner, uncle, with Bassett and me, we could all be partners. Only, you'd have to promise, honor bright, uncle, not to let it go beyond us three. Bassett and I are lucky, and you must be lucky, because it was your ten shillings I started winning with. . . ."

Uncle Oscar took both Bassett and Paul into Richmond Park for an afternoon, and there they talked.

"It's like this, you see, sir," Bassett said. "Master Paul would get me talking about racing events, spinning yarns, you know, sir. And he was always keen on knowing if I'd made or if I'd lost. It's about a year since, now, that I put five shillings on Blush of Dawn for him — and we lost. Then the luck turned, and with that ten shillings he had from you, that we put on Singhalese. And since that time, it's been pretty steady, all things considering. What do you say, Master Paul?"

"We're all right when we're sure," said Paul. "It's when we're not quite sure that we go down."

"Oh, but we're careful then," said Bassett.

"But when are you *sure?*" smiled Uncle Oscar.

"It's Master Paul, sir," said Bassett, in a secret, religious voice. "It's as if he had it from heaven. Like Daffodil, now, for the Lincoln. That was as sure as eggs."

"Did you put anything on Daffodil?" asked Oscar Cresswell.

"Yes, sir. I made my bit."

"And my nephew?"

Bassett was obstinately silent, looking at Paul.

"I made twelve hundred, didn't I, Bassett? I told uncle I was putting three hundred on Daffodil."

"That's right," said Bassett, nodding.

"But where's the money?" asked the uncle.

"I keep it safe locked up, sir. Master Paul he can have it any minute he likes to ask for it."

"What, fifteen hundred pounds?"

"And twenty! And *forty,* that is, with the twenty he made on the course."

"It's amazing!" said the uncle.

"If Master Paul offers you to be partners, sir, I would, if I were you; if you'll excuse me," said Bassett.

Oscar Cresswell thought about it.

"I'll see the money," he said.

They drove home again, and sure enough, Bassett came round to the garden-house with fifteen hundred pounds in notes. The twenty pounds reserve was left with Joe Glee, in the Turf Commission deposit.

"You see, it's all right, uncle, when I'm *sure!* Then we go strong, for all we're worth. Don't we, Bassett?"

"We do that, Master Paul."

"And when are you sure?" said the uncle, laughing.

"Oh, well, sometimes I'm *absolutely* sure, like about Daffodil," said the boy; "and sometimes I have an idea; and sometimes I haven't even an idea, have I, Bassett? Then we're careful, because we mostly go down."

"You do, do you! And when you're sure, like about Daffodil, what makes you sure, sonny?"

"Oh, well, I don't know," said the boy uneasily. "I'm sure, you know, uncle; that's all." 140

"It's as if he had it from heaven, sir," Bassett reiterated.

"I should say so!" said the uncle.

But he became a partner. And when the Leger was coming on, Paul was "sure" about Lively Spark, which was a quite inconsiderable horse. The boy insisted on putting a thousand on the horse, Bassett went for five hundred, and Oscar Cresswell two hundred. Lively Spark came in first, and the betting had been ten to one against him. Paul had made ten thousand.

"You see," he said, "I was absolutely sure of him."

Even Oscar Cresswell had cleared two thousand. 145

"Look here, son," he said, "this sort of thing makes me nervous."

"It needn't, uncle! Perhaps I shan't be sure again for a long time."

"But what are you going to do with your money?" asked the uncle.

"Of course," said the boy, "I started it for mother. She said she had no luck, because father is unlucky, so I thought if *I* was lucky, it might stop whispering."

"What might stop whispering?" 150

"Our house. I *hate* our house for whispering."

"What does it whisper?"

"Why — why" — the boy fidgeted — "why, I don't know. But it's always short of money, you know, uncle."

"I know it, son, I know it."

"You know people send mother writs, don't you, uncle?" 155

"I'm afraid I do," said the uncle.

"And then the house whispers, like people laughing at you behind your back. It's awful, that is! I thought if I was lucky . . ."

"You might stop it," added the uncle.

The boy watched him with big blue eyes, that had an uncanny cold fire in them, and he said never a word.

"Well, then!" said the uncle. "What are we doing?" 160

"I shouldn't like mother to know I was lucky," said the boy.

"Why not, son?"

"She'd stop me."

"I don't think she would."

"Oh!" — and the boy writhed in an odd way — "I *don't* want her to know, uncle." 165

"All right, son! We'll manage it without her knowing."

They managed it very easily. Paul, at the other's suggestion, handed over five thousand pounds to his uncle, who deposited it with the family lawyer, who was then to inform Paul's mother that a relative had put five thousand pounds into his hands, which sum was to be paid out a thousand pounds at a time, on the mother's birthday, for the next five years.

"So she'll have a birthday present of a thousand pounds for five successive years," said Uncle Oscar. "I hope it won't make it all the harder for her later."

Paul's mother had her birthday in November. The house had been "whispering" worse than ever lately, and, even in spite of his luck, Paul could not bear up against it. He was very anxious to see the effect of the birthday letter, telling his mother about the thousand pounds.

When there were no visitors, Paul now took his meals with his parents, as he was beyond the nursery control. His mother went into town nearly every day. She had discovered that she had an odd knack of sketching furs and dress materials, so she worked secretly in the studio of a friend who was the chief "artist" for the leading drapers. She drew the figures of ladies in furs and ladies in silk and sequins for the newspaper advertisements. This young woman artist earned several thousand pounds a year, but Paul's mother only made several hundreds, and she was again dissatisfied. She so wanted to be first in something, and she did not succeed, even in making sketches for drapery advertisements.

She was down to breakfast on the morning of her birthday. Paul watched her face as she read the letters. He knew the lawyer's letter. As his mother read it, her face hardened and became more expressionless. Then a cold, determined look came on her mouth. She hid the letter under the pile of others, and said not a word about it.

"Didn't you have anything nice in the post for your birthday, mother?" said Paul.

"Quite moderately nice," she said, her voice cold and absent.

She went away to town without saying more.

But in the afternoon Uncle Oscar appeared. He said Paul's mother had had a long interview with the lawyer, asking if the whole five thousand could not be advanced at once, as she was in debt.

"What do you think, uncle?" said the boy.

"I leave it to you, son."

"Oh, let her have it, then! We can get some more with the other," said the boy.

"A bird in the hand is worth two in the bush, laddie!" said Uncle Oscar.

"But I'm sure to *know* for the Grand National; or the Lincolnshire; or else the Derby. I'm sure to know for *one* of them," said Paul.

So Uncle Oscar signed the agreement, and Paul's mother touched the whole five thousand. Then something very curious happened. The voices in the house suddenly went mad, like a chorus of frogs on a spring evening. There were certain new furnishings, and Paul had a tutor. He was *really* going to Eton, his father's school, in the following autumn. There were flowers in the winter, and a blossoming of the luxury Paul's mother had been used to. And yet the voices in the house, behind the sprays of mimosa and almond blossom, and from under the piles of iridescent cushions, simply trilled and screamed in a sort of ecstasy: "There *must* be more money! Oh-h-h; there *must* be more money. Oh, now, now-w! Now-w-w — there *must* be more money! — more than ever! More than ever!"

It frightened Paul terribly. He studied away at his Latin and Greek with his tutors. But his intense hours were spent with Bassett. The Grand National had gone by: he had not "known," and had lost a hundred pounds. Summer

170

175

180

was at hand. He was in agony for the Lincoln. But even for the Lincoln he didn't "know," and he lost fifty pounds. He became wild-eyed and strange, as if something were going to explode in him.

"Let it alone, son! Don't you bother about it!" urged Uncle Oscar. But it was as if the boy couldn't really hear what his uncle was saying.

"I've got to know for the Derby! I've got to know for the Derby!" the child reiterated, his big blue eyes blazing with a sort of madness.

His mother noticed how overwrought he was.   185

"You'd better go to the seaside. Wouldn't you like to go now to the seaside, instead of waiting? I think you'd better," she said, looking down at him anxiously, her heart curiously heavy because of him.

But the child lifted his uncanny blue eyes.

"I couldn't possibly go before the Derby, mother!" he said. "I couldn't possibly!"

"Why not?" she said, her voice becoming heavy when she was opposed. "Why not? You can still go from the seaside to see the Derby with your Uncle Oscar, if that's what you wish. No need for you to wait here. Besides, I think you care too much about these races. It's a bad sign. My family has been a gambling family, and you won't know till you grow up how much damage it has done. But it has done damage. I shall have to send Bassett away, and ask Uncle Oscar not to talk racing to you, unless you promise to be reasonable about it; go away to the seaside and forget it. You're all nerves!"

"I'll do what you like, mother, so long as you don't send me away till   190
after the Derby," the boy said.

"Send you away from where? Just from this house?"

"Yes," he said, gazing at her.

"Why, you curious child, what makes you care about this house so much, suddenly? I never knew you loved it."

He gazed at her without speaking. He had a secret within a secret, something he had not divulged, even to Bassett or to his Uncle Oscar.

But his mother, after standing undecided and a little bit sullen for some   195
moments, said:

"Very well, then! Don't go to the seaside till after the Derby, if you don't wish it. But promise me you won't let your nerves go to pieces. Promise you won't think so much about horse-racing and *events,* as you call them!"

"Oh, no," said the boy casually. "I won't think much about them, mother. You needn't worry. I wouldn't worry, mother, if I were you."

"If you were me and I were you," said his mother, "I wonder what we *should* do!"

"But you know you needn't worry, mother, don't you?" the boy repeated.

"I should be awfully glad to know it," she said wearily.   200

"Oh, well, you *can,* you know. I mean, you *ought* to know you needn't worry," he insisted.

"Ought I? Then I'll see about it," she said.

Paul's secret of secrets was his wooden horse, that which had no name. Since he was emancipated from a nurse and a nursery-governess, he had had his rocking-horse removed to his own bedroom at the top of the house.

"Surely, you're too big for a rocking-horse!" his mother had remonstrated.

"Well, you see, mother, till I can have a *real* horse, I like to have *some* sort of animal about," had been his quaint answer.

"Do you feel he keeps you company?" she laughed.

"Oh, yes! He's very good, he always keeps me company, when I'm there," said Paul.

So the horse, rather shabby, stood in an arrested prance in the boy's bedroom.

The Derby was drawing near, and the boy grew more and more tense. He hardly heard what was spoken to him, he was very frail, and his eyes were really uncanny. His mother had sudden strange seizures of uneasiness about him. Sometimes, for half-an-hour, she would feel a sudden anxiety about him that was almost anguish. She wanted to rush to him at once, and know he was safe.

Two nights before the Derby, she was at a big party in town, when one of her rushes of anxiety about her boy, her first-born, gripped her heart till she could hardly speak. She fought with the feeling, might and main, for she believed in common-sense. But it was too strong. She had to leave the dance and go downstairs to telephone to the country. The children's nursery-governess was terribly surprised and startled at being rung up in the night.

"Are the children all right, Miss Wilmot?"

"Oh, yes, they are quite all right."

"Master Paul? Is he all right?"

"He went to bed as right as a trivet. Shall I run up and look at him?"

"No," said Paul's mother reluctantly. "No! Don't trouble. It's all right. Don't sit up. We shall be home fairly soon." She did not want her son's privacy intruded upon.

"Very good," said the governess.

It was about one o'clock when Paul's mother and father drove up to their house. All was still. Paul's mother went to her room and slipped off her white fur cloak. She had told her maid not to wait up for her. She heard her husband downstairs, mixing a whisky-and-soda.

And then, because of the strange anxiety at her heart, she stole upstairs to her son's room. Noiselessly she went along the upper corridor. Was there a faint noise? What was it?

She stood, with arrested muscles, outside his door, listening. There was a strange, heavy, and yet not loud noise. Her heart stood still. It was a soundless noise, yet rushing and powerful. Something huge, in violent, hushed motion. What was it? What in God's name was it? She ought to know. She felt that she knew the noise. She knew what it was.

Yet she could not place it. She couldn't say what it was. And on and on it went, like a madness.

Softly, frozen with anxiety and fear, she turned the door-handle.

The room was dark. Yet in the space near the window, she heard and saw something plunging to and fro. She gazed in fear and amazement.

Then suddenly she switched on the light, and saw her son, in his green pajamas, madly surging on the rocking-horse. The blaze of light suddenly lit him up, as he urged the wooden horse, and lit her up, as she stood, blonde, in her dress of pale green and crystal, in the doorway.

"Paul!" she cried. "Whatever are you doing?"

"It's Malabar!" he screamed, in a powerful, strange voice. "It's Malabar!"

His eyes blazed at her for one strange and senseless second, as he ceased urging his wooden horse. Then he fell with a crash to the ground, and she, all her tormented motherhood flooding upon her, rushed to gather him up.

But he was unconscious, and unconscious he remained, with some brainfever. He talked and tossed, and his mother sat stonily by his side.

"Malabar! It's Malabar! Bassett, Bassett, I *know!* It's Malabar!"

So the child cried, trying to get up and urge the rocking-horse that gave him his inspiration.

"What does he mean by Malabar?" asked the heart-frozen mother.

"I don't know," said the father stonily.

"What does he mean by Malabar?" she asked her brother Oscar.

"It's one of the horses running for the Derby," was the answer.

And, in spite of himself, Oscar Cresswell spoke to Bassett, and himself put a thousand on Malabar: at fourteen to one.

The third day of the illness was critical: they were waiting for a change. The boy, with his rather long, curly hair, was tossing ceaselessly on the pillow. He neither slept nor regained consciousness, and his eyes were like blue stones. His mother sat, feeling her heart had gone, turned actually into a stone.

In the evening, Oscar Cresswell did not come, but Bassett sent a message, saying could he come up for one moment, just one moment? Paul's mother was very angry at the intrusion, but on second thought she agreed. The boy was the same. Perhaps Bassett might bring him to consciousness.

The gardener, a shortish fellow with a little brown moustache, and sharp little brown eyes, tiptoed into the room, touched his imaginary cap to Paul's mother, and stole to the bedside, staring with glittering, smallish eyes, at the tossing, dying child.

"Master Paul!" he whispered. "Master Paul! Malabar came in first all right, a clean win. I did as you told me. You've made over seventy thousand pounds, you have; you've got over eighty thousand. Malabar came in all right, Master Paul."

"Malabar! Malabar! Did I say Malabar, mother? Did I say Malabar? Do you think I'm lucky, mother? I knew Malabar, didn't I? Over eighty thousand pounds! I call that lucky, don't you, mother? Over eighty thousand pounds! I knew, didn't I know I knew? Malabar came in all right. If I ride my horse till I'm sure, then I tell you, Bassett, you can go as high as you like. Did you go for all you were worth, Bassett?"

"I went a thousand on it, Master Paul."

"I never told you, mother, that if I can ride my horse, and *get there,* then I'm absolutely sure — oh, absolutely! Mother, did I ever tell you? I *am* lucky!"

"No, you never did," said the mother.

But the boy died in the night.

And even as he lay dead, his mother heard her brother's voice saying to her: "My God, Hester, you're eighty-odd thousand to the good, and a poor devil of a son to the bad. But, poor devil, poor devil, he's best gone out of a life where he rides his rocking-horse to find a winner."

Edith Wharton

ROMAN FEVER

Edith Wharton (1862 – 1937), born Edith Newbold Jones, grew up in a world she later dissected in her fiction: that of wealthy New York socialites. Although her parents frowned on her ambition to write — after all, why would she need money? — young Edith set out to perfect her own elegant, forceful prose style. In her early twenties she began placing stories in popular magazines, and kept on to become America's most celebrated woman author. A long, unhappy marriage to Edward Wharton, a rich nonreader thirteen years her senior, was cheered by the building of The Manse, a stately home in the Berkshires outside Lenox, Massachusetts. Divorced in 1913, she settled permanently in France. During World War I, she worked tirelessly to aid refugees. Friendship with American novelist Henry James inspired Wharton still more thoroughly to study her craft. Among her twenty-seven books of fiction are the novels The House of Mirth *(1905),* The Custom of the Country *(1913),* Summer *(1917), and* The Age of Innocence *(1920). Today her best-known novel may be that short, powerful tale of thwarted lovers in a New England village,* Ethan Frome *(1911). Besides, Wharton wrote fine ghost stories, memoirs, and a critical study,* The Writing of Fiction *(1925). As her biographer R. W. B. Lewis has shown in* Edith Wharton *(1975), she was a generous, wise, and impassioned woman whose best stories refuse to go away.*

I

From the table at which they had been lunching two American ladies of ripe but well-cared-for middle age moved across the lofty terrace of the Roman restaurant and, leaning on its parapet, looked first at each other, and then down on the outspread glories of the Palatine and the Forum, with the same expression of vague but benevolent approval.

As they leaned there a girlish voice echoed up gaily from the stairs leading to the court below. "Well, come along, then," it cried, not to them but to an invisible companion, "and let's leave the young things to their knitting"; and a voice as fresh laughed back: "Oh, look here, Babs, not actually *knitting* — " "Well, I mean figuratively," rejoined the first. "After all, we haven't left our poor parents much else to do. . . ." and at that point the turn of the stairs engulfed the dialogue.

The two ladies looked at each other again, this time with a tinge of smiling embarrassment, and the smaller and paler one shook her head and colored slightly.

"Barbara!" she murmured, sending an unheard rebuke after the mocking voice in the stairway.

The other lady, who was fuller, and higher in color, with a small determined nose supported by vigorous black eyebrows, gave a good-humored laugh. "That's what our daughters think of us!" 5

Her companion replied by a deprecating gesture. "Not of us individually. We must remember that. It's just the collective modern idea of Mothers. And you see — " Half-guiltily she drew from her handsomely mounted black handbag a twist of crimson silk run through by two fine knitting needles. "One never knows," she murmured. "The new system has certainly given us a good deal of time to kill; and sometimes I get tired just looking — even at this." Her gesture was now addressed to the stupendous scene at their feet.

The dark lady laughed again, and they both relapsed upon the view, contemplating it in silence, with a sort of diffused serenity which might have been borrowed from the spring effulgence of the Roman skies. The luncheon hour was long past, and the two had their end of the vast terrace to themselves. At its opposite extremity a few groups, detained by a lingering look at the outspread city, were gathering up guidebooks and fumbling for tips. The last of them scattered, and the two ladies were alone on the air-washed height.

"Well, I don't see why we shouldn't just stay here," said Mrs. Slade, the lady of the high color and energetic brows. Two derelict basket chairs stood near, and she pushed them into the angle of the parapet, and settled herself in one, her gaze upon the Palatine. "After all, it's still the most beautiful view in the world."

"It always will be, to me," assented her friend Mrs. Ansley, with so slight a stress on the "me" that Mrs. Slade, though she noticed it, wondered if it were not merely accidental, like the random underlinings of old-fashioned letter writers.

"Grace Ansley was always old-fashioned," she thought; and added 10
aloud, with a retrospective smile: "It's a view we've both been familiar with for a good many years. When we first met here we were younger than our girls are now. You remember?"

"Oh, yes, I remember," murmured Mrs. Ansley, with the same undefinable stress. "There's that headwaiter wondering," she interpolated. She was evidently far less sure than her companion of herself and of her rights in the world.

"I'll cure him of wondering," said Mrs. Slade, stretching her hand toward a bag as discreetly opulent-looking as Mrs. Ansley's. Signing to the head-waiter, she explained that she and her friend were old lovers of Rome, and would like to spend the end of the afternoon looking down on the view — that is, if it did not disturb the service? The headwaiter, bowing over her gratuity, assured her that the ladies were most welcome, and would be still more so if they would condescend to remain for dinner. A full-moon night, they would remember. . . .

Mrs. Slade's black brows drew together, as though references to the moon were out of place and even unwelcome. But she smiled away her frown as the headwaiter retreated. "Well, why not? We might do worse. There's no knowing, I suppose, when the girls will be back. Do you even know back from *where?* I don't!"

Mrs. Ansley again colored slightly. "I think those young Italian aviators we met at the Embassy invited them to fly to Tarquinia for tea. I suppose they'll want to wait and fly back by moonlight."

"Moonlight — moonlight! What a part it still plays. Do you suppose 15
they're as sentimental as we were?"

"I've come to the conclusion that I don't in the least know what they are," said Mrs. Ansley. "And perhaps we didn't know much more about each other."

"No; perhaps we didn't."

Her friend gave her a shy glance. "I never should have supposed you were sentimental, Alida."

"Well, perhaps I wasn't." Mrs. Slade drew her lids together in retrospect; and for a few moments the two ladies, who had been intimate since childhood, reflected how little they knew each other. Each one, of course, had a label ready to attach to the other's name; Mrs. Delphin Slade, for instance, would have told herself, or anyone who asked her, that Mrs. Horace Ansley, twenty-five years ago, had been exquisitely lovely — no, you wouldn't believe it, would you? . . . though, of course, still charming, distinguished. . . . Well, as a girl she had been exquisite; far more beautiful than her daughter Barbara, though certainly Babs, according to the new standards at any rate, was more effective — had more *edge,* as they say. Funny where she got it, with those two nullities as parents. Yes; Horace Ansley was — well, just the duplicate of his wife. Museum specimens of old New York. Good-looking, irreproachable, exemplary. Mrs. Slade and Mrs. Ansley had lived opposite each other — actually as well as figuratively — for years. When the drawing-room curtains in No. 20 East 73rd Street were renewed, No. 23, across the way, was always aware of it. And of all the movings, buyings, travels, anniversaries, illnesses — the tame chronicle of an estimable pair. Little of it escaped Mrs. Slade. But she had grown bored with it by the time her husband made his big *coup* in Wall Street, and when they bought in upper Park Avenue had already begun to think: "I'd rather live opposite a speakeasy for a change; at least one might see it raided." The idea of seeing Grace raided was so amusing that (before the move) she launched it at a woman's lunch. It made a hit, and went the rounds — she sometimes wondered if it had crossed the street, and reached Mrs. Ansley. She hoped not, but didn't much mind. Those were the days when respectability was at a discount, and it did the irreproachable no harm to laugh at them a little.

A few years later, and not many months apart, both ladies lost their husbands. There was an appropriate exchange of wreaths and condolences, and a brief renewal of intimacy in the half-shadow of their mourning; and now, after another interval, they had run across each other in Rome, at the same hotel, each of them the modest appendage of a salient daughter. The similarity of their lot had again drawn them together, lending itself to mild jokes, and the mutual confession that, if in old days it must have been tiring to "keep up" with daughters, it was now, at times, a little dull not to.

No doubt, Mrs. Slade reflected, she felt her unemployment more than poor Grace ever would. It was a big drop from being the wife of Delphin Slade to being his widow. She had always regarded herself (with a certain conjugal pride) as his equal in social gifts, as contributing her full share to the making of the exceptional couple they were: but the difference after his death was irremediable. As the wife of the famous corporation lawyer, always with an international case or two on hand, every day brought its exciting and unexpected obligation: the impromptu entertaining of eminent colleagues from abroad, the hurried dashes on legal business to London, Paris or Rome, where the entertaining was so handsomely reciprocated; the amusement of hearing in her wake: "What, that handsome woman with the good clothes and the eyes is Mrs. Slade — *the* Slade's wife? Really? Generally the wives of celebrities are such frumps."

Yes; being *the* Slade's widow was a dullish business after that. In living up to such a husband all her faculties had been engaged; now she had only her daughter to live up to, for the son who seemed to have inherited his father's gifts had died suddenly in boyhood. She had fought through that agony because her husband was there, to be helped and to help; now, after the father's death, the thought of the boy had become unbearable. There was nothing left but to mother her daughter; and dear Jenny was such a perfect daughter that she needed no excessive mothering. "Now with Babs Ansley I don't know that I *should* be so quiet," Mrs. Slade sometimes half-enviously reflected; but Jenny, who was younger than her brilliant friend, was that rare accident, an extremely pretty girl who somehow made youth and prettiness seem as safe as their absence. It was all perplexing — and to Mrs. Slade a little boring. She wished that Jenny would fall in love — with the wrong man, even; that she might have to be watched, out-maneuvered, rescued. And instead, it was Jenny who watched her mother, kept her out of drafts, made sure that she had taken her tonic. . . .

Mrs. Ansley was much less articulate than her friend, and her mental portrait of Mrs. Slade was slighter, and drawn with fainter touches. "Alida Slade's awfully brilliant; but not as brilliant as she thinks," would have summed it up; though she would have added, for the enlightenment of strangers, that Mrs. Slade had been an extremely dashing girl; much more so than her daughter, who was pretty, of course, and clever in a way, but had none of her mother's — well, "vividness," someone had once called it. Mrs. Ansley would take up current words like this, and cite them in quotation marks, as unheard-of audacities. No; Jenny was not like her mother. Sometimes Mrs. Ansley thought Alida Slade was disappointed; on the whole she had had a sad life. Full of failures and mistakes; Mrs. Ansley had always been rather sorry for her. . . .

So these two ladies visualized each other, each through the wrong end of her little telescope.

II

For a long time they continued to sit side by side without speaking. It seemed as though, to both, there was a relief in laying down their somewhat futile activities in the presence of the vast Memento Mori which faced them. Mrs. Slade sat quite still, her eyes fixed on the golden slope of the Palace of the Caesars, and after a while Mrs. Ansley ceased to fidget with her bag, and she too sank into meditation. Like many intimate friends, the two ladies had never before had occasion to be silent together, and Mrs. Ansley was slightly embarrassed by what seemed, after so many years, a new stage in their intimacy, and one with which she did not yet know how to deal.

Suddenly the air was full of that deep clangor of bells which periodically covers Rome with a roof of silver. Mrs. Slade glanced at her wristwatch. "Five o'clock already," she said, as though surprised.

Mrs. Ansley suggested interrogatively: "There's bridge at the Embassy at five." For a long time Mrs. Slade did not answer. She appeared to be lost in contemplation, and Mrs. Ansley thought the remark had escaped her. But after a while she said, as if speaking out of a dream: "Bridge, did you say? Not unless you want to. . . . But I don't think I will, you know."

"Oh, no," Mrs. Ansley hastened to assure her. "I don't care to at all. It's so lovely here; and so full of old memories, as you say." She settled herself in her chair, and almost furtively drew forth her knitting. Mrs. Slade took sideway note of this activity, but her own beautifully cared-for hands remained motionless on her knee.

"I was just thinking," she said slowly, "what different things Rome stands for to each generation of travelers. To our grandmothers, Roman fever; to our mothers, sentimental dangers — how we used to be guarded! — to our daughters, no more dangers than the middle of Main Street. They don't know it — but how much they're missing!"

The long golden light was beginning to pale, and Mrs. Ansley lifted her   30
knitting a little closer to her eyes. "Yes; how we were guarded!"

"I always used to think," Mrs. Slade continued, "that our mothers had a much more difficult job than our grandmothers. When Roman fever stalked the streets it must have been comparatively easy to gather in the girls at the danger hour; but when you and I were young, with such beauty calling us, and the spice of disobedience thrown in, and no worse risk than catching cold during the cool hour after sunset, the mothers used to be put to it to keep us in — didn't they?"

She turned again toward Mrs. Ansley, but the latter had reached a delicate point in her knitting. "One, two, three — slip two; yes, they must have been," she assented, without looking up.

Mrs. Slade's eyes rested on her with a deepened attention. "She can knit — in the face of *this!* How like her. . . ."

Mrs. Slade leaned back, brooding, her eyes ranging from the ruins which faced her to the long green hollow of the Forum, the fading glow of the church fronts beyond it, and the outlying immensity of the Colosseum. Suddenly she thought: "It's all very well to say that our girls have done away with sentiment and moonlight. But if Babs Ansley isn't out to catch that young aviator — the one who's a Marchese — then I don't know anything. And Jenny has no chance beside her. I know that too. I wonder if that's why Grace Ansley likes the two girls to go everywhere together? My poor Jenny as a foil — !" Mrs. Slade gave a hardly audible laugh, and at the sound Mrs. Ansley dropped her knitting.

"Yes — ?"   35

"I — oh, nothing. I was only thinking how your Babs carries everything before her. That Campolieri boy is one of the best matches in Rome. Don't look so innocent, my dear — you know he is. And I was wondering, ever so respectfully, you understand . . . wondering how two such exemplary characters as you and Horace had managed to produce anything quite so dynamic." Mrs. Slade laughed again, with a touch of asperity.

Mrs. Ansley's hands lay inert across her needles. She looked straight out at the great accumulated wreckage of passion and splendor at her feet. But her small profile was almost expressionless. At length she said: "I think you overrate Babs, my dear."

Mrs. Slade's tone grew easier. "No; I don't. I appreciate her. And perhaps envy you. Oh, my girl's perfect; if I were a chronic invalid I'd — well, I think I'd rather be in Jenny's hands. There must be times . . . but there! I always wanted a brilliant daughter . . . and never quite understood why I got an angel instead."

Mrs. Ansley echoed her laugh in a faint murmur. "Babs is an angel too."

"Of course — of course! But she's got rainbow wings. Well, they're wandering by the sea with their young men; and here we sit . . . and it all brings back the past a little too acutely."

40

Mrs. Ansley had resumed her knitting. One might almost have imagined (if one had known her less well, Mrs. Slade reflected) that, for her also, too many memories rose from the lengthening shadows of those august ruins. But no; she was simply absorbed in her work. What was there for her to worry about? She knew that Babs would almost certainly come back engaged to the extremely eligible Campolieri. "And she'll sell the New York house, and settle down near them in Rome, and never be in their way . . . she's much too tactful. But she'll have an excellent cook, and just the right people in for bridge and cocktails . . . and a perfectly peaceful old age among her grandchildren."

Mrs. Slade broke off this prophetic flight with a recoil of self-disgust. There was no one of whom she had less right to think unkindly than of Grace Ansley. Would she never cure herself of envying her? Perhaps she had begun too long ago.

She stood up and leaned against the parapet, filling her troubled eyes with the tranquilizing magic of the hour. But instead of tranquilizing her the sight seemed to increase her exasperation. Her gaze turned toward the Colosseum. Already its golden flank was drowned in purple shadow, and above it the sky curved crystal clear, without light or color. It was the moment when afternoon and evening hang balanced in midheaven.

Mrs. Slade turned back and laid her hand on her friend's arm. The gesture was so abrupt that Mrs. Ansley looked up, startled.

"The sun's set. You're not afraid, my dear?"

45

"Afraid — ?"

"Of Roman fever or pneumonia? I remember how ill you were that winter. As a girl you had a very delicate throat, hadn't you?"

"Oh, we're all right up here. Down below, in the Forum, it does get deathly cold, all of a sudden . . . but not here."

"Ah, of course you know because you had to be so careful." Mrs. Slade turned back to the parapet. She thought: "I must make one more effort not to hate her." Aloud she said: "Whenever I look at the Forum from up here, I remember that story about a great-aunt of yours, wasn't she? A dreadfully wicked great-aunt?"

"Oh, yes; great-aunt Harriet. The one who was supposed to have sent her young sister out to the Forum after sunset to gather a night-blooming flower for her album. All our great-aunts and grandmothers used to have albums of dried flowers."

50

Mrs. Slade nodded. "But she really sent her because they were in love with the same man —"

"Well, that was the family tradition. They said Aunt Harriet confessed it years afterward. At any rate, the poor little sister caught the fever and died. Mother used to frighten us with the story when we were children."

"And you frightened *me* with it, that winter when you and I were here as girls. The winter I was engaged to Delphin."

Mrs. Ansley gave a faint laugh. "Oh, did I? Really frightened you? I don't believe you're easily frightened."

"Not often; but I was then. I was easily frightened because I was too happy. I wonder if you know what that means?" 55

"I — yes . . ." Mrs. Ansley faltered.

"Well, I suppose that was why the story of your wicked aunt made such an impression on me. And I thought: "There's no more Roman fever, but the Forum is deathly cold after sunset — especially after a hot day. And the Colosseum's even colder and damper."

"The Colosseum — ?"

"Yes. It wasn't easy to get in, after the gates were locked for the night. Far from easy. Still, in those days it could be managed; it *was* managed, often. Lovers met there who couldn't meet elsewhere. You knew that?"

"I — I dare say. I don't remember." 60

"You don't remember? You don't remember going to visit some ruins or other one evening, just after dark, and catching a bad chill? You were supposed to have gone to see the moon rise. People always said that expedition was what caused your illness."

There was a moment's silence; then Mrs. Ansley rejoined: "Did they? It was all so long ago."

"Yes. And you got well again — so it didn't matter. But I suppose it struck your friends — the reason given for your illness, I mean — because everybody knew you were so prudent on account of your throat, and your mother took such care of you. . . . You *had* been out late sight-seeing, hadn't you, that night?"

"Perhaps I had. The most prudent girls aren't always prudent. What made you think of it now?"

Mrs. Slade seemed to have no answer ready. But after a moment she broke out: "Because I simply can't bear it any longer — !" 65

Mrs. Ansley lifted her head quickly. Her eyes were wide and very pale. "Can't bear what?"

"Why — your not knowing that I've always known why you went."

"Why I went — ?"

"Yes. You think I'm bluffing, don't you? Well, you went to meet the man I was engaged to — and I can repeat every word of the letter that took you there."

While Mrs. Slade spoke Mrs. Ansley had risen unsteadily to her feet. Her bag, her knitting and gloves, slid in a panic-stricken heap to the ground. She looked at Mrs. Slade as though she were looking at a ghost. 70

"No, no — don't," she faltered out.

"Why not? Listen, if you don't believe me. 'My one darling, things can't go on like this. I must see you alone. Come to the Colosseum immediately after dark tomorrow. There will be somebody to let you in. No one whom you need fear will suspect' — but perhaps you've forgotten what the letter said?"

Mrs. Ansley met the challenge with an unexpected composure. Steadying herself against the chair she looked at her friend, and replied: "No; I know it by heart too."

"And the signature? 'Only *your* D.S.' Was that it? I'm right, am I? That was the letter that took you out that evening after dark?"

Mrs. Ansley was still looking at her. It seemed to Mrs. Slade that a slow struggle was going on behind the voluntarily controlled mask of her small quiet face. "I shouldn't have thought she had herself so well in hand," Mrs. Slade reflected, almost resentfully. But at this moment Mrs. Ansley spoke. "I don't know how you knew. I burnt that letter at once."

"Yes; you would, naturally — you're so prudent!" The sneer was open now. "And if you burnt the letter you're wondering how on earth I know what was in it. That's it, isn't it?"

Mrs. Slade waited, but Mrs. Ansley did not speak.

"Well, my dear, I know what was in the letter because I wrote it!"

"You wrote it?"

"Yes."

The two women stood for a minute staring at each other in the last golden light. Then Mrs. Ansley dropped back into her chair. "Oh," she murmured, and covered her face with her hands.

Mrs. Slade waited nervously for another word or movement. None came, and at length she broke out: "I horrify you."

Mrs. Ansley's hands dropped to her knee. The face they uncovered was streaked with tears. "I wasn't thinking of you. I was thinking — it was the only letter I ever had from him!"

"And I wrote it. Yes; I wrote it! But I was the girl he was engaged to. Did you happen to remember that?"

Mrs. Ansley's head drooped again. "I'm not trying to excuse myself . . . I remembered. . . ."

"And still you went?"

"Still I went."

Mrs. Slade stood looking down on the small bowed figure at her side. The flame of her wrath had already sunk, and she wondered why she had ever thought there would be any satisfaction in inflicting so purposeless a wound on her friend. But she had to justify herself.

"You do understand? I'd found out — and I hated you, hated you. I knew you were in love with Delphin — and I was afraid; afraid of you, of your quiet ways, your sweetness . . . your . . . well, I wanted you out of the way, that's all. Just for a few weeks; just till I was sure of him. So in a blind fury I wrote that letter. . . . I don't know why I'm telling you now."

"I suppose," said Mrs. Ansley slowly, "it's because you've always gone on hating me."

"Perhaps. Or because I wanted to get the whole thing off my mind." She paused. "I'm glad you destroyed the letter. Of course I never thought you'd die."

Mrs. Ansley relapsed into silence, and Mrs. Slade, leaning above her, was conscious of a strange sense of isolation, of being cut off from the warm current of human communion. "You think me a monster!"

"I don't know. . . . It was the only letter I had, and you say he didn't write it?"

"Ah, how you care for him still!"

"I cared for that memory," said Mrs. Ansley.

Mrs. Slade continued to look down on her. She seemed physically reduced by the blow — as if, when she got up, the wind might scatter her like a puff of dust. Mrs. Slade's jealousy suddenly leapt up again at the sight. All these years the woman had been living on that letter. How she must have loved him, to treasure the mere memory of its ashes! The letter of the man her friend was engaged to. Wasn't it she who was the monster?

"You tried your best to get him away from me, didn't you? But you failed; and I kept him. That's all."

"Yes. That's all."

"I wish now I hadn't told you. I'd no idea you'd feel about it as you do; I thought you'd be amused. It all happened so long ago, as you say; and you must do me the justice to remember that I had no reason to think you'd ever taken it seriously. How could I, when you were married to Horace Ansley two months afterward? As soon as you could get out of bed your mother rushed you off to Florence and married you. People were rather surprised — they wondered at its being done so quickly; but I thought I knew. I had an idea you did it out of *pique* — to be able to say you'd got ahead of Delphin and me. Girls have such silly reasons for doing the most serious things. And your marrying so soon convinced me that you'd never really cared."

"Yes. I suppose it would," Mrs. Ansley assented. 100

The clear heaven overhead was emptied of all its gold. Dusk spread over it, abruptly darkening the Seven Hills. Here and there lights began to twinkle through the foliage at their feet. Steps were coming and going on the deserted terrace — waiters looking out of the doorway at the head of the stairs, then reappearing with trays and napkins and flasks of wine. Tables were moved, chairs straightened. A feeble string of electric lights flickered out. Some vases of faded flowers were carried away, and brought back replenished. A stout lady in a dust coat suddenly appeared, asking in broken Italian if anyone had seen the elastic band which held together her tattered Baedeker. She poked with her stick under the table at which she had lunched, the waiters assisting.

The corner where Mrs. Slade and Mrs. Ansley sat was still shadowy and deserted. For a long time neither of them spoke. At length Mrs. Slade began again: "I suppose I did it as a sort of joke — "

"A joke?"

"Well, girls are ferocious sometimes, you know. Girls in love especially. And I remember laughing to myself all that evening at the idea that you were waiting around there in the dark, dodging out of sight, listening for every sound, trying to get in — Of course I was upset when I heard you were so ill afterward."

Mrs. Ansley had not moved for a long time. But now she turned slowly 105 toward her companion. "But I didn't wait. He'd arranged everything. He was there. We were let in at once," she said.

Mrs. Slade sprang up from her leaning position. "Delphin there? They let you in? — Ah, now you're lying!" she burst out with violence.

Mrs. Ansley's voice grew clearer, and full of surprise. "But of course he was there. Naturally he came — "

"Came? How did he know he'd find you there? You must be raving!"

Mrs. Ansley hesitated, as though reflecting. "But I answered the letter. I told him I'd be there. So he came."

Mrs. Slade flung her hands up to her face. "Oh, God — you answered! 110
I never thought of your answering. . . ."

"It's odd you never thought of it, if you wrote the letter."

"Yes. I was blind with rage."

Mrs. Ansley rose, and drew her fur scarf about her. "It is cold here. We'd better go. . . . I'm sorry for you," she said, as she clasped the fur about her throat.

The unexpected words sent a pang through Mrs. Slade. "Yes; we'd better go." She gathered up her bag and cloak. "I don't know why you should be sorry for me," she muttered.

Mrs. Ansley stood looking away from her toward the dusky secret mass 115
of the Colosseum. "Well — because I didn't have to wait that night."

Mrs. Slade gave an unquiet laugh. "Yes; I was beaten there. But I oughtn't to begrudge it to you, I suppose. At the end of all these years. After all, I had everything; I had him for twenty-five years. And you had nothing but that one letter that he didn't write."

Mrs. Ansley was again silent. At length she turned toward the door of the terrace. She took a step, and turned back, facing her companion.

"I had Barbara," she said, and began to move ahead of Mrs. Slade toward the stairway.

Eudora Welty

A WORN PATH   1941

Eudora Welty was born in 1909 in Jackson, Mississippi, daughter of an insurance company president. She grew up within a stone's throw of the state capitol and still lives in her childhood home. Like William Faulkner, another Mississippi writer, she has stayed close to her roots for practically all her life, except for short sojourns at the University of Wisconsin, where she took her B.A., and in New York City, where she studied advertising. Although she is a novelist distinguished for The Robber Bridegroom *(1942),* Delta Wedding *(1946),* The Ponder Heart *(1954), and* Losing Battles *(1970), many critics think her finest work is in the short-story form.* The Collected Stories of Eudora Welty *(1980) gathers the work of more than forty years. Welty's other books include memoirs,* The Optimist's Daughter *(1972) and* One Writer's Beginnings *(1984), and* The Eye of the Story *(1977), a book of sympathetic criticism on the fiction of writers including Willa Cather, Virginia Woolf, Katherine Anne Porter, and Isak Dinesen.*

It was December — a bright frozen day in the early morning. Far out in the country there was an old Negro woman with her head tied in a red rag, coming along a path through the pinewoods. Her name was Phoenix Jackson. She was very old and small and she walked slowly in the dark pine shadows, moving a little from side to side in her steps, with the balanced heaviness and lightness of a pendulum in a grandfather clock. She carried a thin, small cane made from an umbrella, and with this she kept tapping the frozen earth in front of her. This made a grave and persistent noise in the still air, that seemed meditative like the chirping of a solitary little bird.

She wore a dark striped dress reaching down to her shoe tops, and an equally long apron of bleached sugar sacks, with a full pocket: all neat and tidy, but every time she took a step she might have fallen over her shoelaces, which dragged from her unlaced shoes. She looked straight ahead. Her eyes were blue with age. Her skin had a pattern all its own of numberless branching wrinkles and as though a whole little tree stood in the middle of her forehead, but a golden color ran underneath, and the two knobs of her cheeks were illumined by a yellow burning under the dark. Under the red rag her hair came down on her neck in the frailest of ringlets, still black, and with an odor like copper.

Now and then there was a quivering in the thicket. Old Phoenix said, "Out of my way, all you foxes, owls, beetles, jack rabbits, coons and wild animals! . . . Keep out from under these feet, little bobwhites. . . . Keep the big wild hogs out of my path. Don't let none of those come running my direction. I got a long way." Under her small black-freckled hand her cane, limber as a buggy whip, would switch at the brush as if to rouse up any hiding things.

On she went. The woods were deep and still. The sun made the pine needles almost too bright to look at, up where the wind rocked. The cones dropped as light as feathers. Down in the hollow was the mourning dove — it was not too late for him.

The path ran up a hill. "Seem like there is chains about my feet, time I get this far," she said, in the voice of argument old people keep to use with themselves. "Something always take a hold of me on this hill — pleads I should stay."

After she got to the top she turned and gave a full, severe look behind her where she had come. "Up through pines," she said at length. "Now down through oaks."

Her eyes opened their widest, and she started down gently. But before she got to the bottom of the hill a bush caught her dress.

Her fingers were busy and intent, but her skirts were full and long, so that before she could pull them free in one place they were caught in another. It was not possible to allow the dress to tear. "I in the thorny bush," she said. "Thorns, you doing your appointed work. Never want to let folks pass, no sir. Old eyes thought you was a pretty little *green* bush."

Finally, trembling all over, she stood free, and after a moment dared to stoop for her cane.

"Sun so high!" she cried, leaning back and looking, while the thick tears went over her eyes. "The time getting all gone here."

At the foot of this hill was a place where a log was laid across the creek.

"Now comes the trial," said Phoenix.

Putting her right foot out, she mounted the log and shut her eyes. Lifting her skirt, leveling her cane fiercely before her, like a festival figure in some parade, she began to march across. Then she opened her eyes and she was safe on the other side.

"I wasn't as old as I thought," she said.

But she sat down to rest. She spread her skirts on the bank around her 15
and folded her hands over her knees. Up above her was a tree in a pearly cloud
of mistletoe. She did not dare to close her eyes, and when a little boy brought
her a plate with a slice of marble-cake on it she spoke to him. "That would
be acceptable," she said. But when she went to take it there was just her own
hand in the air.

So she left that tree, and had to go through a barbed-wire fence. There
she had to creep and crawl, spreading her knees and stretching her fingers like
a baby trying to climb the steps. But she talked loudly to herself: she could
not let her dress be torn now, so late in the day, and she could not pay for
having her arm or her leg sawed off if she got caught fast where she was.

At last she was safe through the fence and risen up out in the clearing.
Big dead trees, like black men with one arm, were standing in the purple stalks
of the withered cotton field. There sat a buzzard.

"Who you watching?"

In the furrow she made her way along.

"Glad this not the season for bulls," she said, looking sideways, "and the 20
good Lord made his snakes to curl up and sleep in the winter. A pleasure I don't
see no two-headed snake coming around that tree, where it come once. It took
a while to get by him, back in the summer."

She passed through the old cotton and went into a field of dead corn. It
whispered and shook and was taller than her head. "Through the maze now,"
she said, for there was no path.

Then there was something tall, black, and skinny there, moving before
her.

At first she took it for a man. It could have been a man dancing in the
field. But she stood still and listened, and it did not make a sound. It was as
silent as a ghost.

"Ghost," she said sharply, "who be you the ghost of? For I have heard
of nary death close by."

But there was no answer — only the ragged dancing in the wind. 25

She shut her eyes, reached out her hand, and touched a sleeve. She found
a coat and inside that an emptiness, cold as ice.

"You scarecrow," she said. Her face lighted. "I ought to be shut up for
good," she said with laughter. "My senses is gone. I too old. I the oldest people
I ever know. Dance, old scarecrow," she said, "while I dancing with you."

She kicked her foot over the furrow, and with mouth drawn down,
shook her head once or twice in a little strutting way. Some husks blew down
and whirled in streamers about her skirts.

Then she went on, parting her way from side to side with the cane,
through the whispering field. At last she came to the end, to a wagon track
where the silver grass blew between the red ruts. The quail were walking
around like pullets, seeming all dainty and unseen.

"Walk pretty," she said. "This the easy place. This the easy going." 30

She followed the track, swaying through the quiet bare fields, through
the little strings of trees silver in their dead leaves, past cabins silver from
weather, with the doors and windows boarded shut, all like old women under
a spell sitting there. "I walking in their sleep," she said, nodding her head
vigorously.

In a ravine she went where a spring was silently flowing through a hollow log. Old Phoenix bent and drank. "Sweet-gum makes the water sweet," she said, and drank more. "Nobody know who made this well, for it was here when I was born."

The track crossed a swampy part where the moss hung as white as lace from every limb. "Sleep on, alligators, and blow your bubbles." Then the track went into the road.

Deep, deep the road went down between the high green-colored banks. Overhead the live-oaks met, and it was as dark as a cave.

A black dog with a lolling tongue came up out of the weeds by the ditch. [35] She was meditating, and not ready, and when he came at her she only hit him a little with her cane. Over she went in the ditch, like a little puff of milkweed.

Down there, her senses drifted away. A dream visited her, and she reached her hand up, but nothing reached down and gave her a pull. So she lay there and presently went to talking. "Old woman," she said to herself, "that black dog come up out of the weeds to stall you off, and now there he sitting on his fine tail, smiling at you."

A white man finally came along and found her — a hunter, a young man, with his dog on a chain.

"Well, Granny!" he laughed. "What are you doing there?"

"Lying on my back like a June-bug waiting to be turned over, mister," she said, reaching up her hand.

He lifted her up, gave her a swing in the air, and set her down. "Anything [40] broken, Granny?"

"No sir, them old dead weeds is springy enough," said Phoenix, when she had got her breath. "I thank you for your trouble."

"Where do you live, Granny?" he asked, while the two dogs were growling at each other.

"Away back yonder, sir, behind the ridge. You can't even see it from here."

"On your way home?"

"No sir, I going to town." [45]

"Why, that's too far! That's as far as I walk when I come out myself, and I get something for my trouble." He patted the stuffed bag he carried, and there hung down a little closed claw. It was one of the bob-whites, with its beak hooked bitterly to show it was dead. "Now you go on home, Granny!"

"I bound to go to town, mister," said Phoenix. "The time come around."

He gave another laugh, filling the whole landscape. "I know you old colored people! Wouldn't miss going to town to see Santa Claus!"

But something held old Phoenix very still. The deep lines in her face went into a fierce and different radiation. Without warning, she had seen with her own eyes a flashing nickel fall out of the man's pocket onto the ground.

"How old are you, Granny?" he was saying. [50]

"There is no telling, mister," she said, "no telling."

Then she gave a little cry and clapped her hands and said, "Git on away from here, dog! Look! Look at that dog!" She laughed as if in admiration. "He ain't scared of nobody. He a big black dog." She whispered, "Sic him!"

"Watch me get rid of that cur," said the man. "Sic him, Pete! Sic him!"

Phoenix heard the dogs fighting, and heard the man running and throwing sticks. She even heard a gunshot. But she was slowly bending forward by that time, further and further forward, the lids stretched down over her eyes, as if she were doing this in her sleep. Her chin was lowered almost to her knees. The yellow palm of her hand came out from the fold of her apron. Her fingers slid down and along the ground under the piece of money with the grace and care they would have in lifting an egg from under a setting hen. Then she slowly straightened up, she stood erect, and the nickel was in her apron pocket. A bird flew by. Her lips moved. "God watching me the whole time. I come to stealing."

The man came back, and his own dog panted about them. "Well, I scared him off that time," he said, and then he laughed and lifted his gun and pointed it at Phoenix.

She stood straight and faced him.

"Doesn't the gun scare you?" he said, still pointing it.

"No, sir, I seen plenty go off closer by, in my day, and for less than what I done," she said, holding utterly still.

He smiled, and shouldered the gun. "Well, Granny," he said, "you must be a hundred years old, and scared of nothing. I'd give you a dime if I had any money with me. But you take my advice and stay home, and nothing will happen to you."

"I bound to go on my way, mister," said Phoenix. She inclined her head in the red rag. Then they went in different directions, but she could hear the gun shooting again and again over the hill.

She walked on. The shadows hung from the oak trees to the road like curtains. Then she smelled wood-smoke, and smelled the river, and she saw a steeple and the cabins on their steep steps. Dozens of little black children whirled around her. There ahead was Natchez shining. Bells were ringing. She walked on.

In the paved city it was Christmas time. There were red and green electric lights strung and crisscrossed everywhere, and all turned on in the daytime. Old Phoenix would have been lost if she had not distrusted her eyesight and depended on her feet to know where to take her.

She paused quietly on the sidewalk where people were passing by. A lady came along in the crowd, carrying an armful of red-, green- and silver-wrapped presents; she gave off perfume like the red roses in hot summer, and Phoenix stopped her.

"Please, missy, will you lace up my shoe?" She held up her foot.

"What do you want, Grandma?"

"See my shoe," said Phoenix. "Do all right for out in the country, but wouldn't look right to go in a big building."

"Stand still then, Grandma," said the lady. She put her packages down on the sidewalk beside her and laced and tied both shoes tightly.

"Can't lace 'em with a cane," said Phoenix. "Thank you, missy. I doesn't mind asking a nice lady to tie up my shoe, when I gets out on the street."

Moving slowly and from side to side, she went into the big building, and into a tower of steps, where she walked up and around and around until her feet knew to stop.

She entered a door, and there she saw nailed up on the wall the document   70
that had been stamped with the gold seal and framed in the gold frame, which
matched the dream that was hung up in her head.

"Here I be," she said. There was a fixed and ceremonial stiffness over her
body.

"A charity case, I suppose," said an attendant who sat at the desk before
her.

But Phoenix only looked above her head. There was sweat on her face,
the wrinkles in her skin shone like a bright net.

"Speak up, Grandma," the woman said. "What's your name? We must
have your history, you know. Have you been here before? What seems to be
the trouble with you?"

Old Phoenix only gave a twitch to her face as if a fly were bothering her.   75

"Are you deaf?" cried the attendant.

But then the nurse came in.

"Oh, that's just old Aunt Phoenix," she said. "She doesn't come for
herself — she has a little grandson. She makes these trips just as regular as
clockwork. She lives away back off the Old Natchez Trace." She bent down.
"Well, Aunt Phoenix, why don't you just take a seat? We won't keep you
standing after your long trip." She pointed.

The old woman sat down, bolt upright in the chair.

"Now, how is the boy?" asked the nurse.   80

Old Phoenix did not speak.

"I said, how is the boy?"

But Phoenix only waited and stared straight ahead, her face very solemn
and withdrawn into rigidity.

"Is his throat any better?" asked the nurse. "Aunt Phoenix, don't you
hear me? Is your grandson's throat any better since the last time you came for
the medicine?"

With her hands on her knees, the old woman waited, silent, erect and   85
motionless, just as if she were in armor.

"You mustn't take up our time this way, Aunt Phoenix," the nurse said.
"Tell us quickly about your grandson, and get it over. He isn't dead, is he?"

At last there came a flicker and then a flame of comprehension across her
face, and she spoke.

"My grandson. It was my memory had left me. There I sat and forgot
why I made my long trip."

"Forgot?" The nurse frowned. "After you came so far?"

Then Phoenix was like an old woman begging a dignified forgiveness for   90
waking up frightened in the night. "I never did go to school, I was too old at
the Surrender," she said in a soft voice. "I'm an old woman without an education. It was my memory fail me. My little grandson, he is just the same, and
I forgot it in the coming."

"Throat never heals, does it?" said the nurse, speaking in a loud, sure
voice to old Phoenix. By now she had a card with something written on it, a
little list. "Yes. Swallowed lye. When was it? — January — two, three years
ago — "

Phoenix spoke unasked now. "No, missy, he not dead, he just the same.
Every little while his throat begin to close up again, and he not able to swallow.

He not get his breath. He not able to help himself. So the time come around, and I go on another trip for the soothing medicine."

"All right. The doctor said as long as you came to get it, you could have it," said the nurse. "But it's an obstinate case."

"My little grandson, he sit up there in the house all wrapped up, waiting by himself," Phoenix went on. "We is the only two left in the world. He suffer and it don't seem to put him back at all. He got a sweet look. He going to last. He wear a little patch quilt and peep out holding his mouth open like a little bird. I remembers so plain now. I not going to forget him again, no, the whole enduring time. I could tell him from all the others in creation."

"All right." The nurse was trying to hush her now. She brought her a bottle of medicine. "Charity," she said, making a check mark in a book. 95

Old Phoenix held the bottle close to her eyes, and then carefully put it into her pocket.

"I thank you," she said.

"It's Christmas time, Grandma," said the attendant. "Could I give you a few pennies out of my purse?"

"Five pennies is a nickel," said Phoenix stiffly.

"Here's a nickel," said the attendant. 100

Phoenix rose carefully and held out her hand. She received the nickel and then fished the other nickel out of her pocket and laid it beside the new one. She stared at her palm closely, with her head on one side.

Then she gave a tap with her cane on the floor.

"This is what come to me to do," she said. "I going to the store and buy my child a little windmill they sells, made out of paper. He going to find it hard to believe there such a thing in the world. I'll march myself back where he waiting, holding it straight up in this hand."

She lifted her free hand, gave a little nod, turned around, and walked out of the doctor's office. Then her slow step began on the stairs, going down.

Walter Van Tilburg Clark
THE PORTABLE PHONOGRAPH 1942

Walter Van Tilburg Clark (1909 – 1971), born in Maine, moved at age eight to Reno, where his father, Walter Ernest Clark, was president of the state university. As a young man he taught English and coached sports for ten years in the public schools of Cazenovia, New York, while taking his Ph.D. at Colgate University. In 1945 he went back West, living in Taos, New Mexico; Virginia City, Nevada; and Reno, where he ended his days as writer-in-residence back at the University of Nevada, his alma mater. Though Clark's writing career began with poetry, he is best remembered for his fiction, all published in one decade. The first of three novels, The Ox-Bow Incident *(1940), was declared a minor classic as soon as it appeared. Clark sets it in Nevada cattle country, and explores events that follow the lynching of three men wrongly accused of murder. Hollywood turned it into a notable movie.* The City of Trembling Leaves *(1945), evidently autobi-*

ographical, traces the boyhood of an aspiring composer. The Track of the Cat *(1949), a novel about the hunt for a marauding panther, and a volume of short stories,* The Watchful Gods *(1950), closed his major work. Clark's fiction wholly identifies with the American West, and its themes are those of the frontier: survival in the face of hostile nature, imposition of law upon anarchy.*

The red sunset, with narrow, black cloud strips like threats across it, lay on the curved horizon of the prairie. The air was still and cold, and in it settled the mute darkness and greater cold of night. High in the air there was wind, for through the veil of the dusk the clouds could be seen gliding rapidly south and changing shapes. A sensation of torment, of two-sided, unpredictable nature, arose from the stillness of the earth air beneath the violence of the upper air. Out of the sunset, through the dead, matted grass and isolated weed stalks of the prairie, crept the narrow and deeply rutted remains of a road. In the road, in places, there were crusts of shallow, brittle ice. There were little islands of an old oiled pavement in the road too, but most of it was mud, now frozen rigid. The frozen mud still bore the toothed impress of great tanks, and a wanderer on the neighboring undulations might have stumbled, in this light, into large, partially filled-in and weed-grown cavities, their banks channeled and beginning to spread into badlands. These pits were such as might have been made by falling meteors, but they were not. They were the scars of gigantic bombs, their rawness already made a little natural by rain, seed and time. Along the road there were rakish remnants of fence. There was also, just visible, one portion of tangled and multiple barbed wire still erect, behind which was a shelving ditch with small caves, now very quiet and empty, at intervals in its back wall. Otherwise there was no structure or remnant of a structure visible over the dome of the darkling earth, but only, in sheltered hollows, the darker shadows of young trees trying again.

Under the wuthering arch of the high wind a V of wild geese fled south. The rush of their pinions sounded briefly, and the faint, plaintive notes of their expeditionary talk. Then they left a still greater vacancy. There was the smell and expectation of snow, as there is likely to be when the wild geese fly south. From the remote distance, toward the red sky, came faintly the protracted howl and quick yap-yap of a prairie wolf.

North of the road, perhaps a hundred yards, lay the parallel and deeply intrenched course of a small creek, lined with leafless alders and willows. The creek was already silent under ice. Into the bank above it was dug a sort of cell, with a single opening, like the mouth of a mine tunnel. Within the cell there was a little red of fire, which showed dully through the opening, like a reflection or a deception of the imagination. The light came from the chary burning of four blocks of poorly aged peat, which gave off a petty warmth and much acrid smoke. But the precious remnants of wood, old fence posts and timbers from the long-deserted dugouts, had to be saved for the real cold, for the time when a man's breath blew white, the moisture in his nostrils stiffened at once when he stepped out, and the expansive blizzards paraded for days over the vast open, swirling and settling and thickening, till the dawn of the cleared day when the sky was a thin blue-green and the terrible cold, in which a man could not live for three hours unwarmed, lay over the uniformly drifted swell of the plain.

Around the smoldering peat four men were seated cross-legged. Behind them, traversed by their shadows, was the earth bench, with two old and dirty army blankets, where the owner of the cell slept. In a niche in the opposite wall were a few tin utensils which caught the glint of the coals. The host was rewrapping in a piece of daubed burlap, four fine, leather-bound books. He worked slowly and very carefully, and at last tied the bundle securely with a piece of grass-woven cord. The other three looked intently upon the process, as if a great significance lay in it. As the host tied the cord, he spoke. He was an old man, his long, matted beard and hair gray to nearly white. The shadows made his brows and cheekbones appear gnarled, his eyes and cheeks deeply sunken. His big hands, rough with frost and swollen by rheumatism, were awkward but gentle at their task. He was like a prehistoric priest performing a fateful ceremonial rite. Also his voice had in it a suitable quality of deep, reverent despair, yet perhaps, at the moment, a sharpness of selfish satisfaction.

"When I perceived what was happening," he said, "I told myself, 'It is   5
the end. I cannot take much; I will take these.'

"Perhaps I was impractical," he continued. "But for myself, I do not regret, and what do we know of those who will come after us? We are the doddering remnant of a race of mechanical fools. I have saved what I love; the soul of what was good in us here; perhaps the new ones will make a strong enough beginning not to fall behind when they become clever."

He rose with slow pain and placed the wrapped volumes in the niche with his utensils. The others watched him with the same ritualistic gaze.

"Shakespeare, the Bible, *Moby-Dick, The Divine Comedy,*" one of them said softly. "You might have done worse; much worse."

"You will have a little soul left until you die," said another harshly. "That is more than is true of us. My brain becomes thick, like my hands." He held the big, battered hands, with their black nails, in the glow to be seen.

"I want paper to write on," he said. "And there is none."   10

The fourth man said nothing. He sat in the shadow farthest from the fire, and sometimes his body jerked in its rags from the cold. Although he was still young, he was sick, and coughed often. Writing implied a greater future than he now felt able to consider.

The old man seated himself laboriously, and reached out, groaning at the movement, to put another block of peat on the fire. With bowed heads and averted eyes, his three quests acknowledged his magnanimity.

"We thank you, Doctor Jenkins, for the reading," said the man who had named the books.

They seemed then to be waiting for something. Doctor Jenkins understood, but was loath to comply. In an ordinary moment he would have said nothing. But the words of *The Tempest,* which he had been reading, and the religious attention of the three, made this an unusual occasion.

"You wish to hear the phonograph," he said grudgingly.   15

The two middle-aged men stared into the fire, unable to formulate and expose the enormity of their desire.

The young man, however, said anxiously, between suppressed coughs, "Oh, please," like an excited child.

The old man rose again in his difficult way, and went to the back of the cell. He returned and placed tenderly upon the packed floor, where the firelight might fall upon it, an old, portable phonograph in a black case. He smoothed the top with his hand, then opened it. The lovely green-felt-covered disk became visible.

"I have been using thorns as needles," he said. "But tonight, because we have a musician among us" — he bent his head to the young man, almost invisible in the shadow — "I will use a steel needle. There are only three left."

The two middle-aged men stared at him in speechless adoration. The one with the big hands, who wanted to write, moved his lips, but the whisper was not audible.

"Oh, don't," cried the young man, as if he were hurt. "The thorns will do beautifully."

"No," the old man said. "I have become accustomed to the thorns — but they are not really good. For you, my young friend, we will have good music tonight.

"After all," he added generously, and beginning to wind the phonograph, which creaked, "they can't last forever."

"No, nor we," the man who needed to write said harshly. "The needle, by all means."

"Oh, thanks," said the young man. "Thanks," he said again, in a low, excited voice, and then stifled his coughing with a bowed head.

"The records, though," said the old man when he had finished winding, "are a different matter. Already they are very worn. I do not play them more than once a week. One, once a week, that is what I allow myself.

"More than a week I cannot stand it; not to hear them," he apologized.

"No, how could you?" cried the young man. "And with them here like this."

"A man can stand anything," said the man who wanted to write, in his harsh, antagonistic voice.

"Please, the music," said the young man.

"Only the one," said the old man. "In the long run we will remember more that way."

He had a dozen records with luxuriant gold and red seals. Even in that light the others could see that the threads of the records were becoming worn. Slowly he read out the titles, and the tremendous, dead names of the composers and the artists and the orchestras. The three worked upon the names in their minds, carefully. It was difficult to select from such a wealth what they would at once most like to remember. Finally the man who wanted to write named Gershwin's "New York."

"Oh, no," cried the sick young man, and then could say nothing more because he had to cough. The others understood him, and the harsh man withdrew his selection and waited for the musician to choose.

The musician begged Doctor Jenkins to read the titles again, very slowly, so that he could remember the sounds. While they were read, he lay back against the wall, his eyes closed, his thin, horny hand pulling at his light beard, and listened to the voices and the orchestras and the single instruments in his mind.

When the reading was done he spoke despairingly. "I have forgotten," he complained. "I cannot hear them clearly.

"There are things missing," he explained.

"I know," said Doctor Jenkins. "I thought that I knew all of Shelley by heart. I should have brought Shelley."

"That's more soul than we can use," said the harsh man. "Moby-Dick is better.

"By God, we can understand that," he emphasized.

The doctor nodded.

"Still," said the man who had admired the books, "we need the absolute if we are to keep a grasp on anything.

"Anything but these sticks and peat clods and rabbit snares," he said bitterly.

"Shelley desired an ultimate absolute," said the harsh man. "It's too much," he said. "It's no good; no earthly good."

The musician selected a Debussy nocturne. The others considered and approved. They rose to their knees to watch the doctor prepare for the playing, so that they appeared to be actually in an attitude of worship. The peat glow showed the thinness of their bearded faces, and the deep lines in them, and revealed the condition of their garments. The other two continued to kneel as the old man carefully lowered the needle onto the spinning disk, but the musician suddenly drew back against the wall again, with his knees up, and buried his face in his hands.

At the first notes of the piano the listeners were startled. They stared at each other. Even the musician lifted his head in amazement, but then quickly bowed it again, strainingly, as if he were suffering from a pain he might not be able to endure. They were all listening deeply, without movement. The wet, blue-green notes tinkled forth from the old machine, and were individual, delectable presences in the cell. The individual, delectable presences swept into a sudden tide of unbearably beautiful dissonance, and then continued fully the swelling and ebbing of that tide, the dissonant inpourings, and the resolutions, and the diminishments, and the little, quiet wavelets of interlude lapping between. Every sound was piercing and singularly sweet. In all the men except the musician, there occurred rapid sequences of tragically heightened recollection. He heard nothing but what was there. At the final, whispering disappearance, but moving quietly, so that the others would not hear him and look at him, he let his head fall back in agony, as if it were drawn there by the hair, and clenched the fingers of one hand over his teeth. He sat that way while the others were silent, and until they began to breathe again normally. His drawn-up legs were trembling violently.

Quickly Doctor Jenkins lifted the needle off, to save it, and not to spoil the recollection with scraping. When he had stopped the whirling of the sacred disk, he courteously left the phonograph open and by the fire, in sight.

The others, however, understood. The musician rose last, but then abruptly, and went quickly out at the door without saying anything. The others stopped at the door and gave their thanks in low voices. The doctor nodded magnificently.

"Come again," he invited, "in a week. We will have the 'New York.'"

When the two had gone together, out toward the rimmed road, he stood in the entrance, peering and listening. At first there was only the resonant boom of the wind overhead, and then, far over the dome of the dead, dark plain, the wolf cry lamenting. In the rifts of clouds the doctor saw four stars flying. It impressed the doctor that one of them had just been obscured by the beginning of a flying cloud at the very moment he heard what he had been listening for, a sound of suppressed coughing. It was not near by, however. He believed that down against the pale alders he could see the moving shadow.

With nervous hands he lowered the piece of canvas which served as his door, and pegged it at the bottom. Then quickly and quietly, looking at the piece of canvas frequently, he slipped the records into the case, snapped the lid shut, and carried the phonograph to his couch. There, pausing often to stare at the canvas and listen, he dug earth from the wall and disclosed a piece of board. Behind this there was a deep hole in the wall, into which he put the phonograph. After a moment's consideration, he went over and reached down his bundle of books and inserted it also. Then, guardedly, he once more sealed up the hole with the board and the earth. He also changed his blankets, and the grass-stuffed sack which served as a pillow, so that he could lie facing the entrance. After carefully placing two more blocks of peat on the fire, he stood for a long time watching the stretched canvas, but it seemed to billow naturally with the first gusts of a lowering wind. At last he prayed, and got in under his blankets, and closed his smoke-smarting eyes. On the inside of the bed, next the wall, he could feel with his hand, the comfortable piece of lead pipe.

Isak Dinesen
A SAILOR BOY'S TALE
1942

Isak Dinesen was the pen name of Karen Dinesen von Blixen (1885 – 1962), Danish author who wrote in English. In 1913 she married her distant cousin, Baron Bror Blixen, and began a seventeen-year-long attempt to grow coffee in Kenya — a world she recalls beautifully in Out of Africa *(1937). (This memoir omits the love life made graphic in the 1985 film version with Meryl Streep.) Syphilis contracted from her husband, though temporarily arrested, later recurred; it was gradually to waste her to death. In 1931, divorced, shattered in health, her English lover killed in an air crash, her coffee plantation lost on the auction block, Dinesen returned to Denmark. There at age forty-six she turned to writing to pay her debts, determinedly signing her stories Isak ("he who laughs"). Elegant in style, rich in surprise, shining with arch wit and a disturbing sense of the macabre, Dinesen's work quickly attained a large American audience. She wrote* Seven Gothic Tales *(1934);* Winter's Tales *(1942);* The Angelic Avengers *(1944), a novel subtly protesting against the Nazi occupation, published in wartime under the pen name Pierre Andrezel;* Last Tales *(1957); and* Shadows on the Grass *(1961), a later view of Africa. Her mission as a storyteller, she wrote, was "to make others confound fiction and reality in order to render them, for an hour, mysteriously happy."*

The barque *Charlotte* was on her way from Marseille to Athens, in grey weather, on a high sea, after three days' heavy gale. A small sailor-boy, named Simon, stood on the wet, swinging deck, held on to a shroud, and looked up towards the drifting clouds, and to the upper top-gallant yard of the mainmast.

A bird, that had sought refuge upon the mast, had got her feet entangled in some loose tackle-yarn of the halliard, and, high up there, struggled to get free. The boy on the deck could see her wings flapping and her head turning from side to side.

Through his own experience of life he had come to the conviction that in this world everyone must look after himself, and expect no help from others. But the mute, deadly fight kept him fascinated for more than an hour. He wondered what kind of bird it would be. These last days a number of birds had come to settle in the barque's rigging: swallows, quails, and a pair of peregrine falcons; he believed that this bird was a peregrine falcon. He remembered how, many years ago, in his own country and near his home, he had once seen a peregrine falcon quite close, sitting on a stone and flying straight up from it. Perhaps this was the same bird. He thought: "That bird is like me. Then she was there, and now she is here."

At that a fellow-feeling rose in him, a sense of common tragedy; he stood looking at the bird with his heart in his mouth. There were none of the sailors about to make fun of him; he began to think out how he might go up by the shrouds to help the falcon out. He brushed his hair back and pulled up his sleeves, gave the deck round him a great glance, and climbed up. He had to stop a couple of times in the swaying rigging.

It was indeed, he found when he got to the top of the mast, a peregrine falcon. As his head was on a level with hers, she gave up her struggle, and looked at him with a pair of angry, desperate yellow eyes. He had to take hold of her with one hand while he got his knife out, and cut off the tackle-yarn. He was scared as he looked down, but at the same time he felt that he had been ordered up by nobody, but that this was his own venture, and this gave him a proud, steadying sensation, as if the sea and the sky, the ship, the bird and himself were all one. Just as he had freed the falcon, she hacked him in the thumb, so that the blood ran, and he nearly let her go. He grew angry with her, and gave her a clout on the head, then he put her inside his jacket, and climbed down again.

When he reached the deck the mate and the cook were standing there, looking up; they roared to him to ask what he had had to do in the mast. He was so tired that the tears were in his eyes. He took the falcon out and showed her to them, and she kept still within his hands. They laughed and walked off. Simon set the falcon down, stood back and watched her. After a while he reflected that she might not be able to get up from the slippery deck, so he caught her once more, walked away with her and placed her upon a bolt of canvas. A little after she began to trim her feathers, made two or three sharp jerks forward, and then suddenly flew off. The boy could follow her flight above the troughs of the grey sea. He thought: "There flies my falcon."

When the *Charlotte* came home, Simon signed aboard another ship, and two years later he was a light hand on the schooner *Hebe* lying at Bodø, high up on the coast of Norway, to buy herrings.

To the great herring-markets of Bodø ships came together from all corners of the world; here were Swedish, Finnish and Russian boats, a forest of masts, and on shore a turbulent, irregular display of life, with many languages spoken, and mighty fights. On the shore booths had been set up, and the Lapps, small yellow people, noiseless in their movements, with watchful eyes, whom Simon had never seen before, came down to sell bead-embroidered leather-goods. It was April, the sky and the sea were so clear that it was difficult to hold one's eyes up against them — salt, infinitely wide, and filled with bird-shrieks — as if someone were incessantly whetting invisible knives, on all sides, high up in Heaven.

Simon was amazed at the lightness of these April evenings. He knew no geography, and did not assign it to the latitude, but he took it as a sign of an unwonted good-will in the Universe, a favor. Simon had been small for his age all his life, but this last winter he had grown, and had become strong of limb. That good luck, he felt, must spring from the very same source as the sweetness of the weather, from a new benevolence in the world. He had been in need of such encouragement, for he was timid by nature; now he asked for no more. The rest he felt to be his own affair. He went about slowly, and proudly.

One evening he was ashore with land-leave, and walked up to the booth of a small Russian trader, a Jew who sold gold watches. All the sailors knew that his watches were made from bad metal, and would not go, still they bought them, and paraded them about. Simon looked at these watches for a long time, but did not buy. The old Jew had divers goods in his shop, and amongst others a case of oranges. Simon had tasted oranges on his journeys; he bought one and took it with him. He meant to go up on a hill, from where he could see the sea, and suck it there.

As he walked on, and had got to the outskirts of the place, he saw a little girl in a blue frock, standing at the other side of a fence and looking at him. She was thirteen or fourteen years old, as slim as an eel, but with a round, clear, freckled face, and a pair of long plaits. The two looked at one another.

"Who are you looking out for?" Simon asked, to say something. The girl's face broke into an ecstatic, presumptuous smile. "For the man I am going to marry, of course," she said. Something in her countenance made the boy confident and happy; he grinned a little at her. "That will perhaps be me," he said. "Ha, ha," said the girl, "he is a few years older than you, I can tell you." "Why," said Simon, "you are not grown up yourself." The little girl shook her head solemnly. "Nay," she said, "but when I grow up I will be exceedingly beautiful, and wear brown shoes with heels, and a hat." "Will you have an orange?" asked Simon, who could give her none of the things she had named. She looked at the orange and at him. "They are very good to eat," said he. "Why do you not eat it yourself then?" she asked. "I have eaten so many already," said he, "when I was in Athens. Here I had to pay a mark for it." "What is your name?" asked she. "My name is Simon," said he. "What is yours?" "Nora," said the girl. "What do you want for your orange now, Simon?"

When he heard his name in her mouth Simon grew bold. "Will you give

10

me a kiss for the orange?" he asked. Nora looked at him gravely for a moment. "Yes," she said, "I should not mind giving you a kiss." He grew as warm as if he had been running quickly. When she stretched out her hand for the orange he took hold of it. At that moment somebody in the house called out for her. "That is my father," said she, and tried to give him back the orange, but he would not take it. "Then come again tomorrow," she said quickly, "then I will give you a kiss." At that she slipped off. He stood and looked after her, and a little later went back to his ship.

Simon was not in the habit of making plans for the future, and now he did not know whether he would be going back to her or not.

The following evening he had to stay aboard, as the other sailors were going ashore, and he did not mind that either. He meant to sit on the deck with the ship's dog, Balthasar, and to practise upon a concertina that he had purchased some time ago. The pale evening was all around him, the sky was faintly roseate, the sea was quite calm, like milk-and-water, only in the wake of the boats going inshore it broke into streaks of vivid indigo. Simon sat and played; after a while his own music began to speak to him so strongly that he stopped, got up and looked upwards. Then he saw that the full moon was sitting high on the sky.

The sky was so light that she hardly seemed needed there; it was as if she had turned up by a caprice of her own. She was round, demure and presumptuous. At that he knew that he must go ashore, whatever it was to cost him. But he did not know how to get away, since the others had taken the yawl with them. He stood on the deck for a long time, a small lonely figure of a sailor-boy on a boat, when he caught sight of a yawl coming in from a ship farther out, and hailed her. He found that it was the Russian crew from a boat named *Anna*, going ashore. When he could make himself understood to them, they took him with them; they first asked him for money for his fare, then, laughing, gave it back to him. He thought: "These people will be believing that I am going in to town, wenching." And then he felt, with some pride, that they were right, although at the same time they were infinitely wrong, and knew nothing about anything.

When they came ashore they invited him to come in and drink in their company, and he would not refuse, because they had helped him. One of the Russians was a giant, as big as a bear; he told Simon that his name was Ivan. He got drunk at once, and then fell upon the boy with a bear-like affection, pawed him, smiled and laughed into his face, made him a present of a gold watch-chain, and kissed him on both cheeks. At that Simon reflected that he also ought to give Nora a present when they met again, and as soon as he could get away from the Russians he walked up to a booth that he knew of, and bought a small blue silk handkerchief, the same color as her eyes.

It was Saturday evening, and there were many people amongst the houses; they came in long rows, some of them singing, all keen to have some fun that night. Simon, in the midst of this rich, bawling life under the clear moon, felt his head light with the flight from the ship and the strong drinks. He crammed the handkerchief in his pocket; it was silk, which he had never touched before, a present for his girl.

He could not remember the path up to Nora's house, lost his way, and came back to where he had started. Then he grew deadly afraid that he should be too late, and began to run. In a small passage between two wooden huts he ran straight into a big man, and found that it was Ivan once more. The Russian folded his arms round him and held him. "Good! Good!" he cried in high glee, "I have found you, my little chicken. I have looked for you everywhere, and poor Ivan has wept because he lost his friend." "Let me go, Ivan," cried Simon. "Oho," said Ivan, "I shall go with you and get you what you want. My heart and my money are all yours, all yours; I have been seventeen years old myself, a little lamb of God, and I want to be so again tonight." "Let me go," cried Simon, "I am in a hurry." Ivan held him so that it hurt, and patted him with his other hand. "I feel it, I feel it," he said. "Now trust to me, my little friend. Nothing shall part you and me. I hear the others coming; we will have such a night together as you will remember when you are an old grandpapa."

Suddenly he crushed the boy to him, like a bear that carries off a sheep.   20 The odious sensation of male bodily warmth and the bulk of a man close to him made the lean boy mad. He thought of Nora waiting, like a slender ship in the dim air, and of himself, here, in the hot embrace of a hairy animal. He struck Ivan with all his might. "I shall kill you, Ivan," he cried out, "if you do not let me go." "Oh, you will be thankful to me later on," said Ivan, and began to sing. Simon fumbled in his pocket for his knife, and got it opened. He could not lift his hand, but he drove the knife, furiously, in under the big man's arm. Almost immediately he felt the blood spouting out, and running down in his sleeve. Ivan stopped short in the song, let go his hold of the boy and gave two long deep grunts. The next second he tumbled down on his knees. "Poor Ivan, poor Ivan," he groaned. He fell straight on his face. At that moment Simon heard the other sailors coming along, singing, in the by-street.

He stood still for a minute, wiped his knife, and watched the blood spread into a dark pool underneath the big body. Then he ran. As he stopped for a second to choose his way, he heard the sailors behind him scream out over their dead comrade. He thought: "I must get down to the sea, where I can wash my hand." But at the same time he ran the other way. After a little while he found himself on the path that he had walked on the day before, and it seemed as familiar to him as if he had walked it many hundred times in his life.

He slackened his pace to look around, and suddenly saw Nora standing on the other side of the fence; she was quite close to him when he caught sight of her in the moonlight. Wavering and out of breath he sank down on his knees. For a moment he could not speak. The little girl looked down at him. "Good evening, Simon," she said in her small coy voice. "I have waited for you a long time," and after a moment she added: "I have eaten your orange."

"Oh, Nora," cried the boy. "I have killed a man." She stared at him, but did not move. "Why did you kill a man?" she asked after a moment. "To get here," said Simon. "Because he tried to stop me. But he was my friend." Slowly he got on to his feet. "He loved me!" the boy cried out, and at that burst into tears. "Yes," said she slowly and thoughtfully. "Yes, because you must be here in time." "Can you hide me?" he asked. "For they are after me." "Nay," said Nora, "I cannot hide you. For my father is the parson here at Bodø, and he would be sure to hand you over to them, if he knew that you had killed a man." "Then," said Simon, "give me something to wipe my hands on." "What is the matter with your hands?" she asked, and took a little step forward. He stretched out his hands to her. "Is that your own blood?" she asked. "No," said he, "it is his." She took the step back again. "Do you hate me now?" he asked. "No, I do not hate you," said she. "But do put your hands at your back."

As he did so she came up close to him, at the other side of the fence, and clasped her arms round his neck. She pressed her young body to his, and kissed him tenderly. He felt her face, cool as the moonlight, upon his own, and when she released him, his head swam, and he did not know if the kiss had lasted a second or an hour. Nora stood up straight, her eyes wide open. "Now," she said slowly and proudly, "I promise you that I will never marry anybody, as long as I live." The boy kept standing with his hands on his back, as if she had tied them there. "And now," she said, "you must run, for they are coming." They looked at one another. "Do not forget Nora," said she. He turned and ran.

He leapt over a fence, and when he was down amongst the houses he walked. He did not know at all where to go. As he came to a house, from where music and noise streamed out, he slowly went through the door. The room was full of people; they were dancing in here. A lamp hung from the ceiling, and shone down on them; the air was thick and brown with the dust rising from the floor. There were some women in the room, but many of the men danced with each other, and gravely or laughingly stamped the floor. A moment after Simon had come in the crowd withdrew to the walls to clear the floor for two sailors, who were showing a dance from their own country.

Simon thought: "Now, very soon, the men from the boat will come round to look for their comrade's murderer, and from my hands they will know that I have done it." These five minutes during which he stood by the wall of the dancing-room, in the midst of the gay, sweating dancers, were of great significance to the boy. He himself felt it, as if during this time he grew up, and became like other people. He did not entreat his destiny, nor complain. Here he was, he had killed a man, and had kissed a girl. He did not demand any more from life, nor did life now demand more from him. He was Simon, a man like the men round him, and going to die, as all men are going to die.

He only became aware of what was going on outside him, when he saw that a woman had come in, and was standing in the midst of the cleared floor, looking round her. She was a short, broad old woman, in the clothes of the Lapps, and she took her stand with such majesty and fierceness as if she owned the whole place. It was obvious that most of the people knew her, and were a little afraid of her, although a few laughed; the din of the dancing-room stopped when she spoke.

"Where is my son?" she asked in a high shrill voice, like a bird's. The next moment her eyes fell on Simon himself, and she steered through the crowd, which opened up before her, stretched out her old skinny, dark hand, and took him by the elbow. "Come home with me now," she said. "You need not dance here tonight. You may be dancing a high enough dance soon."

Simon drew back, for he thought that she was drunk. But as she looked him straight in the face with her yellow eyes, it seemed to him that he had met her before, and that he might do well in listening to her. The old woman pulled him with her across the floor, and he followed her without a word. "Do not birch your boy too badly, Sunniva," one of the men in the room cried to her. "He has done no harm, he only wanted to look at the dance."

At the same moment as they came out through the door, there was an ³⁰ alarm in the street, a flock of people came running down it, and one of them, as he turned into the house, knocked against Simon, looked at him and the old woman, and ran on.

While the two walked along the street, the old woman lifted up her skirt, and put the hem of it into the boy's hand. "Wipe your hand on my skirt," she said. They had not gone far before they came to a small wooden house, and stopped; the door to it was so low that they must bend to get through it. As the Lapp-woman went in before Simon, still holding on to his arm, the boy looked up for a moment. The night had grown misty; there was a wide ring round the moon.

The old woman's room was narrow and dark, with but one small window to it; a lantern stood on the floor and lighted it up dimly. It was all filled with reindeer skins and wolf skins, and with reindeer horn, such as the Lapps use to make their carved buttons and knife-handles, and the air in here was rank and stifling. As soon as they were in, the woman turned to Simon, took hold of his head, and with her crooked fingers parted his hair and combed it down in Lapp fashion. She clapped a Lapp cap on him and stood back to glance at him. "Sit down on my stool, now," she said. "But first take out your knife." She was so commanding in voice and manner that the boy could not but choose to do as she told him; he sat down on the stool, and he could not take his eyes off her face, which was flat and brown, and as if smeared with dirt in its net of fine wrinkles. As he sat there he heard many people come along outside, and stop by the house; then someone knocked at the door, waited a moment and knocked again. The old woman stood and listened, as still as a mouse.

"Nay," said the boy and got up. "This is no good, for it is me that they are after. It will be better for you to let me go out to them." "Give me your knife," said she. When he handed it to her, she stuck it straight into her thumb, so that the blood spouted out, and she let it drip all over her skirt. "Come in, then," she cried.

The door opened, and two of the Russian sailors came and stood in the opening; there were more people outside. "Has anybody come in here?" they asked. "We are after a man who has killed our mate, but he has run away from us. Have you seen or heard anybody this way?" The old Lapp-woman turned upon them, and her eyes shone like gold in the lamplight. "Have I seen or heard anyone?" she cried. "I have heard you shriek murder all over the town. You frightened me, and my poor silly boy there, so that I cut my thumb as I was ripping the skin-rug that I sew. The boy is too scared to help me, and the rug is all ruined. I shall make you pay me for that. If you are looking for a murderer, come in and search my house for me, and I shall know you when we meet again." She was so furious that she danced where she stood, and jerked her head like an angry bird of prey.

The Russian came in, looked round the room, and at her and her blood- ³⁵ stained hand and skirt. "Do not put a curse on us now, Sunniva," he said timidly. "We know that you can do many things when you like. Here is a mark to pay you for the blood you have spilled." She stretched out her hand, and he placed a piece of money in it. She spat on it. "Then go, and there shall be no bad blood between us," said Sunniva, and shut the door after them. She stuck her thumb in her mouth, and chuckled a little.

The boy got up from his stool, stood straight up before her and stared into her face. He felt as if he were swaying high up in the air, with but a small hold. "Why have you helped me?" he asked her. "Do you not know?" she answered. "Have you not recognized me yet? But you will remember the peregrine falcon which was caught in the tackle-yarn of your boat, the *Charlotte,* as she sailed in the Mediterranean. That day you climbed up by the shrouds of the top-gallantmast to help her out, in a stiff wind, and with a high sea. That falcon was me. We Lapps often fly in such a manner, to see the world. When I first met you I was on my way to Africa, to see my younger sister and her children. She is a falcon too, when she chooses. By that time she was living at Takaunga, within an old ruined tower, which down there they call a minaret." She swathed a corner of her skirt round her thumb, and bit at it. "We do not forget," she said. "I hacked your thumb, when you took hold of me; it is only fair that I should cut my thumb for you tonight."

She came close to him, and gently rubbed her two brown, claw-like fingers against his forehead. "So you are a boy," she said, "who will kill a man rather than be late to meet your sweetheart? We hold together, the females of this earth. I shall mark your forehead now, so that the girls will know of that, when they look at you, and they will like you for it." She played with the boy's hair, and twisted it round her finger.

"Listen now, my little bird," said she. "My great grandson's brother-in-law is lying with his boat by the landing-place at this moment; he is to take a consignment of skins out to a Danish boat. He will bring you back to your boat, in time, before your mate comes. The *Hebe* is sailing tomorrow morning, is it not so? But when you are aboard, give him back my cap for me." She took up his knife, wiped it in her skirt and handed it to him. "Here is your knife," she said. "You will stick it into no more men; you will not need to, for from now you will sail the seas like a faithful seaman. We have enough trouble with our sons as it is."

The bewildered boy began to stammer his thanks to her. "Wait," said she, "I shall make you a cup of coffee, to bring back your wits, while I wash your jacket." She went and rattled an old copper kettle upon the fireplace. After a while she handed him a hot, strong, black drink in a cup without a handle to it. "You have drunk with Sunniva now," she said; "you have drunk down a little wisdom, so that in the future all your thoughts shall not fall like raindrops into the salt sea."

When he had finished and set down the cup, she led him to the door and opened it for him. He was surprised to see that it was almost clear morning. The house was so high up that the boy could see the sea from it, and a milky mist about it. He gave her his hand to say good-bye. 40

She stared into his face. "We do not forget," she said. "And you, you knocked me on the head there, high up in the mast. I shall give you that blow back." With that she smacked him on the ear as hard as she could, so that his head swam. "Now we are quits," she said, gave him a great, mischievous, shining glance, and a little push down the doorstep, and nodded to him.

In this way the sailor-boy got back to his ship, which was to sail the next morning, and lived to tell the story.

Nagai Tatsuo

BRIEF ENCOUNTER   1948

Translated by Edward Seidensticker

Nagai Tatsuo (born in 1904) has written novels and essays over his long literary career, but is most highly esteemed in Japan as a writer of the short story. When poor health obliged him to drop out of school in his early teens, he set to work perfecting his craft as a writer. For decades he worked as an editor for Bungei Shunju, a major publishing firm, eventually becoming a director of the company and founding its branch in Manchuria. Expelled by the Red Chinese occupation in 1947, he returned to his native Tokyo. Nagai's stories portray, with gentle humor, touching moments in the lives of ordinary citizens in swiftly changing, Westernized, postwar Japan.

I must ask you to read a part of my letter before you begin the story proper:

> I received your letter and the enclosed money order. Thank you very much.
>
> Thank you for the remarkable news that the ring I left with you has joined your engagement ring and been reborn as a tooth. I find myself less surprised and sorry than wanting to tell how much it helped with the fresh, new view of life I mentioned to you.
>
> As you have shown in your own person, the gold tooth artlessly in place somewhere behind an eyetooth is especially pleasing when glimpsed in the smile of a woman in her middle twenties. (Was yours perhaps one into which your husband himself put all his affection and skill? Forgive me. I will say no more about your false tooth. Even by way of sympathy.) I only hope this: that the two rings, the symbol of your gloom and the symbol of my new, fresh mood, will become admirable new teeth for the good of the people of Tokyo.
>
> It occurs to me, as I stop writing for a minute to light a cigarette, that letter-writing scenes are disappearing from the movies. To be sure, telephones and telegraphs are relieving the race of the troublesome chore; but I feel a certain nostalgia for the expression on her face for those few seconds when, having laid down the pen, she raises the envelope to her lips.
>
> What was I going to say? At first, not used to the work, I was exhausted; but now a month has gone by, and, sound and healthy again, I am in with the youngsters, having the experience of life in the mines . . .

I had quite cleaned out the room.

The medium-sized Boston bag that held my belongings lay in the middle of the alcove, and twenty or thirty books were stacked against the wall. There was a newspaper on the desk by the window. The bedding was folded neatly in front of the cupboard, with the pillow on top, as if to weigh it down.

I said good-by at the main house, and when I came back to my six-mat room, somehow cut off, amputated from the human world, the red kitten was curled by the pillow.

I felt myself smiling. "And what do you think *you're* doing here?" In my hat and coat, I knelt by the bedding and stroked the animal softly. Its eyes still closed, it rolled over on its back, and, in a most excellent mood, purred for me.

It had been in the main house for three months or so, and it would come to see me several times every day. Although nearly forty, I had never kept a cat or a dog. This was the first time I had ever lived near a cat.

I put my ear to its stomach and listened for a moment to the purring. Then, going out to the corridor that faced the garden and led to the main house, I put on my shoes. I had a raincoat over my arm. They had told me in the main house that the forecast was for rain.

Since they had agreed to store everything I did not immediately need, the disposition of my assets could not have been simpler.

I left the door open a little, for the kitten.

Several days earlier I had told my brother that I thought I might go to see a foreign movie — I would be off in the mines for a while, and would not have another chance. This morning a note had come by messenger.

"I was not able to get tickets for *The Best Years of Our Lives*°. I enclose instead tickets for an English movie that is said to be very good, and with them an express ticket. The latter is for tomorrow. I will see you at the station."

The note was in my pocket when I got off at Shimbashi. I had come in from Hodogaya on the electric line, and I had been wondering all the way what to do. There were two tickets to *Brief Encounter*°, with the Japanese title *Aibiki*, "Assignation." I had no idea what sort of movie it was, but that was the title. It seemed to tease me, to jeer at me, to prod me.

My brother was too serious a sort to be teasing me with the two tickets, that much was sure; but it was ironical all the same, sending two tickets to a bachelor in his late thirties. What was I to do with the other?

As I walked down the stairs at Shimbashi I decided to invite A, who worked in an office behind the Ginza°.

I thought I would make a joke of it: "Someone gave me tickets to a movie called *Aibiki*, and I have them to get rid of. I know it's a little behind the times for two grown men to go to that sort of movie together, but I won't be seeing you again for a while. Come on along."

Unfortunately, A was out. Very well; I would give the ticket to someone in front of the theater. I crossed the bridge in the direction of the H Theater.

There were three or four people at the ticket window. I walked briskly up — and then changed my mind. There was a couple, and there were young

The Best Years of Our Lives: 1946 Samuel Goldwyn movie about American service people returning home from World War II.

Brief Encounter: This classic postwar English film (1945) portrays the fleeting, poignant, but unconsummated love between two middle-aged people already married. Rather than betray their mates, the two finally part, keeping stiff upper lips. Directed by David Lean with screenplay by Noel Coward, the film has touching performances by Celia Johnson and Trevor Howard as the almost-lovers.

the Ginza: busy shopping and entertainment area in Tokyo, concentrated on mile-long Ginza Street.

girls. The expression "a man in his forties" had come into my mind, and the image of middle-age accosting youth. After it, derisively, came those other terms that seemed applicable: "ex-soldier," "broken-down soldier," and the rest.

I went into the theater. The girl showed me to my seat. The next seat of course was vacant. As if asking them to sit down, I gave it to my hat and raincoat.

There was no reason at all to invite someone else just because I had two tickets. This was much better — I could spread out. The trouble with me was that I was still a prisoner of inflexible concepts.

People came in, the theater filled. The bell rang. The news went dizzy-ingly in review. 25

Why was it, my brother had remarked the other day, that there was always something stale and musty about newsreels even when they had the latest scoops? The destruction after the storm was the same, whether the scene was Japan or America. The American woman, blown down the street, clung precariously to a telephone pole, and, frowning into the storm, she turned to the camera and smiled a childlike smile, as if to say that people *did* have interesting experiences.

The lights went on again when the newsreel was over. I felt somehow isolated from the crowd, but then the lights dimmed and the words "Brief Encounter" flashed against the rising curtain. I planted my elbow firmly on the arm of the vacant seat.

I had the aisle seat, and I felt a sort of pressure on my right. Someone, bent slightly forward, was standing there in the dark, waiting to be allowed past.

Automatically I looked back, but the only vacant seat was the one beside me. The ticket for it was in my pocket. I picked up my coat and hat nonetheless and put them on my knee.

The person bowed and slipped adroitly past. It was a woman in foreign dress, leaving a faint perfume behind her. I heard her open her handbag. She seemed to be taking out her glasses. I felt even after she had sat down that she was fairly tall for a woman. 30

Life was new and fresh, clearly it was — I reaffirmed the philosophy I had acquired during the preceding half year. But how to explain the mystery of the seat beside me?

The dull confession of a plain, tired wife, in an atmosphere of indescrib-able gloom. It began to pull at me. At first I resisted, but presently I was caught up in it.

There is no need here to recount the plot or to give my reactions, and indeed I am not qualified to. When I thought of it again some days later on the train, I suddenly thought too of *Earth,* that somber Japanese novel of peasant life, a cheap edition of which I had borrowed from a young comrade when I was stationed on the southern front. The movie was about a secret affair of a nameless woman in a small town, and the views of an ex-soldier are of no importance.

Yet I must mention something I would rather not: I thought again, for the first time in a great while, of my ex-wife, whom, a year before, I had let go without a shade of regret. Although no one could know that I had thought of her, I felt most ashamed of myself afterwards.

I was slightly dissatisfied with the last scene, in which the amiable husband forgave the wife. She had not committed the final error, it is true, but the affair had left her an empty shell. Perhaps that was what made me remember my wife. On that point, at least, I was superior to the husband of the movie.

Brief Encounter was over. I seem to have lost myself in thought, for the woman was asking to be let by. I stood up. I followed her, and we were the last to leave the theater.

The weather forecast had been accurate. The exit was screened by a white curtain, a May rain. There were some ten young people caught without umbrellas.

I stepped beyond them and lighted a cigarette. I was ready for the rain, but felt no need to hurry. The woman too took a cigarette from a silver case. There was a subtle quickness in her gestures, the movement from gesture to gesture. She had on a dark green suit, and she was indeed tall for a woman. I had glanced at her as she looked up into the sky, and been struck by the lashes of the slightly narrowed eyes. A woman's age is among the things I am incapable of judging, but she was not yet thirty, of that I was sure. Perhaps twenty-four or twenty-five, perhaps twenty-seven.

"It's not going to stop, either," she said suddenly. The black eyes moved toward me as she spoke.

"I'm afraid not." I looked at the rain hitting the pavement. Now and then a couple under a single umbrella stumbled through the spray.

"I thought it was so near, and I wouldn't need an umbrella. Stupid of me." A mischievous laugh came into the eyes. There was a trace of lipstick on her cigarette. I had not realized that it was possible to color the lips such a calm, tranquil color.

"It's near, is it?"

"Just over there." The eyes, still smiling, and a finger pointed to the left. "Next door to the curio shop."

I spread open my raincoat. "I have this. I'm going in that direction anyway — suppose I stop by and have someone come with an umbrella."

"Please don't bother. It's so near. I'll run on when I've made up my mind to get wet. Really." She spoke briskly, but with no suggestion of wanting to brush me aside.

"Suppose I do it this way." I pulled the coat over my head like a photographer, and smiled at her. The people who were waiting for a lull in the rain looked at us curiously.

Cocking her head a little to one side, she smiled back. I seemed to have put her at ease.

"Really? I shouldn't ask you to — but may I?" She came a step or two nearer. "The building next to the curio shop. A dentist named Suematsu. If you could ask the girl at the reception desk to come with a coat and an umbrella, I'd really be most grateful."

It pleased me to think that I was helping someone I would never see again. I ran through the rain. But I still did not understand about that seat.

There was a compact little building some two hundred yards away, around the corner from the curio shop. I had no trouble finding the dentist's office on the second floor. "Suematsu Shingo, Doctor of Dental Surgery; Suematsu Akira, Dentist," the sign said in horizontal characters. It also said that

Sunday was a holiday, and that the office was open only until two on Saturdays. Today was a Saturday.

Just inside the door there was a little window over the reception desk, where a girl of eighteen or nineteen was sitting. I told her my business, and she answered quietly.

Feeling somewhat nostalgic at the antiseptic smell of the office, I closed the door behind me. As I started down I could hear the rain below.

"Excuse me." Someone was calling from the head of the stairs.

It was the reception girl. Two umbrellas and an oil-cloth coat in hand, she stood by the wall, waiting for me to come up again.

"If I leave there will be no one here. Would you mind waiting till I get back?"   55

"Not at all, not at all."

She seemed to think that I was a friend of the woman's. Such a simple girl — should she be so trusting? There was something heart-warming about her. I walked slowly up and down before the Suematsu door.

"What a rain, and no sign of letting up. When did it begin?" The bright voice of the woman came from the stairs. Then she saw me, and once more I looked closely into her eyes. "Well! What a bother for you! That's our Miss Tateno, as easygoing as ever. She had you watch the place, did she? Come on in, now that you've gone to so much trouble. For just a minute. It would be strange to let him go like this, wouldn't it, Miss Tateno?"

Turning from me to the receptionist, she pushed open the door without letting me answer.

"It's strange to think it would be strange."   60

She laughed, and opened another door, to a clean little waiting room that could accommodate perhaps three or four people.

"Have a seat. I'll be back in a minute." I took off my wet coat and sat on the sofa.

In the quiet I could hear water, and, faintly, the sound of a comb running through someone's hair.

"What about the coffee in the thermos bottle? Yes, let's have that. You have some too." She spoke to the girl in a voice so quiet that I wondered how it could come from the same person. "It was a gloomy, gloomy movie. I'm exhausted." I next heard someone opening a can. "I don't say it wasn't interesting, but I wonder how it would be for a young person."

Miss Tateno looked much brighter when she came in with coffee. She   65
had changed from her office uniform. The place seemed more like a parlor.

"I shouldn't have asked you to wait. You must forgive me." She had on a blouse, I suppose you would call it — a clear, pale cerulean blue. (I know, having investigated these colors.) The sleeves were short, and the brooch was an ivory flower set in gold. I stood up.

"There was a terrible rainstorm in *Brief Encounter* too."

"Yes. I must look a little like the doctor."

"Maybe it feels good when you get as wet as that." The woman sat down lightly in the chair opposite me.

If one had praised the fairness of her complexion, she would probably   70
have answered: "Oh? And I've never done a thing for it. You should praise my father and mother."

But since in her hair, for all the careful attention that had gone into dressing it, there was a faint touch of calculated disarray, as of a keystone pulled slightly loose, so that the hair set off the beauty of the throat — since there was this air about her whole person, one could not doubt that a considerable sum had been invested in the almost unpowdered whiteness of the skin.

"You're going shopping in the rain?" She cast a quiet glance over my shoulder. "You are? Well, don't worry about me. I'll sit here with this gentleman a little longer, and then close the office."

Miss Tateno said nothing, but I gathered that she was leaving. The woman got up and went toward her.

"I'm sorry I had to say such unpleasant things. You must forgive me."

"Please don't apologize." 75

"You're not to worry. Understand? I'm completely over it now. I'll be in early Monday morning, looking very cheerful." She laughed softly. "Bye-bye."

I sensed that she had taken the girl's hand by way of apology. The "Bye-bye" had a high, clear ring to it.

"Something unpleasant happened, and I ran out to the movie. I felt dreadful, it was such a dismal movie." She had sat down again, and her eyes were still on the silver case after she had offered me a cigarette and taken one herself.

I wondered what the unpleasantness might have been, but did not feel that I could ask. Instead I turned the conversation to the matter that puzzled me. "I had two tickets to the movie, and the second one was a problem. It made me feel very useless."

"You should have taken your wife." 80

"Well, you see, as a matter of fact — " It was not a subject I found easy to talk about.

"May I ask if you were in the service? In the Navy, perhaps?"

"Precisely."

"I had two cousins in the Navy. Up until a few years ago I was rather popular with the young officers." But I did not want to talk about the past.

"And what did you do with the other ticket?" she asked. 85

"I wanted to invite a friend — a man, of course — but he was out. I went by myself."

"What a pity. And for a *Brief Encounter,* too."

"But here I am drinking coffee with you. Why did you take that seat?"

"That seat?" Her eyes narrowed questioningly, and there was a pause. "Oh! I took the wrong seat. How stupid of me!" For the first time I felt a touch of coquetry.

"I thought it a great privilege." 90

"I was upset and a little excited, and there was no usher. I go there often, it's so close, and I thought my seat ought to be about there. And I'm a little nearsighted."

"I see." I saw everything. I saw too that a slight case of myopia could make a woman's eyes rather seductive.

"I think it's letting up. You said you had business on the Ginza?"

"Nothing of any importance." I too looked out the window.

"If you're in no hurry, stay as long as you like. I have nothing to do   95
myself."

"I go away tomorrow."

"How I envy you. Where are you going?"

"I'll be in Kyushu for a while."

"Men have all the advantages. On business."

"No money in it, as they say. I'm going to work. In a coal mine."   100

"Oh?"

"I've done all sorts of things to keep myself alive since I came back. I've
come to the conclusion that it's not too difficult if keeping yourself alive is all
you want. But everything seems so strange, now that the military blinkers are
off. Everything seems so fresh and new, so alive, from the time I get up in the
morning till I go to bed at night."

"You were a commander?"

"A lieutenant-commander at the end of the war. I didn't do so well when
it came to promotions." I spoke rapidly. I did not want to talk about the past.
"There was a kitten that used to come and see me all the time. It was very
interesting. I had never liked cats — so cold and willful. But then I would
watch that kitten, and it seemed strange that such an animal could have been
born. Everything was interesting to it, even its own tail. It was never bored.
If that liveliness to new impressions could go on say four or five years, a cat
would be a remarkable beast."

"Isn't it the truth. They get so fat and sluggish when they are older. I   105
kept three cats once, but then it came to me that it was not very good form
for a childless woman to be fond of cats, and I gave them away."

"I want to have all the experiences I can before I get fat and sluggish
myself. I'm in a great hurry."

"And that's why you're going into a coal mine?"

"I want to do away with the ex-soldier."

"You'll join the Communist Party, then, and the labor movement?"

"Possibly. But the Party is too much like the service. It has no respect   110
for you as an individual." I sensed that I was being asked leading questions.
And so I made a leading remark: "To someone like me it's a fairy story, a
well-matched husband and wife running a clean little office together."

"A fairy story — it was at first." She looked at me again with that slightly
quizzical expression, and immediately lowered her eyes. Her manner changed
abruptly. She evidently did not mean to be taken by my lead. "You're kept
busy, that's all, repairing bad teeth day after day. Unless someone has to have
a difficult bridge made, you can hardly breathe for the boredom. I'd like to use
heaps of gold and platinum on something really good."

With that, I remembered my business on the Ginza. I hesitated a second,
then took a little wad of paper from my pocket. I had found it in the desk
drawer when I cleaned the room that morning. "It's a little sudden, but could
you use this?"

The delicately manicured hand took up the paper, and from it came an
engagement ring.

I explained in some confusion: "I found it this morning when I was
cleaning up. I wondered if I might be able to sell it on the Ginza. I know it
would be more dashing if I were to drop it into the river from Kachidoki Bridge

or somewhere, but I've never been much for romantic things, and I thought I'd put it up for sale instead."

"I could take it for you. Shall I?"

"It's been no use for a year — no, for much longer than that. It's not a question of the money," I added, when I saw a cloud come over her face.

The curve of her neck, slightly arched against the back of the chair, turned toward the window. She fingered the ring languidly. "Three grams, maybe four? Well, let me take it for you. I think the rain has stopped."

I too had been looking uncomfortably at the faint yellowish sunlight coming through the window. It was time to leave.

As the hand with the ring dropped to her lap, she took a deep breath, and two points came to life on her blouse. Then her face, propped on her other hand, turned to me with a delicate quickness, as if to dismiss something. "Excuse me. Here I am brooding when I have company." She hunched over, and the smiling face came nearer. "When I'm busy I usually have lunch just up the street. I've left a supply of rice there. I thought of having something today before I go home, and if you have nothing else to do, suppose you come along." Without waiting for my answer, she took her handbag from the little table. "The price of gold changes every day, but let me give you a thousand yen anyway. Business is business. I'll send the rest to your mine when I know exactly how much it comes to."

The frankness of the smooth-flowing words helped a little.

I waited in the hall.

She came out, her lips alive, and the office door closed sharply.

In the evening sunlight after the May rain, we crossed the bridge toward the Ginza. It is pointless, at such times, to describe life as "new and fresh."

She exchanged quiet greetings with the waiters and sat down opposite me.

"They say beer doesn't go well with it, but — " We emptied our glasses.

"Your husband?" The talk of drink gave me courage to mention something that had puzzled me.

"Oh, don't worry about 'your husband.' " As she poured more beer for me — indeed, by pouring more beer — she fended off my question. "Were you on the southern front for a long time?"

"Here and there for two years."

"And you were separated from your wife a year after you came back?"

"I guessed everything immediately. It wasn't fun, but I wanted to be rid of the past, and I made a clean break with her. But that isn't a very pleasant subject."

"I'm sorry. That last scene of *Brief Encounter* — remember? Where the husband forgives the wife? It bothered me. It made me very sad to think how they would pass the years afterward. And so I brought it up. But no more."

True, that ending was no ending. Might we not better have left the matter to the critics, however?

"We got nothing at all from military life. Or one thing only. We islanders with our island minds can still remember Java or Luzon° when we see a sunset

Java or Luzon: islands in Indonesia and in the Philippines, both of which the Japanese army occupied in World War II.

like this. The sunrise some morning makes us all think of sunrises on the continent, while we plow our fields and row our boats. That is the one thing it gave us."

"Men have all the advantages." Her long eyelashes lowered, she watched the shining beads that rose from the bottom of the glass. It is dangerous to be too impressed by feminine poses at certain times. "Oh, yes. You mustn't forget to give me your Kyushu address."

I took out my card case. A long, narrow piece of paper came out with it.

She opened her handbag.

"I have a pen."

"Thank you." Idly, I turned over the piece of paper. It was the second theater ticket.

"Oh, good! Write on the back of that."

I looked at her and we laughed.

With a delicate fountain pen I wrote down the name of the mine and the dormitory.

"When I was in the south, the boys under me all had pictures of their girlfriends and their fiancées and their brides, and whenever they had a spare minute they would take out their pictures and look at them and show them off to the others. It was very strange, though — the habit would make them forget the real women."

She did not answer.

" 'Hey! What was my old woman's face like?' someone would say, and someone else would say, 'Now that you mention it, I can't remember my girl's face either. Be quiet a minute while I close my eyes and think.' It happened all the time."

"Interesting."

"How shall I describe it? The impulse to beautify women is always at work, and it builds up an image that moves away from the actual person. Even at my age."

"May I ask you to do the same with your image of me?" She tilted her head slightly and smiled.

"It may well happen."

Amused, I had my longest look into her eyes.

We parted at Tokyo Station, she to take the Central Line, I the Yokosuka Line. The next day I left for this mine.

A month later I had a registered letter from her:

First, our business.

The enclosed money order covers what I owe you for the item you left with me. I talked with a man we do business with, and bought it at the price he quoted.

It is becoming the cap for a young lady's second molar. She is a very pretty young lady and she is soon to be married. The lower bicuspid next to it will be capped with platinum, and for that I mean to use my own engagement ring.

The day I met you in that strange way was the day I decided on

135

140

145

150

155

a divorce, after a great deal of unpleasantness. The reason is a most ordinary one, which I shall leave to your imagination.

I hesitated for a time about capping the teeth of a young girl soon to be married with two unlucky engagement rings, but then I came to think that they might be a sort of mascot for her in her new life.

I work hard, all day long. It is new and fresh, this not being anyone's wife.

I trust that you are taking care of yourself.

Have you noted any tendency to beautify my image?

The letter with which I began was my answer. 160

That is all there is to the story.

It would please me beyond measure if, among my readers, there should be some who felt like going back to reread the beginning.

Gabriel García Márquez
THE NIGHT OF THE CURLEWS 1953

Translated by Gregory Rabassa

Gabriel García Márquez, among the most eminent of living Latin American writers, was born in 1929 in Aracataca, a Caribbean port in Colombia, one of sixteen children of an impoverished telegraph operator. For a time he studied law in Bogotá, then became a reporter for a newspaper. Although he never joined the Communist party, García Márquez outspokenly advocated many left-wing proposals for reform. In 1954, despairing of any prospect for political change, he left Colombia to live in Mexico City. Though at nineteen he had completed a book of short stories, La hojorasca (Leafstorm), *he waited until 1955 to publish it. Soon he began to build a towering reputation among readers of Spanish. His celebrated novel,* Cien años de soledad *(1967), published in English as* One Hundred Years of Solitude *(1969), traces the history of a Colombian family through six generations. Called by Chilean poet Pablo Neruda "the greatest revelation in the Spanish language since* Don Quixote," *it has sold more than twelve million copies in thirty languages. In 1982 García Márquez was awarded the Nobel prize for literature. His fiction, rich in myth and invention, has reminded American readers of that of William Faulkner, another explorer of his native turf; indeed, García Márquez has called Faulkner "my master." Recently, he wrote the screenplay for* Eréndira *(1984), a film based on the title story from* Innocent Eréndira *(1978). "The Night of the Curlews" comes from the same collection.*

We were sitting, the three of us, around the table, when someone put a coin in the slot and the Wurlitzer played once more the record that had been going all night. The rest happened so fast that we didn't have time to think. It happened before we could remember where we were, before we could get back our sense of location. One of us reached his hand out over the counter, groping (we couldn't see the hand, we heard it), bumped into a glass, and then was still, with both hands resting on the hard surface. Then the three of us looked for ourselves in the darkness and found ourselves there, in the joints of the thirty fingers piled up on the counter. One of us said:

"Let's go."

And we stood up as if nothing had happened. We still hadn't had time to get upset.

In the hallway, as we passed, we heard the nearby music spinning out at us. We caught the smell of sad women sitting and waiting. We felt the prolonged emptiness of the hall before us while we walked toward the door, before the other smell came out to greet us, the sour smell of the woman sitting by the door. We said:

"We're leaving." 5

The woman didn't answer anything. We heard the creak of a rocking chair, rising up as she stood. We heard the footsteps on the loose board and the return of the woman again, when the hinges creaked once more and the door closed behind us.

We turned around. Right there, behind us, there was a harsh, cutting breeze of an invisible dawn, and a voice that said:

"Get out of the way, I'm coming through with this."

We moved back. And the voice spoke again:

"You're still against the door." 10

And only then, when we'd moved to all sides and had found the voice everywhere, did we say:

"We can't get out of here. The curlews have pecked out our eyes."

Then we heard several doors open. One of us let go of the other hands and we heard him dragging along in the darkness, weaving, bumping into the things that surrounded us. He spoke from somewhere in the darkness.

"We must be close," he said. "There's a smell of piled-up trunks around here."

We felt the contact of his hands again. We leaned against the wall and 15 another voice passed by then, but in the opposite direction.

"They might be coffins," one of us said.

The one who had dragged himself into the corner and was breathing beside us now said:

"They're trunks. Ever since I was little I've been able to tell the smell of stored clothing."

Then we moved in that direction. The ground was soft and smooth, fine earth that had been walked on. Someone held out a hand. We felt the contact with long, live skin, but we no longer felt the wall opposite.

"This is a woman," we said. 20

The other one, the one who had spoken of trunks, said:

"I think she's asleep."

The body shook under our hands, trembled, we felt it slip away, not as if it had got out of our reach, but as if it had ceased to exist. Still, after an instant in which we remained motionless, stiffened, leaning against each other's shoulders, we heard her voice.

"Who's there?" it said.

"It's us," we replied without moving.

The movement of the bed could be heard, the creaking and the shuffling of feet looking for slippers in the darkness. Then we pictured the seated woman, looking at us as when she still hadn't awakened completely.

"What are you doing here?" she asked.

And we answered.

"We don't know. The curlews pecked out our eyes."

The voice said that she'd heard something about that. That the newspapers had said that three men had been drinking in a courtyard where there were five or six curlews. Seven curlews. One of the men began singing like a curlew, imitating them.

"The worst was that he was an hour behind," she said. "That was when the birds jumped on the table and pecked out their eyes."

She said that's what the newspapers had said, but nobody had believed them. We said:

"If people had gone there, they'd have seen the curlews."

And the woman said:

"They did. The courtyard was full of people the next day, but the woman had already taken the curlews somewhere else."

When he turned around, the woman stopped speaking. There was the wall again. By just turning around we would find the wall. Around us, surrounding us, there was always a wall. One let go of our hands again. We heard him crawling again, smelling the ground, saying:

"Now I don't know where the trunks are. I think we're somewhere else now."

And we said:

"Come here. Somebody's here next to us."

We heard him come close. We felt him stand up beside us and again his warm breath hit us in the face.

"Reach out that way," we told him. "There's someone we know there."

He must have reached out, he must have moved toward the place we indicated, because an instant later he came back to tell us:

"I think it's a boy."

And we told him:

"Fine. Ask him if he knows us."

He asked the question. We heard the apathetic and simple voice of the boy, who said:

"Yes, I know you. You're the three men whose eyes were pecked out by the curlews."

Then an adult voice spoke. The voice of a woman who seemed to be behind a closed door, saying:

"You're talking to yourself again."

And the child's voice, unconcerned, said:

"No. The men who had their eyes pecked out by the curlews are here again."

There was a sound of hinges and then the adult voice, closer than the first time.

"Take them home," she said.

And the boy said:

"I don't know where they live." 55

And the adult voice said:

"Don't be mean. Everybody knows where they live ever since the night the curlews pecked their eyes out."

Then she went on in a different tone, as if she were speaking to us:

"What happened is that nobody wanted to believe it and they say it was a fake item made up by the papers to boost their circulation. No one has seen the curlews."

And he said: 60

"But nobody would believe me if I led them along the street."

We didn't move. We were still, leaning against the wall, listening to her. And the woman said:

"If this one wants to take you it's different. After all, nobody would pay much attention to what a boy says."

The child's voice cut in:

"If I go out onto the street with them and say that they're the men who 65 had their eyes pecked out by the curlews, the boys will throw stones at me. Everybody on the street says it couldn't have happened."

There was a moment of silence. Then the door closed again and the boy spoke:

"Besides, I'm reading *Terry and the Pirates*° right now."

Someone said in our ear:

"I'll convince him."

He crawled over to where the voice was. 70

"I like it," he said. "At least tell us what happened to Terry this week."

He's trying to gain his confidence, we thought. But the boy said:

"That doesn't interest me. The only thing I like are the colors."

"Terry's in a maze," we said.

And the boy said: 75

"That was Friday. Today's Sunday and what I like are the colors," and he said it with a cold, dispassionate, indifferent voice.

When the other one came back, we said:

"We've been lost for almost three days and we haven't had a moment's rest."

And one said:

"All right. Let's rest awhile, but without letting go of each other's 80 hands."

We sat down. An invisible sun began to warm us on the shoulders. But not even the presence of the sun interested us. We felt it there, everywhere, having already lost the notion of distance, time, direction. Several voices passed.

"The curlews pecked out our eyes," we said.

And one of the voices said:

Terry and the Pirates: newspaper comic strip of swashbuckling adventures in China.

"These here took the newspapers seriously."

The voices disappeared. And we kept on sitting, like that, shoulder to 85
shoulder, waiting, in that passing of voices, in that passing of images, for a
smell or a voice that was known to us to pass. The sun was above our heads,
still warming us. Then someone said:

"Let's go toward the wall again."

And the others, motionless, their heads lifted toward the invisible light:
"Not yet. Let's just wait till the sun begins to burn us on the face."

Tillie Olsen
I STAND HERE IRONING   1961

*Tillie Olsen was born in Omaha in 1912, into a family of blue-collar
workers who had fled Czarist Russia to escape persecution. Olsen grew up
in poverty and quit school in eleventh grade to work. She later declared,
"Public libraries were my college." As a member of the Young Communist
League, she strove to organize Kansas City meat-packers, and was once
thrown into jail. After her first husband deserted her, leaving her with one
child, she married a printer and labor activist, Jack Olsen, by whom she had
three more children. Although in the 1930s she published fiction in a
distinguished little magazine,* Partisan Review, *the demands of motherhood, political activity, and factory and office jobs left her scant time to write
until 1955. Then her youngest daughter began school and Olsen was
awarded a creative-writing fellowship at Stanford University. Long a cru-
sader for causes, she has been active in the recent feminist movement. "I Stand
Here Ironing," from her first book,* Tell Me a Riddle *(1961), reads like
autobiography. Olsen has since published* Yonnondio *(1974) an unfinished
novel begun at age nineteen, and* Silences *(1978), a study of why writers
— especially women writers — dry up. She holds several honorary degrees.
In 1981 the city of San Francisco, where she has long resided, designated
a Tillie Olsen day.*

I stand here ironing, and what you asked me moves tormented back and
forth with the iron.

"I wish you would manage the time to come in and talk with me about
your daughter. I'm sure you can help me understand her. She's a youngster
who needs help and whom I'm deeply interested in helping."

"Who needs help." . . . Even if I came, what good would it do? You think
because I am her mother I have a key, or that in some way you could use me
as a key? She has lived for nineteen years. There is all that life that has
happened outside of me, beyond me.

And when is there time to remember, to sift, to weigh, to estimate, to
total? I will start and there will be an interruption and I will have to gather
it all together again. Or I will become engulfed with all I did or did not do,
with what should have been and what cannot be helped.

She was a beautiful baby. The first and only one of our five that was   5
beautiful at birth. You do not guess how new and uneasy her tenancy in her
now-loveliness. You did not know her all those years she was thought homely,
or see her poring over her baby pictures, making me tell her over and over how
beautiful she had been — and would be, I would tell her — and was now, to
the seeing eye. But the seeing eyes were few or nonexistent. Including mine.

I nursed her. They feel that's important nowadays. I nursed all the
children, but with her, with all the fierce rigidity of first motherhood, I did like
the books then said. Though her cries battered me to trembling and my breasts
ached with swollenness, I waited till the clock decreed.

Why do I put that first? I do not even know if it matters, or if it explains
anything.

She was a beautiful baby. She blew shining bubbles of sound. She loved
motion, loved light, loved color and music and textures. She would lie on the
floor in her blue overalls patting the surface so hard in ecstasy her hands and
feet would blur. She was a miracle to me, but when she was eight months old
I had to leave her daytimes with the woman downstairs to whom she was no
miracle at all, for I worked or looked for work and for Emily's father, who
"could no longer endure" (he wrote in his good-bye note) "sharing want with
us."

I was nineteen. It was the pre-relief, pre-WPA world of the depression.
I would start running as soon as I got off the streetcar, running up the stairs,
the place smelling sour, and awake or asleep to startle awake, when she saw
me she would break into a clogged weeping that could not be comforted, a
weeping I can hear yet.

After a while I found a job hashing at night so I could be with her days,   10
and it was better. But it came to where I had to bring her to his family and
leave her.

It took a long time to raise the money for her fare back. Then she got
chicken pox and I had to wait longer. When she finally came, I hardly knew
her, walking quick and nervous like her father, looking like her father, thin,
and dressed in a shoddy red that yellowed her skin and glared at the pock-
marks. All the baby loveliness gone.

She was two. Old enough for nursery school they said, and I did not
know then what I know now — the fatigue of the long day, and the lacerations
of group life in the kinds of nurseries that are only parking places for children.

Except that it would have made no difference if I had known. It was the
only place there was. It was the only way we could be together, the only way
I could hold a job.

And even without knowing, I knew. I knew the teacher that was evil
because all these years it has curdled into my memory, the little boy hunched
in the corner, her rasp, "why aren't you outside, because Alvin hits you? that's
no reason, go out, scaredy." I knew Emily hated it even if she did not clutch
and implore "don't go Mommy" like the other children, mornings.

She always had a reason why we should stay home. Momma, you look   15
sick. Momma, I feel sick. Momma, the teachers aren't there today, they're sick.
Momma, we can't go, there was a fire there last night. Momma, it's a holiday
today, no school, they told me.

But never a direct protest, never rebellion. I think of our others in their three-, four-year-oldness — the explosions, the tempers, the denunciations, the demands — and I feel suddenly ill. I put the iron down. What in me demanded that goodness in her? And what was the cost, the cost to her of such goodness?

The old man living in the back once said in his gentle way: "You should smile at Emily more when you look at her." What *was* in my face when I looked at her? I loved her. There were all the acts of love.

It was only with the others I remembered what he said, and it was the face of joy, and not of care or tightness or worry I turned to them — too late for Emily. She does not smile easily, let alone almost always as her brothers and sisters do. Her face is closed and sombre, but when she wants, how fluid. You must have seen it in her pantomimes, you spoke of her rare gift for comedy on the stage that rouses laughter out of the audience so dear they applaud and applaud and do not want to let her go.

Where does it come from, that comedy? There was none of it in her when she came back to me that second time, after I had had to send her away again. She had a new daddy now to learn to love, and I think perhaps it was a better time.

Except when we left her alone nights, telling ourselves she was old enough. 20

"Can't you go some other time, Mommy, like tomorrow?" she would ask. "Will it be just a little while you'll be gone? Do you promise?"

The time we came back, the front door open, the clock on the floor in the hall. She rigid awake. "It wasn't just a little while. I didn't cry. Three times I called you, just three times, and then I ran downstairs to open the door so you could come faster. The clock talked loud. I threw it away, it scared me what it talked."

She said the clock talked loud again that night I went to the hospital to have Susan. She was delirious with the fever that comes before red measles, but she was fully conscious all the week I was gone and the week after we were home when she could not come near the new baby or me.

She did not get well. She stayed skeleton thin, not wanting to eat, and night after night she had nightmares. She would call for me, and I would rouse from exhaustion to sleepily call back: "You're all right, darling, go to sleep, it's just a dream," and if she still called, in a sterner voice, "now go to sleep, Emily, there's nothing to hurt you." Twice, only twice, when I had to get up for Susan anyhow, I went in to sit with her.

Now when it is too late (as if she would let me hold and comfort her like 25 I do the others) I get up and go to her at once at her moan or restless stirring. "Are you awake, Emily? Can I get you something?" And the answer is always the same: "No, I'm all right, go back to sleep, Mother."

They persuaded me at the clinic to send her away to a convalescent home in the country where "she can have the kind of food and care you can't manage for her, and you'll be free to concentrate on the new baby." They still send children to that place. I see pictures on the society page of sleek young women planning affairs to raise money for it, or dancing at the affairs, or decorating Easter eggs or filling Christmas stockings for the children.

They never have a picture of the children so I do not know if the girls still wear those gigantic red bows and the ravaged looks on the every other

Sunday when parents can come to visit "unless otherwise notified" — as we were notified the first six weeks.

Oh it is a handsome place, green lawns and tall trees and fluted flower beds. High up on the balconies of each cottage the children stand, the girls in their red bows and white dresses, the boys in white suits and giant red ties. The parents stand below shrieking up to be heard and the children shriek down to be heard, and between them the invisible wall: "Not to Be Contaminated by Parental Germs or Physical Affection."

There was a tiny girl who always stood hand in hand with Emily. Her parents never came. One visit she was gone. "They moved her to Rose Cottage," Emily shouted in explanation. "They don't like you to love anybody here."

She wrote once a week, the labored writing of a seven-year-old. "I am 30 fine. How is the baby. If I write my leter nicly I will have a star. Love." There never was a star. We wrote every other day, letters she could never hold or keep but only hear read — once. "We simply do not have room for children to keep any personal possessions," they patiently explained when we pieced one Sunday's shrieking together to plead how much it would mean to Emily, who loved so to keep things, to be allowed to keep her letters and cards.

Each visit she looked frailer. "She isn't eating," they told us.

(They had runny eggs for breakfast or mush with lumps, Emily said later, I'd hold it in my mouth and not swallow. Nothing ever tasted good, just when they had chicken.)

It took us eight months to get her released home, and only the fact that she gained back so little of her seven lost pounds convinced the social worker.

I used to try to hold and love her after she came back, but her body would stay stiff, and after a while she'd push away. She ate little. Food sickened her, and I think much of life too. Oh she had physical lightness and brightness, twinkling by on skates, bouncing like a ball up and down up and down over the jump rope, skimming over the hill; but these were momentary.

She fretted about her appearance, thin and dark and foreign-looking at 35 a time when every little girl was supposed to look or thought she should look a chubby blonde replica of Shirley Temple. The doorbell sometimes rang for her, but no one seemed to come and play in the house or be a best friend. Maybe because we moved so much.

There was a boy she loved painfully through two school semesters. Months later she told me how she had taken pennies from my purse to buy him candy. "Licorice was his favorite and I brought him some every day, but he still liked Jennifer better'n me. Why, Mommy?" The kind of question for which there is no answer.

School was a worry to her. She was not glib or quick in a world where glibness and quickness were easily confused with ability to learn. To her overworked and exasperated teachers she was an overconscientious "slow learner" who kept trying to catch up and was absent entirely too often.

I let her be absent, though sometimes the illness was imaginary. How different from my now-strictness about attendance with the others. I wasn't working. We had a new baby, I was home anyhow. Sometimes, after Susan grew old enough, I would keep her home from school, too, to have them all together.

Mostly Emily had asthma, and her breathing, harsh and labored, would fill the house with a curiously tranquil sound. I would bring the two old dresser mirrors and her boxes of collections to her bed. She would select beads and single earrings, bottle tops and shells, dried flowers and pebbles, old postcards and scraps, all sorts of oddments; then she and Susan would play Kingdom, setting up landscapes and furniture, peopling them with action.

Those were the only times of peaceful companionship between her and Susan. I have edged away from it, that poisonous feeling between them, that terrible balancing of hurts and needs I had to do between the two, and did so badly, those earlier years.

Oh there are conflicts between the others too, each one human, needing, demanding, hurting, taking — but only between Emily and Susan, no, Emily toward Susan that corroding resentment. It seems so obvious on the surface, yet it is not obvious. Susan, the second child, Susan, golden- and curly-haired and chubby, quick and articulate and assured, everything in appearance and manner Emily was not; Susan, not able to resist Emily's precious things, losing or sometimes clumsily breaking them; Susan telling jokes and riddles to company for applause while Emily sat silent (to say to me later: that was *my* riddle, Mother, I told it to Susan); Susan, who for all the five years' difference in age was just a year behind Emily in developing physically.

I am glad for that slow physical development that widened the difference between her and her contemporaries, though she suffered over it. She was too vulnerable for that terrible world of youthful competition, of preening and parading, of constant measuring of yourself against every other, of envy, "If I had that copper hair," "If I had that skin. . . ." She tormented herself enough about not looking like the others, there was enough of the unsureness, the having to be conscious of words before you speak, the constant caring — what are they thinking of me? without having it all magnified by the merciless physical drives.

Ronnie is calling. He is wet and I change him. It is rare there is such a cry now. That time of motherhood is almost behind me when the ear is not one's own but must always be racked and listening for the child cry, the child call. We sit for a while and I hold him, looking out over the city spread in charcoal with its soft aisles of light. "*Shoogily,*" he breathes and curls closer. I carry him back to bed, asleep. *Shoogily.* A funny word, a family word, inherited from Emily, invented by her to say: *comfort.*

In this and other ways she leaves her seal, I say aloud. And startle at my saying it. What do I mean? What did I start to gather together, to try and make coherent? I was at the terrible, growing years. War years. I do not remember them well. I was working, there were four smaller ones now, there was not time for her. She had to help be a mother, and housekeeper, and shopper. She had to set her seal. Mornings of crisis and near hysteria trying to get lunches packed, hair combed, coats and shoes found, everyone to school or Child Care on time, the baby ready for transportation. And always the paper scribbled on by a smaller one, the book looked at by Susan then mislaid, the homework not done. Running out to that huge school where she was one, she was lost, she was a drop; suffering over the unpreparedness, stammering and unsure in her classes.

There was so little time left at night after the kids were bedded down.

She would struggle over books, always eating (it was in those years she developed her enormous appetite that is legendary in our family) and I would be ironing, or preparing food for the next day, or writing V-mail to Bill, or tending the baby. Sometimes, to make me laugh, or out of her despair, she would imitate happenings or types at school.

I think I said once: "Why don't you do something like this in the school amateur show?" One morning she phoned me at work, hardly understandable through the weeping: "Mother, I did it. I won, I won; they gave me first prize; they clapped and clapped and wouldn't let me go."

Now suddenly she was Somebody, and as imprisoned in her difference as she had been in anonymity.

She began to be asked to perform at other high schools, even in colleges, then at city and statewide affairs. The first one we went to, I only recognized her that first moment when thin, shy, she almost drowned herself into the curtains. Then: Was this Emily? The control, the command, the convulsing and deadly clowning, the spell, then the roaring, stamping audience, unwilling to let this rare and precious laughter out of their lives.

Afterwards: You ought to do something about her with a gift like that — but without money or knowing how, what does one do? We have left it all to her, and the gift has as often eddied inside, clogged and clotted, as been used and growing.

She is coming. She runs up the stairs two at a time with her light graceful   50
step, and I know she is happy tonight. Whatever it was that occasioned your call did not happen today.

"Aren't you ever going to finish the ironing, Mother? Whistler painted his mother in a rocker. I'd have to paint mine standing over an ironing board." This is one of her communicative nights and she tells me everything and nothing as she fixes herself a plate of food out of the icebox.

She is so lovely. Why did you want me to come in at all? Why were you concerned? She will find her way.

She starts up the stairs to bed. "Don't get me up with the rest in the morning." "But I thought you were having midterms." "Oh, those," she comes back in, kisses me, and says quite lightly, "in a couple of years when we'll all be atom-dead they won't matter a bit."

She has said it before. She *believes* it. But because I have been dredging the past, and all that compounds a human being is so heavy and meaningful in me, I cannot endure it tonight.

I will never total it all. I will never come in to say: She was a child seldom   55
smiled at. Her father left me before she was a year old. I had to work her first six years when there was work, or I sent her home and to his relatives. There were years she had care she hated. She was dark and thin and foreign-looking in a world where the prestige went to blondeness and curly hair and dimples, she was slow where glibness was prized. She was a child of anxious, not proud, love. We were poor and could not afford for her the soil of easy growth. I was a young mother, I was a distracted mother. There were other children pushing up, demanding. Her younger sister seemed all that she was not. There were years she did not want me to touch her. She kept too much in herself, her life was such she had to keep too much in herself. My wisdom came too late. She has much to her and probably little will come of it. She is a child of her age, of depression, of war, of fear.

Let her be. So all that is in her will not bloom — but in how many does it? There is still enough left to live by. Only help her to know — help make it so there is cause for her to know — that she is more than this dress on the ironing board, helpless before the iron.

Philip Roth

THE CONVERSION OF THE JEWS 1959

Philip Roth, called "the inventor of the Jewish novel of manners," was born in 1933 in Newark, New Jersey. He first attended college on the local campus of Rutgers University, later transferred to Bucknell, completed his M.A. degree at the University of Chicago, and served a year in the Army. Although now a writer full time, he has taught fiction writing at three universities: Iowa, Pennsylvania, and Princeton. Roth's first book, the collection of stories Goodbye, Columbus *(1955), from which we take "The Conversion of the Jews," won him immediate fame.* Portnoy's Complaint, *a sardonically comic novel of a man's sexual obsession, topped the bestseller list in 1969. Three novels about a writer named Zuckerman have been collected as* Zuckerman Bound *(1985). Roth has also written plays and literary criticism, notably* Reading Myself and Others *(1975).*

"You're a real one for opening your mouth in the first place," Itzie said. "What do you open your mouth all the time for?"

"I didn't bring it up, Itz, I didn't," Ozzie said.

"What do you care about Jesus Christ for anyway?"

"I didn't bring up Jesus Christ. He did. I didn't even know what he was talking about. Jesus is historical, he kept saying. Jesus is historical." Ozzie mimicked the monumental voice of Rabbi Binder.

"Jesus was a person that lived like you and me," Ozzie continued. "That's what Binder said — "

"Yeah? . . . So what! What do I give two cents whether he lived or not. And what do you gotta open your mouth!" Itzie Lieberman favored closed-mouthedness, especially when it came to Ozzie Freedman's questions. Mrs. Freedman had to see Rabbi Binder twice before about Ozzie's questions and this Wednesday at four-thirty would be the third time. Itzie preferred to keep *his* mother in the kitchen; he settled for behind-the-back subtleties such as gestures, faces, snarls and other less delicate barnyard noises.

"He was a real person, Jesus, but he wasn't like God, and we don't believe he is God." Slowly, Ozzie was explaining Rabbi Binder's position to Itzie, who had been absent from Hebrew School the previous afternoon.

"The Catholics," Itzie said helpfully, "they believe in Jesus Christ, that he's God." Itzie Lieberman used "the Catholics" in its broadest sense — to include the Protestants.

Ozzie received Itzie's remark with a tiny head bob, as though it were a footnote, and went on. "His mother was Mary, and his father probably was Joseph," Ozzie said. "But the New Testament says his real father was God."

"His *real* father?"

"Yeah," Ozzie said, "that's the big thing, his father's supposed to be God."

"Bull."

"That's what Rabbi Binder says, that it's impossible — "

"Sure it's impossible. That stuff's all bull. To have a baby you gotta get laid," Itzie theologized. "Mary hadda get laid."

"That's what Binder says: 'The only way a woman can have a baby is to have intercourse with a man.' "

"He said *that,* Ozz?" For a moment it appeared that Itzie had put the theological question aside. "He said that, intercourse?" A little curled smile shaped itself in the lower half of Itzie's face like a pink mustache. "What you guys do, Ozz, you laugh or something?"

"I raised my hand."

"Yeah? Whatja say?"

"That's when I asked the question."

Itzie's face lit up. "Whatja ask about — intercourse?"

"No, I asked the question about God, how if He could create the heaven and earth in six days, and make all the animals and the fish and the light in six days — the light especially, that's what always gets me, that He could make the light. Making fish and animals, that's pretty good — "

"That's damn good." Itzie's appreciation was honest but unimaginative: it was as though God had just pitched a one-hitter.

"But making light . . . I mean when you think about it, it's really something," Ozzie said. "Anyway, I asked Binder if He could make all that in six days, and He could *pick* the six days He wanted right out of nowhere, why couldn't He let a woman have a baby without having intercourse."

"You said intercourse, Ozz, to Binder?"

"Yeah."

"Right in class?"

"Yeah."

Itzie smacked the side of his head.

"I mean, no kidding around," Ozzie said, "that'd really be nothing. After all that other stuff, that'd practically be nothing."

Itzie considered a moment. "What'd Binder say?"

"He started all over again explaining how Jesus was historical and how he lived like you and me but he wasn't God. So I said I understood that. What I wanted to know was different."

What Ozzie wanted to know was always different. The first time he had wanted to know how Rabbi Binder could call the Jews "The Chosen People" if the Declaration of Independence claimed all men to be created equal. Rabbi Binder tried to distinguish for him between political equality and spiritual legitimacy, but what Ozzie wanted to know, he insisted vehemently, was different. That was the first time his mother had to come.

Then there was the plane crash. Fifty-eight people had been killed in a plane crash at La Guardia°. In studying a casualty list in the newspaper his mother had discovered among the list of those dead eight Jewish names (his

La Guardia: a New York City airport.

grandmother had nine but she counted Miller as a Jewish name); because of the eight she said the plane crash was "a tragedy." During free-discussion time on Wednesday Ozzie had brought to Rabbi Binder's attention this matter of "some of his relations" always picking out the Jewish names. Rabbi Binder had begun to explain cultural unity and some other things when Ozzie stood up at his seat and said that what he wanted to know was different. Rabbi Binder insisted that he sit down and it was then that Ozzie shouted that he wished all fifty-eight were Jews. That was the second time his mother came.

"And he kept explaining about Jesus being historical, and so I kept asking him. No kidding, Itz, he was trying to make me look stupid."

"So what he finally do?"

"Finally he starts screaming that I was deliberately simple-minded and a wise guy, and that my mother had to come, and this was the last time. And that I'd never get bar-mitzvahed if he could help it. Then, Itz, then he starts talking in that voice like a statue, real slow and deep, and he says that I better think over what I said about the Lord. He told me to go to his office and think it over." Ozzie leaned his body towards Itzie. "Itz, I thought it over for a solid hour, and now I'm convinced God could do it."

Ozzie had planned to confess his latest transgression to his mother as soon as she came home from work. But it was a Friday night in November and already dark, and when Mrs. Freedman came through the door she tossed off her coat, kissed Ozzie quickly on the face, and went to the kitchen table to light the three yellow candles, two for the Sabbath and one for Ozzie's father.

When his mother lit the candles she would move her two arms slowly towards her, dragging them through the air, as though persuading people whose minds were half made up. And her eyes would get glassy with tears. Even when his father was alive Ozzie remembered that her eyes had gotten glassy, so it didn't have anything to do with his dying. It had something to do with lighting the candles.

As she touched the flaming match to the unlit wick of a Sabbath candle, the phone rang, and Ozzie, standing only a foot from it, plucked it off the receiver and held it muffled to his chest. When his mother lit candles Ozzie felt there should be no noise; even breathing, if you could manage it, should be softened. Ozzie pressed the phone to his breast and watched his mother dragging whatever she was dragging, and he felt his own eyes get glassy. His mother was a round, tired, gray-haired penguin of a woman whose gray skin had begun to feel the tug of gravity and the weight of her own history. Even when she was dressed up she didn't look like a chosen person. But when she lit candles she looked like something better; like a woman who knew momentarily that God could do anything.

After a few mysterious minutes she was finished. Ozzie hung up the phone and walked to the kitchen table where she was beginning to lay the two places for the four-course Sabbath meal. He told her that she would have to see Rabbi Binder next Wednesday at four-thirty, and then he told her why. For the first time in their life together she hit Ozzie across the face with her hand.

All through the chopped liver and chicken soup part of the dinner Ozzie cried; he didn't have any appetite for the rest.

On Wednesday, in the largest of the three basement classrooms of the synagogue, Rabbi Marvin Binder, a tall, handsome, broad-shouldered man of thirty with thick strong-fibered black hair, removed his watch from his pocket and saw that it was four o'clock. At the rear of the room Yakov Blotnik, the seventy-one-year-old custodian, slowly polished the large window, mumbling to himself, unaware that it was four o'clock or six o'clock, Monday or Wednesday. To most of the students Yakov Blotnik's mumbling, along with his brown curly beard, scythe nose, and two heel-trailing black cats, made of him an object of wonder, a foreigner, a relic, towards whom they were alternately fearful and disrespectful. To Ozzie the mumbling had always seemed a monotonous, curious prayer; what made it curious was that old Blotnik had been mumbling so steadily for so many years, Ozzie suspected he had memorized the prayers and forgotten all about God.

"It is now free-discussion time," Rabbi Binder said. "Feel free to talk about any Jewish matter at all — religion, family, politics, sports — "

There was silence. It was a gusty, clouded November afternoon and it did not seem as though there ever was or could be a thing called baseball. So nobody this week said a word about that hero from the past, Hank Greenberg — which limited free discussion considerably.

And the soul-battering Ozzie Freedman had just received from Rabbi 45 Binder had imposed its limitation. When it was Ozzie's turn to read aloud from the Hebrew book the rabbi had asked him petulantly why he didn't read more rapidly. He was showing no progress. Ozzie said he could read faster but that if he did he was sure not to understand what he was reading. Nevertheless, at the rabbi's repeated suggestion Ozzie tried, and showed a great talent, but in the midst of a long passage he stopped short and said he didn't understand a word he was reading, and started in again at a drag-footed pace. Then came the soul-battering.

Consequently when free-discussion time rolled around none of the students felt too free. The rabbi's invitation was answered only by the mumbling of feeble old Blotnik.

"Isn't there anything at all you would like to discuss?" Rabbi Binder asked again, looking at his watch. "No questions or comments?"

There was a small grumble from the third row. The rabbi requested that Ozzie rise and give the rest of the class the advantage of his thought.

Ozzie rose. "I forget it now," he said, and sat down in his place.

Rabbi Binder advanced a seat towards Ozzie and poised himself on the 50 edge of the desk. It was Itzie's desk and the rabbi's frame only a dagger's-length away from his face snapped him to sitting attention.

"Stand up again, Oscar," Rabbi Binder said calmly, "and try to assemble your thoughts."

Ozzie stood up. All his classmates turned in their seats and watched as he gave an unconvincing scratch to his forehead.

"I can't assemble any," he announced, and plunked himself down.

"Stand up!" Rabbi Binder advanced from Itzie's desk to the one directly in front of Ozzie; when the rabbinical back was turned Ozzie gave it five-fingers off the tip of his nose, causing a small titter in the room. Rabbi Binder was too absorbed in squelching Ozzie's nonsense once and for all to bother with titters. "Stand up, Oscar. What's your question about?"

Ozzie pulled a word out of the air. It was the handiest word. "Religion." 55
"Oh, now you remember?"
"Yes."
"What is it?"
Trapped, Ozzie blurted the first thing that came to him. "Why can't He make anything He wants to make!"
As Rabbi Binder prepared an answer, a final answer, Itzie, ten feet behind 60 him, raised one finger on his left hand, gestured it meaningfully towards the rabbi's back, and brought the house down.
Binder twisted quickly to see what had happened and in the midst of the commotion Ozzie shouted into the rabbi's back what he couldn't have shouted to his face. It was a loud, toneless sound that had the timbre of something stored inside for about six days.
"You don't know! You don't know anything about God!"
The rabbi spun back towards Ozzie. "What?"
"You don't know — you don't — "
"Apologize, Oscar, apologize!" It was a threat. 65
"You don't — "
Rabbi Binder's hand flicked out at Ozzie's cheek. Perhaps it had only been meant to clamp the boy's mouth shut, but Ozzie ducked and the palm caught him squarely on the nose.
The blood came in a short, red spurt on to Ozzie's shirt front.
The next moment was all confusion. Ozzie screamed, "You bastard, you bastard!" and broke for the classroom door. Rabbi Binder lurched a step backwards, as though his own blood had started flowing violently in the opposite direction, then gave a clumsy lurch forward and bolted out the door after Ozzie. The class followed after the rabbi's huge blue-suited back, and before old Blotnik could turn from his window, the room was empty and everyone was headed full speed up the three flights leading to the roof.

If one should compare the light of the day to the life of man: sunrise to 70 birth; sunset — the dropping down over the edge — to death; then as Ozzie Freedman wiggled through the trapdoor of the synagogue roof, his feet kicking backwards bronco-style at Rabbi Binder's outstretched arms — at that moment the day was fifty years old. As a rule, fifty or fifty-five reflects accurately the age of late afternoons in November, for it is in that month, during those hours, that one's awareness of light seems no longer a matter of seeing, but of hearing: light begins clicking away. In fact, as Ozzie locked shut the trapdoor in the rabbi's face, the sharp click of the bolt into the lock might momentarily have been mistaken for the sound of the heavier gray that had just throbbed through the sky.
With all his weight Ozzie kneeled on the locked door; any instant he was certain that Rabbi Binder's shoulder would fling it open, splintering the wood into shrapnel and catapulting his body into the sky. But the door did not move and below him he heard only the rumble of feet, first loud then dim, like thunder rolling away.
A question shot through his brain. "Can this be *me?*" For a thirteen-year-old who had just labeled his religious leader a bastard, twice, it was not an improper question. Louder and louder the question came to him — "Is it me?

Is it me?" — until he discovered himself no longer kneeling, but racing crazily towards the edge of the roof, his eyes crying, his throat screaming, and his arms flying everywhichway as though not his own.

"Is it me? Is it me ME ME ME ME! It has to be me — but is it!"

It is the question a thief must ask himself the night he jimmies open his first window, and it is said to be the question with which bridegrooms quiz themselves before the altar.

In the few wild seconds it took Ozzie's body to propel him to the edge of the roof, his self-examination began to grow fuzzy. Gazing down at the street, he became confused as to the problem beneath the question: was it, is-it-me-who-called-Binder-a-bastard? or, is-it-me-prancing-around-on-the-roof? However, the scene below settled all, for there is an instant in any action when whether it is you or somebody else is academic. The thief crams the money in his pockets and scoots out the window. The bridegroom signs the hotel register for two. And the boy on the roof finds a streetful of people gaping at him, necks stretched backwards, faces up, as though he were the ceiling of the Hayde Planetarium. Suddenly you know it's you.

"Oscar! Oscar Freedman!" A voice rose from the center of the crowd, a voice that, could it have been seen, would have looked like the writing on scroll. "Oscar Freedman, get down from there. Immediately!" Rabbi Binder was pointing one arm stiffly up at him; and at the end of that arm, one finger aimed menacingly. It was the attitude of a dictator, but one — the eyes confessed all — whose personal valet had spit neatly in his face.

Ozzie didn't answer. Only for a blink's length did he look towards Rabbi Binder. Instead his eyes began to fit together the world beneath him, to sort out people from places, friends from enemies, participants from spectators. In little jagged starlike clusters his friends stood around Rabbi Binder, who was still pointing. The topmost point on a star compounded not of angels but of five adolescent boys was Itzie. What a world it was, with those stars below, Rabbi Binder below . . . Ozzie, who a moment earlier hadn't been able to control his own body, started to feel the meaning of the word control: he felt Peace and he felt Power.

"Oscar Freedman, I'll give you three to come down."

Few dictators give their subjects three to do anything; but, as always, Rabbi Binder only looked dictatorial.

"Are you ready, Oscar?"

Ozzie nodded his head yes, although he had no intention in the world — the lower one or the celestial one he'd just entered — of coming down even if Rabbi Binder should give him a million.

"All right then," said Rabbi Binder. He ran a hand through his black Samson hair as though it were the gesture prescribed for uttering the first digit. Then, with his other hand cutting a circle out of the small piece of sky around him, he spoke. "One!"

There was no thunder. On the contrary, at that moment, as though "one" was the cue for which he had been waiting, the world's least thunderous person appeared on the synagogue steps. He did not so much come out the synagogue door as lean out, onto the darkening air. He clutched at the door-knob with one hand and looked up at the roof.

"Oy!"

Yakov Blotnik's old mind hobbled slowly, as if on crutches, and though he couldn't decide precisely what the boy was doing on the roof, he knew it wasn't good — that is, it wasn't-good-for-the-Jews. For Yakov Blotnik life had fractionated itself simply: things were either good-for-the-Jews or no-good-for-the-Jews.

He smacked his free hand to his in-sucked cheek, gently. "Oy, Gut!" And then quickly as he was able, he jacked down his head and surveyed the street. There was Rabbi Binder (like a man at an auction with only three dollars in his pocket, he had just delivered a shaky "Two!"); there were the students, and that was all. So far it-wasn't-so-bad-for-the-Jews. But the boy had to come down immediately, before anybody saw. The problem: how to get the boy off the roof?

Anybody who has ever had a cat on the roof knows how to get him down. You call the fire department. Or first you call the operator and you ask her for the fire department. And the next thing there is great jamming of brakes and clanging of bells and shouting of instructions. And then the cat is off the roof. You do the same thing to get a boy off the roof.

That is, you do the same thing if you are Yakov Blotnik and you once had a cat on the roof.

When the engines, all four of them, arrived, Rabbi Binder had four times given Ozzie the count of three. The big hook-and-ladder swung around the corner and one of the firemen leaped from it, plunging headlong towards the yellow fire hydrant in front of the synagogue. With a huge wrench he began to unscrew the top nozzle. Rabbi Binder raced over to him and pulled at his shoulder.

"There's no fire . . ." 90

The fireman mumbled back over his shoulder and, heatedly, continued working at the nozzle.

"But there's no fire, there's no fire . . ." Binder shouted. When the fireman mumbled again, the rabbi grasped his face with both his hands and pointed it up at the roof.

To Ozzie it looked as though Rabbi Binder was trying to tug the fire-man's head out of his body, like a cork from a bottle. He had to giggle at the picture they made: it was a family portrait — rabbi in black skullcap, fireman in red fire hat, and the little yellow hydrant squatting beside like a kid brother, bareheaded. From the edge of the roof Ozzie waved at the portrait, a one-handed, flapping, mocking wave; in doing it his right foot slipped from under him. Rabbi Binder covered his eyes with his hands.

Firemen work fast. Before Ozzie had even regained his balance, a big, round, yellowed net was being held on the synagogue lawn. The firemen who held it looked up at Ozzie with stern, feelingless faces.

One of the firemen turned his head towards Rabbi Binder. "What, is the 95 kid nuts or something?"

Rabbi Binder unpeeled his hands from his eyes, slowly, painfully, as if they were tape. Then he checked: nothing on the sidewalk, no dents in the net.

"Is he gonna jump, or what?" the fireman shouted.

In a voice not at all like a statue, Rabbi Binder finally answered. "Yes, yes, I think so . . . He's been threatening to . . ."

Threatening to? Why, the reason he was on the roof, Ozzie remembered, was to get away; he hadn't even thought about jumping. He had just run to get away, and the truth was that he hadn't really headed for the roof as much as he'd been chased there.

"What's his name, the kid?"

"Freedman," Rabbi Binder answered. "Oscar Freedman."

The fireman looked up at Ozzie. "What is it with you, Oscar? You gonna jump, or what?"

Ozzie did not answer. Frankly, the question had just arisen.

"Look, Oscar, if you're gonna jump, jump — and if you're not gonna jump, don't jump. But don't waste our time, willya?"

Ozzie looked at the fireman and then at Rabbi Binder. He wanted to see Rabbi Binder cover his eyes one more time.

"I'm going to jump."

And then he scampered around the edge of the roof to the corner, where there was no net below, and he flapped his arms at his sides, swishing the air and smacking his palms to his trousers on the downbeat. He began screaming like some kind of engine, "Wheeeee . . . wheeeeee," and leaning way out over the edge with the upper half of his body. The firemen whipped around to cover the ground with the net. Rabbi Binder mumbled a few words to Somebody and covered his eyes. Everything happened quickly, jerkily, as in a silent movie. The crowd, which had arrived with the fire engines, gave out a long, Fourth-of-July fireworks oooh-aahhh. In the excitement no one had paid the crowd much heed, except, of course, Yakov Blotnik, who swung from the doorknob counting heads. "Fier und tsvansik . . . finf und tsvantsik . . . Oy, Gut!°" It wasn't like this with the cat.

Rabbi Binder peeked through his fingers, checked the sidewalk and net. Empty. But there was Ozzie racing to the other corner. The firemen raced with him but were unable to keep up. Whenever Ozzie wanted to he might jump and splatter himself upon the sidewalk, and by the time the firemen scooted to the spot all they could do with their net would be to cover the mess.

"Wheeeee . . . wheeee . . ."

"Hey, Oscar," the winded fireman yelled, "What the hell is this, a game or something?"

"Wheeeee . . . wheeee . . ."

"Hey, Oscar — "

But he was off now to the other corner, flapping his wings fiercely. Rabbi Binder couldn't take it any longer — the fire engines from nowhere, the screaming suicidal boy, the net. He fell to his knees, exhausted, and with his hands curled together in front of his chest like a little dome, he pleaded, "Oscar, stop it, Oscar. Don't jump, Oscar. Please come down . . . Please don't jump."

And further back in the crowd a single voice, a single young voice, shouted a lone word to the boy on the roof.

"Jump!"

It was Itzie. Ozzie momentarily stopped flapping.

"Go ahead, Ozz — jump!" Itzie broke off his point of the star and courageously, with the inspiration not of a wise-guy but of a disciple, stood alone. "Jump, Ozz, jump!"

Still on his knees, his hands still curled, Rabbi Binder twisted his body back. He looked at Itzie, then, agonizingly, back to Ozzie.

Fier . . . Gut! Yiddish: "Twenty-four . . . twenty-five . . . Oh, God!"

"Oscar, Don't jump! Please, Don't Jump . . . please please . . ."

"Jump!" This time it wasn't Itzie but another point of the star. By the time Mrs. Freedman arrived to keep her four-thirty appointment with Rabbi Binder, the whole little upside down heaven was shouting and pleading for Ozzie to jump, and Rabbi Binder no longer was pleading with him not to jump, but was crying into the dome of his hands.

Understandably Mrs. Freedman couldn't figure out what her son was doing on the roof. So she asked.

"Ozzie, my Ozzie, what are you doing? My Ozzie, what is it?"

Ozzie stopped wheeeeeing and slowed his arms down to a cruising flap, the kind birds use in soft winds, but he did not answer. He stood against the low, clouded, darkening sky — light clicked down swiftly now, as on a small gear — flapping softly and gazing down at the small bundle of a woman who was his mother.

"What are you doing, Ozzie?" She turned towards the kneeling Rabbi Binder and rushed so close that only a paper-thickness of dusk lay between her stomach and his shoulders.

"What is my baby doing?"

Rabbi Binder gaped up at her but he too was mute. All that moved was the dome of his hands; it shook back and forth like a weak pulse.

"Rabbi, get him down! He'll kill himself. Get him down, my only baby . . ."

"I can't," Rabbi Binder said, "I can't . . ." and he turned his handsome head towards the crowd of boys behind him. "It's them. Listen to them."

And for the first time Mrs. Freedman saw the crowd of boys, and she heard what they were yelling.

"He's doing it for them. He won't listen to me. It's them." Rabbi Binder spoke like one in a trance.

"For them?"

"Yes."

"Why for them?"

"They want him to . . ."

Mrs. Freedman raised her two arms upward as though she were conducting the sky. "For them he's doing it!" And then in a gesture older than pyramids, older than prophets and floods, her arms came slapping down to her sides. "A martyr I have. Look!" She tilted her head to the roof. Ozzie was still flapping softly. "My martyr."

"Oscar, come down, *please*," Rabbi Binder groaned.

In a startlingly even voice Mrs. Freedman called to the boy on the roof. "Ozzie, come down, Ozzie. Don't be a martyr, my baby."

As though it were a litany, Rabbi Binder repeated her words. "Don't be a martyr, my baby. Don't be a martyr."

"Gawhead, Ozz — *be* a Martin!" It was Itzie. "Be a Martin, be a Martin," and all the voices joined in singing for Martindom, whatever *it* was. "Be a Martin, be a Martin . . ."

Somehow when you're on a roof the darker it gets the less you can hear. All Ozzie knew was that two groups wanted two new things; his friends were spirited and musical about what they wanted; his mother and the rabbi were even-toned, chanting, about what they didn't want. The rabbi's voice was without tears now and so was his mother's.

The big net stared up at Ozzie like a sightless eye. The big, clouded sky pushed down. From beneath it looked like a gray corrugated board. Suddenly, looking up into that unsympathetic sky, Ozzie realized all the strangeness of what these people, his friends, were asking: they wanted him to jump, to kill himself; they were singing about it now — it made them that happy. And there was an even greater strangeness: Rabbi Binder was on his knees, trembling. If there was a question to be asked now it was not "Is it me?" but rather "Is it us? . . . Is it us?"

Being on the roof, it turned out, was a serious thing. If he jumped would the singing become dancing? Would it? What would jumping stop? Yearningly, Ozzie wished he could rip open the sky, plunge his hands through, and pull out the sun; and on the sun, like a coin, would be stamped JUMP or DON'T JUMP.

Ozzie's knees rocked and sagged a little under him as though they were setting him for a dive. His arms tightened, stiffened, froze, from shoulders to fingernails. He felt as if each part of his body were going to vote as to whether he should kill himself or not — and each part as though it were independent of *him.*

The light took an unexpected click down and the new darkness, like a gag, hushed the friends singing for this and the mother and rabbi chanting for that.

Ozzie stopped counting votes, and in a curiously high voice, like one who   145
wasn't prepared for speech, he spoke.

"Mamma?"

"Yes, Oscar."

"Mamma, get down on your knees, like Rabbi Binder."

"Oscar — "

"Get down on your knees," he said, "or I'll jump."   150

Ozzie heard a whimper, then a quick rustling, and when he looked down where his mother had stood he saw the top of a head and beneath that a circle of dress. She was kneeling beside Rabbi Binder.

He spoke again. "Everybody kneel." There was the sound of everybody kneeling.

Ozzie looked around. With one hand he pointed towards the synagogue entrance. "Make *him* kneel."

There was a noise, not of kneeling, but of body-and-cloth stretching. Ozzie could hear Rabbi Binder saying in a gruff whisper, ". . . or he'll *kill* himself," and when next he looked there was Yakov Blotnik off the doorknob and for the first time in his life upon his knees in the Gentile posture of prayer.

As for the firemen — it is not as difficult as one might imagine to hold   155
a net taut while you are kneeling.

Ozzie looked around again; and then he called to Rabbi Binder.

"Rabbi?"

"Yes, Oscar."

"Rabbi Binder, do you believe in God?"

"Yes."   160

"Do you believe God can do Anything?" Ozzie leaned his head out into the darkness. "Anything?"

"Oscar, I think — "

"Tell me you believe God can do Anything."

There was a second's hesitation. Then: "God can do Anything."

"Tell me you believe God can make a child without intercourse."   165

"He can."

"Tell me!"

"God," Rabbi Binder admitted, "can make a child without intercourse."

"Mamma, you tell me."

"God can make a child without intercourse," his mother said.   170

"Make *him* tell me." There was no doubt who *him* was.

In a few moments Ozzie heard an old comical voice say something to the increasing darkness about God.

Next, Ozzie made everybody say it. And then he made them all say they believed in Jesus Christ — first one at a time, then all together.

When the catechizing was through it was the beginning of evening. From the street it sounded as if the boy on the roof might have sighed.

"Ozzie?" A woman's voice dared to speak. "You'll come down now?"   175

There was no answer, but the woman waited, and when a voice finally did speak it was thin and crying, and exhausted as that of an old man who has just finished pulling the bells.

"Mamma, don't you see — you shouldn't hit me. He shouldn't hit me. You shouldn't hit me about God, Mamma. You should never hit anybody about God — "

"Ozzie, please come down now."

"Promise me, promise me you'll never hit anybody about God."

He had asked only his mother, but for some reason everyone kneeling   180
in the street promised he would never hit anybody about God.

Once again there was silence.

"I can come down now, Mamma," the boy on the roof finally said. He turned his head both ways as though checking the traffic lights. "Now I can come down . . ."

And he did, right into the center of the yellow net that glowed in the evening's edge like an overgrown halo.

Joyce Carol Oates

WHERE ARE YOU GOING, WHERE HAVE YOU BEEN?   1970

Joyce Carol Oates was born in 1938 into a blue-collar family in Lockport, New York. As a college student she won a Mademoiselle *magazine award for fiction. After graduation from Syracuse with top honors, she took a master's degree in English at the University of Wisconsin and went on to teach at universities: Detroit, Windsor (Ontario), and Princeton. She now lives in New Jersey, where together with her husband, Raymond Smith, she directs the Ontario Review Press, literary publishers. An amazingly prolific writer, Oates so far has produced forty-four books of stories; novels including* Them, *winner of a National Book Award in 1970,* Solstice *(1985), and* Marya *(1986); poetry, plays, and literary criticism. Violence and the macabre inhabit the world of her best stories, but Oates has insisted that these elements in her work are never gratuitous.*

For Bob Dylan

Her name was Connie. She was fifteen and she had a quick nervous giggling habit of craning her neck to glance into mirrors, or checking other people's faces to make sure her own was all right. Her mother, who noticed everything and knew everything and who hadn't much reason any longer to look at her own face, always scolded Connie about it. "Stop gawking at yourself, who are you? You think you're so pretty?" she would say. Connie would raise her eyebrows at these familiar complaints and look right through her mother, into a shadowy vision of herself as she was right at that moment: she knew she was pretty and that was everything. Her mother had been pretty once too, if you could believe those old snapshots in the album, but now her looks were gone and that was why she was always after Connie.

"Why don't you keep your room clean like your sister? How've you got your hair fixed — what the hell stinks? Hair spray? You don't see your sister using that junk."

Her sister June was twenty-four and still lived at home. She was a secretary in the high school Connie attended, and if that wasn't bad enough — with her in the same building — she was so plain and chunky and steady that Connie had to hear her praised all the time by her mother and her mother's sisters. June did this, June did that, she saved money and helped clean the house and cooked and Connie couldn't do a thing, her mind was all filled with trashy daydreams. Their father was away at work most of the time and when he came home he wanted supper and he read the newspaper at supper and after supper he went to bed. He didn't bother talking much to them, but around his bent head Connie's mother kept picking at her until Connie wished her mother was dead and she herself was dead and it was all over. "She makes me want to throw up sometimes," she complained to her friends. She had a high, breathless, amused voice which made everything she said sound a little forced, whether it was sincere or not.

There was one good thing: June went places with girl friends of hers, girls who were just as plain and steady as she, and so when Connie wanted to do that her mother had no objections. The father of Connie's best girl friend drove the girls the three miles to town and left them off at a shopping plaza, so that they could walk through the stores or go to a movie, and when he came to pick them up again at eleven he never bothered to ask what they had done.

They must have been familiar sights, walking around that shopping plaza in their shorts and flat ballerina slippers that always scuffed the sidewalk, with charm bracelets jingling on their thin wrists; they would lean together to whisper and laugh secretly if someone passed by who amused or interested them. Connie had long dark blond hair that drew anyone's eye to it, and she wore part of it pulled up on her head and puffed out and the rest of it she let

5

fall down her back. She wore a pull-over jersey blouse that looked one way when she was at home and another way when she was away from home. Everything about her had two sides to it, one for home and one for anywhere that was not home: her walk that could be childlike and bobbing, or languid enough to make anyone think she was hearing music in her head, her mouth which was pale and smirking most of the time, but bright and pink on these evenings out, her laugh which was cynical and drawling at home — "Ha, ha, very funny" — but high-pitched and nervous anywhere else, like the jingling of the charms on her bracelet.

Sometimes they did go shopping or to a movie, but sometimes they went across the highway, ducking fast across the busy road, to a drive-in restaurant where older kids hung out. The restaurant was shaped like a big bottle, though squatter than a real bottle, and on its cap was a revolving figure of a grinning boy who held a hamburger aloft. One night in mid-summer they ran across, breathless with daring, and right away someone leaned out a car window and invited them over, but it was just a boy from high school they didn't like. It made them feel good to be able to ignore him. They went up through the maze of parked and cruising cars to the bright-lit, fly-infested restaurant, their faces pleased and expectant as if they were entering a sacred building that loomed out of the night to give them what haven and what blessing they yearned for. They sat at the counter and crossed their legs at the ankles, their thin shoulders rigid with excitement, and listened to the music that made everything so good: the music was always in the background like music at a church service, it was something to depend upon.

A boy named Eddie came in to talk with them. He sat backwards on his stool, turning himself jerkily around in semi-circles and then stopping and turning again, and after a while he asked Connie if she would like something to eat. She said she did and so she tapped her friend's arm on her way out — her friend pulled her face up into a brave droll look — and Connie said she would meet her at eleven, across the way. "I just hate to leave her like that," Connie said earnestly, but the boy said that she wouldn't be alone for long. So they went out to his car and on the way Connie couldn't help but let her eyes wander over the windshields and faces all around her, her face gleaming with a joy that had nothing to do with Eddie or even this place; it might have been the music. She drew her shoulders up and sucked in her breath with the pure pleasure of being alive, and just at that moment she happened to glance at a face just a few feet from hers. It was a boy with shaggy black hair, in a convertible jalopy painted gold. He stared at her and then his lips widened into a grin. Connie slit her eyes at him and turned away, but she couldn't help glancing back and there he was still watching her. He wagged a finger and laughed and said, "Gonna get you, baby," and Connie turned away again without Eddie noticing anything.

She spent three hours with him, at the restaurant where they ate hamburgers and drank Cokes in wax cups that were always sweating, and then down an alley a mile or so away, and when he left her off at five to eleven only the movie house was still open at the plaza. Her girl friend was there, talking with a boy. When Connie came up the two girls smiled at each other and Connie said, "How was the movie?" and the girl said, "*You* should know." They rode off with the girl's father, sleepy and pleased, and Connie couldn't help but look at the darkened shopping plaza with its big empty parking lot and its signs that were faded and ghostly now, and over at the drive-in restaurant where cars were still circling tirelessly. She couldn't hear the music at this distance.

Next morning June asked her how the movie was and Connie said, "So-so."

She and that girl and occasionally another girl went out several times a 10
week that way, and the rest of the time Connie spent around the house — it was summer vacation — getting in her mother's way and thinking, dreaming, about the boys she met. But all the boys fell back and dissolved into a single face that was not even a face, but an idea, a feeling, mixed up with the urgent insistent pounding of the music and the humid night air of July. Connie's mother kept dragging her back to the daylight by finding things for her to do or saying, suddenly, "What's this about the Pettinger girl?"

And Connie would say nervously, "Oh, her. That dope." She always drew thick clear lines between herself and such girls, and her mother was simple and kindly enough to believe her. Her mother was so simple, Connie thought, that it was maybe cruel to fool her so much. Her mother went scuffling around the house in old bedroom slippers and complained over the telephone to one sister about the other, then the other called up and the two of them complained about the third one. If June's name was mentioned her mother's tone was approving, and if Connie's name was mentioned it was disapproving. This did not really mean she disliked Connie and actually Connie thought that her mother preferred her to June because she was prettier, but the two of them kept up a pretense of exasperation, a sense that they were tugging and struggling over something of little value to either of them. Sometimes, over coffee, they were almost friends, but something would come up — some vexation that was like a fly buzzing suddenly around their heads — and their faces went hard with contempt.

One Sunday Connie got up at eleven — none of them bothered with church — and washed her hair so that it could dry all day long, in the sun. Her parents and sister were going to a barbecue at an aunt's house and Connie said no, she wasn't interested, rolling her eyes to let her mother know just what she thought of it. "Stay home alone then," her mother said sharply. Connie sat out back in a lawn chair and watched them drive away, her father quiet and bald, hunched around so that he could back the car out, her mother with a look that was still angry and not at all softened through the windshield, and in the back seat poor old June all dressed up as if she didn't know what a barbecue was, with all the running yelling kids and the flies. Connie sat with her eyes closed in the sun, dreaming and dazed with the warmth about her as if this were a kind of love, the caresses of love, and her mind slipped over onto thoughts of the boy she had been with the night before and how nice he had been, how sweet it always was, not the way someone like June would suppose but sweet, gentle, the way it was in movies and promised in songs; and when she opened her eyes she hardly knew where she was, the back yard ran off into weeds and a fence-line of trees and behind it the sky was perfectly blue and still. The asbestos "ranch house" that was now three years old startled her — it looked small. She shook her head as if to get awake.

It was too hot. She went inside the house and turned on the radio to drown out the quiet. She sat on the edge of her bed, barefoot, and listened for an hour and a half to a program called XYZ Sunday Jamboree, record after record of hard, fast, shrieking songs she sang along with, interspersed by exclamations from "Bobby King": "An' look here you girls at Napoleon's — Son and Charley want you to pay real close attention to this song coming up!"

And Connie paid close attention herself, bathed in a glow of slow-pulsed joy that seemed to rise mysteriously out of the music itself and lay languidly about the airless little room, breathed in and breathed out with each gentle rise and fall of her chest.

After a while she heard a car coming up the drive. She sat up at once, startled, because it couldn't be her father so soon. The gravel kept crunching all the way in from the road — the driveway was long — and Connie ran to the window. It was a car she didn't know. It was an open jalopy, painted a bright gold that caught the sunlight opaquely. Her heart began to pound and her fingers snatched at her hair, checking it, and she whispered "Christ. Christ," wondering how bad she looked. The car came to a stop at the side door and the horn sounded four short taps as if this were a signal Connie knew.

She went into the kitchen and approached the door slowly, then hung out the screen door, her bare toes curling down off the step. There were two boys in the car and now she recognized the driver: he had shaggy, shabby black hair that looked crazy as a wig and he was grinning at her.

"I ain't late, am I?" he said.

"Who the hell do you think you are?" Connie said.

"Toldja I'd be out, didn't I?"

"I don't even know who you are."

She spoke sullenly, careful to show no interest or pleasure, and he spoke in a fast bright monotone. Connie looked past him to the other boy, taking her time. He had fair brown hair, with a lock that fell onto his forehead. His sideburns gave him a fierce, embarrassed look, but so far he hadn't even bothered to glance at her. Both boys wore sunglasses. The driver's glasses were metallic and mirrored everything in miniature.

"You wanta come for a ride?" he said.

Connie smirked and let her hair fall loose over one shoulder.

"Don'tcha like my car? New paint job," he said. "Hey."

"What?"

"You're cute."

She pretended to fidget, chasing flies away from the door.

"Don'tcha believe me, or what?" he said.

"Look, I don't even know who you are," Connie said in disgust.

"Hey, Ellie's got a radio, see. Mine's broke down." He lifted his friend's arm and showed her the little transistor the boy was holding, and now Connie began to hear the music. It was the same program that was playing inside the house.

"Bobby King?" she said.

"I listen to him all the time. I think he's great."

"He's kind of great," Connie said reluctantly.

"Listen, that guy's *great*. He knows where the action is."

Connie blushed a little, because the glasses made it impossible for her to see just what this boy was looking at. She couldn't decide if she liked him or if he was just a jerk, and so she dawdled in the doorway and wouldn't come down or go back inside. She said, "What's all that stuff painted on your car?"

"Can'tcha read it?" He opened the door very carefully, as if he was afraid it might fall off. He slid out just as carefully, planting his feet firmly on the ground, the tiny metallic world in his glasses slowing down like gelatine hardening and in the midst of it Connie's bright green blouse. "This here is my name, to begin with," he said. ARNOLD FRIEND was written in tarlike black letters on the side, with a drawing of a round grinning face that reminded Connie of a pumpkin, except it wore sunglasses. "I wanta introduce myself, I'm Arnold Friend and that's my real name and I'm gonna be your friend, honey, and inside the car's Ellie Oscar, he's kinda shy." Ellie brought his transistor radio up to his shoulder and balanced it there. "Now these numbers are a secret code, honey," Arnold Friend explained. He read off the numbers 33, 19, 17 and raised his eyebrows at her to see what she thought of that, but she didn't think much of it. The left rear fender had been smashed and around it was written, on the gleaming gold background: DONE BY CRAZY WOMAN DRIVER. Connie had to laugh at that. Arnold Friend was pleased at her laughter and looked up at her. "Around the other side's a lot more — you wanta come and see them?"

"No."

"Why not?"

"Why should I?"

"Don'tcha wanta see what's on the car? Don'tcha wanta go for a ride?"   40

"I don't know."

"Why not?"

"I got things to do."

"Like what?"

"Things."   45

He laughed as if she had said something funny. He slapped his thighs. He was standing in a strange way, leaning back against the car as if he were balancing himself. He wasn't tall, only an inch or so taller than she would be if she came down to him. Connie liked the way he was dressed, which was the way all of them dressed: tight faded jeans stuffed into black, scuffed boots, a belt that pulled his waist in and showed how lean he was, and a white pull-over shirt that was a little soiled and showed the hard small muscles of his arms and shoulders. He looked as if he probably did hard work, lifting and carrying things. Even his neck looked muscular. And his face was a familiar face, somehow: the jaw and chin and cheeks slightly darkened, because he hadn't shaved for a day or two, and the nose long and hawk-like, sniffing as if she were a treat he was going to gobble up and it was all a joke.

"Connie, you ain't telling the truth. This is your day set aside for a ride with me and you know it," he said, still laughing. The way he straightened and recovered from his fit of laughing showed that it had been all fake.

"How do you know what my name is?" she said suspiciously.

"It's Connie."

"Maybe and maybe not."   50

"I know my Connie," he said, wagging his finger. Now she remembered him even better, back at the restaurant, and her cheeks warmed at the thought of how she sucked in her breath just at the moment she passed him — how she must have looked to him. And he had remembered her. "Ellie and I come out here especially for you," he said. "Ellie can sit in back. How about it?"

"Where?"

"Where what?"

"Where're we going?"

He looked at her. He took off the sunglasses and she saw how pale the skin around his eyes was, like holes that were not in shadow but instead in light. His eyes were chips of broken glass that catch the light in an amiable way. He smiled. It was as if the idea of going for a ride somewhere, to some place, was a new idea to him.

"Just for a ride, Connie sweetheart."

"I never said my name was Connie," she said.

"But I know what it is. I know your name and all about you, lots of things," Arnold Friend said. He had not moved yet but stood still leaning back against the side of his jalopy. "I took a special interest in you, such a pretty girl, and found out all about you like I know your parents and sister are gone somewhere and I know where and how long they're going to be gone, and I know who you were with last night, and your best girl friend's name is Betty. Right?"

He spoke in a simple lilting voice, exactly as if he were reciting the words to a song. His smile assured her that everything was fine. In the car Ellie turned up the volume on his radio and did not bother to look around at them.

"Ellie can sit in the back seat," Arnold Friend said. He indicated his friend with a casual jerk of his chin, as if Ellie did not count and she should not bother with him.

"How'd you find out all that stuff?" Connie said.

"Listen: Betty Schultz and Tony Fitch and Jimmy Pettinger and Nancy Pettinger," he said, in a chant. "Raymond Stanley and Bob Hutter — "

"Do you know all those kids?"

"I know everybody."

"Look, you're kidding. You're not from around here."

"Sure."

"But — how come we never saw you before?"

"Sure you saw me before," he said. He looked down at his boots, as if he were a little offended. "You just don't remember."

"I guess I'd remember you," Connie said.

"Yeah?" He looked up at this, beaming. He was pleased. He began to mark time with the music from Ellie's radio, tapping his fists lightly together. Connie looked away from his smile to the car, which was painted so bright it almost hurt her eyes to look at it. She looked at that name, ARNOLD FRIEND. And up at the front fender was an expression that was familiar — MAN THE FLYING SAUCERS. It was an expression kids had used the year before, but didn't use this year. She looked at it for a while as if the words meant something to her that she did not yet know.

"What're you thinking about? Huh?" Arnold Friend demanded. "Not worried about your hair blowing around in the car, are you?"

"No."

"Think I maybe can't drive good?"

"How do I know?"

"You're a hard girl to handle. How come?" he said. "Don't you know I'm 75
your friend? Didn't you see me put my sign in the air when you walked by?"

"What sign?"

"My sign." And he drew an X in the air, leaning out toward her. They were
maybe ten feet apart. After his hand fell back to his side the X was still in the air,
almost visible. Connie let the screen door close and stood perfectly still inside it,
listening to the music from her radio and the boy's blend together. She stared at
Arnold Friend. He stood there so stiffly relaxed, pretending to be relaxed, with
one hand idly on the door handle as if he were keeping himself up that way and
had no intention of ever moving again. She recognized most things about him,
the tight jeans that showed his thighs and buttocks and the greasy leather boots
and the tight shirt, and even that slippery friendly smile of his, that sleepy
dreamy smile that all the boys used to get across ideas they didn't want to put
into words. She recognized all this and also the singsong way he talked, slightly
mocking, kidding, but serious and a little melancholy, and she recognized the
way he tapped one fist against the other in homage to the perpetual music
behind him. But all these things did not come together.

She said suddenly, "Hey, how old are you?"

His smile faded. She could see then that he wasn't a kid, he was much
older — thirty, maybe more. At this knowledge her heart began to pound
faster.

"That's a crazy thing to ask. Can'tcha see I'm your own age?" 80

"Like hell you are."

"Or maybe a coupla years older, I'm eighteen."

"Eighteen?" she said doubtfully.

He grinned to reassure her and lines appeared at the corners of his mouth.
His teeth were big and white. He grinned so broadly his eyes became slits and
she saw how thick the lashes were, thick and black as if painted with a black
tarlike material. Then he seemed to become embarrassed, abruptly, and looked
over his shoulder at Ellie. "*Him,* he's crazy," he said. "Ain't he a riot, he's a
nut, a real character." Ellie was still listening to the music. His sunglasses told
nothing about what he was thinking. He wore a bright orange shirt unbuttoned halfway to show his chest, which was a pale, bluish chest and not
muscular like Arnold Friend's. His shirt collar was turned up all around and
the very tips of the collar pointed out past his chin as if they were protecting
him. He was pressing the transistor radio up against his ear and sat there in
a kind of daze, right in the sun.

"He's kinda strange," Connie said. 85

"Hey, she says you're kinda strange! Kinda strange!" Arnold Friend
cried. He pounded on the car to get Ellie's attention. Ellie turned for the first
time and Connie saw with shock that he wasn't a kid either — he had a fair,
hairless face, cheeks reddened slightly as if the veins grew too close to the
surface of his skin, the face of a forty-year-old baby. Connie felt a wave of
dizziness rise in her at this sight and she stared at him as if waiting for
something to change the shock of the moment, make it all right again. Ellie's
lips kept shaping words, mumbling along with the words blasting in his ear.

"Maybe you two better go away," Connie said faintly.

"What? How come?" Arnold Friend cried. "We come out here to take you for a ride. It's Sunday." He had the voice of the man on the radio now. It was the same voice, Connie thought. "Don'tcha know it's Sunday all day and honey, no matter who you were with last night today you're with Arnold Friend and don't you forget it! — Maybe you better step out here," he said, and this last was in a different voice. It was a little flatter, as if the heat was finally getting to him.

"No. I got things to do."

"Hey." 90

"You two better leave."

"We ain't leaving until you come with us."

"Like hell I am — "

"Connie, don't fool around with me. I mean, I mean, don't fool *around,*" he said, shaking his head. He laughed incredulously. He placed his sunglasses on top of his head, carefully, as if he were indeed wearing a wig, and brought the stems down behind his ears. Connie stared at him, another wave of dizziness and fear rising in her so that for a moment he wasn't even in focus but was just a blur, standing there against his gold car, and she had the idea that he had driven up the driveway all right but had come from nowhere before that and belonged nowhere and that everything about him and even about the music that was so familiar to her was only half real.

"If my father comes and sees you — " 95

"He ain't coming. He's at a barbecue."

"How do you know that?"

"Aunt Tillie's. Right now they're — uh — they're drinking. Sitting around," he said vaguely, squinting as if he were staring all the way to town and over to Aunt Tillie's backyard. Then the vision seemed to get clear and he nodded energetically. "Yeah. Sitting around. There's your sister in a blue dress, huh? And high heels, the poor sad bitch — nothing like you, sweetheart! And your mother's helping some fat woman with the corn, they're cleaning the corn — husking the corn — "

"What fat woman?" Connie cried.

"How do I know what fat woman. I don't know every goddam fat 100 woman in the world!" Arnold Friend laughed.

"Oh, that's Mrs. Hornby. . . . Who invited her?" Connie said. She felt a little light-headed. Her breath was coming quickly.

"She's too fat. I don't like them fat. I like them the way you are, honey," he said, smiling sleepily at her. They stared at each other for a while, through the screen door. He said softly, "Now what you're going to do is this: you're going to come out that door. You're going to sit up front with me and Ellie's going to sit in the back, the hell with Ellie, right? This isn't Ellie's date. You're my date. I'm your lover, honey."

"What? You're crazy — "

"Yes, I'm your lover. You don't know what that is but you will," he said. "I know that too. I know all about you. But look: it's real nice and you couldn't ask for nobody better than me, or more polite. I always keep my word. I'll tell you how it is, I'm always nice at first, the first time. I'll hold you so tight you won't think you have to try to get away or pretend anything because you'll know you can't. And I'll come inside you where it's all secret and you'll give in to me and you'll love me — "

Joyce Carol Oates   381

"Shut up! You're crazy!" Connie said. She backed away from the door.   105
She put her hands against her ears as if she'd heard something terrible, something not meant for her. "People don't talk like that, you're crazy," she muttered. Her heart was almost too big now for her chest and its pumping made
sweat break out all over her. She looked out to see Arnold Friend pause and
then take a step toward the porch lurching. He almost fell. But, like a clever
drunken man, he managed to catch his balance. He wobbled in his high boots
and grabbed hold of one of the porch posts.

"Honey?" he said. "You still listening?"

"Get the hell out of here!"

"Be nice, honey. Listen."

"I'm going to call the police — "

He wobbled again and out of the side of his mouth came a fast spat curse,   110
an aside not meant for her to hear. But even this "Christ!" sounded forced.
Then he began to smile again. She watched this smile come, awkward as if he
were smiling from inside a mask. His whole face was a mask, she thought
wildly, tanned down onto his throat but then running out as if he had plastered
make-up on his face but had forgotten about his throat.

"Honey — ? Listen, here's how it is. I always tell the truth and I promise
you this: I ain't coming in that house after you."

"You better not! I'm going to call the police if you — if you
don't — "

"Honey," he said, talking right through her voice, "honey, I'm not coming in there but you are coming out here. You know why?"

She was panting. The kitchen looked like a place she had never seen
before, some room she had run inside but which wasn't good enough, wasn't
going to help her. The kitchen window had never had a curtain, after three
years, and there were dishes in the sink for her to do — probably — and if you
ran your hand across the table you'd probably feel something sticky there.

"You listening, honey? Hey?"   115

" — going to call the police — "

"Soon as you touch the phone I don't need to keep my promise and can
come inside. You won't want that."

She rushed forward and tried to lock the door. Her fingers were shaking.
"But why lock it," Arnold Friend said gently, talking right into her face. "It's
just a screen door. It's just nothing." One of his boots was at a strange angle,
as if his foot wasn't in it. It pointed out to the left, bent at the ankle. "I mean,
anybody can break through a screen door and glass and wood and iron or
anything else if he needs to, anybody at all and specially Arnold Friend. If the
place got lit up with a fire honey you'd come running out into my arms, right
into my arms and safe at home — like you knew I was your lover and'd
stopped fooling around. I don't mind a nice shy girl but I don't like no fooling
around." Part of those words were spoken with a slight rhythmic lilt, and
Connie somehow recognized them — the echo of a song from last year, about
a girl rushing into her boy friend's arms and coming home again —

Connie stood barefoot on the linoleum floor, staring at him. "What do
you want?" she whispered.

"I want you," he said.   120

"What?"

"Seen you that night and thought, that's the one, yes sir. I never needed to look any more."

"But my father's coming back. He's coming to get me. I had to wash my hair first — " She spoke in a dry, rapid voice, hardly raising it for him to hear.

"No, your daddy is not coming and yes, you had to wash your hair and you washed it for me. It's nice and shining and all for me, I thank you, sweetheart," he said, with a mock bow, but again he almost lost his balance. He had to bend and adjust his boots. Evidently his feet did not go all the way down; the boots must have been stuffed with something so that he would seem taller. Connie stared out at him and behind him Ellie in the car, who seemed to be looking off toward Connie's right, into nothing. This Ellie said, pulling the words out of the air one after another as if he were just discovering them, "You want me to pull out the phone?"

"Shut your mouth and keep it shut," Arnold Friend said, his face red   125
from bending over or maybe from embarrassment because Connie had seen his boots. "This ain't none of your business."

"What — what are you doing? What do you want?" Connie said. "If I call the police they'll get you, they'll arrest you — "

"Promise was not to come in unless you touch that phone, and I'll keep that promise," he said. He resumed his erect position and tried to force his shoulders back. He sounded like a hero in a movie, declaring something important. He spoke too loudly and it was as if he were speaking to someone behind Connie. "I ain't made plans for coming in that house where I don't belong but just for you to come out to me, the way you should. Don't you know who I am?"

"You're crazy," she whispered. She backed away from the door but did not want to go into another part of the house, as if this would give him permission to come through the door. "What do you. . . . You're crazy, you . . ."

"Huh? What're you saying, honey?"

Her eyes darted everywhere in the kitchen. She could not remember   130
what it was, this room.

"This is how it is, honey: you come out and we'll drive away, have a nice ride. But if you don't come out we're gonna wait till your people come home and then they're all going to get it."

"You want that telephone pulled out?" Ellie said. He held the radio away from his ear and grimaced, as if without the radio the air was too much for him.

"I toldja shut up, Ellie," Arnold Friend said, "you're deaf, get a hearing aid, right? Fix yourself up. This little girl's no trouble and's gonna be nice to me, so Ellie keep to yourself, this ain't your date — right? Don't hem in on me. Don't hog. Don't crush. Don't bird dog. Don't trail me," he said in a rapid meaningless voice, as if he were running through all the expressions he'd learned but was no longer sure which one of them was in style, then rushing on to new ones, making them up with his eyes closed, "Don't crawl under my fence, don't squeeze in my chipmunk hole, don't sniff my glue, suck my popsicle, keep your own greasy fingers on yourself!" He shaded his eyes and peered in at Connie, who was backed against the kitchen table. "Don't mind him honey he's just a creep. He's a dope. Right? I'm the boy for you and like I said you come out here nice like a lady and give me your hand, and nobody else gets hurt, I mean, your nice old bald-headed daddy and your mummy and your sister in her high heels. Because listen: why bring them in this?"

"Leave me alone," Connie whispered.

"Hey, you know that old woman down the road, the one with the chickens and stuff — you know her?" 135

"She's dead!"

"Dead? What? You know her?" Arnold Friend said.

"She's dead —"

"Don't you like her?"

"She's dead — she's — she isn't here any more — " 140

"But don't you like her, I mean, you got something against her? Some grudge or something?" Then his voice dipped as if he were conscious of a rudeness. He touched the sunglasses perched on top of his head as if to make sure they were still there. "Now you be a good girl."

"What are you going to do?"

"Just two things, or maybe three," Arnold Friend said. "But I promise it won't last long and you'll like me that way you get to like people you're close to. You will. It's all over for you here, so come on out. You don't want your people in any trouble, do you?"

She turned and bumped against a chair or something, hurting her leg, but she ran into the back room and picked up the telephone. Something roared in her ear, a tiny roaring, and she was so sick with fear that she could do nothing but listen to it — the telephone was clammy and very heavy and her fingers groped down to the dial but were too weak to touch it. She began to scream into the phone, into the roaring. She cried out, she cried for her mother, she felt her breath start jerking back and forth in her lungs as if it were something Arnold Friend were stabbing her with again and again with no tenderness. A noisy sorrowful wailing rose all about her and she was locked inside it the way she was locked inside the house.

After a while she could hear again. She was sitting on the floor with her wet back against the wall. 145

Arnold Friend was saying from the door, "That's a good girl. Put the phone back."

She kicked the phone away from her.

"No, honey. Pick it up. Put it back right."

She picked it up and put it back. The dial tone stopped.

"That's a good girl. Now you come outside." 150

She was hollow with what had been fear, but what was now just an emptiness. All that screaming had blasted it out of her. She sat, one leg cramped under her, and deep inside her brain was something like a pinpoint of light that kept going and would not let her relax. She thought, I'm not going to see my mother again. She thought, I'm not going to sleep in my bed again. Her bright green blouse was all wet.

Arnold Friend said, in a gentle-loud voice that was like a stage voice, "The place where you came from ain't there any more, and where you had in mind to go is cancelled out. This place you are now — inside your daddy's house — is nothing but a cardboard box I can knock down any time. You know that and always did know it. You hear me?"

She thought, I have got to think. I have to know what to do.

"We'll go out to a nice field, out in the country here where it smells so nice and it's sunny," Arnold Friend said. "I'll have my arms around you so you won't need to try to get away and I'll show you what love is like, what it does. The hell with this house! It looks solid all right," he said. He ran a fingernail down the screen and the noise did not make Connie shiver, as it would have the day before. "Now put your hand on your heart, honey. Feel that? That feels solid too but we know better, be nice to me, be sweet like you can because what else is there for a girl like you but to be sweet and pretty and give in? — and get away before her people come back?"

She felt her pounding heart. Her hand seemed to enclose it. She thought for the first time in her life that it was nothing that was hers, that belonged to her, but just a pounding, living thing inside this body that wasn't really hers either.

"You don't want them to get hurt," Arnold Friend went on. "Now get up, honey. Get up all by yourself."

She stood.

"Now turn this way. That's right. Come over here to me — Ellie, put that away, didn't I tell you? You dope. You miserable creepy dope," Arnold Friend said. His words were not angry but only part of an incantation. The incantation was kindly. "Now come out through the kitchen to me honey and let's see a smile, try it, you're a brave sweet little girl and now they're eating corn and hotdogs cooked to bursting over an outdoor fire, and they don't know one thing about you and never did and honey you're better than them because not a one of them would have done this for you."

Connie felt the linoleum under her feet; it was cool. She brushed her hair back out of her eyes. Arnold Friend let go of the post tentatively and opened his arms for her, his elbows pointing in toward each other and his wrists limp, to show that this was an embarrassed embrace and a little mocking, he didn't want to make her self-conscious.

She put out her hand against the screen. She watched herself push the door slowly open as if she were safe back somewhere in the other doorway, watching this body and this head of long hair moving out into the sunlight where Arnold Friend waited.

"My sweet little blue-eyed girl," he said, in a half-sung sigh that had nothing to do with her brown eyes but was taken up just the same by the vast sunlit reaches of the land behind him and on all sides of him, so much land that Connie had never seen before and did not recognize except to know that she was going to it.

Toni Cade Bambara

MY MAN BOVANNE   1972

> *Toni Cade Bambara, born in New York in 1939, grew up on low-rent streets in Harlem and the city's Bedford-Stuyvesant district. After taking her master's degree at City College, she worked for the New York State Welfare Department as a case investigator. Later, she studied dance and film-making,*

and directed a recreation program for psychiatric patients at New York City's Metropolitan Hospital. When her fiction began to spread her fame, she received (and accepted) invitations to teach at Duke, Stephens, and Emory. In recent years she has served Spelman College in Atlanta as writer-in-residence. Bambara's fiction books include Gorilla, My Love *(1972),* The Sea Birds Are Still Alive: Collected Stories *(1977), and* The Salt Eaters *(1980). As a storyteller, Bambara has been especially devoted to correcting stereotyped images of black women.*

Blind people got a hummin jones° if you notice. Which is understandable completely once you been around one and notice what no eyes will force you into to see people, and you get past the first time, which seems to come out of nowhere, and it's like you in church again with fat-chest ladies and old gents gruntin a hum low in the throat to whatever the preacher be saying. Shakey Bee bottom lip all swole up with Sweet Peach° and me explainin how come the sweet-potato bread was a dollar-quarter this time stead of dollar regular and he say uh hunh he understand, then he break into this *thizzin* kind of hum which is quiet, but fiercesome just the same, if you ain't ready for it. Which I wasn't. But I got used to it and the onliest time I had to say somethin bout it was when he was playin checkers on the stoop one time and he commenst to hummin quite churchy seem to me. So I says, "Look here Shakey Bee, I can't beat you and Jesus too." He stop.

So that's how come I asked My Man Bovanne to dance. He ain't my man mind you, just a nice ole gent from the block that we all know cause he fixes things and the kids like him. Or used to fore Black Power° got hold their minds and mess em around till they can't be civil to ole folks. So we at this benefit for my niece's cousin who's runnin for somethin with this Black party somethin or other behind her. And I press up close to dance with Bovanne who blind and I'm hummin and he hummin, chest to chest like talkin. Not jammin my breasts into the man. Wasn't bout tits. Was bout vibrations. And he dug it and asked me what color dress I had on and how my hair was fixed and how I was doin without a man, not nosy but nice-like, and who was at this affair and was the canapés dainty-stingy or healthy enough to get hold of proper. Comfy and cheery is what I'm tryin to get across. Touch talkin like the heel of the hand on the tambourine or on a drum.

But right away Joe Lee come up on us and frown for dancin so close to the man. My own son who knows what kind of warm I am about; and don't grown men all call me long distance and in the middle of the night for a little Mama comfort? But he frown. Which ain't right since Bovanne can't see and defend himself. Just a nice old man who fixes toasters and busted irons and bicycles and things and changes the lock on my door when my men friends get messy. Nice man. Which is not why they invited him. Grass roots you see. Me and Sister

a hummin jones: the habit of humming to express a craving for satisfaction.
Sweet Peach: snuff.
Black Power: militant civil rights movement that in the 1960s began gaining influence, especially among the young.

Taylor and the woman who does heads° at Mamies and the man from the barber shop, we all there on account of we grass roots. And I ain't never been souther than Brooklyn Battery and no more country than the window box on my fire escape. And just yesterday my kids tellin me to take them countrified rags off my head and be cool. And now can't get Black enough to suit 'em. So everybody passin sayin My Man Bovanne. Big deal, keep steppin and don't even stop a minute to get the man a drink or one of them cute sandwiches or tell him what's goin on. And him standin there with a smile ready case someone do speak he want to be ready. So that's how come I pull him on the dance floor and we dance squeezin past the tables and chairs and all them coats and people standin round up in each other face talkin bout this and that but got no use for this blind man who mostly fixed skates and skooters for all these folks when they were just kids. So I'm pressed up close and we touch talkin with the hum. And here come my daughter cuttin her eye at me° like she do when she tell me about my "apolitical" self like I got hoof and mouf disease and there ain't no hope at all. And I don't pay her no mind and just look up in Bovanne shadow face and tell him his stomach like a drum and he laugh. Laugh real loud. And here come my youngest, Task, with a tap on my elbow like he the third grade monitor and I'm cuttin up on the line to assembly.

"I was just talkin on the drums," I explained when they hauled me into the kitchen. I figured drums was my best defense. They can get ready for drums what with all this heritage business. And Bovanne stomach just like that drum Task give me when he come back from Africa. You just touch it and it hum thizzm, thizzm. So I stuck to the drum story. "Just drummin that's all."

"Mama, what are you talkin about?"   5

"She had too much to drink," say Elo to Task cause she don't hardly say nuthin to me direct no more since that ugly argument about my wigs.

"Look here Mama," say Task, the gentle one. "We just trying to pull your coat. You were makin a spectacle of yourself out there dancing like that."

"Dancin like what?"

Task run a hand over his left ear like his father for the world and his father before that.

"Like a bitch in heat," say Elo.   10

"Well uhh, I was goin to say like one of them sex-starved ladies gettin on in years and not too discriminating. Know what I mean?"

I don't answer cause I'll cry. Terrible thing when your own children talk to you like that. Pullin me out the party and hustlin me into some stranger's kitchen in the back of a bar just like the damn police. And ain't like I'm old old. I can still wear me some sleeveless dresses without the meat hangin off my arm. And I keep up with some thangs through my kids. Who ain't kids no more. To hear them tell it. So I don't say nuthin.

"Dancin with that tom°," say Elo to Joe Lee, who leanin on the folks'

---

does heads: fixes hair in a beauty shop.

cuttin her eye at me: throwing me a look that could kill.

tom: an Uncle Tom, slang for a black who, like the stereotyped good old loyal slave in Harriet Beecher Stowe's pre-Civil War novel of plantation life, *Uncle Tom's Cabin,* obligingly submits to mistreatment and white rule.

freezer. "His feet can smell a cracker° a mile away and go into their shuffle number post haste. And them eyes. He could be a little considerate and put on some shades. Who wants to look into them blown-out fuses that — "

"Is this what they call the generation gap?" I say.

"Generation gap," spits Elo, like I suggested castor oil and fricassee   15
possum in the milk-shakes or somethin. "That's a white concept for a white phenomenon. There's no generation gap among Black people. We are a col — "

"Yeh, well never mind," says Joe Lee. "The point is Mama . . . well, it's pride. You embarrass yourself and us too dancin like that."

"I wasn't shame." Then nobody say nuthin. Them standin there in they pretty clothes with drinks in they hands and gangin up on me, and me in the third-degree chair and nary a olive to my name. Felt just like the police got hold to me.

"First of all," Task say, holdin up his hand and tickin off the offenses, "the dress. Now that dress is too short, Mama, and too low-cut for a woman your age. And Tamu's going to make a speech tonight to kick off the campaign and will be introducin you and expecting you to organize the council of elders — "

"Me? Didn nobody ask me nuthin. You mean Nisi? She change her name?"

"Well, Norton was supposed to tell you about it. Nisi wants to introduce   20
you and then encourage the older folks to form a Council of the Elders to act as an advisory — "

"And you going to be standing there with your boobs out and that wig on your head and that hem up to your ass. And people'll say, 'Ain't that the horny bitch that was grindin with the blind dude?' "

"Elo, be cool a minute," say Task, gettin to the next finger. "And then there's the drinkin. Mama, you know you can't drink cause next thing you know you be laughin loud and carryin on," and he grab another finger for the loudness. "And then there's the dancin. You been tattooed on the man for four records straight and slow draggin even on the fast numbers. How you think that look for a woman your age?"

"What's my age?"

"What?"

"I'm axin you all a simple question. You keep talkin bout what's proper   25
for a woman my age. How old am I anyhow?" And Joe Lee slams his eyes shut and squinches up his face to figure. And Task run a hand over his ear and stare into his glass like the ice cubes goin calculate for him. And Elo just starin at the top of my head like she goin rip the wig off any minute now.

"Is your hair braided up under that thing? If so, why don't you take it off? You always did do a neat cornroll°."

"Uh huh," cause I'm thinkin how she couldn't undo her hair fast enough talking bout cornroll so countrified. None of which was the subject. "How old, I say?"

"Sixtee-one or — "

___

cracker: a rural white supremacist.
cornroll: a style of braided hair.

"You a damn lie Joe Lee Peoples."

"And that's another thing," say Task on the fingers.

"You know what you all can kiss," I say, gettin up and brushin the wrinkles out my lap.

"Oh, Mama," Elo say, puttin a hand on my shoulder like she hasn't done since she left home and the hand landin light and not sure it supposed to be there. Which hurt me to my heart. Cause this was the child in our happiness fore Mr. Peoples die. And I carried that child strapped to my chest till she was nearly two. We was close is what I'm tryin to tell you. Cause it was more me in the child than the others. And even after Task it was the girlchild I covered in the night and wept over for no reason at all less it was she was a chub-chub like me and not very pretty, but a warm child. And how did things get to this, that she can't put a sure hand on me and say Mama we love you and care about you and you entitled to enjoy yourself cause you a good woman?

"And then there's Reverend Trent," say Task, glancin from left to right like they hatchin a plot and just now lettin me in on it. "You were suppose to be talking with him tonight, Mama, about giving us his basement for campaign headquarters and — "

"Didn nobody tell me nuthin. If grass roots mean you kept in the dark I can't use it. I really can't. And Reven Trent a fool anyway the way he tore into the widow man up there on Edgecomb cause he wouldn't take in three of them foster children and the woman not even comfy in the ground yet and the man's mind messed up and — "

"Look here," say Task. "What we need is a family conference so we can
get all this stuff cleared up and laid out on the table. In the meantime I think we better get back into the other room and tend to business. And in the meantime, Mama, see if you can't get to Reverend Trent and — "

"You want me to belly rub with the Reven, that it?"

"Oh damn," Elo say and go through the swingin door.

"We'll talk about all this at dinner. How's tomorrow night, Joe Lee?" While Joe Lee being self-important I'm wonderin who's doin the cookin and how come no body ax me if I'm free and do I get a corsage and things like that. Then Joe nod that it's O.K. and he go through the swingin door and just a little hubbub come through from the other room. Then Task smile his smile, lookin just like his daddy, and he leave. And it just me and this stranger's kitchen, which was a mess I wouldn't never let my kitchen look like. Poison you just to look at the pots. Then the door swing the other way and it's My Man Bovanne standin there sayin Miss Hazel but lookin at the deep fry and then at the steam table, and most surprised when I come up on him from the other direction and take him on out of there. Pass the folks pushin up towards the stage where Nisi and some other people settin and ready to talk, and folks gettin to the last of the sandwiches and the booze fore they settle down in one spot and listen serious. And I'm thinkin bout tellin Bovanne what a lovely long dress Nisi got on and the earrings and her hair piled up in a cone and the people bout to hear how we all gettin screwed and gotta form our own party and everybody there listenin and lookin. But instead I just haul the man on out of there, and Joe Lee and his wife look at me like I'm terrible, but they ain't said boo to the man yet. Cause he blind and old and don't nobody there need him since they grown up and don't need they skates fixed no more.

"Where we goin, Miss Hazel?" Him knowin all the time.

"First we gonna buy you some dark sunglasses. Then you comin with me to the supermarket so I can pick up tomorrow's dinner, which is going to be a grand thing proper and you invited. Then we going to my house." 40

"That be fine. I surely would like to rest my feet." Bein cute, but you got to let men play out they little show, blind or not. So he chat on bout how tired he is and how he appreciate me takin him in hand this way. And I'm thinkin I'll have him change the lock on my door first thing. Then I'll give the man a nice warm bath with jasmine leaves in the water and a little Epsom salt on the sponge to do his back. And then a good rubdown with rose water and olive oil. Then a cup of lemon tea with a taste in it. And a little talcum, some of that fancy stuff Nisi mother sent over last Christmas. And then a massage, a good face massage round the forehead which is the worrying part. Cause you gots to take care of the older folks. And let them know they still needed to run the mimeo machine° and keep the spark plugs clean and fix the mailboxes for folks who might help us get the breakfast program goin, and the school for the little kids and the campaign and all. Cause old folks in the nation. That what Nisi was sayin and I mean to do my part.

"I imagine you are a very pretty woman, Miss Hazel."

"I surely am," I say just like the hussy my daughter always say I was.

Ursula K. LeGuin
THE WIFE'S STORY   1982

Ursula K. LeGuin was born in 1929 in Berkeley, California, the daughter of Theodora Kroeber, a folklorist, and Alfred L. Kroeber, an anthropologist. After graduation from Radcliffe, she took an M.A. degree at Columbia. LeGuin, who launched her successful career as a writer while rearing three children and holding a job, first won a devoted following for her stories in science fiction magazines. Roncannon's World *(1966) was her first book; another early novel,* The Left Hand of Darkness *(1969), has been called a classic in its field. Like the novels of Kurt Vonnegut, Jr., LeGuin's work has appealed beyond science fiction fandom to a wider audience. (LeGuin remarks that she did not at first regard herself as a science fiction writer; it was only when she began reading that genre herself that she realized the label would apply.) Bringing a feminine sensibility to science fiction, she has employed science fiction to criticize her own civilization. Many of her stories create whole new cultures and civilizations, with some anthropological authority. Besides, she has written poetry and juvenile fiction, including the trilogy of Earthsea novels beginning with* Wizard of Earthsea *(1968), given a Globe-Hornbook children's book award. She lives in Portland, Oregon. "The Wife's Tale" was originally written for an anthology entitled* Changes.

---

mimeo machine: Mimeograph stencil duplicator, an inexpensive means to turn out propaganda.

He was a good husband, a good father. I don't understand it. I don't believe in it. I don't believe that it happened. I saw it happen but it isn't true. It can't be. He was always gentle. If you'd have seen him playing with the children, anybody who saw him with the children would have known that there wasn't any bad in him, not one mean bone. When I first met him he was still living with his mother, over near Spring Lake, and I used to see them together, the mother and the sons, and think that any young fellow that was that nice with his family must be one worth knowing. Then one time when I was walking in the woods I met him by himself coming back from a hunting trip. He hadn't got any game at all, not so much as a field mouse, but he wasn't cast down about it. He was just larking along enjoying the morning air. That's one of the things I first loved about him. He didn't take things hard, he didn't grouch and whine when things didn't go his way. So we got to talking that day. And I guess things moved right along after that, because pretty soon he was over here pretty near all the time. And my sister said — see, my parents had moved out the year before and gone south, leaving us the place — my sister said, kind of teasing but serious, "Well! If he's going to be here every day and half the night, I guess there isn't room for me!" And she moved out — just down the way. We've always been real close, her and me. That's the sort of thing doesn't ever change. I couldn't ever have got through this bad time without my sis.

Well, so he come to live here. And all I can say is, it was the happy year of my life. He was just purely good to me. A hard worker and never lazy, and so big and fine-looking. Everybody looked up to him, you know, young as he was. Lodge Meeting nights, more and more often they had him to lead the singing. He had such a beautiful voice, and he'd lead off strong, and the others following and joining in, high voices and low. It brings the shivers on me now to think of it, hearing it, nights when I'd stayed home from meeting when the children was babies — the singing coming up through the trees there, and the moonlight, summer nights, the full moon shining. I'll never hear anything so beautiful. I'll never know a joy like that again.

It was the moon, that's what they say. It's the moon's fault, and the blood. It was in his father's blood. I never knew his father, and now I wonder what become of him. He was from up Whitewater way, and had no kin around here. I always thought he went back there, but now I don't know. There was some talk about him, tales, that come out after what happened to my husband. It's something runs in the blood, they say, and it may never come out, but if it does, it's the change of the moon that does it. Always it happens in the dark of the moon. When everybody's home and asleep. Something comes over the one that's got the curse in his blood, they say, and he gets up because he can't sleep, and goes out into the glaring sun, and goes off all alone — drawn to find those like him.

And it may be so, because my husband would do that. I'd half rouse and say, "Where you going to?" and he'd say, "Oh, hunting, be back this evening," and it wasn't like him, even his voice was different. But I'd be so sleepy, and not wanting to wake the kids, and he was so good and responsible, it was no call of mine to go asking "Why?" and "Where?" and all like that.

So it happened that way maybe three times or four. He'd come back late, and worn out, and pretty near cross for one so sweet-tempered — not wanting to talk about it. I figured everybody got to bust out now and then, and nagging never helped anything. But it did begin to worry me. Not so much that he went, but that he come back so tired and strange. Even, he smelled strange. It made my hair stand up on end. I could not endure it and I said, "What is that — those smells on you? All over you!" And he said, "I don't know," real short, and made like he was sleeping. But he went down when he thought I wasn't noticing, and washed and washed himself. But those smells stayed in his hair, and in our bed, for days.

And then the awful thing. I don't find it easy to tell about this. I want to cry when I have to bring it to my mind. Our youngest, the little one, my baby, she turned from her father. Just overnight. He come in and she got scared-looking, stiff, with her eyes wide, and then she begun to cry and try to hide behind me. She didn't yet talk plain but she was saying over and over, "Make it go away! Make it go away!"

The look in his eyes, just for one moment, when he heard that. That's what I don't want ever to remember. That's what I can't forget. The look in his eyes looking at his own child.

I said to the child, "Shame on you, what's got into you!" — scolding, but keeping her right up close to me at the same time, because I was frightened too. Frightened to shaking.

He looked away then and said something like, "Guess she just waked up dreaming," and passed it off that way. Or tried to. And so did I. And I got real mad with my baby when she kept on acting crazy scared of her own dad. But she couldn't help it and I couldn't change it.

He kept away that whole day. Because he knew, I guess. It was just   10 beginning dark of the moon.

It was hot and close inside, and dark, and we'd all been asleep some while, when something woke me up. He wasn't there beside me. I heard a little stir in the passage, when I listened. So I got up, because I could bear it no longer. I went out into the passage, and it was light there, hard sunlight coming in from the door. And I saw him standing just outside, in the tall grass by the entrance. His head was hanging. Presently he sat down, like he felt weary, and looked down at his feet. I held still, inside, and watched — I didn't know what for.

And I saw what he saw. I saw the changing. In his feet, it was, first. They got long, each foot got longer, stretching out, the toes stretching out and the foot getting long, and fleshy, and white. And no hair on them.

The hair begun to come away all over his body. It was like his hair fried away in the sunlight and was gone. He was white all over then, like a worm's skin. And he turned his face. It was changing while I looked. It got flatter and flatter, the mouth flat and wide, and the teeth grinning flat and dull, and the nose just a knob of flesh with nostril holes, and the ears gone, and the eyes gone blue — blue, with white rims around the blue — staring at me out of that flat, soft, white face.

He stood up then on two legs.

I saw him, I had to see him, my own dear love, turned into the hateful   15 one.

I couldn't move, but as I crouched there in the passage staring out into the day I was trembling and shaking with a growl that burst out into a crazy, awful howling. A grief howl and a terror howl and a calling howl. And the others heard it, even sleeping, and woke up.

It stared and peered, that thing my husband had turned into, and shoved its face up to the entrance of our house. I was still bound by mortal fear, but behind me the children had waked up, and the baby was whimpering. The mother anger come into me then, and I snarled and crept forward.

The man thing looked around. It had no gun, like the ones from the man places do. But it picked up a heavy fallen tree branch in its long white foot, and shoved the end of that down into our house, at me. I snapped the end of it in my teeth and started to force my way out, because I knew the man would kill our children if it could. But my sister was already coming. I saw her running at the man with her head low and her mane high and her eyes yellow as the winter sun. It turned on her and raised up that branch to hit her. But I come out of the doorway, mad with the mother anger, and the others all were coming answering my call, the whole pack gathering, there in that blind glare and heat of the sun at noon.

The man looked round at us and yelled out loud, and brandished the branch it held. Then it broke and ran, heading for the cleared fields and plowlands, down the mountainside. It ran, on two legs, leaping and weaving, and we followed it.

I was last, because love still bound the anger and the fear in me. I was running when I saw them pull it down. My sister's teeth were in its throat. I got there and it was dead. The others were drawing back from the kill, because of the taste of the blood, and the smell. The younger ones were cowering and some crying, and my sister rubbed her mouth against her forelegs over and over to get rid of the taste. I went up close because I thought if the thing was dead the spell, the curse must be done, and my husband could come back — alive, or even dead, if I could only see him, my true love, in his true form, beautiful. But only the dead man lay there white and bloody. We drew back and back from it, and turned and ran, back up into the hills, back to the woods of the shadows and the twilight and the blessed dark.

20

12 Criticism: On Fiction

The critical power is of lower rank than the creative. True, but in assenting to this proposition, one or two things are to be kept in mind. It is undeniable that the exercise of a creative power, that of a free creative activity, is the true function of man; it is proved to be so by man's finding in it his true happiness. But it is undeniable, also, that men may have the sense of exercising this free creative activity in other ways than in producing great works of literature or art; if it were not so, all but a very few men would be shut out from the true happiness of all men; they may have it in well-doing, they may have it in learning, they may have it even in criticizing.
— Matthew Arnold, "The Function of Criticism"

Edgar Allan Poe (1809 – 1849)
THE TALE AND ITS EFFECT   1842

Were we called upon, however, to designate that class of composition which, next to [a short lyric poem], should best fulfill the demands of high genius — should offer it the most advantageous field of exertion — we should unhesitatingly speak of the prose tale, as Mr. Hawthorne has here exemplified it. We allude to the short prose narrative, requiring from a half-hour to one or two hours in its perusal. The ordinary novel is objectionable, from its length, for reasons already stated in substance. As it cannot be read at one sitting, it deprives itself, of course, of the immense force derivable from *totality*. Worldly interests intervening during the pauses of perusal, modify, annul, or counteract, in a greater or less degree, the impressions of the book. But simple cessation in reading would, of itself, be sufficient to destroy the true unity. In the brief tale, however, the author is enabled to carry out the fullness of his intention, be it what it may. During the hour of perusal the soul of the reader is at the writer's control. There are no external or extrinsic influences — resulting from weariness or interruption.

A skillful literary artist has constructed a tale. If wise, he has not fashioned his thoughts to accommodate his incidents; but having conceived, with deliberate care, a certain unique or single *effect* to be wrought out, he then invents such incidents — he then combines such events as may best aid him in establishing this preconceived effect. If his very initial sentence tend not to the outbringing of this effect, then he has failed in his first step. In the whole composition there should be no word written, of which the tendency, direct or indirect, is not to the one pre-established design. And by such means, with such care and skill, a picture is at length painted which leaves in the mind of him who contemplates it with a kindred art, a sense of the fullest satisfaction. The idea of the tale has been presented unblemished, because undisturbed; and this is an end unattainable by the novel. Undue brevity is just as exceptionable here as in the poem; but undue length is yet more to be avoided.

— *Twice-Told Tales,* by Nathaniel Hawthorne: A Review

Charlotte Brontë (1816 – 1855)
THE WRITER'S PASSIVE WORK   1850

Whether it is right or advisable to create beings like Heathcliff°, I do not know: I scarcely think it is. But this I know: the writer who possesses the creative gift owns something of which he is not always master — something that, at times, strangely wills and works for itself. He may lay down rules and devise principles, and to rules and principles it will perhaps for years lie in subjection; and then, haply without any warning of revolt, there comes a time when it will no longer consent to "harrow the valleys, or be bound with a band

THE WRITER'S PASSIVE WORK. *Heathcliff:* Central character of the novel *Wuthering Heights:* "a man's shape animated by demon life" (in Charlotte Brontë's view).

in the furrow" — when it "laughs at the multitude of the city, and regards not the crying of the driver" — when, refusing absolutely to make ropes out of sea-sand any longer, it sets to work on statue-hewing, and you have a Pluto or Jove, a Tisiphone or a Psyche, a Mermaid or a Madonna, as Fate or Inspiration direct. Be the work grim or glorious, dread or divine, you have little choice left but quiescent adoption. As for you — the nominal artist — your share in it has been to work passively under dictates you neither delivered nor could question — that would not be uttered at your prayer, nor suppressed nor changed at your caprice. If the result be attractive, the World will praise you, who little deserve praise; if it be repulsive, the same World will blame you, who almost as little deserve blame.

— Preface to the Second Edition of *Wuthering Heights* (by Emily Brontë)

Gustave Flaubert (1821 – 1880)

THE LABOR OF STYLE   1854

Translated by Francis Steegmuller

I have just made a fresh copy of what I have written since New Year, or rather since the middle of February, for on my return from Paris I burned all my January work. It amounts to thirteen pages, no more, no less, thirteen pages in seven weeks. However, they are in shape, I think, and as perfect as I can make them. There are only two or three repetitions of the same word which must be removed, and two turns of phrase that are still too much alike. At last something is completed. It was a difficult transition: the reader had to be led gradually and imperceptibly from psychology to action. Now I am about to begin the dramatic, eventful part. Two or three more big pushes and the end will be in sight. By July or August I hope to tackle the denouement. What a struggle it has been! My God, what a struggle! Such drudgery! Such discouragement! I spent all last evening frantically poring over surgical texts. I am studying the theory of clubfeet. In three hours I devoured an entire volume on this interesting subject and took notes. I came upon some really fine sentences. "The maternal breast is an impenetrable and mysterious sanctuary, where . . . etc." An excellent treatise, incidentally. Why am I not young? How I should work! One ought to know everything, to write. All of us scribblers are monstrously ignorant. If only we weren't so lacking in stamina, what a rich field of ideas and similes we could tap! Books that have been the source of entire literatures, like Homer and Rabelais, contain the sum of all the knowledge of their times. They knew everything, those fellows, and we know nothing. Ronsard's poetics contain a curious precept: he advises the poet to become well versed in the arts and crafts — to frequent blacksmiths, goldsmiths, locksmiths, etc. — in order to enrich his stock of metaphors. And indeed that is the sort of thing that makes for rich and varied language. The sentences in a book must quiver like the leaves in a forest, all dissimilar in their similarity.

— Letter to Louise Colet, April 7, 1854,
during the writing of *Madame Bovary*

Nathaniel Hawthorne (1804 – 1864)

AMERICA AND THE LANDSCAPE OF ROMANCE   1860

The author proposes to himself merely to write a fanciful story, evolving a thoughtful moral, and did not purpose attempting a portraiture of Italian manners and character. . . . Italy, as the site of his Romance, was chiefly valuable to him as affording a sort of poetic or fairy precinct, where actualities would not be so terribly insisted upon as they are, and must needs be, in America. No author, without a trial, can conceive of the difficulty of writing a romance about a country where there is no shadow, no antiquity, no mystery, no picturesque and gloomy wrong, nor anything but a commonplace prosperity, in broad and simple daylight, as is happily the case with my dear native land. It will be very long, I trust, before romance-writers may find congenial and easily handled themes, either in the annals of our stalwart republic, or in any characteristic and probable events of our individual lives. Romance and poetry, like ivy, lichens, and wall-flowers, need ruin to make them grow.

— Preface to *The Marble Faun*

Thomas Hardy (1840 – 1928)

"THE WHOLE SECRET OF A LIVING STYLE"   1874

The whole secret of a living style and the difference between it and a dead style, lies in not having too much style — being, in fact, a little careless, or rather seeming to be, here and there. It brings wonderful life into the writing. . . .

Otherwise your style is like worn half-pence — all the fresh images rounded off by rubbing, and no crispness or movement at all.

It is, of course, simply a carrying into prose the knowledge I have acquired in poetry — that inexact rhymes and rhythms now and then are far more pleasing than correct ones.

— Note to himself, quoted by Florence Emily Hardy,
The Early Life of Thomas Hardy (London: Macmillan, 1928)

Henry James (1843 – 1916)

THE MIRROR OF A CONSCIOUSNESS   1908

This in fact I have ever found rather terribly the point — that the figures in any picture, the agents in any drama, are interesting only in proportion as they feel their respective situations; since the consciousness, on their part, of the complication exhibited forms for us their link of connection with it. But there are degrees of feeling — the muffled, the faint, the just sufficient, the barely intelligent, as we may say; and the acute, the intense, the complete, in a word — the power to be finely aware and richly responsible. It is those moved in this latter fashion who "get most" out of all that happens to them and who in so doing enable us, as readers of their record, as participators by a fond attention, also to get most. Their being finely aware — as Hamlet and Lear, say, are finely aware — *makes* absolutely the intensity of their adventure, gives the maximum of sense to what befalls them. We care, our curiosity and our sympathy care, comparatively little for what happens to the stupid, the coarse and the blind; care for it, and for the effects of it, at the most as helping to precipitate what happens to the more deeply wondering, to the really sentient. Hamlet and Lear are surrounded, amid their complications, by the stupid and the blind, who minister in all sorts of ways to their recorded fate. . . .

Verily even, I think, no "story" is possible without its fools — as most of the fine painters of life, Shakespeare, Cervantes and Balzac, Fielding, Scott, Thackeray, Dickens, George Meredith, George Eliot, Jane Austen, have abundantly felt. At the same time I confess I never see the *leading* interest of any human hazard but in a consciousness (on the part of the moved and moving creature) subject to fine intensification and wide enlargement. It is as mirrored in that consciousness that the gross fools, the headlong fools, the fatal fools play their part for us — they have much less to show us in themselves. The troubled life mostly at the center of our subject — whatever our subject, for the artistic hour, happens to be — embraces them and deals with them for its amusement and its anguish: they are apt largely indeed, on a near view, to be all the cause of its trouble. This means, exactly, that the person capable of feeling in the given case more than another of what is to be felt for it, and so serving in the highest degree to *record* it dramatically and objectively, is the only sort of person on whom we can count not to betray, to cheapen or, as we say, give away, the value and beauty of the thing. By so much as the affair matters *for* some such individual, by so much do we get the best there is of it, and by so much as it falls within the scope of a denser and duller, a more vulgar and more shallow capacity, do we get a picture dim and meager.

The great chroniclers have clearly always been aware of this; they have at least always either placed a mind of some sort — in the sense of a reflecting and coloring medium — in possession of the general adventure . . . or else paid signally, as to the interest created for their failure to do so.

— Preface to *The Princess Casamassima*

James Joyce (1882 – 1941)

Epiphanies   1904 – 1906

He° was passing through Eccles Street one evening, one misty evening, with all these thoughts dancing the dance of unrest in his brain when a trivial incident set him composing some ardent verses which he entitled a 'Villanelle of the Temptress.' A young lady was standing on the steps of one of those brown brick houses which seem the very incarnation of Irish paralysis. A young gentleman was leaning on the rusty railings of the area. Stephen as he

Epiphanies. *He:* Stephen Dedalus, protagonist of Joyce's novel (an early version of *Portrait of the Artist as a Young Man*), a young Dublin intellectual resembling Joyce himself.

passed on his quest heard the following fragment of colloquy out of which he received an impression keen enough to afflict his sensitiveness very severely.

THE YOUNG LADY — (drawling discreetly) . . . O, yes . . . I was . . . at the . . . cha . . . pel. . . .

THE YOUNG GENTLEMAN — (inaudibly) . . . I . . . (again inaudibly) . . . I . . .

THE YOUNG LADY — (softly) . . . O . . . but you're . . . ve . . . ry . . . wick . . . ed. . . .

This triviality made him think of collecting many such moments together in a book of epiphanies. By an epiphany he meant a sudden spiritual manifestation, whether in the vulgarity of speech or of gesture or in a memorable phase of the mind itself. He believed that it was for the man of letters to record these epiphanies with extreme care, seeing that they themselves are the most delicate and evanescent of moments. He told Cranly° that the clock of the Ballast Office was capable of an epiphany. Cranly questioned the inscrutable dial of the Ballast Office with his no less inscrutable countenance.

— Yes, said Stephen. I will pass it time after time, allude to it, refer to it, catch a glimpse of it. It is only an item in the catalogue of Dublin's street furniture. Then all at once I see it and I know at once what it is: epiphany . . .

— Stephen Hero

Virginia Woolf (1882 – 1941)
"A LUMINOUS HALO"   1919

Examine for a moment an ordinary mind on an ordinary day. The mind receives a myriad impressions — trivial, fantastic, evanescent, or engraved with the sharpness of steel. From all sides they come, an incessant shower of innumerable atoms; and as they fall, as they shape themselves into the life of Monday or Tuesday, the accent falls differently from of old; the moment of importance came not here but there; so that if a writer were a free man and not a slave, if he could write what he chose, not what he must, if he could base his work upon his own feeling and not upon convention, there would be no plot, no comedy, no tragedy, no love interest or catastrophe in the accepted style, and perhaps not a single button sewn on as the Bond Street tailors would have it. Life is not a series of gig lamps symmetrically arranged; but a luminous halo, a semi-transparent envelope surrounding us from the beginning of consciousness to the end. Is it not the task of the novelist to convey this varying, this unknown and uncircumscribed spirit, whatever aberration or complexity it may display, with as little mixture of the alien and external as possible? We are not pleading merely for courage and sincerity; we are suggesting that the proper stuff of fiction is a little other than custom would have us believe it.

It is, at any rate, in some such fashion as this that we seek to define the quality which distinguishes the work of several young writers, among whom Mr. James Joyce is the most notable, from that of their predecessors. They

Cranly: a fellow student.

attempt to come closer to life, and to preserve more sincerely and exactly what interests and moves them, even if to do so they must discard most of the conventions which are commonly observed by the novelist. Let us record the atoms as they fall upon the mind in the order in which they fall, let us trace the pattern, however disconnected and incoherent in appearance, which each sight or incident scores upon the consciousness. Let us not take it for granted that life exists more fully in what is commonly thought big than in what is commonly thought small.

— Modern Fiction, *The Common Reader*

Edith Wharton (1862 – 1937)
THE SHORT STORY AND THE NOVEL   1925

A curious distinction between the successful tale and the successful novel at once presents itself. It is safe to say (since the surest way of measuring achievement in art is by survival) that the test of the novel is that its people should be *alive.* No subject in itself, however fruitful, appears to be able to keep a novel alive; only the characters in it can. Of the short story the same cannot be said. Some of the greatest short stories owe their vitality entirely to the dramatic rendering of a situation. Undoubtedly the characters engaged must be a little more than puppets; but apparently, also, they may be a little less than individual human beings. In this respect the short story, rather than the novel, might be called the direct descendant of the old epic or ballad — of those earlier forms of fiction in all of which action was the chief affair, and the characters, if they did not remain mere puppets, seldom or never became more than types — such as the people, for instance, in Molière. The reason for the difference is obvious. Type, general character, may be set forth in a few strokes, but the progression, the unfolding of personality, of which the reader instinctively feels the need if the actors in the tale are to retain their individuality for him through a succession of changing circumstances — this slow but continuous growth requires space, and therefore belongs by definition to a larger, a symphonic plan.

The chief technical difference between the short story and the novel may therefore be summed up by saying that situation is the main concern of the short story, character of the novel; and it follows that the effect produced by the short story depends almost entirely on its form, or presentation. Even more — yes, and much more — than in the construction of the novel, the impression of vividness, of *presentness,* in the affair narrated, has to be sought, and made sure of beforehand, by that careful artifice which is the real carelessness of art. The short-story writer must not only know from what angle to present his anecdote if it is to give out all its fires, but must understand just *why* that particular angle and no other is the right one. He must therefore have turned his subject over and over, walked around it, so to speak, and applied to it those laws of perspective which Paolo Uccello called "so beautiful," before it can be offered to the reader as a natural unembellished fragment of experience, detached like a ripe fruit from the tree.

— *The Writing of Fiction*

William Faulkner (1897 – 1962)
"THE HUMAN HEART IN CONFLICT WITH ITSELF" 1950

Our tragedy today is a general and universal physical fear so long sustained by now that we can even bear it. There are no longer problems of the spirit. There is only the question: When will I be blown up? Because of this, the young man or woman writing today has forgotten the problems of the human heart in conflict with itself which alone can make good writing because only that is worth writing about, worth the agony and the sweat.

He must learn them again. He must teach himself that the basest of all things is to be afraid; and, teaching himself that, forget it forever, leaving no room in his workshop for anything but the old verities and truths of the heart, the old universal truths lacking which any story is ephemeral and doomed — love and honor and pity and pride and compassion and sacrifice. Until he does so, he labors under a curse. He writes not of love but of lust, of defeats in which nobody loses anything of value, of victories without hope and, worst of all, without pity or compassion. His griefs grieve on no universal bones, leaving no scars. He writes not of the heart but of the glands.

Until he relearns these things, he will write as though he stood among and watched the end of man. I decline to accept the end of man. It is easy enough to say that man is immortal simply because he will endure; that when the last ding-dong of doom has clanged and faded from the last worthless rock hanging tideless in the last red and dying evening, that even then there will still be one more sound: that of his puny inexhaustible voice, still talking. I refuse to accept this. I believe that man will not merely endure: he will prevail. He is immortal, not because he alone among creatures has an inexhaustible voice, but because he has a soul, a spirit capable of compassion and sacrifice and endurance. The poet's, the writer's, duty is to write about these things. It is his privilege to help man endure by lifting his heart, by reminding him of the courage and honor and hope and pride and compassion and pity and sacrifice which have been the glory of his past. The poet's voice need not merely be the record of man, it can be one of the props, the pillars to help him endure and prevail.

— Speech of Acceptance for the award
of the Nobel Prize for Literature

Frank O'Connor (1903 – 1966)
THE GREATEST ESSENTIAL OF A STORY 1957

INTERVIEWER: What is the greatest essential of a story?

O'CONNOR: You have to have a theme, a story to tell. Here's a man at the other side of the table and I'm talking to him; I'm going to tell him something that will interest him. As you know perfectly well, our principal difficulty at Harvard was a number of people who'd had affairs with girls or had had another interesting experience, and wanted to come in and tell about it, straight away. That is not a theme. A theme is something that is worth something to everybody. In fact, you wouldn't, if you'd ever been involved in a thing like this, grab a man in a pub and say, "Look, I had a girl out last night, under the Charles Bridge." That's the last thing you'd do. You grab somebody and say, "Look, an extraordinary thing happened to me yesterday — I met a man — he said this to me — " and that, to me, is a theme. The moment you grab somebody by the lapels and you've got something to tell, that's a real story. It means you want to tell him and think the story is interesting in itself. If you start describing your own personal experiences, something that's only of interest to yourself, then you can't express yourself, you cannot say, ultimately, what you think about human beings. The moment you say this, you're committed.

I'll tell you what I mean. We were down on the south coast of Ireland for a holiday and we got talkin' to this old farmer and he said his son, who was dead now, had gone to America. He'd married an American girl and she had come over for a visit, alone. Apparently her doctor had told her a trip to Ireland would do her good. And she stayed with the parents, had gone around to see his friends and other relations, and it wasn't till after she'd gone that they learned that the boy had died. Why didn't she tell them? There's your story. Dragging the reader in, making the reader a part of the story . . .

— *Writers at Work: The Paris Review Interviews*

Stanley Fish (b. 1938)

An eskimo "a rose for emily" 1980

The fact that it remains easy to think of a reading that most of us would dismiss out of hand does not mean that the text excludes it but that there is as yet no elaborated interpretive procedure for producing that text. . . . Norman Holland's analysis of Faulkner's "A Rose for Emily" is a case in point. Holland is arguing for a kind of psychoanalytic pluralism. The text, he declares, is "at most a matrix of psychological possibilities for its readers," but, he insists, "only some possibilities . . . truly fit the matrix": "One would not say, for example, that a reader of . . . 'A Rose for Emily' who thought the 'tableau' [of Emily and her father in the doorway] described an Eskimo was really responding to the story at all — only pursuing some mysterious inner exploration."

Holland is making two arguments: first, that anyone who proposes an Eskimo reading of "A Rose for Emily" will not find a hearing in the literary community. And that, I think, is right. ("We are right to rule out at least some readings.") His second argument is that the unacceptability of the Eskimo reading is a function of the text, of what he calls its "sharable promptuary" (p. 287), the public "store of structured language" (p. 287) that sets limits to the interpretations the words can accommodate. And that, I think, is wrong. The Eskimo reading is unacceptable because there is at present no interpretive strategy for producing it, no way of "looking" or reading (and remember, all acts of looking or reading are "ways") that would result in the emergence of obviously Eskimo meanings. This does not mean, however, that no such strategy could ever come into play, and it is not difficult to imagine the circumstances under which it would establish itself. One such circumstance would be the discovery of a letter in which Faulkner confides that he has always believed himself to be an Eskimo changeling. (The example is absurd only if one forgets Yeats's *Vision* or Blake's Swedenborgianism or James Miller's recent elaboration of a homosexual reading of *The Waste Land*). Immediately the workers in the Faulkner industry would begin to reinterpret the canon in the light of this newly revealed "belief" and the work of reinterpretation would involve the elaboration of a symbolic or allusive system (not unlike mythological or typological criticism) whose application would immediately transform the text into one informed everywhere by Eskimo meanings. It might seem that I am admitting that there is a text to be transformed, but the object of transformation would be the text (or texts) given by whatever interpretive strategies the Eskimo strategy was in the process of dislodging or expanding. The result would be that whereas we now have a Freudian "A Rose for Emily," a mythological "A Rose for Emily," a Christological "A Rose for Emily," a regional "A Rose for Emily," a sociological "A Rose for Emily," a linguistic "A Rose for Emily," we would in addition have an Eskimo "A Rose for Emily," existing in some relation of compatibility or incompatibility with the others.

Again the point is that while there are always mechanisms for ruling out readings, their source is not the text but the presently recognized interpretive strategies for producing the text. It follows, then, that no reading, however outlandish it might appear, is inherently an impossible one.

— *Is There a Text in This Class?*

POETRY

To the Muse

Give me leave, Muse, in plain view to array
Your shift and bodice by the light of day.
I would have brought an epic. Be not vexed
Instead to grace a niggling schoolroom text;
Let down your sanction, help me to oblige
Him who would lead fresh devots to your liege,
And at your altar, grant that in a flash
They, he and I know incense from dead ash.
— X.J.K.

What is poetry? Pressed for an answer, Robert Frost made a classic reply: "Poetry is the kind of thing poets write." In all likelihood, Frost was not trying merely to evade the question but to chide his questioner into thinking for himself. A trouble with definitions is that they may stop thought. If Frost had said, "Poetry is a rhythmical composition of words expressing an attitude, designed to surprise and delight, and to arouse an emotional response," the questioner might have settled back in his chair, content to have learned the truth about poetry. He would have learned nothing, or not so much as he might learn by continuing to wonder.

The nature of poetry eludes simple definitions. (In this respect it is rather like jazz. Asked after one of his concerts, "What is jazz?" Louis Armstrong replied, "Man, if you gotta ask, you'll never know.") Definitions will be of little help at first, if we are to know poetry and respond to it. We have to go to it willing to see and hear. For this reason, you are asked in reading this book not to be in any hurry to decide what poetry is, but instead to study poems and to let them grow in your mind. At the end of our discussions of poetry, the problem of definition will be taken up again (for those who may wish to pursue it).

Confronted with a formal introduction to poetry, you may be wondering, "Who needs it?" and you may well be right. You hardly can have avoided meeting poetry before; and perhaps you already have a friendship, or at least a fair acquaintance, with some of the great English-speaking poets of all time. What this book provides is an introduction to the *study* of poetry. It tries to help you look at a poem closely, to offer you a wider and more accurate vocabulary with which to express what poems say to you. It will suggest ways to judge for yourself the poems you read. It may set forth some poems new to you.

A frequent objection is that poetry ought not to be studied at all. In this view, a poem is either a series of gorgeous noises to be funneled through one ear and out the other without being allowed to trouble the mind, or an experience so holy that to analyze it in a classroom is as cruel and mechanical as dissecting a hummingbird. To the first view, it might be countered that a good poem has something to say that is well worth listening to. To the second view, it might be argued that poems are much less perishable than hummingbirds, and luckily, we can study them in flight. The risk of a poem's dying from observation is not nearly so great as the risk of not really seeing it at all. It is doubtful that any excellent poem has ever vanished from human memory because people have read it too closely. More likely, poems that vanish are poems that no one reads closely, for no one cares.

Good poetry is something to care about. In fact, an ancient persuasion of mankind is that the hearing of a poem, as well as the making of a poem, can be a religious act. Poetry, in speech and song, was part of classic Greek drama, which for playwright, actor, and spectator alike was a holy-day ceremony. The Greeks' belief that a poet writes a poem only by supernatural assistance is clear from the invocations to the Muse that begin the *Iliad* and the *Odyssey* and from the opinion of Socrates (in Plato's *Ion*) that a poet has no powers of invention until divinely inspired. Among the ancient Celts, poets were regarded as magicians and priests, and whoever insulted one of them might expect to receive a curse in rime potent enough to afflict him with boils and to curdle the milk of his cows. Such identifications between the poet and the magician are less common these days, although we know that poetry is involved in the primitive white-magic of children, who bring themselves good luck in a game with the charm "Roll, roll, Tootsie-roll! / Roll the marble in the hole!" and who warn against a hex while jumping along a sidewalk: "Step on a crack, / Break your mother's back." But in this age when we pride ourselves that a computer may solve the riddle of all creation as soon as it is programmed, magic seems to some people of small importance and so too does poetry. It is dangerous, however, to dismiss what we do not logically understand. To read a poem at all, we have to be willing to offer it responses *besides* a logical understanding. Whether we attribute the effect of a poem to a divine spirit or to the reactions of our glands and cortexes, we have to take the reading of poetry seriously (not solemnly), if only because — as some of the poems in this book may demonstrate — few other efforts can repay us so generously, both in wisdom and in joy.

If, as I hope you will do, you sometimes browse in the book for fun, you may be annoyed to see so many questions following the poems. Should you feel this way, try reading with a slip of paper to cover up the questions. You will then — if the Muse should inspire you — have paper in hand to write a poem.

13 Reading a Poem

How do you read a poem? The literal-minded might say, "Just let your eye light on it"; but there is more to poetry than meets the eye. What Shakespeare called "the mind's eye" also plays a part. Many a reader who has no trouble understanding and enjoying prose finds poetry difficult. This is to be expected. At first glance, a poem usually will make some sense and give some pleasure, but it may not yield everything at once. Sometimes it only hints at meaning still to come if we will keep after it. Poetry is not to be galloped over like the daily news: a poem differs from most prose in that it is to be read slowly, carefully, and attentively. Not all poems are difficult, of course, and some can be understood and enjoyed on first seeing. But good poems yield more if read twice; and the best poems — after ten, twenty, or a hundred readings — still go on yielding.

Approaching a thing written in lines and surrounded with white space, we need not expect it to be a poem just because it is **verse**. (Any composition in lines of more or less regular rhythm, usually ending in rimes, is verse.) Here, for instance, is a specimen of verse that few will call poetry:

> Thirty days hath September,
> April, June, and November;
> All the rest have thirty-one
> Excepting February alone,
> To which we twenty-eight assign
> Till leap year makes it twenty-nine.

To a higher degree than that classic memory-tickler, poetry appeals to the mind and arouses feelings. Poetry may state facts, but, more important, it makes imaginative statements that we may value even if its facts are incorrect. Coleridge's error in placing a star within the horns of the crescent moon in "The Rime of the Ancient Mariner" does not stop the passage from being good poetry, though it is faulty astronomy. According to one poet, Gerard Manley Hopkins, poetry is "to be heard for its own sake and interest even over and above its interest of meaning." There are other elements in a poem besides plain prose sense: sounds, images, rhythms, figures of speech. These may strike us and please us even before we ask, "But what does it all mean?"

This is a truth not readily grasped by anyone who regards a poem as a kind of puzzle written in secret code with a message slyly concealed. The effect of a poem (one's whole mental and emotional response to it) consists in much more than simply a message. By its musical qualities, by its suggestions, it can work on the reader's unconscious. T. S. Eliot put it well when he said in *The Use of Poetry and the Use of Criticism* that the prose sense of a poem is chiefly useful in keeping the reader's mind "diverted and quiet, while the poem does its work upon him." Eliot went on to liken the meaning of a poem to the bit of meat a burglar brings along to throw to the family dog. What is the work of a poem? To touch us, to stir us, to make us glad, and possibly even to tell us something.

How to set about reading a poem? Here are a few suggestions.

To begin with, read the poem once straight through, with no particular expectations; read open-mindedly. Let yourself experience whatever you find, without worrying just yet about the large general and important ideas the poem contains (if indeed it contains any). Don't dwell on a troublesome word or difficult passage — just push on. Some of the difficulties may seem smaller when you read the poem for a second time; at least, they will have become parts of a whole for you.

On second reading, read for the exact sense of all the words; if there are words you don't understand, look them up in a dictionary. Dwell on any difficult parts as long as you need to.

If you read the poem silently to yourself, sound its words in your mind. (This is a technique that will get you nowhere in a speed-reading course, but it may help the poem to do its work on you.) Better still, read the poem aloud, or hear someone else read it. You may discover meanings you didn't perceive in it before. Even if you are no actor, to decide how to speak a poem can be an excellent method of getting to understand it. Some poems, like bells, seem heavy till heard. Listen while reading the following lines from Alexander Pope's *Dunciad.* Attacking the minor poet James Ralph, who had sung the praises of a mistress named Cynthia, Pope makes the goddess of Dullness exclaim:

"Silence, ye wolves! while Ralph to Cynthia howls,
And makes night hideous — answer him, ye owls!"

When *ye owls* slide together and become *yowls,* poor Ralph's serenade is turned into the nightly outcry of a cat.

Try to **paraphrase** the poem as a whole, or perhaps just the more difficult lines. In paraphrasing, we put into our own words what we understand the poem to say, restating ideas that seem essential, coming out and stating what the poem may only suggest. This may sound like a heartless thing to do to a poem, but good poems can stand it. In fact, to compare a poem to its paraphrase is a good way to see the distance between poetry and prose. In making a paraphrase, we generally work through a poem or a passage line by line. The statement that results may take as many words as the original, if not more. A paraphrase, then, is ampler than a **summary**, a brief condensation of gist, main idea, or story. (Summary of a horror film in *TV Guide:* "Demented biologist, coveting power over New York, swells sewer rats to hippopotamus-size.") Here is a poem worth considering line by line.

A. E. Housman (1859 – 1936)*
Loveliest of trees, the cherry now   1896

Loveliest of trees, the cherry now
Is hung with bloom along the bough,
And stands about the woodland ride
Wearing white for Eastertide.

Now, of my threescore years and ten,   5
Twenty will not come again,
And take from seventy springs a score,
It only leaves me fifty more.

And since to look at things in bloom
Fifty springs are little room,   10
About the woodlands I will go
To see the cherry hung with snow.

Though simple, Housman's poem is far from simple-minded, and it contains at least one possible problem: what, in this instance, is a *ride*? If we guess, we won't be far wrong; but a dictionary helps: "a road or path through the woods, especially for horseback riding." A paraphrase of the poem might say something like this (in language easier to forget than the original): "Now it is Easter time, and the cherry tree in the woods by the path is in blossom. I'm twenty, my life is passing. I expect to live the average life-span of seventy. That means I'm going to see only fifty more springs, so I had better go out into the woods and start looking." And the paraphrase might add, to catch the deeper implication, "Life is brief and fleeting: I must enjoy beauty while I may."

These dull remarks, roughly faithful to what Housman is saying, are clearly as far from being poetry as a cherry pit is far from being a cherry. Still, they can help whoever makes the paraphrase to see the main argument of Housman's poem: its **theme** or central thought. Theme isn't the same thing as **subject,** the central topic. In "Loveliest of trees," the subject is cherry blossoms, or the need to look at them, but the theme is "Time flies: enjoy beauty now!" Not all poems clearly assert a proposition, but many do; some even declare their themes in their very first lines: "Gather ye rose-buds while ye may" — enjoy love before it's too late. The theme stated in that famous opening line (from Robert Herrick's "To the Virgins, to Make Much of Time," page 727) is so familiar that it has a name: **carpe diem** (Latin for "seize the day"), a favorite argument of poets from Horace to Housman.

A paraphrase, of course, never tells *all* that a poem contains; nor will every reader agree that a particular paraphrase is accurate. We all make our own interpretations; and sometimes the total meaning of a poem evades even the poet who wrote it. Asked to explain his difficult *Sordello*, Robert Browning replied that when he had written the poem only God and he knew what it meant; but "Now, only God knows." Still, to analyze a poem *as if* we could be certain of its meaning is, in general, more fruitful than to proceed as if no certainty could ever be had. The latter approach is likely to end in complete subjectivity: the attitude of the reader who says, "Housman's 'Loveliest of trees' is really about a walk in the snow; it is, because I think it is. How can you prove me wrong?"

All of us bring to our readings of poems certain personal associations, as Housman's "Loveliest of trees" might convey a particular pleasure to a reader who had climbed cherry trees when he was small. To some extent, these associations are inevitable, even to be welcomed. But we need to distinguish between irrelevant, tangential responses and those the poem calls for. The reader who can't stand "Loveliest of trees" because cherries remind him of blood, is reading a poem of his own, not Housman's.

Housman's poem is a **lyric:** a short poem expressing the thoughts and feelings of a single speaker. (As its Greek name suggests, a lyric originally was sung to the music of a lyre.) Often a lyric is written in the first person ("About the woodlands *I* will go"), but not always. It may be, for instance, a description of an object or an experience in which the poet isn't even mentioned. Housman's first stanza, printed by itself as a complete poem, would still be a lyric. Though a lyric may relate an incident, we tend to think of it as a reflective poem in which little physical action takes place — unlike a **narrative poem,** one whose main concern is to tell a story.

At the moment, it is a safe bet that, in English and other Western languages, lyrics are more plentiful than other kinds of poetry (novels having virtually replaced the long narrative poems esteemed from the time of Homer's *Odyssey* to the time of Tennyson's *Idylls of the King*). **Didactic poetry,** to mention one other kind, is poetry apparently written to teach or to state a message. In a lyric, the speaker may express sadness; in a didactic poem, he may explain that sadness is inherent in life. Poems that impart a body of knowledge, like Ovid's *Art of Love* and Lucretius's *On the Nature of Things,* are didactic. Such instructive poetry was favored especially by classical Latin poets and by English poets of the eighteenth century. In *The Fleece* (1757), John Dyer celebrated the British woolen industry and included practical advice on raising sheep:

> In cold stiff soils the bleaters oft complain
> Of gouty ails, by shepherds termed the halt:

Those let the neighboring fold or ready crook
Detain, and pour into their cloven feet
Corrosive drugs, deep-searching arsenic,
Dry alum, verdegris, or vitriol keen.

One might agree with Dr. Johnson's comment on Dyer's effort: "The subject, Sir, cannot be made poetical." But it may be argued that didactic poetry (to quote a recent view) "is not intrinsically any less poetic because of its subject-matter than lines about a rose fluttering in the breeze are intrinsically more poetic because of their subject-matter."[1] John Milton also described sick sheep in "Lycidas," a poem few readers have thought unpoetic:

The hungry sheep look up, and are not fed,
But, swoll'n with wind and the rank mist they draw,
Rot inwardly, and foul contagion spread . . .

What makes Milton's lines better poetry than Dyer's is, among other things, a difference in attitude. Sick sheep to Dyer mean the loss of a few shillings and pence; to Milton, whose sheep stand for English Christendom, they mean a moral catastrophe.

Now and again we meet a poem — perhaps startling and memorable — into which the method of paraphrase won't take us far. Some portion of any deep poem resists explanation, but certain poems resist it almost entirely. Many poems of religious mystics seem closer to dream than waking. So do poems that record hallucinations or drug experiences, such as Coleridge's "Kubla Khan" (page 702), as well as poems that embody some private system of beliefs, such as Blake's "The Sick Rose" (page 691), or the same poet's lines from *Jerusalem,*

For a Tear is an Intellectual thing,
And a Sigh is the Sword of an Angel King.

So do nonsense poems, translations of primitive folk songs, and surreal poems.[2] Such poetry may move us and give pleasure (although not, perhaps, the pleasure of mental understanding). We do it no harm by trying to paraphrase it, though we may fail. Whether logically clear or strangely opaque, good poems appeal to the intelligence and do not shrink from it.

So far, we have taken it for granted that poetry differs from prose; yet all our strategies for reading poetry — plowing straight on through and then going back, isolating difficulties, trying to paraphrase, reading aloud, using a dictionary — are no different from those we might employ in unraveling a complicated piece of prose. Poetry, after all, is similar to prose

[1]Sylvan Barnet, Morton Berman, and William Burto, *A Dictionary of Literary, Dramatic, and Cinematic Terms,* 2nd ed. (Boston: Little, Brown, 1971).
[2]The French poet André Breton, founder of **surrealism,** a movement in art and writing, declared that a higher reality exists, which to mortal eyes looks absurd. To mirror that reality, surrealist poets are fond of bizarre and dreamlike objects such as soluble fish and white-haired revolvers.

in most respects; at the very least, it is written in the same language. And like prose, poetry imparts knowledge. It tells us, for instance, something about the season and habitat of cherry trees and how one can feel toward them. Maybe a poet knows no more of cherry trees than a writer of seed-catalog descriptions, if as much. And yet Housman's perception of cherry blossoms as snow, with the implication that they too will soon melt and disappear, indicates a kind of knowledge that seed catalogs do not ordinarily reveal.

Robert Hayden (1913 – 1980)
THOSE WINTER SUNDAYS   1962

Sundays too my father got up early
and put his clothes on in the blueblack cold,
then with cracked hands that ached
from labor in the weekday weather made
banked fires blaze. No one ever thanked him.   5

I'd wake and hear the cold splintering, breaking.
When the rooms were warm, he'd call,
and slowly I would rise and dress,
fearing the chronic angers of that house,

Speaking indifferently to him,   10
who had driven out the cold
and polished my good shoes as well.
What did I know, what did I know
of love's austere and lonely offices?

QUESTIONS

1. Is the speaker a boy or a man? How do you know?
2. Summarize the poem's theme — its main idea.
3. What do you understand from "the chronic angers of that house"?
4. How does this poet's choice of words differ from that of most writers of prose? Suggestion: Read the opening five lines aloud.

Linda Pastan (b. 1932)*
ETHICS   1980

In ethics class so many years ago
our teacher asked this question every fall:
if there were a fire in a museum
which would you save, a Rembrandt painting

or an old woman who hadn't many 5
years left anyhow? Restless on hard chairs
caring little for pictures or old age
we'd opt one year for life, the next for art
and always half-heartedly. Sometimes
the woman borrowed my grandmother's face 10
leaving her usual kitchen to wander
some drafty, half imagined museum.
One year, feeling clever, I replied
why not let the woman decide herself?
Linda, the teacher would report, eschews 15
the burdens of responsibility.
This fall in a real museum I stand
before a real Rembrandt, old woman,
or nearly so, myself. The colors
within this frame are darker than autumn, 20
darker even than winter — the browns of earth,
though earth's most radiant elements burn
through the canvas. I know now that woman
and painting and season are almost one
and all beyond saving by children. 25

QUESTIONS

1. How has the passage of time influenced the speaker's attitude toward her teacher's question? Paraphrase her conclusion that "woman and painting and season are almost one and all beyond saving by children."
2. What is the subject of "Ethics"? What is its theme? Is the theme *carpe diem?* Is she saying, with Housman, "Life is fleeting; I'd better enjoy beauty while I may"?
3. Does the main impulse of the poem seem lyric, or narrative?
4. In what ways does "Ethics" differ from prose?

Robert Francis (b. 1901)

CATCH 1950

Two boys uncoached are tossing a poem together,
Overhand, underhand, backhand, sleight of hand, every hand,
Teasing with attitudes, latitudes, interludes, altitudes,
High, make him fly off the ground for it, low, make him stoop,
Make him scoop it up, make him as-almost-as-possible miss it, 5
Fast, let him sting from it, now, now fool him slowly,
Anything, everything tricky, risky, nonchalant,
Anything under the sun to outwit the prosy,
Over the tree and the long sweet cadence down,
Over his head, make him scramble to pick up the meaning, 10
And now, like a posy, a pretty one plump in his hands.

1. Who are the two boys in this poem?
2. Point out a few of the most important similarities in this extended comparison.
3. Consider especially line 8: *Anything under the sun to outwit the prosy.* What, in your own words, does Robert Francis mean?

Andrew Marvell (1621 – 1678)

TO HIS COY MISTRESS   1681

Had we but world enough and time,
This coyness°, lady, were no crime.   *modesty, reluctance*
We would sit down and think which way
To walk, and pass our long love's day.
Thou by the Indian Ganges' side   5
Should'st rubies find; I by the tide
Of Humber would complain°. I would   *sing sad songs*
Love you ten years before the Flood,
And you should, if you please, refuse
Till the conversion of the Jews.   10
My vegetable° love should grow   *vegetative, flourishing*
Vaster than empires, and more slow.
An hundred years should go to praise
Thine eyes, and on thy forehead gaze,
Two hundred to adore each breast,   15
But thirty thousand to the rest.
An age at least to every part,
And the last age should show your heart.
For, lady, you deserve this state°,   *pomp, ceremony*
Nor would I love at lower rate.   20
   But at my back I always hear
Time's wingèd chariot hurrying near,
And yonder all before us lie
Deserts of vast eternity.
Thy beauty shall no more be found,   25
Nor in thy marble vault shall sound
My echoing song; then worms shall try
That long preserved virginity,
And your quaint honor turn to dust,
And into ashes all my lust.   30
The grave's a fine and private place,
But none, I think, do there embrace.
   Now therefore, while the youthful hue
Sits on thy skin like morning glew°   *glow*
And while thy willing soul transpires   35
At every pore with instant° fires,   *eager*
Now let us sport us while we may;
And now, like amorous birds of prey,

Rather at once our time devour
Than languish in his slow-chapped° power.   *slow-jawed*   40
Let us roll all our strength and all
Our sweetness up into one ball
And tear our pleasures with rough strife
Thorough° the iron gates of life.   *through*
Thus, though we cannot make our sun
                                                                                  45
Stand still, yet we will make him run.

To His Coy Mistress. 7. *Humber:* a river that flows by Marvell's town of Hull (on the side of
the world opposite from the Ganges). 10. *conversion of the Jews:* an event that, according to St.
John the Divine, is to take place just before the end of the world. 35. *transpires:* exudes, as
a membrane lets fluid or vapor pass through it.

Questions

1. "All this poet does is feed some woman a big line. There's no time for romance,
   so he says, 'Quick, let's hit the bed before we hit the dirt.'" Discuss this
   summary. Then try making your own, more accurate one. (Suggestion: The
   poem is divided into three parts, each beginning with an indented line. Take
   these parts one at a time, putting the speaker's main thoughts into your own
   words.)
2. In part one, how much space would be "world enough" for the lovers? Exactly
   how much time would be enough time?
3. What is the main idea of part two? How is this theme similar to that of Housman's "Loveliest of trees"?
4. Paraphrase with special care lines 37 – 44. Is Marvell urging violence?
5. Considering the poem as a whole, does the speaker seem playful, or serious?

Suggestion for Writing

Write a concise, accurate paraphrase of a poem from Chapter 29, "Poems for
Further Reading," (pages 679 – 792). Your instructor may wish to suggest a poem
or poems. Although your paraphrase should take in the entire poem, it need not
mention everything. Just try to include the points that seem most vital and try to
state the poem's main thought, or *theme.* Be ready to share your paraphrase with
the rest of the class and to compare it with other paraphrases of the same poem.
You may then be able to test yourself as a reader of poetry. What in the poem
whizzed by you that other students noticed? What did you discover that others
ignored?

14 Listening to a Voice

TONE

In late-show Westerns, when one hombre taunts another, it is customary for the second to drawl, "Smile when you say that, pardner" or "Mister, I don't like your tone of voice." Sometimes in reading a poem, although we neither can see a face nor hear a voice, we can infer the poet's attitude from other evidence.

Like tone of voice, **tone** in literature often conveys an attitude toward the person addressed. Like the manner of a person, the manner of a poem may be friendly or belligerent toward its reader, condescending or respectful. Again like tone of voice, the tone of a poem may tell us how the speaker feels about himself or herself: cocksure or humble, sad or glad. But usually when we ask, "What is the tone of a poem?" we mean, "What attitude does the poet take toward a theme or a subject?" Is the poet being affectionate, hostile, earnest, playful, sarcastic, or what? We may never be able to know, of course, the poet's personal feelings. All we need know is how to feel when we read a poem.

Strictly speaking, tone isn't an attitude; it is whatever in the poem makes an attitude clear to us: the choice of certain words instead of others, the picking out of certain details. In Housman's "Loveliest of trees," for example, the poet communicates his admiration for a cherry tree's beauty by singling out for attention its white blossoms; had he wanted to show his dislike for the tree, he might have concentrated on its broken branches, birdlime, or snails. Rightly to perceive the tone of a poem, we need to read the poem carefully, paying attention to whatever suggestions we find in it.

Theodore Roethke (1908 – 1963)*
My Papa's Waltz   1948

The whiskey on your breath
Could make a small boy dizzy;
But I hung on like death:
Such waltzing was not easy.

We romped until the pans   5
Slid from the kitchen shelf;
My mother's countenance
Could not unfrown itself.

The hand that held my wrist
Was battered on one knuckle;   10
At every step you missed
My right ear scraped a buckle.

You beat time on my head
With a palm caked hard by dirt,
Then waltzed me off to bed   15
Still clinging to your shirt.

What is the tone of this poem? Most readers find the speaker's attitude toward his father affectionate, and take this recollection of childhood to be a happy one. But at least one reader, concentrating on certain details, once wrote: "Roethke expresses his resentment for his father, a drunken brute with dirty hands and a whiskey breath who carelessly hurt the child's ear and manhandled him." Although this reader accurately noticed some of the events in the poem and perceived that in the son's hanging on to the father "like death" there is something desperate, he missed the tone of the poem and so misunderstood it altogether. Among other things, this reader didn't notice the rollicking rhythms of the poem; the playfulness of a rime like *dizzy* and *easy;* the joyful suggestions of the words *waltz, waltzing,* and *romped.* Probably the reader didn't stop to visualize this scene in all its comedy, with kitchen pans falling and the father happily using his son's head for a drum. Nor did he stop to feel the suggestions in the last line, with the boy *still clinging* with persistent love.

Such a poem, though it includes lifelike details that aren't pretty, has a tone relatively easy to recognize. So does **satiric poetry,** a kind of comic poetry that generally conveys a message. Usually its tone is one of detached amusement, withering contempt, and implied superiority. In a satiric poem, the poet ridicules some person or persons (or perhaps some kind of human behavior), examining the victim by the light of certain principles and implying that the reader, too, ought to feel contempt for the victim.

Countee Cullen (1903 – 1946)
For a Lady I Know   1925

She even thinks that up in heaven
  Her class lies late and snores,
While poor black cherubs rise at seven
  To do celestial chores.

1. What is Cullen's message?
2. How would you characterize the tone of this poem? Wrathful? Amused?

In some poems the poet's attitude may be plain enough; while in other poems attitudes may be so mingled that it is hard to describe them tersely without doing injustice to the poem. Does Andrew Marvell in "To His Coy Mistress" (page 418) take a serious or playful attitude toward the fact that he and his lady are destined to be food for worms? No one-word answer will suffice. And what of T. S. Eliot's "Love Song of J. Alfred Prufrock" (page 713)? In his attitude toward his redemption-seeking hero who wades with trousers rolled, Eliot is seriously funny. Such a mingled tone may be seen in the following poem by the wife of a governor of the Massachusetts Bay Colony and the earliest American poet of note. Anne Bradstreet's first book, *The Tenth Muse Lately Sprung Up in America* (1650), had been published in England without her consent. She wrote these lines to preface a second edition:

Anne Bradstreet (1612? – 1672)
THE AUTHOR TO HER BOOK   1678

Thou ill-formed offspring of my feeble brain,
Who after birth did'st by my side remain,
Till snatched from thence by friends, less wise than true,
Who thee abroad exposed to public view;
Made thee in rags, halting, to the press to trudge,   5
Where errors were not lessened, all may judge.
At thy return my blushing was not small,
My rambling brat (in print) should mother call;
I cast thee by as one unfit for light,
Thy visage was so irksome in my sight;   10
Yet being mine own, at length affection would
Thy blemishes amend, if so I could:
I washed thy face, but more defects I saw,
And rubbing off a spot, still made a flaw.
I stretched thy joints to make thee even feet,   15
Yet still thou run'st more hobbling than is meet;
In better dress to trim thee was my mind,
But nought save homespun cloth in the house I find.
In this array, 'mongst vulgars may'st thou roam;
In critics' hands beware thou dost not come;   20
And take thy way where yet thou are not known.

If for thy Father asked, say thou had'st none;
And for thy Mother, she alas is poor,
Which caused her thus to send thee out of door.

In the author's comparison of her book to an illegitimate ragamuffin, we may be struck by the details of scrubbing and dressing a child: details that might well occur to a mother who had scrubbed and dressed many. As she might feel toward such a child, so she feels toward her book. She starts by deploring it but, as the poem goes on, cannot deny it her affection. Humor enters (as in the pun in line 15). She must dress the creature in *homespun cloth,* something both crude and serviceable. By the end of her poem, Mrs. Bradstreet seems to regard her book-child with tenderness, amusement, and a certain indulgent awareness of its faults. To read this poem is to sense its mingling of several attitudes. Simultaneously, a poet can be merry and in earnest.

Walt Whitman (1819 – 1892)*
To a Locomotive in Winter   1881

Thee for my recitative,
Thee in the driving storm even as now, the snow, the winter-day
    declining,
Thee in thy panoply°, thy measur'd dual throbbing and thy   *suit of*
    beat convulsive,   *armor*
Thy black cylindric body, golden brass and silvery steel,
Thy ponderous side-bars, parallel and connecting rods, gyrating,
    shuttling at thy sides,   5
Thy metrical, now swelling pant and roar, now tapering in the
    distance,
Thy great protruding head-light fix'd in front,
Thy long, pale, floating vapor-pennants, tinged with delicate purple,
The dense and murky clouds out-belching from thy smoke-stack,
Thy knitted frame, thy springs and valves, the tremulous twinkle of
    thy wheels,   10
Thy train of cars behind, obedient, merrily following,
Through gale or calm, now swift, now slack, yet steadily careering;
Type of the modern — emblem of motion and power — pulse of the
    continent,
For once come serve the Muse and merge in verse, even as here I see
    thee,
With storm and buffeting gusts of wind and falling snow,   15
By day thy warning ringing bell to sound its notes,
By night thy silent signal lamps to swing.

Fierce-throated beauty!
Roll through my chant with all thy lawless music, thy swinging
    lamps at night,
Thy madly-whistled laughter, echoing, rumbling like an earthquake,
    rousing all,   20
Law of thyself complete, thine own track firmly holding,
(No sweetness debonair of tearful harp or glib piano thine,)
Thy trills of shrieks by rocks and hills return'd,
Launch'd o'er the prairies wide, across the lakes,
To the free skies unpent and glad and strong.   25

Emily Dickinson (1830 – 1886)*

I LIKE TO SEE IT LAP THE MILES   (about 1862)

I like to see it lap the Miles –
And lick the Valleys up –
And stop to feed itself at Tanks –
And then – prodigious step

Around a Pile of Mountains –   5
And supercilious peer
In Shanties – by the sides of Roads –
And then a Quarry pare

To fit its Ribs
And crawl between   10
Complaining all the while
In horrid – hooting stanza –
Then chase itself down Hill –

And neigh like Boanerges –
Then – punctual as a Star   15
Stop – docile and omnipotent
At its own stable door –

QUESTIONS

1. What differences in tone do you find between Whitman's and Emily Dickinson's poems? Point out in each poem whatever contributes to these differences.
2. *Boanerges* in Emily Dickinson's last stanza means "sons of thunder," a name given by Jesus to the disciples John and James (see Mark 3:17). How far should the reader work out the particulars of this comparison? Does it make the tone of the poem serious?
3. In Whitman's opening line, what is a *recitative?* What other specialized terms from the vocabulary of music and poetry does each poem contain? How do they help underscore Whitman's theme?
4. Poets and song-writers probably have regarded the locomotive with more affection than they have shown most other machines. Why do you suppose this to be? Can you think of any other poems or songs for example?

5. What do these two poems tell you about locomotives that you would not be likely to find in a technical book on railroading?
6. Are the subjects of the two poems identical? Discuss.

John Milton (1608 – 1674)*
ON THE LATE MASSACRE IN PIEMONT (1655)

Avenge, O Lord, thy slaughtered saints, whose bones
  Lie scattered on the Alpine mountains cold;
  Even them who kept thy truth so pure of old,
When all our fathers worshiped stocks and stones,
Forget not: in thy book record their groans   5
  Who were thy sheep, and in their ancient fold
  Slain by the bloody Piemontese, that rolled
Mother with infant down the rocks. Their moans
The vales redoubled to the hills, and they
  To heaven. Their martyred blood and ashes sow   10
O'er all the Italian fields, where still doth sway
  The triple Tyrant; that from these may grow
  A hundredfold, who, having learnt thy way,
Early may fly the Babylonian woe.

ON THE LATE MASSACRE IN PIEMONT. Despite hostility between Catholics and Protestants, the Waldenses, members of a Puritan sect, had been living in the Piemont, that region in northwest Italy bounded by the crests of the Alps. In 1655, ignoring a promise to observe religious liberty, troops of the Roman Catholic ruler of the Piemont put to death several members of the sect. 4. *When . . . stones:* Englishmen had been Catholics, worshiping stone and wooden statues (so Milton charges) when the Waldensian sect was founded in the twelfth century. 12. *The triple Tyrant:* The Pope, to whom is attributed authority over earth, heaven, and hell. 14. *Babylonian woe:* Destruction expected to befall the city of Babylon at the world's end as punishment for its luxury and other wickedness (see Revelation 18:1 – 24). Protestants took Babylon to mean the Church of Rome.

QUESTION

What is Milton's attitude toward the massacre? Does he express a single feeling, or a mingling of feelings?

THE PERSON IN THE POEM

The tone of a poem, we said, is like tone of voice in that both communicate feelings. Still, this comparison raises a question: when we read a poem, whose "voice" speaks to us?

"The poet's" is one possible answer; and in the case of many a poem, that answer may be right. Reading Anne Bradstreet's "The Author to Her Book," we can be reasonably sure that the poet speaks of her very own book, and of her own experiences. In order to read a poem, we seldom need to read a poet's biography; but in truth there are certain poems whose full effect depends upon our knowing at least a fact or two of the poet's life. In this poem, surely the poet refers to himself:

Trumbull Stickney (1874 – 1904)

SIR, SAY NO MORE   1905

Sir, say no more,
Within me 'tis as if
The green and climbing eyesight of a cat
Crawled near my mind's poor birds.

The subject of Stickney's poem is not some nightmare or hallucination. The poem may mean more to you if you know that Stickney, who wrote it shortly before his death, had been afflicted by cancer of the brain. But the poem is not a prosaic entry in the diary of a dying man, nor is it a good poem because a dying man wrote it. Not only does it tell truth from experience, it speaks in memorable words.

Most of us can tell the difference between a person we meet in life and a person we meet in a work of art — unlike the moviegoer in the Philippines who, watching a villain in an exciting film, pulled out a revolver and peppered the screen. And yet, in reading poems, we are liable to temptation. When the poet says "I," we may want to assume that he, like Trumbull Stickney, is making a personal statement. But reflect: do all poems have to be personal? Here is a brief poem inscribed on the tombstone of an infant in Burial Hill cemetery, Plymouth, Massachusetts:

Since I have been so quickly done for,
I wonder what I was begun for.

We do not know who wrote those lines, but it is clear that the poet was not a short-lived infant writing from personal experience. In other poems, the speaker is obviously a **persona** or fictitious character: not the poet, but the poet's creation. As a grown man, William Blake, a skilled professional engraver, wrote a poem in the voice of a boy, an illiterate chimney sweeper. (The poem appears on page 441.) No law decrees that the speaker in a poem even has to be human: good poems have been uttered by clouds, pebbles, and cats. A **dramatic monologue** is a poem written as a speech made at some decisive or revealing moment. It is usually addressed by the speaker to some other character (who remains silent). Robert Browning, who developed the form, liked to put words into the mouths of characters stupider, weaker, or nastier than he: for instance see "My Last Duchess" (page 696), in which the speaker is an arrogant Renaissance duke. Browning himself, from all reports, was neither domineering nor merciless.

Let's consider a poem spoken not by a poet but by a persona — in this case, a child. To understand the poem, you need to pay attention not only to what the child says, but also to how the poet seems to feel about it.

Randall Jarrell (1914 – 1965)*

A Sick Child 1951

The postman comes when I am still in bed.
"Postman, what do you have for me today?"
I say to him. (But really I'm in bed.)
Then he says — what shall I have him say?

"This letter says that you are president 5
Of — this word here; it's a republic."
Tell them I can't answer right away.
"It's your duty." No, I'd rather just be sick.

Then he tells me there are letters saying everything
That I can think of that I want for them to say. 10
I say, "Well, thank you very much. Good-bye."
He is ashamed, and turns and walks away.

If I can think of it, it isn't what I want.
I want . . . I want a ship from some near star
To land in the yard, and beings to come out 15
And think to me: "So this is where you are!

Come." Except that they won't do,
I thought of them. . . . And yet somewhere there must be
Something that's different from everything.
All that I've never thought of — think of me! 20

Questions

1. Would you call the speaker unfeeling or sensitive? Unimaginative or imaginative? How do you know?
2. Why is the postman *ashamed?*
3. Besides sickness, what is bothering the child? What does the child long for?
4. Do you think Jarrell sympathizes with the child's wishes and longings? By what means does he indicate his own attitude?

In a famous definition, William Wordsworth calls poetry "the spontaneous overflow of powerful feelings . . . recollected in tranquillity."[1] But in the case of the following poem, Wordsworth's feelings weren't all his; they didn't just overflow spontaneously; and the process of tranquil recollection had to go on for years.

[1]For a fuller text of Wordsworth's statement, see page 826.

William Wordsworth (1770 – 1850)*

I WANDERED LONELY AS A CLOUD

1807

I wandered lonely as a cloud
  That floats on high o'er vales and hills,
When all at once I saw a crowd,
  A host, of golden daffodils,
Beside the lake, beneath the trees,   5
Fluttering and dancing in the breeze.

Continuous as the stars that shine
  And twinkle on the milky way,
They stretched in never-ending line
  Along the margin of a bay: 10
Ten thousand saw I at a glance,
Tossing their heads in sprightly dance.

The waves beside them danced; but they
  Out-did the sparkling waves in glee;
A poet could not but be gay,   15
  In such a jocund company;
I gazed — and gazed — but little thought
What wealth the show to me had brought:

For oft, when on my couch I lie
  In vacant or in pensive mood,   20
They flash upon that inward eye
  Which is the bliss of solitude;
And then my heart with pleasure fills,
And dances with the daffodils.

Between the first printing of the poem in 1807 and the version of 1815 given here, Wordsworth made several deliberate improvements. He changed *dancing* to *golden* in line 4, *Along* to *Beside* in line 5, *Ten thousand* to *Fluttering and* in line 6, *laughing* to *jocund* in line 16, and he added a whole stanza (the second). In fact, the writing of the poem was unspontaneous enough for Wordsworth, at a loss for lines 21 – 22, to take them from his wife Mary. It is likely that the experience of daffodil-watching was not entirely his to begin with but was derived in part from the recollections his sister Dorothy Wordsworth had set down in her journal of April 15, 1802, two years before he first drafted his poem:

> When we were in the woods beyond Gowbarrow Park we saw a few daffodils close to the water-side. We fancied that the lake had floated the seeds ashore, and that the little colony had so sprung up. But as we went along there were more and yet more; and at last, under the boughs of the trees, we saw that there was a long belt of them along the shore, about the breadth of a country turnpike road. I never saw daffodils so beautiful. They grew among the mossy stones about and about them; some rested their heads upon these stones as on a pillow for weariness; and the rest tossed and reeled and danced, and seemed as if they verily laughed with

the wind, that flew upon them over the Lake; they looked so gay, ever glancing, ever changing. This wind blew directly over the Lake to them. There was here and there a little knot, and a few stragglers a few yards higher up; but they were so few as not to disturb the simplicity, unity, and life of that one busy highway.

Notice that Wordsworth's poem echoes a few of his sister's observations. Weaving poetry out of their mutual memories, Wordsworth has offered the experience as if altogether his own, made himself lonely, and left Dorothy out. The point is not that Wordsworth is a liar or a plagiarist but that, like any other good poet, he has transformed ordinary life into art. A process of interpreting, shaping, and ordering had to intervene between the experience of looking at daffodils and the finished poem.

We need not deny that a poet's experience can contribute to a poem nor that the emotion in the poem can indeed be the poet's. Still, to write a good poem one has to do more than live and feel. It seems a pity that, as Randall Jarrell has said, a cardinal may write verses worse than his youngest choirboy's. But writing poetry takes skill and imagination — qualities that extensive travel and wide experience do not necessarily give. For much of her life, Emily Dickinson seldom strayed from her family's house and grounds in Amherst, Massachusetts; yet her rimed lifestudies of a snake, a bee, and a hummingbird contain more poetry than we find in any firsthand description (so far) of the surface of the moon.

Edwin Arlington Robinson (1869 – 1935)*
HOW ANNANDALE WENT OUT   1910

"They called it Annandale — and I was there
To flourish, to find words, and to attend:
Liar, physician, hypocrite, and friend,
I watched him; and the sight was not so fair
As one or two that I have seen elsewhere: 5
An apparatus not for me to mend —
A wreck, with hell between him and the end,
Remained of Annandale; and I was there.

"I knew the ruin as I knew the man;
So put the two together, if you can,   10
Remembering the worst you know of me.
Now view yourself as I was, on the spot —
With a slight kind of engine. Do you see?
Like this . . . You wouldn't hang me? I thought not."

QUESTIONS

1. Who is the speaker? What does he reveal about himself?
2. Who do you suppose to be his audience?

3. What took place during that ellipsis in the last line?
4. What could that "slight kind of engine" have been?
5. How do you think Edwin Arlington Robinson feels toward the speaker and his deed? From exactly what in this poem can you detect any hints of the poet's own attitude?

Paul Zimmer (b. 1934)
THE DAY ZIMMER LOST RELIGION   1976

The first Sunday I missed Mass on purpose
I waited all day for Christ to climb down
Like a wiry flyweight from the cross and
Club me on my irreverent teeth, to wade into
My blasphemous gut and drop me like a   5
Red hot thurible, the devil roaring in
Reserved seats until he got the hiccups.

It was a long cold way from the old days
When cassocked and surpliced I mumbled Latin
At the old priest and rang his obscure bell.   10
A long way from the dirty wind that blew
The soot like venial sins across the school yard
Where God reigned as a threatening,
One-eyed triangle high in the fleecy sky.

The first Sunday I missed Mass on purpose   15
I waited all day for Christ to climb down
Like the playground bully, the cuts and mice
Upon his face agleam, and pound me
Till my irreligious tongue hung out.
But of course He never came, knowing that   20
I was grown up and ready for Him now.

QUESTIONS

1. Who is the person in this poem? The mature poet? The poet as a child? Some fictitious character?
2. What do you understand to be the speaker's attitude toward religion at the present moment?

Richard Hugo (1923 – 1982)
IN YOUR YOUNG DREAM   1977

You are traveling to play basketball. Your team's
a good one, boys you knew when you were young.
A game's in Wyoming, a small town, a gym
in a grammar school. You go in to practice.
No nets on the hoops. You say to the coach,   5
a small man, mean face, "We need nets on the rims."

He sneers as if you want luxury. You explain
how this way you can't see the shots go in.
You and another player, vaguely seen, go out
to buy nets. A neon sign on a local tavern   10
gives directions to the next town, a town
a woman you loved lives in. You go to your room
to phone her, to tell her you're here just
one town away to play ball. She's already
waiting in your room surrounded by children.   15
She says, "I'll come watch you play ball."
Though young in the dream you know you are old.
You are troubled. You know you need nets on the rims.

QUESTION

Who is the *you* in this poem?

EXPERIMENT: *Reading with and without Biography*

Read the following poem and state what you understand from it. Then consider
the circumstances in which it probably came to be written. (Some information is
offered in a note on page 442.) Does the meaning of the poem change? To what
extent does an appreciation of the poem need the support of biography?

William Carlos Williams (1883 – 1963)*
THE RED WHEELBARROW   1923

so much depends
upon

a red wheel
barrow

glazed with rain
water

beside the white
chickens.

IRONY

To see a distinction between the poet and the words of a fictitious
character — between Randall Jarrell and "A Sick Child" — is to be aware
of **irony:** a manner of speaking that implies a discrepancy. If the mask says
one thing and we sense that the writer is in fact saying something else, the
writer has adopted an **ironic point of view.** No finer illustration exists in
English than Jonathan Swift's "A Modest Proposal," an essay in which
Swift speaks as an earnest, humorless citizen who sets forth his reasonable
plan to aid the Irish poor. The plan is so monstrous no sane reader can
assent to it: the poor are to sell their children as meat for the tables of their

landlords. From behind his falseface, Swift is actually recommending not cannibalism but love and Christian charity.

A poem is often made complicated and more interesting by another kind of irony. **Verbal irony** occurs whenever words say one thing but mean something else, usually the opposite. The word *love* means *hate* here: "I just *love* to stay home and do my hair on a Saturday night!" If the verbal irony is conspicuously bitter, heavy-handed, and mocking, it is **sarcasm:** "Oh, he's the biggest spender in the world, all right!" (The sarcasm, if that statement were spoken, would be underscored by the speaker's tone of voice.) A famous instance of sarcasm is Mark Antony's line in his oration over the body of slain Julius Caesar: "Brutus is an honorable man." Antony repeats this line until the enraged populace begins shouting exactly what he means to call Brutus and the other conspirators: traitors, villains, murderers. We had best be alert for irony on the printed page, for if we miss it, our interpretations of a poem may go wild.

Robert Creeley (b. 1926)
OH NO   1959

If you wander far enough
you will come to it
and when you get there
they will give you a place to sit

for yourself only, in a nice chair,   5
and all your friends will be there
with smiles on their faces
and they will likewise all have places.

This poem is rich in verbal irony. The title helps point out that between the speaker's words and attitude lie deep differences. In line 2, what is *it?* Old age? The wandering suggests a conventional metaphor: the journey of life. Is *it* literally a rest home for "senior citizens," or perhaps some naïve popular concept of heaven (such as we meet in comic strips: harps, angels with hoops for halos) in which the saved all sit around in a ring, smugly congratulating one another? We can't be sure, but the speaker's attitude toward this final sitting-place is definite. It is a place for the selfish, as we infer from the phrase *for yourself only.* And *smiles on their faces* may hint that the smiles are unchanging and forced. There is a difference between saying "They had smiles on their faces" and "They smiled": the latter suggests that the smiles came from within. The word *nice* is to be regarded with distrust. If we see through this speaker, as Creeley implies we can do, we realize that, while pretending to be sweet-talking us into a seat, actually he is revealing the horror of a little hell. And the title is the poet's reaction to it (or the speaker's unironic, straightforward one): "Oh no! Not *that!*"

Dramatic irony, like verbal irony, contains an element of contrast, but it usually refers to a situation in a play wherein a character, whose knowledge is limited, says, does, or encounters something of greater significance than he or she knows. We, the spectators, realize the meaning of this speech or action, for the playwright has afforded us superior knowledge. In Sophocles' *King Oedipus,* when Oedipus vows to punish whoever has brought down a plague upon the city of Thebes, we know — as he does not — that the man he would punish is himself. (Referring to such a situation that precedes the downfall of a hero in a tragedy, some critics speak of **tragic irony** instead of dramatic irony.) Superior knowledge can be enjoyed not only by spectators in a theater but by readers of poetry as well. In *Paradise Lost,* we know in advance that Adam will fall into temptation, and we recognize his overconfidence when he neglects a warning. The situation of Oedipus contains also **cosmic irony,** or **irony of fate:** some Fate with a grim sense of humor seems cruelly to trick a human being. Cosmic irony clearly exists in poems in which fate or the Fates are personified and seen as hostile, as in Thomas Hardy's "The Convergence of the Twain" (page 721); and it may be said to occur too in Robinson's "Richard Cory" (page 518). Evidently it is a twist of fate for the most envied man in town to kill himself.

To sum up: the effect of irony depends upon the reader's noticing some incongruity or discrepancy between two things. In *verbal irony,* there is a contrast between the speaker's words and meaning; in an *ironic point of view,* between the writer's attitude and what is spoken by a fictitious character; in *dramatic irony,* between the limited knowledge of a character and the fuller knowledge of the reader or spectator; in *cosmic irony,* between a character's aspiration and the treatment he or she receives at the hands of Fate. Although in the work of an inept poet irony can be crude and obvious sarcasm, it is invaluable to a poet of more complicated mind, who imagines more than one perspective.

W. H. Auden (1907 – 1973)*
THE UNKNOWN CITIZEN   1940

*(To JS/07/M/378
This Marble Monument
Is Erected by the State)*

He was found by the Bureau of Statistics to be
One against whom there was no official complaint,
And all the reports on his conduct agree
That, in the modern sense of an old-fashioned word, he was a saint,
For in everything he did he served the Greater Community.   5
Except for the War till the day he retired
He worked in a factory and never got fired,

But satisfied his employers, Fudge Motors Inc.
Yet he wasn't a scab or odd in his views,
For his Union reports that he paid his dues,   10
(Our report on his Union shows it was sound)
And our Social Psychology workers found
That he was popular with his mates and liked a drink.
The Press are convinced that he bought a paper every day
And that his reactions to advertisements were normal in every way.   15
Policies taken out in his name prove that he was fully insured,
And his Health-card shows he was once in hospital but left it cured.
Both Producers Research and High-Grade Living declare
He was fully sensible to the advantages of the Installment Plan
And had everything necessary to the Modern Man,   20
A phonograph, a radio, a car and a frigidaire.
Our researchers into Public Opinion are content
That he held the proper opinions for the time of year;
When there was peace, he was for peace; when there was war, he
    went.
He was married and added five children to the population,   25
Which our Eugenist says was the right number for a parent of his
    generation,
And our teachers report that he never interfered with their education.
Was he free? Was he happy? The question is absurd:
Had anything been wrong, we should certainly have heard.

QUESTIONS

1. Read the three-line epitaph at the beginning of the poem as carefully as you read what follows. How does the epitaph help establish the voice by which the rest of the poem is spoken?
2. Who is speaking?
3. What ironic discrepancies do you find between the speaker's attitude toward the subject and that of the poet himself? By what is the poet's attitude made clear?
4. In the phrase "The Unknown Soldier" (of which "The Unknown Citizen" reminds us), what does the word *unknown* mean? What does it mean in the title of Auden's poem?
5. What tendencies in our civilization does Auden satirize?
6. How would you expect the speaker to define a Modern Man, if a phonograph, a radio, a car, and a refrigerator are "everything" a Modern Man needs?

John Betjeman (1906 – 1984)
IN WESTMINSTER ABBEY   1940

Let me take this other glove off
  As the *vox humana* swells,
And the beauteous fields of Eden
  Bask beneath the Abbey bells.
Here, where England's statesmen lie,   5
Listen to a lady's cry.

Gracious Lord, oh bomb the Germans.
  Spare their women for Thy Sake,
And if that is not too easy
  We will pardon Thy Mistake.   10
But, gracious Lord, whate'er shall be,
Don't let anyone bomb me.

Keep our Empire undismembered,
  Guide our Forces by Thy Hand,
Gallant blacks from far Jamaica,   15
  Honduras and Togoland;
Protect them Lord in all their fights,
And, even more, protect the whites.

Think of what our Nation stands for:
  Books from Boots' and country lanes,   20
Free speech, free passes, class distinction,
  Democracy and proper drains.
Lord, put beneath Thy special care
One-eighty-nine Cadogan Square.

Although dear Lord I am a sinner,   25
  I have done no major crime;
Now I'll come to Evening Service
  Whensoever I have the time.
So, Lord, reserve for me a crown,
And do not let my shares° go down.   *stocks*   30

I will labor for Thy Kingdom,
  Help our lads to win the war,
Send white feathers to the cowards,
  Join the Women's Army Corps,
Then wash the Steps around ·Thy Throne   35
In the Eternal Safety Zone.

Now I feel a little better,
  What a treat to hear Thy Word,
Where the bones of leading statesmen
  Have so often been interred.   40
And now, dear Lord, I cannot wait
Because I have a luncheon date.

IN WESTMINSTER ABBEY. First printed during World War II. 2. *vox humana:* an organ stop that
makes tones similar to those of the human voice. 20. *Boots':* a chain of pharmacies whose
branches had lending libraries.

QUESTIONS

1. Who is the speaker? What do we know about her life style? About her prejudices?
2. Point out some of the places in which she contradicts herself.

3. How would you describe the speaker's attitude toward religion?
4. Through the medium of irony, what positive points do you believe Betjeman makes?

Sarah N. Cleghorn (1876 – 1959)
THE GOLF LINKS 1917

The golf links lie so near the mill
   That almost every day
The laboring children can look out
   And see the men at play.

QUESTIONS

1. Is this brief poem satiric? Does it contain any verbal irony? Is the poet making a matter-of-fact statement in words that mean just what they say?
2. What other kind of irony is present in the poem?
3. Sarah N. Cleghorn's poem dates from before the enactment of legislation against child labor. Is it still a good poem, or is it hopelessly dated?
4. How would you state its theme?
5. Would you call this poem lyric, narrative, or didactic?

EXERCISE: *Detecting Irony*

Point out the kinds of irony that occur in the following poem.

Thomas Hardy (1840 – 1928)*
THE WORKBOX 1914

"See, here's the workbox, little wife,
   That I made of polished oak."
He was a joiner°, of village life;   *carpenter*
   She came of borough folk.

He holds the present up to her   5
   As with a smile she nears
And answers to the profferer,
   " 'Twill last all my sewing years!"

"I warrant it will. And longer too.
   'Tis a scantling that I got   10
Off poor John Wayward's coffin, who
   Died of they knew not what.

"The shingled pattern that seems to cease
   Against your box's rim
Continues right on in the piece   15
   That's underground with him.

"And while I worked it made me think
  Of timber's varied doom:
One inch where people eat and drink,
  The next inch in a tomb.   20

"But why do you look so white, my dear,
  And turn aside your face?
You knew not that good lad, I fear,
  Though he came from your native place?"

"How could I know that good young man,   25
  Though he came from my native town,
When he must have left far earlier than
  I was a woman grown?"

"Ah, no. I should have understood!
  It shocked you that I gave   30
To you one end of a piece of wood
  Whose other is in a grave?"

"Don't, dear, despise my intellect,
  Mere accidental things
Of that sort never have effect   35
  On my imaginings."

Yet still her lips were limp and wan,
  Her face still held aside,
As if she had known not only John,
  But known of what he died.   40

FOR REVIEW AND FURTHER STUDY

EXERCISE: *Telling Tone*

Here are two radically different poems on a similar subject. Try stating the theme
of each poem in your own words. How is tone (the speaker's attitude) different in
the two poems?

Richard Lovelace (1618 – 1658)
TO LUCASTA   1649

On Going to the Wars

Tell me not, Sweet, I am unkind
  That from the nunnery
Of thy chaste breast and quiet mind,
  To war and arms I fly.

True, a new mistress now I chase,   5
   The first foe in the field;
And with a stronger faith embrace
   A sword, a horse, a shield.

Yet this inconstancy is such
   As you too shall adore;   10
I could not love thee, Dear, so much,
   Loved I not Honor more.

Wilfred Owen (1893 – 1918)*
DULCE ET DECORUM EST   1920

Bent double, like old beggars under sacks,
Knock-kneed, coughing like hags, we cursed through sludge,
Till on the haunting flares we turned our backs
And towards our distant rest began to trudge.
Men marched asleep. Many had lost their boots   5
But limped on, blood-shod. All went lame; all blind;
Drunk with fatigue; deaf even to the hoots
Of tired, outstripped Five-Nines° that dropped behind.   *gas-shells*

Gas! Gas! Quick, boys! — An ecstasy of fumbling,
Fitting the clumsy helmets just in time;   10
But someone still was yelling out and stumbling
And flound'ring like a man in fire or lime . . .
Dim, through the misty panes and thick green light,
As under a green sea, I saw him drowning.
In all my dreams, before my helpless sight,   15
He plunges at me, guttering, choking, drowning.

If in some smothering dreams you too could pace
Behind the wagon that we flung him in,
And watch the white eyes writhing in his face,
His hanging face, like a devil's sick of sin;   20
If you could hear, at every jolt, the blood
Come gargling from the froth-corrupted lungs,
Obscene as cancer, bitter as the cud
Of vile, incurable sores on innocent tongues, —
My friend, you would not tell with such high zest   25
To children ardent for some desperate glory,
The old Lie: Dulce et decorum est
Pro patria mori.

DULCE ET DECORUM EST. A British infantry officer in World War I, Owen was killed in action. 17. *you too:* Some manuscript versions of this poem carry the dedication "To Jessie Pope" (a writer of patriotic verse) or "To a certain Poetess." 27 – 28. *Dulce et . . . mori:* a quotation from the Latin poet Horace, "It is sweet and fitting to die for one's country."

James Stephens (1882 – 1950)*
A GLASS OF BEER
1918

The lanky hank of a she in the inn over there
Nearly killed me for asking the loan of a glass of beer;
May the devil grip the whey-faced slut by the hair,
And beat bad manners out of her skin for a year.

That parboiled ape, with the toughest jaw you will see   5
On virtue's path, and a voice that would rasp the dead,
Came roaring and raging the minute she looked at me,
And threw me out of the house on the back of my head!

If I asked her master he'd give me a cask a day;
But she, with the beer at hand, not a gill° would arrange!   *quarter-pint*   10
May she marry a ghost and bear him a kitten, and may
The High King of Glory permit her to get the mange.

QUESTIONS

1. Who do you take to be the speaker? Is it the poet? The speaker may be angry,
   but what is the tone of this poem?
2. Would you agree with a commentator who said, "To berate anyone in truly
   memorable language is practically a lost art in America"? How well does the
   speaker (an Irishman) succeed? Which of his epithets and curses strike you as
   particularly imaginative?

Jonathan Swift (1667 – 1745)*
ON STELLA'S BIRTHDAY
(1718 – 1719)

Stella this day is thirty-four
(We shan't dispute a year or more) —
However, Stella, be not troubled,
Although thy size and years are doubled,
Since first I saw thee at sixteen,   5
The brightest virgin on the green,
So little is thy form declined,
Made up so largely in thy mind.
Oh, would it please the gods, to split
Thy beauty, size, and years, and wit,   10
No age could furnish out a pair
Of nymphs so graceful, wise, and fair,
With half the luster of your eyes,
With half your wit, your years, and size.
And then, before it grew too late,   15
How should I beg of gentle Fate
(That either nymph might have her swain)
To split my worship too in twain.

ON STELLA'S BIRTHDAY. For many years Swift made an annual birthday gift of a poem to his close friend Mrs. Esther Johnson, the degree of whose nearness to the proud and lonely Swift remains an enigma to biographers. 18. *my worship:* as Dean of St. Patrick's in Dublin, Swift was addressed as "Your Worship."

QUESTIONS

1. If you were Stella, would you be amused or insulted by the poet's references to your *size?*
2. According to Swift in lines 7 – 8, what has compensated Stella for what the years have taken away?
3. Comment on the last four lines. Does Swift exempt himself from growing old?
4. How would you describe the tone of this poem? Offensive (like the speaker's complaints in "A Glass of Beer")? Playfully tender? Sad over Stella's growing fat and old?

A. E. Housman (1859 – 1936)*
EPITAPH ON AN ARMY OF MERCENARIES   1922

These, in the day when heaven was falling,
  The hour when earth's foundations fled,
Followed their mercenary calling
  And took their wages and are dead.

Their shoulders held the sky suspended;   5
  They stood, and earth's foundations stay;
What God abandoned, these defended,
  And saved the sum of things for pay.

Hugh MacDiarmid
[Christopher Murray Grieve] (1892 – 1978)*
ANOTHER EPITAPH ON AN ARMY OF MERCENARIES   1935

In reply to A. E. Housman's

It is a God-damned lie to say that these
Saved, or knew, anything worth any man's pride.
They were professional murderers and they took
Their blood money and their impious risks and died.
In spite of all their kind some elements of worth
With difficulty persist here and there on earth.

1. What attitude or attitudes toward its subject does Housman's poem express?
2. In MacDiarmid's reply, what is the attitude toward the mercenaries? Toward Housman's poem?

Bettie Sellers (b. 1926)

IN THE COUNSELOR'S WAITING ROOM   1981

The terra cotta girl
with the big flat farm feet
traces furrows in the rug
with her toes,
reads an existentialist paperback   5
from psychology class,
finds no ease there
from the guilt of loving
the quiet girl down the hall.
Their home soil has seen to this visit,   10
their Baptist mothers,
who weep for the waste of sturdy hips
ripe for grandchildren.

IN THE COUNSELOR'S WAITING ROOM. The poet is a teacher and administrator at a small college in Georgia. 1. *terra cotta:* fired clay, light brownish orange in hue. 5. *existentialist:* of the twentieth-century school of philosophy that holds (among other tenets) that an individual is alone and isolated, free and yet responsible, and ordinarily subject to guilt, anxiety, and dread.

QUESTIONS

1. For what sort of counseling is this girl waiting?
2. Point out all the words that refer to plowing, to clay and earth. Why are the mothers called "home soil"? How do these references to earth relate to the idea in the last line?
3. What irony inheres in this situation?
4. Does the poet appear to sympathize with the girls? With their weeping mothers? In what details does this poem hint at any of the poet's own attitude or attitudes?

William Blake (1757 – 1827)*

THE CHIMNEY SWEEPER   1789

When my mother died I was very young,
And my father sold me while yet my tongue
Could scarcely cry " 'weep! 'weep! 'weep! 'weep!"
So your chimneys I sweep, and in soot I sleep.

There's little Tom Dacre, who cried when his head,   5
That curled like a lamb's back, was shaved: so I said
"Hush, Tom! never mind it, for when your head's bare
You know that the soot cannot spoil your white hair."

And so he was quiet, and that very night,
As Tom was a-sleeping, he had such a sight!   10
That thousands of sweepers, Dick, Joe, Ned, and Jack,
Were all of them locked up in coffins of black.

And by came an Angel who had a bright key,
And he opened the coffins and set them all free;
Then down a green plain leaping, laughing, they run,   15
And wash in a river, and shine in the sun.

Then naked and white, all their bags left behind,
They rise upon clouds and sport in the wind;
And the Angel told Tom, if he'd be a good boy,
He'd have God for his father, and never want joy.   20

And so Tom awoke; and we rose in the dark,
And got with our bags and our brushes to work.
Though the morning was cold, Tom was happy and warm;
So if all do their duty they need not fear harm.

Questions

1. What does Blake's poem reveal about conditions of life in the London of his day?
2. What does this poem have in common with "The Golf Links" (page 436)?
3. How does "The Chimney Sweeper" resemble "A Sick Child" (page 427)? In what ways does Blake's poem seem much different?
4. Sum up your impressions of the speaker's character. What does he say and do that displays it to us?
5. What pun do you find in line 3? Is its effect comic or serious?
6. In Tom Dacre's dream (lines 11 – 20), what wishes come true? Do you understand them to be the wishes of the chimney sweepers, of the poet, or of both?
7. In the last line, what is ironic in the speaker's assurance that the dutiful *need not fear harm*? What irony is there in his urging all to *do their duty*? (Who have failed in their duty to *him*?)
8. What is the tone of Blake's poem? Angry? Hopeful? Sorrowful? Compassionate? (Don't feel obliged to sum it up in a single word.)

Information for Experiment: *Reading with and without Biography*

The Red Wheelbarrow (p. 431). Dr. Williams's poem reportedly contains a personal experience: he was gazing from the window of the house where one of his patients, a small girl, lay suspended between life and death. (This account, from the director of the public library in Williams's native Rutherford, N.J., is given by Geri M. Rhodes in "The Paterson Metaphor in William Carlos Williams' *Paterson*," master's essay, Tufts University, June 1965.)

Suggestions for Writing

1. In a paragraph, sum up your initial reactions to "The Red Wheelbarrow." Then, taking another look at the poem in light of information noted above, write a second paragraph summing up your further reactions.
2. Write a short essay titled "What Thomas Hardy in 'The Workbox' Leaves Unsaid."
3. Write a verbal profile or short character sketch of the speaker of John Betjeman's "In Westminster Abbey."
4. In a brief essay, consider the tone of two poems on a similar subject. Compare and contrast Walt Whitman and Emily Dickinson as locomotive-fanciers; or, in the poems by Richard Lovelace and Wilfred Owen, compare and contrast attitudes toward war. (For advice on writing about poetry by the method of comparison and contrast, see page 1381.)

15 Words

LITERAL MEANING: WHAT A POEM SAYS FIRST

Although successful as a painter, Edgar Degas struggled to produce sonnets, and found poetry discouragingly hard to write. To his friend, the poet Stéphane Mallarmé, he complained, "What a business! My whole day gone on a blasted sonnet, without getting an inch further . . . and it isn't ideas I'm short of . . . I'm full of them, I've got too many . . ."

"But Degas," said Mallarmé, "you can't make a poem with ideas — you make it with *words*!"[1]

Like the celebrated painter, some people assume that all it takes to make a poem is a bright idea. Poems state ideas, to be sure, and sometimes the ideas are invaluable; and yet the most impressive idea in the world will not make a poem unless its words are selected and arranged with loving art. Some poets take great pains to find the right word. Unable to fill a two-syllable gap in an unfinished line that went, "The seal's wide – – gaze toward Paradise," Hart Crane paged through an unabridged dictionary. When he reached *S,* he found the object of his quest in *spindrift:* "spray skimmed from the sea by a strong wind." The word is exact and memorable. Any word can be the right word, however, if artfully chosen and placed. It may be a word as ordinary as *from.* Consider the difference between "The sedge is withered *on* the lake" (a misquotation of a line by Keats) and "The sedge is withered *from* the lake" (what Keats in fact wrote). Keats's original line suggests, as the altered line doesn't, that because the sedge (a growth of grasslike plants) has withered *from* the lake, it has withdrawn mysteriously.

In reading a poem, some people assume that its words can be skipped over rapidly, and they try to leap at once to the poem's general theme. It is as if they fear being thought clods unless they can find huge ideas in the poem (whether or not there are any). Such readers often ignore the literal meanings of words: the ordinary, matter-of-fact sense to be found in a

---

[1]Paul Valéry, *Degas . . . Manet . . . Morisot,* translated by David Paul (New York: Pantheon, 1960) 62.

dictionary. (As you will see in Chapter Sixteen, "Saying and Suggesting," words possess not only dictionary meanings — **denotations** — but also many associations and suggestions — **connotations**.) Consider the following poem and see what you make of it.

William Carlos Williams (1883 – 1963)*
THIS IS JUST TO SAY   1934

I have eaten
the plums
that were in
the icebox
and which   5
you were probably
saving
for breakfast

Forgive me
they were delicious   10
so sweet
and so cold

Some readers distrust a poem so simple and candid. They think, "What's wrong with me? There has to be more to it than this!" But poems seldom are puzzles in need of solutions. We can begin by accepting the poet's statements, without suspecting him of trying to hoodwink us. On later reflection, of course, we might possibly decide that the poet is playfully teasing or being ironic; but Williams gives us no reason to think that. There seems no need to look beyond the literal sense of his words, no profit in speculating that the plums symbolize worldly joys and that the icebox stands for the universe. Clearly, a reader who held such a grand theory would have overlooked (in eagerness to find a significant idea) the plain truth that the poet makes clear to us: that ice-cold plums are a joy to taste, especially if one knows they'll be missed the next morning.

To be sure, Williams's small poem is simpler than most poems are; and yet in reading any poem, no matter how complicated, you will do well to reach slowly and reluctantly for generalizations. An adept reader of poetry reads with open mind — with (in Richard L. McGuire's phrase) "as much innocence as he can muster." For in order to experience a poem, you first have to pay attention to its words; and only if you see what the words are saying are you likely to come to the poem's true theme. Recall Housman's "Loveliest of trees" (page 413): a poem that contains a message (how rapidly life passes, how vital it is to make the most of every spring). Yet before you can realize that theme, you have to notice the color, the quantity, and the weight (*hung with bloom*) of Housman's imagined cherry blossoms.

Poets often strive for words that point to physical details and solid objects. They may do so even when speaking of an abstract idea:

Beauty is but a flower
Which wrinkles will devour;
Brightness falls from the air,
Queens have died young and fair,
Dust hath closed Helen's eye.
I am sick, I must die:
   Lord, have mercy on us!

In these lines by Thomas Nashe, the abstraction *beauty* has grown petals that shrivel. Brightness may be a general name for light, but Nashe succeeds in giving it the weight of a falling body.

If a poem reads *daffodils* instead of *vegetation, diaper years* instead of *infancy,* and *eighty-four* instead of *numerous,* we call its **diction** — its choice of words — **concrete,** or particular, rather than **abstract,** or general. In an apt criticism, William Butler Yeats once took to task the poems of W. E. Henley for being "abstract, as even an actor's movement can be when the thought of doing is plainer to his mind than the doing itself: the straight line from cup to lip, let us say, more plain than the hand's own sensation weighed down by that heavy spillable cup."[2] To convey the sense of that heavy spillable cup was to Yeats a goal, one that surely he attained in "Among School Children" by describing a woman's stark face: "Hollow of cheek as though it drank the wind / And took a mess of shadows for its meat." A more abstract-minded poet might have written "Her hollow cheek and wasted, hungry look." Ezra Pound gave a famous piece of advice to his fellow poets: "Go in fear of abstractions." This is not to say that a poet cannot employ abstract words, nor that all poems have to be about physical things. Much of T. S. Eliot's *Four Quartets* is concerned with time, eternity, history, language, reality, and other things that cannot be handled. But Eliot, however high he may soar for a general view, keeps returning to earth. He makes us aware of *things,* as Thomas Carlyle said a good writer has to do: "Wonderful it is with what cutting words, now and then, he severs asunder the confusion; shears it down, were it furlongs deep, into the true center of the matter; and there not only hits the nail on the head, but with crushing force smites it home, and buries it." Like other good writers, good poets remind us of that smitten nail and that spillable cup. "Perhaps indeed," wrote Walt Whitman in *Specimen Days,* "the efforts of the true poets, founders, religions, literatures, all ages, have been, and ever will be, our time and times to come, essentially the same — to bring people back from their persistent strayings and sickly abstractions, to the costless, average, divine, original concrete."

[2] *The Trembling of the Veil* (1922), reprinted in *The Autobiography of William Butler Yeats* (New York: Macmillan, 1953) 177.

Knute Skinner (b. 1929)

The Cold Irish Earth   1968

I shudder thinking
of the cold Irish earth.
The firelighter flares
in the kitchen range,
but a cold rain falls   5
all around Liscannor.
It scours the Hag's face
on the Cliffs of Moher.
It runs through the bog
and seeps up into mounds   10
of abandoned turf.
My neighbor's fields are chopped
by the feet of cattle
sinking down to the roots
of winter grass.   15
That coat hangs drying now
by the kitchen range,
but down at Healy's cross
the Killaspuglonane graveyard
is wet to the bone.   20

QUESTIONS

1. To what familiar phrase does Skinner's poem lend fresh meaning? What is its
   usual meaning?
2. What details in the poem show us that, in using the old phrase, Skinner literally
   means what he says?

Henry Taylor (b. 1942)

Riding a One-Eyed Horse   1975

One side of his world is always missing.
You may give it a casual wave of the hand
or rub it with your shoulder as you pass,
but nothing on his blind side ever happens.

Hundreds of trees slip past him into darkness,   5
drifting into a hollow hemisphere
whose sounds you will have to try to explain.
Your legs will tell him not to be afraid

if you learn never to lie. Do not forget
to turn his head and let what comes come seen: 10
he will jump the fences he has to if you swing
toward them from the side that he can see

and hold his good eye straight. The heavy dark
will stay beside you always; let him learn
to lean against it. It will steady him   15
and see you safely through diminished fields.

QUESTION

Do you read this poem as a fable in which the horse stands for something, or as
a set of instructions for riding a one-eyed horse?

Robert Graves (1895 – 1985)
DOWN, WANTON, DOWN!   1933

Down, wanton, down! Have you no shame
That at the whisper of Love's name,
Or Beauty's, presto! up you raise
Your angry head and stand at gaze?

Poor bombard-captain, sworn to reach   5
The ravelin and effect a breach —
Indifferent what you storm or why,
So be that in the breach you die!

Love may be blind, but Love at least
Knows what is man and what mere beast;   10
Or Beauty wayward, but requires
More delicacy from her squires.

Tell me, my witless, whose one boast
Could be your staunchness at the post,
When were you made a man of parts   15
To think fine and profess the arts?

Will many-gifted Beauty come
Bowing to your bald rule of thumb,
Or Love swear loyalty to your crown?
Be gone, have done! Down, wanton, down!   20

DOWN, WANTON, DOWN! 5. *bombard-captain:* officer in charge of a bombard, an early type of
cannon that hurled stones. 6. *ravelin:* fortification with two faces that meet in a protruding
angle. *effect a breach:* break an opening through (a fortification). 15. *man of parts:* man of talent
or ability.

QUESTIONS

1. How do you define a wanton?
2. What wanton does the poet address?
3. Explain the comparison drawn in the second stanza.
4. In line 14, how many meanings do you find in *staunchness at the post*?
5. Explain any other puns you find in lines 15 – 19.

6. Do you take this to be a cynical poem making fun of Love and Beauty, or is Graves making fun of stupid, animal lust?

Peter Davison (b. 1928)
THE LAST WORD   1970

When I saw your head bow, I knew I had beaten you.
You shed no tears — not near me — but held your neck
Bare for the blow I had been too frightened
Ever to deliver, even in words. And now,
In spite of me, plummeting it came.   5
Frozen we both waited for its fall.

Most of what you gave me I have forgotten
With my mind but taken into my body,
But this I remember well: the bones of your neck
And the strain in my shoulders as I heaved up that huge   10
Double blade and snapped my wrists to swing
The handle down and hear the axe's edge
Nick through your flesh and creak into the block.

QUESTIONS

1. "The Last Word" stands fourth in a series titled "Four Love Poems." Sum up what happens in this poem. Do you take this to be *merely* a literal account of an execution? Explain the comparison.
2. Which words embody concrete things and show us physical actions? Which words have sounds that especially contribute to the poem's effectiveness?

David B. Axelrod (b. 1943)
ONCE IN A WHILE A PROTEST POEM   1976

Over and over again the papers print
the dried-out tit of an African woman
holding her starving child. Over
and over, cropping it each time to one
prominent, withered tit, the feeble   5
infant face. Over and over to toughen
us, teach us to ignore the foam turned
dusty powder on the infant's lips,
the mother's sunken face (is cropped)
and filthy dress. The tit remains;   10
the tit held out for everyone to see,
reminding us only that we are not so hungry
ogling the tit, admiring it and in our
living rooms, making it a symbol of starving
millions; our sympathy as real as silicone.   15

1. Why is the last word in this poem especially meaningful?
2. What does the poet protest?

Miller Williams (b. 1930)

ON THE SYMBOLIC CONSIDERATION OF HANDS
AND THE SIGNIFICANCE OF DEATH   1973

Watch people stop by bodies in funeral homes.
You know their eyes will fix on the hands and they do.
Because a hand that has no desire to make
a fist again or cut bread or lay stones
is among those things most difficult to believe.
It is believed for a fact by a very few
old nuns in France who carve beads out of knuckle bones.

QUESTIONS

1. Why, according to the poet, is it hard for us to believe in the literal fact of death? Why isn't such belief a problem for the nuns?
2. From just the title of the poem, would you expect the poem to be written in plain, simple language, or in very abstract, general language? In what kind of language *is* it written?
3. What possible reason could the poet have for choosing such a title? (Besides being a poet, Miller Williams is a critic and teacher of poetry. He probably knows many readers and students of poetry who expect poems *necessarily* to deal in symbolic considerations and large significances.)

John Donne (1572 – 1631)*

BATTER MY HEART, THREE-PERSONED GOD, FOR YOU   (about 1610)

Batter my heart, three-personed God, for You
As yet but knock, breathe, shine, and seek to mend.
That I may rise and stand, o'erthrow me, and bend
Your force to break, blow, burn, and make me new.
I, like an usurped town to another due,   5
Labor to admit You, but Oh! to no end.
Reason, Your viceroy in me, me should defend,
But is captived, and proves weak or untrue.
Yet dearly I love You, and would be lovèd fain,
But am betrothed unto Your enemy;   10
Divorce me, untie or break that knot again;
Take me to You, imprison me, for I,
Except You enthrall me, never shall be free,
Nor ever chaste, except You ravish me.

1. In the last line of this sonnet, to what does Donne compare the onslaught of God's love? Do you think the poem weakened by the poet's comparing a spiritual experience to something so grossly carnal? Discuss.
2. Explain the seeming contradiction in the last line: in what sense can a ravished person be *chaste?* Explain the seeming contradictions in lines 3 – 4 and 12 – 13: how can a person thrown down and destroyed be enabled to *rise and stand;* an imprisoned person be *free?*
3. In lines 5 – 6 the speaker compares himself to a *usurped town* trying to throw off its conqueror by admitting an army of liberation. Who is the "usurper" in this comparison?
4. Explain the comparison of *Reason* to a *viceroy* (lines 7 – 8).
5. Sum up in your own words the message of Donne's poem. In stating its theme, did you have to read the poem for literal meanings, figurative comparisons, or both?

THE VALUE OF A DICTIONARY

If a poet troubles to seek out the best words available, the least we can do is to find out what the words mean. The dictionary is a firm ally in reading poems; if the poems are more than a century old, it is indispensable. Meanings change. When the Elizabethan poet George Gascoigne wrote, "O Abraham's brats, O brood of blessed seed," the word *brats* implied neither irritation nor contempt. When in the seventeenth century Andrew Marvell imagined two lovers' "vegetable love," he referred to a vegetative or growing love, not one resembling a lettuce. And when King George III called a building an "awful artificial spectacle," he was not condemning it but praising it as an awe-inspiring work of art.

In reading poetry, there is nothing to be done about this inevitable tendency of language except to watch out for it. If you suspect that a word has shifted in meaning over the years, most standard desk dictionaries will be helpful, an unabridged dictionary more helpful yet, and most helpful of all the *Oxford English Dictionary (OED),* which gives, for each definition, successive examples of the word's written use down through the past thousand years. You need not feel a grim obligation to keep interrupting a poem in order to rummage the dictionary; but if the poem is worth reading very closely, you may wish any aid you can find.

One of the valuable services of poetry is to recall for us the concrete, physical sense that certain words once had, but since have lost. As the English critic H. Coombes has remarked in *Literature and Criticism,*

> We use a word like *powerful* without feeling that it is really "power-full." We do not seem today to taste the full flavor of words as we feel that Falstaff (and Shakespeare, and probably his audience) tasted them when he was applauding the virtues of "good sherris-sack," which makes the brain "apprehensive, quick, forgetive, full of nimble, fiery, and delectable shapes." And being less aware of the life and substantiality of words, we are probably less aware of the things . . . that these words stand for.

"Every word which is used to express a moral or intellectual fact," said Emerson in *The Conduct of Life,* "if traced to its root, is found to be borrowed from some material appearance. *Right* means straight; *wrong* means twisted. *Spirit* primarily means wind; *transgression,* the crossing of a line; *supercilious,* the raising of an eyebrow." Browse in a dictionary and you will discover such original concretenesses. These are revealed in your dictionary's etymologies, or brief notes on the derivation of words, given in most dictionaries near the beginning of an entry on a word; in some dictionaries, at the end of the entry. Look up *squirrel,* for instance, and you will find it comes from two Greek words meaning "shadow-tail." For another example of a common word that originally contained a poetic metaphor, look up the origin of the word *daisy.*

EXPERIMENT: *Seeing Words' Origins*

Much of the effect of the following poem depends upon our awareness of the precision with which the poet has selected his words. We can better see this by knowing their derivations. For instance, *potpourri* comes from French: *pot* plus *pourri.* What do these words mean? (If you do not know French, look up the etymology of the word in a dictionary.) Look up the definitions and etymologies of *revenance, circumstance, inspiration, conceptual, commotion, cordial,* and *azure;* and try to state the meanings these words have in Wilbur's poem.

Richard Wilbur (b. 1921)*
IN THE ELEGY SEASON   1950

Haze, char, and the weather of All Souls':
A giant absence mopes upon the trees:
Leaves cast in casual potpourris
Whisper their scents from pits and cellar-holes.

Or brewed in gulleys, steeped in wells, they spend   5
In chilly steam their last aromas, yield
From shallow hells a revenance of field
And orchard air. And now the envious mind

Which could not hold the summer in my head
While bounded by that blazing circumstance   10
Parades these barrens in a golden trance,
Remembering the wealthy season dead,

And by an autumn inspiration makes
A summer all its own. Green boughs arise
Through all the boundless backward of the eyes,   15
And the soul bathes in warm conceptual lakes.

Less proud than this, my body leans an ear
Past cold and colder weather after wings'
Soft commotion, the sudden race of springs,
The goddess' tread heard on the dayward stair,   20

Longs for the brush of the freighted air, for smells
Of grass and cordial lilac, for the sight
Of green leaves building into the light
And azure water hoisting out of wells.

An **allusion** is an indirect reference to any person, place, or thing —
fictitious, historical, or actual. Sometimes, to understand an allusion in a
poem, we have to find out something we didn't know before. But usually
the poet asks of us only common knowledge. When Edgar Allan Poe refers
to "the glory that was Greece / And the grandeur that was Rome," he
assumes that we have heard of those places, and that we will understand
his allusion to the cultural achievement of those nations (implicit in *glory*
and *grandeur*).

Allusions not only enrich the meaning of a poem, they also save
space. In "The Love Song of J. Alfred Prufrock" (page 713), T. S. Eliot, by
giving a brief introductory quotation from the speech of a damned soul in
Dante's *Inferno,* is able to suggest that his poem will be the confession of
a soul in torment, who sees no chance of escape.

Often in reading a poem you will meet a name you don't recognize,
on which the meaning of a line (or perhaps a whole poem) seems to
depend. In this book, most such unfamiliar references and allusions are
glossed or footnoted, but when you venture out on your own in reading
poems, you may find yourself needlessly perplexed unless you look up
such names, the way you look up any other words. Unless the name is one
that the poet made up, you will probably find it in one of the larger desk
dictionaries, such as *Webster's New Collegiate Dictionary, The American Heritage
Dictionary,* or *Webster's II.* If you don't solve your problem there, try an
encyclopedia, a world atlas, or *The New Century Cyclopedia of Names.*

Some allusions are quotations from other poems. In L. E. Sissman's
"In and Out: A Home Away from Home," the narrator, a male college
student, describes his sleeping love,

> This Sally now does like a garment wear
> The beauty of the evening; silent, bare,
> Hips, shoulders, arms, tresses, and temples lie.

(For the source of these lines, see Wordsworth's "Composed upon Westminster Bridge," page 788.)

EXERCISE: *Catching Allusions*

From your knowledge, supplemented by a dictionary or other reference work if
need be, explain the allusions in the following five poems.

Cid Corman (b. 1924)

THE TORTOISE

1964

Always to want to
go back, to correct
an error, ease a

guilt, see how a friend
is doing. And yet
one doesnt, except 5

in memory, in
dreams. The land remains
desolate. Always

the feeling is of 10
terrible slowness
overtaking haste.

J. V. Cunningham (1911 – 1985)*

FRIEND, ON THIS SCAFFOLD THOMAS MORE LIES DEAD

1960

Friend, on this scaffold Thomas More lies dead
Who would not cut the Body from the Head.

Herman Melville (1819 – 1891)

THE PORTENT

(1859)

Hanging from the beam,
  Slowly swaying (such the law),
Gaunt the shadow on your green,
  Shenandoah!

The cut is on the crown 5
  (Lo, John Brown),
And the stabs shall heal no more.

Hidden in the cap
  Is the anguish none can draw;
So your future veils its face, 10
  Shenandoah!

But the streaming beard is shown
  (Weird John Brown),
The meteor of the war.

John Dryden (1631 – 1700)*

Lines Printed Under the Engraved Portrait of Milton
1668

Three poets, in three distant ages born,
Greece, Italy, and England did adorn.
The first in loftiness of thought surpassed,
The next in majesty, in both the last:
The force of Nature could no farther go;
To make a third she joined the former two.

Lines Printed Under the Engraved Portrait of Milton. These lines appeared in Tonson's folio edition of *Paradise Lost* (1668).

Laurence Perrine (b. 1915)

Janus
1984

Janus writes books for women's liberation;
His wife types up the scripts from his dictation.

John Clare (1793 – 1864)

Mouse's Nest
(about 1835)

I found a ball of grass among the hay
And progged it as I passed and went away;
And when I looked I fancied something stirred,
And turned again and hoped to catch the bird —
When out an old mouse bolted in the wheats   5
With all her young ones hanging at her teats;
She looked so odd and so grotesque to me,
I ran and wondered what the thing could be,
And pushed the knapweed bunches where I stood;
Then the mouse hurried from the craking° brood.   *crying*   10
The young ones squeaked, and as I went away
She found her nest again among the hay.
The water o'er the pebbles scarce could run
And broad old cesspools glittered in the sun.

Questions

1. "To prog" (line 2) means "to poke about for food, to forage." In what ways does this word fit more exactly here than *prodded, touched,* or *searched?*
2. Is *craking* (line 10) better than *crying?* Which word better fits the poem? Why?
3. What connections do you find between the last two lines and the rest of the poem? To what are water that *scarce could run* and *broad old cesspools* (lines 13 and 14) likened?

Lewis Carroll
[Charles Lutwidge Dodgson] (1832 – 1898)

JABBERWOCKY   1871

'Twas brillig, and the slithy toves
   Did gyre and gimble in the wabe:
All mimsy were the borogoves,
   And the mome raths outgrabe.

"Beware the Jabberwock, my son!   5
   The jaws that bite, the claws that catch!
Beware the Jubjub bird, and shun
   The frumious Bandersnatch!"

He took his vorpal sword in hand;
   Long time the manxome foe he sought —   10
So rested he by the Tumtum tree
   And stood awhile in thought.

And, as in uffish thought he stood,
   The Jabberwock, with eyes of flame,
Came whiffling through the tulgey wood,   15
   And burbled as it came!

One, two! One, two! And through and through
   The vorpal blade went snicker-snack!
He left it dead, and with its head
   He went galumphing back.   20

"And hast thou slain the Jabberwock?
   Come to my arms, my beamish boy!
O frabjous day! Callooh, Callay!"
   He chortled in his joy.

'Twas brillig, and the slithy toves   25
   Did gyre and gimble in the wabe:
All mimsy were the borogoves,
   And the mome raths outgrabe.

JABBERWOCKY. Fussy about pronunciation, Carroll in his preface to *The Hunting of the Snark* declares: "The first 'o' in 'borogoves' is pronounced like the 'o' in 'borrow.' I have heard people try to give it the sound of the 'o' in 'worry.' Such is Human Perversity." *Toves,* he adds, rimes with *groves.*

QUESTIONS

1. Look up *chortled* (line 24) in your dictionary and find out its definition and origin.
2. In *Through the Looking-Glass,* Alice seeks the aid of Humpty Dumpty to decipher the meaning of this nonsense poem. *"Brillig,"* he explains, "means four o'clock in the afternoon — the time when you begin *broiling* things for dinner." Does *brillig* sound like any other familiar word?

3. *"Slithy,"* the explanation goes on, "means 'lithe and slimy.' 'Lithe' is the same as 'active.' You see it's like a portmanteau — there are two meanings packed up into one word." *Mimsy* is supposed to pack together both "flimsy" and "miserable." In the rest of the poem, what other portmanteau — or packed suitcase — words can you find?

Wallace Stevens (1879 – 1955)*

METAMORPHOSIS   1942

Yillow, yillow, yillow,
Old worm, my pretty quirk,
How the wind spells out
Sep - tem - ber. . . .

Summer is in bones.   5
Cock-robin's at Caracas.
Make o, make o, make o,
Oto - otu - bre.

And the rude leaves fall.
The rain falls. The sky   10
Falls and lies with the worms.
The street lamps

Are those that have been hanged.
Dangling in an illogical
To and to and fro   15
Fro Niz - nil - imbo.

QUESTIONS

1. Explain the title. Of the several meanings of *metamorphosis* given in a dictionary, which best applies to the process that Stevens sees in the natural world?
2. What metamorphosis is also taking place in the *language* of the poem? How does it continue from line 4 to line 8 to line 16?
3. In the last line, which may recall the thickening drone of a speaker lapsing into sleep, *Niz - nil - imbo* seems not only a pun on the name of a month, but also a portmanteau word into which at least two familiar words are packed. Say it aloud. What are they?
4. What dictionary definitions of the word *quirk* seem relevant to line 2? How can a worm be a quirk? What else in this poem seems quirky?

WORD CHOICE AND WORD ORDER

Even if Samuel Johnson's famous *Dictionary* of 1755 had been as thick as Webster's unabridged, an eighteenth-century poet searching through it for words to use would have had a narrower choice. For in English literature of the **neoclassical period** or **Augustan age** — that period from about

1660 into the late eighteenth century — many poets subscribed to a belief in **poetic diction:** "A system of words," said Dr. Johnson, "refined from the grossness of domestic use." The system admitted into a serious poem only certain words and subjects, excluding others as violations of **decorum** (propriety). Accordingly such common words as *rat, cheese, big, sneeze,* and *elbow,* although admissible to satire, were thought inconsistent with the loftiness of tragedy, epic, ode, and elegy. Dr. Johnson's biographer, James Boswell, tells how a poet writing an epic reconsidered the word "rats" and instead wrote "the whiskered vermin race." Johnson himself objected to Lady Macbeth's allusion to her "keen knife," saying that "we do not immediately conceive that any crime of importance is to be committed with a knife; or who does not, at last, from the long habit of connecting a knife with sordid offices, feel aversion rather than terror?" Probably Johnson was here the victim of his age, and Shakespeare was right, but Johnson in one of his assumptions was right too: there are inappropriate words as well as appropriate ones.

Neoclassical poets chose their classical models more often from Roman writers than from Greek, as their diction suggests by the frequency of Latin derivatives. For example, a *net,* according to Dr. Johnson's dictionary, is "any thing reticulated or decussated, at equal distances, with interstices between the intersections." In company with Latinate words often appeared fixed combinations of adjective and noun ("finny prey" for "fish"), poetic names (a song to a lady named Molly might rechristen her Parthenia), and allusions to classical mythology. Neoclassical poetic diction was evidently being abused when, instead of saying "uncork the bottle," a poet could write,

> Apply thine engine to the spongy door,
> Set *Bacchus* from his glassy prison free,

in some bad lines ridiculed by Alexander Pope in *Peri Bathous, or, Of the Art of Sinking in Poetry.*

Not all poetic diction is excess baggage. To a reader who knew at first hand both living sheep and the pastoral poems of Virgil — as most readers nowadays do not — such a fixed phrase as "the fleecy care," which seems stilted to us, conveyed pleasurable associations. But "fleecy care" was more than a highfalutin way of saying "sheep"; as one scholar has pointed out, "when they wished, our poets could say 'sheep' as clearly and as often as anybody else. In the first place, 'fleecy' drew attention to wool, and demanded the appropriate visual image of sheep; for aural imagery the poets would refer to 'the bleating kind'; it all depended upon what was happening in the poem."[3]

Other poets have found some special kind of poetic language valu-

---

[3]Bonamy Dobrée, *English Literature in the Early Eighteenth Century, 1700 – 1740* (New York: Oxford UP, 1959) 161.

able: Old English poets, with their standard figures of speech ("whale-road" for the sea, "ring-giver" for a ruler); makers of folk ballads who, no less than neoclassicists, love fixed epithet-noun combinations ("milk-white steed," "blood-red wine," "steel-driving man"); and Edmund Spenser, whose example made popular the adjective ending in -y (*fleecy, grassy, milky*).

When Wordsworth, in his Preface to *Lyrical Ballads,* asserted that "the language really spoken by men," especially by humble rustics, is plainer, more emphatic, and conveys "elementary feelings . . . in a state of greater simplicity," he was, in effect, advocating a new poetic diction. Wordsworth's ideas invited freshness into English poetry and, by admitting words that neoclassical poets would have called "low" ("His poor old *ankles* swell"), helped rid poets of the fear of being thought foolish for mentioning a commonplace.

This theory of the superiority of rural diction was, as Coleridge pointed out, hard to adhere to, and, in practice, Wordsworth was occasionally to write a language as Latinate and citified as these lines on yew trees:

> Huge trunks! — and each particular trunk a growth
> Of intertwisted fibers serpentine
> Up-coiling, and inveterately convolved . . .

Language so Latinate sounds pedantic to us, especially the phrase *inveterately convolved.* In fact, some poets, notably Gerard Manley Hopkins, have subscribed to the view that English words derived from Anglo-Saxon (Old English) have more force and flavor than their Latin equivalents. *Kingly,* one may feel, has more power than *regal.* One argument for this view is that so many words of Old English origin — *man, wife, child, house, eat, drink, sleep* — are basic to our living speech. It may be true that a language closer to Old English is particularly fit for rendering abstract notions concretely — as does the memorable title of a medieval work of piety, the *Ayenbite of Inwit* ("again-bite of inner wisdom" or "remorse of conscience"). And yet this view, if accepted at all, must be accepted with reservations. Some words of Latin origin carry meanings both precise and physical. In the King James Bible is the admonition, "See then that ye walk circumspectly, not as fools, but as wise" (Ephesians 5:15). To be *circumspect* (a word from two Latin roots meaning "to look" and "around") is to be watchful on all sides — a meaning altogether lost in a modernized wording of the passage once printed on a subway poster for a Bible society: "Be careful how you live, not thoughtlessly but thoughtfully."

When E. E. Cummings begins a poem, "mr youse needn't be so spry / concernin questions arty," we recognized another kind of diction available to poetry: **vulgate** (speech not much affected by schooling). Handbooks of grammar sometimes distinguish various **levels of usage.** A sort of ladder is imagined, on whose rungs words, phrases, and sentences may be ranked in an ascending order of formality, from the curses of an illiterate thug to the commencement-day address of a doctor of divinity. These levels range from vulgate through **colloquial** (the casual conversation or informal writing of literate people) and **general English** (most literate speech and writing, more studied than colloquial but not pretentious), up to **formal English** (the impersonal language of educated persons, usually only written, possibly spoken on dignified occasions). Recently, however, lexicographers have been shunning such labels. The designation *colloquial* has been expelled (*bounced* would be colloquial; *trun out,* vulgate) from *Webster's Third New International Dictionary* on the grounds that "it is impossible to know whether a word out of context is colloquial or not" and that the diction of Americans nowadays is more fluid than the labels suggest. Aware that we are being unscientific, we may find the labels useful. They may help roughly to describe what happens when, as in the following poem, a poet shifts from one level of usage to another. This poem employs, incidentally, a colloquial device throughout: omitting the subjects of sentences. In keeping the characters straight, it may be helpful to fill in the speaker for each *said* and for the verbs *saw* and *ducked* (lines 9 and 10).

Josephine Miles (1911 – 1985)
REASON   1955

Said, Pull her up a bit will you, Mac, I want to unload there.
Said, Pull her up my rear end, first come first serve.
Said, Give her the gun, Bud, he needs a taste of his own bumper.
Then the usher came out and got into the act:
Said, Pull her up, pull her up a bit, we need this space, sir.   5
Said, For God's sake, is this still a free country or what?
You go back and take care of Gary Cooper's horse
And leave me handle my own car.

Saw them unloading the lame old lady,
Ducked out under the wheel and gave her an elbow,   10
Said, All you needed to do was just explain;
Reason, Reason is my middle name.

Language on more than one level enlivens this miniature comedy; the vulgate of the resentful driver ("Pull her up my rear end," "leave me handle my own car") and the colloquial of the bystander ("Give her the gun"). There is also a contrast in formality between the old lady's driver, who says "Mac," and the usher, who says "sir." These varied levels of language distinguish the speakers in the poem from one another.

The diction of "Reason" is that of speech; that of Coleridge's "Kubla Khan" (page 702) is more bookish. Coleridge is not at fault, however: the language of Josephine Miles's reasonable driver might not have contained Kubla Khan's stately pleasure dome. At present, most poetry in English appears to be shunning expressions such as "fleecy care" in favor of general

English and the colloquial. In Scotland, there has been an interesting development: the formation of an active group of poets who write in Scots, a **dialect** (variety of language spoken by a social group or spoken in a certain locality). Perhaps, whether poets write in language close to speech or in language of greater formality, their poems will ring true if they choose appropriate words.

EXPERIMENT: *Wheeshts into Hushes*

Reword the following poem from Scots dialect into general English, using the closest possible equivalents. Then try to assess what the poem has gained or lost. (In line 4, a "ploy," as defined by *Webster's Third New International Dictionary*, is a pursuit or activity, "especially one that requires eagerness or finesse.")

Hugh MacDiarmid
[Christopher Murray Grieve] (1892 – 1978)*

WHEESHT, WHEESHT   1926

Wheesht°, wheesht, my foolish hert,	*hush*
For weel ye ken°	*know*
I widna ha'e ye stert	
Auld ploys again.	
It's guid to see her lie	
Sae snod° an' cool,	*smooth*
A' lust o' lovin' by –	
Wheesht, wheesht, ye fule!	

Not only the poet's choice of words makes a poem seem more formal, or less, but also the way the words are arranged into sentences. Compare these lines,

> Jack and Jill went up the hill
> To fetch a pail of water.
> Jack fell down and broke his crown
> And Jill came tumbling after.

with Milton's account of a more significant downfall:

> Earth trembled from her entrails, as again
> In pangs, and Nature gave a second groan;
> Sky loured, and, muttering thunder, some sad drops
> Wept at completing of the mortal sin
> Original; while Adam took no thought
> Eating his fill, nor Eve to iterate
> Her former trespass feared, the more to soothe
> Him with her loved society, that now
> As with new wine intoxicated both
> They swim in mirth, and fancy that they feel

Divinity within them breeding wings
Wherewith to scorn the Earth.

Not all the words in Milton's lines are bookish: indeed, many of them can be found in nursery rimes. What helps, besides diction, to distinguish this account of the Biblical fall from "Jack and Jill" is that Milton's nonstop sentence seems further removed from usual speech in its length (83 words), in its complexity (subordinate clauses), and in its word order ("with new wine intoxicated both" rather than "both intoxicated with new wine"). Should we think less (or more highly) of Milton for choosing a style so elaborate and formal? No judgment need be passed: both Mother Goose and the author of *Paradise Lost* use language appropriate to their purposes.

Among languages, English is by no means the most flexible. English words must be used in fairly definite and inviolable patterns, and whoever departs too far from them will not be understood. In the sentence "Cain slew Abel," if you change the word order, you change the meaning: "Abel slew Cain." Such inflexibility was not true of Latin, in which a poet could lay down words in almost any sequence and, because their endings (inflections) showed what parts of speech they were, could trust that no reader would mistake a subject for an object or a noun for an adjective. (E. E. Cummings has striven, in certain of his poems, for the freedom of Latin. One such poem, "anyone lived in a pretty how town," appears on page 463.)

The rigidity of English word order invites the poet to defy it and to achieve unusual effects by inverting it. It is customary in English to place adjective in front of noun *(a blue mantle, new pastures)*. But an unusual emphasis is achieved when Milton ends "Lycidas" by reversing the pattern:

At last he rose, and twitched his mantle blue:
Tomorrow to fresh woods, and pastures new.

Perhaps the inversion in *mantle blue* gives more prominence to the color associated with heaven (and in "Lycidas," heaven is of prime importance). Perhaps the inversion in *pastures new,* stressing the *new,* heightens the sense of a rebirth.

Coleridge offered two "homely definitions of prose and poetry; that is, *prose:* words in their best order; *poetry:* the best words in the best order." If all goes well, a poet may fasten the right word into the right place, and the result may be — as T. S. Eliot said in "Little Gidding" — a "complete consort dancing together."

Thomas Hardy (1840 – 1928)*
The Ruined Maid   1901

"O 'Melia, my dear, this does everything crown!
Who could have supposed I should meet you in Town?
And whence such fair garments, such prosperi-ty?" —
"O didn't you know I'd been ruined?" said she.

— "You left us in tatters, without shoes or socks,   5
Tired of digging potatoes, and spudding up docks°;   *spading up dockweed*
And now you've gay bracelets and bright feathers three!" —
"Yes: that's how we dress when we're ruined," said she.

— "At home in the barton° you said 'thee' and 'thou,'   *farmyard*
And 'thik oon,' and 'theäs oon,' and 't'other'; but now   10
Your talking quite fits 'ee for high compa-ny!" —
"Some polish is gained with one's ruin," said she.

— "Your hands were like paws then, your face blue and bleak
But now I'm bewitched by your delicate cheek,
And your little gloves fit as on any la-dy!" —   15
"We never do work when we're ruined," said she.

— "You used to call home-life a hag-ridden dream,
And you'd sigh, and you'd sock°; but at present you seem   *groan*
To know not of megrims° or melancho-ly!" —   *blues*
"True. One's pretty lively when ruined," said she.   20

— "I wish I had feathers, a fine sweeping gown,
And a delicate face, and could strut about Town!" —
"My dear — a raw country girl, such as you be,
Cannot quite expect that. You ain't ruined," said she.

QUESTIONS

1. Where does this dialogue take place? Who are the two speakers?
2. Comment on Hardy's use of the word *ruined*. What is the conventional meaning of the word when applied to a girl? As 'Melia applies it to herself what is its meaning?
3. Sum up the attitude of each speaker toward the other. What details of the new 'Melia does the first speaker most dwell upon? Would you expect Hardy to be so impressed by all these details, or is there, between his view of the characters and their view of themselves, any hint of an ironic discrepancy?
4. In losing her country dialect (*thik oon* and *theäs oon* for *this one* and *that one*), 'Melia is presumed to have gained in sophistication. What does Hardy suggest by her *ain't* in the last line?

E. E. Cummings (1894 – 1962)*

ANYONE LIVED IN A PRETTY HOW TOWN   1940

anyone lived in a pretty how town
(with up so floating many bells down)
spring summer autumn winter
he sang his didn't he danced his did.

Women and men (both little and small)   5
cared for anyone not at all
they sowed their isn't they reaped their same
sun moon stars rain

children guessed (but only a few
and down they forgot as up they grew
autumn winter spring summer)
that noone loved him more by more

when by now and tree by leaf
she laughed his joy she cried his grief
bird by snow and stir by still
anyone's any was all to her

someones married their everyones
laughed their cryings and did their dance
(sleep wake hope and then) they
said their nevers they slept their dream

stars rain sun moon
(and only the snow can begin to explain
how children are apt to forget to remember
with up so floating many bells down)

one day anyone died i guess
(and noone stooped to kiss his face)
busy folk buried them side by side
little by little and was by was

all by all and deep by deep
and more by more they dream their sleep
noone and anyone earth by april
wish by spirit and if by yes.

Women and men (both dong and ding)
summer autumn winter spring
reaped their sowing and went their came
sun moon stars rain

10

15

20

25

30

35

Questions

1. Summarize the story told in this poem. Who are the characters?
2. Rearrange the words in the two opening lines into the order you would expect them usually to follow. What effect does Cummings obtain by his unconventional word order?
3. Another of Cummings's strategies is to use one part of speech as if it were another; for instance, in line 4, *didn't* and *did* ordinarily are verbs, but here they are used as nouns. What other words in the poem perform functions other than their expected ones?

James Emanuel (b. 1921)

THE NEGRO   1968

Never saw him.
Never can.
Hypothetical,
Haunting man.

Eyes a-saucer,   5
Yessir bossir,
Dice a-clicking,
Razor flicking.

The-ness froze him
In a dance.   10
A-ness never
had a chance.

QUESTIONS

1. How do you think the poet would define his coined words *the-ness* and *a-ness*?
2. In your own words, sum up the theme of this poem.

Richard Eberhart (b. 1904)

THE FURY OF AERIAL BOMBARDMENT   1947

You would think the fury of aerial bombardment
Would rouse God to relent; the infinite spaces
Are still silent. He looks on shock-pried faces.
History, even, does not know what is meant.

You would feel that after so many centuries   5
God would give man to repent; yet he can kill
As Cain could, but with multitudinous will,
No farther advanced than in his ancient furies.

Was man made stupid to see his own stupidity?
Is God by definition indifferent, beyond us all?   10
Is the eternal truth man's fighting soul
Wherein the Beast ravens in its own avidity?

Of Van Wettering I speak, and Averill,
Names on a list, whose faces I do not recall
But they are gone to early death, who late in school   15
Distinguished the belt feed lever from the belt holding pawl.

1. As a naval officer during World War II, Richard Eberhart was assigned for a time as an instructor in a gunnery school. How has this experience apparently contributed to the diction of his poem?
2. In his *Life of John Dryden,* complaining about a description of a sea fight Dryden had filled with nautical language, Samuel Johnson argued that technical terms should be excluded from poetry. Is this criticism applicable to Eberhart's last line? Can a word succeed for us in a poem, even though we may not be able to define it? (For more evidence, see also the technical terms in Henry Reed's "Naming of Parts," p. 758.)
3. Some readers have found a contrast in tone between the first three stanzas of this poem and the last stanza. How would you describe this contrast? What does diction contribute to it?

EXERCISE: *Different Kinds of English*

Read the following poems and see what kinds of diction and word order you find in them. Which poems are least formal in their language and which most formal? Is there any use of vulgate English? Any dialect? What does each poem achieve that its own kind of English makes possible?

Anonymous (American oral verse)
CARNATION MILK   (about 1900?)

Carnation Milk is the best in the land;
Here I sit with a can in my hand —
No tits to pull, no hay to pitch,
You just punch a hole in the son of a bitch.

CARNATION MILK. "This quatrain is imagined as the caption under a picture of a rugged-looking cowboy seated upon a bale of hay," notes William Harmon in his *Oxford Book of American Light Verse* (New York: Oxford UP, 1979). Possibly the first to print this work was David Ogilvy (b. 1911), who quotes it in his *Confessions of an Advertising Man* (New York: Atheneum, 1963).

A. R. Ammons (b. 1926)
SPRING COMING   1970

The caryophyllaceae
like a scroungy
frost are
rising through the lawn:
many-fingered as leggy   5
  copepods:
a suggestive delicacy,

lacework, like
the scent of wild plum
   thickets: 10
also the grackles
with their incredible
vertical, horizontal,
reversible
tails have arrived: 15
such nice machines.

William Wordsworth (1770 – 1850)*
My heart leaps up when I behold   1807

My heart leaps up when I behold
   A rainbow in the sky:
So was it when my life began;
So is it now I am a man;
So be it when I shall grow old,   5
   Or let me die!
The Child is father of the Man;
And I could wish my days to be
Bound each to each by natural piety.

William Wordsworth (1770 – 1850)*
Mutability   1822

From low to high doth dissolution climb,
And sink from high to low, along a scale
Of awful notes, whose concord shall not fail;
A musical but melancholy chime,
Which they can hear who meddle not with crime,   5
Nor avarice, nor over-anxious care.
Truth fails not; but her outward forms that bear
The longest date do melt like frosty rime°,   *frozen dew*
That in the morning whitened hill and plain
And is no more; drop like the tower sublime   10
Of yesterday, which royally did wear
His crown of weeds, but could not even sustain
Some casual shout that broke the silent air,
Or the unimaginable touch of Time.

John Malcolm Brinnin (b. 1916)

THE ASCENSION: 1925   1963

Step on it, said Aunt Alice, *for God's sake,*
The bloody thing is going up at four!
She crammed two broilers in a paper sack,
Harnessed the dog and pushed us out the door.
Flapping like a witch, our touring car   5
Ate black macadam toward Fort Frontenac
Where, trembling in her ropes, the ship of air
Rolled easy as a fifty-cent cigar.

Jesus, said Uncle Lester, *what a beaut!*
Chomping on Juicy Fruit, we eyed her close   10
As, nuzzling upward from her stake, she rose
In strict submission to the absolute.
We hit the highway sixty on the nose
And jettisoned our chicken bones en route.

Anonymous

SCOTTSBORO   1936

Paper come out — done strewed de news
Seven po' chillun moan deat' house blues,
Seven po' chillun moanin' deat' house blues.
Seven nappy° heads wit' big shiny eye   *frizzy*
All boun' in jail and framed to die,   5
All boun' in jail and framed to die.

Messin' white woman — snake lyin' tale
Hang and burn and jail wit' no bail.
Dat hang and burn and jail wit' no bail.
Worse ol' crime in white folks' lan'   10
Black skin coverin' po' workin' man,
Black skin coverin' po' workin' man.

Judge and jury — all in de stan'
Lawd, biggety name for same lynchin' ban',
Lawd, biggety name for same lynchin' ban'.   15
White folks and nigger in great co't house
Like cat down cellar wit' nohole mouse.
Like cat down cellar wit' nohole mouse.

SCOTTSBORO. This folk blues, collected by Lawrence Gellert in *Negro Songs of Protest* (New York: Carl Fischer, Inc., 1936), is a comment on the Scottsboro case. In 1931 nine black youths of Scottsboro, Alabama, were arrested and charged with the rape of two white women. Though eventually, after several trials, they were found not guilty, some of them at the time this song was composed had been convicted and sentenced to death.

SUGGESTIONS FOR WRITING

1. Choosing a poem that strikes you as particularly inventive or unusual in its language, such as Wallace Stevens's "Metamorphosis" (page 457), E. E. Cummings's "anyone lived in a pretty how town" (page 463), or Gerard Manley Hopkins's "The Windhover" (page 730), write a brief analysis of it. Concentrate on the diction of the poem and its word order. For what possible purposes does the poet depart from standard English? (To find some pointers on writing about poetry by the method of analysis, see page 1378.)

2. In a short essay, set forth the pleasures of browsing in a dictionary. As you browse, see if you can discover any "found poems" (discussed on pages 573 – 575).

3. "Printing poetry in dialect, such as 'Scottsboro,' insults the literacy of a people." Think about this critical charge and comment on it.

4. Write a short defense of a poet's right to employ the language of science and technology. Alternatively, point out some of the dangers and drawbacks of using such language in poetry. For evidence, see the poems in this chapter by Richard Eberhart and A. R. Ammons and those in the Anthology by James Merrill (page 746) and Henry Reed (page 758).

16 Saying and Suggesting

To write so clearly that they might bring "all things as near the mathematical plainness" as possible — that was the goal of scientists according to Bishop Thomas Sprat, who lived in the seventeenth century. Such an effort would seem bound to fail, because words, unlike numbers, are ambiguous indicators. Although it may have troubled Bishop Sprat, the tendency of a word to have multiplicity of meaning rather than mathematical plainness opens broad avenues to poetry.

Every word has at least one **denotation:** a meaning as defined in a dictionary. But the English language has many a common word with so many denotations that a reader may need to think twice to see what it means in a specific context. The noun *field,* for instance, can denote a piece of ground, a sports arena, the scene of a battle, part of a flag, a profession, and a number system in mathematics. Further, the word can be used as a verb ("he fielded a grounder") or an adjective ("field trip," "field glasses").

A word also has **connotations:** overtones or suggestions of additional meaning that it gains from all the contexts in which we have met it in the past. The word *skeleton,* according to a dictionary, denotes "the bony framework of a human being or other vertebrate animal, which supports the flesh and protects the organs." But by its associations, the word can rouse thoughts of war, of disease and death, or (possibly) of one's plans to go to medical school. Think, too, of the difference between "Old Doc Jones" and "Abner P. Jones, M.D." In the mind's eye, the former appears in his shirtsleeves; the latter has a gold nameplate on his door. That some words denote the same thing but have sharply different connotations is pointed out in this anonymous Victorian jingle:

> Here's a little ditty that you really ought to know:
> Horses "sweat" and men "perspire," but ladies only "glow."

The terms *druggist, pharmacist,* and *apothecary* all denote the same occupation, but apothecaries lay claim to special distinction.

Poets aren't the only people who care about the connotations of language. Advertisers know that connotations make money. Recently a Boston automobile dealer advertised his secondhand cars not as "used" but as "pre-owned," as if fearing that "used car" would connote an old heap with soiled upholstery and mysterious engine troubles that somebody couldn't put up with. "Pre-owned," however, suggests that the previous owner has taken the trouble of breaking in the car for you. Not long ago prune-packers, alarmed by a slump in sales, sponsored a survey to determine the connotations of prunes in the public consciousness. Asked, "What do you think of when you hear the word *prunes?*" most people replied, "dried up," "wrinkled," or "constipated." Dismayed, the packers hired an advertising agency to create a new image for prunes, in hopes of inducing new connotations. Soon, advertisements began to show prunes in brightly colored settings, in the company of bikinied bathing beauties.[1]

In imaginative writing, connotations are as crucial as they are in advertising. Consider this sentence: "A new brand of journalism is being born, or spawned" (Dwight Macdonald writing in *The New York Review of Books*). The last word, by its associations with fish and crustaceans, suggests that this new journalism is scarcely the product of human beings. And what do we make of Romeo's assertion that Juliet "is the sun"? Surely even a lovesick boy cannot mean that his sweetheart is "the incandescent body of gases about which the earth and other planets revolve" (a dictionary definition). He means, of course, that he thrives in her sight, that he feels warm in her presence or even at the thought of her, that she illumines his world and is the center of his universe. Because in the mind of the hearer these and other suggestions are brought into play, Romeo's statement, literally absurd, makes excellent sense.

Here is a famous poem that groups together things with similar connotations: certain ships and their cargoes. (A *quinquireme,* by the way, was an ancient Assyrian vessel propelled by sails and oars.)

John Masefield (1878 – 1967)

Cargoes   1902

Quinquireme of Nineveh from distant Ophir,
Rowing home to haven in sunny Palestine,
With a cargo of ivory,
And apes and peacocks,
Sandalwood, cedarwood, and sweet white wine.   5

Stately Spanish galleon coming from the Isthmus,
Dipping through the Tropics by the palm-green shores,
With a cargo of diamonds,
Emeralds, amethysts,
Topazes, and cinnamon, and gold moidores°.   *Portuguese coins*   10

[1]For this and other instances of connotation-engineering, see Vance Packard's *The Hidden Persuaders* (New York: McKay, 1958) chap. 13.

Dirty British coaster with a salt-caked smoke stack,
Butting through the Channel in the mad March days,
With a cargo of Tyne coal,
Road-rails, pig-lead,
Firewood, iron-ware, and cheap tin trays.   15

To us, as well as to the poet's original readers, the place-names in the first
two stanzas suggest the exotic and faraway. Ophir, a vanished place, may
have been in Arabia; according to the Bible, King Solomon sent there for
its celebrated pure gold, also for ivory, apes, peacocks, and other luxury
items. (See I Kings 9 – 10.) In his final stanza, Masefield groups commonplace things (mostly heavy and metallic), whose suggestions of crudeness,
cheapness, and ugliness he deliberately contrasts with those of the precious stuffs he has listed earlier. For British readers, the Tyne is a stodgy
and familiar river; the English Channel in March, choppy and likely to
upset a stomach. The quinquireme is *rowing*, the galleon is *dipping*, but the
dirty British freighter is *butting*, aggressively pushing. Conceivably, the
poet could have described firewood and even coal as beautiful, but evidently he wants them to convey sharply different suggestions here, to go
along with the rest of the coaster's cargo. In drawing such a sharp contrast
between past and present, Masefield does more than merely draw up
bills-of-lading. Perhaps he even implies a wry and unfavorable comment
upon life in the present day. His meaning lies not so much in the dictionary
definitions of his words (*"moidores:* Portuguese gold coins formerly worth
approximately five pounds sterling") as in their rich and vivid connotations.

William Blake (1757 – 1827)*

LONDON   1794

I wander through each chartered street,
Near where the chartered Thames does flow,
And mark in every face I meet
Marks of weakness, marks of woe.

In every cry of every man,   5
In every infant's cry of fear,
In every voice, in every ban,
The mind-forged manacles I hear.

How the chimney-sweeper's cry
Every black'ning church appalls;   10
And the hapless soldier's sigh
Runs in blood down palace walls.

But most through midnight streets I hear
How the youthful harlot's curse

Blasts the new born infant's tear,   15
And blights with plagues the marriage hearse.

Here are only a few of the possible meanings of three of Blake's
words:

chartered (lines 1, 2)
  Denotations: Established by a charter (a written grant or a certificate
     of incorporation); leased or hired.
  Connotations: Defined, limited, restricted, channeled, mapped,
     bound by law; bought and sold (like a slave or an inanimate
     object); Magna Charta; charters given crown colonies by the King.
  Other Words in the Poem with Similar Connotations: *Ban,* which can
     denote (1) a legal prohibition; (2) a churchman's curse or maledic-
     tion; (3) in medieval times, an order summoning a king's vassals
     to fight for him. *Manacles,* or shackles, restrain movement. *Chimney-
     sweeper, soldier,* and *harlot* are all hirelings.
  Interpretation of the Lines: The street has had mapped out for it the
     direction in which it must go; the Thames has had laid down to
     it the course it must follow. Street and river are channeled, impris-
     oned, enslaved (like every inhabitant of London).

black'ning (line 10)
  Denotation: Becoming black.
  Connotations: The darkening of something once light, the defilement
     of something once clean, the deepening of guilt, the gathering of
     darkness at the approach of night.
  Other Words in the Poem with Similar Connotations: Objects
     becoming marked or smudged (*marks of weakness, marks of woe* in the
     faces of passers-by; bloodied walls of a palace; marriage blighted
     with plagues); the word *appalls* (denoting not only "to overcome
     with horror" but "to make pale" and also "to cast a pall or shroud
     over"); *midnight streets.*
  Interpretation of the Line: Literally, every London church grows
     black from soot and hires a chimney-sweeper (a small boy) to help
     clean it. But Blake suggests too that by profiting from the suffering
     of the child laborer, the church is soiling its original purity.

Blasts, blights (lines 15 – 16)
  Denotations: Both *blast* and *blight* mean "to cause to wither" or "to
     ruin and destroy." Both are terms from horticulture. Frost *blasts* a
     bud and kills it; disease *blights* a growing plant.
  Connotations: Sickness and death; gardens shriveled and dying; gusts
     of wind and the ravages of insects; things blown to pieces or rotted
     and warped.
  Other Words in the Poem with Similar Connotations: Faces marked

with weakness and woe; the child become a chimney-sweep; the soldier killed by war; blackening church and bloodied palace; young girl turned harlot; wedding carriage transformed into a hearse.

Interpretation of the Lines: Literally, the harlot spreads the plague of syphilis, which, carried into marriage, can cause a baby to be born blind. In a larger and more meaningful sense, Blake sees the prostitution of even one young girl corrupting the entire institution of matrimony and endangering every child.

Some of these connotations are more to the point than others; the reader of a poem nearly always has the problem of distinguishing relevant associations from irrelevant ones. We need to read a poem in its entirety and, when a word leaves us in doubt, look for other things in the poem to corroborate or refute what we think it means. Relatively simple and direct in its statement, Blake's account of his stroll through the city at night becomes an indictment of a whole social and religious order. The indictment could hardly be this effective if it were "mathematically plain," its every word restricted to one denotation clearly spelled out.

Wallace Stevens (1879 – 1955)*
DISILLUSIONMENT OF TEN O'CLOCK   1923

The houses are haunted
By white night-gowns.
None are green,
Or purple with green rings,
Or green with yellow rings,   5
Or yellow with blue rings.
None of them are strange,
With socks of lace
And beaded ceintures.
People are not going   10
To dream of baboons and periwinkles.
Only, here and there, an old sailor,
Drunk and asleep in his boots,
Catches tigers
In red weather.   15

QUESTIONS

1. What are *beaded ceintures?* What does the phrase suggest?
2. What contrast does Stevens draw between the people who live in these houses and the old sailor? What do the connotations of *white night-gowns* and *sailor* add to this contrast?
3. What is lacking in these people who wear white night-gowns? Why should the poet's view of them be a "disillusionment"?

Samuel Johnson (1709 – 1784)

A Short Song of Congratulation (1780)

Long-expected one and twenty
  Ling'ring year at last is flown,
Pomp and pleasure, pride and plenty,
  Great Sir John, are all your own.

Loosened from the minor's tether;   5
  Free to mortgage or to sell,
Wild as wind, and light as feather
  Bid the slaves of thrift farewell.

Call the Bettys, Kates, and Jennys
  Every name that laughs at care,   10
Lavish of your grandsire's guineas,
  Show the spirit of an heir.

All that prey on vice and folly
  Joy to see their quarry fly:
Here the gamester light and jolly,   15
  There the lender grave and sly.

Wealth, Sir John, was made to wander,
  Let it wander as it will;
See the jockey, see the pander,
  Bid them come, and take their fill.   20

When the bonny blade carouses,
  Pockets full, and spirits high,
What are acres? What are houses?
  Only dirt, or° wet or dry.   *either*

If the guardian or the mother   25
  Tell the woes of willful waste,
Scorn their counsel and their pother,
  You can hang or drown at last.

Questions

1. In line 5, what does *tether* denote? What does the word suggest?
2. Why are *Bettys, Kates,* and *Jennys* more meaningful names as Johnson uses them than Elizabeths, Katherines, and Genevieves would be?
3. Johnson states in line 24 the connotations that *acres* and *houses* have for the young heir. What connotations might these terms have for Johnson himself?

Timothy Steele (b. 1948)*

Epitaph   1979

Here lies Sir Tact, a diplomatic fellow
Whose silence was not golden, but just yellow.

1. To what famous saying does the poet allude?
2. What are the connotations of *golden?* Of *yellow?*

Richard Snyder (1925 – 1986)
A MONGOLOID CHILD HANDLING SHELLS ON THE BEACH   1971

She turns them over in her slow hands,
as did the sea sending them to her;
broken bits from the mazarine maze,
they are the calmest things on this sand.

The unbroken children splash and shout,   5
rough as surf, gay as their nesting towels.
But she plays soberly with the sea's
small change and hums back to it its slow vowels.

QUESTIONS

1. In what ways is the phrase *the mazarine maze* more valuable to this poem than if
   the poet had said "the deep blue sea"?
2. What is suggested by calling the other children *unbroken?* By saying that their
   towels are *nesting?*
3. How is the child like the sea? How are the other children like the surf? What
   do the differences between sea and surf contribute to Richard Snyder's poem?
4. What is the poet's attitude toward the child? How can you tell?
5. Since 1971, when this poem first appeared, the congenital condition once commonly named *mongolism* has come to be called *Down's syndrome,* after the physician
   who first identified its characteristics. The denotations of *mongolism* and *Down's
   syndrome* are identical. What connotations of the word *mongoloid* seem responsible
   for the word's fall from favor?

Geoffrey Hill (b. 1932)
MERLIN   1959

I will consider the outnumbering dead:
For they are the husks of what was rich seed.
Now, should they come together to be fed,
They would outstrip the locusts' covering tide.

Arthur, Elaine, Mordred; they are all gone   5
Among the raftered galleries of bone.
By the long barrows of Logres they are made one,
And over their city stands the pinnacled corn.

MERLIN. In medieval legend, Merlin was a powerful magician and a seer, an aide of King
Arthur. 5. *Elaine:* in Arthurian romance, the beloved of Sir Launcelot. *Mordred:* Arthur's
treacherous nephew by whose hand the king died. 7. *barrows:* earthworks for burial of the

dead. *Logres:* name of an ancient British kingdom, according to the twelfth-century historian Geoffrey of Monmouth, who gathered legends of King Arthur.

QUESTIONS

1. What does the title "Merlin" contribute to this poem? Do you prefer to read the poem as though it is Merlin who speaks to us — or the poet?
2. Line 4 alludes to the plague of locusts that God sent upon Egypt (Exodus 10): "For they covered the face of the whole earth, so that the land was darkened . . ." With this allusion in mind, explain the comparison of the dead to locusts.
3. Why are the suggestions inherent in the names of *Arthur, Elaine,* and *Mordred* more valuable to this poem than those we might find in the names of other dead persons called, say, Gus, Tessie, and Butch?
4. Explain the phrase in line 6: *the raftered galleries of bone.*
5. In the last line, what *city* does the poet refer to? Does he mean some particular city, or is he making a comparison?
6. What is interesting in the adjective *pinnacled?* How can it be applied to corn?

Wallace Stevens (1879 – 1955)*
THE EMPEROR OF ICE-CREAM   1923

Call the roller of big cigars,
The muscular one, and bid him whip
In kitchen cups concupiscent curds.
Let the wenches dawdle in such dress
As they are used to wear, and let the boys   5
Bring flowers in last month's newspapers.
Let be be finale of seem.
The only emperor is the emperor of ice-cream.

Take from the dresser of deal,
Lacking the three glass knobs, that sheet   10
On which she embroidered fantails once
And spread it so as to cover her face.
If her horny feet protrude, they come
To show how cold she is, and dumb.
Let the lamp affix its beam.   15
The only emperor is the emperor of ice-cream.

THE EMPEROR OF ICE-CREAM. 9. *deal:* fir or pine wood used to make cheap furniture.

QUESTIONS

1. What scene is taking place in the first stanza? Describe it in your own words. What are your feelings about it?
2. Who do you suppose to be the dead person in the second stanza? What can you infer about her? What do you know about her for sure?
3. Make a guess about this mysterious emperor. Who do you take him to be?
4. What does ice cream mean to you? In this poem, what do you think it means to Stevens?

Walter de la Mare (1873 – 1956)

THE LISTENERS 1912

"Is there anybody there?" said the Traveller,
  Knocking on the moonlit door;
And his horse in the silence champed the grasses
  Of the forest's ferny floor:
And a bird flew up out of the turret,   5
  Above the Traveller's head:
And he smote upon the door again a second time;
  "Is there anybody there?" he said.
But no one descended to the Traveller;
  No head from the leaf-fringed sill   10
Leaned over and looked into his grey eyes,
  Where he stood perplexed and still.
But only a host of phantom listeners
  That dwelt in the lone house then
Stood listening in the quiet of the moonlight   15
  To that voice from the world of men:
Stood thronging the faint moonbeams on the dark stair
  That goes down to the empty hall,
Hearkening in an air stirred and shaken
  By the lonely Traveller's call.   20
And he felt in his heart their strangeness,
  Their stillness answering his cry,
While his horse moved, cropping the dark turf,
  'Neath the starred and leafy sky;
For he suddenly smote on the door, even   25
  Louder, and lifted his head: —
"Tell them I came, and no one answered,
  That I kept my word," he said.
Never the least stir made the listeners,
  Though every word he spake   30
Fell echoing through the shadowiness of the still house
  From the one man left awake:
Ay, they heard his foot upon the stirrup,
  And the sound of iron on stone,
And how the silence surged softly backward,   35
  When the plunging hoofs were gone.

QUESTIONS

1. Before you had read this poem, what suggestions did its title bring to mind?
2. Now that you have read the poem, what do you make of these "listeners"? Who or what do you imagine them to be?
3. Why is *the moonlit door* (in line 2) a phrase more valuable to this poem than if the poet had written simply "the door"?
4. What does *turret* (in line 5) suggest?
5. Reconstruct some earlier events that might have preceded the Traveller's visit.

Who might this Traveller be? Who are the unnamed persons — "them" (line 27) — for whom the Traveller leaves a message? What promise has he kept? (The poet doesn't tell us; we can only guess.)

6. Do you think this poem any the worse for the fact that its setting, characters, and action are so mysterious? What does "The Listeners" gain from not telling us all?

Robert Frost (1874 – 1963)*
FIRE AND ICE   1923

Some say the world will end in fire,
Some say in ice.
From what I've tasted of desire
I hold with those who favor fire.
But if it had to perish twice,   5
I think I know enough of hate
To say that for destruction ice
Is also great
And would suffice.

QUESTIONS

1. To whom does Frost refer in line 1? In line 2?
2. What connotations of *fire* and *ice* contribute to the richness of Frost's comparison?

SUGGESTIONS FOR WRITING

1. In a short essay, analyze a poem full of words that radiate suggestions. Looking into the Anthology that begins on page 679, you might consider T. S. Eliot's "The Love Song of J. Alfred Prufrock," John Keats's "To Autumn," Sylvia Plath's "Daddy," or many others. Focus on particular words: explain their connotations and show how these suggestions are part of the poem's meaning. (For guidelines on writing about poetry by the method of analysis, see page 1378.)

2. In a current newspaper or magazine, select an advertisement that tries to surround a product with an aura. A new car, for instance, might be described in terms of some powerful jungle cat ("purring power, ready to spring"). Likely hunting-grounds for such ads are magazines that cater to the affluent (*New Yorker, Playboy, Vogue,* and others). Clip or photocopy the ad and circle words in it that seem especially suggestive. Then, in an accompanying paper, unfold the suggestions in these words and try to explain the ad's appeal. How is the purpose of connotative language used in advertising copy different from that of such language when used in poetry?

17 Imagery

Ezra Pound (1885 – 1972)[*]
In a Station of the Metro   1916

The apparition of these faces in the crowd;
Petals on a wet, black bough.

     Pound said he wrote this poem to convey an experience: emerging one day from a train in the Paris subway *(Métro)*, he beheld "suddenly a beautiful face, and then another and another." Originally he had described his impression in a poem thirty lines long. In this final version, each line contains an **image,** which, like a picture, may take the place of a thousand words.

     Though the term *image* suggests a thing seen, when speaking of images in poetry we generally mean *a word or sequence of words that refers to any sensory experience.* Often this experience is a sight (**visual imagery,** as in Pound's poem), but it may be a sound (**auditory imagery**) or a touch (**tactile imagery,** as a perception of roughness or smoothness). It may be an odor or a taste or perhaps a bodily sensation such as pain, the prickling of gooseflesh, the quenching of thirst, or — as in the following brief poem — the perception of something cold.

Taniguchi Buson (1715 – 1783)
The piercing chill I feel   (about 1760)

The piercing chill I feel:
  my dead wife's comb, in our bedroom,
    under my heel . . .
              — Translated by Harold G. Henderson

As in this **haiku** (in Japanese, a poem of about seventeen syllables) an image can convey a flash of understanding. Had he wished, the poet might have spoken of the dead woman, of the contrast between her death and his memory of her, of his feelings toward death in general. But such a discussion would be quite different from the poem he actually wrote. Striking his bare foot against the comb, now cold and motionless but associated with the living wife (perhaps worn in her hair), the widower feels a shock as if he had touched the woman's corpse. A literal, physical sense of death is conveyed; the abstraction "death" is understood through the senses. To render the abstract in concrete terms is what poets often try to do; in this attempt, an image can be valuable.

An image may occur in a single word, a phrase, a sentence, or, as in this case, an entire short poem. To speak of the **imagery** of a poem — all its images taken together — is often more useful than to speak of separate images. To divide Buson's haiku into five images — *chill, wife, comb, bedroom, heel* — is possible, for any noun that refers to a visible object or a sensation is an image, but this is to draw distinctions that in themselves mean little and to disassemble a single experience.

Does an image cause a reader to experience a sense impression? Not quite. Reading the word *petals,* no one literally sees petals; but the occasion is given for imagining them. The image asks to be seen with the mind's eye. And although "In a Station of the Metro" records what Ezra Pound saw, it is of course not necessary for a poet actually to have lived through a sensory experience in order to write it. Keats may never have seen a newly discovered planet through a telescope, despite the image in his sonnet on Chapman's Homer (p. 737).

It is tempting to think of imagery as mere decoration, particularly when we read Keats, who fills his poems with an abundance of sights, sounds, odors, and tastes. But a successful image is not just a dab of paint or a flashy bauble. When Keats opens "The Eve of St. Agnes" with what have been called the coldest lines in literature, he evokes by a series of images a setting and a mood:

> St. Agnes' eve — Ah, bitter chill it was!
> The owl, for all his feathers, was a-cold;
> The hare limped trembling through the frozen grass,
> And silent was the flock in woolly fold:
> Numb were the Beadsman's fingers, while he told
> His rosary, and while his frosted breath,
> Like pious incense from a censer old,
> Seemed taking flight for heaven, without a death, . . .

Indeed, some literary critics look for much of the meaning of a poem in its imagery, wherein they expect to see the mind of the poet more truly revealed than in whatever the poet explicitly claims to believe. In his investigation of Wordsworth's "Ode: Intimations of Immortality," the critic Cleanth Brooks devotes his attention to the imagery of light and darkness, which he finds carries on and develops Wordsworth's thought.[1]

Though Shakespeare's Theseus (in *A Midsummer Night's Dream*) ac-

---

[1] "Wordsworth and the Paradox of the Imagination," in *The Well Wrought Urn* (New York: Harcourt, 1956).

cuses poets of being concerned with "airy nothings," poets are usually very much concerned with what is in front of them. This concern is of use to us. Perhaps, as Alan Watts has remarked, Americans are not the materialists they are sometimes accused of being. How could anyone taking a look at an American city think that its inhabitants deeply cherish material things? Involved in our personal hopes and apprehensions, anticipating the future so hard that much of the time we see the present through a film of thought across our eyes, perhaps we need a poet occasionally to remind us that even the coffee we absentmindedly sip comes in (as Yeats put it) a "heavy spillable cup."

Theodore Roethke (1908 – 1963)*
ROOT CELLAR   1948

Nothing would sleep in that cellar, dank as a ditch,
Bulbs broke out of boxes hunting for chinks in the dark,
Shoots dangled and drooped,
Lolling obscenely from mildewed crates,
Hung down long yellow evil necks, like tropical snakes.   5
And what a congress of stinks! —
Roots ripe as old bait,
Pulpy stems, rank, silo-rich,
Leaf-mold, manure, lime, piled against slippery planks.
Nothing would give up life: 10
Even the dirt kept breathing a small breath.

QUESTIONS

1. As a boy growing up in Saginaw, Michigan, Theodore Roethke spent much of his time in a large commercial greenhouse run by his family. What details in his poem show more than a passing acquaintance with growing things?
2. What varieties of image does "Root Cellar" contain? Point out examples.
3. Which lines contain personifications, metaphors, or similes? How large a part of this poem is composed of these figures of speech?
4. What do you understand to be Roethke's attitude toward the root cellar? Does he view it as a disgusting chamber of horrors? Pay special attention to the last two lines.

Elizabeth Bishop (1911 – 1979)*
THE FISH   1946

I caught a tremendous fish
and held him beside the boat
half out of water, with my hook
fast in a corner of his mouth.

He didn't fight.
He hadn't fought at all.
He hung a grunting weight,
battered and venerable
and homely. Here and there
his brown skin hung in strips
like ancient wall-paper,
and its pattern of darker brown
was like wall-paper:
shapes like full-blown roses
stained and lost through age.
He was speckled with barnacles,
fine rosettes of lime,
and infested
with tiny white sea-lice,
and underneath two or three
rags of green weed hung down.
While his gills were breathing in
the terrible oxygen
— the frightening gills,
fresh and crisp with blood,
that can cut so badly —
I thought of the coarse white flesh
packed in like feathers,
the big bones and the little bones,
the dramatic reds and blacks
of his shiny entrails,
and the pink swim-bladder
like a big peony.
I looked into his eyes
which were far larger than mine
but shallower, and yellowed,
the irises backed and packed
with tarnished tinfoil
seen through the lenses
of old scratched isinglass.
They shifted a little, but not
to return my stare.
— It was more like the tipping
of an object toward the light.
I admired his sullen face,
the mechanism of his jaw,
and then I saw
that from his lower lip
— if you could call it a lip —
grim, wet, and weapon-like,
hung five old pieces of fish-line,
or four and a wire leader
with the swivel still attached,

with all their five big hooks
grown firmly in his mouth.   55
A green line, frayed at the end
where he broke it, two heavier lines,
and a fine black thread
still crimped from the strain and snap
when it broke and he got away.   60
Like medals with their ribbons
frayed and wavering,
a five-haired beard of wisdom
trailing from his aching jaw.
I stared and stared   65
and victory filled up
the little rented boat,
from the pool of bilge
where oil had spread a rainbow
around the rusted engine   70
to the bailer rusted orange,
the sun-cracked thwarts,
the oarlocks on their strings,
the gunnels — until everything
was rainbow, rainbow, rainbow!   75
And I let the fish go.

QUESTIONS

1. How many abstract words does this poem contain? What proportion of the poem is imagery?
2. What is the speaker's attitude toward the fish? Comment in particular on lines 61–64.
3. What attitude do the images of the rainbow of oil (line 69), the orange bailer (bailing bucket, line 71), the *sun-cracked thwarts* (line 72) convey? Does the poet expect us to feel mournful because the boat is in such sorry condition?
4. What is meant by *rainbow, rainbow, rainbow*?
5. How do these images prepare us for the conclusion? Why does the speaker let the fish go?

Jean Toomer (1894 – 1967)

REAPERS   1923

Black reapers with the sound of steel on stones
Are sharpening scythes. I see them place the hones
In their hip-pockets as a thing that's done,
And start their silent swinging, one by one.

Black horses drive a mower through the weeds,
And there, a field rat, startled, squealing bleeds,
His belly close to ground. I see the blade,
Blood-stained, continue cutting weeds and shade.

QUESTIONS

1. Imagine the scene Jean Toomer describes. Which particulars most vividly strike the mind's eye?
2. What kind of image is *silent swinging*?
3. Read the poem aloud. Notice especially the effect of the words *sound of steel on stones* and *field rat, startled, squealing bleeds.* What interesting sounds are present in the very words that contain these images?
4. What feelings do you get from this poem as a whole? Would you agree with someone who said, "This poem gives us a sense of happy, carefree life down on the farm, close to nature"? Exactly what in "Reapers" makes you feel the way you do? Besides appealing to our auditory and visual imagination, what do the images contribute?

Gerard Manley Hopkins (1844 – 1889)*
PIED BEAUTY (1877)

Glory be to God for dappled things —
    For skies of couple-color as a brinded° cow;   *streaked*
        For rose-moles all in stipple upon trout that swim;
Fresh-firecoal chestnut-falls; finches' wings;
    Landscape plotted and pieced — fold, fallow, and plow;   5
        And áll trádes, their gear and tackle and trim°.   *equipment*

All things counter, original, spare, strange;
    Whatever is fickle, freckled (who knows how?)
        With swift, slow; sweet, sour; adazzle, dim;
He fathers-forth whose beauty is past change: 10
            Praise him.

QUESTIONS

1. What does the word *pied* mean? (Hint: what does a Pied Piper look like?)
2. According to Hopkins, what do *skies, cow, trout, ripe chestnuts, finches' wings,* and *landscapes* all have in common? What landscapes can the poet have in mind? (Have you ever seen any *dappled* landscape while looking down from an airplane, or from a mountain or high hill?)
3. What do you make of line 6: what can carpenters' saws and ditch-diggers' spades possibly have in common with the dappled things in lines 2 – 4?
4. Does Hopkins refer only to contrasts that meet the eye? What other kinds of variation interest him?
5. Try to state in your own words the theme of this poem. How essential to our understanding of this theme are Hopkins's images?

ABOUT HAIKU

> On the one-ton temple bell
> a moonmoth, folded into sleep,
> sits still.
> — Taniguchi Buson

The name *haiku* means "beginning-verse" — perhaps because the form may have originated in a game. Players, given a haiku, were supposed to extend its three lines into a longer poem. Haiku (the word can also be plural) tend to consist mainly of imagery, but as we saw in Buson's lines on the cold comb, their imagery is not always only pictorial.

> Heat-lightning streak —
> through darkness pierces
> the heron's shriek.
> — Matsuo Basho

In the poet's account of his experience, are sight and sound neatly distinguished from each other?

Note that a haiku has little room for abstract thoughts or general observations. The following attempt, though in seventeen syllables, is far from haiku in spirit:

> Now that our love is gone
> I feel within my soul
> a nagging distress.

Unlike the author of those lines, haiku poets look out upon a literal world, seldom looking inward to *discuss* their feelings. Japanese haiku tend to be seasonal in subject, but because they are so highly compressed, they usually just *imply* a season: a blossom indicates spring; a crow on a branch, autumn; snow, winter. Not just pretty little sketches of nature (as some Westerners think), haiku assume a view of the universe in which observer and nature are not separated.

A haiku in Japanese is rimeless, its seventeen syllables usually arranged in three lines, often following a pattern of five, seven, and five syllables. Haiku written in English frequently ignore such a pattern; they may be rimed or unrimed as the poet prefers.

If you care to try your hand at haiku-writing, here are a few suggestions. Make every word matter. Include few adjectives, shun needless conjunctions. Set your poem in the present — "Haiku," said Basho, "is simply what is happening in this place at this moment." Confine your poem to what can be seen, heard, smelled, tasted, or touched. Mere sensory reports, however, will be meaningless unless they make the reader feel something — as a contemporary American writer points out in this spoof.

Richard Brautigan (1935 – 1985)

HAIKU AMBULANCE   1968

A piece of green pepper
  fell
off the wooden salad bowl:
so what?

Here, freely translated, are two more Japanese haiku to inspire you.
The first is by master poet Basho (1644 – 1694), sometimes called the
Shakespeare of the haiku.

In the old stone pool
a frogjump:
splishhhhh.

The second (in a translation by Cid Corman) is by Issa (1763 – 1827), a poet
noted for wit.

only one guy and
only one fly trying to
make the guest room do

Finally, here are eight more recent haiku written in English. (Don't expect
them all to observe a strict arrangement of seventeen syllables.) As in
Japanese, haiku is an art of few words, many suggestions. A haiku starts
us thinking and feeling. "So the reader," Raymond Roseliep wrote, "keeps
getting on where the poet got off."

Sprayed with strong poison
my roses are crisp this year
  in the crystal vase
          — Paul Goodman

After weeks of watching the roof leak
          I fixed it tonight
by moving a single board
          — Gary Snyder

Dusk over the lake;
  a turtle's head emerges
    then silently sinks
          — Virgil Hutton

The moving shadows
  of the oil well pumps;
    winter afternoon
          — Virgil Hutton

campfire extinguished,
the woman washing dishes
in a pan of stars
          — Raymond Roseliep

Into the blinding sun . . .
  the funeral procession's
    glaring headlights.
          — Nicholas Virgilio

The green cockleburs
Caught in the thick woolly hair
Of the black boy's head.
          — Richard Wright

A dawn in a tree of birds.
Another.
And then another.
          — Kenneth Rexroth

John Keats (1795 – 1821)*
BRIGHT STAR! WOULD I WERE STEADFAST AS THOU ART (1819)

Bright star! would I were steadfast as thou art —
  Not in lone splendor hung aloft the night,
And watching, with eternal lids apart,
  Like nature's patient, sleepless Eremite°   *hermit*
The moving waters at their priest-like task   5
  Of pure ablution round earth's human shores,
Or gazing on the new soft-fallen mask
  Of snow upon the mountains and the moors —
No — yet still steadfast, still unchangeable,
  Pillowed upon my fair love's ripening breast,   10
To feel for ever its soft fall and swell,
  Awake for ever in a sweet unrest,
Still, still to hear her tender-taken breath,
And so live ever — or else swoon to death.

QUESTIONS

1. Stars are conventional symbols for love and a loved one. (Love, Shakespeare tells us in a sonnet, "is the star to every wandering bark.") In this sonnet, why is it not possible for the star to have this meaning? How does Keats use it?
2. What seems concrete and particular in the speaker's observations?
3. Suppose Keats had said *slow and easy* instead of *tender-taken* in line 13? What would have been lost?

Carl Sandburg (1878 – 1967)
FOG 1916

The fog comes
on little cat feet.
It sits looking
over harbor and city
on silent haunches
and then moves on.

QUESTION

In lines 15–22 of "The Love Song of J. Alfred Prufrock" (page 713), T.S. Eliot also likens fog to a cat. Compare Sandburg's lines and Eliot's. Which passage tells us more about fogs and cats?

EXPERIMENT: *Writing with Images*

Taking the following poems as examples from which to start rather than as models to be slavishly copied, try to compose a brief poem that consists largely of imagery.

Walt Whitman (1819 – 1892)*
THE RUNNER   1867

On a flat road runs the well-train'd runner;
He is lean and sinewy, with muscular legs;
He is thinly clothed — he leans forward as he runs,
With lightly closed fists, and arms partially rais'd.

T. E. Hulme (1883 – 1917)
IMAGE   (about 1910)

Old houses were scaffolding once
            and workmen whistling.

William Carlos Williams (1883 – 1963)*
THE GREAT FIGURE   1921

Among the rain
and lights
I saw the figure 5
in gold
on a red   5
firetruck
moving
tense
unheeded
to gong clangs   10
siren howls
and wheels rumbling
through the dark city.

Robert Bly (b. 1926)*
DRIVING TO TOWN LATE TO MAIL A LETTER   1962

It is a cold and snowy night. The main street is deserted.
The only things moving are swirls of snow.
As I lift the mailbox door, I feel its cold iron.
There is a privacy I love in this snowy night.
Driving around, I will waste more time.

Gary Snyder (b. 1930)
MID-AUGUST AT SOURDOUGH MOUNTAIN LOOKOUT   1959

Down valley a smoke haze
Three days heat, after five days rain
Pitch glows on the fir-cones
Across rocks and meadows
Swarms of new flies.   5

I cannot remember things I once read
A few friends, but they are in cities.
Drinking cold snow-water from a tin cup
Looking down for miles
Through high still air.   10

MID-AUGUST AT SOURDOUGH MOUNTAIN LOOKOUT. *Sourdough Mountain:* in the state of Washington, where the poet's job at the time was to watch for forest fires.

H. D. [Hilda Doolittle] (1886 – 1961)
HEAT   1916

O wind, rend open the heat,
cut apart the heat,
rend it to tatters.

Fruit cannot drop
through this thick air —   5
fruit cannot fall into heat
that presses up and blunts
the points of pears
and rounds the grapes.

Cut the heat —   10
plough through it,
turning it on either side
of your path.

James Preston (b. 1951)

SUNFISH RACES   1986

A kaleidoscope
Of gliding
Triangles

Mary Oliver (b. 1935)

RAIN IN OHIO   1983

The robin cries: *rain!*
The crow calls: *plunder!*

The blacksnake climbing
in the vines halts
his long ladder of muscle   5

while the thunderheads whirl up
out of the white west,

their dark hooves nicking
the tall trees as they come.

Rain, rain, rain! sings the robin   10
frantically, then flies for cover.

The crow hunches.
The blacksnake

pours himself swift and heavy
into the ground.   15

SUGGESTIONS FOR WRITING

1. Choose, from the Anthology in Chapter 29, a poem that appeals to you. Then write a brief account of your experience in reading it, paying special notice to its imagery. What images strike you, and why? What do they contribute to the poem as a whole? Poems rich in imagery include Samuel Taylor Coleridge's "Kubla Khan," Robert Frost's "The Wood-Pile," John Keats's "Ode on Melancholy," Charlotte Mew's "Fame," William Carlos Williams's "Spring and All (By the road to the contagious hospital)" and many more.
2. After you have read the haiku and the discussion of haiku-writing in this chapter, write three or four haiku of your own. Then write a brief prose account of your experience in writing them. What, if anything, did you find out?
3. Reflect on Samuel Johnson's famous remarks on "the business of the poet" (page 389). Try applying Johnson's view to some recent poem — say, Elizabeth Bishop's "The Fish" (in this chapter). Would Johnson find Bishop a seer of "general and transcendental truths" or a counter of tulip-streaks? Then, in a short critical statement of your own, support or attack Johnson's view.

18 Figures of Speech

WHY SPEAK FIGURATIVELY?

"I will speak daggers to her, but use none," says Hamlet, preparing to confront his mother. His statement makes sense only because we realize that *daggers* is to be taken two ways: literally (denoting sharp, pointed weapons) and nonliterally (referring to something that can be used *like* weapons — namely, words). Reading poetry, we often meet comparisons between two things whose similarity we have never noticed before. When Marianne Moore observes that a fir tree has "an emerald turkey-foot at the top," the result is a pleasure that poetry richly affords: the sudden recognition of likenesses.

A treetop like a turkey-foot, words like daggers — such comparisons are called **figures of speech.** In its broadest definition, a figure of speech may be said to occur whenever a speaker or writer, for the sake of freshness or emphasis, departs from the usual denotations of words. Certainly, when Hamlet says he will speak daggers, no one expects him to release pointed weapons from his lips, for *daggers* is not to be read solely for its denotation. Its connotations — sharp, stabbing, piercing, wounding — also come to mind, and we see ways in which words and daggers work alike. (Words too can hurt: by striking through pretenses, possibly, or by wounding their hearer's self-esteem.) In the statement "A razor is sharper than an ax," there is no departure from the usual denotations of *razor* and *ax,* and no figure of speech results. Both objects are of the same class; the comparison is not offensive to logic. But in "How sharper than a serpent's tooth it is to have a thankless child," the objects — snake's tooth (fang) and ungrateful offspring — are so unlike that no reasonable comparison may be made between them. To find similarity, we attend to the connotations of *serpent's tooth* — biting, piercing, venom, pain — rather than to its denotations. If we are aware of the connotations of *red rose* (beauty, softness, freshness, and so forth), then the line "My love is like a red, red rose" need not call to mind a woman with a scarlet face and a thorny neck.

Figures of speech are not devices to state what is demonstrably untrue. Indeed they often state truths that more literal language cannot communicate; they call attention to such truths; they lend them emphasis.

Alfred, Lord Tennyson (1809 – 1892)*

THE EAGLE

1851

He clasps the crag with crooked hands;
Close to the sun in lonely lands,
Ringed with the azure world, he stands.

The wrinkled sea beneath him crawls;
He watches from his mountain walls,
And like a thunderbolt he falls.

    This brief poem is rich in figurative language. In the first line, the phrase *crooked hands* may surprise us. An eagle does not have hands, we might protest; but the objection would be a quibble, for evidently Tennyson is indicating exactly how an eagle clasps a crag, in the way that human fingers clasp a thing. By implication, too, the eagle is a person. *Close to the sun,* if taken literally, is an absurd exaggeration, the sun being a mean distance of 93,000,000 miles from the earth. For the eagle to be closer to it by the altitude of a mountain is an approach so small as to be insignificant. But figuratively, Tennyson conveys that the eagle stands above the clouds, perhaps silhouetted against the sun, and for the moment belongs to the heavens rather than to the land and sea. The word *ringed* makes a circle of the whole world's horizons and suggests that we see the world from the eagle's height; the sea becomes an aged, sluggish animal; *mountain walls,* possibly literal, also suggests a fort or castle; and finally the eagle itself is likened to a thunderbolt in speed and in power, perhaps also in that its beak is — like our abstract conception of a lightning bolt — pointed. How much of the poem can be taken literally? Only *he clasps the crag, he stands, he watches, he falls.* The rest is made of figures of speech. The result is that, reading Tennyson's poem, we gain a bird's-eye view of sun, sea, and land — and even of bird. Like imagery, figurative language refers us to the physical world.

William Shakespeare (1564 – 1616)*

SHALL I COMPARE THEE TO A SUMMER'S DAY?

1609

Shall I compare thee to a summer's day?
Thou art more lovely and more temperate.
Rough winds do shake the darling buds of May,
And summer's lease hath all too short a date.
Sometime too hot the eye of heaven shines,   5
And often is his gold complexion dimmed;
And every fair° from fair sometimes declines,   *fair one*
By chance, or nature's changing course, untrimmed.
But thy eternal summer shall not fade,

Nor lose possession of that fair thou ow'st°;   *ownest, have*   10
Nor shall death brag thou wand'rest in his shade,
When in eternal lines to time thou grow'st.
   So long as men can breathe or eyes can see,
   So long lives this, and this gives life to thee.

Howard Moss (b. 1922)

SHALL I COMPARE THEE TO A SUMMER'S DAY?   1976

Who says you're like one of the dog days?
You're nicer. And better.
Even in May, the weather can be gray,
And a summer sub-let doesn't last forever.
Sometimes the sun's too hot;   5
Sometimes it is not.
Who can stay young forever?
People break their necks or just drop dead!
But you? Never!
If there's just one condensed reader left   10
Who can figure out the abridged alphabet,
   After you're dead and gone,
   In this poem you'll live on!

QUESTIONS

1. In Howard Moss's streamlined version of Shakespeare, from a series called "Modified Sonnets (Dedicated to adapters, abridgers, digesters, and condensers everywhere)," to what extent does he use figurative language? In Shakespeare's original sonnet, how high a proportion of Shakespeare's language is figurative?
2. Compare some of Moss's lines to the corresponding lines in Shakespeare's sonnet. Why is *Even in May, the weather can be gray* less interesting than the original? In the lines on the sun (5 – 6 in both versions), what has Moss's modification deliberately left out? Why is Shakespeare's seeing death as a braggart memorable? Why aren't you greatly impressed by Moss's last two lines?
3. Can you explain Shakespeare's play on the word *untrimmed* (line 8)? Evidently the word can mean "divested of trimmings," but what other suggestions do you find in it?
4. How would you answer someone who argued, "Maybe Moss's language isn't as good as Shakespeare's, but the meaning is still there. What's wrong with putting Shakespeare into up-to-date words that can be understood by everybody?"

METAPHOR AND SIMILE

   Life, like a dome of many-colored glass,
   Stains the white radiance of Eternity.

The first of these lines (from Shelley's "Adonais") is a **simile:** a comparison of two things, indicated by some connective, usually *like, as, than,* or a verb such as *resembles.* A simile expresses a similarity. Still, for a simile to exist, the things compared have to be dissimilar in kind. It is no simile to say, "Your fingers are like mine," it is a literal observation. But to say, "Your fingers are like sausages" is to use a simile. Omit the connective — say, "Your fingers are sausages" — and the result is a **metaphor,** a statement that one thing *is* something else, which, in a literal sense, it is not. In the second of Shelley's lines, it is *assumed* that Eternity is light or radiance, and we have an **implied metaphor,** one that uses neither a connective nor the verb *to be.* Here are examples:

Oh, my love is like a red, red rose.	*Simile*
Oh, my love resembles a red, red rose.	*Simile*
Oh, my love is redder than a rose.	*Simile*
Oh, my love is a red, red rose.	*Metaphor*
Oh, my love has red petals and sharp thorns.	*Implied metaphor*
Oh, I placed my love into a long-stem vase	
And I bandaged my bleeding thumb.	*Implied metaphor*

Often you can tell a metaphor from a simile by much more than just the presence or absence of a connective. In general, a simile refers to only one characteristic that two things have in common, while a metaphor is not plainly limited in the number of resemblances it may indicate. To use the simile "He eats like a pig" is to compare man and animal in one respect: eating habits. But to say "He's a pig" is to use a metaphor that might involve comparisons of appearance and morality as well.

In everyday speech, simile and metaphor occur frequently. We use metaphors ("She's a doll"), and similes ("The tickets are selling like hot-cakes") without being fully conscious of them. If, however, we are aware that words possess literal meanings as well as figurative ones, we do not write *died in the wool* for *dyed in the wool* or *tow the line* for *toe the line,* nor do we use **mixed metaphors** as did the writer who advised, "Water the spark of knowledge and it will bear fruit," or the speaker who urged, "To get ahead, keep your nose to the grindstone, your shoulder to the wheel, your ear to the ground, and your eye on the ball." Perhaps the unintended humor of these statements comes from our seeing that the writer, busy stringing together stale metaphors, was not aware that they had any physical reference.

Unlike a writer who thoughtlessly mixes metaphors, a good poet can join together incongruous things and still keep the reader's respect. In his ballad "Thirty Bob a Week," John Davidson has a British workingman tell how it feels to try to support a large family on small wages:

> It's a naked child against a hungry wolf;
>   It's playing bowls upon a splitting wreck;
> It's walking on a string across a gulf
>   With millstones fore-and-aft about your neck;
> But the thing is daily done by many and many a one;
>   And we fall, face forward, fighting, on the deck.

Like the man with his nose to the grindstone, Davidson's wage-earner is in an absurd fix; but his balancing act seems far from merely nonsensical. For every one of the poet's comparisons — of workingman to child, to bowler, to tight-rope walker, and to seaman — offer suggestions of a similar kind. All help us see (and imagine) the workingman's hard life: a brave and unyielding struggle against impossible odds.

A poem may make a series of comparisons, like Davidson's, or the whole poem may be one extended comparison:

Richard Wilbur (b. 1917)*
A SIMILE FOR HER SMILE
1950

Your smiling, or the hope, the thought of it,
Makes in my mind such pause and abrupt ease
As when the highway bridgegates fall,
Balking the hasty traffic, which must sit
On each side massed and staring, while   5
Deliberately the drawbridge starts to rise:

Then horns are hushed, the oilsmoke rarifies,
Above the idling motors one can tell
The packet's smooth approach, the slip,
Slip of the silken river past the sides,   10
The ringing of clear bells, the dip
And slow cascading of the paddle wheel.

How much life metaphors bring to poetry may be seen by comparing two poems by Tennyson and Blake.

Alfred, Lord Tennyson (1809 – 1892)*
FLOWER IN THE CRANNIED WALL
1869

Flower in the crannied wall,
I pluck you out of the crannies,
I hold you here, root and all, in my hand,
Little flower — but *if* I could understand
What you are, root and all, and all in all,
I should know what God and man is.

How many metaphors does this poem contain? None. Compare it with a briefer poem on a similar theme: the quatrain that begins Blake's "Auguries of Innocence." (We follow here the opinion of W. B. Yeats who, in editing Blake's poems, thought the lines ought to be printed separately.)

William Blake (1757 – 1827)*

TO SEE A WORLD IN A GRAIN OF SAND (about 1803)

To see a world in a grain of sand
And a heaven in a wild flower,
Hold infinity in the palm of your hand
And eternity in an hour.

Set beside Blake's poem, Tennyson's — short though it is — seems lengthy. What contributes to the richness of "To see a world in a grain of sand" is Blake's use of a metaphor in every line. And every metaphor is loaded with suggestion. Our world does indeed resemble a grain of sand: in being round, in being stony, in being one of a myriad (the suggestions go on and on). Like Blake's grain of sand, a metaphor holds much, within a small circumference.

Sylvia Plath (1932 – 1963)*

METAPHORS 1960

I'm a riddle in nine syllables,
An elephant, a ponderous house,
A melon strolling on two tendrils.
O red fruit, ivory, fine timbers!
This loaf's big with its yeasty rising.   5
Money's new-minted in this fat purse.
I'm a means, a stage, a cow in calf.
I've eaten a bag of green apples,
Boarded the train there's no getting off.

QUESTIONS

1. To what central fact do all the metaphors in this poem refer?
2. In the first line, what has the speaker in common with a riddle? Why does she say she has *nine* syllables?
3. How would you describe the tone of this poem? (Perhaps the poet expresses more than one attitude.) What attitude is conveyed in the metaphors of an elephant, "a ponderous house," "a melon strolling on two tendrils"? By the metaphors of red fruit, ivory, fine timbers, new-minted money? By the metaphor in the last line?

Jane Kenyon (b. 1947)

THE SUITOR 1978

We lie back to back. Curtains
lift and fall,

like the chest of someone sleeping.
Wind moves the leaves of the box elder;
they show their light undersides,   5
turning all at once
like a school of fish.
Suddenly I understand that I am happy.
For months this feeling
has been coming closer, stopping   10
for short visits, like a timid suitor.

QUESTION

In each simile you find in this poem, exactly what is the similarity?

Emily Dickinson (1830 – 1886)*
IT DROPPED SO LOW – IN MY REGARD   (about 1863)

It dropped so low – in my Regard –
I heard it hit the Ground –
And go to pieces on the Stones
At bottom of my Mind –

Yet blamed the Fate that flung it-*less*
Than I denounced Myself,
For entertaining Plated Wares
Upon My Silver Shelf –

QUESTIONS

1. What is *it*? What two things are compared?
2. How much of the poem develops and amplifies this comparison?

Ruth Whitman (b. 1922)
CASTOFF SKIN   1973

She lay in her girlish sleep at ninety-six,
small as a twig.
Pretty good figure.

for an old lady, she said to me once.
Then she crawled away, leaving   5
a tiny stretched transparence

behind her. When I kissed her paper cheek
I thought of the snake,
of his quick motion.

1. Explain the central metaphor in "Castoff Skin."
2. What other figures of speech does the poem contain?

Denise Levertov (b. 1923)*

LEAVING FOREVER
1964

He says the waves in the ship's wake
are like stones rolling away.
I don't see it that way.
But I see the mountain turning,
turning away its face as the ship
takes us away.

QUESTIONS

1. What do you understand to be the man's feelings about leaving forever? How does the speaker feel? With what two figures of speech does the poet express these conflicting views?
2. Suppose that this poem had ended in another simile (instead of its three last lines):

   I see the mountain as a suitcase
   left behind on the shore
   as the ship takes us away.

   How is Denise Levertov's choice of a figure of speech a much stronger one?

Peter Williams (b. 1937)

WHEN SHE WAS HERE, LI BO, SHE WAS LIKE COLD SUMMER
LAGER
1978

Her presence was a roomful of flowers,
Her absence is an empty bed.
           — Li Bo (701 – 762)

When she was here, Li Bo, she was like cold
        summer lager,
Like hot pastrami at Katz's on Houston Street,
Like a bright nickname on my downtown express,
Like every custardy honey from the old art books:
She was quadraphonic° Mahler   *four-channeled*   5
And the perfect little gymnast.

Now she's gone, it's like flat Coke on Sunday morning,
Like a melted Velveeta on white, eaten
Listening to Bobby Vinton —
Like the Philadelphia Eagles.   10

Questions

1. What do the lines from the Chinese poet Li Bo (in the **epigraph** or introductory quotation) have to do with the poem that ensues?
2. In the first six lines of the poem, what quality or qualities does the poet find in the things he likens to the presence of his lover? In the last lines, how are the four things that resemble her absence all alike?
3. This poem is full of allusions: in the first part, to a famous New York delicatessen and to a much-admired Austrian composer. Explain the allusions in part two.
4. What is the tone of the poem? (Sorrowful? Bitter? Or what?) How do the similes help communicate the poet's attitude?

Experiment: *Likening*

Write a two-part poem that follows the method of Peter Williams, finding your own similes to express a joyful experience in terms of things you admire, and a glum experience in terms of things you dislike. Possible subjects: Before meeting a loved one and after. Having a dull, badly paid job and then quitting it. Losing weight and putting it back on.

Exercise: *What Is Similar?*

Each of these quotations contains a simile or a metaphor. In each of these figures of speech, what two things is the poet comparing? Try to state exactly what you understand the two things to have in common: the most striking similarity or similarities that the poet sees.

1. Think of the storm roaming the sky uneasily
   like a dog looking for a place to sleep in,
   listen to it growling.
   > — Elizabeth Bishop, "Little Exercise"
2. When the hounds of spring are on winter's traces . . .
   > — Algernon Charles Swinburne, "Atalanta in Calydon"
3. The scarlet of the maples can shake me like a cry
   Of bugles going by.
   > — Bliss Carman, "A Vagabond Song"
4. "Hope" is the thing with feathers –
   That perches in the soul –
   And sings the tune without the words –
   And never stops – at all –
   > — Emily Dickinson, an untitled poem
5. Work without Hope draws nectar in a sieve . . .
   > —Samuel Taylor Coleridge, "Work Without Hope"
6. A new electric fence,
   Its five barbed wires tight
   As a steel-stringed banjo.
   > — Van K. Brock, "Driving at Dawn"
7. Spring stirs Gossamer Beynon schoolmistress like a spoon.
   > — Dylan Thomas, *Under Milk Wood*

OTHER FIGURES

When Shakespeare asks, in a sonnet,

O! how shall summer's honey breath hold out
Against the wrackful siege of batt'ring days,

it might seem at first that he mixes metaphors. How can a *breath* confront the battering ram of an invading army? But it is summer's breath and, by giving it to summer, Shakespeare makes the season a man or woman. It is as if the fragrance of summer were the breath within a person's body, and winter were the onslaught of old age.

Such is one instance of **personification:** a figure of speech in which a thing, an animal, or an abstract term *(truth, nature)* is made human. A personification extends throughout this whole short poem:

James Stephens (1882 – 1950)*
THE WIND   1915

The wind stood up and gave a shout.
He whistled on his fingers and

Kicked the withered leaves about
And thumped the branches with his hand

And said he'd kill and kill and kill,
And so he will and so he will.

The wind is a wild man, and evidently it is not just any autumn breeze but a hurricane or at least a stiff gale. In poems that do not work as well as this one, personification may be employed mechanically. Hollow-eyed personifications walk the works of lesser English poets of the eighteenth century: Coleridge has quoted the beginning of one such neoclassical ode, "Inoculation! heavenly Maid, descend!" It is hard for the contemporary reader to be excited by William Collins's "The Passions, An Ode for Music" (1747), which personifies, stanza by stanza, Fear, Anger, Despair, Hope, Revenge, Pity, Jealousy, Love, Hate, Melancholy, and Cheerfulness, and has them listen to Music, until even "Brown Exercise rejoiced to hear, / And Sport leapt up, and seized his beechen spear." Still, the portraits of the Seven Deadly Sins in the fourteenth-century *Vision of Piers Plowman* remain memorable: "Thanne come Slothe al bislabered, with two slimy eiyen. . . ." In "Two Sonnets on Fame" John Keats makes an abstraction come alive in seeing Fame as "a wayward girl."

Hand in hand with personification often goes **apostrophe:** a way of addressing someone or something invisible or not ordinarily spoken to. In an apostrophe, a poet (in these examples Wordsworth) may address an inanimate object ("Spade! with which Wilkinson hath tilled his lands"), some dead or absent person ("Milton! thou shouldst be living at this hour"), an abstract thing ("Return, Delights!"), or a spirit ("Thou Soul that art the eternity of thought"). More often than not, the poet uses apostrophe to announce a lofty and serious tone. An "O" may even be put in front of it ("O moon!") since, according to W. D. Snodgrass, every poet has a right to do so at least once in a lifetime. But apostrophe doesn't have to be highfalutin. It is a means of giving life to the inanimate. It is a way of giving body to the intangible, a way of speaking to it person to person, as in the words of a moving American spiritual: "Death, ain't you got no shame?"

Most of us, from time to time, emphasize a point with a statement containing exaggeration: "Faster than greased lightning," "I've told him a thousand times." We speak, then, not literal truth but use a figure of speech called **overstatement** (or **hyperbole**). Poets too, being fond of emphasis, often exaggerate for effect. Instances are Marvell's profession of a love that should grow "Vaster than empires, and more slow" and Burgon's description of Petra: "A rose-red city, half as old as Time." Overstatement can be used also for humorous purposes, as in a fat woman's boast (from a blues song): "Every time I shake, some skinny gal loses her home."[1] The opposite is **understatement,** implying more than is said. Mark Twain in *Life on the Mississippi* recalls how, as an apprentice steamboat-pilot asleep when supposed to be on watch, he was roused by the pilot and sent clambering to the pilot house: "Mr. Bixby was close behind, commenting." Another example is Robert Frost's line "One could do worse than be a swinger of birches" — the conclusion of a poem that has suggested that to swing on a birch tree is one of the most deeply satisfying activities in the world.

In **metonymy,** the name of a thing is substituted for that of another closely associated with it. For instance, we say "The White House decided," and mean the president did. When John Dyer writes in "Grongar Hill,"

A little rule, a little sway,
A sun beam on a winter's day,
Is all the proud and mighty have
Between the cradle and the grave,

we recognize that *cradle* and *grave* signify birth and death. A kind of metonymy, **synecdoche** is the use of a part of a thing to stand for the whole of it or vice versa. We say "She lent a hand," and mean that she lent her entire presence. Similarly, Milton in "Lycidas" refers to greedy clergymen as "blind mouths." Another kind of metonymy is the **transferred epithet:** a device of emphasis in which the poet attributes some characteristic of a thing to another thing closely associated with it. When Thomas Gray observes that, in the evening pastures, "drowsy tinklings lull the distant

---

[1]Quoted by Amiri Baraka [LeRoi Jones] in *Blues People* (New York: Morrow, 1963).

folds," he well knows that sheep's bells do not drowse, but sheep do. When Hart Crane, describing the earth as seen from an airplane, speaks of "nimble blue plateaus," he attributes the airplane's motion to the earth.

Paradox occurs in a statement that at first strikes us as self-contradictory but that on reflection makes some sense. "The peasant," said G. K. Chesterton, "lives in a larger world than the globe-trotter." Here, two different meanings of *larger* are contrasted: "greater in spiritual values" versus "greater in miles." Some paradoxical statements, however, are much more than plays on words. In a moving sonnet, the blind John Milton tells how one night he dreamed he could see his dead wife. The poem ends in a paradox:

> But oh, as to embrace me she inclined,
> I waked, she fled, and day brought back my night.

EXERCISE: *Paradox*

What paradoxes do you find in the following poem? For each, explain the sense that underlies the statement.

Chidiock Tichborne (1568? – 1586)
ELEGY, WRITTEN WITH HIS OWN HAND
IN THE TOWER BEFORE HIS EXECUTION   1586

My prime of youth is but a frost of cares,
  My feast of joy is but a dish of pain,
My crop of corn is but a field of tares°,   weeds
  And all my good is but vain hope of gain:
The day is past, and yet I saw no sun,   5
And now I live, and now my life is done.

My tale was heard, and yet it was not told,
  My fruit is fall'n, and yet my leaves are green,
My youth is spent, and yet I am not old,
  I saw the world, and yet I was not seen: 10
My thread is cut, and yet it is not spun,
And now I live, and now my life is done.

I sought my death, and found it in my womb,
  I looked for life, and saw it was a shade,
I trod the earth, and knew it was my tomb,   15
  And now I die, and now I was but made:
My glass is full, and now my glass is run,
And now I live, and now my life is done.

ELEGY, WRITTEN WITH HIS OWN HAND. Accused of taking part in the Babington Conspiracy, a plot by Roman Catholics against the life of Queen Elizabeth I, eighteen-year-old Chidiock Tichborne was hanged, drawn, and quartered at the Tower of London. That is virtually all we know about him.

Asked to tell the difference between men and women, Samuel Johnson replied, "I can't conceive, madam, can you?" The great dictionary-maker was using a figure of speech known to classical rhetoricians as *paronomasia,* better known to us as a **pun** or play on words. How does a pun operate? It reminds us of another word (or other words) of similar or identical sound but of very different denotation. Although puns at their worst can be mere piddling quibbles, at best they can sharply point to surprising but genuine resemblances. The name of a dentist's country estate, Tooth Acres, is accurate: aching teeth paid for the property. In his novel *Moby-Dick,* Herman Melville takes up questions about whales that had puzzled scientists: for instance, are the whale's spoutings water or gaseous vapor? And when Melville speaks pointedly of the great whale "sprinkling and mistifying the gardens of the deep," we catch his pun, and conclude that the creature both mistifies and mystifies at once.

In poetry, a pun may be facetious, as in Thomas Hood's ballad of "Faithless Nelly Gray":

> Ben Battle was a soldier bold,
>   And used to war's alarms;
> But a cannon-ball took off his legs,
>   So he laid down his arms!

Or it may be serious, as in these lines on war by E. E. Cummings:

> the bigness of cannon
> is skillful,

(*is skillful* becoming *is kill-ful* when read aloud), or perhaps, as in Shakespeare's song in *Cymbeline,* "Fear no more the heat o' th' sun," both facetious and serious at once:

> Golden lads and girls all must,
> As chimney-sweepers, come to dust.

George Herbert (1593 – 1633)*
THE PULLEY   1633

  When God at first made man,
Having a glass of blessings standing by —
Let us (said he) pour on him all we can;
Let the world's riches, which dispersèd lie,
  Contract into a span.   5

  So strength first made a way,
Then beauty flowed, then wisdom, honor, pleasure:
When almost all was out, God made a stay,
Perceiving that, alone of all His treasure,
  Rest in the bottom lay.   10

For if I should (said he)
Bestow this jewel also on My creature,
He would adore My gifts instead of Me,
And rest in Nature, not the God of Nature:
So both should losers be.   15

Yet let him keep the rest,
But keep them with repining restlessness;
Let him be rich and weary, that at least,
If goodness lead him not, yet weariness
May toss him to My breast.   20

QUESTIONS

1. What different senses of the word *rest* does Herbert bring into this poem?
2. How do God's words in line 16, *Yet let him keep the rest,* seem paradoxical?
3. What do you feel to be the tone of Herbert's poem? Does the punning make
   the poem seem comic?
4. Why is the poem called "The Pulley"? What is its implied metaphor?

To sum up: even though figures of speech are not to be taken *only*
literally, they refer us to a tangible world. By *personifying* an eagle, Tennyson reminds us that the bird and humankind have certain characteristics
in common. Through *metonymy,* a poet can focus our attention on a particular detail in a larger object; through *hyperbole* and *understatement,* make us see
the physical actuality in back of words. *Pun* and *paradox* cause us to realize
this actuality, too, and probably surprise us enjoyably at the same time.
Through *apostrophe,* the poet animates the inanimate and asks it to listen
— speaks directly to an immediate god or to the revivified dead. Put to
such uses, figures of speech have power. They are more than just ways of
playing with words.

Edmund Waller (1606 – 1687)
ON A GIRDLE   1645

That which her slender waist confined,
Shall now my joyful temples bind;
No monarch but would give his crown,
His arms might do what this has done.

It was my heaven's extremest sphere,   5
The pale° which held that lovely deer;   *enclosure*
My joy, my grief, my hope, my love,
Did all within this circle move!

A narrow compass! and yet there
Dwelt all that's good, and all that's fair!   10
Give me but what this riband bound,
Take all the rest the sun goes round!

On a Girdle. This girdle is a waistband or sash — not, of course, a modern "foundation garment." 1 – 2. *That which . . . temples bind:* A courtly lover might bind his brow with a lady's ribbon, to signify he was hers. 5. *extremest sphere:* In Ptolemaic astronomy, the outermost of the concentric spheres that surround the earth. In its wall the farthest stars are set.

Questions

1. To what things is the girdle compared?
2. Explain the pun in line 4. What effect does it have upon the tone of the poem?
3. Why is the effect of this pun different from that of Thomas Hood's play on the same word in "Faithless Nelly Gray" (quoted on p. 504)?
4. What does *compass* denote in line 9?
5. What paradox occurs in lines 9 – 10?
6. How many of the poem's statements are hyperbolic? Is the compliment the speaker pays his lady too grandiose to be believed? Explain.

Theodore Roethke (1908 – 1963)*

I Knew a Woman   1958

I knew a woman, lovely in her bones,
When small birds sighed, she would sigh back at them;
Ah, when she moved, she moved more ways than one:
The shapes a bright container can contain!
Of her choice virtues only gods should speak,   5
Or English poets who grew up on Greek
(I'd have them sing in chorus, cheek to cheek).

How well her wishes went! She stroked my chin,
She taught me Turn, and Counter-turn, and Stand;
She taught me Touch, that undulant white skin;   10
I nibbled meekly from her proffered hand;
She was the sickle; I, poor I, the rake,
Coming behind her for her pretty sake
(But what prodigious mowing we did make).

Love likes a gander, and adores a goose: 15
Her full lips pursed, the errant note to seize;
She played it quick, she played it light and loose;
My eyes, they dazzled at her flowing knees;
Her several parts could keep a pure repose,
Or one hip quiver with a mobile nose   20
(She moved in circles, and those circles moved).

Let seed be grass, and grass turn into hay:
I'm martyr to a motion not my own;
What's freedom for? To know eternity.
I swear she cast a shadow white as stone.   25
But who would count eternity in days?
These old bones live to learn her wanton ways:
(I measure time by how a body sways).

1. What outrageous puns do you find in Roethke's poem? Describe the effect of them.
2. What kind of figure of speech occurs in all three lines: *Of her choice virtues only gods should speak; My eyes, they dazzled at her flowing knees;* and *I swear she cast a shadow white as stone?*
3. What sort of figure is the poet's reference to himself as *old bones?*
4. Do you take *Let seed be grass, and grass turn into hay* as figurative language, or literal statement?
5. If you agree that the tone of this poem is witty and playful, do you think the poet is making fun of the woman? What is his attitude toward her? What part do figures of speech play in communicating it?

FOR REVIEW AND FURTHER STUDY

Robert Frost (1874 – 1963)*
THE SILKEN TENT   1942

She is as in a field a silken tent
At midday when a sunny summer breeze
Has dried the dew and all its ropes relent,
So that in guys° it gently sways at ease,   *attachments that steady it*
And its supporting central cedar pole,   5
That is its pinnacle to heavenward
And signifies the sureness of the soul,
Seems to owe naught to any single cord,
But strictly held by none, is loosely bound
By countless silken ties of love and thought   10
To everything on earth the compass round,
And only by one's going slightly taut
In the capriciousness of summer air
Is of the slightest bondage made aware.

QUESTIONS

1. Is Frost's comparison of woman and tent a simile or a metaphor?
2. What are the ropes or cords?
3. Does the poet convey any sense of this woman's character? What sort of person do you believe her to be?
4. Paraphrase the poem, trying to state its implied meaning. (If you need to be refreshed about paraphrase, turn back to pages 412 – 414.) Be sure to include the implications of the last three lines.

James C. Kilgore (b. 1928)

THE WHITE MAN PRESSED THE LOCKS 1970

Driving down the concrete artery,
Away from the smoky heart,
Through the darkening, blighted body,
Pausing at varicose veins,
The white man pressed the locks   5
    on all the sedan's doors,
Sped toward the white corpuscles
    in the white arms
        hugging the black city.

QUESTIONS

1. Explain the two implied metaphors in this poem: what are the two bodies?
2. How do you take the word *hugging?* Is this a loving embrace or a stranglehold?
3. What, in your own words, is the poet's theme?

Ogden Nash (1902 – 1971)

VERY LIKE A WHALE 1934

One thing that literature would be greatly the better for
Would be a more restricted employment by authors of simile and
    metaphor.
Authors of all races, be they Greeks, Romans, Teutons or Celts,
Can't seem just to say that anything is the thing it is but have to go
    out of their way to say that it is like something else.
What does it mean when we are told   5
That the Assyrian came down like a wolf on the fold?
In the first place, George Gordon Byron had had enough experience
To know that it probably wasn't just one Assyrian, it was a lot of
    Assyrians.
However, as too many arguments are apt to induce apoplexy and
    thus hinder longevity,
We'll let it pass as one Assyrian for the sake of brevity.   10
Now then, this particular Assyrian, the one whose cohorts were
    gleaming in purple and gold,
Just what does the poet mean when he says he came down like a
    wolf on the fold?
In heaven and earth more than is dreamed of in our philosophy there
    are a great many things,
But I don't imagine that among them there is a wolf with purple and
    gold cohorts or purple and gold anythings.
No, no, Lord Byron, before I'll believe that this Assyrian was actually
    like a wolf I must have some kind of proof;   15
Did he run on all fours and did he have a hairy tail and a big red
    mouth and big white teeth and did he say Woof woof woof?

Frankly I think it very unlikely, and all you were entitled to say, at
    the very most,
Was that the Assyrian cohorts came down like a lot of Assyrian
    cohorts about to destroy the Hebrew host.
But that wasn't fancy enough for Lord Byron, oh dear me no,
    he had to invent a lot of figures of speech and then interpolate
    them,
With the result that whenever you mention Old Testament soldiers
    to people they say Oh yes, they're the ones that a lot of wolves
    dressed up in gold and purple ate them.   20
That's the kind of thing that's being done all the time by poets, from
    Homer to Tennyson;
They're always comparing ladies to lilies and veal to venison.
How about the man who wrote,
Her little feet stole in and out like mice beneath her petticoat?
Wouldn't anybody but a poet think twice   25
Before stating that his girl's feet were mice?
Then they always say things like that after a winter storm
The snow is a white blanket. Oh it is, is it, all right then, you sleep
    under a six-inch blanket of snow and I'll sleep under a
    half-inch blanket of unpoetical blanket material and we'll see
    which one keeps warm,
And after that maybe you'll begin to comprehend dimly
What I mean by too much metaphor and simile.   30

VERY LIKE A WHALE. The title is from *Hamlet* (Act III, scene 2): Feigning madness, Hamlet likens
the shape of a cloud to a whale. "Very like a whale," says Polonius, who, to humor his prince,
will agree to the accuracy of any figure at all. Nash's art has been described by Max Eastman
in *Enjoyment of Laughter* (New York: Simon and Schuster, 1936):

If you have ever tried to write rimed verse, you will recognize in Nash's writing every naïve
crime you were ever tempted to commit — artificial inversions, pretended rimes, sentences
wrenched and mutilated to bring the rime-word to the end of the line, words assaulted and
battered into riming whether they wanted to or not, ideas and whole dissertations dragged
in for the sake of a rime, the metrical beat delayed in order to get all the necessary words
in, the metrical beat speeded up unconscionably because there were not enough words to put
in.

QUESTIONS

1. Nash alludes to the opening lines of Byron's poem "The Destruction of Sen-
nacherib":

The Assyrian came down like the wolf on the fold,
And his cohorts were gleaming in purple and gold;

and to Sir John Suckling's portrait of a bride in "A Ballad Upon a Wedding":

Her feet beneath her petticoat,
Like little mice stole in and out,
As if they feared the light: . . .

How can these metaphors be defended against Nash's quibbles?
2. What valuable functions of simile and metaphor in poetry is Nash pretending
to ignore?

In each of these poems, what figures of speech do you notice? For each metaphor or simile, try to state what is compared. In any use of metonymy, what is represented?

Richard Wilbur (b. 1921)*
SLEEPLESS AT CROWN POINT   1976

All night, this headland
Lunges into the rumpling
Capework of the wind.

Anonymous (English)
THE FORTUNES OF WAR, I TELL YOU PLAIN   (1854 – 1856)

The fortunes of war, I tell you plain,
Are a wooden leg — or a golden chain.

Robert Frost (1874 – 1963)*
THE SECRET SITS   1936

We dance round in a ring and suppose,
But the Secret sits in the middle and knows.

Margaret Atwood (b. 1939)
YOU FIT INTO ME   1971

you fit into me
like a hook into an eye

a fish hook
an open eye

John Tagliabue (b. 1923)
MAINE VASTLY COVERED WITH MUCH SNOW   1984

4 squirrels
are as busy as monks
looking for seeds; inside the seeds is a
        scripture;
nourishing themselves they trace their pre-history   5
        and future;

is theology something like the flourish of their tails?
    alert, aware of changing seasons,
    aware of other blokes about
    they persist in their   10
    scrutiny of syllables.

John Ashbery (b. 1927)*
THE CATHEDRAL IS   1979

Slated for demolition.

Etheridge Knight (b. 1931)
FOR BLACK POETS WHO THINK OF SUICIDE   1973

Black Poets should live — not leap
From steel bridges (like the white boys do).
Black Poets should live — not lay
Their necks on railroad tracks (like the white boys do).
Black Poets should seek — but not search too much   5
In sweet dark caves, nor hunt for snipe
Down psychic trails (like the white boys do).

For Black Poets belong to Black People. Are
The Flutes of Black Lovers. Are
The Organs of Black Sorrows. Are   10
The Trumpets of Black Warriors.
Let All Black Poets die as Trumpets,
And be buried in the dust of marching feet.

W. S. Merwin (b. 1927)
SONG OF MAN CHIPPING AN ARROWHEAD   1973

Little children you will all go
but the one you are hiding
will fly

Robert Burns (1759 – 1796)*
OH, MY LOVE IS LIKE A RED, RED ROSE   (about 1788)

Oh, my love is like a red, red rose
  That's newly sprung in June;
My love is like the melody
  That's sweetly played in tune.

So fair art thou, my bonny lass,
    So deep in love am I;
And I will love thee still, my dear,
    Till a' the seas gang° dry.   *go*

Till a' the seas gang dry, my dear,
    And the rocks melt wi' the sun;   10
And I will love thee still, my dear,
    While the sands o' life shall run.

And fare thee weel, my only love!
    And fare thee weel awhile!
And I will come again, my love   15
    Though it were ten thousand mile.

Gibbons Ruark (b. 1941)
THE ROSE GROWING INTO THE HOUSE   1978

Lately I think of my love for you and the rose
Growing into the house, springing up from under the eaves
And spiraling upward to pierce the chink in the corner
Where the walls come together to keep out everything,
Weather, mongrel dogs, and the rose coming on like a thief.   5
But I mean to let it grow forever if it wants to,
For lately I think of my love for you and the rose invading the
        darkness,
And I long never to learn the difference.

SUGGESTIONS FOR WRITING

1. Freely using your imagination, write a paragraph in which you make as many
   hyperbolic statements as possible. Then write another version, changing all your
   exaggeration to understatement. Then, in a concluding paragraph, sum up what
   this experiment shows you about figurative language. Some possible topics are
   "The Most Gratifying (or Terrifying) Moment of My Life," "The Job I Almost
   Landed," "The Person I Most Admire."
2. Write a poem in the free-wheeling form of Ogden Nash's "Very Like a Whale,"
   allowing your lines to ramble on for as long as necessary to land on a rime. Fill
   your poem (or whatever it turns out to be) with as many metaphors and similes
   as you can discover.
3. Choose a short poem rich in figurative language: Sylvia Plath's "Metaphors,"
   say, or Burns's "Oh, my love is like a red, red rose." Rewrite the poem, taking
   for your model Howard Moss's deliberately bepiddling version of "Shall I
   compare thee to a summer's day?" Eliminate every figure of speech. Turn the
   poem into language as flat and unsuggestive as possible. (Just ignore any rime
   or rhythm in the original.) Then, in a paragraph, indicate lines in your revised
   version that seem glaringly worsened. In conclusion, sum up what your barbaric
   rewrite tells you about the nature of poetry.

19 Song

SINGING AND SAYING

Most poems are more memorable than most ordinary speech, and when music is combined with poetry the result can be more memorable still. The differences between speech, poetry, and song may appear if we consider, first of all, this fragment of an imaginary conversation between two lovers:

> Let's not drink; let's just sit here and look at each other. Or put a kiss inside my goblet and I won't want anything to drink.

Forgettable language, we might think; but let's try to make it a little more interesting:

> Drink to me only with your eyes, and I'll pledge my love to you with my eyes;
> Or leave a kiss within the goblet, that's all I'll want to drink.

The passage is closer to poetry, but still has a distance to go. At least we now have a figure of speech — the metaphor that love is wine, implied in the statement that one lover may salute another by lifting an eye as well as by lifting a goblet. But the sound of the words is not yet especially interesting. Here is another try, by Ben Jonson:

> Drink to me only with thine eyes,
>   And I will pledge with mine;
> Or leave a kiss but in the cup,
>   And I'll not ask for wine.

In these opening lines from Jonson's poem "To Celia," the improvement is noticeable. These lines are poetry; their language has become special. For one thing, the lines rime (with an additional rime sound on *thine*). There is interest, too, in the proximity of the words *kiss* and *cup:* the repetition (or alliteration) of the *k* sound. The rhythm of the lines has become regular; generally every other word (or syllable) is stressed:

> DRINK to me ON-ly WITH thine EYES,
>   And I will PLEDGE with MINE;
> OR LEAVE a KISS but IN the CUP,
>   And I'LL not ASK for WINE.

All these devices of sound and rhythm, together with metaphor, produce a pleasing effect — more pleasing than the effect of "Let's not drink; let's look at each other." But the words became more pleasing still when later set to music:

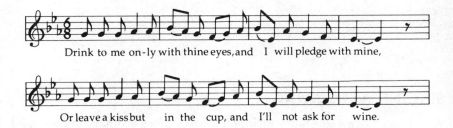

Drink to me on-ly with thine eyes, and I will pledge with mine,

Or leave a kiss but in the cup, and I'll not ask for wine.

In this memorable form, the poem is still alive today.

Ben Jonson (1573? – 1637)*
To Celia   1616

Drink to me only with thine eyes,
  And I will pledge with mine;
Or leave a kiss but in the cup,
  And I'll not ask for wine.
The thirst that from the soul doth rise   5
  Doth ask a drink divine;
But might I of Jove's nectar sup,
  I would not change for thine.

I sent thee late a rosy wreath,
  Not so much honoring thee   10
As giving it a hope that there
  It could not withered be.
But thou thereon didst only breathe,
  And sent'st it back to me;
Since when it grows, and smells, I swear,   15
  Not of itself but thee.

A compliment to a lady has rarely been put in language more graceful, more wealthy with interesting sounds. Other figures of speech besides metaphor make them unforgettable: for example, the hyperbolic tributes to the power of the lady's sweet breath, which can start picked roses growing again, and her kisses, which even surpass the nectar of the gods.

This song falls into stanzas — as many poems that resemble songs also do. A **stanza** (Italian for "station," "stopping-place," or "room") is a group of lines whose pattern is repeated throughout the poem. Most songs have more than one stanza. When printed, the stanzas of songs and poems usually are set off from one another by space. When sung, stanzas of songs are indicated by a pause or by the introduction of a refrain, or chorus (a line or lines repeated). The word **verse,** which strictly refers to one line of a poem, is sometimes loosely used to mean a whole stanza: "All join in and sing the second verse!" In speaking of a stanza, whether sung or read, it is customary to indicate by a convenient algebra its **rime scheme,** the order in which rimed words recur. For instance, the rime scheme of this stanza by Herrick is *a b a b;* the first and third lines rime and so do the second and fourth:

> Round, round, the roof doth run;
>   And being ravished thus,
> Come, I will drink a tun
>   To my Propertius.

Refrains are words, phrases, or lines repeated at intervals in a song or songlike poem. A refrain usually follows immediately after a stanza, and when it does, it is called **terminal refrain.** A refrain whose words change slightly with each recurrence is called an **incremental refrain.** Sometimes we also hear an **internal refrain:** one that appears within a stanza, generally in a position that stays fixed throughout a poem. Both internal refrains and terminal refrains are used to great effect in the traditional song "The Cruel Mother":

Anonymous (traditional Scottish ballad)
THE CRUEL MOTHER

She sat down below a thorn,
   Fine flowers in the valley,
And there she has her sweet babe born
   And the green leaves they grow rarely.

"Smile na sae° sweet, my bonny babe,"   *so* 5
   Fine flowers in the valley,
"And° ye smile sea sweet, ye'll smile me dead."   *if*
   And the green leaves they grow rarely.

She's taen out her little pen-knife,
   Fine flowers in the valley,   10
And twinned° the sweet babe o' its life,   *severed*
   And the green leaves they grow rarely.

She's howket° a grave by the light of the moon,   *dug*
   Fine flowers in the valley,
And there she's buried her sweet babe in   15
   And the green leaves they grow rarely.

As she was going to the church,
    Fine flowers in the valley,
She saw a sweet babe in the porch
    And the green leaves they grow rarely.   20

"O sweet babe, and thou were mine,"
    Fine flowers in the valley,
"I wad cleed° thee in the silk so fine."   *dress*
    And the green leaves they grow rarely.

"O mother dear, when I was thine,"   25
    Fine flowers in the valley,
"You did na prove to me sae kind."
    And the green leaves they grow rarely.

Taken by themselves, the refrain lines might seem mere pretty nonsense. But interwoven with the story of the murdered child, they form a terrible counterpoint. What do they come to mean? Possibly that Nature keeps going about her chores, unmindful of sin and suffering. The effect is an ironic contrast. It is the repetitiveness of a refrain, besides, that helps to give it power.

Songs tend to be written in language simple enough to be understood on first hearing. Even the witty, trickful lyrics of Cole Porter, master songsmith for the Broadway stage, seem designed — for all their allusions — to be taken in at once. Here, for instance, is a stanza of "You're the Top," from the musical *Anything Goes* (1934):

> You're the top! You're an Arrow collar.
> You're the top! You're a Coolidge dollar.
> You're the nimble tread of the feet of Fred Astaire.
> You're an O'Neill drama,
> You're Whistler's mama,
> You're Camembert.
> You're a rose,
> You're Inferno's Dante,
> You're the nose
> Of the great Durante.
> I'm just in the way, as the French would say,
> "De trop,"
> But if, baby, I'm the bottom you're the top.

More recently, songwriters have assumed that their listeners would pay close attention to their words. Bob Dylan, Leonard Cohen, Don McLean, Bruce Springsteen, and others have written lyrics both complex and demanding, requiring listeners to play recordings many times, with trebles turned up all the way.

Many familiar poems began life as songs, but today, their tunes forgotten, they survive only in poetry anthologies. Shakespeare studded his plays with songs, and many of his contemporaries wrote verse to fit existing tunes. Some poets, themselves musicians (like Thomas Campion), composed both words and music. In Shakespeare's day, **madrigals,** short secular songs for three or more voice-parts arranged in counterpoint, enjoyed great favor. A madrigal by Chidiock Tichborne is given on page 503 and another by an anonymous poet, "The Silver Swan," on page 526.

Some poets who were not composers printed their work in madrigal books for others to set to music. In the seventeenth century, however, poetry and song seem to have fallen away from each other. By the end of the century, much new poetry, other than songs for plays, was written to be printed and to be silently read. Poets who wrote popular songs — like Thomas D'Urfey, compiler of the collection *Pills to Purge Melancholy* — were considered somewhat disreputable. With the notable exceptions of John Gay, who took existing popular tunes for *The Beggar's Opera,* and Robert Burns, who rewrote folk songs or made completely new words for them, few important English poets since Campion have been first-rate song-writers.

Occasionally, a poet has learned a thing or two from music. "But for the opera I could never have written *Leaves of Grass,"* said Walt Whitman, who loved the Italian art form for its expansiveness. Coleridge, Hardy, Auden, and many others have learned from folk ballads, and T. S. Eliot patterned his thematically repetitive *Four Quartets* after the structure of a quartet in classical music. "Poetry," said Ezra Pound, "begins to atrophy when it gets too far from music." Still, even in the twentieth century, the poet has been more often a corrector of printer's proofs than a tunesmith or performer.

Some people think that to make a poem and to travel about singing it, as many rock singer-composers now do, is a return to the venerable tradition of the **troubadours,** minstrels of the late Middle Ages. But there are differences. No doubt the troubadours had to please their patrons, but for better or worse their songs were not affected by a stopwatch in a producer's hand or by the technical resources of a sound studio. Bob Dylan has denied that he is a poet, and Paul Simon once told an interviewer, "If you want poetry read Wallace Stevens." Nevertheless, much has been made lately of current song lyrics as poetry.[1] Are rock songs poems? Clearly some, but not all, are. That the lyrics of a song cannot stand the scrutiny of a reader does not necessarily invalidate them, though; song-writers do not usually write in order to be read. Pete Seeger has quoted a saying of his father: "A printed folk song is like a photograph of a bird in flight." Still there is no reason not to photograph birds, or to read song

---

[1]See the anthologies *The Poetry of Rock,* ed. Richard Goldstein (New York: Bantam, 1969), and *Rock Is Beautiful,* ed. Stephanie Spinner (New York: Dell, 1970).

lyrics. If the words seem rich and interesting, we may possibly increase our
enjoyment of them and perhaps be able to sing them more accurately. Like
most poems and songs of the past, most current songs may end in the trash
can of time. And yet, certain memorable rimed and rhythmic lines may live
on, especially if music has served them for a base and if singers have given
them wide exposure.

EXERCISE: *Comparing Poem and Song*

Compare the following poem by Edwin Arlington Robinson and a popular song
lyric based on it. Notice what Paul Simon had to do to Robinson's original in order
to make it into a song, and how Simon altered Robinson's conception.

Edwin Arlington Robinson (1869 – 1935)*

RICHARD CORY   1897

Whenever Richard Cory went down town,
We people on the pavement looked at him:
He was a gentleman from sole to crown,
Clean favored, and imperially slim.

And he was always quietly arrayed,   5
And he was always human when he talked;
But still he fluttered pulses when he said,
"Good-morning," and he glittered when he walked.

And he was rich — yes, richer than a king —
And admirably schooled in every grace: 10
In fine°, we thought that he was everything   *in short*
To make us wish that we were in his place.

So on we worked, and waited for the light,
And went without the meat, and cursed the bread;
And Richard Cory, one calm summer night,   15
Went home and put a bullet through his head.

Paul Simon (b. 1942)

RICHARD CORY   1966

With Apologies to E. A. Robinson

They say that Richard Cory owns
One half of this old town,
With elliptical connections

RICHARD CORY by Paul Simon. If possible, listen to the ballad sung by Simon and Garfunkel
on *Sounds of Silence* (Columbia recording CL 2469, stereo CS 9269). © 1966 by Paul Simon. Used
by permission.

To spread his wealth around.
Born into Society,   5
A banker's only child,
He had everything a man could want:
Power, grace and style.

Refrain:

But I, I work in his factory
And I curse the life I'm livin'   10
And I curse my poverty
And I wish that I could be
Oh I wish that I could be
Oh I wish that I could be
Richard Cory.   15

The papers print his picture
Almost everywhere he goes:
Richard Cory at the opera,
Richard Cory at a show
And the rumor of his party   20
And the orgies on his yacht —
Oh he surely must be happy
With everything he's got.   *(Refrain.)*

He really gave to charity,
He had the common touch,   25
And they were grateful for his patronage
And they thanked him very much,
So my mind was filled with wonder
When the evening headlines read:
    "Richard Cory went home last night   30
    And put a bullet through his head."   *(Refrain.)*

BALLADS

Any narrative song, like Paul Simon's "Richard Cory," may be called
a **ballad.** In English, some of the most famous ballads are **folk ballads,**
loosely defined as anonymous story-songs transmitted orally before they
were ever written down. Sir Walter Scott, a pioneer collector of Scottish
folk ballads, drew the ire of an old woman whose songs he had transcribed:
"They were made for singing and no' for reading, but ye ha'e broken the
charm now and they'll never be sung mair." The old singer had a point.
Print freezes songs and tends to hold them fast to a single version. If Scott
and others had not written them down, however, many would have been
lost.

In his monumental work *The English and Scottish Popular Ballads* (1882 –
1898), the American scholar Francis J. Child winnowed out 305 folk ballads
he considered authentic — that is, creations of illiterate or semiliterate

people who had preserved them orally. Child, who worked by insight as well as by learning, did such a good job of telling the difference between folk ballads and other kinds that later scholars have added only about a dozen ballads to his count. Often called **Child ballads,** his texts include "The Three Ravens," "Sir Patrick Spence," "The Twa Corbies," "Edward," "The Cruel Mother," and many others still on the lips of singers. Here is one of the best-known Child ballads.

Anonymous (traditional Scottish ballad)
Bonny Barbara Allan

It was in and about the Martinmas time,
  When the green leaves were afalling,
That Sir John Graeme, in the West Country,
  Fell in love with Barbara Allan.

He sent his men down through the town,   5
  To the place where she was dwelling;
"O haste and come to my master dear,
  Gin° ye be Barbara Allan."   *if*

O hooly°, hooly rose she up,   *slowly*
  To the place where he was lying,   10
And when she drew the curtain by:
  "Young man, I think you're dying."

"O it's I'm sick, and very, very sick,
  And 'tis a' for Barbara Allan." —
"O the better for me ye's never be,   15
  Tho your heart's blood were aspilling.

"O dinna ye mind°, young man," said she,   *don't you remember*
  "When ye was in the tavern adrinking,
That ye made the health° gae round and round,   *toasts*
  And slighted Barbara Allan?"   20

He turned his face unto the wall,
  And death was with him dealing:
"Adieu, adieu, my dear friends all,
  And be kind to Barbara Allan."

And slowly, slowly raise she up,   25
  And slowly, slowly left him,
And sighing said she could not stay,
  Since death of life had reft him.

She had not gane a mile but twa,
  When she heard the dead-bell ringing,   30
And every jow° that the dead-bell geid,   *stroke*
  It cried, "Woe to Barbara Allan!"

"O mother, mother, make my bed!
  O make it saft and narrow!
Since my love died for me today, 35
  I'll die for him tomorrow."

BONNY BARBARA ALLAN. 1. *Martinmas:* Saint Martin's day, November 11.

QUESTIONS

1. In any line does the Scottish dialect cause difficulty? If so, try reading the line aloud.
2. Without ever coming out and explicitly calling Barbara hard-hearted, this ballad reveals that she is. In which stanza and by what means is her cruelty demonstrated?
3. At what point does Barbara evidently have a change of heart? Again, how does the poem dramatize this change without explicitly talking about it?
4. In many American versions of this ballad, noble knight John Graeme becomes an ordinary citizen. The gist of the story is the same, but at the end are these further stanzas, incorporated from a different ballad:

   They buried Willie in the old churchyard
     And Barbara in the choir;
   And out of his grave grew a red, red rose,
     And out of hers a briar.

   They grew and grew to the steeple top
     Till they could grow no higher;
   And there they locked in a true love's knot,
     The red rose round the briar.

   Do you think this appendage heightens or weakens the final impact of the story? Can the American ending be defended as an integral part of a new song? Explain.
5. Paraphrase lines 9, 15 – 16, 22, 25 – 28. By putting these lines into prose, what has been lost?

As you can see from "Bonny Barbara Allan," in a traditional English or Scottish folk ballad the storyteller speaks of the lives and feelings of others. Even if the pronoun "I" occurs, it rarely has much personality. Characters often exchange dialogue, but no one character speaks all the way through. Events move rapidly, perhaps because some of the dull transitional stanzas have been forgotten. The events themselves, as ballad scholar Albert B. Friedman has said, are frequently "the stuff of tabloid journalism — sensational tales of lust, revenge and domestic crime. Unwed mothers slay their newborn babes; lovers unwilling to marry their pregnant mistresses brutally murder the poor women, for which, without fail, they are justly punished."[2] There are also many ballads of the supernatural ("The Twa Corbies") and of gallant knights ("Sir Patrick Spence"), and there are a few humorous ballads, usually about unhappy marriages.

[2]Introduction to *The Viking Book of Folk Ballads of the English-Speaking World,* edited by Albert B. Friedman (New York: Viking, 1956).

The ballad-spinner has at hand a fund of ready-made epithets: steeds are usually "milk-white" or "berry-brown," lips "rosy" or "ruby-red," corpses and graves "clay-cold," beds (like Barbara Allan's) "soft and narrow." At the least, these conventional phrases are terse and understandable. Sometimes they add meaning: the king who sends Sir Patrick Spence to his doom drinks "blood-red wine." The clothing, steeds, and palaces of ladies and lords are always luxurious: a queen may wear "grass-green silk" or "Spanish leather" and ride a horse with "fifty silver bells and nine." Such descriptions are naive, for as Friedman points out, ballad-singers were probably peasants imagining what they had seen only from afar: the life of the nobility. This may be why the skin of ladies in folk ballads is ordinarily "milk-white," "lily-white," or "snow-white." In an agrarian society, where most people worked in the fields, not to be suntanned was a sign of gentility.

A favorite pattern of ballad-makers is the so-called **ballad stanza,** four lines rimed *a b c b,* tending to fall into 8, 6, 8, and 6 syllables:

> Clerk Saunders and Maid Margaret
>   Walked owre yon garden green,
> And deep and heavy was the love
>   That fell thir twa between°.   *between those two*

Though not the only possible stanza for a ballad, this easily singable quatrain has continued to attract poets since the Middle Ages. Close kin to the ballad stanza is **common meter,** a stanza found in hymns, such as "Amazing Grace," by the eighteenth-century English hymnist John Newton:

> Amazing grace! how sweet the sound
>   That saved a wretch like me!
> I once was lost, but now am found,
>   Was blind, but now I see.

Notice that its pattern is that of the ballad stanza except for its *two* pairs of rimes. That all its lines rime is probably a sign of more literate artistry than we usually hear in folk ballads. Another sign of schoolteachers' influence is that Newton's rimes are exact. (Rimes in folk ballads are often rough-and-ready, as if made by ear, rather than polished and exact, as if the riming words had been matched for their similar spellings. In "Barbara Allan," for instance, the hard-hearted lover's name rimes with *afalling, dwelling, aspilling, dealing,* and even with *ringing* and *adrinking.*) That so many hymns were written in common meter may have been due to convenience. If a congregation didn't know the tune to a hymn in common meter, they readily could sing its words to the tune of another such hymn they knew. Besides hymnists, many poets have favored common meter, among them

A. E. Housman and Emily Dickinson. (For a well-known hymn to compare with some Dickinson poetry, see page 704.)

Related to traditional folk ballads but displaying characteristics of their own, **broadside ballads** (so called because they were printed on one sheet of paper) often were set to traditional tunes. Most broadside ballads were an early form of journalism made possible by the development of cheap printing and by the growth of audiences who could read, just barely. Sometimes merely humorous or tear-jerking, often they were rimed accounts of sensational news events. That they were widespread and often scorned in Shakespeare's day is attested by the character of Autolycus in *A Winter's Tale,* an itinerant hawker of ballads about sea monsters and strange pregnancies ("a usurer's wife was brought to bed of twenty money-bags"). Although many broadsides tend to be **doggerel** (verse full of irregularities due not to skill but to incompetence), many excellent poets had their work taken up and peddled in the streets — among them Marvell, Swift, and Byron.[3]

Literary ballads, not meant for singing, are written by sophisticated poets for book-educated readers who enjoy being reminded of folk ballads. Literary ballads imitate certain features of folk ballads: they may tell of dramatic conflicts or of mortals who encounter the supernatural; they may use conventional figures of speech or ballad stanzas. Well-known poems of this kind include Keats's "La Belle Dame Sans Merci," Coleridge's "Rime of the Ancient Mariner," and (in our time) Dudley Randall's "Ballad of Birmingham" (page 757).

John Lennon (1940 – 1980)
Paul McCartney (b. 1942)

ELEANOR RIGBY   1966

Ah, look at all the lonely people!
Ah, look at all the lonely people!

Eleanor Rigby
Picks up the rice in the church where a wedding has been,
Lives in a dream,   5
Waits at the window
Wearing the face that she keeps in a jar by the door.
Who is it for?

---

[3]A generous collection of broadsides has been assembled by Vivian de Sola Pinto and A. E. Rodway in *The Common Muse: An Anthology of Popular British Ballad Poetry, XVth – XXth Century* (St. Clair Shores, Mich.: Scholarly Press, 1957). See also *Irish Street Ballads,* edited by Colm O. Lochlainn (New York: Corinth Books, 1960), and Olive Woolley Burt, *American Murder Ballads and Their Stories* (New York: Oxford UP, 1958).

All the lonely people,
Where do they all come from?   10
All the lonely people,
Where do they all belong?

Father McKenzie,
Writing the words of a sermon that no one will hear,
No one comes near   15
Look at him working,
Darning his socks in the night when there's nobody there.
What does he care?

All the lonely people
Where do they all come from?   20
All the lonely people
Where do they all belong?

Eleanor Rigby
Died in the church and was buried along with her name.
Nobody came.   25
Father McKenzie,
Wiping the dirt from his hands as he walks from the grave,
No one was saved.

All the lonely people,
Where do they all come from?   30
All the lonely people,
Where do they all belong?

Ah, look at all the lonely people!
Ah, look at all the lonely people!

QUESTION

Is there any reason to call this famous song lyric a ballad? Compare it with a traditional ballad, such as "Bonny Barbara Allan." Do you notice any similarity? What are the differences?

EXPERIMENT *Seeing the Traits of Ballads*

In the Anthology at the back of this book, read the Child ballads "Edward," "Sir Patrick Spence," "The Three Ravens," and "The Twa Corbies" (pages 681 – 684). With these ballads in mind, consider one or more of these modern poems:

W. H. Auden, "As I Walked Out One Evening" (page 687)
Dudley Randall, "Ballad of Birmingham" (page 757)
William Jay Smith, "American Primitive" (page 771)
William Butler Yeats, "Crazy Jane Talks with the Bishop" (page 790).

What characteristics of folk ballads do you find in them? In what ways do these modern poets depart from the traditions of folk ballads of the Middle Ages?

FOR REVIEW AND FURTHER STUDY

Adrienne Rich (b. 1929)*
SONG   1973

You're wondering if I'm lonely:
OK then, yes, I'm lonely
as a plane rides lonely and level
on its radio beam, aiming
across the Rockies   5
for the blue-strung aisles
of an airfield on the ocean

You want to ask, am I lonely?
Well, of course, lonely
as a woman driving across country   10
day after day, leaving behind
mile after mile
little towns she might have stopped
and lived and died in, lonely

If I'm lonely   15
it must be the loneliness
of waking first, of breathing
dawn's first cold breath on the city
of being the one awake
in a house wrapped in sleep   20

If I'm lonely
it's with the rowboat ice-fast on the shore
in the last red light of the year
that knows what it is, that knows it's neither
ice nor mud nor winter light   25
but wood, with a gift for burning

QUESTION

This "Song" is a lyric poem, not to be sung but to be read on the page. What songlike elements do you find in it?

Consider each of the following song lyrics. Which do you think can stand not only to be sung but to be read as poetry? Which probably should not be seen but only heard?

Anonymous (English madrigal)

FA, MI, FA, RE, LA, MI   1609

   Fa, mi, fa, re, la, mi,
Begin, my son, and follow me;
    Sing flat, fa mi,
  So shall we well agree.
    Hey tro loly lo.
    Hold fast, good son,
  With hey tro lily lo.
O sing this once again, lustily.

Anonymous (English madrigal)

THE SILVER SWAN, WHO LIVING HAD NO NOTE   1612

The silver swan, who living had no note,
When death approached unlocked her silent throat;
Leaning her breast against the reedy shore,
Thus sung her first and last, and sung no more.
Farewell, all joys; O death, come close mine eyes;
More geese than swans now live, more fools than wise.

Willie Nelson (b. 1933)

HEAVEN AND HELL   1974

Well, sometimes it's Heaven, and sometimes it's Hell,
And sometimes I don't even know;
And sometimes I take it as far as I can,
And sometimes I don't even go.

My front tracks are bound for a cold water well,   5
My back tracks are covered with snow;
And sometimes it's Heaven, and sometimes it's Hell,
And sometimes I don't even know.

Heaven ain't walking on a street paved with gold,
And Hell ain't a mountain of fire;   10
Heaven is laying in my sweet Baby's arms,
And Hell is when Baby's not there.

Well, my front tracks are bound for a cold water well
And my back tracks are covered with snow;
And sometimes it's Heaven, and sometimes it's Hell,   15
And sometimes I don't even know.

Well, sometimes it's Heaven, and sometimes it's Hell,
And sometimes I don't even know.

Bruce Springsteen (b. 1949)
BORN TO RUN   1975

In the day we sweat it out in the streets
        of a runaway American dream
At night we ride through mansions of
        glory in suicide machines
Sprung from cages out on Highway 9
Chrome wheeled, fuel injected
And steppin' out over the line   5
Baby this town rips the bones from your back
It's a death trap, it's a suicide rap
We gotta get out while we're young
'Cause tramps like us, baby we were born to run.

Wendy, let me in, I wanna be your friend   10
I want to guard your dreams and visions
Just wrap your legs round these velvet rims
And strap your hands across my engines
Together we could break this trap
We'll run till we drop, baby we'll never go back   15
Will you walk with me out on the wire
'Cause baby I'm just a scared and lonely rider
But I gotta know how it feels
I want to know if your love is wild
Girl I want to know if love is real   20

Beyond the Palace hemi-powered drones
        scream down the boulevard
The girls comb their hair in rear-view mirrors
And the boys try to look so hard
The amusement park rises bold and stark
Kids are huddled on the beach in a mist   25
I wanna die with you out on the streets tonight
In an everlasting kiss

The highways jammed with broken heroes
On a last chance power drive
Everybody's out on the run tonight   30
But there's no place left to hide
Together, Wendy, we can live with the sadness

I'll love you with all the madness in my soul
Someday girl, I don't know when,
    we're gonna get to that place
Where we really want to go
And we'll walk in the sun
But till then tramps like us
Baby we were born to run

35

Suggestions for Writing

1. Write a short study of a lyric (or lyrics) by a recent popular song-writer. Show why you believe the song-writer's work deserves the name of poetry.
2. Compare and contrast the English folk ballad "The Three Ravens" with the Scottish folk ballad "The Twa Corbies" (both in the Anthology).
3. How do the poems of Emily Dickinson resemble hymns? Consider this question in a brief essay (see pages 704 – 707).
4. Compare the versions of "Richard Cory" by Edwin Arlington Robinson and by Paul Simon. Point out changes Simon apparently made in the poem to render it singable. What other changes did he make? How did he alter Robinson's story and its characters?

20 Sound

SOUND AS MEANING

Isak Dinesen, in a memoir of her life on a plantation in East Africa, tells how some Kikuyu tribesmen reacted to their first hearing of rimed verse:

> The Natives, who have a strong sense of rhythm, know nothing of verse, or at least did not know anything before the times of the schools, where they were taught hymns. One evening out in the maize-field, where we had been harvesting maize, breaking off the cobs and throwing them on to the ox-carts, to amuse myself, I spoke to the field laborers, who were mostly quite young, in Swahili verse. There was no sense in the verses, they were made for the sake of rime — "Ngumbe na-penda chumbe, Malaya mbaya. Wakamba na-kula mamba." The oxen like salt — whores are bad — The Wakamba eat snakes. It caught the interest of the boys, they formed a ring round me. They were quick to understand that meaning in poetry is of no consequence, and they did not question the thesis of the verse, but waited eagerly for the rime, and laughed at it when it came. I tried to make them themselves find the rime and finish the poem when I had begun it, but they could not, or would not, do that, and turned away their heads. As they had become used to the idea of poetry, they begged: "Speak again. Speak like rain." Why they should feel verse to be like rain I do not know. It must have been, however, an expression of applause, since in Africa rain is always longed for and welcomed.[1]

What the tribesmen had discovered is that poetry, like music, appeals to the ear. However limited it may be in comparison with the sound of an orchestra — or a tribal drummer — the sound of words in itself gives pleasure. However, we might doubt Isak Dinesen's assumption that "meaning in poetry is of no consequence." "Hey nonny-nonny" and such nonsense has a place in song lyrics and other poems, and we might take pleasure in hearing rimes in Swahili; but most good poetry has meaningful sound as well as musical sound. Certainly the words of a song have an

[1] Isak Dinesen, *Out of Africa* (New York: Random, 1972).

effect different from that of wordless music: they go along with their music and, by making statements, add more meaning. The French poet Isidore Isou, founder of a literary movement called *lettrisme,* maintained that poems can be written not only in words but in letters (sample lines: *xyl, xyl, / prprali dryl / znglo trpylo pwi*). But the sound of letters alone, without denotation and connotation, has not been enough to make Letterist poems memorable. In the response of the Kikuyu tribesmen, there may have been not only the pleasure of hearing sounds but also the agreeable surprise of finding that things not usually associated had been brought together.

More powerful when in the company of meaning, not apart from it, the sounds of consonants and vowels can contribute greatly to a poem's effect. The sound of *s,* which can suggest the swishing of water, has rarely been used more accurately than in Surrey's line "Calm is the sea, the waves work less and less." When, in a poem, the sound of words working together with meaning pleases mind and ear, the effect is **euphony,** as in the following lines from Tennyson's "Come down, O maid":

> Myriads of rivulets hurrying through the lawn,
> The moan of doves in immemorial elms,
> And murmuring of innumerable bees.

Its opposite is **cacophony:** a harsh, discordant effect. It too is chosen for the sake of meaning. We hear it in Milton's scornful reference in "Lycidas" to corrupt clergymen whose songs "Grate on their scrannel pipes of wretched straw." (Read that line and one of Tennyson's aloud and see which requires lips, teeth, and tongue to do more work.) But note that although Milton's line is harsh in sound, the line (when we meet it in his poem) is pleasing because it is artful. In a famous passage from his *Essay on Criticism,* Pope has illustrated both euphony and cacophony. (Given here as Pope printed it, the passage relies heavily on italics and capital letters, for particular emphasis. If you will read these lines aloud, dwelling a little longer or harder on the words italicized, you will find that Pope has given you very good directions for a meaningful reading.)

Alexander Pope (1688 – 1744)*
TRUE EASE IN WRITING COMES FROM ART, NOT CHANCE   1711

True Ease in Writing comes from Art, not Chance,
As those move easiest who have learned to dance.
'Tis not enough no Harshness gives Offence,
The *Sound* must seem an *Echo* to the *Sense.*
Soft is the strain when *Zephyr*° gently blows,   *the west wind*   5
And the *smooth Stream* in *smoother Numbers*° flows;   *metrical rhythm*
But when loud Surges lash the sounding Shore,
The *hoarse, rough Verse* should like the *Torrent* roar.

When *Ajax* strives, some Rock's vast Weight to throw,
The Line too *labors,* and the Words move *slow;*　　　　　10
Not so, when swift *Camilla* scours the Plain,
Flies o'er th' unbending Corn, and skims along the Main°. *expanse (of sea)*
Hear how *Timotheus'* varied Lays surprise,
And bid Alternate Passions fall and rise!
While, at each Change, the Son of *Lybian Jove*　　　　15
Now *burns* with Glory, and then *melts* with Love;
Now his *fierce Eyes* with *sparkling Fury* glow;
Now *Sighs* steal out, and *Tears begin to flow:*
Persians and Greeks like *Turns of Nature* found,
And the *World's Victor* stood subdued by *Sound!*　　　　20
The Pow'rs of Music all our Hearts allow;
And what *Timotheus* was, is *Dryden* now.

TRUE EASE IN WRITING COMES FROM ART, NOT CHANCE (*An Essay on Criticism,* lines 362 – 383). 9. *Ajax:* Greek hero, almost a superman, who in Homer's account of the siege of Troy hurls an enormous rock that momentarily flattens Hector, the Trojan prince (*Iliad* VII, 268 – 272). 11. *Camilla:* a kind of Amazon or warrior woman of the Volcians, whose speed and lightness of step are praised by the Roman poet Virgil: "She could have skimmed across an unmown grainfield / Without so much as bruising one tender blade; / She could have sped across an ocean's surge / Without so much as wetting her quicksilver soles" (*Aeneid* VII, 808 – 811). 13. *Timotheus:* favorite musician of Alexander the Great. In "Alexander's Feast, or The Power of Music," John Dryden imagines him: "Timotheus, placed on high / Amid the tuneful choir, / With flying fingers touched the lyre: / The trembling notes ascend the sky, / And heavenly joys inspire." 15. *Lybian Jove:* name for Alexander. A Libyan oracle had declared the king to be the son of the god Zeus Ammon.

Notice the pleasing effect of all the *s* sounds in the lines about the west wind and the stream, and in another meaningful place, the effect of the consonants in *Ajax strives,* a phrase that makes our lips work almost as hard as Ajax throwing the rock.

Is sound identical with meaning in lines such as these? Not quite. In the passage from Tennyson, for instance, the cooing of doves is not *exactly* a moan. As John Crowe Ransom pointed out, the sound would be almost the same but the meaning entirely different in "The murdering of innumerable beeves." While it is true that the consonant sound *sl-* will often begin a word that conveys ideas of wetness and smoothness — *slick, slimy, slippery, slush* — we are so used to hearing it in words that convey nothing of the kind — *slave, slow, sledgehammer* — that it is doubtful whether, all by itself, the sound communicates anything definite. The most beautiful phrase in the English language, according to Dorothy Parker, is *cellar door.* Another wit once nominated, as our most euphonious word, not *sunrise* or *silvery* but *syphilis.*

Relating sound more closely to meaning, the device called **onomatopoeia** is an attempt to represent a thing or action by a word that imitates the sound associated with it: *zoom, whiz, crash, bang, ding-dong, pitter-patter, yakety-yak.* Onomatopoeia is often effective in poetry, as in Emily Dickinson's line about the fly with its "uncertain stumbling Buzz," in which the nasal sounds *n, m, ng* and the sibilants *c, s,* help make a droning buzz, and in Robert Lowell's transcription of a bird call, "yuck-a, yuck-a, yuck-a" (in "Falling Asleep over the Aeneid").

Like the Kikuyu tribesmen, others who care for poetry have discovered in the sound of words something of the refreshment of cool rain. Dylan Thomas, telling how he began to write poetry, said that from early childhood words were to him "as the notes of bells, the sounds of musical instruments, the noises of wind, sea, and rain, the rattle of milkcarts, the clopping of hooves on cobbles, the fingering of branches on the window pane, might be to someone, deaf from birth, who has miraculously found his hearing."[2] For readers, too, the sound of words can have a magical spell, most powerful when it points to meaning. James Weldon Johnson in *God's Trombones* has told of an old-time preacher who began his sermon, "Brothers and sisters, this morning I intend to explain the unexplainable — find out the indefinable — ponder over the imponderable — and unscrew the inscrutable!" The repetition of sound in *unscrew* and *inscrutable* has appeal, but the magic of the words is all the greater if they lead us to imagine the mystery of all Creation as an enormous screw that the preacher's mind, like a screw-driver, will loosen. Though the sound of a word or the meaning of a word may have value all by itself, both become more memorable when taken together.

William Butler Yeats (1865 – 1939)*
WHO GOES WITH FERGUS?   1892

Who will go drive with Fergus now,
And pierce the deep wood's woven shade,
And dance upon the level shore?
Young man, lift up your russet brow,
And lift your tender eyelids, maid,   5
And brood on hopes and fear no more.

And no more turn aside and brood
Upon love's bitter mystery;
For Fergus rules the brazen cars°,   *chariots*
And rules the shadows of the wood,   10
And the white breast of the dim sea
And all dishevelled wandering stars.

WHO GOES WITH FERGUS? *Fergus:* Irish king who gave up his throne to be a wandering poet.

2"Notes on the Art of Poetry," *Modern Poetics,* ed. James Scully (New York: McGraw-Hill, 1965).

1. In what lines do you find euphony?
2. In what line do you find cacophony?
3. How do the sounds of these lines stress what is said in them?

EXERCISE: *Listening to Meaning*

Read aloud the following brief poems. In the sounds of which particular words are meanings well captured? In which of the poems below do you find onomatopoeia?

John Updike (b. 1932)*
WINTER OCEAN   1960

Many-maned scud-thumper, tub
of male whales, maker of worn wood, shrub-
ruster, sky-mocker, rave!
portly pusher of waves, wind-slave.

Frances Cornford (1886 – 1960)
THE WATCH   1923

I wakened on my hot, hard bed,
Upon the pillow lay my head;
Beneath the pillow I could hear
My little watch was ticking clear.
I thought the throbbing of it went   5
Like my continual discontent.
I thought it said in every tick:
I am so sick, so sick, so sick.
O death, come quick, come quick, come quick,
Come quick, come quick, come quick, come quick!   10

William Wordsworth (1770 – 1850)*
A SLUMBER DID MY SPIRIT SEAL   1800

A slumber did my spirit seal;
  I had no human fears —
She seemed a thing that could not feel
  The touch of earthly years.

No motion has she now, no force;
  She neither hears nor sees;
Rolled round in earth's diurnal course,
  With rocks, and stones, and trees.

Emanuel di Pasquale (b. 1943)
RAIN   1971

Like a drummer's brush,
the rain hushes the surface of tin porches.

ALLITERATION AND ASSONANCE

Listening to a symphony in which themes are repeated throughout
each movement, we enjoy both their recurrence and their variation. We
take similar pleasure in the repetition of a phrase or a single chord. Something like this pleasure is afforded us frequently in poetry.

Analogies between poetry and wordless music, it is true, tend to
break down when carried far, since poetry — to mention a single difference
— has denotation. But like musical compositions, poems have patterns of
sounds. Among such patterns long popular in English poetry is **alliteration**, which has been defined as a succession of similar sounds. Alliteration occurs in the repetition of the same consonant sound at the beginning
of successive words — "round and round the rugged rocks the ragged
rascal ran" — or inside the words, as in Milton's description of the gates
of Hell:

> On a sudden open fly
> With impetuous recoil and jarring sound
> The infernal doors, and on their hinges grate
> Harsh thunder, that the lowest bottom shook
> Of Erebus.

The former kind is called **initial alliteration**, the latter **internal alliteration**
or **hidden alliteration**. We recognize alliteration by sound, not by spelling:
know and *nail* alliterate, *know* and *key* do not. In a line by E. E. Cummings,
"colossal hoax of clocks and calendars," the sound of *x* within *hoax* alliterates with the *cks* in clo*cks*. Incidentally, the letter *r* does not *always* lend
itself to cacophony: elsewhere in *Paradise Lost* Milton said that

> Heaven opened wide
> Her ever-during gates, harmonious sound
> On golden hinges moving . . .

By itself, a letter-sound has no particular meaning. This is a truth forgotten
by people who would attribute the effectiveness of Milton's lines on the
Heavenly Gates to, say, "the mellow *o*'s and liquid *l* of *harmonious* and
golden." Mellow *o*'s and liquid *l*'s occur also in the phrase *moldy cold oatmeal*,
which may have a quite different effect. Meaning depends on larger units
of language than letters of the alphabet.

Today good prose writers usually avoid alliteration; in the past, some
cultivated it. "There is nothing more swifter than time, nothing more

sweeter," wrote John Lyly in *Euphues* (1579), and he went on — playing especially with the sounds of *v, n, t, s, l,* and *b* — "we have not, as Seneca saith, little time to live, but we lose much; neither have we a short life by nature, but we make it shorter by naughtiness." Poetry, too, formerly contained more alliteration than it usually contains today. In Old English verse, each line was held together by alliteration, a basic pattern still evident in the fourteenth century, as in the following description of the world as a "fair field" in *Piers Plowman:*

> A *f*eir *f*eld *f*ul of *f*olk *f*ond I ther bi-twene,
> Of alle *m*aner of *m*en, the *m*ene and the riche . . .

Most poets nowadays save alliteration for special occasions. They may use it to give emphasis, as Edward Lear does: "*F*ar and *f*ew, *f*ar and *f*ew, / Are the *l*ands where the Jumblies *l*ive." With its aid they can point out the relationship between two things placed side by side, as in Pope's line on things of little worth: "The courtier's *p*romises, and sick man's *p*rayers." Alliteration, too, can be a powerful aid to memory. It is hard to forget such tongue twisters as "Peter Piper picked a peck of pickled peppers," or common expressions like "green as grass," "tried and true," and "from stem to stern." In fact, because alliteration directs our attention to something, it had best be used neither thoughtlessly nor merely for decoration, lest it call attention to emptiness. A case in point may be a line by Philip James Bailey, a reaction to a lady's weeping: "I saw, but *sp*ared to *sp*eak." If the poet chose the word *spared* for any meaningful reason other than that it alliterates with *speak,* the reason is not clear.

As we have seen, to repeat the sound of a consonant is to produce alliteration, but to repeat the sound of a *vowel* is to produce **assonance.** Like alliteration, assonance may occur either initially — "*a*ll the *a*wful *a*uguries"[3] — or internally — Edmund Spenser's "Her goodly *eye*s l*i*ke sapph*i*res sh*i*ning br*i*ght, / Her forehead *i*vory wh*i*te . . ." and it can help make common phrases unforgettable: "eager beaver," "holy smoke." Like alliteration, it slows the reader down and focuses attention.

A. E. Housman (1859 – 1936)*
Eight O'Clock   1922

He stood, and heard the steeple
    Sprinkle the quarters on the morning town.
One, two, three, four, to market-place and people
    It tossed them down.

---

[3]Some prefer to call the repetition of an initial vowel-sound by the name of alliteration: "apt alliteration's artful aid."

Strapped, noosed, nighing his hour,
    He stood and counted them and cursed his luck;
And then the clock collected in the tower
    Its strength, and struck.

QUESTIONS

1. Why does the protagonist in this brief drama curse his luck? What is his situation?
2. For so short a poem, "Eight O'Clock" carries a great weight of alliteration. What patterns of initial alliteration do you find? What patterns of internal alliteration? What effect is created by all this heavy emphasis?

Robert Herrick (1591 – 1674)*
UPON JULIA'S VOICE   1648

So smooth, so sweet, so silv'ry is thy voice,
As, could they hear, the damned would make no noise,
But listen to thee (walking in thy chamber)
Melting melodious words, to lutes of amber.

UPON JULIA'S VOICE. 4. *amber:* either the fossilized resin from which pipestems are sometimes made today, and which might have inlaid the body of a lute; or an alloy of four parts silver and one part gold.

QUESTIONS

1. Is Julia speaking or singing? How do we know for sure?
2. In what moments in this brief poem does the sound of words especially help convey meaning?
3. Does Herrick's reference to *the damned* (presumably howling from Hell's torments) seem out of place?

Janet Lewis (b. 1899)
GIRL HELP   1927

Mild and slow and young,
She moves about the room,
And stirs the summer dust
With her wide broom.

In the warm, lofted air,   5
Soft lips together pressed,
Soft wispy hair,
She stops to rest,

And stops to breathe,
Amid the summer hum,   10
The great white lilac bloom
Scented with days to come.

1. What assonance and alliteration do you find in this poem? (Suggestion: It may help to read the poem aloud.)
2. In this particular poem, how are these repetitions (or echoes) of sound valuable?

EXERCISE: *Hearing How Sound Helps*

Which of these translations of the same passage from Petrarch do you think is better poetry? Why? What do assonance and alliteration have to do with your preference?

1. Love that liveth and reigneth in my thought,
   That built his seat within my captive breast,
   Clad in the arms wherein with me he fought,
   Oft in my face he doth his banner rest.
   —Henry Howard, Earl of Surrey (1517? – 1547)
2. The long love that in my thought doth harbor,
   And in mine heart doth keep his residence,
   Into my face presseth with bold pretense
   And therein campeth, spreading his banner.
   —Sir Thomas Wyatt (1503? – 1542)

EXPERIMENT: *Reading for Assonance*

Try reading aloud as rapidly as possible the following poem by Tennyson. From the difficulties you encounter, you may be able to sense the slowing effect of assonance. Then read the poem aloud a second time, with consideration.

Alfred, Lord Tennyson (1809 – 1892)*

THE SPLENDOR FALLS ON CASTLE WALLS   1850

The splendor falls on castle walls
  And snowy summits old in story;
The long light shakes across the lakes,
  And the wild cataract leaps in glory.
Blow, bugle, blow, set the wild echoes flying,   5
Blow, bugle; answer, echoes, dying, dying, dying.

O hark, O hear! how thin and clear,
  And thinner, clearer, farther going!
O sweet and far from cliff and scar°   *jutting rock*
  The horns of Elfland faintly blowing!   10
Blow, let us hear the purple glens replying:
Blow, bugle; answer, echoes, dying, dying, dying.

O love, they die in yon rich sky,
  They faint on hill or field or river;
Our echoes roll from soul to soul,   15
  And grow for ever and for ever.
Blow, bugle, blow, set the wild echoes flying,
And answer, echoes, answer, dying, dying, dying.

RIME

Isak Dinesen's tribesmen, to whom rime was a new phenomenon, recognized at once that rimed language is special language. So do we, for, although much English poetry is unrimed, rime is one means to set poetry apart from ordinary conversation and bring it closer to music. A **rime** (or rhyme), defined most narrowly, occurs when two or more words or phrases contain an identical or similar vowel-sound, usually accented, and the consonant-sounds (if any) that follow the vowel-sound are identical: *hay* and *sleigh, prairie schooner* and *piano tuner.* [4] From these examples it will be seen that rime depends not on spelling but on sound.

Excellent rimes surprise. It is all very well that a reader may anticipate which vowel-sound is coming next, for patterns of rime give pleasure by satisfying expectations; but riming becomes dull clunking if, at the end of each line, the reader can predict the word that will end the next. Hearing many a jukebox song for the first time, a listener can do so: *charms* lead to *arms, skies above* to *love.* As Alexander Pope observes of the habits of dull rimesters,

> Where'er you find "the cooling western breeze,"
> In the next line it "whispers through the trees";
> If crystal streams "with pleasing murmurs creep,"
> The reader's threatened (not in vain) with "sleep" . . .

But who — given the opening line of this children's jingle — could predict the lines that follow?

Anonymous (English)

JULIUS CAESAR
(about 1940?)

Julius Caesar,
The Roman geezer,
Squashed his wife with a lemon-squeezer.

Here rimes combine things unexpectedly. Robert Herrick, too, made good use of rime to indicate a startling contrast:

> Then while time serves, and we are but decaying,
> Come, my Corinna, come, let's go a-Maying.

Though good rimes seem fresh, not all will startle, and probably few will call to mind things so unlike as *May* and *decay, Caesar* and *lemon-squeezer.*

---

[4] Some definitions of *rime* would apply the term to the repetition of any identical or similar sound, not only a vowel-sound. In this sense, assonance is a kind of rime; so is alliteration (called **initial rime**).

Some masters of rime often link words that, taken out of text, might seem common and unevocative. Here, for instance, is Alexander Pope's comment on a trifling courtier:

> Yet let me flap this bug with gilded wings,
> This painted child of dirt, that stinks and stings;
> Whose buzz the witty and the fair annoys,
> Yet wit ne'er tastes, and beauty ne'er enjoys:
> So well-bred spaniels civilly delight
> In mumbling of the game they dare not bite.
> Eternal smiles his emptiness betray,
> As shallow streams run dimpling all the way.

Pope's rime-words are not especially memorable — and yet these lines are, because (among other reasons) they rime. Wit may be driven home without rime, but it is rime that rings the doorbell. Admittedly, some rimes wear thin from too much use. More difficult to use freshly than before the establishment of Tin Pan Alley, rimes such as *moon, June, croon* seem leaden and to ring true would need an extremely powerful context. *Death* and *breath* are a rime that poets have used with wearisome frequency; another is *birth, earth, mirth.* And yet we cannot exclude these from the diction of poetry, for they might be the very words a poet would need in order to say something new and original. The following brief poem seems fresher than its rimes (if taken out of context) would lead us to expect.

William Blake (1757 – 1827)*
THE ANGEL THAT PRESIDED O'ER MY BIRTH   (1808 – 1811)

The Angel that presided o'er my birth
Said, "Little creature, formed of Joy and Mirth,
Go love without the help of any thing on earth."

What matters to rime is freshness — not of a word but of the poet's way of seeing.

Good poets, said John Dryden, learn to make their rime "so properly a part of the verse, that it should never mislead the sense, but itself be led and governed by it." The comment may remind us that skillful rime — unlike poor rime — is never a distracting ornament. "Rime the rudder is of verses, / With which, like ships, they steer their courses," wrote the seventeenth-century poet Samuel Butler. Like other patterns of sound, rime can help a poet to group ideas, emphasize particular words, and weave a poem together. It can start reverberations between words and can point to connections of meaning.

To have an **exact rime,** sounds following the vowel sound have to be the same: *red* and *bread, wealthily* and *stealthily, walk to her* and *talk to her.* If final consonant sounds are the same but the vowel sounds are different, the result is **slant rime,** also called **near rime, off rime,** or **partial rime:** *sun* riming with *bone, moon, rain, green, gone, thin.* By not satisfying the reader's expectation of an exact chime, but instead giving a clunk, a slant rime can help a poet say some things in a particular way. It works especially well for disappointed let-downs, negations, and denials, as in Blake's couplet:

He who the ox to wrath has moved
Shall never be by woman loved.

Consonance, a kind of slant rime, occurs when the rimed words or phrases have the same consonant sounds but a different vowel, as in *chitter* and *chatter.* It is used in a traditional nonsense poem, "The Cutty Wren": " 'O where are you going?' says *Milder* to *Malder.* " (W. H. Auden wrote a variation on it that begins, " 'O where are you going?' said *reader* to *rider,* " thus keeping the consonance.)

End rime, as its name indicates, comes at the ends of lines, **internal rime** within them. Most rime tends to be end rime. Few recent poets have used internal rime so heavily as Wallace Stevens in the beginning of "Bantams in Pine-Woods": "Chieftain Iffucan of Azcan in caftan / Of tan with henna hackles, halt!" (lines also heavy on alliteration). A poet may employ both end rime and internal rime in the same poem, as in Robert Burns's satiric ballad "The Kirk's Alarm":

Orthodox, Orthodox, wha believe in John Knox,
   Let me sound an alarm to your conscience:
There's a heretic blast has been blawn i' the wast°,   *west*
   "That what is not sense must be nonsense."

Masculine rime is a rime of one-syllable words *(jail, bail)* or (in words of more than one syllable) stressed final syllables: *di-VORCE, re-MORSE,* or *horse, re-MORSE.* **Feminine rime** is a rime of two or more syllables, with stress on a syllable other than the last: *TUR-tle, FER-tile,* or (to take an example from Byron) *in-tel-LECT-u-al, hen-PECKED you all.* Often it lends itself to comic verse, but can occasionally be valuable to serious poems, as in Wordsworth's "Resolution and Independence":

We poets in our youth begin in gladness,
But thereof come in the end despondency and madness.

or as in Anne Sexton's seriously witty "Eighteen Days Without You":

and of course we're not married, we are a pair of scissors
who come together to cut, without towels saying His. Hers.

Serious poems containing feminine rimes of three syllables have been attempted, notably by Thomas Hood in "The Bridge of Sighs":

Take her up tenderly,
Lift her with care;
Fashioned so slenderly,
Young, and so fair!

But the pattern is hard to sustain without lapsing into unintended comedy, as in the same poem:

Still, for all slips of hers,
One of Eve's family —
Wipe those poor lips of hers,
Oozing so clammily.

It works better when comedy is wanted:

Hilaire Belloc (1870 – 1953)

THE HIPPOPOTAMUS   1896

I shoot the Hippopotamus
  with bullets made of platinum,
Because if I use leaden ones
  his hide is sure to flatten 'em.

In **eye rime,** spellings look alike but pronunciations differ — *rough* and *dough, idea* and *flea, Venus* and *menus.* Strictly speaking, eye rime is not rime at all.

In the early 1960s in American poetry, rime suffered a tremendous fall from favor. A new generation of poets took for models the open forms of Whitman and William Carlos Williams. Only lately has skilled rime prominently reappeared in the work of new poets such as R. L. Barth, Amy Clampitt, Marilyn Hacker, Brad Leithauser, Gjertrud Schnackenberg, and Timothy Steele. Here is a recent sample:

Brad Leithauser (b. 1953)

TRAUMA   1982

You will carry this suture
  Into the future.
The past never passes.
  It simply amasses.

Still, most American poets don't write in rime; some even consider it exhausted. Such a view may be a reaction against the wearing-thin of rimes by overuse or the mechanical and meaningless application of a rime scheme. Yet anyone who listens to children skipping rope in the street, making up rimes to delight themselves as they go along, may doubt that the pleasures of rime are ended; and certainly the practice of Yeats and Emily Dickinson, to name only two, suggests that the possibilities of slant rime may be nearly infinite. If successfully employed, as it has been at times by a majority of English-speaking poets whose work we care to save, rime runs through its poem like a spine: the creature moves by means of it.

James Hayford (b. 1913)
MASON'S TRICK $\qquad$ 1983

From masons laying up brick
To build a rosy wall
Level and square and tall,

We borrow a mason's trick,
Or at least a builder's term: 5
Rhymes keep our corners firm.

Robert Frost (1874 – 1963)*
DESERT PLACES $\qquad$ 1936

Snow falling and night falling fast, oh, fast
In a field I looked into going past,
And the ground almost covered smooth in snow,
But a few weeds and stubble showing last.

The woods around it have it — it is theirs.   5
All animals are smothered in their lairs,
I am too absent-spirited to count;
The loneliness includes me unawares.

And lonely as it is, that loneliness
Will be more lonely ere it will be less —   10
A blanker whiteness of benighted snow
With no expression, nothing to express.

They cannot scare me with their empty spaces
Between stars — on stars where no human race is.
I have it in me so much nearer home   15
To scare myself with my own desert places.

QUESTIONS

1. What are these desert places that the speaker finds in himself? (More than one theory is possible. What is yours?)

2. Notice how many times, within the short space of lines 8 – 10, Frost says *lonely* (or *loneliness*). What other words in the poem contain similar sounds that reinforce these words?
3. In the closing stanza, the feminine rimes *spaces, race is,* and *places* might well occur in light or comic verse. Does "Desert Places" leave you laughing? If not, what does it make you feel?

William Butler Yeats (1865 – 1939)*
LEDA AND THE SWAN   1924

A sudden blow: the great wings beating still
Above the staggering girl, her thighs caressed
By the dark webs, her nape caught in his bill,
He holds her helpless breast upon his breast.

How can those terrified vague fingers push   5
The feathered glory from her loosening thighs?
And how can body, laid in that white rush,
But feel the strange heart beating where it lies?

A shudder in the loins engenders there
The broken wall, the burning roof and tower   10
And Agamemnon dead.
                            Being so caught up,
So mastered by the brute blood of the air,
Did she put on his knowledge with his power
Before the indifferent beak could let her drop?

QUESTIONS

1. According to Greek mythology, the god Zeus in the form of a swan descended upon Leda, a Spartan queen. Among the offspring of this union were Clytemnestra, Agamemnon's unfaithful wife who conspired in his murder, and Helen, on whose account the Trojan war was fought. What does a knowledge of these allusions contribute to our understanding of the poem's last two lines?
2. The slant rime *up / drop* (lines 11, 14) may seem accidental or inept. Is it? Would this poem have ended nearly so well if Yeats had made an exact rime like *up / cup* or like *stop / drop?*

Gerard Manley Hopkins (1844 – 1889)*
GOD'S GRANDEUR   (1877)

The world is charged with the grandeur of God.
    It will flame out, like shining from shook foil;
    It gathers to a greatness, like the ooze of oil
Crushed. Why do men then now not reck his rod?
Generations have trod, have trod, have trod;   5
    And all is seared with trade; bleared, smeared with toil;
    And wears man's smudge and shares man's smell: the soil
Is bare now, nor can foot feel, being shod.

And for all this, nature is never spent;
   There lives the dearest freshness deep down things;   10
And though the last lights off the black West went
   Oh, morning, at the brown brink eastward, springs —
Because the Holy Ghost over the bent
   World broods with warm breast and with ah! bright wings.

QUESTIONS

1. In a letter Hopkins explained *shook foil* (line 2): "I mean foil in its sense of leaf or tinsel. . . . Shaken goldfoil gives off broad glares like sheet lightning and also, and this is true of nothing else, owing to its zigzag dints and creasings and network of small many cornered facets, a sort of fork lightning too." What do you think he meant by *ooze of oil* (line 3)? Is this phrase an example of alliteration?
2. What instances of internal rime does the poem contain? How would you describe their effects?
3. Point out some of the poet's uses of alliteration and assonance. Does Hopkins go too far in his heavy use of devices of sound, or would you defend his practice?
4. Why do you suppose Hopkins, in the last two lines, says *over the bent / World* instead of (as we might expect) *bent over the world*? How can the world be bent? Can you make any sense out of this wording, or is Hopkins just trying to get his rime scheme to work out?

Emily Dickinson (1830 – 1886)*
THE SOUL SELECTS HER OWN SOCIETY   (1862)

The Soul selects her own Society –
Then – shuts the Door –
To her divine Majority –
Present no more –

Unmoved – she notes the Chariots – pausing –   5
At her low Gate –
Unmoved – an Emperor be kneeling
Upon her Mat –

I've known her – from an ample nation –
Choose One –   10
Then – close the Valves of her attention –
Like Stone –

QUESTIONS

1. What kinds of rime do you find in this poem?
2. Try to describe the effect of the closing rime, *One / Stone.*
3. Who or what is the *One* chosen in line 10? Is this a living soul or a dying one? (Don't expect all readers of this poem to agree.)

READING AND HEARING POEMS ALOUD

Thomas Moore's "The light that lies in women's eyes" — a line rich in internal rime, alliteration, and assonance — is harder to forget than "The light burning in the gaze of a woman." Because of sound, it is possible to remember the obscure line Christopher Smart wrote while in an insane asylum: "Let Ross, house of Ross rejoice with the Great Flabber Dabber Flat Clapping Fish with hands." Such lines, striking as they are even when read silently, become still more effective when said out loud. Reading poems aloud is a way to understand them. For this reason, practice the art of lending poetry your voice.

Before trying to read a poem aloud to other people, understand its meaning as thoroughly as possible. If you know what the poet is saying and the poet's attitude toward it, you will be able to find an appropriate tone of voice and to give each part of the poem a proper emphasis.

Except in the most informal situations and in some class exercises, read a poem to yourself before trying it on an audience. No actor goes before the footlights without first having studied the script, and the language of poems usually demands even more consideration than the language of most contemporary plays. Prepare your reading in advance. Check pronunciations you are not sure of. Underline things to be emphasized.

Read deliberately, more slowly than you would read aloud from a newspaper. Keep in mind that you are saying something to somebody. Don't race through the poem as if you are eager to get it over with.

Don't lapse into singsong. A poem may have a definite swing, but swing should never be exaggerated at the cost of sense. If you understand what the poem is saying and utter the poem as if you do, the temptation to fall into such a mechanical intonation should not occur. Observe the punctuation, making slight pauses for commas, longer pauses for full stops (periods, question marks, exclamation points).

If the poem is rimed, don't raise your voice and make the rimes stand out unnaturally. They should receive no more volume than other words in the poem, though a faint pause at the end of each line will call the listener's attention to them. This advice is contrary to a school that holds that, if a line does not end in any punctuation, one should not pause but run it together with the line following. The trouble is that, from such a reading, a listener may not be able to identify the rimes; besides, the line, that valuable unit of rhythm, is destroyed.

In some older poems rimes that look like slant rimes may have been exact rimes in their day:

Still so perverse and opposite,
As if they worshiped God for spite.
— Samuel Butler, *Hudibras* (1663)

Soft yielding minds to water glide away,
And sip, with nymphs, their elemental tea.
— Alexander Pope, "The Rape of the Lock" (1714)

You may wish to establish a consistent policy toward such shifting usage: is it worthwhile to distort current pronunciation for the sake of the rime?

Listening to a poem, especially if it is unfamiliar, calls for concentration. Merciful people seldom read poetry uninterruptedly to anyone for more than a few minutes at a time. Robert Frost, always kind to his audiences, used to intersperse poems with many silences and seemingly casual remarks — shrewdly giving his hearers a chance to rest from their labors and giving his poems a chance to settle in.

If, in first listening to a poem, you don't take in all its meaning, don't be discouraged. With more practice in listening, your attention span and your ability to understand poems read aloud will increase. Incidentally, following the text of poems in a book while hearing them read aloud may increase your comprehension, but it may not necessarily help you to *listen*. At least some of the time, close your book and let your ears make the poems welcome. That way, their sounds may better work for you.

Hearing recordings of poets reading their work can help both your ability to read aloud and your ability to listen. Not all poets read their poems well, but there is much to be relished in both the highly dramatic reading style of a Dylan Thomas and the quiet underplay of a Robert Frost. You need feel no obligation, of course, to imitate the poet's reading of a poem. You have to feel about the poem in your own way, in order to read it with conviction and naturalness.

Even if you don't have an audience, the act of speaking poetry can have its own rewards. Perhaps that is what James Wright is driving at in the following brief prose poem.

James Wright (1927 – 1980)*
SAYING DANTE ALOUD   1976

You can feel the muscles and veins rippling in widening and rising
    circles,
like a bird in flight under your tongue.

EXERCISE: *Reading for Sound and Meaning*

Read these brief poems aloud. What devices of sound do you find in each of them? Try to explain what sound contributes to the total effect of the poem and how it reinforces what the poet is saying.

Michael Stillman (b. 1940)

IN MEMORIAM JOHN COLTRANE

1972

Listen to the coal
rolling, rolling through the cold
    steady rain, wheel on

wheel, listen to the
turning of the wheels this night   5
    black as coal dust, steel

on steel, listen to
these cars carry coal, listen
    to the coal train roll.

IN MEMORIAM JOHN COLTRANE. John Coltrane (1926 – 1967) was the saxophonist whose originality, passion, and technical wizardry have had a deep influence on the history of modern jazz.

William Shakespeare (1564 – 1616)*

FULL FATHOM FIVE THY FATHER LIES

(ABOUT 1611)

Full fathom five thy father lies;
    Of his bones are coral made;
Those are pearls that were his eyes:
    Nothing of him that doth fade,
But doth suffer a sea change   5
Into something rich and strange.
Sea nymphs hourly ring his knell:
    Ding-dong.
Hark! now I hear them — *Ding-dong, bell.*

FULL FATHOM FIVE THY FATHER LIES. The spirit Ariel sings this song in *The Tempest* to Ferdinand, prince of Naples, who mistakenly thinks his father is drowned.

A. E. Housman (1859 – 1936)*

WITH RUE MY HEART IS LADEN

1896

With rue my heart is laden
    For golden friends I had,
For many a rose-lipt maiden
    And many a lightfoot lad.

By brooks too broad for leaping   5
    The lightfoot boys are laid;
The rose-lipt girls are sleeping
    In fields where roses fade.

T. S. Eliot (1888 – 1965)*

VIRGINIA   1934

Red river, red river,
Slow flow heat is silence
No will is still as a river
Still. Will heat move
Only through the mocking-bird   5
Heard once? Still hills
Wait. Gates wait. Purple trees,
White trees, wait, wait,
Delay, decay. Living, living,
Never moving. Ever moving   10
Iron thoughts came with me
And go with me:
Red river, river, river.

VIRGINIA. This poem is one of a series entitled "Landscapes."

Galway Kinnell (b. 1927)*

BLACKBERRY EATING   1980

I love to go out in late September
among the fat, overripe, icy, black blackberries
to eat blackberries for breakfast,
the stalks very prickly, a penalty
they earn for knowing the black art   5
of blackberry-making; and as I stand among them
lifting the stalks to my mouth, the ripest berries
fall almost unbidden to my tongue,
as words sometimes do, certain peculiar words
like *strengths* or *squinched*,   10
many-lettered, one-syllabled lumps,
which I squeeze, squinch open, and splurge well
in the silent, startled, icy, black language
of blackberry-eating in late September.

SUGGESTIONS FOR WRITING

1. Write about a personal experience with reading poems aloud.
2. Explain why contemporary poets are right (or wrong) to junk rime.
3. Consider the verbal music in W. H. Auden's "As I Walked Out One Evening"
   (or another selection from the Anthology). Analyze the poem for language with
   ear-appeal and show how the poem's sound is of a piece with its meaning.

21 Rhythm

STRESSES AND PAUSES

Rhythms affect us powerfully. We are lulled by a hammock's sway, awakened by an alarm clock's repeated yammer. Long after we come home from a beach, the rising and falling of waves and tides continue in memory. How powerfully the rhythms of poetry also move us may be felt in folk songs of railroad workers and chain gangs whose words were chanted in time to the lifting and dropping of a sledgehammer, and in verse that marching soldiers shout, putting a stress on every word that coincides with a footfall:

> Your LEFT! TWO! THREE! FOUR!
> Your LEFT! TWO! THREE! FOUR!
> You LEFT your WIFE and TWEN-ty-one KIDS
> And you LEFT! TWO! THREE! FOUR!
> You'll NEV-er get HOME to-NIGHT!

A rhythm is produced by a series of recurrences: the returns and departures of the seasons, the repetitions of an engine's stroke, the beats of the heart. A rhythm may be produced by the recurrence of a sound (the throb of a drum, a telephone's busy-signal), but rhythm and sound are not identical. A totally deaf man at a parade can sense rhythm from the motions of the marchers' arms and feet, from the shaking of the pavement as they tramp. Rhythms inhere in the motions of the moon and stars, even though when they move we hear no sound.

In poetry, several kinds of recurrent *sound* are possible, including (as we saw in the last chapter) rime, alliteration, and assonance. But most often when we speak of the **rhythm** of a poem we mean the recurrence of stresses and pauses in it. When we hear a poem read aloud, stresses and pauses are, of course, part of its sound. It is possible to be aware of rhythms in poems read silently, too.

A **stress** (or **accent**) is a greater amount of force given to one syllable in speaking than is given to another. We favor a stressed syllable with a little more breath and emphasis, with the result that it comes out slightly louder, higher in pitch, or longer in duration than other syllables. In this manner we place a stress on the first syllable of words such as *eagle, impact, open,* and *statue,* and on the second syllable in *cigar, mystique, precise,* and *until.* Each word in English carries at least one stress, except (usually) for the articles *a, an,* and *the,* and one-syllable prepositions: *at, by, for, from, of, to, with.* Even these, however, take a stress once in a while: "Get WITH it!" "You're not THE Dolly Parton?" One word by itself is seldom long enough for us to notice a rhythm in it. Usually a sequence of at least a few words is needed for stresses to establish their pattern: a line, a passage, a whole poem. Strong rhythms may be seen in most Mother Goose rimes, to which children have been responding for hundreds of years. This rime is for an adult to chant while jogging a child up and down on a knee:

> Here goes my lord
> A trot, a trot, a trot, a trot!
> Here goes my lady
> A canter, a canter, a canter, a canter!
> Here goes my young master
> Jockey-hitch, jockey-hitch, jockey-hitch, jockey-hitch!
> Here goes my young miss
> An amble, an amble, an amble, an amble!
> The footman lags behind to tipple ale and wine
> And goes gallop, a gallop, a gallop, to make up his time.

More than one rhythm occurs in these lines, as the make-believe horse changes pace. How do these rhythms differ? From one line to the next, the interval between stresses lengthens or grows shorter. In "a TROT a TROT a TROT a TROT," the stress falls on every other syllable. But in the middle of the line "A CAN-ter a CAN-ter a CAN-ter a CAN-ter," the stress falls on every third syllable. When stresses recur at fixed intervals as in these lines, the result is called a **meter.** The line "A trot a trot a trot a trot" is in **iambic** meter, a succession of alternate unstressed and stressed syllables.[1] Of all rhythms in the English language, this one is most familiar; most of our traditional poetry is written in it and ordinary speech tends to resemble it. Most poems, less obvious in rhythm than nursery rimes are, rarely stick to their meters with such jog-trot regularity. The following lines also contain a horseback-riding rhythm. (The poet, Gerard Manley Hopkins, is comparing the pell-mell plunging of a burn — Scottish word for a brook — to the motion of a wild horse.)

> This darksome burn, horseback brown,
> His rollrock highroad roaring down,
> In coop and in comb the fleece of his foam
> Flutes and low to the lake falls home.

---

[1]Another kind of meter is possible, in which the intervals between stresses vary. This is **accentual** meter, not often found in contemporary poetry. It is discussed in the second part of this chapter.

In the third line, when the brook courses through coop and comb ("hollow" and "ravine"), the passage breaks into a gallop; then, with the two-beat *falls home,* almost seems reined to a sudden halt.

Stresses embody meanings. Whenever two or more fall side by side, words gain in emphasis. Consider these hard-hitting lines from John Donne, in which accent marks have been placed, dictionary-fashion, to indicate the stressed syllables:

> Bat'ter my heart', three'-per'soned God', for You'
> As yet' but knock', breathe', shine', and seek' to mend';
> That I may rise' and stand', o'er'throw' me, and bend'
> Your force' to break', blow', burn', and make' me new'.

Unstressed (or **slack**) syllables also can direct our attention to what the poet means. In a line containing few stresses and a great many unstressed syllables, there can be an effect not of power and force but of hesitation and uncertainty. Yeats asks in "Among School Children" what young mother, if she could see her baby grown to be an old man, would think him

> A com'pen·sa'tion for the pang' of his birth'
> Or the un·cer'tain·ty of his set'ting forth'?

When unstressed syllables recur in pairs, the result is a rhythm that trips and bounces, as in Robert Service's rollicking line:

> A bunch' of the boys' were whoop'ing it up' in the Mal'a·mute
>   sa·loon' . . .

or in Poe's lines — also light but probably supposed to be serious:

> For the moon' nev·er beams' with·out bring'ing me dreams'
> Of the beau'ti·ful An'na·bel Lee'.

Apart from the words that convey it, the rhythm of a poem has no meaning. There are no essentially sad rhythms, nor any essentially happy ones. But some rhythms enforce certain meanings better than others do. The bouncing rhythm of Service's line seems fitting for an account of a merry night in a Klondike saloon; but it may be distracting when encountered in Poe's wistful elegy.

EXERCISE: *Appropriate and Inappropriate Rhythms*

In each of the following passages decide whether rhythm enforces meaning and tone or works against these elements and consequently against the poem's effectiveness.

1. Alfred, Lord Tennyson, "Break, break, break":

> Break, break, break,
> On thy cold gray stones, O Sea!

2. Edgar Allan Poe, "Ulalume":

Then my heart it grew ashen and sober
  As the leaves that were crispèd and sere —
  As the leaves that were withering and sere,
And I cried: "It was surely October
    On *this* very night of last year
    That I journey — I journeyed down here —
    That I brought a dread burden down here —
    On this night of all nights in the year,
    Ah, what demon has tempted me here?"

3. Greg Keeler, "There Ain't No Such Thing as a Montana Cowboy" (a song lyric):

I couldn't be cooler, I come from Missoula,
And I rope and I chew and I ride.
But I'm a heroin dealer, and I drive a four-wheeler
With stereo speakers inside.
My ol' lady Phoebe's out rippin' off C.B.'s
From the rigs at the Wagon Wheel Bar,
Near a Montana truck stop and a shit-outta-luck stop
For a trucker who's driven too far.

4. Eliza Cook, "Song of the Sea-Weed":

Many a lip is gaping for drink,
  And madly calling for rain;
And some hot brains are beginning to think
  Of a messmate's opened vein.

5. William Shakespeare, song from *The Tempest:*

The master, the swabber, the boatswain, and I,
The gunner and his mate
Loved Moll, Meg, and Marian, and Margery,
But none of us cared for Kate;
For she had a tongue with a tang
Would cry to a sailor "Go hang!" —
She loved not the savor of tar nor of pitch
Yet a tailor might scratch her where'er she did itch;
Then to sea, boys, and let her go hang!

Rhythms in poetry are due not only to stresses but also to pauses. "Every nice ear," observed Alexander Pope (*nice* meaning "finely tuned"), "must, I believe, have observed that in any smooth English verse of ten syllables, there is naturally a pause either at the fourth, fifth, or sixth syllable." Such a light but definite pause within a line is called a **cesura** (or caesura), "a cutting." More liberally than Pope, we apply the name to any pause in a line of any length, after any word in the line. In studying a poem, we often indicate a cesura by double lines(‖). Usually, a cesura will occur at a mark of punctuation, but there can be a cesura even if no punctuation is present. Sometimes you will find it at the end of a phrase or clause or, as in these lines by William Blake, after an internal rime:

And priests in black gowns‖were walking their rounds
And binding with briars‖my joys and desires.

Lines of ten or twelve syllables (as Pope knew) tend to have just one cesura, though sometimes there are more:

> Cover her face:‖mine eyes dazzle:‖she died young.

Pauses also tend to recur at more prominent places — namely, after each line. At the end of a verse (from *versus,* "a turning"), the reader's eye, before turning to go on to the next line, makes a pause, however brief. If a line ends in a full pause — usually indicated by some mark of punctuation — we call it **end-stopped.** All the lines in this stanza by Theodore Roethke are end-stopped:

> Let seed be grass and grass turn into hay:
> I'm martyr to a motion not my own;
> What's freedom for? To know eternity.
> I swear she cast a shadow white as stone.
> But who would count eternity in days?
> These old bones live to learn her wanton ways:
> (I measure time by how a body sways).[2]

A line that does not end in punctuation and that therefore is read with only a slight pause after it is called a **run-on line.** Because a run-on line gives us only part of a phrase, clause, or sentence, we have to read on to the line or lines following, in order to complete a thought. All these lines from Robert Browning are run-on lines:

> . . . Sir, 'twas not
> Her husband's presence only, called that spot
> Of joy into the Duchess' cheek: perhaps
> Frà Pandolf chanced to say "Her mantle laps
> Over my lady's wrist too much," or "Paint
> Must never hope to reproduce the faint
> Half-flush that dies along her throat." Such stuff
> Was courtesy, she thought . . .[3]

A passage in run-on lines has a rhythm different from that of a passage like Roethke's in end-stopped lines. When emphatic pauses occur in the quotation from Browning, they fall within a line rather than at the end of one. The passage by Roethke and that by Browning are in lines of the same meter (iambic) and the same length (ten syllables). What makes the big difference in their rhythms is the running on, or lack of it.

To sum up: rhythm is recurrence. In poems, it is made of stresses and pauses. The poet can produce it by doing any of several things: making the intervals between stresses fixed or varied, long or short; indicating pauses (cesuras) within lines; end-stopping lines or running them over; writing in short or long lines. Rhythm in itself cannot convey meaning. And yet if a poet's words have meaning, their rhythm must be one with it.

[2]The complete poem, "I Knew a Woman," appears on page 506.
[3]The complete poem, "My Last Duchess," appears on page 696.

Gwendolyn Brooks (b. 1917)*
We Real Cool   1960

The Pool Players.
Seven at the Golden Shovel.

We real cool. We
Left school. We

Lurk late. We
Strike straight. We

Sing sin. We
Thin gin. We

Jazz June. We
Die soon.

Question

Describe the rhythms of this poem. By what techniques are they produced?

Robert Frost (1874 – 1963)*
Never Again Would Birds' Song Be the Same   1942

He would declare and could himself believe
That the birds there in all the garden round
From having heard the daylong voice of Eve
Had added to their own an oversound,
Her tone of meaning but without the words.   5
Admittedly an eloquence so soft
Could only have had an influence on birds
When call or laughter carried it aloft.
Be that as may be, she was in their song.
Moreover her voice upon their voices crossed   10
Had now persisted in the woods so long
That probably it never would be lost.
Never again would birds' song be the same.
And to do that to birds was why she came.

Questions

1. Who is *he?*
2. In reading aloud line 9, do you stress *may?* (Do you say "as MAY be" or "as may BE"?) What guide do we have to the poet's wishes here?
3. Which lines does Frost cast mostly or entirely into monosyllables? How would you describe the impact of these lines?
4. In his *Essay on Criticism,* Alexander Pope made fun of poets who wrote mechanically, without wit: "And ten low words oft creep in one dull line." Do you think this criticism applicable to Frost's lines of monosyllables? Explain.

Ben Jonson (1573? – 1637)*

SLOW, SLOW, FRESH FOUNT, KEEP TIME
WITH MY SALT TEARS   1600

Slow, slow, fresh fount, keep time with my salt tears;
   Yet slower yet, oh faintly, gentle springs;
List to the heavy part the music bears,
    Woe weeps out her division° when she sings.   *a part in a song*
      Droop herbs and flowers,   5
      Fall grief in showers;
      Our beauties are not ours;
        Oh, I could still,
Like melting snow upon some craggy hill,
   Drop, drop, drop, drop,   10
Since nature's pride is now a withered daffodil.

SLOW, SLOW, FRESH FOUNT. The nymph Echo sings this lament over the youth Narcissus in Jonson's play *Cynthia's Revels.* In mythology, Nemesis, goddess of vengeance, to punish Narcissus for loving his own beauty, caused him to pine away and then transformed him into a narcissus (another name for a *daffodil,* line 11).

QUESTIONS

1. Read the first line aloud rapidly. Why is it difficult to do so?
2. Which lines rely most heavily on stressed syllables?
3. In general, how would you describe the rhythm of this poem? How is it appropriate to what is said?

Alexander Pope (1688 – 1744)*

ATTICUS   1735

How did they fume, and stamp, and roar, and chafe!
And swear, not Addison himself was safe.
   Peace to all such! but were there one whose fires
True genius kindles, and fair fame inspires;
Blest with each talent, and each art to please,   5
And born to write, converse, and live with ease,
Should such a man, too fond to rule alone,
Bear, like the Turk, no brother near the throne,
View him with scornful, yet with jealous eyes,
And hate for arts that caused himself to rise;   10
Damn with faint praise, assent with civil leer,
And, without sneering, teach the rest to sneer;
Willing to wound, and yet afraid to strike,
Just hint a fault, and hesitate dislike;
Alike reserved to blame, or to commend,   15
A timorous foe, and a suspicious friend;
Dreading e'en fools, by flatterers besieged,
And so obliging, that he ne'er obliged;

Like Cato, give his little Senate laws,
And sit attentive to his own applause: 20
While wits and Templars every sentence raise,
And wonder with a foolish face of praise —
Who but must laugh, if such a man there be?
Who would not weep, if Atticus were he?

ATTICUS. In this selection from "An Epistle to Dr. Arbuthnot," Pope has been referring to dull
versifiers and their angry reception of his satiric thrusts at them. With *Peace to all such!* (line
3) he turns to his celebrated portrait of a rival man of letters, Joseph Addison. 19. *Cato:* Roman
senator about whom Addison had written a tragedy. 21. *Templars:* London lawyers who
dabbled in literature.

QUESTIONS

1. In these lines — one of the most famous damnations in English poetry — what
   positive virtues, in Pope's view, does Addison lack?
2. Which lines are end-stopped? What is the effect of these lines upon the rhythm
   of this passage? (Suggestion: Read "Atticus" aloud.)

EXERCISE: *Two Kinds of Rhythm*

The following compositions in verse have lines of similar length, yet they differ
greatly in rhythm. Explain how they differ and why.

Sir Thomas Wyatt (1503? – 1542)*

WITH SERVING STILL   (1528 – 1536)

With serving still°   *continually*
   This have I won,
For my goodwill
   To be undone;

And for redress   5
   Of all my pain,
Disdainfulness
   I have again°;   *in return*

And for reward
   Of all my smart   10
Lo, thus unheard,
   I must depart!

Wherefore all ye
   That after shall
By fortune be,   15
   As I am, thrall,

Example take
   What I have won,
Thus for her sake
   To be undone!   20

Dorothy Parker (1893 – 1967)
Résumé   1926

Razors pain you;
Rivers are damp;
Acids stain you;
And drugs cause cramp.
Guns aren't lawful;   5
Nooses give;
Gas smells awful;
You might as well live.

METER

To enjoy the rhythms of a poem, no special knowledge of meter is necessary. All you need do is pay attention to stresses and where they fall; and you will perceive the basic pattern, if there is any. However, there is nothing occult about the study of meter. Most people find they can master its essentials in no more time than it takes to learn a complicated game such as chess. If you take the time, you will then have the pleasure of knowing what is happening in the rhythms of many a fine poem, and pleasurable knowledge may even deepen your insight into poetry. The following discussion, then, will be of interest only to those who care to go deeper into **prosody**, the study of metrical structures in poetry.

Far from being artificial constructions found only in the minds of poets, meters occur in everyday speech and prose. As the following example will show, they may need only a poet to recognize them. The English satirist Max Beerbohm, after contemplating the title page of his first book, took his pen and added two more lines.

Max Beerbohm (1872 – 1956)
On the imprint of the first English edition of The Works of Max Beerbohm   (1896)

"London: John Lane, *The Bodley Head*
   New York: Charles Scribner's Sons."
This plain announcement, nicely read,
   Iambically runs.

In everyday life, nobody speaks or writes in perfect iambic rhythm, except at moments: "a HAM on RYE and HIT the MUStard HARD!" (As we have seen, iambic rhythm consists of a series of syllables alternately unstressed and stressed.) Poets rarely speak in it for long, either — at least, not with absolute consistency. If you read aloud Max Beerbohm's lines, you'll hear an iambic rhythm, but not an unvarying one. And yet all of us speak with a rising and falling of stress *somewhat like* iambic meter. Perhaps, as the poet and scholar John Thompson has maintained, "The iambic metrical pattern has dominated English verse because it provides the best symbolic model of our language."[4]

To make ourselves aware of a meter, we need only listen to a poem, or sound its words to ourselves. If we care to work out exactly what a poet is doing, we *scan* a line or a poem by indicating the stresses in it. **Scansion,** the art of so doing, is not just a matter of pointing to syllables; it is also a matter of listening to a poem and making sense of it. To scan a poem is one way to indicate how to read it aloud; in order to see where stresses fall, you have to see the places where the poet wishes to put emphasis. That is why, when scanning a poem, you may find yourself suddenly understanding it.

An objection might be raised against scanning: isn't it too simple to pretend that all language (and poetry) can be divided neatly into stressed syllables and unstressed syllables? Indeed it is. As the linguist Otto Jespersen has said, "In reality there are infinite gradations of stress, from the most penetrating scream to the faintest whisper."[5] However, the idea in scanning a poem is not to reproduce the sound of a human voice. For that we would do better to buy a tape recorder. To scan a poem, rather, is to make a diagram of the stresses (and absences of stress) we find in it. Various marks are used in scansion; in this book we use ' for a stressed syllable and ˘ for an unstressed syllable. Some scanners, wishing a little more precision, also use the **half-stress** (ˋ); this device can be helpful in many instances when a syllable usually not stressed comes at a place where it takes some emphasis, as in the last syllable in a line:

Bŏund eách tŏ eách with nát·ŭ·răl pí·e·ty.

Here, with examples, are some of the principal meters we find in English poetry. Each is named for its basic **foot,** or molecule (usually one stressed and one or two unstressed syllables).

1. **Iambic** (foot: the **iamb,** ˘'):

   Thĕ fáll·ĭng oút ŏf fáith·fŭl friénds, rĕ·néw·ĭng ís ŏf lóve

2. **Anapestic** (foot: the **anapest,** ˘˘'):

   Ĭ ăm món·ărch ŏf áll Ĭ sŭr·véy

---

[4] *The Founding of English Metre* (New York: Columbia UP, 1966) 12.
[5] "Notes on Metre," (1933), reprinted in *The Structure of Verse: Modern Essays on Prosody,* ed. Harvey Gross, 2nd ed. (New York: Echo Press, 1978).

3. **Trochaic** (foot: the **trochee,** '˘):

Dóu·ble˘, dóu·ble˘, tóil a˘nd tróu·ble˘

4. **Dactylic** (foot: the **dactyl,** '˘˘):

Táke he˘r u˘p tén·de˘r·ly˘

Iambic and anapestic meters are called **rising** meters because their movement rises from unstressed syllable (or syllables) to stress; trochaic and dactylic meters are called **falling.** In the twentieth century, the bouncing meters — anapestic and dactylic — have been used more often for comic verse than for serious poetry. Called feet, though they contain no unaccented syllables, are the **monosyllabic foot** (') and the **spondee** ("). Meters are not ordinarily made up of them; if one were, it would be like the steady impact of nails being hammered into a board — no pleasure to hear or to dance to. But inserted now and then, they can lend emphasis and variety to a meter, as Yeats well knew when he broke up the predominantly iambic rhythm of "Who Goes with Fergus?" (page 532) with the line,

A˘nd the˘ whíte breást o˘f the˘ dím séa,

in which occur two spondees. Meters are classified also by line lengths: *trochaic monometer,* for instance, is a line one trochee long, as in this anonymous brief comment on microbes:

Adam
Had 'em.

A frequently heard metrical description is **iambic pentameter:** a line of five iambs, a meter especially familiar because it occurs in all blank verse (such as Shakespeare's plays and Milton's *Paradise Lost*), heroic couplets, and sonnets. The commonly used names for line lengths follow:

monometer	one foot	**pentameter**	five feet
dimeter	two feet	**hexameter**	six feet
trimeter	three feet	**heptameter**	seven feet
tetrameter	four feet	**octameter**	eight feet

Lines of more than eight feet are possible but are rare. They tend to break up into shorter lengths in the listening ear.

When Yeats chose the spondees *white breast* and *dim sea,* he was doing what poets who write in meter do frequently for variety — using a foot other than the expected one. Often such a substitution will be made at the very beginning of a line, as in the third line of this passage from Christopher Marlowe's *Tragical History of Doctor Faustus:*

Wa˘s thís the˘ fáce tha˘t láunched a˘ thoú·sa˘nd shíps
A˘nd búrnt the˘ tóp·le˘ss tów'rs o˘f Íl·i˘·um?
Swéet Hél·e˘n, máke me˘ i˘m·mór·ta˘l wíth a˘ kíss.

How, we might wonder, can that last line be called iambic at all? But it is, just as a waltz that includes an extra step or two, or leaves a few steps out, remains a waltz. In the preceding lines the basic iambic pentameter is established, and though in the third line the regularity is varied from, it does not altogether disappear. It continues for a while to run on in the reader's mind, where (if the poet does not stay away from it for too long) the meter will be when the poem comes back to it.

Like a basic dance step, a meter is not to be slavishly adhered to. The fun in reading a metrical poem often comes from watching the poet continually departing from perfect regularity, giving a few heel-kicks to display a bit of joy or ingenuity, then easing back into the basic step again. Because meter is orderly and the rhythms of living speech are unruly, poets can play one against the other, in a sort of counterpoint. Robert Frost, a master at pitting a line of iambs against a very natural-sounding and irregular sentence, declared, "I am never more pleased than when I can get these into strained relation. I like to drag and break the intonation across the meter as waves first comb and then break stumbling on a shingle."[6]

Evidently Frost's skilled effects would be lost to a reader who, scanning a Frost poem or reading it aloud, distorted its rhythms to fit the words exactly to the meter. With rare exceptions, a good poem can be read and scanned the way we would speak its sentences if they were ours. This, for example, is an unreal scansion:

That's my last Duch·ess paint·ed on the wall.

— because no speaker of English would say that sentence in that way. We are likely to stress *That's* and *last.*

Variety in rhythm is not merely desirable in poetry, it is a necessity, and the poem that fails to depart often enough from absolute regularity is in trouble. If the beat of its words slips into a mechanical pattern, the poem marches robot-like right into its grave. Luckily, few poets, except writers of greeting cards, favor rhythms that go "a TROT a TROT a TROT a TROT" for very long. Robert Frost told an audience one time that if when writing a poem he found its rhythm becoming monotonous, he knew that the poem was going wrong and that he himself didn't believe what it was saying.

Although in good poetry we seldom meet a very long passage of absolute metrical regularity, we sometimes find (in a line or so) a monotonous rhythm that is effective. Words fall meaningfully in Macbeth's famous statement of world-weariness: "Tomorrow and tomorrow and tomorrow . . ." and in the opening lines of Thomas Gray's "Elegy":

[6]Letter to John Cournos in 1914, in *Selected Letters of Robert Frost,* ed. Lawrance Thompson (New York: Holt, 1964) 128.

The cúr·fĕw tólls thĕ knéll ŏf párt·ĭng dáy,

The lów·ĭng hérd wínd slów·lў o'ér thĕ léa,

The plów·măn hóme·wărd plóds hĭs weár·ў wáy,

Ănd leáves thĕ wórld tŏ dárk·nĕss ănd tŏ mé.[7]

Although certain unstressed syllables in these lines seem to call for more emphasis than others — you might, for instance, care to throw a little more weight on the second syllable of *curfew* in the opening line — we can still say the lines are notably iambic. Their almost unvarying rhythm seems just right to convey the tolling of a bell and the weary setting down of one foot after the other.

Besides the two rising meters (iambic, anapestic) and the two falling meters (trochaic, dactylic), English poets have another valuable meter. It is **accentual meter,** in which the poet does not write in feet (as in the other meters) but instead counts accents (stresses). The idea is to have the same number of stresses in every line. The poet may place them anywhere in the line and may include practically any number of unstressed syllables, which do not count. In "Christabel," for instance, Coleridge keeps four stresses to a line, though the first line has only eight syllables and the last line has eleven:

There is nót wínd e·nóugh to twírl

The óne red léaf, the lást of its clán,

That dán·ces as óf·ten as dánce it cán,

Háng·ing so líght, and háng·ing so hígh,

On the tóp-most twíg that looks úp at the sky.

The history of accentual meter is long and honorable. Old English poetry was written in a kind of accentual meter, but its line was more rule-bound than Coleridge's: four stresses arranged two on either side of a cesura, plus alliteration of three of the stressed syllables. In "Junk," Richard Wilbur revives the pattern:

An áxe án·gles ‖ from my néigh·bor's ásh·can . . .

Many poets, from the authors of Mother Goose rimes to Gerard Manley Hopkins, have sometimes found accentual meters congenial.

It has been charged that the importation of Greek names for meters and of the classical notion of feet was an unsuccessful attempt to make a Parthenon out of English wattles. The charge is open to debate, but at least it is certain that Greek names for feet cannot mean to us what they meant to Aristotle. Greek and Latin poetry is measured not by stressed and unstressed syllables but by long and short vowel sounds. An iamb in

[7]The complete poem, "Elegy Written in a Country Churchyard," appears on page 667.

classical verse is one short syllable followed by a long syllable. Such a meter constructed on the principle of vowel length is called a **quantitative** meter. Campion's "Rose-cheeked Laura" was an attempt to demonstrate it in English, but probably we enjoy the rhythm of the poem's well-placed stresses whether or not we notice its vowel sounds.

Thomas Campion (1567 – 1620)*
Rose-cheeked Laura, come 1602

Rose-cheeked Laura, come,
Sing thou smoothly with thy beauty's
Silent music, either other
    Sweetly gracing.

Lovely forms do flow 5
From concent° divinely framèd; *harmony*
Heav'n is music, and thy beauty's
    Birth is heavenly.

These dull notes we sing
Discords need for helps to grace them; 10
Only beauty purely loving
    Knows no discord,

But still moves delight,
Like clear springs renewed by flowing,
Ever perfect, ever in them- 15
    Selves eternal.

Although less popular among poets today than formerly, meter endures. Major poets from Shakespeare through Yeats have fashioned their work by it, and if we are to read their poems with full enjoyment, we need to be aware of it. To enjoy metrical poetry — even to write it — you do not have to slice lines into feet; you do need to recognize when a meter is present in a line, and when the line departs from it. An argument in favor of meter is that it reminds us of body rhythms such as breathing, walking, the beating of the heart. In an effective metrical poem, these rhythms cannot be separated from what the poet is saying — or, in the words of an old jazz song, "It don't mean a thing if you ain't got that swing." A critic, Paul Fussell, has put it: "No element of a poem is more basic — and I mean physical — in its effect upon the reader than the metrical element, and perhaps no technical triumphs reveal more readily than the metrical the poet's sympathy with that universal human nature . . . which exists outside his own."[8]

[8]*Poetic Meter and Poetic Form* (New York: Random, 1965) 110.

Walter Savage Landor (1775 – 1864)

On Seeing a Hair of Lucretia Borgia   (1825)

Borgia, thou once wert almost too august
And high for adoration; now thou'rt dust.
All that remains of thee these plaits unfold,
Calm hair, meandering in pellucid gold.

Questions

1. Who was Lucretia Borgia and when did she live? Because of her reputation,
   what connotations does her name add to Landor's poem?
2. What does *meander* mean? How can a hair meander?
3. Scan the poem, indicating stressed syllables. What is the basic meter of most of
   the poem? What happens to this meter in the last line? Note especially *meandering
   in pel-*. How many light, unstressed syllables are there in a row? Does rhythm
   in any way reinforce what Landor is saying?

Exercise: *Meaningful Variation*

At what place or places in each of these passages does the poet depart from basic
iambic meter? How does each departure help underscore the meaning?

1. John Dryden, "Mac Flecknoe" (speech of Flecknoe, prince of Nonsense, referring to Thomas Shadwell, poet and playwright):

   Shadwell alone of all my sons is he
   Who stands confirmed in full stupidity.
   The rest to some faint meaning make pretense,
   But Shadwell never deviates into sense.

2. Alexander Pope, *An Essay on Criticism:*

   A needless Alexandrine ends the song
   That, like a wounded snake, drags its slow length along.

3. Henry King, "The Exequy" (an apostrophe to his wife):

   'Tis true, with shame and grief I yield,
   Thou like the van° first tookst the field,   vanguard
   And gotten hath the victory
   In thus adventuring to die
   Before me, whose more years might crave
   A just precedence in the grave.
   But hark! my pulse like a soft drum
   Beats my approach, tells thee I come;
   And slow howe'er my marches be,
   I shall at last sit down by thee.

4. Henry Wadsworth Longfellow, "Mezzo Cammin":

   Half-way up the hill, I see the Past
      Lying beneath me with its sounds and sights, —
   A city in the twilight dim and vast,
      With smoking roofs, soft bells, and gleaming lights, —
   And hear above me on the autumnal blast
      The cataract of Death far thundering from the heights.

5. Wallace Stevens, "Sunday Morning":

> Deer walk upon our mountains, and the quail
> Whistle about us their spontaneous cries;
> Sweet berries ripen in the wilderness;
> And, in the isolation of the sky,
> At evening, casual flocks of pigeons make
> Ambiguous undulations as they sink,
> Downward to darkness, on extended wings.

EXERCISE: *Recognizing Rhythms*

Which of the following poems contain predominant meters? Which poems are not wholly metrical, but are metrical in certain lines? Point out any such lines. What reasons do you see, in such places, for the poet's seeking a metrical effect?

Edna St. Vincent Millay (1892 – 1950)
COUNTING-OUT RHYME   1928

Silver bark of beech, and sallow
Bark of yellow birch and yellow
  Twig of willow.

Stripe of green in moosewood maple,
Color seen in leaf of apple,   5
  Bark of popple.

Wood of popple pale as moonbeam,
Wood of oak for yoke and barn-beam,
  Wood of hornbeam.

Silver bark of beech, and hollow   10
Stem of elder, tall and yellow
  Twig of willow.

A. E. Housman (1859 – 1936)*
WHEN I WAS ONE-AND-TWENTY   1896

When I was one-and-twenty
  I heard a wise man say,
"Give crowns and pounds and guineas
  But not your heart away;
Give pearls away and rubies   5
  But keep your fancy free."
But I was one-and-twenty,
  No use to talk to me.

When I was one-and-twenty
    I heard him say again,   10
"The heart out of the bosom
    Was never given in vain;
'Tis paid with sighs a plenty
    And sold for endless rue."
And I am two-and-twenty,   15
    And oh, 'tis true, 'tis true.

William Carlos Williams (1883 – 1963)*
THE DESCENT OF WINTER (SECTION 10/30)   1934

To freight cars in the air

all the slow
   clank, clank
   clank, clank
moving about the treetops   5

the
   wha, wha
of the hoarse whistle

   pah, pah, pah
   pah, pah, pah, pah, pah   10
   piece and piece
   piece and piece
moving still trippingly
through the morningmist

long after the engine   15
has fought by
        and disappeared
in silence
       to the left

Walt Whitman (1819 – 1892)*
BEAT! BEAT! DRUMS!   (1861)

Beat! beat! drums! — blow! bugles! blow!
Through the windows — through doors — burst like a ruthless force,
Into the solemn church, and scatter the congregation,
Into the school where the scholar is studying;
Leave not the bridegroom quiet — no happiness must he have now
    with his bride,   5

Nor the peaceful farmer any peace, ploughing his field or gathering
    his grain,
So fierce you whirr and pound you drums — so shrill you bugles
    blow.

Beat! beat! drums! — blow! bugles! blow!
Over the traffic of cities — over the rumble of wheels in the streets;
Are beds prepared for sleepers at night in the houses? no sleepers
    must sleep in those beds,   10
No bargainer's bargains by day — no brokers or speculators — would
    they continue?
Would the talkers be talking? would the singer attempt to sing?
Would the lawyer rise in the court to state his case before the judge?
Then rattle quicker, heavier drums — you bugles wilder blow.

Beat! beat! drums! — blow! bugles! blow!   15
Make no parley — stop for no expostulation,
Mind not the timid — mind not the weeper or prayer,
Mind not the old man beseeching the young man,
Let not the child's voice be heard, nor the mother's entreaties,
Make even the trestles to shake the dead where they lie awaiting the
    hearses.   20
So strong you thump O terrible drums — so loud you bugles blow.

SUGGESTIONS FOR WRITING

1. When has a rhythm of any kind (whether or not in poetry) stirred you, picked
   you up, and carried you along with it? Write an account of your experience.
2. The fact that most contemporary poets have given up meter, in the view of
   Stanley Kunitz, has made poetry "easier to write, but harder to remember."
   Why so? Comment on Kunitz's remark, or quarrel with it, in two or three
   paragraphs.
3. Ponder Robert Frost's idea of "the sound of sense" (page 829). Then, in a
   paragraph or two, try to show what light this idea sheds upon Frost's "Never
   Again Would Birds' Song Be the Same" (or any other Frost poem in this book).

22 Closed Form, Open Form

Form, as a general idea, is the design of a thing as a whole, the configuration of all its parts. No poem can escape having some kind of form, whether its lines are as various in length as broomstraws, or all in hexameter. To put this point in another way: if you were to listen to a poem read aloud in a language unknown to you, or if you saw the poem printed in that foreign language, whatever in the poem you could see or hear would be the form of it.[1]

Writing in **closed form,** a poet follows (or finds) some sort of pattern, such as that of a sonnet with its rime scheme and its fourteen lines of iambic pentameter. On a page, poems in closed form tend to look regular and symmetrical. Along with William Butler Yeats, who held that a successful poem will "come shut with a click, like a closing box," the poet who writes in closed form apparently strives for a kind of perfection — seeking, perhaps, to lodge words so securely in place that no word can be budged without a worsening. For the sake of meaning, though, a competent poet often will depart from a symmetrical pattern. As Robert Frost observed, there is satisfaction to be found in things not mechanically regular: "We enjoy the straight crookedness of a good walking stick."

The poet who writes in **open form** usually seeks no final click. Often, such a poet views the writing of a poem as a process, rather than a quest for an absolute. Free to use white space for emphasis, able to shorten or lengthen lines as the sense seems to require, the poet lets the poem discover its shape as it goes along, moving as water flows downhill, adjusting to its terrain, engulfing obstacles.

Right now, most American poets prefer open form to closed. But although less fashionable than they were, rime and meter are still in evidence. Most poetry of the past is in closed form. The reader who seeks a wide understanding of poetry will want to know both closed and open varieties.

---

[1]For a good summary of the uses of the term **form** in criticism of poetry, see the article "Form" by G. N. G. Orsini in *Princeton Encyclopedia of Poetry and Poetics,* 2nd ed., eds. Preminger, Warnke, and Hardison (Princeton: Princeton UP, 1975).

CLOSED FORM: BLANK VERSE, STANZA, SONNET

Closed form gives some poems a valuable advantage: it makes them more easily memorable. The **epic** poems of nations — long narratives tracing the adventures of popular heroes: the Greek *Iliad* and *Odyssey,* the French *Song of Roland,* the Spanish *Cid* — tend to occur in patterns of fairly consistent line length or number of stresses because these works were sometimes transmitted orally. Sung to the music of a lyre or chanted to a drumbeat, they may have been easier to memorize because of their patterns. If a singer forgot something, the song would have a noticeable hole in it, so rime or fixed meter probably helped prevent an epic from deteriorating when passed along from one singer to another. It is no coincidence that so many English playwrights of Shakespeare's day favored iambic pentameter. Companies of actors, often called upon to perform a different play daily, could count on a fixed line length to aid their burdened memories.

Some poets complain that closed form is a straitjacket, a limit to free expression. Other poets, however, feel that, like fires held fast in a narrow space, thoughts stated in a tightly binding form may take on a heightened intensity. "Limitation makes for power," according to one contemporary practitioner of closed form, Richard Wilbur; "the strength of the genie comes of his being confined in a bottle." Compelled by some strict pattern to arrange and rearrange words, delete, and exchange them, poets must focus on them the keenest attention. Often they stand a chance of discovering words more meaningful than the ones they started out with. And at times, in obedience to a rime scheme, the poet may be surprised by saying something quite unexpected. Composing a poem is like walking blindfolded down a dark road, with one's hand in the hand of an inexorable guide. With the conscious portion of the mind, the poet may wish to express what seems to be a good idea. But a line ending in *year* must be followed by another ending in *atmosphere, beer, bier, bombardier, cashier, deer, frictiongear, frontier,* or some other rime word that otherwise might not have entered the poem. That is why rime schemes and stanza patterns can be mighty allies and valuable disturbers of the unconscious. As Rolfe Humphries has said about a strict form: "It makes you think of better things than you would all by yourself."

The best-known one-line pattern for a poem in English is **blank verse:** unrimed iambic pentameter. (This pattern is not a stanza: stanzas have more than one line.) Most portions of Shakespeare's plays are in blank verse, and so are Milton's *Paradise Lost,* Tennyson's "Ulysses," certain dramatic monologues of Browning and Frost, and thousands of other poems. Here is a poem in blank verse that startles us by dropping out of its pattern in the final line. Keats appears to have written it late in his life to his fiancée Fanny Brawne.

John Keats (1795 – 1821)*
THIS LIVING HAND, NOW WARM AND CAPABLE   (1819?)

This living hand, now warm and capable
Of earnest grasping, would, if it were cold
And in the icy silence of the tomb,
So haunt thy days and chill thy dreaming nights
That thou wouldst wish thine own heart dry of blood   5
So in my veins red life might stream again,
And thou be conscience-calmed — see here it is —
I hold it towards you.

The **couplet** is a two-line stanza, usually rimed. Its lines often tend to be equal in length, whether short or long. Here are two examples:

Blow,
Snow!

As I in hoary winter's night stood shivering in the snow,
Surprised I was with sudden heat which made my heart to glow.

(Actually, any pair of rimed lines that contains a complete thought is called a couplet, even if it is not a stanza, such as the couplet that ends a sonnet by Shakespeare.) Unlike other stanzas, couplets are often printed solid, one couplet not separated from the next by white space. This practice is usual in printing the **heroic couplet** — or **closed couplet** — two rimed lines of iambic pentameter, the first ending in a light pause, the second more heavily end-stopped. George Crabbe, in *The Parish Register,* described a shotgun wedding:

Next at our altar stood a luckless pair,
Brought by strong passions and a warrant there:
By long rent cloak, hung loosely, strove the bride,
From every eye, what all perceived, to hide;
While the boy bridegroom, shuffling in his place,
Now hid awhile and then exposed his face.
As shame alternately with anger strove
The brain confused with muddy ale to move,
In haste and stammering he performed his part,
And looked the rage that rankled in his heart.

Though employed by Chaucer, the heroic couplet was named from its later use by Dryden and others in poems, translations of classical epics, and verse plays of epic heroes. It continued in favor through most of the eighteenth century. Much of our pleasure in reading good heroic couplets comes from the seemingly easy precision with which a skilled poet unites statements and strict pattern. In doing so, the poet may place a pair of words, phrases, clauses, or sentences side by side in agreement or similarity, forming a **parallel,** or in contrast and opposition, forming an **antithesis.** The effect is neat. For such skill in manipulating parallels and antitheses, John Denham's lines on the river Thames were much admired:

> O could I flow like thee, and make thy stream
> My great example, as it is my theme!
> Though deep, yet clear; though gentle, yet not dull;
> Strong without rage, without o'erflowing full.

These lines were echoed by Pope, ridiculing a poetaster, in two heroic couplets in *The Dunciad:*

> Flow, Welsted, flow! like thine inspirer, Beer:
> Though stale, not ripe; though thin, yet never clear;
> So sweetly mawkish, and so smoothly dull;
> Heady, not strong; o'erflowing, though not full.

Reading long poems in so exact a form, one may feel like a spectator at a ping-pong match unless the poet skillfully keeps varying rhythms. (Among much else, this skill distinguishes the work of Dryden and Pope from that of a lockstep horde of coupleteers who followed them.) One way of escaping such metronome-like monotony is to keep the cesura (see page 552) shifting about from place to place — now happening early in a line, now happening late — and at times unexpectedly to hurl in a second or third cesura. Try working through these lines from *The Narcissiad,* a recent satiric poem by R. S. Gwynn, in which a poetaster is depicted; and notice where — with lively variety — the cesuras fall.

> With Flair in hand he takes the poet's stance
> To write, instead of sonnets, sheaves of grants
> Which touch the bureaucrats and move their hearts
> To turn the spigot on and flood the arts
> With cold cash, carbon copies, calculators,
> And, for each poet, two administrators.
> In brief, his every effort at creation
> Is one more act of self-perpetuation
> To raise the towering babble of his Reputation.

Gwynn's passage ends in a **tercet,** a group of three lines that, if rimed, usually keep to one rime sound. **Terza rima,** the form Dante employs for *The Divine Comedy,* is made of tercets linked together by the rime scheme *a b a, b c b, c d c, d e d, e f e,* and so on. Harder to do in English than in Italian — with its greater resources of riming words — the form nevertheless has been managed by Shelley in "Ode to the West Wind" (with the aid of some slant rimes):

> Make me thy lyre, even as the forest is:
> What if my leaves are falling like its own!
> The tumult of thy mighty harmonies

Will take from both a deep, autumnal tone,
Sweet though in sadness. Be thou, spirit fierce,
My spirit! Be thou me, impetuous one!

The workhorse of English stanzas is the **quatrain,** used for more rimed poems than any other form. It comes in many line lengths, and sometimes contains lines of varying length, as in the ballad stanza (see Chapter 19).

Longer and more complicated stanzas are, of course, possible, but couplet, tercet, and quatrain have been called the building blocks of our poetry because most longer stanzas are made up of them. What short stanzas does John Donne mortar together to make the longer stanza of his "Song"?

John Donne (1572 – 1631)*
Song   1633

Go and catch a falling star,
  Get with child a mandrake root,
Tell me where all past years are,
  Or who cleft the Devil's foot,
Teach me to hear mermaids singing,   5
  Or to keep off envy's stinging,
      And find
      What wind
Serves to advance an honest mind.

If thou be'st borne to strange sights,   10
  Things invisible to see,
Ride ten thousand days and nights,
  Till age snow white hairs on thee,
Thou, when thou return'st, wilt tell me
  All strange wonders that befell thee,   15
      And swear
      Nowhere
Lives a woman true, and fair.

If thou findst one, let me know,
  Such a pilgrimage were sweet —   20
Yet do not, I would not go,
  Though at next door we might meet;
Though she were true, when you met her,
  And last, till you write your letter,
      Yet she   25
      Will be
False, ere I come, to two, or three.

Recently in vogue is a form known as **syllabic verse** in which the poet establishes a pattern of a certain number of syllables to a line. Either rimed or rimeless but usually stanzaic, syllabic verse has been hailed as a way for poets to escape "the tyranny of the iamb" and discover less conventional rhythms, since, if they take as their line length an *odd* number of syllables, then iambs, being feet of *two* syllables, cannot fit perfectly into it. Offbeat victories have been scored in syllabics by such poets as W. H. Auden, W. D. Snodgrass, Donald Hall, Thom Gunn, and Marianne Moore. A well-known syllabic poem is Dylan Thomas's "Fern Hill" (page 779). Notice its shape on the page, count the syllables in its lines, and you'll perceive its perfect symmetry. Although like playing a game, the writing of such a poem is apparently more than finger exercise: the discipline can help a poet to sing well, though (with Thomas) singing "in . . . chains like the sea."

Poets who write in demanding forms seem to enjoy taking on an arbitrary task for the fun of it, as ballet dancers do, or weightlifters. Much of our pleasure in reading such poems comes from watching words fall into a shape. It is the pleasure of seeing any hard thing done skillfully — a leap executed in a dance, a basketball swished through a basket. Still, to be excellent, a poem needs more than skill; and to enjoy a poem it isn't always necessary for the reader to be aware of the skill that went into it. Unknowingly, the editors of *The New Yorker* once printed an **acrostic** — a poem in which the initial letter of each line, read downward, spells out a word or words — that named (and insulted) a well-known anthologist. Evidently, besides being ingenious, the acrostic was a printable poem. In the Old Testament book of Lamentations, profoundly moving songs tell of the sufferings of the Jews after the destruction of Jerusalem. Four of the songs are written as an alphabetical acrostic, every stanza beginning with a letter of the Hebrew alphabet. However ingenious, such sublime poetry cannot be dismissed as merely witty; nor can it be charged that a poet who writes in such a form does not express deep feeling.

Patterns of sound and rhythm can, however, be striven after in a dull mechanical way, for which reason many poets today think them dangerous. Swinburne, who loved alliterations and tripping meters, had enough detachment to poke fun at his own excessive patterning:

> From the depth of the dreamy decline of the dawn through a notable
>   nimbus of nebulous noonshine,
> Pallid and pink as the palm of the flag-flower that flickers with fear
>   of the flies as they float,
> Are the looks of our lovers that lustrously lean from a marvel of mystic
>   miraculous moonshine,
> These that we feel in the blood of our blushes that thicken and
>   threaten with throbs through the throat?

This is bad, but bad deliberately. If any good at all, a poem in a fixed pattern, such as a sonnet, is created not only by the craftsman's chipping away at it but by the explosion of a sonnet-shaped *idea*. Viewed mechanically, as so many empty boxes somehow to be filled up, stanzas can impose the most hollow sort of discipline, and a poem written in these stanzas becomes no more than finger-exercise. This comment (although on fiction) may be appropriate:

Roy Campbell (1901 – 1957)
ON SOME SOUTH AFRICAN NOVELISTS   1930

You praise the firm restraint with which they write —
    I'm with you there, of course.
They use the snaffle and the curb all right;
    But where's the bloody horse?

Not only firm restraint marks the rimed poems of Shakespeare, Emily Dickinson, and William Butler Yeats, but also strong emotion. Such poets ride with certain hand upon a sturdy horse.

Ronald Gross (b. 1935)
YIELD   1967

Yield.
No Parking.
Unlawful to Pass.
Wait for Green Light.
Yield.   5

Stop.
Narrow Bridge.
Merging Traffic Ahead
Yield.

Yield.   10

QUESTIONS

1. This poem by Ronald Gross is a "found poem." After reading it, how would you define **found poetry**?
2. Does "Yield" have a theme? If so, how would you state it?
3. What makes "Yield" mean more than traffic signs ordinarily mean to us?

Ronald Gross, who produces his "found poetry" by arranging prose from such unlikely places as traffic signs and news stories into poem-like lines, has told of making a discovery:

> As I worked with labels, tax forms, commercials, contracts, pin-up captions, obituaries, and the like, I soon found myself rediscovering all the traditional verse forms in found materials: ode, sonnet, epigram, haiku, free verse. Such finds made me realize that these forms are not mere artifices, but shapes that language naturally takes when carrying powerful thoughts or feelings.[2]

Though Gross is a playful experimenter, his remark is true of serious poetry. Traditional verse forms like sonnets and haiku aren't a lot of hollow pillowcases for a poet to stuff with verbiage. At best, in the hands of a skilled poet, they can be shapes into which living language seems to fall naturally.

It is fun to see words tumble gracefully into such a shape. Consider, for instance, one famous "found poem," a sentence discovered in a physics textbook: "And so no force, however great, can stretch a cord, however fine, into a horizontal line which shall be absolutely straight."[3] What a good clear sentence containing effective parallels ("however great . . . however fine"), you might say, taking pleasure in it. Yet this plain statement gives extra pleasure if arranged like this:

And so no force, however great,
  Can stretch a cord, however fine,
  Into a horizontal line
Which shall be absolutely straight.

So spaced, in lines that reveal its built-in rimes and rhythms, the sentence would seem one of those "shapes that language naturally takes" that Ronald Gross finds everywhere. (It is possible, of course, that the textbook writer was gleefully planting a quatrain for someone to find; but perhaps it is more likely that he knew much rimed, metrical poetry by heart and couldn't help writing it unconsciously.) Inspired by pop artists who reveal fresh vistas in Brillo boxes and comic strips, found poetry has had a recent flurry of activity. Earlier practitioners include William Carlos Williams, whose long poem *Paterson* quotes historical documents and statistics. Prose, wrote Williams, can be a "laboratory" for poetry: "It throws up jewels which may be cleaned and grouped." Such a jewel may be the sentence Rosmarie Waldrop found in *The Joy of Cooking* and arranged as verse.

[2]"Speaking of Books: Found Poetry," *The New York Times Book Review,* June 11, 1967. See also Gross's *Pop Poems* (New York: Simon, 1967).
[3]William Whewell, *Elementary Treatise on Mechanics* (Cambridge, England, 1819).

Rosmarie Waldrop (b. 1935)

THE RELAXED ABALONE 1970

Abalone, like inkfish,
needs prodigious pounding
if it has died in a state
of tension.

EXPERIMENT: *Finding a Poem*

In a newspaper, magazine, catalogue, textbook, or advertising throwaway, find a
sentence or passage that (with a little artistic manipulation on your part) shows
promise of becoming a poem. Copy it into lines like poetry, being careful to place
what seem to be the most interesting words at the ends of lines to give them
greatest emphasis. According to the rules of found poetry, you may excerpt, delete,
repeat, and rearrange elements but not add anything. What does this experiment
tell you about poetic form? About ordinary prose?

When we speak, with Ronald Gross, of "traditional verse forms," we
usually mean **fixed forms.** If written in a fixed form a poem inherits from
other poems certain familiar elements of structure: an unvarying number
of lines, say, or a stanza pattern. In addition, it may display certain **conventions:** expected features such as themes, subjects, attitudes, or figures of
speech. In medieval folk ballads a "milk-white steed" is a conventional
figure of speech; and if its rider be a cruel and beautiful witch who kidnaps
mortals, she is a conventional character. (*Conventional* doesn't necessarily
mean uninteresting.)

In the poetry of western Europe and America, the **sonnet** is the fixed
form that has attracted for the longest time the largest number of noteworthy practitioners. Originally an Italian form (*sonnetto:* "little song"), the
sonnet owes much of its prestige to Petrarch (1304 – 1374), who wrote in
it of his love for the unattainable Laura. So great was the vogue for sonnets
in England at the end of the sixteenth century that a gentleman might have
been thought a boor if he couldn't turn out a decent one. Not content to
adopt merely the sonnet's fourteen-line pattern, English poets also tried on
its conventional mask of the tormented lover. They borrowed some of
Petrarch's similes (a lover's heart, for instance, is like a storm-tossed boat)
and invented others. (If you would like more illustrations of Petrarchan
conventions, see Shakespeare's sonnet on page 664.)

Soon after English poets imported the sonnet in the middle of the
sixteenth century, they worked out their own rime scheme — one easier
for them to follow than Petrarch's, which calls for a greater number of
riming words than English can readily provide. (In Italian, according to an
exaggerated report, practically everything rimes.) In the following **English
sonnet,** sometimes called a **Shakespearean sonnet,** the rimes cohere in

four clusters: *a b a b, c d c d, e f e f, g g.* Because a rime scheme tends to shape the poet's statements to it, the English sonnet has three places where the procession of thought is likely to turn in another direction. Within its form, a poet may pursue one idea throughout the three quatrains and then in the couplet end with a surprise.

Michael Drayton (1563 – 1631)
SINCE THERE'S NO HELP, COME LET US KISS AND PART   1619

Since there's no help, come let us kiss and part;
Nay, I have done, you get no more of me,
And I am glad, yea, glad with all my heart
That thus so cleanly I myself can free;
Shake hands for ever, cancel all our vows,   5
And when we meet at any time again,
Be it not seen in either of our brows
That we one jot of former love retain.
Now at the last gasp of Love's latest breath,
When, his pulse failing, Passion speechless lies,   10
When Faith is kneeling by his bed of death,
And Innocence is closing up his eyes,
     Now if thou wouldst, when all have given him over,
     From death to life thou mightst him yet recover.

Less frequently met in English poetry, the **Italian sonnet,** or **Petrarchan sonnet,** follows the rime scheme *a b b a, a b b a* in its first eight lines, the **octave,** and then adds new rime sounds in the last six lines, the **sestet.** The sestet may rime *c d c d c d, c d e c d e, c d c c d c,* or in almost any other variation that doesn't end in a couplet. This organization into two parts sometimes helps arrange the poet's thoughts. In the octave, the poet may state a problem, and then, in the sestet, may offer a resolution. A lover, for example, may lament all octave long that a loved one is neglectful, then in line 9 begin to foresee some outcome: the speaker will die, or accept unhappiness, or trust that the beloved will have a change of heart.

Elizabeth Barrett Browning (1806 – 1861)*
GRIEF   1844

I tell you, hopeless grief is passionless;
     That only men incredulous of despair,
     Half-taught in anguish, through the midnight air
Beat upward to God's throne in loud access
Of shrieking and reproach. Full desertness   5

In souls, as countries, lieth silent-bare
  Under the blanching, vertical eye-glare
Of the absolute Heavens. Deep-hearted man, express
Grief for the Dead in silence like to death:
  Most like a monumental statue set   10
In everlasting watch and moveless woe
Till itself crumble to the dust beneath.
  Touch it: the marble eyelids are not wet —
If it could weep, it could arise and go.

In this Italian sonnet, the division in thought comes a bit early — in the
middle of line 8. Few English-speaking poets who have used the form seem
to feel strictly bound by it.

"The sonnet," in the view of Robert Bly, a modern critic, "is where
old professors go to die." And yet the use of the form by such twentieth-
century poets as Yeats, Frost, Auden, Thomas, Pound, Cummings, Berry-
man, and Lowell suggests that it may be far from exhausted. Like the hero
of the popular ballad "Finnegan's Wake," literary forms (though not
professors) declared dead have a habit of springing up again. No law
compels sonnets to adopt an exalted tone, or confines them to an Elizabethan vocabulary.

Archibald MacLeish (1892 – 1982)
THE END OF THE WORLD   1926

Quite unexpectedly as Vasserot
The armless ambidextrian was lighting
A match between his great and second toe,
And Ralph the lion was engaged in biting
The neck of Madame Sossman while the drum   5
Pointed, and Teeny was about to cough
In waltz-time swinging Jocko by the thumb —
Quite unexpectedly the top blew off:

And there, there overhead, there, there hung over
Those thousands of white faces, those dazed eyes,   10
There in the starless dark the poise, the hover,
There with vast wings across the canceled skies,
There in the sudden blackness the black pall
Of nothing, nothing, nothing — nothing at all.

QUESTIONS

1. Where does the action of this poem take place?
2. To see for yourself how the sonnet is organized, sum up what happens in the
   octave. Then sum up what happens in the sestet.

3. How does the tone of the octave contrast with that of the sestet? (If you need to review *tone,* see pages 10 – 13.) Comment in particular on the clause in line 8: *the top blew off.* How do those words make you feel? Grim? Horrified? Or what?
4. Now read the closing couplet aloud. Try to describe (and account for) its effectiveness. Suppose MacLeish had wanted to write an Italian sonnet; he might have arranged the lines in the sestet like this —

And there, there overhead, there, there hung over
Those thousands of white faces, those dazed eyes,
There in the sudden blackness the black pall,
There in the starless dark the poise, the hover,
There with vast wings across the canceled skies
Of nothing, nothing, nothing — nothing at all.

Would that have been as effective?

EXERCISE: *Knowing Two Kinds of Sonnet*

Find other sonnets in this book. Which are English in form? Which are Italian? Which are variations on either form or combinations of the two? You may wish to try your hand at writing both kinds of sonnet and experience the difference for yourself.

Oscar Wilde said that a cynic is "a man who knows the price of everything and the value of nothing." Such a terse, pointed statement is called an epigram. In poetry, however, an **epigram** is a form: "A short poem ending in a witty or ingenious turn of thought, to which the rest of the composition is intended to lead up" (according to the *Oxford English Dictionary*). Often it is a malicious gibe with an unexpected stinger in the final line — perhaps in the very last word:

Alexander Pope (1688 – 1744)*
EPIGRAM ENGRAVED ON THE COLLAR OF A DOG
WHICH I GAVE TO HIS ROYAL HIGHNESS   1738

I am his Highness' dog at Kew;
Pray tell me, sir, whose dog are you?

Cultivated by the Roman poet Martial — for whom the epigram was a short poem, sometimes satiric but not always — this form has been especially favored by English poets who love Latin. Few characteristics of the English epigram seem fixed. Its pattern tends to be brief and rimed, its tone playfully merciless.

Martial (A.D. 40? – 102?)
YOU SERVE THE BEST WINES ALWAYS, MY DEAR SIR   A.D. 90

You serve the best wines always, my dear sir,
And yet they say your wines are not so good.
They say you are four times a widower.
They say . . . A drink? I don't believe I would.

Translated by J. V. Cunningham

Sir John Harrington (1561? – 1612)
OF TREASON   1618

Treason doth never prosper; what's the reason?
For if it prosper, none dare call it treason.

William Blake (1757 – 1827)*
HER WHOLE LIFE IS AN EPIGRAM   (1793)

Her whole life is an epigram: smack smooth°, and   *perfectly smooth*
    neatly penned,
Platted° quite neat to catch applause, with a sliding   *plaited, woven*
    noose at the end.

E. E. Cummings (1894 – 1962)*
A POLITICIAN   1944

a politician is an arse upon
which everyone has sat except a man

J. V. Cunningham (1911 – 1985)*
THIS HUMANIST WHOM NO BELIEFS CONSTRAINED   1947

This *Humanist* whom no beliefs constrained
Grew so broad-minded he was scatter-brained.

John Frederick Nims (b. 1914)*
CONTEMPLATION   1967

"I'm Mark's alone!" you swore. Given cause to doubt you,
I think less of you, dear. But more about you.

Robert Crawford (b. 1959)
MY IAMBIC PENTAMETER LINES   1986

Three drunks, a leg on one quite gone, bereft
Of sense, and traveling on five feet, all left.

Paul Ramsey (b. 1924)
A POET DEFENDED   1984

You claim his poems are garbage. Balderdash!
Garbage includes some meat. His poems are trash.

Bruce Bennett (b. 1940)
LEADER   1984

      A man shot himself
in the foot.

      "OW!" he howled,
hopping this way and
that. "Do something!
Do something!"

      "We are! We are!"
shouted those around
him. "We're hopping!
We're hopping!"

EXPERIMENT: *Expanding an Epigram*

Rewrite any of the preceding epigrams, taking them out of rime (if they are in rime)
and adding a few more words to them. See if your revisions have nearly the same
effect as the originals.

EXERCISE: *Reading for Couplets*

Read all the sonnets by Shakespeare in this book. How do the final couplets of
some of them resemble epigrams? Does this similarity diminish their effect of
"seriousness"?

In English the only other fixed form to rival the sonnet and the
epigram in favor is the **limerick:** five anapestic lines usually riming *a a b
b a.* Here is a sample, attributed to W. R. Inge (1860 – 1954):

There was an old man of Khartoum
Who kept a tame sheep in his room,
  "To remind me," he said,
  "Of someone who's dead,
But I never can recollect whom."

The limerick was made popular by Edward Lear (1812 – 1888), English painter and author of nonsense, whose own custom was to make the last line hark back to the first: "That oppressive old man of Khartoum."

Mark Twain [Samuel Langhorne Clemens] (1835 – 1910)
A LIMERICK   1901

A man hired by John Smith and Co.
Loudly declared that he'd tho.
   Men that he saw
   Dumping dirt near his store.
The drivers, therefore, didn't do.

EXPERIMENT: *Contriving a Clerihew*

The **clerihew,** a fixed form named for its inventor, Edmund Clerihew Bentley (1875 – 1956), has straggled behind the limerick in popularity. Here are four examples: how would you define the form and what are its rules? Who or what is its conventional subject matter? Try writing your own example.

James Watt
Was the hard-boiled kind of Scot:
He thought any dream.
Sheer waste of steam.
         — W. H. Auden

Sir Christopher Wren
Said, "I am going to dine with some men.
If anybody calls
Say I am designing St. Paul's."
         — Edmund Clerihew Bentley

Etienne de Silhouette
(It's a good bet)
Has the shadiest claim
To fame.
         — Cornelius J. Ter Maat

Dylan Thomas (1914 – 1953)*
DO NOT GO GENTLE INTO THAT GOOD NIGHT   1952

Do not go gentle into that good night,
Old age should burn and rave at close of day;
Rage, rage against the dying of the light.

Though wise men at their end know dark is right,
Because their words had forked no lightning they
Do not go gentle into that good night.

5

Good men, the last wave by, crying how bright
Their frail deeds might have danced in a green bay,
Rage, rage against the dying of the light.

Wild men who caught and sang the sun in flight,   10
And learn, too late, they grieved it on its way,
Do not go gentle into that good night.

Grave men, near death, who see with blinding sight
Blind eyes could blaze like meteors and be gay,
Rage, rage against the dying of the light.   15

And you, my father, there on the sad height,
Curse, bless, me now with your fierce tears, I pray,
Do not go gentle into that good night.
Rage, rage against the dying of the light.

QUESTIONS

1. "Do not go gentle into that good night" is a **villanelle:** a fixed form originated
   by French courtly poets of the Middle Ages. (For another villanelle, see Theodore Roethke's "The Waking," page 762.) What are its rules?
2. Is Thomas's poem, like many another villanelle, just an elaborate and trivial
   exercise? Whom does the poet address? What is he saying?

OPEN FORM

Writing in **open form**, a poet seeks to discover a fresh and individual
arrangement for words in every poem. Such a poem, generally speaking,
has neither a rime scheme nor a basic meter informing the whole of it.
Doing without those powerful (some would say hypnotic) elements, the
poet who writes in open form relies on other means to engage and to
sustain the reader's attention. Novice poets often think that open form
looks easy, not nearly so hard as riming everything; but in truth, formally
open poems are easy to write only if written carelessly. To compose lines
with keen awareness of open form's demands, and of its infinite possibilities, calls for skill: at least as much as that needed to write in meter and
rime, if not more. Should the poet succeed, then the discovered arrangement will seem exactly right for what the poem is saying. Words will seem
at home in their positions, as naturally as the words of a decent sonnet.

Denise Levertov (b. 1923)*
SIX VARIATIONS (PART III)   1961

Shlup, shlup, the dog
as it laps up
water
makes intelligent

music, resting
now and then to take breath in irregular
measure.

Open form, in this brief poem, affords Denise Levertov certain advantages. Able to break off a line at whatever point she likes (a privilege not available to the poet writing, say, a conventional sonnet, who has to break off each line after its tenth syllable), she selects her pauses artfully. Line-breaks lend emphasis: a word or phrase at the end of a line takes a little more stress (and receives a little more attention), because the ending of the line compels the reader to make a slight pause, if only for the brief moment it takes to sling back one's eyes (like a typewriter carriage) and fix them on the line following. Slight pauses, then, follow the words and phrases *the dog / laps up / water / intelligent / resting / irregular / measure* — all of these being elements that apparently the poet wishes to call our attention to. (The pause after a line-break also casts a little more weight upon the *first* word or phrase of each succeeding line.) Levertov makes the most of white space — another means of calling attention to things, as any good picture-framer knows. By setting a word all alone on a line *(water / measure),* she makes it stand out more than it would do in a line of pentameter. She feels free to include a bit of rime *(Shlup, shlup / up).* She creates rhythms: if you will read aloud the phrases *intelligent / music* and *irregular / measure,* you will sense that in each phrase the arrangement of pauses and stresses is identical. Like the dog's halts to take breath, the lengths of the lines seem naturally irregular. The result is a fusion of meaning and form: indeed, an "intelligent music."

Poetry in open form used to be called **free verse** (from the French **vers libre**), suggesting a kind of verse liberated from the shackles of rime and meter. "Writing free verse," said Robert Frost, who wasn't interested in it, "is like playing tennis with the net down." And yet, as Denise Levertov and many other poets demonstrate, high scores can be made in such an unconventional game, provided it doesn't straggle all over the court. For a successful poem in open form, the term *free verse* seems inaccurate. "Being an art form," said William Carlos Williams, "verse cannot be 'free' in the sense of having *no* limitations or guiding principles."[4] Various substitute names have been suggested: organic poetry, composition by field, raw (as against cooked) poetry, open form poetry. "But what does it matter what you call it?" remark the editors of an anthology called *Naked Poetry.* The best poems of the last twenty years "don't rhyme (usually) and don't move on feet of more or less equal duration (usually). That nondescription moves toward the only technical principle they all have in common."[5]

[4]"Free Verse," article in *Princeton Encyclopedia of Poetry and Poetics.*
[5]Stephen Berg and Robert Mezey, eds., foreword to *Naked Poetry: Recent American Poetry in Open Forms* (Indianapolis: Bobbs-Merrill, 1969).

And yet many poems in open form have much more in common than absences and lacks. One positive principle has been Ezra Pound's famous suggestion that poets "compose in the sequence of the musical phrase, not in the sequence of the metronome" — good advice, perhaps, even for poets who write inside fixed forms. In Charles Olson's influential theory of **projective verse**, poets compose by listening to their own breathing. On paper, they indicate the rhythms of a poem by using a little white space or a lot, a slight indentation or a deep one, depending on whether a short pause or a long one is intended. Words can be grouped in clusters on the page (usually no more words than a lungful of air can accommodate). Heavy cesuras are sometimes shown by breaking a line in two and lowering the second part of it.[6] (An Olson poem appears on page 602.)

To the poet working in open form, no less than to the poet writing a sonnet, line length can be valuable. Walt Whitman, who loved to expand vast sentences for line after line, knew well that an impressive rhythm can accumulate if the poet will keep long lines approximately the same length, causing a pause to recur at about the same interval after every line. Sometimes, too, Whitman repeats the same words at each line's opening. An instance is the masterly sixth section of "When Lilacs Last in the Dooryard Bloom'd," an elegy for Abraham Lincoln:

> Coffin that passes through lanes and streets,
> Through day and night with the great cloud darkening the land,
> With the pomp of the inloop'd flags with the cities draped in black,
> With the show of the States themselves as of crape-veil'd women standing,
> With processions long and winding and the flambeaus of the night,
> With the countless torches lit, with the silent sea of faces and the unbared heads,
> With the waiting depot, the arriving coffin, and the somber faces,
> With dirges through the night, with the thousand voices rising strong and solemn,
> With all the mournful voices of the dirges pour'd around the coffin,
> The dim-lit churches and the shuddering organs — where amid these you journey,
> With the tolling tolling bells' perpetual clang,
> Here, coffin that slowly passes,
> I give you my sprig of lilac.

There is music in such solemn, operatic arias. Whitman's lines echo another model: the Hebrew **psalms**, or sacred songs, as translated in the King James Version of the Bible. In Psalm 150, repetition also occurs inside of lines:

[6]See Olson's essays "Projective Verse" and "Letter to Elaine Feinstein" in *Selected Writings,* edited by Robert Creeley (New York: New Directions, 1966). Olson's letters to Cid Corman are fascinating: *Letters for Origin, 1950 – 1955,* edited by Albert Glover (New York: Grossman, 1970).

Praise ye the Lord. Praise God in his sanctuary: praise him in the firmament of his power.

Praise him for his mighty acts: praise him according to his excellent greatness.

Praise him with the sound of the trumpet: praise him with the psaltery and harp.

Praise him with the timbrel and dance: praise him with stringed instruments and organs.

Praise him upon the loud cymbals: praise him upon the high sounding cymbals.

Let every thing that hath breath praise the Lord. Praise ye the Lord.

In Biblical Psalms, we are in the presence of (as Robert Lowell has said) "supreme poems, written when their translators merely intended prose and were forced by the structure of their originals to write poetry."[7]

Whitman was a more deliberate craftsman than he let his readers think, and to anyone interested in writing in open form, his work will repay close study. He knew that repetitions of any kind often make memorable rhythms, as in this passage from "Song of Myself," with every line ending on an *-ing* word (a stressed syllable followed by an unstressed syllable):

Here and there with dimes on the eyes walking,
To feed the greed of the belly the brains liberally spooning,
Tickets buying, taking, selling, but in to the feast never once going,
Many sweating, ploughing, thrashing, and then the chaff for payment
    receiving,
A few idly owning, and they the wheat continually claiming.

Much more than simply repetition, of course, went into the music of those lines — the internal rime *feed, greed,* the use of assonance, the trochees that begin the third and fourth lines, whether or not they were calculated.

In such classics of open form poetry, sound and rhythm are positive forces. When speaking a poem in open form, you often may find that it makes a difference for the better if you pause at the end of each line. Try pausing there, however briefly; but don't allow your voice to drop. Read just as you would normally read a sentence in prose (except for the pauses, of course). Why do the pauses matter? Open form poetry usually has no meter to lend it rhythm. *Some* lines in an open form poem, as we have seen in Whitman's "dimes on the eyes" passage, do fall into metrical feet; sometimes the whole poem does. Usually lacking meter's aid, however, open form, in order to have more and more noticeable rhythms, has need of all the recurring pauses it can get. When reading their own work aloud, open form poets like Robert Creeley and Allen Ginsberg often pause very definitely at each line break. Such a habit makes sense only in reading artful poems.

[7]"On Freedom in Poetry," in Berg and Mezey, *Naked Poetry.*

Some poems, to be sure, seem more widely open in form than others. A poet, for instance, may employ rime, but have the rimes recur at various intervals; or perhaps rime lines of various lengths. (See T. S. Eliot's famous "Love Song of J. Alfred Prufrock" on page 713. Is it a closed poem left ajar or an open poem trying to slam itself?) No law requires a poet to split thoughts into verse lines at all. Charles Baudelaire, Rainer Maria Rilke, Jorge Luis Borges, Alexander Solzhenitsyn, T. S. Eliot, and many others have written **prose poems**, in which, without caring that eye appeal and some of the rhythm of a line structure may be lost, the poet prints words in a block like a prose paragraph. For an example see Karl Shapiro's "The Dirty Word" (page 767).[8]

The great majority of poems appearing at present in American literary magazines are in open form. "Farewell, pale skunky pentameters (the only honest English meter, gloop! gloop!)," Kenneth Koch has gleefully exclaimed. Many poets have sought reasons for turning away from patterns and fixed forms. Some hold that it is wrong to fit words into any pattern that already exists and instead believe in letting a poem seek its own shape as it goes along. (Traditionalists might say that that is what all good poems do anyway: sonnets rarely know they are going to be sonnets until the third line has been written. However, there is no doubt that the sonnet form already exists, at least in the back of the head of any poet who has ever read sonnets.) Some open form poets offer a historical motive: they want to reflect the nervous, staccato, disconnected pace of our bumper-to-bumper society. Others see open form as an attempt to suit thoughts and words to a more spontaneous order than the traditional verse forms allow. "Better," says Gary Snyder, quoting from Zen, "the perfect, easy discipline of the swallow's dip and swoop, 'without east or west.' "[9]

E. E. Cummings (1894 – 1962)*

Buffalo Bill's   1923

Buffalo Bill's
defunct
    who used to
    ride a watersmooth-silver
          stallion   5
and break onetwothreefourfive pigeonsjustlikethat
               Jesus
he was a handsome man
        and what i want to know is
how do you like your blueeyed boy   10
Mister Death

[8]For more examples see *The Prose Poem, An International Anthology*, edited by Michael Benedikt (New York: Dell, 1976).
[9]"Some Yips & Barks in the Dark," in Berg and Mezey, *Naked Poetry*.

Cummings's poem would look like this if given conventional punctuation and set in a solid block like prose:

Buffalo Bill's defunct, who used to ride a water-smooth silver stallion and break one, two, three, four, five pigeons just like that. Jesus, he was a handsome man. And what I want to know is: "How do you like your blue-eyed boy, Mister Death?"

If this were done, by what characteristics would it still be recognizable as poetry? But what would be lost?

Emily Dickinson (1830 – 1886)*

VICTORY COMES LATE   (1861)

Victory comes late –
And is held low to freezing lips –
Too rapt with frost
To take it –
How sweet it would have tasted –   5
Just a Drop –
Was God so economical?
His Table's spread too high for Us –
Unless We dine on tiptoe –
Crumbs – fit such little mouths –   10
Cherries – suit Robins –
The Eagle's Golden Breakfast strangles – Them –
God keep His Oath to Sparrows –
Who of little Love – know how to starve –

QUESTIONS

1. In this specimen of poetry in open form, can you see any other places at which the poet might have broken off any of her lines? To place a word last in a line gives it a greater emphasis; she might, for instance, have ended line 12 with *Breakfast* and begun a new line with the word *strangles.* Do you think she knows what she is doing here or does the pattern of this poem seem decided by whim? Discuss.
2. Read the poem aloud. Try pausing for a fraction of a second at every dash. Is there any justification for the poet's unorthodox punctuation?

Robert Herrick (1591 – 1674)*

UPON A CHILD THAT DIED   1648

Here she lies, a pretty bud,
Lately made of flesh and blood.
Who as soon fell fast asleep
As her little eyes did peep.
Give her strewings, but not stir
The earth that lightly covers her.

Saint Geraud [Bill Knott] (b. 1940)
POEM

1968

The only response
to a child's grave is
to lie down before it and play dead

QUESTION

What differences do you find between the effect of Herrick's poem and that of
Saint Geraud's? Try to explain how the pattern (or lack of pattern) in each poem
contributes to these differences.

William Carlos Williams (1883 – 1963)*
THE DANCE

1944

In Breughel's great picture, The Kermess,
the dancers go round, they go round and
around, the squeal and the blare and the
tweedle of bagpipes, a bugle and fiddles
tipping their bellies (round as the thick-
sided glasses whose wash they impound)

5

their hips and their bellies off balance
to turn them. Kicking and rolling about
the Fair Grounds, swinging their butts, those
shanks must be sound to bear up under such 10
rollicking measures, prance as they dance
in Breughel's great picture, The Kermess.

THE DANCE. Pieter Breughel (1520? – 1569), a Flemish painter known for his scenes of peasant activities, represented in "The Kermess" a celebration on the feast day of a local patron saint.

QUESTIONS

1. Scan this poem and try to describe the effect of its rhythms.
2. Williams, widely admired for his free verse, insisted for many years that what he sought was a form not in the least bit free. What effect does he achieve by ending lines on such weak words as the articles *and* and *the?* By splitting *thick-/sided?* By splitting a prepositional phrase with the break at the end of line 8? By using line breaks to split *those* and *such* from what they modify? What do you think he is trying to convey?
3. Is there any point in his making line 12 a repetition of the opening line?
4. Look at the reproduction of Breughel's painting "The Kermess" (also called "Peasants Dancing"). Aware that the rhythms of dancers, the rhythms of a painting, and the rhythms of a poem are not all the same, can you put in your own words what Breughel's dancing figures have in common with Williams's descriptions of them?
5. Compare with "The Dance" another poem that refers to a Breughel painting: W. H. Auden's "Musée des Beaux Arts" on page 689. What seems to be each poet's main concern: to convey in words a sense of the painting, or to visualize the painting in order to state some theme?

Stephen Crane (1871 – 1900)
THE HEART
1895

In the desert
I saw a creature, naked, bestial,
Who, squatting upon the ground,
Held his heart in his hands,
And ate of it. 5

I said, "Is it good, friend?"
"It is bitter — bitter," he answered;
"But I like it
Because it is bitter,
And because it is my heart." 10

Walt Whitman (1819 – 1892)*
CAVALRY CROSSING A FORD (1865)

A line in long array where they wind betwixt green islands,
They take a serpentine course, their arms flash in the sun — hark to
    the musical clank,
Behold the silvery river, in it the splashing horses loitering stop to
    drink,
Behold the brown-faced men, each group, each person a picture, the
    negligent rest on the saddles,
Some emerge on the opposite bank, others are just entering the ford
    — while,
Scarlet and blue and snowy white,
The guidon flags flutter gayly in the wind.

QUESTIONS

The following nit-picking questions are intended to help you see exactly what
makes these two open form poems by Crane and Whitman so different in their
music.
1. What devices of sound occur in Whitman's phrase *silvery river* (line 3)? Where
   else in his poem do you find these devices?
2. Does Crane use any such devices?
3. In number of syllables, Whitman's poem is almost twice as long as Crane's.
   Which poem has more pauses in it? (Count pauses at the ends of lines, at marks
   of punctuation.)
4. Read the two poems aloud. In general, how would you describe the effect of
   their sounds and rhythms? Is Crane's poem necessarily an inferior poem for
   having less music?

Wallace Stevens (1879 – 1955)*
THIRTEEN WAYS OF LOOKING AT A BLACKBIRD 1923

I

Among twenty snowy mountains,
The only moving thing
Was the eye of the blackbird.

II

I was of three minds,
Like a tree
In which there are three blackbirds.

III

The blackbird whirled in the autumn winds.
It was a small part of the pantomime.

IV

A man and a woman
Are one.
A man and a woman and a blackbird
Are one.

V

I do not know which to prefer,
The beauty of inflections
Or the beauty of innuendoes,
The blackbird whistling
Or just after.

VI

Icicles filled the long window
With barbaric glass.
The shadow of the blackbird
Crossed it, to and fro.
The mood
Traced in the shadow
An indecipherable cause.

VII

O thin men of Haddam,
Why do you imagine golden birds?
Do you not see how the blackbird
Walks around the feet
Of the women about you?

VIII

I know noble accents
And lucid, inescapable rhythms;
But I know, too,
That the blackbird is involved
In what I know.

IX

When the blackbird flew out of sight,
It marked the edge
Of one of many circles.

X

At the sight of blackbirds
Flying in a green light,
Even the bawds of euphony
Would cry out sharply.

XI

He rode over Connecticut
In a glass coach.
Once, a fear pierced him,
In that he mistook   45
The shadow of his equipage
For blackbirds.

XII

The river is moving.
The blackbird must be flying.

XIII

It was evening all afternoon.   50
It was snowing
And it was going to snow.
The blackbird sat
In the cedar-limbs.

THIRTEEN WAYS OF LOOKING AT A BLACKBIRD. 25. *Haddam:* This Biblical-sounding name is that
of a town in Connecticut.

QUESTIONS

1. What is the speaker's attitude toward the men of Haddam? What attitude
   toward this world does he suggest they lack? What is implied by calling them
   thin (line 25)?
2. What do the landscapes of winter contribute to the poem's effectiveness? If
   Stevens had chosen images of summer lawns, what would have been lost?
3. In which sections of the poem does Stevens suggest that a unity exists between
   human being and blackbird, between blackbird and the entire natural world?
   Can we say that Stevens "philosophizes"? What role does imagery play in
   Stevens's statement of his ideas?
4. What sense can you make of Part X? Make an enlightened guess.
5. Consider any one of the thirteen parts. What patterns of sound and rhythm do
   you find in it? What kind of structure does it have?
6. If the thirteen parts were arranged in some different order, would the poem be
   just as good? Or can we find a justification for its beginning with Part I and
   ending with Part XIII?
7. Does the poem seem an arbitrary combination of thirteen separate poems? Or
   is there any reason to call it a whole?

Gary Gildner (b. 1938)

FIRST PRACTICE   1969

After the doctor checked to see
we weren't ruptured,
the man with the short cigar took us
under the grade school,

where we went in case of attack   5
or storm, and said
he was Clifford Hill, he was
a man who believed dogs
ate dogs, he had once killed
for his country, and if   10
there were any girls present
for them to leave now.
                         No one
left. OK, he said, he said I take
that to mean you are hungry
men who hate to lose as much   15
as I do. OK. Then
he made two lines of us
facing each other,
and across the way, he said,
is the man you hate most   20
in the world,
and if we are to win
that title I want to see how.
But I don't want to see
any marks when you're dressed,   25
he said. He said, *Now.*

Questions

1. What do you make of Hill and his world-view?
2. How does the speaker reveal his own view? Why, instead of quoting Hill directly ("This is a dog-eat-dog world"), does he call him *a man who believed dogs ate dogs* (lines 8 – 9)?
3. What effect is made by breaking off and lowering *No one* at the end of line 12?
4. What is gained by having a rime on the poem's last word?
5. For the sake of understanding how right the form of Gildner's poem is for it, imagine the poem in meter and a rime scheme, and condensed into two stanzas:

   Then he made two facing lines of us
   And he said, Across the way,
   Of all the men there are in the world
   Is the man you most want to slay,

   And if we are to win that title, he said,
   I want you to show me how.
   But I don't want to see any marks when you're dressed,
   He said. Go get him. *Now.*

   Why would that rewrite be so unfaithful to what Gildner is saying?
6. How would you answer someone who argued, "This can't be a poem — its subject is ugly and its language isn't beautiful"?

Leonard Cohen (b. 1934)

ALL THERE IS TO KNOW ABOUT ADOLPH EICHMANN

EYES: .... Medium
HAIR: .... Medium
WEIGHT: .... Medium
HEIGHT: .... Medium
DISTINGUISHING FEATURES: .... None
NUMBER OF FINGERS: .... Ten
NUMBER OF TOES: .... Ten
INTELLIGENCE: .... Medium

What did you expect?

Talons?

Oversize incisors?

Green saliva?

Madness?

ALL THERE IS TO KNOW ABOUT ADOLPH EICHMANN. During World War II Eichmann, a colonel in Hitler's secret police, directed the deportation to concentration camps of some 6,000,000 Jews from Germany and Nazi-occupied countries. After the war Eichmann was arrested in Argentina by Israeli agents. Tried in Israel on charges of mass murder, he was found guilty, sentenced to death, and hanged in 1962.

QUESTIONS

1. How does this work resemble a "found poem"?
2. How does it recall poetry in closed form? (Suggestion: Read it aloud.)
3. What is it saying? Try to state its theme.

Bruce Guernsey (b. 1944)

LOUIS B. RUSSELL

Louis B. Russell, a shop teacher from Indianapolis, died Wednesday after living for more than six years with a transplanted heart — longer than anyone else in history . . . he had received the heart of a 17 year-old boy killed in a hunting accident.

—The Associated Press

At night
he'd lie in bed
listening
to his new heart thump,
the blood pumping like strong legs   5

in a race
around the body's track,
its quick steps the echo
of his own young heart
as he reached for her hand   10
years ago,
that first kiss.

And falling asleep
he'd dream of the rifle, lifting it
slowly, slowly,   15
to his cheek,
his heart wild with death:
his first buck
square in the crosshairs
as he squeezes forever the blue steel   20
of the trigger,
his own head in another's sights
exploding like a melon
under the blood-bright cap.

Suddenly awake,   25
he'd listen for hours to the clock's tick
quick as a sprinter's breath,
its bright circle of numbers
grinning in the dark,
and think   30
of the shop class he'd teach tomorrow,
the powerful young men,
hammers
tight in their fists.

QUESTIONS

1. What does the poet indicate by dividing his poem into three parts?
2. In the third part, what comparison is implied in the image of *the clock's tick*? In
   the young men's *hammers tight in their fists*?
3. It doesn't make sense for a poem about a heart to be written in jerky little short
   uneven lines like these. Guernsey ought to have written it in meter, in lines with
   a regular heart-like beat." Would you side with this critic, or with the poet?
   Why?

Christopher Bursk (b. 1943)

FIRST AID AT 4 A.M.   1983

In the one light on
in the house, he is choking,
he is banging on the kitchen counter to call his family down
from sleep. He holds his throat,

sinks to his knees.   5
The cats circle around him, meowing,
waiting to be fed.
How odd it seems.
Two weeks ago he nearly drove a car full of children into
another car. To die on the way to Pinocchio.   10
To choke to death on aspirin.
Then his thirteen year old's arms are reaching around him
from the back — they are astonishingly strong.
He feels the child's angry sobs
against his own weakening body,   15
the boy shouting, "Breathe, damn you,
breathe, daddy,"
the boy half-saving his father,
half-hanging on to him.

QUESTIONS

1. In what lines does Bursk, by breaking off the lines at specific places, emphasize
   particular things?
2. From whose point of view is this brief story told — the poet's, the father's, or
   the child's?

FOR REVIEW AND FURTHER STUDY

Leigh Hunt (1784 – 1859)

RONDEAU   1838

Jenny kissed me when we met,
    Jumping from the chair she sat in;
Time, you thief, who love to get
    Sweets into your list, put that in:
Say I'm weary, say I'm sad,
    Say that health and wealth have missed me,
Say I'm growing old, but add,
    Jenny kissed me.

QUESTION

Here is a fresh contemporary version of Hunt's "Rondeau" that yanks open the
form of the rimed original:

Jenny kissed me when we met,
jumping from her chair;
Time, you thief, who love to add
sweets into your list, put that in:
say I'm weary, say I'm sad,
say I'm poor and in ill health,
say I'm growing old — but note, too,
Jenny kissed me.

That revised version says approximately the same thing as Hunt's original, doesn't it? Why is it less effective?

Stevie Smith (1902 – 1971)
I Remember   1957

It was my bridal night I remember,
An old man of seventy-three
I lay with my young bride in my arms,
A girl with t.b.
It was wartime, and overhead   5
The Germans were making a particularly heavy raid on Hampstead.
What rendered the confusion worse, perversely
Our bombers had chosen that moment to set out for Germany.
Harry, do they ever collide?
I do not think it has ever happened,   10
Oh my bride, my bride.

QUESTIONS

1. From the opening three lines, you might expect a rollicking, roughly metrical ballad or song. But as this poem goes on, how does its form surprise you?
2. What besides form, by the way, is odd or surprising here? Why can't this be called a conventional love lyric?
3. Lewis Turco has proposed the name *Nashers* for a certain kind of line (or couplet) found in the verse of Ogden Nash (whose "Very Like a Whale" appears on page 98). Nashers, according to Turco, are "usually long, of flat free verse or prose with humorous, often multisyllabic endings utilizing wrenched rhymes" (Lewis Turco, *The Book of Forms*, New York: Dutton, 1968). What Nashers can you find in "I Remember"?
4. What does the poet achieve by ending her poem in an exact rime *(collide/bride)*? Suppose she had ended it with another long, sprawling, unrimed line; for example, "As far as I know from reading the newspapers, O my poor coughing dear." What would be lost?
5. What do you understand to be the *tone* of this poem (the poet's implied attitude toward her material)? Would you call it tender and compassionate? Sorrowful? Grim? Playful and humorous? Earnest?
6. How does noticing the form of this poem help you to understand the tone of it?

Keith Waldrop (b. 1932)*
Proposition II   1975

Each grain of sand has an architecture, but
a desert displays the structure of the wind.

QUESTIONS

1. How is this poem like an epigram?
2. How is it dissimilar?

Elizabeth Bishop (1911 – 1979)*

SESTINA

September rain falls on the house.
In the failing light, the old grandmother
sits in the kitchen with the child
beside the Little Marvel Stove,
reading the jokes from the almanac,   5
laughing and talking to hide her tears.

She thinks that her equinoctial tears
and the rain that beats on the roof of the house
were both foretold by the almanac,
but only known to a grandmother.   10
The iron kettle sings on the stove.
She cuts some bread and says to the child,

It's time for tea now; but the child
is watching the teakettle's small hard tears
dance like mad on the hot black stove,   15
the way the rain must dance on the house.
Tidying up, the old grandmother
hangs up the clever almanac

on its string. Birdlike, the almanac
hovers half open above the child,   20
hovers above the old grandmother
and her teacup full of dark brown tears.
She shivers and says she thinks the house
feels chilly, and puts more wood in the stove.

It was to be, says the Marvel Stove.   25
I know what I know, says the almanac.
With crayons the child draws a rigid house
and a winding pathway. Then the child
puts in a man with buttons like tears
and shows it proudly to the grandmother.   30

But secretly, while the grandmother
busies herself about the stove,
the little moons fall down like tears
from between the pages of the almanac
into the flower bed the child   35
has carefully placed in the front of the house.

Time to plant tears, says the almanac.
The grandmother sings to the marvellous stove
and the child draws another inscrutable house.

SESTINA. As its title indicates, this poem is written in the trickiest of medieval fixed forms, that of the **sestina** (or "song of sixes"), said to have been invented in Provence in the thirteenth century by the troubadour poet Arnaut Daniel. In six six-line stanzas, the poet repeats six end-words (in a prescribed order), then reintroduces the six repeated words (in any order) in a closing **envoy** of three lines. Elizabeth Bishop strictly follows the troubadour rules for the order in which the end-words recur. (If you care, you can figure out the formula: in the first stanza, the six words are arranged A B C D E F; in the second, F A E B D C; and so on.) Memorable sestinas in English have been written also by Sir Philip Sidney, Algernon Charles Swinburne, and Rudyard Kipling, more recently by Ezra Pound ("Sestina: Altaforte"), by W. H. Auden ("Hearing of Harvests Rotting in the Valleys" and others), and by contemporary poets, among them John Ashbery, Dana Gioia, Marilyn Hacker, Donald Justice, Peter Klappert, William Meredith, Howard Nemerov, John Frederick Nims, Robert Pack, and Mona Van Duyn.

QUESTIONS

1. A perceptive comment from a student: "Something seems to be going on here that the child doesn't understand. Maybe some terrible loss has happened." Test this guess by reading the poem closely.
2. Then consider this possibility. We don't know that "Sestina" is autobiographical; still, does any information about the poet's early life contribute to your reading of the poem? In fact, Elizabeth Bishop (whose widowed mother suffered from a recurrent mental illness and had a final breakdown when the poet was five) herself lived until age six with her grandmother in a coastal village in Nova Scotia.
3. In the "little moons" that fall from the almanac (line 33), does the poem introduce dream or fantasy, or do you take these to be small round pieces of paper?
4. What is the tone of this poem — the speaker's apparent attitude toward the scene described?
5. In an essay, "The Sestina," in *A Local Habitation* (U of Michigan P, 1985), John Frederick Nims defends the form against an obvious complaint against it:

   A shallow view of the sestina might suggest that the poet writes a stanza, and then is stuck with six words which he has to juggle into the required positions through five more stanzas and an envoy — to the great detriment of what passion and sincerity would have him say. But in a good sestina the poet has six words, six images, six ideas so urgently in his mind that he cannot get away from them; he wants to test them in all possible combinations and come to a conclusion about their relationship.

   How well does this description of a good sestina fit Elizabeth Bishop's poem?

EXPERIMENT: *Urgent Repetition*

Write a sestina and see what you find out by doing so. (Even if you fail in the attempt, you just might learn something interesting.) To start, pick six words you won't mind repeating six times. Here is a word of encouragement from a poet and critic, John Heath-Stubbs: "I have never read a sestina that seemed to me a total failure."

Geoffrey Chaucer (1340? – 1400)

YOUR ẎEN TWO WOL SLEE ME SODENLY (late fourteenth century)

Your ẏen° two wol slee° me sodenly;   *eyes; slay*
I may the beautee of hem° not sustene°,   *them; resist*
So woundeth hit thourghout my herte kene.

And but° your word wol helen° hastily   *unless, heal*
My hertes wounde, while that hit is grene°,   *new*   5
    Your ÿen two wol slee me sodenly;
    I may the beautee of hem not sustene.

Upon my trouthe° I sey you feithfully   *word*
That ye ben of my lyf and deeth the quene;
For with my deeth the trouthe° shal be sene.   *truth*   10
    Your ÿen two wol slee me sodenly;
    I may the beautee of hem not sustene,
    So woundeth it thourghout my herte kene.

YOUR ÿEN TWO WOL SLEE ME SODENLY. This poem is one of a group of three in the same fixed form, entitled "Merciles Beaute." 3. *so woundeth . . . kene:* "So deeply does it wound me through the heart."

QUESTIONS

1. This is a **roundel** (or **rondel**), an English form. What are its rules? How does it remind you of French courtly forms such as the villanelle and the triolet?
2. Try writing a roundel of your own in modern English. Although tricky, the form isn't extremely difficult: write only three lines and your poem is already eight-thirteenths finished. Here are some possible opening lines:

Baby, your eyes will slay me. Shut them tight.
Against their glow, I can't hold out for long. . . .

Your eyes present a pin to my balloon:
One pointed look and I start growing small. . . .

Since I escaped from love, I've grown so fat,
I barely can remember being thin. . . .

EXERCISE: *Seeing the Logic of Open Form Verse*

Read the following poems in open form silently to yourself, noticing what each poet does with white space, repetitions, line breaks, and indentations. Then read the poems aloud, trying to indicate by slight pauses where lines end and also pausing slightly at any space inside a line. Can you see any reasons for the poet's placing his words in this arrangement rather than in a prose paragraph? Do any of these poets seem to care also about visual effect? (As with other kinds of poetry, there may not be any obvious logical reason for everything that happens in these poems.)

E. E. Cummings (1894 – 1962)*

IN JUST –   1923

in Just –
spring   when the world is mud –
luscious the little
lame balloonman

whistles   far   and wee   5

and eddieandbill come
running from marbles and
piracies and it's
spring

when the world is puddle-wonderful   10

the queer
old balloonman whistles
far   and   wee
and bettyandisbel come dancing

from hop-scotch and jump-rope and   15

it's
spring
and
    the

        goat-footed   20

balloonMan   whistles
far
and
wee

Linda Pastan (b. 1932)*
JUMP CABLING   1984

When our cars	touched
When you lifted the hood	of mine
To see the intimate workings	underneath,
When we were bound	together
By a pulse of pure	energy, 5
When my car like the	princess
In the tale woke with a	start,

I thought why not ride the rest of the way together?

Donald Finkel (b. 1929)
GESTURE   1970

My arm sweeps down
    a pliant arc
        whatever I am
            streams through my
                negligent wrist: 5

```
the poem
            uncoils
                    like a
                            whip, and
snaps                                                                    10
softly      an inch from your enchanted face.
```

Charles Olson (1910 – 1970)

LA CHUTE   1967

```
my drum, hollowed out thru the thin slit,
carved from the cedar wood, the base I took
when the tree was felled

o my lute, wrought from the tree's crown

my drum, whose lustiness                                                 5
was not to be resisted
                        my lute,

from whose pulsations
not one could turn away

                                    They                                 10
are where the dead are, my drum fell
where the dead are, who
will bring it up, my lute
who will bring it up where it fell in the face of them
where they are, where my lute and drum have fallen?                      15
```

LA CHUTE. The French title means "The Fall."

SUGGESTIONS FOR WRITING

1. Ponder the blast at sonnets delivered by William Carlos Williams (in "The crab and the box," page 831) and, in a two-page essay, defend the modern American sonnet against Williams's charge. Or instead, open fire on the modern sonnet, using Williams's view for ammunition. Some sonnets to consider before you write: Archibald MacLeish's "The End of the World" (page 577), the sonnets of Robert Frost (pages 507, 554, 1374), Gwendolyn Brooks's "The Rites for Cousin Vit" (page 694), John Malcolm Brinnin's "The Ascension: 1925" (page 468), Anne Sexton's "To a Friend Whose Work Has Come to Triumph" (page 764).
2. Write an unserious argument for or against the abolition of limericks. Give illustrations of limericks you think worthy of abolition (or preservation).
3. Is "free verse" totally free? Argue this question in a short essay, drawing evidence from open-form poems that interest you.

23 Poems for the Eye

Let's look at a famous poem with a distinctive visible shape. In the seventeenth century, ingenious poets trimmed their lines into the silhouettes of altars and crosses, pillars and pyramids. Here is one. Is it anything more than a demonstration of ingenuity?

George Herbert (1593 – 1633)*
EASTER WINGS   1633

Lord, who createdst man in wealth and store,
Though foolishly he lost the same,
Decaying more and more
Till he became
Most poor;
With thee
Oh, let me rise
As larks, harmoniously,
And sing this day thy victories;
Then shall the fall further the flight in me.

My tender age in sorrow did begin;
And still with sicknesses and shame
Thou didst so punish sin,
That I became
Most thin.
With thee
Let me combine,
And feel this day thy victory;
For if I imp my wing on thine,
Affliction shall advance the flight in me.

In the next-to-last line, *imp* is a term from falconry meaning to repair the wing of an injured bird by grafting feathers into it.

If we see it merely as a picture, we will have to admit that Herbert's word design does not go far. It renders with difficulty shapes that a sketcher's pencil could set down in a flash, in more detail, more accurately. Was Herbert's effort wasted? It might have been, were there not more to his poem than meets the eye. The mind, too, is engaged by the visual pattern, by the realization that the words *most thin* are given emphasis by their narrow form. Here, visual pattern points out meaning. Heard aloud, too, "Easter Wings" gives further pleasure. Its rimes, its rhythm are perceptible.

Ever since George Herbert's day, poets have continued to experiment with the looks of printed poetry. Notable efforts to entertain the eye are Lewis Carroll's rimed mouse's tail in *Alice in Wonderland;* and the *Calligrammes* of Guillaume Apollinaire, who arranged words in the shapes of a necktie, of the Eiffel Tower, of spears of falling rain. Here is a bird-shaped poem of more recent inspiration than Herbert's. What does its visual form have to do with what the poet is saying?

John Hollander (b. 1929)
SWAN AND SHADOW   1969

```
                    Dusk
              Above the
        water hang the
                  loud
                  flies
                  Here
                  O so
                  gray
                  then
                  What              A pale signal will appear
                  When          Soon before its shadow fades
                  Where         Here in this pool of opened eye
                  In us      No Upon us As at the very edges
              of where we take shape in the dark air
                this object bares its image awakening
                    ripples of recognition that will
                      brush darkness up into light
      even after this bird this hour both drift by atop the perfect sad instant now
                      already passing out of sight
                    toward yet—untroubled reflection
                  this image bears its object darkening
                  into memorial shades Scattered bits of
              light      No of water Or something across
              water         Breaking up No Being regathered
              soon            Yet by then a swan will have
              gone               Yes out of mind into what
                  vast
                  pale
                  hush
                  of a
                  place
                  past
        sudden dark as
              if a swan
                  sang
```


604   Poems for the Eye

A whole poem doesn't need to be such a verbal silhouette, of course, for its appearance on the page to seem meaningful. In some lines of a longer poem, William Carlos Williams has conveyed the way an energetic bellhop (or hotel porter) runs downstairs:

> ta tuck a
>   ta tuck a
>   ta tuck a
>   ta tuck a
>   ta tuck a

This is not only good onomatopoeia and an accurate description of a rhythm; the steplike appearance of the lines goes together with their meaning.

At least some of our pleasure in silently reading a poem derives from the way it looks upon its page. A poem in an open form can engage the eye with snowfields of white space and thickets of close-set words. A poem in stanzas can please us by its visual symmetry. And, far from being merely decorative, the visual devices of a poem can be meaningful, too. White space — as poets demonstrate who work in open forms — can indicate pauses. If white space entirely surrounds a word or phrase or line, then that portion of the poem obviously takes special emphasis. Typographical devices such as capital letters and italics also can lay stress upon words. In most traditional poems, a capital letter at the beginning of each new line helps indicate the importance the poet places upon line-divisions, whose regular intervals make a rhythm out of pauses. And the poet may be trying to show us that certain lines rime by indenting them.

Though too much importance can be given to the visual element of poetry and though many poets seem hardly to care about it, it can be another dimension that sets apart poetry from prose. It is at least arguable that some of Walt Whitman's long-line, page-filling descriptions of the wide ocean, open landscapes, and broad streets of his America, which meet the eye as wide expanses of words, would lose something — besides rhythm — if couched in lines only three or four syllables long. Another poet who deeply cared about visual appearance was William Blake (1757 – 1827), graphic artist and engraver as well as a master artist in words. By publishing his *Songs of Innocence* and *Songs of Experience* (among other works) with illustrations and accompanying hand-lettered poems, often interwoven with the lines of the poems, Blake apparently strove to make poem and appearance of poem a unity, striking mind and eye at the same time.

Some poets who write in English have envied poets who write in Chinese, a language in which certain words look like the things they represent. Consider this Chinese poem:

Wang Wei (701 – 761)
BIRD-SINGING STREAM   (about 750)

人靜月時　閒夜出鳴　桂春驚春　花山山澗　落空鳥中

Substituting English words for ideograms, the poem becomes:

man	leisure	cassia	flower	fall
quiet	night	spring	mountain	empty
moon	rise	startle	mountain	bird
at times	sing	spring	stream	middle

Even without the aid of English crib-notes, all of us can read some Chinese if we can recognize a picture of a man. What resemblances can you see between any of the other ideograms and the things they stand for?[1]

Wai-lim Yip, the poet and critic who provided the Chinese text and translation, has also translated the poem into more usual English word order, still keeping close to the original sequence of ideas:

Man at leisure. Cassia flowers fall.
Quiet night. Spring mountain is empty.
Moon rises. Startles — a mountain bird.
It sings at times in the spring stream.

One envious Western poet was Ezra Pound, who included a few Chinese ideograms in his *Cantos* as illustrations. From the scholar Ernest Fenollosa, Pound said he had come to understand why a language written in ideograms "simply *had to stay poetic;* simply couldn't help being and staying poetic in a way that a column of English type might very well not stay poetic."[2] Having an imperfect command of Chinese, Pound greatly overestimated the tendency of the language to depict things. (Only a small number of characters in modern Chinese are pictures; Chinese characters, like Western alphabets, also indicate the sounds of words.) Still, Pound's misunderstanding was fruitful. Thanks to his influence, many other recent poets were encouraged to consider the appearance of words.[3] E. E. Cummings, in a poem that begins "mOOn Over tOwns mOOn," has reveled in the fact that O's are moonshaped. Aram Saroyan, in a poem entitled "crickets," makes capital of the fact that the word *cricket* somewhat resembles the snub-nosed insect of approximately the same length. The poem begins,

crickets
crickets
crickets
crickets

[1]To help you compare English and Chinese, the Chinese original has been arranged in Western word-order. (Ordinarily, in Chinese, the word for "man" would appear at the upper right.)

[2]*The ABC of Reading* (Norfolk, Conn., 1960) 22.

[3]For a brief discussion of Pound's misunderstanding and its influence, see Milton Klonsky's introduction to his anthology *Speaking Pictures: A Gallery of Pictorial Poetry from the Sixteenth Century to the Present* (New York: Harmony, 1975).

and goes on down its page like that, for thirty-seven lines. (Read aloud, by the way, the poem sounds somewhat like crickets chirping!)

In recent years, a movement called **concrete poetry** has traveled far and wide. Though practitioners of the art disagree over its definition, what most concretists seem to do is make designs out of letters and words. Other concrete poets wield typography like a brush dipped in paint, using such techniques as blow-up, montage, and superimposed elements (the same words printed many times on top of the same impression, so that the result is blurriness). They may even keep words in a usual order, perhaps employing white space as freely as any writer of open form verse. (More freely sometimes — Aram Saroyan has a concrete poem that consists of a page blank except for the word *oxygen.*) Richard Kostelanetz has suggested that a more accurate name for concrete poetry might be "word-imagery." He sees it occupying an area somewhere between conventional poetry and visual art.[4]

Admittedly, some concrete poems mean less than meets the eye. That many pretentious doodlers have taken up concretism may have caused a *Time* writer to sneer: did Joyce Kilmer miss all that much by never having seen a poem lovely as a

```
    t
   ttt
  rrrrr
 rrrrrrr
eeeeeeee
   ???
```

Like other structures of language, however, concrete poems evidently can have the effect of poetry, if written by poets. Whether or not it ought to be dubbed "poetry," this art can do what poems traditionally have done: use language in delightful ways that reveal meanings to us.

Edwin Morgan (b. 1920)

SIESTA OF A HUNGARIAN SNAKE   1968

s   sz   sz   SZ   sz   SZ   sz   ZS   zs   ZS   zs   zs   z

QUESTIONS

1. What do you suppose Morgan is trying to indicate by reversing the order of the two letters in mid line?
2. What, if anything, about this snake seems Hungarian?
3. Does the sound of its consonants matter?

[4]Introduction to his anthology *Imaged Words and Worded Images* (New York: Outerbridge and Dienstfrey, 1970).

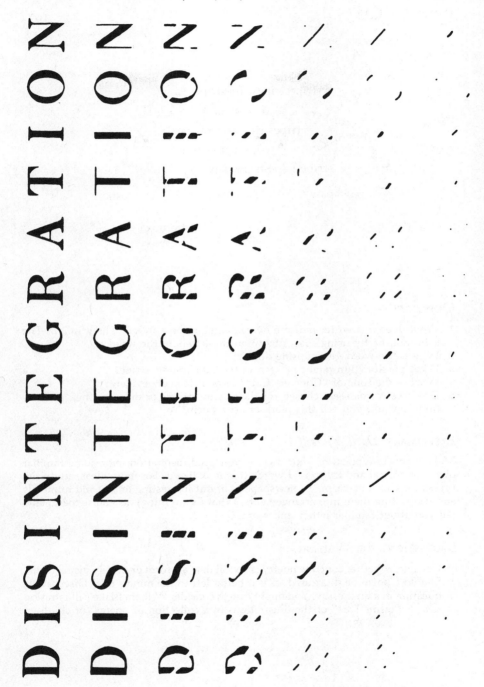

Dorthi Charles (b. 1963)

CONCRETE CAT

1971

```
     A        A
   e   r    e   r

  e Y e    e Y e      stripestripestripestripe
                        stripestripestripe  ə
whisker        whisker   stripestripestripestripes    i   l   t   a   i   l
                                                          l   t
whisker  m   h whisker   stripestripestripe
         o   t          stripestripestripestripe
       U
       stripestripestripestripe

     paw paw      paw paw          əsnoɯ

 dishdish                    litterbox
                             litterbox
```

QUESTIONS

1. What does this writer indicate by capitalizing the *a* in *ear?* The *y* in *eye?* The *u* in mouth? By using spaces between the letters in the word *tail?*
2. Why is the word *mouse* upside down?
3. What possible pun might be seen in the cat's middle stripe?
4. What is the tone of "Concrete Cat"? How is it made evident?
5. Do these words seem chosen for their connotations or only for their denotations? Would you call this work of art a poem?

EXPERIMENT: *Do It Yourself*

Make a concrete poem of your own. If you need inspiration, pick some familiar object or animal and try to find words that look like it. For more ideas, study the typography of a magazine or newspaper; cut out interesting letters and numerals and try pasting them into arrangements. What (if anything) do your experiments tell you about familiar letters and words?

SUGGESTIONS FOR WRITING

1. Consider whether concrete poetry is a vital new art form or merely visual trivia.
2. Should a poem be illustrated, or is it better left to the mind's eye? Discuss this question in a brief essay. You might care to consider William Blake's illustration for "A Poison Tree" or the illustrations in a collection of poems for children.

24 Symbol

The national flag is supposed to bestir our patriotic feelings. When a black cat crosses his path, a superstitious man shivers, foreseeing bad luck. To each of these, by custom, our society expects a standard response. A flag, a black cat's crossing one's path — each is a **symbol:** a visible object or action that suggests some further meaning in addition to itself. In literature, a symbol might be the word *flag* or the words *a black cat crossed his path* or every description of flag or cat in an entire novel, story, play, or poem.

A flag and the crossing of a black cat may be called **conventional symbols,** since they can have a conventional or customary effect on us. Conventional symbols are also part of the language of poetry, as we know when we meet the red rose, emblem of love, in a lyric, or the Christian cross in the devotional poems of George Herbert. More often, however, symbols in literature have no conventional, long-established meaning, but particular meanings of their own. In Melville's novel *Moby-Dick,* to take a rich example, whatever we associate with the great white whale is *not* attached unmistakably to white whales by custom. Though Melville tells us that men have long regarded whales with awe and relates Moby Dick to the celebrated fish that swallowed Jonah, the reader's response is to one particular whale, the creature of Herman Melville. Only the experience of reading the novel in its entirety can give Moby Dick his particular meaning.

We should say *meanings,* for as Eudora Welty has observed, it is a good thing Melville made Moby Dick a whale, a creature large enough to contain all that critics have found in him. A symbol in literature, if not conventional, has more than just one meaning. In "The Raven," by Edgar Allan Poe, the appearance of a strange black bird in the narrator's study is sinister; and indeed, if we take the poem seriously, we may even respond with a sympathetic shiver of dread. Does the bird mean death, fate, melancholy, the loss of a loved one, knowledge in the service of evil? All these, perhaps. Like any well-chosen symbol, Poe's raven sets going within the reader an unending train of feelings and associations.

We miss the value of a symbol, however, if we think it can mean absolutely anything we wish. If a poet has any control over our reactions, the poem will guide our responses in a certain direction.

T. S. Eliot (1888 – 1965)*
THE BOSTON EVENING TRANSCRIPT   1917

The readers of the *Boston Evening Transcript*
Sway in the wind like a field of ripe corn.

When evening quickens faintly in the street,
Wakening the appetites of life in some
And to others bringing the *Boston Evening Transcript,*
I mount the steps and ring the bell, turning
Wearily, as one would turn to nod good-bye to La Rochefoucauld,
If the street were time and he at the end of the street,
And I say, "Cousin Harriet, here is the *Boston Evening Transcript.*"

The newspaper, whose name Eliot purposely repeats so monotonously, indicates what this poem is about. Now defunct, the *Transcript* covered in detail the slightest activity of Boston's leading families and was noted for the great length of its obituaries. Eliot, then, uses the newspaper as a symbol for an existence of boredom, fatigue *(Wearily)*, petty and unvarying routine (since an evening newspaper, like night, arrives on schedule). The *Transcript* evokes a way of life without zest or passion, for, opposed to people who read it, Eliot sets people who do not: those whose desires revive, not expire, when the working day is through. Suggestions abound in the ironic comparison of the *Transcript*'s readers to a cornfield late in summer. To mention only a few: the readers sway because they are sleepy; they vegetate; they are drying up; each makes a rattling sound when turning a page. It is not necessary that we know the remote and similarly disillusioned friend to whom the speaker might nod: La Rochefoucauld, whose cynical *Maxims* entertained Parisian society under Louis XIV (sample: "All of us have enough strength to endure the misfortunes of others"). We understand that the nod is symbolic of an immense weariness of spirit. We know nothing about Cousin Harriet, whom the speaker addresses, but imagine from the greeting she inspires that she is probably a bore.

If Eliot wishes to say that certain Bostonians lead lives of sterile boredom, why does he couch his meaning in symbols? Why doesn't he tell us directly what he means? These questions imply two assumptions not necessarily true: first, that Eliot has a message to impart; second, that he is concealing it. We have reason to think that Eliot did not usually have a message in mind when beginning a poem, for as he once told a critic: "The conscious problems with which one is concerned in the actual writing are more those of a quasi musical nature . . . than of a conscious exposition of ideas." Poets sometimes discover what they have to say while in the act of saying it. And it may be that in his *Transcript* poem, Eliot is saying exactly what he means. By communicating his meaning through symbols instead of statements, he may be choosing the only kind of language appropriate to an idea of great subtlety and complexity. (The paraphrase "Certain Bostonians are bored" hardly begins to describe the poem in all its possible meaning.) And by his use of symbolism, Eliot affords us the pleasure of finding our own entrances to his poem. Another great strength of a symbol is that, like some figures of speech, it renders the abstract in concrete terms, and, like any other image, refers to what we can perceive — an object like a newspaper, a gesture like a nod. Eliot might, like Robert Frost, have called himself a "synecdochist." Frost explained: "Always a larger significance. A little thing touches a larger thing."

This power of suggestion that a symbol contains is, perhaps, its greatest advantage. Sometimes, as in the following poem by Emily Dickinson, a symbol will lead us from a visible object to something too vast to be perceived.

Emily Dickinson (1830 – 1886)*
THE LIGHTNING IS A YELLOW FORK   (about 1870)

The Lightning is a yellow Fork
From Tables in the sky
By inadvertent fingers dropt
The awful Cutlery

Of mansions never quite disclosed
And never quite concealed
The Apparatus of the Dark
To ignorance revealed.

If the lightning is a fork, then whose are the fingers that drop it, the table from which it slips, the household to which it belongs? The poem implies this question without giving an answer. An obvious answer is "God," but can we be sure? We wonder, too, about these partially lighted mansions: if our vision were clearer, what would we behold?[1]

---

[1]In its suggestion of an infinite realm that mortal eyes cannot quite see, but whose nature can be perceived fleetingly through things visible, Emily Dickinson's poem, by coincidence, resembles the work of late-nineteenth-century French poets called **symbolists.** To a symbolist the shirt-tail of Truth is continually seen disappearing around a corner. With their Neoplatonic view of ideal realities existing in a great beyond, whose corresponding symbols are the perceptible cats that bite us and tangible stones we stumble over, French poets such as Charles Baudelaire, Jules Laforgue, and Stéphane Mallarmé were profoundly to affect poets writing in English, notably Yeats (who said a poem "entangles . . . a part of the Divine essence") and Eliot. But we consider in this chapter symbolism as an element in certain poems, not Symbolism, the literary movement.

"But how am I supposed to know a symbol when I see one?" The best approach is to read poems closely, taking comfort in the likelihood that it is better not to notice symbols at all than to find significance in every literal stone and huge meanings in every thing. In looking for the symbols in a poem, pick out all the references to concrete objects — newspapers, black cats, twisted pins. Consider these with special care. Notice any that the poet emphasizes by detailed description, by repetition, or by placing at the very beginning or end of the poem. Ask: What is the poem about, what does it add up to? If, when the poem is paraphrased, the paraphrase depends primarily upon the meaning of certain concrete objects, these richly suggestive objects may be the symbols.

There are some things a literary symbol usually is *not*. A symbol is not an abstraction. Such terms as *truth, death, love,* and *justice* cannot work as symbols (unless personified, as in the traditional figure of Justice holding a scale). Most often, a symbol is something we can see in the mind's eye: a newspaper, a lightning bolt, a gesture of nodding good-bye.

In narratives, a well-developed character who speaks much dialogue and is not the least bit mysterious is usually not a symbol. But watch out for an executioner in a black hood; a character, named for a Biblical prophet, who does little but utter a prophecy; a trio of old women who resemble the Three Fates. (It has been argued, with good reason, that Milton's fully rounded character of Satan in *Paradise Lost* is a symbol embodying evil and human pride, but a narrower definition of symbol is more frequently useful.) A symbol *may* be a part of a person's body (the baleful eye of the murder victim in Poe's story "The Tell-Tale Heart") or a look, a voice, a mannerism.

A symbol usually is not the second term of a metaphor. In the line "The lightning is a yellow fork," the symbol is the lightning, not the fork.

Sometimes a symbol addresses a sense other than sight: the sound of a mysterious harp at the end of Chekhov's play *The Cherry Orchard;* or, in William Faulkner's tale "A Rose for Emily," the odor of decay that surrounds the house of the last survivor of a town's leading family — suggesting not only physical dissolution but also the decay of a social order. A symbol is a special kind of image, for it exceeds the usual image in the richness of its connotations. The dead wife's cold comb in the haiku of Buson (discussed on pages 480 – 481) works symbolically, suggesting among other things the chill of the grave, the contrast between the living and the dead.

Holding a narrower definition than that used in this book, some readers of poetry prefer to say that a symbol is always a concrete object, never an act. They would deny the label "symbol" to Ahab's breaking his tobacco pipe before setting out to pursue Moby Dick (suggesting, perhaps, his determination to allow no pleasure to distract him from the chase) or to any large motion (as Ahab's whole quest). This distinction, while confining, does have the merit of sparing one from seeing all motion to be possibly symbolic. Some would call Ahab's gesture not a symbol but a **symbolic act.**

To sum up: a symbol radiates hints or casts long shadows (to use Henry James's metaphor). We are unable to say it "stands for" or "represents" a meaning. It evokes, it suggests, it manifests. It demands no single necessary interpretation, such as the interpretation a driver gives to a red traffic light. Rather, like Emily Dickinson's lightning bolt, it points toward an indefinite meaning, which may lie in part beyond the reach of words. In a symbol, as Thomas Carlyle said in *Sartor Resartus,* "the Infinite is made to blend with the Finite, to stand visible, and as it were, attainable there."

Thomas Hardy (1840 – 1928)*
Neutral Tones
1898

We stood by a pond that winter day,
And the sun was white, as though chidden of God,
And a few leaves lay on the starving sod;
   — They had fallen from an ash, and were gray.

Your eyes on me were as eyes that rove   5
Over tedious riddles of years ago;
And some words played between us to and fro
    On which lost the more by our love.

The smile on your mouth was the deadest thing
Alive enough to have strength to die;   10
And a grin of bitterness swept thereby
    Like an ominous bird a-wing. . . .

Since then, keen lessons that love deceives,
And wrings with wrong, have shaped to me
Your face, and the God-curst sun, and a tree,   15
    And a pond edged with grayish leaves.

Questions

1. Sum up the story told in this poem. In lines 1 – 12, what is the dramatic situation? What has happened in the interval between the experience related in these lines and the reflection in the last stanza?
2. What meanings do you find in the title?
3. Explain in your own words the metaphor in line 2.
4. What connotations appropriate to this poem does the *ash* (line 4) have, that *oak* or *maple* would lack?
5. What visible objects in the poem function symbolically? What actions or gestures?

If we read of a ship, its captain, its sailors, and the rough seas, and we realize we are reading about a commonwealth and how its rulers and workers keep it going even in difficult times, then we are reading an **allegory.** Closely akin to symbolism, allegory is a description — usually narrative — in which persons, places, and things are employed in a continuous system of equivalents.

Although more strictly limited in its suggestions than symbolism, allegory need not be thought inferior. Few poems continue to interest readers more than Dante's allegorical *Divine Comedy.* Sublime evidence of the appeal of allegory may be found in Christ's use of the **parable:** a brief narrative — usually allegorical but sometimes not — that teaches a moral.

Matthew 13:24–30 (Authorized or King James Version, 1611)
The Parable of the Good Seed

The kingdom of heaven is likened unto a man which sowed good seed in his field:
But while men slept, his enemy came and sowed tares among the wheat, and went his way.
But when the blade was sprung up, and brought forth fruit, then appeared the tares also.
So the servants of the householder came and said unto him, Sir, didst not thou sow good seed in thy field? From whence then hath it tares?
He said unto them, An enemy hath done this. The servants said unto him, Wilt thou then that we go and gather them up?
But he said, Nay; lest while ye gather up the tares, ye root up also the wheat with them.
Let both grow together until the harvest: and in the time of harvest I will say to the reapers, Gather ye together first the tares, and bind them in bundles to burn them: but gather the wheat into my barn.

The sower is the Son of man, the field is the world, the good seed are the children of the Kingdom, the tares are the children of the wicked one, the enemy is the devil, the harvest is the end of the world, the reapers are angels. "As therefore the tares are gathered and burned in the fire; so shall it be in the end of this world" (Matthew 13:36 – 42).

Usually, as in this parable, the meanings of an allegory are plainly labeled or thinly disguised. In John Bunyan's allegorical narrative *The Pilgrim's Progress,* it is clear that the hero Christian, on his journey through places with such pointed names as Vanity Fair, the Valley of the Shadow of Death, and Doubting Castle, is the soul, traveling the road of life on the way toward Heaven. An allegory, when carefully built, is systematic. It makes one principal comparison, the working out of whose details may lead to further comparisons, then still further comparisons: Christian, thrown by Giant Despair into the dungeon of Doubting Castle, escapes by means of a key called Promise. Such a complicated design may take great length to unfold, as in Spenser's *Faerie Queene;* but the method may be seen in a short poem:

George Herbert (1593 – 1633)*
REDEMPTION 1633

Having been tenant long to a rich Lord,
   Not thriving, I resolvèd to be bold,
And make a suit unto him to afford
   A new small-rented lease and cancel th' old.
In Heaven at his manor I him sought. 5
   They told me there that he was lately gone
About some land which he had dearly bought
   Long since on earth, to take possessiòn.
I straight returned, and knowing his great birth,
   Sought him accordingly in great resorts, 10
   In cities, theaters, gardens, parks, and courts.
At length I heard a ragged noise and mirth
   Of thieves and murderers; there I him espied,
   Who straight "Your suit is granted," said, and died.

QUESTIONS

1. In this allegory, what equivalents does Herbert give each of these terms: *tenant, Lord, not thriving, suit, new lease, old lease, manor, land, dearly bought, take possession, his great birth?*
2. What scene is depicted in the last three lines?

An object in allegory is like a bird whose cage is clearly lettered with its identity — "RAVEN, *Corvus corax;* habitat of specimen, Maine." A symbol, by contrast, is a bird with piercing eyes that mysteriously appears one evening in your library. It is there; you can touch it. But what does it mean? You look at it. It continues to look at you.

Whether an object in literature is a symbol, part of an allegory, or no such thing at all, it has at least one sure meaning. Moby Dick is first a whale, the *Boston Evening Transcript* a newspaper. Besides deriving a multitude of intangible suggestions from the title symbol in Eliot's long poem *The Waste Land,* its readers cannot fail to carry away a sense of the land's physical appearance: a river choked with sandwich papers and cigarette ends, London Bridge "under the brown fog of a winter dawn." A virtue of *The Pilgrim's Progress* is that its walking abstractions are no mere abstractions but are also human: Giant Despair is a henpecked husband. The most vital element of a literary work may pass us by, unless before seeking further depths in a thing, we look to the thing itself.

Sir Philip Sidney (1554 – 1586)

You that with allegory's curious frame
   Of others' children changelings use to make,
   With me those pains, for God's sake, do not take;
I list not° dig so deep for brazen fame.   *I do not choose to*
When I say Stella, I do mean the same   5
   Princess of beauty for whose only sake
   The reins of love I love, though never slake,
And joy therein, though nations count it shame.
I beg no subject to use eloquence,
   Nor in hid ways do guide philosophy;   —10
Look at my hands for no such quintessence,
   But know that I in pure simplicity
   Breathe out the flames which burn within my heart,
   Love only reading unto me this art.

Emily Dickinson (1830 – 1886)*

I heard a Fly buzz – when I died –
The Stillness in the Room
Was like the Stillness in the Air –
Between the Heaves of Storm –

The Eyes around – had wrung them dry –   5
And Breaths were gathering firm
For that last Onset – when the King
Be witnessed – in the Room –

I willed my Keepsakes – Signed away
What portion of me be   10
Assignable – and then it was
There interposed a Fly –

With Blue – uncertain stumbling Buzz –
Between the light – and me –
And then the Windows failed – and then   15
I could not see to see –

QUESTIONS

1. Why is the poem written in the past tense? Where is the speaker at present?
2. What do you understand from the repetition of the word *see* in the last line?
3. What does the poet mean by *Eyes around* (line 5), *that last Onset* (line 7), *the King* (line 7), and *What portion of me be / Assignable* (lines 10 – 11)?
4. In line 13, how can a sound be called *Blue* and *stumbling?*

5. What further meaning might *the Windows* (line 15) suggest, in addition to denoting the windows of the room?
6. What connotations of the word *fly* seem relevant to an account of a death?
7. Summarize your interpretation of the poem. What does the fly mean?

Gjertrud Schnackenberg (b. 1953)

Signs   1985

Threading the palm, a web of little lines
Spells out the lost money, the heart, the head,
The wagging tongues, the sudden deaths, in signs
We would smooth out, like imprints on a bed,

In signs that can't be helped, geese heading south,   5
In signs read anxiously, like breath that clouds
A mirror held to a barely open mouth,
Like telegrams, the gathering of crowds —

The plane's X in the sky, spelling disaster:
Before the whistle and hit, a tracer flare;   10
Before rubble, a hairline crack in plaster
And a housefly's panicked scribbling on the air.

Questions

1. What are "signs" in this poet's sense of the word?
2. The poem gives a list of signs. What unmistakable meaning does each indicate?
3. Compare Schnackenberg's fly and Emily Dickinson's (page 618). Which insect seems loaded with more suggestions?
4. Can you think of any familiar signs that *aren't* ominous?

Louis Simpson (b. 1923)

The Boarder   1959

The time is after dinner. Cigarettes
    Glow on the lawn;
Glasses begin to tinkle; TV sets
    Have been turned on.

The moon is brimming like a glass of beer   5
    Above the town,
And love keeps her appointments — "Harry's here!"
    "I'll be right down."

But the pale stranger in the furnished room
    Lies on his back   10
Looking at paper roses, how they bloom,
    And ceilings crack.

1. What symbolism do you find in this poem, if any? Back up your claims with evidence.
2. For what possible effect does Simpson bring together (in one tightly rimed stanza) the simile of the moon as beer and the quoted conversation?
3. Compare "The Boarder" with T. S. Eliot's "The *Boston Evening Transcript*" (page 612). In what respects are the two poems similar?

Christina Rossetti (1830 – 1894)

UPHILL   1862

Does the road wind uphill all the way?
   Yes, to the very end.
Will the day's journey take the whole long day?
   From morn to night, my friend.

But is there for the night a resting-place?   5
   A roof for when the slow dark hours begin.
May not the darkness hide it from my face?
   You cannot miss that inn.

Shall I meet other wayfarers at night?
   Those who have gone before.   10
Then must I knock, or call when just in sight?
   They will not keep you standing at that door.

Shall I find comfort, travel-sore and weak?
   Of labor you shall find the sum.
Will there be beds for me and all who seek?   15
   Yea, beds for all who come.

QUESTIONS

1. At what line in reading this poem did you tumble to the fact that the poet is building an allegory?
2. For what does each thing stand?
3. What does the title of the poem suggest to you?
4. Recast the meaning of line 14, a knotty line, in your own words.
5. Discuss the possible identities of the two speakers — the apprehensive traveler and the character with all the answers. Are they specific individuals? Allegorical figures?
6. Compare "Uphill" with Robert Creeley's "Oh No" (page 432). What striking similarities do you find in these two dissimilar poems?

Philip Dow (b. 1937)

DRUNK LAST NIGHT WITH FRIENDS, I GO TO WORK   1979
ANYWAY

The boss knows what shape I'm in. He tells me
about the twenties, when he was my age,

how he drank all night and woke up in strange rooms
with strange dolls. He tells me *Get lost.*

Out back, a weedbank I'd never noticed —   5
I head for it in cold air, remembering
dogs and cats eating grass when sick.

I sit shoulder deep in weeds. Beneath the leaves
in green air black beetles shoulder
enormous stems, dew quivering   10
between stalk and leaf. In the pale moss I see
ants the size of salt grains,
and budding red flowers
smaller than these ants. A snail
dreaming in the throat of an old wine bottle.   15

QUESTIONS

Is the snail in the throat of a wine bottle a symbol? A simple image from nature?
An implied metaphor expressing how the speaker himself feels?

EXERCISE: *Symbol Hunting*

After you have read each of these poems, decide which description best suits it:
1. The poem has a central symbol.
2. The poem contains no symbolism, but is to be taken literally.

William Carlos Williams (1883 – 1963)*
POEM   1934

As the cat
climbed over
the top of

the jamcloset
first the right   5
forefoot

carefully
then the hind
stepped down
into the pit of   10
the empty
flowerpot

Theodore Roethke (1908 – 1963)*
NIGHT CROW   1948

When I saw that clumsy crow
Flap from a wasted tree,

A shape in the mind rose up:
Over the gulfs of dream
Flew a tremendous bird   5
Further and further away
Into a moonless black,
Deep in the brain, far back.

John Donne (1572 – 1631)*
A Burnt Ship   1633

Out of a fired ship which by no way
But drowning could be rescued from the flame
Some men leaped forth, and ever as they came
Near the foe's ships, did by their shot decay;
So all were lost, which in the ship were found,
  They in the sea being burnt, they in the burnt ship drowned.

Wallace Stevens (1879 – 1955)*
Anecdote of the Jar   1923

I placed a jar in Tennessee,
And round it was, upon a hill.
It made the slovenly wilderness
Surround that hill.

The wilderness rose up to it,   5
And sprawled around, no longer wild.
The jar was round upon the ground
And tall and of a port in air.

It took dominion everywhere.
The jar was gray and bare.   10
It did not give of bird or bush,
Like nothing else in Tennessee.

Suggestions for Writing

1. Write a paraphrase of Emily Dickinson's "I heard a Fly buzz — when I died."
   Make clear whatever meanings you find in the fly (and other concrete objects).
2. Discuss the symbolism in a poem by Adrienne Rich, either "Aunt Jennifer's
   Tigers" or "Diving into the Wreck," both in Chapter 29 (pages 759 – 762).
3. Take some relatively simple, straightforward poem, such as William Carlos
   Williams's "This Is Just to Say" (page 445), and write a burlesque critical interpretation of it. Claim to discover symbols in the poem that it doesn't contain.
   While letting your ability to "read into" a poem run wild, don't invent anything
   that you can't somehow support from the text of the poem itself. At the end
   of your burlesque, add a paragraph summing up what this exercise indicates
   about how to read poems, or how not to.

25 Myth

Poets have long been fond of retelling **myths,** narrowly defined as traditional stories of immortal beings. Such stories taken collectively may also be called **myth** or **mythology.** In one of the most celebrated collections of myth ever assembled, the *Metamorphoses,* the poet Ovid has told — to take one example from many — how Phaeton, child of the sun god, rashly tried to drive his father's fiery chariot on its daily round, lost control of the horses, and caused disaster both to himself and to the world. Our use of the term *myth* in discussing poetry, then, differs from its use in expressions such as "the myth of communism" and "the myth of democracy." In these examples, myth, in its broadest sense, is any idea people believe in, whether true or false. Nor do we mean — to take another familiar use of the word — a cock-and-bull story: "Judge Rapp doesn't roast speeders alive; that's just a *myth.*" In the following discussion, *myth* will mean — as critic Northrop Frye has put it — "the imitation of actions near or at the conceivable limits of desire." Myths tell us of the exploits of the gods — their battles, the ways in which they live, love, and perhaps suffer — all on a scale of magnificence larger than our life. We envy their freedom and power; they enact our wishes and dreams. Whether we believe in them or not, their adventures are myths: Ovid, it seems, placed no credence in the stories he related, for he declared, "I prate of ancient poets' monstrous lies."

And yet it is characteristic of a myth that it *can* be believed. Throughout history, myths have accompanied religious doctrines and rituals. They have helped sanction or recall the reasons for religious observances. A sublime instance is the New Testament account of the Last Supper. Because of it and its record of the words of Jesus, "This do in remembrance of Me," Christians have continued to re-enact the offering and partaking of the body and blood of their Lord, under the appearances of bread and wine. It is essential to recall that, just because a myth narrates the acts of a god, we do not necessarily mean by the term a false or fictitious narrative. When we speak of the "myth of Islam" or "the Christian myth," we do so without implying either belief or disbelief. Myths can also help sanction customs and institutions other than religious ones. At the same time as the baking of bread was introduced to ancient Greece — one theory goes — there was introduced the myth of Demeter, goddess of grain, who had kindly sent her emissary Triptolemus to teach humankind this valuable art — thus helping to persuade the distrustful that bread was a good thing. Some myths seem made to divert and regale, not to sanction anything. Such may be the story of the sculptor Pygmalion, who fell in love with his statue of a woman; so exquisite was his work, so deep was his feeling, that Aphrodite brought the statue to life. And yet perhaps the story goes deeper than mere diversion: perhaps it is a way of saying that works of art achieve a reality of their own, that love can transform or animate its object.

How does a myth begin? Several theories have been proposed, none universally accepted. One is that a myth is a way to explain some natural phenomenon. Winter comes and the vegetation perishes because Persephone, child of Demeter, must return to the underworld for four months every year. This theory, as classical scholar Edith Hamilton has pointed out, may lead us to think incorrectly that Greek mythology was the creation of a primitive people. Tales of the gods of Mount Olympus may reflect an earlier inheritance, but Greek myths known to us were transcribed in an era of high civilization. Anthropologists have questioned whether primitive people generally find beauty in the mysteries of nature. "From my own study of living myths among savages," wrote Bronislaw Malinowski, "I should say that primitive man has to a very limited extent the purely artistic or scientific interest in nature; there is but little room for symbolism in his ideas and tales; and myth, in fact, is not an idle rhapsody . . . but a hard-working, extremely important cultural force."[1] Such a practical function was seen by Sir James Frazer in *The Golden Bough:* myths were originally expressions of human hope that nature would be fertile. Still another theory is that, once upon a time, heroes of myth were human prototypes. The Greek philosopher Euhemerus declared myths to be tales of real persons, which poets had exaggerated. Most present-day historians of myth would seek no general explanation but would say that different myths probably have different origins.

Poets have many coherent mythologies on which to draw; perhaps those most frequently consulted by British and American poets are the classical, the Christian, the Norse, and folk myth of the American frontier (embodying the deeds of superhuman characters such as Paul Bunyan). Some poets have taken inspiration from other myths as well: T. S. Eliot's *The Waste Land,* for example, is enriched by allusions to Buddhism and to pagan vegetation-cults.

As a tour through any good art museum will demonstrate, myth pervades much of the graphic art of Western civilization. In literature, one evidence of its continuing value to recent poets and storytellers is the frequency with which myths — both primitive and civilized — are retold. William Faulkner's story "The Bear" recalls tales of Indian totem animals; John Updike's novel *The Centaur* presents the horse-man Chiron as a mod-

---

[1]Bronislaw Malinowski, *Myth in Primitive Psychology* (1926); reprinted in *Magic, Science and Religion* (New York: Doubleday, 1954) 97.

ern high school teacher; Hart Crane's poem "For the Marriage of Faustus and Helen" unites two figures of different myths, who dance to jazz; T. S. Eliot's plays bring into the drawing room the myths of Alcestis *(The Cocktail Party)* and the Eumenides *(The Family Reunion);* Jean Cocteau's film *Orphée* shows us Eurydice riding to the underworld with an escort of motorcycles. Popular interest in such works may testify to the profound appeal myths continue to hold for us. Like any other large body of knowledge that can be alluded to, myth offers the poet an instant means of communication — if the reader also knows the particular myth cited. Writing "Lycidas," John Milton could depend upon his readers — mostly persons of similar classical learning — to understand him without footnotes. Today, a poet referring to a traditional myth must be sure to choose a reasonably well-known one, or else write as well as T. S. Eliot, whose work has compelled his readers to single out his allusions and look them up. Like other varieties of poetry, myth is a kind of knowledge, not at odds with scientific knowledge but existing in addition to it.

D. H. Lawrence (1885 – 1930)*
BAVARIAN GENTIANS   1932

Not every man has gentians in his house
in soft September, at slow, sad Michaelmas.

Bavarian gentians, big and dark, only dark
darkening the daytime, torch-like with the smoking blueness of
      Pluto's gloom,
ribbed and torch-like, with their blaze of darkness spread blue   5
down flattening into points, flattened under the sweep of white day
torch-flower of the blue-smoking darkness, Pluto's dark-blue daze,
black lamps from the halls of Dis, burning dark blue,
giving off darkness, blue darkness, as Demeter's pale lamps give off
      light,
lead me then, lead the way.   10

Reach me a gentian, give me a torch!
let me guide myself with the blue, forked torch of this flower
down the darker and darker stairs, where blue is darkened on
      blueness
even where Persephone goes, just now, from the frosted September
to the sightless realm where darkness is awake upon the dark   15
and Persephone herself is but a voice
or a darkness invisible enfolded in the deeper dark
of the arms Plutonic, and pierced with the passion of dense gloom,
among the splendor of torches of darkness, shedding darkness on the
      lost bride and her groom.

BAVARIAN GENTIANS. 4. *Pluto:* Roman name for Hades, in Greek mythology the ruler of the underworld, who abducted Persephone to be his bride. Each spring Persephone returns to earth and is welcomed by her mother Demeter, goddess of fruitfulness; each winter she departs again, to dwell with her husband below. 8. *Dis:* Pluto's realm.

QUESTIONS

1. Read this poem aloud. What devices of sound do you hear in it?
2. What characteristics of gentians appear to remind Lawrence of the story of Persephone? What significance do you attach to the poem's being set in September? How does the fact of autumn matter to the gentians and to Persephone?

Thomas Hardy (1840 – 1928)*
THE OXEN   1915

Christmas Eve, and twelve of the clock.
   "Now they are all on their knees,"
An elder said as we sat in a flock
   By the embers in hearthside ease.

We pictured the meek mild creatures where   5
   They dwelt in their strawy pen,
Nor did it occur to one of us there
   To doubt they were kneeling then.

So fair a fancy few would weave
   In these years! Yet, I feel,   10
If someone said on Christmas Eve,
   "Come; see the oxen kneel

"In the lonely barton° by yonder coomb°   *farmyard; a hollow*
   Our childhood used to know,"
I should go with him in the gloom,   15
   Hoping it might be so.

THE OXEN. This ancient belief has had wide currency among peasants and farmers of Western Europe. Some also say that on Christmas Eve the beasts can speak.

QUESTIONS

1. What body of myth is Hardy's subject and what are his speaker's attitudes toward it? Perhaps, in Hardy's view, the pious report about oxen is only part of it.
2. Read this poem aloud and notice its sound and imagery. What contrast do you find between the sounds of the first stanza and the sounds of the last stanza? Which words make the difference? What images enforce a contrast in tone between the beginning of the poem and its ending?
3. G. K. Chesterton, writing as a defender of Christian faith, called Hardy's writings "the mutterings of the village atheist." See other poems by Hardy (particularly "Five Satires of Circumstance," page 723). What do you think Chesterton might have meant? Can "The Oxen" be called a hostile mutter?

William Wordsworth (1770 – 1850)*
The World Is Too Much with Us

The world is too much with us; late and soon,
Getting and spending, we lay waste our powers;
Little we see in Nature that is ours;
We have given our hearts away, a sordid boon!
This Sea that bares her bosom to the moon;   5
The winds that will be howling at all hours,
And are up-gathered now like sleeping flowers;
For this, for everything, we are out of tune;
It moves us not. Great God! I'd rather be
A Pagan suckled in a creed outworn;   10
So might I, standing on this pleasant lea,
Have glimpses that would make me less forlorn;
Have sight of Proteus rising from the sea;
Or hear old Triton blow his wreathèd horn.

Questions

1. In this sonnet by Wordsworth what condition does the poet complain about?
   To what does he attribute this condition?
2. How does it affect him as an individual?

When Plato in *The Republic* relates the Myth of Er, he introduces supernatural characters he himself originated. Poets, too, have been inspired to make up myths of their own, for their own purposes. "I must create a system or be enslaved by another man's," said William Blake, who in his "prophetic books" peopled the cosmos with supernatural beings having names like Los, Urizen, and Vala (side by side with recognizable figures from the Old Testament and New Testament). This kind of system-making probably has advantages and drawbacks. T. S. Eliot, in his essay on Blake, wishes that the author of *The Four Zoas* had accepted traditional myths, and he compares Blake's thinking to a piece of homemade furniture whose construction diverted valuable energy from the writing of poems. Others have found Blake's untraditional cosmos an achievement — notably William Butler Yeats, himself the author of an elaborate personal mythology. Although we need not know all of Yeats's mythology to enjoy his poems, to know of its existence can make a few great poems deeper for us and less difficult.

William Butler Yeats (1865 – 1939)*
The Second Coming

Turning and turning in the widening gyre°   *spiral*
The falcon cannot hear the falconer;
Things fall apart; the center cannot hold;

Mere anarchy is loosed upon the world,
The blood-dimmed tide is loosed, and everywhere   5
The ceremony of innocence is drowned;
The best lack all conviction, while the worst
Are full of passionate intensity.

Surely some revelation is at hand;
Surely the Second Coming is at hand;   10
The Second Coming! Hardly are those words out
When a vast image out of *Spiritus Mundi*
Troubles my sight: somewhere in sands of the desert
A shape with lion body and the head of a man,
A gaze blank and pitiless as the sun,   15
Is moving its slow thighs, while all about it
Reel shadows of the indignant desert birds.
The darkness drops again; but now I know
That twenty centuries of stony sleep
Were vexed to nightmare by a rocking cradle,   20
And what rough beast, its hour come round at last,
Slouches towards Bethlehem to be born?

What kind of Second Coming does Yeats expect? Evidently it is not
to be a Christian one. Yeats saw human history as governed by the turning
of a Great Wheel, whose phases influence events and determine human
personalities — rather like the signs of the Zodiac in astrology. Every two
thousand years comes a horrendous moment: the Wheel completes a turn;
one civilization ends and another begins. Strangely, a new age is always
announced by birds and by acts of violence. Thus the Greek-Roman world
arrives with the descent of Zeus in swan's form and the burning of Troy,
the Christian era with the descent of the Holy Spirit — traditionally depicted as a dove — and the Crucifixion. In 1919 when Yeats wrote "The
Second Coming," his Ireland was in the midst of turmoil and bloodshed;
the Western Hemisphere had been severely shaken by World War I. A new
millennium seemed imminent. What sphinxlike, savage deity would next
appear, with birds proclaiming it angrily? Yeats thinks he imagines it
emerging from *Spiritus Mundi,* Soul of the World, a collective unconscious
from which a human being (since the individual soul touches it) receives
dreams, nightmares, and racial memories.[2]

It is hard to say whether a poet who discovers a personal myth does
so to have something to live by or to have something to write about. Robert
Graves, who professes his belief in a White Goddess ("Mother of All
Living, the ancient power of love and terror"), has said that he has written
poetry in a trance, inspired by his Goddess-Muse.[3] Luckily, we do not have

[2]Yeats fully explains his system in *A Vision* (1938; reprinted New York: Macmillan, 1956).
[3]See Graves's *The White Goddess,* rev. ed. (New York: Farrar, 1966), or for a terser statement
of his position, see his lecture "The Personal Muse" in *On Poetry: Collected Talks and Essays* (New
York: Doubleday, 1969).

to know a poet's religious affiliation before we can read the poems. Perhaps most personal myths that enter poems are not acts of faith but works of art: stories that resemble traditional mythology.

John Milton (1608 – 1674)*

LYCIDAS   1637

In this monody the author bewails a learned friend, unfortunately drowned in his passage from Chester on the Irish Seas, 1637. And by occasion foretells the ruin of our corrupted clergy then in their height.

Yet once more, O ye laurels, and once more,	
Ye myrtles brown°, with ivy never sere,	*dark*
I come to pluck your berries harsh and crude°,	*immature*
And with forced fingers rude	
Shatter your leaves before the mellowing year.	5
Bitter constraint and sad occasion dear	
Compels me to disturb your season due;	
For Lycidas is dead, dead ere his prime,	
Young Lycidas, and hath not left his peer.	
Who would not sing for Lycidas? he knew	10
Himself to sing, and build the lofty rhyme.	
He must not float upon his wat'ry bier	
Unwept, and welter° to the parching wind,	*toss about*
Without the meed° of some melodious tear.	*tribute*
Begin, then, Sisters of the Sacred Well	15
That from beneath the seat of Jove doth spring,	
Begin, and somewhat loudly sweep the string.	
Hence with denial vain and coy excuse:	
So may some gentle Muse°	*poet*
With lucky words favor my destined urn,	20
And, as he passes, turn,	
And bid fair peace be to my sable shroud!	
For we were nursed upon the self-same hill,	
Fed the same flocks, by fountain, shade, and rill;	
Together both, ere the high lawns appeared	25
Under the opening eyelids of the Morn,	
We drove a-field, and both together heard	
What time the gray-fly winds° her sultry horn,	*sounds*
Batt'ning° our flocks with the fresh dews of night,	*feeding*
Oft till the star that rose at evening bright	30

LYCIDAS. A *monody* is a song for a single voice, generally a lament. Milton's *learned friend* was Edward King, scholar and poet, a fellow student at Cambridge University, where King had been preparing for the ministry. In calling him Lycidas, Milton employs a conventional name for a young shepherd in **pastoral poetry** (which either portrays the world of shepherds with some realism, as in Virgil's *Eclogues*, or makes it a prettified Eden, as in Marlowe's "The Passionate Shepherd to His Love"). 1 – 2. *laurels, myrtles:* Evergreens in the crowns traditionally bestowed upon poets.

Toward Heav'n's descent had sloped his westering wheel.
Meanwhile the rural ditties were not mute,
Tempered to the oaten° flute,   *made of an oat stalk*
Rough satyrs danced, and fauns with cloven heel
From the glad sound would not be absent long;   35
And old Damoetas loved to hear our song.
   But, O the heavy change, now thou art gone,
Now thou art gone, and never must return!
Thee, Shepherd, thee the woods and desert caves,
With wild thyme and the gadding° vine o'ergrown,   *wandering*   40
And all their echoes mourn.
The willows, and the hazel copses green,
Shall now no more be seen
Fanning their joyous leaves to thy soft lays.
As killing as the canker to the rose,   45
Or taint-worm to the weanling herds that graze,
Or frost to flowers, that their gay wardrobe wear
When first the white thorn blows°;   *blossoms*
Such, Lycidas, thy loss to shepherd's ear.
   Where were ye, Nymphs, when the remorseless deep   50
Closed o'er the head of your loved Lycidas?
For neither were ye playing on the steep
Where your old bards, the famous Druids, lie,
Nor on the shaggy top of Mona high,
Nor yet where Deva spreads her wizard stream.   55
Ay me! I fondly° dream!   *foolishly*
"Had ye been there" — for what could that have done?
What could the Muse herself that Orpheus bore,
The Muse herself, for her enchanting son,
Whom universal Nature did lament,   60
When, by the rout° that made the hideous roar,   *mob*
His gory visage down the stream was sent,
Down the swift Hebrus to the Lesbian shore?
   Alas! What boots it° with uncessant care   *what good does it do*
To tend the homely, slighted shepherd's trade,   65
And strictly meditate the thankless Muse?
Were it not better done, as others use°,   *do*
To sport with Amaryllis in the shade,
Or with the tangles of Neaera's hair?
Fame is the spur that the clear spirit doth raise   70
(That last infirmity of noble mind)
To scorn delights and live laborious days;
But the fair guerdon when we hope to find,

36. *Damoetas:* Perhaps some Cambridge tutor. 53. *Druids:* priests and poets of the Celts in pre-Christian Britain. 54. *Mona:* Roman name for the Isle of Man, near which King was drowned. 55. *Deva:* the River Dee, flowing between England and Wales. Its shifts in course were said to augur good luck for one country or the other. 68 – 69. *Amaryllis, Neaera:* conventional names for shepherdesses. 70. *the clear spirit doth raise:* doth raise the clear spirit.

And think to burst out into sudden blaze
Comes the blind Fury with th' abhorrèd shears,   75
And slits the thin-spun life. "But not the praise,"
Phoebus replied, and touched my trembling ears:
"Fame is no plant that grows on mortal soil,
Nor in the glistering° foil,   *glittering*
Set off to the world, nor in broad rumor° lies,   *reputation*   80
But lives and spreads aloft by those pure eyes
And perfect witness of all-judging Jove;
As he pronounces lastly on each deed,
Of so much fame in Heav'n expect thy meed."

    O fountain Arethuse, and thou honored flood,   85
Smooth-sliding Mincius, crowned with vocal reeds,
That strain I heard was of a higher mood:
But now my oat proceeds,
And listens to the Herald of the Sea,
That came in Neptune's plea.   90
He asked the waves, and asked the felon winds,
What hard mishap hath doomed this gentle swain?
And questioned every gust of rugged wings
That blows from off each beakèd promontory:
They knew not of his story;   95
And sage Hippotades their answer brings,
That not a blast was from his dungeon strayed:
The air was calm, and on the level brine
Sleek Panope with all her sisters played.
It was that fatal and perfidious bark,   100
Built in th' eclipse, and rigged with curses dark,
That sunk so low that sacred head of thine.

    Next, Camus, reverend sire, went footing slow,
His mantle hairy, and his bonnet sedge,
Inwrought with figures dim, and on the edge   105
Like to that sanguine flower inscribed with woe.
"Ah! who hath reft," quoth he, "my dearest pledge?"
Last came, and last did go,
The pilot of the Galilean lake;
Two massy keys he bore of metals twain   110
(The golden opes, the iron shuts amain°).   *with force*
He shook his mitered locks, and stern bespake: —
"How well could I have spared for thee, young swain,

77. *touched . . . ears:* gesture signifying "Remember!" 79. *foil:* a setting of gold or silver leaf, used
to make a gem appear more brilliant. 85 – 86. *Arethuse, Minicius:* a fountain and river near the
birthplaces of Theocritus and Virgil, respectively, hence recalling the most celebrated writer
of pastorals in Greek and the most celebrated in Latin. 90. *in Neptune's plea:* bringing the
sea-god's plea, "not guilty." 99. *Panope:* a sea nymph. Her name means "one who sees all."
101. *eclipse:* thought to be an omen of evil fortune. 103. *Camus:* spirit of the river Cam and
personification of Cambridge University. 109 – 112. *pilot:* Saint Peter, once a fisherman in
Galilee, to whom Jesus gave the *keys* of Heaven (Matthew 16:19). As first Bishop of Rome,
he wears the miter, a bishop's emblematic head-covering.

Enow° of such as for their bellies' sake,   *enough*
Creep, and intrude, and climb into the fold!   115
Of other care they little reck'ning make
Than how to scramble at the shearers' feast,
And shove away the worthy bidden guest.
Blind mouths! that scarce themselves know how to hold
A sheep-hook, or have learned aught else the least   120
That to the faithful herdsman's art belongs!
What recks it them? What need they? they are sped°;   *prosperous*
And, when they list°, their lean and flashy songs   *so incline*
Grate on their scrannel° pipes of wretched straw;   *feeble, harsh*
The hungry sheep look up, and are not fed,   125
But, swoll'n with wind and the rank mist they draw,
Rot inwardly, and foul contagion spread;
Besides what the grim wolf with privy° paw   *stealthy*
Daily devours apace, and nothing said;
But that two-handed engine at the door   130
Stands ready to smite once, and smite no more."
      Return, Alpheus; the dread voice is past
That shrunk thy streams; return, Sicilian Muse,
And call the vales, and bid them hither cast
Their bells and flow'rets of a thousand hues.   135
Ye valleys low, where the mild whispers use°   *resort*
Of shades, and wanton winds, and gushing brooks,
On whose fresh lap the swart star sparely looks,
Throw hither all your quaint enameled eyes,
That on the green turf suck the honied showers,   140
And purple all the ground with vernal flowers.
Bring the rathe° primrose that forsaken dies,   *early*
The tufted crow-toe, and pale jessamine,
The white pink, and the pansy freaked° with jet,   *streaked*
The glowing violet,   145
The musk-rose, and the well-attired woodbine,
With cowslips wan that hang the pensive head,
And every flower that sad embroidery wears;
Bid amaranthus all his beauty shed,
And daffadillies fill their cups with tears,   150
To strew the laureate hearse where Lycid lies.
For so, to interpose a little ease,
Let our frail thoughts dally with false surmise,

115. *fold:* the Church of England. 120. *sheep-hook:* a bishop's staff or crozier, which resembles a shepherd's crook. 128. *wolf:* probably the Church of Rome. Jesuits in England at the time were winning converts. 130. *two-handed engine:* This disputed phrase may refer (among other possibilities) to the punishing sword of The Word of God (Revelation 19:13 – 15 and Hebrews 4:12). Perhaps Milton sees it as a lightning bolt, as does Spenser, to whom Jove's wrath is a "three-forked engine" (*Faerie Queene,* VIII, 9). 131. *smite once . . . no more:* Because, in the proverb, lightning never strikes twice in the same place. 133. *Sicilian Muse:* who inspired Theocritus, a native of Sicily. 138. *swart star:* Sirius, at its zenith in summer, was thought to turn vegetation black. 153. *false surmise:* futile hope that the body of Lycidas could be recovered.

Ay me! whilst thee the shores and sounding seas
Wash far away, where'er thy bones are hurled;　　　　　　　　155
Whether beyond the stormy Hebrides,
Where thou, perhaps, under the whelming tide
Visit'st the bottom of the monstrous° world;　　　　*full of sea monsters*
Or whether thou, to our moist vows° denied,　　　　　　*prayers*
Sleep'st by the fable of Bellerus old,　　　　　　　　　160
Where the great Vision of the guarded mount
Looks toward Namancos and Bayona's hold°:　　　　　*stronghold*
Look homeward, angel, now, and melt with ruth°;　　　　*pity*
And, O ye dolphins, waft the hapless youth.

　　Weep no more, woeful shepherds, weep no more,　　　165
For Lycidas, your sorrow, is not dead,
Sunk though he be beneath the wat'ry floor:
So sinks the day-star in the ocean bed
And yet anon repairs his drooping head,
And tricks° his beams, and with new-spangled ore°　*arrays; gold* 170
Flames in the forehead of the morning sky:
So Lycidas sunk low, but mounted high,
Through the dear might of Him that walked the waves,
Where, other groves and other streams along,
With nectar pure his oozy locks he laves,　　　　　　　175
And hears the unexpressive nuptial song,
In the blest kingdoms meek of Joy and Love.
There entertain him all the Saints above,
In solemn troops, and sweet societies,
That sing, and singing in their glory move,　　　　　　180
And wipe the tears forever from his eyes.
Now, Lycidas, the shepherds weep no more;
Henceforth thou art the Genius° of the shore,　　　*guardian spirit*
In thy large recompense, and shalt be good
To all that wander in that perilous flood.　　　　　　　185

　　Thus sang the uncouth° swain to th' oaks and rills,　*rustic (or little-known)*
While the still Morn went out with sandals gray;
He touched the tender stops of various quills°,　*reeds of a shepherd's pipe*
With eager thought warbling his Doric lay:
And now the sun had stretched out all the hills,　　　190
And now was dropped into the western bay.
At last he rose, and twitched° his mantle blue:　　　　*donned*
Tomorrow to fresh woods and pastures new.

160. *Bellerus:* legendary giant of Land's End, the far tip of Cornwall. 161. *guarded mount:* Saint Michael's Mount, off Land's End, said to be under the protection of the archangel. 162. *Namancos, Bayona:* on the coast of Spain. 164. *dolphins:* In Greek legend, these kindly mammals carried the spirits of the dead to the Blessed Isles. 176. *unexpressive nuptial song:* inexpressibly beautiful song for the marriage feast of the Lamb (Revelation 19:9). 189. *Doric lay:* pastoral poem. Doric is the dialect of Greek employed by Theocritus.

Questions and Exercises

1. With the aid of an encyclopedia or a handbook of classical mythology (such as Bulfinch's *Mythology*, Edith Hamilton's *Mythology*, or H. J. Rose's *Handbook of Greek Mythology*) learn more about the following myths or mythical figures and places to which Milton alludes:

   Line 15 Sisters of the Sacred Well (Muses)
        16 seat of Jove (Mount Olympus)
        58 the Muse . . . that Orpheus bore (Calliope)
    61 – 63 (the death of Orpheus)
        75 Fury with the . . . shears (Atropos, one of the three Fates)
        77 Phoebus
        89 Herald of the Sea (Triton)
        90 Neptune
        96 Hippotades
      106 (Hyacinthus)
      132 Alpheus

   Then reread Milton's poem. As a result of your familiarity with these myths, what details become clear?

2. Read the parable of the Good Shepherd (John 10:1 – 18). What relationships does Milton draw between the Christian idea of the shepherd and pastoral poetry?

3. "With these trifling fictions [allusions to classical mythology]," wrote Samuel Johnson about "Lycidas," "are mingled the most awful and sacred truths, such as ought never to be polluted with such irreverend combinations." Does this mingling of paganism and Christianity detract from Milton's poem? Discuss.

4. In "Lycidas" does Milton devise any new myth or myths?

Suggestions for Writing

1. Write an explication of D. H. Lawrence's "Bavarian Gentians" or Thomas Hardy's "The Oxen." (For hints on writing about poetry by the method of explication, see page 1373.)

2. In a brief essay, either serious or otherwise, invent a brand new personal myth.

26 Alternatives

THE POET'S REVISIONS

"He / Who casts to write a living line must sweat, / . . . and strike the second heat / Upon the Muse's anvil," wrote Ben Jonson. Indeed, few if any immortal poems can have been perfected with the first blow. As a result, a poet may leave us two or more versions of a poem — perhaps (as Robert Graves has said of his work drafts) "hatched and cross-hatched by puzzling layers of ink."

We need not, of course, rummage the poet's wastebasket in order to evaluate a poem. If we wish, we can follow a suggestion of the critic Austin Warren: take any fine poem and make changes in it. Then compare the changes with the original. We may then realize why the poem is as it is instead of something else. However, there is a certain undeniable pleasure in watching a poem go through its growth stages. Some readers have claimed that the study of successive versions gives them insight into the process by which poems come to be. More important to a reader whose concern is to read poems with appreciation, we stand to learn something about the rightness of a finished poem from seeing what alternatives occurred to the poet. To a critic who protested two lines in Wordsworth's "The Thorn," a painfully flat description of an infant's grave,

> I've measured it from side to side;
> 'Tis three feet long and two feet wide,

Wordsworth retorted, "They ought to be liked." However, he thought better of them and later made this change:

> Though but of compass small, and bare
> To thirsty suns and parching air.

William Butler Yeats, who enjoyed revision, kept trying to improve the poems of his youth. A merciless self-critic, Yeats discarded lines that a lesser poet would have been grateful for. In some cases his final version was practically a new poem.

William Butler Yeats (1865 – 1939)*

THE OLD PENSIONER   1890

I had a chair at every hearth,
When no one turned to see
With "Look at that old fellow there;
And who may he be?"
And therefore do I wander on,   5
And the fret is on me.

The road-side trees keep murmuring —
Ah, wherefore murmur ye
As in the old days long gone by,
Green oak and poplar tree!   10
The well-known faces are all gone,
And the fret is on me.

THE LAMENTATION OF THE OLD PENSIONER   1939

Although I shelter from the rain
Under a broken tree
My chair was nearest to the fire
In every company
That talked of love or politics,   5
Ere Time transfigured me.

Though lads are making pikes again
For some conspiracy,
And crazy rascals rage their fill
At human tyranny,   10
My contemplations are of Time
That has transfigured me.

There's not a woman turns her face
Upon a broken tree,
And yet the beauties that I loved   15
Are in my memory;
I spit into the face of Time
That has transfigured me.

QUESTIONS

1. "The Old Pensioner" is this poem's first printed version; "Lamentation," its last. From the original, what elements has Yeats in the end retained?
2. What does the final version add to our knowledge of the old man (his character, attitudes, circumstances)?
3. Compare in sound and rhythm the refrain in the "Lamentation" with the original refrain.
4. Why do the statements in the final version seem to follow one another more naturally, and the poem as a whole seem more tightly woven together?

Yeats's practice seems to document the assertion of critic A. F. Scott that "the work of correction is often quite as inspired as the first onrush of words and ideas." Yeats made a revealing comment on his methods of revision:

> In dream poetry, in "Kubla Khan," . . . every line, every word can carry its unanalyzable, rich associations; but if we dramatize some possible singer or speaker we remember that he is moved by one thing at a time, certain words must be dull and numb. Here and there in correcting my early poems I have introduced such numbness and dullness, turned, for instance, the "curd-pale moon" into the "brilliant moon," that all might seem, as it were, remembered with indifference, except some one vivid image. When I began to rehearse a play I had the defects of my early poetry; I insisted upon obvious all-pervading rhythm. Later on I found myself saying that only in those lines or words where the beauty of the passage came to its climax, must rhythm be obvious.[1]

In changing words for "dull and numb" ones, in breaking up and varying rhythms, Yeats evidently is trying for improvement not necessarily in a particular line, but in an entire poem.

Not all revisions are successful. An instance might be the alterations Keats made in "La Belle Dame sans Merci," in which a stanza with "wild wild eyes" and exactly counted kisses,

> She took me to her elfin grot,
>   And there she wept and sighed full sore,
> And there I shut her wild wild eyes
>   With kisses four.

was scrapped in favor of:

> She took me to her elfin grot,
>   And there she gazed and sighèd deep,
> And there I shut her wild sad eyes —
>   So kissed to sleep.

When Mark Antony begins his funeral oration, "Friends, Romans, countrymen: lend me your ears," Shakespeare makes him ask something quite different from the modernized version in one high school English textbook: "Friends, Romans, countrymen: listen to me." Strictly speaking, any revised version of a poem is a different poem, even if its only change is a single word.

EXERCISE: *Early and Late Versions*

In each of the following pairs, which details of the revised version show an improvement of the earlier one? Exactly what makes the poet's second thoughts seem

---

[1]"Dramatis Personae, 1896 – 1902," in *The Autobiography of William Butler Yeats* (New York: Macmillan, 1953).

better (if you agree that they are)? Italics indicate words of one text not found in the other. Notice that in some cases, the poet has also changed word order.

1. Samuel Taylor Coleridge, "The Rime of the Ancient Mariner," from Part III:

   a. One after one, by the hornèd Moon
         (Listen, O Stranger! to me)
      Each turn'd his face with a ghastly pang
         And curs'd me with his *ee.*

   (1799 version)

   b. One after one, by the *star-dogged* Moon,
         Too quick for groan or sigh,
      Each turned his face with a ghastly pang
      And cursed me with his *eye.*

   (1817 version)

2. William Blake, last stanza of "London" (complete poem given on 472):

   a. But most the midnight harlot's curse
      From every *dismal* street I hear,
      Weaves around the marriage hearse
      And blasts the new born infant's tear.

   (first draft, 1793)

   b. But most *through* midnight streets I hear
      How the *youthful* harlot's curse
      Blasts the new born infant's tear
      And *blights with plagues* the marriage hearse.

   (1794 version)

3. Edward FitzGerald, *The Rubáiyát of Omar Khayyám,* a quatrain:

   a. *For in and out, above, about, below,*
         'Tis nothing but a Magic Shadow-show,
            Play'd in a Box whose Candle is the Sun,
      Round *which* we *Phantom Figures* come and go.

   (first version, 1859 edition)

   b. We *are no other than a moving row*
         Of Magic Shadow-*shapes that* come and go
      Round *with* the Sun-*illumined Lantern held*
      In Midnight by the Master of the Show; . . .

   (fifth version, 1889 edition)

Walt Whitman (1819 – 1892)*

A Noiseless Patient Spider

A noiseless patient spider,
I mark'd where on a little promontory it stood isolated,
Mark'd how to explore the vacant vast surrounding,
It launch'd forth filament, filament, filament, out of itself,
Ever unreeling them, ever tirelessly speeding them.   5
And you O my soul where you stand,
Surrounded, detached, in measureless oceans of space,

Ceaselessly musing, venturing, throwing, seeking the spheres to
    connect them,
Till the bridge you will need be form'd, till the ductile anchor hold,
Till the gossamer thread you fling catch somewhere, O my soul.   10

The Soul, reaching, throwing out for love

The Soul, reaching, throwing out for love,
As the spider, from some little promontory, throwing out filament
    after filament, tirelessly out of itself, that one at least may catch
    and form a link, a bridge, a connection
O I saw one passing along, saying hardly a word — yet full of love I
    detected him, by certain signs
O eyes wishfully turning! O silent eyes!
For then I thought of you o'er the world,   5
O latent oceans, fathomless oceans of love!
O waiting oceans of love! yearning and fervid! and of you sweet
    souls perhaps in the future, delicious and long:
But Death, unknown on the earth — ungiven, dark here, unspoken,
    never born:
You fathomless latent souls of love — you pent and unknown oceans
    of love!

Questions

1. One of these two versions of a poem by Whitman is an early draft from the poet's notebook. The other is the final version completed in 1871, about ten years later. Which is the final version?
2. In the final version, what has Whitman done to render his central metaphor (the comparison of soul and spider) more vivid and exact? What proportion of the final version is devoted to this metaphor?
3. In the early draft, what lines seem distracting or nonessential?

TRANSLATIONS

Poetry, said Robert Frost, is what gets lost in translation. If absolutely true, the comment is bad news for most of us, who have to depend on translations for our only knowledge of great poems in some other languages. However, some translators seem able to save a part of their originals and bring it across the language gap. At times they may even add more poetry of their own, as if to try to compensate for what is lost.

Unlike the writer of an original poem, the translator begins with a meaning that already exists. To convey it, the translator may decide to stick closely to the denotations of the original words or else to depart from them, more or less freely, after something he or she values more. The latter aim is evident in the *Imitations* of Robert Lowell, who said he had been "reckless with literal meaning" and instead had "labored hard to get the tone." Particularly defiant of translation are poems in dialect, uneducated speech, and slang: what can be used for English equivalents? Ezra Pound, in a bold move, translates the song of a Chinese peasant in *The Classic Anthology Defined by Confucius:*

> Yaller bird, let my corn alone,
> Yaller bird, let my crawps alone,
> These folks here won't let me eat,
> I wanna go back whaar I can meet
> the folks I used to know at home,
>   I got a home an' I wanna' git goin'.

Here, it is our purpose to judge a translation not by its fidelity to its original, but by the same standards we apply to any other poem written in English. To do so may be another way to see the difference between appropriate and inappropriate words.

Federico García Lorca (1899 – 1936)

LA GUITARRA   (1921)   GUITAR   1967

Empieza el llanto	Begins the crying
de la guitarra.	of the guitar.
Se rompen las copas	From earliest dawn
de la madrugada.	the strokes are breaking.
Empieza el llanto	Begins the crying 5
de la guitarra.	of the guitar.
Es inútil	It is futile
callarla.	to stop its sound.
Es imposible	It is impossible
callarla.	to stop its sound. 10
Llora monótona	It is crying a monotone
como llora el agua,	like the crying of water,
como llora el viento	like the crying of wind
sobre la nevada.	over fallen snow.
Es imposible	It is impossible 15
callarla.	to stop its sound.
Llora por cosas	It is crying over things
lejanas.	far off.
Arena del Sur caliente	Burning sand of the South
que pide camelias blancas.	which covets white camelias. 20
Llora flecha sin blanco,	It is crying the arrow without aim,
la tarde sin mañana,	the evening without tomorrow,
y el primer pájaro muerto	and the first dead bird on the branch.
sobre la rama.	O guitar!
¡Oh, guitarra!	Heart heavily wounded 25
Corazón malherido	by five sharp swords.
por cinco espadas.	

— Translated by Keith Waldrop

1. Someone who knows Spanish should read aloud the original and the translation. Although it is impossible for any translation fully to capture the resonance of García Lorca's poem, in what places is the English version most nearly able to approximate it?
2. Another translation renders line 21: "It mourns for the targetless arrow." What is the difference between mourning for something and being the cry of it?
3. Throughout his translation, Waldrop closely follows the line divisions of the original, but in line 23 he combines García Lorca's lines 23 and 24. Can you see any point in his doing so? Would "on the branch" by itself be a strong line of English poetry?

EXERCISE: *Comparing Translations*

Which English translation of each of the following poems is the best poetry? The originals may be of interest to some. For those who do not know the foreign language, the editor's line-by-line prose paraphrases may help indicate what the translator had to work with and how much of the translation is the translator's own idea. In which do you find the diction most felicitous? In which do pattern and structure best move as one? What differences in tone are apparent? It is doubtful that any one translation will surpass the others in every detail.

Horace (65 – 8 B.C.)
ODES I (38)
(about 20 B.C.)

Persicos odi, puer, apparatus,
Displicent nexae philyra coronae;
Mitte sectari, rosa quo locorum
      Sera moretur.
Simplici myrto nihil allabores   5
Sedulus curo: neque te ministrum
Dedecet myrtus neque me sub arta
      Vite bibentem.

ODES I (38). Prose translation: (1) Persian pomp, boy, I detest, (2) garlands woven of linden bark displease me; (3 – 4) give up searching for the place where the late-blooming rose is. (5 – 6) Put no laborious trimmings on simple myrtle: (6 – 7) for myrtle is unbecoming neither to you, a servant, nor to me, under the shade of this (8) vine, drinking.

  1. SIMPLICITY   (about 1782)

    Boy, I hate their empty shows,
      Persian garlands I detest,
    Bring me not the late-blown rose
      Lingering after all the rest:
    Plainer myrtle pleases me   5
      Thus outstretched beneath my vine,
    Myrtle more becoming thee,
      Waiting with thy master's wine.
          — William Cowper

2. FIE ON EASTERN LUXURY!   (about 1830)

Nay, nay, my boy — 'tis not for me,
    This studious pomp of Eastern luxury;
Give me no various garlands — fine
    With linden twine,
Nor seek, where latest lingering blows,   5
    The solitary rose.

Earnest I beg — add not with toilsome pain,
One far-sought blossom to the myrtle plain,
For sure, the fragrant myrtle bough
    Looks seemliest on thy brow;   10
Nor me mis-seems, while, underneath the vine,
Close interweaved, I quaff the rosy wine.
          — Hartley Coleridge

3. THE PREFERENCE DECLARED   1892

Boy, I detest the Persian pomp;
    I hate those linden-bark devices;
And as for roses, holy Moses!
    They can't be got at living prices!
Myrtle is good enough for us, —   5
    For *you,* as bearer of my flagon;
For *me,* supine beneath this vine,
    Doing my best to get a jag on!
          — Eugene Field

Charles Baudelaire (1821 – 1867)
RECUEILLEMENT   1866

Sois sage, ô ma Douleur, et tiens-toi plus tranquille.
Tu réclamais le Soir; il descend; le voici:
Une atmosphère obscure enveloppe la ville,
Aux uns portant la paix, aux autres le souci.

Pendant que des mortels la multitude vile,   5
Sous le fouet du Plaisir, ce bourreau sans merci,
Va cueillir des remords dans la fête servile,
Ma Douleur, donne-moi la main; viens par ici,

Loin d'eux. Vois se pencher les défuntes Années,
Sur les balcons du ciel, en robes surannées;   10
Surgir du fond des eaux le Regret souriant;

Le Soleil moribond s'endormir sous une arche,
Et, comme un long linceul traînant à l'Orient,
Entends, ma chère, entends la douce Nuit qui marche.

"MEDITATION." Prose translation: (1) Behave yourself [as a mother would say to her child],
O my Sorrow, and keep calmer. (2) You called for Evening; it descends; here it is: (3) a dim
atmosphere envelops the city, (4) Bringing peace to some; to others anxiety. (5) While the
vile multitude of mortals (6) under the whip of Pleasure, that merciless executioner, (7) go
to gather remorse in the servile festival, (8) my Sorrow, give me your hand; come this way,

(9) far from them. See the dead years lean (10) on the balconies of the sky, in old-fashioned dresses; (11) [see] Regret, smiling, emerge from the depths of the waters; (12) [see] the dying Sun go to sleep under an arch; (13) and like a long shroud trailing in the East, (14) hear, my darling, hear the soft Night who is walking.

1. Peace, be at peace, O thou my heaviness   1919

> Peace, be at peace, O thou my heaviness,
> Thou callèdst for the evening, lo! 'tis here,
> The City wears a somber atmosphere
> That brings repose to some, to some distress.
> Now while the heedless throng make haste to press   5
> Where pleasure drives them, ruthless charioteer,
> To pluck the fruits of sick remorse and fear,
> Come thou with me, and leave their fretfulness.
> See how they hang from heaven's high balconies,
> The old lost years in faded garments dressed,   10
> And see Regret with faintly smiling mouth;
> And while the dying sun sinks in the west,
> Hear how, far off, Night walks with velvet tread,
> And her long robe trails all about the south.
>   — Lord Alfred Douglas

2. Inward Conversation   1961

> Be reasonable, my pain, and think with more detachment.
> You asked to see the dusk; it descends; it is here:
> A sheath of dark light robes the city,
> To some bringing peace, to some the end of peace.
> Now while the rotten herds of mankind,   5
> Flogged by pleasure, that lyncher without touch,
> Go picking remorse in their filthy holidays,
> Let us join hands, my pain; come this way,
>
> Far from them. Look at the dead years that lean on
> The balconies of the sky, in their clothes long out of date;   10
> The sense of loss that climbs from the deep waters with a smile;
>
> The sun, nearly dead, that drops asleep beneath an arch;
> And listen to the night, like a long shroud being dragged
> Toward the east, my love, listen, the soft night is moving.
>   — Robert Bly

3. Meditation   1961

> Calm down, my Sorrow, we must move with care.
> You called for evening; it descends; it's here.
> The town is coffined in its atmosphere,
> bringing relief to some, to others care.
>
> Now while the common multitude strips bare,   5
> feels pleasure's cat o' nine tails on its back,
> and fights off anguish at the great bazaar,
> give me your hand, my Sorrow. Let's stand back;
>
> back from these people! Look, the dead years dressed
> in old clothes crowd the balconies of the sky.   10
> Regret emerges smiling from the sea,

the sick sun slumbers underneath an arch,
and like a shroud strung out from east to west,
listen, my Dearest, hear the sweet night march!
— Robert Lowell

4. MEDITATION   1982

Behave, my Sorrow! let's have no more scenes.
Evening's what you wanted — Evening's here:
a gradual darkness overtakes the town,
bringing peace to some, to others pain.

Now, while humanity racks up remorse   5
in low distractions under Pleasure's lash,
grovelling for a ruthless master — come
away, my Sorrow, leave them! Give me your hand . . .

See how the dear departed dowdy years
crowd the balconies of heaven, leaning down,   10
while smiling out of the sea appears Regret;

the Sun will die in its sleep beneath a bridge,
and trailing westward like a winding-sheet —
listen, my dear — how softly Night arrives.
— Richard Howard

PARODY

In a **parody,** one writer imitates — and pokes fun at — another.
Skillfully wrought, a parody can be a devastating form of literary criticism.
Usually the parodist imitates the characteristic tone, form, language, and
other elements of the original model, but sometimes applies them to a
ludicrously uncharacteristic subject.

Rather than merely flinging abuse at another poet, the wise parodist
imitates with understanding — perhaps with sympathy. The many crude
parodies of T. S. Eliot's difficult poem *The Waste Land* show parodists
mocking what they cannot fathom, with the result that, instead of illuminating the original, they belittle it (and themselves). Good parodists
have an ear for the sounds and rhythms of their originals, as does James
Camp, who echoes Walt Whitman's stately "Out of the Cradle Endlessly
Rocking" in his line "Out of the crock endlessly ladling" (what a weary
teacher feels he is doing). William Harmon has imagined Emily Dickinson
as a college student keeping a diary that begins:

The Soul selects her own Sorority –
Then – shuts the Dorm –
From her elite Majority
Black balls – eclectic – swarm –

(Compare Emily Dickinson's original on page 544.) Parody can be aimed
at poems good or bad; yet there are poems of such splendor and dignity
that no parodist seems able to touch them without looking like a small dog
defiling a cathedral, and others so illiterate that good parody would be

squandered on them. In the following original by T. E. Brown, what failings does the parodist, J. A. Lindon, jump upon? (*God wot,* by the way, is an archaism for "God knows.")

T. E. Brown (1830 – 1897)

My Garden 1887

A garden is a lovesome thing,
  God wot!
Rose plot,
Fringed pool,
Ferned grot —
The veriest school
Of peace; and yet the fool
Contends that God is not —
Not God! in gardens! when the eve
  is cool?
Nay, but I have a sign;
'Tis very sure God walks in mine.

J. A. Lindon (b. 1914)

My Garden 1959

A garden is a *lovesome* thing?
  What rot!
Weed plot,
Scum pool,
Old pot,
Snail-shiny stool
In pieces; yet the fool
Contends that snails are not —
Not snails! in gardens! when
  the eve is cool?
Nay, but I see their trails!
'Tis very sure *my* garden's full
  of snails!

Hugh Kingsmill
[Hugh Kingsmill Lunn] (1889 – 1949)

What, still alive at twenty-two? (about 1920)

What, still alive at twenty-two,
A clean, upstanding chap like you?
Sure, if your throat 'tis hard to slit,
Slit your girl's, and swing for it.

Like enough, you won't be glad
When they come to hang you, lad:
But bacon's not the only thing
That's cured by hanging from a string.

So, when the spilt ink of the night
Spreads o'er the blotting-pad of light,
Lads whose job is still to do
Shall whet their knives, and think of you.

Questions

1. A. E. Housman considered this the best of many parodies of his poetry. Read his poems in this book, particularly "Terence, this is stupid stuff" and "To an Athlete Dying Young" (pages 731 – 733). What characteristics of theme, form, and language does Hugh Kingsmill's parody convey?
2. What does Kingsmill exaggerate?

Kenneth Koch (b. 1925)

MENDING SUMP

"Hiram, I think the sump is backing up.
The bathroom floor boards for above two weeks
Have seemed soaked through. A little bird, I think,
Has wandered in the pipes, and all's gone wrong."
"Something there is that doesn't hump a sump,"   5
He said; and through his head she saw a cloud
That seemed to twinkle. "Hiram, well," she said,
"Smith is come home! I saw his face just now
While looking through your head. He's come to die
Or else to laugh, for hay is dried-up grass   10
When you're alone." He rose, and sniffed the air.
"We'd better leave him in the sump," he said.

QUESTIONS

1. What poet is the object of this parody? Which of his poems are echoed in it?
2. Koch gains humor by making outrageous statements in the tone and language
   of his original. Looking at other poems in this book by the poet being parodied,
   how would you describe their tone? Their language?
3. Suppose, instead of casting his parody into blank verse, Koch had written:

   "Hiram, the sump is backing up.
   The bathroom floor boards
   For above two weeks
   Have been soaking through. A little bird,
   I think, has wandered in
   The pipes, and all's gone wrong."

   Why would the biting edge of his parody have been blunted?
4. What, by the way, is a *sump?*

EXERCISE: *Spotting the Originals*

In the following parody, what poem or poet is being kidded? Does the parodist
seem only to be having fun, or is he making any critical point?

George Starbuck (b. 1931)

MARGARET ARE YOU DRUG

Cool it Mag.
Sure it's a drag
With all that green flaked out.
Next thing you know they'll be changing the color of bread.

But look, Chick,   5
Why panic?
Sevennyeighty years, we'll *all* be dead.

Roll with it, Kid.
I did.
Give it the old benefit of the doubt.   10

I mean leaves
Schmeaves.
You sure you aint just feeling sorry for yourself?

MARGARET ARE YOU DRUG. This is one of a series of "Translations from the English."

SUGGESTIONS FOR WRITING

1. Write a poem in the manner of Emily Dickinson, William Carlos Williams, E. E. Cummings, or any other modern poet whose work interests you and which you feel able to imitate. Decide, before you start, whether to write a serious imitation (that could be slipped into the poet's *Collected Poems* without anyone being the wiser), or a humorous parody. Read all the poet's poems included in this book; perhaps you will find it helpful also to consult a larger selection or collection of the poet's work. It might be simplest to choose a particular poem as your model; but, if you like, you may echo any number of poems. Choose a model within the range of your own skill: to imitate a sonnet, for instance, you need to be able to rime and to write in meter. Probably, if your imitation is serious, and not a parody, it is a good idea to pick a subject or theme characteristic of the poet. This is a difficult project, but if you can do it even fairly well, you will know a great deal more about poetry and your poet.
2. Compare and contrast the earlier version of Robert Frost's poem originally titled "In White" (page 1389) with the finished version "Design" (page 1374). What specific improvements did the poet make? Why do you think he made them? What was the matter with his first thoughts?
3. Word-processing systems, it is claimed, now enable writers to revise swiftly and efficiently. If you are familiar with word processors or computers, point out any possible advantages and disadvantages to poetry that may result from this recent development in technology.

27 Evaluating a Poem

TELLING GOOD FROM BAD

Why do we call some poems "bad"? We are talking not about their moral implications. Rather, we mean that, for one or more of many possible reasons, the poem has failed to move us or to engage our sympathies. Instead, it has made us doubt that the poet is in control of language and vision; perhaps it has aroused our antipathies or unwittingly appealed to our sense of the comic, though the poet is serious. Some poems can be said to succeed despite burdensome faults. But in general such faults are symptoms of deeper malady: some weakness in a poem's basic conception or in the poet's competence.

Nearly always, a bad poem reveals only a dim and distorted awareness of its probable effect on its audience. Perhaps the sound of words may clash with what a poem is saying, as in the jarring last word of this opening line of a tender lyric (author unknown, quoted by Richard Wilbur): "Come into the tent, my love, and close the flap." Perhaps a metaphor may fail by calling to mind more differences than similarities, as in Emily Dickinson's lines "Our lives are Swiss — / So still — so cool." A bad poem usually overshoots or falls short of its mark by the poet's thinking too little or too much. Thinking much, a poet contrives such an excess of ingenuity as that quoted by Alexander Pope in *Peri Bathous,* or *Of the Art of Sinking in Poetry:* a hounded stag who "Hears his own feet, and thinks they sound like more; / And fears the hind feet will o'ertake the fore." Thinking little, a poet writes redundantly, as Wordsworth in "The Thorn": "And they had fixed the wedding-day, / The morning that must wed them both."

In a poem that has a rime scheme or a set line length, when all is well, pattern and structure move inseparably with the rest of their poem, the way a tiger's skin and bones move with their tiger. But sometimes, in a poem that fails, the poet evidently has had difficulty in fitting the statements into a formal pattern. English poets have long felt free to invert word order for a special effect (Milton: "ye myrtles brown"), but the poet having trouble keeping to a rime scheme may invert words for no apparent reason but convenience. Needing a rime for *barge* may lead to ending a line with a *policedog large* instead of *a large policedog.* Another sign of trouble is a profusion of adjectives. If a line of iambic pentameter reads, "Her lovely skin, like dear sweet white old silk," we suspect the poet of stuffing the line to make it long enough. (But no one suspects Matthew Arnold of padding the last line of "To Marguerite": "The unplumbed, salt, estranging sea.")

Because, over his dead body, even a poet's slightest and feeblest efforts may be collected, some lines in the canon of celebrated bards make us wonder, "How could he have written this?" Wordsworth, Shelley, Whitman, and Browning are among the great whose failures can be painful, and sometimes an excellent poem will have a bad spot in it. To be unwilling to read them, though, would be as ill advised as to refuse to see Venice just because the Grand Canal is said to contain impurities. The seasoned reader of poetry thinks no less of Tennyson for having written, "Form, Form, Riflemen Form! . . . Look to your butts, and take good aims!" The collected works of a duller poet may contain no such lines of unconscious double meaning, but neither do they contain any poem as good as "Ulysses." If the duller poet never had a spectacular failure, it may be because of failure to take risks. "In poetry," said Ronsard, "the greatest vice is mediocrity."

Often, inept poems fall into familiar categories. At one extreme is the poem written entirely in conventional diction, dimly echoing Shakespeare, Wordsworth, and the Bible, but garbling them. Couched in a rhythm that ticks along like a metronome, this kind of poem shows no sign that its author has ever taken a hard look at anything that can be tasted, handled, and felt. It employs loosely and thoughtlessly the most abstract of words: *love, beauty, life, death, time, eternity.* Littered with old-fashioned contractions *('tis, o'er, where'er),* it may end in a simple preachment or platitude. George Orwell's complaint against much contemporary writing (not only poetry) is applicable: "As soon as certain topics are raised" — and one thinks of such standard topics for poetry as spring, a first kiss, and stars — "the concrete melts into the abstract and no one seems able to think of turns of speech that are not hackneyed." Writers, Orwell charged, too often make their sentences out of tacked-together phrases "like the sections of a prefabricated hen-house."[1] Versifiers often do likewise.

At the opposite extreme is the poem that displays no acquaintance with poetry of the past but manages, instead, to fabricate its own clichés. Slightly paraphrased, a manuscript once submitted to *The Paris Review* began:

---

[1]George Orwell, "Politics and the English Language," from *Shooting an Elephant and Other Essays* (New York: Harcourt, 1945).

Vile
        rottenflush
            o   — *screaming* —
            f CORPSEBLOOD!!   ooze
    STRANGLE my
            eyes . . .
                        HELL's
            O, ghastly   stench**!!!

At most, such a work has only a private value. The writer has vented
personal frustrations upon words, instead of kicking stray dogs. In its way,
"Vile Rottenflush" is as self-indulgent as the oldfangled "first kiss in
spring" kind of poem. "I dislike," said John Livingston Lowes, "poems that
black your eyes, or put up their mouths to be kissed."

As jewelers tell which of two diamonds is fine by seeing which
scratches the other, two poems may be tested by comparing them. This
method works only on poems similar in length and kind: an epigram
cannot be held up to test an epic. Most poems we meet are neither sheer
trash nor obvious masterpieces. Because good diamonds to be proven need
softer ones to scratch, in this chapter you will find a few clear-cut gems
and a few clinkers.

Anonymous (English)

O MOON, WHEN I GAZE ON THY BEAUTIFUL FACE   (about 1900)

O Moon, when I gaze on thy beautiful face,
Careering along through the boundaries of space,
The thought has often come into my mind
If I ever shall see thy glorious behind.

O MOON. Sir Edmund Gosse, the English critic (1849 – 1928), offered this quatrain as the work
of his maidservant, but there is reason to suspect him of having written it.

QUESTIONS

1. To what fact of astronomy does the last line refer?
2. Which words seem chosen with too little awareness of their denotations and
   connotations?
3. Even if you did not know that these lines probably were deliberately bad, how
   would you argue with someone who maintained that the opening *O* in the poem
   was admirable as a bit of concrete poetry? (See the quotation from E. E. Cummings on page 607.)

Grace Treasone

LIFE   (about 1963)

Life is like a jagged tooth
that cuts into your heart;
fix the tooth and save the root,
and laughs, not tears, will start.

QUESTIONS

1. Try to paraphrase this poem. What is the poet saying?
2. How consistent is the working out of the comparison of life to a tooth?

M. Krishnamurti (b. 1912)

THE SPIRIT'S ODYSSEY   1950

I saw her first in gleams,
As one might see in dreams
   A moonmaiden undrape
   Her opalescent shape
Midst moveless lunar streams!   5

Now fierce and sudden-truth'd,
She smites me, saber-tooth'd:
   As sunlight, snarling, crawls
   Into the bower and mauls
The waker, slumber-sooth'd!   10

QUESTIONS

1. What is the effect of this poet's rimes? Suggestion: Read "The Spirit's Odyssey" aloud.
2. To what do you attribute the moonmaiden's surprising metamorphosis into an angry saber-toothed tiger?
3. Can you defend this poem? Try being a devil's advocate.

Stephen Tropp (b. 1930)

MY WIFE IS MY SHIRT   1960

My wife is my shirt
I put my hands through her armpits
slide my head through her mouth
& finally button her blood around my hands

1. How consistently is the metaphor elaborated?
2. Why can this metaphor be said to work in exactly the opposite way from a personification?
3. A paraphrase might discover this simile: "My wife is as intimate, familiar, and close to me as the shirt on my back." If this is the idea and the poem is supposed to be a love poem, how precisely is its attitude expressed?

Emily Dickinson (1830 – 1886)*

A DYING TIGER – MOANED FOR DRINK (ABOUT 1862)

A Dying Tiger – moaned for Drink –
I hunted all the Sand –
I caught the Dripping of a Rock
And bore it in my Hand –

His Mighty Balls – in death were thick – 5
But searching – I could see
A Vision on the Retina
Of Water – and of me –

'Twas not my blame – who sped too slow –
'Twas not his blame – who died 10
While I was reaching him –
But 'twas – the fact that He was dead –

QUESTION

How does this poem compare in success with other poems of Emily Dickinson that you know? Justify your opinion by pointing to some of this poem's particulars.

EXERCISE: *Seeing What Went Wrong*

Here is a small anthology of bad moments in poetry. For what reasons does each selection fail? In which passages do you attribute the failure to inappropriate sound or diction? To awkward word order? To inaccurate metaphor? To excessive overstatement? To forced rime? To monotonous rhythm? To redundancy? To simplemindedness or excessive ingenuity?

1. "I'm Glad," in its entirety, author unknown:

   I'm glad the sky is painted blue,
   And the earth is painted green,
   With such a lot of nice fresh air
   All sandwiched in between.

2. A lover's lament, from Harry Edward Mills's *Select Sunflowers:*

   I see her in my fondest moods,
     She haunts the parlor hallway;
   And yet her form my clasp eludes,
     Her lips my kisses alway.

3. A suffering swain makes a vow, from "the poem of a young tradesman" quoted by Coleridge in *Biographia Literaria:*

   No more will I endure love's pleasing pain,
   Or round my heart's leg tie his galling chain.

4. From an elegy for Queen Victoria by one of her subjects:

   Dust to dust, and ashes to ashes,
   Into the tomb the Great Queen dashes.

5. The opening lines of Alice Meynell's "The Shepherdess":

   She walks — the lady of my delight —
   A shepherdess of sheep.

6. From a juvenile poem of John Dryden, "Upon the Death of the Lord Hastings" (a victim of smallpox):

   Blisters with pride swelled; which through's flesh did sprout
   Like rose-buds, stuck i' th'lily-skin about.
   Each little pimple had a tear in it,
   To wail the fault its rising did commit . . .

7. From a classified advertisement on the obituary page, Boston *Globe,* January 8, 1980:

   1977 — ELVIS PRESLEY — 1980
   Today is your birthday
   And although you're not here,
   There are, no doubt, many more
   Than I who still miss you and care.
   And every time we see your pictures
   Or hear your special songs,
   We'll feel a pain deep
   In our hearts, still so strong.
   We will never forget you.
   You remain on our minds.
   Forever, our love, Elvis.
   You were one of a kind.
   A loving fan.
   Diane.

8. A metaphor from Edgar A. Guest's "The Crucible of Life":

   Sacred and sweet is the joy that must come
   From the furnace of life when you've poured off the scum.

9. A stanza composed by Samuel Johnson as a deliberately bad example:

   I put my hat upon my head
   And walked into the Strand;
   And there I met another man
   Whose hat was in his hand.

10. A lover describes his lady, from Thomas Holley Chivers's "Rosalie Lee":

    Many mellow Cydonian suckets,
       Sweet apples, anthosmial, divine,
    From the ruby-rimmed beryline buckets,
       Star-gemmed, lily-shaped, hyaline:
    Like the sweet golden goblet found growing

On the wild emerald cucumber-tree,
Rich, brilliant, like chrysoprase glowing,
Was my beautiful Rosalie Lee.

11. Lines on a sick gypsy, author unknown, quoted in *The Stuffed Owl: An Anthology of Bad Verse,* edited by D. B. Wyndham Lewis and Charles Lee:

There we leave her,
There we leave her,
Far from where her swarthy kindred roam,
In the Scarlet Fever,
Scarlet Fever,
Scarlet Fever Convalescent Home.

Sentimentality is a failure of writers who seem to feel a great emotion but who fail to give us sufficient grounds for sharing it. The emotion may be an anger greater than its object seems to call for, as in these lines to a girl who caused scandal (the exact nature of her act never being specified): "The gossip in each hall / Will curse your name . . . / Go! better cast yourself right down the falls!"[2] Or it may be an enthusiasm quite unwarranted by its subject: in *The Fleece* John Dyer temptingly describes the pleasures of life in a workhouse for the poor. The sentimental poet is especially prone to tenderness. Great tears fill his eyes at a glimpse of an aged grandmother sitting by a hearth. For all the poet knows, she may be the manager of a casino in Las Vegas, who would be startled to find herself an object of pity, but the sentimentalist doesn't care to know about the woman herself. She is a general excuse for feeling maudlin. Any other conventional object will serve as well: a faded valentine, the strains of an old song, a baby's cast-off pacifier. An instance of such emotional self-indulgence is "The Old Oaken Bucket," by Samuel Woodworth, a stanza of which goes:

How sweet from the green, mossy brim to receive it,
    As, poised on the curb, it inclined to my lips!
Not a full-flushing goblet could tempt me to leave it,
    Tho' filled with the nectar that Jupiter sips.
And now, far removed from the loved habitation,
    The tear of regret will intrusively swell,
As fancy reverts to my father's plantation,
    And sighs for the bucket that hung in the well.

The staleness of the phrasing and imagery (Jove's nectar, *tear of regret*) suggests that the speaker is not even seeing the actual physical bucket, and the tripping meter of the lines is inappropriate to an expression of tearful regret. Perhaps the poet's nostalgia is genuine. Indeed, as Keith Waldrop has put it, "a bad poem is always sincere." However sincere in their

[2]Ali. S. Hilmi, "The Preacher's Sermon," in *Verse at Random* (Larnaca, Cyprus: Ohanian Press, 1953).

feelings, sentimental poets are insincere in their art — otherwise, wouldn't they trouble to write better poems? Wet-eyed and sighing for a bucket, Woodworth achieves not pathos but **bathos:** a description that can move us to laughter instead of tears.[3]

Tears, of course, can be shed for good reason. A piece of sentimentality is not to be confused with a well-wrought poem whose tone is tenderness. At first glance, the following poem by Burns might strike you as sentimental. It is a rare poet who can speak honestly on the theme that love grows deeper as lovers grow old. Many a popular songwriter has seen the process of aging as valuable: "Darling, I am growing old, / Silver threads among the gold — " as if to grow decrepit were a privilege. What is fresh in Burns's poem, however, is his refusal to gloss over the ravages of age and the inevitability of death. The speaker expresses no self-pity, no comment *about* her feelings, only a simple account of what has befallen her and her John and what is still to follow.

Robert Burns (1759 – 1796)*

JOHN ANDERSON MY JO, JOHN   1790

John Anderson my jo°, John,	*dear*
When we were first acquent°,	*acquainted*
Your locks were like the raven,	
Your bonny brow was brent°;	*unwrinkled*
But now your brow is beld°, John,	*bald* 5
Your locks are like the snaw;	
But blessings on your frosty pow°,	*head*
John Anderson my jo.	
John Anderson my jo, John,	
We clamb the hill thegither;	10
And mony a canty° day, John,	*happy*
We've had wi' ane anither:	
Now we maun° totter down, John,	*must*
And hand in hand we'll go,	
And sleep together at the foot,	15
John Anderson my jo.	

---

[3]*Bathos* in poetry can also mean an abrupt fall from the sublime to the trivial or incongruous. A sample, from Nicholas Rowe's play *The Fair Penitent:* "Is it the voice of thunder, or my father?" Another, from John Close, a minor Victorian: "Around their heads a dazzling halo shone, / No need of mortal robes, or any hat." When, however, such a letdown is used for a *desirable* effect of humor or contrast, it is usually called an **anticlimax:** as in Alexander Pope's lines on the queen's palace, "Here thou, great Anna! whom three realms obey, / Dost sometimes counsel take — and sometimes tea."

Rod McKuen (b. 1933)
THOUGHTS ON CAPITAL PUNISHMENT   1954

There ought to be capital punishment for cars
that run over rabbits and drive into dogs
and commit the unspeakable, unpardonable crime
of killing a kitty cat still in his prime.

Purgatory, at the very least   5
                      should await the driver
   driving over a beast.

Those hurrying headlights coming out of the dark
that scatter the scampering squirrels in the park
should await the best jury that one might compose   10
of fatherless chipmunks and husbandless does.

And then found guilty, after too fair a trial
should be caged in a cage with a hyena's smile
or maybe an elephant with an elephant gun
should shoot out his eyes when the verdict is done.   15

There ought to be something, something that's fair
to avenge Mrs. Badger as she waits in her lair
for her husband who lies with his guts spilling out
cause he didn't know what automobiles are about.

Hell on the highway, at the very least   20
                      should await the driver
   driving over a beast.

Who kills a man kills a bit of himself
But a cat too is an extension of God.

William Stafford (b. 1914)*
TRAVELING THROUGH THE DARK   1962

Traveling through the dark I found a deer
dead on the edge of the Wilson River road.
It is usually best to roll them into the canyon:
that road is narrow; to swerve might make more dead.

By glow of the tail-light I stumbled back of the car   5
and stood by the heap, a doe, a recent killing;
she had stiffened already, almost cold.
I dragged her off; she was large in the belly.

My fingers touching her side brought me the reason —
her side was warm; her fawn lay there waiting,   10
alive, still, never to be born.
Beside that mountain road I hesitated.

The car aimed ahead its lowered parking lights;
under the hood purred the steady engine.
I stood in the glare of the warm exhaust turning red;   15
around our group I could hear the wilderness listen.

I thought hard for us all — my only swerving —
then pushed her over the edge into the river.

QUESTIONS

1. Compare these poems by Rod McKuen and William Stafford. How are they similar?
2. Explain Stafford's title. Who are all those traveling through the dark?
3. Comment on McKuen's use of language. Consider especially: *unspeakable, unpardonable crime* (line 3), *kitty cat* (4), *scatter the scampering squirrels* (9), and *cause he didn't know* (19).
4. Compare the meaning of Stafford's last two lines and McKuen's last two. Does either poem have a moral? Can either poem be said to moralize?
5. Which poem might be open to the charge of sentimentality? Why?

EXERCISE: *Fine or Shoddy Tenderness*

Which of the following four poems do you find sentimental? Which would you defend? At least one kind of evidence to look for is minute, detailed observation of physical objects. In a successful poem, the poet is likely at least occasionally to notice the world beyond his or her own skin; in a sentimental poem, this world is likely to be ignored.

Hart Crane (1899 – 1932)
MY GRANDMOTHER'S LOVE LETTERS   1926

There are no stars to-night
But those of memory.
Yet how much room for memory there is
In the loose girdle of soft rain.

There is even room enough   5
For the letters of my mother's mother,
Elizabeth,
That have been pressed so long
Into a corner of the roof
That they are brown and soft,
And liable to melt as snow.   10

Over the greatness of such space
Steps must be gentle.
It is all hung by an invisible white hair.
It trembles as birch limbs webbing the air.   15

And I ask myself:

"Are your fingers long enough to play
Old keys that are but echoes:
Is the silence strong enough
To carry back the music to its source   20
And back to you again
As though to her?"

Yet I would lead my grandmother by the hand
Through much of what she would not understand;
And so I stumble. And the rain continues on the roof   25
With such a sound of gently pitying laughter.

Eliza Cook (1818 – 1889)
The Old Arm-Chair   (about 1870)

I love it, I love it! and who shall dare
To chide me for loving that old arm-chair?
I've treasured it long as a sainted prize,
I've bedewed it with tears, I've embalmed it with sighs,
'Tis bound by a thousand bands to my heart;   5
Not a tie will break, not a link will start.
Would you know the spell? — a mother sat there!
And a sacred thing is that old arm-chair.

In childhood's hour I lingered near
The hallowed seat with listening ear;   10
And gentle words that mother would give
To fit me to die and teach me to live.
She told me that shame would never betide
With truth for my creed, and God for my guide;
She taught me to lisp my earliest prayer,   15
As I knelt beside that old arm-chair.

I sat and watched her many a day,
When her eyes grew dim, and her locks were gray;
And I almost worshipped her when she smiled,
And turned from her Bible to bless her child.   20
Years rolled on, but the last one sped, —
My idol was shattered, my earth-star fled!
I learned how much the heart can bear,
When I saw her die in her old arm-chair.

'Tis past, 'tis past! but I gaze on it now,   25
With quivering breath and throbbing brow;
'Twas there she nursed me, 'twas there she died,
And memory flows with a lava tide.
Say it is folly, and deem me weak,

Whilst scalding drops start down my cheek;   30
But I love it, I love it! and cannot tear
My soul from a mother's old arm-chair.

D. H. Lawrence (1885 – 1930)*
PIANO   1918

Softly, in the dusk, a woman is singing to me;
Taking me back down the vista of years, till I see
A child sitting under the piano, in the boom of the tingling strings
And pressing the small, poised feet of a mother who smiles as she sings.

In spite of myself, the insidious mastery of song   5
Betrays me back, till the heart of me weeps to belong
To the old Sunday evenings at home, with winter outside
And hymns in the cozy parlor, the tinkling piano our guide.

So now it is vain for the singer to burst into clamor
With the great black piano appassionato. The glamor   10
Of childish days is upon me, my manhood is cast
Down in the flood of remembrance, I weep like a child for the past.

Alfred, Lord Tennyson (1809 – 1892)*
TEARS, IDLE TEARS   1847

   Tears, idle tears, I know not what they mean,
Tears from the depth of some divine despair
Rise in the heart, and gather to the eyes,
In looking on the happy autumn-fields,
And thinking of the days that are no more.   5

   Fresh as the first beam glittering on a sail,
That brings our friends up from the underworld,
Sad as the last which reddens over one
That sinks with all we love below the verge;
So sad, so fresh, the days that are no more.   10

   Ah, sad and strange as in dark summer dawns
The earliest pipe of half-awakened birds
To dying ears, when unto dying eyes
The casement slowly grows a glimmering square;
So sad, so strange, the days that are no more.   15

   Dear as remembered kisses after death,
And sweet as those by hopeless fancy feigned
On lips that are for others; deep as love,
Deep as first love, and wild with all regret;
O Death in Life, the days that are no more!   20

KNOWING EXCELLENCE

How can we tell an excellent poem from any other? To give reasons for excellence in poetry is harder than to give reasons for failure in poetry (so often due to familiar kinds of imprecision and sentimentality). A bad poem tends to be stereotyped, an excellent poem unique. In judging either, we can have no absolute specifications. A poem is not like an electric toaster that an inspector can test by a check-off list. It has to be judged on the basis of what it is trying to be and how well it succeeds in the effort.

To judge a poem, we first have to understand it. At least, we need to understand it *almost* all the way; there is, to be sure, a poem such as Hopkins's "The Windhover" (page 730), which most readers probably would call excellent even though its meaning is still being debated. Although it is a good idea to give a poem at least a couple of considerate readings before judging it, sometimes our first encounter starts turning into an act of evaluation. Moving along into the poem, becoming more deeply involved in it, we may begin forming an opinion. In general, the more a poem contains for us to understand, the more rewarding we are likely to find it. Of course, an obscure and highly demanding poem is not always to be preferred to a relatively simple one. Difficult poems can be pretentious and incoherent; still, there is something to be said for the poem complicated enough to leave us something to discover on our fifteenth reading (unlike most limericks, which yield their all at a look). Here is such a poem, one not readily fathomed and exhausted.

William Butler Yeats (1865 – 1939)*

SAILING TO BYZANTIUM   1927

That is no country for old men. The young
In one another's arms, birds in the trees
— Those dying generations — at their song,
The salmon-falls, the mackerel-crowded seas,
Fish, flesh, or fowl, commend all summer long   5
Whatever is begotten, born, and dies.
Caught in that sensual music all neglect
Monuments of unaging intellect.

An aged man is but a paltry thing,
A tattered coat upon a stick, unless   10
Soul clap its hands and sing, and louder sing
For every tatter in its mortal dress,
Nor is there singing school but studying
Monuments of its own magnificence;
And therefore I have sailed the seas and come   15
To the holy city of Byzantium.

O sages standing in God's holy fire
As in the gold mosaic of a wall,
Come from the holy fire, perne in a gyre°,   *spin down a spiral*
And be the singing-masters of my soul.   20
Consume my heart away; sick with desire
And fastened to a dying animal
It knows not what it is; and gather me
Into the artifice of eternity.

Once out of nature I shall never take   25
My bodily form from any natural thing,
But such a form as Grecian goldsmiths make
Of hammered gold and gold enameling
To keep a drowsy Emperor awake;
Or set upon a golden bough to sing   30
To lords and ladies of Byzantium
Of what is past, or passing, or to come.

SAILING TO BYZANTIUM. Byzantium was the capital of the Byzantine Empire, the city now called
Istanbul. Yeats means, though, not merely the physical city. Byzantium is also a name for
his conception of paradise.

Though *salmon-falls* (line 4) suggests Yeats's native Ireland, the poem,
as we find out in line 25, is about escaping from the entire natural world.
If the poet desires this escape, then probably the *country* mentioned in the
opening line is no political nation but the cycle of birth and death in which
human beings are trapped; and, indeed, the poet says his heart is "fastened
to a dying animal." Imaginary landscapes, it would seem, are merging with
the historical Byzantium. Lines 17 – 18 refer to mosaic images, adornments
of the Byzantine cathedral of St. Sophia, in which the figures of saints are
inlaid against backgrounds of gold. The clockwork bird of the last stanza
is also a reference to something actual. Yeats noted: "I have read somewhere that in the Emperor's palace at Byzantium was a tree made of gold
and silver, and artificial birds that sang." This description of the role the
poet would seek — that of a changeless, immortal singer — directs us back
to the earlier references to music and singing. Taken all together, they
point toward the central metaphor of the poem: the craft of poetry can be
a kind of singing. One kind of everlasting monument is a great poem. To
study masterpieces of poetry is the only "singing school" — the only way
to learn to write a poem.

We have no more than skimmed through a few of this poem's
suggestions, enough to show that, out of allusion and imagery, Yeats has
woven at least one elaborate metaphor. Surely one thing the poem achieves
is that, far from merely puzzling us, it makes us aware of relationships
between what a person can imagine and the physical world. There is the
statement that a human heart is bound to the body that perishes, and yet
it is possible to see consciousness for a moment independent of flesh, to
sing with joy at the very fact that the body is crumbling away. Expressing

a similar view of mortality, the Japanese artist Hokusai has shown a withered tree letting go of its few remaining leaves, while under it two gray-beards shake with laughter. Like Hokusai's view, that of Yeats is by no means simple. Much of the power of Yeats's poem comes from the physical terms with which he states the ancient quarrel between body and spirit, body being a "tattered coat upon a stick." There is all the difference in the world between the work of the poet like Yeats whose eye is on the living thing and whose mind is awake and passionate, and that of the slovenly poet whose dull eye and sleepy mind focus on nothing more than some book read hastily long ago. The former writes a poem out of compelling need, the latter as if it seems a nice idea to write something.

Yeats's poem has the three qualities essential to beauty, according to the definition of Thomas Aquinas: wholeness, harmony, and radiance. The poem is all one; its parts move in peace with one another; it shines with emotional intensity. There is an orderly progression going on in it: from the speaker's statement of his discontent with the world of "sensual music," to his statement that he is quitting this world, to his prayer that the sages will take him in, and his vision of future immortality. And the images of the poem relate to one another — *dying generations* (line 3), *dying animal* (line 22), and the undying golden bird (lines 27 – 32) — to mention just one series of related things. "Sailing to Byzantium" is not the kind of poem that has, in Pope's words, "One simile, that solitary shines / In the dry desert of a thousand lines." Rich in figurative language, Yeats's whole poem develops a metaphor, with further metaphors as its tributaries.

"Sailing to Byzantium" has a theme that matters to us. What human being does not long, at times, to shed timid, imperfect flesh, to live in a state of absolute joy, unperishing? Being human, perhaps we too are stirred by Yeats's prayer: "Consume my heart away, sick with desire / And fastened to a dying animal. . . ." If it is true that in poetry (as Ezra Pound declared) "only emotion endures," then Yeats's poem ought to endure. (No reasons to be moved by a poem, however, can be of much use. If you happen not to feel moved by this poem, try another — but come back to "Sailing to Byzantium" after a while.)

Most excellent poems, it might be argued, contain significant themes, as does "Sailing to Byzantium." But the presence of such a theme is not enough to render a poem excellent. That classic tear-jerker "The Old Arm-Chair" (page 658) expresses in its way, too, faith in a kind of immortality. Not theme alone makes an excellent poem, but how well a theme is stated.

Yeats's poem, some would say, is the match for any lyric in our language. Some might call it inferior to an epic (to Milton's *Paradise Lost,* say, or to the *Iliad*), but this claim is to lead us into a different argument: whether certain genres are innately better than others. Such an argument usually leads to a dead end. Evidently, *Paradise Lost* has greater range, variety, matter, length, and ambitiousness. But any poem — whether an epic or an epigram — may be judged by how well it fulfills the design it undertakes. God, who created both fleas and whales, pronounced all good. Fleas, like epigrams, have no reason to feel inferior.

EXERCISE: *Two Poems to Compare*

Here are two poems with a similar theme. Which contains more qualities of excellent poetry? Decide whether the other is bad or whether it may be praised for achieving something different.

Arthur Guiterman (1871 – 1943)
ON THE VANITY OF EARTHLY GREATNESS 1936

The tusks that clashed in mighty brawls
Of mastodons, are billiard balls.

The sword of Charlemagne the Just
Is ferric oxide, known as rust.

The grizzly bear whose potent hug   5
Was feared by all, is now a rug.

Great Caesar's bust is on the shelf,
And I don't feel so well myself.

Percy Bysshe Shelley (1792 – 1822)
OZYMANDIAS 1818

I met a traveler from an antique land
Who said: Two vast and trunkless legs of stone
Stand in the desert. Near them, on the sand,
Half sunk, a shattered visage lies, whose frown,
And wrinkled lip, and sneer of cold command,   5
Tell that its sculptor well those passions read
Which yet survive, stamped on these lifeless things,
The hand that mocked° them and the heart that fed;   *imitated*
And on the pedestal these words appear:
"My name is Ozymandias, king of kings: 10
Look on my works, ye Mighty, and despair!"
Nothing beside remains. Round the decay
Of that colossal wreck, boundless and bare
The lone and level sands stretch far away.

Some excellent poems of the past will remain sealed to us unless we are willing to sympathize with their conventions. Pastoral poetry, for instance — Marlowe's "Passionate Shepherd" and Milton's "Lycidas" — asks us to accept certain conventions and situations that may seem old-fashioned: idle swains, oaten flutes. We are under no grim duty, of course, to admire poems whose conventions do not appeal to us. But there is no point in blaming a poet for playing a particular game or for observing its rules.

Bad poems, of course, can be woven together out of conventions, like patchwork quilts made of old unwanted words. In Shakespeare's England, poets were busily imitating the sonnets of Petrarch, the Italian poet whose praise of his beloved Laura had become well known. The result of their industry was a surplus of Petrarchan **conceits,** or elaborate comparisons (from the Italian *concetto:* concept, bright idea). In the following sonnet, Shakespeare, who at times helped himself generously from the Petrarchan stockpile, pokes fun at poets who thoughtlessly use such handed-down figures of speech.

William Shakespeare (1564 – 1616)*
MY MISTRESS' EYES ARE NOTHING LIKE THE SUN   1609

My mistress' eyes are nothing like the sun;
Coral is far more red than her lips' red;
If snow be white, why then her breasts are dun;
If hairs be wires, black wires grow on her head.
I have seen roses damasked red and white,   5
But no such roses see I in her cheeks;
And in some perfumes is there more delight
Than in the breath that from my mistress reeks.
I love to hear her speak, yet well I know
That music hath a far more pleasing sound;   10
I grant I never saw a goddess go:
My mistress, when she walks, treads on the ground.
   And yet, by heaven, I think my love as rare
   As any she°, belied with false compare.   *woman*

Contrary to what you might expect, for years after Shakespeare's time, poets continued to write fine poems with Petrarchan conventions.

Thomas Campion (1567 – 1620)*
THERE IS A GARDEN IN HER FACE   1617

  There is a garden in her face
Where roses and white lilies grow;
  A heav'nly paradise is that place
Wherein all pleasant fruits do flow.
   There cherries grow which none may buy   5
   Till "Cherry-ripe" themselves do cry.

Those cherries fairly do enclose
Of orient pearl a double row,
  Which when her lovely laughter shows,
They look like rose-buds filled with snow;
    Yet them nor° peer nor prince can buy,   *neither*
    Till "Cherry-ripe" themselves do cry.

  Her eyes like angels watch them still;
Her brows like bended bows do stand,
  Threat'ning with piercing frowns to kill   15
All that attempt, with eye or hand
    Those sacred cherries to come nigh
    Till "Cherry-ripe" themselves do cry.

THERE IS A GARDEN IN HER FACE. 6. *"Cherry-ripe"*: cry of fruit-peddlers in London streets.

QUESTIONS

1. What does Campion's song owe to Petrarchan tradition?
2. What in it strikes you as fresh observation of actual life?
3. Comment in particular on the last stanza. Does the comparison of eyebrows to threatening bowmen seem too silly or far-fetched? What sense do you find in it?
4. Try to describe the tone of this poem. What do you understand, from this portrait of a young girl, to be the poet's feelings?

     Excellent poetry might be easier to recognize if each poet had a fixed position on the slopes of Mount Parnassus, but from one century to the next, the reputations of some poets have taken humiliating slides, or made impressive clambers. We decide for ourselves which poems to call excellent, but readers of the future may reverse our opinions. Most of us no longer would share this popular view of Walt Whitman by one of his contemporaries:

> Walt Whitman (1819 – 1892), by some regarded as a great poet; by others, as no poet at all. Most of his so-called poems are mere catalogues of things, without meter or rime, but in a few more regular poems and in lines here and there he is grandly poetical, as in "O Captain! My Captain!"[1]

---

[1]J. Willis Westlake, A.M., in *Common-school Literature, English and American, with Several Hundred Extracts to be Memorized* (Philadelphia, 1898).

Walt Whitman (1819 – 1892)*

O CAPTAIN! MY CAPTAIN! 1865

O Captain! my Captain! our fearful trip is done,
The ship has weather'd every rack, the prize we sought is won,
The port is near, the bells I hear, the people all exulting,
While follow eyes the steady keel, the vessel grim and daring;
    But O heart! heart! heart!   5
      O the bleeding drops of red,
        Where on the deck my Captain lies,
          Fallen cold and dead.

O Captain! my Captain! rise up and hear the bells;
Rise up — for you the flag is flung — for you the bugle trills,   10
For you bouquets and ribbon'd wreaths — for you the shores
    a-crowding,
For you they call, the swaying mass, their eager faces turning;
      Here Captain! dear father!
      This arm beneath your head!
        It is some dream that on the deck,   15
        You've fallen cold and dead.

My Captain does not answer, his lips are pale and still,
My father does not feel my arm, he has no pulse nor will,
The ship is anchor'd safe and sound, its voyage closed and done,
From fearful trip the victor ship comes in with object won;   20
      Exult O shores, and ring O bells!
      But I with mournful tread,
        Walk the deck my Captain lies,
          Fallen cold and dead.

O CAPTAIN! MY CAPTAIN! Written soon after the death of Abraham Lincoln, this was, in Whitman's lifetime, by far the most popular of his poems.

QUESTIONS

1. Compare this with other Whitman poems. (See another elegy for Lincoln, "When Lilacs Last in the Dooryard Bloom'd," quoted in part on page 584.) In what ways is "O Captain! My Captain!" uncharacteristic of his works? Do you agree with J. Willis Westlake that this is one of the few occasions on which Whitman is "grandly poetical?"
2. Comment on the appropriateness to its subject of the poem's rhythms.
3. Do you find any evidence in this poem that an excellent poet wrote it?

There is nothing to do but commit ourselves and praise or blame and, if need be, let time erase our error. In a sense, all readers of poetry are constantly reexamining the judgments of the past by choosing those poems they care to go on reading. In the end, we have to admit that the critical principles set forth in this chapter are all very well for admiring excellent poetry we already know, but they cannot be carried like a yardstick in the hand, to go out looking for it. As Ezra Pound said in his *ABC of Reading,* "A classic is classic not because it conforms to certain structural rules, or fits certain definitions (of which its author had quite probably never heard). It is classic because of a certain eternal and irrepressible freshness."

The best poems, like "Sailing to Byzantium," may offer a kind of religious experience. In the eighth decade of the twentieth century, some of us rarely set foot outside an artificial environment. Whizzing down four-lane superhighways, we observe lakes and trees in the distance. In a way our cities are to us as anthills are to ants: no less than anthills, they are "natural" structures. But the "unnatural" world of school or business is, as Wordsworth says, too much with us. Locked in the shells of our ambitions, our self-esteem, we forget our kinship to earth and sea. We fabricate self-justifications. But a great poem shocks us into another order of perception. It points beyond language to something still more essential. It ushers us into an experience so moving and true that we feel (to quote King Lear) "cut to the brain." In bad or indifferent poetry, words are all there is.

Thomas Gray (1716 – 1771)*
Elegy Written in a Country Churchyard 1753

The curfew tolls the knell of parting day,
   The lowing herd wind slowly o'er the lea,
The plowman homeward plods his weary way,
   And leaves the world to darkness and to me.

Now fades the glimmering landscape on the sight,   5
   And all the air a solemn stillness holds,
Save where the beetle wheels his droning flight,
   And drowsy tinklings lull the distant folds;

Save that from yonder ivy-mantled tower
   The moping owl does to the moon complain   10
Of such, as wand'ring near her secret bower,
   Molest her ancient solitary reign.

Beneath those rugged elms, that yew tree's shade,
   Where heaves the turf in many a mold'ring heap,
Each in his narrow cell forever laid,   15
   The rude° forefathers of the hamlet sleep.   *simple, ignorant*

The breezy call of incense-breathing morn,
   The swallow twitt'ring from the straw-built shed,
The cock's shrill clarion, or the echoing horn°,   *fox-hunters' horn*
   No more shall rouse them from their lowly bed.   20

For them no more the blazing hearth shall burn,
   Or busy housewife ply her evening care;
No children run to lisp their sire's return,
   Or climb his knees the envied kiss to share.

Oft did the harvest to their sickle yield,   25
   Their furrow oft the stubborn glebe° has broke;   *turf*
How jocund did they drive their team afield!
   How bowed the woods beneath their sturdy stroke!

Let not Ambition mock their useful toil,
   Their homely joys, and destiny obscure;   30
Nor Grandeur hear with a disdainful smile
   The short and simple annals of the poor.

The boast of heraldry°, the pomp of pow'r,   *noble birth*
   And all that beauty, all that wealth e'er gave,
Awaits alike th' inevitable hour.   35
   The paths of glory lead but to the grave.

Nor you, ye proud, impute to these the fault,
   If Mem'ry o'er their tomb no trophies raise,
Where through the long-drawn aisle and fretted° vault   *inlaid with designs*
   The pealing anthem swells the note of praise.   40

Can storied urn or animated bust
   Back to its mansion call the fleeting breath?
Can Honor's voice provoke the silent dust,
   Or Flatt'ry soothe the dull cold ear of Death?

Perhaps in this neglected spot is laid   45
   Some heart once pregnant with celestial fire;
Hands that the rod of empire might have swayed,
   Or waked to ecstasy the living lyre.

But knowledge to their eyes her ample page
   Rich with the spoils of time did ne'er unroll;   50
Chill Penury° repressed their noble rage,   *Poverty*
   And froze the genial current of the soul.

Full many a gem of purest ray serene,
   The dark unfathomed caves of ocean bear:
Full many a flower is born to blush unseen,   55
   And waste its sweetness on the desert air.

Some village Hampden, that with dauntless breast
   The little tyrant of his field withstood;
Some mute inglorious Milton here may rest,
   Some Cromwell, guiltless of his country's blood.   60

Th' applause of list'ning senates to command,
   The threats of pain and ruin to despise,
To scatter plenty o'er a smiling land,
   And read their hist'ry in a nation's eyes,

Their lot forbade; nor circumscribed alone   65
    Their growing virtues, but their crimes confined;
Forbade to wade through slaughter to a throne,
    And shut the gates of mercy on mankind,

The struggling pangs of conscious truth to hide,
    To quench the blushes of ingenuous° shame,   *innocent* 70
Or heap the shrine of Luxury and Pride
    With incense kindled at the Muse's flame.

Far from the madding° crowd's ignoble strife,   *frenzied*
    Their sober wishes never learned to stray;
Along the cool sequestered vale of life   75
    They kept the noiseless tenor° of their way.   *ongoing motion*

Yet ev'n these bones from insult to protect
    Some frail memorial still erected nigh,
With uncouth rhymes and shapeless sculpture decked,
    Implores the passing tribute of a sigh.   80

Their name, their years, spelt by th' unlettered Muse,
    The place of fame and elegy supply:
And many a holy text around she strews,
    That teach the rustic moralist to die.

For who to dumb Forgetfulness a prey,   85
    This pleasing anxious being e'er resigned,
Left the warm precincts of the cheerful day,
    Nor cast one longing ling'ring look behind?

On some fond breast the parting soul relies,
    Some pious drops the closing eye requires;   90
Ev'n from the tomb the voice of Nature cries,
    Ev'n in our ashes live their wonted° fires.   *customary*

For thee, who mindful of th' unhonored dead
    Dost in these lines their artless tale relate;
If chance°, by lonely contemplation led,   *if by chance* 95
    Some kindred spirit shall inquire thy fate,

Haply° some hoary-headed swain° may say,   *perhaps; gray-haired shepherd*
    "Oft have we seen him at the peep of dawn
Brushing with hasty steps the dews away
    To meet the sun upon the upland lawn.   100

"There at the foot of yonder nodding beech
    That wreathes its old fantastic roots so high,
His listless length at noontide would he stretch,
    And pore upon the brook that babbles by.

"Hard by yon wood, now smiling as in scorn,   105
    Mutt'ring his wayward fancies he would rove,
Now drooping, woeful wan, like one forlorn,
    Or crazed with care, or crossed in hopeless love.

"One morn I missed him, on the customed hill,
   Along the heath and near his fav'rite tree;   110
Another came; not yet beside the rill°,   *brook*
   Nor up the lawn, nor at the wood was he;

"The next with dirges due in sad array
   Slow through the churchway path we saw him borne.
Approach and read (for thou canst read) the lay°,   *song or poem* 115
   Graved on the stone beneath yon aged thorn."

The Epitaph

Here rests his head upon the lap of Earth
   A youth to Fortune and to Fame unknown.
Fair Science° frowned not on his humble birth,   *Knowledge*
   And Melancholy marked him for her own.   120

Large was his bounty, and his soul sincere,
   Heav'n did a recompense as largely send:
He gave to Mis'ry all he had, a tear,
   He gained from Heav'n ('twas all he wished) a friend.

No farther seek his merits to disclose,   125
   Or draw his frailties from their dread abode,
(There they alike in trembling hope repose),
   The bosom of His Father and his God.

ELEGY WRITTEN IN A COUNTRY CHURCHYARD. In English poetry, an **elegy** has come to mean a lament or a sadly meditative poem, sometimes written on the occasion of a death. Other elegies in this book include Chidiock Tichborne's "Elegy," Milton's "Lycidas," A. E. Housman's "To an Athlete Dying Young," and in more recent poetry, "The Rites for Cousin Vit" by Gwendolyn Brooks and "Elegy for Jane" by Theodore Roethke. 41. *storied urn:* vessel holding the ashes of the dead after cremation. *Storied* can mean (1) decorated with scenes; (2) inscribed with a life's story; or (3) celebrated in story or history. The *animated bust* is a lifelike sculpture of the dead, placed on a tomb. 57. *Hampden:* John Hampden (1594 – 1643), member of Parliament, had resisted illegal taxes on his lands imposed by Charles I. 60. *Cromwell . . . his country's blood:* Gray blames Oliver Cromwell (1599 – 1658) for strife and tyranny. As general of the armies of Parliament, Cromwell had won the Civil War against Charles I and had signed the king's death warrant. As Lord Protector of England (1653 – 1658), he had ruled with an iron hand. 71 – 72: *heap the shrine . . . Muse's flame:* Gray chides mercenary poets who write poems to please their rich, high-living patrons.

QUESTIONS

1. In contrasting the unknown poor buried in this village churchyard and famous men buried in cathedrals (in *fretted vault,* line 39), what is Gray's theme? What do you understand from the line, *The paths of glory lead but to the grave?*
2. Carl J. Weber thinks that Gray's compassion for the village poor anticipates the democratic sympathies of the American Revolution: "Thomas Gray is the pioneer literary spokesman for the Ordinary Man." But another critic, Lyle Glazier, argues that the "Elegy" isn't political at all: that we misread if we think the poet meant "to persuade the poor and obscure that their barren lives are meaningful"; and also misread if we think he meant to assure the privileged classes "in whose ranks Gray was proud to consider himself" that they need not worry about the poor, "who have already all essential riches." How much truth do you find in either of these views?

3. Cite lines and phrases that show Gray's concern for the musical qualities of words.
4. Who is the *youth* of the closing Epitaph? By *thee* (line 93) does Gray mean himself? Does he mean some fictitious poet supposedly writing the "Elegy" — the first-person speaker (line 4)? Does he mean some village stonecutter, a crude poet whose illiterate Muse (line 81) inspired him to compose tombstone epitaphs? Or could the Epitaph possibly refer to Gray's close friend of school and undergraduate days, the promising poet Richard West, who had died in 1742? Which interpretation seems to you the most reasonable? (Does our lack of absolute certainty negate the value of the poem?)
5. Walter Savage Landor called the Epitaph a tin kettle tied to the tail of a noble dog. Do you agree that the Epitaph is inferior to what has gone before it? What is its function in Gray's poem?
6. Many sources for Gray's phrases and motifs have been found in earlier poets: Virgil, Horace, Dante, Milton, and many more. Even if it could be demonstrated that Gray's poem has not one original line in it, would it be possible to dismiss the "Elegy" as a mere rag-bag of borrowings?
7. Gray's poem, a pastoral elegy, is in the same genre as another famous English poem: John Milton's "Lycidas." What conventions are common to both?
8. In the earliest surviving manuscript of Gray's poem, lines 73 – 76 read:

No more with Reason and thyself at strife;
Give anxious cares and endless wishes room
But through the cool sequester'd vale of Life
Pursue the silent tenor of thy doom.

In what ways does the final version of those lines seem superior?
9. Perhaps the best-known poem in English, Gray's "Elegy" has inspired hundreds of imitations, countless parodies, and translations into eighteen or more languages. (Some of these languages contain dozens of attempts to translate it.) To what do you attribute the poem's fame? What do you suppose has proved so universally appealing in it?
10. Compare Gray's "Elegy" with Shelley's "Ozymandias" and Arthur Guiterman's "On the Vanity of Earthly Greatness." What do the three poems have in common? How would you rank them in order of excellence?

David Bottoms (b. 1949)
SMOKING IN AN OPEN GRAVE   1980

We bury ourselves to get high.
Huddled in this open crypt we lay the bottle,
the lantern, the papers, the bag on a marble slab,
tune the guitar to a mouth harp
and choir out the old spirituals.   5
When the shadows of this life have grown, I'll fly away.

Across Confederate Row an owl hoots our departure
and half-fallen brick becomes a porthole filled with stars.
We lay our ears against the clay wall;
at the foot of the hill the river whispers on its track.   10
It's a strange place where graves go,
so much of us already geared for the journey.

1. What ironies do you detect in this poem? What contrasts between past and present?
2. "Like Thomas Gray, David Bottoms speaks for the Graveyard School in poetry. As does Gray in his celebrated 'Elegy,' Bottoms both affirms truth about the dead and appears to be making his own personal statement." Discuss this critical opinion.
3. How would you evaluate "Smoking in an Open Grave" — good, bad, indifferent, or excellent? Refer to the poem in supporting your evaluation.

Maria Lowell (1821 – 1853)

AN OPIUM FANTASY   (1853)

Soft hangs the opiate in the brain,
And lulling soothes the edge of pain,
Till harshest sound, far off or near,
Sings floating in its mellow sphere.

What wakes me from my heavy dream?   5
    Or am I still asleep?
Those long and soft vibrations seem
    A slumberous charm to keep.

The graceful play, a moment stopped,
    Distance again unrolls,   10
Like silver balls, that, softly dropped,
    Ring into golden bowls.

I question of the poppies red,
    The fairy flaunting band,
While I a weed, with drooping head,   15
    Within their phalanx stand.

"Some airy one, with scarlet cap,
    The name unfold to me
Of this new minstrel, who can lap
    Sleep in his melody?"   20

Bright grew their scarlet-kerchiefed heads,
    As freshening winds had blown,
And from their gently swaying beds
    They sang in undertone,

"Oh, he is but a little owl,   25
    The smallest of his kin,
Who sits beneath the midnight's cowl,
    And makes this airy din."

"Deceitful tongues, of fiery tints,
    Far more than this you know, —   30
That he is your enchanted prince,
    Doomed as an owl to go;

"Nor his fond play for years hath stopped,
    But nightly he unrolls
His silver balls, that, softly dropped,   35
    Ring into golden bowls."

AN OPIUM FANTASY. Maria White Lowell, born into a distinguished, intellectually vigorous
New England family, became the first wife of a poet widely admired in his time, James Russell
Lowell. Her health, never robust, sharply deteriorated following the early deaths of three of
her four children. In her last years she became an invalid, no doubt a taker of opium, then
commonly prescribed to induce sleep. Only after her death (at thirty-two) was her work
collected, but obscurely: in a book her husband had printed privately in an edition of fifty
copies. (In 1936 Hope Jillson Vernon edited a scholarly edition, *The Poems of Maria Lowell;*
Providence: Brown University Studies.) Another poet of the same family, Amy Lowell,
remarked of "An Opium Fantasy": "That is *poetry*! It is better than anything her husband ever
wrote, and he always said that she was a better poet than he."

QUESTIONS

1. What imagery do you find in "An Opium Fantasy"? What one image particularly stands out?
2. In the fifth stanza ("'Some airy one . . .'"), who is speaking? Who drops the
   silver balls into the golden bowls?
3. What does this poem have in common with David Bottoms's "Smoking in an
   Open Grave"? How is it dissimilar?
4. Do you call this poem bad, good, or (with Amy Lowell) excellent? Give reasons
   for your evaluation.

SUGGESTIONS FOR WRITING

1. Concoct the worst poem you can write and, in a brief accompanying essay,
   recount the difficulties you met and overcame in writing it. Quote, for instance,
   any lines you thought of but had to discard for not being bad enough.
2. Selecting from the exercise "Fine or Shoddy Tenderness" a poem by Hart Crane,
   Eliza Cook, D. H. Lawrence, or Alfred, Lord Tennyson, attack it on the grounds
   that it is sentimental — or argue that it successfully communicates deep feelings.
3. In Chapter 29, "Poems for Further Reading," find a poem you especially admire,
   or dislike. In a brief essay (300 – 500 words), evaluate it. Refer to particulars in
   the poem to support your opinion of it.

28 What Is Poetry?

Archibald MacLeish (1892 – 1982)

Ars Poetica°   *Art of Poetry*   1926

A poem should be palpable and mute
As a globed fruit,

Dumb
As old medallions to the thumb,

Silent as the sleeve-worn stone   5
Of casement ledges where the moss has grown —

A poem should be wordless
As the flight of birds.

A poem should be motionless in time
As the moon climbs,   10

Leaving, as the moon releases
Twig by twig the night-entangled trees,

Leaving, as the moon behind the winter leaves,
Memory by memory the mind —

A poem should be motionless in time   15
As the moon climbs.

A poem should be equal to:
Not true.

For all the history of grief
An empty doorway and a maple leaf.   20

For love
The leaning grasses and two lights above the sea —

A poem should not mean
But be.

What is poetry? By now, perhaps, you have formed your own idea, whether or not you feel you can define it. Robert Frost made an attempt at a definition: "A poem is an idea caught in the act of dawning." Just in case further efforts at definition can be useful, here are a few memorable ones (including, for a second look, some given earlier):

> the art of uniting pleasure with truth by calling imagination to the help of reason.
> — Samuel Johnson

> the best words in the best order.
> — Samuel Taylor Coleridge

> the record of the best and happiest moments of the happiest and best minds.
> — Percy Bysshe Shelley

> musical Thought.
> — Thomas Carlyle

> at bottom a criticism of life.
> — Matthew Arnold

> If I read a book and it makes my whole body so cold no fire can ever warm me, I know that it is poetry. If I feel physically as if the top of my head were taken off, I know that it is poetry. These are the only ways I know it. Is there any other way?
> — Emily Dickinson

> speech framed . . . to be heard for its own sake and interest even over and above its interest of meaning.
> — Gerard Manley Hopkins

> a revelation in words by means of the words.
> — Wallace Stevens

> not the assertion that something is true, but the making of that truth more fully real to us.
> — T. S. Eliot

> the body of linguistic constructions that men usually refer to as poems.
> — J. V. Cunningham

> the clear expression of mixed feelings.
> — W. H. Auden

A poem differs from most prose in several ways. For one, both writer and reader tend to regard it differently. The poet's attitude is something like this: I offer this piece of writing to be read not as prose but as a poem — that is, more perceptively, thoughtfully, and considerately, with more attention to sounds and connotations. This is a great deal to expect, but in return, the reader, too, has a right to certain expectations. Approaching the poem in the anticipation of out-of-the-ordinary knowledge and pleasure, the reader assumes that the poem may use certain enjoyable devices not available to prose: rime, alliteration, meter, and rhythms — definite, various, or emphatic. (The poet may not *always* decide to use these things.) The reader expects the poet to make greater use, perhaps, of resources of meaning such as figurative language, allusion, symbol, and imagery. As readers of prose we might seek no more than meaning: no more than what could be paraphrased without serious loss. Meeting any figurative language or graceful turns of word order, we think them pleasant extras. But in poetry all these "extras" matter as much as the paraphraseable content, if not more. For, when we finish reading a good poem, we cannot explain precisely to ourselves what we have experienced — without repeating, word for word, the language of the poem itself.

"Poetry is to prose as dancing is to walking," remarked Paul Valéry. It is doubtful, however, that anyone can draw an immovable boundary between poetry and prose. Certain prose needs only to be arranged in lines to be seen as poetry — especially prose that conveys strong emotion in vivid, physical imagery and in terse, figurative, rhythmical language. Even in translation the words of Chief Joseph of the Nez Percé tribe, at the moment of his surrender to the U.S. Army in 1877, still move us and are memorable:

> Hear me, my warriors, my heart is sick and sad:
> Our chiefs are killed,
> The old men all are dead,
> It is cold and we have no blankets.
>
> The little children freeze to death.
>
> Hear me, my warriors, my heart is sick and sad:
> From where the sun now stands I will fight no more forever.

It may be that a poem can point beyond words to something still more essential. Language has its limits, and probably Edgar Allan Poe was the only poet ever to claim he could always find words for whatever he wished to express. For, of all a human being can experience and imagine, words say only part. "Human speech," said Flaubert, who strove after the best of it, "is like a cracked kettle on which we hammer out tunes to make bears dance, when what we long for is the compassion of the stars."

Like Yeats's chestnut-tree in "Among School Children" (which when asked whether it is leaf, blossom, or bole, has no answer), a poem is to be seen not as a confederation of form, rime, image, metaphor, tone, and theme, but as a whole. We study a poem one element at a time because the intellect best comprehends what it can separate. But only our total attention, involving the participation of our blood and marrow, can see all elements in a poem fused, all dancing together. Yeats knew how to make poems and how to read them:

> God guard me from those thoughts men think
> In the mind alone;
> He that sings a lasting song
> Thinks in a marrow-bone.

Throughout this book, we have been working on the assumption that the patient and conscious explication of poems will sharpen unconscious perceptions. We can only hope that it will; the final test lies in whether you care to go on by yourself, reading other poems, finding in them pleasure and enlightenment. Pedagogy must have a stop; so too must the viewing of poems as if their elements fell into chapters. For the total experience of reading a poem surpasses the mind's categories. The wind in the grass, says a proverb, cannot be taken into the house.

29 Poems for Further Reading

Sit a while dear son,
Here are biscuits to eat and here is milk to drink,
But as soon as you sleep and renew yourself in sweet clothes,
I kiss you with a good-by kiss and open the gates for your egress
    hence.

Long enough have you dream'd contemptible dreams,
Now I wash the gum from your eyes,
You must habit yourself to the dazzle of the light and of every
    moment of your life.

Long have you timidly waded holding a plank by the shore,
Now I will you to be a bold swimmer,
To jump off in the midst of the sea, rise again, nod to me, shout, and
    laughingly dash with your hair.
        — Walt Whitman, "Song of Myself"

Anonymous (traditional Scottish ballad)

EDWARD

"Why dois your brand° sae° drap wi' bluid,   *sword; so*
      Edward, Edward?
Why dois your brand sae drap wi' bluid?
  And why sae sad gang° yee, O?"   *go*
"O, I hae killed my hauke sae guid,   5
      Mither, mither,
O, I hae killed my hauke sae guid,
  And I had nae mair bot° hee, O."   *but*

"Your haukis bluid was nevir sae reid,
      Edward, Edward,   10
Your haukis bluid was nevir sae reid,
  My deir son I tell thee, O."
"O, I hae killed my reid-roan steid,
      Mither, mither,
O, I hae killed my reid-roan steid,   15
  That erst° was sa fair and frie°, O."   *once; free*

"Your steid was auld, and ye hae gat mair,
      Edward, Edward,
Your steid was auld, and ye hae gat mair,
  Sum other dule° ye drie°, O."   *sorrow; suffer* 20
"O, I hae killed my fadir deir,
      Mither, mither,
O, I hae killed my fadir deir,
  Alas, and wae° is mee, O!"   *woe*

"And whatten penance wul ye drie for that,   25
      Edward, Edward?
And whatten penance will ye drie for that?
  My deir son, now tell me, O."
"Ile set my feit in yonder boat,
      Mither, mither,   30
Ile set my feit in yonder boat,
  And Ile fare ovir the sea, O."

"And what wul ye doe wi' your towirs and your ha'°,   *hall*
      Edward, Edward,
And what wul ye doe wi' your towirs and your ha',   35
  That were sae fair to see, O?"
"Ile let thame stand tul they doun fa',
      Mither, mither,
Ile let thame stand tul they doun fa',
  For here nevir mair maun° I bee, O."   *must* 40

"And what wul ye leive to your bairns° and your wife,   *children*
   Edward, Edward?
And what wul ye leive to your bairns and your wife,
   When ye gang ovir the sea, O?"
"The warldis° room, late° them beg thrae° life,   *world's; let; through* 45
   Mither, mither
The warldis room, late them beg thrae life,
   For thame nevir mair wul I see, O."

"And what wul ye leive to your ain° mither deir,   *own*
   Edward, Edward?   50
And what wul ye leive to your ain mither deir?
   My deir son, now tell me, O."
"The curse of hell frae me sall ye beir,
   Mither, mither,
The curse of hell frae me sall ye beir,   55
   Sic° counseils° ye gave to me, O."   *such; counsel*

Anonymous (traditional Scottish ballad)
SIR PATRICK SPENCE

The king sits in Dumferling toune,
   Drinking the blude-reid wine:
"O whar will I get guid sailor
   To sail this schip of mine?"

Up and spak an eldern knicht,   5
   Sat at the kings richt kne:
"Sir Patrick Spence is the best sailor
   That sails upon the se."

The king has written a braid letter,
   And signed it wi' his hand,   10
And sent it to Sir Patrick Spence,
   Was walking on the sand.

The first line that Sir Patrick red,
   A loud lauch lauchèd he;
The next line that Sir Patrick red,   15
   The teir blinded his ee.

"O wha° is this has don this deid,   *who*
   This ill deid don to me,
To send me out this time o' the yeir,
   To sail upon the se!   20

"Mak haste, mak haste, my mirry men all,
   Our guid schip sails the morne."
"O say na sae°, my master deir,   *so*
   For I feir a deadlie storme.

"Late late yestreen I saw the new moone,   25
    Wi' the auld moone in hir arme,
And I feir, I feir, my deir master,
    That we will cum to harme."

O our Scots nobles wer richt laith°   *loath*
    To weet° their cork-heild schoone°;   *wet; shoes* 30
Bot lang owre° a' the play wer playd,   *before*
    Their hats they swam aboone°.   *above (their heads)*

O lang, lang may their ladies sit,
    Wi' their fans into their hand,
Or ere° they se Sir Patrick Spence   *long before* 35
    Cum sailing to the land.

O lang, lang may the ladies stand,
    Wi' their gold kems° in their hair,   *combs*
Waiting for their ain° deir lords,   *own*
    For they'll se thame na mair.   40

Haf owre°, haf owre to Aberdour,   *halfway over*
    It's fiftie fadom deip,
And thair lies guid Sir Patrick Spence,
    Wi' the Scots lords at his feit.

Sir Patrick Spence. 9. *braid:* Broad, but broad in what sense? Among guesses are *plain-spoken, official,* and *on wide paper.*

Anonymous (traditional English ballad)

The Three Ravens

There were three ravens sat on a tree,
    Down a down, hay down, hay down,
There were three ravens sat on a tree,
    With a down,
There were three ravens sat on a tree,   5
They were as black as they might be.
    With a down derry, derry, derry, down, down.

The one of them said to his mate,
"Where shall we our breakfast take?"

"Down in yonder greene field,   10
There lies a knight slain under his shield.

"His hounds they lie down at his feet,
So well they can their master keep.

"His hawks they fly so eagerly,
There's no fowl dare him come nigh."   15

Down there comes a fallow doe,
As great with young as she might go.

She lift up his bloody head,
And kist his wounds that were so red.

She got him up upon her back,   20
And carried him to earthen lake°.   *the grave*

She buried him before the prime,
She was dead herself ere evensong time.

God send every gentleman
Such hawks, such hounds, and such a leman°.   *lover* 25

THE THREE RAVENS. The lines of refrain are repeated in each stanza. "Perhaps in the folk mind
the doe is the form the soul of a human mistress, now dead, has taken," Albert B. Friedman
has suggested (in *The Viking Book of Folk Ballads*). "Most probably the knight's beloved was
understood to be an enchanted woman who was metamorphosed at certain times into an
animal." 22 – 23. *prime, evensong:* two of the canonical hours set aside for prayer and worship.
Prime is at dawn, evensong at dusk.

Anonymous (traditional Scottish ballad)
THE TWA CORBIES

As I was walking all alane,
I heard twa corbies° making a mane°;   *ravens; moan*
The tane° unto the t'other say,   *one*
"Where sall we gang° and dine today?"   *go*

"In behint yon auld fail dyke°,   *turf wall* 5
I wot° there lies a new slain knight;   *know*
And naebody kens° that he lies there,   *knows*
But his hawk, his hound, and lady fair.

"His hound is to the hunting gane,
His hawk to fetch the wild-fowl hame,   10
His lady's ta'en another mate,
So we may mak our dinner sweet.

"Ye'll sit on his white hause-bane°,   *neck bone*
And I'll pike out his bonny blue een;
Wi' ae° lock o' his gowden hair   *one* 15
We'll theek° our nest when it grows bare.   *thatch*

"Mony a one for him makes mane,
But nane sall ken where he is gane;
O'er his white banes, when they are bare,
The wind sall blaw for evermair."   20

THE TWA CORBIES. Sir Walter Scott, the first to print this ballad in his *Minstrelsy of the Scottish
Border* (1802 – 1803), calls it "rather a counterpart than a copy" of "The Three Ravens." M.
J. C. Hodgart and other scholars think he may have written most of it himself.

Anonymous (English lyric)

SUMER IS ICUMEN IN   (thirteenth century)

Sumer is icumen in	Summer is acoming in —
Lhude sing cuccu	Loudly sing, cuckoo!
Groweþ sed and bloweþ med	Groweth seed and bloweth mead
and springþ þe wde nu	And springeth the wood new.
Sing cuccu	Sing, cuckoo! 5
Awe bleteþ after lomb	Ewe bleateth after lamb,
Ihouþ after calue cu	Loweth after calf cow,
Bulluc sterteþ bucke uerteþ	Bullock starteth, buck farteth —
Murie sing cuccu	Merrily sing, cuckoo!
Cuccu cuccu	Cuckoo, cuckoo, 10
Wel singes þu cuccu	Well singest thou, cuckoo!
ne swik þu nauer nu	Cease thou never now.
Sing cuccu nu Sing cuccu	Sing, cuckoo now! Sing, cuckoo!
Sing cuccu Sing cuccu nu	Sing, cuckoo! Sing, cuckoo, now!

SUMER IS ICUMEN IN. On the left, this famous song is printed as it appears in a thirteenth-century manuscript: a commonplace book, or book of songs and obituaries set down by various monks at Reading Abbey (Harley manuscript 978, now in the British Museum). On the right, words and spellings have been modernized and punctuation added, but word-order kept unaltered. In the opening line, *acoming* is not quite a faithful translation: *is icumen* means "has come." Summer is already here. The character þ is called a *thorn,* and is pronounced like the spelling *th.* 8. *starteth:* starts, jumps up and runs.

Anonymous (English lyric)

I SING OF A MAIDEN   (fifteenth century)

I sing of a maiden	that is makeless°,	*matchless (or mateless)*
King of alle kinges	to° her son che ches°.	*to be; she chose*
He cam all so stille	there° his moder was	*where*
As dew in Aprille	that falleth on the grass.	
He cam all so stille	to his moderes bower	5
As dew in Aprille	that falleth on the flower.	
He cam all so stille	there his moder lay	
As dew in Aprille	that falleth on the spray.	
Moder and maiden	was never none but she —	
Well may swich° a lady	Godes moder be.	*such* 10

I SING OF A MAIDEN. To keep the rhythm, pronounce the final *e* in *alle, stille,* and *Aprille* like *e* in *the.* 5. *bower:* dwelling place, room, or bedchamber.

Anonymous (English lyric)

WESTERN WIND

(about 1500)

Western wind, when wilt thou blow,
The° small rain down can rain?   *(so that) the*
Christ, if my love were in my arms,
And I in my bed again!

Matthew Arnold (1822 – 1888)

DOVER BEACH

1867

The sea is calm tonight.
The tide is full, the moon lies fair
Upon the straits; — on the French coast the light
Gleams and is gone; the cliffs of England stand,
Glimmering and vast, out in the tranquil bay.   5
Come to the window, sweet is the night-air!
Only, from the long line of spray
Where the sea meets the moon-blanched land,
Listen! you hear the grating roar
Of pebbles which the waves draw back, and fling,   10
At their return, up the high strand,
Begin, and cease, and then again begin,
With tremulous cadence slow, and bring
The eternal note of sadness in.

Sophocles long ago   15
Heard it on the Aegean, and it brought
Into his mind the turbid ebb and flow
Of human misery; we
Find also in the sound a thought,
Hearing it by this distant northern sea.   20

The Sea of Faith
Was once, too, at the full, and round earth's shore
Lay like the folds of a bright girdle furled.
But now I only hear
Its melancholy, long, withdrawing roar,   25
Retreating, to the breath
Of the night-wind, down the vast edges drear
And naked shingles° of the world.   *gravel beaches*

Ah, love, let us be true
To one another! for the world, which seems   30
To lie before us like a land of dreams,
So various, so beautiful, so new,
Hath really neither joy, nor love, nor light,
Nor certitude, nor peace, nor help for pain;

And we are here as on a darkling° plain   *darkened or darkening*   35
Swept with confused alarms of struggle and flight,
Where ignorant armies clash by night.

John Ashbery (b. 1927)*
CITY AFTERNOON   1975

A veil of haze protects this
Long-ago afternoon forgotten by everybody
In this photograph, most of them now
Sucked screaming through old age and death.

If one could seize America   5
Or at least a fine forgetfulness
That seeps into our outline
Defining our volumes with a stain
That is fleeting too
But commemorates   10
Because it does define, after all:
Gray garlands, that threesome
Waiting for the light to change,
Air lifting the hair of one
Upside down in the reflecting pool.   15

W. H. Auden (1907 – 1973)*
AS I WALKED OUT ONE EVENING   1940

As I walked out one evening,
    Walking down Bristol Street,
The crowds upon the pavement
    Were fields of harvest wheat.

And down by the brimming river   5
    I heard a lover sing
Under an arch of the railway:
    "Love has no ending.

"I'll love you, dear, I'll love you
    Till China and Africa meet,   10
And the river jumps over the mountain
    And the salmon sing in the street,

"I'll love you till the ocean
    Is folded and hung up to dry
And the seven stars go squawking   15
    Like geese about the sky.

"The years shall run like rabbits,
   For in my arms I hold
The Flower of the Ages,
   And the first love of the world."   20

But all the clocks in the city
   Began to whirr and chime:
"O let not Time deceive you,
   You cannot conquer Time.

"In the burrows of the Nightmare   25
   Where Justice naked is,
Time watches from the shadow
   And coughs when you would kiss.

"In headaches and in worry
   Vaguely life leaks away,   30
And Time will have his fancy
   Tomorrow or today.

"Into many a green valley
   Drifts the appalling snow;
Time breaks the threaded dances   35
   And the diver's brilliant bow.

"O plunge your hands in water,
   Plunge them in up to the wrist;
Stare, stare in the basin
   And wonder what you've missed.   40

"The glacier knocks in the cupboard,
   The desert sighs in the bed,
And the crack in the teacup opens
   A lane to the land of the dead.

"Where the beggars raffle the banknotes   45
   And the Giant is enchanting to Jack,
And the Lily-white Boy is a Roarer,
   And Jill goes down on her back.

"O look, look in the mirror,
   O look in your distress;   50
Life remains a blessing
   Although you cannot bless.

"O stand, stand at the window
   As the tears scald and start;
You shall love your crooked neighbor   55
   With your crooked heart."

It was late, late in the evening,
   The lovers they were gone;
The clocks had ceased their chiming,
   And the deep river ran on.   60

W. H. Auden (1907 – 1973)*

MUSÉE DES BEAUX ARTS   1940

About suffering they were never wrong,
The Old Masters: how well they understood
Its human position; how it takes place
While someone else is eating or opening a window or just walking
    dully along;
How, when the aged are reverently, passionately waiting   5
For the miraculous birth, there always must be
Children who did not specially want it to happen, skating
On a pond at the edge of the wood:
They never forgot
That even the dreadful martyrdom must run its course   10
Anyhow in a corner, some untidy spot
Where the dogs go on with their doggy life and the torturer's horse
Scratches its innocent behind on a tree.

In Brueghel's *Icarus,* for instance: how everything turns away
Quite leisurely from the disaster; the ploughman may   15
Have heard the splash, the forsaken cry,
But for him it was not an important failure; the sun shone
As it had to on the white legs disappearing into the green
Water; and the expensive delicate ship that must have seen
Something amazing, a boy falling out of the sky,   20
Had somewhere to get to and sailed calmly on.

COMPARE:

"Musée des Beaux Arts" with "The Dance" by William Carlos Williams (page 588) and the painting by Pieter Breughel (1502? – 1569) to which each poem refers. Also with "To a Friend Whose Work Has Come to Triumph" by Anne Sexton (page 764).

R. L. Barth (b. 1947)
THE INSERT   1981

Courage is of two kinds: First, physical courage . . .;
and next, moral courage. We speak only of the first.
                        — von Clausewitz

Our view of sky, jungle, and fields constricts
Into a sink hole covered with saw-grass

Undulating, soon whipped slant as the chopper
Hovers at four feet. Rapt, boot deep in slime,

We deploy ourselves in loose perimeter,   5
Listening for incoming rockets above

The thump of rotor blades; edgy for contact,
Junkies of terror impatient to shoot up.

Nothing moves, nothing sounds; then, single file,
We move across a stream-bed toward high ground.   10

The terror of the insert's quickly over.
Too quickly . . . And more quickly every time . . .

THE INSERT. R. L. Barth, a U.S. Marine in 1966 – 69, served as a long-range reconnaissance leader in Vietnam. An *insert* is the dropping of troops into an area by helicopter. The epigraph comes from *On War,* the major work of Karl von Clausewitz (1780 – 1831), Prussian officer and writer on military subjects.

COMPARE:

"The Insert" with the poems of Wilfred Owen: "Dulce et Decorum Est" (page 438) and "Anthem for Doomed Youth" (page 751).

Elizabeth Bishop (1911 – 1979)*
FILLING STATION   1965

Oh, but it is dirty!
— this little filling station,
oil-soaked, oil-permeated
to a disturbing, over-all
black translucency.   5
Be careful with that match!

690   Poems for Further Reading

Father wears a dirty,
oil-soaked monkey suit
that cuts him under the arms,
and several quick and saucy   10
and greasy sons assist him
(it's a family filling station),
all quite thoroughly dirty.

Do they live in the station?
It has a cement porch   15
behind the pumps, and on it
a set of crushed and grease-
impregnated wickerwork;
on the wicker sofa
a dirty dog, quite comfy.   20

Some comic books provide
the only note of color —
of certain color. They lie
upon a big dim doily
draping a taboret   25
(part of the set), beside
a big hirsute begonia.

Why the extraneous plant?
Why the taboret?
Why, oh why, the doily?   30
(Embroidered in daisy stitch
with marguerites, I think,
and heavy with gray crochet.)

Somebody embroidered the doily.
Somebody waters the plant,   35
or oils it, maybe. Somebody
arranges the rows of cans
so that they softly say:
ESSO — SO — SO — SO
to high-strung automobiles.   40
Somebody loves us all.

William Blake (1757 – 1827)*
The Sick Rose   1794

O Rose, thou art sick!
The invisible worm
That flies in the night,
In the howling storm,

Has found out thy bed   5
Of crimson joy,
And his dark secret love
Does thy life destroy.

William Blake (1757 – 1827)*
THE TYGER   1794

Tyger! Tyger! burning bright
In the forests of the night,
What immortal hand or eye
Could frame thy fearful symmetry?

In what distant deeps or skies   5
Burnt the fire of thine eyes?
On what wings dare he aspire?
What the hand dare seize the fire?

And what shoulder, and what art,
Could twist the sinews of thy heart?   10
And when thy heart began to beat,
What dread hand? and what dread feet?

What the hammer? what the chain?
In what furnace was thy brain?
What the anvil? what dread grasp   15
Dare its deadly terrors clasp?

When the stars threw down their spears,
And watered heaven with their tears,
Did he smile his work to see?
Did he who made the Lamb make thee?   20

Tyger! Tyger! burning bright
In the forests of the night,
What immortal hand or eye
Dare frame thy fearful symmetry?

Louise Bogan (1897 – 1970)
THE DREAM   1941

O God, in the dream the terrible horse began
To paw at the air, and make for me with his blows.
Fear kept for thirty-five years poured through his mane,
And retribution equally old, or nearly, breathed through his nose.

Coward complete, I lay and wept on the ground 5
When some strong creature appeared, and leapt for the rein.
Another woman, as I lay half in a swound,
Leapt in the air, and clutched at the leather and chain.

Give him, she said, something of yours as a charm.
Throw him, she said, some poor thing you alone claim. 10
No, no, I cried, he hates me; he's out for harm,
And whether I yield or not, it is all the same.

But, like a lion in a legend, when I flung the glove
Pulled from my sweating, my cold right hand,
The terrible beast, that no one may understand, 15
Came to my side, and put down his head in love.

Mark Alexander Boyd (1563 – 1601)

CUPID AND VENUS   (late sixteenth century)

Fra bank to bank, fra wood to wood I rin°,	*run*
Ourhailit° with my feeble fantasie,	*overcome*
Like til° a leaf that fallis from a tree	*to*
Or til a reed ourblawin with the win.	
Twa gods guides me: the ane of them is blin,	5
Yea, and a bairn° brocht up in vanitie,	*child*
The next a wife ingenrit° of the sea,	*engendered, born*
And lichter nor° a dauphin° with her fin.	*than; dolphin*
Unhappy is the man for evermair	
That tills the sand and sawis° in the air;	*sows* 10
But twice unhappier is he, I lairn,	
That feidis° in his hairt a mad desire	*feeds*
And follows on a woman thro the fire,	
Led by a blind and teachit by a bairn.	

Emily Brontë (1818 – 1848)

LOVE AND FRIENDSHIP   (1839)

Love is like the wild rose-briar,
Friendship like the holly-tree —
The holly is dark when the rose-briar blooms
But which will bloom most constantly?

The wild rose-briar is sweet in spring, 5
Its summer blossoms scent the air;
Yet wait till winter comes again
And who will call the wild-briar fair?

Then scorn the silly rose-wreath now
And deck thee with the holly's sheen,   10
That when December blights thy brow
He still may leave thy garland green.

Gwendolyn Brooks (b. 1917)*
THE RITES FOR COUSIN VIT   1949

Carried her unprotesting out the door.
Kicked back the casket-stand. But it can't hold her,
That stuff and satin aiming to enfold her,
The lid's contrition nor the bolts before.
Oh oh. Too much. Too much. Even now, surmise,   5
She rises in the sunshine. There she goes,
Back to the bars she knew and the repose
In love-rooms and the things in people's eyes.
Too vital and too squeaking. Must emerge.
Even now she does the snake-hips with a hiss,   10
Slops the bad wine across her shantung, talks
Of pregnancy, guitars and bridgework, walks
In parks or alleys, comes haply on the verge
Of happiness, haply hysterics. Is.

Gwendolyn Brooks (b. 1917)*
SADIE AND MAUD   1945

Maud went to college.
Sadie stayed at home.
Sadie scraped life
With a fine-tooth comb.

She didn't leave a tangle in.   5
Her comb found every strand.
Sadie was one of the livingest chits
In all the land.

Sadie bore two babies
Under her maiden name.   10
Maud and Ma and Papa
Nearly died of shame.

When Sadie said her last so-long
Her girls struck out from home.
(Sadie had left as heritage   15
Her fine-tooth comb.)

Maud, who went to college,
Is a thin brown mouse.
She is living all alone
In this old house.   20

Olga Broumas (b. 1949)

CINDERELLA   1977

> . . . *the joy that isn't shared*
> *I heard, dies young.*
> Anne Sexton, 1928 – 1974

Apart from my sisters, estranged
from my mother, I am a woman alone
in a house of men
who secretly
call themselves princes, alone   5
with me usually, under cover of dark. I am the one allowed in

to the royal chambers, whose small foot conveniently
fills the slipper of glass. The woman writer, the lady
umpire, the madam chairman, anyone's wife.
I know what I know.   10
And I once was glad

of the chance to use it, even alone
in a strange castle, doing overtime on my own, cracking
the royal code. The princes spoke
in their fathers' language, were eager to praise me   15
my nimble tongue. I am a woman in a state of siege, alone

as one piece of laundry, strung on a windy clothesline a
mile long. A woman co-opted by promises: the lure
of a job, the ruse of a choice, a woman forced
to bear witness, falsely   20
against my kind, as each
other sister was judged inadequate, bitchy, incompetent,
jealous, too thin, too fat. I know what I know.
What sweet bread I make

for myself in this prosperous house   25
is dirty, what good soup I boil turns
in my mouth to mud. Give
me my ashes. A cold stove, a cinder-block pillow, wet
canvas shoes in my sisters', my sisters' hut. Or I swear

I'll die young   30
like those favored before me, hand-picked each one
for her joyful heart.

Elizabeth Barrett Browning (1806 – 1861)*
HOW DO I LOVE THEE? LET ME COUNT THE WAYS   1850

How do I love thee? Let me count the ways.
I love thee to the depth and breadth and height
My soul can reach, when feeling out of sight
For the ends of being and ideal grace.
I love thee to the level of every day's   5
Most quiet need, by sun and candle-light.
I love thee freely, as men strive for right.
I love thee purely, as they turn from praise.
I love thee with the passion put to use
In my old griefs, and with my childhood's faith.   10
I love thee with a love I seemed to lose
With my lost saints. I love thee with the breath,
Smiles, tears, of all my life; and, if God choose,
I shall but love thee better after death.

Robert Browning (1812 – 1889)*
MY LAST DUCHESS   1842

Ferrara

That's my last Duchess painted on the wall,
Looking as if she were alive. I call
That piece a wonder, now; Frà Pandolf's hands
Worked busily a day, and there she stands.
Will 't please you sit and look at her? I said   5
"Frà Pandolf" by design, for never read
Strangers like you that pictured countenance,
The depth and passion of its earnest glance,
But to myself they turned (since none puts by
The curtain I have drawn for you, but I)   10
And seemed as they would ask me, if they durst,
How such a glance came there; so, not the first
Are you to turn and ask thus. Sir, 'twas not
Her husband's presence only, called that spot
Of joy into the Duchess' cheek; perhaps   15
Frà Pandolf chanced to say, "Her mantle laps
Over my lady's wrist too much," or "Paint

Must never hope to reproduce the faint
Half-flush that dies along her throat." Such stuff
Was courtesy, she thought, and cause enough   20
For calling up that spot of joy. She had
A heart — how shall I say? — too soon made glad,
Too easily impressed; she liked whate'er
She looked on, and her looks went everywhere.
Sir, 'twas all one! My favor at her breast,   25
The dropping of the daylight in the West,
The bough of cherries some officious fool
Broke in the orchard for her, the white mule
She rode with round the terrace — all and each
Would draw from her alike the approving speech,   30
Or blush, at least. She thanked men, — good! but thanked
Somehow — I know not how — as if she ranked
My gift of a nine-hundred-years' old name
With anybody's gift. Who'd stoop to blame
This sort of trifling? Even had you skill   35
In speech — which I have not — to make your will
Quite clear to such an one, and say "Just this
Or that in you disgusts me; here you miss,
Or there exceed the mark" — and if she let
Herself be lessoned so, nor plainly set   40
Her wits to yours, forsooth, and made excuse —
E'en then would be some stooping; and I choose
Never to stoop. Oh, sir, she smiled, no doubt,
Whene'er I passed her; but who passed without
Much the same smile? This grew; I gave commands;   45
Then all smiles stopped together. There she stands
As if alive. Will·'t please you rise? We'll meet
The company below, then. I repeat,
The Count your master's known munificence
Is ample warrant that no just pretense   50
Of mine for dowry will be disallowed;
Though his fair daughter's self, as I avowed
At starting, is my object. Nay, we'll go
Together down, sir. Notice Neptune, though,
Taming a sea-horse, thought a rarity,   55
Which Claus of Innsbruck cast in bronze for me!

My Last Duchess. Ferrara, a city in northern Italy, is the scene. Browning may have modeled
his speaker after Alonzo, Duke of Ferrara (1533 – 1598). 3. *Frà Pandolf* and 56. *Claus of Innsbruck:*
fictitious names of artists.

Robert Browning (1812 – 1889)*
SOLILOQUY OF THE SPANISH CLOISTER
1842

Gr-r-r — there go, my heart's abhorrence!
   Water your damned flower-pots, do!
If hate killed men, Brother Lawrence,
   God's blood, would not mine kill you!
What? your myrtle-bush wants trimming?   5
   Oh, that rose has prior claims —
Needs its leaden vase filled brimming?
   Hell dry you up with its flames!

At the meal we sit together;
   Salve tibi!° I must hear   *Hail to thee!* 10
Wise talk of the kind of weather,
   Sort of season, time of year:
Not a plenteous cork-crop: scarcely
   Dare we hope oak-galls, I doubt;
What's the Latin name for "parsley"?   15
   What's the Greek name for "swine's snout"?

Whew! We'll have our platter burnished,
   Laid with care on our own shelf!
With a fire-new spoon we're furnished,
   And a goblet for ourself,   20
Rinsed like something sacrificial
   Ere 'tis fit to touch our chaps —
Marked with L. for our initial!
   (He-he! There his lily snaps!)

Saint, forsooth! While Brown Dolores   25
   Squats outside the Convent bank
With Sanchicha, telling stories,
   Steeping tresses in the tank,
Blue-black, lustrous, thick like horsehairs,
   — Can't I see his dead eye glow,   30
Bright as 'twere a Barbary corsair's?
   (That is, if he'd let it show!)

When he finishes refection,
   Knife and fork he never lays
Cross-wise, to my recollection,   35
   As I do, in Jesu's praise.
I the Trinity illustrate,
   Drinking watered orange-pulp —
In three sips the Arian frustrate;
   While he drains his at one gulp!   40

Oh, those melons! if he's able
  We're to have a feast; so nice!
One goes to the Abbot's table,
  All of us get each a slice.
How go on your flowers? None double?   45
  Not one fruit-sort can you spy?
Strange! — And I, too, at such trouble,
  Keep them close-nipped on the sly!

There's a great text in Galatians,
  Once you trip on it, entails   50
Twenty-nine distinct damnations,
  One sure, if another fails;
If I trip him just a-dying,
  Sure of heaven as sure can be,
Spin him round and send him flying   55
  Off to hell, a Manichee?

Or, my scrofulous French novel
  On grey paper with blunt type!
Simply glance at it, you grovel
  Hand and foot in Belial's gripe;   60
If I double down its pages
  At the woeful sixteenth print,
When he gathers his greengages,
  Ope a sieve and slip it in't?

Or, there's Satan! — one might venture   65
  Pledge one's soul to him, yet leave
Such a flaw in the indenture
  As he'd miss till, past retrieve,
Blasted lay that rose-acacia
  We're so proud of! *Hy, Zy, Hine. . . .*   70
'St, there's Vespers! *Plena gratia*
  Ave, Virgo!° Gr-r-r — you swine!   *Hail, Virgin, full of grace!*

SOLILOQUY OF THE SPANISH CLOISTER. 3. *Brother Lawrence:* one of the speaker's fellow monks. 31. *Barbary corsair:* a pirate operating off the Barbary coast of Africa. 39. *Arian:* a follower of Arius, heretic who denied the doctrine of the Trinity. 49. *a great text in Galatians:* a difficult verse in this book of the Bible. Brother Lawrence will be damned as a heretic if he wrongly interprets it. 56. *Manichee:* another kind of heretic, one who (after the Persian philosopher Mani) sees in the world a constant struggle between good and evil, neither able to win. 60. *Belial:* Here, not specifically Satan but (as used in the Old Testament) a name for wickedness. 70. *Hy, Zy, Hine:* Possibly the sound of a bell to announce evening devotions.

Thomas Carew (1594? – 1640)

ASK ME NO MORE WHERE JOVE BESTOWS   1640

Ask me no more where Jove bestows,
When June is past, the fading rose;
For in your beauty's orient deep
These flowers, as in their causes, sleep.

Ask me no more whither do stray   5
The golden atoms of the day;
For in pure love heaven did prepare
Those powders to enrich your hair.

Ask me no more whither doth haste
The nightingale when May is past,   10
For in your sweet dividing throat
She winters, and keeps warm her note.

Ask me no more where those stars light
That downwards fall in dead of night,
For in your eyes they sit, and there   15
Fixèd become, as in their sphere.

Ask me no more if east or west
The phoenix builds her spicy nest,
For unto you at last she flies
And in your fragrant bosom dies.   20

ASK ME NO MORE WHERE JOVE BESTOWS. 3. *orient:* radiant, glowing. (In our time, this sense of the word is obsolete.) 4. *These flowers . . . sleep:* as they slept before they came into existence. (A *cause,* that which gives being, is a term from Aristotle and the Scholastic philosophers.) 11. *dividing:* singing, uttering a **"division"** or melodic phrase added to a basic tune. 18. *phoenix:* In legend, an Arabian bird believed to subsist on incense and perfumes. It was supposed to reproduce by going up in flames, to rise again out of its ashes.

Fred Chappell (b. 1936)

SKIN FLICK   1971

The selfsame surface that billowed once with
The shapes of Trigger and Gene. New faces now
Are in the saddle. Tits and buttocks
Slide rattling down the beam as down
A coal chute; in the splotched light   5
The burning bush strikes dumb.
Different sort of cattle drive:
No water for miles and miles.

In the aisles, new bugs and rats
Though it's the same Old Paint. 10
Audience of lepers, hopeless and homeless,
Or like the buffalo, at home
In the wind only. No
Mushy love stuff for them.

They eye the violent innocence they always knew. 15
Is that the rancher's palomino daughter?
Is this her eastern finishing school?
Same old predicament:
No water for miles and miles,
The horizon breeds no cavalry. 20

Men, draw your wagons in a circle. Be ready.

G. K. Chesterton (1874 – 1936)
THE DONKEY 1900

When fishes flew and forests walked
    And figs grew upon thorn,
Some moment when the moon was blood
    Then surely I was born;

With monstrous head and sickening cry 5
    And ears like errant wings,
The devil's walking parody
    On all four-footed things.

The tattered outlaw of the earth,
    Of ancient crooked will; 10
Starve, scourge, deride me: I am dumb,
    I keep my secret still.

Fools! For I also had my hour;
    One far fierce hour and sweet:
There was a shout about my ears, 15
    And palms before my feet.

THE DONKEY. For more details of the donkey's hour of triumph see Matthew 21:1 – 8.

Amy Clampitt (b. 1924)
THE CORMORANT IN HIS ELEMENT 1983

That bony potbellied arrow, wing-pumping along
implacably, with a ramrod's rigid adherence,
airborne, to the horizontal, discloses talents
one would never have guessed at. Plummeting

waterward, big black feet splayed for a landing
gear, slim head turning and turning, vermilion-
strapped, this way and that, with a lightning glance
over the shoulder, the cormorant astounding- 5

ly, in one sleek involuted arabesque, a vertical
turn on a dime, goes into that inimitable 10
vanishing-and-emerging-from-under-the-briny-

deep act which, unlike the works of Homo Houdini,
is performed for reasons having nothing at all
to do with ego, guilt, ambition, or even money.

Lucille Clifton (b. 1936)

TO THE UNBORN AND WAITING CHILDREN 1980

i went into my mother as
some souls go into a church,
for the rest only. but there,
even there, from the belly of a
poor woman who could not save herself 5
i was pushed without my permission
into a tangle of birthdays.
listen, eavesdroppers, there is no such thing
as a bed without affliction;
the bodies all may open wide but 10
you enter at your own risk.

Samuel Taylor Coleridge (1772 – 1834)

KUBLA KHAN (1797 – 1798)

Or, a Vision in a Dream. A Fragment.

In Xanadu did Kubla Khan
A stately pleasure-dome decree:
Where Alph, the sacred river, ran
Through caverns measureless to man
    Down to a sunless sea. 5
So twice five miles of fertile ground
With walls and towers were girdled round;
And there were gardens bright with sinuous rills,
Where blossomed many an incense-bearing tree;
And here were forests ancient as the hills, 10
Enfolding sunny spots of greenery.

But oh! that deep romantic chasm which slanted
Down the green hill athwart a cedarn cover!
A savage place! as holy and enchanted
As e'er beneath a waning moon was haunted   15
By woman wailing for her demon-lover!
And from this chasm, with ceaseless turmoil seething,
As if this earth in fast thick pants were breathing,
A mighty fountain momently was forced:
Amid whose swift half-intermitted burst   20
Huge fragments vaulted like rebounding hail,
Or chaffy grain beneath the thresher's flail:
And 'mid these dancing rocks at once and ever
It flung up momently the sacred river.
Five miles meandering with a mazy motion   25
Through wood and dale the sacred river ran,
Then reached the caverns measureless to man,
And sank in tumult to a lifeless ocean:
And 'mid this tumult Kubla heard from far
Ancestral voices prophesying war!   30

    The shadow of the dome of pleasure
    Floated midway on the waves;
    Where was heard the mingled measure
    From the fountain and the caves.
It was a miracle of rare device,   35
A sunny pleasure-dome with caves of ice!

    A damsel with a dulcimer
    In a vision once I saw:
    It was an Abyssinian maid,
    And on her dulcimer she played,   40
    Singing of Mount Abora.
    Could I revive within me
    Her symphony and song,
    To such a deep delight 'twould win me,
That with music loud and long,   45
I would build that dome in air,
That sunny dome! those caves of ice!
And all who heard should see them there,
And all should cry, Beware! Beware!
His flashing eyes, his floating hair!   50
Weave a circle round him thrice,
And close your eyes with holy dread,
For he on honey-dew hath fed,
And drunk the milk of Paradise.

KUBLA KHAN. There was an actual Kublai Khan, a thirteenth-century Mongol emperor, and
a Chinese city of Xamdu; but Coleridge's dream vision also borrows from travelers' descriptions of such other exotic places as Abyssinia and America. 51. *circle:* a magic circle drawn
to keep away evil spirits.

William Cowper (1731 – 1800)*
PRAISE FOR THE FOUNTAIN OPENED   1779

There is a fountain filled with blood
  Drawn from Emmanuel's veins;
And sinners, plunged beneath that flood,
  Lose all their guilty stains.

The dying thief rejoiced to see   5
  That fountain in his day;
And there have I, as vile as he,
  Washed all my sins away.

Dear dying Lamb, thy precious blood
  Shall never lose its pow'r;   10
Till all the ransomed church of God
  Be saved, to sin no more.

E'er since, by faith, I saw the stream
  Thy flowing wounds supply,
Redeeming love has been my theme   15
  And shall be till I die.

Then in a nobler sweeter song
  I'll sing thy power to save;
When this poor lisping stammering tongue
  Lies silent in the grave.   20

Lord, I believe thou hast prepared
  (Unworthy though I be)
For me a blood-bought free reward,
  A golden harp for me!

'Tis strung, and tuned, for endless years,   25
  And formed by pow'r divine
To sound in God the Father's ears
  No other name but thine.

PRAISE FOR THE FOUNTAIN OPENED. This hymn is based on the Biblical prophecy of the cleansing fountain (Zechariah 13:1): "In that day there shall be a fountain opened to the house of David and to the inhabitants of Jerusalem for sin and for uncleanness." Cowper, although his works were various, was most widely famed in late eighteenth-century England as the poet of a new evangelical religious movement, Methodism. For a collection, the *Olney Hymns,* written together with the Reverend John Newton, Cowper supplied this and sixty-six other hymns including "Oh! For a Closer Walk with God" and "Light Shining Out of Darkness" ("God moves in a mysterious way, / His wonders to perform").

COMPARE:

Compare the language and stanza form of Cowper's hymn with "Because I could not stop for Death" (below) and other poems by Emily Dickinson.

Emily Dickinson (1830 – 1886)*

Because I could not stop for Death (1863)

Because I could not stop for Death –
He kindly stopped for me –
The Carriage held but just Ourselves –
And Immortality.

We slowly drove – He knew no haste   5
And I had put away
My labor and my leisure too,
For His Civility –

We passed the School, where Children strove
At Recess – in the Ring –   10
We passed the Fields of Gazing Grain –
We passed the Setting Sun –

Or rather – He passed Us –
The Dews drew quivering and chill –
For only Gossamer, my Gown –   15
My Tippet° – only Tulle –   *cape*

We paused before a House that seemed
A Swelling of the Ground –
The Roof was scarcely visible –
The Cornice – in the Ground –   20

Since then – 'tis Centuries – and yet
Feels shorter than the Day
I first surmised the Horses' Heads
Were toward Eternity –

Because I could not stop for Death. In the version of this poem printed by Emily Dickinson's first editors in 1890, stanza four was left out. In line 9 *strove* was replaced by *played;* line 10 was made to read "Their lessons scarcely done"; line 20, "The cornice but a mound"; line 21, "Since then 'tis centuries, but each"; and capitalization and punctuation were made conventional.

Compare:

"Because I could not stop for Death" and other poems in common meter by Emily Dickinson (such as "I heard a Fly buzz – when I died," page 618, and "My Life had stood – a Loaded Gun," page 706) with "Praise for the Fountain Opened" by William Cowper (page 704).

Emily Dickinson (1830 – 1886)*
I started Early – Took my Dog

(1862)

I started Early – Took my Dog –
And visited the Sea –
The Mermaids in the Basement
Came out to look at me –

And Frigates – in the Upper Floor   5
Extended Hempen Hands –
Presuming Me to be a Mouse –
Aground – upon the Sands –

But no Man moved Me – till the Tide
Went past my simple Shoe –   10
And past my Apron – and my Belt
And past my Bodice – too –

And made as He would eat me up –
As wholly as a Dew
Upon a Dandelion's Sleeve –   15
And then – I started – too –

And He – He followed – close behind –
I felt His Silver Heel
Upon my Ankle – Then my Shoes
Would overflow with Pearl –   20

Until We met the Solid Town –
No One He seemed to know –
And bowing – with a Mighty look –
At me – The Sea withdrew –

Emily Dickinson (1830 – 1886)*
My Life had stood – a Loaded Gun

(about 1863)

My Life had stood – a Loaded Gun –
In Corners – till a Day
The Owner passed – identified –
And carried Me away –

And now We roam in Sovreign Woods –   5
And now We hunt the Doe –
And every time I speak for Him –
The Mountains straight reply –

And do I smile, such cordial light
Upon the Valley glow –   10
It is as a Vesuvian face
Had let its pleasure through –

And when at Night – Our good Day done –
I guard My Master's Head –
'Tis better than the Eider-Duck's
Deep Pillow – to have shared –

To foe of His – I'm deadly foe –
None stir the second time –
On whom I lay a Yellow Eye –
Or an emphatic Thumb –

Though I than He – may longer live
He longer must – than I –
For I have but the power to kill,
Without – the power to die –

John Donne (1572 – 1631)*

The Bait (about 1600?)

Come live with me and be my love,
And we will some new pleasures prove°,   *try*
Of golden sands and crystal brooks,
With silken lines and silver hooks.

There will the river whispering run,   5
Warmed by thy eyes more than the sun;
And there the enamored fish will stay,
Begging themselves they may betray.

When thou wilt swim in that live bath,
Each fish, which every channel hath,   10
Will amorously to thee swim,
Gladder to catch thee, than thou him.

If thou to be so seen be'st loath,
By sun or moon, thou dark'nest both;
And if myself have leave to see,   15
I need not their light, having thee.

Let others freeze with angling reeds°,   *rods*
And cut their legs with shells and weeds,
Or treacherously poor fish beset
With strangling snare or windowy net.   20

Let coarse bold hands from slimy nest
The bedded fish in banks out-wrest,
Or curious traitors, sleave-silk flies,
Bewitch poor fishes' wand'ring eyes.

For thee, thou need'st no such deceit,   25
For thou thyself art thine own bait;
That fish that is not catched thereby,
Alas, is wiser far than I.

COMPARE:

"The Bait" with "The Passionate Shepherd to His Love" by Christopher Marlowe (page 745) and with "The Nymph's Reply to the Shepherd" by Sir Walter Raleigh (page 756).

John Donne (1572 – 1631)*
DEATH BE NOT PROUD (about 1610)

Death be not proud, though some have callèd thee
Mighty and dreadful, for thou art not so;
For those whom thou think'st thou dost overthrow
Die not, poor death, nor yet canst thou kill me.
From rest and sleep, which but thy pictures be,   5
Much pleasure, then from thee much more must flow,
And soonest our best men with thee do go,
Rest of their bones, and soul's delivery.
Thou art slave to fate, chance, kings, and desperate men,
And dost with poison, war, and sickness dwell,   10
And poppy, or charms can make us sleep as well,
And better than thy stroke; why swell'st thou then?
One short sleep past, we wake eternally,
And death shall be no more; death, thou shalt die.

John Donne (1572 – 1631)*
THE FLEA 1633

Mark but this flea, and mark in this
How little that which thou deny'st me is;
It sucked me first, and now sucks thee,
And in this flea our two bloods mingled be;
Thou know'st that this cannot be said   5
A sin, nor shame, nor loss of maidenhead,
   Yet this enjoys before it woo,
   And pampered swells with one blood made of two,
   And this, alas, is more than we would do.

Oh stay, three lives in one flea spare,   10
Where we almost, yea more than married are.
This flea is you and I, and this
Our marriage bed, and marriage temple is;
Though parents grudge, and you, we're met
And cloistered in these living walls of jet.   15
   Though use° make you apt to kill me,   *custom*
   Let not to that, self-murder added be,
   And sacrilege, three sins in killing three.

Cruel and sudden, hast thou since
Purpled thy nail in blood of innocence?   20
Wherein could this flea guilty be,
Except in that drop it sucked from thee?
Yet thou triumph'st, and say'st that thou
Find'st not thyself, nor me, the weaker now;
  'Tis true; then learn how false, fears be;   25
  Just so much honor, when thou yield'st to me,
  Will waste, as this flea's death took life from thee.

John Donne (1572 – 1631)*

A Valediction: Forbidding Mourning   (1611)

As virtuous men pass mildly away,
  And whisper to their souls to go,
Whilst some of their sad friends do say
  The breath goes now, and some say no:

So let us melt, and make no noise,   5
  No tear-floods, nor sigh-tempests move;
'Twere profanation of our joys
  To tell the laity° our love.   *common people*

Moving of th' earth° brings harms and fears;   *earthquake*
  Men reckon what it did and meant;   10
But trepidation of the spheres,
  Though greater far, is innocent°.   *harmless*

Dull sublunary lovers' love
  (Whose soul is sense) cannot admit
Absence, because it doth remove   15
  Those things which elemented° it.   *constituted*

But we, by a love so much refined
  That ourselves know not what it is,
Inter-assurèd of the mind,
  Care less, eyes, lips, and hands to miss.   20

Our two souls, therefore, which are one,
  Though I must go, endure not yet
A breach, but an expansìon,
  Like gold to airy thinness beat.

If they be two, they are two so   25
  As stiff twin compasses are two:
Thy soul, the fixed foot, makes no show
  To move, but doth, if th' other do.

And though it in the center sit,
  Yet when the other far doth roam,   30
It leans and harkens after it,
  And grows erect as that comes home.

Such wilt thou be to me, who must,
    Like th' other foot, obliquely run;
Thy firmness makes my circle just°,   *perfect* 35
    And makes me end where I begun.

A VALEDICTION: FORBIDDING MOURNING. According to Donne's biographer Izaak Walton, Donne's wife received this poem as a gift before the poet departed on a journey to France. 11. *spheres:* In Ptolemaic astronomy, the concentric spheres surrounding the earth. The trepidation or motion of the ninth sphere was thought to change the date of the equinox. 19. *Inter-assurèd of the mind:* each sure in mind that the other is faithful. 24. *gold to airy thinness:* Gold is so malleable that, if beaten to the thickness of gold leaf (1/250,000 of one inch), one ounce of gold would cover 250 square feet.

John Dryden (1631 – 1700)*
TO THE MEMORY OF MR. OLDHAM   1684

Farewell, too little and too lately known,
Whom I began to think and call my own;
For sure our souls were near allied, and thine
Cast in the same poetic mold with mine.
One common note on either lyre did strike,   5
And knaves and fools we both abhorred alike.
To the same goal did both our studies drive:
The last set out the soonest did arrive.
Thus Nissus fell upon the slippery place,
While his young friend performed and won the race.   10
O early ripe! to thy abundant store
What could advancing age have added more?
It might (what Nature never gives the young)
Have taught the numbers° of thy native tongue.   *meters*
But satire needs not those, and wit will shine   15
Through the harsh cadence of a rugged line.
A noble error, and but seldom made,
When poets are by too much force betrayed.
Thy gen'rous fruits, though gathered ere their prime,
Still showed a quickness; and maturing time   20
But mellows what we write to the dull sweets of rhyme.
Once more, hail, and farewell! farewell, thou young
But ah! too short, Marcellus of our tongue!
Thy brows with ivy and with laurels bound;
But fate and gloomy night encompass thee around.   25

TO THE MEMORY OF MR. OLDHAM. John Oldham, poet best remembered for his *Satires upon the Jesuits,* had died at thirty. 9 – 10. *Nissus; his young friend:* These two close friends, as Virgil tells us in the *Aeneid,* ran a race for the prize of an olive crown. 23. *Marcellus:* Had he not died in his twentieth year, he would have succeeded the Roman emperor Augustus. 25. This line echoes the *Aeneid* (VI, 886), in which Marcellus is seen walking under the black cloud of his impending doom.

Norman Dubie (b. 1945)

THE FUNERAL

1985

It felt like the zero in brook ice.
She was my youngest aunt, the summer before
We had stood naked
While she stiffened and giggled, letting the minnows
Nibble at her toes. I was almost four —   5
That evening she took me
To the springhouse where on the scoured planks
There were rows of butter in small bricks, a mold
Like ermine on the cheese,
And cut onions to rinse the air   10
Of the black, sickly-sweet meats of rotting pecans.

She said butter was colored with marigolds
Plucked down by the marsh
With its tall grass and miner's-candles.
We once carried the offal's pail beyond the barn   15
To where the fox could be caught in meditation.
Her bed linen smelled of camphor. We went

In late March for her burial. I heard the men talk.
I saw the minnows nibble at her toe.
And Uncle Peter, in a low voice, said   20
The cancer ate her like horse piss eats deep snow.

Alan Dugan (b. 1923)

LOVE SONG: I AND THOU

1961

Nothing is plumb, level or square:
    the studs are bowed, the joists
are shaky by nature, no piece fits
    any other piece without a gap
or pinch, and bent nails   5
    dance all over the surfacing
like maggots. By Christ
    I am no carpenter, I built
the roof for myself, the walls
    for myself, the floors   10
for myself, and got
    hung up in it myself. I
danced with a purple thumb
    at this house-warming, drunk
with my prime whiskey: rage.   15
    Oh I spat rage's nails
into the frame-up of my work:
    it held. It settled plumb,

level, solid, square and true
    for that great moment. Then   20
it screamed and went on through,
    skewing as wrong the other way.
God damned it. This is hell,
    but I planned it, I sawed it,
I nailed it, and I   25
    will live in it until it kills me.
I can nail my left palm
    to the left-hand cross-piece but
I can't do everything myself.
    I need a hand to nail the right,   30
a help, a love, a you, a wife.

COMPARE:

"Love Song: I and Thou" with "Love Poem" by John Frederick Nims (page 750).

T. S. Eliot (1888 – 1965)*
JOURNEY OF THE MAGI   1927

"A cold coming we had of it,
Just the worst time of the year
For a journey, and such a long journey:
The ways deep and the weather sharp,
The very dead of winter."   5
And the camels galled, sore-footed, refractory,
Lying down in the melting snow.
There were times we regretted
The summer palaces on slopes, the terraces,
And the silken girls bringing sherbet.   10
Then the camel men cursing and grumbling
And running away, and wanting their liquor and women,
And the night-fires going out, and the lack of shelters,
And the cities hostile and the towns unfriendly
And the villages dirty and charging high prices: 15
A hard time we had of it.
At the end we preferred to travel all night,
Sleeping in snatches,
With the voices singing in our ears, saying
That this was all folly.   20

Then at dawn we came down to a temperate valley,
Wet, below the snow line, smelling of vegetation;
With a running stream and a water-mill beating the darkness,
And three trees on the low sky,
And an old white horse galloped away in the meadow.   25
Then we came to a tavern with vine-leaves over the lintel,

Six hands at an open door dicing for pieces of silver,
And feet kicking the empty wine-skins.
But there was no information, and so we continued
And arrived at evening, not a moment too soon   30
Finding the place; it was (you may say) satisfactory.
All this was a long time ago, I remember,
And I would do it again, but set down
This set down
This: were we led all that way for   35
Birth or Death? There was a Birth, certainly,
We had evidence and no doubt. I had seen birth and death,
But had thought they were different; this Birth was
Hard and bitter agony for us, like Death, our death.
We returned to our places, these Kingdoms,   40
But no longer at ease here, in the old dispensation,
With an alien people clutching their gods.
I should be glad of another death.

JOURNEY OF THE MAGI. The story of the Magi, the three wise men who traveled to Bethlehem to behold the baby Jesus, is told in Matthew 2:1 – 12. That the three were kings is a later tradition. 1 – 5. *A cold coming . . . winter:* Eliot quotes with slight changes from a sermon preached on Christmas day, 1622, by Bishop Lancelot Andrewes. 24. *three trees:* foreshadowing the three crosses on Calvary (see Luke 23:32 – 33). 25. *white horse:* perhaps the steed that carried the conquering Christ in the vision of St. John the Divine (Revelation 19:11 – 16). 41. *old dispensation:* older, pagan religion about to be displaced by Christianity.

COMPARE:

"Journey of the Magi" with "The Magi" by William Butler Yeats (page 792).

T. S. Eliot (1888 – 1965)*
THE LOVE SONG OF J. ALFRED PRUFROCK   1917

S'io credessi che mia risposta fosse
A persona che mai tornasse al mondo,
Questa fiamma staria senza piu scosse.
Ma perciocche giammai di questo fondo
Non torno vivo alcun, s'i'odo il vero,
Senza tema d'infamia ti rispondo.

Let us go then, you and I,
When the evening is spread out against the sky
Like a patient etherized upon a table;
Let us go, through certain half-deserted streets,
The muttering retreats   5
Of restless nights in one-night cheap hotels
And sawdust restaurants with oyster-shells:
Streets that follow like a tedious argument
Of insidious intent

To lead you to an overwhelming question . . .   10
Oh, do not ask, "What is it?"
Let us go and make our visit.

In the room the women come and go
Talking of Michelangelo.

The yellow fog that rubs its back upon the window-panes,
The yellow smoke that rubs its muzzle on the window-panes   15
Licked its tongue into the corners of the evening,
Lingered upon the pools that stand in drains,
Let fall upon its back the soot that falls from chimneys,
Slipped by the terrace, made a sudden leap,   20
And seeing that it was a soft October night,
Curled once about the house, and fell asleep.

And indeed there will be time
For the yellow smoke that slides along the street,
Rubbing its back upon the window-panes;   25
There will be time, there will be time
To prepare a face to meet the faces that you meet;
There will be time to murder and create,
And time for all the works and days of hands
That lift and drop a question on your plate;   30
Time for you and time for me,
And time yet for a hundred indecisions,
And for a hundred visions and revisions,
Before the taking of a toast and tea.

In the room the women come and go   35
Talking of Michelangelo.

And indeed there will be time
To wonder, "Do I dare?" and, "Do I dare?"
Time to turn back and descend the stair,
With a bald spot in the middle of my hair —   40
(They will say: "How his hair is growing thin!")
My morning coat, my collar mounting firmly to the chin,
My necktie rich and modest, but asserted by a simple pin —
(They will say: "But how his arms and legs are thin!")
Do I dare   45
Disturb the universe?
In a minute there is time
For decisions and revisions which a minute will reverse.

For I have known them all already, known them all: —
Have known the evenings, mornings, afternoons,   50
I have measured out my life with coffee spoons;
I know the voices dying with a dying fall
Beneath the music from a farther room.
    So how should I presume?

And I have known the eyes already, known them all —   55
The eyes that fix you in a formulated phrase,
And when I am formulated, sprawling on a pin,
When I am pinned and wriggling on the wall,
Then how should I begin
To spit out all the butt-ends of my days and ways?   60
    And how should I presume?

And I have known the arms already, known them all —
Arms that are braceleted and white and bare
(But in the lamplight, downed with light brown hair!)
Is it perfume from a dress   65
That makes me so digress?
Arms that lie along a table, or wrap about a shawl.
    And should I then presume?
    And how should I begin?

                    . . . . . .

Shall I say, I have gone at dusk through narrow streets   70
And watched the smoke that rises from the pipes
Of lonely men in shirt-sleeves, leaning out of windows? . . .

I should have been a pair of ragged claws
Scuttling across the floors of silent seas.

And the afternoon, the evening, sleeps so peacefully!   75
Smoothed by long fingers,
Asleep . . . tired . . . or it malingers,
Stretched on the floor, here beside you and me.
Should I, after tea and cakes and ices,
Have the strength to force the moment to its crisis?   80
But though I have wept and fasted, wept and prayed,
Though I have seen my head (grown slightly bald) brought in upon a
        platter,
I am no prophet — and here's no great matter;
I have seen the moment of my greatness flicker,
And I have seen the eternal Footman hold my coat, and snicker,   85
And in short, I was afraid.

And would it have been worth it, after all,
After the cups, the marmalade, the tea,
Among the porcelain, among some talk of you and me,
Would it have been worth while,   90
To have bitten off the matter with a smile,
To have squeezed the universe into a ball
To roll it toward some overwhelming question,
To say: "I am Lazarus, come from the dead,
Come back to tell you all, I shall tell you all" —   95
If one, settling a pillow by her head,
    Should say: "That is not what I meant at all.
    That is not it, at all."

And would it have been worth it, after all,
Would it have been worth while,   100
After the sunsets and the dooryards and the sprinkled streets,
After the novels, after the teacups, after the skirts that trail along the
    floor —
And this, and so much more? —
It is impossible to say just what I mean!
But as if a magic lantern threw the nerves in patterns on a screen: 105
Would it have been worth while
If one, settling a pillow or throwing off a shawl,
And turning toward the window, should say:
    "That is not it at all,
    That is not what I meant, at all."   110

                        .   .   .   .   .

No! I am not Prince Hamlet, nor was meant to be;
Am an attendant lord, one that will do
To swell a progress, start a scene or two,
Advise the prince; no doubt, an easy tool,
Deferential, glad to be of use,   115
Politic, cautious, and meticulous;
Full of high sentence, but a bit obtuse;
At times, indeed, almost ridiculous —
Almost, at times, the Fool.

I grow old . . . I grow old . . .   120
I shall wear the bottoms of my trousers rolled.

Shall I part my hair behind? Do I dare to eat a peach?
I shall wear white flannel trousers, and walk upon the beach.
I have heard the mermaids singing, each to each.

I do not think that they will sing to me.   125

I have seen them riding seaward on the waves
Combing the white hair of the waves blown back
When the wind blows the water white and black.

We have lingered in the chambers of the sea
By sea-girls wreathed with seaweed red and brown   130
Till human voices wake us, and we drown.

THE LOVE SONG OF J. ALFRED PRUFROCK. The epigraph, from Dante's *Inferno,* is the speech of one
dead and damned, who thinks that his hearer also is going to remain in Hell. Count Guido
da Montefeltro, whose sin has been to give false counsel after a corrupt prelate had offered
him prior absolution and whose punishment is to be wrapped in a constantly burning flame,
offers to tell Dante his story: "If I thought my reply were to someone who could ever return
to the world, this flame would waver no more. But since, I'm told, nobody ever escapes from
this pit, I'll tell you without fear of ill fame." 29. *works and days:* title of a poem by Hesiod
(eighth century B.C.), depicting his life as a hard-working Greek farmer and exhorting his
brother to be like him. 82. *head . . . platter:* like that of John the Baptist, prophet and praiser
of chastity, whom King Herod beheaded at the demand of Herodias, his unlawfully wedded
wife (see Mark 6:17 – 28). 92 – 93. *squeezed . . . To roll it:* an echo from Marvell's "To His Coy

Mistress," lines 41 – 42 (see p. 418). 94. *Lazarus:* Probably the Lazarus whom Jesus called forth from the tomb (John 11:1 – 44), but possibly the beggar seen in Heaven by the rich man in Hell (Luke 16:19 – 25).

Robert Frost (1874 – 1963)*
STOPPING BY WOODS ON A SNOWY EVENING 1923

Whose woods these are I think I know.
His house is in the village though;
He will not see me stopping here
To watch his woods fill up with snow.

My little horse must think it queer   5
To stop without a farmhouse near
Between the woods and frozen lake
The darkest evening of the year.

He gives his harness bells a shake
To ask if there is some mistake.   10
The only other sound's the sweep
Of easy wind and downy flake.

The woods are lovely, dark and deep,
But I have promises to keep,
And miles to go before I sleep,   15
And miles to go before I sleep.

COMPARE:

"Stopping by Woods on a Snowy Evening" with "Desert Places" by Robert Frost (page 542).

Robert Frost (1874 – 1963)*
THE WOOD-PILE 1914

Out walking in the frozen swamp one grey day,
I paused and said, "I will turn back from here.
No, I will go on farther — and we shall see,"
The hard snow held me, save where now and then
One foot went through. The view was all in lines   5
Straight up and down of tall slim trees
Too much alike to mark or name a place by
So as to say for certain I was here
Or somewhere else: I was just far from home.
A small bird flew before me. He was careful   10
To put a tree between us when he lighted,
And say no word to tell me who he was
Who was so foolish as to think what *he* thought.

He thought that I was after him for a feather —
The white one in his tail; like one who takes   15
Everything said as personal to himself.
One flight out sideways would have undeceived him.
And then there was a pile of wood for which
I forgot him and let his little fear
Carry him off the way I might have gone,   20
Without so much as wishing him good-night.
He went behind it to make his last stand.
It was a cord of maple, cut and split
And piled — and measured, four by four by eight.
And not another like it could I see.   25
No runner tracks in this year's snow looped near it.
And it was older sure than this year's cutting,
Or even last year's or the year's before.
The wood was grey and the bark warping off it
And the pile somewhat sunken. Clematis   30
Had wound strings round and round it like a bundle.
What held it though on one side was a tree
Still growing, and on one a stake and prop,
These latter about to fall. I thought that only
Someone who lived in turning to fresh tasks   35
Could so forget his handiwork on which
He spent himself, the labor of his axe,
And leave it there far from a useful fireplace
To warm the frozen swamp as best it could
With the slow smokeless burning of decay.   40

Tess Gallagher (b. 1943)
UNDER STARS   1978

The sleep of this night deepens
because I have walked coatless from the house
carrying the white envelope.
All night it will say one name
in its little tin house by the roadside.   5

I have raised the metal flag
so its shadow under the roadlamp
leaves an imprint on the rain-heavy bushes.
Now I will walk back
thinking of the few lights still on   10
in the town a mile away.

In the yellowed light of a kitchen
the millworker has finished his coffee,
his wife has laid out the white slices of bread
on the counter. Now while the bed they have left   15

is still warm, I will think of you, you
who are so far away
you have caused me to look up at the stars.

Tonight they have not moved
from childhood, those games played after dark.   20
Again I walk into the wet grass
toward the starry voices. Again, I
am the found one, intimate, returned
by all I touch on the way.

Allen Ginsberg (b. 1926)

A SUPERMARKET IN CALIFORNIA   1950

What thoughts I have of you tonight, Walt Whitman, for I walked
down the sidestreets under the trees with a headache self-conscious
looking at the full moon.

In my hungry fatigue, and shopping for images, I went into the
neon fruit supermarket, dreaming of your enumerations!

What peaches and what penumbras! Whole families shopping at
night! Aisles full of husbands! Wives in the avocados, babies in the
tomatoes! — and you, Garcia Lorca, what were you doing down by the
watermelons?

I saw you, Walt Whitman, childless, lonely old grubber, poking
among the meats in the refrigerator and eyeing the grocery boys.

I heard you asking questions of each: Who killed the pork chops?
What price bananas? Are you my Angel?   5

I wandered in and out of the brilliant stacks of cans following you,
and followed in my imagination by the store detective.

We strode down the open corridors together in our solitary fancy
tasting artichokes, possessing every frozen delicacy, and never passing
the cashier.

Where are we going, Walt Whitman? The doors close in an hour.
Which way does your beard point tonight?

(I touch your book and dream of our odyssey in the supermarket
and feel absurd.)

Will we walk all night through solitary streets? The trees add shade
to shade, lights out in the houses, we'll both be lonely.   10

Will we stroll dreaming of the lost America of love past blue
automobiles in driveways, home to our silent cottage?

Ah, dear father, graybeard, lonely old courage-teacher, what
American did you have when Charon quit poling his ferry and you got
out on a smoking bank and stood watching the boat disappear on the
black waters of Lethe?

A SUPERMARKET IN CALIFORNIA. 2. *enumerations:* Many of Whitman's poems contain lists of
observed details. 3. *Garcia Lorca:* modern Spanish poet who wrote an "Ode to Walt Whitman"

in his booklength sequence *Poet in New York.* (A poem by Lorca appears on page 640.) 12. *Charon . . . Lethe:* Is the poet confusing two underworld rivers? Charon, in Greek and Roman mythology, is the boatman who ferries the souls of the dead across the River Styx. The River Lethe also flows through Hades, and a drink of its waters makes the dead lose their painful memories of loved ones thay have left behind.

COMPARE:

"A Supermarket in California" with Walt Whitman's "To a Locomotive in Winter" (page 423) and "I Saw in Louisiana a Live-Oak Growing" (page 785).

Dana Gioia (b. 1950)
CALIFORNIA HILLS IN AUGUST   1982

I can imagine someone who found
these fields unbearable, who climbed
the hillside in the heat, cursing the dust,
cracking the brittle weeds underfoot,
wishing a few more trees for shade.   5

An Easterner especially, who would scorn
the meagreness of summer, the dry
twisted shapes of black elm,
scrub oak, and chaparral — a landscape
August has already drained of green.   10

One who would hurry over the clinging
thistle, foxtail, golden poppy,
knowing everything was just a weed,
unable to conceive that these trees
and sparse brown bushes were alive.   15

And hate the bright stillness of the noon,
without wind, without motion,
the only other living thing
a hawk, hungry for prey, suspended
in the blinding, sunlit blue.   20

And yet how gentle it seems to someone
raised in a landscape short of rain —
the skyline of a hill broken by no more
trees than one can count, the grass,
the empty sky, the wish for water.   25

Donald Hall (b. 1928)
NAMES OF HORSES   1978

All winter your brute shoulders strained against collars, padding
and steerhide over the ash hames, to haul

sledges of cordwood for drying through spring and summer,
for the Glenwood stove next winter, and for the simmering range.

In April you pulled cartloads of manure to spread on the fields,   5
dark manure of Holsteins, and knobs of your own clustered with
    oats.
All summer you mowed the grass in meadow and hayfield, the
    mowing machine
clacketing beside you, while the sun walked high in the morning;

and after noon's heat, you pulled a clawed rake through the same
    acres,
gathering stacks, and dragged the wagon from stack to stack,   10
and the built hayrack back, uphill to the chaffy barn,
three loads of hay a day from standing grass in the morning.

Sundays you trotted the two miles to church with the light load
of a leather quartertop buggy, and grazed in the sound of hymns.
Generation on generation, your neck rubbed the windowsill   15
of the stall, smoothing the wood as the sea smooths glass.

When you were old and lame, when your shoulders hurt bending to
    graze,
one October the man, who fed you and kept you, and harnessed you
    every morning,
led you through corn stubble to sandy ground above Eagle Pond,
and dug a hole beside you where you stood shuddering in your skin,   20

and lay the shotgun's muzzle in the boneless hollow behind your ear,
and fired the slug into your brain, and felled you into your grave,
shoveling sand to cover you, setting goldenrod upright above you,
where by next summer a dent in the ground made your monument.

For a hundred and fifty years, in the pasture of dead horses,   25
roots of pine trees pushed through the pale curves of your ribs,
yellow blossoms flourished above you in autumn, and in winter
frost heaved your bones in the ground — old toilers, soil makers:

O Roger, Mackerel, Riley, Ned, Nellie, Chester, Lady Ghost.

Thomas Hardy (1840 – 1928)*
THE CONVERGENCE OF THE TWAIN   1912

Lines on the Loss of the "Titanic"

I

      In a solitude of the sea
      Deep from human vanity,
And the Pride of Life that planned her, stilly couches she.

II

        Steel chambers, late the pyres
        Of her salamandrine fires,   5
Cold currents thrid°, and turn to rhythmic tidal lyres.   *thread*

III

        Over the mirrors meant
        To glass the opulent
The sea-worm crawls — grotesque, slimed, dumb, indifferent.

IV

        Jewels in joy designed   10
        To ravish the sensuous mind
Lie lightless, all their sparkles bleared and black and blind.

V

        Dim moon-eyed fishes near
        Gaze at the gilded gear
And query: "What does this vaingloriousness down here?"   15

VI

        Well: while was fashioning
        This creature of cleaving wing,
The Immanent Will that stirs and urges everything

VII

        Prepared a sinister mate
        For her — so gaily great —   20
A Shape of Ice, for the time far and dissociate.

VIII

        And as the smart ship grew
        In stature, grace, and hue,
In shadowy silent distance grew the Iceberg too.

IX

        Alien they seemed to be: 25
        No mortal eye could see
The intimate welding of their later history,

X

        Or sign that they were bent
        By paths coincident
On being anon twin halves of one august event.   30

XI

        Till the Spinner of the Years
        Said "Now!" And each one hears,
And consummation comes, and jars two hemispheres.

THE CONVERGENCE OF THE TWAIN. The luxury liner *Titanic,* supposedly unsinkable, went down in 1912 after striking an iceberg, on its first Atlantic voyage. 5. *salamandrine:* like the salamander, a lizard that supposedly thrives in fires, or like a spirit of the same name that inhabits fire (according to alchemists).

Thomas Hardy (1840 – 1928)*

FIVE SATIRES OF CIRCUMSTANCE

1914

In Church

"And now to God the Father," he ends,
And his voice thrills up to the topmost tiles:
Each listener chokes as he bows and bends,
And emotion pervades the crowded aisles.
Then the preacher glides to the vestry-door,   5
And shuts it, and thinks he is seen no more.

The door swings softly ajar meanwhile,
And a pupil of his in the Bible class,
Who adores him as one without gloss or guile
Sees her idol stand with a satisfied smile   10
And re-enact at the vestry-glass
Each pulpit gesture in deft dumb-show
That had moved the congregation so.

In the Room of the Bride-elect

"Would it had been the man of our wish!"
Sighs her mother. To whom with vehemence she   15
In the wedding-dress — the wife to be —
"Then why were you so mollyish
As not to insist on him for me!"
The mother, amazed: "Why, dearest one,
Because you pleaded for this or none!"   20

"But Father and you should have stood out strong!
Since then, to my cost, I have lived to find
That you were right and that I was wrong;
This man is a dolt to the one declined. . . .
Ah! — here he comes with his button-hole rose.   25
Good God — I must marry him I suppose!"

In the Cemetery

"You see those mothers squabbling there?"
Remarks the man of the cemetery.
"One says in tears, ' 'Tis mine lies here!'
Another, 'Nay, mine, you Pharisee°!'   *hypocrite*   30
Another, 'How dare you move my flowers
And put your own on this grave of ours!'
But all their children were laid therein
At different times, like sprats in a tin°.   *sardines in a can*

"And then the main drain had to cross,   35
And we moved the lot some nights ago,
And packed them away in the general foss°   *ditch*
With hundreds more. But their folks don't know,
And as well cry over a new-laid drain
As anything else, to ease your pain!"   40

In the Nuptial Chamber

"O that mastering tune!" And up in the bed
Like a lace-robed phantom springs the bride;
"And why?" asks the man she had that day wed,
With a start, as the band plays on outside.
"It's the townsfolk's cheery compliment   45
Because of our marriage, my Innocent."

"O but you don't know! 'Tis the passionate air
To which my old Love waltzed with me,
And I swore as we spun that none should share
My home, my kisses, till death, save he!   50
And he dominates me and thrills me through,
And it's he I embrace while embracing you!"

Over the Coffin

They stand confronting, the coffin between,
His wife of old, and his wife of late,
And the dead man whose they both had been   55
Seems listening aloof, as to things past date.
— "I have called," says the first. "Do you marvel or not?"
"In truth," says the second, "I do — somewhat."

"Well, there was a word to be said by me! . . .
I divorced that man because of you —   60
It seemed I must do it, boundenly;
But now I am older, and tell you true,
For life is little, and dead lies he;
I would I had let alone you two!
And both of us, scorning parochial ways,   65
Had lived like the wives in the patriarchs' days."

FIVE SATIRES OF CIRCUMSTANCE. The series "Satires of Circumstance" consists of fifteen short
poems; this is a sampling of them. 66. *like the wives in the patriarchs' days:* in bigamy, as in the
times of Solomon and other forefathers recorded in Scripture.

Seamus Heaney (b. 1939)
SUNLIGHT   1975

There was a sunlit absence.
The helmeted pump in the yard

heated its iron,
water honeyed

in the slung bucket
and the sun stood
like a griddle cooling
against the wall

of each long afternoon.
So, her hands scuffled
over the bakeboard,
the reddening stove

sent its plaque of heat
against her where she stood
in a floury apron
by the window.

Now she dusts the board
with a goose's wing,
now sits, broad-lapped,
with whitened nails

and measling shins:
here is a space
again, the scone rising
to the tick of two clocks.

And here is love
like a tinsmith's scoop
sunk past its gleam
in the meal-bin.

5

10

15

20

25

SUNLIGHT. This portrait of a woman at work in an Irish country kitchen comes from "Moss-bawn: Two Poems in Dedication for Mary Heaney." Mossbawn is the farm in Derry, North-ern Ireland, where the poet was born. 23. *scone:* a quick, faintly sweet bread made of oatmeal and barley flour. Usually rolled, cut into quarters, and baked on a hot griddle, it looks like a baking-powder biscuit.

Anthony Hecht (b. 1923)
THE VOW
1967

In the third month, a sudden flow of blood.
The mirth of tabrets ceaseth, and the joy
Also of the harp. The frail image of God
Lay spilled and formless. Neither girl nor boy,
But yet blood of my blood, nearly my child.
        All that long day
Her pale face turned to the window's mild
        Featureless grey.

And for some nights she whimpered as she dreamed
The dead thing spoke, saying: "Do not recall

5

10

Pleasure at my conception. I am redeemed
From pain and sorrow. Mourn rather for all
Who breathlessly issue from the bone gates,
      The gates of horn,
For truly it is best of all the fates   15
      Not to be born.

"Mother, a child lay gasping for bare breath
On Christmas Eve when Santa Claus had set
Death in the stocking, and the lights of death
Flamed in the tree. O, if you can, forget   20
You were the child, turn to my father's lips
      Against the time
When his cold hand puts forth its fingertips
      Of jointed lime."

Doctors of Science, what is man that he   25
Should hope to come to a good end? *The best*
Is not to have been born. And could it be
That Jewish diligence and Irish jest
The consent of flesh and a midwinter storm
      Had reconciled,   30
Was yet too bold a mixture to inform
      A simple child?

Even as gold is tried, Gentile and Jew.
If that ghost was a girl's, I swear to it:
Your mother shall be far more blessed than you.   35
And if a boy's, I swear: The flames are lit
That shall refine us; they shall not destroy
      A living hair.
Your younger brothers shall confirm in joy
      This that I swear.   40

THE VOW. 2. *tabrets:* small drums used to accompany traditional Jewish dances. 14. *gates of horn:*
According to Homer and Virgil pleasant, lying dreams emerge from the underworld through
gates of ivory; ominous, truth-telling dreams, through gates of horn.

George Herbert (1593 – 1633)*
LOVE   1633

Love bade me welcome; yet my soul drew back,
      Guilty of dust and sin.
But quick-eyed Love, observing me grow slack
      From my first entrance in,
Drew nearer to me, sweetly questioning   5
      If I lacked anything.

"A guest," I answered, "worthy to be here";
      Love said, "You shall be he."

"I, the unkind, ungrateful? Ah, my dear,
     I cannot look on Thee."
Love took my hand, and smiling did reply,   10
     "Who made the eyes but I?"

"Truth, Lord, but I have marred them; let my shame
     Go where it doth deserve."
"And know you not," says Love, "who bore the blame?"   15
     "My dear, then I will serve."
"You must sit down," says Love, "and taste My meat."
     So I did sit and eat.

COMPARE

"Love" with "Batter my heart, three-personed God, for You" by John Donne (page 450).

Robert Herrick (1591 – 1674)*
DELIGHT IN DISORDER   1648

A sweet disorder in the dress
Kindles in clothes a wantonness.
A lawn° about the shoulders thrown   *linen*
Into a fine distractión;
An erring lace, which here and there   5
Enthralls the crimson stomacher;
A cuff neglectful, and thereby
Ribbons to flow confusedly;
A winning wave, deserving note,
In the tempestuous petticoat;   10
A careless shoestring, in whose tie
I see a wild civility;
Do more bewitch me than when art
Is too precise in every part.

Robert Herrick (1591 – 1674)*
TO THE VIRGINS, TO MAKE MUCH OF TIME   1648

Gather ye rose-buds while ye may,
  Old Time is still a-flying;
And this same flower that smiles today,
  Tomorrow will be dying.

The glorious lamp of heaven, the sun,   5
  The higher he's a-getting,
The sooner will his race be run,
  And nearer he's to setting.

That age is best which is the first,
   When youth and blood are warmer;   10
But being spent, the worse, and worst
   Times still succeed the former.

Then be not coy, but use your time,
   And while ye may, go marry;
For having lost but once your prime,   15
   You may for ever tarry.

COMPARE:

"To the Virgins, to Make Much of Time" with "To His Coy Mistress" by Andrew
Marvell (page 418) and "Go, Lovely Rose" by Edmund Waller (page 784).

Michael Hogan (b. 1943)

SPRING   1976

Ice has been cracking all day
and small boys on the shore
pretending it is the booming of artillery
lie prone clutching imaginary carbines.

Inside the compound returning birds   5
peck at bread scraps from the mess hall.

Old cons shiver in cloth jackets
as they cross the naked quadrangle.
They know the inside perimeter is exactly
two thousand eighty-four steps   10
and they can walk it five more times
before the steam whistle blows for count.

Above them a tower guard dips his rifle
then raises it again dreamily.
He imagines a speckled trout   15
coming up shining and raging with life.

SPRING. This poem was written in Arizona State Prison.

Garrett Kaoru Hongo (b. 1951)

THE HONGO STORE
29 MILES VOLCANO
HILO, HAWAII   1982

From a photograph

My parents felt those rumblings
Coming deep from the earth's belly,

Thudding like the bell of the Buddhist Church.
Tremors in the ground swayed the bathinette
Where I lay squalling in soapy water.   5

My mother carried me around the house,
Back through the orchids, ferns, and plumeria
Of that greenhouse world behind the store,
And jumped between gas pumps into the car.

My father gave it the gun   10
And said, "Be quiet," as he searched
The frequencies, flipping for the right station
(The radio squealing more loudly than I could cry).

And then even the echoes stopped —
The only sound the Edsel's grinding   15
And the bark and crackle of radio news
Saying stay home or go to church.

"Dees time she no blow!"
My father said, driving back
Over the red ash covering the road.   20
"I worried she went go for broke already!"

So in this print the size of a matchbook,
The dark skinny man, shirtless and grinning,
A toothpick in the corner of his smile,
Lifts a naked baby above his head —   25
Behind him the plate glass of the store only cracked.

Gerard Manley Hopkins (1844 – 1889)*
SPRING AND FALL   (1880)

To a Young Child

Márgarét, are you grieving
Over Goldengrove unleaving°?   *shedding its leaves*
Leáves, like the things of man, you
With your fresh thoughts care for, can you?
Ah! ás the heart grows older   5
It will come to such sights colder
By and by, nor spare a sigh
Though worlds of wanwood leafmeal lie;
And yet you will weep and know why.
Now no matter, child, the name: 10
Sórrow's springs áre the same.
Nor mouth had, no nor mind, expressed
What heart heard of, ghost° guessed: *spirit*
It is the blight man was born for,
It is Margaret you mourn for.   15

COMPARE:

"Spring and Fall" with "Margaret Are You Drug" by George Starbuck (page 646).

Gerard Manley Hopkins (1844 – 1889)*
THOU ART INDEED JUST, LORD, IF I CONTEND   (1889)

*Justus quidem tu es, Domine, si disputem tecum: verumtamen justa loquar
ad te: Quare via impiorum prosperatur? &c.*

Thou art indeed just, Lord, if I contend
With thee; but, sir, so what I plead is just.
Why do sinners' ways prosper? and why must
Disappointment all I endeavor end?
Wert thou my enemy, O thou my friend,   5
How wouldst thou worse, I wonder than thou dost
Defeat, thwart me? Oh, the sots and thralls of lust
Do in spare hours more thrive than I that spend,

Sir, life upon thy cause. See, banks and brakes°   *ferny marshes*
Now, levèd how thick! lacèd they are again   10
With fretty chervil°, look, and fresh wind shakes   *wild herb*

Them; birds build — but not I build; no, but strain,
Time's eunuch, and not breed one work that wakes.
Mine, O thou lord of life, send my roots rain.

THOU ART INDEED JUST, LORD, IF I CONTEND. In the first two sentences of this poem, Hopkins
translates the Latin quotation from the Vulgate Bible (Jeremiah 12:1).

COMPARE:

"Thou art indeed just, Lord . . ." with "When I consider how my light is spent"
by John Milton (page 747).

Gerard Manley Hopkins (1844 – 1889)*
THE WINDHOVER   (1877)

To Christ Our Lord

I caught this morning morning's minion, kingdom of daylight's
    dauphin, dapple-dawn-drawn Falcon, in his riding
    Of the rolling level underneath him steady air, and striding
High there, how he rung upon the rein of a wimpling wing
In his ecstasy! then off, off forth on swing,   5
    As a skate's heel sweeps smooth on a bow-bend: the hurl and
        gliding
    Rebuffed the big wind. My heart in hiding
Stirred for a bird, — the achieve of, the mastery of the thing!

Brute beauty and valor and act, oh, air, pride, plume, here
    Buckle! and the fire that breaks from thee then, a billion   10
Times told lovelier, more dangerous, O my chevalier!

    No wonder of it: shéer plód makes plow down sillion°   *furrow*
Shine, and blue-bleak embers, ah my dear,
    Fall, gall themselves, and gash gold-vermilion.

THE WINDHOVER. A windhover is a kestrel, or small falcon, so called because it can hover upon the wind. 4. *rung . . . wing:* A horse is "rung upon the rein" when its trainer holds the end of a long rein and has the horse circle him. The possible meanings of *wimpling* include (1) curving; (2) pleated, arranged in many little folds one on top of another; (3) rippling or undulating like the surface of a flowing stream.

A. E. Housman (1859 – 1936)*

TERENCE, THIS IS STUPID STUFF   1896

"Terence, this is stupid stuff:
You eat your victuals fast enough;
There can't be much amiss, 'tis clear,
To see the rate you drink your beer.
But oh, good Lord, the verse you make,   5
It gives a chap the belly-ache.
The cow, the old cow, she is dead;
It sleeps well, the horned head:
We poor lads, 'tis our turn now
To hear such tunes as killed the cow.   10
Pretty friendship 'tis to rhyme
Your friends to death before their time
Moping melancholy mad:
Come, pipe a tune to dance to, lad."

    Why, if 'tis dancing you would be,   15
There's brisker pipes than poetry.
Say, for what were hop-yards meant,
Or why was Burton built on Trent?
Oh many a peer of England brews
Livelier liquor than the Muse,   20
And malt does more than Milton can
To justify God's ways to man.
Ale, man, ale's the stuff to drink
For fellows whom it hurts to think:
Look into the pewter pot   25
To see the world as the world's not.
And faith, 'tis pleasant till 'tis past:
The mischief is that 'twill not last.
Oh I have been to Ludlow fair
And left my necktie God knows where,   30
And carried half-way home, or near,
Pints and quarts of Ludlow beer:

Then the world seemed none so bad,
And I myself a sterling lad;
And down in lovely muck I've lain,   35
Happy till I woke again.
Then I saw the morning sky:
Heigho, the tale was all a lie;
The world, it was the old world yet,
I was I, my things were wet,   40
And nothing now remained to do
But begin the game anew.

    Therefore, since the world has still
Much good, but much less good than ill,
And while the sun and moon endure   45
Luck's a chance, but trouble's sure,
I'd face it as a wise man would,
And train for ill and not for good.
'Tis true, the stuff I bring for sale
Is not so brisk a brew as ale: 50
Out of a stem that scored the hand
I wrung it in a weary land.
But take it: if the smack is sour,
The better for the embittered hour;
It should do good to heart and head   55
When your soul is in my soul's stead;
And I will friend you, if I may,
In the dark and cloudy day.

    There was a king reigned in the East:
There, when kings will sit to feast,   60
They get their fill before they think
With poisoned meat and poisoned drink.
He gathered all that springs to birth
From the many-venomed earth;
First a little, thence to more,   65
He sampled all her killing store;
And easy, smiling, seasoned sound,
Sate the king when healths went round.
They put arsenic in his meat
And stared aghast to watch him eat;   70
They poured strychnine in his cup
And shook to see him drink it up:
They shook, they stared as white's their shirt:
Them it was their poison hurt.
—I tell the tale that I heard told.   75
Mithridates, he died old.

TERENCE, THIS IS STUPID STUFF. 1. *Terence:* As a name for himself, Housman takes that of a Roman poet, author of satiric comedies. 18. *why was Burton built on Trent?* The answer is: to use the river's water in the town's brewing industry.

A. E. Housman (1859 – 1936)*
TO AN ATHLETE DYING YOUNG 1896

The time you won your town the race
We chaired you through the market-place;
Man and boy stood cheering by,
And home we brought you shoulder-high.

Today, the road all runners come, 5
Shoulder-high we bring you home,
And set you at your threshold down,
Townsman of a stiller town.

Smart lad, to slip betimes away
From fields where glory does not stay, 10
And early though the laurel grows
It withers quicker than the rose.

Eyes the shady night has shut
Cannot see the record cut,
And silence sounds no worse than cheers 15
After earth has stopped the ears.

Now you will not swell the rout
Of lads that wore their honors out,
Runners whom renown outran
And the name died before the man. 20

So set, before its echoes fade,
The fleet foot on the sill of shade,
And hold to the low lintel up
The still-defended challenge-cup.

And round that early-laureled head 25
Will flock to gaze the strengthless dead,
And find unwithered on its curls
The garland briefer than a girl's.

COMPARE:

"To an Athlete Dying Young" with "Ex-Basketball Player" by John Updike (page 780).

Langston Hughes (1902 – 1967)*
DREAM DEFERRED 1951

What happens to a dream deferred?

Does it dry up
like a raisin in the sun?

Or fester like a sore —
And then run?   5
Does it stink like rotten meat?
Or crust and sugar over —
like a syrupy sweet?

Maybe it just sags
like a heavy load.   10

Or does it explode?

COMPARE:

"Dream Deferred" with "Ballad of Birmingham" by Dudley Randall (page 757).

Langston Hughes (1902 – 1967)*
SUBWAY RUSH HOUR   1951

Mingled
breath and smell
so close
mingled
black and white   5
so near
no room for fear

David Ignatow (b. 1914)
GET THE GASWORKS   1948

Get the gasworks into a poem,
and you've got the smoke and smokestacks,
the mottled red and yellow tenements,
and grimy kids who curse with the pungency
of the odor of gas. You've got America, boy.   5

Sketch in the river and barges,
all dirty and slimy.
How do the seagulls stay so white?
And always cawing like little mad geniuses?
You've got the kind of living   10
that makes the kind of thinking we do:
gaswork smokestack whistle tooting wisecracks.
They don't come because we like it that way,
but because we find it outside our window each morning,
in soot on the furniture,   15
and trucks carrying coal for gas,
the kid hot after the ball under the wheel.

He gets it over the belly, all right.
He dies there.

So the kids keep tossing the ball around   20
after the funeral.
So the cops keep chasing them,
so the mamas keep hollering,
and papa flings his newspaper outward,
in disgust with discipline.   25

Randall Jarrell (1914 – 1965)*
THE DEATH OF THE BALL TURRET GUNNER   1945

From my mother's sleep I fell into the State
And I hunched in its belly till my wet fur froze.
Six miles from earth, loosed from its dream of life,
I woke to black flak and the nightmare fighters.
When I died they washed me out of the turret with a hose.

THE DEATH OF THE BALL TURRET GUNNER. Jarrell has written: "A ball turret was a plexiglass
sphere set into the belly of a B-17 or B-24, and inhabited by two .50 caliber machine-guns
and one man, a short small man. When this gunner tracked with his machine-guns a fighter
attacking his bomber from below, he revolved with the turret; hunched in his little sphere,
he looked like the fetus in the womb. The fighters which attacked him were armed with
cannon firing explosive shells. The hose was a steam hose."

COMPARE:

"The Death of the Ball Turret Gunner" with "Dulce et Decorum Est" by Wilfred
Owen (page 438).

Randall Jarrell (1914 – 1965)*
WELL WATER   1965

What a girl called "the dailiness of life"
(Adding an errand to your errand. Saying,
"Since you're up . . ." Making you a means to
A means to a means to) is well water
Pumped from an old well at the bottom of the world.   5
The pump you pump the water from is rusty
And hard to move and absurd, a squirrel-wheel
A sick squirrel turns slowly, through the sunny
Inexorable hours. And yet sometimes
The wheel turns of its own weight, the rusty   10
Pump pumps over your sweating face the clear
Water, cold, so cold! you cup your hands
And gulp from them the dailiness of life.

Ben Jonson (1573? – 1637)*
ON MY FIRST SON   (1603)

Farewell, thou child of my right hand, and joy.
My sin was too much hope of thee, loved boy;
Seven years thou wert lent to me, and I thee pay,
Exacted by thy fate, on the just day.
Oh, could I lose all father° now. For why   *fatherhood*   5
Will man lament the state he should envỳ? —
To have so soon 'scaped world's and flesh's rage,
And, if no other misery, yet age.
Rest in soft peace, and asked, say, "Here doth lie
Ben Jonson his best piece of poetry,"   10
For whose sake henceforth all his vows be such
As what he loves may never like° too much.   *thrive*

ON MY FIRST SON. 1. *child of my right hand:* Jonson's son was named Benjamin; this phrase translates the Hebrew name. 4. *the just day:* the very day. The boy had died on his seventh birthday.

Donald Justice (b. 1925)
ON THE DEATH OF FRIENDS IN CHILDHOOD   1960

We shall not ever meet them bearded in heaven,
Nor sunning themselves among the bald of hell;
If anywhere, in the deserted schoolyard at twilight,
Forming a ring, perhaps, or joining hands
In games whose very names we have forgotten.   5
Come, memory, let us seek them there in the shadows.

COMPARE:

"On the Death of Friends in Childhood" with the poem that precedes it, "On My First Son" by Ben Jonson; also with A. E. Housman's "With rue my heart is laden" (page 547).

John Keats (1795 – 1821)*
ODE ON MELANCHOLY   1820

No, no, go not to Lethe, neither twist
    Wolf's-bane, tight-rooted, for its poisonous wine;
Nor suffer thy pale forehead to be kissed
    By nightshade, ruby grape of Proserpine;
Make not your rosary of yew-berries,   5
    Nor let the beetle, nor the death-moth be
        Your mournful Psyche, nor the downy owl

A partner in your sorrow's mysteries;
    For shade to shade will come too drowsily,
        And drown the wakeful anguish of the soul.   10

But when the melancholy fit shall fall
    Sudden from heaven like a weeping cloud,
That fosters the droop-headed flowers all,
    And hides the green hill in an April shroud;
Then glut thy sorrow on a morning rose,   15
    Or on the rainbow of the salt sand-wave,
        Or on the wealth of globèd peonies;
Or if thy mistress some rich anger shows,
    Emprison her soft hand, and let her rave,
        And feed deep, deep upon her peerless eyes.   20

She dwells with beauty — beauty that must die;
    And joy, whose hand is ever at his lips
Bidding adieu; and aching pleasure nigh,
    Turning to poison while the bee-mouth sips:
Ay, in the very temple of delight   25
    Veiled Melancholy has her sovran shrine,
        Though seen of none save him whose strenuous tongue
Can burst joy's grape against his palate fine;
His soul shall taste the sadness of her might,
        And be among her cloudy trophies hung.   30

ODE ON MELANCHOLY. 1. *Lethe:* in ancient Greek belief, a river in Hades. The dead, on drinking its waters, forget past life. 2, 4. *Wolf's-bane, nightshade:* plants, sources of opiates (drugs to induce sleep). 4. *Proserpine:* (also spelled Persephone), Hades' queen. 5. *yew-berries:* To this day, the yew tree, a conventional symbol of mourning, is sometimes planted in graveyards. 6 – 7. *death-moth . . . Psyche:* Psyche is a personification of the human soul (the name means "soul" in Greek). Ancients believed that the soul quits the body of a dying person in the form of a moth. Keats makes the insect a "death's-head moth," whose dark-spotted wings seem to depict a skull.

John Keats (1795 – 1821)*
ON FIRST LOOKING INTO CHAPMAN'S HOMER   1816

Much have I traveled in the realms of gold,
    And many goodly states and kingdoms seen;
    Round many western islands have I been
Which bards in fealty to Apollo hold.
Oft of one wide expanse had I been told   5
    That deep-browed Homer ruled as his demesne°,   *domain*
    Yet did I never breathe its pure serene
Till I heard Chapman speak out loud and bold.
Then felt I like some watcher of the skies
    When a new planet swims into his ken;   10
Or like stout Cortez when with eagle eyes
    He stared at the Pacific — and all his men
Looked at each other with a wild surmise —
    Silent, upon a peak in Darien.

ON FIRST LOOKING INTO CHAPMAN'S HOMER. When one evening in October 1816 Keats's friend and former teacher Cowden Clarke introduced the young poet to George Chapman's vigorous Elizabethan translations of the *Iliad* and the *Odyssey*, Keats stayed up all night reading and discussing them in high excitement; then went home at dawn to compose this sonnet, which Clarke received at his breakfast table. 4. *fealty:* in feudalism, the loyalty of a vassal to his lord; *Apollo:* classical god of poetic inspiration. 11. *stout Cortez:* the best-known boner in English poetry. (What Spanish explorer *was* the first European to view the Pacific?) 14. *Darien:* old name for the Isthmus of Panama.

John Keats (1795 – 1821)*

TO AUTUMN

1820

I

Season of mists and mellow fruitfulness,
  Close bosom-friend of the maturing sun;
Conspiring with him how to load and bless
  With fruit the vines that round the thatch-eves run;
To bend with apples the mossed cottage-trees,   5
  And fill all fruit with ripeness to the core;
    To swell the gourd, and plump the hazel shells
With a sweet kernel; to set budding more,
And still more, later flowers for the bees,
Until they think warm days will never cease,   10
    For Summer has o'er-brimmed their clammy cells.

II

Who hath not seen thee oft amid thy store?
  Sometimes whoever seeks abroad may find
Thee sitting careless on a granary floor,
  Thy hair soft-lifted by the winnowing wind;   15
Or on a half-reaped furrow sound asleep,
  Drowsed with the fume of poppies, while thy hook
    Spares the next swath and all its twinèd flowers:
And sometimes like a gleaner thou dost keep
  Steady thy laden head across a brook;   20
  Or by a cider-press, with patient look,
    Thou watchest the last oozings hours by hours.

III

Where are the songs of Spring? Ay, where are they?
  Think not of them, thou hast thy music too, —
While barrèd clouds bloom the soft-dying day,   25
  And touch the stubble-plains with rosy hue;
Then in a wailful choir the small gnats mourn
  Among the river sallows°, borne aloft   *willows*
    Or sinking as the light wind lives or dies;
And full-grown lambs loud bleat from hilly bourn;   30
  Hedge-crickets sing; and now with treble soft
The red-breast whistles from a garden-croft°   *garden plot*
  And gathering swallows twitter in the skies.

COMPARE:

"To Autumn" with "In the Elegy Season" by Richard Wilbur (page 452).

Galway Kinnell (b. 1927)*
SAINT FRANCIS AND THE SOW

1980

The bud
stands for all things,
even for those things that don't flower,
for everything flowers, from within, of self-blessing;
though sometimes it is necessary   5
to reteach a thing its loveliness,
to put a hand on its brow
of the flower
and retell it in words and in touch
it is lovely   10
until it flowers again from within, of self-blessing;
as Saint Francis
put his hand on the creased forehead
of the sow, and told her in words and in touch
blessings of earth on the sow, and the sow   15
began remembering all down her thick length,
from the earthen snout all the way
through the fodder and slops to the spiritual curl of the tail,
from the hard spininess spiked out from the spine
down through the great broken heart   20
to the blue milken dreaminess spurting and shuddering
from the fourteen teats into the fourteen mouths sucking and
        blowing beneath them:
the long, perfect loveliness of sow.

Carolyn Kizer (b. 1925)
THE INTRUDER

1971

My mother — preferring the strange to the tame:
Dove-note, bone marrow, deer dung,
Frog's belly distended with finny young,
Leaf-mould wilderness, hare-bell, toadstool,
Odd, small snakes roving through the leaves,   5
Metallic beetles rambling over stones: all
Wild and natural! — flashed out her instinctive love, and quick, she
Picked up the fluttering, bleeding bat the cat laid at her feet,
And held the little horror to the mirror, where
He gazed on himself, and shrieked like an old screen door far off.   10

Depended from her pinched thumb, each wing
Came clattering down like a small black shutter.
Still tranquil, she began, "It's rather sweet. . . ."
The soft mouse body, the hard feral glint
In the caught eyes. Then we saw,   15
And recoiled: lice, pallid, yellow,
Nested within the wing-pits, cosily sucked and snoozed.
The thing dropped from her hands, and with its thud,
Swiftly, the cat, with a clean careful mouth
Closed on the soiled webs, growling, took them out to the back stoop.   20

But still, dark blood, a sticky puddle on the floor
Remained, of all my mother's tender, wounding passion
For a whole wild, lost, betrayed and secret life
Among its dens and burrows, its clean stones,
Whose denizens can turn upon the world.   25
With spitting tongue, an odor, talon, claw,
To sting or soil benevolence, alien
As our clumsy traps, our random scatter of shot.
She swept to the kitchen. Turning on the tap,
She washed and washed the pity from her hands.   30

Ted Kooser (b. 1939)
FLYING AT NIGHT   1985

Above us, stars. Beneath us, constellations.
Five billion miles away, a galaxy dies
like a snowflake falling on water. Below us,
some farmer, feeling the chill of that distant death,
snaps on his yard light, drawing his sheds and barn   5
back into the little system of his care.
All night, the cities, like shimmering novas,
tug with bright streets at lonely lights like his.

Philip Larkin (1922 – 1985)*
HOME IS SO SAD   1964

Home is so sad. It stays as it was left,
Shaped to the comfort of the last to go
As if to win them back. Instead, bereft
Of anyone to please, it withers so,
Having no heart to put aside the theft   5

And turn again to what it started as,
A joyous shot at how things ought to be,
Long fallen wide. You can see how it was:
Look at the pictures and the cutlery.
The music in the piano stool. That vase.   10

Philip Larkin (1922 – 1985)*
A STUDY OF READING HABITS   1964

When getting my nose in a book
Cured most things short of school,
It was worth ruining my eyes
To know I could still keep cool,
And deal out the old right hook   5
To dirty dogs twice my size.

Later, with inch-thick specs,
Evil was just my lark:
Me and my cloak and fangs
Had ripping times in the dark.   10
The women I clubbed with sex!
I broke them up like meringues.

Don't read much now: the dude
Who lets the girl down before
The hero arrives, the chap   15
Who's yellow and keeps the store,
Seem far too familiar. Get stewed:
Books are a load of crap.

D. H. Lawrence (1885 – 1930)*
A YOUTH MOWING   1917

There are four men mowing down by the Isar;
I can hear the swish of the scythe-strokes, four
Sharp breaths taken: yea, and I
Am sorry for what's in store.

The first man out of the four that's mowing   5
Is mine, I claim him once and for all;
Though it's sorry I am, on his young feet, knowing
None of the trouble he's led to stall.

As he sees me bringing the dinner, he lifts
His head as proud as a deer that looks   10
Shoulder-deep out of the corn; and wipes
His scythe-blade bright, unhooks

The scythe-stone and over the stubble to me.
Lad, thou has gotten a child in me,
Laddie, a man thou'lt ha'e to be,   15
Yea, though I'm sorry for thee.

A YOUTH MOWING. 1. *Isar:* river in Austria and Germany that flows into the Danube.

Irving Layton (b. 1912)

THE BULL CALF   1959

The thing could barely stand. Yet taken
from his mother and the barn smells
he still impressed with his pride,
with the promise of sovereignty in the way
his head moved to take us in.   5
The fierce sunlight tugging the maize from the ground
licked at his shapely flanks.
He was too young for all that pride.
I thought of the deposed Richard II.

"No money in bull calves," Freeman had said.   10
The visiting clergyman rubbed the nostrils
now snuffing pathetically at the windless day.
"A pity," he sighed.
My gaze slipped off his hat toward the empty sky
that circled over the black knot of men,   15
over us and the calf waiting for the first blow.

Struck,
the bull calf drew in his thin forelegs
as if gathering strength for a mad rush . . .
tottered . . . raised his darkening eyes to us,   20
and I saw we were at the far end
of his frightened look, growing smaller and smaller
till we were only the ponderous mallet
that flicked his bleeding ear
and pushed him over on his side, stiffly,   25
like a block of wood.

Below the hill's crest
the river snuffled on the improvised beach.
We dug a deep pit and threw the dead calf into it.
It made a wet sound, a sepulchral gurgle,   30
as the warm sides bulged and flattened.
Settled, the bull calf lay as if asleep,
one foreleg over the other,
bereft of pride and so beautiful now,
without movement, perfectly still in the cool pit,   35
I turned away and wept.

Denise Levertov (b. 1923)*
THE ACHE OF MARRIAGE   1964

The ache of marriage:

thigh and tongue, beloved,
are heavy with it,
it throbs in the teeth

We look for communion   5
and are turned away, beloved,
each and each

It is Leviathan and we
in its belly
looking for joy, some joy   10
not to be known outside it

two by two in the ark of
the ache of it.

THE ACHE OF MARRIAGE. 8. *Leviathan:* Biblical sea monster, sometimes said to be the great fish that swallowed Jonah.

Philip Levine (b. 1928)
TO A CHILD TRAPPED IN A BARBER SHOP   1966

You've gotten in through the transom
        and you can't get out
till Monday morning or, worse,
        till the cops come.

That six-year-old red face   5
        calling for mama
is yours; it won't help you
        because your case

is closed forever, hopeless.
        So don't drink   10
the Lucky Tiger, don't
        fill up on grease

because that makes it a lot worse,
        that makes it a crime
against property and the state   15
        and that costs time.

We've all been here before,
        we took our turn
under the electric storm
        of the vibrator   20

and stiffened our wills to meet
          the close clippers
and heard the true blade mowing
          back and forth

on a strip of dead skin,   25
          and we stopped crying.
You think your life is over?
          It's just begun.

Robert Lowell (1917 – 1977)*
Skunk Hour   1959

For Elizabeth Bishop

Nautilus Island's hermit
heiress still lives through winters in her Spartan cottage;
her sheep still graze above the sea.
Her son's a bishop. Her farmer
is first selectman in our village;   5
she's in her dotage.

Thirsting for
the hierarchic privacy
of Queen Victoria's century,
she buys up all   10
the eyesores facing her shore,
and lets them fall.

The season's ill —
we've lost our summer millionaire,
who seemed to leap from an L. L. Bean   15
catalogue. His nine-knot yawl
was auctioned off to lobstermen.
A red fox stain covers Blue Hill.

And now our fairy
decorator brightens his shop for fall;   20
his fishnet's filled with orange cork,
orange, his cobbler's bench and awl;
there is no money in his work,
he'd rather marry.

One dark night,   25
my Tudor Ford climbed the hill's skull;
I watched for love-cars. Lights turned down,
they lay together, hull to hull,
where the graveyard shelves on the town. . . .
My mind's not right.   30

A car radio bleats,
"Love, O careless Love. . . ." I hear
my ill-spirit sob in each blood cell,
as if my hand were at its throat. . . .
I myself am hell;   35
nobody's here —

only skunks, that search
in the moonlight for a bite to eat.
They march on their soles up Main Street:
white stripes, moonstruck eyes' red fire   40
under the chalk-dry and spar spire
of the Trinitarian Church.

I stand on top
of our back steps and breathe the rich air —
a mother skunk with her column of kittens swills the garbage pail.   45
She jabs her wedge-head in a cup
of sour cream, drops her ostrich tail,
and will not scare.

Christopher Marlowe (1564 – 1593)
The Passionate Shepherd to His Love   1600

Come live with me and be my love,
And we will all the pleasures prove
That valleys, groves, hills, and fields,
Woods, or steepy mountain yields.

And we will sit upon the rocks,   5
Seeing the shepherds feed their flocks
By shallow rivers, to whose falls
Melodious birds sing madrigals.

And I will make thee beds of roses
And a thousand fragrant posies,   10
A cap of flowers and a kirtle°   *skirt*
Embroidered all with leaves of myrtle;

A gown made of the finest wool
Which from our pretty lambs we pull;
Fair-linèd slippers for the cold,   15
With buckles of the purest gold;

A belt of straw and ivy buds,
With coral clasps and amber studs.
And if these pleasures may thee move,
Come live with me and be my love.   20

The shepherds' swains shall dance and sing
For thy delight each May morning.
If these delights thy mind may move,
Then live with me and be my love.

COMPARE:

"The Passionate Shepherd to His Love" with "The Nymph's Reply to the Shepherd" by Sir Walter Raleigh (page 756) and another reply, "The Bait" by John Donne (page 707).

George Meredith (1828 – 1909)

LUCIFER IN STARLIGHT   1883

On a starred night Prince Lucifer uprose,
  Tired of his dark dominion, swung the fiend
  Above the rolling ball in cloud part screened,
Where sinners hugged their specter of repose.
Poor prey to his hot fit of pride were those.   5
  And now upon his western wing he leaned,
  Now his huge bulk o'er Afric's sands careened,
Now the black planet shadowed Arctic snows.
Soaring through wider zones that pricked his scars
  With memory of the old revolt from Awe,   10
He reached a middle height, and at the stars,
Which are the brain of heaven, he looked, and sank.
Around the ancient track marched, rank on rank,
  The army of unalterable law.

James Merrill (b. 1926)

LABORATORY POEM   1958

Charles used to watch Naomi, taking heart
And a steel saw, open up turtles, live.
While she swore they felt nothing, he would gag
At blood, at the blind twitching, even after
The murky dawn of entrails cleared, revealing   5
Contours he knew, egg-yellows like lamps paling.

Well then. She carried off the beating heart
To the kymograph and rigged it there, a rag
In fitful wind, now made to strain, now stopped
By her solutions tonic or malign   10
Alternately in which it would be steeped.
What the heart bore, she noted on a chart,

For work did not stop only with the heart.
He thought of certain human hearts, their climb
Through violence into exquisite disciplines   15
Of which, as it now appeared, they all expired.
Soon she would fetch another and start over,
Easy in the presence of her lover.

LABORATORY POEM. 8. *kymograph:* device to record wavelike motions or pulsations on a piece
of paper fastened to a revolving drum.

Charlotte Mew (1869 – 1928)

FAME   1916

Sometimes in the over-heated house, but not for long,
     Smirking and speaking rather loud,
   I see myself among the crowd,
Where no one fits the singer to his song,
Or sifts the unpainted from the painted faces   5
Of the people who are always on my stair;
They were not with me when I walked in heavenly places;
       But could I spare
In the blind Earth's great silences and spaces,
   The din, the scuffle, the long stare   10
   If I went back and it was not there?
Back to the old known things that are the new,
The folded glory of the gorse, the sweet-briar air,
To the larks that cannot praise us, knowing nothing of what we do
   And the divine, wise trees that do not care.   15
Yet, to leave Fame, still with such eyes and that bright hair!
God! If I might! And before I go hence
     Take in her stead
     To our tossed bed,
One little dream, no matter how small, how wild.   20
Just now, I think I found it in a field, under a fence —
A frail, dead, new-born lamb, ghostly and pitiful and white,
     A blot upon the night,
     The moon's dropped child!

John Milton (1608 – 1674)*

WHEN I CONSIDER HOW MY LIGHT IS SPENT   (1655?)

When I consider how my light is spent,
  Ere half my days in this dark world and wide,
  And that one talent which is death to hide
Lodged with me useless, though my soul more bent
To serve therewith my Maker, and present   5

My true account, lest He returning chide;
  "Doth God exact day-labor, light denied?"
I fondly° ask. But Patience, to prevent   *foolishly*
That murmur, soon replies, "God doth not need
  Either man's work or His own gifts. Who best   10
  Bear His mild yoke, they serve Him best. His state
Is kingly: thousands at His bidding speed,
  And post o'er land and ocean without rest;
  They also serve who only stand and wait."

WHEN I CONSIDER HOW MY LIGHT IS SPENT. 1. *my light is spent:* Milton had become blind. 3. *that one talent:* For Jesus's parable of the talents (measures of money), see Matthew 25:14 – 30.

COMPARE:

"When I consider how my light is spent" with "Thou art indeed just, Lord, if I contend" by Gerard Manley Hopkins (page 730).

N. Scott Momaday (b. 1934)
THE DELIGHT SONG OF TSOAI-TALEE   1974

I am a feather on the bright sky
I am the blue horse that runs in the plain
I am the fish that rolls, shining, in the water
I am the shadow that follows a child
I am the evening light, the lustre of meadows   5
I am an eagle playing with the wind
I am a cluster of bright beads
I am the farthest star
I am the cold of the dawn
I am the roaring of the rain   10
I am the glitter on the crust of the snow
I am the long track of the moon in a lake
I am a flame of four colors
I am a deer standing away in the dusk
I am a field of sumac and the pomme blanche   15
I am an angle of geese in the winter sky
I am the hunger of a young wolf
I am the whole dream of these things

You see, I am alive, I am alive
I stand in good relation to the earth   20
I stand in good relation to the gods
I stand in good relation to all that is beautiful
I stand in good relation to the daughter of Tsen-tainte
You see, I am alive, I am alive

THE DELIGHT SONG OF TSOAI-TALEE. The poet is a Kiowa Indian.

Marianne Moore (1887 – 1972)

THE MIND IS AN ENCHANTING THING   1944

is an enchanted thing
    like the glaze on a
katydid-wing
        subdivided by sun
        till the nettings are legion.   5
Like Gieseking playing Scarlatti;

like the apteryx-awl
    as a beak, or the
kiwi's rain-shawl
        of haired feathers, the mind   10
        feeling its way as though blind,
walks along with its eyes on the ground.

It has memory's ear
    that can hear without
having to hear.   15
        Like the gyroscope's fall,
        truly unequivocal
because trued by regnant certainty,

it is a power of
    strong enchantment. It   20
is like the dove-
        neck animated by
        sun; it is memory's eye;
it's conscientious inconsistency.

It tears off the veil; tears   25
    the temptation, the
mist the heart wears,
        from its eyes, — if the heart
        has a face; it takes apart
dejection. It's fire in the dove-neck's   30

iridescence; in the
    inconsistencies
of Scarlatti.
        Unconfusion submits
        its confusion to proof; it's   35
not a Herod's oath that cannot change.

THE MIND IS AN ENCHANTING THING. 6. *Gieseking . . . Scarlatti:* Walter Gieseking (1895 – 1956), German pianist, was a celebrated performer of the difficult sonatas of Italian composer Domenico Scarlatti (1685 – 1757). 7. *apteryx-awl:* awl-shaped beak of the apteryx, one of the kiwi family. (An awl is a pointed tool for piercing wood or leather.) 36. *Herod's oath:* King Herod's order condemning to death all infants in Bethlehem (Matthew 2:1 – 16). In one medieval English version of the Herod story, a pageant play, the king causes the death of his own child by refusing to withdraw his command.

Howard Nemerov (b. 1920)
Storm Windows   1958

People are putting up storm windows now,
Or were, this morning, until the heavy rain
Drove them indoors. So, coming home at noon,
I saw storm windows lying on the ground,
Frame-full of rain; through the water and glass   5
I saw the crushed grass, how it seemed to stream
Away in lines like seaweed on the tide
Or blades of wheat leaning under the wind.
The ripple and splash of rain on the blurred glass
Seemed that it briefly said, as I walked by,   10
Something I should have liked to say to you,
Something . . . the dry grass bent under the pane
Brimful of bouncing water . . . something of
A swaying clarity which blindly echoes
This lonely afternoon of memories   15
And missed desires, while the wintry rain
(Unspeakable, the distance in the mind!)
Runs on the standing windows and away.

John Frederick Nims (b. 1914)*
Love Poem   1947

My clumsiest dear, whose hands shipwreck vases,
At whose quick touch all glasses chip and ring,
Whose palms are bulls in china, burs in linen,
And have no cunning with any soft thing

Except all ill-at-ease fidgeting people: 5
The refugee uncertain at the door
You make at home; deftly you steady
The drunk clambering on his undulant floor.

Unpredictable dear, the taxi drivers' terror,
Shrinking from far headlights pale as a dime   10
Yet leaping before red apoplectic streetcars —
Misfit in any space. And never on time.

A wrench in clocks and the solar system. Only
With words and people and love you move at ease.
In traffic of wit expertly manoeuvre   15
And keep us, all devotion, at your knees.

Forgetting your coffee spreading on our flannel,
Your lipstick grinning on our coat,
So gayly in love's unbreakable heaven
Our souls on glory of split bourbon float.   20

Be with me, darling, early and late. Smash glasses —
I will study wry music for your sake.
For should your hands drop white and empty
All the toys of the world would break.

COMPARE:

"Love Poem" with "Love Song: I and Thou" by Alan Dugan (page 711).

Sharon Olds (b. 1942)
THE ONE GIRL AT THE BOYS PARTY 1983

When I take my girl to the swimming party
I set her down among the boys. They tower and
bristle, she stands there smooth and sleek,
her math scores unfolding in the air around her.
They will strip to their suits, her body hard and   5
indivisible as a prime number,
they'll plunge in the deep end, she'll subtract
her height from ten feet, divide it into
hundreds of gallons of water, the numbers
bouncing in her mind like molecules of chlorine   10
in the bright blue pool. When they climb out,
her ponytail will hang its pencil lead
down her back, her narrow silk suit
with hamburgers and french fries printed on it
will glisten in the brilliant air, and they will   15
see her sweet face, solemn and
sealed, a factor of one, and she will
see their eyes, two each,
their legs, two each, and the curves of their sexes,
one each, and in her head she'll be doing her   20
wild multiplying, as the drops
sparkle and fall to the power of a thousand from her body.

Wilfred Owen (1893 – 1918)*
ANTHEM FOR DOOMED YOUTH (1917?)

What passing-bells for these who die as cattle?
    Only the monstrous anger of the guns.
Only the stuttering rifles' rapid rattle
Can patter out their hasty orisons.
No mockeries now for them; no prayers nor bells,   5
    Nor any voice of mourning save the choirs, —
The shrill, demented choirs of wailing shells;
    And bugles calling for them from sad shires°.   *counties*

What candles may be held to speed them all?
  Not in the hands of boys, but in their eyes   10
  Shall shine the holy glimmers of good-byes.
The pallor of girls' brows shall be their pall;
Their flowers the tenderness of patient minds,
And each slow dusk a drawing-down of blinds.

Robert Phillips (b. 1938)
RUNNING ON EMPTY   1981

As a teenager I would drive Father's
Chevrolet cross-county, given me

reluctantly: "Always keep the tank
half full, boy, half full, ya hear?"

The fuel gauge dipping, dipping   5
toward Empty, hitting Empty, then

— thrilling! — 'way below Empty,
myself driving cross-county

mile after mile, faster and faster,
all night long, this crazy kid driving   10

the earth's rolling surface,
against all laws, defying chemistry,

rules, and time, riding on nothing
but fumes, pushing luck harder

than anyone pushed before, the wind   15
screaming past like the Furies . . .

I stranded myself only once, a white
night with no gas station open, ninety miles

from nowhere. Panicked for a while,
at standstill, myself stalled.   20

At dawn the car and I both refilled. But,
Father, I am running on empty still.

RUNNING ON EMPTY. 16. *Furies:* In Greek mythology, deities who pursue and torment evildoers.

Sylvia Plath (1932 – 1963)*
DADDY   1965

You do not do, you do not do
Any more, black shoe
In which I have lived like a foot

For thirty years, poor and white,
Barely daring to breathe or Achoo.   5

Daddy, I have had to kill you.
You died before I had time —
Marble-heavy, a bag full of God,
Ghastly statue with one grey toe
Big as a Frisco seal   10

And a head in the freakish Atlantic
Where it pours bean green over blue
In the waters off beautiful Nauset.
I used to pray to recover you.
Ach, du.   15

In the German tongue, in the Polish town
Scraped flat by the roller
Of wars, wars, wars.
But the name of the town is common.
My Polack friend   20

Says there are a dozen or two.
So I never could tell where you
Put your foot, your root,
I never could talk to you.
The tongue stuck in my jaw.   25

It stuck in a barb wire snare.
Ich, ich, ich, ich,
I could hardly speak.
I thought every German was you.
And the language obscene   30

An engine, an engine
Chuffing me off like a Jew.
A Jew to Dachau, Auschwitz, Belsen.
I began to talk like a Jew.
I think I may well be a Jew.   35

The snows of the Tyrol, the clear beer of Vienna
Are not very pure or true.
With my gypsy ancestress and my weird luck
And my Taroc pack and my Taroc pack
I may be a bit of a Jew.   40

I have always been scared of *you,*
With your Luftwaffe, your gobbledygoo.
And your neat moustache
And your Aryan eye, bright blue.
Panzer-man, panzer-man, O You —   45

Not God but a swastika
So black no sky could squeak through.

Every woman adores a Fascist,
The boot in the face, the brute
Brute heart of a brute like you.   50

You stand at the blackboard, daddy,
In the picture I have of you,
A cleft in your chin instead of your foot
But no less a devil for that, no not
Any less the black man who   55

Bit my pretty red heart in two.
I was ten when they buried you.
At twenty I tried to die
And get back, back, back at you.
I thought even the bones will do.   60

But they pulled me out of the sack,
And they stuck me together with glue.
And then I knew what to do.
I made a model of you,
A man in black with a Meinkampf look   65

And a love of the rack and the screw.
And I said I do, I do.
So daddy, I'm finally through.
The black telephone's off at the root,
The voices just can't worm through.   70

If I've killed one man, I've killed two —
The vampire who said he was you
And drank my blood for a year,
Seven years, if you want to know.
Daddy, you can lie back now.   75

There's a stake in your fat black heart
And the villagers never liked you.
They are dancing and stamping on you.
They always *knew* it was you.
Daddy, daddy, you bastard, I'm through.   80

DADDY. Introducing this poem in a reading, Sylvia Plath remarked:

The poem is spoken by a girl with an Electra complex. Her father died while she thought he
was God. Her case is complicated by the fact that her father was also a Nazi and her mother
very possibly part Jewish. In the daughter the two strains marry and paralyze each other —
she has to act out the awful little allegory before she is free of it.

(Quoted by A. Alvarez, *Beyond All This Fiddle*, New York, 1971.) In some details "Daddy" is
autobiography: the poet's father, Otto Plath, a German, had come to the United States from
Grabow, Poland. He had died following amputation of a gangrened foot and leg, when Sylvia
was eight years old. Politically, Otto Plath was a Republican, not a Nazi; but was apparently
a somewhat domineering head of the household. (See the recollections of the poet's mother,
Aurelia Schober Plath, in her edition of *Letters Home* by Sylvia Plath, New York, 1975.) 15.
Ach, du: Oh, you. 27. *Ich, ich, ich, ich:* I, I, I, I. 51. *blackboard:* Otto Plath had been a professor
of biology at Boston University. 65. *Meinkampf:* Adolf Hitler entitled his autobiography *Mein
Kampf* ("My Struggle").

COMPARE:

"Daddy" with "American Primitive" by William Jay Smith (page 771).

Sylvia Plath (1932 – 1963)*
MORNING SONG
1965

Love set you going like a fat gold watch.
The midwife slapped your footsoles, and your bald cry
Took its place among the elements.

Our voices echo, magnifying your arrival. New statue.
In a drafty museum, your nakedness   5
Shadows our safety. We stand round blankly as walls.

I'm no more your mother
Than the cloud that distills a mirror to reflect its own slow
Effacement at the wind's hand.

All night your moth-breath   10
Flickers among the flat pink roses. I wake to listen:
A far sea moves in my ear.

One cry, and I stumble from bed, cow-heavy and floral
In my Victorian nightgown.
Your mouth opens clean as a cat's. The window square   15

Whitens and swallows its dull stars. And now you try
Your handful of notes;
The clear vowels rise like balloons.

Ezra Pound (1885 – 1972)*
THE RIVER-MERCHANT'S WIFE: A LETTER
1915

While my hair was still cut straight across my forehead
I played about the front gate, pulling flowers.
You came by on bamboo stilts, playing horse,
You walked about my seat, playing with blue plums.
And we went on living in the village of Chokan: 5
Two small people, without dislike or suspicion.
At fourteen I married My Lord you.
I never laughed, being bashful.
Lowering my head, I looked at the wall.
Called to, a thousand times, I never looked back.   10

At fifteen I stopped scowling,
I desired my dust to be mingled with yours
Forever and forever and forever.
Why should I climb the lookout?

At sixteen you departed,   15
You went into far Ku-to-yen, by the river of swirling eddies,
And you have been gone five months.
The monkeys make sorrowful noise overhead.

You dragged your feet when you went out.
By the gate now, the moss is grown, the different mosses,   20
Too deep to clear them away!
The leaves fall early this autumn, in wind.
The paired butterflies are already yellow with August
Over the grass in the West garden;
They hurt me. I grow older.   25
If you are coming down through the narrows of the river Kiang,
Please let me know before hand,
And I will come out to meet you
        As far as Cho-fu-sa.

THE RIVER-MERCHANT'S WIFE: A LETTER. A free translation from the Chinese poet Li Po (eighth century).

Sir Walter Raleigh (1552? – 1618)
THE NYMPH'S REPLY TO THE SHEPHERD   (1589?)

If all the world and love were young,
And truth in every shepherd's tongue,
These pretty pleasures might me move
To live with thee and be thy love.

Time drives the flocks from field to fold,   5
When rivers rage and rocks grow cold;
And Philomel° becometh dumb;   *the nightingale*
The rest complains of cares to come.

The flowers do fade, and wanton fields
To wayward winter reckoning yields: 10
A honey tongue, a heart of gall,
Is fancy's spring, but sorrow's fall.

Thy gowns, thy shoes, thy beds of roses,
Thy cap, thy kirtle°, and thy posies   *long dress*
Soon break, soon wither, soon forgotten,   15
In folly ripe, in reason rotten.

Thy belt of straw and ivy buds,
Thy coral clasps and amber studs,
All these in me no means can move
To come to thee and be thy love.   20

But could youth last, and love still breed,
Had joys no date, nor age no need,

Then these delights my mind might move
To live with thee and be thy love.

COMPARE:

"The Nymph's Reply to the Shepherd" with Christopher Marlowe's "The Passion-ate Shepherd to His Love" (page 745) and another reply to Marlowe's poem, "The Bait" by John Donne (page 707).

Dudley Randall (b. 1914)

BALLAD OF BIRMINGHAM   1966

*(On the Bombing of a Church in
Birmingham, Alabama, 1963)*

"Mother dear, may I go downtown
Instead of out to play,
And march the streets of Birmingham
In a Freedom March today?"

"No, baby, no, you may not go,   5
For the dogs are fierce and wild,
And clubs and hoses, guns and jail
Aren't good for a little child."

"But, mother, I won't be alone.
Other children will go with me,   10
And march the streets of Birmingham
To make our country free."

"No, baby, no, you may not go,
For I fear those guns will fire.
But you may go to church instead   15
And sing in the children's choir."

She has combed and brushed her night-dark hair,
And bathed rose petal sweet,
And drawn white gloves on her small brown hands,
And white shoes on her feet.   20

The mother smiled to know her child
Was in the sacred place,
But that smile was the last smile
To come upon her face.

For when she heard the explosion,   25
Her eyes grew wet and wild.
She raced through the streets of Birmingham
Calling for her child.

She clawed through bits of glass and brick,
Then lifted out a shoe.   30
"O here's the shoe my baby wore,
But, baby, where are you?"

COMPARE:

"Ballad of Birmingham" with traditional ballads such as "Edward" (page 681) or
"The Cruel Mother" (page 515).

John Crowe Ransom (1888 – 1974)
BELLS FOR JOHN WHITESIDE'S DAUGHTER   1924

There was such speed in her little body,
And such lightness in her footfall,
It is no wonder her brown study
Astonishes us all.

Her wars were bruited in our high window.   5
We looked among orchard trees and beyond,
Where she took arms against her shadow,
Or harried unto the pond

The lazy geese, like a snow cloud
Dripping their snow on the green grass,   10
Tricking and stopping, sleepy and proud,
Who cried in goose, Alas,

For the tireless heart within the little
Lady with rod that made them rise
From their noon apple-dreams, and scuttle   15
Goose-fashion under the skies!

But now go the bells, and we are ready;
In one house we are sternly stopped
To say we are vexed at her brown study,
Lying so primly propped.   20

COMPARE:

"Bells for John Whiteside's Daughter" with "Elegy for Jane" by Theodore Roethke
(page 762).

Henry Reed (b. 1914)
NAMING OF PARTS   1946

Today we have naming of parts. Yesterday,
We had daily cleaning. And tomorrow morning,
We shall have what to do after firing. But today,

Today we have naming of parts. Japonica
Glistens like coral in all of the neighboring gardens,   5
        And today we have naming of parts.

This is the lower sling swivel. And this
Is the upper sling swivel, whose use you will see,
When you are given your slings. And this is the piling swivel,
Which in your case you have not got. The branches   10
Hold in the gardens their silent, eloquent gestures,
        Which in our case we have not got.

This is the safety-catch, which is always released
With an easy flick of the thumb. And please do not let me
See anyone using his finger. You can do it quite easy   15
If you have any strength in your thumb. The blossoms
Are fragile and motionless, never letting anyone see
        Any of them using their finger.

And this you can see is the bolt. The purpose of this
Is to open the breech, as you see. We can slide it   20
Rapidly backwards and forwards: we call this
Easing the spring. And rapidly backwards and forwards
The early bees are assaulting and fumbling the flowers:
        They call it easing the Spring.

They call it easing the Spring: it is perfectly easy   25
If you have any strength in your thumb: like the bolt,
And the breech, and the cocking-piece, and the point of balance,
Which in our case we have not got; and the almond-blossom
Silent in all of the gardens and the bees going backwards and
        forwards,
        For today we have naming of parts.   30

Compare:

"Naming of Parts" with "The Fury of Aerial Bombardment" by Richard Eberhart
(page 465).

Adrienne Rich (b. 1929)*

Aunt Jennifer's Tigers   1951

Aunt Jennifer's tigers prance across a screen,
Bright topaz denizens of a world of green.
They do not fear the men beneath the tree;
They pace in sleek chivalric certainty.

Aunt Jennifer's fingers fluttering through her wool   5
Find even the ivory needle hard to pull.
The massive weight of Uncle's wedding band
Sits heavily upon Aunt Jennifer's hand.

When Aunt is dead, her terrified hands will lie
Still ringed with ordeals she was mastered by.   10
The tigers in the panel that she made
Will go on prancing, proud and unafraid.

Adrienne Rich (b. 1929)*
DIVING INTO THE WRECK   1973

First having read the book of myths,
and loaded the camera,
and checked the edge of the knife-blade,
I put on
the body-armor of black rubber   5
the absurd flippers
the grave and awkward mask.
I am having to do this
not like Cousteau with his
assiduous team   10
aboard the sun-flooded schooner
but here alone.

There is a ladder.
The ladder is always there
hanging innocently   15
close to the side of the schooner.
We know what it is for,
we who have used it.
Otherwise
it's a piece of maritime floss   20
some sundry equipment.

I go down.
Rung after rung and still
the oxygen immerses me
the blue light   25
the clear atoms
of our human air.
I go down.
My flippers cripple me,
I crawl like an insect down the ladder   30
and there is no one
to tell me when the ocean
will begin.

First the air is blue and then
it is bluer and then green and then   35
black I am blacking out and yet
my mask is powerful
it pumps my blood with power
the sea is another story

the sea is not a question of power   40
I have to learn alone
to turn my body without force
in the deep element.

And now: it is easy to forget
what I came for   45
among so many who have always
lived here
swaying their crenellated fans
between the reefs
and besides   50
you breathe differently down here.

I came to explore the wreck.
The words are purposes.
The words are maps.
I came to see the damage that was done   55
and the treasures that prevail.
I stroke the beam of my lamp
slowly along the flank
of something more permanent
than fish or weed   60

the thing I came for:
the wreck and not the story of the wreck
the thing itself and not the myth
the drowned face always staring
toward the sun   65
the evidence of damage
worn by salt and sway into this threadbare beauty
the ribs of the disaster
curving their assertion
among the tentative haunters.   70

This is the place.
And I am here, the mermaid whose dark hair
streams black, the merman in his armored body
We circle silently
about the wreck   75
we dive into the hold.
I am she: I am he

whose drowned face sleeps with open eyes
whose breasts still bear the stress
whose silver, copper, vermeil cargo lies   80
obscurely inside barrels
half-wedged and left to rot
we are the half-destroyed instruments
that once held to a course
the water-eaten log   85
the fouled compass

We are, I am, you are
by cowardice or courage
the one who find our way
back to this scene   90
carrying a knife, a camera
a book of myths
in which
our names do not appear.

Theodore Roethke (1908 – 1963)*
ELEGY FOR JANE   1953

My Student, Thrown by a Horse

I remember the neckcurls, limp and damp as tendrils;
And her quick look, a sidelong pickerel smile;
And how, once startled into talk, the light syllables leaped for her,
And she balanced in the delight of her thought,
A wren, happy, tail into the wind,   5
Her song trembling the twigs and small branches.
The shade sang with her;
The leaves, their whispers turned to kissing;
And the mold sang in the bleached valleys under the rose.

Oh, when she was sad, she cast herself down into such a pure depth,   10
Even a father could not find her:
Scraping her cheek against straw;
Stirring the clearest water.

My sparrow, you are not here,
Waiting like a fern, making a spiny shadow.   15
The sides of wet stones cannot console me,
Nor the moss, wound with the last light.

If only I could nudge you from this sleep,
My maimed darling, my skittery pigeon.
Over this damp grave I speak the words of my love: 20
I, with no rights in this matter,
Neither father nor lover.

Theodore Roethke (1908 – 1963)*
THE WAKING   1953

I wake to sleep, and take my waking slow.
I feel my fate in what I cannot fear.
I learn by going where I have to go.

We think by feeling. What is there to know?
I hear my being dance from ear to ear. 5
I wake to sleep, and take my waking slow.

Of those so close beside me, which are you?
God bless the Ground! I shall walk softly there,
And learn by going where I have to go.

Light takes the Tree; but who can tell us how? 10
The lowly worm climbs up a winding stair;
I wake to sleep, and take my waking slow.

Great Nature has another thing to do
To you and me; so take the lively air,
And, lovely, learn by going where to go. 15

This shaking keeps me steady. I should know.
What falls away is always. And is near.
I wake to sleep, and take my waking slow.
I learn by going where I have to go.

COMPARE:

"The Waking" with "Do not go gentle into that good night" by Dylan Thomas
(page 581).

Paul Ruffin (b. 1941)

HOTEL FIRE: NEW ORLEANS 1980

From first light we fear falling:
after the fever of birth, impetus
toward that natural window, we
reach, cling, our fingers and toes
curled to grip, after the fire 5
that tempers us for the sun.

There I saw them — I see them still —
thrust from windows,
flailing like children
who know the earth has failed them: 10
they snatch at chinks, to ledges,
tumble to the wet street below,
the fire an old and certain death,
the leap the only faith that's left.

Winfield Townley Scott (1910 – 1968)

MRS. SEVERIN 1959

Mrs. Severin came home from the Methodist Encampment,
Climbed naked to the diningroom table and lay down.

She was alone at the time but naturally told of it afterward.
"Lord! Lord!" she had called out. "Thou seest me. Wherein is my
    fault?"

When she heard of it, second-hand, Mrs. Birchfield laughed till she
    cried.   5
"My God!" she said, "I'd like to've seen her getting up there!"
For Mrs. Severin, you see, was a very stout old lady,
A spilling mass by buttons, shawls, pins and ribboned eyeglasses
    held together.

The eyeglasses were a shift of drama: hoisted for reading aloud,
    lowered for talking;
They were not interruption. Mrs. Severin's soft incessant sibilance   10
Through all the days she visited and rocked by the window
Braided inextricably Bible and autobiography. Jesus was near.

"The morning Encampment began the Lord suddenly told me to go.
Ran all the way down-street to the cars for Canobie Lake,
Didn't fasten my dress or tie my shoes. Left the house open.   15
    Young ones at the neighbors.
'Lord,' I said, 'I am thy servant' — and stayed the whole beautiful,
    blessed week."

On the listening child her showers of quotation pattered a drugged
    dream.
" 'Thought becomes word. Word becomes act. Act becomes character.
    Character becomes destiny.'
Remember that. And praise the Lord," she said, giving off also
Odor of camphor, old rose jars and muttonleg sleeves. "Amen!"   20

The husband long gone who wasted her inheritance; the irritable
    children
Who hated to have to have her now; the friends who took her in
    now and again: gone.
Here in her false hair and handmedowns, patiently talking — talking:
Old Mrs. Severin who once, brave on a diningroom table, naked
    confronted her unanswering Lord.

Anne Sexton (1928 – 1974)
To a Friend Whose Work Has Come to Triumph   1962

Consider Icarus, pasting those sticky wings on,
testing that strange little tug at his shoulder blade,
and think of that first flawless moment over the lawn
of the labyrinth. Think of the difference it made!
There below are the trees, as awkward as camels;   5
and here are the shocked starlings pumping past
and think of innocent Icarus who is doing quite well.

larger than a sail, over the fog and the blast
of the plushy ocean, he goes. Admire his wings!
Feel the fire at his neck and see how casually   10
he glances up and is caught, wondrously tunneling
into that hot eye. Who cares that he fell back to the sea?
See him acclaiming the sun and come plunging down
while his sensible daddy goes straight into town.

COMPARE:

"To a Friend Whose Work Has Come to Triumph" with "Musée des Beaux Arts"
by W. H. Auden (page 689). Also compare "To a Friend Whose Work Has Come
to Nothing" by William Butler Yeats (page 791).

William Shakespeare (1564 – 1616)*
THAT TIME OF YEAR THOU MAYST IN ME BEHOLD   1609

That time of year thou mayst in me behold
When yellow leaves, or none, or few, do hang
Upon those boughs which shake against the cold,
Bare ruined choirs where late the sweet birds sang.
In me thou see'st the twilight of such day   5
As after sunset fadeth in the west,
Which by-and-by black night doth take away,
Death's second self that seals up all in rest.
In me thou see'st the glowing of such fire
That on the ashes of his youth doth lie,   10
As the deathbed whereon it must expire,
Consumed with that which it was nourished by.
    This thou perceiv'st, which makes thy love more strong,
    To love that well which thou must leave ere long.

William Shakespeare (1564 – 1616)*
WHEN, IN DISGRACE WITH FORTUNE AND MEN'S EYES   1609

When, in disgrace with Fortune and men's eyes,
I all alone beweep my outcast state,
And trouble deaf heaven with my bootless° cries,   *futile*
And look upon myself and curse my fate,
Wishing me like to one more rich in hope,   5
Featured like him, like him with friends possessed,
Desiring this man's art, and that man's scope,
With what I most enjoy contented least,
Yet in these thoughts myself almost despising,
Haply° I think on thee, and then my state,   *luckily* 10
Like to the lark at break of day arising

From sullen earth, sings hymns at heaven's gate;
  For thy sweet love rememb'red such wealth brings
  That then I scorn to change my state with kings.

William Shakespeare (1564 – 1616)*
WHEN DAISIES PIED AND VIOLETS BLUE   1598

When daisies pied and violets blue
  And lady-smocks all silver-white
And cuckoo-buds° of yellow hue   *buttercups*
  Do paint the meadows with delight,
The cuckoo then, on every tree,   5
Mocks married men; for thus sings he,
          "Cuckoo,
Cuckoo, cuckoo!" — O word of fear,
Unpleasing to a married ear!

When shepherds pipe on oaten straws,   10
  And merry larks are ploughmen's clocks,
When turtles tread°, and rooks, and daws,   *turtledoves mate*
  And maidens bleach their summer smocks,
The cuckoo then, on every tree,
Mocks married men; for thus sings he,   15
          "Cuckoo,
Cuckoo, cuckoo!" — O word of fear,
Unpleasing to a married ear!

WHEN DAISIES PIED. This song and "When icicles hang by the wall" conclude the play *Love's Labor's Lost.* 2. *lady-smocks:* also named cuckoo-flowers. 8. *O word of fear:* because it sounds like *cuckold,* a man whose wife has deceived him.

William Shakespeare (1564 – 1616)*
WHEN ICICLES HANG BY THE WALL   1598

When icicles hang by the wall,
  And Dick the shepherd blows his nail,
And Tom bears logs into the hall,
  And milk comes frozen home in pail,
When blood is nipped and ways° be foul,   *roads* 5
  Then nightly sings the staring owl:
          "Tu-whit, to-who!"
          A merry note,
While greasy Joan doth keel° the pot.   *cool (as by skimming or stirring)*

When all aloud the wind doth blow,   10
  And coughing drowns the parson's saw°,   *old saw, platitude*
And birds sit brooding in the snow,

And Marian's nose looks red and raw,
When roasted crabs° hiss in the bowl,   *crab apples*
    Then nightly sings the staring owl: 15
        "Tu-whit, to-who!"
            A merry note,
While greasy Joan doth keel the pot.

Karl Shapiro (b. 1913)
THE DIRTY WORD   1947

The dirty word hops in the cage of the mind like the Pondicherry
vulture, stomping with its heavy left claw on the sweet meat of the brain
and tearing it with its vicious beak, ripping and chopping the flesh.
Terrified, the small boy bears the big bird of the dirty word into the
house, and grunting, puffing, carries it up the stairs to his own room in   5
the skull. Bits of black feather cling to his clothes and his hair as he locks
the staring creature in the dark closet.

All day the small boy returns to the closet to examine and feed the
bird, to caress and kick the bird, that now snaps and flaps its wings
savagely whenever the door is opened. How the boy trembles and de-   10
lights at the sight of the white excrement of the bird! How the bird leaps
and rushes against the walls of the skull, trying to escape from the zoo
of the vocabulary! How wildly snaps the sweet meat of the brain in its
rage.

And the bird outlives the man, being freed at the man's death-funeral   15
by a word from the rabbi.

(But I one morning went upstairs and opened the door and entered the
closet and found in the cage of my mind the great bird dead. Softly I wept
it and softly removed it and softly buried the body of the bird in the
hollyhock garden of the house I lived in twenty years before. And out   20
of the worn black feathers of the wing have I made these pens to write
these elegies, for I have outlived the bird, and I have murdered it in my
early manhood.)

Stephen Shu-ning Liu (b. 1930)
MY FATHER'S MARTIAL ART   1982

When he came home Mother said he looked
like a monk and stank of green fungus.
At the fireside he told us about life
at the monastery: his rock pillow,
his cold bath, his steel-bar lifting   5
and his wood-chopping. He didn't see
a woman for three winters, on Mountain O Mei.

"My Master was both light and heavy.
He skipped over treetops like a squirrel.
Once he stood on a chair, one foot tied
to a rope. We four pulled; we couldn't
move him a bit. His kicks could split
a cedar's trunk."

I saw Father break into a pumpkin
with his fingers. I saw him drop a hawk
with bamboo arrows. He rose before dawn, filled
our backyard with a harsh sound *hah, hah, hah:*
there was his Black Dragon Sweep, his Crane Stand,
his Mantis Walk, his Tiger Leap, his Cobra Coil . . .
Infrequently he taught me tricks and made me
fight the best of all the village boys.

From a busy street I brood over high cliffs
on O Mei, where my father and his Master sit:
shadows spread across their faces as the smog
between us deepens into a funeral pyre.

But don't retreat into night, my father.
Come down from the cliffs. Come
with a single Black Dragon Sweep and hush
this oncoming traffic with your *hah, hah, hah.*

Charles Simic (b. 1938)

Butcher Shop   1971

Sometimes walking late at night
I stop before a closed butcher shop.
There is a single light in the store
Like the light in which the convict digs his tunnel.

An apron hangs on the hook:
The blood on it smeared into a map
Of the great continents of blood,
The great rivers and oceans of blood.

There are knives that glitter like altars
In a dark church
Where they bring the cripple and the imbecile
To be healed.

There's a wooden block where bones are broken,
Scraped clean — a river dried to its bed
Where I am fed,
Where deep in the night I hear a voice.

Christopher Smart (1722 – 1771)

For I will consider my Cat Jeoffry (1759 – 1763)

For I will consider my Cat Jeoffry.

For he is the servant of the Living God, duly and daily serving him.

For at the first glance of the glory of God in the East he worships in
    his way.

For is this done by wreathing his body seven times round with
    elegant quickness.

For then he leaps up to catch the musk°, which is the   *catnip*
    blessing of God upon his prayer.   5

For he rolls upon prank to work it in.

For having done duty and received blessing he begins to consider
    himself.

For this he performs in ten degrees.

For first he looks upon his fore-paws to see if they are clean.

For secondly he kicks up behind to clear away there.   10

For thirdly he works it upon stretch° with the fore-paws   *he works his*
    extended.   *muscles, stretching*

For fourthly he sharpens his paws by wood.

For fifthly he washes himself.

For sixthly he rolls upon wash.

For seventhly he fleas himself, that he may not be interrupted upon
    the beat°.   *his patrol* 15

For eighthly he rubs himself against a post.

For ninthly he looks up for his instructions.

For tenthly he goes in quest of food.

For having considered God and himself he will consider his neighbor.

For if he meets another cat he will kiss her in kindness.   20

For when he takes his prey he plays with it to give it a chance.

For one mouse in seven escapes by his dallying.

For when his day's work is done his business more properly begins.

For he keeps the Lord's watch in the night against the Adversary.

For he counteracts the powers of darkness by his electrical skin and
    glaring eyes.   25

For he counteracts the Devil, who is death, by brisking about the life.

For in his morning orisons he loves the sun and the sun loves him.

For he is of the tribe of Tiger.

For the Cherub Cat is a term of the Angel Tiger.

For he has the subtlety and hissing of a serpent, which in goodness
    he suppresses.   30

For he will not do destruction if he is well-fed, neither will he spit
    without provocation.

For he purrs in thankfulness when God tells him he's a good Cat.

For he is an instrument for the children to learn benevolence upon.

For every house is incomplete without him, and a blessing is lacking
    in the spirit.

For the Lord commanded Moses concerning the cats at the departure
    of the Children of Israel from Egypt.   35

For every family had one cat at least in the bag.
For the English cats are the best in Europe.
For he is the cleanest in the use of his fore-paws of any quadruped.
For the dexterity of his defense is an instance of the love of God to
      him exceedingly.
For he is the quickest to his mark of any creature.   40
For he is tenacious of his point.
For he is a mixture of gravity and waggery.
For he knows that God is his Savior.
For there is nothing sweeter than his peace when at rest.
For there is nothing brisker than his life when in motion.   45
For he is of the Lord's poor, and so indeed is he called by
      benevolence perpetually — Poor Jeoffry! poor Jeoffry! the rat
      has bit thy throat.
For I bless the name of the Lord Jesus that Jeoffry is better.
For the divine spirit comes about his body to sustain it in complete
      cat.
For his tongue is exceeding pure so that it has in purity what it
      wants in music.
For he is docile and can learn certain things.   50
For he can sit up with gravity which is patience upon approbation.
For he can fetch and carry, which is patience in employment.
For he can jump over a stick which is patience upon proof positive.
For he can spraggle upon waggle at the word of command.
For he can jump from an eminence into his master's bosom.   55
For he can catch the cork and toss it again.
For he is hated by the hypocrite and miser.
For the former is afraid of detection.
For the latter refuses the charge.
For he camels his back to bear the first notion of business.   60
For he is good to think on, if a man would express himself neatly.
For he made a great figure in Egypt for his signal services.
For he killed the Icneumon-rat, very pernicious by land.
For his ears are so acute that they sting again.
For from this proceeds the passing quickness of his attention.   65
For by stroking of him I have found out electricity.
For I perceived God's light about him both wax and fire.
For the electrical fire is the spiritual substance which God sends from
      heaven to sustain the bodies both of man and beast.
For God has blessed him in the variety of his movements.
For, though he cannot fly, he is an excellent clamberer.   70
For his motions upon the face of the earth are more than any other
      quadruped.
For he can tread to all the measures upon the music.
For he can swim for life.
For he can creep.

For I will consider my Cat Jeoffry. This is a self-contained extract from Smart's long poem
Jubilate Agno ("Rejoice in the Lamb"), written during his confinement for insanity. 35. *For the*

Lord commanded Moses concerning the cats: No such command is mentioned in Scripture. 54. *spraggle upon waggle:* W. F. Stead, in his edition of Smart's poem, suggests that this means Jeoffry will sprawl when his master waggles a finger or a stick. 59. *the charge:* perhaps the cost of feeding a cat.

William Jay Smith (b. 1918)

AMERICAN PRIMITIVE   1953

Look at him there in his stovepipe hat,
His high-top shoes, and his handsome collar;
Only my Daddy could look like that,
And I love my Daddy like he loves his Dollar.

The screen door bangs, and it sounds so funny —   5
There he is in a shower of gold;
His pockets are stuffed with folding money,
His lips are blue, and his hands feel cold.

He hangs in the hall by his black cravat,
The ladies faint, and the children holler: 10
Only my Daddy could look like that,
And I love my Daddy like he loves his Dollar.

COMPARE:

"American Primitive" with "Daddy" by Sylvia Plath (page 752).

W. D. Snodgrass (b. 1926)

THE OPERATION   1959

From stainless steel basins of water
They brought warm cloths and they washed me,
From spun aluminum bowls, cold Zephiran sponges, fuming;
Gripped in the dead yellow glove, a bright straight razor
Inched on my stomach, down my groin,   5
Paring the brown hair off. They left me
White as a child, not frightened. I was not
Ashamed. They clothed me, then,
In the thin, loose, light, white garments,
The delicate sandals of poor Pierrot,   10
A schoolgirl first offering her sacrament.

I was drifting, inexorably, on toward sleep.
In skullcaps, masked, in blue-green gowns, attendants
Towed my cart, afloat in its white cloths,
The body with its tributary poisons borne   15
Down corridors of the diseased, thronging:
The scrofulous faces, contagious grim boys,

The huddled families, weeping, a staring woman
Arched to her gnarled stick, — a child was somewhere
Screaming, screaming — then, blind silence, the elevator rising   20
To the arena, humming, vast with lights; blank hero,
Shackled and spellbound, to enact my deed.
Into flowers, into women, I have awakened.
Too weak to think of strength, I have thought all day,
Or dozed among standing friends. I lie in night, now,   25
A small mound under linen like the drifted snow.
Only by nurses visited, in radiance, saying, Rest.
Opposite, ranked office windows glare; headlamps, below,
Trace out our highways; their cargoes under dark tarpaulins,
Trucks climb, thundering, and sirens may   30
Wail for the fugitive. It is very still. In my brandy bowl
Of sweet peas at the window, the crystal world
Is inverted, slow and gay.

THE OPERATION. 3. *Zephiran:* like Zephirus, Greek personification of the west wind: gentle, cool, and soothing. Also the name of an antiseptic, so named to indicate that it does not sting. 10. *Pierrot:* traditional clown in French pantomime, white-faced, wearing loose pantaloons.

Gary Soto (b. 1952)
BLACK HAIR   1985

At eight I was brilliant with my body.
In July, that ring of heat
We all jumped through, I sat in the bleachers
Of Romain Playground, in the lengthening
Shade that rose from our dirty feet.   5
The game before us was more than baseball.
It was a figure — Hector Moreno
Quick and hard with turned muscles,
His crouch the one I assumed before an altar
Of worn baseball cards, in my room.   10

I came here because I was Mexican, a stick
Of brown light in love with those
Who could do it — the triple and hard slide,
The gloves eating balls into double plays.
What could I do with 50 pounds, my shyness,   15
My black torch of hair, about to go out?
Father was dead, his face no longer
Hanging over the table or our sleep,
And mother was the terror of mouths
Twisting hurt by butter knives.   20

In the bleachers I was brilliant with my body,
Waving players in and stomping my feet,
Growing sweaty in the presence of white shirts.

I chewed sunflower seeds. I drank water
And bit my arm through the late innings.   25
When Hector lined balls into deep
Center, in my mind I rounded the bases
With him, my face flared, my hair lifting
Beautifully, because we were coming home
To the arms of brown people.   30

William Stafford (b. 1914)*

AT THE KLAMATH BERRY FESTIVAL   1966

The war chief danced the old way —
the eagle wing he held before his mouth —
and when he turned the boom-boom
stopped. He took two steps. A sociologist
was there; the Scout troop danced.   5
I envied him the places where he had not been.

The boom began again. Outside he heard
the stick game, and the Blackfoot gamblers
arguing at poker under lanterns.
Still-moccasined and bashful, holding   10
the eagle wing before his mouth,
listening and listening, he danced after others stopped.

He took two steps, the boom caught up,
the mountains rose, the still deep river
slid but never broke its quiet.   15
I looked back when I left:
he took two steps, he took two steps,
past the sociologist.

AT THE KLAMATH BERRY FESTIVAL. The Klamath Indians have a reservation at the base of the
Cascade Range in southern Oregon.

Timothy Steele (b. 1948)*

TIMOTHY   1984

Although the field lay cut in swaths,
Grass at the edge survived the crop:
Stiff stems, with lateral blades of leaf,
Dense cat-tail flower-spikes at the top.

If there was breeze and open sky,   5
We raked each swath into a row;
If not, we took the hay to dry
To the barn's golden-showering mow.

The hay we forked there from the truck
Was thatched resilience where it fell,   10
And I took pleasure in the thought
The fresh hay's name was mine as well.

Work was a soothing, rhythmic ache;
Hay stuck where skin or clothes were damp.
At length, the pick-up truck would shake   15
Its last stack up the barn's wood ramp.

Pumping a handpump's iron arm,
I washed myself as best I could,
Then watched the acres of the farm
Draw lengthening shadows from the wood   20

Across the grass, which seemed a thing
In which the lonely and concealed
Had risen from its sorrowing
And flourished in the open field.

Wallace Stevens (1879 – 1955)*
PETER QUINCE AT THE CLAVIER   1923

I

Just as my fingers on these keys
Make music, so the selfsame sounds
On my spirit make a music, too.

Music is feeling, then, not sound;
And thus it is that what I feel,   5
Here in this room, desiring you,

Thinking of your blue-shadowed silk,
Is music. It is like the strain
Waked in the elders by Susanna.

Of a green evening, clear and warm,   10
She bathed in her still garden, while
The red-eyed elders watching, felt

The basses of their beings throb
In witching chords, and their thin blood
Pulse pizzicati of Hosanna.   15

II

In the green water, clear and warm,
Susanna lay.
She searched
The touch of springs,

And found
Concealed imaginings.
She sighed,
For so much melody.   20

Upon the bank, she stood
In the cool
Of spent emotions.   25
She felt, among the leaves,
The dew
Of old devotions.

She walked upon the grass,
Still quavering.   30
The winds were like her maids,
On timid feet,
Fetching her woven scarves,
Yet wavering.   35

A breath upon her hand
Muted the night.
She turned —
A cymbal crashed,
And roaring horns.   40

III

Soon, with a noise like tambourines,
Came her attendant Byzantines.

They wondered why Susanna cried
Against the elders by her side;

And as they whispered, the refrain   45
Was like a willow swept by rain.

Anon, their lamps' uplifted flame
Revealed Susanna and her shame.

And then, the simpering Byzantines
Fled, with a noise like tambourines.   50

IV

Beauty is momentary in the mind —
The fitful tracing of a portal;
But in the flesh it is immortal.

The body dies; the body's beauty lives.
So evenings die, in their green going,   55
A wave, interminably flowing.
So gardens die, their meek breath scenting
The cowl of winter, done repenting.
So maidens die, to the auroral
Celebration of a maiden's choral.   60

Susanna's music touched the bawdy strings
Of those white elders; but, escaping,
Left only Death's ironic scraping.
Now, in its immortality, it plays
On the clear viol of her memory,   65
And makes a constant sacrament of praise.

PETER QUINCE AT THE CLAVIER. In Shakespeare's *Midsummer Night's Dream,* Peter Quince is a clownish carpenter who stages a mock-tragic play. In The Book of Susanna in the Apocrypha, two lustful elders who covet Susanna, a virtuous married woman, hide in her garden, spy on her as she bathes, then threaten to make false accusations against her unless she submits to them. When she refuses, they cry out, and her servants come running. All ends well when the prophet Daniel cross-examines the elders and proves them liars. 15. *pizzicati:* thin notes made by plucking a stringed instrument. 42. *Byzantines:* Susanna's maidservants.

May Swenson (b. 1919)
QUESTION   1954

Body my house
my horse my hound
what will I do
when you are fallen

Where will I sleep   5
How will I ride
What will I hunt

Where can I go
without my mount
all eager and quick   10
How will I know
in thicket ahead
is danger or treasure
when Body my good
bright dog is dead   15

How will it be
to lie in the sky
without roof or door
and wind for an eye

With cloud for shift   20
how will I hide?

Jonathan Swift (1667 – 1745)*
A DESCRIPTION OF THE MORNING   1711

Now hardly here and there an hackney-coach°,   *horse-drawn cab*
Appearing, showed the ruddy morn's approach.

Now Betty from her master's bed had flown
And softly stole to discompose her own.
The slipshod 'prentice from his master's door   5
Had pared the dirt, and sprinkled round the floor.
Now Moll had whirled her mop with dextrous airs,
Prepared to scrub the entry and the stairs.
The youth with broomy stumps began to trace
The kennel°-edge, where wheels had worn the place.   *gutter*   10
The small-coal man was heard with cadence deep
Till drowned in shriller notes of chimneysweep,
Duns° at his lordship's gate began to meet,   *bill-collectors*
And Brickdust Moll had screamed through half the street.
The turnkey° now his flock returning sees,   *jailkeeper*   15
Duly let out a-nights to steal for fees;
The watchful bailiffs° take their silent stands;   *constables*
And schoolboys lag with satchels in their hands.

A DESCRIPTION OF THE MORNING. 9. *youth with broomy stumps:* a young man sweeping the gutter's edge with worn-out brooms, looking for old nails fallen from wagonwheels, which were valuable. 14. *Brickdust Moll:* woman selling brickdust to be used for scouring.

Alfred, Lord Tennyson (1809 – 1892)*
DARK HOUSE, BY WHICH ONCE MORE I STAND   1850

Dark house, by which once more I stand
  Here in the long unlovely street,
  Doors, where my heart was used to beat
So quickly, waiting for a hand,

A hand that can be clasped no more —   5
  Behold me, for I cannot sleep,
  And like a guilty thing I creep
At earliest morning to the door.

He is not here; but far away
  The noise of life begins again,   10
  And ghastly through the drizzling rain
On the bald street breaks the blank day.

DARK HOUSE. This poem is one part of the series *In Memoriam,* an elegy for Tennyson's friend Arthur Henry Hallam.

Alfred, Lord Tennyson (1809 – 1892)*
ULYSSES   (1833)

It little profits that an idle king,
By this still hearth, among these barren crags,
Matched with an agèd wife, I mete and dole

Unequal laws unto a savage race
That hoard, and sleep, and feed, and know not me.   5
I cannot rest from travel; I will drink
Life to the lees. All times I have enjoyed
Greatly, have suffered greatly, both with those
That loved me, and alone; on shore, and when
Through scudding drifts the rainy Hyades   10
Vexed the dim sea. I am become a name;
For always roaming with a hungry heart
Much have I seen and known — cities of men
And manners, climates, councils, governments,
Myself not least, but honored of them all —   15
And drunk delight of battle with my peers,
Far on the ringing plains of windy Troy.
I am a part of all that I have met;
Yet all experience is an arch wherethrough
Gleams that untraveled world whose margin fades   20
Forever and forever when I move.
How dull it is to pause, to make an end,
To rust unburnished, not to shine in use!
As though to breathe were life! Life piled on life
Were all too little, and of one to me   25
Little remains; but every hour is saved
From that eternal silence, something more,
A bringer of new things; and vile it were
For some three suns to store and hoard myself,
And this grey spirit yearning in desire   30
To follow knowledge like a sinking star,
Beyond the utmost bound of human thought.
     This is my son, mine own Telemachus,
To whom I leave the scepter and the isle —
Well-loved of me, discerning to fulfill   35
This labor, by slow prudence to make mild
A rugged people, and through soft degrees
Subdue them to the useful and the good.
Most blameless is he, centered in the sphere
Of common duties, decent not to fail   40
In offices of tenderness, and pay
Meet adoration to my household gods,
When I am gone. He works his work, I mine.
     There lies the port; the vessel puffs her sail;
There gloom the dark, broad seas. My mariners,   45
Souls that have toiled, and wrought, and thought with me —
That ever with a frolic welcome took
The thunder and the sunshine, and opposed
Free hearts, free foreheads — you and I are old;
Old age hath yet his honor and his toil.   50
Death closes all; but something ere the end,
Some work of noble note, may yet be done,

Not unbecoming men that strove with Gods.
The lights begin to twinkle from the rocks;
The long day wanes; the low moon climbs; the deep   55
Moans round with many voices. Come, my friends,
'Tis not too late to seek a newer world.
Push off, and sitting well in order smite
The sounding furrows; for my purpose holds
To sail beyond the sunset, and the baths   60
Of all the western stars, until I die.
It may be that the gulfs will wash us down;
It may be we shall touch the Happy Isles,
And see the great Achilles, whom we knew.
Though much is taken, much abides; and though   65
We are not now that strength which in old days
Moved earth and heaven, that which we are, we are —
One equal temper of heroic hearts,
Made weak by time and fate, but strong in will
To strive, to seek, to find, and not to yield.   70

ULYSSES. 10. *Hyades:* daughters of Atlas, who were transformed into a group of stars. Their rising with the sun was thought to be a sign of rain. 63. *Happy Isles:* Elysium, a paradise believed to be attainable by sailing west.

COMPARE:

"Ulysses" with "Sir Patrick Spence" (page 682).

Dylan Thomas (1914 – 1953)*
FERN HILL   1946

Now as I was young and easy under the apple boughs
About the lilting house and happy as the grass was green,
     The night above the dingle° starry,   *wooded valley*
       Time let me hail and climb
       Golden in the heydays of his eyes,   5
And honored among wagons I was prince of the apple towns
And once below a time I lordly had the trees and leaves
       Trail with daisies and barley
       Down the rivers of the windfall light.

And as I was green and carefree, famous among the barns   10
About the happy yard and singing as the farm was home,
       In the sun that is young once only,
        Time let me play and be
       Golden in the mercy of his means,
And green and golden I was huntsman and herdsman, the calves   15
Sang to my horn, the foxes on the hills barked clear and cold,
       And the sabbath rang slowly
       In the pebbles of the holy streams.

All the sun long it was running, it was lovely, the hay
Fields high as the house, the tunes from the chimneys, it was air   20
     And playing, lovely and watery
        And fire green as grass.
     And nightly under the simple stars
As I rode to sleep the owls were bearing the farm away,
All the moon long I heard, blessed among stables, the nightjars   25
     Flying with the ricks, and the horses
        Flashing into the dark.

And then to awake, and the farm, like a wanderer white
With the dew, come back, the cock on his shoulder: it was all
     Shining, it was Adam and maiden,   30
        The sky gathered again
     And the sun grew round that very day.
So it must have been after the birth of the simple light
In the first, spinning place, the spellbound horses walking warm
     Out of the whinnying green stable   35
        On to the fields of praise.

And honored among foxes and pheasants by the gay house
Under the new made clouds and happy as the heart was long,
     In the sun born over and over,
        I ran my heedless ways,   40
     My wishes raced through the house high hay
And nothing I cared, at my sky blue trades, that time allows
In all his tuneful turning so few and such morning songs
     Before the children green and golden
        Follow him out of grace,   45

Nothing I cared, in the lamb white days, that time would take me
Up to the swallow thronged loft by the shadow of my hand,
     In the moon that is always rising,
        Nor that riding to sleep
     I should hear him fly with the high fields   50
And wake to the farm forever fled from the childless land.
Oh as I was young and easy in the mercy of his means,
     Time held me green and dying
     Though I sang in my chains like the sea.

John Updike (b. 1932)*
Ex-Basketball Player   1958

Pearl Avenue runs past the high-school lot,
Bends with the trolley tracks, and stops, cut off
Before it has a chance to go two blocks,
At Colonel McComsky Plaza. Berth's Garage
Is on the corner facing west, and there,   5
Most days, you'll find Flick Webb, who helps Berth out.

Flick stands tall among the idiot pumps —
Five on a side, the old bubble-head style,
Their rubber elbows hanging loose and low.
One's nostrils are two S's, and his eyes   10
An E and O. And one is squat, without
A head at all — more of a football type.

Once Flick played for the high-school team, the Wizards.
He was good: in fact, the best. In '46
He bucketed three hundred ninety points,   15
A county record still. The ball loved Flick.
I saw him rack up thirty-eight or forty
In one home game. His hands were like wild birds.

He never learned a trade, he just sells gas,
Checks oil, and changes flats. Once in a while,   20
As a gag, he dribbles an inner tube,
But most of us remember anyway.
His hands are fine and nervous on the lug wrench.
It makes no difference to the lug wrench, though.

Off work, he hangs around Mae's luncheonette.   25
Grease-gray and kind of coiled, he plays pinball,
Smokes those thin cigars, nurses lemon phosphates.
Flick seldom says a word to Mae, just nods
Beyond her face toward bright applauding tiers
Of Necco Wafers, Nibs, and Juju Beads.   30

COMPARE:

"Ex-Basketball Player" with "To an Athlete Dying Young" by A. E. Housman
(page 733).

Henry Vaughan (1621? – 1695)

The Retreat   1650

    Happy those early days! when I
Shined in my angel-infancy.
Before I understood this place
Appointed for my second race,
Or taught my soul to fancy aught   5
But a white celestial thought;
When yet I had not walked above
A mile or two from my first love,
And looking back, at that short space,
Could see a glimpse of His bright face;   10
When on some gilded cloud, or flower
My gazing soul would dwell an hour,
And in those weaker glories spy

Some shadows of eternity;
Before I taught my tongue to wound   15
My conscience with a sinful sound,
Or had the black art to dispense
A several sin to every sense,
But felt through all this fleshly dress
Bright shoots of everlastingness.   20
        Oh how I long to travel back
And tread again that ancient track!
That I might once more reach that plain
Where first I left my glorious train,
From whence the enlightened spirit sees   25
That shady city of palm trees.
But, ah! my soul with too much stay
Is drunk, and staggers in the way.
Some men a forward motion love,
But I by backward steps would move,   30
And when this dust falls to the urn,
In that state I came return.

THE RETREAT. 24. *glorious train:* band of attendants — the angels who accompanied the soul in
its former life.

David Wagoner (b. 1926)
STAYING ALIVE   1966

Staying alive in the woods is a matter of calming down
At first and deciding whether to wait for rescue,
Trusting to others,
Or simply to start walking and walking in one direction
Till you come out — or something happens to stop you.   5
By far the safer choice
Is to settle down where you are, and try to make a living
Off the land, camping near water, away from shadows.
Eat no white berries:
Spit out all bitterness. Shooting at anything   10
Means hiking further and further every day
To hunt survivors;
It may be best to learn what you have to learn without a gun,
Not killing but watching birds and animals go
In and out of shelter   15
At will. Following their example, build for a whole season:
Facing across the wind in your lean-to,
You may feel wilder,
But nothing, not even you, will have to stay in hiding.
If you have no matches, a stick and a fire-bow   20
Will keep you warmer,

Or the crystal of your watch, filled with water, held up to the sun
Will do the same in time. In case of snow
Drifting toward winter,
Don't try to stay awake through the night, afraid of freezing —   25
The bottom of your mind knows all about zero;
It will turn you over
And shake you till you waken. If you have trouble sleeping
Even in the best of weather, jumping to follow
With eyes strained to their corners   30
The unidentifiable noises of the night and feeling
Bears and packs of wolves nuzzling your elbow,
Remember the trappers
Who treated them indifferently and were left alone.
If you hurt yourself, no one will comfort you   35
Or take your temperature,
So stumbling, wading, and climbing are as dangerous as flying.
But if you decide, at last, you must break through
In spite of all danger,
Think of yourself by time and not by distance, counting   40
Wherever you're going by how long it takes you;
No other measure
Will bring you safe to nightfall. Follow no streams: they run
Under the ground or fall into wilder country.
Remember the stars   45
And moss when your mind runs into circles. If it should rain
Or the fog should roll the horizon in around you,
Hold still for hours
Or days if you must, or weeks, for seeing is believing
In the wilderness. And if you find a pathway,   50
Wheel-rut, or fence-wire,
Retrace it left or right: someone knew where he was going
Once upon a time, and you can follow
Hopefully, somewhere,
Just in case. There may even come, on some uncanny evening,   55
A time when you're warm and dry, well fed, not thirsty,
Uninjured, without fear,
When nothing, either good or bad, is happening.
This is called staying alive. It's temporary.
What occurs after   60
Is doubtful. You must always be ready for something to come
        bursting
Through the far edge of a clearing, running toward you,
Grinning from ear to ear
And hoarse with welcome. Or something crossing and hovering
Overhead, as light as air, like a break in the sky,   65
Wondering what you are.
Here you are face to face with the problem of recognition.
Having no time to make smoke, too much to say,
You should have a mirror

With a tiny hole in the back for better aiming, for reflecting 70
Whatever disaster you can think of, to show
The way you suffer.
These body signals have universal meaning: If you are lying
Flat on your back with arms outstretched behind you,
You say you require 75
Emergency treatment; if you are standing erect and holding
Arms horizontal, you mean you are not ready;
If you hold them over
Your head, you want to be picked up. Three of anything
Is a sign of distress. Afterward, if you see 80
No ropes, no ladders,
No maps or messages falling, no searchlights or trails blazing,
Then, chances are, you should be prepared to burrow
Deep for a deep winter.

Edmund Waller (1606 – 1687)
Go, Lovely Rose 1645

    Go, lovely rose,
Tell her that wastes her time and me
    That now she knows,
When I resemble° her to thee, *compare*
How sweet and fair she seems to be. 5

    Tell her that's young
And shuns to have her graces spied,
    That hadst thou sprung
In deserts where no men abide,
Thou must have uncommended died. 10

    Small is the worth
Of beauty from the light retired:
    Bid her come forth,
Suffer herself to be desired,
And not blush so to be admired. 15

    Then die, that she
The common fate of all things rare
    May read in thee,
How small a part of time they share
That are so wondrous sweet and fair. 20

COMPARE:

"Go, Lovely Rose" with "To the Virgins, to Make Much of Time" by Robert
Herrick (page 727) and "To His Coy Mistress" by Andrew Marvell (page 418).

Walt Whitman (1819 – 1892)*

I Saw in Louisiana a Live-Oak Growing

1867

I saw in Louisiana a live-oak growing,
All alone stood it and the moss hung down from the branches,
Without any companion it grew there uttering joyous leaves of dark
    green,
And its look, rude, unbending, lusty, made me think of myself,
But I wonder'd how it could utter joyous leaves standing alone there
    without its friend near, for I knew I could not,   5
And I broke off a twig with a certain number of leaves upon it, and
    twined around it a little moss,
And brought it away, and I have placed it in sight in my room,
It is not needed to remind me as of my own dear friends,
(For I believe lately I think of little else than of them,)
Yet it remains to me a curious token, it makes me think of manly
    love;   10
For all that, and though the live-oak glistens there in Louisiana
    solitary in a wide flat space,
Uttering joyous leaves all its life without a friend a lover near,
I know very well I could not.

COMPARE:

"I Saw in Louisiana a Live-Oak Growing" with "A Supermarket in California" by
Allen Ginsberg (page 719).

Richard Wilbur (b. 1921)*

Museum Piece

1950

The good gray guardians of art
Patrol the halls on spongy shoes,
Impartially protective, though
Perhaps suspicious of Toulouse.

Here dozes one against the wall,   5
Disposed upon a funeral chair.
A Degas dancer pirouettes
Upon the parting of his hair.

See how she spins! The grace is there,
But strain as well is plain to see.   10
Degas loved the two together:
Beauty joined to energy.

Edgar Degas purchased once
A fine El Greco, which he kept
Against the wall beside his bed   15
To hang his pants on while he slept.

MUSEUM PIECE. 4. *Toulouse:* Henri Marie Raymond de Toulouse-Lautrec, French painter and lithographer (1864 – 1901), who roomed in a Paris brothel and whose work depicted life in circuses, music halls, and cabarets. 7. *Degas:* Hilaire Germain Edgar Degas, French Impressionist painter and sculptor (1834 – 1917), particularly famed for his representations of ballet dancers. 14. *El Greco:* "The Greek," Spanish painter, originally named Domenicos Theotocopoulos (1541? – 1614).

William Carlos Williams (1883 – 1963)*

SPRING AND ALL   1923

By the road to the contagious hospital
under the surge of the blue
mottled clouds driven from the
northeast — a cold wind. Beyond, the
waste of broad, muddy fields   5
brown with dried weeds, standing and fallen

patches of standing water
the scattering of tall trees

All along the road the reddish
purplish, forked, upstanding, twiggy   10
stuff of bushes and small trees
with dead, brown leaves under them
leafless vines —

Lifeless in appearance, sluggish
dazed spring approaches —   15

They enter the new world naked,
cold, uncertain of all
save that they enter. All about them
the cold, familiar wind —

Now the grass, tomorrow   20
the stiff curl of wildcarrot leaf
One by one objects are defined —
It quickens: clarity, outline of leaf

But now the stark dignity of
entrance — Still, the profound change   25
has come upon them: rooted, they
grip down and begin to awaken

COMPARE:

"Spring and All" with "in Just-" by E. E. Cummings (page 600) and "Root Cellar" by Theodore Roethke (page 482).

William Carlos Williams (1883 – 1963)*
To Waken an Old Lady   1921

Old age is
a flight of small
cheeping birds
skimming
bare trees   5
above a snow glaze.
Gaining and failing
they are buffeted
by a dark wind —
But what?   10
On harsh weedstalks
the flock has rested,
the snow
is covered with broken
seedhusks   15
and the wind tempered
by a shrill
piping of plenty.

COMPARE:

"To Waken an Old Lady" with "Castoff Skin" by Ruth Whitman (page 498).

Yvor Winters (1900 – 1968)
At the San Francisco Airport   1960

To My Daughter, 1954

This is the terminal: the light
Gives perfect vision, false and hard;
The metal glitters, deep and bright.
Great planes are waiting in the yard —
They are already in the night.   5

And you are here beside me, small,
Contained and fragile, and intent
On things that I but half recall —
Yet going whither you are bent.
I am the past, and that is all.   10

But you and I in part are one:
The frightened brain, the nervous will,
The knowledge of what must be done,
The passion to acquire the skill
To face that which you dare not shun.   15

The rain of matter upon sense
Destroys me momently. The score:
There comes what will come. The expense
Is what one thought, and something more —
One's being and intelligence.   20

This is the terminal, the break.
Beyond this point, on lines of air,
You take the way that you must take;
And I remain in light and stare —
In light, and nothing else, awake.   25

William Wordsworth (1770 – 1850)*
COMPOSED UPON WESTMINSTER BRIDGE   1807

Earth has not anything to show more fair:
Dull would he be of soul who could pass by
A sight so touching in its majesty:
This City now doth, like a garment, wear
The beauty of the morning; silent, bare,   5
Ships, towers, domes, theatres, and temples lie
Open unto the fields, and to the sky;
All bright and glittering in the smokeless air.
Never did sun more beautifully steep
In his first splendor, valley, rock, or hill;   10
Ne'er saw I, never felt, a calm so deep!
The river glideth at his own sweet will:
Dear God! the very houses seem asleep;
And all that mighty heart is lying still!

James Wright (1927 – 1980)*
A BLESSING   1961

Just off the highway to Rochester, Minnesota,
Twilight bounds softly forth on the grass.
And the eyes of those two Indian ponies
Darken with kindness.
They have come gladly out of the willows   5
To welcome my friend and me.
We step over the barbed wire into the pasture
Where they have been grazing all day, alone.
They ripple tensely, they can hardly contain their happiness
That we have come.   10
They bow shyly as wet swans. They love each other.
There is no loneliness like theirs.
At home once more,
They begin munching the young tufts of spring in the darkness.

I would like to hold the slenderer one in my arms,   15
For she has walked over to me
And nuzzled my left hand.
She is black and white,
Her mane falls wild on her forehead,
And the light breeze moves me to caress her long ear   20
That is delicate as the skin over a girl's wrist.
Suddenly I realize
That if I stepped out of my body I would break
Into blossom.

James Wright (1927 – 1980)*
AUTUMN BEGINS IN MARTINS FERRY, OHIO   1963

In the Shreve High football stadium,
I think of Polacks nursing long beers in Tiltonsville,
And gray faces of Negroes in the blast furnace at Benwood,
And the ruptured night watchman of Wheeling Steel,
Dreaming of heroes.   5

All the proud fathers are ashamed to go home.
Their women cluck like starved pullets,
Dying for love.

Therefore,
Their sons grow suicidally beautiful   10
At the beginning of October,
And gallop terribly against each other's bodies.

Sir Thomas Wyatt (1503? – 1542)*
THEY FLEE FROM ME THAT SOMETIME DID ME SEKË   (ABOUT 1535)

They flee from me that sometime did me sekë
   With naked fotë° stalking in my chamber.   *foot*
I have seen them gentle, tame and mekë
   That now are wild, and do not remember
   That sometime they put themself in danger   5
To take bread at my hand; and now they range
Busily seeking with a continual change.

Thankèd be fortune, it hath been otherwise
   Twenty times better; but once in speciàll,
In thin array, after a pleasant guise,   10
   When her loose gown from her shoulders did fall,
   And she me caught in her armës long and small,
Therëwith all sweetly did me kiss,
And softly said, *Dear heart, how like you this?*

It was no dremë: I lay broadë waking. 15
    But all is turned thorough° my gentleness *through*
Into a strangë fashion of forsaking;
    And I have leave to go of her goodness,
    And she also to use newfangleness°. *to seek novelty*
But since that I so kindëly am served 20
I would fain knowë what she hath deserved.

THEY FLEE FROM ME THAT SOMETIME DID ME SEKË. Some latter-day critics have called Sir Thomas Wyatt a careless poet because some of his lines appear faltering and metrically inconsistent; others have thought he knew what he was doing. It is uncertain whether the final *e*'s in English spelling were still pronounced in Wyatt's day as they were in Chaucer's, but if they were, perhaps Wyatt has been unjustly blamed. In this text, spellings have been modernized except in words where the final *e* would make a difference in rhythm. To sense how it matters, try reading the poem aloud leaving out the *e*'s and then putting them in wherever indicated. Sound them like the *a* in *sofa*. 20. *kindëly:* according to my kind (or hers); that is, as befits the nature of man (or woman). Perhaps there is also irony here, and the word means "unkindly."

William Butler Yeats (1865 – 1939)*
CRAZY JANE TALKS WITH THE BISHOP 1933

I met the Bishop on the road
And much said he and I.
"Those breasts are flat and fallen now,
Those veins must soon be dry;
Live in a heavenly mansion, 5
Not in some foul sty."

"Fair and foul are near of kin,
And fair needs foul," I cried.
"My friends are gone, but that's a truth
Nor° grave nor bed denied, *neither* 10
Learned in bodily lowliness
And in the heart's pride.

"A woman can be proud and stiff
When on love intent;
But Love has pitched his mansion in 15
The place of excrement;
For nothing can be sole or whole
That has not been rent."

William Butler Yeats (1865 – 1939)*
FOR ANNE GREGORY 1933

"Never shall a young man,
Thrown into despair
By those great honey-colored
Ramparts at your ear,

Love you for yourself alone
And not your yellow hair."   5

"But I can get a hair-dye
And set such color there,
Brown, or black, or carrot,
That young men in despair   10
May love me for myself alone
And not my yellow hair."

"I heard an old religious man
But yesternight declare
That he had found a text to prove   15
That only God, my dear,
Could love you for yourself alone
And not your yellow hair."

William Butler Yeats (1865 – 1939)*
THE LAKE ISLE OF INNISFREE   1892

I will arise and go now, and go to Innisfree,
And a small cabin build there, of clay and wattles made:
Nine bean-rows will I have there, a hive for the honey-bee,
And live alone in the bee-loud glade.

And I shall have some peace there, for peace comes dropping slow,   5
Dropping from the veils of the morning to where the cricket sings;
There midnight's all a glimmer, and noon a purple glow,
And evening full of the linnet's wings.

I will arise and go now, for always night and day
I hear lake water lapping with low sounds by the shore;   10
While I stand on the roadway, or on the pavements grey,
I hear it in the deep heart's core.

THE LAKE ISLE OF INNISFREE. Yeats refers to an island in Lough (Lake) Gill, in County Sligo in the west of Ireland. 2. *wattles:* frameworks of interwoven sticks or branches, used to make walls and roofs.

COMPARE:

"The Lake Isle of Innisfree" with Yeats's "Sailing to Byzantium" (page 660).

William Butler Yeats (1865 – 1939)*
TO A FRIEND WHOSE WORK HAS COME TO NOTHING   1914

Now all the truth is out,
Be secret and take defeat
From any brazen throat,

For how can you compete,
Being honor bred, with one   5
Who, were it proved he lies,
Were neither shamed in his own
Nor in his neighbors' eyes?
Bred to a harder thing
Than Triumph, turn away   10
And like a laughing string
On which mad fingers play
Amid a place of stone,
Be secret and exult,
Because of all things known   15
That is most difficult.

To a Friend Whose Work Has Come to Nothing. The friend was Lady Gregory, who had
worked to persuade the City of Dublin to build an art museum. Her nephew, Hugh Lane,
had offered Dublin his famous collection of French paintings, provided the city would house
it. 5. *one:* William Martin Murphy, proprietor of a popular daily newspaper, enemy of the
proposed museum.

Compare:

"To a Friend Whose Work Has Come to Nothing" with "To a Friend Whose Work
Has Come to Triumph" by Anne Sexton (page 764).

William Butler Yeats (1865 – 1939)*
The Magi   1914

Now as at all times I can see in the mind's eye,
In their stiff, painted clothes, the pale unsatisfied ones
Appear and disappear in the blue depth of the sky
With all their ancient faces like rain-beaten stones,
And all their helms of silver hovering side by side,   5
And all their eyes still fixed, hoping to find once more,
Being by Calvary's turbulence unsatisfied,
The uncontrollable mystery on the bestial floor.

Compare:

"The Magi" with "Journey of the Magi" by T. S. Eliot (page 712).

30 Lives of the Poets

Here you will find a brief biographical note for each poet represented in the book by more than one poem. There is also a note for Thomas Gray, author of the long poem "Elegy in a Country Churchyard." (Brief poems given as examples, such as haiku and limericks, did not qualify a poet for a biography.)

John Ashbery

John Ashbery, born in Rochester, New York, in 1927, was educated at Deerfield Academy, Harvard, and Columbia. In 1960 he became an art critic in Paris for the *New York Herald Tribune,* and from 1966 to 1972 served as executive editor of the magazine *Art News* in New York. His first full collection of poetry, *Some Trees* (1956), was chosen by W. H. Auden for publication in the Yale Series of Younger Poets; his *Self-Portrait in a Convex Mirror* (1976) garnered praise and three leading literary prizes, and sold well for a book of serious poetry. Ashbery has written plays and a novel (with James Schuyler), *A Nest of Ninnies* (1969). He now lives in New York and teaches part time in the writing program at Brooklyn College. Some critics have speculated that Ashbery's experience as an art critic has tinged his poetry: that he performs in words what an abstract expressionist performs on canvas in oils. His work can annoy readers who expect poems to make clear statements to be taken in only one way; others think him the foremost living American poet and major heir to the tradition of Wallace Stevens — that is, to the art of suggesting rather than depicting, of arranging words primarily for their own sake.

W. H. Auden

W. H. Auden (1907 – 1973), born in York, England, in 1907, as a young man in the 1930s became the acknowledged spokesman for a generation of English poets that included Stephen Spender, C. Day Lewis, Christopher Isherwood, and Louis MacNeice. His early work was characterized by blithe wit, a Marxist outlook, and a knowledge of Freudian psychology; in later life, he professed Christianity and (in his views of poetry) increasing conservatism. In 1939 Auden emigrated to America, and in 1946 became a United States citizen. A prolific editor, anthologist, and translator of poetry, he collaborated on verse plays, travel memoirs, and (with his longtime friend Chester Kallman) librettos for operas, including Igor Stravinsky's *The Rake's Progress* (1951). He wrote influential criticism, notably that collected in *The Dyer's Hand* (1962). Auden divided his last years among England, Italy, Austria, and New York.

Elizabeth Bishop

Elizabeth Bishop (1911 – 1979) was born in Worcester, Massachusetts. After her father died (in her first year) and her mother was stricken with mental illness, she spent her early childhood with her grandparents in a village in Nova Scotia. A sufferer from asthma, she received scant elementary schooling, but she read widely and deeply at home. At sixteen she entered Walnut Hill, a boarding school, and later graduated from Vassar. Her undergraduate poems won her the friendship of the poet Marianne Moore, who persuaded her not to go on to medical school, but instead to write. Fond of travel and flower-filled climates, Bishop lived for nine years in Key West, Florida, then for fifteen years in Brazil, dividing her time between the mountains and Rio de Janeiro. In 1966 she returned to the United States to teach: first at the University of Washington, then at Harvard from 1969 until 1977, when she retired. Most of her sparely disciplined work is contained in two volumes: *Complete Poems 1927 – 1979* (1983) and *Collected Prose* (1984). Her sharp-eyed poems, full of vivid images and apt metaphors, have affected the work of other poets, among them her friends Randall Jarrell and Robert Lowell.

William Blake

William Blake (1757 – 1827), poet, painter, and visionary, was born in the Soho district of London and early in life was apprenticed to an engraver. Becoming a skilled craftsman, he earned his living illustrating books, among them Dante's *Divine Comedy,* Milton's poems, and the Book of Job. A remarkable and original graphic artist whose only formal training came from a few months at the Royal Academy, Blake published his own poems, engraving them in a careful script embellished with hand-colored illustrations and decorations. His wife Catherine Boucher, whom he taught to read and write, shared his visions and helped him do the coloring. *Songs of Innocence* (1789) and *Songs of Experience* (1794), brief lyrics written from a child's point of view, are easy to enjoy; but anyone deeply interested in Blake copes also with the longer, more demanding "Prophetic Books," among them *The Book of Thel* (1789), *The Marriage of Heaven and Hell* (1790), and *Jerusalem* (1804 – 20). In these later works, out of his readings in alchemy, the Bible, and the works of Plato and Swedenborg, Blake derived support for his lifelong hatred of scientific rationalism and created his own mythology, complete with devils and deities. A sympathizer with both American and French revolutions, Blake was once accused of sedition, but the charges were dismissed. In his lifetime, Wordsworth and Coleridge were among the few admirers of his short lyrics; his "Prophetic Books" have had to wait until our century for compassionate readers.

Robert Bly

Robert Bly was born on a farm in Madison, Minnesota, in 1926, and continued to live there for most of his life. He was graduated from Harvard, where he began studies in mathematics before deciding to devote his life to poetry. Rather than teaching, Bly has preferred to support himself and his family by giving poetry readings and by translating books and poems from Scandinavian and other languages. In 1958 he launched a poetry magazine, *The Fifties* (later renamed, as decades went by, *The Sixties* and *The Seventies*). In it he spoofed academic critics, urged American poets to open their work to dream and surrealism, and introduced in translation the work of important poets of Europe and Latin America. Bly has vitally influenced the work of James Wright, Donald Hall, and many younger poets. His readings, in which he sometimes chants and dons primitive masks, have drawn throngs. In the 1960s he organized (with David Ray) American Writers Against the Vietnam War, and over the years has championed many causes, usually pacifist and antinuclear. Lately he has been leading retreats for men, trying to help them understand their male natures.

Gwendolyn Brooks

Gwendolyn Brooks, born in 1917 in Topeka, Kansas, moved early in life to Chicago's South Side, whose people she has commemorated in her poetry and in a novel, *Maud Martha* (1953). Recipient of the Pulitzer prize for poetry in 1950, for *Annie Allen*, Brooks has long been recognized as a leading voice in modern American letters. She has combined several teaching positions with raising two children. Since 1967, when she took part in a conference for black writers at Fisk University and was impressed with young black poets' views, she has increasingly been an activist, teaching teen-age black writers in Chicago and addressing her work especially to black audiences. Instead of continuing to publish with a mainstream New York publishing house, she switched her work to Broadside, a small literary press in Detroit founded by black poet Dudley Randall. Her memoir *Report from Part One* (1972) discusses her altered outlook. In 1985 she was named Consultant in Poetry to the Library of Congress. Her goals in life, she has declared, are "to be clean of heart, clear of mind, and claiming of what is right and just."

Elizabeth Barrett Browning

Elizabeth Barrett Browning (1806 – 1861), was born in Durham, England, into a large family dominated by a father whose wealth came from plantations in Jamaica. At thirty-two, following a "nervous collapse," still suffering from an earlier spinal injury, she became an invalid. Her first book, *Poems* (1844) drew a fan letter from a younger poet, Robert Browning, who called and paid her court. Two years later, at forty, defying father's and doctor's orders, she secretly married Browning and ran off with him to Florence, Italy. There she gained in strength, bore a son, and presided over a circle of English artists and writers. Her flight from home is retold in Rudolf Bessier's slightly exaggerated play *The Barretts of Wimpole Street* (1930). But as a poet, Elizabeth Barrett earned her own laurels. In her day, her work was far more popular than her husband's, and more highly regarded. A wide audience welcomed her *Sonnets from the Portuguese* (1850) (not translations: "my little Portuguese" was a name Browning gave her for her dark complexion) and her novel in verse, *Aurora Leigh* (1857). She was a learned translator from the Greek, a pioneer feminist, an abolitionist, an outspoken advocate of Italian unification. In fact, Sandra M. Gilbert and Susan Gubar write in *The Norton Anthology of Literature by Women,* nothing could be less truthful than to imagine her "a swooning Victorian invalid, languishing on a sofa, smelling-salts in one hand and sentimental verses in the other."

Robert Browning

Robert Browning (1812 – 1889), born in a suburb of London, was educated mainly in his father's six-thousand-volume library. With *Pauline* (1833), he began to print his poetry. After the death of his wife Elizabeth Barrett Browning (see previous note), he returned to England to begin his final period as (Henry James wrote) an "accomplished, saturated, sane, sound man of the London world." There, as he neared sixty, he enjoyed late but loud applause and the adulation of the Browning Society: faithful readers whose local groups met over their teacups to explicate him. Readers have most greatly favored Browning's story-poems in a form he perfected, the dramatic monologue — such as "My Last Duchess" and "Soliloquy of the Spanish Cloister" — in which he brings to life persons from the past (some of them famous), has them speak their inmost thoughts and reveal their characters. His masterpiece, *The Ring and the Book* (1868 – 69), is a long narrative poem in twelve monologues, based on a seventeenth-century Roman murder trial. Browning also wrote several plays, among them *A Blot in the 'Scutcheon* (1842). Through the praise and emulation of his later admirers Ezra Pound and T. S. Eliot, Browning has profoundly affected modern poetry. A formal experimenter, he speaks to us in energetic, punchy words — and like many later poets he introduces learning into his poems without apology. More important, Browning is among the great yea-sayers in English poetry: an affirmer and celebrant of life.

Robert Burns

Robert Burns (1759 – 1796), the preeminent poet of Scotland, was born in a two-room farm cottage in Alloway, a hamlet on the River Doon, the son of a farmer who worked himself to death. For most of his days Burns too struggled to farm poor soil. Though his schooling lasted only three years, he eagerly read Shakespeare and Pope as a boy and let poetry pour from his own pen. Only in 1786, when he felt he needed money to emigrate to Jamaica, did he publish his *Poems, Chiefly in the Scottish Dialect,* depicting Scottish rural life with warm humor, tender compassion, and rugged exuberance. The book scored an immediate hit and Burns remained in Scotland for the rest of his days. After Edinburgh's stylish society, which had lionized him for a time, let him drop, he returned to his plough, married Jean Armour (who earlier had borne him two sets of twins), and continued to farm until 1791, when he retired to the easier life of a tax official. But worn from toil, hardship, and poverty, Burns died at thirty-seven. Among his legacies are songs, such as "Flow Gently, Sweet Afton," "Comin' Through the Rye," and a song still heard in this country each New Year's eve, "Auld Lang Syne." Like Hugh MacDiarmid, Burns wrote poetry in both standard English and Scots dialect — in the latter whenever, as in "The Jolly Beggars" and "Address to the Unco Guid," he expressed defiantly unconventional views.

Thomas Campion

Thomas Campion (1567 – 1620), Elizabethan courtier, physician, musician, and poet, was the author of several books of solo songs with lute accompaniment, much admired for their masterly unifying of words and music. In 1602 Campion wrote a tract, *Observations in the Art of English Poesy,* in which he argued in favor of writing quantitative verse in English, after the example of the ancient Greek and Latin poets. "Rose-cheeked Laura" was apparently written to illustrate his theories. In the same tract, he opposed the writing of any more poetry in rime and traditional English meters — in which, however, he excelled.

E. E. Cummings

E[dward] E[stlin] Cummings (1894 – 1962) was born in Cambridge, Massachusetts, the son of a minister. As a young man at Harvard, he studied Greek and Latin. In World War I, while serving as an ambulance driver, he was mistakenly arrested and confined to a French prison — an experience that gave rise to a novel filled with vivid portraits of his fellow prisoners, *The Enormous Room* (1922). Off and on throughout the 1920s, Cummings lived in Paris. In *Eimi* (1933) he scathingly and satirically reported on a trip to the Soviet Union. Although many of his lyric poems revel in typographical experiment, in theme and sentiment they are often more conventional than they appear. Besides poetry Cummings wrote essays, plays including *Him* (1927) and *Santa Claus* (1946), and the ballet *Tom* (1935), and produced substantial work as a painter and a graphic artist. Throughout his career, he upheld simple themes: love is good, pomp is silly, one individual is worth a thousand faceless societies.

William Cowper

William Cowper (1731 – 1800), the son of a clergyman in Hertfordshire, England, was a descendant of John Donne. His mother died when he was six, and afterward Cowper was subject to periods of melancholy. He studied law and was admitted to the bar, but after a suicide attempt at thirty-two was committed for a time to an asylum. In 1767, living with friends, he sought the spiritual guidance of Methodist preacher John Newton, with whom he wrote the *Olney Hymns* (1771 – 79). As long as he led a peaceful life in the country, caring for rabbits and gardening, Cowper was content, although troubled by recurrent fits of his illness and by a persistent conviction that he was damned. His long poem *The Task* (1785) depicts rural life. He is a splendid satirist and writer of epigrams. His letters are among the richest a poet has written in English — along with those of Gray, Keats, Hart Crane, and Dylan Thomas.

J. V. Cunningham

J[ames] V[incent] Cunningham (1911 – 1985) was born in Maryland, but spent his early life in Montana. A Shakespeare scholar with a Stanford Ph.D., Cunningham taught English at Brandeis for many years (1953 – 80) and for eight years served as chairman of the department. A reader of Latin and Greek, he became the modern master of the terse, pithy English verse epigram in the classical manner. All his poems have a similar brevity, firm control, and a cold, hardboiled manner. "Poetry is what looks like poetry, what sounds like poetry," he stated. "It is metrical composition." His relatively slim *Collected Poems and Epigrams* (1971) gathers most of his work in verse; his *Collected Essays* (1976), most of his work in prose, including an earlier study, *Woe and Wonder: The Emotional Effect of Shakespearean Tragedy.* In a late critical work, *Dickinson: Lyric and Legend* (1980), Cunningham took a withering look at the bard of Amherst.

Emily Dickinson

Emily Dickinson (1830 – 1886) passed nearly all her life in her family home in Amherst, Massachusetts. Her father was a prominent lawyer and for a time a United States congressman. One trip to Washington, D.C. and a short, unhappy period as a college student at New England Female Seminary (later Mount Holyoke) were the extent of her distant travels, and as the years passed Dickinson withdrew from town activities and retired into deeper seclusion. Though she wrote more than a thousand poems, she published only seven. The extent of her work was known only after her death, when her manuscripts were discovered in a trunk in the homestead attic, stitched into little booklets and peppered with an idiosyncratic system of punctuation. From 1890 until midcentury, nine posthumous collections of her poems were assembled by friends and relatives, some of whom rewrote her work to make it more conventional. Thomas H. Johnson's three-volume edition of the *Poems* (1955) established a better text. In relatively few and simple forms clearly indebted to the hymns she heard in church, Dickinson succeeded in being a true visionary and a poet of colossal originality.

John Donne

John Donne (1572 – 1631), English poet and divine, wrote his subtle, worldly love lyrics as a young man in the court of Queen Elizabeth I. At the time, he came to be known in London as (wrote his contemporary, Richard

Baker) "a great visitor of ladies, a great frequenter of plays, a great writer of conceited verses." The poems of his *Songs and Sonnets* were first circulated in manuscript, for in his lifetime Donne printed little. When in 1601 he married without the consent of his bride's father, he was dismissed from his secretarial post at court. For several years he endured poverty. His longer poems, *The First Anniversary* and *The Second Anniversary* (1611, 1612), suffused with gloom, see the order of the universe shaken by science and doubt. In 1615 Donne — apparently with some reluctance, for he had been raised a Catholic — became a priest of the Anglican church. From 1621 until he died he was dean of St. Paul's Cathedral in London, where he preached sermons known for their eloquence. His "Holy Sonnets" date from later life. Almost forgotten for two centuries, Donne's work has had much influence in our time. H. J. C. Grierson brought out a great scholarly edition of it in 1912; shortly thereafter it was championed by T. S. Eliot.

John Dryden

John Dryden (1631 – 1700) is usually named with Alexander Pope, Jonathan Swift, and Samuel Johnson as a leading poet of the Neoclassical period in English literature (a time when writers subscribed to classical, usually Latin, influences: roughly from 1660 through the late eighteenth century). He began his career as a poet with an elegy for Oliver Cromwell; then, a year later, wrote a long poem celebrating the restoration of Charles II — thus "changing with the nation," Samuel Johnson approvingly remarked. In 1668 Dryden was appointed poet laureate, in which capacity he wrote poems for state occasions. After the revolution of 1688, he refused to take an oath of loyalty to the new monarchs, William and Mary, and was stripped of his post. Until he was fifty, Dryden supported his family by writing plays, among them the comedy *Marriage à la Mode* (1672) and the splendid verse drama of Antony and Cleopatra, *All for Love* (1677). In the poem *Religio Laici* (1682) he set forth the faith of a Protestant layman; five years later, in another poem, *The Hind and the Panther,* he announced his conversion to Roman Catholicism. Dryden's changes in creed and politics, Louis I. Bredvold wrote, were consistent: always increasingly conservative. One of the great English satiric poets, Dryden pokes fun at aspirants to political power in *Absalom and Achitophel* (1681 – 82) and roasts a bad poet in *MacFlecknoe* (1682).

T. S. Eliot

T[homas] S[tearns] Eliot (1888 – 1965) was born of a New England family who had moved to St. Louis. After study at Harvard, Eliot emigrated to London, became a bank clerk and later an influential editor for the publishing house of Faber. In 1927 he became a British citizen and joined the Church of England. During the fire bombings of London in World War II, he served as an air raid warden. Although Eliot strove to keep his private life private, a recent biographer, Peter Ackroyd in *T. S. Eliot* (1984), throws light upon his troubled early marriage. Early poems such as "The Love Song of J. Alfred Prufrock" (1917) and *The Waste Land* (1922), an allusive and seemingly disconnected complaint about the sterility of contemporary city life, enormously influenced young poets. Eliot was mainly responsible for bringing French Symbolism into English poetry, and as a critic he helped revive interest in John Donne and other Metaphysical poets. In an early essay, "Tradition and the Individual Talent" (1919), he finds a necessary continuity in Western civilization. *Four Quartets,* completed in 1943, was Eliot's last major work of poetry: an attempt to structure a long thematic poem like a work of music. In later years he devoted himself to writing verse plays for the London stage; the best received was *The Cocktail Party* (1950), in which Alec Guinness played a psychiatrist. In 1948 Eliot received the Nobel Prize for Literature.

Robert Frost

Robert Frost (1874 – 1963), though born in San Francisco, came to be popularly known as a spokesman of rural New England. In periods of farming, teaching school, and raising chickens and writing for poultry journals, Frost struggled until his late thirties to support his family and to publish his poems, with little success. Moving to England to write and farm in 1912 – 15, he had his first book published in London: *A Boy's Will* (1913). Returning to America, he settled in New Hampshire, later teaching for many years (in a casual way) at Amherst College in Massachusetts. Audiences responded warmly to the poet's public readings; he was awarded four Pulitzer prizes. In late years the white-haired Frost became a sort of elder statesman and poet laureate of the John F. Kennedy administration: invited to read a poem at President Kennedy's inauguration, dispatched to Russia as a cultural emissary. Frost is sometimes admired for putting colloquial Yankee speech into poetry — and he did, but more essentially he mastered the art of laying conversational American speech along a metrical line. In a three-volume biography (1966 – 76), Lawrance Thompson made Frost out to be an overweening egotist who tormented his family, and we are only now coming around again to seeing him as more than that.

Thomas Gray

Thomas Gray (1716 – 1771), author of the most often quoted poem in English, was born in London into a middle-class home (his father was a scrivener, his mother kept a hat shop). He was the only one of twelve children to survive infancy. He attended Eton and later Cambridge University, where he studied for four years but did not take a degree. After a tour of Europe with his schoolmate Horace Walpole (the first Gothic novelist) and a short sojourn with his mother in the village of Stoke Poges, Gray returned to Cambridge to spend the rest of his life in seclusion as a sort of perpetual graduate student. He stayed around the university so long and became so widely learned in architecture, heraldry, botany, Greek, Old Norse, and other matters that in 1768, at fifty-two, he was appointed Regius Professor of History. So retiring was Gray that he first published his "Elegy in a Country Churchyard" anonymously — and only when friends browbeat him into printing it. He seems to have suffered from a constitutional lack of energy. He dreaded being known, and when the post of poet laureate was offered him, he rejected it. A dilettante, Gray considered himself an amateur in whatever he did. Poetry was only one of his interests, but in his "Elegy" and his Pindaric odes "The Bard" and "The Progress of Poesy," he spurred English poetry to break away from neoclassicism and move toward plainer speech, more various forms, infatuation with the colorful, primitive Old English past, and love of nature and countryside. Gray is buried in Stoke Poges, in the churchyard for which we remember him.

Thomas Hardy

Thomas Hardy (1840 – 1928) was both a major Victorian novelist and a great poet of the twentieth century. After his novel *Jude the Obscure* (1896) was trounced by critics who objected to its dismal morbidity, Hardy, who by then had made a modest fortune from his fiction, switched exclusively to his first love, poetry. Hardy was born in the English county of Dorsetshire ("Wessex" in his fiction and poetry), and as a young man worked as an architect. Determined to be a novelist, he first won success with *Far from the Madding Crowd* (1874), followed by *The Return of the Native* (1878), *The Mayor of Casterbridge* (1886), and his masterpiece *Tess of the D'Urbervilles* (1891). After the death of his first wife Emma, with whom he appears to have had had a rather cold and troubled relationship, Hardy was inspired to write a great spate of love poems in her memory. In old age he wrote a two-volume autobiography and charged his second wife, Florence, to publish it after his death under her own name. In both fiction and poetry, Hardy's view of the universe is somber: God appears to have forgotten us, and happiness usually arrives too late. *The Dynasts* (1903 – 08), a long epic poem, makes amused gods sneer down on the Napoleonic wars. Many modern poets have credited Hardy with teaching them a good deal, probably about irony and the use of spoken language, among them W. H. Auden, Philip Larkin, Dylan Thomas, and W. D. Snodgrass.

George Herbert

George Herbert (1593 – 1633), English devotional poet, the son of an aristocratic family, began writing poems as an undergraduate at Cambridge University. After dabbling for a time in worldly affairs, he entered the priesthood of the Church of England, to live out his days in a country parish. Herbert's poems have many references to music; according to his contemporary John Aubrey, he "had a very good hand on the lute, and set [to music] his own lyrics and sacred poems." Herbert did not publish his poems in his lifetime, but after his death friends collected them in *The Temple* (1633). The book is said to have stimulated Henry Vaughan to follow in Herbert's footsteps as a poet. Herbert makes the religious experience personal, definite, and familiar. For his use of startling "metaphysical" figures of speech, he has been compared with John Donne; but a rare sweetness and plain-spokenness make him unique among religious poets in English.

Robert Herrick

Robert Herrick (1591 – 1674), after serving as a goldsmith's apprentice, entered Cambridge University at twenty-two, then a late age. For nine years he seems to have lived in London, consorting with a group of poets and wits whose chief was Ben Jonson. In 1629 he became parish priest in Dean Prior, in rural Devonshire, where he lived out his days, sometimes chafing about the boorishness of his parishioners. When in 1647 the Puritans temporarily ousted him from his pulpit, Herrick returned to London. There at fifty-six he brought out his first book, *Noble Numbers* (1647), pious poems; then reprinted them together with five times as many sportive, secular poems in *Hesperides* (1648). Unluckily, the books came too late to cause a stir, Herrick's early fame as a poet having withered and the vogue for chiseled classical lyrics having gone by. Like his master Jonson, Herrick writes songlike poems inspired by Greek and Latin pastoral (or shepherd-and-shepherdess) poetry. We go to him not for profound ideas, but for fresh, tough speech and resonant music. Herrick, who remained a bachelor clergyman, probably imagined the mistresses he praised. He declared in *Hesperides,* "To his book's end this last line he'd have placed: / Jocund his Muse was, but his life was chaste."

Gerard Manley Hopkins

Gerard Manley Hopkins (1844 – 1889), born in Essex, England, was, like Emily Dickinson, a major poet not known until our century. At twenty, a student at Oxford, he was converted to Roman Catholicism and received into that church by Cardinal Newman. Ordained a Jesuit, Hopkins at first served as parish priest and teacher in working-class sections of large cities (London, Glasgow, Liverpool, Manchester), where poverty and suffering distressed him. But his sermons were reportedly so strange (in one, he likened the church to a cow we milk and whose moo we follow) that his superiors removed him from public view, making him Professor of Greek at University College, Dublin. Feeling an exile in Ireland, he died of typhoid fever at forty-four. Nearly thirty years after Hopkins's death, his friend Robert Bridges published his *Poems* (1918), having thought them too demanding for earlier readers. That much of Hopkins's work sounds odd to us may be due to the poet's admiration for Old English, with its gutsy monosyllables, and for Welsh poetry, rich in patterns of sound. Hopkins developed his own theory of versification: "sprung rhythm" — in brief, a kind of accentual verse. Though on entering the priesthood he had renounced poetry, he welcomed the suggestion of a superior that he contribute to a Jesuit magazine a poem on the drowning of five Franciscan nuns. The result, "The Wreck of the *Deutschland,*" received a rejection slip. This challenging poem has been called "the dragon guarding the door to Hopkins's poetry," but most readers have gone in by the back door of his more quickly accessible nature poems. In these, the sensuous world bursts forth in irrepressible testimony to its Maker's glory.

A. E. Housman

A. E. Housman (1859 – 1936), English poet and professor of Latin, was born in a village in rural Shropshire, England. Although as a student at Oxford he distinguished himself as a promising scholar of the classics, he failed his exams, apparently because of some inner crisis precipitated by his love for a fellow male student. Determined to overcome this setback, Housman, while working as a clerk in the British Patent Office, at night wrote scholarly articles. Within ten years these academic writings, bristling with cold sarcasms and scathing put-downs of rival scholars, had won him such high repute that he was invited to be Professor of Latin at the University of London. Later he stepped up to Cambridge University, to spend the rest of his days living a retiring academic life befitting his shy temperament. Though Housman published only two slim collections of poems — the instantly and enormously popular *A Shropshire Lad* (1898) and the conclusively titled *Last Poems* (1922) — his place as a minor master of the English lyric seems unshakable. Like many Latin poets he admired, he insists in well-turned lines that life is short and comes to a bad end.

Langston Hughes

Langston Hughes (1902 – 1967), who dropped his first name, James, was born in Joplin, Missouri. As a high school senior in Cleveland, he wrote a poem still often reprinted, "The Negro Speaks of Rivers." When a young man Hughes worked as a merchant seaman, visited Africa, and lived for a time in Rome and Paris. While working as a busboy at a Washington, D.C., hotel, he showed his poems to hotel guest Vachel Lindsay, a poet then celebrated, and Lindsay urged them on a publisher. *The Weary Blues* (1926) earned him a considerable reputation. Hughes's work in poetry won him a scholarship to Lincoln University, from which he was graduated in 1929. He became a major figure in the Harlem Renaissance of the 1920s and early 1930s — a period when that district of New York City became a lively center for black writers, artists, and musicians. A versatile writer and teacher, Hughes, one of the first practicing poets to teach poetry writing in elementary schools, was also among the few poets to earn a living by giving readings and lecturing. Among his other works are novels, stories, plays, song lyrics, children's books, memoirs, translations, and essays reporting conversations with a Harlem dweller called Simple, a streetwise philosopher. *A Langston Hughes Reader* (1958) gives some idea of his richness and variety.

Randall Jarrell

Randall Jarrell (1914 – 1965) was born in Nashville, Tennessee, and served as a private in the army air force in World War II, an experience that gave rise to several of his best early poems. Much of his life was spent in academe. At Vanderbilt, a psychology major, he studied literature with poet-critic John

Crowe Ransom, who changed the direction of Jarrell's career. When Ransom moved to Kenyon College, Jarrell followed as an English instructor. At Kenyon, he formed another lifelong friendship: with a student who was to become a distinguished poet, Robert Lowell. Later Jarrell taught at the University of Texas, Sarah Lawrence, Princeton, Illinois, and for many years (1947 – 65) at the Woman's College of the University of North Carolina (now the U.N.C., Greensboro). His one novel, *Pictures from an Institution* (1954), is a satire set on a campus. As poetry editor for *The Nation* in the mid-1940s, Jarrell drew attention for his witty, astute, outspoken reviews of poetry. *Poetry and the Age* (1953) includes especially brilliant essays on Robert Frost and Wallace Stevens. Jarrell, who loved the German language, translated Goethe's *Faust* (Part I) and some of the Grimm fairy tales. In late years he wrote four books for children (with beautiful drawings by Maurice Sendak) including *The Bat Poet* (1964) and the posthumous *Fly by Night* (1976).

Ben Jonson

Ben Jonson (1573? – 1637), posthumous son of a Scottish minister, was a native Londoner. As a boy he received a firm grounding in Latin and Greek at Westminster School, but instead of enrolling in a university, took up bricklaying, then served as a soldier in Flanders. Home from the wars, he married and became an actor and playwright in London. Although a coolly rational classicist by persuasion, Jonson seems to have been an outspoken hothead, given to quarrels and brawls. In 1598 he killed a fellow actor in a duel and escaped the gallows only by claiming an ancient law that forbade hanging anyone who could read. From about 1606, Jonson frequented the Mermaid Tavern in London's Fleet Street, a favorite hangout of writers and actors. There, on the first Friday of each month, he presided over famed literary discussions; according to one report, his friend Shakespeare would take part at times and match wits with him. Later changing pubs (to the Devil and St. Dunstan), Jonson and his circle became known as the "Tribe of Ben"; Thomas Carew and Robert Herrick were younger members. Later Jonson became the leading writer of masks, elaborate plays with music and dancing produced at court. As a poet Jonson, in his precise Latinate lyrics, odes, and epigrams, helped get rid of worn-out Petrarchan conventions (those Shakespeare mocks in "My mistress' eyes are nothing like the sun"). As a playwright, he excelled; his comedies, especially *Volpone, or The Fox* (1606) and *The Alchemist* (1610), are among the crown jewels of the English stage.

John Keats

John Keats (1795 – 1821), son of a London stable keeper, studied to become a physician and served as a surgeon's apprentice before deciding on poetry as a career. In 1817 he published his first book, *Poems,* including "On First Looking into Chapman's Homer." Despite critics' hostility to his narrative poem *Endymion* (1818), Keats persisted. In 1818 he fell in love with sixteen-year-old Fanny Brawne, but, stricken with tuberculosis, postponed plans for marriage. In 1820, shortly after publication of his third and last book, Keats went to Italy in hopes of regaining his health, but his poetry soon slowed to a stop. In the following year, at twenty-five, he died in Rome and was buried there beneath the epitaph he wrote for himself: "Here lies one whose name was writ in water." His name, however, has continued to endure. No English poet wrote poems richer in sensuous imagery (as in his great odes, among them "Ode on Melancholy" and "To Autumn"), nor quite so beautifully reimagined the Middle Ages (in poems such as "La Belle Dame sans Merci" and "The Eve of St. Agnes"). He wrote several of the finest sonnets in the language, an unfinished epic of great interest, *Hyperion*, hilarious light verse, and scores of superb letters.

Galway Kinnell

Galway Kinnell, born in 1927 in Providence, Rhode Island, served in the U.S. Navy before his graduation from Princeton. He has lived mainly in New York and in Sheffield, Vermont, but also in Chicago, Hawaii, France, and Iran — this last the scene of his one novel, *Black Light* (1966). He has written for children, and has translated the work of François Villon, Yves Bonnefoy, and other French poets. He has received a Pulitzer Prize for poetry, and many other awards. Recently, he has directed the creative writing program at New York University. With "The Avenue Bearing the Initial of Christ into the New World," a long poem set in Brooklyn, in his first book *What a Kingdom It Was* (1960), Kinnell displayed Whitmanlike qualities: openness of form and an all-embracing affirmation of city life. By contrast, *The Book of Nightmares* (1971), a long poem, holds a litany of contemporary horrors.

Philip Larkin

Philip Larkin (1922 – 1985), born in Coventry, England, has been called the most influential British poet since World War II. After studies at Oxford, he drifted into being a librarian, and for many years was head librarian for the University of Hull. Early in his career Larkin wrote two novels, *Jill* (1946) and *A Girl in Winter* (1947). He also reviewed jazz recordings for a London newspaper. A self-declared foe of modernism in music, art, and literature, he published only four slim volumes of poems, traditional in form. The earliest collection was heavily indebted to Yeats: *The North Ship* (1945, reissued in 1966 with a preface making fun of it). With *The Less Deceived* (1955), Larkin hit his characteristic stride, writing most of the poems in the voice of a tough-minded, disillusioned, self-deprecating man facing a dreary urban landscape of quiet frustration. This voice drew an immediate response from readers in postwar England.

D. H. Lawrence

D. H. Lawrence (1885 – 1930), both poet and fiction writer, is the subject of a capsule biography together with his story "The Rocking Horse Winner" on page 305.

Denise Levertov

Denise Levertov was born in 1923 in Essex, England, daughter of a Welsh mother and a Russian Jewish-born priest of the Anglican church. She was educated at home, reading in her father's library. She served as a nurse in World War II. In 1947 she married an American novelist, Mitchell Goodman, and in the following year came to the United States. Her first book, published in England, had observed traditional poetic conventions (including rime and meter), but in America she discovered the work of William Carlos Williams and other open-form poets, and began to write in a different, freer mode. With Robert Creeley and others of the Black Mountain group, she has exerted much influence among younger poets. Her critical essays have been collected in *The Poet in the World* (1973) and *Light up the Cave* (1981). Levertov has been a tireless political activist, prominent in peace movements of the 1960s, 1970s, and 1980s. She now makes her home in Somerville, Massachusetts, and recently has been teaching poetry writing at Stanford on one coast and at Brandeis on the other.

Robert Lowell

Robert Lowell (1917 – 1977), born in Boston, came from a famous New England family that included three distinguished poets: James Russell, Maria, and Amy. He attended Harvard, then on the advice of his psychiatrist transferred to Kenyon, where he studied with poet-critics John Crowe Ransom and Randall Jarrell. During World War II he served time in a federal prison for resisting the draft. Lowell's early poems in *Lord Weary's Castle* (1946) were violent in imagery and tightly traditional in form. With the deliberately looser *Life Studies* (1959), he showed that he had learned from William Carlos Williams and the Beat poets, and his work became more open in form, more colloquial in speech, and more direct in its use of his own experience. Some of these poems were labeled "confessional poetry." As "Skunk Hour" tells us, Lowell's mind was sometimes "not right"; he suffered from recurrent manic depression that required him to spend periods in a hospital. Besides poetry, he wrote plays based on stories by Hawthorne and Melville: *The Old Glory* (1964, enlarged edition 1968) — as well as English versions of the *Phaedra* of Racine (1961) and the *Prometheus Bound* of Aeschylus (1969). Lowell was also a remarkable critic of poetry, though he never troubled to collect his critical writings.

Hugh MacDiarmid

Hugh MacDiarmid (pen name of Christopher Murray Grieve, 1892 – 1978) like Robert Burns wrote poetry in both Scots dialect and in standard English. Born in Dumfriesshire, Scotland, and educated at the University of Edinburgh, he published his first book of verse in 1923 and went on to produce copiously: plays, short stories, biography, autobiography, anthologies, literary criticism, and many volumes of poetry, including the book-length *A Drunk Man Looks at the Thistle* (1926). From time to time Grieve earned his living as a journalist and a broadcaster. He served in both world wars. A Marxist and a Scottish nationalist, he ran for Parliament. The example of his vigorous poetry encouraged a revival of writing in Scots.

John Milton

John Milton (1608 – 1674), author of *Paradise Lost,* the greatest English epic, was born in London, the son of a scrivener who composed music. His mother early began schooling him to be a minister. He studied zealously. As he later recalled: "From my twelfth year I scarcely ever went to bed before midnight, which was the first cause of injury to my eyes." After he received his B.A. from Cambridge University in 1629, his father supported him through eight years of further study. "Lycidas" (1638), a poem of this period, shows his deepening seriousness about religion and his growing resentment of corruptions in the church, which were to lead him to the Puritan cause. Milton wrote much prose in the service of causes. In *Areopagitica* (1644), he argues for freedom of the press and opposes the strict censorship that had been imposed by Parliament. His unhappy marriage to Mary Powell led him to write tracts in favor of divorce. When Oliver Cromwell and the Puritans ousted King Charles and declared England a commonwealth, Milton's writings were remembered, and earned him a post as Cromwell's foreign secretary. His eyesight strained by years of hard study, Milton went blind and had to dictate his correspondence (in Latin) to clerks, one of whom was fellow poet Andrew Marvell. With the Restoration of Charles II in 1660, Milton's world came crashing down. In retirement, at last he turned to a project he had planned as a young man: his major heroic poem, *Paradise Lost* (1667), about Satan's rebellion and the Fall of Adam and Eve. This epic was followed by *Paradise Regained* (1671) and a verse drama modeled on a Greek tragedy, *Samson Agonistes* (1671).

John Frederick Nims

John Frederick Nims, born in 1913 in Muskegon, Michigan, has had a distinguished career as poet and translator, teacher and editor. He has taught at Florida, Illinois (Urbana and Chicago), Missouri, Notre Dame, Toronto, and other universities, and has held visiting professorships at Harvard and in Florence, Milan, and Madrid. The poems in his first book *The Iron Pastoral* (1947) deal wittily with jukeboxes, penny arcades, poolrooms, and other features of the contemporary scene. In *Of Flesh and Bone* (1967) Nims shows his mastery of the epigram. His *Selected Poems* appeared in 1982. A translator of poetry from languages as varied as classical Greek, Catalan, and Galacian, Nims has splendidly rendered into English *The Poems of St. John of the Cross* (1959, revised edition 1968). For several recent years (1978 – 85) he was editor of *Poetry* magazine. He is the author of an introduction to poetry, *Western Wind* (second edition, 1983) and editor of *The Harper Anthology of Poetry* (1981).

Wilfred Owen

Wilfred Owen (1893 – 1918) was, like A. E. Housman, a native of Shropshire, England. He attended London University and for a time served as lay assistant to a minister, helping the sick and poor. In 1916, during World War I, he enlisted in the British army, became a company commander, and in less than two years wrote all his famous antiwar poems of life in the trenches. The army seems suddenly to have changed Owen from a competent minor poet with little to say into a powerful voice of pacifism. At age twenty-five, while trying to get his men across a canal under enemy fire on the French front, he was killed in action only a week before the war ended. Though Owen published only four poems, after his death a collection of his work was edited by another front-line war poet, Siegfried Sassoon (1920). Owen is preeminent among English poets who wrote of that conflict, and the reputation of his work has continued to grow.

Linda Pastan

Linda Pastan was born Linda Olenik in New York in 1932. After her graduation from Radcliffe, she took two master's degrees at Simmons (M.L.S.) and Brandeis (M.A.). She married in 1953 and has a daughter and two sons. Her first book, *A Perfect Circle of the Sun* (1971), established her as an up-and-comer; *Selected Poems* appeared in 1979, confirming her accomplishment. Her subtle, often powerful poems are exceptionally clear and accessible.

Sylvia Plath

Sylvia Plath (1932 – 1963), one of the most remarkable poets in English of the past half-century, was born in Boston, the daughter of German immigrants who both taught at Boston University. The death of her father when the poet was eight came as a trauma from which she seems never quite to have recovered. As a scholarship-winning student at Smith College, Plath revealed early promise, and her work received early publication. Like Esther Greenwood, protagonist of her one novel *The Bell Jar* (1963), Plath won a student contest that sent her to work in New York for a national magazine, and struggled with a year-long siege of mental illness for which she underwent shock treatments. Returning to Smith, she was graduated with top honors. Later she studied at Cambridge University in England, where she met and in 1956 married the poet Ted Hughes. Estranged from her husband, she died a suicide in London, leaving two children and, in manuscript, the intense, powerful poems that went into her posthumous, highly acclaimed collection, *Ariel* (1965).

Alexander Pope

Alexander Pope (1688 – 1744), the leading English poet of the early eighteenth century, was born in London, son of a Roman Catholic linen merchant.

A sickly, stunted, pockmarked child, he suffered from weak health and continual exhaustion throughout his life, and was said to have worn padded clothes to disguise his misshapen frame. Pope early excelled as a poet, composing his *Pastorals* (1709) at age sixteen. His rimed translations of the *Iliad* (1720) and the *Odyssey* (1725 – 26) and his edition of Shakespeare (1725), bestsellers in their day, made him independently wealthy, and he was able to buy an estate at Twickenham and live in style. Pope did not write an epic, but instead translated epics and wrote great mock epics: *The Rape of the Lock* (1714), in which he voices compassion for women transformed into wives, and *The Dunciad* (1728 – 43), in which he mocks his many literary enemies. He was a master satirist and splendid craftsman of the heroic couplet. Romantic critics generally think him no poet at all, but G. K. Chesterton remarked, "If Pope be not a poet, then who is?"

Ezra Pound

Ezra Pound (1885 – 1972), among the most influential (and still controversial) poets of our century, was born in Hailey, Idaho. He readied himself for a teaching career, but when in 1907 he lost his job at Wabash College for sheltering a penniless prostitute, he left America. Settling in England and later in Paris, he wielded influence on the work of T. S. Eliot, whose long poem *The Waste Land* he edited; W. B. Yeats, whom he served as secretary and critic; and James Joyce. Pound was perpetually championing writers then unknown, like Robert Frost. In 1924 Pound settled permanently in Italy, where he came to admire Mussolini's economic policies. During World War II he made broadcasts to America by Italian radio, deemed treasonous. When American armed forces arrested him in 1944, Pound spent three weeks in a cage in an army camp in Pisa. Flown to the United States to stand trial, he was declared incompetent and for twelve years was confined in St. Elizabeth's in Washington, a hospital for the criminally insane. In 1958, at the intervention of Robert Frost, Archibald MacLeish, and other old friends, he was pronounced incurable and allowed to return to Italy to spend his last, increasingly silent years. In his prime, Pound is a swaggeringly confident critic, a berater of smugness and mediocrity, a delectable humorist. Among his lasting books are *Personae* (enlarged edition, 1949), short poems; his *ABC of Reading* (1934), an introduction to poetry; and *Literary Essays* (1954). His *Cantos,* a vast poem woven of historical themes published in instalments over forty years, Pound never finished. He is a great translator of poetry from Italian, Provençal, Chinese, and other languages. Pare away his delusions, and a remarkable human being and splendid poet remains.

Adrienne Rich

Adrienne Rich was born in Baltimore in 1929, into a father-dominated Jewish family of comfortable means. While still an undergraduate at Radcliffe, she published her first book of poems, *A Change of World* (1951), with an introduction by W. H. Auden. Later she studied at Oxford. In 1953 she married an economist and soon bore three sons — an experience she said had been "radicalizing."

During the Vietnam War, she took an active part in the peace movement. In 1970 after the suicide of her estranged husband, perhaps obliquely referred to in the poem "Diving into the Wreck," Rich turned increasingly to feminist matters, expressed not only in poetry but in prose: in *Of Woman Born* (1976), a study of the institution of motherhood. With Michelle Cliff, she has coedited *Sinister Wisdom,* a lesbian little magazine. Rich has taught at City College of New York, Columbia, Brandeis, Smith, Douglass, and elsewhere. Few woman poets in recent years have commanded a more devoted audience.

Edwin Arlington Robinson

Edwin Arlington Robinson (1869 – 1935), who traced his family tree back to Anne Bradstreet, was born in Head Tide, Maine, and attended Harvard for two years until his family ran out of money. Fond of portraying failures, reprobates, and heavy drinkers — the characters with whom he populated his semifictitious Tilbury Town (modeled after Gardiner, Maine, where he grew up) — Robinson viewed life with stoic pessimism. He struggled through a series of ill-paid odd jobs until President Theodore Roosevelt, a reader of poetry, wrote a glowing comment on his work and got him an appointment as a clerk in a New York customs office. *Tristram* (1927), a narrative poem about King Arthur and his knights, was, oddly enough, a commercial success. Robinson brought hard-eyed realism to his New England landscapes and combined tight stanzas with tightlipped colloquial Yankee language long before Robert Frost.

Theodore Roethke

Theodore Roethke (1908 – 1963) was born in Saginaw, Michigan, where his family ran a large greenhouse. (No poet seems wealthier in his knowledge of vegetation.) He went to the University of Michigan and (for a year) to Harvard. As a young poet teaching college at a time when creative writing teachers without Ph.D.s were suspect, Roethke held impermanent jobs before coming to rest at the University of Washington in Seattle. There, from 1947 until his death, he was an influential teacher of poetry and poetry writing; among his students were Carolyn Kizer, David Wagoner, and James Wright. Roethke was a large, heavyset man light on his feet (he once coached varsity tennis at Lafayette), and would sometimes prepare for a poetry reading by pacing the stage like an athlete warming up. His poetry developed from rather conventional and imitative lyrics through a phase of disconnected stream of consciousness into (at the end) a meditative poetry reminiscent in its open lines of Walt Whitman's.

William Shakespeare

William Shakespeare (1565 – 1616) was born in Stratford-on-Avon and made his living as an actor and playwright in London. For a full biography, see page 903. Although he did not worry about the preservation of his plays, he carefully saw his *Sonnets* (1609) and the story-poems *Venus and Adonis* (1593) and *The Rape of Lucrece* (1594) through press.

William Stafford

William Stafford, born in 1914 in Hutchinson, Kansas, was graduated from the University of Kansas and later took a doctorate at the University of Iowa. During World War II he was interned as a conscientious objector, an experience he recalls in his prose memoir *Down in My Heart* (1947). For many years he taught at Lewis and Clark College in Portland, Oregon, and in 1970 – 71 he served as Consultant in Poetry for the Library of Congress. *Traveling Through the Dark* (1962) won the National Book Award, and in 1977 Stafford published a large volume of his collected poems, *Stories That Could Be True.* In much of his work he traces the landscapes of the Midwest and of the Pacific Northwest, where he has long lived. He describes his poetry as "much like talk, with some enhancement."

Timothy Steele

Timothy Steele, born in Burlington, Vermont, in 1948, took his doctorate in English at Brandeis, where he studied literature with J. V. Cunningham. A Californian by adoption, he has taught and held a Wallace Stegner fellowship in creative writing at Stanford, and more recently has been teaching on the University of California's Los Angeles and Santa Barbara campuses. With Gjertrud Schnackenberg, R. L. Barth, and R. S. Gwynn, he is among the few younger poets to write exclusively in traditional forms. His first collection, *Uncertainties and Rest,* appeared in 1979, and his most recent, *Sapphics Against Anger and Other Poems,* in 1986. For a long time Steele has been writing a critical history of the development of modern poetry. If his poems seem to wear a Yankee reticence and a tendency toward precise understatement, they hold much power within their strict limits.

James Stephens

James Stephens (1882 – 1950), born in Dublin, Ireland, was a famous member of the Irish Literary Renaissance, a movement early in the century that included William Butler Yeats and the playwrights Lady Gregory, J. M. Synge, and Sean O'Casey. As a young man Stephens took a job as a typist in a lawyer's office, where access to a typewriter started him writing fantastic fiction, some of it based on Irish folklore, such as his most popular novel, *The Crock of Gold* (1912). Other imaginative novels followed, including *The Demi-Gods* (1914) and *Deirdre* (1923). *Irish Fairy Tales* (1920) retells classic legends for young readers. Although best remembered for such books, Stephens was a considerable poet as well. His first collection appeared in 1909, and in 1926 he published his

Collected Poems. Some of his poems are actually free translations from the Irish: "A Glass of Beer," for instance, is a version of a poem by Dáibhí Ó Bruadair (about 1625 – 98).

Wallace Stevens

Wallace Stevens (1879 – 1955) was born in Reading, Pennsylvania; his father was a successful lawyer; his mother, a former schoolteacher. As a special student at Harvard, he became president of the student literary magazine, the *Harvard Advocate,* but he did not want a liberal arts degree. Instead, he became a lawyer in New York City, and in 1916 joined the legal staff of the Hartford Accident and Indemnity Company. In 1936 he was elected a vice-president. Stevens, who would write poems in his head while walking to work and then dictate them to his secretary, was a leading expert on surety claims. Once asked how he was able to combine poetry and insurance, he replied that the two occupations had an element in common: "calculated risk." As a young man in New York, Stevens made lasting friendships with poets Marianne Moore and William Carlos Williams, but he did not seek literary society. Though his poems are full of references to Europe and remote places, his only travels were annual vacation trips to Key West. He printed his early poems in *Poetry* magazine, but did not publish a book until *Harmonium* appeared in 1923, when he was forty-four. Living quietly in Hartford, Connecticut, Stevens sought to discover order in a chaotic world with his subtle and exotic imagination. His critical essays, collected in *The Necessary Angel* (1951), and his *Letters* (1966), edited by his daughter Holly Stevens, reveal a penetrating, philosophic mind. His *Collected Poems* (1954), published on his seventy-fifth birthday, garnered major prizes and belated recognition for Stevens as a major American poet.

Jonathan Swift

Jonathan Swift (1667 – 1745), Anglo-Irish poet, satirist, journalist, and clergyman, was born in Dublin, said to have been sired by an English steward. Uncles helped him attend Trinity College, Dublin, from which he was graduated "by special grace," having shone only in his studies of the classics. In 1694 Swift entered the Church of England and held parish appointments in Ireland, finally becoming Dean of St. Patrick's Cathedral, Dublin — to his disappointment, for he loved London and had hoped for a position there. His cousin John Dryden (see biographical note) told him, "Cousin Swift, you will never be a poet," a prophecy that time has proved inaccurate. In a life crowded with church duties, political agitation, literary society, and long and perhaps sexless love affairs, especially with his former pupil Esther Johnson (whom he called Stella), Swift found occasion to write much excellent verse. Still, he is best remembered for *Gulliver's Travels* (1726), an affectionate tribute to the reasoning part of "that animal called man," a scathing and scatological rebuke to the rest of him.

Alfred, Lord Tennyson

Alfred, Lord Tennyson (1809 – 1892), was born Alfred Tennyson in Lincoln-shire, England, the son of an alcoholic rural minister. When Queen Victoria made him a baron in 1883 (at seventy-five), he added the "Lord" to his byline. A precocious poet, Tennyson began writing verse at five, and when still in his teens collaborated with his brother Charles on *Poems by Two Brothers* (1827). As a student at Cambridge, he was unusual: he kept a snake for a pet, won a medal for poetry, and went home without taking a degree. But in college he made influential friendships, especially that of Arthur Hallam, whose death in 1833 inspired Tennyson's *In Memoriam* (1850), the elegiac sequence that contains "Dark house by which once more I stand." The year 1850 was a banner one for Tennyson in other ways: he at last felt prosperous enough to marry Emily Sellwood, who had remained engaged to him for fourteen years, and Queen Victoria named him poet laureate, in which capacity he served for four decades, writing poems for state occasions. Between 1859 and 1888 Tennyson completed *Idylls of the King,* a twelve-part narrative poem of Arthur and his Round Table. In his mid-sixties he wrote several plays. A spokesman for the Victorian age and its militant colonialism, Tennyson is still respected as a poet of varied assets, including an excellent ear.

Dylan Thomas

Dylan Thomas (1914 – 1953) was born in the coastal town of Swansea, Wales, the son of an English teacher. Much of Thomas's life was a bitter struggle to support his wife and children, a struggle intensified by fondness for spending freely. Lacking a university education, Thomas found most paying literary work barred to him in Britain, although late in life he received many assignments to write film and radio scripts. A resonant reader-aloud of poetry, he made broadcasts for BBC radio and undertook several immensely popular reading tours of America, preceded by a reputation for heavy drinking and gustatorial lovemaking. He died in a hospital in New York City after drinking a procession of straight whiskeys, apparently court-ing the end. Thomas wrote not only poems (in the early ones he brought surrealism into English poetry), he also wrote remarkable stories and a "play for voices," *Under Milk Wood* (1954), based on memories of his home town in Wales.

John Updike

John Updike, born in 1932, is primarily regarded as a novelist, as indicated in the biographical note on page 12 with his story "A & P." But his first book was verse, *The Carpentered Hen* (1954), from which we take "Ex-Basketball Player"; and ever since, he has continued to produce verse both light and serious.

Keith Waldrop

Keith Waldrop, born in 1932 in Emporia, Kansas, grew up in a family divided by his father's militant atheism and his mother's pious Christian fundamentalism. He took his doctorate at the University of Michigan with a thesis on obscenity in literature, and has since taught at Wesleyan University and at Brown, where he is now director of graduate studies in English. Waldrop has directed and acted in films and plays. His first book of poems, *A Windmill near Calvary* (1968), was nominated for the National Book Award. He lives in Providence, Rhode Island, with his wife, the poet and translator Rosmarie Waldrop, thousands of books and recordings, and a basement printing press that produces more books under the imprint Burning Deck.

Walt Whitman

Walt Whitman (1819 – 1892) was born on Long Island, son of an impoverished farmer. He spent his early years as a school teacher, a temperance propagandist, a carpenter, a printer, and a newspaper editor on the Brooklyn *Eagle.* He began writing poetry in youth, sometimes declaiming his lines above the crash of waves on New York beaches. Apparently he was also inspired to write wide, spacious, confident lines by attending performances of Italian opera. His self-published *Leaves of Grass* (1855) won praise from Ralph Waldo Emerson and gained Whitman readers in England. For the rest of his life, he kept revising and enlarging it, ceasing with a ninth or "deathbed edition" in 1891 – 92. Americans at first were slow to accept Whitman's unconventionally open verse forms, his sexual frankness, and his gregarious egoism. The poet of boundless faith in American democracy, Whitman tempered his vision by his experiences as a volunteer hospital nurse during the Civil War (described in his poems *Drum-Taps* and his wartime letters). After the war, he held secretarial jobs to support himself, and lost one such job when his employer's scandalized eye fell upon the *Leaves.* In old age, a semi-invalid after a stroke, Whitman made his home in Camden, New Jersey. Before he died he saw his work finally winning respect and worldwide acceptance. Whitman's influence on later American poetry has been profound, both by the example of his open forms and by his bold encompassing of subject matter that had formerly been considered unpoetic. (In "Song of the Exposition," read aloud at an industrial show in New York, the poet exclaims of his Muse: "She's here, install'd amid the kitchen ware!")

Richard Wilbur

Richard Wilbur, born in 1917 in New York City, was graduated from Amherst College, then served in the army in World War II. He has taught English at Harvard, Wellesley, Wesleyan, and Smith. With his first two collections, *The Beautiful Changes* (1947) and *Ceremony* (1950), Wilbur acquired a high reputation for a poetry of sensitivity, wit, grace, and command of traditional forms.

Besides writing poetry, for which he has received many prizes, including a Pulitzer Prize and a National Book Award, Wilbur has edited the poetry of Shakespeare and Poe. He has written song lyrics for *Candide,* a Broadway musical by Lillian Hellman and Leonard Bernstein (1956); *Loudmouse,* a story for children (1963); and *Responses,* literary criticism (1976); and he has translated four rimed plays of Molière into wonderfully skillful English verse. He lives in Cummington, Massachusetts, in a home adjacent to an apple orchard.

William Carlos Williams

William Carlos Williams (1883 – 1963) was born in Rutherford, New Jersey, where he remained in later life as a practicing pediatrician. While taking his M.D. degree at the University of Pennsylvania, he made friends with the poets Ezra Pound and H.D. (Hilda Doolittle). Surprisingly prolific for a busy doctor, Williams wrote (besides poetry) novels and short stories, plays, criticism, and essays in history (*In the American Grain,* 1939). He kept a fliptop desk in his office and between patients would haul out his typewriter and dash off poems. His encouragement of younger poets, among them Allen Ginsberg (whose doctor he was when Ginsberg was a baby), and the long-sustained example of his formally open poetry made him an appealing father figure to the generation of the Beat poets and the Black Mountain poets — Ginsberg, Gary Snyder, and Robert Creeley. But he also had great influence on Robert Lowell, and on a whole younger generation of American poets in our day. Williams believed in truthtelling about ordinary life, championed plain speech "out of the mouths of Polish mothers," and insisted that there can be "no ideas but in things." Combining poetry with prose (including documents and statistics), his long poem in five parts, *Paterson* (1946 – 58) explores the past, present, and future of the large New Jersey industrial city near which Williams lived for most of his days.

William Wordsworth

William Wordsworth (1770 – 1850) was born in England's Lake District, whose landscapes and people were to inform many of his poems. As a young man he visited France, sympathized with the Revolution, and met a young Frenchwoman who bore him a child. The Reign of Terror prevented him from returning to France, and he and Annette Vallon never married. With his sister Dorothy (1771 – 1855), his lifelong intellectual companion and the author of remarkable journals, he settled in Dorsetshire. Later they moved to Grasmere, in the Lake District, where Wordsworth lived the rest of his life. In 1798 his friendship with Samuel Taylor Coleridge resulted in their joint publication of *Lyrical Ballads,* a book credited with introducing Romanticism to English poetry. (Wordsworth contributed "Tintern Abbey" and other poems; Coleridge, "Kubla Khan," "Christabel," and "The Rime of the Ancient Mariner.") To the second edition of 1800, Wordsworth supplied a preface calling for a poetry written "in the real language of men." Time brought him a small official job, a conventional marriage, a swing from left to right in his political sentiments, and appointment as poet laureate. Although he kept on writing, readers have more greatly favored his earlier poems. *The Prelude,* a long poem-memoir completed in 1805, did not appear till after the poet's death. One of the most original of writers, Wordsworth — especially for his poems of nature and simple rustics — occupies a popular place in English poetry, much like that of Robert Frost in America.

James Wright

James Wright (1927 – 1980) was born in Martins Ferry, Ohio. After taking his doctorate at the University of Washington, where he studied with Theodore Roethke, he taught at the University of Minnesota, Macalester College, and Hunter College in New York. His first book, *A Green Wall* (1957), in the Yale Series of Younger Poets, established him as a traditional formalist of great skill. With Robert Bly, by whom he was persuaded to branch out of traditional forms, he translated the poems of Cesar Valejo, Pablo Neruda, and George Trakl. In 1972 he received the Pulitzer Prize for his *Collected Poems.* Wright was a memorable teacher, a great quoter of poetry from memory, and a fine critic. "I try and say how I love my country and how I despise the way it is treated," he declared. "I try and speak of the beauty and again of the ugliness in the lives of the poor and neglected."

Sir Thomas Wyatt

Sir Thomas Wyatt (1503? – 1542) was both poet and man of action: diplomat, soldier, and courtier. He was born in his father's castle in Kent, England, and as a boy he was sent to court. In 1516 he entered St. John's College, Cambridge. Wyatt twice saw the inside of prison when he slipped from the favor of King Henry VIII. He is thought to have been a lover of Anne Boleyn, later the King's wife, a fact that perhaps affects some of his remarkable love lyrics. A prominent man in Tudor England, Wyatt carried out diplomatic missions, served as ambassador to Spain, was a member of Parliament and the king's privy council, and was Commander of the Fleet. Wyatt's mission to Italy in 1527 had great consequence for English poetry, for he brought back knowledge of the works of Petrarch and other Italian love poets. In imitation of them, Wyatt wrote some of the first sonnets in our language — also lyrics, rondels, satires, and psalms.

William Butler Yeats

William Butler Yeats (1865 – 1939), poet and playwright, an Irishman of English ancestry, was born in Dublin, the son of painter John Butler Yeats. For a time he studied art himself and was irregularly schooled in Dublin and in London. Early in life Yeats sought to transform Irish folklore and legend into mellifluous poems. He overcame shyness to take an active part in cataclysmic events: he became involved in the movement for an Irish nation (partly drawn into it by his unrequited love for Maud Gonne, a crusading nationalist) and in founding the Irish Literary Theatre (1898) and the Irish National Theatre, which in 1904 moved to the renowned Abbey Theatre in Dublin. Dublin audiences were difficult: in 1899 they jeered Yeats's first play, *The Countess Cathleen,* for portraying a woman who, defying the church, sells her soul to the devil to buy bread for starving peasants. Eventually Yeats retired from the fray, to write plays given in drawing rooms, like *Purgatory.* After the establishment of the Irish Free State, Yeats served as a senator (1922 – 28). His lifelong interest in the occult culminated in his writing of *A Vision* (1937), a view of history as governed by the phases of the moon; Yeats believed the book inspired by spirit masters who dictated communications to his wife, Georgie Hyde-Lees. Had Yeats stopped writing in 1900, he would be remembered as an outstanding minor Victorian. Instead, he went on to become one of the most influential poets of the twentieth century.

31 Criticism: On Poetry

What is a modern Poet's fate?
To write his thoughts upon a slate —
The Critic spits on what is done,
Gives it a wipe — and all is gone.
                    — Thomas Hood, "To the Reviewers"

The critical power is of lower rank than the creative. True, but in assenting to this proposition, one or two things are to be kept in mind. It is undeniable that the exercise of a creative power, that a free creative activity, is the true function of man; it is proved to be so by man's finding in it his true happiness. But it is undeniable, also, that men may have the sense of exercising this free creative activity in other ways than in producing great works of literature or art; if it were not so, all but a very few men would be shut out from the true happiness of all men; they may have it in well-doing, they may have it in learning, they may have it even in criticising.
                    — Matthew Arnold, "The Function of Criticism"

"A poem is a pheasant," said Wallace Stevens. Studying poetry, you may find it useful at times to have before you the exact words of a critic who has described that elusive, easily startled bird. Here then are twenty critical insights. Some are unfamiliar; others are among the best-known, most stimulating remarks about poetry ever made. Included are a few remarks by poets, such as Robert Frost's to his friend about the "sound of sense," which Frost called "the most important thing I know." May they widen your own thinking about poetry and perhaps give you something tough to argue with. Some are controversial. Socrates' case against poets, for instance, remains a fresh and lively opinion still debatable even after twenty-three-hundred-odd years. Nor do these critics chime in perfect harmony. You may hear a certain jangling in their views.

After each passage, its source is indicated. Should one of these ideas capture your interest, why settle for the excerpt given here?

Plato (427? – 347? B.C.)

Inspiration[1]   (about 390 B.C.)

Ion: The world agrees with me in thinking that I do speak better and have more to say about Homer than any other man. But I do not speak equally well about others — tell me the reason for this.

Socrates: I perceive, Ion; and I will proceed to explain to you what I imagine to be the reason for this. The gift which you possess of speaking excellently about Homer is not an art, but, as I was just saying, an inspiration; there is a divinity moving you, like that contained in the stone which Euripides calls a magnet, but which is commonly known as the stone of Heraclea. This stone not only attracts iron rings, but also imparts to them a similar power of attracting other rings; and sometimes you may see a number of pieces of iron and rings suspended from one another so as to form quite a long chain: and all of them derive their power of suspension from the original stone. In like manner the Muse first of all inspires men herself; and from these inspired persons a chain of other persons is suspended, who take the inspiration. For all good poets, epic as well as lyric, compose their beautiful poems not by art, but because they are inspired and possessed. And as the Corybantian revellers when they dance are not in their right mind, so the lyric poets are not in their right mind when they are composing their beautiful strains: but when falling under the power of music and meter they are inspired and possessed; like Bacchic maidens who draw milk and honey from the rivers when they are under the influence of Dionysus but not when they are in their right mind. And the soul of the lyric poet does the same, as they themselves say; for they tell us that they bring songs from honeyed fountains, culling them out of the gardens and dells of the Muses; they, like the bees, winging their way from flower to flower. And this is true. For the poet

[1]Translated by Benjamin Jowett.

is a light and winged and holy thing, and there is no invention in him until he has been inspired and is out of his senses, and the mind is no longer in him: when he has not attained to this state, he is powerless and is unable to utter his oracles. Many are the noble words in which poets speak concerning the actions of men; but like yourself when speaking about Homer, they do not speak of them by any rules of art: they are simply inspired to utter that to which the Muse impels them, and that only; and when inspired, one of them will make dithyrambs, another hymns of praise, another choral strains, another epic or iambic verses — and he who is good at one is not good at any other kind of verse: for not by art does the poet sing, but by power divine. Had he learned by rules of art, he would have known how to speak not of one theme only, but of all; and therefore God takes away the minds of poets, and uses them as his ministers, as he also uses diviners and holy prophets, in order that we who hear them may know them to be speaking not of themselves who utter these priceless words in a state of unconsciousness, but that God himself is the speaker, and that through them he is conversing with us. And Tynnichus the Chalcidian affords a striking instance of what I am saying: he wrote nothing that any one would care to remember but the famous paean which is in every one's mouth, one of the finest poems ever written, simply an invention of the Muses, as he himself says. For in this way the God would seem to indicate to us and not allow us to doubt that these beautiful poems are not human, or the work of man, but divine and the work of God; and that the poets are only the interpreters of the Gods by whom they are severally possessed. Was not this the lesson which the God intended to teach when by the mouth of the worst of poets he sang the best of songs? Am I not right, Ion?

Ion

INSPIRATION. Plato records a dialogue between his master, the philosopher Socrates (469 B.C. – 399 B.C.) and Ion, a young man of Athens. *Corybantian revellers:* The Corybants, priests or attendants of the nature goddess Cybele, deity of the ancient peoples of Asia Minor, were given to orgiastic rites and frenzied dances. *Bacchic maidens:* attendants of the god of wine and fertility, called Dionysus by the Greeks, Bacchus by the Romans. *Muses:* In Greek mythology, nine sister goddesses who presided over poetry and song, the arts and sciences.

Plato (427? – 347? B.C.)
SOCRATES BANISHES POETS
FROM HIS IDEAL STATE[2]   (ABOUT 373 B.C.)

Socrates: Hear and judge: The best of us, I conceive, when we listen to a passage of Homer, or one of the tragedians, in which he represents some pitiful hero who is drawling out his sorrows in a long oration, or weeping, and smiting his breast — the best of us, you know, delight in giving way to sympathy, and are in raptures at the excellence of the poet who stirs our feelings most.
Glaucon: Yes, of course I know.

[2]Translated by Benjamin Jowett.

Socrates: But when any sorrow of our own happens to us, then you may observe that we pride ourselves on the opposite quality — we would fain be quiet and patient; this is the manly part, and the other which delighted us in the recitation is now deemed to be the part of a woman.

Glaucon: Very true.

Socrates: Now can we be right in praising and admiring another who is doing that which any one of us would abominate and be ashamed of in his own person?

Glaucon: No, that is certainly not reasonable.

Socrates: Nay, quite reasonable from one point of view.

Glaucon: What point of view?

Socrates: If you consider that when in misfortune we feel a natural hunger and desire to relieve our sorrow by weeping and lamentation, and that this feeling which is kept under control in our own calamities is satisfied and delighted by the poets; — the better nature in each of us, not having been sufficiently trained by reason or habit, allows the sympathetic element to break loose because the sorrow is another's; and the spectator fancies that there can be no disgrace to himself in praising and pitying any one who comes telling him what a good man he is, and making a fuss about his troubles; he thinks that the pleasure is a gain, and why should he be supercilious and lose this and the poem too? Few persons ever reflect, as I should imagine, that from the evil of other men something of evil is communicated to themselves. And so the feeling of sorrow which has gathered strength at the sight of the misfortunes of others is with difficulty repressed in our own.

Glaucon: How very true!

Socrates: And does not the same hold also of the ridiculous? There are jests which you would be ashamed to make yourself, and yet on the comic stage, or indeed in private, when you hear them, you are greatly amused by them, and are not at all disgusted at their unseemliness; — the case of pity is repeated; — there is a principle in human nature which is disposed to raise a laugh, and this which you once restrained by reason, because you were afraid of being thought a buffoon, is now let out again; and having stimulated the risible faculty at the theater, you are betrayed unconsciously to yourself into playing the comic poet at home.

Glaucon: Quite true.

Socrates: And the same may be said of lust and anger and all the other affections, of desire and pain and pleasure, which are held to be inseparable from every action — in all of them poetry feeds and waters the passions instead of drying them up; she lets them rule, although they ought to be controlled, if mankind are ever to increase in happiness and virtue.

Glaucon: I cannot deny it.

Socrates: Therefore, Glaucon, whenever you meet with any of the eulogists of Homer declaring that he has been the educator of Hellas, and that he is profitable for education and for the ordering of human things, and that you should take him up again and again and get to know him and regulate your whole life according to him, we may love and honor those who say these things — they are excellent people, as far as their lights extend; and we are ready to acknowledge that Homer is the greatest of poets and first of tragedy writers; but we must remain firm in our conviction that hymns to the gods and praises of famous men are the only poetry which ought to be admitted into our State. For if you go beyond this and allow the honeyed muse to enter, either in epic or lyric verse, not law and the reason of mankind, which by common consent have ever been deemed best, but pleasure and pain will be the rulers in our State.

Glaucon: That is most true.

Socrates: And now since we have reverted to the subject of poetry, let this our defense serve to show the reasonableness of our former judgment in sending away out of our State an art having the tendencies which we have described; for reason constrained us. But that she may not impute to us any harshness or want of politeness, let us tell her that there is an ancient quarrel between philosophy and poetry; of which there are many proofs, such as the saying of 'the yelping hound howling at her lord,' or of one 'mighty in the vain talk of fools,' and 'the mob of sages circumventing Zeus,' and the 'subtle thinkers who are beggars after all'; and there are innumerable other signs of ancient enmity between them. Notwithstanding this, let us assure our sweet friend and the sister arts of imitation, that if she will only prove her title to exist in a well-ordered State we shall be delighted to receive her — we are very conscious of her charms; but we may not on that account betray the truth.

The Republic, X

Aristotle (384 – 322 B.C.)

TWO CAUSES OF POETRY[3]   (ABOUT 330 B.C.)

Poetry in general seems to have sprung from two causes, each of them lying deep in our nature. First, the instinct of imitation is implanted in man from childhood, one difference between him and other animals being that he is the most imitative of living creatures; and through imitation he learns his earliest lessons; and no less universal is the pleasure felt in things imitated. We have evidence of this in the facts of experience. Objects which in themselves we view with pain, we delight to contemplate when reproduced with minute fidelity: such as the forms of the most ignoble animals and of dead bodies. The cause of this again is, that to learn gives the liveliest pleasure, not only to philosophers but to men in general; whose capacity, however, of learning is more limited. Thus the reason why men enjoy seeing a likeness is, that in contemplating it they find themselves learning or inferring, and saying perhaps, "Ah, that is he." For if you happen not to have seen the original, the pleasure will be due not to the imitation as such, but to the execution, the coloring, or some such other cause.

Imitation, then, is one instinct of our nature. Next, there is the instinct for "harmony" and rhythm, meters being manifestly sections of rhythm. Persons, therefore, starting with this natural gift developed by degrees their special aptitudes, till their rude improvisations gave birth to Poetry.

Poetics, IV

[3]Translated by S. H. Butcher.

Sir Philip Sidney (1554 – 1586)

NATURE AND THE POET   1595

There is no art delivered unto mankind that hath not the works of nature for [its] principal object, without which they could not consist, and on which they so depend as they become actors and players, as it were, of what nature will have set forth. So doth the astronomer look upon the stars, and, by what he seeth, set down what order nature hath taken therein. . . . The physician weigheth the nature of man's body, and the nature of things helpful or hurtful unto it. And the metaphysician, though it be in the second and abstract notions, and therefore be counted supernatural, yet doth he, indeed, build upon the depth of nature.

Only the poet, disdaining to be tied to any such subjection, lifted up with the vigor of his own invention, doth grow, in effect, into another nature, in making things either better than nature bringeth forth, or, quite anew, forms such as never were in nature, as the heroes, demi-gods, cyclops, chimeras, furies, and such like; so as he goeth hand in hand with nature, not enclosed within the narrow warrant of her gifts, but freely ranging within the zodiac of his own wit. Nature never set forth the earth in so rich tapestry as divers poets have done; neither with pleasant rivers, fruitful trees, sweet-smelling flowers, nor whatsoever else may make the too-much-loved earth more lovely; her world is brazen, the poets only deliver a golden.

The Defense of Poetry

Samuel Johnson (1709 – 1784)

THE BUSINESS OF A POET   1759

The business of a poet is to examine, not the individual, but the species; to remark general properties and large appearances; he does not number the streaks of the tulip, or describe the different shades in the verdure of the forest. He is to exhibit in his portraits of nature such prominent and striking features as recall the original to every mind, and must neglect the minuter discriminations, which one may have remarked and another have neglected, for those characteristics which are alike obvious to vigilance and carelessness.

But the knowledge of nature is only half the task of a poet; he must be acquainted likewise with all the modes of life. His character requires that he estimate the happiness and misery of every condition, observe the power of all the passions in all their combinations, and trace the changes of the human mind as they are modified by various institutions and accidental influences of climate or custom, from the sprightliness of infancy to the despondency of decrepitude. He must divest himself of the prejudices of his age or country; he must consider right and wrong in their abstracted and variable state; he must disregard present laws and opinions, and rise to general and transcendental truths, which will always be the same.

The History of Rasselas,
Prince of Abyssinia

William Wordsworth (1770 – 1850)
EMOTION RECOLLECTED IN TRANQUILLITY   1800

I have said that poetry is the spontaneous overflow of powerful feelings: it takes its origin from emotion recollected in tranquillity: the emotion is contemplated till, by a species of reaction, the tranquillity gradually disappears, and an emotion, kindred to that which was before the subject of contemplation, is gradually produced, and does itself actually exist in the mind. In this mood successful composition generally begins, and in a mood similar to this it is carried on; but the emotion, of whatever kind, and in whatever degree, from various causes, is qualified by various pleasures, so that in describing any passions whatsoever, which are voluntarily described, the mind will, upon the whole, be in a state of enjoyment. If Nature be thus cautious to preserve in a state of enjoyment a being so employed, the Poet ought to profit by the lesson held forth to him, and ought especially to take care, that, whatever passions he communicates to his Reader, those passions, if his Reader's mind be sound and vigorous, should always be accompanied with an overbalance of pleasure. Now the music of harmonious metrical language, the sense of difficulty overcome, and the blind association of pleasure which has been previously received from works of rhyme or meter of the same or similar construction, an indistinct perception perpetually renewed of language closely resembling that of real life, and yet, in the circumstance of meter, differing from it so widely — all these imperceptibly make up a complex feeling of delight, which is of the most important use in tempering the painful feeling always found intermingled with powerful descriptions of the deeper passions. This effect is always produced in pathetic and impassioned poetry; while, in lighter compositions, the ease and gracefulness with which the Poet manages his numbers are themselves confessedly a principal source of the gratification of the Reader. All that it is *necessary* to say, however, upon this subject, may be effected by affirming, what few persons will deny, that, of two descriptions, either of passions, manners, or characters, each of them equally well executed, the one in prose and the other in verse, the verse will be read a hundred times where the prose is read once.

Preface to *Lyrical Ballads,*
second edition

EMOTION RECOLLECTED IN TRANQUILLITY. For information on Wordsworth's methods of composition in his poem "I Wandered Lonely as a Cloud," see pages 428 – 429.

Samuel Taylor Coleridge (1772 – 1834)
IMAGINATION   1817

What is poetry? — is so nearly the same question with, what is a poet? — that the answer to the one is involved in the solution of the other. For it is a distinction resulting from the poetic genius itself, which sustains and modifies the images, thoughts, and emotions of the poet's own mind.

The poet, described in ideal perfection, brings the whole soul of man into activity, with the subordination of its faculties to each other according to their relative worth and dignity. He diffuses a tone and spirit of unity, that blends, and (as it were) *fuses,* each into each, by that synthetic and magical power, to which I would exclusively appropriate the name of Imagination. This power, first put in action by the will and understanding, and retained under their irremissive, though gentle and unnoticed, control, *laxis effertur habenis°,* reveals itself in the balance or reconcilement of opposite or discordant qualities; of sameness, with difference; of the general with the concrete; the idea with the image; the individual with the representative; the sense of novelty and freshness with old and familiar objects; a more than usual state of emotion with more than usual order; judgment ever awake and steady self-possession, with enthusiasm and feeling profound and vehement; and while it blends and harmonizes the natural and the artificial, still subordinates art to nature; the manner to the matter; and our admiration of the poet to our sympathy with the poetry.

Biographia Literaria: or, Biographical Sketches
of My Literary Life and Opinions, Chapter XIV

THAT SYNTHETIC AND MAGICAL POWER. The Latin phrase *laxis effertur habenis* means "is driven with reins relaxed."

Percy Bysshe Shelley (1792 – 1822)

UNACKNOWLEDGED LEGISLATORS   (1821)

The most unfailing herald, companion, and follower of the awakening of a great people to work a beneficial change in opinion or institution, is poetry. At such periods there is an accumulation of the power of communicating and receiving intense and impassioned conceptions respecting man and nature. The persons in whom this power resides, may often, as far as regards many portions of their nature, have little apparent correspondence with that spirit of good of which they are the ministers. But even whilst they deny and abjure, they are yet compelled to serve, the power which is seated on the throne of their own soul. It is impossible to read the compositions of the most celebrated writers of the present day without being startled with the electric life which burns within their words. They measure the circumference and sound the depths of human nature with a comprehensive and all-penetrating spirit, and they are themselves perhaps the most sincerely astonished at its manifestations; for it is less their spirit than the spirit of the age. Poets are the hierophants of an unapprehended inspiration; the mirrors of the gigantic shadows which futurity casts upon the present; the words which express what they understand not; the trumpets which sing to battle, and feel not what they inspire; the influence which is moved not, but moves. Poets are the unacknowledged legislators of the world.

A Defense of Poetry

Ralph Waldo Emerson (1803 – 1882)

METER-MAKING ARGUMENT   1844

I took part in a conversation the other day concerning a recent writer of lyrics, a man of subtle mind, whose head appeared to be a music-box of delicate tunes and rhythms, and whose skill and command of language we could not sufficiently praise. But when the question arose whether he was not only a lyrist but a poet, we were obliged to confess that he is plainly a contemporary, not an eternal man. He does not stand out of our low limitations, like a Chimborazo under the line°, running up from a torrid base through all the climates of the globe, with belts of the herbage of every latitude on its high and mottled sides; but this genius is the landscape-garden of a modern house adorned with fountains and statues, with well-bred men and women standing and sitting in the walks and terraces. We hear, through all the varied music, the ground-tone of conventional life. Our poets are men of talents who sing, and not the children of music. The argument is secondary, the finish of the verses is primary.

For it is not meters, but a meter-making argument that makes a poem, — a thought so passionate and alive that like the spirit of a plant or an animal it has an architecture of its own, and adorns nature with a new thing. The thought and the form are equal in the order of time, but in the order of genesis the thought is prior to the form. The poet has a new thought; he has a whole new experience to unfold; he will tell us how it was with him, and all men will be the richer in his fortune. For the experience of each new age requires a new confession, and the world seems always waiting for its poet.

The Poet

METER-MAKING ARGUMENT. *Chimborazo under the line:* mountain in Ecuador, south of the Equator.

Edgar Allan Poe (1809 – 1849)

A LONG POEM DOES NOT EXIST   1848

I hold that a long poem does not exist. I maintain that the phrase, "a long poem," is simply a flat contradiction in terms.

I need scarcely observe that a poem deserves its title only inasmuch as it excites, by elevating the soul. The value of the poem is in the ratio of its elevative excitement. But all excitements are, through a psychal necessity, transient. That degree of excitement which would entitle a poem to be so called at all cannot be sustained throughout a composition of any great length. After the lapse of half an hour, at the very utmost, its flags — fails — a revulsion ensues — and then the poem is in effect, and in fact, no longer such.

The Poetic Principle

Robert Frost (1874 – 1963)

THE SOUND OF SENSE (1913)

I alone of English writers have consciously set myself to make music out of what I may call the sound of sense. Now it is possible to have sense without the sound of sense (as in much prose that is supposed to pass muster but makes very dull reading) and the sound of sense without sense (as in Alice in Wonderland which makes anything but dull reading). The best place to get the abstract sound of sense is from voices behind a door that cuts off the words. Ask yourself how these sentences would sound without the words in which they are embodied:

You mean to tell me you can't read?
I said no such thing.
Well read then.
You're not my teacher.

. . .

He says it's too late.
Oh, say!
Damn an Ingersoll watch anyway.

. . .

One-two-three — go!
No good! Come back — come back.
Haslam go down there and make those kids get out of the track.

. . .

Those sounds are summoned by the [audial] imagination and they must be positive, strong, and definitely and unmistakably indicated by the context. The reader must be at no loss to give his voice the posture proper to the sentence. The simple declarative sentence used in making a plain statement is one sound. But Lord love ye it mustn't be worked to death. It is against the law of nature that whole poems should be written in it. If they are written they won't be read. The sound of sense, then. You get that. It is the abstract vitality of our speech. It is pure sound — pure form. One who concerns himself with it more than the subject is an artist. But remember we are still talking merely of the raw material of poetry. An ear and an appetite for these sounds of sense is the first qualification of a writer, be it of prose or verse. But if one is to be a poet he must learn to get cadences by skillfully breaking the sounds of sense with all their irregularity of accent across the regular beat of the meter. Verse in which there is nothing but the beat of the meter furnished by the accents of the polysyllabic words we call doggerel. Verse is not that. Neither is it the sound of sense alone. It is a resultant from those two. There are only two or three meters that are worth anything. We depend for variety on the infinite play of accents in the sound of sense. The high possibility of emotional expression all lets in this mingling of sense-sound and word-accent. A curious thing. And all this has its bearing on your prose, me boy. Never if you can help it write down a sentence in which the voice will not know how to posture *specially*.

Letter to John T. Bartlett, from *Selected Letters of Robert Frost,* ed. Lawrance Thompson (New York: Holt, 1964)

Wallace Stevens (1879 – 1955)

PROVERBS 1957

The poet makes silk dresses out of worms.

After one has abandoned a belief in God, poetry is that essence which takes its place as life's redemption.

All poetry is experimental poetry.

One reads poetry with one's nerves.

A poet looks at the world as a man looks at a woman.

Aristotle is a skeleton.

Thought tends to collect in pools.

Poetry must resist the intelligence almost successfully.

One cannot spend one's time in being modern when there are so many more important things to be.

Adagia, Opus Posthumous

William Carlos Williams (1883 – 1963)

THE RHYTHM PERSISTS (1913?)

No action, no creative action is complete but a period from a greater action going in rhythmic course. . . . Imagination creates an image, point by point, piece by piece, segment by segment — into a whole, living. But each part as it plays into its neighbor, each segment into its neighbor segment and every part into every other, causing the whole — exists naturally in rhythm, and as there are waves there are tides and as there are ridges in the sand there are bars after bars. . . .

I do not believe in *vers libre,* this contradiction in terms. Either the motion continues or it does not continue, either there is rhythm or no rhythm. *Vers libre* is prose. In the hands of Whitman it was a good tool, a kind of synthetic chisel — the best he had. In his bag of chunks even lie some of the pieces of rhythmic life of which we must build. This is honor enough. *Vers libre* is finished — Whitman did all that was necessary with it. Verse has nothing to gain here and all to lose. . . .

Each piece of work, rhythmic in whole, is then in essence an assembly of tides, waves, ripples — in short, of greater and lesser rhythmic particles regularly repeated or destroyed.

Essay "Speech Rhythm" quoted by Mike Weaver,
William Carlos Williams, The American Background
(New York: Cambridge University Press, 1971)

William Carlos Williams (1883 – 1963)
THE CRAB AND THE BOX   1952

Forcing twentieth-century America into a sonnet — gosh, how I hate sonnets — is like putting a crab into a square box. You've got to cut his legs off
to make him fit. When you get through, you don't have a crab any more.

Statement to Dorothy Tooker,
Interviews with William Carlos Williams,
edited by Linda Welshimer Wagner
(New York: New Directions, 1976)

Ezra Pound (1885 – 1972)
POETRY AND MUSIC   1934

The great lyric age lasted while Campion made his own music, while Lawes
set Waller's verses, while verses, if not actually sung or set to music, were at
least made with the intention of going to music.

Music rots when it gets *too far* from the dance. Poetry atrophies when it gets
too far from music.

ABC of Reading

T. S. Eliot (1888 – 1965)
EMOTION AND PERSONALITY   1920

It is not in his personal emotions, the emotions provoked by particular
events in his life, that the poet is in any way remarkable or interesting. His
particular emotions may be simple, or crude, or flat. The emotion in his poetry
will be a very complex thing, but not with the complexity of the emotions of
people who have very complex or unusual emotions in life. One error, in fact,
of eccentricity in poetry is to seek for new human emotions to express; and
in this search for novelty in the wrong place it discovers the perverse. The
business of the poet is not to find new emotions, but to use the ordinary ones
and, in working them up into poetry, to express feelings which are not in actual
emotions at all. And emotions which he has never experienced will serve his
turn as well as those familiar to him. Consequently, we must believe that
"emotion recollected in tranquillity" is an inexact formula. For it is neither
emotion, nor recollection, nor, without distortion of meaning, tranquillity. It
is a concentration, and a new thing resulting from the concentration, of a very
great number of experiences which to the practical and active person would
not seem to be experiences at all; it is a concentration which does not happen
consciously or of deliberation. These experiences are not "recollected," and
they finally unite in an atmosphere which is "tranquil" only in that it is a
passive attending upon the event. Of course this is not quite the whole story.
There is a great deal, in the writing of poetry, which must be conscious and
deliberate. In fact, the bad poet is usually unconscious where he ought to be
conscious, and conscious where he ought to be unconscious. Both errors tend

to make him "personal." Poetry is not a turning loose of emotion, but an escape from emotion; it is not the expression of personality, but an escape from personality. But, of course, only those who have personality and emotions know what it means to want to escape from these things.

Tradition and the Individual Talent

Yvor Winters (1900 – 1968)
THE FALLACY OF EXPRESSIVE FORM   1939

I cannot grasp the contemporary notion that the traditional virtues of style are incompatible with a poetry of modern subject matter; it appears to rest on the fallacy of expressive form, the notion that the form of the poem should express the matter. This fallacy results in the writing of chaotic poetry about the traffic; of loose poetry about our sprawling nation; of semi-conscious poetry about our semi-conscious states. But the matter of poetry is and always has been chaotic; it is raw nature. To let the form of the poem succumb to its matter is and always will be the destruction of poetry and may be the destruction of intelligence.

Before Disaster

Randall Jarrell (1914 – 1965)
ON THE CHARGE THAT MODERN POETRY IS OBSCURE   1953

That the poet, the modern poet, is, understandably enough, for all sorts of good reasons, more obscure than even he has any imaginable right to be — this is one of those great elementary (or, as people say nowadays, *elemental*) attitudes about which it is hard to write anything that is not sensible and gloomily commonplace; one might as well talk on faith and works, on heredity and environment, or on that old question: why give the poor bath-tubs when they only use them to put coal in? Anyone knows enough to reply to this question: "They don't; and, even if they did, *that's* not the reason you don't want to help pay for the tubs." Similarly, when someone says, "I don't read modern poetry because it's all stuff that nobody on earth can understand," I know enough to be able to answer, though not aloud: "It isn't; and, even if it were, *that's* not the reason you don't read it." . . . And people who have inherited the custom of not reading poets justify it by referring to the obscurity of the poems they have never read — since most people decide that poets are obscure very much as legislators decide that books are pornographic: by glancing at a few fragments someone has strung together to disgust them. When a person says accusingly that he can't understand Eliot, his tone implies that most of his happiest hours are spent at the fireside among worn copies of the *Agamemnon, Phèdre,* and the Symbolic Books of William Blake; and it is melancholy to find, as one commonly will, that for months at a time he can be found pushing eagerly through the pages of *Gone with the Wind* or *Forever Amber.*°

The Obscurity of the Poet,
Poetry and the Age

ON THE CHARGE THAT MODERN POETRY IS OBSCURE. *Forever Amber:* novel by Kathleen Winsor, a best-seller in its day (1945). Much of its action takes place in bed.

Sylvia Plath (1932 – 1963)

THE MAGIC MOUNTAINS   1957

The artist's life nourishes itself on the particular, the concrete: that came to me last night as I despaired about writing poems on the concept of the seven deadly sins and told myself to get rid of the killing idea: this must be a great work of philosophy. Start with the mat-green fungus in the pine woods yesterday: words about it, describing it — and a poem will come. Daily, simply, and then it won't lower in the distance, an untouchable object. Write about the cow, Mrs. Spaulding's heavy eyelids, the smell of vanilla flavoring in a brown bottle. That's where the magic mountains begin.

Journals

Barbara Herrnstein Smith (b. 1932)

CLOSURE AND ANTI-CLOSURE   1968

"Openness," the "anti-teleological," the positive value placed on the unfinished look or sound — anti-closure, in other words, is evidently a sign of the times in contemporary art; and whether one refers it specifically to a revolution in philosophy or in art history, one suspects that it is ultimately related to even more general developments and crises. . . . We know too much and are skeptical of all that we know, feel, and say. All traditions are equally viable partly because all are equally suspect. Where conviction is seen as self-delusion and all last words are lies, the only resolution may be in the affirmation of irresolution, and conclusiveness may be seen as not only less honest but *less stable* than inconclusiveness. . . .

The song of uncertainty in modern poetry expresses the temper (or distemper) of our times thematically; it also reflects in its very structure. The relation between structure and closure is of considerable importance here, for "anti-closure" in all the arts is a matter not only of how the works terminate but how and whether they are organized throughout. The "openness" and "unfinished" look and sound of *avant-garde* poetry and music is not a quality of their endings only, but affects the audience's entire experience of such works. . . . Whereas the weak closure of much modern poetry can be understood partly as the result of the prevalence of formal and thematic structures that offer minimal resources for closure, the reverse is also likely: the prevalence of free verse, for example, probably reflects, in part, the impulse to anti-closure, the reaction against poems that "click like a box." . . .

But if the anti-teleology of the modern poet is not so thoroughgoing as that of the painter or composer, it may be due more to the conservatism of the materials of his art than to the conservatism of the poet himself. While he may share the general impulse to "radical empiricism," he is confined by the fact that if his empiricism is too radical, his art loses both its identity and, more important, the sources of its characteristic effects. For the material of poetry

Criticism: On Poetry   833

is not words, but *language* — a system of conventions previously determined and continuously mediated by usage in a community — and if the poem divorces itself utterly from the structure of discourse, it ceases to be poetry and ceases to affect us as such. Although traditional *formal* structures may yield to deliberate dissolution, the design of a poem is never wholly formal and a considerable degree of organization is built into it by virtue of its fundamental relation to the structure of discourse. Consequently, to the extent that anti-closure is a matter of anti-structure, the poet cannot go all the way.

Poetic Closure: A Study of How Poems End

DRAMA

Unlike a short story or a novel, a **play** is a work of storytelling in which actors represent the characters. In another essential, a play differs from a work of fiction: it is addressed not to readers but to spectators.

To be part of an audience in a theater is an experience far different from reading a story in solitude. Expectant, as the house lights dim and the curtain rises, we become members of a community. The responses of people around us affect our own responses. We, too, contribute to the community's response whenever we laugh, sigh, applaud, murmur in surprise, and catch our breath in excitement. In contrast, when all alone we watch a movie by means of a videocassette recorder — say, a slapstick comedy — we probably laugh less often than if we were watching the same film in a theater, surrounded by a roaring crowd. Of course, no one is spilling popcorn down the back of our neck. Each kind of theatrical experience, to be sure, has its advantages.

A theater of live actors has another advantage: a sensitive give-and-take between actors and audience. Such rapport, of course, depends on the actors being skilled and the audience perceptive. Although professional actors may try to give a top-class performance on all occasions, it is natural for them to feel more keenly inspired by a lively, appreciative audience than by a dull, lethargic one. No doubt a large turnout of spectators also helps draw the best from performers on stage: the *Othello* you get may be somewhat less inspired if you are part of an audience that may be counted on the fingers of one hand. But at any rate, as veteran playgoers well know, something unique and wonderful can happen when good actors and a good audience respond to each other.

In another sense, a play is more than actors and audience: Like a short story or a poem, a play is a work of art made of words. The playwright devoted thought and care and skill to the selection and arrangement of language. Watching a play, of course, we do not notice the playwright standing between us and the characters. [1] If the play is absorbing, it flows

---

[1] The word *playwright,* by the way, invites misspelling. Notice that it is not *playwrite.* The suffix *-wright* (from Old English) means "one who makes" — like a *boatwright,* a worker in a trade.

before our eyes. In a silent reading, the usual play consists mainly of **dialogue,** exchanges of speech, punctuated by stage directions.[2] In performance, though, stage directions vanish. And although the thoughtful efforts of perhaps a hundred people — actors, director, producer, stage designer, costumer, makeup artist, technicians — may have gone into a production, a successful play makes us forget its artifice. We may even forget that the play is literature, for its gestures, facial expressions, bodily stances, lighting, and special effects are as much a part of it as the playwright's written words. Even though words are not all there is to a living play, they are its bones. And the whole play, the finished production, is the total of whatever transpires on stage.

The sense of immediacy we derive from **drama** is suggested by the root of the word. *Drama* means "action" or "deed" (from the Greek *dran,* "to do"). We use *drama* as a synonym for *plays,* but the word has several meanings. Sometimes it refers to one play ("a stirring drama"); or to the work of a playwright, or **dramatist** ("Ibsen's drama"); or perhaps to a body of plays written in a particular time or place ("Elizabethan drama," "French drama of the seventeenth century"). In yet another familiar sense, *drama* often means events that elicit high excitement: "A real-life drama," a news story might begin, "was enacted today before lunchtime crowds in downtown Manhattan as firemen battled to free two children trapped on the sixteenth floor of a burning building." In this sense, whatever is "dramatic" implies suspense, tension, or conflict. Plays, as we shall see, frequently contain such "dramatic" chains of events; and yet, if we expect all plays to be crackling with suspense or conflict, we may be disappointed. Some plays, such as Edward Albee's *The Zoo Story,* create little suspense. They do, however, compel our attention: perhaps we watch them to satisfy our curiosity. "Good drama," said critic George Jean Nathan, "is anything that interests an intelligently emotional group of persons assembled together in an illuminated hall."

In partaking of the nature of ritual — something to be repeated in front of an audience on a special occasion — drama is akin to a festival (whether a religious festival or a rock festival) or a church service. Twice in the history of Europe, drama has sprung forth as a part of worship: when in ancient Greece, plays were performed on feast days; and when in the Christian church of the Middle Ages, a play was introduced as an adjunct to the Easter mass with the enactment of the meeting between the three Marys and the angel at Christ's empty tomb. Evidently something in drama remains constant over the years — something as old, perhaps, as the deepest desires and highest aspirations of humanity.

[2]Not all plays employ dialogue. There is also **pantomime** — generally, a play without words (sometimes also called a **dumb show**). Originally, in ancient Rome, a pantomime meant an actor who singlehandedly played all the parts. An eminent modern pantomime (or **mime**) is French stage and screen actor Marcel Marceau.

32 Reading a Play

Most plays are written not to be read in books but to be performed. Finding plays in a literature anthology, the student may well ask, isn't there something wrong with the idea of reading plays on the printed page? To do so — to treat them as literature — isn't that a perversion of their nature?

True, plays are meant to be seen on stage, but equally true, reading a play may afford advantages. One is that it is better to know some masterpieces by reading them than never to know them at all. Even if you live in a large city with many theaters, even if you attend a college with many theatrical productions, to succeed in your lifetime in witnessing, say, all the plays of Shakespeare might well be impossible. In print, they are as near-to-hand as a book on a shelf, ready to be enacted (if you like) on the stage of the mind.

After all, a play is literature before it comes alive in a theater; and it might be argued that when we read an unfamiliar play, we meet it in the same form in which it first appears to its actors and its director. If a play is rich and complex, or if it dates from the remote past and contains difficulties of language and allusion, to read it on the page enables us to study it at our leisure, to return to the parts that demand greater scrutiny.

Let us admit, by the way, that some plays, whatever the intentions of their authors, are destined to be read more often than they are acted. Such a play is sometimes called a **closet drama** — "closet" meaning a small, private room. Percy Bysshe Shelley's neo-Shakespearean tragedy *The Cenci* (1819) has seldom escaped from its closet, even though Shelley tried without luck to have it performed on the London stage. Perhaps too rich in talk to please an audience or too sparse in opportunities for actors to use their bodies, such works nevertheless may lead long, respectable lives on their own, solely as literature.

But even if a play may be seen in a theater, sometimes to read it in print may be our only way of knowing it as the author wrote it in its entirety. Far from regarding Shakespeare's words as holy writ, producers of *Hamlet, King Lear, Othello,* and other masterpieces often leave out whole speeches and scenes, or shorten them. Besides, the nature of the play, as far as you can tell from a stage production, may depend upon decisions of the director. Shall *Othello* dress as a Renaissance Moor, or as a jet-set contemporary? Every actor who plays Iago in *Othello* makes his own interpretation of this knotty character. Some see Iago as a figure of pure evil; others, as a madman; still others, as a suffering human being consumed by hatred, jealousy, and pride. What do you think Shakespeare meant? You can always read the play and decide for yourself. If every stage production of a play is a fresh interpretation, so too is every reader's reading of it.

Some readers, when silently reading a play to themselves, try to visualize a stage, imagining the characters in costume and under lights. If such a reader is an actor or a director and is reading the play with an eye to staging it, then that reader may try to imagine every detail of a possible production, even shades of makeup and loudness of sound effects. But the nonprofessional reader, who regards the play as literature, need not attempt such exhaustive imagining. Although some readers find it enjoyable to imagine the play taking place upon a stage, others prefer to imagine the people and events that the play brings vividly to mind. Sympathetically following the tangled life of Nora in *A Doll House* by Henrik Ibsen, we forget that we are reading printed stage directions and instead find ourselves in the presence of human conflict. Thus regarded, a play becomes a form of storytelling, and the playwright's instructions to the actors and the director become a conventional mode of narrative that we accept in much the way as we accept the methods of a novel or short story. In reading *A Doll House* caring more about Nora's fate than the imagined appearance of an actress portraying her, we speed through an ordinary passage such as this (from a scene in which Nora's husband hears the approach of an unwanted caller, Dr. Rank):

> *Helmer (with quiet irritation):* Oh, what does he want now? *(Aloud.)* Hold on. *(Goes and opens the door.)* Oh, how nice that you didn't just pass us by!

We read the passage, if the story absorbs us, as though we were reading a novel whose author, employing the conventional devices for recording speech in fiction, might have written:

> "Oh, what does he want now?" said Helmer under his breath, in annoyance. Aloud, he called, "Hold on," then walked to the door and opened it and greeted Rank with all the cheer he could muster — "Oh, how nice that you didn't just pass us by!"

Such is the power of an excellent play to make us ignore the playwright's artistry that it becomes a window through which the reader's gaze, given focus, encompasses more than language and typography and beholds a scene of imagined life.

Most plays, whether seen in a theater or in print, employ *some* **conventions:** customary methods of presenting an action, usual and recognizable devices that an audience is willing to accept. In reading a great play from the past, such as *Oedipus Rex* or *Othello,* it will help if we know some of the conventions of the classical Greek theater or the Elizabethan theater.

When in *Oedipus Rex* we encounter a character called the Choragos, it may be useful to be aware that he is not exactly a participant in the action, but a leader of the chorus who stands to one side of the action, conversing with the principal character and commenting. In *Othello,* when the sinister Iago, left on stage alone, begins to speak (at the end of Act II, Scene 1), we recognize the conventional device of a **soliloquy,** a dramatic monologue in which we seem to overhear the character's inmost thoughts uttered aloud. Like conventions in poetry, such familiar methods of staging a story afford us a happy shock of recognition. Often, as in these examples, they are ways of making clear to us exactly what the playwright would have us know.

A PLAY IN ITS ELEMENTS

When we read a play on the printed page and find ourselves swept forward by the motion of its story, we need not wonder how — and of what ingredients — the playwright put it together. Still, to analyze the structure of a play is one way to understand and appreciate a playwright's art. Analysis is complicated, however, because in an excellent play the elements (including plot, theme, and characters) do not stand in isolation. Often, deeds clearly follow from the kinds of people the characters are, and from those deeds it is left to the reader to infer the **theme** of the play — the general point or truth about human beings that may be drawn from it. Perhaps the most meaningful way to study the elements of a play (and certainly the most enjoyable) is to consider a play in its entirety.

Here is a short, famous one-act play worth reading for the boldness of its elements — and for its own sake. *Trifles* tells the story of a murder. As you will discover, the "trifles" mentioned in its title are not of trifling stature. In reading the play, you will probably find yourself imagining what you might see on stage if you were in a theater. You may also care to imagine what took place in the lives of the characters before the curtain rose. All this imagining may sound like a tall order, but don't worry. Just read the play for enjoyment the first time through, and then we will consider whatever makes it effective.

Susan Glaspell
TRIFLES   1916

> *Susan Glaspell (1882 – 1948), grew up in her native Davenport, Iowa, daughter of a grain dealer. After four years at Drake University and a reporting job in Des Moines, she settled in New York's Greenwich Village. In 1915, with her husband George Cram Cook, a theatrical director, she founded the Provincetown Players, the first influential noncommercial theater troupe in America. Summers, in a makeshift playhouse on a Cape Cod pier,*

the Players staged the earliest plays of Eugene O'Neill and work by John Reed, Edna St. Vincent Millay, and Glaspell herself. (Later transplanting the company to New York, Glaspell and Cook renamed it the Playwrights' Theater.) Glaspell wrote several still-remembered plays, among them a pioneering work of feminist drama, The Verge (1921), and the Pulitzer prize-winning Alison's House (1930), about the family of a reclusive poet like Emily Dickinson who, after her death, squabble over the right to publish her poems. First widely known for her fiction with an Iowa background, Glaspell wrote ten novels, including Fidelity (1915) and The Morning Is Near Us (1939). Shortly after writing the play Trifles, she rewrote it as a short story, "A Jury of Her Peers."

Characters

George Henderson, county attorney
Henry Peters, sheriff
Lewis Hale, a neighboring farmer
Mrs. Peters
Mrs. Hale

Scene. *The kitchen in the now abandoned farmhouse of John Wright, a gloomy kitchen, and left without having been put in order — unwashed pans under the sink, a loaf of bread outside the breadbox, a dish towel on the table — other signs of incompleted work. At the rear the outer door opens and the Sheriff comes in followed by the County Attorney and Hale. The Sheriff and Hale are men in middle life, the County Attorney is a young man; all are much bundled up and go at once to the stove. They are followed by two women — the Sheriff's wife first; she is a slight wiry woman, a thin nervous face. Mrs. Hale is larger and would ordinarily be called more comfortable looking, but she is disturbed now and looks fearfully about as she enters. The women have come in slowly, and stand close together near the door.*

County Attorney: [*Rubbing his hands.*] This feels good. Come up to the fire, ladies.
Mrs. Peters: [*After taking a step forward.*] I'm not — cold.
Sheriff: [*Unbuttoning his overcoat and stepping away from the stove as if to mark the beginning of official business.*] Now, Mr. Hale, before we move things about, you explain to Mr. Henderson just what you saw when you came here yesterday morning.
County Attorney: By the way, has anything been moved? Are things just as you left them yesterday?
Sheriff: [*Looking about.*] It's just the same. When it dropped below zero last night I thought I'd better send Frank out this morning to make a fire for us — no use getting pneumonia with a big case on, but I told him not to touch anything except the stove — and you know Frank.
County Attorney: Somebody should have been left here yesterday.
Sheriff: Oh — yesterday. When I had to send Frank to Morris Center for that man who went crazy — I want you to know I had my hands full yesterday,

I knew you could get back from Omaha by today and as long as I went over everything here myself —

County Attorney: Well, Mr. Hale, tell just what happened when you came here yesterday morning.

Hale: Harry and I had started to town with a load of potatoes. We came along the road from my place and as I got here I said, "I'm going to see if I can't get John Wright to go in with me on a party telephone." I spoke to Wright about it once before and he put me off, saying folks talked too much anyway, and all he asked was peace and quiet — I guess you know about how much he talked himself; but I thought maybe if I went to the house and talked about it before his wife, though I said to Harry that I didn't know as what his wife wanted made much difference to John —

County Attorney: Let's talk about that later, Mr. Hale. I do want to talk about that, but tell now just what happened when you got to the house.

Hale: I didn't hear or see anything; I knocked at the door, and still it was all quiet inside. I knew they must be up, it was past eight o'clock. So I knocked again, and I thought I heard somebody say, "Come in." I wasn't sure, I'm not sure yet, but I opened the door — this door [*Indicating the door by which the two women are still standing*] and there in that rocker — [*Pointing to it*] sat Mrs. Wright.

[*They all look at the rocker.*]

County Attorney: What — was she doing?

Hale: She was rockin' back and forth. She had her apron in her hand and was kind of — pleating it.

County Attorney: And how did she — look?

Hale: Well, she looked queer.

County Attorney: How do you mean — queer?

Hale: Well, as if she didn't know what she was going to do next. And kind of done up.

County Attorney: How did she seem to feel about your coming?

Hale: Why, I don't think she minded — one way or other. She didn't pay much attention. I said, "How do, Mrs. Wright, it's cold, ain't it?" And she said, "Is it?" — and went on kind of pleating at her apron. Well, I was surprised; she didn't ask me to come up to the stove, or to set down, but just sat there, not even looking at me, so I said, "I want to see John." And then she — laughed. I guess you would call it a laugh. I thought of Harry and the team outside, so I said a little sharp: "Can't I see John?" "No," she says, kind o' dull like. "Ain't he home?" says I. "Yes," says she, "he's home." "Then why can't I see him?" I asked her, out of patience. " 'Cause he's dead," says she. *"Dead?"* says I. She just nodded her head, not getting a bit excited, but rockin' back and forth. "Why — where is he?" says I, not knowing what to say. She just pointed upstairs — like that [*Himself pointing to the room above*]. I got up, with the idea of going up there. I walked from there to here — then I says, "Why, what did he die of?" "He died of a rope round his neck," says she, and just went on pleatin' at her apron. Well, I went out and called Harry. I thought I might — need help. We went upstairs and there he was lyin' —

County Attorney: I think I'd rather have you go into that upstairs, where you can point it all out. Just go on now with the rest of the story.

Hale: Well, my first thought was to get that rope off. It looked . . . [*Stops, his face twitches*] . . . but Harry, he went up to him, and he said, "No, he's dead all right, and we'd better not touch anything." So we went back down stairs. She was still sitting that same way. "Has anybody been notified?" I asked. "No," says she, unconcerned. "Who did this, Mrs. Wright?" said Harry. He said it businesslike — and she stopped pleatin' of her apron. "I don't know," she says. "You don't *know*?" says Harry. "No," says she. "Weren't you sleepin' in the bed with him?" says Harry. "Yes," says she, "but I was on the inside." "Somebody slipped a rope round his neck and strangled him and you didn't wake up?" says Harry. "I didn't wake up," she said after him. We must 'a looked as if we didn't see how that could be, for after a minute she said, "I sleep sound." Harry was going to ask her more questions but I said maybe we ought to let her tell her story first to the coroner, or the sheriff, so Harry went fast as he could to Rivers' place, where there's a telephone.

County Attorney: And what did Mrs. Wright do when she knew that you had gone for the coroner?

Hale: She moved from that chair to this one over here [*Pointing to a small chair in the corner*] and just sat there with her hands held together and looking down. I got a feeling that I ought to make some conversation, so I said I had come in to see if John wanted to put in a telephone, and at that she started to laugh, and then she stopped and looked at me — scared. [*The County Attorney, who has had his notebook out, makes a note.*] I dunno, maybe it wasn't scared. I wouldn't like to say it was. Soon Harry got back, and then Dr. Lloyd came, and you, Mr. Peters, and so I guess that's all I know that you don't.

County Attorney: [*Looking around.*] I guess we'll go upstairs first — and then out to the barn and around there. [*To the Sheriff*] You're convinced that there was nothing important here — nothing that would point to any motive.

Sheriff: Nothing here but kitchen things.

[*The County Attorney, after again looking around the kitchen, opens the door of a cupboard closet. He gets up on a chair and looks on a shelf. Pulls his hand away, sticky.*]

County Attorney: Here's a nice mess.

[*The women draw nearer.*]

Mrs. Peters: [*To the other woman.*] Oh, her fruit; it did freeze. [*To the County Attorney*] She worried about that when it turned so cold. She said the fire'd go out and her jars would break.

Sheriff: Well, can you beat the women! Held for murder and worryin' about her preserves.

County Attorney: I guess before we're through she may have something more serious than preserves to worry about.

Hale: Well, women are used to worrying over trifles.

[*The two women move a little closer together.*]

County Attorney: [With the gallantry of a young politician.] And yet, for all their worries, what would we do without the ladies? [The women do not unbend. He goes to the sink, takes a dipperful of water from the pail and pouring it into a basin, washes his hands. Starts to wipe them on the roller towel, turns it for a cleaner place.] Dirty towels! [Kicks his foot against the pans under the sink.] Not much of a housekeeper, would you say, ladies?

Mrs. Hale: [Stiffly.] There's a great deal of work to be done on a farm.

County Attorney: To be sure. And yet [With a little bow to her] I know there are some Dickson county farmhouses which do not have such roller towels.

[He gives it a pull to expose its full length again.]

Mrs. Hale: Those towels get dirty awful quick. Men's hands aren't always as clean as they might be.

County Attorney: Ah, loyal to your sex, I see. But you and Mrs. Wright were neighbors. I suppose you were friends, too.

Mrs. Hale: [Shaking her head.] I've not seen much of her of late years. I've not been in this house — it's more than a year.

County Attorney: And why was that? You didn't like her?

Mrs. Hale: I liked her all well enough. Farmers' wives have their hands full, Mr. Henderson. And then —

County Attorney: Yes — ?

Mrs. Hale: [Looking about.] It never seemed a very cheerful place.

County Attorney: No — it's not cheerful. I shouldn't say she had the homemaking instinct.

Mrs. Hale: Well, I don't know as Wright had, either.

County Attorney: You mean that they didn't get on very well?

Mrs. Hale: No, I don't mean anything. But I don't think a place'd be any cheerfuller for John Wright's being in it.

County Attorney: I'd like to talk more of that a little later. I want to get the lay of things upstairs now.

[He goes to the left, where three steps lead to a stair door.]

Sheriff: I suppose anything Mrs. Peter does'll be all right. She was to take in some clothes for her, you know, and a few little things. We left in such a hurry yesterday.

County Attorney: Yes, but I would like to see what you take, Mrs. Peters, and keep an eye out for anything that might be of use to us.

Mrs. Peters: Yes, Mr. Henderson.

[The women listen to the men's steps on the stairs, then look about the kitchen.]

Mrs. Hale: I'd hate to have men coming into my kitchen, snooping around and criticising.

[She arranges the pans under sink which the County Attorney had shoved out of place.]

Mrs. Peters: Of course it's no more than their duty.

Mrs. Hale: Duty's all right, but I guess that deputy sheriff that came out to make the fire might have got a little of this on. [Gives the roller towel a pull.] Wish I'd thought of that sooner. Seems mean to talk about her for not having things slicked up when she had to come away in such a hurry.

Mrs. Peters: [*Who has gone to a small table in the left rear corner of the room, and lifted one end of a towel that covers a pan.*] She had bread set.

[*Stands still.*]

Mrs. Hale: [*Eyes fixed on a loaf of bread beside the breadbox, which is on a low shelf at the other side of the room. Moves slowly toward it.*] She was going to put this in there. [*Picks up loaf, then abruptly drops it. In a manner of returning to familiar things.*] It's a shame about her fruit. I wonder if it's all gone. [*Gets up on the chair and looks.*] I think there's some here that's all right, Mrs. Peters. Yes — here; [*Holding it toward the window*] this is cherries, too. [*Looking again.*] I declare I believe that's the only one. [*Gets down, bottle in her hand. Goes to the sink and wipes it off on the outside.*] She'll feel awful bad after all her hard work in the hot weather. I remember the afternoon I put up my cherries last summer.

[*She puts the bottle on the big kitchen table, center of the room. With a sigh, is about to sit down in the rocking-chair. Before she is seated realizes what chair it is; with a slow look at it, steps back. The chair which she has touched rocks back and forth.*]

Mrs. Peters: Well, I must get those things from the front room closet. [*She goes to the door at the right, but after looking into the other room, steps back.*] You coming with me, Mrs. Hale? You could help me carry them.

[*They go in the other room; reappear, Mrs. Peters carrying a dress and skirt, Mrs. Hale following with a pair of shoes.*]

Mrs. Peters: My, it's cold in there.

[*She puts the clothes on the big table, and hurries to the stove.*]

Mrs. Hale: [*Examining her skirt.*] Wright was close. I think maybe that's why she kept so much to herself. She didn't even belong to the Ladies Aid. I suppose she felt she couldn't do her part, and then you don't enjoy things when you feel shabby. She used to wear pretty clothes and be lively, when she was Minnie Foster, one of the town girls singing in the choir. But that — oh, that was thirty years ago. This all you was to take in?

Mrs. Peters: She said she wanted an apron. Funny thing to want, for there isn't much to get you dirty in jail, goodness knows. But I suppose just to make her feel more natural. She said they was in the top drawer in this cupboard. Yes, here. And then her little shawl that always hung behind the door. [*Opens stair door and looks.*] Yes, here it is.

[*Quickly shuts door leading upstairs.*]

Mrs. Hale: [*Abruptly moving toward her.*] Mrs. Peters?

Mrs. Peters: Yes, Mrs. Hale?

Mrs. Hale: Do you think she did it?

Mrs. Peters: [*In a frightened voice.*] Oh, I don't know.

Mrs. Hale: Well, I don't think she did. Asking for an apron and her little shawl. Worrying about her fruit.

Mrs. Peters: [*Starts to speak, glances up, where footsteps are heard in the room above. In a low voice.*] Mr. Peters says it looks bad for her. Mr. Henderson is awful sarcastic in a speech and he'll make fun of her sayin' she didn't wake up.

Mrs. Hale: Well, I guess John Wright didn't wake when they was slipping that rope under his neck.

Mrs. Peters: No, it's strange. It must have been done awful crafty and still. They say it was such a — funny way to kill a man, rigging it all up like that.

Mrs. Hale: That's just what Mr. Hale said. There was a gun in the house. He says that's what he can't understand.

Mrs. Peters: Mr. Henderson said coming out that what was needed for the case was a motive; something to show anger, or — sudden feeling.

Mrs. Hale: [*Who is standing by the table.*] Well, I don't see any signs of anger around here. [*She puts her hand on the dish towel which lies on the table, stands looking down at table, one half of which is clean, the other half messy.*] It's wiped to here. [*Makes a move as if to finish work, then turns and looks at loaf of bread outside the breadbox. Drops towel. In that voice of coming back to familiar things.*] Wonder how they are finding things upstairs. I hope she had it a little more red-up° up there. You know, it seems kind of *sneaking.* Locking her up in town and then coming out here and trying to get her own house to turn against her!

Mrs. Peters: But Mrs. Hale, the law is the law.

Mrs. Hale: I s'pose 'tis. [*Unbuttoning her coat.*] Better loosen up your things, Mrs. Peters. You won't feel them when you go out.

[*Mrs. Peters takes off her fur tippet, goes to hang it on hook at back of room, stands looking at the under part of the small corner table.*]

Mrs. Peters: She was piecing a quilt.

[*She brings the large sewing basket and they look at the bright pieces.*]

Mrs. Hale: It's log cabin pattern. Pretty, isn't it? I wonder if she was goin' to quilt it or just knot it?

[*Footsteps have been heard coming down the stairs. The Sheriff enters followed by Hale and the County Attorney.*]

Sheriff: They wonder if she was going to quilt it or just knot it!

[*The men laugh; the women look abashed.*]

County Attorney: [*Rubbing his hands over the stove.*] Frank's fire didn't do much up there, did it? Well, let's go out to the barn and get that cleared up.

[*The men go outside.*]

Mrs. Hale: [*Resentfully.*] I don't know as there's anything so strange, our takin' up our time with little things while we're waiting for them to get the evidence. [*She sits down at the big table smoothing out a block with decision.*] I don't see as it's anything to laugh about.

---

red-up: (slang) prettified, like a woman who touches up her face with rouge.

Mrs. Peters: [*Apologetically.*] Of course they've got awful important things on their minds.

[*Pulls up a chair and joins Mrs. Hale at the table.*]

Mrs. Hale: [*Examining another block.*] Mrs. Peters, look at this one. Here, this is the one she was working on, and look at the sewing! All the rest of it has been so nice and even. And look at this! It's all over the place! Why, it looks as if she didn't know what she was about!

[*After she has said this they look at each other, then start to glance back at the door. After an instant Mrs. Hale has pulled at a knot and ripped the sewing.*]

Mrs. Peters: Oh, what are you doing, Mrs. Hale?

Mrs. Hale: [*Mildly.*] Just pulling out a stitch or two that's not sewed very good. [*Threading a needle.*] Bad sewing always made me fidgety.

Mrs. Peters: [*Nervously.*] I don't think we ought to touch things.

Mrs. Hale: I'll just finish up this end. [*Suddenly stopping and leaning forward.*] Mrs. Peters?

Mrs. Peters: Yes, Mrs. Hale?

Mrs. Hale: What do you suppose she was so nervous about?

Mrs. Peters: Oh — I don't know. I don't know as she was nervous. I sometimes sew awful queer when I'm just tired. [*Mrs. Hale starts to say something, looks at Mrs. Peters, then goes on sewing.*] Well, I must get these things wrapped up. They may be through sooner than we think. [*Putting apron and other things together.*] I wonder where I can find a piece of paper, and string.

Mrs. Hale: In that cupboard, maybe.

Mrs. Peters: [*Looking in cupboard.*] Why, here's a birdcage. [*Holds it up.*] Did she have a bird, Mrs. Hale?

Mrs. Hale: Why, I don't know whether she did or not — I've not been here for so long. There was a man around last year selling canaries cheap, but I don't know as she took one; maybe she did. She used to sing real pretty herself.

Mrs. Peters: [*Glancing around.*] Seems funny to think of a bird here. But she must have had one, or why would she have a cage? I wonder what happened to it.

Mrs. Hale: I s'pose maybe the cat got it.

Mrs. Peters: No, she didn't have a cat. She's got that feeling some people have about cats — being afraid of them. My cat got in her room and she was real upset and asked me to take it out.

Mrs. Hale: My sister Bessie was like that. Queer, ain't it?

Mrs. Peters: [*Examining the cage.*] Why, look at this door. It's broke. One hinge is pulled apart.

Mrs. Hale: [*Looking too.*] Looks as if someone must have been rough with it.

Mrs. Peters: Why, yes.

[*She brings the cage forward and puts it on the table.*]

Mrs. Hale: I wish if they're going to find any evidence they'd be about it. I don't like this place.

Mrs. Peters: But I'm awful glad you came with me, Mrs. Hale. It would be lonesome for me sitting here alone.

Mrs. Hale: It would, wouldn't it? [*Dropping her sewing.*] But I tell you what I do wish, Mrs. Peters. I wish I had come over sometimes when *she* was here. I — [*Looking around the room*] — wish I had.

Mrs. Peters: But of course you were awful busy, Mrs. Hale — your house and your children.

Mrs. Hale: I could've come. I stayed away because it weren't cheerful — and that's why I ought to have come. I — I've never liked this place. Maybe because it's down in a hollow and you don't see the road. I dunno what it is but it's a lonesome place and always was. I wish I had come over to see Minnie Foster sometimes. I can see now —

[*Shakes her head.*]

Mrs. Peters: Well, you mustn't reproach yourself, Mrs. Hale. Somehow we just don't see how it is with other folks until — something comes up.

Mrs. Hale: Not having children makes less work — but it makes a quiet house, and Wright out to work all day, and no company when he did come in. Did you know John Wright, Mrs. Peters?

Mrs. Peters: Not to know him; I've seen him in town. They say he was a good man.

Mrs. Hale: Yes — good; he didn't drink, and kept his word as well as most, I guess, and paid his debts. But he was a hard man, Mrs. Peters. Just to pass the time of day with him — [*Shivers.*] Like a raw wind that gets to the bone. [*Pauses, her eye falling on the cage.*] I should think she would 'a wanted a bird. But what do you suppose went with it?

Mrs. Peters: I don't know, unless it got sick and died.

[*She reaches over and swings the broken door, swings it again. Both women watch it.*]

Mrs. Hale: You weren't raised round here, were you? [*Mrs. Peters shakes her head.*] You didn't know — her?

Mrs. Peters: Not till they brought her yesterday.

Mrs. Hale: She — come to think of it, she was kind of like a bird herself — real sweet and pretty, but kind of timid and — fluttery. How — she — did — change. [*Silence; then as if struck by a happy thought and relieved to get back to everyday things.*] Tell you what, Mrs. Peters, why don't you take the quilt in with you? It might take up her mind.

Mrs. Peters: Why, I think that's a real nice idea, Mrs. Hale. There couldn't possibly be any objection to it, could there? Now, just what would I take? I wonder if her patches are in here — and her things.

[*They look in the sewing basket.*]

Mrs. Hale: Here's some red. I expect this has got sewing things in it. [*Brings out a fancy box.*] What a pretty box. Looks like something somebody would give you. Maybe her scissors are in here. [*Opens box. Suddenly puts her hand to her nose.*] Why — [*Mrs. Peters bends nearer, then turns her face away.*] There's something wrapped up in this piece of silk.

Mrs. Peters: Why, this isn't her scissors.

Mrs. Hale: [*Lifting the silk.*] Oh, Mrs. Peters — it's —

[Mrs. Peters bends closer.]

Mrs. Peters: It's the bird.
Mrs. Hale: [*Jumping up.*] But, Mrs. Peters — look at it! Its neck! Look at its neck! It's all — other side *to.*
Mrs. Peters: Somebody — wrung — its — neck.

[Their eyes meet. A look of growing comprehension, of horror. Steps are heard outside. Mrs. Hale slips box under quilt pieces, and sinks into her chair. Enter Sheriff and County Attorney. Mrs. Peters rises.]

County Attorney: [*As one turning from serious things to little pleasantries.*] Well, ladies, have you decided whether she was going to quilt it or knot it?
Mrs. Peters: We think she was going to — knot it.
County Attorney: Well, that's interesting, I'm sure. [*Seeing the birdcage.*] Has the bird flown?
Mrs. Hale: [*Putting more quilt pieces over the box.*] We think the — cat got it.
County Attorney: [*Preoccupied.*] Is there a cat?

[Mrs. Hale glances in a quick covert way at Mrs. Peters.]

Mrs. Peters: Well, not *now.* They're superstitious, you know. They leave.
County Attorney: [*To Sheriff Peters, continuing an interrupted conversation.*] No sign at all of anyone having come from the outside. Their own rope. Now let's go up again and go over it piece by piece. [*They start upstairs.*] It would have to have been someone who knew just the —

[Mrs. Peters sits down. The two women sit there not looking at one another, but as if peering into something and at the same time holding back. When they talk now it is in the manner of feeling their way over strange ground, as if afraid of what they are saying, but as if they can not help saying it.]

Mrs. Hale: She liked the bird. She was going to bury it in that pretty box.
Mrs. Peters: [*In a whisper.*] When I was a girl — my kitten — there was a boy took a hatchet, and before my eyes — and before I could get there — [*Covers her face an instant*] If they hadn't held me back I would have — [*Catches herself, looks upstairs where steps are heard, falters weakly*] — hurt him.
Mrs. Hale: [*With a slow look around her.*] I wonder how it would seem never to have had any children around. [*Pause.*] No, Wright wouldn't like the bird — a thing that sang. She used to sing. He killed that, too.
Mrs. Peters: [*Moving uneasily.*] We don't know who killed the bird.
Mrs. Hale: I knew John Wright.
Mrs. Peters: It was an awful thing was done in this house that night, Mrs. Hale. Killing a man while he slept, slipping a rope around his neck that choked the life out of him.
Mrs. Hale: His neck. Choked the life out of him.

[Her hand goes out and rests on the birdcage.]

Mrs. Peters: [*With rising voice.*] We don't know who killed him. We don't know.
Mrs. Hale: [*Her own feeling not interrupted.*] If there'd been years and years of nothing, then a bird to sing to you, it would be awful — still, after the bird was still.

Mrs. Peters: [*Something within her speaking.*] I know what stillness is. When we homesteaded in Dakota, and my first baby died — after he was two years old, and me with no other then —

Mrs. Hale: [*Moving.*] How soon do you suppose they'll be through, looking for the evidence?

Mrs. Peters: I know what stillness is. [*Pulling herself back.*] The law has got to punish crime, Mrs. Hale.

Mrs. Hale: [*Not as if answering that.*] I wish you'd seen Minnie Foster when she wore a white dress with blue ribbons and stood up there in the choir and sang. [*A look around the room.*] Oh, I wish I'd come over here once in a while! That was a crime! That was a crime! Who's going to punish that?

Mrs. Peters: [*Looking upstairs.*] We mustn't — take on.

Mrs. Hale: I might have known she needed help! I know how things can be — for women. I tell you, it's queer, Mrs. Peters. We live close together and we live far apart. We all go through the same things — it's all just a different kind of the same thing. [*Brushes her eyes; noticing the bottle of fruit, reaches out for it.*] If I was you I wouldn't tell her her fruit was gone. Tell her it *ain't.* Tell her it's all right. Take this in to prove it to her. She — she may never know whether it was broke or not.

Mrs. Peters: [*Takes the bottle, looks about for something to wrap it in; takes petticoat from the clothes brought from the other room, very nervously begins winding this around the bottle. In a false voice.*] My, it's a good thing the men couldn't hear us. Wouldn't they just laugh! Getting all stirred up over a little thing like a — dead canary. As if that could have anything to do with — with — wouldn't they *laugh!*

[*The men are heard coming down stairs.*]

Mrs. Hale: [*Under her breath.*] Maybe they would — maybe they wouldn't.

County Attorney: No, Peters, it's all perfectly clear except a reason for doing it. But you know juries when it comes to women. If there was some definite thing. Something to show — something to make a story about — a thing that would connect up with this strange way of doing it —

[*The women's eyes meet for an instant. Enter Hale from outer door.*]

Hale: Well, I've got the team around. Pretty cold out there.

County Attorney: I'm going to stay here a while by myself. [*To the Sheriff.*] You can send Frank out for me, can't you? I want to go over everything. I'm not satisfied that we can't do better.

Sheriff: Do you want to see what Mrs. Peters is going to take in?

[*The County Attorney goes to the table, picks up the apron, laughs.*]

County Attorney: Oh, I guess they're not very dangerous things the ladies have picked out. [*Moves a few things about, disturbing the quilt pieces which cover the box. Steps back.*] No, Mrs. Peters doesn't need supervising. For that matter, a sheriff's wife is married to the law. Ever think of it that way, Mrs. Peters?

Mrs. Peters: Not — just that way.

Sheriff: [*Chuckling.*] Married to the law. [*Moves toward the other room.*] I just want you to come in here a minute, George. We ought to take a look at these windows.

County Attorney: [*Scoffingly.*] Oh, windows!

Sheriff: We'll be right out, Mr. Hale.

> [*Hale goes outside. The Sheriff follows the County Attorney into the other room. Then Mrs. Hale rises, hands tight together, looking intensely at Mrs. Peters, whose eyes make a slow turn, finally meeting Mrs. Hale's. A moment Mrs. Hale holds her, then her own eyes point the way to where the box is concealed. Suddenly Mrs. Peters throws back quilt pieces and tries to put the box in the bag she is wearing. It is too big. She opens box, starts to take bird out, cannot touch it, goes to pieces, stands there helpless. Sound of a knob turning in the other room. Mrs. Hale snatches the box and puts it in the pocket of her big coat. Enter County Attorney and Sheriff.*]

County Attorney: [*Facetiously.*] Well, Henry, at least we found out that she was not going to quilt it. She was going to — what is it you call it, ladies?

Mrs. Hale: [*Her hand against her pocket.*] We call it — knot it, Mr. Henderson.

CURTAIN

QUESTIONS

1. What attitudes toward women do the Sheriff and the County Attorney express? How do Mrs. Hale and Mrs. Peters react to these sentiments?
2. Why does the County Attorney care so much about discovering a motive for the killing?
3. What does Glaspell show us about the position of women in this early twentieth-century community?
4. What do we learn about the married life of the Wrights? By what means is this knowledge revealed to us?
5. What is the setting of this play and how does it help us to understand Mrs. Wright's deed?
6. What do you infer from the wildly stitched block in Minnie's quilt? Why does Mrs. Hale rip out the crazy stitches?
7. What is so suggestive in the ruined birdcage and the dead canary wrapped in silk? What do these objects have to do with Minnie Foster Wright? What similarity do you notice between the way the canary died and John Wright's own death?
8. What thoughts and memories confirm Mrs. Peters and Mrs. Hale in their decision to help Minnie beat the murder rap?
9. In what places does Mrs. Peters show that she is trying to be a loyal, law-abiding sheriff's wife? How do she and Mrs. Hale differ in background and temperament?
10. What ironies does the play contain? Comment on Mrs. Hale's closing speech: "We call it — knot it, Mr. Henderson." Why is that little hesitation before "knot it" such a meaningful pause?
11. Point out some moments in the play when the playwright gives us to understand much without needing a spoken word.
12. How would you sum up the play's major theme?
13. How does this play, first produced in 1916, show its age? In what ways does it seem still remarkably new?
14. *"Trifles* is a lousy mystery. All the action took place before the curtain went up. Almost in the beginning, on the third page, we find out 'who done it.' So there isn't really much reason for us to sit through the rest of the play." Discuss this view.

Some plays endure, perhaps because (among other reasons) actors take pleasure in performing them. *Trifles* is such a play: a showcase for the skills of its two principals. While the men importantly bumble about, trying to discover a motive for the murder and making gibes about women's preoccupation with "trifles," Mrs. Peters and Mrs. Hale solve the case right under their dull noses. The two players in these leading roles face a challenging task: to show both characters growing onstage before us. Discovering a secret that binds them, the two must realize painful truths in their own lives, become aware of all they have in common with Minnie Wright, and gradually resolve to side with the accused against the men. That *Trifles* has lately enjoyed a revival of attention may reflect its evident feminist views, its convincing portrait of two women forced reluctantly to make a moral judgment and to make a defiant move.

Some critics say that the essence of drama is conflict. Evidently, Glaspell's play is rich in this essential, even though its most violent conflict — the war between John and Minnie Wright — takes place earlier, off scene. Right away, when the menfolk barge through the door into the warm room, letting the women trail in after them; right away, when the sheriff makes fun of Minnie for worrying about "trifles" and the county attorney (that slick politician) starts crudely trying to flatter the "ladies," we sense a conflict between officious, self-important men and the women they expect to wait on them. What is the play's *theme*? Surely the title points to it: Women, who men say worry over trifles, can find in those little things large meanings.

Like a carefully constructed traditional short story, *Trifles* has a **plot**, a term sometimes taken to mean whatever happens in a story, but more exactly referring to the unique arrangement of events that the author has made. (For more about plot in a story, see Chapter One.) If Glaspell had elected to tell the story of John and Minnie Wright in chronological order, the sequence in which events took place in time, she might have written a much longer play, opening perhaps with a scene of Minnie's buying her canary and John's cold complaint, "That damned bird keeps twittering all day long!" Then she might show us John strangling the canary and swearing when it beaks him, then the Wrights in their loveless bed while Minnie knots her noose. Then she might show us farmer Hale's entrance after the murder, with Minnie rocking. Only at last might she show us what happened after the crime. That arrangement of events would have made for a quite different play than the short, tight one Glaspell wrote. By telling of events in retrospect, by having the women detectives piece together what happened, Glaspell leads us to focus not only on the murder but, more important, on the developing bond between the two women and their growing compassion for the accused.

If *Trifles* may be said to have a **protagonist**, a leading character — a word we usually save for the primary figure of a larger and more eventful play such as *Othello* or *Death of a Salesman* — then you could call the two women dual protagonists. Both act in unison to make the plot unfold. Or you could argue that Mrs. Hale, because she destroys the wild stitching in the quilt; because she finds the dead canary; because she invents a cat to catch the bird (thus deceiving the county attorney); and because in the end when Mrs. Peters helplessly "goes to pieces," it is she who takes the initiative and seizes the evidence, deserves to be called the protagonist. More than anyone else in the play, you could claim, the more decisive Mrs. Hale makes things happen.

A vital part in most plays is an **exposition**, the part in which we first meet the characters, learn what happened before the curtain rose, and find out what is happening now. For a one-act play, *Trifles* has a fairly long exposition, extending from the opening of the kitchen door through the end of farmer Hale's story. Clearly, this substantial exposition is necessary to set the situation and to fill in the facts of the crime. By comparison, Shakespeare's far longer *Tragedy of Richard III* begins almost abruptly, with its protagonist, a duke who yearns to be king, summing up history in an opening speech and revealing his evil character: "And therefore, since I cannot prove a lover . . . I am determined to prove a villain." But Glaspell, too, knows her craft. In the exposition, we are given a **foreshadowing** (or hint of what is to come) in Hale's dry remark, "I didn't know as what his wife wanted made much difference to John." The remark announces the play's theme that men often ignore women's feelings, and it hints at Minnie Wright's motive, later to be revealed. The county attorney, failing to pick up a valuable clue, tables the discussion. (Still another foreshadowing occurs in Mrs. Hale's ripping out the wild, panicky stitches in Minnie's quilt. In the end, Mrs. Hale will make a similar final move to conceal the evidence.)

With the county attorney's speech to the sheriff, "You're convinced that there was nothing important here — nothing that would point to any motive," we begin to understand what he seeks. As he will make even clearer later, the attorney needs a motive in order to convict the accused wife of murder in the first degree. Will Minnie's motive in killing her husband be discovered? Through the first two-thirds of *Trifles,* this is the play's **dramatic question**. Whether or not we state such a question in our minds, and it is doubtful that we do, our interest quickens as we sense that here is a problem to be solved, an uncertainty to be dissipated. When Mrs. Hale and Mrs. Peters find the dead canary with the twisted neck, the question is answered. We know that Minnie killed John to repay him for his act of gross cruelty. But the playwright now raises a *new* dramatic question. Having discovered Minnie's motive, will the women reveal it to the lawmen? Or (if you care to phrase the new question differently), what will they do with the incriminating evidence? We keep reading, or stay clamped to our theater seats, because we want that question answered. We share the women's secret now, and we want to see what they will do with it.

Tightly packed, the one-act *Trifles* contains but one plot: the story of how two women discover evidence that might hang another woman and then hide it. But some plays, usually longer ones, may be more complicated. They may contain a **double plot** (or **subplot**), a secondary arrangement of incidents, involving not the protagonist but someone less important. In Henrik Ibsen's *A Doll House,* the main plot involves a woman and her husband. But they are joined by a second couple, whose fortunes we also follow with interest and whose futures pose another dramatic question.

Step by step, *Trifles* builds to a **climax**: a moment, usually coming late in a play, when tension reaches its greatest height. At such a moment, we sense that the play's dramatic question (or its final dramatic question, if the writer has posed two or more) is about to be answered. In *Trifles,* this climax occurs when Mrs. Peters finds herself torn between her desire to save Minnie and her duty to the law. "It was an awful thing that was done in this house that night," she reminds herself in one speech, suggesting that Minnie deserves to be punished; then in the next speech she insists, "We don't know who killed him. We don't *know.* " Shortly after that, in one speech she voices two warring attitudes. Remembering the loss of her first child, she sympathizes with Minnie: "I know what stillness is." But in her next breath she recalls once more her duty to be a loyal sheriff's wife: "The law has got to punish crime, Mrs. Hale." For a moment, she is placed in conflict with Mrs. Hale, who knew Minnie personally. The two now stand on the edge of a fateful brink. Which way will they decide?[1]

From this moment of climax, the play, like its protagonist (or if you like, protagonists), will make a final move. Mrs. Peters takes her stand. Mrs. Hale, too, decides. She owes Minnie something to make up for her own "crime" — her failure to visit the desperate woman. The plot now charges ahead to its outcome or **resolution**, also called the **conclusion** or **denouement** (French: untying of a knot). The two women act: they scoop up the damning evidence. Seconds before the very end, Glaspell heightens the **suspense**, our enjoyable anxiety, by making Mrs. Peters fumble with the incriminating box as the sheriff and the county attorney draw near. Mrs. Hale's swift grab for the evidence saves the day, and presumably saves Minnie's life. The sound of the doorknob turning in the next room, as the lawmen return, is a small but effective bit of **stage business** — any nonverbal action that engages the attention of an audience. When Mrs. Hale almost sits down in Minnie's place, the empty chair that ominously

---

[1]You will sometimes hear *climax* used in a different sense: to mean any **crisis** — that is, a moment of tension when one or another outcome is possible. What *crisis* means will be easy to remember if you think of a crisis in medicine: the turning point in a disease when it becomes clear that a patient will either die or recover. In talking about plays, you will probably find both *crisis* and *climax* useful. You can say that a play has more than one crisis, perhaps several. In such a play, the last and most decisive crisis is the climax. A play has only one climax.

starts rocking is another brilliant piece of stage business. Not only does it give us something interesting to watch, it gives us something to think about.

Some critics maintain that events in a plot can be arranged in the outline of a pyramid.[2] In this view, a play begins with a **rising action**, that part of the story (including the exposition) in which events start moving toward a climax. After the climax, the story tapers off in a **falling action**: the subsequent events, including a resolution. In a tragedy, this falling action usually is recognizable: the protagonist's fortunes proceed downhill to an inexorable end.

Some plays indeed have demonstrable pyramids. In *Trifles,* we might claim that in the first two thirds of the play a rising action builds up in intensity. It proceeds through each main incident: the finding of the crazily stitched quilt, Mrs. Hale's ripping out the evidence, the discovery of the birdcage, then the bird itself, and Mrs. Hale's concealing it. At the climax, the peak of the pyramid, the two women seem about to clash as Mrs. Peters wavers uncertainly. The action then falls to a swift resolution. But if you outlined that pyramid on paper, it would look lopsided — a long rise and a short, steep fall. The pyramid metaphor seems more meaningfully to fit longer plays, among them some classic tragedies. Try it on *Oedipus Rex,* or for an even neater fit, on Shakespeare's *Julius Caesar* — an unusual play in that its climax, the assassination of Caesar, occurs exactly in the middle (III, 1), right where a good pyramid's point ought to be. But in most other plays, it is hard to find a symmetrical pyramid. (For a demonstration of another, quite different way to outline *Trifles,* see "Writing a Card Report" on pages 1409 – 1412.)

Brief though it is, *Trifles* has main elements you will find in much longer, more complicated plays. It even has **symbols**, things that hint at large meanings: the broken birdcage and the dead canary, both suggesting the music and the joy that John Wright stifled in Minnie and the terrible stillness that followed his killing the one thing she loves. Perhaps the lone remaining jar of cherries, too, radiates suggestions: it is the one bright, cheerful thing poor Minnie has to show for a whole summer of toil. Symbols in drama may be as large as Prospero's island in *The Tempest,* or they may appear to be trifles. In Glaspell's rich art, such trifles aren't trifling at all.[3]

---

[2]The metaphor of a play as a pyramid was invented by German critic Gustav Freytag in his *Techniques of the Drama,* 1904; reprint ed. New York: Arno (1968).

[3]Plays can also contain symbolic characters (generally flat ones like a prophet who croaks, "Beware the ides of March"), symbolic settings, and symbolic gestures. For more about symbolism, see Chapters Eight and Twenty-four.

33 Tragedy

> A tragedy, then, is an imitation of an action that is serious, complete in itself, and of a certain magnitude; in a language embellished with each kind of artistry . . . cast in the form of drama, not narrative; accomplishing through incidents that arouse pity and fear the purgation of these emotions.
>
> — Aristotle, *Poetics,* Chapter VI

The form of drama we call **tragedy** was born in Greece in the fifth century B.C. Aristotle's famous definition, constructed in the fourth century B.C., has the authority of one who probably saw many classical tragedies performed. In making his observations, Aristotle does not seem to be laying down laws for what a tragedy ought to be. More likely, he is drawing — from tragedies he has seen or read — a general description of them.

Aristotle observes that the protagonist, the hero or chief character of a tragedy, is a person of "high estate," apparently a king or queen or other member of a royal family. In thus being as keenly interested as contemporary dramatists in the private lives of the powerful, Greek dramatists need not be accused of snobbery. It is the nature of tragedy that the protagonist must fall from power and from happiness; his high estate gives him a place of dignity to fall from and perhaps makes his fall seem all the more a calamity in that it involves an entire nation or people. Nor is the protagonist extraordinary merely in his position in society. Oedipus, in the play by Sophocles, is not only a king but a noble soul who suffers profoundly and who employs splendid speech to express his suffering.

But the tragic hero is not a superman; he is fallible. The hero's downfall is the result, as Aristotle said, of his **hamartia**: his error or transgression or (as some translators would have it) his flaw or weakness of character. The notion that a tragic hero has such a **tragic flaw** has often been attributed to Aristotle, but it is by no means clear that Aristotle meant just that. According to this interpretation, every tragic hero has some fatal weakness, some moral Achilles' heel (pride, say, or lust for power) that brings him to a bad end. This interpretation does not fit every tragedy, nor does it unmistakably fit Aristotle's favorite example, *Oedipus Rex,* as we shall see.

Whatever Aristotle had in mind, however, many later critics find value in the idea of the tragic flaw. In this view, the downfall of a hero follows from his very nature. But whatever view we take — whether we find the hero's sufferings due to a flaw of character or to an error of judgment — we will probably find that his downfall results from acts for which he himself is responsible. In a Greek tragedy, the hero is a character amply capable of making choices — capable, too, of accepting the consequences.

It may be useful to take another look at Aristotle's definition of tragedy, with which we began. By **purgation** (or **katharsis**), did the ancient theorist mean that after witnessing a tragedy we feel relief, having released our pent-up emotions? Or did he mean that our feelings are purified, refined into something more ennobling? Scholars continue to argue. Whatever his exact meaning, clearly Aristotle implies that after witnessing a tragedy we feel better, not worse — not depressed, but somehow elated. We take a kind of pleasure in the spectacle of a noble man being abased, but surely this pleasure is a legitimate one. For tragedy, Edith Hamilton wrote, affects us as "pain transmuted into exaltation by the alchemy of poetry."[1]

THE THEATER OF SOPHOCLES

For a citizen of Athens in the fifth century B.C., when the surviving classical Greek tragedies originated, a play was a religious occasion. Plays were given at the Lenaea, or feast of the winepress, in January; or during the Great Dionysia, or feast of Dionysus, god of wine and crops, in the spring. So well did the Athenians love contests that at the spring festival each playwright was to present — in competition — three tragedies on successive days, the last tragedy to be followed by a short comedy of a special sort. The comedy was a **satyr play**, a parody of a mythic story, with a chorus of actors playing *satyrs,* creatures half goat or horse, half man. The costs of the plays (and presumably the prize money) were borne by a wealthy citizen chosen by the state.

Seated in the open air, in a hillside amphitheater, as many as fourteen thousand spectators could watch a performance that must have somewhat resembled an opera or a modern musical. The audience, arranged in rows, looked out across a rounded **orchestra** or dancing-place, where the chorus of fifteen (the number was fixed by Sophocles) sang passages of lyric poetry and executed dance movements. (It is also possible that actors and chorus sometimes shared the orchestra.) In these song and dance interludes may have originated the modern custom of dividing a play into acts and scenes. Besides providing stage business, the chorus had a function in telling the story: in the plays of Sophocles, they converse with the main

[1]"The Idea of Tragedy" in *The Greek Way to Western Civilization* (New York: Norton, 1942).

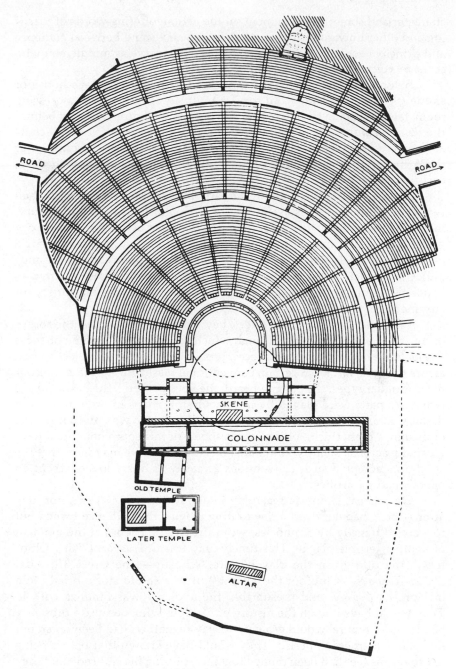

ROAD

ROAD

SKENE

COLONNADE

OLD TEMPLE

LATER TEMPLE

ALTAR

The theater of Dionysus at Athens in the time of Sophocles; a modern drawing
based on scholarly guesswork. From R. C. Flickinger, *The Greek Theater and
Its Drama* (1918).

character and sometimes comment on the action, offering words of warning and other unwanted advice. As they *physically* stand between audience and principal actors, the members of the chorus serve as middlemen who seem to voice the spectators' reactions.

Behind the orchestra stood the actors, in front of a stage house or **skene** (the source of our word *scene*). Originally, the *skene* was a dressing room; later it is believed to have borne a painted backdrop. Directly behind the *skene,* a **colonnade** or row of pillars provided (according to one scholarly guess) a ready-made set for a palace. (This is a rough description of the Athenian theater of Dionysus; several other Greek cities had theaters, each unique in details.)

In the plays of Aeschylus in the early fifth century B.C., no more than two actors occupied the stage at any time. Sophocles, in the midcentury, increased the number to three, making situations of greater complexity possible. Still later in the century, in the time of Euripides (last of the trio of supreme Greek tragic dramatists), the *skene* supported a hook-and-pulley by which actors who played gods could be lowered or lifted — hence the Latin phrase **deus ex machina** ("god out of the machine") for any means of bringing a play quickly to a resolution.

What did the actors look like? They wore **masks** (*personae,* the source of our word *person:* "a thing through which sound comes"); some of these masks had exaggerated mouthpieces, probably designed to project speech across the open air. From certain conventional masks the spectators recognized familiar types: the old graybeard, the young soldier, the beautiful girl (women's parts were played by male actors). Perhaps in order to gain in dignity, actors in the Greek theater eventually came to wear the **cothurnus** or buskin, a high, thick-soled elevator shoe. All this equipment must have given the actors a slightly inhuman appearance, but we may infer that the spectators accepted such conventions as easily as opera lovers accept an opera's natural artifice.

On a Great Dionysia feast day in about the year 430 B.C., not long after Athens had survived a devastating plague, the audience turned out to watch a tragedy by Sophocles, set in the city of Thebes at the moment of another terrible plague. This timely play was *Oedipus Rex* ("King Clubfoot," the title given the play by later scholars — the Greek title was *Oedipus Tyrannos,* "Clubfoot the Tyrant"). It was an old story, briefly told in Homer's *Odyssey,* and presumably the audience was familiar with it. They would have known the history of Oedipus who, because a prophecy had foretold that he would grow up to slay his father, had been taken out into the wilderness to perish. They would have known that before being left to die his feet had been pinned together, causing his clubfoot; and they would have known that later, adopted by King Polybos and grown to maturity, Oedipus won the throne of Thebes as a reward for ridding the city of the Sphinx, a winged, woman-headed lion. All comers to the Sphinx were asked a riddle, and failure to solve it meant death: "What goes on four legs in the morning, two at noon, and three at evening?" Oedipus correctly answered, "Man" (because as a baby he crawls on all fours, then as a man he walks erect, then as an old man he uses a cane). Chagrined, the Sphinx leaped from her rocky perch and dashed herself to death.

Sophocles
OEDIPUS REX

An English Version by Dudley Fitts and Robert Fitzgerald

Sophocles (496? – 406 B.C.), tragic dramatist, priest, for a time one of ten Athenian generals, was among three great ancient Greek writers of tragedy. (The other two were his contemporaries: Aeschylus, his senior, and Euripides, his junior.) Sophocles won his first victory in the Athenian spring drama competition in 468 B.C., when a tragedy he had written defeated a tragedy by Aeschylus. He went on to win many prizes, writing more than 120 plays, of which only seven have survived entire — Ajax, Antigonê, Oedipus Rex, Electra, Philoctetes, The Trachinian Women, *and* Oedipus at Colonus. *(Of the lost plays, about a thousand fragments remain.) In his long life, Sophocles saw Greece rise to supremacy over the Persian Empire. He enjoyed the favor of the statesman Pericles, who, making peace with enemy Sparta, ruled Athens during a Golden Age (461 – 429 B.C.) during which the Parthenon was built and music, art, drama, and philosophy flourished. The playwright lived on to see his native city-state in decline, its strength drained by the disastrous Peloponnesian War. His last play,* Oedipus at Colonus, *set twenty years after the events of* Oedipus Rex, *shows the former king in old age, ragged and blind, cast into exile by his sons, but still accompanied by his faithful daughter Antigonê. It was written when Sophocles was nearly ninety.* Oedipus Rex *is believed to have been first produced in 425 B.C., five years after plague had broken out in Athens.*

Characters°

Oedipus
A Priest
Creon
Teiresias
Iocastê
Messenger
Shepherd of Laïos
Second Messenger
Chorus of Theban Elders

Characters: Some of these names are usually Anglicized: Jocasta, Laius. In this version, the translators prefer spelling names more nearly like the Greek.

The Scene: *Before the palace of Oedipus, King of Thebes. A central door and two lateral doors open onto a platform which runs the length of the façade. On the platform, right and left, are altars; and three steps lead down into the "orchestra," or chorus-ground. At the beginning of the action these steps are crowded by Suppliants° who have brought branches and chaplets of olive leaves and who lie in various attitudes of despair. Oedipus enters.*

PROLOGUE°

Oedipus: My children, generations of the living
    In the line of Kadmos°, nursed at his ancient hearth:
    Why have you strewn yourself before these altars
    In supplication, with your boughs and garlands?
    The breath of incense rises from the city   5
    With a sound of prayer and lamentation.
                                  Children,
    I would not have you speak through messengers,
    And therefore I have come myself to hear you —
    I, Oedipus, who bear the famous name.
    (To a Priest.) You, there, since you are eldest in the company,
    Speak for them all, tell me what preys upon you,   10
    Whether you come in dread, or crave some blessing:
    Tell me, and never doubt that I will help you
    In every way I can; I should be heartless
    Were I not moved to find you suppliant here.
Priest: Great Oedipus, O powerful King of Thebes!   15
    You see how all the ages of our people
    Cling to your altar steps: here are boys
    Who can barely stand alone, and here are priests
    By weight of age, as I am a priest of God,
    And young men chosen from those yet unmarried;   20
    As for the others, all that multitude,
    They wait with olive chaplets in the squares,
    At the two shrines of Pallas°, and where Apollo°
    Speaks in the glowing embers.
                         Your own eyes
    Must tell you: Thebes is in her extremity   25
    And can not lift her head from the surge of death.
    A rust consumes the buds and fruits of the earth;
    The herds are sick; children die unborn,
    And labor is vain. The god of plague and pyre
    Raids like detestable lightning through the city,   30

Suppliants: persons come to ask some favor of the king.
Prologue: portion of the play containing the exposition.
²*line of Kadmos:* according to legend, the city of Thebes, where the play takes place, had been founded by the hero Cadmus.   ²³*Pallas:* title for Athena, goddess of wisdom.   ²³*Apollo:* god of music, poetry, and prophecy. At his shrine near Thebes, the ashes of fires were used to divine the future.

And all the house of Kadmos is laid waste,
All emptied, and all darkened: Death alone
Battens upon the misery of Thebes.

You are not one of the immortal gods, we know;
Yet we have come to you to make our prayer   35
As to the man of all men best in adversity
And wisest in the ways of God. You saved us
From the Sphinx, that flinty singer, and the tribute
We paid to her so long; yet you were never
Better informed than we, nor could we teach you: 40
It was some god breathed in you to set us free.

Therefore, O mighty King, we turn to you:
Find us our safety, find us a remedy,
Whether by counsel of the gods or men.
A king of wisdom tested in the past   45
Can act in a time of troubles, and act well.
Noblest of men, restore
Life to your city! Think how all men call you
Liberator for your triumph long ago;
Ah, when your years of kingship are remembered,   50
Let them not say *We rose, but later fell* —
Keep the State from going down in the storm!
Once, years ago, with happy augury,
You brought us fortune; be the same again!
No man questions your power to rule the land: 55
But rule over men, not over a dead city!
Ships are only hulls, citadels are nothing,
When no life moves in the empty passageways.
Oedipus: Poor children! You may be sure I know
All that you longed for in your coming here.   60
I know that you are deathly sick; and yet,
Sick as you are, not one is as sick as I.
Each of you suffers in himself alone
His anguish, not another's; but my spirit
Groans for the city, for myself, for you.   65

I was not sleeping, you are not waking me.
No, I have been in tears for a long while
And in my restless thought walked many ways.
In all my search, I found one helpful course,
And that I have taken: I have sent Creon,   70
Son of Menoikeus, brother of the Queen,
To Delphi, Apollo's place of revelation°,
To learn there, if he can,

---

⁷²*Delphi . . . revelation:* In the temple of Delphi at the foot of Mount Parnassus, a priestess of Dionysos, while in an ecstatic trance, would speak the wine god's words. Such a priestess was called an *oracle;* the word can also mean a message from the god.

What act or pledge of mine may save the city.
I have counted the days, and now, this very day,   75
I am troubled, for he has overstayed his time.
What is he doing? He has been gone too long.
Yet whenever he comes back, I should do ill
To scant whatever hint the god may give.
Priest: It is a timely promise. At this instant   80
    They tell me Creon is here.
Oedipus: O Lord Apollo!
    May his news be fair as his face is radiant!
Priest: It could not be otherwise: he is crowned with bay,
    The chaplet is thick with berries.
Oedipus: We shall soon know;
    He is near enough to hear us now.

Enter Creon.

                                O Prince: 85
    Brother: son of Menoikeus:
    What answer do you bring us from the god?
Creon: It is favorable. I can tell you, great afflictions
    Will turn out well, if they are taken well.
Oedipus: What was the oracle? These vague words   90
    Leave me still hanging between hope and fear.
Creon: Is it your pleasure to hear me with all these
    Gathered around us? I am prepared to speak,
    But should we not go in?
Oedipus: Let them all hear it.
    It is for them I suffer, more than for myself.   95
Creon: Then I will tell you what I heard at Delphi.

    In plain words
    The god commands us to expel from the land of Thebes
    An old defilement that it seems we shelter.
    It is a deathly thing, beyond expiation.   100
    We must not let it feed upon us longer.
Oedipus: What defilement? How shall we rid ourselves of it?
Creon: By exile or death, blood for blood. It was
    Murder that brought the plague-wind on the city.
Oedipus: Murder of whom? Surely the god has named him?   105
Creon: My lord: long ago Laïos was our king,
    Before you came to govern us.
Oedipus: I know;
    I learned of him from others; I never saw him.
Creon: He was murdered; and Apollo commands us now
    To take revenge upon whoever killed him.   110
Oedipus: Upon whom? Where are they? Where shall we find a clue
    To solve that crime, after so many years?
Creon: Here in this land, he said.
                            If we make enquiry,

We may touch things that otherwise escape us.

Oedipus: Tell me: Was Laïos murdered in his house,   115
   Or in the fields, or in some foreign country?

Creon: He said he planned to make a pilgrimage.
   He did not come home again.

Oedipus: And was there no one,
   No witness, no companion, to tell what happened?

Creon: They were all killed but one, and he got away   120
   So frightened that he could remember one thing only.

Oedipus: What was that one thing? One may be the key
   To everything, if we resolve to use it.

Creon: He said that a band of highwaymen attacked them,
   Outnumbered them, and overwhelmed the King.   125

Oedipus: Strange, that a highwayman should be so daring —
   Unless some faction here bribed him to do it.

Creon: We thought of that. But after Laïos' death
   New troubles arose and we had no avenger.

Oedipus: What troubles could prevent your hunting down the killers?   130

Creon: The riddling Sphinx's song
   Made us deaf to all mysteries but her own.

Oedipus: Then once more I must bring what is dark to light.
   It is most fitting that Apollo shows,
   As you do, this compunction for the dead.   135
   You shall see how I stand by you, as I should,
   To avenge the city and the city's god,
   And not as though it were for some distant friend,
   But for my own sake, to be rid of evil.
   Whoever killed King Laïos might — who knows? —   140
   Decide at any moment to kill me as well.
   By avenging the murdered king I protect myself.
   Come, then, my children: leave the altar steps,
   Lift up your olive boughs!
                                    One of you go
   And summon the people of Kadmos to gather here.   145
   I will do all that I can; you may tell them that.

Exit a Page.

   So, with the help of God,
   We shall be saved — or else indeed we are lost.

Priest: Let us rise, children. It was for this we came,
   And now the King has promised it himself.   150
   Phoibos° has sent us an oracle; may he descend
   Himself to save us and drive out the plague.

*Exeunt Oedipus and Creon into the palace by the central door. The Priest and
the Suppliants disperse right and left. After a short pause the Chorus enters
the orchestra.*

---

[151] *Phoibos:* the sun god Phoebus Apollo.

PARODOS°

Strophe 1

Chorus: What is God singing in his profound
    Delphi of gold and shadow?
    What oracle for Thebes, the sunwhipped city?
    Fear unjoints me, the roots of my heart tremble.
    Now I remember, O Healer, your power, and wonder;   5
    Will you send doom like a sudden cloud, or weave it
    Like nightfall of the past?
    Speak, speak to us, issue of holy sound:
    Dearest to our expectancy: be tender!

Antistrophe 1

    Let me pray to Athenê, the immortal daughter of Zeus,   10
    And to Artemis her sister
    Who keeps her famous throne in the market ring,
    And to Apollo, bowman at the far butts of heaven —

    O gods, descend! Like three streams leap against
    The fires of our grief, the fires of darkness;   15
    Be swift to bring us rest!

    As in the old time from the brilliant house
    Of air you stepped to save us, come again!

Strophe 2

    Now our afflictions have no end,
    Now all our stricken host lies down   20
    And no man fights off death with his mind;

    The noble plowland bears no grain,
    And groaning mothers can not bear —

    See, how our lives like birds take wing,
    Like sparks that fly when a fire soars,   25
    To the shore of the god of evening.

Antistrophe 2

    The plague burns on, it is pitiless,
    Though pallid children laden with death
    Lie unwept in the stony ways,

    And old gray women by every path   30
    Flock to the strand about the altars

Parodos: part to be sung by the chorus on first entering. A *strophe* (according to theory) was sung while the chorus danced from stage right to stage left; an *antistrophe,* while they danced back again.

There to strike their breasts and cry
Worship of Phoibos in wailing prayers:
Be kind, God's golden child!

Strophe 3

There are no swords in this attack by fire,   35
No shields, but we are ringed with cries.
Send the besieger plunging from our homes
Into the vast sea-room of the Atlantic
Or into the waves that foam eastward of Thrace —
For the day ravages what the night spares —   40
Destroy our enemy, lord of the thunder!
Let him be riven by lightning from heaven!

Antistrophe 3

Phoibos Apollo, stretch the sun's bowstring,
That golden cord, until it sing for us,
Flashing arrows in heaven!
                    Artemis, Huntress,   45
Race with flaring lights upon our mountains!

O scarlet god, O golden-banded brow,
O Theban Bacchos in a storm of Maenads°,

Enter Oedipus, center.

Whirl upon Death, that all the Undying hate!
Come with blinding cressets, come in joy!   50

SCENE I

Oedipus: Is this your prayer? It may be answered. Come,
    Listen to me, act as the crisis demands,
    And you shall have relief from all these evils.

    Until now I was a stranger to this tale,
    As I had been a stranger to the crime.   5
    Could I track down the murderer without a clue?
    But now, friends,
    As one who became a citizen after the murder,
    I make this proclamation to all Thebans:
    If any man knows by whose hand Laïos, son of Labdakos,   10
    Met his death, I direct that man to tell me everything,
    No matter what he fears for having so long withheld it.
    Let it stand as promised that no further trouble
    Will come to him, but he may leave the land in safety.

⁴⁸*Bacchos . . . Maenads:* god of wine with his attendant girl revelers.

Moreover: If anyone knows the murderer to be foreign,   15
Let him not keep silent: he shall have his reward from me.
However, if he does conceal it; if any man
Fearing for his friend or for himself disobeys this edict,
Hear what I propose to do:

I solemnly forbid the people of this country,   20
Where power and throne are mine, ever to receive that man
Or speak to him, no matter who he is, or let him
Join in sacrifice, lustration, or in prayer.
I decree that he be driven from every house,
Being, as he is, corruption itself to us: the Delphic   25
Voice of Zeus has pronounced this revelation.
Thus I associate myself with the oracle
And take the side of the murdered king.

As for the criminal, I pray to God —
Whether it be a lurking thief, or one of a number —   30
I pray that that man's life be consumed in evil and wretchedness.
And as for me, this curse applies no less
If it should turn out that the culprit is my guest here,
Sharing my hearth.
                    You have heard the penalty.
I lay it on you now to attend to this   35
For my sake, for Apollo's, for the sick
Sterile city that heaven has abandoned.
Suppose the oracle had given you no command:
Should this defilement go uncleansed for ever?
You should have found the murderer: your king,   40
A noble king, had been destroyed!
                    Now I,
Having the power that he held before me,
Having his bed, begetting children there
Upon his wife, as he would have, had he lived —
Their son would have been my children's brother,   45
If Laïos had had luck in fatherhood!
(But surely ill luck rushed upon his reign) —
I say I take the son's part, just as though
I were his son, to press the fight for him
And see it won! I'll find the hand that brought   50
Death to Labdakos' and Polydoros' child,
Heir of Kadmos' and Agenor's line.
And as for those who fail me,
May the gods deny them the fruit of the earth,
Fruit of the womb, and may they rot utterly!   55
Let them be wretched as we are wretched, and worse!

For you, for loyal Thebans, and for all
Who find my actions right, I pray the favor

Of justice, and of all the immortal gods.

Choragos°: Since I am under oath, my lord, I swear   60
    I did not do the murder, I can not name
    The murderer. Might not the oracle
    That has ordained the search tell where to find him?
Oedipus: An honest question. But no man in the world
    Can make the gods do more than the gods will.   65
Choragos: There is one last expedient —
Oedipus: Tell me what it is.
    Though it seem slight, you must not hold it back.
Choragos: A lord clairvoyant to the lord Apollo,
    As we all know, is the skilled Teiresias.
    One might learn much about this from him, Oedipus.   70
Oedipus: I am not wasting time:
    Creon spoke of this, and I have sent for him —
    Twice, in fact; it is strange that he is not here.
Choragos: The other matter — that old report — seems useless.
Oedipus: Tell me. I am interested in all reports.   75
Choragos: The King was said to have been killed by highwaymen.
Oedipus: I know. But we have no witnesses to that.
Choragos: If the killer can feel a particle of dread,
    Your curse will bring him out of hiding!
Oedipus: No.
    The man who dared that act will fear no curse.   80

Enter the blind seer Teiresias, led by a Page.

Choragos: But there is one man who may detect the criminal.
    This is Teiresias, this is the holy prophet
    In whom, alone of all men, truth was born.
Oedipus: Teiresias: seer: student of mysteries,
    Of all that's taught and all that no man tells,   85
    Secrets of Heaven and secrets of the earth:
    Blind though you are, you know the city lies
    Sick with plague; and from this plague, my lord,
    We find that you alone can guard or save us.

    Possibly you did not hear the messengers?   90
    Apollo, when we sent to him,
    Sent us back word that this great pestilence
    Would lift, but only if we established clearly
    The identity of those who murdered Laïos.
    They must be killed or exiled.
                          Can you use   95
    Birdflight or any art of divination
    To purify yourself, and Thebes, and me
    From this contagion? We are in your hands.
    There is no fairer duty

---

⁶⁰*Choragos:* spokesman for the chorus.

Than that of helping others in distress.   100
Teiresias: How dreadful knowledge of the truth can be
When there's no help in truth! I knew this well,
But did not act on it: else I should not have come.
Oedipus: What is troubling you? Why are your eyes so cold?
Teiresias: Let me go home. Bear your own fate, and I'll   105
Bear mine. It is better so: trust what I say.
Oedipus: What you say is ungracious and unhelpful
To your native country. Do not refuse to speak.
Teiresias: When it comes to speech, your own is neither temperate
Nor opportune. I wish to be more prudent.   110
Oedipus: In God's name, we all beg you —
Teiresias: You are all ignorant.
No; I will never tell you what I know.
Now it is my misery; then, it would be yours.
Oedipus: What! You do know something, and will not tell us?
You would betray us all and wreck the State?   115
Teiresias: I do not intend to torture myself, or you.
Why persist in asking? You will not persuade me.
Oedipus: What a wicked old man you are! You'd try a stone's
Patience! Out with it! Have you no feeling at all?
Teiresias: You call me unfeeling. If you could only see   120
The nature of your own feelings . . .
Oedipus: Why,
Who would not feel as I do? Who could endure
Your arrogance toward the city?
Teiresias: What does it matter!
Whether I speak or not, it is bound to come.
Oedipus: Then, if "it" is bound to come, you are bound to tell me.   125
Teiresias: No, I will not go on. Rage as you please.
Oedipus: Rage? Why not!
                                    And I'll tell you what I think:
You planned it, you had it done, you all but
Killed him with your own hands: if you had eyes,
I'd say the crime was yours, and yours alone.   130
Teiresias: So? I charge you, then,
Abide by the proclamation you have made:
From this day forth
Never speak again to these men or to me;
You yourself are the pollution of this country.   135
Oedipus: You dare say that! Can you possibly think you have
Some way of going free, after such insolence?
Teiresias: I have gone free. It is the truth sustains me.
Oedipus: Who taught you shamelessness? It was not your craft.
Teiresias: You did. You made me speak. I did not want to.   140
Oedipus: Speak what? Let me hear it again more clearly.
Teiresias: Was it not clear before? Are you tempting me?
Oedipus: I did not understand it. Say it again.
Teiresias: I say that you are the murderer whom you seek.

Oedipus: Now twice you have spat out infamy. You'll pay for it! 145
Teiresias: Would you care for more? Do you wish to be really angry?
Oedipus: Say what you will. Whatever you say is worthless.
Teiresias: I say you live in hideous shame with those
    Most dear to you. You can not see the evil.
Oedipus: It seems you can go on mouthing like this for ever. 150
Teiresias: I can, if there is power in truth.
Oedipus: There is:
    But not for you, not for you,
    You sightless, witless, senseless, mad old man!
Teiresias: You are the madman. There is no one here
    Who will not curse you soon, as you curse me. 155
Oedipus: You child of endless night! You can not hurt me
    Or any other man who sees the sun.
Teiresias: True: it is not from me your fate will come.
    That lies within Apollo's competence,
    As it is his concern.
Oedipus: Tell me: 160
    Are you speaking for Creon, or for yourself?
Teiresias: Creon is no threat. You weave your own doom.
Oedipus: Wealth, power, craft of statesmanship!
    Kingly position, everywhere admired!
    What savage envy is stored up against these, 165
    If Creon, whom I trusted, Creon my friend,
    For this great office which the city once
    Put in my hands unsought — if for this power
    Creon desires in secret to destroy me!

    He has brought this decrepit fortune-teller, this 170
    Collector of dirty pennies, this prophet fraud —
    Why, he is no more clairvoyant than I am!
                        Tell us:
    Has your mystic mummery ever approached the truth?
    When that hellcat the Sphinx was performing here,
    What help were you to these people? 175
    Her magic was not for the first man who came along:
    It demanded a real exorcist. Your birds —
    What good were they? or the gods, for the matter of that?
    But I came by,
    Oedipus, the simple man, who knows nothing — 180
    I thought it out for myself, no birds helped me!
    And this is the man you think you can destroy,
    That you may be close to Creon when he's king!
    Well, you and your friend Creon, it seems to me,
    Will suffer most. If you were not an old man, 185
    You would have paid already for your plot.
Choragos: We can not see that his words or yours
    Have been spoken except in anger, Oedipus,
    And of anger we have no need. How can God's will

Be accomplished best? That is what most concerns us.　190
Teiresias: You are a king. But where argument's concerned
　　I am your man, as much a king as you.
　　I am not your servant, but Apollo's.
　　I have no need of Creon to speak for me.

　　Listen to me. You mock my blindness, do you?　195
　　But I say that you, with both your eyes, are blind:
　　You can not see the wretchedness of your life,
　　Nor in whose house you live, no, nor with whom.
　　Who are your father and mother? Can you tell me?
　　You do not even know the blind wrongs　200
　　That you have done them, on earth and in the world below.
　　But the double lash of your parents' curse will whip you
　　Out of this land some day, with only night
　　Upon your precious eyes.
　　Your cries then — where will they not be heard?　205
　　What fastness of Kithairon will not echo them?
　　And that bridal-descant of yours — you'll know it then,
　　The song they sang when you came here to Thebes
　　And found your misguided berthing.
　　All this, and more, that you can not guess at now,　210
　　Will bring you to yourself among your children.

　　Be angry, then. Curse Creon. Curse my words.
　　I tell you, no man that walks upon the earth
　　Shall be rooted out more horribly than you.
Oedipus: Am I to bear this from him? — Damnation　215
　　Take you! Out of this place! Out of my sight!
Teiresias: I would not have come at all if you had not asked me.
Oedipus: Could I have told that you'd talk nonsense, that
　　You'd come here to make a fool of yourself, and of me?
Teiresias: A fool? Your parents thought me sane enough.　220
Oedipus: My parents again! — Wait: who were my parents?
Teiresias: This day will give you a father, and break your heart.
Oedipus: Your infantile riddles! Your damned abracadabra!
Teiresias: You were a great man once at solving riddles.
Oedipus: Mock me with that if you like; you will find it true.　225
Teiresias: It was true enough. It brought about your ruin.
Oedipus: But if it saved this town?
Teiresias (to the Page):　　　　　　　Boy, give me your hand.
Oedipus: Yes, boy; lead him away.
　　　　　　　　　　　　— While you are here
　　We can do nothing. Go; leave us in peace.
Teiresias: I will go when I have said what I have to say.　230
　　How can you hurt me? And I tell you again:
　　The man you have been looking for all this time,
　　The damned man, the murderer of Laïos,
　　That man is in Thebes. To your mind he is foreignborn,
　　But it will soon be shown that he is a Theban,　235

A revelation that will fail to please.
                              A blind man,
Who has his eyes now; a penniless man, who is rich now;
And he will go tapping the strange earth with his staff;
To the children with whom he lives now he will be
Brother and father — the very same; to her   240
Who bore him, son and husband — the very same
Who came to his father's bed, wet with his father's blood.

Enough. Go think that over.
If later you find error in what I have said,
You may say that I have no skill in prophecy.   245

Exit Teiresias, led by his Page. Oedipus goes into the palace.

ODE I°

Strophe 1

Chorus: The Delphic stone of prophecies
        Remembers ancient regicide
        And a still bloody hand.
        That killer's hour of flight has come.
        He must be stronger than riderless   5
        Coursers of untiring wind,
        For the son of Zeus° armed with his father's thunder
        Leaps in lightning after him;
        And the Furies° follow him, the sad Furies.

Antistrophe 1

        Holy Parnassos' peak of snow   10
        Flashes and blinds that secret man,
        That all shall hunt him down:
        Though he may roam the forest shade
        Like a bull gone wild from pasture
        To rage through glooms of stone.   15
        Doom comes down on him; flight will not avail him;
        For the world's heart calls him desolate,
        And the immortal Furies follow, for ever follow.

Strophe 2

        But now a wilder thing is heard
        From the old man skilled at hearing Fate in the wingbeat of a bird.   20
        Bewildered as a blown bird, my soul hovers and can not find
        Foothold in this debate, or any reason or rest of mind.
        But no man ever brought — none can bring

Ode: a choral song. Here again (as in the *parodos*) *strophe* and *antistrophe* probably indicate the movements of a dance.
[7]*son of Zeus:* Apollo.   [9]*Furies:* three horrific female spirits whose task was to seek out and punish evildoers.

Proof of strife between Thebes' royal house,
Labdakos' line,° and the son of Polybos°;   25
And never until now has any man brought word
Of Laïos' dark death staining Oedipus the King.

Divine Zeus and Apollo hold
Perfect intelligence alone of all tales ever told;
And well though this diviner works, he works in his own night;   30
No man can judge that rough unknown or trust in second sight,
For wisdom changes hands among the wise.
Shall I believe my great lord criminal
At a raging word that a blind old man let fall?
I saw him, when the carrion woman faced him of old,   35
Prove his heroic mind! These evil words are lies.

SCENE II

Creon: Men of Thebes:
   I am told that heavy accusations
   Have been brought against me by King Oedipus.

   I am not the kind of man to bear this tamely.

   If in these present difficulties   5
   He holds me accountable for any harm to him
   Through anything I have said or done — why, then,
   I do not value life in this dishonor.
   It is not as though this rumor touched upon
   Some private indiscretion. The matter is grave.   10
   The fact is that I am being called disloyal
   To the State, to my fellow citizens, to my friends.
Choragos: He may have spoken in anger, not from his mind.
Creon: But did you not hear him say I was the one
   Who seduced the old prophet into lying?   15
Choragos: The thing was said; I do not know how seriously.
Creon: But you were watching him! Were his eyes steady?
   Did he look like a man in his right mind?
Choragos: I do not know.
   I can not judge the behavior of great men.
   But here is the King himself.

   Enter Oedipus.

Oedipus: So you dared come back.   20
   Why? How brazen of you to come to my house,

---

²⁵*Labdakos´ line:* descendants of Laïos (true father of Oedipus, although the chorus does not
know it).   ²⁵*Polybos:* king who adopted the child Oedipus.

You murderer!
                    Do you think I do not know
That you plotted to kill me, plotted to steal my throne?
Tell me, in God's name: am I coward, a fool,
That you should dream you could accomplish this?   25
A fool who could not see your slippery game?
A coward, not to fight back when I saw it?
You are the fool, Creon, are you not? hoping
Without support or friends to get a throne?
Thrones may be won or bought: you could do neither.   30
Creon: Now listen to me. You have talked; let me talk, too.
   You can not judge unless you know the facts.
Oedipus: You speak well: there is one fact; but I find it hard
   To learn from the deadliest enemy I have.
Creon: That above all I must dispute with you.   35
Oedipus: That above all I will not hear you deny.
Creon: If you think there is anything good in being stubborn
   Against all reason, then I say you are wrong.
Oedipus: If you think a man can sin against his own kind
   And not be punished for it, I say you are mad.   40
Creon: I agree. But tell me: what have I done to you?
Oedipus: You advised me to send for that wizard, did you not?
Creon: I did. I should do it again.
Oedipus: Very well. Now tell me:
   How long has it been since Laïos —
Creon: What of Laïos?
Oedipus: Since he vanished in that onset by the road?   45
Creon: It was long ago, a long time.
Oedipus: And this prophet,
   Was he practicing here then?
Creon: He was; and with honor, as now.
Oedipus: Did he speak of me at that time?
Creon: He never did;
   At least, not when I was present.
Oedipus: But . . . the enquiry?
   I suppose you held one?
Creon: We did, but we learned nothing.   50
Oedipus: Why did the prophet not speak against me then?
Creon: I do not know; and I am the kind of man
   Who holds his tongue when he has no facts to go on.
Oedipus: There's one fact that you know, and you could tell it.
Creon: What fact is that? If I know it, you shall have it.   55
Oedipus: If he were not involved with you, he could not say
   That it was I who murdered Laïos.
Creon: If he says that, you are the one that knows it! —
   But now it is my turn to question you.
Oedipus: Put your questions. I am no murderer.   60
Creon: First then: You married my sister?
Oedipus: I married your sister.

Creon: And you rule the kingdom equally with her?
Oedipus: Everything that she wants she has from me.
Creon: And I am the third, equal to both of you?
Oedipus: That is why I call you a bad friend. 65
Creon: No. Reason it out, as I have done.
Think of this first. Would any sane man prefer
Power, with all a king's anxieties,
To that same power and the grace of sleep?
Certainly not I. 70
I have never longed for the king's power — only his rights.
Would any wise man differ from me in this?
As matters stand, I have my way in everything
With your consent, and no responsibilities.
If I were king, I should be a slave to policy. 75

How could I desire a scepter more
Than what is now mine — untroubled influence?
No, I have not gone mad; I need no honors,
Except those with the perquisites I have now.
I am welcome everywhere; every man salutes me, 80
And those who want your favor seek my ear,
Since I know how to manage what they ask.
Should I exchange this ease for that anxiety?
Besides, no sober mind is treasonable.
I hate anarchy 85
And never would deal with any man who likes it.

Test what I have said. Go to the priestess
At Delphi, ask if I quoted her correctly.
And as for this other thing: if I am found
Guilty of treason with Teiresias, 90
Then sentence me to death! You have my word
It is a sentence I should cast my vote for —
But not without evidence!
                              You do wrong
When you take good men for bad, bad men for good.
A true friend thrown aside — why, life itself 95
Is not more precious!
                              In time you will know this well:
For time, and time alone, will show the just man,
Though scoundrels are discovered in a day.
Choragos: This is well said, and a prudent man would ponder it.
Judgments too quickly formed are dangerous. 100
Oedipus: But is he not quick in his duplicity?
And shall I not be quick to parry him?
Would you have me stand still, hold my peace, and let
This man win everything, through my inaction?
Creon: And you want — what is it, then? To banish me? 105

Oedipus: No, not exile. It is your death I want,
    So that all the world may see what treason means.
Creon: You will persist, then? You will not believe me?
Oedipus: How can I believe you?
Creon: Then you are a fool.
Oedipus: To save myself?
Creon: In justice, think of me.   110
Oedipus: You are evil incarnate.
Creon: But suppose that you are wrong?
Oedipus: Still I must rule.
Creon: But not if you rule badly.
Oedipus: O city, city!
Creon: It is my city, too!
Choragos: Now, my lords, be still. I see the Queen,
    Iocastê, coming from her palace chambers;   115
    And it is time she came, for the sake of you both.
    This dreadful quarrel can be resolved through her.

    Enter Iocastê.

Iocastê: Poor foolish men, what wicked din is this?
    With Thebes sick to death, is it not shameful
    That you should rake some private quarrel up?   120
    (To Oedipus.) Come into the house.
                        — And you, Creon, go now:
    Let us have no more of this tumult over nothing.
Creon: Nothing? No, sister: what your husband plans for me
    Is one of two great evils: exile or death.
Oedipus: He is right.
               Why, woman, I have caught him squarely   125
    Plotting against my life.
Creon: No! Let me die
    Accurst if ever I have wished you harm!
Iocastê: Ah, believe it, Oedipus!
    In the name of the gods, respect this oath of his
    For my sake, for the sake of these people here!   130

                               Strophe 1
Choragos: Open your mind to her, my lord. Be ruled by her, I beg you!
Oedipus: What would you have me do?
Choragos: Respect Creon's word. He has never spoken like a fool,
    And now he has sworn an oath.
Oedipus: You know what you ask?
Choragos: I do.
Oedipus: Speak on, then.
Choragos: A friend so sworn should not be baited so,   135
    In blind malice, and without final proof.
Oedipus: You are aware, I hope, that what you say
    Means death for me, or exile at the least.

Choragos: No, I swear by Helios, first in Heaven!
    May I die friendless and accurst,   140
  The worst of deaths, if ever I meant that!
    It is the withering fields
      That hurt my sick heart:
    Must we bear all these ills,
      And now your bad blood as well?   145
Oedipus: Then let him go. And let me die, if I must,
  Or be driven by him in shame from the land of Thebes.
  It is your unhappiness, and not his talk,
  That touches me.
            As for him —
  Wherever he is, I will hate him as long as I live.   150
Creon: Ugly in yielding, as you were ugly in rage!
  Natures like yours chiefly torment themselves.
Oedipus: Can you not go? Can you not leave me?
Creon: I can.
  You do not know me; but the city knows me,
  And in its eyes I am just, if not in yours.   155

Exit Creon.

Choragos: Lady Iocastê, did you not ask the King to go to his chambers?
Iocastê: First tell me what has happened.
Choragos: There was suspicion without evidence; yet it rankled
  As even false charges will.
Iocastê: On both sides?
Choragos: On both.
Iocastê: But what was said?
Choragos: Oh let it rest, let it be done with!   160
  Have we not suffered enough?
Oedipus: You see to what your decency has brought you:
  You have made difficulties where my heart saw none.

Choragos: Oedipus, it is not once only I have told you —
  You must know I should count myself unwise   165
  To the point of madness, should I now forsake you —
    You, under whose hand,
      In the storm of another time,
    Our dear land sailed out free.
      But now stand fast at the helm!   170
Iocastê: In God's name, Oedipus, inform your wife as well:
  Why are you so set in this hard anger?
Oedipus: I will tell you, for none of these men deserves
  My confidence as you do. It is Creon's work,
  His treachery, his plotting against me.   175

Iocastê: Go on, if you can make this clear to me.

Oedipus: He charges me with the murder of Laïos.

Iocastê: Has he some knowledge? Or does he speak from hearsay?

Oedipus: He would not commit himself to such a charge,
But he has brought in that damnable soothsayer   180
To tell his story.

Iocastê: Set your mind at rest.
If it is a question of soothsayers, I tell you
That you will find no man whose craft gives knowledge
Of the unknowable.

                              Here is my proof:

An oracle was reported to Laïos once   185
(I will not say from Phoibos himself, but from
His appointed ministers, at any rate)
That his doom would be death at the hands of his own son —
His son, born of his flesh and of mine!

Now, you remember the story: Laïos was killed   190
By marauding strangers where three highways meet;
But his child had not been three days in this world
Before the King had pierced the baby's ankles
And left him to die on a lonely mountainside.

Thus, Apollo never caused that child   195
To kill his father, and it was not Laïos' fate
To die at the hands of his son, as he had feared.
This is what prophets and prophecies are worth!
Have no dread of them.

                              It is God himself
Who can show us what he wills, in his own way.   200

Oedipus: How strange a shadowy memory crossed my mind,
Just now while you were speaking; it chilled my heart.

Iocastê: What do you mean? What memory do you speak of?

Oedipus: If I understand you, Laïos was killed
At a place where three roads meet.

Iocastê: So it was said;   205
We have no later story.

Oedipus: Where did it happen?

Iocastê: Phokis, it is called: at a place where the Theban Way
Divides into the roads toward Delphi and Daulia.

Oedipus: When?

Iocastê: We had the news not long before you came
And proved the right to your succession here.   210

Oedipus: Ah, what net has God been weaving for me?

Iocastê: Oedipus! Why does this trouble you?

Oedipus: Do not ask me yet.
First, tell me how Laïos looked, and tell me
How old he was.

Iocastê: He was tall, his hair just touched
    With white; his form was not unlike your own.   215
Oedipus: I think that I myself may be accurst
    By my own ignorant edict.
Iocastê: You speak strangely.
    It makes me tremble to look at you, my King.
Oedipus: I am not sure that the blind man can not see.
    But I should know better if you were to tell me —   220
Iocastê: Anything — though I dread to hear you ask it.
Oedipus: Was the King lightly escorted, or did he ride
    With a large company, as a ruler should?
Iocastê: There were five men with him in all: one was a herald;
    And a single chariot, which he was driving.   225
Oedipus: Alas, that makes it plain enough!
                                          But who —
    Who told you how it happened?
Iocastê: A household servant,
    The only one to escape.
Oedipus: And is he still
    A servant of ours?
Iocastê: No; for when he came back at last
    And found you enthroned in the place of the dead king,   230
    He came to me, touched my hand with his, and begged
    That I would send him away to the frontier district
    Where only the shepherds go —
    As far away from the city as I could send him.
    I granted his prayer; for although the man was a slave,   235
    He had earned more than this favor at my hands.
Oedipus: Can he be called back quickly?
Iocastê: Easily.
    But why?
Oedipus: I have taken too much upon myself
    Without enquiry; therefore I wish to consult him.
Iocastê: Then he shall come.
                              But am I not one also   240
    To whom you might confide these fears of yours?
Oedipus: That is your right; it will not be denied you,
    Now least of all; for I have reached a pitch
    Of wild foreboding. Is there anyone
    To whom I should sooner speak?   245
    Polybos of Corinth is my father.
    My mother is a Dorian: Meropê.
    I grew up chief among the men of Corinth
    Until a strange thing happened —
    Not worth my passion, it may be, but strange.   250
    At a feast, a drunken man maundering in his cups
    Cries out that I am not my father's son!

    I contained myself that night, though I felt anger

And a sinking heart. The next day I visited
My father and mother, and questioned them. They stormed,   255
Calling it all the slanderous rant of a fool;
And this relieved me. Yet the suspicion
Remained always aching in my mind;
I knew there was talk; I could not rest;
And finally, saying nothing to my parents,   260
I went to the shrine at Delphi.
The god dismissed my question without reply;
He spoke of other things.

                    Some were clear,
Full of wretchedness, dreadful, unbearable:
As, that I should lie with my own mother, breed   265
Children from whom all men would turn their eyes;
And that I should be my father's murderer.

I heard all this, and fled. And from that day
Corinth to me was only in the stars
Descending in that quarter of the sky,   270
As I wandered farther and farther on my way
To a land where I should never see the evil
Sung by the oracle. And I came to this country
Where, so you say, King Laïos was killed.

I will tell you all that happened there, my lady.   275

There were three highways
Coming together at a place I passed;
And there a herald came towards me, and a chariot
Drawn by horses, with a man such as you describe
Seated in it. The groom leading the horses   280
Forced me off the road at his lord's command;
But as this charioteer lurched over towards me
I struck him in my rage. The old man saw me
And brought his double goad down upon my head
As I came abreast.

                  He was paid back, and more!   285
Swinging my club in this right hand I knocked him
Out of his car, and he rolled on the ground.
                         I killed him.

I killed them all.
Now if that stranger and Laïos were — kin,
Where is a man more miserable than I?   290
More hated by the gods? Citizen and alien alike
Must never shelter me or speak to me —
I must be shunned by all.
                And I myself
Pronounced this malediction upon myself!

Think of it: I have touched you with these hands,   295
These hands that killed your husband. What defilement!

Am I all evil, then? It must be so,
Since I must flee from Thebes, yet never again
See my own countrymen, my own country,
For fear of joining my mother in marriage   300
And killing Polybos, my father.
                                          Ah,
If I was created so, born to this fate,
Who could deny the savagery of God?

O holy majesty of heavenly powers!
May I never see that day! Never!   305
Rather let me vanish from the race of men
Than know the abomination destined me!
Choragos: We too, my lord, have felt dismay at this.
    But there is hope: you have yet to hear the shepherd.
Oedipus: Indeed, I fear no other hope is left me.   310
Iocastê: What do you hope from him when he comes?
Oedipus: This much:
    If his account of the murder tallies with yours,
    Then I am cleared.
Iocastê: What was it that I said
    Of such importance?
Oedipus: Why, "marauders," you said,
    Killed the King, according to this man's story.   315
    If he maintains that still, if there were several,
    Clearly the guilt is not mine: I was alone.
    But if he says one man, singlehanded, did it,
    Then the evidence all points to me.
Iocastê: You may be sure that he said there were several;   320
    And can he call back that story now? He can not.
    The whole city heard it as plainly as I.
    But suppose he alters some detail of it:
    He can not ever show that Laïos' death
    Fulfilled the oracle: for Apollo said   325
    My child was doomed to kill him; and my child —
    Poor baby! — it was my child that died first.

No. From now on, where oracles are concerned,
I would not waste a second thought on any.
Oedipus: You may be right.
                                    But come: let someone go   330
For the shepherd at once. This matter must be settled.
Iocastê: I will send for him.
    I would not wish to cross you in anything,
    And surely not in this. — Let us go in.

Exeunt into the palace.

ODE II

Chorus: Let me be reverent in the ways of right,
    Lowly the paths I journey on;
    Let all my words and actions keep
    The laws of the pure universe
    From highest Heaven handed down.   5
    For Heaven is their bright nurse,
    Those generations of the realms of light;
    Ah, never of mortal kind were they begot,
    Nor are they slaves of memory, lost in sleep:
    Their Father is greater than Time, and ages not.   10

Antistrophe 1

    The tyrant is a child of Pride
    Who drinks from his great sickening cup
    Recklessness and vanity,
    Until from his high crest headlong
    He plummets to the dust of hope.   15
    That strong man is not strong.
    But let no fair ambition be denied;
    May God protect the wrestler for the State
    In government, in comely policy,
    Who will fear God, and on His ordinance wait.   20

Strophe 2

    Haughtiness and the high hand of disdain
    Tempt and outrage God's holy law;
    And any mortal who dares hold
    No immortal Power in awe
    Will be caught up in a net of pain: 25
    The price for which his levity is sold.
    Let each man take due earnings, then,
    And keep his hands from holy things,
    And from blasphemy stand apart —
    Else the crackling blast of heaven   30
    Blows on his head, and on his desperate heart;
    Though fools will honor impious men,
    In their cities no tragic poet sings.

Antistrophe 2

    Shall we lose faith in Delphi's obscurities,
    We who have heard the world's core   35
    Discredited, and the sacred wood
    Of Zeus at Elis praised no more?
    The deeds and the strange prophecies
    Must make a pattern yet to be understood.
    Zeus, if indeed you are lord of all,   40
    Throned in light over night and day,

Mirror this in your endless mind:
Our masters call the oracle
Words on the wind, and the Delphic vision blind!
Their hearts no longer know Apollo,   45
And reverence for the gods has died away.

SCENE III

Enter Iocastê.

Iocastê: Princes of Thebes, it has occurred to me
To visit the altars of the gods, bearing
These branches as a suppliant, and this incense.
Our King is not himself: his noble soul
Is overwrought with fantasies of dread,   5
Else he would consider
The new prophecies in the light of the old.
He will listen to any voice that speaks disaster,
And my advice goes for nothing.

She approaches the altar, right.

To you, then, Apollo,
Lycean lord, since you are nearest, I turn in prayer.   10
Receive these offerings, and grant us deliverance
From defilement. Our hearts are heavy with fear
When we see our leader distracted, as helpless sailors
Are terrified by the confusion of their helmsman.

Enter Messenger.

Messenger: Friends, no doubt you can direct me: 15
Where shall I find the house of Oedipus,
Or, better still, where is the King himself?
Choragos: It is this very place, stranger; he is inside.
This is his wife and mother of his children.
Messenger: I wish her happiness in a happy house,   20
Blest in all the fulfillment of her marriage.
Iocastê: I wish as much for you: your courtesy
Deserves a like good fortune. But now, tell me:
Why have you come? What have you to say to us?
Messenger: Good news, my lady, for your house and your husband. 25
Iocastê: What news? Who sent you here?
Messenger: I am from Corinth.
The news I bring ought to mean joy for you,
Though it may be you will find some grief in it.
Iocastê: What is it? How can it touch us in both ways?
Messenger: The people of Corinth, they say,   30
Intend to call Oedipus to be their king.
Iocastê: But old Polybos — is he not reigning still?

Messenger: No. Death holds him in his sepulchre.

Iocastê: What are you saying? Polybos is dead?

Messenger: If I am not telling the truth, may I die myself.   35

Iocastê (to a Maidservant): Go in, go quickly; tell this to your master.

O riddlers of God's will, where are you now!
This was the man whom Oedipus, long ago,
Feared so, fled so, in dread of destroying him —
But it was another fate by which he died.   40

Enter Oedipus, center.

Oedipus: Dearest Iocastê, why have you sent for me?

Iocastê: Listen to what this man says, and then tell me
   What has become of the solemn prophecies.

Oedipus: Who is this man? What is his news for me?

Iocastê: He has come from Corinth to announce your father's death!   45

Oedipus: Is it true, stranger? Tell me in your own words.

Messenger: I can not say it more clearly: the King is dead.

Oedipus: Was it by treason? Or by an attack of illness?

Messenger: A little thing brings old men to their rest.

Oedipus: It was sickness, then?

Messenger: Yes, and his many years.   50

Oedipus: Ah!
   Why should a man respect the Pythian hearth°, or
   Give heed to the birds that jangle above his head?
   They prophesied that I should kill Polybos,
   Kill my own father; but he is dead and buried,   55
   And I am here — I never touched him, never,
   Unless he died of grief for my departure,
   And thus, in a sense, through me. No. Polybos
   Has packed the oracles off with him underground.
   They are empty words.

Iocastê: Had I not told you so?   60

Oedipus: You had; it was my faint heart that betrayed me.

Iocastê: From now on never think of those things again.

Oedipus: And yet — must I not fear my mother's bed?

Iocastê: Why should anyone in this world be afraid,
   Since Fate rules us and nothing can be foreseen?   65
   A man should live only for the present day.

   Have no more fear of sleeping with your mother:
   How many men, in dreams, have lain with their mothers!
   No reasonable man is troubled by such things.

Oedipus: That is true; only —   70
   If only my mother were not still alive!
   But she is alive. I can not help my dread.

Iocastê: Yet this news of your father's death is wonderful.

52*Pythian hearth:* the shrine at Delphi, whose priestess was famous for her prophecies.

Oedipus: Wonderful. But I fear the living woman.
Messenger: Tell me, who is this woman that you fear? 75
Oedipus: It is Meropê, man; the wife of King Polybos.
Messenger: Meropê? Why should you be afraid of her?
Oedipus: An oracle of the gods, a dreadful saying.
Messenger: Can you tell me about it or are you sworn to silence?
Oedipus: I can tell you, and I will. 80

    Apollo said through his prophet that I was the man
    Who should marry his own mother, shed his father's blood
    With his own hands. And so, for all these years
    I have kept clear of Corinth, and no harm has come —
    Though it would have been sweet to see my parents again. 85
Messenger: And is this the fear that drove you out of Corinth?
Oedipus: Would you have me kill my father?
Messenger: As for that
    You must be reassured by the news I gave you.
Oedipus: If you could reassure me, I would reward you.
Messenger: I had that in mind, I will confess: I thought 90
    I could count on you when you returned to Corinth.
Oedipus: No: I will never go near my parents again.
Messenger: Ah, son, you still do not know what you are doing —
Oedipus: What do you mean? In the name of God tell me!
Messenger: — If these are your reasons for not going home. 95
Oedipus: I tell you, I fear the oracle may come true.
Messenger: And guilt may come upon you through your parents?
Oedipus: That is the dread that is always in my heart.
Messenger: Can you not see that all your fears are groundless?
Oedipus: How can you say that? They are my parents, surely? 100
Messenger: Polybos was not your father.
Oedipus: Not my father?
Messenger: No more your father than the man speaking to you.
Oedipus: But you are nothing to me!
Messenger: Neither was he.
Oedipus: Then why did he call me son?
Messenger: I will tell you:
    Long ago he had you from my hands, as a gift. 105
Oedipus: Then how could he love me so, if I was not his?
Messenger: He had no children, and his heart turned to you.
Oedipus: What of you? Did you buy me? Did you find me by chance?
Messenger: I came upon you in the crooked pass of Kithairon.
Oedipus: And what were you doing there?
Messenger: Tending my flocks. 110
Oedipus: A wandering shepherd?
Messenger: But your savior, son, that day.
Oedipus: From what did you save me?
Messenger: Your ankles should tell you that.
Oedipus: Ah, stranger, why do you speak of that childhood pain?
Messenger: I cut the bonds that tied your ankles together.
Oedipus: I have had the mark as long as I can remember. 115

Messenger: That was why you were given the name you bear.

Oedipus: God! Was it my father or my mother who did it?
     Tell me!

Messenger: I do not know. The man who gave you to me
     Can tell you better than I.   120

Oedipus: It was not you that found me, but another?

Messenger: It was another shepherd gave you to me.

Oedipus: Who was he? Can you tell me who he was?

Messenger: I think he was said to be one of Laïos' people.

Oedipus: You mean the Laïos who was king here years ago?   125

Messenger: Yes; King Laïos; and the man was one of his herdsmen.

Oedipus: Is he still alive? Can I see him?

Messenger: These men here
     Know best about such things.

Oedipus: Does anyone here
     Know this shepherd that he is talking about?
     Have you seen him in the fields, or in the town?   130
     If you have, tell me. It is time things were made plain.

Choragos: I think the man he means is that same shepherd
     You have already asked to see. Iocastê perhaps
     Could tell you something.

Oedipus: Do you know anything
     About him, Lady? Is he the man we have summoned?   135
     Is that the man this shepherd means?

Iocastê: Why think of him?
     Forget this herdsman. Forget it all.
     This talk is a waste of time.

Oedipus: How can you say that,
     When the clues to my true birth are in my hands?

Iocastê: For God's love, let us have no more questioning!   140
     Is your life nothing to you?
     My own is pain enough for me to bear.

Oedipus: You need not worry. Suppose my mother a slave,
     And born of slaves: no baseness can touch you.

Iocastê: Listen to me, I beg you: do not do this thing!   145

Oedipus: I will not listen; the truth must be made known.

Iocastê: Everything that I say is for your own good!

Oedipus: My own good
     Snaps my patience, then; I want none of it.

Iocastê: You are fatally wrong! May you never learn who you are!

Oedipus: Go, one of you, and bring the shepherd here.   150
     Let us leave this woman to brag of her royal name.

Iocastê: Ah, miserable!
     That is the only word I have for you now.
     That is the only word I can ever have.

     Exit into the palace.

Choragos: Why has she left us, Oedipus? Why has she gone   155
     In such a passion of sorrow? I fear this silence:

Something dreadful may come of it.

Oedipus: Let it come!
   However base my birth, I must know about it.
   The Queen, like a woman, is perhaps ashamed
   To think of my low origin. But I   160
   Am a child of Luck; I can not be dishonored.
   Luck is my mother; the passing months, my brothers,
   Have seen me rich and poor.
                              If this is so,
   How could I wish that I were someone else?
   How could I not be glad to know my birth?   165

ODE III

                                                            Strophe

Chorus: If ever the coming time were known
      To my heart's pondering,
      Kithairon, now by Heaven I see the torches
      At the festival of the next full moon,
      And see the dance, and hear the choir sing   5
      A grace to your gentle shade:
      Mountain where Oedipus was found,
      O mountain guard of a noble race!
      May the god who heals us lend his aid,
      And let that glory come to pass   10
      For our king's cradling-ground.

                                                       Antistrophe

      Of the nymphs that flower beyond the years,
      Who bore you, royal child,
      To Pan of the hills or the timberline Apollo,
      Cold in delight where the upland clears,   15
      Or Hermês for whom Kyllenê's° heights are piled?
      Or flushed as evening cloud,
      Great Dionysos, roamer of mountains,
      He — was it he who found you there,
      And caught you up in his own proud   20
      Arms from the sweet god-ravisher
      Who laughed by the Muses' fountains?

SCENE IV

Oedipus: Sirs: though I do not know the man,
      I think I see him coming, this shepherd we want:

¹⁶*Kyllenê:* a sacred mountain, birthplace of Hermês, the deities' messenger. The chorus assumes that the mountain was created in order to afford him birth.

He is old, like our friend here, and the men
Bringing him seem to be servants of my house.
But you can tell, if you have ever seen him.   5

Enter Shepherd escorted by servants.

Choragos: I know him, he was Laïos' man. You can trust him.
Oedipus: Tell me first, you from Corinth: is this the shepherd
　　We were discussing?
Messenger:　　　　　　This is the very man.
Oedipus (to Shepherd): Come here. No, look at me. You must answer
　　Everything I ask. — You belonged to Laïos?   10
Shepherd: Yes: born his slave, brought up in his house.
Oedipus: Tell me: what kind of work did you do for him?
Shepherd: I was a shepherd of his, most of my life.
Oedipus: Where mainly did you go for pasturage?
Shepherd: Sometimes Kithairon, sometimes the hills near-by.   15
Oedipus: Do you remember ever seeing this man out there?
Shepherd: What would he be doing there? This man?
Oedipus: This man standing here. Have you ever seen him before?
Shepherd: No. At least, not to my recollection.
Messenger: And that is not strange, my lord. But I'll refresh   20
　　His memory: he must remember when we two
　　Spent three whole seasons together, March to September,
　　On Kithairon or thereabouts. He had two flocks;
　　I had one. Each autumn I'd drive mine home
　　And he would go back with his to Laïos' sheepfold. —   25
　　Is this not true, just as I have described it?
Shepherd: True, yes; but it was all so long ago.
Messenger: Well, then: do you remember, back in those days
　　That you gave me a baby boy to bring up as my own?
Shepherd: What if I did? What are you trying to say?   30
Messenger: King Oedipus was once that little child.
Shepherd: Damn you, hold your tongue!
Oedipus:　　　　　　　　　　　　　No more of that!
　　It is your tongue needs watching, not this man's.
Shepherd: My King, my Master, what is it I have done wrong?
Oedipus: You have not answered his question about the boy.   35
Shepherd: He does not know . . . He is only making trouble . . .
Oedipus: Come, speak plainly, or it will go hard with you.
Shepherd: In God's name, do not torture an old man!
Oedipus: Come here, one of you; bind his arms behind him.
Shepherd: Unhappy king! What more do you wish to learn?   40
Oedipus: Did you give this man the child he speaks of?
Shepherd:　　　　　　　　　　　　　　　　I did.
　　And I would to God I had died that very day.
Oedipus: You will die now unless you speak the truth.
Shepherd: Yet if I speak the truth, I am worse than dead.
Oedipus: Very well; since you insist upon delaying —   45
Shepherd: No! I have told you already that I gave him the boy.

Oedipus: Where did you get him? From your house? From somewhere
        else?
Shepherd: Not from mine, no. A man gave him to me.
Oedipus: Is that man here? Do you know whose slave he was?
Shepherd: For God's love, my King, do not ask me any more!   50
Oedipus: You are a dead man if I have to ask you again.
Shepherd: Then . . . Then the child was from the palace of Laïos.
Oedipus: A slave child? or a child of his own line?
Shepherd: Ah, I am on the brink of dreadful speech!
Oedipus: And I of dreadful hearing. Yet I must hear.   55
Shepherd: If you must be told, then . . .

                  They said it was Laïos' child,
But it is your wife who can tell you about that.
Oedipus: My wife! — Did she give it to you?
Shepherd: My lord, she did.
Oedipus: Do you know why?
Shepherd: I was told to get rid of it.
Oedipus: An unspeakable mother!
Shepherd: There had been prophecies . . .   60
Oedipus: Tell me.
Shepherd: It was said that the boy would kill his own father.
Oedipus: Then why did you give him over to this old man?
Shepherd: I pitied the baby, my King,
And I thought that this man would take him far away
To his own country.

             He saved him — but for what a fate!   65
For if you are what this man says you are,
No man living is more wretched than Oedipus.
Oedipus: Ah God!
    It was true!
          All the prophecies!
                      — Now,
O Light, may I look on you for the last time!   70
I, Oedipus,
Oedipus, damned in his birth, in his marriage damned,
Damned in the blood he shed with his own hand!

He rushes into the palace.

ODE IV

                                            Strophe 1

Chorus: Alas for the seed of men.

What measure shall I give these generations
That breathe on the void and are void
And exist and do not exist?

Who bears more weight of joy 5
Than mass of sunlight shifting in images,
Or who shall make his thought stay on
That down time drifts away?

Your splendor is all fallen.

O naked brow of wrath and tears, 10
O change of Oedipus!
I who say your days call no man blest —
Your great days like ghosts gone.

Antistrophe 1

That mind was a strong bow.
Deep, how deep you drew it then, hard archer, 15
At a dim fearful range,
And brought dear glory down!

You overcame the stranger —
The virgin with her hooking lion claws —
And though death sang, stood like a tower 20
To make pale Thebes take heart.

Fortress against our sorrow!

Divine king, giver of laws,
Majestic Oedipus!
No prince in Thebes had ever such renown, 25
No prince won such grace of power.

Strophe 2

And now of all men ever known
Most pitiful is this man's story:
His fortunes are most changed, his state
Fallen to a low slave's 30
Ground under bitter fate.

O Oedipus, most royal one!
The great door that expelled you to the light
Gave at night — ah, gave night to your glory:
As to the father, to the fathering son. 35

All understood too late.

How could that queen whom Laïos won,
The garden that he harrowed at his height,
Be silent when that act was done?

But all eyes fail before time's eye,   40
All actions come to justice there.
Though never willed, though far down the deep past,
Your bed, your dread sirings,
Are brought to book at last.
Child by Laïos doomed to die,   45
Then doomed to lose that fortunate little death,
Would God you never took breath in this air
That with my wailing lips I take to cry:

For I weep the world's outcast.

I was blind, and now I can tell why: 50
Asleep, for you had given ease of breath
To Thebes, while the false years went by.

EXODOS°

   Enter, from the palace, Second Messenger.

Second Messenger: Elders of Thebes, most honored in this land,
   What horrors are yours to see and hear, what weight
   Of sorrow to be endured, if, true to your birth,
   You venerate the line of Labdakos!
   I think neither Istros nor Phasis, those great rivers,   5
   Could purify this place of the corruption
   It shelters now, or soon must bring to light —
   Evil not done unconsciously, but willed.

   The greatest griefs are those we cause ourselves.
Choragos: Surely, friend, we have grief enough already;   10
   What new sorrow do you mean?
Second Messenger: The Queen is dead.
Choragos: Iocastê? Dead? But at whose hand?
Second Messenger: Her own.
   The full horror of what happened, you can not know,
   For you did not see it; but I, who did, will tell you
   As clearly as I can how she met her death.   15

   When she had left us,
   In passionate silence, passing through the court,
   She ran to her apartment in the house,
   Her hair clutched by the fingers of both hands.
   She closed the doors behind her; then, by that bed   20
   Where long ago the fatal son was conceived —

Exodos: final scene, containing the resolution.

That son who should bring about his father's death —
We heard her call upon Laïos, dead so many years,
And heard her wail for the double fruit of her marriage,
A husband by her husband, children by her child.   25

Exactly how she died I do not know:
For Oedipus burst in moaning and would not let us
Keep vigil to the end: it was by him
As he stormed about the room that our eyes were caught.
From one to another of us he went, begging a sword,   30
Cursing the wife who was not his wife, the mother
Whose womb had carried his own children and himself.
I do not know: it was none of us aided him,
But surely one of the gods was in control!
For with a dreadful cry   35
He hurled his weight, as though wrenched out of himself,
At the twin doors: the bolts gave, and he rushed in.
And there we saw her hanging, her body swaying
From the cruel cord she had noosed about her neck.
A great sob broke from him, heartbreaking to hear,   40
As he loosed the rope and lowered her to the ground.

I would blot out from my mind what happened next!
For the King ripped from her gown the golden brooches
That were her ornament, and raised them, and plunged them down
Straight into his own eyeballs, crying, "No more,   45
No more shall you look on the misery about me,
The horrors of my own doing! Too long you have known
The faces of those whom I should never have seen,
Too long been blind to those for whom I was searching!
From this hour, go in darkness!" And as he spoke,   50
He struck at his eyes — not once, but many times;
And the blood spattered his beard,
Bursting from his ruined sockets like red hail.
So from the unhappiness of two this evil has sprung,
A curse on the man and woman alike. The old   55
Happiness of the house of Labdakos
Was happiness enough: where is it today?
It is all wailing and ruin, disgrace, death — all
The misery of mankind that has a name —
And it is wholly and for ever theirs.   60
Choragos: Is he in agony still? Is there no rest for him?
Second Messenger: He is calling for someone to lead him to the gates
So that all the children of Kadmos may look upon
His father's murderer, his mother's — no,
I can not say it!
                    And then he will leave Thebes,   65
Self-exiled, in order that the curse
Which he himself pronounced may depart from the house.

He is weak, and there is none to lead him,
So terrible is his suffering.
                              But you will see:
Look, the doors are opening; in a moment   70
You will see a thing that would crush a heart of stone.

The central door is opened; Oedipus, blinded, is led in.

Choragos: Dreadful indeed for men to see.
    Never have my own eyes
    Looked on a sight so full of fear.

    Oedipus!   75
    What madness came upon you, what daemon
    Leaped on your life with heavier
    Punishment than a mortal man can bear?
    No: I can not even
    Look at you, poor ruined one.   80
    And I would speak, question, ponder,
    If I were able. No.
    You make me shudder.
Oedipus: God. God.
    Is there a sorrow greater?   85
    Where shall I find harbor in this world?
    My voice is hurled far on a dark wind.
    What has God done to me?
Choragos: Too terrible to think of, or to see.

                                         Strophe 1

Oedipus: O cloud of night,   90
    Never to be turned away: night coming on,
    I can not tell how: night like a shroud!

    My fair winds brought me here.
                              Oh God. Again
    The pain of the spikes where I had sight,
    The flooding pain   95
    Of memory, never to be gouged out.
Choragos: This is not strange.
    You suffer it all twice over, remorse in pain,
    Pain in remorse.

                                      Antistrophe 1

Oedipus: Ah dear friend   100
    Are you faithful even yet, you alone?
    Are you still standing near me, will you stay here,
    Patient, to care for the blind?
                              The blind man!
    Yet even blind I know who it is attends me,
    By the voice's tone —   105

Though my new darkness hide the comforter.
Choragos: Oh fearful act!
  What god was it drove you to rake black
  Night across your eyes?

Strophe 2

Oedipus: Apollo. Apollo. Dear   110
  Children, the god was Apollo.
  He brought my sick, sick fate upon me.
  But the blinding hand was my own!
  How could I bear to see
  When all my sight was horror everywhere?   115
Choragos: Everywhere; that is true.
Oedipus: And now what is left?
  Images? Love? A greeting even,
  Sweet to the senses? Is there anything?
  Ah, no, friends: lead me away.   120
  Lead me away from Thebes.
                        Lead the great wreck
  And hell of Oedipus, whom the gods hate.
Choragos: Your fate is clear, you are not blind to that.
  Would God you had never found it out!

Antistrophe 2

Oedipus: Death take the man who unbound   125
  My feet on that hillside
  And delivered me from death to life! What life?
  If only I had died,
  This weight of monstrous doom
  Could not have dragged me and my darlings down.   130
Choragos: I would have wished the same.
Oedipus: Oh never to have come here
  With my father's blood upon me! Never
  To have been the man they call his mother's husband!
  Oh accurst! Oh child of evil,   135
  To have entered that wretched bed —
                        the selfsame one!
  More primal than sin itself, this fell to me.
Choragos: I do not know how I can answer you.
  You were better dead than alive and blind.
Oedipus: Do not counsel me any more. This punishment   140
  That I have laid upon myself is just.
  If I had eyes,
  I do not know how I could bear the sight
  Of my father, when I came to the house of Death,
  Or my mother: for I have sinned against them both   145
  So vilely that I could not make my peace
  By strangling my own life.
                  Or do you think my children,

Born as they were born, would be sweet to my eyes?
Ah never, never! Nor this town with its high walls,
Nor the holy images of the gods.
                              For I,   150
Thrice miserable! — Oedipus, noblest of all the line
Of Kadmos, have condemned myself to enjoy
These things no more, by my own malediction
Expelling that man whom the gods declared
To be a defilement in the house of Laïos.   155
After exposing the rankness of my own guilt,
How could I look men frankly in the eyes?
No, I swear it,
If I could have stifled my hearing at its source,
I would have done it and made all this body   160
A tight cell of misery, blank to light and sound:
So I should have been safe in a dark agony
Beyond all recollection.
                        Ah Kithairon!
Why did you shelter me? When I was cast upon you,
Why did I not die? Then I should never   165
Have shown the world my execrable birth.

Ah Polybos! Corinth, city that I believed
The ancient seat of my ancestors: how fair
I seemed, your child! And all the while this evil
Was cancerous within me!
                        For I am sick   170
In my daily life, sick in my origin.

O three roads, dark ravine, woodland and way
Where three roads met: you, drinking my father's blood,
My own blood, spilled by my own hand: can you remember
The unspeakable things I did there, and the things   175
I went on from there to do?
                        O marriage, marriage!
The act that engendered me, and again the act
Performed by the son in the same bed —
                                      Ah, the net
Of incest, mingling fathers, brothers, sons,
With brides, wives, mothers: the last evil   180
That can be known by men: no tongue can say
How evil!
        No. For the love of God, conceal me
Somewhere far from Thebes; or kill me; or hurl me
Into the sea, away from men's eyes for ever.

Come, lead me. You need not fear to touch me.   185
Of all men, I alone can bear this guilt.

Enter Creon.

Choragos: We are not the ones to decide; but Creon here
    May fitly judge of what you ask. He only
    Is left to protect the city in your place.
Oedipus: Alas, how can I speak to him? What right have I   190
    To beg his courtesy whom I have deeply wronged?
Creon: I have not come to mock you, Oedipus,
    Or to reproach you, either.
    (To Attendants.)   — You, standing there:
    If you have lost all respect for man's dignity,
    At least respect the flame of Lord Helios: 195
    Do not allow this pollution to show itself
    Openly here, an affront to the earth
    And Heaven's rain and the light of day. No, take him
    Into the house as quickly as you can.
    For it is proper   200
    That only the close kindred see his grief.
Oedipus: I pray you in God's name, since your courtesy
    Ignores my dark expectation, visiting
    With mercy this man of all men most execrable:
    Give me what I ask — for your good, not for mine.   205
Creon: And what is it that you would have me do?
Oedipus: Drive me out of this country as quickly as may be
    To a place where no human voice can ever greet me.
Creon: I should have done that before now — only,
    God's will had not been wholly revealed to me.   210
Oedipus: But his command is plain: the parricide
    Must be destroyed. I am that evil man.
Creon: That is the sense of it, yes; but as things are,
    We had best discover clearly what is to be done.
Oedipus: You would learn more about a man like me?   215
Creon: You are ready now to listen to the god.
Oedipus: I will listen. But it is to you
    That I must turn for help. I beg you, hear me.

    The woman in there —
    Give her whatever funeral you think proper: 220
    She is your sister.
                  — But let me go, Creon!
    Let me purge my father's Thebes of the pollution
    Of my living here, and go out to the wild hills,
    To Kithairon, that has won such fame with me,
    The tomb my mother and father appointed for me,   225
    And let me die there, as they willed I should.
    And yet I know
    Death will not ever come to me through sickness
    Or in any natural way: I have been preserved

For some unthinkable fate. But let that be.   230
As for my sons, you need not care for them.
They are men, they will find some way to live.
But my poor daughters, who have shared my table,
Who never before have been parted from their father —
Take care of them, Creon; do this for me.   235
And will you let me touch them with my hands
A last time, and let us weep together?
Be kind, my lord,
Great prince, be kind!
                    Could I but touch them,
They would be mine again, as when I had my eyes.   240

Enter Antigonê and Ismene, attended.

Ah, God!
Is it my dearest children I hear weeping?
Has Creon pitied me and sent my daughters?
Creon: Yes, Oedipus: I knew that they were dear to you
In the old days, and know you must love them still.   245
Oedipus: May God bless you for this — and be a friendlier
Guardian to you than he has been to me!

Children, where are you?
Come quickly to my hands: they are your brother's —
Hands that have brought your father's once clear eyes   250
To this way of seeing —
                    Ah dearest ones,
I had neither sight nor knowledge then, your father
By the woman who was the source of his own life!
And I weep for you — having no strength to see you —
I weep for you when I think of the bitterness   255
That men will visit upon you all your lives.
What homes, what festivals can you attend
Without being forced to depart again in tears?
And when you come to marriageable age,
Where is the man, my daughters, who would dare   260
Risk the bane that lies on all my children?
Is there any evil wanting? Your father killed
His father; sowed the womb of her who bore him;
Engendered you at the fount of his own existence!
That is what they will say of you.
                              Then, whom   265
Can you ever marry? There are no bridegrooms for you,
And your lives must wither away in sterile dreaming.
O Creon, son of Menoikeus!
You are the only father my daughters have,
Since we, their parents, are both of us gone for ever.   270
They are your own blood: you will not let them

Fall into beggary and loneliness;
You will keep them from the miseries that are mine!
Take pity on them; see, they are only children,
Friendless except for you. Promise me this,   275
Great Prince, and give me your hand in token of it.

Creon clasps his right hand.

Children:
I could say much, if you could understand me,
But as it is, I have only this prayer for you:
Live where you can, be as happy as you can —   280
Happier, please God, than God has made your father!
Creon: Enough. You have wept enough. Now go within.
Oedipus: I must; but it is hard.
Creon: Time eases all things.
Oedipus: But you must promise —
Creon: Say what you desire.
Oedipus: Send me from Thebes!
Creon: God grant that I may!   285
Oedipus: But since God hates me . . .
Creon: No, he will grant your wish.
Oedipus: You promise?
Creon: I can not speak beyond my knowledge.
Oedipus: Then lead me in.
Creon: Come now, and leave your children.
Oedipus: No! Do not take them from me!
Creon: Think no longer
That you are in command here, but rather think   290
How, when you were, you served your own destruction.

*Exeunt into the house all but the Chorus; the Choragos chants directly to the
audience.*

Choragos: Men of Thebes: look upon Oedipus.

This is the king who solved the famous riddle
And towered up, most powerful of men.
No mortal eyes but looked on him with envy,   295
Yet in the end ruin swept over him.
Let every man in mankind's frailty
Consider his last day; and let none
Presume on his good fortune until he find
Life, at his death, a memory without pain.   300

QUESTIONS

1. In Scene I, how explicitly does the prophet Teiresias reveal the guilt of Oedipus?
   Does it seem to you stupidity on the part of Oedipus, or a defect in Sophocles'
   play, that the king takes so long to recognize his guilt and to admit to it?

2. How does Oedipus exhibit weakness of character? Point to scenes that reveal him as imperfectly noble in his words, deeds, or treatment of others.

3. "Oedipus is punished not for any fault in himself, but for his ignorance. Not knowing his family history, unable to recognize his parents on sight, he is blameless; and in slaying his father and marrying his mother, he behaves as any sensible person might behave in the same circumstances." Do you agree with this interpretation?

4. Besides the predictions of Teiresias, what other foreshadowings of the shepherd's revelation does the play contain?

5. Consider the character of Iocastê. Is she a "flat" character — a generalized queen figure — or an individual with distinctive traits of personality? Point to speeches or details in the play to back up your opinion.

6. Do the choral interludes merely interrupt the play with wordy poetry? Other than providing song, dance, and variety, do they have any value to the telling of the story?

7. What is dramatic irony? Besides the example given on page 433, what other instances of dramatic irony do you find in *Oedipus Rex*? What do they contribute to the effectiveness of the play?

8. In the drama of Sophocles, violence and bloodshed take place offstage; thus, the suicide of Iocastê is only reported to us. Nor do we witness Oedipus' removal of his eyes; this horror is only given in the report by the second messenger. Of what advantage or disadvantage to the play is this limitation?

9. For what reason does Oedipus blind himself? What meaning, if any, do you find in his choice of a surgical instrument?

10. What are your feelings toward him as the play ends?

11. Read the famous interpretation of this play offered by Sigmund Freud (page 1319). How well does Freud explain why the play moves you?

12. With what attitude toward the gods does the play leave you? By inflicting a plague upon Thebes, by causing barrenness, by cursing both the people and their king, do the gods seem cruel, unjust, or tyrannical? Does the play show any reverence toward them?

13. Does this play end in total gloom?

14. How readily adaptable to the contemporary stage does *Oedipus Rex* seem? Suppose you were to stage a production of the play with the aim of making it come alive for the playgoer today. What problems would you encounter? How would you deal with them?

In a great tragedy, we sense some overpowering force at work, closing in steadily upon the protagonist. Few spectators of *Oedipus Rex* wonder how the play will turn out, or ask themselves whether it will all end happily. French playwright Jean Anouilh remarks,

> In a tragedy, nothing is in doubt and everyone's destiny is known. That makes for tranquility. There is a sort of fellow-feeling among characters in a tragedy: he who kills is as innocent as he who gets killed: it's all a matter of what part you are playing. Tragedy is restful; and the reason is that hope, that foul, deceitful thing, has no part in it. There isn't any hope. You're trapped. The whole sky has fallen on you, and all you can do about it is shout.[2]

[2]*Antigone,* translated by Lewis Galantière (New York: Random, 1946).

Aristotle, in describing the workings of this inexorable force in *Oedipus Rex,* uses terms that later critics have found valuable. One is **recognition** or discovery *(anagnorisis):* the revelation of some fact not known before, or some person's true identity. Oedipus makes such a discovery: he recognizes that he himself was the child whom his mother had given over to be destroyed. Such a recognition also occurs in Shakespeare's *Macbeth* when Macduff reveals himself to have been "from his mother's womb / Untimely ripped," thus disclosing a double meaning in the witches' prophecy that Macbeth could be harmed by "none of woman born," and sweeping aside Macbeth's last shred of belief that he is infallible. Modern critics have taken the term to mean also the terrible enlightenment that accompanies such a recognition. "To see things plain — that is *anagnorisis,*" Clifford Leech observes, "and it is the ultimate experience we shall have if we have leisure at the point of death. . . . It is what tragedy ultimately is about: the realization of the unthinkable."[3]

Having made his discovery, Oedipus suffers a reversal in his fortunes: he goes off into exile, blinded and dethroned. Such a fall from happiness seems intrinsic to tragedy, but we should know that Aristotle has a more particular meaning for his term **reversal** *(peripeteia,* anglicized as **peripety**). He means an action that turns out to have the opposite effect from the one its doer had intended. One of his illustrations of such an ironic reversal is from *Oedipus Rex:* the first messenger intends to cheer Oedipus with the partially good news that, contrary to the prophecy that Oedipus would kill his father, his father has died of old age. The reversal is in the fact that, when the messenger further reveals that old Polybos was Oedipus' father only by adoption, the king, instead of having his fears allayed, is stirred to new dread.

We are not altogether sorry, perhaps, to see an arrogant man such as Oedipus humbled, and yet it is difficult not to feel that the punishment of Oedipus is greater than he deserves. Possibly this feeling is what Aristotle meant in his observation that a tragedy arouses our pity and our fear: our compassion for Oedipus, and our terror as we sense the remorselessness of a universe in which a man is doomed.

Notice, however, that at the end of the play Oedipus does not curse God and die. Although such a complex play is open to many interpretations, it is probably safe to say that the play is not a bitter complaint against the universe. At last, Oedipus accepts the divine will, prays for blessings upon his children, and prepares to endure his exile — fallen from high estate, but uplifted in moral dignity.

Since the time of Sophocles, tragedy has been shaped by different theatrical conventions and by different philosophies. Still, some of the tragedies of Shakespeare resemble the tragedies of Sophocles in several

[3] *Tragedy* (London: Methuen, 1969) 65.

ways. Othello, like Oedipus, is a person of high estate: "a noble and valiant general." Another resemblance: *Othello,* like *Oedipus Rex,* conveys a sense that we are watching the inevitable.

THE THEATER OF SHAKESPEARE

Compared with the technical resources of a theater of today, those of a London public theater in the time of Queen Elizabeth I seem hopelessly limited. Plays had to be performed by daylight and scenery had to be kept simple: a table, a chair, a throne, perhaps an artificial tree or two to suggest a forest. But these limitations were in a sense advantages. What the theater of today can spell out for us realistically, with massive scenery and electric lighting, Elizabethan playgoers had to imagine and the playwright had to make vivid for them by means of language. Not having a lighting technician to work a panel, Shakespeare had to indicate the dawn by having Horatio, in *Hamlet,* say in a speech rich in metaphor and descriptive detail:

> But look, the morn in russet mantle clad
> Walks o'er the dew of yon high eastward hill.

And yet the theater of Shakespeare was not bare, for the playwright did have *some* valuable technical resources. Costumes could be elaborate, and apparently some costumes conveyed recognized meanings: one theater manager's inventory included "a robe for to go invisible in." There could be musical accompaniment and sound effects such as gunpowder explosions and the beating of a pan to simulate thunder.

The stage itself was remarkably versatile. At its back were doors for exits and entrances and a curtained booth or alcove useful for hiding inside. Above the stage was a higher acting area — perhaps a porch or balcony — useful for a Juliet to stand upon and for a Romeo to raise his eyes to. And in the stage floor was a trapdoor leading to a "hell" or cellar, especially useful for ghosts or devils who had to appear or disappear. The stage itself was a rectangular platform that projected into a yard enclosed by three-storied galleries.

The building was round or octagonal: in *Henry V,* Shakespeare calls it a "wooden O." The audience sat in these galleries or else stood in the yard in front of the stage and at its sides. A roof or awning protected the stage and the high-priced gallery seats, but in a sudden rain, the *groundlings,* who paid a penny to stand in the yard, must have been dampened.

Built by the theatrical company to which Shakespeare belonged, the Globe, most celebrated of Elizabethan theaters, was not in the city of London itself but on the south bank of the Thames River. This location had been chosen because earlier, in 1574, public plays had been banished from the city by an ordinance that blamed them for "corruptions of youth

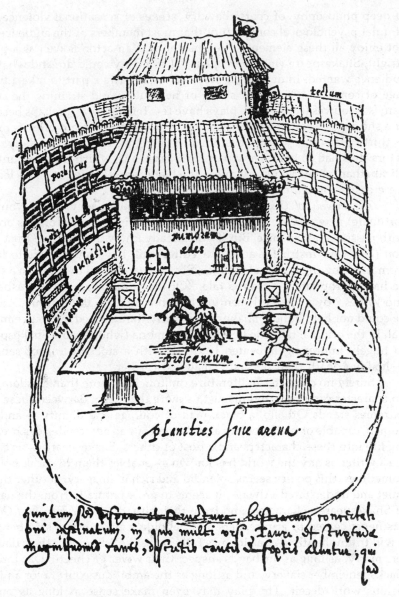

The labels visible in the drawing: tectum, porticus, ædes, orchestra, mimorum, sedilia, ingressus, proscænium, planities sive arena.

Johannes de Witt, a Continental visitor to London, made a drawing of the Swan Theatre about 1596. The original drawing is lost; this is Arend van Buchel's copy of it.

and other enormities" (such as providing opportunities for prostitutes and purse-cutters).

A playwright had to please all members of the audience, not only the mannered and educated. This obligation may help to explain the wide range of matter and tone in an Elizabethan play: passages of subtle poetry, of deep philosophy, of coarse bawdry; scenes of sensational violence and of quiet psychological conflict (not that most members of the audience did not enjoy all these elements). Because he was an actor as well as a playwright, Shakespeare well knew what his company could do, and what his audience wanted. In devising a play, he could write a part to take advantage of some actor's specific skills; or he could avoid straining the company's resources (some of his plays have few female parts, perhaps because of a shortage of competent boy actors). The company might offer as many as thirty plays in a season, customarily changing the program daily. The actors thus had to hold many parts in their heads, which may account for Elizabethan playwrights' fondness for blank verse. Lines of fixed length were easier for actors to commit to memory.

The Tragedy of Othello, here offered for study, may be (if you are fortunate) new to you. It is seldom taught in high school, for it is ablaze with passion and violence. But if you already know the play, we trust that you (like your instructor and your editor) still have much more to learn from it. Following his usual practice, Shakespeare based the play on a story he had appropriated — from a tale, "Of the Unfaithfulness of Husbands and Wives," by a sixteenth-century Italian writer, Giraldi Cinthio. And as he could not help but do, Shakespeare freely transformed his source material. In the original tale, the heroine Disdemona (whose name Shakespeare so hugely improved) is beaten to death with a stocking full of sand — a shoddier death than the Bard imagined for her.

Surely no character in literature can touch us more than Desdemona, no character can shock and disgust us more than Iago. Between these two extremes stands Othello, a black man of courage and dignity — and yet human, capable of being fooled, a pushover for bad advice. Besides breathing life into these characters and a host of others, Shakespeare — as capable a writer as any the world has known — enables them to speak poetry. Sometimes, this poetry seems splendid and rich in imagery; at other times, quiet and understated. Always, it seems to grow naturally from the nature of Shakespeare's characters and from their situations. *The Tragedy of Othello* has never ceased to grip readers and beholders alike. It is a safe bet that it will triumphantly live as long as fathers dislike whomever their daughters marry, as long as husbands suspect their wives of cheating, as long as blacks remember slavery, and as long as the ambitious court favor and the jealous work deceit. The play may even make sense as long as public officials connive behind smiling faces, and it may even endure as long as the world makes room for the kind, the true, the beautiful — the blessed pure in heart.

William Shakespeare
THE TRAGEDY OF OTHELLO   1604?

The Moor of Venice

Edited by Alvin Kernan°

> *William Shakespeare (1564 – 1616), the supreme writer of English, was born, baptized, and buried in the market town of Stratford-on-Avon, eighty miles from London. Son of a glovemaker and merchant who was high bailiff (or mayor) of the town, he probably attended grammar school and learned to read Latin authors in the original. At eighteen he married Anne Hathaway, twenty-six, by whom he had three children, including twins. By 1592 he had become well known and envied as an actor and playwright in London. From 1594 until he retired, he belonged to the same theatrical company, the Lord Chamberlain's Men (later renamed the King's Men in honor of their patron, James I), for whom he wrote thirty-six plays — some of them, such as* Hamlet *and* King Lear, *profound reworkings of old plays. As an actor, Shakespeare is believed to have played supporting roles, such as Hamlet's father's ghost. The company prospered, moved into the Globe in 1599, and in 1608 bought the fashionable Blackfriars as well; Shakespeare owned an interest in both theaters. When plagues shut down the theaters from 1592 to 1594, Shakespeare turned to story poems; his great* Sonnets *(published only in 1609) probably also date from the 1590s. Plays were regarded as entertainments of little literary merit, like comic books today, and Shakespeare did not bother to supervise their publication. After* The Tempest *(1611), the last play entirely from his hand, he retired to Stratford, where since 1597 he had owned the second largest house in town. Most critics agree that when he wrote* Othello, *about 1604, Shakespeare was at the height of his powers.*

Characters

Othello, the Moor
Brabantio, father to Desdemona
Cassio, an honorable lieutenant
Iago, a villain
Roderigo, a Venetian gentleman

°Edited by Alvin Kernan: This text of *Othello* is based on that of the First Folio, or large collection, of Shakespeare's plays (1623). But there are many differences between the Folio text and that of the play's first printing in the Quarto, or small volume, of 1621 (eighteen or nineteen years after the play's first performance). Some readings from the Quarto are included. For the reader's convenience, some material has been added by the editor (some indications of scene, some stage directions). Such additions are enclosed in brackets. Mr. Kernan's text and notes were prepared for the edition of *Othello* in the Signet Classic Shakespeare series (New York: NAL, 1963), under the general editorship of Sylvan Barnet.

Duke of Venice
Senators
Montano, Governor of Cyprus
Gentlemen of Cyprus
Lodovico and Gratiano, two noble Venetians
Sailors
Clown
Desdemona, wife to Othello
Emilia, wife to Iago
Bianca, a courtesan
[Messenger, Herald, Officers, Gentlemen, Musicians, Attendants]

Scene. Venice and Cyprus.

ACT I

Scene I [Venice. A street.]

Roderigo: Tush! Never tell me? I take it much unkindly
    That thou, Iago, who hast had my purse
    As if the strings were thine, shouldst know of this.
Iago: 'Sblood°, but you'll not hear me! If ever I did dream
    Of such a matter, abhor me.
Roderigo: Thou told'st me   5
    Thou didst hold him in thy hate.
Iago: Despise me
    If I do not. Three great ones of the city,
    In personal suit to make me his lieutenant,
    Off-capped° to him; and, by the faith of man,
    I know my price; I am worth no worse a place.   10
    But he, as loving his own pride and purposes,
    Evades them with a bombast circumstance°,
    Horribly stuffed with epithets of war;
    Nonsuits° my mediators. For, "Certes," says he,
    "I have already chose my officer." And what was he?   15
    Forsooth, a great arithmetician°,
    One Michael Cassio, a Florentine,
    (A fellow almost damned in a fair wife)°
    That never set a squadron in the field,
    Nor the division of a battle knows   20
    More than a spinster; unless the bookish theoric,

I.i. ⁴'Sblood: by God's blood.   ⁹Off-capped: doffed their caps — as a mark of respect.   ¹²bombast circumstance: stuffed, roundabout speech.   ¹⁴Nonsuits: rejects.   ¹⁶arithmetician: theorist (rather than practical).   ¹⁸A . . . wife: (a much-disputed passage, probably best taken as a general sneer at Cassio as a dandy and a ladies' man. But in the story from which Shakespeare took his plot the counterpart of Cassio is married, and it may be that at the beginning of the play Shakespeare had decided to keep him married but later changed his mind).

Wherein the tonguèd° consuls can propose
As masterly as he. Mere prattle without practice
Is all his soldiership. But he, sir, had th' election;
And I, of whom his eyes had seen the proof   25
At Rhodes, at Cyprus, and on other grounds
Christian and heathen, must be belee'd and calmed
By debitor and creditor. This counter-caster°,
He, in good time, must his lieutenant be,
And I — God bless the mark! — his Moorship's ancient°.   30
Roderigo: By heaven, I rather would have been his hangman.
Iago: Why, there's no remedy. 'Tis the curse of service:
Preferment goes by letter and affection°,
And not by old gradation°, where each second
Stood heir to th' first. Now, sir, be judge yourself,   35
Whether I in any just term am affined°
To love the Moor.
Roderigo: I would not follow him then.
Iago: O, sir, content you.
I follow him to serve my turn upon him.
We cannot all be masters, nor all masters   40
Cannot be truly followed. You shall mark
Many a duteous and knee-crooking° knave
That, doting on his own obsequious bondage,
Wears out his time, much like his master's ass,
For naught but provender; and when he's old, cashiered.   45
Whip me such honest knaves! Others there are
Who, trimmed in forms and visages of duty,
Keep yet their hearts attending on themselves,
And, throwing but shows of service on their lords,
Do well thrive by them, and when they have lined their coats, 50
Do themselves homage. These fellows have some soul;
And such a one do I profess myself. For, sir,
It is as sure as you are Roderigo,
Were I the Moor, I would not be Iago.
In following him, I follow but myself.   55
Heaven is my judge, not I for love and duty,
But seeming so, for my peculiar° end;
For when my outward action doth demonstrate
The native° act and figure of my heart
In complement extern°, 'tis not long after   60
But I will wear my heart upon my sleeve
For daws to peck at; I am not what I am.
Roderigo: What a full fortune does the thick-lips owe°

---

²²*tonguèd:* eloquent.   ²⁸*counter-caster:* i.e., a bookkeeper who *casts* (reckons up) figures on a
counter (abacus).   ³⁰*ancient:* standard-bearer; an under-officer.   ³³*letter and affection:* recommen-
dations (from men of power) and personal preference.   ³⁴*old gradation:* seniority.   ³⁶*affined:*
bound.   ⁴²*knee-crooking:* bowing.   ⁵⁷*peculiar:* personal.   ⁵⁹*native:* natural, innate.   ⁶⁰*complement extern:* outward appearance.   ⁶³*owe:* own.

If he can carry't thus!

Iago: Call up her father,
Rouse him. Make after him, poison his delight, 65
Proclaim him in the streets, incense her kinsmen,
And though he in a fertile climate dwell,
Plague him with flies; though that his joy be joy,
Yet throw such chances of vexation on't
As it may lose some color. 70

Roderigo: Here is her father's house. I'll call aloud.

Iago: Do, with like timorous° accent and dire yell
As when, by night and negligence, the fire
Is spied in populous cities.

Roderigo: What, ho, Brabantio! Signior Brabantio, ho! 75

Iago: Awake! What, ho, Brabantio! Thieves! Thieves!
Look to your house, your daughter, and your bags!
Thieves! Thieves!

Brabantio above° [*at a window*].

Brabantio: What is the reason of this terrible summons?
What is the matter there? 80

Roderigo: Signior, is all your family within?

Iago: Are your doors locked?

Brabantio: Why, wherefore ask you this?

Iago: Zounds, sir, y'are robbed! For shame. Put on your gown!
Your heart is burst, you have lost half your soul.
Even now, now, very now, an old black ram 85
Is tupping your white ewe. Arise, arise!
Awake the snorting citizens with the bell,
Or else the devil will make a grandsire of you.
Arise, I say!

Brabantio: What, have you lost your wits?

Roderigo: Most reverend signior, do you know my voice? 90

Brabantio: Not I. What are you?

Roderigo: My name is Roderigo.

Brabantio: The worser welcome!
I have charged thee not to haunt about my doors.
In honest plainness thou hast heard me say
My daughter is not for thee; and now, in madness, 95
Being full of supper and distemp'ring draughts°,
Upon malicious knavery dost thou come
To start° my quiet.

Roderigo: Sir, sir, sir —

Brabantio: But thou must needs be sure
My spirits and my place° have in their power 100

---

⁷²*timorous:* frightening. ⁷⁸*above:* (i.e., on the small upper stage above and to the rear of the main platform stage, which resembled the projecting upper story of an Elizabethan house). ⁹⁶*distemp'ring draughts:* unsettling drinks. ⁹⁸*start:* disrupt. ¹⁰⁰*place:* rank, i.e., of senator.

To make this bitter to thee.

Roderigo: Patience, good sir.

Brabantio: What tell'st thou me of robbing? This is Venice,
  My house is not a grange°.

Roderigo: Most grave Brabantio,
  In simple and pure soul I come to you.

Iago: Zounds, sir, you are one of those that will not serve God if the devil   105
  bid you. Because we come to do you service and you think we are
  ruffians, you'll have your daughter covered with a Barbary° horse,
  you'll have your nephews° neigh to you, you'll have coursers for
  cousins°, and gennets for germans°.

Brabantio: What profane wretch art thou?   110

Iago: I am one, sir, that comes to tell you your daughter and the Moor
  are making the beast with two backs.

Brabantio: Thou art a villain.

Iago: You are — a senator.

Brabantio: This thou shalt answer. I know thee, Roderigo.

Roderigo: Sir, I will answer anything. But I beseech you,   115
  If't be your pleasure and most wise consent,
  As partly I find it is, that your fair daughter,
  At this odd-even° and dull watch o' th' night,
  Transported, with no worse nor better guard
  But with a knave of common hire, a gondolier,   120
  To the gross clasps of a lascivious Moor —
  If this be known to you, and your allowance,
  We then have done you bold and saucy wrongs;
  But if you know not this, my manners tell me
  We have your wrong rebuke. Do not believe   125
  That from the sense of all civility°
  I thus would play and trifle with your reverence.
  Your daughter, if you have not given her leave,
  I say again, hath made a gross revolt,
  Tying her duty, beauty, wit, and fortunes   130
  In an extravagant° and wheeling stranger
  Of here and everywhere. Straight satisfy yourself.
  If she be in her chamber, or your house,
  Let loose on me the justice of the state
  For thus deluding you.

Brabantio: Strike on the tinder, ho!   135
  Give me a taper! Call up all my people!
  This accident° is not unlike my dream.
  Belief of it oppresses me already.
  Light, I say! Light!   *Exit* [*above*].

---

¹⁰³*grange:* isolated house.   ¹⁰⁷*Barbary:* Arabian, i.e., Moorish.   ¹⁰⁸*nephews:* i.e., grandsons.
¹⁰⁹*cousins:* relations.   ¹⁰⁹*gennets for germans:* Spanish horses for blood relatives.   ¹¹⁸*odd-even:*
between night and morning.   ¹²⁶*sense of all civility:* feeling of what is proper.   ¹³¹*extravagant:*
vagrant, wandering (Othello is not Venetian and thus may be considered a wandering soldier
of fortune).   ¹³⁷*accident:* happening.

Iago: Farewell, for I must leave you.
It seems not meet, nor wholesome to my place,   140
To be produced — as, if I stay, I shall —
Against the Moor. For I do know the State,
However this may gall him with some check°,
Cannot with safety cast° him; for he's embarked
With such loud reason to the Cyprus wars,   145
Which even now stands in act°, that for their souls
Another of his fathom° they have none
To lead their business; in which regard,
Though I do hate him as I do hell-pains,
Yet, for necessity of present life,   150
I must show out a flag and sign of love,
Which is indeed but sign. That you shall surely find him,
Lead to the Sagittary° that raisèd search:
And there will I be with him. So farewell.   [_Exit._]

Enter Brabantio [in his nightgown], with Servants and torches.

Brabantio: It is too true an evil. Gone she is;   155
And what's to come of my despisèd time
Is naught but bitterness. Now, Roderigo,
Where didst thou see her? — O unhappy girl! —
With the Moor, say'st thou? — Who would be a father? —
How didst thou know 'twas she? — O, she deceives me   160
Past thought! — What said she to you? Get moe° tapers!
Raise all my kindred! — Are they married, think you?
Roderigo: Truly I think they are.
Brabantio: O heaven! How got she out? O treason of the blood!
Fathers, from hence trust not your daughters' minds   165
By what you see them act°. Is there not charms
By which the property° of youth and maidhood
May be abused? Have you not read, Roderigo,
Of some such thing?
Roderigo: Yes, sir, I have indeed.
Brabantio: Call up my brother. — O, would you had had her! —   170
Some one way, some another. — Do you know
Where we may apprehend her and the Moor?
Roderigo: I think I can discover him, if you please
To get good guard and go along with me.
Brabantio: Pray you lead on. At every house I'll call;   175
I may command at most. — Get weapons, ho!
And raise some special officers of night. —
On, good Roderigo; I will deserve your pains°.   [_Exeunt°._]

---

¹⁴³_check:_ restraint.   ¹⁴⁴_cast:_ dismiss.   ¹⁴⁶_stands in act:_ takes place.   ¹⁴⁷_fathom:_ ability.
¹⁵³_Sagittary:_ (probably the name of an inn).   ¹⁶¹_moe:_ more.   ¹⁶⁶_act:_ do.   ¹⁶⁷_property:_ true
nature.   ¹⁷⁸_deserve your pains:_ be worthy of (and reward) your efforts.   ¹⁷⁸_Exeunt:_ Latin, "They
go out," a direction indicating that all characters leave the stage.

Scene II [*A street.*]

Enter Othello, Iago, Attendants with torches.

Iago: Though in the trade of war I have slain men,
Yet do I hold it very stuff° o' th' conscience
To do no contrived murder. I lack iniquity
Sometime to do me service. Nine or ten times
I had thought t' have yerked° him here, under the ribs.   5
Othello: 'Tis better as it is.
Iago: Nay, but he prated,
And spoke such scurvy and provoking terms
Against your honor, that with the little godliness I have
I did full hard forbear him. But I pray you, sir,
Are you fast married? Be assured of this,   10
That the magnifico° is much beloved,
And hath in his effect a voice potential
As double as the Duke's°. He will divorce you,
Or put upon you what restraint or grievance
The law, with all his might to enforce it on,   15
Will give him cable°.
Othello: Let him do his spite.
My services which I have done the Signiory°
Shall out-tongue his complaints. 'Tis yet to know° —
Which when I know that boasting is an honor
I shall promulgate — I fetch my life and being   20
From men of royal siege°, and my demerits°
May speak unbonneted to as proud a fortune
As this that I have reached°. For know, Iago,
But that I love the gentle Desdemona,
I would not my unhousèd° free condition   25
Put into circumscription and confine
For the seas' worth. But look, what lights come yond?

Enter Cassio, with [Officers and] torches.

Iago: Those are the raisèd father and his friends.
You were best go in.
Othello: Not I. I must be found.
My parts, my title, and my perfect soul°   30
Shall manifest me rightly. Is it they?
Iago: By Janus, I think no.
Othello: The servants of the Duke? And my lieutenant?
The goodness of the night upon you, friends.

I.ii. ²*stuff:* essence. ⁵*yerked:* stabbed. ¹¹*magnifico:* nobleman. ¹²⁻¹³*hath . . . Duke's:* i.e., can be as effective as the Duke. ¹⁶*cable:* range, scope. ¹⁷*Signiory:* the rulers of Venice. ¹⁸*yet to know:* unknown as yet. ²¹*siege:* rank. ²¹*demerits:* deserts. ²²⁻²³*May . . . reached:* i.e., are the equal of the family I have married into. ²⁵*unhousèd:* unconfined. ³⁰*perfect soul:* clear, unflawed conscience.

What is the news?

Cassio: The Duke does greet you, general;   35
And he requires your haste-posthaste appearance
Even on the instant.

Othello: What is the matter, think you?

Cassio: Something from Cyprus, as I may divine.
It is a business of some heat. The galleys
Have sent a dozen sequent° messengers   40
This very night at one another's heels,
And many of the consuls, raised and met,
Are at the Duke's already. You have been hotly called for.
When, being not at your lodging to be found,
The Senate hath sent about three several° quests   45
To search you out.

Othello: 'Tis well I am found by you.
I will but spend a word here in the house,
And go with you.   [*Exit.*]

Cassio: Ancient, what makes he here?

Iago: Faith, he tonight hath boarded a land carack°.
If it prove lawful prize, he's made forever.   50

Cassio: I do not understand.

Iago: He's married.

Cassio: To who?

[*Enter Othello.*]

Iago: Marry°, to — Come captain, will you go?

Othello: Have with you.

Cassio: Here comes another troop to seek for you.

Enter Brabantio, Roderigo, with Officers and torches.

Iago: It is Brabantio. General, be advised.
He comes to bad intent.

Othello: Holla! Stand there!   55

Roderigo: Signior, it is the Moor.

Brabantio: Down with him, thief! [*They draw swords.*]

Iago: You, Roderigo? Come, sir, I am for you.

Othello: Keep up your bright swords, for the dew will rust them.
Good signior, you shall more command with years
Than with your weapons.   60

Brabantio: O thou foul thief, where hast thou stowed my daughter?
Damned as thou art, thou hast enchanted her!
For I'll refer me to all things of sense°,
If she in chains of magic were not bound,
Whether a maid so tender, fair, and happy,   65
So opposite to marriage that she shunned

---

⁴⁰*sequent:* successive. ⁴⁵*several:* separate. ⁴⁹*carack:* treasure ship. ⁵²*Marry:* By Mary (an interjection). ⁶³*refer . . . sense:* i.e., base (my argument) on all ordinary understanding of nature.

The wealthy, curlèd darlings of our nation,
Would ever have, t'incur a general mock°,
Run from her guardage to the sooty bosom
Of such a thing as thou — to fear, not to delight.   70
Judge me the world if 'tis not gross in sense°
That thou hast practiced° on her with foul charms,
Abused her delicate youth with drugs or minerals
That weaken motion°. I'll have't disputed on;
'Tis probable, and palpable to thinking.   75
I therefore apprehend and do attach° thee
For an abuser of the world, a practicer
Of arts inhibited and out of warrant°.
Lay hold upon him. If he do resist,
Subdue him at his peril.
Othello: Hold your hands,   80
Both you of my inclining and the rest.
Were it my cue to fight, I should have known it
Without a prompter. Whither will you that I go
To answer this your charge?
Brabantio: To prison, till fit time
Of law and course of direct session   85
Call thee to answer.
Othello: What if I do obey?
How may the Duke be therewith satisfied,
Whose messengers are here about my side
Upon some present° business of the state
To bring me to him?
Officer: 'Tis true, most worthy signior.   90
The Duke's in council, and your noble self
I am sure is sent for.
Brabantio: How? The Duke in council?
In this time of the night? Bring him away.
Mine's not an idle cause. The Duke himself,
Or any of my brothers° of the state,   95
Cannot but feel this wrong as 'twere their own;
For if such actions may have passage free,
Bondslaves and pagans shall our statesmen be.   *Exeunt.*

Scene III [*A council chamber.*]

Enter Duke, Senators, and Officers [*set at a table, with lights and Attendants*].

Duke: There's no composition° in this news
That gives them credit°.

---

⁶⁸*general mock:* public shame.   ⁷¹*gross in sense:* obvious.   ⁷²*practiced:* used tricks.   ⁷⁴*motion:* thought, i.e., reason.   ⁷⁶*attach:* arrest.   ⁷⁸*inhibited . . . warrant:* prohibited and illegal (black magic).   ⁸⁹*present:* immediate.   ⁹⁵*brothers:* i.e., the other senators.   I.iii. ¹*composition:* agreement.   ²*gives them credit:* makes them believable.

First Senator:　　　　　　　Indeed, they are disproportioned.
　　My letters say a hundred and seven galleys.
Duke: And mine a hundred forty.
Second Senator:　　　　　　　And mine two hundred.
　　But though they jump° not on a just accompt° —　　　　　5
　　As in these cases where the aim° reports
　　'Tis oft with difference — yet do they all confirm
　　A Turkish fleet, and bearing up to Cyprus.
Duke: Nay, it is possible enough to judgment°.
　　I do not so secure me in the error,　　　　　　　　　10
　　But the main article I do approve
　　In fearful sense°.

Sailor (Within):　　　　　　What, ho! What, ho! What, ho!

　　Enter Sailor.

Officer: A messenger from the galleys.
Duke:　　　　　　　　　　Now? What's the business?
Sailor: The Turkish preparation makes for Rhodes.
　　So was I bid report here to the State　　　　　　　15
　　By Signior Angelo.
Duke: How say you by this change?
First Senator:　　　　　　　　This cannot be
　　By no assay of reason. 'Tis a pageant°
　　To keep us in false gaze°. When we consider
　　Th' importancy of Cyprus to the Turk,　　　　　　20
　　And let ourselves again but understand
　　That, as it more concerns the Turk than Rhodes,
　　So may he with more facile question° bear it,
　　For that it stands not in such warlike brace°,
　　But altogether lacks th' abilities　　　　　　　　　25
　　That Rhodes is dressed in. If we make thought of this,
　　We must not think the Turk is so unskillful
　　To leave that latest which concerns him first,
　　Neglecting an attempt of ease and gain
　　To wake and wage a danger profitless.　　　　　　30
Duke: Nay, in all confidence he's not for Rhodes.
Officer: Here is more news.

　　Enter a Messenger.

Messenger: The Ottomites, reverend and gracious,
　　Steering with due course toward the isle of Rhodes,
　　Have there injointed them with an after° fleet.　　　35
First Senator: Ay, so I thought. How many, as you guess?

---

⁵*jump:* agree.　⁵*just accompt:* exact counting.　⁶*aim:* approximation.　⁹*to judgment:* when carefully considered.　¹⁰⁻¹²*I do . . . sense:* i.e., just because the numbers disagree in the reports, I do not doubt that the principal information (that the Turkish fleet is out) is fearfully true.　¹⁸*pageant:* show, pretense.　¹⁹*in false gaze:* looking the wrong way.　²³*facile question:* easy struggle.　²⁴*warlike brace:* "military posture."　³⁵*after:* following.

Messenger: Of thirty sail; and now they do restem
    Their backward course, bearing with frank appearance
    Their purposes toward Cyprus. Signior Montano,
    Your trusty and most valiant servitor,   40
    With his free duty° recommends° you thus,
    And prays you to believe him.
Duke: 'Tis certain then for Cyprus.
    Marcus Luccicos, is not he in town?
First Senator: He's now in Florence.   45
Duke: Write from us to him; post-posthaste dispatch.
First Senator: Here comes Brabantio and the valiant Moor.

    Enter Brabantio, Othello, Cassio, Iago, Roderigo, and Officers.

Duke: Valiant Othello, we must straight° employ you
    Against the general° enemy Ottoman.
    [To Brabantio] I did not see you. Welcome, gentle signior.   50
    We lacked your counsel and your help tonight.
Brabantio: So did I yours. Good your grace, pardon me.
    Neither my place, nor aught I heard of business,
    Hath raised me from my bed; nor doth the general care
    Take hold on me; for my particular grief   55
    Is of so floodgate and o'erbearing nature
    That it engluts and swallows other sorrows,
    And it is still itself.
Duke: Why, what's the matter?
Brabantio: My daughter! O, my daughter!
Senators: Dead?
Brabantio: Ay, to me.
    She is abused, stol'n from me, and corrupted   60
    By spells and medicines bought of mountebanks;
    For nature so prepost'rously to err,
    Being not deficient, blind, or lame of sense,
    Sans° witchcraft could not.
Duke: Whoe'er he be that in this foul proceeding   65
    Hath thus beguiled your daughter of herself,
    And you of her, the bloody book of law
    You shall yourself read in the bitter letter
    After your own sense; yea, though our proper° son
    Stood in your action°.
Brabantio: Humbly I thank your Grace.   70
    Here is the man — this Moor, whom now, it seems,
    Your special mandate for the state affairs
    Hath hither brought.
All: We are very sorry for't.
Duke [To Othello]: What in your own part can you say to this?
Brabantio: Nothing, but this is so.   75

---

⁴¹*free duty:* unlimited respect.   ⁴¹*recommends:* informs.   ⁴⁸*straight:* at once.   ⁴⁹*general:* universal.   ⁶⁴*Sans:* without.   ⁶⁹*proper:* own.   ⁷⁰*Stood in your action:* were the accused in your suit.

Othello: Most potent, grave, and reverend signiors,
My very noble and approved° good masters,
That I have ta'en away this old man's daughter,
It is most true; true I have married her.
The very head and front° of my offending   80
Hath this extent, no more. Rude am I in my speech,
And little blessed with the soft phrase of peace.
For since these arms of mine had seven years' pith°
Till now some nine moons wasted°, they have used
Their dearest° action in the tented field;   85
And little of this great world can I speak
More than pertains to feats of broils and battle;
And therefore little shall I grace my cause
In speaking for myself. Yet, by your gracious patience,
I will a round° unvarnished tale deliver   90
Of my whole course of love — what drugs, what charms,
What conjuration, and what mighty magic,
For such proceeding I am charged withal,
I won his daughter —
Brabantio: A maiden never bold,
Of spirit so still and quiet that her motion   95
Blushed at herself°, and she, in spite of nature,
Of years, of country, credit, everything,
To fall in love with what she feared to look on!
It is a judgment maimed and most imperfect
That will confess perfection so could err   100
Against all rules of nature, and must be driven
To find out practices of cunning hell
Why this should be. I therefore vouch again
That with some mixtures pow'rful o'er the blood,
Or with some dram, conjured to this effect,   105
He wrought upon her.
Duke: To vouch this is no proof,
Without more wider and more overt test
Than these thin habits° and poor likelihoods
Of modern° seeming do prefer against him.
First Senator: But, Othello, speak.   110
Did you by indirect and forcèd courses
Subdue and poison this young maid's affections?
Or came it by request, and such fair question°
As soul to soul affordeth?
Othello: I do beseech you,
Send for the lady to the Sagittary   115
And let her speak of me before her father.

---

[77]*approved:* tested, proven by past performance.   [80]*head and front:* extreme form (*front* = forehead).   [83]*pith:* strength.   [84]*wasted:* past.   [85]*dearest:* most important.   [90]*round:* blunt.
[95-96]*her motion / Blushed at herself:* i.e., she was so modest that she blushed at every thought (and movement).   [108]*habits:* clothing.   [109]*modern:* trivial.   [113]*question:* discussion.

If you do find me foul in her report,
The trust, the office, I do hold of you
Not only take away, but let your sentence
Even fall upon my life.

Duke: Fetch Desdemona hither.   120

Othello: Ancient, conduct them; you best know the place.

[*Exit Iago, with two or three Attendants.*]

And till she come, as truly as to heaven
I do confess the vices of my blood,
So justly to your grave ears I'll present
How I did thrive in this fair lady's love,   125
And she in mine.

Duke: Say it, Othello.

Othello: Her father loved me; oft invited me;
Still° questioned me the story of my life
From year to year, the battle, sieges, fortune
That I have passed.   130
I ran it through, even from my boyish days
To th' very moment that he bade me tell it.
Wherein I spoke of most disastrous chances,
Of moving accidents by flood and field,
Of hairbreadth scapes i' th' imminent° deadly breach,   135
Of being taken by the insolent foe
And sold to slavery, of my redemption thence
And portance° in my travel's history,
Wherein of anters° vast and deserts idle°,
Rough quarries, rocks, and hills whose heads touch heaven,   140
It was my hint to speak. Such was my process.
And of the Cannibals that each other eat,
The Anthropophagi°, and men whose heads
Grew beneath their shoulders. These things to hear
Would Desdemona seriously incline;   145
But still the house affairs would draw her thence;
Which ever as she could with haste dispatch,
She'd come again, and with a greedy ear
Devour up my discourse. Which I observing,
Took once a pliant hour, and found good means   150
To draw from her a prayer of earnest heart
That I would all my pilgrimage dilate°,
Whereof by parcels she had something heard,
But not intentively°. I did consent,
And often did beguile her of her tears   155
When I did speak of some distressful stroke
That my youth suffered. My story being done,

128*Still:* regularly.   135*imminent:* threatening.   138*portance:* manner of acting.   139*anters:* caves.
139*idle:* empty, sterile.   143*Anthropophagi:* maneaters.   152*dilate:* relate in full.   154*intentively:* at
length and in sequence.

She gave me for my pains a world of kisses.
She swore in faith 'twas strange, 'twas passing° strange;
'Twas pitiful, 'twas wondrous pitiful.   160
She wished she had not heard it; yet she wished
That heaven had made her such a man. She thanked me,
And bade me, if I had a friend that loved her,
I should but teach him how to tell my story,
And that would woo her. Upon this hint I spake.   165
She loved me for the dangers I had passed,
And I loved her that she did pity them.
This only is the witchcraft I have used.
Here comes the lady. Let her witness it.

Enter Desdemona, Iago, Attendants.

Duke: I think this tale would win my daughter too.   170
  Good Brabantio, take up this mangled matter at the best°.
  Men do their broken weapons rather use
  Than their bare hands.
Brabantio: I pray you hear her speak.
  If she confess that she was half the wooer,
  Destruction on my head if my bad blame   175
  Light on the man. Come hither, gentle mistress.
  Do you perceive in all this noble company
  Where most you owe obedience?
Desdemona: My noble father,
  I do perceive here a divided duty.
  To you I am bound for life and education;   180
  My life and education both do learn me
  How to respect you. You are the lord of duty,
  I am hitherto your daughter. But here's my husband,
  And so much duty as my mother showed
  To you, preferring you before her father,   185
  So much I challenge° that I may profess
  Due to the Moor my lord.
Brabantio: God be with you. I have done.
  Please it your Grace, on to the state affairs.
  I had rather to adopt a child than get° it.
  Come hither, Moor.   190
  I here do give thee that with all my heart
  Which, but thou hast already, with all my heart
  I would keep from thee. For your sake°, jewel,
  I am glad at soul I have no other child,
  For thy escape would teach me tyranny,   195
  To hang clogs on them. I have done, my lord.
Duke: Let me speak like yourself and lay a sentence°

---

¹⁵⁹*passing:* surpassing.   ¹⁷¹*take . . . best:* i.e., make the best of this disaster.   ¹⁸⁶*challenge:* claim as right.   ¹⁸⁹*get:* beget.   ¹⁹³*For your sake:* because of you.   ¹⁹⁷*lay a sentence:* provide a maxim.

Which, as a grise° or step, may help these lovers.
When remedies are past, the griefs are ended
By seeing the worst, which late on hopes depended°.   200
To mourn a mischief that is past and gone
Is the next° way to draw new mischief on.
What cannot be preserved when fortune takes,
Patience her injury a mock'ry makes.
The robbed that smiles, steals something from the thief;   205
He robs himself that spends a bootless° grief.
Brabantio: So let the Turk of Cyprus us beguile:
We lose it not so long as we can smile.
He bears the sentence well that nothing bears
But the free comfort which from thence he hears;   210
But he bears both the sentence and the sorrow
That to pay grief must of poor patience borrow.
These sentences, to sugar, or to gall,
Being strong on both sides, are equivocal.
But words are words. I never yet did hear   215
That the bruisèd heart was piercèd° through the ear.
I humbly beseech you, proceed to th' affairs of state.
Duke: The Turk with a most mighty preparation makes for Cyprus.
Othello, the fortitude° of the place is best known to you; and though
we have there a substitute° of most allowed sufficiency°, yet opinion,   220
a more sovereign mistress of effects, throws a more safer voice on
you°. You must therefore be content to slubber° the gloss of your
new fortunes with this more stubborn and boisterous° expedition.
Othello: The tyrant Custom, most grave senators,
Hath made the flinty and steel couch of war   225
My thrice-driven° bed of down. I do agnize°
A natural and prompt alacrity
I find in hardness and do undertake
These present wars against the Ottomites.
Most humbly, therefore, bending to your state,   230
I crave fit disposition for my wife,
Due reference of place, and exhibition°,
With such accommodation and besort
As levels with° her breeding.
Duke: Why, at her father's.
Brabantio: I will not have it so.

---

[198]*grise:* step. [200]*late on hopes depended:* was supported by hope (of a better outcome) until
lately. [202]*next:* closest, surest. [206]*bootless:* valueless. [216]*piercèd:* (some editors emend to
piecèd, i.e., "healed." But *piercèd* makes good sense: Brabantio is saying in effect that his heart
cannot be further hurt [pierced] by the indignity of the useless, conventional advice the Duke
offers him. *Pierced* can also mean, however, "lanced" in the medical sense, and would then
mean "treated"). [219]*fortitude:* fortification. [220]*substitute:* viceroy. [220]*most allowed sufficiency:*
generally acknowledged capability. [220 – 222]*opinion . . . you:* i.e., the general opinion, which
finally controls affairs, is that you would be the best man in this situation. [222]*slubber:*
besmear. [223]*stubborn and boisterous:* rough and violent. [226]*thrice-driven:* i.e., softest. [226]*agnize:*
know in myself. [232]*exhibition:* grant of funds. [234]*levels with:* is suitable to.

Othello: Nor I.   235

Desdemona: Nor would I there reside,
    To put my father in impatient thoughts
    By being in his eye. Most gracious Duke,
    To my unfolding° lend your prosperous° ear,
    And let me find a charter° in your voice,   240
    T' assist my simpleness.

Duke: What would you, Desdemona?

Desdemona: That I love the Moor to live with him,
    My downright violence, and storm of fortunes,
    May trumpet to the world. My heart's subdued
    Even to the very quality of my lord.°   245
    I saw Othello's visage in his mind,
    And to his honors and his valiant parts
    Did I my soul and fortunes consecrate.
    So that, dear lords, if I be left behind,
    A moth of peace, and he go to the war,   250
    The rites° for why I love him are bereft me,
    And I a heavy interim shall support
    By his dear absence. Let me go with him.

Othello: Let her have your voice°.
    Vouch with me, heaven, I therefore beg it not   255
    To please the palate of my appetite,
    Nor to comply with heat° — the young affects°
    In me defunct — and proper satisfaction°;
    But to be free and bounteous to her mind;
    And heaven defend° your good souls that you think   260
    I will your serious and great business scant
    When she is with me. No, when light-winged toys
    Of feathered Cupid seel° with wanton° dullness
    My speculative and officed instrument°,
    That my disports corrupt and taint my business,   265
    Let housewives make a skillet of my helm,
    And all indign° and base adversities
    Make head° against my estimation°! —

Duke: Be it as you shall privately determine,
    Either for her stay or going. Th' affair cries haste,   270
    And speed must answer it.

First Senator: You must away tonight.

Othello: With all my heart.

Duke: At nine i' th' morning here we'll meet again.
    Othello, leave some officer behind,

---

²³⁹*unfolding:* explanation. ²³⁹*prosperous:* favoring. ²⁴⁰*charter:* permission. ²⁴⁴⁻²⁴⁵*My . . . lord:* i.e., I have become one in nature and being with the man I married (therefore, I too would go to the wars like a soldier). ²⁵¹*rites:* (may refer either to the marriage rites or to the rites, formalities, of war). ²⁵⁴*voice:* consent. ²⁵⁷*heat:* lust. ²⁵⁷*affects:* passions. ²⁵⁸*proper satisfaction:* i.e., consummation of the marriage. ²⁶⁰*defend:* forbid. ²⁶³*seel:* sew up. ²⁶³*wanton:* lascivious. ²⁶⁴*speculative . . . instrument:* i.e., sight (and, by extension, the mind). ²⁶⁷*indign:* unworthy. ²⁶⁸*Make head:* form an army, i.e., attack. ²⁶⁸*estimation:* reputation.

And he shall our commission bring to you,   275
And such things else of quality and respect
As doth import you.
Othello: So please your grace, my ancient;
A man he is of honesty and trust.
To his conveyance I assign my wife,
With what else needful your good grace shall think   280
To be sent after me.
Duke: Let it be so.
Good night to every one. [*To Brabantio*] And, noble signior,
If virtue no delighted° beauty lack,
Your son-in-law is far more fair than black.
First Senator: Adieu, brave Moor. Use Desdemona well.   285
Brabantio: Look to her, Moor, if thou hast eyes to see:
She has deceived her father, and may thee.

> [*Exeunt Duke, Senators, Officers, &c.*]

Othello: My life upon her faith! Honest Iago,
My Desdemona must I leave to thee.
I prithee let thy wife attend on her,   290
And bring them after in the best advantage°.
Come, Desdemona. I have but an hour
Of love, of worldly matter, and direction
To spend with thee. We must obey the time.

> *Exit* [*Moor. with Desdemona*].

Roderigo: Iago?   295
Iago: What say'st thou, noble heart?
Roderigo: What will I do, think'st thou?
Iago: Why, go to bed and sleep.
Roderigo: I will incontinently° drown myself.
Iago: If thou dost, I shall never love thee after. Why, thou silly gentle-   300
man?
Roderigo: It is silliness to live when to live is torment; and then have we
a prescription to die when death is our physician.
Iago: O villainous! I have looked upon the world for four times seven
years, and since I could distinguish betwixt a benefit and an injury,   305
I never found man that knew how to love himself. Ere I would say
I would drown myself for the love of a guinea hen, I would change
my humanity with a baboon.
Roderigo: What should I do? I confess it is my shame to be so fond, but
it is not in my virtue° to amend it.   310
Iago: Virtue? A fig! 'Tis in ourselves that we are thus, or thus. Our bodies
are our gardens, to the which our wills are gardeners; so that if we
will plant nettles or sow lettuce, set hyssop and weed up thyme,
supply it with one gender of herbs or distract° it with many — either

---

²⁸³*delighted:* delightful. ²⁹¹*advantage:* opportunity. ²⁹⁹*incontinently:* at once. ³¹⁰*virtue:*
strength (Roderigo is saying that his nature controls him). ³¹⁴*distract:* vary.

to have it sterile with idleness or manured with industry — why, the 315
power and corrigible° authority of this lies in our wills. If the balance
of our lives had not one scale of reason to poise another of sensuality, the blood and baseness of our natures would conduct us to most
prepost'rous conclusions°. But we have reason to cool our raging
motions, our carnal sting or unbitted° lusts, whereof I take this that 320
you call love to be a sect or scion°.

Roderigo: It cannot be.

Iago: It is merely a lust of the blood and a permission of the will. Come,
be a man! Drown thyself? Drown cats and blind puppies! I have
professed me thy friend, and I confess me knit to thy deserving with 325
cables of perdurable toughness. I could never better stead° thee than
now. Put money in thy purse. Follow thou the wars; defeat thy
favor° with an usurped° beard. I say, put money in thy purse. It
cannot be long that Desdemona should continue her love to the
Moor. Put money in thy purse. Nor he his to her. It was a violent 330
commencement in her and thou shalt see an answerable° sequestra-
tion — put but money in thy purse. These Moors are changeable in
their wills — fill thy purse with money. The food that to him now
is as luscious as locusts° shall be to him shortly as bitter as colo-
quintida°. She must change for youth; when she is sated with his 335
body, she will find the errors of her choice. Therefore, put money
in thy purse. If thou wilt needs damn thyself, do it a more delicate
way than drowning. Make all the money thou canst. If sanc-
timony° and a frail vow betwixt an erring° barbarian and supersubtle
Venetian be not too hard for my wits, and all the tribe of hell, thou 340
shalt enjoy her. Therefore, make money. A pox of drowning thyself,
it is clean out of the way. Seek thou rather to be hanged in com-
passing° thy joy than to be drowned and go without her.

Roderigo: Wilt thou be fast to my hopes, if I depend on the issue?

Iago: Thou art sure of me. Go, make money. I have told thee often, and 345
I retell thee again and again, I hate the Moor. My cause is
hearted°; thine hath no less reason. Let us be conjunctive° in our
revenge against him. If thou canst cuckold him, thou dost thyself a
pleasure, me a sport. There are many events in the womb of time,
which will be delivered. Traverse, go, provide thy money! We will 350
have more of this tomorrow. Adieu.

Roderigo: Where shall we meet i' th' morning?

Iago: At my lodging.

Roderigo: I'll be with thee betimes.

Iago: Go to, farewell. Do you hear, Roderigo? 355

Roderigo: I'll sell all my land. *Exit.*

Iago: Thus do I ever make my fool my purse;

---

³¹⁶*corrigible:* corrective. ³¹⁹*conclusions:* ends. ³²⁰*unbitted:* i.e., uncontrolled. ³²¹*sect or scion:*
off-shoot. ³²⁶*stead:* serve. ³²⁷⁻³²⁸*defeat thy favor:* disguise your face. ³²⁸*usurped:* assumed.
³³¹*answerable:* similar. ³³⁴*locusts:* (a sweet fruit). ³³⁵*coloquintida:* a purgative derived from a
bitter apple. ³³⁹*sanctimony:* sacred bond (of marriage). ³³⁹*erring:* wandering. ³⁴³*compassing:*
encompassing, achieving. ³⁴⁷*hearted:* deepseated in the heart. ³⁴⁷*conjunctive:* joined.

For I mine own gained knowledge° should profane
If I would time expend with such a snipe
But for my sport and profit. I hate the Moor,   360
And it is thought abroad that 'twixt my sheets
H'as done my office. I know not if't be true,
But I, for mere suspicion in that kind,
Will do, as if for surety°. He holds me well;
The better shall my purpose work on him.   365
Cassio's a proper° man. Let me see now:
To get his place, and to plume up my will°
In double knavery. How? How? Let's see.
After some time, to abuse Othello's ears   370
That he is too familiar with his wife.
He hath a person and a smooth dispose°
To be suspected — framed° to make women false.
The Moor is of a free and open nature
That thinks men honest that but seem to be so;
And will as tenderly be led by th' nose   375
As asses are.
I have't! It is engendered! Hell and night
Must bring this monstrous birth to the world's light.   [*Exit.*]

ACT II

Scene I [*Cyprus.*]

Enter Montano and two Gentlemen [one above]°.

Montano: What from the cape can you discern at sea?
First Gentleman: Nothing at all, it is a high-wrought flood.
    I cannot 'twixt the heaven and the main
    Descry a sail.
Montano: Methinks the wind hath spoke aloud at land;   5
    A fuller blast ne'er shook our battlements.
    If it hath ruffianed so upon the sea,
    What ribs of oak, when mountains melt on them,
    Can hold the mortise? What shall we hear of this?
Second Gentleman: A segregation° of the Turkish fleet.   10
    For do but stand upon the foaming shore,
    The chidden billow seems to pelt the clouds;
    The wind-shaked surge, with high and monstrous main°,

---

³⁵⁸*gained knowledge:* i.e., practical, worldly wisdom.   ³⁶⁴*surety:* certainty.   ³⁶⁶*proper:* handsome.
³⁶⁷*plume up my will:* (many explanations have been offered for this crucial line, which in Q_1
reads "make up my will." The general sense is something like "to make more proud and
gratify my ego").   ³⁷¹*dispose:* manner.   ³⁷²*framed:* designed.   °II.i. stage direction (the Folio
text requires that the First Gentleman stand above — on the upper stage — and act as a
lookout reporting sights that cannot be seen by Montano standing below on the main stage).
¹⁰*segregation:* separation.   ¹³*main:* (both "ocean" and "strength").

Seems to cast water on the burning Bear
And quench the guards of th' ever-fixèd pole.°   15
I never did like molestation view
On the enchafèd flood.
Montano: If that the Turkish fleet
Be not ensheltered and embayed, they are drowned;
It is impossible to bear it out.

Enter a [third] Gentleman.

Third Gentleman: News, lads! Our wars are done.   20
The desperate tempest hath so banged the Turks
That their designment halts. A noble ship of Venice
Hath seen a grievous wrack and sufferance°
On most part of their fleet.
Montano: How? Is this true?
Third Gentleman: The ship is here put in,   25
A Veronesa; Michael Cassio,
Lieutenant to the warlike Moor Othello,
Is come on shore; the Moor himself at sea,
And is in full commission here for Cyprus.
Montano: I am glad on't. 'Tis a worthy governor.   30
Third Gentleman: But this same Cassio, though he speak of comfort
Touching the Turkish loss, yet he looks sadly
And prays the Moor be safe, for they were parted
With foul and violent tempest.
Montano: Pray heavens he be;
For I have served him, and the man commands   35
Like a full soldier. Let's to the seaside, ho!
As well to see the vessel that's come in
As to throw out our eyes for brave Othello,
Even till we make the main and th' aerial blue
An indistinct regard°.
Third Gentleman: Come, let's do so;   40
For every minute is expectancy
Of more arrivancie°.

Enter Cassio.

Cassio: Thanks, you the valiant of the warlike isle,
That so approve° the Moor. O, let the heavens
Give him defense against the elements,   45
For I have lost him on a dangerous sea.
Montano: Is he well shipped?
Cassio: His bark is stoutly timbered, and his pilot
Of very expert and approved allowance°;
Therefore my hopes, not surfeited to death°,   50

---

¹⁴⁻¹⁵*Seems . . . pole:* (the constellation Ursa Minor contains two stars that are the *guards,* or companions, of the *pole,* or North Star).   ²³*sufferance:* damage.   ³⁹⁻⁴⁰*the main . . . regard:* i.e., the sea and sky become indistinguishable.   ⁴²*arrivancie:* arrivals.   ⁴⁴*approve:* ("honor" or, perhaps, "are as warlike and valiant as your governor").   ⁴⁹*approved allowance:* known and tested.   ⁵⁰*not surfeited to death:* i.e., not so great as to be in danger.

Stand in bold cure°. (*Within:* A sail, a sail, a sail!)
Cassio: What noise?
First Gentleman: The town is empty; on the brow o' th' sea
Stand ranks of people, and they cry, "A sail!"
Cassio: My hopes do shape him for the governor.   [*A shot.*]   55
Second Gentleman: They do discharge their shot of courtesy:
Our friends at least.
Cassio: I pray you, sir, go forth
And give us truth who 'tis that is arrived.
Second Gentleman: I shall.   [*Exit.*]
Montano: But, good lieutenant, is your general wived?   60
Cassio: Most fortunately. He hath achieved a maid
That paragons° description and wild fame°;
One that excels the quirks of blazoning pens°,
And in th' essential vesture of creation°
Does tire the ingener°.

Enter [Second] Gentleman.

                    How now? Who has put in?   65
Second Gentleman: 'Tis one Iago, ancient to the general.
Cassio: H'as had most favorable and happy speed:
Tempests themselves, high seas, and howling winds,
The guttered° rocks and congregated° sands,
Traitors ensteeped° to enclog the guiltless keel,   70
As having sense° of beauty, do omit
Their mortal° natures, letting go safely by
The divine Desdemona.
Montano: What is she?
Cassio: She that I spake of, our great captain's captain,
Left in the conduct of the bold Iago,   75
Whose footing° here anticipates our thoughts
A se'nnight's° speed. Great Jove, Othello guard,
And swell his sail with thine own pow'rful breath,
That he may bless this bay with his tall° ship,
Make love's quick pants in Desdemona's arms,   80
Give renewed fire to our extincted spirits.

Enter Desdemona, Iago, Roderigo, and Emilia.

O, behold! The riches of the ship is come on shore!
You men of Cyprus, let her have your knees.   [*Kneeling.*]
Hail to thee, lady! and the grace of heaven,
Before, behind thee, and on every hand,   85
Enwheel thee round.
Desdemona: I thank you, valiant Cassio.

---

[51]*Stand in bold cure:* i.e., are likely to be restored.   [62]*paragons:* exceeds.   [62]*wild fame:* extravagant
report.   [63]*quirks of blazoning pens:* ingenuities of praising pens.   [64]*essential vesture of creation:*
essential human nature as given by the Creator.   [65]*tire the ingener:* a difficult line that probably
means something like "outdo the human ability to imagine and picture."   [69]*guttered:* jagged.
[69]*congregated:* gathered.   [70]*ensteeped:* submerged.   [71]*sense:* awareness.   [72]*mortal:* deadly.
[76]*footing:* landing.   [77]*se'nnight's:* week's.   [79]*tall:* brave.

What tidings can you tell me of my lord?

Cassio: He is not yet arrived, nor know I aught
But that he's well and will be shortly here.

Desdemona: O but I fear. How lost you company?   90

Cassio: The great contention of sea and skies
Parted our fellowship. (*Within:* A sail, a sail!)   [*A shot.*]
But hark. A sail!

Second Gentleman: They give this greeting to the citadel;
This likewise is a friend.

Cassio: See for the news.   [*Exit Gentleman.*]   95
Good ancient, you are welcome. [*To Emilia*] Welcome, mistress.
Let it not gall your patience, good Iago,
That I extend° my manners. 'Tis my breeding°
That gives me this bold show of courtesy.   [*Kisses Emilia.*]

Iago: Sir, would she give you so much of her lips   100
As of her tongue she oft bestows on me,
You would have enough.

Desdemona: Alas, she has no speech.

Iago: In faith, too much.
I find it still when I have leave to sleep°.
Marry, before your ladyship°, I grant,   105
She puts her tongue a little in her heart
And chides with thinking.

Emilia: You have little cause to say so.

Iago: Come on, come on! You are pictures° out of door,
Bells in your parlors, wildcats in your kitchens,
Saints in your injuries°, devils being offended,   110
Players in your housewifery°, and housewives in your beds.

Desdemona: O, fie upon thee, slanderer!

Iago: Nay, it is true, or else I am a Turk:
You rise to play, and go to bed to work.

Emilia: You shall not write my praise.

Iago: No, let me not.   115

Desdemona: What wouldst write of me, if thou shouldst praise me?

Iago: O gentle lady, do not put me to't.
For I am nothing if not critical.

Desdemona: Come on, assay. There's one gone to the harbor?

Iago: Ay, madam.   120

Desdemona [*Aside*]: I am not merry; but I do beguile
The thing I am by seeming otherwise. —
Come, how wouldst thou praise me?

Iago: I am about it; but indeed my invention

---

⁹⁸*extend:* stretch.   ⁹⁸*breeding:* careful training in manners (Cassio is considerably more the polished gentleman than Iago, and aware of it).   ¹⁰⁴*still . . . sleep:* i.e., even when she allows me to sleep she continues to scold.   ¹⁰⁵*before your ladyship:* in your presence.   ¹⁰⁸*pictures:* models (of virtue).   ¹¹⁰*in your injuries:* when you injure others.   ¹¹¹*housewifery:* this word can mean "careful, economical household management," and Iago would then be accusing women of only pretending to be good housekeepers, while in bed they are either (1) economical of their favors, or more likely (2) serious and dedicated workers.

Comes from my pate as birdlime° does from frieze° —   125
It plucks out brains and all. But my Muse labors,
And thus she is delivered:
If she be fair° and wise: fairness and wit,
The one's for use, the other useth it.
Desdemona: Well praised. How if she be black° and witty?   130
Iago: If she be black, and thereto have a wit,
    She'll find a white that shall her blackness fit.
Desdemona: Worse and worse!
Emilia: How if fair and foolish?
Iago: She never yet was foolish that was fair,   135
    For even her folly helped her to an heir.
Desdemona: Those are old fond° paradoxes to make fools laugh i' th'
    alehouse. What miserable praise hast thou for her that's foul and
    foolish?
Iago: There's none so foul, and foolish thereunto,   140
    But does foul pranks which fair and wise ones do.
Desdemona: O heavy ignorance. Thou praisest the worst best. But what
    praise couldst thou bestow on a deserving woman indeed — one that
    in the authority of her merit did justly put on the vouch of very
    malice itself°?   145
Iago: She that was ever fair, and never proud;
    Had tongue at will, and yet was never loud;
    Never lacked gold, and yet went never gay;
    Fled from her wish, and yet said "Now I may";
    She that being angered, her revenge being nigh,   150
    Bade her wrong stay, and her displeasure fly;
    She that in wisdom never was so frail
    To change the cod's head for the salmon's tail°;
    She that could think, and nev'r disclose her mind;
    See suitors following, and not look behind: 155
    She was a wight° (if ever such wights were) —
Desdemona: To do what?
Iago: To suckle fools and chronicle small beer.°
Desdemona: O most lame and impotent conclusion. Do not learn of him,
    Emilia, though he be thy husband. How say you, Cassio? Is he not   160
    a most profane and liberal° counselor?
Cassio: He speaks home°, madam. You may relish him more in° the soldier
    than in the scholar. [*Takes Desdemona's hand.*]
Iago [*Aside*]: He takes her by the palm. Ay, well said, whisper! With as
    little a web as this will I ensnare as great a fly as Cassio. Ay, smile 165
    upon her, do! I will gyve° thee in thine own courtship. — You say

---

¹²⁵*birdlime:* a sticky substance put on branches to catch birds.   ¹²⁵*frieze:* rough cloth.   ¹²⁸*fair:*
light-complexioned.   ¹³⁰*black:* brunette.   ¹³⁷*fond:* foolish.   ¹⁴³⁻⁴⁵*one . . . itself:* i.e., a woman
so honest and deserving that even malice would be forced to approve of her.   ¹⁵³*To . . . tail:*
i.e., to exchange something valuable for something useless.   ¹⁵⁶*wight:* person.   ¹⁵⁸*chronicle
small beer:* i.e., keep household accounts (the most trivial of occupations in Iago's opinion).
¹⁶¹*liberal:* licentious.   ¹⁶²*speaks home:* thrusts deeply with his speech.   ¹⁶²*relish him more in:*
enjoy him more as.   ¹⁶⁶*gyve:* bind.

true; 'tis so, indeed! — If such tricks as these strip you out of your
lieutenantry, it had been better you had not kissed your three fingers
so oft — which now again you are most apt to play the sir° in. Very
good! Well kissed! An excellent curtsy°! 'Tis so, indeed. Yet again   170
your fingers to your lips? Would they were clyster pipes° for your
sake! [*Trumpets within.*] The Moor! I know his trumpet°.

Cassio: 'Tis truly so.

Desdemona: Let's meet him and receive him.

Cassio: Lo, where he comes.   175

    Enter Othello and Attendants.

Othello: O my fair warrior!

Desdemona: My dear Othello.

Othello: It gives me wonder great as my content
To see you here before me. O my soul's joy!
If after every tempest come such calms,
May the winds blow till they have wakened death.   180
And let the laboring bark climb hills of seas
Olympus-high, and duck again as low
As hell's from heaven. If it were now to die,
'Twere now to be most happy; for I fear
My soul hath her content so absolute   185
That not another comfort like to this
Succeeds in unknown fate.

Desdemona: The heavens forbid
But that our loves and comforts should increase
Even as our days do grow.

Othello: Amen to that, sweet powers!
I cannot speak enough of this content: 190
It stops me here [*touches his heart*]; it is too much of joy.
And this, and this, the greatest discords be   [*They kiss.*]
That e'er our hearts shall make!

Iago [*Aside*]:   O, you are well tuned now!
But I'll set down the pegs° that make this music,
As honest as I am.

Othello: Come, let us to the castle.   195
News, friends! Our wars are done; the Turks are drowned.
How does my old acquaintance of this isle?
Honey, you shall be well desired in Cyprus;
I have found great love amongst them. O my sweet,
I prattle out of fashion, and I dote   200
In mine own comforts. I prithee, good Iago,
Go to the bay and disembark my coffers.
Bring thou the master to the citadel;
He is a good one and his worthiness

---

[169] *the sir:* the fashionable gentleman. [170] *curtsy:* courtesy, i.e., bow. [171] *clyster pipes:* enema
tubes. [172] *his trumpet:* (great men had their own distinctive calls). [194] *set down the pegs:* loosen
the strings (to produce discord).

Does challenge° much respect. Come, Desdemona,   205
Once more well met at Cyprus.

Exit Othello and Desdemona [and all but Iago and Roderigo].

Iago [To an Attendant]: Do thou meet me presently at the harbor. [*To
Roderigo*] Come hither. If thou be'st valiant (as they say base men
being in love have then a nobility in their natures more than is native
to them), list me. The lieutenant tonight watches on the court of   210
guard°. First, I must tell thee this: Desdemona is directly in love with
him.
Roderigo: With him? Why, 'tis not possible.
Iago: Lay thy finger thus [*puts his finger to his lips*], and let thy soul be
instructed. Mark me with what violence she first loved the Moor but   215
for bragging and telling her fantastical lies. To love him still for
prating? Let not thy discreet heart think it. Her eye must be fed. And
what delight shall she have to look on the devil? When the blood
is made dull with the act of sport, there should be a game° to inflame
it and to give satiety a fresh appetite, loveliness in favor°, sympathy   220
in years°, manners, and beauties; all which the Moor is defective in.
Now for want of these required conveniences°, her delicate tenderness will find itself abused, begin to heave the gorge°, disrelish and
abhor the Moor. Very nature will instruct her in it and compel her
to some second choice. Now sir, this granted — as it is a most   225
pregnant° and unforced position — who stands so eminent in the
degree of this fortune as Cassio does? A knave very voluble; no
further conscionable° than in putting on the mere form of civil and
humane° seeming for the better compass of his salt° and most hidden
loose° affection. Why, none! Why, none! A slipper° and subtle knave,   230
a finder of occasion, that has an eye can stamp and counterfeit
advantages, though true advantage never present itself. A devilish
knave. Besides, the knave is handsome, young, and hath all those
requisites in him that folly and green minds look after. A pestilent
complete knave, and the woman hath found him already.   235
Roderigo: I cannot believe that in her; she's full of most blessed condition.
Iago: Blessed fig's-end! The wine she drinks is made of grapes. If she had
been blessed, she would never have loved the Moor. Blessed pudding! Didst thou not see her paddle with the palm of his hand? Didst
not mark that?   240
Roderigo: Yes, that I did; but that was but courtesy.
Iago: Lechery, by this hand! [*Extends his index finger.*] An index° and obscure
prologue to the history of lust and foul thoughts. They met so near
with their lips that their breaths embraced together. Villainous
thoughts, Roderigo. When these mutualities so marshal the way,   245

---

²⁰⁵*challenge:* require, exact.   ²¹¹*court of guard:* guardhouse.   ²¹⁹*game:* sport (with the added
sense of "gamey," "rank").   ²²⁰*favor:* countenance, appearance.   ²²⁰⁻²¹*sympathy in years:*
sameness of age.   ²²²*conveniences:* advantages.   ²²³*heave the gorge:* vomit.   ²²⁶*pregnant:* likely.
²²⁷⁻²⁸*no further conscionable:* having no more conscience.   ²²⁹*humane:* polite.   ²²⁹*salt:* lecherous.
²³⁰*loose:* immoral.   ²³⁰*slipper:* slippery.   ²⁴²*index:* pointer.

hard at hand comes the master and main exercise, th' incorpo-
rate° conclusion: Pish! But, sir, be you ruled by me. I have brought
you from Venice. Watch you tonight; for the command, I'll lay't
upon you. Cassio knows you not. I'll not be far from you. Do you
find some occasion to anger Cassio, either by speaking too loud, or   250
tainting° his discipline, or from what other course you please which
the time shall more favorably minister.

Roderigo: Well.

Iago: Sir, he's rash and very sudden in choler°, and haply may strike at
you. Provoke him that he may; for even out of that will I cause these   255
of Cyprus to mutiny, whose qualification shall come into no true
taste° again but by the displanting of Cassio. So shall you have a
shorter journey to your desires by the means I shall then have to
prefer them; and the impediment most profitably removed without
the which there were no expectation of our prosperity.   260

Roderigo: I will do this if you can bring it to any opportunity.

Iago: I warrant thee. Meet me by and by at the citadel. I must fetch his
necessaries ashore. Farewell.

Roderigo: Adieu.   *Exit.*

Iago: That Cassio loves her, I do well believe't;   265
That she loves him, 'tis apt and of great credit.
The Moor, howbeit that I endure him not,
Is of a constant, loving, noble nature,
And I dare think he'll prove to Desdemona
A most dear° husband. Now I do love her too;   270
Not out of absolute° lust, though peradventure°
I stand accountant for as great a sin,
But partly led to diet° my revenge,
For that I do suspect the lusty Moor
Hath leaped into my seat; the thought whereof   275
Doth, like a poisonous mineral, gnaw my inwards;
And nothing can or shall content my soul
Till I am evened with him, wife for wife.
Or failing so, yet that I put the Moor
At least into a jealousy so strong   280
That judgment cannot cure. Which thing to do,
If this poor trash of Venice, whom I trace°
For his quick hunting, stand the putting on,
I'll have our Michael Cassio on the hip,
Abuse him to the Moor in the right garb°   285
(For I fear Cassio with my nightcap too),
Make the Moor thank me, love me, and reward me

---

²⁴⁶⁻⁴⁷*incorporate:* carnal.   ²⁵¹*tainting:* discrediting.   ²⁵⁴*choler:* anger.   ²⁵⁶⁻⁵⁷*qualification . . .
taste:* i.e., appeasement will not be brought about (wine was "qualified" by adding water).
²⁷⁰*dear:* expensive.   ²⁷¹*out of absolute:* absolutely out of.   ²⁷¹*peradventure:* perchance.   ²⁷³*diet:*
feed.   ²⁸²*trace:* (most editors emend to "trash," meaning to hang weights on a dog to slow
his hunting: but "trace" clearly means something like "put on the trace" or "set on the track").
²⁸⁵*right garb:* i.e., "proper fashion."

For making him egregiously an ass
And practicing upon° his peace and quiet,
Even to madness. 'Tis here, but yet confused: 290
Knavery's plain face is never seen till used.   *Exit.*

Scene II [*A street.*]

Enter Othello's Herald, with a proclamation.

Herald: It is Othello's pleasure, our noble and valiant general, that upon
certain tidings now arrived importing the mere perdition° of the
Turkish fleet, every man put himself into triumph. Some to dance,
some to make bonfires, each man to what sport and revels his
addition° leads him. For, besides these beneficial news, it is the   5
celebration of his nuptial. So much was his pleasure should be proclaimed. All offices° are open, and there is full liberty of feasting
from this present hour of five till the bell have told eleven. Bless the
isle of Cyprus and our noble general Othello!   *Exit.*

Scene III [*The citadel of Cyprus.*]

Enter Othello, Desdemona, Cassio, and Attendants.

Othello: Good Michael, look you to the guard tonight.
Let's teach ourselves that honorable stop,
Not to outsport direction.
Cassio: Iago hath discretion what to do;
But notwithstanding, with my personal eye   5
Will I look to't.
Othello: Iago is most honest.
Michael, good night. Tomorrow with your earliest
Let me have speech with you. [*To Desdemona*] Come, my dear love,
The purchase made, the fruits are to ensue.
That profit's yet to come 'tween me and you.   10
Good night.   *Exit* [*Othello with Desdemona and Attendants*].

Enter Iago.

Cassio: Welcome, Iago. We must to the watch.
Iago: Not this hour, lieutenant; 'tis not yet ten o' th' clock. Our general
cast° us thus early for the love of his Desdemona; who let us not
therefore blame. He hath not yet made wanton the night with her,   15
and she is sport for Jove.
Cassio: She's a most exquisite lady.
Iago: And, I'll warrant her, full of game.
Cassio: Indeed, she's a most fresh and delicate creature.
Iago: What an eye she has! Methinks it sounds a parley to provocation.   20

---

²⁸⁹*practicing upon:* scheming to destroy. II.ii. ²*mere perdition:* absolute destruction. ⁵*addition:*
rank. ⁷*offices:* kitchens and storerooms of food. II.iii. ¹⁴*cast:* dismissed.

Cassio: An inviting eye; and yet methinks right modest.

Iago: And when she speaks, is it not an alarum° to love?

Cassio: She is indeed perfection.

Iago: Well, happiness to their sheets! Come, lieutenant, I have a stoup° of wine, and here without are a brace of Cyprus gallants that 25
would fain have a measure to the health of black Othello.

Cassio: Not tonight, good Iago. I have very poor and unhappy brains for drinking; I could well wish courtesy would invent some other custom of entertainment.

Iago: O, they are our friends. But one cup! I'll drink for you. 30

Cassio: I have drunk but one tonight, and that was craftily qualified° too; and behold what innovation it makes here. I am unfortunate in the infirmity and dare not task my weakness with any more.

Iago: What, man! 'Tis a night of revels, the gallants desire it.

Cassio: Where are they? 35

Iago: Here, at the door. I pray you call them in.

Cassio: I'll do't, but it dislikes me.   *Exit.*

Iago: If I can fasten but one cup upon him
With that which he hath drunk tonight already,
He'll be as full of quarrel and offense   40
As my young mistress' dog. Now, my sick fool Roderigo,
Whom love hath turned almost the wrong side out,
To Desdemona hath tonight caroused
Potations pottle-deep°; and he's to watch.
Three else° of Cyprus, noble swelling spirits,   45
That hold their honors in a wary distance°,
The very elements of this warlike isle,
Have I tonight flustered with flowing cups,
And they watch too. Now, 'mongst this flock of drunkards
Am I to put our Cassio in some action   50
That may offend the isle. But here they come.

Enter Cassio, Montano, and Gentlemen.

If consequence do but approve my dream,
My boat sails freely, both with wind and stream.

Cassio: 'Fore God, they have given me a rouse° already.

Montano: Good faith, a little one; not past a pint, as I am a soldier. 55

Iago: Some wine, ho!
[*Sings*] And let me the canakin clink, clink;
        And let me the canakin clink.
        A soldier's a man;
        O man's life's but a span.   60
        Why then, let a soldier drink.
Some wine, boys!

Cassio: 'Fore God, an excellent song!

---

²²*alarum:* the call to action, "general quarters." ²⁵*stoup:* two-quart tankard. ³¹*qualified:* diluted. ⁴⁴*pottle-deep:* to the bottom of the cup. ⁴⁵*else:* others. ⁴⁶*hold . . . distance:* are scrupulous in maintaining their honor. ⁵⁴*rouse:* drink.

Iago: I learned it in England, where indeed they are most potent in potting. Your Dane, your German, and your swag-bellied° Hollander — Drink, ho! — are nothing to your English. 65

Cassio: Is your Englishman so exquisite° in his drinking?

Iago: Why, he drinks you with facility your Dane dead drunk; he sweats not to overthrow your Almain; he gives your Hollander a vomit ere the next pottle can be filled. 70

Cassio: To the health of our general!

Montano: I am for it, lieutenant, and I'll do you justice.

Iago: O sweet England!

> [*Sings*] King Stephen was and a worthy peer;
>> His breeches cost him but a crown; 75
>> He held them sixpence all too dear,
>> With that he called the tailor lown°.
> He was a wight of high renown,
> And thou art but of low degree:
> 'Tis pride that pulls the country down; 80
> And take thine auld cloak about thee.

Some wine, ho!

Cassio: 'Fore God, this is a more exquisite song than the other.

Iago: Will you hear't again?

Cassio: No, for I hold him to be unworthy of his place that does those 85 things. Well, God's above all; and there be souls must be saved, and there be souls must not be saved.

Iago: It's true, good lieutenant.

Cassio: For mine own part — no offense to the general, nor any man of quality — I hope to be saved. 90

Iago: And so do I too, lieutenant.

Cassio: Ay, but, by your leave, not before me. The lieutenant is to be saved before the ancient. Let's have no more of this; let's to our affairs. — God forgive us our sins! — Gentlemen, let's look to our business. Do not think, gentlemen, I am drunk. This is my ancient; 95 this is my right hand, and this is my left. I am not drunk now. I can stand well enough, and I speak well enough.

Gentlemen: Excellent well!

Cassio: Why, very well then. You must not think then that I am drunk.

Exit.

Montano: To th' platform, masters. Come, let's set the watch. 100

Iago: You see this fellow that is gone before.
> He's a soldier fit to stand by Caesar
> And give direction; and do but see his vice.
> 'Tis to his virtue a just equinox°,
> The one as long as th' other. 'Tis pity of him. 105
> I fear the trust Othello puts him in,
> On some odd time of his infirmity,
> Will shake this island.

---

65 *swag-bellied:* pendulous-bellied. 67 *exquisite:* superb. 77 *lown:* lout. 104 *just equinox:* exact balance (of dark and light).

Montano: But is he often thus?
Iago: 'Tis evermore his prologue to his sleep:
     He'll watch the horologe a double set°   110
     If drink rock not his cradle.
Montano: It were well
     The general were put in mind of it.
     Perhaps he sees it not, or his good nature
     Prizes the virtue that appears in Cassio
     And looks not on his evils. Is not this true?   115

     Enter Roderigo.

Iago [Aside]: How now, Roderigo?
     I pray you after the lieutenant, go!   [Exit Roderigo.]
Montano: And 'tis great pity that the noble Moor
     Should hazard such a place as his own second
     With one of an ingraft° infirmity.   120
     It were an honest action to say so
     To the Moor.
Iago: Not I, for this fair island!
     I do love Cassio well and would do much
     To cure him of this evil.   (Help! Help! Within.)
     But hark! What noise?   125

     Enter Cassio, pursuing Roderigo.

Cassio: Zounds, you rogue! You rascal!
Montano: What's the matter, lieutenant?
Cassio: A knave teach me my duty? I'll beat the knave into a twig-
     gen° bottle.
Roderigo: Beat me?   130
Cassio: Dost thou prate, rogue?   [Strikes him.]
Montano: Nay, good lieutenant! I pray you, sir, hold your hand.

                                        [Stays him.]

Cassio: Let me go, sir, or I'll knock you o'er the mazzard°.
Montano: Come, come, you're drunk!
Cassio: Drunk?   [They fight.]   135
Iago [Aside to Roderigo]: Away, I say! Go out and cry a mutiny!

                                        [Exit Roderigo.]

     Nay, good lieutenant. God's will, gentlemen!
     Help, ho! Lieutenant. Sir. Montano.
     Help, masters! Here's a goodly watch indeed!   [A bell rung.]
     Who's that which rings the bell? Diablo, ho!   140
     The town will rise. God's will, lieutenant,
     You'll be ashamed forever.

---

¹¹⁰*watch . . . set:* stay awake twice around the clock.   ¹²⁰*ingraft:* ingrained.   ¹³⁰⁻³¹*twiggen:*
wicker-covered.   ¹³³*mazzard:* head.

Enter Othello and Attendants.

Othello: What is the matter here?
Montano: Zounds, I bleed still. I am hurt to the death.
    He dies.   [*He and Cassio fight again.*]
Othello: Hold for your lives!   145
Iago: Hold, ho! Lieutenant. Sir. Montano. Gentlemen!
    Have you forgot all place of sense and duty?
    Hold! The general speaks to you. Hold, for shame!
Othello: Why, how now, ho? From whence ariseth this?
    Are we turned Turks, and to ourselves do that   150
    Which heaven hath forbid the Ottomites°?
    For Christian shame put by this barbarous brawl!
    He that stirs next to carve for his own rage
    Holds his soul light°; he dies upon his motion.
    Silence that dreadful bell! It frights the isle   155
    From her propriety°. What is the matter, masters?
    Honest Iago, that looks dead with grieving,
    Speak. Who began this? On thy love, I charge thee.
Iago: I do not know. Friends all, but now, even now,
    In quarter° and in terms like bride and groom   160
    Devesting them for bed; and then, but now —
    As if some planet had unwitted men —
    Swords out, and tilting one at other's breasts
    In opposition bloody. I cannot speak
    Any beginning to this peevish odds°,   165
    And would in action glorious I had lost
    Those legs that brought me to a part of it!
Othello: How comes it, Michael, you are thus forgot?
Cassio: I pray you pardon me; I cannot speak.
Othello: Worthy Montano, you were wont to be civil;   170
    Thy gravity and stillness of your youth
    The world hath noted, and your name is great
    In mouths of wisest censure°. What's the matter
    That you unlace° your reputation thus
    And spend your rich opinion° for the name   175
    Of a night-brawler? Give me answer to it.
Montano: Worthy Othello, I am hurt to danger.
    Your officer, Iago, can inform you.
    While I spare speech, which something now offends° me,
    Of all that I do know; nor know I aught   180
    By me that's said or done amiss this night,
    Unless self-charity be sometimes a vice,

---

¹⁵¹*heaven . . . Ottomites:* i.e., by sending the storm which dispersed the Turks.   ¹⁵⁴*Holds his soul light:* values his soul lightly.   ¹⁵⁶*propriety:* proper order.   ¹⁶⁰*In quarter:* on duty.   ¹⁶⁵*odds:* quarrel.   ¹⁷³*censure:* judgment.   ¹⁷⁴*unlace:* undo (the term refers specifically to the dressing of a wild boar killed in the hunt).   ¹⁷⁵*opinion:* reputation.   ¹⁷⁹*offends:* harms, hurts.

And to defend ourselves it be a sin
When violence assails us.
Othello: Now, by heaven,
My blood begins my safer guides to rule,   185
And passion, having my best judgment collied°,
Assays to lead the way. If I once stir
Or do but lift this arm, the best of you
Shall sink in my rebuke. Give me to know
How this foul rout began, who set it on;   190
And he that is approved in this offense,
Though he had twinned with me, both at a birth,
Shall lose me. What? In a town of war
Yet wild, the people's hearts brimful of fear,
To manage° private and domestic quarrel?   195
In night, and on the court and guard of safety?
'Tis monstrous. Iago, who began't?
Montano: If partially affined, or leagued in office°,
Thou dost deliver more or less than truth,
Thou art no soldier.
Iago: Touch me not so near.   200
I had rather have this tongue cut from my mouth
Than it should do offense to Michael Cassio.
Yet I persuade myself to speak the truth
Shall nothing wrong him. This it is, general.
Montano and myself being in speech,   205
There comes a fellow crying out for help,
And Cassio following him with determined sword
To execute upon him. Sir, this gentleman
Steps in to Cassio and entreats his pause.
Myself the crying fellow did pursue,   210
Lest by his clamor — as it so fell out —
The town might fall in fright. He, swift of foot,
Outran my purpose; and I returned then rather
For that I heard the clink and fall of swords,
And Cassio high in oath; which till tonight   215
I ne'er might say before. When I came back —
For this was brief — I found them close together
At blow and thrust, even as again they were
When you yourself did part them.
More of this matter cannot I report;   220
But men are men; the best sometimes forget.
Though Cassio did some little wrong to him,
As men in rage strike those that wish them best,
Yet surely Cassio I believe received
From him that fled some strange indignity,   225
Which patience could not pass°.

---

¹⁸⁶*collied:* darkened.   ¹⁹⁵*manage:* conduct.   ¹⁹⁸*If . . . office:* if you are partial because you are
related ("affined") or the brother officer (of Cassio).   ²²⁶*pass:* allow to pass.

Othello: I know, Iago,
  Thy honesty and love doth mince° this matter,
  Making it light to Cassio. Cassio, I love thee;
  But never more be officer of mine.

Enter Desdemona, attended.

  Look if my gentle love be not raised up.   130
  I'll make thee an example.
Desdemona: What is the matter, dear?
Othello: All's well, sweeting; come away to bed.
  [*To Montano*] Sir, for your hurts, myself will be your surgeon.
  Lead him off.   [*Montano led off.*]
  Iago, look with care about the town   135
  And silence those whom this vile brawl distracted.
  Come, Desdemona: 'tis the soldiers' life
  To have their balmy slumbers waked with strife.

                         Exit [with all but Iago and Cassio].

Iago: What, are you hurt, lieutenant?
Cassio: Ay, past all surgery.   140
Iago: Marry, God forbid!
Cassio: Reputation, reputation, reputation! O, I have lost my reputation!
  I have lost the immortal part of myself, and what remains is bestial.
  My reputation, Iago, my reputation.
Iago: As I am an honest man, I had thought you had received some bodily   145
  wound. There is more sense° in that than in reputation. Reputation
  is an idle and most false imposition°, oft got without merit and lost
  without deserving. You have lost no reputation at all unless you
  repute yourself such a loser. What, man, there are more ways to
  recover the general again. You are but now cast in his mood° —   150
  a punishment more in policy° than in malice — even so as one would
  beat his offenseless dog to affright an imperious lion. Sue to him
  again, and he's yours.
Cassio: I will rather sue to be despised than to deceive so good a commander with so slight, so drunken, and so indiscreet an officer. Drunk!   155
  And speak parrot°! And squabble! Swagger! Swear! and discourse
  fustian° with one's own shadow! O thou invisible spirit of wine, if
  thou hast no name to be known by, let us call thee devil!
Iago: What was he that you followed with your sword?   160
  What had he done to you?
Cassio: I know not.
Iago: Is't possible?
Cassio: I remember a mass of things, but nothing distinctly: a quarrel, but
  nothing wherefore. O God, that men should put an enemy in their

---

¹²⁷*mince:* cut up (i.e., tell only part of).   ¹⁴⁶*sense:* physical feeling.   ¹⁴⁷*imposition:* external
thing.   ¹⁵⁰*cast in his mood:* dismissed because of his anger.   ¹⁵¹*in policy:* politically necessary.
¹⁵⁶*speak parrot:* gabble without sense.   ^{156 – 57}*discourse fustian:* speak nonsense ("fustian" was a
coarse cotton cloth used for stuffing).

mouths to steal away their brains! that we should with joy, pleas- 165
ance, revel, and applause transform ourselves into beasts!

Iago: Why, but you are now well enough. How came you thus recovered?

Cassio: It hath pleased the devil drunkenness to give place to the devil
wrath. One unperfectness shows me another, to make me frankly
despise myself. 170

Iago: Come, you are too severe a moraler. As the time, the place, and the
condition of this country stands, I could heartily wish this had not
befall'n; but since it is as it is, mend it for your own good.

Cassio: I will ask him for my place again: he shall tell me I am a drunkard.
Had I as many mouths as Hydra, such an answer would stop them 175
all. To be now a sensible man, by and by a fool, and presently a
beast! O strange! Every inordinate cup is unblest, and the ingredient
is a devil.

Iago: Come, come, good wine is a good familiar creature if it be well used.
Exclaim no more against it. And, good lieutenant, I think you think 180
I love you.

Cassio: I have well approved it, sir. I drunk?

Iago: You or any man living may be drunk at a time, man. I tell you what
you shall do. Our general's wife is now the general. I may say so in
this respect, for all he hath devoted and given up himself to the 185
contemplation, mark, and devotement of her parts° and graces. Confess yourself freely to her; importune her help to put you in your
place again. She is of so free, so kind, so apt, so blessed a disposition
she holds it a vice in her goodness not to do more than she is
requested. This broken joint between you and her husband entreat 190
her to splinter°; and my fortunes against any lay° worth naming, this
crack of your love shall grow stronger than it was before.

Cassio: You advise me well.

Iago: I protest, in the sincerity of love and honest kindness.

Cassio: I think it freely; and betimes in the morning I will beseech the 195
virtuous Desdemona to undertake for me. I am desperate of my
fortunes if they check° me.

Iago: You are in the right. Good night, lieutenant; I must to the watch.

Cassio: Good night, honest Iago. *Exit Cassio.*

Iago: And what's he then that says I play the villain, 200
When this advice is free° I give, and honest,
Probal to° thinking, and indeed the course
To win the Moor again? For 'tis most easy
Th' inclining° Desdemona to subdue
In any honest suit; she's framed as fruitful° 205
As the free elements°. And then for her
To win the Moor — were't to renounce his baptism,
All seals and symbols of redeemèd sin —
His soul is so enfettered to her love

---

[186]*devotement of her parts:* devotion to her qualities.   [191]*splinter:* splint.   [191]*lay:* wager.   [197]*check:*
repulse.   [201]*free:* generous and open.   [202]*Probal to:* provable by.   [204]*inclining:* inclined (to be
helpful).   [205]*framed as fruitful:* made as generous.   [206]*elements:* i.e., basic nature.

That she may make, unmake, do what she list,   210
Even as her appetite° shall play the god
With his weak function°. How am I then a villain
To counsel Cassio to this parallel course,
Directly to his good? Divinity of hell!
When devils will the blackest sins put on°,   215
They do suggest at first with heavenly shows°,
As I do now. For whiles this honest fool
Plies Desdemona to repair his fortune,
And she for him pleads strongly to the Moor,
I'll pour this pestilence into his ear: 220
That she repeals him 221 for her body's lust;
And by how much she strives to do him good,
She shall undo her credit with the Moor.
So will I turn her virtue into pitch,
And out of her own goodness make the net   225
That shall enmesh them all. How now, Roderigo?

Enter Roderigo.

Roderigo: I do not follow here in the chase, not like a hound that hunts,
but one that fills up the cry°. My money is almost spent; I have been
tonight exceedingly well cudgeled; and I think the issue will be, I
shall have so much experience for my pains; and so, with no money   230
at all, and a little more wit, return again to Venice.

Iago: How poor are they that have not patience!
What wound did ever heal but by degrees?
Thou know'st we work by wit, and not by witchcraft;
And wit depends on dilatory time.   235
Does't not go well? Cassio hath beaten thee,
And thou by that small hurt hath cashiered Cassio.
Though other things grow fair against the sun,
Yet fruits that blossom first will first be ripe.
Content thyself awhile. By the mass, 'tis morning!   240
Pleasure and action make the hours seem short.
Retire thee, go where thou art billeted.
Away, I say! Thou shalt know more hereafter.
Nay, get thee gone!   *Exit Roderigo.*
                    Two things are to be done:
My wife must move° for Cassio to her mistress;   245
I'll set her on;
Myself awhile° to draw the Moor apart
And bring him jump° when he may Cassio find
Soliciting his wife. Ay, that's the way!
Dull not device by coldness and delay.   *Exit.*   250

---

²¹¹*appetite:* liking.   ²¹²*function:* thought.   ²¹⁵*put on:* advance, further.   ²¹⁶*shows:* appearances.
²²¹*repeals him:* asks for (Cassio's reinstatement).   ²²⁸*fills up the cry:* makes up one of the hunting
pack, adding to the noise but not actually tracking.   ²⁴⁵*move:* petition.   ²⁴⁷*awhile:* at the same
time.   ²⁴⁸*jump:* at the precise moment and place.

ACT III

Scene I [*A street.*]

Enter Cassio [and] Musicians.

Cassio: Masters, play here. I will content your pains°.
Something that's brief; and bid "Good morrow, general."

[*They play.*]

[*Enter Clown°.*]

Clown: Why, masters, have your instruments been in Naples° that they
speak i' th' nose thus?
Musician: How, sir, how?   5
Clown: Are these, I pray you, wind instruments?
Musician: Ay, marry, are they, sir.
Clown: O, thereby hangs a tale.
Musician: Whereby hangs a tale, sir?
Clown: Marry, sir, by many a wind instrument that I know. But, masters,   10
here's money for you; and the general so likes your music that he
desires you, for love's sake, to make no more noise with it.
Musician: Well, sir, we will not.
Clown: If you have any music that may not be heard, to't again. But, as
they say, to hear music the general does not greatly care.   15
Musician: We have none such, sir.
Clown: Then put up your pipes in your bag, for I'll away. Go, vanish into
air, away!   *Exit Musicians.*
Cassio: Dost thou hear me, mine honest friend?
Clown: No. I hear not your honest friend. I hear you.   20
Cassio: Prithee keep up thy quillets°. There's a poor piece of gold for thee.
If the gentlewoman that attends the general's wife be stirring, tell
her there's one Cassio entreats her a little favor of speech. Wilt thou
do this?
Clown: She is stirring, sir. If she will stir hither, I shall seem to notify unto   25
her°.   *Exit Clown.*

Enter Iago.

Cassio: In happy time, Iago.
Iago: You have not been abed then?
Cassio: Why no, the day had broke before we parted.
I have made bold, Iago, to send in to your wife;
My suit to her is that she will to virtuous Desdemona   30
Procure me some access.
Iago: I'll send her to you presently,

III.i. ¹*content your pains:* reward your efforts.   s.d. *Clown:* fool.   ³*Naples:* this may refer either
to the Neapolitan nasal tone, or to syphilis — rife in Naples — which breaks down the nose.
²¹*quillets:* puns.   ²⁵⁻²⁶*seem . . . her:* (the Clown is mocking Cassio's overly elegant manner of
speaking).

And I'll devise a mean to draw the Moor
Out of the way, that your converse and business
May be more free.
Cassio: I humbly thank you for't.   *Exit* [*Iago*].
                              I never knew   35
A Florentine° more kind and honest.

Enter Emilia.

Emilia: Good morrow, good lieutenant. I am sorry
For your displeasure°; but all will sure be well.
The general and his wife are talking of it,
And she speaks for you stoutly. The Moor replies   40
That he you hurt is of great fame in Cyprus
And great affinity°, and that in wholesome wisdom
He might not but refuse you. But he protests he loves you.
And needs no other suitor but his likings
To bring you in again.
Cassio: Yet I beseech you,   45
If you think fit, or that it may be done,
Give me advantage of some brief discourse
With Desdemona alone.
Emilia: Pray you come in.
I will bestow you where you shall have time
To speak your bosom° freely.   50
Cassio: I am much bound to you.   [*Exeunt.*]

Scene II [*The citadel.*]

Enter Othello, Iago, and Gentlemen.

Othello: These letters give, Iago, to the pilot
And by him do my duties to the Senate.
That done, I will be walking on the works;
Repair° there to me.
Iago: Well, my good lord, I'll do't.
Othello: This fortification, gentlemen, shall we see't?   5
Gentlemen: We'll wait upon your lordship.   *Exeunt.*

Scene III [*The citadel.*]

Enter Desdemona, Cassio, and Emilia.

Desdemona: Be thou assured, good Cassio, I will do
All my abilities in thy behalf.
Emilia: Good madam, do. I warrant it grieves my husband
As if the cause were his.
Desdemona: O, that's an honest fellow. Do not doubt, Cassio,   5

---

³⁶*Florentine:* i.e., Iago is as kind as if he were from Cassio's home town, Florence.   ³⁸*displeasure:*
discomforting.   ⁴²*affinity:* family.   ⁵⁰*bosom:* inmost thoughts.   III.ii.   ⁴*Repair:* go.

But I will have my lord and you again
As friendly as you were.
Cassio: Bounteous madam,
Whatever shall become of Michael Cassio,
He's never anything but your true servant.
Desdemona: I know't; I thank you. You do love my lord.   10
You have known him long, and be you well assured
He shall in strangeness stand no farther off
Than in a politic distance.°
Cassio: Ay, but, lady,
That policy may either last so long,
Or feed upon such nice° and waterish diet,   15
Or breed itself so out of circumstances°,
That, I being absent, and my place supplied°,
My general will forget my love and service.
Desdemona: Do not doubt° that; before Emilia here
I give thee warrant of thy place. Assure thee,   20
If I do vow a friendship, I'll perform it
To the last article. My lord shall never rest;
I'll watch him tame° and talk him out of patience;
His bed shall seem a school, his board a shrift°;
I'll intermingle everything he does   25
With Cassio's suit. Therefore be merry, Cassio,
For thy solicitor shall rather die
Than give thy cause away.

     Enter Othello and Iago [at a distance].

Emilia: Madam, here comes my lord.
Cassio: Madam, I'll take my leave.   30
Desdemona: Why, stay, and hear me speak.
Cassio: Madam, not now. I am very ill at ease,
Unfit for mine own purposes.
Desdemona: Well, do your discretion.   *Exit Cassio.*
Iago: Ha! I like not that.
Othello: What dost thou say?
Iago: Nothing, my lord; or if — I know not what.   35
Othello: Was not that Cassio parted from my wife?
Iago: Cassio, my lord? No, sure, I cannot think it
That he would steal away so guilty-like,
Seeing you coming.
Othello: I do believe 'twas he.   40
Desdemona [Coming to them]: How now, my lord?
I have been talking with a suitor here,
A man that languishes in your displeasure.

III.iii. ¹²⁻¹³*He . . . distance:* i.e., he shall act no more distant to you than is necessary for political
reasons. ¹⁵*nice:* trivial. ¹⁶*Or . . . circumstances:* i.e., or grow so on the basis of accidental
happenings and political needs. ¹⁷*supplied:* filled. ¹⁹*doubt:* imagine. ²³*watch him tame:* (animals were tamed by being kept awake). ²⁴*board a shrift:* table (seem) a confessional.

Othello: Who is't you mean?

Desdemona: Why, your lieutenant, Cassio. Good my lord, 45
 If I have any grace or power to move you,
 His present° reconciliation take.
 For if he be not one that truly loves you,
 That errs in ignorance, and not in cunning,
 I have no judgment in an honest face. 50
 I prithee call him back.

Othello: Went he hence now?

Desdemona: I' sooth so humbled
 That he hath left part of his grief with me
 To suffer with him. Good love, call him back.

Othello: Not now, sweet Desdemon; some other time. 55

Desdemona: But shall't be shortly?

Othello: The sooner, sweet, for you.

Desdemona: Shall't be tonight at supper?

Othello: No, not tonight.

Desdemona: Tomorrow dinner then?

Othello: I shall not dine at home;
 I meet the captains at the citadel.

Desdemona: Why then, tomorrow night, on Tuesday morn, 60
 On Tuesday noon, or night, on Wednesday morn.
 I prithee name the time, but let it not
 Exceed three days. In faith, he's penitent;
 And yet his trespass, in our common reason
 (Save that, they say, the wars must make example 65
 Out of her best), is not almost a fault
 T' incur a private check.° When shall he come?
 Tell me, Othello. I wonder in my soul
 What you would ask me that I should deny
 Or stand so mamm'ring° on. What? Michael Cassio, 70
 That came awooing with you, and so many a time,
 When I have spoke of you dispraisingly,
 Hath ta'en your part — to have so much to do
 To bring him in? By'r Lady, I could do much —

Othello: Prithee no more. Let him come when he will! 75
 I will deny thee nothing.

Desdemona: Why, this is not a boon;
 'Tis as I should entreat you wear your gloves,
 Or feed on nourishing dishes, or keep you warm,
 Or sue to you to do a peculiar profit°
 To your own person. Nay, when I have a suit 80
 Wherein I mean to touch your love indeed,
 It shall be full of poise° and difficult weight,
 And fearful to be granted.

---

⁴⁷*present:* immediate. ⁶⁶⁻⁶⁷*is . . . check:* is almost not serious enough for a private rebuke (let alone a public disgrace). ⁷⁰*mamm'ring:* hesitating. ⁷⁹*peculiar profit:* particularly personal good. ⁸²*poise:* weight.

Othello: I will deny thee nothing!
    Whereon I do beseech thee grant me this,
    To leave me but a little to myself.   85
Desdemona: Shall I deny you? No. Farewell, my lord.
Othello: Farewell, my Desdemona: I'll come to thee straight°.
Desdemona: Emilia, come. Be as your fancies teach you;
    Whate'er you be, I am obedient.   *Exit [with Emilia].*
Othello: Excellent wretch! Perdition catch my soul   90
    But I do love thee! And when I love thee not,
    Chaos is come again.
Iago: My noble lord —
Othello: What dost thou say, Iago?
Iago: Did Michael Cassio, when you wooed my lady,
    Know of your love?   95
Othello: He did, from first to last. Why dost thou ask?
Iago: But for a satisfaction of my thought,
    No further harm.
Othello: Why of thy thought, Iago?
Iago: I did not think he had been acquainted with her.
Othello: O, yes, and went between us° very oft.   100
Iago: Indeed?
Othello: Indeed? Ay, indeed! Discern'st thou aught in that?
    Is he not honest?
Iago: Honest, my lord?
Othello: Honest? Ay, honest.
Iago: My lord, for aught I know.
Othello: What dost thou think?
Iago: Think, my lord?
Othello: Think, my lord?   105
    By heaven, thou echoest me,
    As if there were some monster in thy thought
    Too hideous to be shown. Thou dost mean something.
    I heard thee say even now, thou lik'st not that,
    When Cassio left my wife. What didst not like?   110
    And when I told thee he was of my counsel°
    Of my whole course of wooing, thou cried'st "Indeed?"
    And didst contract and purse thy brow together,
    As if thou then hadst shut up in thy brain
    Some horrible conceit°. If thou dost love me,   115
    Show me thy thought.
Iago: My lord, you know I love you.
Othello: I think thou dost;
    And, for I know thou'rt full of love and honesty
    And weigh'st thy words before thou giv'st them breath,
    Therefore these stops° of thine fright me the more;   120
    For such things in a false disloyal knave

---

[87]*straight:* at once.   [100]*between us:* i.e., as messenger.   [111]*of my counsel:* in my confidence.
[115]*conceit:* thought.   [120]*stops:* interruptions.

Are tricks of custom°; but in a man that's just
They're close dilations°, working from the heart
That passion cannot rule.
Iago: For Michael Cassio,
I dare be sworn, I think that he is honest.
Othello: I think so too.
Iago: Men should be what they seem;
Or those that be not, would they might seem none!
Othello: Certain, men should be what they seem.
Iago: Why then, I think Cassio's an honest man.
Othello: Nay, yet there's more in this?   130
I prithee speak to me as to thy thinkings,
As thou dost ruminate, and give thy worst of thoughts
The worst of words.
Iago: Good my lord, pardon me:
Though I am bound to every act of duty,
I am not bound to that all slaves are free to.   135
Utter my thoughts? Why, say they are vile and false,
As where's that palace whereinto foul things
Sometimes intrude not? Who has that breast so pure
But some uncleanly apprehensions
Keep leets and law days°, and in sessions sit   140
With meditations lawful?
Othello: Thou dost conspire against thy friend, Iago,
If thou but think'st him wronged, and mak'st his ear
A stranger to thy thoughts.
Iago: I do beseech you —
Though I perchance am vicious in my guess   145
(As I confess it is my nature's plague
To spy into abuses, and of my jealousy
Shape faults that are not), that your wisdom
From one that so imperfectly conceits
Would take no notice, nor build yourself a trouble   150
Out of his scattering and unsure observance.
It were not for your quiet nor your good,
Nor for my manhood, honesty, and wisdom,
To let you know my thoughts.
Othello: What dost thou mean?
Iago: Good name in man and woman, dear my lord,   155
Is the immediate jewel of their souls.
Who steals my purse steals trash; 'tis something, nothing;
'Twas mine, 'tis his, and has been slave to thousands;
But he that filches from me my good name
Robs me of that which not enriches him   160
And makes me poor indeed.
Othello: By heaven, I'll know thy thoughts!

---

122 *of custom:* customary.   123 *close dilations:* expressions of hidden thoughts.   140 *leets and law days:*
meetings of local courts.

Iago: You cannot, if my heart were in your hand;
　　　Nor shall not whilst 'tis in my custody.
Othello: Ha!
Iago: 　　　O, beware, my lord, of jealousy! 165
　　　It is the green-eyed monster, which doth mock
　　　The meat it feeds on. That cuckold lives in bliss
　　　Who, certain of his fate, loves not his wronger;
　　　But O, what damnèd minutes tells° he o'er
　　　Who dotes, yet doubts — suspects, yet fondly° loves! 170
Othello: O misery.
Iago: Poor and content is rich, and rich enough;
　　　But riches fineless° is as poor as winter
　　　To him that ever fears he shall be poor.
　　　Good God the souls of all my tribe defend 175
　　　From jealousy!
Othello: 　　　　Why? Why is this?
　　　Think'st thou I'd make a life of jealousy,
　　　To follow still° the changes of the moon
　　　With fresh suspicions? No! To be once in doubt
　　　Is to be resolved. Exchange me for a goat 180
　　　When I shall turn the business of my soul
　　　To such exsufflicate and blown° surmises,
　　　Matching thy inference. 'Tis not to make me jealous
　　　To say my wife is fair, feeds well, loves company,
　　　Is free of speech, sings, plays, and dances; 185
　　　Where virtue is, these are more virtuous.
　　　Nor from mine own weak merits will I draw
　　　The smallest fear or doubt of her revolt,
　　　For she had eyes, and chose me. No, Iago;
　　　I'll see before I doubt; when I doubt, prove; 190
　　　And on the proof there is no more but this:
　　　Away at once with love or jealousy!
Iago: I am glad of this; for now I shall have reason
　　　To show the love and duty that I bear you
　　　With franker spirit. Therefore, as I am bound, 195
　　　Receive it from me. I speak not yet of proof.
　　　Look to your wife; observe her well with Cassio;
　　　Wear your eyes thus: not jealous nor secure.
　　　I would not have your free and noble nature
　　　Out of self-bounty° be abused. Look to't. 200
　　　I know our country disposition well:
　　　In Venice they do let heaven see the pranks
　　　They dare not show their husbands; their best conscience
　　　Is not to leave't undone, but kept unknown.°

---

¹⁶⁹*tells:* counts. ¹⁷⁰*fondly:* foolishly. ¹⁷³*fineless:* infinite. ¹⁷⁸*To follow still:* to change always (as the phases of the moon). ¹⁸²*exsufflicate and blown:* inflated and flyblown. ²⁰⁰*self-bounty:* innate kindness (which attributes his own motives to others). ²⁰³⁻⁴*their . . . unknown:* i.e., their morality does not forbid adultery, but it does forbid being found out.

Othello: Dost thou say so?   205

Iago: She did deceive her father, marrying you;
And when she seemed to shake and fear your looks,
She loved them most.

Othello: And so she did.

Iago: Why, go to then!
She that so young could give out such a seeming
To seel° her father's eyes up close as oak° —   210
He thought 'twas witchcraft. But I am much to blame.
I humbly do beseech you of your pardon
For too much loving you.

Othello: I am bound to thee forever.

Iago: I see this hath a little dashed your spirits.

Othello: Not a jot, not a jot.

Iago: Trust me, I fear it has.   215
I hope you will consider what is spoke
Comes from my love. But I do see y' are moved.
I am to pray you not to strain° my speech
To grosser issues nor to larger reach°
Than to suspicion.   220

Othello: I will not.

Iago: Should you do so, my lord,
My speech should fall into such vile success
Which my thoughts aimed not. Cassio's my worthy friend —
My lord, I see y' are moved.

Othello: No, not much moved.
I do not think but Desdemona's honest.   225

Iago: Long live she so. And long live you to think so.

Othello: And yet, how nature erring from itself —

Iago: Ay, there's the point, as (to be bold with you)
Not to affect many proposèd matches
Of her own clime, complexion, and degree°,   230
Whereto we see in all things nature tends° —
Foh! one may smell in such a will most rank,
Foul disproportions, thoughts unnatural.
But, pardon me, I do not in position°
Distinctly° speak of her; though I may fear   235
Her will, recoiling to her better judgment,
May fall to match° you with her country forms°,
And happily° repent.

Othello: Farewell, farewell!
If more thou dost perceive, let me know more.
Set on thy wife to observe. Leave me, Iago.   240

---

²¹⁰*seel:* hoodwink.   ²¹⁰*oak:* (a close-grained wood).   ²¹⁸*strain:* enlarge the meaning.
²¹⁹*reach:* meaning.   ²³⁰*degree:* social station.   ²³¹*in . . . tends:* i.e., all things in nature seek out
their own kind.   ²³⁴*position:* general argument.   ²³⁵*Distinctly:* specifically.   ²³⁷*fall to match:*
happen to compare.   ²³⁷*country forms:* i.e., the familiar appearance of her countrymen.
²³⁸*happily:* by chance.

Iago: My lord, I take my leave.   *[Going.]*
Othello: Why did I marry? This honest creature doubtless
    Sees and knows more, much more, than he unfolds.
Iago [Returns]: My lord, I would I might entreat your honor
    To scan this thing no farther. Leave it to time.   245
    Although 'tis fit that Cassio have his place,
    For sure he fills it up with great ability,
    Yet, if you please to hold him off awhile,
    You shall by that perceive him and his means.
    Note if your lady strains his entertainment°   250
    With any strong or vehement importunity;
    Much will be seen in that. In the meantime
    Let me be thought too busy in my fears
    (As worthy cause I have to fear I am)
    And hold her free, I do beseech your honor.   255
Othello: Fear not my government°.
Iago: I once more take my leave.   *Exit.*
Othello: This fellow's of exceeding honesty,
    And knows all qualities°, with a learnèd spirit
    Of human dealings. If I do prove her haggard°,
    Though that her jesses° were my dear heartstrings,   260
    I'd whistle her off and let her down the wind°
    To prey at fortune. Haply for° I am black
    And have not those soft parts° of conversation
    That chamberers° have, or for I am declined
    Into the vale of years — yet that's not much —   265
    She's gone. I am abused, and my relief
    Must be to loathe her. O curse of marriage,
    That we can call these delicate creatures ours,
    And not their appetites! I had rather be a toad
    And live upon the vapor of a dungeon   270
    Than keep a corner in the thing I love
    For others' uses. Yet 'tis the plague to great ones;
    Prerogatived are they less than the base.
    'Tis destiny unshunnable, like death.
    Even then this forkèd° plague is fated to us   275
    When we do quicken°. Look where she comes.

Enter Desdemona and Emilia.

    If she be false, heaven mocked itself!
    I'll not believe't.
Desdemona: How now, my dear Othello?

---

[250] *strains his entertainment:* urge strongly that he be reinstated.   [256] *government:* self-control.
[258] *qualities:* natures, types of people.   [259] *haggard:* a partly trained hawk which has gone wild
again.   [260] *jesses:* straps which held the hawk's legs to the trainer's wrist.   [261] *I'd . . . wind:* I
would release her (like an untamable hawk) and let her fly free.   [262] *Haply for:* it may be
because.   [263] *soft parts:* gentle qualities and manners.   [264] *chamberers:* courtiers — or, perhaps,
accomplished seducers.   [275] *forkèd:* horned (the sign of the cuckold was horns).   [276] *do quicken:*
are born.

Your dinner, and the generous islanders
By you invited, do attend° your presence.   280
Othello: I am to blame.
Desdemona: Why do you speak so faintly?
    Are you not well?
Othello: I have a pain upon my forehead, here°.
Desdemona: Why, that's with watching; 'twill away again,
    Let me but bind it hard, within this hour   285
    It will be well.
Othello: Your napkin° is too little;

    [*He pushes the handkerchief away, and it falls.*]

    Let it° alone. Come, I'll go in with you
Desdemona: I am very sorry that you are not well.   *Exit* [*with Othello*].
Emilia: I am glad I have found this napkin;
    This was her first remembrance from the Moor.   290
    My wayward husband hath a hundred times
    Wooed me to steal it; but she so loves the token
    (For he conjured her she should ever keep it)
    That she reserves it evermore about her
    To kiss and talk to. I'll have the work ta'en out°   295
    And give't Iago. What he will do with it,
    Heaven knows, not I; I nothing° but to please his fantasy°.

    Enter Iago.

Iago: How now? What do you here alone?
Emilia: Do not you chide; I have a thing for you.
Iago: You have a thing for me? It is a common thing —   300
Emilia: Ha?
Iago: To have a foolish wife.
Emilia: O, is that all? What will you give me now
    For that same handkerchief?
Iago: What handkerchief?
Emilia: What handkerchief!   305
    Why, that the Moor first gave to Desdemona,
    That which so often you did bid me steal.
Iago: Hast stol'n it from her?
Emilia: No, but she let it drop by negligence,
    And to th' advantage°, I, being here, took't up.   310
    Look, here't is.
Iago: A good wench. Give it me.
Emilia: What will you do with't, that you have been so earnest
    To have me filch it?

---

²⁸⁰*attend:* wait.   ²⁸³*here:* (he points to his imaginary horns).   ²⁸⁶*napkin:* elaborately worked
handkerchief.   ²⁸⁷*it:* (it makes a considerable difference in the interpretation of later events
whether this "it" refers to Othello's forehead or to the handkerchief; nothing in the text
makes the reference clear).   ²⁹⁵*work ta'en out:* needlework copied.   ²⁹⁷*I nothing:* I wish nothing.   ²⁹⁷*fantasy:* fancy, whim.   ³¹⁰*to th' advantage:* being lucky.

Iago: Why, what is that to you?   *[Takes it.]*

Emilia: If it be not for some purpose of import°,

    Give't me again. Poor lady, she'll run mad   315

    When she shall lack° it.

Iago: Be not acknown on't°.

    I have use for it. Go, leave me.   *Exit Emilia.*

    I will in Cassio's lodging lose this napkin

    And let him find it. Trifles light as air

    Are to the jealous confirmations strong   320

    As proofs of Holy Writ. This may do something.

    The Moor already changes with my poison:

    Dangerous conceits are in their natures poisons,

    Which at the first are scarce found to distaste°,

    But with a little°, act upon the blood,   325

    Burn like the mines of sulfur. I did say so.

Enter Othello.

    Look where he comes! Not poppy nor mandragora°,

    Nor all the drowsy syrups of the world,

    Shall ever medicine thee to that sweet sleep

    Which thou owedst° yesterday.

Othello: Ha! ha! False to me?   330

Iago: Why, how now, general? No more of that.

Othello: Avaunt! be gone! Thou hast set me on the rack.

    I swear 'tis better to be much abused

    Than but to know't a little.

Iago: How now, my lord?

Othello: What sense had I of her stol'n hours of lust?   335

    I saw't not, thought it not, it harmed not me;

    I slept the next night well, fed well, was free and merry;

    I found not Cassio's kisses on her lips.

    He that is robbed, not wanting° what is stol'n,

    Let him not know't, and he's not robbed at all.   340

Iago: I am sorry to hear this.

Othello: I had been happy if the general camp,

    Pioners° and all, had tasted her sweet body,

    So I had nothing known. O now, forever

    Farewell the tranquil mind! Farewell content!   345

    Farewell the plumèd troops, and the big wars

    That make ambition virtue! O, farewell!

    Farewell the neighing steed and the shrill trump,

    The spirit-stirring drum, th' ear-piercing fife,

    The royal banner, and all quality,   350

    Pride, pomp, and circumstance° of glorious war!

---

[314]*import:* importance.   [316]*lack:* miss.   [316]*Be not acknown on't:* forget you ever saw it.   [324]*are scarce found to distaste:* scarcely can be tasted.   [325]*with a little:* in a short time.   [327]*poppy nor mandragora:* soporifics.   [330]*owedst:* possessed.   [339]*wanting:* missing.   [343]*Pioners:* the basest manual laborers in the army, who dug trenches and mines.   [351]*circumstance:* pageantry.

And O you mortal engines° whose rude throats
Th' immortal Jove's dread clamors° counterfeit,
Farewell! Othello's occupation's gone!

Iago: Is't possible, my lord?   355
Othello: Villain, be sure thou prove my love a whore!
Be sure of it; give me the ocular proof;
Or, by the worth of mine eternal soul,
Thou hadst been better have been born a dog
Than answer my waked wrath!

Iago: Is't come to this?   360
Othello: Make me to see't; or at the least so prove it
That the probation° bear no hinge nor loop
To hang a doubt on — or woe upon thy life!

Iago: My noble lord —
Othello: If thou dost slander her and torture me,   365
Never pray more; abandon all remorse;
On horror's head horrors accumulate;
Do deeds to make heaven weep, all earth amazed;
For nothing canst thou to damnation add
Greater than that.

Iago: O grace! O heaven forgive me!   370
Are you a man? Have you a soul or sense?
God b' wi' you! Take mine office. O wretched fool,
That lov'st to make thine honesty a vice!
O monstrous world! Take note, take note, O world,
To be direct and honest is not safe.   375
I thank you for this profit, and from hence
I'll love no friend, sith° love breeds such offense.

Othello: Nay, stay. Thou shouldst be honest.
Iago: I should be wise; for honesty's a fool
And loses that it works for.

Othello: By the world,   380
I think my wife be honest, and think she is not;
I think that thou art just, and think thou are not.
I'll have some proof. My name, that was as fresh
As Dian's° visage, is now begrimed and black
As mine own face. If there be cords, or knives,   385
Poison, or fire, or suffocating streams,
I'll not endure it. Would I were satisfied!

Iago: I see you are eaten up with passion.
I do repent me that I put it to you.
You would be satisfied?

Othello: Would? Nay, and I will.   390
Iago: And may; but how? How satisfied, my lord?
Would you, the supervisor°, grossly gape on?

---

³⁵²*mortal engines:* lethal weapons, i.e., cannon.   ³⁵³*clamors:* i.e., thunder.   ³⁶²*probation:* proof.
³⁷⁷*sith:* since.   ³⁸⁴*Dian's:* Diana's (goddess of the moon and of chastity).   ³⁹²*supervisor:* on-looker.

Behold her topped?

Othello: Death and damnation! O!

Iago: It were a tedious° difficulty, I think,
To bring them to that prospect°. Damn them then,   395
If ever mortal eyes do see them bolster°
More than their own! What then? How then?
What shall I say? Where's satisfaction?
It is impossible you should see this,
Were they as prime° as goats, as hot as monkeys,   400
As salt° as wolves in pride°, and fools as gross
As ignorance made drunk. But yet, I say,
If imputation and strong circumstances
Which lead directly to the door of truth
Will give you satisfaction, you might hav't.   405

Othello: Give me a living reason she's disloyal.

Iago: I do not like the office°.
But sith I am entered in this cause so far,
Pricked° to't by foolish honesty and love,
I will go on. I lay with Cassio lately,   410
And being troubled with a raging tooth,
I could not sleep.
There are a kind of men so loose of soul
That in their sleeps will mutter their affairs.
One of this kind is Cassio.   415
In sleep I heard him say, "Sweet Desdemona,
Let us be wary, let us hide our loves!"
And then, sir, would he gripe° and wring my hand,
Cry "O sweet creature!" Then kiss me hard,
As if he plucked up kisses by the roots   420
That grew upon my lips; laid his leg o'er my thigh,
And sigh, and kiss, and then cry, "Cursèd fate
That gave thee to the Moor!"

Othello: O monstrous! monstrous!

Iago: Nay, this was but his dream.

Othello: But this denoted a foregone conclusion°,   425
'Tis a shrewd doubt°, though it be but a dream.

Iago: And this may help to thicken other proofs
That do demonstrate° thinly.

Othello: I'll tear her all to pieces!

Iago: Nay, yet be wise. Yet we see nothing done;
She may be honest yet. Tell me but this: 430
Have you not sometimes seen a handkerchief
Spotted with strawberries in your wife's hand?

Othello: I gave her such a one; 'twas my first gift.

---

³⁹⁴*tedious:* hard to arrange.   ³⁹⁵*prospect:* sight (where they can be seen).   ³⁹⁶*bolster:* go to bed with.   ⁴⁰⁰⁻⁰¹*prime, salt:* lustful.   ⁴⁰¹*pride:* heat.   ⁴⁰⁷*office:* duty.   ⁴⁰⁹*Pricked:* spurred. ⁴¹⁸*gripe:* seize.   ⁴²⁵*foregone conclusion:* consummated fact.   ⁴²⁶*shrewd doubt:* penetrating guess. ⁴²⁸*demonstrate:* show, appear.

Iago: I know not that; but such a handkerchief —
  I am sure it was your wife's — did I today   435
  See Cassio wipe his beard with.
Othello: If it be that —
Iago: If it be that or any that was hers,
  It speaks against her with the other proofs.
Othello: O, that the slave had forty thousand lives!
  One is too poor, too weak for my revenge.   440
  Now do I see 'tis true. Look here, Iago:
  All my fond love thus do I blow to heaven.
  'Tis gone.
  Arise, black vengeance, from the hollow hell!
  Yield up, O love, thy crown and hearted° throne   445
  To tyrannous hate! Swell, bosom, with thy fraught°,
  For 'tis of aspics'° tongues.
Iago: Yet be content°.
Othello: O, blood, blood, blood!
Iago: Patience, I say. Your mind may change.
Othello: Never, Iago. Like to the Pontic Sea°,   450
  Whose icy current and compulsive course
  Nev'r keeps retiring ebb, but keeps due on
  To the Propontic and the Hellespont,
  Even so my bloody thoughts, with violent pace,
  Shall nev'r look back, nev'r ebb to humble love,   455
  Till that a capable and wide° revenge
  Swallow them up. [*He kneels.*] Now, by yond marble heaven,
  In the due reverence of a sacred vow
  I here engage my words.
Iago: Do not rise yet.   [*Iago kneels.*]
  Witness, you ever-burning lights above,   460
  You elements that clip° us round about,
  Witness that here Iago doth give up
  The execution° of his wit, hands, heart
  To wronged Othello's service! Let him command,
  And to obey shall be in me remorse°,   465
  What bloody business ever°.   [*They rise.*]
Othello: I greet thy love,
  Not with vain thanks but with acceptance bounteous°,
  And will upon the instant put thee to 't°.
  Within these three days let me hear thee say
  That Cassio's not alive.   470
Iago: My friend is dead. 'Tis done at your request.
  But let her live.

---

[445] *hearted:* seated in the heart.   [446] *fraught:* burden.   [447] *aspics':* asps'.   [447] *content:* patient, quiet.   [450] *Pontic Sea:* the Black Sea (famous for the strong and constant current with which it flows through the Bosporus into the Mediterranean, where the water level is lower). [456] *capable and wide:* sufficient and far-reaching.   [461] *clip:* enfold.   [463] *execution:* workings, action. [465] *remorse:* pity.   [466] *ever:* soever.   [467] *bounteous:* absolute.   [468] *to 't:* i.e., to the work you have said you are prepared to do.

Othello: Damn her, lewd minx! O, damn her! Damn her!
   Come, go with me apart. I will withdraw
   To furnish me with some swift means of death
   For the fair devil. Now art thou my lieutenant.   475
Iago: I am your own forever.   *Exeunt.*

Scene IV [*A street.*]

   Enter Desdemona, Emilia, and Clown.

Desdemona: Do you know, sirrah, where Lieutenant Cassio lies°?
Clown: I dare not say he lies anywhere.
Desdemona: Why, man?
Clown: He's a soldier, and for me to say a soldier lies, 'tis stabbing.
Desdemona: Go to. Where lodges he?   5
Clown: To tell you where he lodges is to tell you where I lie.
Desdemona: Can anything be made of this?
Clown: I know not where he lodges, and for me to devise a lodging, and
   say he lies here or he lies there, were to lie in mine own throat°.
Desdemona: Can you enquire him out, and be edified° by report?   10
Clown: I will catechize the world for him; that is, make questions, and
   by them answer.
Desdemona: Seek him, bid him come hither. Tell him I have moved° my
   lord on his behalf and hope all will be well.
Clown: To do this is within the compass° of man's wit, and therefore I   15
   will attempt the doing it.   *Exit Clown.*
Desdemona: Where should° I lose the handkerchief, Emilia?
Emilia: I know not, madam.
Desdemona: Believe me, I had rather have lost my purse
   Full of crusadoes°. And but my noble Moor   20
   Is true of mind, and made of no such baseness
   As jealous creatures are, it were enough
   To put him to ill thinking.
Emilia: Is he not jealous?
Desdemona: Who? He? I think the sun where he was born
   Drew all such humors° from him.
Emilia: Look where he comes.   25

   Enter Othello.

Desdemona: I will not leave him now till Cassio
   Be called to him. How is't with you, my lord?
Othello: Well, my good lady. [*Aside*] O, hardness to
   dissemble°! —

III.iv. ¹*lies:* lodges. ⁹*lie in mine own throat:* (to lie in the throat is to lie absolutely and completely). ¹⁰*edified:* enlightened (Desdemona mocks the Clown's overly elaborate diction).
¹³*moved:* pleaded with. ¹⁵*compass:* reach. ¹⁷*should:* might. ²⁰*crusadoes:* Portuguese gold
coins. ²⁴*humors:* characteristics. ²⁹*hardness to dissemble:* (Othello may refer here either to the
difficulty he has in maintaining his appearance of composure, or to what he believes to be
Desdemona's hardened hypocrisy).

How do you, Desdemona?

Desdemona: Well, my good lord.   30

Othello: Give me your hand. This hand is moist°, my lady.

Desdemona: It hath felt no age nor known no sorrow.

Othello: This argues° fruitfulness and liberal° heart.
    Hot, hot, and moist. This hand of yours requires
    A sequester° from liberty; fasting and prayer;   35
    Much castigation; exercise devout;
    For here's a young and sweating devil here
    That commonly rebels. 'Tis a good hand,
    A frank one.

Desdemona: You may, indeed, say so;
    For 'twas that hand that gave away my heart.   40

Othello: A liberal hand! The hearts of old gave hands,
    But our new heraldry° is hands, not hearts.

Desdemona: I cannot speak of this. Come now, your promise!

Othello: What promise, chuck?

Desdemona: I have sent to bid Cassio come speak with you.   45

Othello: I have a salt and sorry rheum° offends me.
    Lend me thy handkerchief.

Desdemona: Here, my lord.

Othello: That which I gave you.

Desdemona: I have it not about me.

Othello: Not?

Desdemona: No, indeed, my lord.

Othello: That's a fault.   50
    That handkerchief
    Did an Egyptian to my mother give.
    She was a charmer°, and could almost read
    The thoughts of people. She told her, while she kept it
    'Twould make her amiable° and subdue my father   55
    Entirely to her love; but if she lost it
    Or made a gift of it, my father's eye
    Should hold her loathèd, and his spirits should hunt
    After new fancies. She, dying, gave it me,
    And bid me, when my fate would have me wived,   60
    To give it her. I did so; and take heed on't;
    Make it a darling like your precious eye.
    To lose't or give't away were such perdition
    As nothing else could match.

Desdemona: Is't possible?

Othello: 'Tis true. There's magic in the web° of it.   65
    A sibyl that had numbered in the world

---

³¹*moist:* (a moist, hot hand was taken as a sign of a lustful nature).   ³³*argues:* suggests.
³³*liberal:* free, open (but also with a suggestion of "licentious"; from here on in this scene
Othello's words bear a double meaning, seeming to be normal but accusing Desdemona of
being unfaithful).   ³⁵*sequester:* separation.   ⁴²*heraldry:* heraldic symbolism.   ⁴⁶*a salt and sorry*
rheum: a heavy, running head cold.   ⁵³*charmer:* magician.   ⁵⁵*amiable:* desirable.   ⁶⁵*web:*
weaving.

The sun to course two hundred compasses,
In her prophetic fury° sewed the work;
The worms were hallowed that did breed the silk,
And it was dyed in mummy° which the skillful   70
Conserved of maidens' hearts.
Desdemona: Indeed? Is't true?
Othello: Most veritable. Therefore look to't well.
Desdemona: Then would to God that I had never seen't!
Othello: Ha! Wherefore?
Desdemona: Why do you speak so startingly and rash?   75
Othello: Is't lost? Is't gone? Speak, is it out o' th' way?
Desdemona: Heaven bless us!
Othello: Say you?
Desdemona: It is not lost. But what an if it were?
Othello: How?   80
Desdemona: I say it is not lost.
Othello: Fetch't, let me see't!
Desdemona: Why, so I can; but I will not now.
    This is a trick to put me from my suit:
    Pray you let Cassio be received again.   85
Othello: Fetch me the handkerchief! My mind misgives.
Desdemona: Come, come!
    You'll never meet a more sufficient° man —
Othello: The handkerchief!
Desdemona: A man that all his time
    Hath founded his good fortunes on your love,   90
    Shared dangers with you —
Othello: The handkerchief!
Desdemona: I'faith, you are to blame.
Othello: Away!   *Exit Othello.*
Emilia: Is not this man jealous?   95
Desdemona: I nev'r saw this before.
    Sure there's some wonder in this handkerchief;
    I am most unhappy in the loss of it.
Emilia: 'Tis not a year or two shows us a man.
    They are all but stomachs, and we all but food;   100
    They eat us hungerly, and when they are full,
    They belch us.

    Enter Iago and Cassio.

                Look you, Cassio and my husband.
Iago: There is no other way; 'tis she must do't.
    And lo the happiness! Go and importune her.
Desdemona: How now, good Cassio? What's the news with you?   105
Cassio: Madam, my former suit. I do beseech you
    That by your virtuous means I may again

---

⁶⁸*prophetic fury:* seized by the spirit and able to prophesy.   ⁷⁰*mummy:* liquid drained from embalmed bodies.   ⁸⁸*sufficient:* complete, with all proper qualities.

Exist, and be a member of his love
Whom I with all the office° of my heart
Entirely honor. I would not be delayed.   110
If my offense be of such mortal kind
That nor my service past, nor present sorrows,
Nor purposed merit in futurity,
Can ransom me into his love again,
But to know so must be my benefit°.   115
So shall I clothe me in a forced content,
And shut myself up in some other course
To fortune's alms.

Desdemona: Alas, thrice-gentle Cassio,
My advocation° is not now in tune.
My lord is not my lord; nor should I know him   120
Were he in favor° as in humor altered.
So help me every spirit sanctified
As I have spoken for you all my best
And stood within the blank° of his displeasure
For my free speech. You must awhile be patient.   125
What I can do I will; and more I will
Than for myself I dare. Let that suffice you.

Iago: Is my lord angry?

Emilia: He went hence but now,
And certainly in strange unquietness.

Iago: Can he be angry? I have seen the cannon   130
When it hath blown his ranks into the air
And, like the devil, from his very arm
Puffed his own brother. And is he angry?
Something of moment° then. I will go meet him.
There's matter in't indeed if he be angry.   135

Desdemona: I prithee do so.   *Exit* [*Iago.*]
                         Something sure of state°,
Either from Venice or some unhatched practice°
Made demonstrable here in Cyprus to him,
Hath puddled° his clear spirit; and in such cases
Men's natures wrangle with inferior things,   140
Though great ones are their object. 'Tis even so.
For let our finger ache, and it endues°
Our other, healthful members even to a sense
Of pain. Nay, we must think men are not gods,
Nor of them look for such observancy   145
As fits the bridal. Beshrew me much, Emilia,
I was, unhandsome warrior as I am,
Arraigning his unkindness with my soul;
But now I find I had suborned the witness,

---

¹⁰⁹*office:* duty.   ¹¹⁵*benefit:* good.   ¹¹⁹*advocation:* advocacy.   ¹²¹*favor:* countenance.   ¹²⁴*blank:*
bull's-eye of a target.   ¹³⁴*moment:* importance.   ¹³⁶*of state:* state affairs.   ¹³⁷*unhatched practice:*
undisclosed plot.   ¹³⁹*puddled:* muddied.   ¹⁴²*endues:* leads.

And he's indicted falsely.

Emilia: Pray heaven it be   150
     State matters, as you think, and no conception
     Nor no jealous toy° concerning you.

Desdemona: Alas the day! I never gave him cause.

Emilia: But jealous souls will not be answered so;
     They are not ever jealous for the cause,   155
     But jealous for they're jealous. It is a monster
     Begot upon itself, born on itself.

Desdemona: Heaven keep the monster from Othello's mind!

Emilia: Lady, amen.

Desdemona: I will go seek him. Cassio, walk here about.   160
     If I do find him fit°, I'll move your suit
     And seek to effect it to my uttermost.

Cassio: I humbly thank your ladyship.   *Exit [Desdemona with Emilia].*

     Enter Bianca.

Bianca: Save you, friend Cassio!

Cassio: What make you from home?
     How is't with you, my most fair Bianca?   165
     I' faith, sweet love, I was coming to your house.

Bianca: And I was going to your lodging, Cassio.
     What, keep a week away? Seven days and nights?
     Eightscore eight hours? And lovers' absent hours
     More tedious than the dial eightscore times?   170
     O weary reck'ning°.

Cassio: Pardon me, Bianca.
     I have this while with leaden thoughts been pressed,
     But I shall in a more continuate° time
     Strike off this score° of absence. Sweet Bianca,

             [Gives her Desdemona's handkerchief.]

     Take me this work out.

Bianca: O Cassio, whence came this?   175
     This is some token from a newer friend.
     To the felt absence now I feel a cause.
     Is't come to this? Well, well.

Cassio: Go to, woman!
     Throw your vile guesses in the devil's teeth,
     From whence you have them. You are jealous now   180
     That this is from some mistress, some remembrance.
     No, by my faith, Bianca.

Bianca: Why, whose is it?

Cassio: I know not neither; I found it in my chamber.
     I like the work well; ere it be demanded°,

---

¹⁵²*toy:* trifle.   ¹⁶¹*fit:* receptive.   ¹⁷¹*reck'ning:* addition.   ¹⁷³*continuate:* uninterrupted.
¹⁷⁴*Strike off this score:* i.e., pay this bill (the *score* being the account of drinks kept in a tavern).
¹⁸⁴*demanded:* asked for (by the person who lost it).

As like enough it will, I would have it copied.   185
Take it and do't, and leave me for this time.
Bianca: Leave you? Wherefore?
Cassio: I do attend here on the general
    And think it no addition, nor my wish,
    To have him see me womaned.
Bianca: Why, I pray you?   190
Cassio: Not that I love you not.
Bianca: But that you do not love me!
    I pray you bring° me on the way a little,
    And say if I shall see you soon at night.
Cassio: 'Tis but a little way that I can bring you,
    For I attend here; but I'll see you soon.   195
Bianca: 'Tis very good. I must be circumstanced°.   *Exeunt omnes.*

ACT IV

Scene I [*A street.*]

    Enter Othello and Iago.

Iago: Will you think so?
Othello: Think so, Iago?
Iago: What,
    To kiss in private?
Othello: An unauthorized° kiss?
Iago: Or to be naked with her friend in bed
    An hour or more, not meaning any harm?
Othello: Naked in bed, Iago, and not mean harm?   5
    It is hypocrisy against the devil.
    They that mean virtuously, and yet do so,
    The devil their virtue tempts, and they tempt heaven.
Iago: If they do nothing, 'tis a venial slip.
    But if I give my wife a handkerchief —   10
Othello: What then?
Iago: Why, then 'tis hers, my lord; and being hers,
    She may, I think, bestow't on any man.
Othello: She is protectress of her honor too.
    May she give that?   15
Iago: Her honor is an essence that's not seen;
    They have it very oft that have it not.
    But for the handkerchief —
Othello: By heaven, I would most gladly have forgot it!
    Thou said'st — O, it comes o'er my memory   20
    As doth the raven° o'er the infected house,

---

¹⁹²*bring:* accompany.   ¹⁹⁶*be circumstanced:* accept things as they are.   IV.i.   ²*unauthorized:* illicit.
²¹*raven:* (a harbinger of death).

Boding to all — he had my handkerchief.
Iago: Ay, what of that?
Othello: That's not so good now.
Iago: What if I had said I had seen him do you wrong?
 Or heard him say — as knaves be such abroad°   25
 Who having, by their own importunate suit,
 Or voluntary dotage° of some mistress,
 Convincèd or supplied° them, cannot choose
 But they must blab —
Othello: Hath he said anything?
Iago: He hath, my lord; but be you well assured,   30
 No more than he'll unswear.
Othello: What hath he said?
Iago: Why, that he did — I know not what he did.
Othello: What? what?
Iago: Lie —
Othello: With her?
Iago: With her, on her; what you will.   35
Othello: Lie with her? Lie on her? — We say lie on her when they belie
 her. — Lie with her! Zounds, that's fulsome°. — Handkerchief —
 confessions — handkerchief! — To confess, and be hanged for his
 labor — first to be hanged, and then to confess! I tremble at it.
 Nature would not invest herself in such shadowing passion without   40
 some instruction°. It is not words that shakes me thus. — Pish!
 Noses, ears, and lips? Is't possible? — Confess? — Handkerchief?
 — O devil!   *Falls in a trance.*
Iago: Work on.
 My med'cine works! Thus credulous fools are caught,   45
 And many worthy and chaste dames even thus,
 All guiltless, meet reproach°. What, ho! My lord!
 My lord, I say! Othello!

 Enter Cassio.

      How now, Cassio?

Cassio: What's the matter?
Iago: My lord is fall'n into an epilepsy.   50
 This is his second fit; he had one yesterday.
Cassio: Rub him about the temples.
Iago: The lethargy° must have his quiet course.
 If not, he foams at mouth, and by and by
 Breaks out to savage madness. Look, he stirs.   55
 Do you withdraw yourself a little while.

---

²⁵*abroad:* i.e., in the world.   ²⁷*voluntary dotage:* weakness of the will.   ²⁸*Convincèd or supplied:*
persuaded or gratified (the mistress).   ³⁷*fulsome:* foul, repulsive.   ⁴⁰⁻⁴¹*Nature . . . instruction:*
i.e., my mind would not become so darkened (with anger) unless there were something in
this (accusation); remember that Othello believes in the workings of magic and supernatural
forces).   ⁴⁷*reproach:* shame.   ⁵³*lethargy:* coma.

He will recover straight. When he is gone,
I would on great occasion° speak with you.   [*Exit Cassio.*]
How is it, general? Have you not hurt your head?
Othello: Dost thou mock° me?
Iago: I mock you not, by heaven.   60
Would you would bear your fortune like a man.
Othello: A hornèd man's a monster and a beast.
Iago: There's many a beast then in a populous city,
And many a civil° monster.
Othello: Did he confess it?
Iago: Good, sir, be a man.   65
Think every bearded fellow that's but yoked
May draw° with you. There's millions now alive
That nightly lie in those unproper° beds
Which they dare swear peculiar.° Your case is better.
O, 'tis the spite of hell, the fiend's arch-mock,   70
To lip a wanton in a secure couch,
And to suppose her chaste. No, let me know;
And knowing what I am, I know what she shall be.
Othello: O, thou art wise! 'Tis certain.
Iago: Stand you awhile apart;
Confine yourself but in a patient list.°   75
Whilst you were here, o'erwhelmèd with your grief —
A passion most unsuiting such a man —
Cassio came hither. I shifted him away°
And laid good 'scuses upon your ecstasy°,
Bade him anon return, and here speak with me;   80
The which he promised. Do but encave° yourself
And mark the fleers°, the gibes, and notable° scorns
That dwell in every region of his face.
For I will make him tell the tale anew:
Where, how, how oft, how long ago, and when   85
He hath, and is again to cope your wife.
I say, but mark his gesture. Marry patience,
Or I shall say you're all in all in spleen°,
And nothing of a man.
Othello: Dost thou hear, Iago?
I will be found most cunning in my patience;   90
But — dost thou hear? — most bloody.
Iago: That's not amiss;
But yet keep time in all. Will you withdraw?

---

⁵⁸*great occasion:* very important matter.   ⁶⁰*mock:* (Othello takes Iago's comment as a reference
to his horns — which it is).   ⁶⁴*civil:* city-dwelling.   ⁶⁷*draw:* i.e., like the horned ox.
⁶⁸*unproper:* i.e., not exclusively the husband's.   ⁶⁹*peculiar:* their own alone.   ⁷⁵*a patient list:* the
bounds of patience.   ⁷⁸*shifted him away:* got rid of him by a stratagem.   ⁷⁹*ecstasy:* trance (the
literal meaning, "outside oneself," bears on the meaning of the change Othello is undergoing).
⁸¹*encave:* hide.   ⁸²*fleers:* mocking looks or speeches.   ⁸²*notable:* obvious.   ⁸⁸*spleen:* passion,
particularly anger.

[Othello moves to one side, where his remarks are not audible to Cassio and Iago.]

Now will I question Cassio of Bianca,
A huswife° that by selling her desires
Buys herself bread and cloth. It is a creature   95
That dotes on Cassio, as 'tis the strumpet's plague
To beguile many and be beguiled by one.
He, when he hears of her, cannot restrain
From the excess of laughter. Here he comes.

Enter Cassio.

As he shall smile, Othello shall go mad: 100
And his unbookish° jealousy must conster°
Poor Cassio's smiles, gestures, and light behaviors
Quite in the wrong. How do you, lieutenant?
Cassio: The worser that you give me the addition°
Whose want even kills me.   105
Iago: Ply Desdemona well, and you are sure on't.
Now, if this suit lay in Bianca's power,
How quickly should you speed!
Cassio: Alas, poor caitiff!°
Othello: Look how he laughs already!
Iago: I never knew woman love man so.   110
Cassio: Alas, poor rogue! I think, i' faith, she loves me.
Othello: Now he denies it faintly, and laughs it out.
Iago: Do you hear, Cassio?
Othello: Now he importunes him
To tell it o'er. Go to! Well said, well said!
Iago: She gives it out that you shall marry her.   115
Do you intend it?
Cassio: Ha, ha, ha!
Othello: Do ye triumph, Roman? Do you triumph?
Cassio: I marry? What, a customer°? Prithee bear some charity to my wit;
do not think it so unwholesome. Ha, ha, ha!   120
Othello: So, so, so, so. They laugh that win.
Iago: Why, the cry goes that you marry her.
Cassio: Prithee, say true.
Iago: I am a very villain else.
Othello: Have you scored° me? Well.   125
Cassio: This is the monkey's own giving out. She is persuaded I will marry
her out of her own love and flattery, not out of my promise.
Othello: Iago beckons me; now he begins the story.

[Othello moves close enough to hear.]

Cassio: She was here even now; she haunts me in every place. I was the

---

⁹⁴*huswife:* housewife (but with the special meaning here of "prostitute"). ¹⁰¹*unbookish:* ignorant. ¹⁰¹*conster:* construe. ¹⁰⁴*addition:* title. ¹⁰⁸*caitiff:* wretch. ¹¹⁹*customer:* one who sells, a merchant (here, a prostitute). ¹²⁵*scored:* marked, defaced.

other day talking on the sea bank with certain Venetians, and thither   130
comes the bauble°, and falls me thus about my neck —

Othello: Crying "O dear Cassio!" as it were. His gesture imports it.

Cassio: So hangs, and lolls, and weeps upon me; so shakes and pulls me!
Ha, ha, ha!

Othello: Now he tells how she plucked him to my chamber. O, I see that   135
nose of yours, but not that dog I shall throw it to.

Cassio: Well, I must leave her company.

Iago: Before me!° Look where she comes.

Enter Bianca.

Cassio: 'Tis such another fitchew!° Marry a perfumed one? What do you
mean by this haunting of me?   140

Bianca: Let the devil and his dam haunt you! What did you mean by that
same handkerchief you gave me even now? I was a fine fool to take
it. I must take out the work? A likely piece of work that you should
find it in your chamber and know not who left it there! This is some
minx's token, and I must take out the work? There! [*She throws down*   145
the handkerchief.] Give it your hobbyhorse°. Wheresoever you had it,
I'll take out no work on't.

Cassio: How now, my sweet Bianca? How now? how now?

Othello: By heaven, that should be my handkerchief!

Bianca: If you'll come to supper tonight, you may; if you will not, come   150
when you are next prepared for°.   *Exit.*

Iago: After her, after her!

Cassio: Faith, I must; she'll rail in the streets else.

Iago: Will you sup there?

Cassio: Yes, I intend so.   155

Iago: Well, I may chance to see you, for I would very fain speak with you.

Cassio: Prithee come. Will you?

Iago: Go to, say no more.   [*Exit Cassio.*]

Othello [*Comes forward*]: How shall I murder him, Iago?

Iago: Did you perceive how he laughed at his vice?   160

Othello: O Iago!

Iago: And did you see the handkerchief?

Othello: Was that mine?

Iago: Yours, by this hand! And to see how he prizes the foolish woman
your wife! She gave it him, and he hath giv'n it his whore.   165

Othello: I would have him nine years a-killing! — A fine woman, a fair
woman, a sweet woman?

Iago: Nay, you must forget that.

Othello: Ay, let her rot, and perish, and be damned tonight; for she shall
not live. No, my heart is turned to stone; I strike it, and it hurts my   170
hand. O, the world hath not a sweeter creature! She might lie by an
emperor's side and command him tasks.

131*bauble:* plaything.   138*Before me!:* (an exclamation of surprise).   139*fitchew:* polecat, i.e.,
strong-smelling creature.   146*hobbyhorse:* prostitute.   151*next prepared for:* next expected —
i.e., never.

Iago: Nay, that's not your way°.

Othello: Hang her! I do but say what she is. So delicate with her needle. An admirable musician. O, she will sing the savageness out of a bear! 175 Of so high and plenteous wit and invention° —

Iago: She's the worse for all this.

Othello: O, a thousand, a thousand times. And then, of so gentle a condition°?

Iago: Ay, too gentle. 180

Othello: Nay, that's certain. But yet the pity of it, Iago. O Iago, the pity of it, Iago.

Iago: If you are so fond over her iniquity, give her patent to offend; for if it touch° not you, it comes near nobody.

Othello: I will chop her into messes°. Cuckold me! 185

Iago: O, 'tis foul in her.

Othello: With mine officer!

Iago: That's fouler.

Othello: Get me some poison, Iago, this night. I'll not expostulate with her, lest her body and beauty unprovide my mind° again. This night, 190 Iago!

Iago: Do it not with poison. Strangle her in her bed, even the bed she hath contaminated.

Othello: Good, good! The justice of it pleases. Very good!

Iago: And for Cassio, let me be his undertaker°. You shall hear more by 195 midnight.

Othello: Excellent good!   [*A trumpet.*]
            What trumpet is that same?

Iago: I warrant something from Venice.

Enter Lodovico, Desdemona, and Attendants.

                              'Tis Lodovico.
This comes from the Duke. See, your wife's with him.

Lodovico: God save you, worthy general.

Othello: With° all my heart, sir. 200

Lodovico: The Duke and the senators of Venice greet you.

                           [*Gives him a letter.*]

Othello: I kiss the instrument of their pleasures.

                         [*Opens the letter and reads.*]

Desdemona: And what's the news, good cousin Lodovico?

Iago: I am very glad to see you, signior.
      Welcome to Cyprus. 205

Lodovico: I thank you. How does Lieutenant Cassio?

Iago: Lives, sir.

---

[173]*way:* proper course.   [176]*invention:* imagination.   [178–79]*gentle a condition:* (1) well born (2) of a gentle nature.   [184]*touch:* affects.   [185]*messes:* bits.   [190]*unprovide my mind:* undo my resolution. [195]*undertaker:* (not "burier" but "one who undertakes to do something").   [200]*With:* i.e., I greet you with.

Desdemona: Cousin, there's fall'n between him and my lord
    An unkind° breach; but you shall make all well.
Othello: Are you sure of that?
Desdemona: My lord? 110
Othello [*Reads*]: "This fail you not to do, as you will —"
Lodovico: He did not call; he's busy in the paper.
    Is there division 'twixt my lord and Cassio?
Desdemona: A most unhappy one. I would do much
    T' atone° them, for the love I bear to Cassio. 115
Othello: Fire and brimstone!
Desdemona: My lord?
Othello: Are you wise?
Desdemona: What, is he angry?
Lodovico: May be th' letter moved him;
    For, as I think, they do command him home,
    Deputing Cassio in his government°.
Desdemona: Trust me, I am glad on't.
Othello: Indeed?
Desdemona: My lord? 120
Othello: I am glad to see you mad.
Desdemona: Why, sweet Othello —
Othello: Devil!   [*Strikes her.*]
Desdemona: I have not deserved this.
Lodovico: My lord, this would not be believed in Venice,
    Though I should swear I saw't. 'Tis very much. 125
    Make her amends; she weeps.
Othello: O devil, devil!
    If that the earth could teem° with woman's tears,
    Each drop she falls° would prove a crocodile°.
    Out of my sight!
Desdemona: I will not stay to offend you.   [*Going.*]
Lodovico: Truly, an obedient lady. 130
    I do beseech your lordship call her back.
Othello: Mistress!
Desdemona: My lord?
Othello: What would you with her, sir?
Lodovico: Who? I, my lord?
Othello: Ay! You did wish that I would make her turn.
    Sir, she can turn, and turn, and yet go on 135
    And turn again; and she can weep, sir, weep;
    And she's obedient; as you say, obedient.
    Very obedient. Proceed you in your tears.
    Concerning this, sir — O well-painted passion!
    I am commanded home. — Get you away; 140
    I'll send for you anon. — Sir, I obey the mandate
    And will return to Venice. — Hence, avaunt!   [*Exit Desdemona.*]

---

[108] *unkind:* unnatural.   [115] *atone:* reconcile.   [119] *government:* office.   [127] *teem:* conceive.   [128] *falls:*
drops.   [128] *crocodile:* (the crocodile was supposed to shed false tears to lure its victims).

Cassio shall have my place. And, sir, tonight
I do entreat that we may sup together.
You are welcome, sir, to Cyprus. — Goats and monkeys!   *Exit.*   145
Lodovico: Is this the noble Moor whom our full Senate
Call all in all sufficient? Is this the nature
Whom passion could not shake? whose solid virtue
The shot of accident nor dart of chance
Could neither graze nor pierce?
Iago: He is much changed.   150
Lodovico: Are his wits safe? Is he not light of brain?
Iago: He's that he is; I may not breathe my censure.
What he might be (if, what he might, he is not)
I would to heaven he were!
Lodovico: What, strike his wife?
Iago: Faith, that was not so well; yet would I knew   155
That stroke would prove the worst.
Lodovico: Is it his use?°
Or did the letters work upon his blood°
And new-create his fault?
Iago: Alas, alas!
It is not honesty in me to speak
What I have seen and known. You shall observe him,   160
And his own courses° will denote him so
That I may save my speech. Do but go after
And mark how he continues.
Lodovico: I am sorry that I am deceived in him.   *Exeunt.*

Scene II [*The citadel.*]

Enter Othello and Emilia.

Othello: You have seen nothing then?
Emilia: Nor ever heard, nor ever did suspect.
Othello: Yes, you have seen Cassio and she together.
Emilia: But then I saw no harm, and then I heard
Each syllable that breath made up° between them.   5
Othello: What, did they never whisper?
Emilia: Never, my lord.
Othello: Nor send you out o' th' way?
Emilia: Never.
Othello: To fetch her fan, her gloves, her mask, nor nothing?
Emilia: Never, my lord.   10
Othello: That's strange.
Emilia: I durst, my lord, to wager she is honest,
Lay down my soul at stake°. If you think other,
Remove your thought. It doth abuse your bosom.

156*use:* habit. 157*blood:* passion. 161*courses:* actions. IV.ii. 5*that breath made up:* spoken.
13*at stake:* as the wager.

If any wretch have put this in your head,   15
Let heaven requite it with the serpent's curse°,
For if she be not honest°, chaste, and true,
There's no man happy. The purest of their wives
Is foul as slander.
Othello: Bid her come hither. Go.   *Exit Emilia.*
She says enough; yet she's a simple bawd°   20
That cannot say as much. This is a subtle whore,
A closet lock and key of villainous secrets,
And yet she'll kneel and pray; I have seen her do't.

Enter Desdemona and Emilia.

Desdemona: My lord, what is your will?
Othello: Pray you, chuck, come hither.
Desdemona: What is your pleasure?
Othello: Let me see your eyes.   25
Look in my face.
Desdemona: What horrible fancy's this?
Othello [*To Emilia*]: Some of your function°, mistress:
Leave procreants alone and shut the door;
Cough or cry hem if anybody come.
Your mystery°, your mystery! Nay, dispatch!   *Exit Emilia.*   30
Desdemona: Upon my knee, what doth your speech import?
I understand a fury in your words°.
Othello: Why, what art thou?
Desdemona: Your wife, my lord; your true
And loyal wife.
Othello: Come, swear it, damn thyself;
Lest, being like one of heaven, the devils themselves   35
Should fear to seize thee. Therefore be doubledamned:
Swear thou art honest.
Desdemona: Heaven doth truly know it.
Othello: Heaven truly knows that thou art false as hell.
Desdemona: To whom, my lord? With whom? How am I false?
Othello: Ah, Desdemon! Away! Away! Away!   40
Desdemona: Alas the heavy day! Why do you weep?
Am I the motive° of these tears, my lord?
If haply° you my father do suspect
An instrument of this your calling back,
Lay not your blame on me. If you have lost him,   45
I have lost him too.
Othello: Had it pleased heaven
To try me with affliction, had they rained
All kinds of sores and shames on my bare head,

---

¹⁶*serpent's curse:* (God's curse on the serpent after the fall in Eden).   ¹⁷*honest:* chaste.   ²⁰*bawd:*
procuress.   ²⁷*Some of your function:* do your proper work (as the operator of a brothel).
³⁰*mystery:* trade.   ³²*words:* (Q1 adds to this line, "But not the words").   ⁴²*motive:* cause.
⁴³*haply:* by chance.

Steeped° me in poverty to the very lips,
Given to captivity me and my utmost hopes,　　　　　　　　50
I should have found in some place of my soul
A drop of patience. But alas, to make me
The fixèd figure for the time of scorn°
To point his slow and moving finger at.
Yet could I bear that too, well, very well.　　　　　　　　55
But there where I have garnered up my heart,
Where either I must live or bear no life,
The fountain from the which my current runs
Or else dries up — to be discarded thence,
Or keep it as a cistern for foul toads　　　　　　　　60
To knot and gender° in — turn thy complexion there,
Patience, thou young and rose-lipped cherubin!
I here look grim as hell!°
Desdemona: I hope my noble lord esteems me honest.
Othello: O, ay, as summer flies are in the shambles°,　　　　　65
That quicken even with blowing°. O thou weed,
Who art so lovely fair, and smell'st so sweet,
That the sense aches at thee, would thou hadst never been born!
Desdemona: Alas, what ignorant° sin have I committed?
Othello: Was this fair paper, this most goodly book,　　　　　70
Made to write "whore" upon? What committed?
Committed? O thou public commoner°,
I should make very forges of my cheeks
That would to cinders burn up modesty,
Did I but speak thy deeds. What committed?　　　　　75
Heaven stops the nose at it, and the moon winks°;
The bawdy wind that kisses all it meets
Is hushed within the hollow mine of earth
And will not hear't. What committed?
Desdemona: By heaven, you do me wrong!　　　　　　　　80
Othello: Are not you a strumpet?
Desdemona:　　　　　　　　　No, as I am a Christian!
If to preserve this vessel for my lord
From any other foul unlawful touch
Be not to be a strumpet, I am none.
Othello: What, not a whore?
Desdemona:　　　　　　　　　No, as I shall be saved!　　　　85
Othello: Is't possible?
Desdemona: O, heaven forgive us!
Othello:　　　　　　　　　I cry you mercy° then.
I took you for that cunning whore of Venice
That married with Othello. [*Calling*] You, mistress,

---

⁴⁹*Steeped:* submerged.　⁵³*The . . . scorn:* the very image of scorn in our time.　⁶¹*knot and gender:*
twist in bunches and procreate.　⁶¹⁻⁶³*turn . . . hell:* (the rough sense would seem to be "even
Patience would grow pale, turn complexion, at Desdemona's perfidy, but that Othello looks
grimly on").　⁶⁵*shambles:* abattoirs.　⁶⁶*quicken even with blowing:* become impregnated as soon
as they lay their eggs.　⁶⁹*ignorant:* unknowing.　⁷²*commoner:* prostitute.　⁷⁶*winks:* closes its
eyes (the moon was the symbol of chastity).　⁸⁷*cry you mercy:* ask your pardon.

Enter Emilia.

That have the office opposite to Saint Peter   90
And keep the gate of hell! You, you, ay, you!
We have done our course; there's money for your pains.

                                    [*Throws her some coins.*]

I pray you turn the key and keep our counsel.   *Exit.*
Emilia: Alas, what does this gentleman conceive?
    How do you, madam? How do you, my good lady?   95
Desdemona: Faith, half asleep.
Emilia: Good madam, what's the matter with my lord?
Desdemona: With who?
Emilia: Why, with my lord, madam.
Desdemona: Who is thy lord?
Emilia: He that is yours, sweet lady.   100
Desdemona: I have none. Do not talk to me, Emilia.
    I cannot weep, nor answers have I none
    But what should go by water°. Prithee tonight
    Lay on my bed my wedding sheets, remember;
    And call thy husband hither.
Emilia: Here's a change indeed!   *Exit.*   105
Desdemona: 'Tis meet I should be used so, very meet.
    How have I been behaved, that he might stick
    The small'st opinion on my least misuse°?

    Enter Iago and Emilia.

Iago: What is your pleasure, madam? How is't with 'you?
Desdemona: I cannot tell. Those that do teach young babes   110
    Do it with gentle means and easy tasks.
    He might have chid me so; for, in good faith,
    I am a child to chiding.
Iago   What is the matter, lady?
Emilia: Alas, Iago, my lord hath so bewhored her,
    Thrown such despite° and heavy terms upon her   115
    That true hearts cannot bear it.
Desdemona: Am I that name, Iago?
Iago.   What name, fair lady?
Desdemona: Such as she said my lord did say I was.
Emilia: He called her whore. A beggar in his drink
    Could not have laid such terms upon his callet°.   120
Iago: Why did he so?
Desdemona: I do not know; I am sure I am none such.
Iago: Do not weep, do not weep. Alas the day.
Emilia: Hath she forsook so many noble matches,
    Her father and her country, and her friends,   125
    To be called whore? Would it not make one weep?

---

^{103}*water:* tears. $^{107-08}$*stick . . . misuse:* base any doubt on my smallest fault. ^{115}*despite:* abuse.
^{120}*callet:* slut.

Desdemona: It is my wretched fortune.
Iago: Beshrew° him for't!
  How comes this trick upon him?
Desdemona: Nay, heaven doth know.
Emilia: I will be hanged if some eternal villain,
  Some busy and insinuating rogue,   130
  Some cogging°, cozening slave, to get some office,
  Have not devised this slander. I will be hanged else.
Iago: Fie, there is no such man! It is impossible.
Desdemona: If any such there be, heaven pardon him.
Emilia: A halter pardon him! And hell gnaw his bones!   135
  Why should he call her whore? Who keeps her company?
  What place? What time? What form? What likelihood?
  The Moor's abused by some most villainous knave,
  Some base notorious knave, some scurvy fellow.
  O heavens, that such companions° thou'dst unfold°,   140
  And put in every honest hand a whip
  To lash the rascals naked through the world
  Even from the east to th' west!
Iago: Speak within door°.
Emilia: O, fie upon them! Some such squire° he was
  That turned your wit the seamy side without   145
  And made you to suspect me with the Moor.
Iago: You are a fool. Go to.
Desdemona   Alas, Iago,
  What shall I do to win my lord again?
  Good friend, go to him, for, by this light of heaven,
  I know not how I lost him. Here I kneel: 150
  If e'er my will did trespass 'gainst his love
  Either in discourse of thought° or actual deed,
  Or that mine eyes, mine ears, or any sense
  Delighted them in any other form;
  Or that I do not yet, and ever did,   155
  And ever will (though he do shake me off
  To beggarly divorcement) love him dearly,
  Comfort forswear me. Unkindness may do much,
  And his unkindness may defeat° my life,
  But never taint my love. I cannot say "whore."   160
  It does abhor me now I speak the word;
  To do the act that might the addition earn
  Not the world's mass of vanity could make me.
Iago: I pray you be content. 'Tis but his humor°.
  The business of the state does him offense.   165
Desdemona: If 'twere no other.
Iago: It is but so, I warrant. [*Trumpets within.*]

127*Beshrew:* curse.   131*cogging:* cheating.   140*companions:* fellows, rogues.   140*unfold:* disclose.
143*within door:* more quietly and moderately.   144*squire:* (a term of contempt).   152*discourse of
thought:* thinking.   159*defeat:* destroy.   164*humor:* mood.

Hark how these instruments summon to supper.
The messengers of Venice stay the meat°.
Go in, and weep not. All things shall be well.

[*Exeunt Desdemona and Emilia.*]

Enter Roderigo.

How now, Roderigo? 170
Roderigo: I do not find that thou deal'st justly with me.
Iago: What in the contrary?
Roderigo: Every day thou daff'st° me with some device,° Iago, and rather,
   as it seems to me now, keep'st from me all conveniency° than suppli-
   est me with the least advantage of hope. I will indeed no longer 175
   endure it; nor am I yet persuaded to put up° in peace what already
   I have foolishly suffered.
Iago: Will you hear me, Roderigo?
Roderigo: I have heard too much, and your words and performances are
   no kin together. 180
Iago: You charge me most unjustly.
Roderigo: With naught but truth. I have wasted myself out of my means.
   The jewels you have had from me to deliver Desdemona would half
   have corrupted a votarist°. You have told me she hath received them,
   and returned me expectations and comforts of sudden respect° and 185
   acquaintance; but I find none.
Iago: Well, go to; very well.
Roderigo: Very well? Go to? I cannot go to, man; nor 'tis not very well.
   Nay, I think it is scurvy, and begin to find myself fopped° in it.
Iago: Very well. 190
Roderigo: I tell you 'tis not very well. I will make myself known to
   Desdemona. If she will return me my jewels, I will give over my suit
   and repent my unlawful solicitation. If not, assure yourself I will
   seek satisfaction of you.
Iago: You have said now? 195
Roderigo: Ay, and said nothing but what I protest° intendment of doing.
Iago: Why, now I see there's mettle° in thee, and even from this instant
   do build on thee a better opinion than ever before. Give me thy
   hand, Roderigo. Thou hast taken against me a most just excep-
   tion°, but yet I protest I have dealt most directly° in thy affair. 200
Roderigo: It hath not appeared.
Iago: I grant indeed it hath not appeared, and your suspicion is not
   without wit and judgment. But, Roderigo, if thou hast that in thee
   indeed which I have greater reason to believe now than ever —
   I mean purpose, courage, and valor — this night show it. If thou the 205
   next night following enjoy not Desdemona, take me from this world
   with treachery and devise engines for° my life.

---

¹⁶⁸*stay the meat:* await the meal.   ¹⁷³*daff'st:* put off.   ¹⁷³*device:* scheme.   ¹⁷⁴*conveniency:* what is
needful.   ¹⁷⁶*put up:* accept.   ¹⁸⁴*votarist:* nun.   ¹⁸⁵*sudden respect:* immediate consideration.
¹⁸⁹*fopped:* duped.   ¹⁹⁶*protest:* aver.   ¹⁹⁷*mettle:* spirit.   ¹⁹⁹⁻²⁰⁰*exception:* objection.   ²⁰⁰*directly:*
straightforwardly.   ²⁰⁷*engines for:* schemes against.

Roderigo: Well, what is it? Is it within reason and compass°?

Iago: Sir, there is especial commission come from Venice to depute Cassio
in Othello's place. 210

Roderigo: Is that true? Why, then Othello and Desdemona return again
to Venice.

Iago: O, no; he goes into Mauritania and taketh away with him the fair
Desdemona, unless his abode be lingered here by some accident;
wherein none can be so determinate° as the removing of Cassio. 215

Roderigo: How do you mean, removing him?

Iago: Why, by making him uncapable of Othello's place — knocking out
his brains.

Roderigo: And that you would have me to do?

Iago: Ay, if you dare do yourself a profit and a right. He sups tonight with 220
a harlotry°, and thither will I go to him. He knows not yet of his
honorable fortune. If you will watch his going thence, which I will
fashion to fall out° between twelve and one, you may take him at
your pleasure. I will be near to second° your attempt, and he shall
fall between us. Come, stand not amazed at it, but go along with me. 225
I will show you such a necessity in his death that you shall think
yourself bound to put it on him. It is now high supper time, and the
night grows to waste. About it.

Roderigo: I will hear further reason for this.

Iago: And you shall be satisfied. *Exeunt.* 230

Scene III [*The citadel.*]

Enter Othello, Lodovico, Desdemona, Emilia, and Attendants.

Lodovico: I do beseech you, sir, trouble yourself no further.

Othello: O, pardon me; 'twill do me good to walk.

Lodovico: Madam, good night. I humbly thank your ladyship.

Desdemona: Your honor is most welcome.

Othello: Will you walk, sir? O, Desdemona. 5

Desdemona: My lord?

Othello: Get you to bed on th' instant; I will be returned forthwith.
Dismiss your attendant there. Look't be done.

Desdemona: I will, my lord. *Exit [Othello, with Lodovico and Attendants].*

Emilia: How goes it now? He looks gentler than he did. 10

Desdemona: He says he will return incontinent°,
And hath commanded me to go to bed.
And bade me to dismiss you.

Emilia: Dismiss me?

Desdemona: It was his bidding; therefore, good Emilia,
Give me my nightly wearing, and adieu. 15
We must not now displease him.

Emilia: I would you had never seen him!

---

²⁰⁸*compass:* possibility. ²¹⁵*determinate:* effective. ²²¹*harlotry:* female. ²²³*fall out:* occur.
²²⁴*second:* support. IV.iii. ¹¹*incontinent:* at once.

Desdemona: So would not I. My love doth so approve him
    That even his stubbornness, his checks°, his frowns —
    Prithee unpin me — have grace and favor.   20
Emilia: I have laid these sheets you bade me on the bed.
Desdemona: All's one°. Good Father, how foolish are our minds!
    If I do die before, prithee shroud me
    In one of these same sheets.
Emilia: Come, come! You talk.   25
Desdemona: My mother had a maid called Barbary.
    She was in love; and he she loved proved mad
    And did forsake her. She had a song of "Willow";
    An old thing 'twas, but it expressed her fortune,
    And she died singing it. That song tonight   30
    Will not go from my mind; I have much to do
    But to go hang my head all at one side
    And sing it like poor Barbary. Prithee dispatch.
Emilia: Shall I go fetch your nightgown?
Desdemona: No, unpin me here.   35
    This Lodovico is a proper man.
Emilia: A very handsome man.
Desdemona: He speaks well.
Emilia: I know a lady in Venice would have walked barefoot to Palestine
    for a touch of his nether lip.   40
Desdemona [*Sings*]:
    "The poor soul sat singing by a sycamore tree,
        Sing all a green willow;
      Her hand on her bosom, her head on her knee,
        Sing willow, willow, willow.
    The fresh streams ran by her and murmured her moans;   45
        Sing willow, willow, willow;
      Her salt tears fell from her, and soft'ned the stones —
        Sing willow, willow, willow — "
    Lay by these.   [*Gives Emilia her clothes.*]
      "Willow, Willow" —   50
    Prithee hie° thee; he'll come anon°.
      "Sing all a green willow must be my garland
      Let nobody blame him; his scorn I approve" —
    Nay, that's not next. Hark! Who is't that knocks?
Emilia: It is the wind.   55
Desdemona [*Sings*]:
    "I called my love false love; but what said he then?
        Sing willow, willow, willow:
    If I court moe° women, you'll couch with moe men."
    So, get thee gone; good night. Mine eyes do itch.
    Doth that bode weeping?
Emilia: 'Tis neither here nor there.   60
Desdemona: I have heard it said so. O, these men, these men.

---

[19]*checks:* rebukes.   [22]*All's one:* no matter.   [51]*hie:* hurry.   [51]*anon:* at once.   [58]*moe:* more.

Dost thou in conscience think, tell me, Emilia,
That there be women do abuse their husbands
In such gross kind?

Emilia: There be some such, no question.

Desdemona: Wouldst thou do such a deed for all the world?   65

Emilia: Why, would not you?

Desdemona: No, by this heavenly light!

Emilia: Nor I neither by this heavenly light.
I might do't as well i' th' dark.

Desdemona: Wouldst thou do such a deed for all the world?

Emilia: The world's a huge thing; it is a great price for a small vice.   70

Desdemona: In troth, I think thou wouldst not.

Emilia: In troth, I think I should; and undo't when I had done. Marry,
I would not do such a thing for a joint-ring°, nor for measures of
lawn°, nor for gowns, petticoats, nor caps, nor any petty exhibi-
tion°, but for all the whole world? Why, who would not make her   75
husband a cuckold to make him a monarch? I should venture purga-
tory for't.

Desdemona: Beshrew me if I would do such a wrong for the whole world.

Emilia: Why, the wrong is but a wrong i' th' world; and having the world
for your labor, 'tis a wrong in your own world, and you might   80
quickly make it right.

Desdemona: I do not think there is any such woman.

Emilia: Yes, a dozen; and as many to th' vantage as would store° the world
they played for.
But I do think it is their husbands' faults   85
If wives do fall. Say that they slack their duties
And pour our treasures into foreign° laps;
Or else break out in peevish jealousies,
Throwing restraint upon us; or say they strike us,
Or scant our former having in despite° —   90
Why, we have galls; and though we have some grace,
Yet have we some revenge. Let husbands know
Their wives have sense like them. They see, and smell,
And have their palates both for sweet and sour,
As husbands have. What is it that they do   95
When they change° us for others? Is it sport?
I think it is. And doth affection° breed it?
I think it doth. Is't frailty that thus errs?
It is so too. And have not we affections?
Desires for sport? and frailty? as men have?   100
Then let them use us well; else let them know,
The ills we do, their ills instruct us so°.

Desdemona: Good night, good night. Heaven me such uses° send,
Not to pick bad from bad, but by bad mend.   *Exeunt.*

---

⁷³*joint-ring:* (a ring with interlocking halves).   ⁷⁴*lawn:* fine linen.   ⁷⁴⁻⁷⁵*exhibition:* payment.
⁸³*to . . . store:* in addition as would fill.   ⁸⁷*foreign:* alien, i.e., other than the wife.   ⁹⁰*scant*
. . . despite: reduce, in spite, our household allowance (?).   ⁹⁶*change:* exchange.   ⁹⁷*affection:*
strong feeling, desire.   ¹⁰²*instruct us so:* teach us to do likewise.   ¹⁰³*uses:* practices.

ACT V

Scene I [*A street.*]

Enter Iago and Roderigo.

Iago: Here, stand behind this bulk°; straight will he come.
Wear thy good rapier bare, and put it home.
Quick, quick! Fear nothing; I'll be at thy elbow.
It makes us, or it mars us, think on that,
And fix most firm thy resolution.   5
Roderigo: Be near at hand; I may miscarry in't.
Iago: Here, at thy hand. Be bold, and take thy stand.

                                            [*Moves to one side.*]

Roderigo: I have no great devotion to the deed,
And yet he hath given me satisfying reasons.
'Tis but a man gone. Forth my sword! He dies!   10
Iago: I have rubbed this young quat° almost to the sense°,
And he grows angry. Now, whether he kill Cassio,
Or Cassio him, or each do kill the other,
Every way makes my gain. Live Roderigo,
He calls me to a restitution large   15
Of gold and jewels that I bobbed° from him
As gifts to Desdemona.
It must not be. If Cassio do remain,
He hath a daily beauty in his life
That makes me ugly; and besides, the Moor   20
May unfold me to him; there stand I in much peril.
No, he must die. But so, I hear him coming.

    Enter Cassio.

Roderigo: I know his gait. 'Tis he. Villain, thou diest!

                                            [*Thrusts at Cassio.*]

Cassio: That thrust had been mine enemy indeed
But that my coat° is better than thou know'st.   25
I will make proof of thine.   [*Fights with Roderigo.*]
Roderigo: O, I am slain!°
Cassio: I am maimed forever. Help, ho! Murder! Murder!

    Enter Othello [*to one side*].

Othello: The voice of Cassio. Iago keeps his word.

V.i. ¹*bulk:* projecting stall of a shop.   ¹¹*quat:* pimple.   ¹¹*to the sense:* raw.   ¹⁶*bobbed:* swindled.
²⁵*coat:* i.e., a mail shirt or bulletproof vest.   ²⁶*slain:* most editors add here a stage direction
that has Iago wounding Cassio in the leg from behind, but remaining unseen. However,
nothing in the text requires this expedient, and Cassio's wound can be given him in the fight
with Roderigo, for presumably when Cassio attacks Roderigo the latter would not simply
accept the thrust but would parry. Iago enters again at line 46, so that he must exit after line
22.

Roderigo: O, villain that I am!

Othello: It is even so.

Cassio: O help, ho! Light! A surgeon!   30

Othello: 'Tis he. O brave Iago, honest and just,

    That hast such noble sense of thy friend's wrong!

    Thou teachest me. Minion°, your dear lies dead,

    And your unblest° fate hies°. Strumpet, I come.

    Forth of my heart those charms, thine eyes, are blotted.   35

    Thy bed, lust-stained, shall with lust's blood be spotted.

Exit Othello.

    Enter Lodovico and Gratiano.

Cassio: What, ho? No watch? No passage°? Murder! Murder!

Gratiano: 'Tis some mischance. The voice is very direful.

Cassio: O, help!

Lodovico: Hark!   40

Roderigo: O wretched villain!

Lodovico: Two or three groan. 'Tis heavy night.

    These may be counterfeits. Let's think't unsafe

    To come into the cry without more help.

Roderigo: Nobody come? Then shall I bleed to death.   45

Lodovico: Hark!

    Enter Iago [with a light].

Gratiano: Here's one comes in his shirt, with light and weapons.

Iago: Who's there? Whose noise is this that cries on murder?

Lodovico: We do not know.

Iago: Do not you hear a cry?

Cassio: Here, here! For heaven's sake, help me!

Iago: What's the matter?   50

Gratiano: This is Othello's ancient, as I take it.

Lodovico: The same indeed, a very valiant fellow.

Iago: What are you here that cry so grievously?

Cassio: Iago? O, I am spoiled, undone by villains.

    Give me some help.   55

Iago: O me, lieutenant! What villains have done this?

Cassio: I think that one of them is hereabout

    And cannot make away.

Iago: O treacherous villains!

    [*To Lodovico and Gratiano*] What are you there?

    Come in, and give some help.

Roderigo: O, help me here!   60

Cassio: That's one of them.

Iago: O murd'rous slave! O villain!

    [*Stabs Roderigo.*]

---

³³*Minion:* hussy, i.e., Desdemona. ³⁴*unblest:* unsanctified. ³⁴*hies:* approaches swiftly. ³⁷*passage:* passers-by.

Roderigo: O damned Iago! O inhuman dog!

Iago: Kill men i' th' dark? — Where be these bloody thieves? —
How silent is this town! — Ho! Murder! Murder! —
What may you be? Are you of good or evil? 65

Lodovico: As you shall prove us, praise us.

Iago: Signior Lodovico?

Lodovico: He, sir.

Iago: I cry you mercy. Here's Cassio hurt by villains.

Gratiano: Cassio? 70

Iago: How is't, brother?

Cassio: My leg is cut in two.

Iago: Marry, heaven forbid!
Light, gentlemen. I'll bind it with my shirt.

Enter Bianca.

Bianca: What is the matter, ho? Who is't that cried?

Iago: Who is't that cried? 75

Bianca: O my dear Cassio! My sweet Cassio!
O Cassio, Cassio, Cassio!

Iago: O notable strumpet! — Cassio, may you suspect
Who they should be that have thus mangled you?

Cassio: No. 80

Gratiano: I am sorry to find you thus. I have been to seek you.

Iago: Lend me a garter. So. O for a chair
To bear him easily hence.

Bianca: Alas, he faints! O Cassio, Cassio, Cassio!

Iago: Gentlemen all, I do suspect this trash 85
To be a party in this injury. —
Patience awhile, good Cassio. — Come, come.
Lend me a light. Know we this face or no?
Alas, my friend and my dear countryman
Roderigo? No. — Yes, sure. — Yes, 'tis Roderigo! 90

Gratiano: What, of Venice?

Iago: Even he, sir. Did you know him?

Gratiano: Know him? Ay.

Iago: Signior Gratiano? I cry your gentle pardon.
These bloody accidents must excuse my manners
That so neglected you.

Gratiano: I am glad to see you. 95

Iago: How do you, Cassio? — O, a chair, a chair!

Gratiano: Roderigo?

Iago: He, he, 'tis he! [*A chair brought in.*] O, that's well said°; the chair.
Some good man bear him carefully from hence.
I'll fetch the general's surgeon. [*To Bianca*] For you, mistress, 100
Save you your labor. [*To Cassio*] He that lies slain here, Cassio,
Was my dear friend. What malice was between you?

Cassio: None in the world; nor do I know the man.

---

⁹⁸*well said:* well done.

Iago: What, look you pale? — O, bear him out o' th' air.

[Cassio is carried off.]

Stay you, good gentlemen. — Look you pale, mistress?   105
Do you perceive the gastness° of her eye?
Nay, if you stare, we shall hear more anon.
Behold her well; I pray you look upon her.
Do you see, gentlemen? Nay, guiltiness will speak,
Though tongues were out of use°.   110

[Enter Emilia.]

Emilia: Alas, what is the matter? What is the matter, husband?
Iago: Cassio hath here been set on in the dark
　　By Roderigo and fellows that are scaped.
　　He's almost slain, and Roderigo quite dead.
Emilia: Alas, good gentleman! Alas, good Cassio!   115
Iago: This is the fruits of whoring. Prithee, Emilia,
　　Go know of Cassio where he supped tonight.
　　[To Bianca] What, do you shake at that?
Bianca: He supped at my house; but I therefore shake not.
Iago: O, did he so? I charge° you go with me.   120
Emilia: Oh fie upon thee, strumpet!
Bianca: I am no strumpet, but of life as honest
　　As you that thus abuse me.
Emilia:　　　　　　　　　　As I? Fie upon thee!
Iago: Kind gentlemen, let's go see poor Cassio dressed°.
　　[To Bianca] Come, mistress, you must tell's another tale. 125
　　Emilia, run you to the citadel
　　And tell my lord and lady what hath happed.   *[Exit Emilia.]*
　　Will you go on afore?   *Exeunt [all but Iago].*
　　　　　　　　This is the night
　　That either makes me or fordoes me quite°.   *[Exit.]*

Scene II. *[Desdemona's chamber.]*

Enter Othello [with a light]; and Desdemona in her bed.

Othello: It is the cause, it is the cause, my soul.
　　Let me not name it to you, you chaste stars.
　　It is the cause. Yet I'll not shed her blood,
　　Nor scar that whiter skin of hers than snow
　　And smooth as monumental alabaster.   5
　　Yet she must die, else she'll betray more men.
　　Put out the light, and then put out the light.
　　If I quench thee, thou flaming minister°,
　　I can again thy former light restore,
　　Should I repent me; but once put out thy light,   10

---

[106]*gastness:* terror. [110]*tongues were out of use:* men no longer spoke. [120]*charge:* command.
[124]*dressed:* bandaged. [129]*fordoes me quite:* completely ruins me.   V.ii. [8]*minister:* worker, servant.

Thou cunning'st° pattern of excelling nature,
I know not where is that Promethean heat°
That can thy light relume°. When I have plucked the rose,
I cannot give it vital° growth again;
It needs must wither. I'll smell thee on the tree.   [*He kisses her.*]   15
O balmy breath, that dost almost persuade
Justice to break her sword. One more, one more!
Be thus when thou art dead, and I will kill thee,
And love thee after. One more, and that's the last!
So sweet was ne'er so fatal. I must weep,   20
But they are cruel tears. This sorrow's heavenly;
It strikes where it doth love. She wakes.
Desdemona: Who's there? Othello?
Othello: Ay, Desdemona.
Desdemona: Will you come to bed, my lord?
Othello: Have you prayed tonight, Desdemon?
Desdemona: Ay, my lord.   25
Othello: If you bethink yourself of any crime
     Unreconciled as yet to heaven and grace,
     Solicit for it straight.
Desdemona: Alack, my lord, what may you mean by that?
Othello: Well, do it, and be brief; I will walk by°.   30
     I would not kill thy unpreparèd spirit.
     No, heavens forfend! I would not kill thy soul.
Desdemona: Talk you of killing?
Othello: Ay, I do.
Desdemona: Then heaven
     Have mercy on me!
Othello: Amen, with all my heart.
Desdemona: If you say so, I hope you will not kill me.   35
Othello: Humh.
Desdemona: And yet I fear you; for you're fatal then
     When your eyes roll so. Why I should fear I know not,
     Since guiltiness I know not; but yet I feel I fear.
Othello: Think on thy sins.
Desdemona: They are loves I bear to you.   40
Othello: Ay, and for that thou diest.
Desdemona: That death's unnatural that kills for loving.
     Alas, why gnaw you so your nether lip?
     Some bloody passion shakes your very frame.
     These are portents; but yet I hope, I hope,   45
     They do not point on me.
Othello: Peace and be still.
Desdemona: I will so. What's the matter?
Othello: That handkerchief which I so loved and gave thee,

---

[11]*cunning'st:* most intricate and skillfully wrought (by nature excelling itself).   [12]*Promethean heat:* divine fire (Prometheus is the Titan who stole fire from heaven and gave it to man).   [13]*relume:* relight.   [14]*vital:* living.   [30]*by:* nearby.

Thou gav'st to Cassio.
Desdemona: No, by my life and soul!
Send for the man and ask him.
Othello: Sweet soul, take heed, 50
Take heed of perjury; thou art on thy deathbed.
Desdemona: Ay, but not yet to die.
Othello: Presently°.
Therefore confess thee freely of thy sin,
For to deny each article° with oath
Cannot remove nor choke the strong conception 55
That I do groan withal. Thou art to die.
Desdemona: Then Lord have mercy on me.
Othello: I say, amen.
Desdemona: And have you mercy too. I never did
Offend you in my life; never loved Cassio
But with such general warranty° of heaven 60
As I might love. I never gave him token.
Othello: By heaven, I saw my handkerchief in's hand!
O perjured woman! thou dost stone° my heart,
And mak'st me call what I intend to do
A murder, which I thought a sacrifice. 65
I saw the handkerchief.
Desdemona: He found it then.
I never gave it him. Send for him hither.
Let him confess a truth.
Othello: He hath confessed.
Desdemona: What, my lord?
Othello: That he hath used thee.
Desdemona: How? Unlawfully?
Othello: Ay. 70
Desdemona: He will not say so.
Othello: No, his mouth is stopped.
Honest Iago hath ta'en order for't°.
Desdemona: O, my fear interprets. What, is he dead?
Othello: Had all his hairs been lives, my great revenge
Had stomach° for them all. 75
Desdemona: Alas, he is betrayed, and I undone!
Othello: Out, strumpet! Weep'st thou for him to my face?
Desdemona: O, banish me, my lord, but kill me not!
Othello: Down, strumpet!
Desdemona: Kill me tomorrow; let me live tonight! 80
Othello: Nay, if you strive —
Desdemona: But half an hour!
Othello: Being done, there is no pause.
Desdemona: But while I say one prayer!

---

[52]*Presently:* immediately. [54]*article:* item (of the charge of adultery. Othello makes heavy use of legal terms in this scene). [60]*warranty:* allowance. [63]*stone:* turn to stone. [72]*ta'en order for't:* made sure of it. [75]*stomach:* appetite.

Othello: It is too late.   *Smothers her.*

    Emilia at the door.

Emilia [*Calls within*]: My lord, my lord! What, ho, my lord, my lord!
Othello: What noise is this? Not dead? Not yet quite dead?   85
    I that am cruel am yet merciful;
    I would not have thee linger in thy pain.
Emilia [*Within*]: What, ho! My lord, my lord!
Othello: So, so. Who's there?
Emilia [*Within*]: O, good my lord, I would speak a word with you.
Othello: Yes, 'tis Emilia. — By and by. — She's dead. —   90
    'Tis like she comes to speak of Cassio's death.
    The noise was high.° Ha! No more moving?
    Still as the grave. — Shall she come in? Were't good? —
    I think she stirs again. No. — What's best to do?
    If she come in, she'll sure speak to my wife.   95
    My wife! My wife! What wife? I have no wife.
    O, insupportable! O heavy hour!
    Methinks it should be now a huge eclipse
    Of sun and moon, and that th' affrighted globe
    Should yawn° at alteration.
Emilia [*Within*]:   I do beseech you   100
    That I may speak with you, O good my lord!
Othello: I had forgot thee. O, come in, Emilia.
    Soft, by and by. — Let me the curtains draw. —

        [*Draws the bed hangings and then opens the door.*]

    Where art thou?

    Enter Emilia.

          What's the matter with thee now?
Emilia: O my good lord, yonder's foul murders done!   105
Othello: What? Now?
Emilia: But now, my lord.
Othello: It is the very error° of the moon.
    She comes more nearer earth than she was wont
    And makes men mad.   110
Emilia: Cassio, my lord, hath killed a young Venetian
    Called Roderigo.
Othello: Roderigo killed?
    And Cassio killed?
Emilia: No, Cassio is not killed.
Othello: Not Cassio killed? Then murder's out of tune,
    And sweet revenge grows harsh.   115

---

⁹²*high:* loud (Q1 reads "here"). ⁹⁸⁻¹⁰⁰*Methinks . . . alteration:* (the Elizabethans believed that
great changes in human affairs were reflected by disorders in nature). ¹⁰⁰*yawn:* gape open
(as in an earthquake). ¹⁰⁸*error:* wandering out of regular course (disorders in the heavens
were believed by some to cause disorders on earth, as well as vice versa).

Desdemona: O, falsely, falsely murdered!

Emilia: O Lord! What cry is that?

Othello: That? What?

Emilia: Out and alas! that was my lady's voice.
Help! Help, ho! Help! O lady, speak again!
Sweet Desdemona! O sweet mistress, speak!   120

Desdemona: A guiltless death I die.

Emilia: O, who hath done this deed?

Desdemona: Nobody — I myself. Farewell.
Commend me to my kind lord. O, farewell!   [*She dies.*]

Othello: Why, how should she be murd'red?

Emilia: Alas, who knows?   125

Othello: You heard her say herself, it was not I.

Emilia: She said so. I must needs report the truth.

Othello: She's like a liar gone to burning hell!
'Twas I that killed her.

Emilia: O, the more angel she,
And you the blacker devil!   130

Othello: She turned to folly, and she was a whore.

Emilia: Thou dost belie her, and thou art a devil.

Othello: She was false as water.

Emilia: Thou art rash as fire to say
That she was false. O, she was heavenly true!

Othello: Cassio did top her. Ask thy husband else.   135
O, I were damned beneath all depth in hell
But that I did proceed upon just grounds
To this extremity. Thy husband knew it all.

Emilia: My husband?

Othello: Thy husband.

Emilia: That she was false to wedlock?

Othello: Ay, with Cassio. Had she been true,   140
If heaven would make me such another world
Of one entire and perfect chrysolite°,
I'd not have sold her for it.

Emilia: My husband?

Othello: Ay, 'twas he that told me on her first.
An honest man he is, and hates the slime   145
That sticks on filthy deeds.

Emilia: My husband?

Othello: What needs this iterance? Woman, I say thy husband.

Emilia: O mistress, villainy hath made mocks with love!
My husband say she was false?

Othello: He, woman.
I say, thy husband. Dost understand the word?   150
My friend, thy husband; honest, honest Iago.

Emilia: If he say so, may his pernicious soul
Rot half a grain a day! He lies to th' heart.

---

¹⁴²*chrysolite:* topaz.

She was too fond of her most filthy bargain.
Othello: Hah?   155
Emilia: Do thy worst.
　　This deed of thine is no more worthy heaven
　　Than thou wast worthy her.
Othello:　　　　　　　　　　　Peace, you were best°.
Emilia: Thou hast not half that pow'r to do me harm
　　As I have to be hurt. O gull! O dolt!   160
　　As ignorant as dirt! Thou hast done a deed —

　　　　　　　　　　[*Othello moves to draw his sword.*]

　　I care not for thy sword; I'll make thee known,
　　Though I lost twenty lives. Help! Help! Ho! Help!
　　The Moor hath killed my mistress! Murder! murder!

Enter Montano, Gratiano, and Iago [and Others].

Montano: What is the matter? How now, general?   165
Emilia: O, are you come, Iago? You have done well,
　　That men must lay their murders on your neck.
Gratiano: What is the matter?
Emilia: Disprove this villain, if thou be'st a man.
　　He says thou told'st him that his wife was false.   170
　　I know thou didst not; thou'rt not such a villain.
　　Speak, for my heart is full.
Iago: I told him what I thought, and told no more
　　Than what he found himself was apt and true.
Emilia: But did you ever tell him she was false?   175
Iago: I did.
Emilia: You told a lie, an odious damnèd lie!
　　Upon my soul, a lie! A wicked lie!
　　She false with Cassio? Did you say with Cassio?
Iago: With Cassio, mistress. Go to, charm° your tongue.   180
Emilia: I will not charm my tongue; I am bound to speak:
　　My mistress here lies murdered in her bed.
All: O heavens forfend!
Emilia: And your reports have set the murder on.
Othello: Nay, stare not, masters. It is true indeed.   185
Gratiano: 'Tis a strange truth.
Montano: O monstrous act!
Emilia:　　　　　　　　Villainy, villainy, villainy!
　　I think upon't — I think I smell't! — O villainy!
　　I thought so then. — I'll kill myself for grief. —
　　O villainy, villainy!   190
Iago: What, are you mad? I charge you get you home.
Emilia: Good gentlemen, let me have leave to speak.
　　'Tis proper I obey him, but not now.
　　Perchance, Iago, I will ne'er go home.

---

[158]*Peace, you were best:* i.e., you had better be silent.　[180]*charm:* control.

Othello: O! O! O!   *[Falls on the bed.]*
Emilia: Nay, lay thee down and roar,   195
    For thou hast killed the sweetest innocent
    That e'er did lift up eye.
Othello: O, she was foul!   *[Rises.]*
    I scarce did know you, uncle. There lies your niece,
    Whose breath, indeed, these hands have newly stopped.
    I know this act shows horrible and grim.   200
Gratiano: Poor Desdemon! I am glad thy father's dead.
    Thy match was mortal to him, and pure grief
    Shore his old thread in twain. Did he live now,
    This sight would make him do a desperate turn;
    Yea, curse his better angel from his side,   205
    And fall to reprobation°.
Othello: 'Tis pitiful; but yet Iago knows
    That she with Cassio hath the act of shame
    A thousand times committed. Cassio confessed it;
    And she did gratify his amorous works   210
    With that recognizance and pledge of love,
    Which I first gave her. I saw it in his hand.
    It was a handkerchief, an antique token
    My father gave my mother.
Emilia: O God! O heavenly God!   215
Iago: Zounds, hold your peace!
Emilia: 'Twill out, 'twill out! I peace?
    No, I will speak as liberal as the north°.
    Let heaven and men and devils, let them all,
    All, all, cry shame against me, yet I'll speak.
Iago: Be wise, and get you home.
Emilia: I will not.   220

                    [Iago draws and threatens Emilia.]

Gratiano: Fie! Your sword upon a woman?
Emilia: O thou dull Moor, that handkerchief thou speak'st of
    I found by fortune, and did give my husband;
    For often with a solemn earnestness —
    More than indeed belonged to such a trifle —   225
    He begged of me to steal 't.
Iago: Villainous whore!
Emilia: She give it Cassio? No, alas, I found it,
    And I did give 't my husband.
Iago: Filth, thou liest!
Emilia: By heaven, I do not, I do not, gentlemen.
    O murd'rous coxcomb! What should such a fool   230
    Do with so good a wife?
Othello: Are there no stones° in heaven
    But what serves for the thunder? Precious villain!

²⁰⁶*reprobation:* damnation.   ²¹⁷*liberal as the north:* freely (and bitingly) as the north wind blows.
²³¹*stones:* thunderbolts.

[*The Moor runs at Iago, but is disarmed by Montano. Iago kills his wife.*]

Gratiano: The woman falls. Sure he hath killed his wife.

Emilia: Ay, ay. O, lay me by my mistress' side. [*Exit Iago.*]

Gratiano: He's gone, but his wife's killed. 235

Montano: 'Tis a notorious° villain. Take you this weapon,
     Which I have recovered from the Moor.
     Come, guard the door without. Let him not pass,
     But kill him rather. I'll after that same villain,
     For 'tis a damnèd slave.   Exit [*with all but Othello and Emilia*].

Othello: I am not valiant neither; 240
     But every puny whipster° gets my sword.
     But why should honor outlive honesty?
     Let it go all.

Emilia: What did thy song bode, lady?
     Hark, canst thou hear me? I will play the swan,
     And die in music. [*Sings*] "Willow, willow, willow." 245
     Moor, she was chaste. She loved thee, cruel Moor,
     So come my soul to bliss as I speak true.
     So speaking as I think, alas, I die.   [*She dies.*]

Othello: I have another weapon in this chamber;
     It was a sword of Spain, the ice-brook's temper. 250
     O, here it is. — Uncle, I must come forth.

Gratiano [*Within*]: If thou attempt it, it will cost thee dear.
     Thou hast no weapon, and perforce must suffer.

Othello: Look in upon me then and speak with me,
     Or, naked as I am, I will assault thee. 255

[*Enter Gratiano.*]

Gratiano: What is the matter?

Othello: Behold, I have a weapon;
     A better never did itself sustain
     Upon a soldier's thigh. I have seen the day
     That with this little arm and this good sword
     I have made my way through more impediments 260
     Than twenty times your stop. But O vain boast!
     Who can control his fate? 'Tis not so now.
     Be not afraid, though you do see me weaponed.
     Here is my journey's end, here is my butt°,
     And very seamark of my utmost sail°. 265
     Do you go back dismayed? 'Tis a lost fear.
     Man but a rush° against Othello's breast.
     And he retires. Where should Othello go?
     Now, how dost thou look now? O ill-starred wench!
     Pale as thy smock! When we shall meet at compt°, 270
     This look of thine will hurl my soul from heaven,

²³⁶*notorious:* out-and-out.   ²⁴¹*puny whipster:* small top-whipping boy (?).   ²⁶⁴*butt:* target, stopping place.   ²⁶⁵*seamark of my utmost sail:* maker of my farthest journey.   ²⁶⁷*Man but a rush:* attack with only a reed.   ²⁷⁰*compt:* Judgment Day.

And fiends will snatch at it. Cold, cold, my girl?
Even like thy chastity.
O cursèd, cursèd slave! Whip me, ye devils,
From the possession of° this heavenly sight!   275
Blow me about in winds! roast me in sulfur!
Wash me in steep-down gulfs of liquid fire!
O Desdemon! Dead Desdemon; dead. O! O!

Enter Lodovico, Cassio, Montano, and Iago [as prisoner], with Officers.

Lodovico: Where is this rash and most unfortunate man?
Othello: That's he that was Othello? Here I am.   280
Lodovico: Where is that viper? Bring the villain forth.
Othello: I look down towards his feet° — but that's a fable.
    If that thou be'st a devil, I cannot kill thee.   [*Wounds Iago.*]
Lodovico: Wrench his sword from him.   [*Othello is disarmed.*]
Iago: I bleed, sir, but not killed.
Othello: I am not sorry neither. I'd have thee live;   285
    For in my sense, 'tis happiness to die.
Lodovico: O thou Othello that was once so good,
    Fall'n in the practice° of a cursèd slave,
    What shall be said to thee?
Othello: Why, anything:
    An honorable murderer, if you will;   290
    For naught I did in hate, but all in honor.
Lodovico: This wretch hath part confessed his villainy.
    Did you and he consent in Cassio's death?
Othello: Ay.
Cassio: Dear general, I never gave you cause.   295
Othello: I do believe it, and I ask your pardon.
    Will you, I pray, demand that demi-devil
    Why he hath thus ensnared my soul and body?
Iago: Demand me nothing. What you know, you know.
    From this time forth I never will speak word.   300
Lodovico: What, not to pray?
Gratiano: Torments will open your lips.
Othello: Well, thou dost best.
Lodovico: Sir, you shall understand what hath befall'n,
    Which, as I think, you know not. Here is a letter
    Found in the pocket of the slain Roderigo;   305
    And here another. The one of them imports
    The death of Cassio to be undertook
    By Roderigo.
Othello: O villain!
Cassio: Most heathenish and most gross!
Lodovico: Now here's another discontented paper   310
    Found in his pocket too; and this, it seems,

---

²⁷⁵*the possession of:* being possessed by.   ²⁸²*towards his feet:* i.e., for his cloven hoofs.   ²⁸⁸*practice:* plotting.

984   Tragedy

Roderigo meant t' have sent this damnèd villain;
But that, belike, Iago in the interim
Came in and satisfied him.
Othello: O thou pernicious caitiff!
How came you, Cassio, by that handkerchief   315
That was my wife's?
Cassio: I found it in my chamber;
And he himself confessed it but even now
That there he dropped it for a special purpose
Which wrought to his desire.
Othello: O fool! Fool! Fool!
Cassio: There is besides in Roderigo's letter,   320
How he upbraids Iago that he made him
Brave me upon the watch; whereon it came
That I was cast; and even but now he spake,
After long seeming dead — Iago hurt him,
Iago set him on.   325
Lodovico: You must forsake this room and go with us.
Your power and your command is taken off,
And Cassio rules in Cyprus. For this slave,
If there be any cunning cruelty
That can torment him much and hold him long,   330
It shall be his. You shall close prisoner rest
Till that the nature of your fault be known
To the Venetian state. Come, bring away.
Othello: Soft you, a word or two before you go.
I have done the state some service and they know't.   335
No more of that. I pray you, in your letters,
When you shall these unlucky deeds relate,
Speak of me as I am. Nothing extenuate,
Nor set down aught in malice. Then must you speak
Of one that loved not wisely, but too well;   340
Of one not easily jealous, but, being wrought,
Perplexed in the extreme; of one whose hand,
Like the base Judean°, threw a pearl away
Richer than all his tribe; of one whose subdued eyes,
Albeit unusèd to the melting mood,   345
Drops tears as fast as the Arabian trees
Their med'cinable gum. Set you down this.
And say besides that in Aleppo once,
Where a malignant and a turbaned Turk
Beat a Venetian and traduced the state,   350
I took by th' throat the circumcisèd dog
And smote him — thus.   [*He stabs himself.*]
Lodovico: O bloody period!°
Gratiano: All that is spoke is marred.

---

³⁴³*Judean:* (most editors use the Q1 reading, "Indian," here, but F is clear: both readings point toward the infidel, the unbeliever. ³⁵³*period:* end.

Othello: I kissed thee ere I killed thee. No way but this,
   Killing myself, to die upon a kiss.

                              [*He falls over Desdemona and dies.*]   355

Cassio: This did I fear, but thought he had no weapon;
   For he was great of heart.
Lodovico [*To Iago*]:   O Spartan dog,
   More fell³⁵⁸ than anguish, hunger, or the sea!
   Look on the tragic loading of this bed.
   This is thy work. The object poisons sight;   360
   Let it be hid.   [*Bed curtains drawn.*]
              Gratiano, keep° the house,
   And seize upon the fortunes of the Moor,
   For they succeed on you. To you, lord governor,
   Remains the censure of this hellish villain,
   The time, the place, the torture. O, enforce it!   365
   Myself will straight aboard, and to the state
   This heavy act with heavy heart relate.   *Exeunt.*

QUESTIONS

ACT I

1. What is Othello's position in society? How is he regarded by those who know him? By his own words, when we first meet him in Scene II, what traits of character does he manifest?
2. How do you account for Brabantio's dismay on learning of his daughter's marriage, despite the fact that Desdemona has married a man so generally honored and admired?
3. What is Iago's view of human nature? In his fondness for likening men to animals (as in I, i, 44 – 45; I, i, 85 – 86; and I, iii, 374 – 375), what does he tell us about himself?
4. What reasons does Iago give for his hatred of Othello?
5. In Othello's defense before the senators (Scene III), how does he explain Desdemona's gradual falling in love with him?
6. Is Brabantio's warning to Othello (I, iii, 286 – 287) an accurate or an inaccurate prophecy?
7. By what strategy does Iago enlist Roderigo in his plot against the Moor? In what lines do we learn Iago's true feelings toward Roderigo?

ACT II

1. What do the Cypriots think of Othello? Do their words (in Scene I) make him seem to us a lesser man, or a larger one?
2. What cruelty does Iago display toward Emilia? How well founded is his distrust of his wife's fidelity?
3. In II, iii, 227, Othello speaks of Iago's "honesty and love." How do you account for Othello's being so totally deceived?

---

³⁵⁸*fell:* cruel.   ³⁶¹*keep:* remain in.

4. For what major events does the merrymaking (proclaimed in Scene II) give opportunity?

ACT III

1. Trace the steps by which Iago rouses Othello to suspicion. Is there anything in Othello's character or circumstances that renders him particularly susceptible to Iago's wiles?
2. In III, iv, 96 – 97, Emilia knows of Desdemona's distress over the lost handkerchief. At this moment, how do you explain her failure to relieve Desdemona's mind? Is Emilia aware of her husband's villainy?

ACT IV

1. In this act, what circumstantial evidence is added to Othello's case against Desdemona?
2. How plausible do you find Bianca's flinging the handkerchief at Cassio just when Othello is looking on? How important is the handkerchief in this play? What does it represent? What suggestions or hints do you find in it?
3. What prevents Othello from being moved by Desdemona's appeal (IV, ii, 34 – 87)?
4. When Roderigo grows impatient with Iago (IV, ii, 171 – 196), how does Iago make use of his fellow plotter's discontent?
5. What does the conversation between Emilia and Desdemona (Scene III) tell us about the nature of each? Someone has called Emilia's concluding speech (84 – 101) a Renaissance plea for women's liberation. Do you agree? How timely is it?
6. In this act, what scenes (or speeches) contain memorable dramatic irony?

ACT V

1. Summarize the events that lead to Iago's unmasking.
2. How does Othello's mistaken belief that Cassio is slain (V, i, 27 – 33) affect the outcome of the play?
3. What is Iago's motive in stabbing Roderigo?
4. In your interpretation of the play, exactly what impels Othello to kill Desdemona? Jealousy? Desire for revenge? Excess idealism? A wish to be a public avenger who punishes, "else she'll betray more men"?
5. What do you understand by Othello's calling himself "one that loved not wisely but too well" (V, ii, 340)?
6. In your view, does Othello's long speech in V, ii, 334 – 352 succeed in restoring his original dignity and nobility? Do you agree with Cassio (V, ii, 357) that Othello was "great of heart"?

GENERAL QUESTIONS

1. What motivates Iago to carry out his schemes? Do you find him a devil incarnate, a madman, or a rational human being?
2. Who besides Othello does Iago deceive? What is Desdemona's opinion of him? Emilia's? Cassio's (before Iago is found out)? To what do you attribute Iago's success as a deceiver?
3. How essential to the play is the fact that Othello is a black man, a Moor, and not a native of Venice?

4. In the introduction to his edition of the play in *The Complete Signet Classic Shakespeare,* Alvin Kernan remarks:

> *Othello* is probably the most neatly, the most formally constructed of Shakespeare's plays. Every character is, for example, balanced by another similar or contrasting character. Desdemona is balanced by her opposite, Iago; love and concern for others at one end of the scale, hatred and concern for self at the other.

Besides Desdemona and Iago, what other pairs of characters seem to strike balances?

5. "Never was any play fraught, like this of *Othello,* with improbabilities," wrote Thomas Rymer in a famous attack (*A Short View of Tragedy,* 1692). Discuss Rymer's objections to the play (see page 1321).

6. Consider any passage of the play in which there is a shift from verse to prose, or from prose to verse. What is the effect of this shift?

7. Indicate a passage that you consider memorable for its poetry. Does the passage seem introduced for its own sake? Does it in any way advance the action of the play, express theme, or demonstrate character?

8. Does the play contain any tragic *recognition* — as discussed on page 899, a moment of terrible enlightenment, a "realization of the unthinkable"?

9. Does the downfall of Othello proceed from any flaw in his nature, or is his downfall entirely the work of Iago?

SUGGESTIONS FOR WRITING

1. "The downfall of Oedipus is the work of the gods; the downfall of Othello is self-inflicted." Test this comment against the two plays, and report your findings.

2. Write a defense of Iago.

3. Compare the Fitts and Fitzgerald version of *Oedipus Rex,* given in this book, with a different English translation of the play. See, for example, the versions by Gilbert Murray, J. T. Sheppard, and H. D. F. Kitto; by Paul Roché (in a Signet paperback); by W. B. Yeats (in his *Collected Plays*); and by Stephen Berg and Diskin Clay (Oxford UP, 1978). Point to some of the major differences between the two texts. What decisions have the translators had to make? Which version do you prefer? Why?

4. Suppose you had the assignment of directing and producing a new stage production of either *Oedipus Rex* or *Othello.* (Take your choice.) Decide how you would go about your task. Would you set the play in contemporary North America?

5. Consider Arthur Miller's *Death of a Salesman* (in "Plays for Further Reading") and his essay "Tragedy and the Common Man" (page 1328). Then decide how well Miller succeeds in making the decline and fall of Willy Loman into a tragedy. In your view, is tragedy still possible today?

34 Comedy

Comedy, from the Greek *komos,* "a revel," is thought to have originated in festivities to celebrate spring: ritual performances in praise of Dionysus, god of fertility and wine. No one knows the origin of comedy for sure, but at least we do know that one ancient comic play, the *Cyclops* of Euripides, includes the jovial, drunken character of Silenus — the foster father of Dionysus — and a chorus garbed as goatlike satyrs, who tipple wine, sing, and dance. In drama, comedy may be broadly defined as whatever makes us laugh. A comedy may be a name for one entire play, or we may say that there is comedy in only part of a play — as in a comic character or a comic situation.

The best-known traditional emblem of drama — a pair of masks, one sorrowful (representing tragedy) and one smiling (representing comedy) — suggests that tragedy and comedy, although opposites, are close relatives. Often, comedy shows people getting into trouble through error or weakness; in this respect it is akin to tragedy. But an important difference between comedy and tragedy lies in the attitude toward human failing that is expected of us. When a main character in a comedy suffers from overweening pride, as does Oedipus, or if he fails to recognize that his bride-to-be is actually his mother, we laugh — something we would never do in watching a competent performance of *Oedipus Rex.* In a tragedy, some force — fate or the gods or the nature of things — relentlessly decrees suffering or death for the protagonist. In a comedy, the force impels the protagonist to realize, against all odds, eventual good fortune: success in love, sudden wealth, the humiliation of his enemies.

If Jean Anouilh is right in saying that one effect of a tragic situation is a certain serenity for the character or characters trapped in a hopeless bind,[1] then perhaps a comic situation generates serenity too — but certainly not for the characters embroiled in it. They may struggle as hard as Charles Chaplin trying to rescue a drunk from drowning, getting tangled in a rope, then slipping and falling into the water (in a classic film comedy, *City Lights*). In comedy, the characters usually achieve serenity only in the

[1]See Anouilh's comment quoted in the discussion of tragedy, page 898.

final moments, when at last the bullies are exposed, the money turns up, and the "nice guys" triumph. If we want to find serenity in comedy, we can probably find it in the audience, who know that somehow the character's struggles will turn out all right. Characters in silent movie comedies lead a charmed existence. When the Keystone Kops whip their car across a railroad track a split second before a train roars by, the moviegoer does not worry about their safety. Even a horrible crash will not kill anyone, though it may turn tall men into midgets, or produce a few characters whose heads are interchanged.

Many theories have been propounded to explain why we laugh; most of these are likely to be of a few familiar types. One school, maintained by French philosopher Henri Bergson, sees laughter as a form of ridicule, implying a feeling of disinterested superiority: all jokes are *on* somebody. Bergson suggests that laughter springs from situations in which we sense a conflict between some mechanical or rigid pattern of behavior and our sense of a more natural or "organic" kind of behavior that is possible. [2] An example occurs in Buster Keaton's comic film *The Boat:* having launched a little boat that springs a leak, Keaton rigidly goes down with it, with frozen face. (The more natural and organic thing to do would be to swim for shore.) Other thinkers view laughter as our response to expectations fulfilled, or to expectations set up but then suddenly frustrated. Some hold it to be the expression of our delight in seeing our suppressed urges acted out (as when a comedian hurls an egg at a pompous stuffed shirt); some, to be our defensive reaction to a painful and disturbing truth.

"There are all kinds of humor," film comic Groucho Marx declared. "Some is derisive, some sympathetic, and some merely whimsical. That is just what makes comedy so much harder to create than serious drama; people laugh in many different ways, and they cry only in one." [3] Whether or not it is correct to say that we have only one way of crying, the great film clown is right in saying that humor is various, and he accurately distinguishes one kind of comedy from another.

Derisive humor is basic to **satiric comedy**, in which human weakness or folly is ridiculed from a vantage point of supposedly enlightened superiority. Satiric comedy may be coolly malicious and gently biting, but it is always fundamentally hostile. An obvious illustration of hostility, from Ben Jonson's *Epicene; or, The Silent Woman* (1609), is this speech of the henpecked sea captain Otter, berating his wife:

> A most vile face! and yet she spends me forty pound a year in mercury and hogs' bones. All her teeth were made in the Blackfriars, both her eyebrows in the Strand, and her hair in Silver-street. Every part of the town owns a piece of her. . . . She takes herself asunder still when she

[2] See Bergson's essay *Le Rire* (1900), translated as "Laughter" in *Comedy*, ed. Wylie Sypher (New York: Anchor, 1956).
[3] Statement attributed to Max Eastman, *The Enjoyment of Laughter* (New York: Simon, 1936).

goes to bed, into some twenty boxes; and about next day noon is put together again, like a great German clock: and so comes forth, and rings a tedious larum [4] to the whole house, and then is quiet again for an hour, but for her quarters.

The satirist is castigating not only some women's excessive reliance on makeup, but men's greed in marrying for money: Otter had previously revealed that he didn't love his wife; he loved her six thousand pounds in dowry.

Satiric comedy is at least as old as the classic plays of Aristophanes (about 448 – 380 B.C.), whose *Lysistrata* is another attack on human greed and on men who delude themselves that they wage war for unselfish reasons. Satiric playwrights, from Molière in seventeenth-century France to Jules Feiffer in twentieth-century America, have claimed that their satire has a corrective function: that by exposing vice or pretense they cause the spectators to avoid behavior of the sort pilloried on the stage. It is doubtful, however, that many playgoers have recognized their own follies in satiric plays and have then reformed.

Comedy is sometimes divided into "high" and "low" categories. **High comedy** relies on wit and verbal humor rather than physical action. It appeals to a sophisticated audience fond of epigrams ("A fellow that lives in a windmill has not a more whimsical dwelling than the heart of a man that is lodged in a woman" — an **epigram,** or short, sententious statement, from William Congreve's *The Way of the World,* 1700). A species of high comedy, the **comedy of manners,** or witty satire set in high society, was written not only by Molière but also by Congreve and other English playwrights of the **Restoration period** (the period following the year 1660, when Charles II, restored to the throne, reopened the London theaters, which had been closed by the Puritans). In more recent times, splendid comedies of manners have been written by Oscar Wilde — notably *The Importance of Being Earnest* (1895) — and by Bernard Shaw, whose play *Pygmalion* (1913) contrasts life in the streets with life in aristocratic drawing rooms and suggests that a flower peddler differs from a duchess in little except manners and habits of speech.

Low comedy (the opposite extreme) places greater emphasis on physical action, and its verbal jokes do not require much intellect to appreciate. ("I've got a goat with no nose." — "No nose, eh? How does the poor thing smell?" — "Just terrible.") Low comedy includes several distinct types. One is the **burlesque,** a broadly humorous parody or travesty of another play or kind of play. (In America, *burlesque* is something else: a form of show business once popular featuring stripteases interspersed with bits of ribald low comedy.)

Another valuable type of low comedy is the **farce,** a broadly humorous play whose plot is usually improbable. Molière, a master of high

[4] alarm.

comedy, was also a masterly writer of farces. Recently making a comeback in popularity, the farces of another French playwright, Georges Feydeau (1862 – 1921), are practically all plot, with only the flattest of characters: mindless ninnies who play frantic games of hide-and-seek in order not to be discovered by their spouses. **Slapstick comedy** (such as that of the Keystone Kops) is a kind of farce. Featuring violent physical action, it takes its name from a circus clown's device: a bat with two boards that loudly clap together when one clown swats another. Although called "low," farce can have high-reaching implications. In a classic moment in a silent movie, *We Faw Down* (1928), when Laurel and Hardy's wives catch their husbands with two girl friends and chase the two buffoons down a street lined with apartment houses, one wife fires a gun. Suddenly the street is thick with dozens of pantsless men leaping out of every bedroom window. The joke, as Henry James said of symbols, "casts long shadows": it assumes a society in which infidelity is the norm, not the exception.

Another traditional sort of comedy, **romantic comedy,** prefers sympathetic humor (another of Groucho Marx's categories). Its main characters are generally lovers, and its plot unfolds their successful attempt to be united. Unlike satiric comedy, romantic comedy portrays people with kindly indulgence, not withering contempt. It may take place in the everyday world or in some never-never land, such as the forest of Arden in Shakespeare's *As You Like It* or Prospero's island in *The Tempest.* Though a romantic comedy may depict folly and vice (especially in its villains and minor characters), entertainment, not moral correction, is usually its apparent business. The writer of such a play seems to agree with George Meredith that "to love Comedy you must know the real world, and know men and women well enough not to expect too much of them, though you may still hope for good."[5]

Though a play may be a comedy, it can search depths and scale heights — as *The Tempest* does. Here is the story of Prospero, statesman turned magician, the ruler of a remote island and its supernatural spirits; of his daughter Miranda and her lover Ferdinand; of subhuman Caliban, begotten on a witch by a devil, and Ariel, who travels in the wind — two of the oddest and most memorable characters in literature. Like many a work of science fiction, *The Tempest* plunges us into a "brave new world." Indeed, Prospero may well remind you of that familiar figure, the man of learning whose studies have gained him the power to work wonders — in a way, like Aylmer in Nathaniel Hawthorne's tale "The Birthmark," like Victor Frankenstein in Mary Shelley's classic novel, or like the superscientist in H. G. Wells's early novel of science fiction, *The Island of Dr. Moreau.* The theme that a human being may have fearful powers on call will be familiar to us all, since Hiroshima.

[5]"An Essay on Comedy" (1877) in Sypher, *Comedy.*

Although in some respects *The Tempest* may strike us as startlingly contemporary, it mirrors its own time as well. No less than Prospero's mysterious island, the new world of America, still being mapped and explored in Shakespeare's day, reportedly teemed with marvels. In 1610 news reached England of the rescue of the crew and passengers of a ship lost earlier in a hurricane. To the great surprise of all London, the castaways had landed in the Bermudas, islands whose rough surrounding seas had caused earlier sailors to avoid them. And the survivors bore good news: the much-feared islands had proved warm and welcoming. Shakespeare may well have had this news in mind in writing *The Tempest* — his last great play, perhaps the summing-up of his art, surely the most amazing of all romantic comedies.

William Shakespeare

The Tempest   1611

Edited by Robert Langbaum

> *William Shakespeare (1564 – 1616), whose life is sketched in a note on page 903 at the start of* Othello, *wrote* The Tempest *late in his career. Scholars believe it to be the last play he wrote entirely by himself (though later he may have collaborated with John Fletcher on* The Two Noble Kinsmen *in 1613). Many have seen* The Tempest *as Shakespeare's autobiographical farewell to the theater and the world. Sylvan Barnet offers a caution to readers intent on seeing it in this light (in his comment on page 1323).*

Characters

Alonso, king of Naples
Sebastian, his brother
Prospero, the right duke of Milan
Antonio, his brother, the usurping duke of Milan
Ferdinand, son to the king of Naples
Gonzalo, an honest old councilor
Adrian and *Francisco,* lords
Caliban, a savage and deformed slave
Trinculo, a jester
Stephano, a drunken butler
Master of a ship
Boatswain
Mariners
Miranda, daughter to Prospero
Ariel, an airy spirit

Iris
Ceres
Juno } [presented by] spirits
Nymphs
Reapers
Other spirits attending on Prospero

Scene: *An uninhabited island.*

ACT I

Scene I. [*On a ship at sea.*]

   A tempestuous noise of thunder and lightning heard. Enter a Shipmaster and a Boatswain.

Master: Boatswain!
Boatswain: Here, master. What cheer?
Master: Good°, speak to th' mariners! Fall to't yarely°, or we run ourselves
   aground. Bestir, bestir! *Exit.*

   Enter Mariners.

Boatswain: Heigh, my hearts! Cheerly, cheerly, my hearts! Yare, yare!   5
   Take in the topsail! Tend to th' master's whistle! Blow till thou burst
   thy wind, if room enough°!

   Enter Alonso, Sebastian, Antonio, Ferdinand, Gonzalo, and others.

Alonso: Good boatswain, have care. Where's the master? Play the
   men°.
Boatswain: I pray now, keep below.   10
Antonio: Where is the master, bos'n?
Boatswain: Do you not hear him? You mar our labor. Keep your cabins;
   you do assist the storm.
Gonzalo: Nay, good, be patient.
Boatswain: When the sea is. Hence! What care these roarers for the name   15
   of king? To cabin! Silence! Trouble us not!
Gonzalo: Good, yet remember whom thou hast aboard.
Boatswain: None that I more love than myself. You are a councilor; if you
   can command these elements to silence and work the peace of the
   present°, we will not hand° a rope more. Use your authority. If you   20
   cannot, give thanks you have lived so long, and make yourself ready
   in your cabin for the mischance of the hour, if it so hap. Cheerly,
   good hearts! Out of our way, I say. *Exit.*
Gonzalo: I have great comfort from this fellow. Methinks he hath no

---

I.i. ³*Good:* good fellow. ³*yarely:* briskly. ⁶⁻⁷*Blow . . . enough:* The storm can blow and split
itself as long as there is open sea, without rocks, to maneuver in. ⁸⁻⁹*Play the men:* Act like
men. ¹⁹⁻²⁰*work . . . present:* restore the present to peace (because as a councilor his job is to
quell disorder). ²⁰*hand:* handle.

drowning mark upon him; his complexion is perfect gallows°. Stand   25
fast, good Fate, to his hanging! Make the rope of his destiny our
cable, for our own doth little advantage°. If he be not born to be
hanged, our case is miserable.   *Exit* [*with the rest*].

Enter Boatswain.

Boatswain: Down with the topmast! Yare! Lower, lower! Bring her to try
with main course°! (*A cry within.*) A plague upon this howling! They   30
are louder than the weather or our office°.

Enter Sebastian, Antonio, and Gonzalo.

Yet again? What do you here? Shall we give o'er° and drown? Have
you a mind to sink?
Sebastian: A pox o' your throat, you bawling, blasphemous, incharitable
dog!   35
Boatswain: Work you, then.
Antonio: Hang, cur! Hang, you whoreson, insolent noisemaker! We are
less afraid to be drowned than thou art.
Gonzalo: I'll warrant him for° drowning, though the ship were no stronger
than a nutshell and as leaky as an unstanched° wench.   40
Boatswain: Lay her ahold, ahold! Set her two courses°! Off to sea again!
Lay her off°!

Enter Mariners wet.

Mariners: All lost! To prayers, to prayers! All lost!   [*Exeunt.*]°
Boatswain: What, must our mouths be cold?
Gonzalo: The king and prince at prayers! Let's assist them,   45
For our case is as theirs.
Sebastian: I am out of patience.
Antonio: We are merely° cheated of our lives by drunkards.
This wide-chopped° rascal — would thou mightst lie drowning
The washing of ten tides°!
Gonzalo: He'll be hanged yet,
Though every drop of water swear against it   50
And gape at wid'st to glut him.
           A confused noise within: "Mercy on us!"
"We split, we split!" "Farewell, my wife and children!"
"Farewell, brother!" "We split, we split, we split!"

                                        [*Exit Boatswain.*]

---

²⁴⁻²⁵*no drowning . . . gallows:* alluding to the proverb, "He that's born to be hanged need fear
no drowning." ²⁷*doth little advantage:* gives us little advantage. ²⁹⁻³⁰*Bring . . . course:* Heave
to, under the mainsail. ³⁰⁻³¹*They . . . office:* These passengers make more noise than the
tempest or than we do at our work. ³²*give o'er:* give up trying to run the ship. ³⁹*warrant
him for:* guarantee him against. ⁴⁰*unstanched:* wide-open. ⁴¹*Lay . . . courses:* the ship is still
being blown dangerously close to shore, and so the boatswain orders that the foresail be set
in addition to the mainsail; but the ship still moves toward shore. ⁴²*Lay her off:* i.e., away
from the shore. ⁴³*Exeunt:* Latin, "They go out," a direction indicating that all or some
characters leave the stage. ⁴⁷*merely:* completely. ⁴⁸*wide-chopped:* big-mouthed. ⁴⁹*ten tides:*
pirates were hanged on the shore and left there until three tides had washed over them.

Antonio: Let's all sink wi' th' king.

Sebastian: Let's take leave of him.

Exit [with Antonio].

Gonzalo: Now would I give a thousand furlongs of sea for an acre of   55
barren ground — long heath°, brown furze, anything. The wills
above be done, but I would fain die a dry death.   *Exit.*

Scene II. [*The island. In front of Prospero's cell.*]

Enter Prospero and Miranda.

Miranda: If by your art, my dearest father, you have
Put the wild waters in this roar, allay them.
The sky, it seems, would pour down stinking pitch
But that the sea, mounting to th' welkin's cheek°,
Dashes the fire out. O, I have suffered   5
With those that I saw suffer! A brave° vessel
(Who had no doubt some noble creature in her)
Dashed all to pieces! O, the cry did knock
Against my very heart! Poor souls, they perished!
Had I been any god of power, I would   10
Have sunk the sea within the earth or ere
It should the good ship to have swallowed and
The fraughting° souls within her.

Prospero: Be collected.
No more amazement°. Tell your piteous heart
There's no harm done.

Miranda: O, woe the day!

Prospero: No harm.   15
I have done nothing but in care of thee,
Of thee my dear one, thee my daughter, who
Art ignorant of what thou art, naught knowing
Of whence I am, nor that I am more better
Than Prospero, master of a full poor cell,   20
And thy no greater father°.

Miranda: More to know
Did never meddle° with my thoughts.

Prospero: 'Tis time
I should inform thee farther. Lend thy hand
And pluck my magic garment from me. So.

[*Lays down his robe.*]

Lie there, my art. Wipe thou thine eyes; have comfort.   25
The direful spectacle of the wrack, which touched
The very virtue° of compassion in thee,

---

⁵⁶*heath:* heather.   I.ii. ⁴*welkin's cheek:* face of the sky.   ⁶*brave:* fine, gallant (the word often has
this meaning in the play). ¹³*fraughting:* forming her freight. ¹⁴*amazement:* consternation.
²¹*thy . . . father:* thy father, no greater than the Prospero just described. ²²*meddle:* mingle.
²⁷*virtue:* essence.

I have with such provision° in mine art
So safely ordered that there is no soul —
No, not so much perdition° as an hair   30
Betid° to any creature in the vessel
Which thou heard'st cry, which thou saw'st sink. Sit down;
For thou must now know farther.
Miranda: You have often
Begun to tell me what I am; but stopped
And left me to a bootless inquisition,   35
Concluding, "Stay; not yet."
Prospero: The hour's now come;
The very minute bids thee ope thine ear.
Obey, and be attentive. Canst thou remember
A time before we came unto this cell?
I do not think thou canst, for then thou wast not   40
Out° three years old.
Miranda: Certainly, sir, I can.
Prospero: By what? By any other house or person?
Of anything the image tell me that
Hath kept with thy remembrance.
Miranda: 'Tis far off,
And rather like a dream than an assurance   45
That my remembrance warrants°. Had I not
Four or five women once that tended me?
Prospero: Thou hadst, and more, Miranda. But how is it
That this lives in thy mind? What see'st thou else
In the dark backward and abysm of time?   50
If thou rememb'rest aught ere thou cam'st here,
How thou cam'st here thou mayst.
Miranda: But that I do not.
Prospero: Twelve year since, Miranda, twelve year since,
Thy father was the Duke of Milan° and
A prince of power.
Miranda: Sir, are not you my father?   55
Prospero: Thy mother was a piece° of virtue, and
She said thou wast my daughter; and thy father
Was Duke of Milan; and his only heir
And princess, no worse issued.°
Miranda: O the heavens!
What foul play had we that we came from thence?   60
Or blessèd was't we did?
Prospero: Both, both, my girl!
By foul play, as thou say'st, were we heaved thence,
But blessedly holp° hither.
Miranda: O, my heart bleeds
To think o' th' teen that I have turned you to°,

---

²⁸*provision:* foresight.   ³⁰*perdition:* loss.   ³¹*Betid:* happened.   ⁴¹*Out:* fully.   ⁴⁶*remembrance war-*
rants: memory guarantees.   ⁵⁴*Milan:* pronounced "Milan."   ⁵⁶*piece:* masterpiece.   ⁵⁹*no worse*
issued: of no meaner lineage than he.   ⁶³*holp:* helped.   ⁶⁴*teen . . . to:* sorrow I have caused you
to remember.

Which is from° my remembrance! Please you, farther. 65
Prospero: My brother and thy uncle, called Antonio —
I pray thee mark me — that a brother should
Be so perfidious — he whom next thyself
Of all the world I loved, and to him put
The manage of my state°, as at that time 70
Through all the signories° it was the first,
And Prospero the prime duke, being so reputed
In dignity, and for the liberal arts
Without a parallel. Those being all my study,
The government I cast upon my brother 75
And to my state grew stranger, being transported
And rapt in secret studies. Thy false uncle —
Dost thou attend me?
Miranda: Sir, most heedfully.
Prospero: Being once perfected° how to grant suits,
How to deny them, who t' advance, and who 80
To trash for overtopping,° new-created
The creatures that were mine, I say — or changed 'em,
Or else new-formed 'em° — having both the key°
Of officer and office, set all hearts i' th' state
To what tune pleased his ear, that now he was 85
The ivy which had hid my princely trunk
And sucked my verdure out on't. Thou attend'st not?
Miranda: O, good sir, I do.
Prospero: I pray thee mark me.
I thus neglecting worldly ends, all dedicated
To closeness° and the bettering of my mind — 90
With that which, but by being so retired,
O'erprized all popular rate, in my false brother
Awaked an evil nature°, and my trust,
Like a good parent°, did beget of him
A falsehood in its contrary as great 95
As my trust was, which had indeed no limit,
A confidence sans bound. He being thus lorded —
Not only with what my revenue° yielded
But what my power might else exact, like one
Who having into truth — by telling of it° — 100
Made such a sinner of his memory

---

⁶⁵*from:* out of.   ⁷⁰*manage . . . state:* management of my domain.   ⁷¹*signories:* lordships (of Italy).
⁷⁹*perfected:* grown skillful.   ⁸¹*trash for overtopping:* (1) check the speed of (as of hounds) (2) cut
down to size (as of over-tall trees) the aspirants for political favor who are growing too bold.
⁸¹⁻⁸³*new-created . . . 'em:* he recreated my following — either exchanging my adherents for his
own, or else transforming my adherents into different people.   ⁸³*key:* a pun leading to the
musical metaphor.   ⁹⁰*closeness:* seclusion.   ⁹¹⁻⁹³*With . . . nature:* with that dedication to the
mind which, were it not that it kept me from exercising the duties of my office would surpass
in value all ordinary estimate, I awakened evil in my brother's nature.   ⁹⁴*good parent:* alluding
to the proverb cited by Miranda in line 120.   ⁹⁸*revenue:* pronounced "revènue."   ⁹⁹⁻¹⁰⁰*like
. . . it:* like one who really had these things — by repeatedly saying he had them ("into"
— unto).

To° credit his own lie, he did believe
He was indeed the duke, out o' th' substitution
And executing th' outward face of royalty
With all prerogative°. Hence his ambition growing — 105
Dost thou hear?

Miranda:　　　　　　Your tale, sir, would cure deafness.

Prospero: To have no screen between this part he played
And him he played it for, he needs will be
Absolute Milan°. Me (poor man) my library
Was dukedom large enough. Of temporal royalties 110
He thinks me now incapable; confederates
(So dry° he was for sway) wi' th' King of Naples
To give him annual tribute, do him homage,
Subject his coronet to his crown, and bend
The dukedom, yet unbowed (alas, poor Milan!), 115
To most ignoble stooping.

Miranda:　　　　　　O the heavens!

Prospero: Mark his condition°, and th' event°, then tell me
If this might be a brother.

Miranda:　　　　　　I should sin
To think but nobly of my grandmother.
Good wombs have borne bad sons.

Prospero:　　　　　　Now the condition. 120
This King of Naples, being an enemy
To me inveterate, hearkens my brother's suit;
Which was, that he, in lieu o' th' premises°
Of homage and I know not how much tribute,
Should presently extirpate me and mine 125
Out of the dukedom and confer fair Milan,
With all the honors, on my brother. Whereon,
A treacherous army levied, one midnight
Fated to th' purpose, did Antonio open
The gates of Milan; and, i' th' dead of darkness, 130
The ministers° for th' purpose hurried thence
Me and thy crying self.

Miranda:　　　　　　Alack, for pity!
I, not rememb'ring how I cried out then,
Will cry it o'er again; it is a hint°
That wrings mine eyes to't.

Prospero:　　　　　　Hear a little further, 135
And then I'll bring thee to the present business
Which now's upon's; without the which this story
Were most impertinent°.

---

¹⁰²*To:* as to. ¹⁰³⁻⁰⁵*out . . . prerogative:* as a result of his acting as my substitute and performing the outward functions of royalty with all its prerogatives. ¹⁰⁹*Absolute Milan:* Duke of Milan in fact. ¹¹²*dry:* thirsty. ¹¹⁷*condition:* terms of his pact with Naples. ¹¹⁷*event:* outcome. ¹²³*in . . . premises:* in return for the guarantees. ¹³¹*ministers:* agents. ¹³⁴*hint:* occasion. ¹³⁸*impertinent:* inappropriate.

Miranda: Wherefore did they not
    That hour destroy us?
Prospero: Well demanded, wench.
    My tale provokes that question. Dear, they durst not,   140
    So dear the love my people bore me; nor set
    A mark so bloody on the business; but,
    With colors fairer, painted their foul ends.
    In few°, they hurried us aboard a bark;
    Bore us some leagues to sea, where they prepared   145
    A rotten carcass of a butt°, not rigged,
    Nor tackle, sail, nor mast; the very rats
    Instinctively have quit it. There they hoist us,
    To cry to th' sea that roared to us; to sigh
    To th' winds, whose pity, sighing back again,   150
    Did us but loving wrong.
Miranda: Alack, what trouble
    Was I then to you!
Prospero: O, a cherubin
    Thou wast that did preserve me! Thou didst smile,
    Infusèd with a fortitude from heaven,
    When I have decked° the sea with drops full salt,   155
    Under my burden groaned; which° raised in me
    An undergoing stomach°, to bear up
    Against what should ensue.
Miranda: How came we ashore?
Prospero: By providence divine.
    Some food we had, and some fresh water, that   160
    A noble Neapolitan, Gonzalo,
    Out of his charity, who being then appointed
    Master of this design, did give us, with
    Rich garments, linens, stuffs, and necessaries
    Which since have steaded° much. So, of his gentleness,   165
    Knowing I loved my books, he furnished me
    From mine own library with volumes that
    I prize above my dukedom.
Miranda: Would I might
    But ever see that man!
Prospero: Now I arise.
    Sit still, and hear the last of our sea sorrow.   170
    Here in this island we arrived; and here
    Have I, thy schoolmaster, made thee more profit
    Than other princess' can°, that have more time
    For vainer hours, and tutors not so careful.
Miranda: Heavens thank you for't! And now I pray you, sir —   175
    For still 'tis beating in my mind — your reason

144*few:* few words. 146*butt:* tub. 155*decked:* covered (wept salt tears into the sea). 156*which:* Miranda's smile. 157*undergoing stomach:* spirit of endurance. 165*steaded:* been of use. 173*princess' can:* princesses can have.

For raising this sea storm?

Prospero: Know thus far forth.
    By accident most strange, bountiful Fortune
    (Now my dear lady)° hath mine enemies
    Brought to this shore; and by my prescience   180
    I find my zenith° doth depend upon
    A most auspicious star, whose influence
    If now I court not, but omit°, my fortunes
    Will ever after droop. Here cease more questions.
    Thou art inclined to sleep. 'Tis a good dullness,   185
    And give it way. I know thou canst not choose.

    [*Miranda sleeps.*]

    Come away°, servant, come! I am ready now.
    Approach, my Ariel! Come!

    Enter Ariel.

Ariel: All hail, great master! Grave sir, hail! I come
    To answer thy best pleasure; be't to fly,   190
    To swim, to dive into the fire, to ride
    On the curled clouds. To thy strong bidding task°
    Ariel and all his quality.°

Prospero: Hast thou, spirit,
    Performed, to point°, the tempest that I bade thee?

Ariel: To every article.   195
    I boarded the king's ship. Now on the beak°,
    Now in the waist°, the deck°, in every cabin,
    I flamed amazement°. Sometime I'd divide
    And burn in many places; on the topmast,
    The yards, and boresprit° would I flame distinctly°,   200
    Then meet and join. Jove's lightnings, the precursors
    O' th' dreadful thunderclaps, more momentary
    And sight-outrunning were not. The fire and cracks
    Of sulfurous roaring the most mighty Neptune
    Seem to besiege, and make his bold waves tremble;   205
    Yea, his dread trident shake.

Prospero: My brave spirit!
    Who was so firm, so constant, that this coil°
    Would not infect his reason?

Ariel: Not a soul
    But felt a fever of the mad and played
    Some tricks of desperation. All but mariners   210

---

[179]*Now . . . lady:* i.e., formerly my foe, now my patroness. [181]*zenith:* apex of fortune.
[183]*omit:* neglect. [187]*Come away:* come from where you are; come here. [192]*task:* tax to the
utmost. [193]*quality:* cohorts (Ariel is leader of a band of spirits). [194]*to point:* in every detail.
[196]*beak:* prow. [197]*waist:* amidships. [197]*deck:* poop. [198]*flamed amazement:* struck terror by
appearing as (Saint Elmo's) fire. [200]*boresprit:* bowsprit. [200]*distinctly:* in different places.
[207]*coil:* uproar.

Plunged in the foaming brine and quit the vessel,
Then all afire with me. The king's son Ferdinand,
With hair up-staring° (then like reeds, not hair),
Was the first man that leapt; cried, "Hell is empty,
And all the devils are here!"

Prospero: Why, that's my spirit!   215
But was not this nigh shore?

Ariel: Close by, my master.

Prospero: But are they, Ariel, safe?

Ariel: Not a hair perished.
On their sustaining° garments not a blemish,
But fresher than before; and as thou bad'st me,
In troops I have dispersed them 'bout the isle.   220
The king's son have I landed by himself,
Whom I left cooling of the air with sighs
In an odd angle of the isle, and sitting,
His arms in this sad knot.

  [*Illustrates with a gesture.*]

Prospero: Of the king's ship,
The mariners, say how thou hast disposed,   225
And all the rest o' th' fleet.

Ariel: Safely in harbor
Is the king's ship; in the deep nook where once
Thou call'dst me up at midnight to fetch dew
From the still-vexed Bermoothes°, there she's hid;
The mariners all under hatches stowed,   230
Who, with a charm joined to their suff'red° labor,
I have left asleep. And for the rest o'th' fleet,
Which I dispersed, they all have met again,
And are upon the Mediterranean flote°
Bound sadly home for Naples,   235
Supposing that they saw the king's ship wracked
And his great person perish.

Prospero: Ariel, thy charge
Exactly is performed; but there's more work.
What is the time o' th' day?

Ariel: Past the mid season°.

Prospero: At least two glasses.° The time 'twixt six and now   240
Must by us both be spent most preciously.

Ariel: Is there more toil? Since thou dost give me pains°,
Let me remember° thee what thou hast promised,
Which is not yet performed me.

Prospero: How now? Moody?
What is't thou canst demand?

---

²¹³*up-staring:* standing on end.   ²¹⁸*sustaining:* buoying them up.   ²²⁹*Bermoothes:* Bermudas.
²³¹*suff'red:* undergone.   ²³⁴*flote:* sea.   ²³⁹*mid season:* noon.   ²⁴⁰*two glasses:* two o'clock.
²⁴²*pains:* hard tasks.   ²⁴³*remember:* remind.

Ariel: My liberty.   245
Prospero: Before the time be out? No more!
Ariel: I prithee,
   Remember I have done thee worthy service,
   Told thee no lies, made thee no mistakings, served
   Without or grudge or grumblings. Thou did promise
   To bate me° a full year.
Prospero: Dost thou forget   250
   From what a torment I did free thee?
Ariel: No.
Prospero: Thou dost; and think'st it much to tread the ooze
   Of the salt deep,
   To run upon the sharp wind of the North,
   To do me business in the veins° o' th' earth   255
   When it is baked° with frost.
Ariel: I do not, sir.
Prospero: Thou liest, malignant thing! Hast thou forgot
   The foul witch Sycorax°, who with age and envy°
   Was grown into a hoop? Hast thou forgot her?
Ariel: No, sir.
Prospero: Thou hast. Where was she born? Speak!   260
   Tell me!
Ariel: Sir, in Argier°.
Prospero: O, was she so? I must
   Once in a month recount what thou hast been,
   Which thou forget'st. This damned witch Sycorax,
   For mischiefs manifold, and sorceries terrible   265
   To enter human hearing, from Argier,
   Thou know'st, was banished. For one thing she did
   They would not take her life. Is not this true?
Ariel: Ay, sir.
Prospero: This blue-eyed° hag was hither brought with child   270
   And here was left by th' sailors. Thou, my slave,
   As thou report'st thyself, wast then her servant.
   And, for thou wast a spirit too delicate
   To act her earthy and abhorred commands,
   Refusing her grand hests°, she did confine thee,   275
   By help of her more potent ministers°,
   And in her most unmitigable rage,
   Into a cloven pine; within which rift
   Imprisoned thou didst painfully remain
   A dozen years; within which space she died   280

---

²⁵⁰*bate me:* reduce my term of service.   ²⁵⁵*veins:* streams.   ²⁵⁶*baked:* caked.   ²⁵⁸*Sycorax:* name not found elsewhere; probably derived from Greek *sys,* "sow," and *korax,* which means both "raven" — see line 324 — and "hook" — hence perhaps "hoop."   ²⁵⁸*envy:* malice.   ²⁶²*Argier:* Algiers.   ²⁷⁰*blue-eyed:* referring to the livid color of the eyelid, a sign of pregnancy.   ²⁷⁵*hests:* commands.   ²⁷⁶*her . . . ministers:* her agents, spirits more powerful than thou.

And left thee there, where thou didst vent thy groans
As fast as millwheels strike. Then was this island
(Save for the son that she did litter here,
A freckled whelp, hagborn) not honored with
A human shape.
Ariel: Yes, Caliban her son.   285
Prospero: Dull thing, I say so! He, that Caliban
Whom now I keep in service. Thou best know'st
What torment I did find thee in; thy groans
Did make wolves howl and penetrate the breasts
Of ever-angry bears. It was a torment   290
To lay upon the damned, which Sycorax
Could not again undo. It was mine art,
When I arrived and heard thee, that made gape
The pine, and let thee out.
Ariel: I thank thee, master.
Prospero: If thou more murmur'st, I will rend an oak   295
And peg thee in his° knotty entrails till
Thou hast howled away twelve winters.
Ariel: Pardon, master.
I will be correspondent° to command
And do my spriting gently°.
Prospero: Do so; and after two days
I will discharge thee.
Ariel: That's my noble master!   300
What shall I do? Say what? What shall I do?
Prospero: Go make thyself like a nymph o' th' sea. Be subject
To no sight but thine and mine, invisible
To every eyeball else°. Go take this shape
And hither come in't. Go! Hence with diligence!   *Exit [Ariel].* 305
Awake, dear heart, awake! Thou hast slept well.
Awake!
Miranda: The strangeness of your story put
Heaviness in me.
Prospero: Shake it off. Come on.
We'll visit Caliban, my slave, who never   310
Yields us kind answer.
Miranda: 'Tis a villain, sir,
I do not love to look on.
Prospero: But as 'tis,
We cannot miss° him. He does make our fire,
Fetch in our wood, and serves in offices
That profit us. What, ho! Slave! Caliban!   315
Thou earth, thou! Speak!

---

[296] *his:* its.   [298] *correspondent:* obedient.   [299] *do . . . gently:* render graciously my services as a
spirit.   [303–04] *invisible . . . else:* Ariel is invisible to everyone in the play except Prospero;
Henslowe's *Diary,* an Elizabethan stage account, lists "a robe for to go invisible."   [313] *miss:*
do without.

Caliban [*Within.*]:   There's wood enough within.
Prospero: Come forth, I say! There's other business for thee.
        Come, thou tortoise! When°?

        Enter Ariel like a water nymph.

        Fine apparition! My quaint° Ariel,
        Hark in thine ear. [*Whispers.*]
Ariel: My lord, it shall be done.   *Exit.*   320
Prospero: Thou poisonous slave, got by the devil himself
        Upon thy wicked dam, come forth!

        Enter Caliban.

Caliban: As wicked dew as e'er my mother brushed
        With raven's feather from unwholesome fen
        Drop on you both! A southwest blow on ye   325
        And blister you all o'er!
Prospero: For this, be sure, tonight thou shalt have cramps,
        Side-stitches that shall pen thy breath up. Urchins°
        Shall, for that vast of night that they may work°,
        All exercise on thee; thou shalt be pinched   330
        As thick as honeycomb, each pinch more stinging
        Than bees that made 'em.
Caliban: I must eat my dinner.
        This island's mine by Sycorax my mother,
        Which thou tak'st from me. When thou cam'st first,
        Thou strok'st me and made much of me; wouldst give me   335
        Water with berries in't; and teach me how
        To name the bigger light, and how the less,
        That burn by day and night. And then I loved thee
        And showed thee all the qualities o' th' isle,
        The fresh springs, brine pits, barren place and fertile.   340
        Cursed be I that did so! All the charms
        Of Sycorax — toads, beetles, bats, light on you!
        For I am all the subjects that you have,
        Which first was mine own king; and here you sty me
        In this hard rock, whiles you do keep from me   345
        The rest o' th' island.
Prospero: Thou most lying slave,
        Whom stripes° may move, not kindness! I have used thee
        (Filth as thou art) with humane care, and lodged thee
        In mine own cell till thou didst seek to violate
        The honor of my child.   350
Caliban: O ho, O ho! Would't had been done!
        Thou didst prevent me; I had peopled else
        This isle with Calibans.

---

[318] *When:* expression of impatience.   [319] *quaint:* ingenious.   [328] *Urchins:* goblins in the shape
of hedgehogs.   [329] *vast . . . work:* the long, empty stretch of night during which malignant
spirits are allowed to be active.   [347] *stripes:* lashes.

Miranda:°   Abhorrèd slave,
Which any print of goodness wilt not take,
Being capable of all ill°! I pitied thee,   355
Took pains to make thee speak, taught thee each hour
One thing or other. When thou didst not, savage,
Know thine own meaning, but wouldst gabble like
A thing most brutish, I endowed thy purposes
With words that made them known. But thy vile race,   360
Though thou didst learn, had that in't which good natures
Could not abide to be with. Therefore wast thou
Deservedly confined into this rock, who hadst
Deserved more than a prison.
Caliban: You taught me language, and my profit on't   365
Is, I know how to curse. The red plague rid° you
For learning me your language!
Prospero: Hagseed, hence!
Fetch us in fuel. And be quick, thou'rt best°,
To answer other business. Shrug'st thou, malice?
If thou neglect'st or dost unwillingly   370
What I command, I'll rack thee with old° cramps,
Fill all thy bones with aches°, make thee roar
That beasts shall tremble at thy din.
Caliban: No, pray thee.

[*Aside.*]

I must obey. His art is of such pow'r
It would control my dam's god, Setebos,   375
And make a vassal of him.
Prospero: So, slave; hence!   *Exit Caliban.*

Enter Ferdinand; and Ariel (invisible), playing and singing.

              Ariel's song.
         Come unto these yellow sands,
            And then take hands.
         Curtsied when you have and kissed
            The wild waves whist°,   380
         Foot it featly° here and there;
         And, sweet sprites, the burden bear.
            Hark, hark!

Burden, dispersedly°. Bow, wow!

---

[353]*Miranda:* many editors transfer this speech to Prospero as inappropriate to Miranda.
[355]*capable . . . ill:* susceptible only to evil impressions.   [366]*rid:* destroy.   [368]*thou'rt best:* you'd
better.   [371]*old:* plenty of (with an additional suggestion, "such as old people have").
[372]*aches:* pronounced "aitches."   [379–80]*kissed . . . whist:* when you have, through the harmony
of kissing in the dance, kissed the wild waves into silence (?) when you have kissed in the
dance, the wild waves being silenced (?).   [381]*featly:* nimbly.   [384]*Burden, dispersedly:* an under-
song, coming from all parts of the stage; it imitates the barking of dogs and perhaps at the
end the crowing of a cock.

Burden, dispersedly. Bow, wow!

        Hark, hark! I hear
        The strain of strutting chanticleer
        Cry cock-a-diddle-dow.

Ferdinand: Where should this music be? I' th' air or th' earth?   390
It sounds no more; and sure it waits upon
Some god o' th' island. Sitting on a bank,
Weeping again the King my father's wrack,
This music crept by me upon the waters,
Allaying both their fury and my passion°   395
With its sweet air. Thence I have followed it,
Or it hath drawn me rather; but 'tis gone.
No, it begins again.

                Ariel's song.
        Full fathom five thy father lies;
          Of his bones are coral made;   400
        Those are pearls that were his eyes;
          Nothing of him that doth fade
        But doth suffer a sea change
        Into something rich and strange.
        Sea nymphs hourly ring his knell: 405

Burden. Ding-dong.

        Hark! Now I hear them — ding-dong bell.
Ferdinand: The ditty does remember my drowned father.
This is no mortal business, nor no sound
That the earth owes°. I hear it now above me.   410
Prospero: The fringèd curtains of thine eye advance°
And say what thou see'st yond.
Miranda: What is't? A spirit?
Lord, how it looks about! Believe me, sir,
It carries a brave form. But 'tis a spirit.
Prospero: No, wench; it eats, and sleeps, and hath such senses   415
As we have, such. This gallant which thou see'st
Was in the wrack; and, but he's something stained
With grief (that's beauty's canker), thou mightst call him
A goodly person. He hath lost his fellows
And strays about to find 'em.
Miranda: I might call him   420
A thing divine; for nothing natural
I ever saw so noble.
Prospero [*Aside.*]:   It goes on, I see,
As my soul prompts it. Spirit, fine spirit, I'll free thee
Within two days for this.

---

[395]*passion:* grief.   [410]*owes:* owns.   [411]*advance:* raise.

Ferdinand: Most sure, the goddess
On whom these airs attend! Vouchsafe my prayer   425
May know if you remain° upon this island,
And that you will some good instruction give
How I may bear me° here. My prime request,
Which I do last pronounce, is (O you wonder!)
If you be maid or no?
Miranda: No wonder, sir,   430
But certainly a maid.
Ferdinand: My language? Heavens!
I am the best of them that speak this speech,
Were I but where 'tis spoken.
Prospero: How? The best?
What wert thou if the King of Naples heard thee?
Ferdinand: A single° thing, as I am now, that wonders   435
To hear thee speak of Naples. He does hear me;
And that he does I weep. Myself am Naples,
Who with mine eyes, never since at ebb, beheld
The king my father wracked.
Miranda: Alack, for mercy!
Ferdinand: Yes, faith, and all his lords, the Duke of Milan   440
And his brave son° being twain.°
Prospero [Aside.]:   The Duke of Milan
And his more braver daughter could control° thee,
If now 'twere fit to do't. At the first sight
They have changed eyes°. Delicate Ariel,
I'll set thee free for this. [*To Ferdinand.*] A word, good sir.   445
I fear you have done yourself some wrong°. A word!
Miranda: Why speaks my father so ungently? This
Is the third man that e'er I saw; the first
That e'er I sighed for. Pity move my father
To be inclined my way!
Ferdinand: O, if a virgin,   450
And your affection not gone forth, I'll make you
The queen of Naples.
Prospero: Soft, sir! One word more.

[*Aside.*]

They are both in either's pow'rs. But this swift business
I must uneasy make, lest too light winning
Make the prize light. [*To Ferdinand.*] One word more! I charge thee   455
That thou attend me. Thou dost here usurp
The name thou ow'st° not, and hast put thyself
Upon this island as a spy, to win it

425–26 *Vouchsafe . . . remain:* may my prayer induce you to inform me whether you dwell.
428 *bear me:* conduct myself.   435 *single:* (1) solitary (2) helpless.   441 *son:* the only time Antonio's son is mentioned.   441 *twain:* two (of these lords).   442 *control:* refute.   444 *changed eyes:*
i.e., fallen in love.   446 *done . . . wrong:* said what is not so.   457 *ow'st:* ownest.

From me, the lord on't.

Ferdinand: No, as I am a man!

Miranda: There's nothing ill can dwell in such a temple.   460
If the ill spirit have so fair a house,
Good things will strive to dwell with't.

Prospero: Follow me.

[*To Miranda.*]

Speak not you for him; he's a traitor. [*To Ferdinand.*] Come!
I'll manacle thy neck and feet together;
Sea water shalt thou drink; thy food shall be   465
The fresh-brook mussels, withered roots, and husks
Wherein the acorn cradled. Follow!

Ferdinand: No.
I will resist such entertainment till
Mine enemy has more pow'r.

He draws, and is charmed from moving.

Miranda: O dear father,
Make not too rash a trial of him, for   470
He's gentle and not fearful°.

Prospero: What, I say,
My foot my tutor°? [*To Ferdinand.*] Put thy sword up, traitor —
Who mak'st a show but dar'st not strike, thy conscience
Is so possessed with guilt! Come, from thy ward°!
For I can here disarm thee with this stick°   475
And make thy weapon drop.

Miranda: Beseech you, father!

Prospero: Hence! Hang not on my garments.

Miranda: Sir, have pity.
I'll be his surety.

Prospero: Silence! One word more
Shall make me chide thee, if not hate thee. What,
An advocate for an impostor? Hush!   480
Thou think'st there is no more such shapes as he,
Having seen but him and Caliban. Foolish wench!
To th' most of men this is a Caliban,
And they to him are angels.

Miranda: My affections
Are then most humble. I have no ambition   485
To see a goodlier man.

Prospero [*To Ferdinand.*]: Come on, obey!
Thy nerves° are in their infancy again
And have no vigor in them.

Ferdinand: So they are.
My spirits, as in a dream, are all bound up.   490

---

[471] *gentle . . . fearful:* of noble birth and no coward.   [472] *My . . . tutor?:* am I to be instructed by my inferior?   [474] *ward:* fighting posture.   [475] *stick:* his wand.   [488] *nerves:* sinews.

My father's loss, the weakness which I feel,
The wrack of all my friends, not this man's threats
To whom I am subdued, are but light to me,
Might I but through my prison once a day
Behold this maid. All corners else o' th' earth   495
Let liberty make use of. Space enough
Have I in such a prison.
Prospero [*Aside.*]: It works. [*To Ferdinand.*] Come on.

[*To Ariel.*]

Thou hast done well, fine Ariel! [*To Ferdinand.*] Follow me.

[*To Ariel.*] Hark what thou else shalt do me.

Miranda: Be of comfort.   500
My father's of a better nature, sir,
Than he appears by speech. This is unwonted
Which now came from him.
Prospero: Thou shalt be as free
As mountain winds; but then° exactly do
All points of my command.
Ariel: To th' syllable.   505
Prospero [*To Ferdinand.*]:
Come, follow. [*To Miranda.*] Speak not for him.   *Exeunt.*

ACT II

Scene I. [*Another part of the island.*]

Enter Alonso, Sebastian, Antonio, Gonzalo, Adrian, Francisco, and others.

Gonzalo: Beseech you, sir, be merry. You have cause
(So have we all) of joy; for our escape
Is much beyond our loss. Our hint of° woe
Is common; every day some sailor's wife,
The master of some merchant°, and the merchant,   5
Have just our theme of woe. But for the miracle,
I mean our preservation, few in millions
Can speak like us. Then wisely, good sir, weigh
Our sorrow with° our comfort.
Alonso: Prithee, peace.
Sebastian [*Aside to Antonio.*]: He receives comfort like cold porridge°.   10
Antonio [*Aside to Sebastian.*]: The visitor° will not give him o'er so.°
Sebastian: Look, he's winding up the watch of his wit; by and by it will
strike.
Gonzalo: Sir —

504*then:* till then. II.i. 3*hint of:* occasion for. 5*master . . . merchant:* captain of some merchant
ship. 9*with:* against. 10*He . . . porridge:* "He" is Alonso; pun on "peace," for porridge
contained peas. 11*visitor:* spiritual comforter. 11*give . . . so:* release him so easily.

Sebastian [*Aside to Antonio.*]: One. Tell°.   15
Gonzalo: When every grief is entertained, that's° offered
    Comes to th' entertainer —
Sebastian: A dollar.
Gonzalo: Dolor comes to him, indeed. You have spoken truer than you
    purposed.   20
Sebastian: You have taken it wiselier° than I meant you should.
Gonzalo: Therefore, my lord —
Antonio: Fie, what a spendthrift is he of his tongue!
Alonso: I prithee, spare°.
Gonzalo: Well, I have done. But yet —   25
Sebastian: He will be talking.
Antonio: Which, of he or Adrian, for a good wager, first° begins to crow?
Sebastian: The old cock°.
Antonio: The cock'rel°.
Sebastian: Done! The wager?   30
Antonio: A laughter°.
Sebastian: A match!
Adrian: Though this island seem to be desert —
Antonio: Ha, ha, ha!
Sebastian: So, you're paid.   35
Adrian: Uninhabitable and almost inaccessible —
Sebastian: Yet —
Adrian: Yet —
Antonio: He could not miss't.
Adrian: It must needs be of subtle, tender, and delicate temperance°.   40
Antonio: Temperance was a delicate wench.
Sebastian: Ay, and a subtle, as he most learnedly delivered.
Adrian: The air breathes upon us here most sweetly.
Sebastian: As if it had lungs, and rotten ones.
Antonio: Or as 'twere perfumed by a fen.   45
Gonzalo: Here is everything advantageous to life.
Antonio: True; save means to live.
Sebastian: Of that there's none, or little.
Gonzalo: How lush and lusty the grass looks! How green!
Antonio: The ground indeed is tawny.   50
Sebastian: With an eye° of green in't.
Antonio: He misses not much.
Sebastian: No; he doth but mistake the truth totally.
Gonzalo: But the rarity of it is — which is indeed almost beyond
    credit —   55
Sebastian: As many vouched rarities are.
Gonzalo: That our garments, being, as they were, drenched in the sea,

---

¹⁵*One. Tell:* He has struck one. Keep count. ¹⁶*that's:* that which is. ²¹*wiselier:* i.e., under-
stood my pun. ²⁴*spare:* spare your words. ²⁷*Which . . . first:* let's wager which of the two,
Gonzalo or Adrian, will first. ²⁸*old cock:* Gonzalo. ²⁹*cock'rel:* young cock; i.e., Adrian.
³¹*laughter:* the winner will have the laugh on the loser. ⁴⁰*temperance:* climate (in the next line,
a girl's name). ⁵¹*eye:* spot (also perhaps Gonzalo's eye).

hold, notwithstanding, their freshness and glosses, being rather
new-dyed than stained with salt water.

Antonio: If but one of his pockets could speak, would it not say he   60
lies°?

Sebastian: Ay, or very falsely pocket up his report°.

Gonzalo: Methinks our garments are now as fresh as when we put them
on first in Afric, at the marriage of the king's fair daughter Claribel
to the King of Tunis.   65

Sebastian: 'Twas a sweet marriage, and we prosper well in our return.

Adrian: Tunis was never graced before with such a paragon to° their
queen.

Gonzalo: Not since widow Dido's time.

Antonio: Widow? A pox o' that! How came that "widow" in? Widow   70
Dido!

Sebastian: What if he had said "widower Aeneas"° too? Good Lord, how
you take it!

Adrian: "Widow Dido," said you? You make me study of that. She was
of Carthage, not of Tunis.   75

Gonzalo: This Tunis, sir, was Carthage.

Adrian: Carthage?

Gonzalo: I assure you, Carthage.

Antonio: His word is more than the miraculous harp°.

Sebastian: He hath raised the wall and houses too.   80

Antonio: What impossible matter will he make easy next?

Sebastian: I think he will carry this island home in his pocket and give
it his son for an apple.

Antonio: And, sowing the kernels of it in the sea, bring forth more islands.

Gonzalo: Ay!   85

Antonio: Why, in good time°.

Gonzalo [To Alonso.]: Sir, we were talking that our garments seem now as
fresh as when we were at Tunis at the marriage of your daughter,
who is now queen.

Antonio: And the rarest that e'er came there.   90

Sebastian: Bate°, I beseech you, widow Dido.

Antonio: O, widow Dido? Ay, widow Dido!

Gonzalo: Is not, sir, my doublet as fresh as the first day I wore it? I mean,
in a sort°.

Antonio: That "sort" was well fished for.   95

Gonzalo: When I wore it at your daughter's marriage.

Alonso: You cram these words into mine ears against

---

⁶⁰⁻⁶¹*If . . . lies:* i.e., the insides of Gonzalo's pockets are stained.   ⁶²*Ay . . . report:* unless the
pocket were, like a false knave, to receive without resentment the imputation that it is
unstained.   ⁶⁷*to:* for.   ⁷⁰⁻⁷²*Widow Dido . . . "widower Aeneas":* the point of the joke is that Dido
was a widow, but one does not ordinarily think of her in that way; and the same with Aeneas.
⁷⁹*miraculous harp:* of Amphion, which raised only the *walls* of Thebes; whereas Gonzalo has
rebuilt the whole ancient city of Carthage by identifying it mistakenly with modern Tunis.
⁸⁶*Why . . . time:* hearing Gonzalo reaffirm his false statement about Tunis and Carthage,
Antonio suggests that Gonzalo will indeed, at the first opportunity, carry this island home
in his pocket.   ⁹¹*Bate:* except.   ⁹⁴*in a sort:* so to speak.

The stomach of my sense°. Would I had never
Married my daughter there! For, coming thence,
My son is lost; and, in my rate°, she too,   100
Who is so far from Italy removed
I ne'er again shall see her. O thou mine heir
Of Naples and of Milan, what strange fish
Hath made his meal on thee?
Francisco: Sir, he may live.
I saw him beat the surges under him   105
And ride upon their backs. He trod the water,
Whose enmity he flung aside, and breasted
The surge most swol'n that met him. His bold head
'Bove the contentious waves he kept, and oared
Himself with his good arms in lusty stroke   110
To th' shore, that o'er his° wave-worn basis bowed°,
As stooping to relieve him. I not doubt
He came alive to land.
Alonso: No, no, he's gone.
Sebastian [*To Alonso.*]: Sir, you may thank yourself for this great loss,
That would not bless our Europe with your daughter,
But rather loose her to an African,   115
Where she, at least, is banished from your eye
Who hath cause to wet the grief on't.
Alonso: Prithee, peace.
Sebastian: You were kneeled to and importuned otherwise
By all of us; and the fair soul herself   120
Weighed, between loathness and obedience, at
Which end o' th' beam should bow°. We have lost your son,
I fear, forever. Milan and Naples have
Moe° widows in them of this business' making
Than we bring men to comfort them.   125
The fault's your own.
Alonso: So is the dear'st° o' th' loss.
Gonzalo: My Lord Sebastian,
The truth you speak doth lack some gentleness,
And time to speak it in. You rub the sore
When you should bring the plaster.
Sebastian: Very well.   130
Antonio: And most chirurgeonly°.
Gonzalo [*To Alonso.*]: It is foul weather in us all, good sir,
When you are cloudy.
Sebastian [*Aside to Antonio.*]: Foul weather?
Antonio [*Aside to Sebastian.*]:   Very foul.

97–98*against . . . sense:* though my mind (or feelings) have no appetite for them.   100*rate:*
opinion.   111*his:* its.   111*wave-worn basis bowed:* the image is of a guardian cliff on the shore.
121–22*Weighed . . . bow:* Claribel's unwillingness to marry was outweighed by her obedience
to her father.   124*Moe:* more.   126*dear'st:* intensifies the meaning of the noun.   131*chirur-
geonly:* like a surgeon.

Gonzalo: Had I plantation° of this isle, my lord —
Antonio: He'd sow't with nettle seed.
Sebastian: Or docks, or mallows.   135
Gonzalo: And were the king on't, what would I do?
Sebastian: Scape being drunk for want of wine.
Gonzalo: I' th' commonwealth I would by contraries°
    Execute all things. For no kind of traffic°
    Would I admit; no name of magistrate;   140
    Letters° should not be known; riches, poverty,
    And use of service°, none; contract, succession°,
    Bourn°, bound of land, tilth°, vineyard, none;
    No use of metal, corn, or wine, or oil;
    No occupation; all men idle, all;   145
    And women too, but innocent and pure;
    No sovereignty.
Sebastian: Yet he would be king on't.
Antonio: The latter end of his commonwealth forgets the beginning.
Gonzalo: All things in common nature should produce
    Without sweat or endeavor. Treason, felony,   150
    Sword, pike, knife, gun, or need of any engine°
    Would I not have; but nature should bring forth,
    Of it° own kind, all foison°, all abundance,
    To feed my innocent people.
Sebastian: No marrying 'mong his subjects?   155
Antonio: None, man, all idle — whores and knaves.
Gonzalo: I would with such perfection govern, sir,
    T' excel the Golden Age.
Sebastian [*Loudly.*]:   Save his majesty!
Antonio [*Loudly.*]: Long live Gonzalo!
Gonzalo: And — do you mark me, sir?
Alonso: Prithee, no more. Thou dost talk nothing to me.   160
Gonzalo: I do well believe your highness; and did it to minister occa-
    sion° to these gentlemen, who are of such sensible° and nimble lungs
    that they always use to laugh at nothing.
Antonio: 'Twas you we laughed at.
Gonzalo: Who in this kind of merry fooling am nothing to you; so you   165
    may continue, and laugh at nothing still.
Antonio: What a blow was there given!
Sebastian: And° it had not fall'n flatlong°.
Gonzalo: You are gentlemen of brave mettle; you would lift the moon
    out of her sphere if she would continue in it five weeks without   170
    changing.

    Enter Ariel [invisible] playing solemn music.

---

¹³⁴*plantation:* colonization (Antonio then puns by taking the word in its other sense).   ¹³⁸*con-traries:* in contrast to the usual customs.   ¹³⁹*traffic:* trade.   ¹⁴¹*Letters:* learning.   ¹⁴²*service:* servants.   ¹⁴²*succession:* inheritance.   ¹⁴³*Bourn:* boundary.   ¹⁴³*tilth:* agriculture.   ¹⁵¹*engine:* weapon.   ¹⁵³*it* its.   ¹⁵³*foison:* abundance.   ¹⁶¹⁻¹⁶²*minister occasion:* afford opportunity.   ¹⁶²*sensible:* sensitive.   ¹⁶⁸*And:* if.   ¹⁶⁸*flatlong:* with the flat of the sword.

Sebastian: We would so, and then go a-batfowling°.

Antonio: Nay, good my lord, be not angry.

Gonzalo: No, I warrant you; I will not adventure my discretion so
    weakly°. Will you laugh me asleep? For I am very heavy.   175

Antonio: Go sleep, and hear us.

    [*All sleep except Alonso, Sebastian, and Antonio.*]

Alonso: What, all so soon asleep? I wish mine eyes
    Would, with themselves, shut up my thoughts. I find
    They are inclined to do so.

Sebastian: Please you, sir,
    Do not omit° the heavy offer of it.   180
    It seldom visits sorrow; when it doth,
    It is a comforter.

Antonio: We two, my lord,
    Will guard your person while you take your rest,
    And watch your safety.

Alonso: Thank you. Wondrous heavy.

    [*Alonso sleeps. Exit Ariel.*]

Sebastian: What a strange drowsiness possesses them!   185

Antonio: It is the quality o' th' climate.

Sebastian: Why
    Doth it not then our eyelids sink? I find not
    Myself disposed to sleep.

Antonio: Nor I: my spirits are nimble.
    They fell together all, as by consent.
    They dropped as by a thunderstroke. What might,   190
    Worthy Sebastian — O, what might? — No more!
    And yet methinks I see it in thy face,
    What thou shouldst be. Th' occasion speaks° thee, and
    My strong imagination sees a crown
    Dropping upon thy head.

Sebastian: What? Art thou waking?   195

Antonio: Do you not hear me speak?

Sebastian: I do; and surely
    It is a sleepy language, and thou speak'st
    Out of thy sleep. What is it thou didst say?
    This is a strange repose, to be asleep
    With eyes wide open; standing, speaking, moving,   200
    And yet so fast asleep.

Antonio: Noble Sebastian,
    Thou let'st thy fortune sleep — die, rather; wink'st°
    Whiles thou art waking.

Sebastian: Thou dost snore distinctly;

---

¹⁷²*We . . . a-batfowling:* We would use the moon for a lantern in order to hunt birds at night
by attracting them with a light and beating them down with bats; i.e., in order to gull
simpletons like you (?).   ¹⁷⁴⁻⁷⁵*adventure . . . weakly:* risk my reputation for good sense because
of your weak wit.   ¹⁸⁰*omit:* neglect.   ¹⁹³*speaks:* speaks to.   ²⁰²*wink'st:* dost shut thine eyes.

There's meaning in thy snores.

Antonio: I am more serious than my custom. You   205
     Must be so too, if heed° me; which to do
     Trebles thee o'er°.

Sebastian: Well, I am standing water.

Antonio: I'll teach you how to flow.

Sebastian: Do so. To ebb
     Hereditary sloth instructs me.

Antonio: O,
     If you but knew how you the purpose cherish   210
     Whiles thus you mock it; how, in stripping it,
     You more invest it°! Ebbing men, indeed,
     Most often do so near the bottom run
     By their own fear or sloth.

Sebastian: Prithee, say on.
     The setting of thine eye and cheek proclaim   215
     A matter° from thee; and a birth, indeed,
     Which throes thee much° to yield.

Antonio: Thus, sir:
     Although this lord of weak remembrance°, this
     Who shall be of as little memory°
     When he is earthed°, hath here almost persuaded   220
     (For he's a spirit of persuasion, only
     Professes to persuade°) the king his son's alive,
     'Tis as impossible that he's undrowned
     As he that sleeps here swims.

Sebastian: I have no hope
     That he's undrowned.

Antonio: O, out of that no hope   225
     What great hope have you! No hope that way is
     Another way so high a hope that even
     Ambition cannot pierce a wink beyond,
     But doubt discovery there°. Will you grant with me
     That Ferdinand is drowned?

Sebastian: He's gone.

Antonio: Then tell me,   230
     Who's the next heir of Naples?

Sebastian: Claribel.

Antonio: She that is Queen of Tunis; she that dwells
     Ten leagues beyond man's life°; she that from Naples
     Can have no note — unless the sun were post°;

---

²⁰⁶*if heed:* if you heed.   ²⁰⁷*Trebles thee o'er:* makes thee three times what thou now art.
²¹¹⁻¹²*in stripping . . . invest it:* in stripping the purpose off you, you clothe yourself with it all
the more.   ²¹⁶*matter:* matter of importance.   ²¹⁷*throes thee much:* costs thee much pain.
²¹⁸*remembrance:* memory   ²¹⁹*of . . . memory:* as little remembered.   ²²⁰*earthed:* buried.
²²¹⁻²²*only . . . persuade:* his only profession is to persuade.   ²²⁸⁻²⁹*Ambition . . . there:* the eye
of ambition can reach no further, but must even doubt the reality of what it discerns thus
far.   ²³³*Ten . . . life:* it would take a lifetime to get within ten leagues of the place.   ²³⁴*post:*
messenger.

The man i' th' moon's too slow — till newborn chins   235
Be rough and razorable°; she that from whom
We all were sea-swallowed°, though some cast° again,
And, by that destiny, to perform an act
Whereof what's past is prologue, what to come,
In yours and my discharge.
Sebastian: What stuff is this? How say you?   240
'Tis true my brother's daughter's Queen of Tunis;
So is she heir of Naples; 'twixt which regions
There is some space.
Antonio: A space whose ev'ry cubit
Seems to cry out, "How shall that Claribel
Measure us back to Naples? Keep in Tunis,   245
And let Sebastian wake!" Say this were death
That now hath seized them, why, they were no worse
Than now they are. There be that can rule Naples
As well as he that sleeps; lords that can prate
As amply and unnecessarily   250
As this Gonzalo; I myself could make
A chough° of as deep chat. O, that you bore
The mind that I do! What a sleep were this
For your advancement! Do you understand me?
Sebastian: Methinks I do.
Antonio: And how does your content   255
Tender° your own good fortune?
Sebastian: I remember
You did supplant your brother Prospero.
Antonio: True.
And look how well my garments sit upon me,
Much feater° than before. My brother's servants
Were then my fellows; now they are my men.   260
Sebastian: But, for your conscience —
Antonio: Ay, sir, where lies that? If 'twere a kibe°,
'Twould put me to my slipper; but I feel not
This deity in my bosom. Twenty consciences
That stand 'twixt me and Milan, candied be they   265
And melt, ere they molest! Here lies your brother,
No better than the earth he lies upon —
If he were that which now he's like, that's dead° —
Whom I with this obedient steel (three inches of it)
Can lay to bed forever; whiles you, doing thus,   270
To the perpetual wink° for aye might put
This ancient morsel, this Sir Prudence, who
Should not upbraid our course. For all the rest,

235–36*till . . . razorable:* till babies just born be ready to shave.   236–37*she . . . sea-swallowed:* she
who is separated from Naples by so dangerous a sea that we were ourselves swallowed up
by it.   237*cast:* cast upon the shore (with a suggestion of its theatrical meaning that leads to
the next metaphor).   252*chough:* jackdaw (a bird that can be taught to speak a few words).
256*Tender:* regard (i.e., Do you like your good fortune?).   259*feater:* more becomingly.
262*kibe:* chilblain on the heel.   268*that's dead:* that is, if he were dead.   271*wink:* eye-shut.

They'll take suggestion as a cat laps milk;
They'll tell the clock° to any business that   275
We say befits the hour.
Sebastian: Thy case, dear friend,
Shall be my precedent. As thou got'st Milan,
I'll come by Naples. Draw thy sword. One stroke
Shall free thee from the tribute which thou payest,
And I the king shall love thee.
Antonio: Draw together;   280
And when I rear my hand, do you the like,
To fall it on Gonzalo. [They draw.]
Sebastian: O, but one word!

Enter Ariel [invisible] with music and song.

Ariel: My master through his art foresees the danger
That you, his friend, are in, and sends me forth
(For else his project dies) to keep them living.   285

Sings in Gonzalo's ear.

        While you here do snoring lie,
        Open-eyed conspiracy
          His time doth take.
        If of life you keep a care,
        Shake off slumber and beware.   290
          Awake, awake!
Antonio: Then let us both be sudden.
Gonzalo [Wakes.]:   Now good angels
Preserve the king!

[The others wake.]

Alonso: Why, how now? Ho, awake! Why are you drawn?
Wherefore this ghastly looking?
Gonzalo: What's the matter?   295
Sebastian: Whiles we stood here securing your repose,
Even now, we heard a hollow burst of bellowing
Like bulls, or rather lions. Did't not wake you?
It struck mine ear most terribly.
Alonso: I heard nothing.
Antonio: O, 'twas a din to fright a monster's ear,   300
To make an earthquake! Sure it was the roar
Of a whole herd of lions.
Alonso: Heard you this, Gonzalo?
Gonzalo: Upon mine honor, sir, I heard a humming,
And that a strange one too, which did awake me.
I shaked you, sir, and cried. As mine eyes opened,   305
I saw their weapons drawn. There was a noise,
That's verily°. 'Tis best we stand upon our guard,
Or that we quit this place. Let's draw our weapons.

---

²⁷⁵*tell the clock:* say yes. ³⁰⁷*verily:* the truth.

Alonso: Lead off this ground, and let's make further search
    For my poor son.
Gonzalo: Heavens keep him from these beasts!   310
    For he is, sure, i' th' island.
Alonso: Lead away.
Ariel: Prospero my lord shall know what I have done.
    So, king, go safely on to seek thy son.   *Exeunt.*

Scene II. [*Another part of the island.*]

   Enter Caliban with a burden of wood. A noise of thunder heard.

Caliban: All the infections that the sun sucks up
    From bogs, fens, flats, on Prosper fall, and make him
    By inchmeal° a disease! His spirits hear me,
    And yet I needs must curse. But they'll nor pinch,
    Fright me with urchin shows°, pitch me i' th' mire,   5
    Nor lead me, like a firebrand°, in the dark
    Out of my way, unless he bid 'em. But
    For every trifle are they set upon me;
    Sometime like apes that mow° and chatter at me,
    And after bite me; then like hedgehogs which   10
    Lie tumbling in my barefoot way and mount
    Their pricks at my footfall; sometime am I
    All wound with adders, who with cloven tongues
    Do hiss me into madness.

   Enter Trinculo.

                Lo, now, lo!
    Here comes a spirit of his, and to torment me   15
    For bringing wood in slowly. I'll fall flat.
    Perchance he will not mind me.

   [*Lies down.*]

Trinculo: Here's neither bush nor shrub to bear off° any weather at all,
and another storm brewing; I hear it sing i' th' wind. Yond same
black cloud, yond huge one, looks like a foul bombard° that would   20
shed his liquor. If it should thunder as it did before, I know not
where to hide my head. Yond same cloud cannot choose but fall by
pailfuls. What have we here? A man or a fish? Dead or alive? A fish!
He smells like a fish; a very ancient and fishlike smell; a kind of not
of the newest Poor John°. A strange fish! Were I in England now, as   25
once I was, and had but this fish painted°, not a holiday fool there
but would give a piece of silver. There would this monster make a
man°; any strange beast there makes a man. When they will not give
a doit° to relieve a lame beggar, they will lay out ten to see a dead

---

II.ii. ³*By inchmeal:* inch by inch.   ⁵*urchin shows:* impish apparitions.   ⁶*like a firebrand:* in the
form of a will-o'-the-wisp.   ⁹*mow:* make faces.   ¹⁸*bear off:* ward off.   ²⁰*bombard:* large leather
jug.   ²⁵*Poor John:* dried hake.   ²⁶*painted:* i.e., as a sign hung outside a booth at a fair.
²⁷⁻²⁸*make a man:* pun: make a man's fortune.   ²⁹*doit:* smallest coin.

Indian. Legged like a man! And his fins like arms! Warm, o' my troth! 30
I do now let loose my opinion, hold it no longer. This is no fish, but
an islander, that hath lately suffered by a thunderbolt. [*Thunder.*]
Alas, the storm is come again! My best way is to creep under his
gaberdine; there is no other shelter hereabout. Misery acquaints a
man with strange bedfellows. I will here shroud till the dregs of the 35
storm be past.

[*Creeps under Caliban's garment.*]

Enter Stephano, singing, [*a bottle in his hand.*]

Stephano: I shall no more to sea, to sea;
          Here shall I die ashore.
This is a very scurvy tune to sing at a man's funeral.
Well, here's my comfort. 40

[*Drinks.*]

          The master, the swabber, the boatswain, and I,
               The gunner, and his mate,
          Loved Moll, Meg, and Marian, and Margery,
               But none of us cared for Kate.
          For she had a tongue with a tang, 45
               Would cry to a sailor, "Go hang!"
     She loved not the savor of tar nor of pitch;
          Yet a tailor might scratch her where'er she did itch.
          Then to sea, boys, and let her go hang!
This is a scurvy tune too; but here's my comfort. 50

     [*Drinks.*]

Caliban: Do not torment me! O!
Stephano: What's the matter? Have we devils here? Do you put tricks
     upon's with savages and men of Inde, ha? I have not 'scaped drown-
     ing to be afeard now of your four legs. For it hath been said, "As
     proper a man as ever went on four legs cannot make him give 55
     ground"; and it shall be said so again, while Stephano breathes at'
     nostrils°.
Caliban: The spirit torments me. O!
Stephano: This is some monster of the isle, with four legs, who hath got,
     as I take it, an ague. Where the devil should he learn our language? 60
     I will give him some relief, if it be but for that. If I can recover° him,
     and keep him tame, and get to Naples with him, he's a present for
     any emperor that ever trod on neat's leather°.
Caliban: Do not torment me, prithee; I'll bring my wood home faster.
Stephano: He's in his fit now and does not talk after the wisest. He shall 65
     taste of my bottle; if he have never drunk wine afore, it will go near
     to remove his fit. If I can recover him and keep him tame, I will not
     take too much° for him. He shall pay for him that hath him, and that
     soundly.

_____

56–57*at' nostrils:* at the nostrils.   61*recover:* cure.   63*neat's leather:* cowhide.   67–68*not . . . much:*
too much will not be enough.

1020 Comedy

Caliban: Thou dost me yet but little hurt. Thou wilt anon°; I know it by   70
  thy trembling°. Now Prosper works upon thee.
Stephano: Come on your ways, open your mouth; here is that which will
  give language to you, cat°. Open your mouth. This will shake your
  shaking, I can tell you, and that soundly. [*Gives Caliban drink.*] You
  cannot tell who's your friend. Open your chaps° again.   75
Trinculo: I should know that voice. It should be — but he is drowned; and
  these are devils. O, defend me!
Stephano: Four legs and two voices — a most delicate monster! His forward voice now is to speak well of his friend; his backward voice
  is to utter foul speeches and to detract. If all the wine in my bottle   80
  will recover him, I will help his ague. Come! [*Gives drink.*] Amen! I
  will pour some in thy other mouth.
Trinculo: Stephano!
Stephano: Doth thy other mouth call me? Mercy, mercy! This is a devil,
  and no monster. I will leave him; I have no long spoon°.   85
Trinculo: Stephano! If thou beest Stephano, touch me and speak to me;
  for I am Trinculo — be not afeard — thy good friend Trinculo.
Stephano: If thou beest Trinculo, come forth. I'll pull thee by the lesser
  legs. If any be Trinculo's legs, these are they. [*Draws him out from under
  Caliban's garment.*] Thou art very Trinculo indeed! How cam'st thou   90
  to be the siege° of this mooncalf°? Can he vent Trinculos?
Trinculo: I took him to be killed with a thunderstroke. But art thou not
  drowned, Stephano? I hope now thou art not drowned. Is the storm
  overblown? I hid me under the dead mooncalf's gaberdine for fear
  of the storm. And art thou living, Stephano? O Stephano, two   95
  Neapolitans scaped!
Stephano: Prithee do not turn me about; my stomach is not constant.
Caliban [*Aside.*]: These be fine things, and if° they be not sprites.
  That's a brave god and bears celestial liquor.
  I will kneel to him.   100
Stephano: How didst thou scape? How cam'st thou hither? Swear by this
  bottle how thou cam'st hither. I escaped upon a butt of sack which
  the sailors heaved o'erboard — by this bottle which I made of the
  bark of a tree with mine own hands since I was cast ashore.
Caliban: I'll swear upon that bottle to be thy true subject, for the liquor   105
  is not earthly.
Stephano: Here! Swear then how thou escap'dst.
Trinculo: Swum ashore, man, like a duck. I can swim like a duck, I'll be
  sworn.
Stephano: Here, kiss the book. [*Gives him drink.*] Though thou canst swim   110
  like a duck, thou art made like a goose.
Trinculo: O Stephano, hast any more of this?
Stephano: The whole butt, man. My cellar is in a rock by th' seaside, where
  my wine is hid. How now, mooncalf? How does thine ague?

---

[70]*anon:* soon.   [71]*trembling:* Trinculo is shaking with fear.   [73]*cat:* alluding to the proverb
"Liquor will make a cat talk."   [75]*chaps:* jaws.   [85]*long spoon:* alluding to the proverb "He who
sups with (i.e., from the same dish as) the devil must have a long spoon."   [91]*siege:* excrement.
[91]*mooncalf:* monstrosity.   [98]*and if:* if.

Caliban: Hast thou not dropped from heaven?   115
Stephano: Out o' th' moon, I do assure thee. I was the Man i' th' Moon
   when time was°.
Caliban: I have seen thee in her, and I do adore thee.
   My mistress showed me thee, and thy dog, and thy bush°.
Stephano: Come, swear to that; kiss the book. [*Gives him drink.*] I will   120
   furnish it anon with new contents. Swear.

   [*Caliban drinks.*]

Trinculo: By this good light, this is a very shallow monster! I afeard of
   him? A very weak monster! The Man i' th' Moon? A most poor
   credulous monster! Well drawn°, monster, in good sooth!
Caliban: I'll show thee every fertile inch o' th' island;   125
   And I will kiss thy foot. I prithee, be my god.
Trinculo: By this light, a most perfidious and drunken monster! When's
   god's asleep, he'll rob his bottle.
Caliban: I'll kiss thy foot. I'll swear myself thy subject.
Stephano: Come on then. Down, and swear!   130
Trinculo: I shall laugh myself to death at this puppyheaded monster. A
   most scurvy monster! I could find in my heart to beat him —
Stephano: Come, kiss.
Trinculo: But that the poor monster's in drink. An abominable monster!
Caliban: I'll show thee the best springs; I'll pluck thee berries;   135
   I'll fish for thee, and get thee wood enough.
   A plague upon the tyrant that I serve!
   I'll bear him no more sticks, but follow thee,
   Thou wondrous man.
Trinculo: A most ridiculous monster, to make a wonder of a poor   140
   drunkard!
Caliban: I prithee let me bring thee where crabs° grow;
   And I with my long nails will dig thee pignuts°,
   Show thee a jay's nest, and instruct thee how
   To snare the nimble marmoset. I'll bring thee   145
   To clust'ring filberts, and sometimes I'll get thee
   Young scamels° from the rock. Wilt thou go with me?
Stephano: I prithee now, lead the way without any more talking. Trinculo,
   the king and all our company else being drowned, we will inherit
   here. Here, bear my bottle. Fellow Trinculo, we'll fill him by and by   150
   again.

   Caliban sings drunkenly.

Caliban: Farewell, master; farewell, farewell!
Trinculo: A howling monster! A drunken monster!

---

¹¹⁷*when time was:* once upon a time.   ¹¹⁸⁻¹⁹*thee . . . bush:* the Man in the Moon was banished
there, according to legend, for gathering brushwood with his dog on Sunday.   ¹²⁴*Well drawn:*
a good pull at the bottle.   ¹⁴²*crabs:* crabapples.   ¹⁴³*pignuts:* earthnuts.   ¹⁴⁷*scamels:* perhaps a
misprint for "seamels" or "seamews," a kind of sea bird.

Caliban: No more dams° I'll make for fish,
                  Nor fetch in firing   155
                     At requiring,
                  Nor scrape trenchering°, nor wash dish.
                     'Ban, 'Ban, Ca — Caliban
                  Has a new master. Get a new man!
        Freedom, high day! High day, freedom! Freedom, high day, freedom!   160
Stephano: O brave monster! Lead the way.   *Exeunt.*

ACT III

Scene I. [*In front of Prospero's cell.*]

Enter Ferdinand, bearing a log.

Ferdinand: There be some sports are painful, and their labor
        Delight in them sets off°; some kinds of baseness
        Are nobly undergone, and most poor matters
        Point to rich ends. This my mean task
        Would be as heavy to me as odious, but   5
        The mistress which I serve quickens° what's dead
        And makes my labors pleasures. O, she is
        Ten times more gentle than her father's crabbed;
        And he's composed of harshness. I must remove
        Some thousands of these logs and pile them up,`   10
        Upon a sore injunction°. My sweet mistress
        Weeps when she sees me work, and says such baseness
        Had never like executor. I forget°;
        But these sweet thoughts do even refresh my labors,
        Most busiest when I do it°.

        Enter Miranda; and Prospero [behind, unseen].

Miranda: Alas, now pray you,   15
        Work not so hard! I would the lightning had
        Burnt up those logs that you are enjoined to pile!
        Pray set it down and rest you. When this burns,
        'Twill weep° for having wearied you. My father
        Is hard at study; pray now rest yourself;   20
        He's safe for these three hours.
Ferdinand: O most dear mistress,
        The sun will set before I shall discharge
        What I must strive to do.

---

¹⁵⁴*dams:* to catch fish and keep them.   ¹⁵⁷*trenchering:* trenchers, wooden plates.   III.i. ²*sets off:*
cancels.   ⁶*quickens:* brings to life.   ¹¹*sore injunction:* severe command.   ¹³*forget:* i.e., my task.
¹⁵*Most . . . it:* i.e., my thoughts are busiest when I am (the Folio's "busie lest" has been
variously emended; "it" may refer to "task," line 4, the understood object in line 13).
¹⁹*weep:* i.e., exude resin.

Miranda: If you'll sit down,
    I'll bear your logs the while. Pray give me that;
    I'll carry it to the pile.
Ferdinand: No, precious creature,   25
    I had rather crack my sinews, break my back,
    Than you should such dishonor undergo
    While I sit lazy by.
Miranda: It would become me
    As well as it does you; and I should do it
    With much more ease; for my good will is to it,   30
    And yours it is against.
Prospero [Aside.]:   Poor worm, thou art infected!
    This visitation° shows it.
Miranda: You look wearily.
Ferdinand: No, noble mistress, 'tis fresh morning with me
    When you are by at night°. I do beseech you,
    Chiefly that I might set it in my prayers,   35
    What is your name?
Miranda: Miranda. O my father,
    I have broke your hest° to say so!
Ferdinand: Admired Miranda°!
    Indeed the top of admiration, worth
    What's dearest to the world! Full many a lady
    I have eyed with best regard, and many a time   40
    Th' harmony of their tongues hath into bondage
    Brought my too diligent ear. For several virtues
    Have I liked several women; never any
    With so full soul but some defect in her
    Did quarrel with the noblest grace she owed°,   45
    And put it to the foil°. But you, O you,
    So perfect and so peerless, are created
    Of every creature's best.
Miranda: I do not know
    One of my sex; no woman's face remember,
    Save, from my glass, mine own. Nor have I seen   50
    More that I may call men than you, good friend,
    And my dear father. How features are abroad
    I am skilless° of; but, by my modesty
    (The jewel in my dower), I would not wish
    Any companion in the world but you;   55
    Nor can imagination form a shape,
    Besides yourself, to like of°. But I prattle
    Something too wildly, and my father's precepts

---

³²*visitation:* (1) visit (2) attack of plague (referring to metaphor of "infected").   ³⁴*at night:* i.e.,
even at night when I am very tired.   ³⁷*hest:* command, *Admired Miranda: admired* means "to
be wondered at", the Latin *Miranda* means "wonderful."   ³⁷*hest:* command; *Admired Miranda:*
admired means "to be wondered at"; the Latin *Miranda* means "wonderful."   ⁴⁵*owed:* owned.
⁴⁶*put . . . foil:* defeated it.   ⁵³*skilless:* ignorant.   ⁵⁷*like of:* like.

I therein do forget.

Ferdinand: I am, in my condition,
A prince, Miranda; I do think, a king   60
(I would not so), and would no more endure
This wooden slavery than to suffer
The fleshfly blow my mouth. Hear my soul speak!
The very instant that I saw you, did
My heart fly to your service; there resides,   65
To make me slave to it; and for your sake
Am I this patient log-man.

Miranda: Do you love me?

Ferdinand: O heaven, O earth, bear witness to this sound,
And crown what I profess with kind event°
If I speak true! If hollowly, invert   70
What best is boded me° to mischief! I,
Beyond all limit of what else i' th' world,
Do love, prize, honor you.

Miranda: I am a fool
To weep at what I am glad of.

Prospero [*Aside.*]:   Fair encounter
Of two most rare affections! Heavens rain grace   75
On that which breeds between 'em!

Ferdinand: Wherefore weep you?

Miranda: At mine unworthiness, that dare not offer
What I desire to give, and much less take
What I shall die to want°. But this is trifling°;
And all the more it seeks to hide itself,   80
The bigger bulk it shows. Hence, bashful cunning,
And prompt me, plain and holy innocence!
I am your wife, if you will marry me;
If not, I'll die your maid. To be your fellow°
You may deny me; but I'll be your servant,   85
Whether you will or no.

Ferdinand: My mistress, dearest,
And I thus humble ever.

Miranda: My husband then?

Ferdinand: Ay, with a heart as willing
As bondage e'er of freedom°. Here's my hand.

Miranda: And mine, with my heart in't; and now farewell   90
Till half an hour hence.

Ferdinand: A thousand thousand!

Exeunt [*Ferdinand and Miranda in different directions*].

Prospero: So glad of this as they I cannot be,
Who are surprised withal°; but my rejoicing

---

⁶⁹*event:* outcome.   ⁷¹*What . . . me:* whatever good fortune fate has in store for me.   ⁷⁹*to want:*
if I lack.   ⁷⁹*trifling:* i.e., to speak in riddles like this.   ⁸⁴*fellow:* equal.   ⁸⁹*of freedom:* i.e., to win
freedom.   ⁹³*withal:* by it.

At nothing can be more. I'll to my book;
For yet ere suppertime must I perform   95
Much business appertaining°.   *Exit.*

Scene II. [*Another part of the island.*]

Enter Caliban, Stephano, and Trinculo.

Stephano: Tell not me! When the butt is out, we will drink water; not a
   drop before. Therefore bear up and board 'em°! Servant monster,
   drink to me.

Trinculo: Servant monster? The folly of this island! They say there's but
   five upon this isle; we are three of them. If th' other two be brained   5
   like us, the state totters.

Stephano: Drink, servant monster, when I bid thee; thy eyes are almost
   set in thy head.

Trinculo: Where should they be set else? He were a brave monster indeed
   if they were set in his tail.   10

Stephano: My man-monster hath drowned his tongue in sack. For my
   part, the sea cannot drown me. I swam, ere I could recover the shore,
   five-and-thirty leagues off and on, by this light. Thou shalt be my
   lieutenant, monster, or my standard°.

Trinculo: Your lieutenant, if you list°; he's no standard.   15

Stephano: We'll not run°, Monsieur Monster.

Trinculo: Nor go° neither; but you'll lie° like dogs, and yet say nothing
   neither.

Stephano: Mooncalf, speak once in thy life, if thou beest a good mooncalf.

Caliban: How does thy honor? Let me lick thy shoe. I'll not serve him;   20
   he is not valiant.

Trinculo: Thou liest, most ignorant monster; I am in case° to justle° a
   constable. Why, thou deboshed° fish thou, was there ever man a
   coward that hath drunk so much sack as I today? Wilt thou tell a
   monstrous lie, being but half a fish and half a monster?   25

Caliban: Lo, how he mocks me! Wilt thou let him, my lord?

Trinculo: "Lord" quoth he? That a monster should be such a natural°!

Caliban:
   Lo, lo, again! Bite him to death, I prithee.

Stephano: Trinculo, keep a good tongue in your head. If you prove a
   mutineer — the next tree°! The poor monster's my subject, and he   30
   shall not suffer indignity.

Caliban: I thank my noble lord. Wilt thou be pleased
   To hearken once again to the suit I made to thee?

---

⁹⁶*appertaining:* i.e., to my plan. III.ii. ²*bear . . . 'em:* i.e., drink up. ¹⁴*standard:* standard-bearer,
ensign (pun, for Caliban is so drunk he cannot stand). ¹⁵*if you list:* if it please you (with pun
on *list* as pertaining to a ship that leans over to one side). ¹⁶⁻¹⁷*run, 'lie:* with puns on
secondary meanings: "make water," "excrete." ¹⁷*go:* walk. ²²*case:* fit condition. ²²*justle:*
jostle. ²³*deboshed:* debauched. ²⁷*natural:* idiot. ³⁰*the next tree:* i.e., you will be hanged.

Stephano: Marry°, will I. Kneel and repeat it; I will stand, and so shall
  Trinculo.   35

  Enter Ariel, invisible.

Caliban: As I told thee before, I am subject to a tyrant,
  A sorcerer, that by his cunning hath
  Cheated me of the island.
Ariel: Thou liest.
Caliban: Thou liest, thou jesting monkey thou!
  I would my valiant master would destroy thee.   40
  I do not lie.
Stephano: Trinculo, if you trouble him any more in's tale, by this hand,
  I will supplant some of your teeth.
Trinculo: Why, I said nothing.
Stephano: Mum then, and no more. Proceed.   45
Caliban: I say by sorcery he got this isle;
  From me he got it. If thy greatness will
  Revenge it on him — for I know thou dar'st,
  But this thing° dare not —
Stephano: That's most certain.   50
Caliban: Thou shalt be lord of it, and I'll serve thee.
Stephano: How now shall this be compassed?
  Canst thou bring me to the party?
Caliban: Yea, yea, my lord! I'll yield him thee asleep,
  Where thou mayst knock a nail into his head.   55
Ariel: Thou liest; thou canst not.
Caliban: What a pied° ninny's this! Thou scurvy patch°!
  I do beseech thy greatness, give him blows
  And take his bottle from him. When that's gone,
  He shall drink naught but brine, for I'll not show him   60
  Where the quick freshes° are.
Stephano: Trinculo, run into no further danger! Interrupt the monster one
  word further and, by this hand, I'll turn my mercy out o' doors and
  make a stockfish° of thee.
Trinculo: Why, what did I? I did nothing. I'll go farther off.   65
Stephano: Didst thou not say he lied?
Ariel: Thou liest.
Stephano: Do I so? Take thou that! [*Strikes Trinculo.*] As you like this, give
  me the lie another time.
Trinculo: I did not give the lie. Out o' your wits, and hearing too? A pox 70
  o' your bottle! This can sack and drinking do. A murrain° on your
  monster, and the devil take your fingers!
Caliban: Ha, ha, ha!

---

³⁴*Marry:* an expletive, from "By the Virgin Mary." ⁴⁹*this thing:* Trinculo. ⁵⁷*pied:* referring
to Trinculo's parti-colored jester's costume. ⁵⁷*patch:* clown. ⁶¹*quick freshes:* living springs of
fresh water. ⁶⁴*stockfish:* dried cod, softened by beating. ⁷¹*murrain:* plague (that infects cattle).

Stephano: Now forward with your tale. [*To Trinculo.*] Prithee, stand further off. 75

Caliban: Beat him enough. After a little time
I'll beat him too.

Stephano: Stand farther. Come, proceed.

Caliban: Why, as I told thee, 'tis a custom with him
I' th' afternoon to sleep. There thou mayst brain him,
Having first seized his books, or with a log 80
Batter his skull, or paunch° him with a stake,
Or cut his wezand° with thy knife. Remember
First to possess his books; for without them
He's but a sot°, as I am, nor hath not
One spirit to command. They all do hate him 85
As rootedly as I. Burn but his books.
He has brave utensils° (for so he calls them)
Which, when he has a house, he'll deck withal.
And that most deeply to consider is
The beauty of his daughter. He himself 90
Calls her a nonpareil. I never saw a woman
But only Sycorax my dam and she;
But she as far surpasseth Sycorax
As great'st does least.

Stephano: Is it so brave a lass?

Caliban: Ay, lord. She will become thy bed, I warrant, 95
And bring thee forth brave brood.

Stephano: Monster, I will kill this man. His daughter and I will be king
and queen — save our graces! — and Trinculo and thyself shall be
viceroys. Dost thou like the plot, Trinculo?

Trinculo: Excellent. 100

Stephano: Give me thy hand. I am sorry I beat thee; but while thou liv'st,
keep a good tongue in thy head.

Caliban: Within this half hour will he be asleep.
Wilt thou destroy him then?

Stephano: Ay, on mine honor.

Ariel: This will I tell my master. 105

Caliban: Thou mak'st me merry; I am full of pleasure.
Let us be jocund. Will you troll the catch°
You taught me but whilere°?

Stephano: At thy request, monster, I will do reason, any reason°. Come on,
Trinculo, let us sing. 110

[*Sings.*]

Flout 'em and scout° 'em
And scout 'em and flout 'em!
Thought is free.

81*paunch:* stab in the belly.   82*wezand:* windpipe.   84*sot:* fool.   87*brave utensils:* fine furnishings
(pronounced "útensils").   107*troll the catch:* sing the round.   108*but whilere:* just now.
109*reason, any reason:* i.e., anything within reason.   111*scout:* jeer at.

Caliban: That's not the tune.

Ariel [*plays the tune on a tabor° and pipe*].

Stephano: What is this same?   115
Trinculo: This is the tune of our catch, played by the picture of
      Nobody°.
Stephano: If thou beest a man, show thyself in thy likeness. If thou beest
      a devil, take't as thou list.
Trinculo: O, forgive me my sins!   120
Stephano: He that dies pays all debts. I defy thee. Mercy upon us!
Caliban: Art thou afeard?
Stephano: No, monster, not I.
Caliban: Be not afeard; the isle is full of noises,
      Sounds and sweet airs that give delight and hurt not.
      Sometimes a thousand twangling instruments   125
      Will hum about mine ears; and sometime voices
      That, if I then had waked after long sleep,
      Will make me sleep again; and then, in dreaming,
      The clouds methought would open and show riches
      Ready to drop upon me, that, when I waked,   130
      I cried to dream again.
Stephano: This will prove a brave kingdom to me, where I shall have my
      music for nothing.
Caliban: When Prospero is destroyed.
Stephano: That shall be by and by; I remember the story.   135
Trinculo: The sound is going away; let's follow it, and after do our work.
Stephano: Lead, monster; we'll follow. I would I could see this taborer; he
      lays it on.
Trinculo [*To Caliban.*]: Wilt come°? I'll follow Stephano.   *Exeunt.*

Scene III. [*Another part of the island.*]

Enter Alonso, Sebastian, Antonio, Gonzalo, Adrian, Francisco, &c.

Gonzalo: By'r Lakin°, I can go no further, sir;
      My old bones aches. Here's a maze trod indeed
      Through forthrights and meanders°. By your patience,
      I needs must rest me.
Alonso: Old lord, I cannot blame thee,
      Who am myself attached° with weariness   5
      To th' dulling of my spirits. Sit down and rest.
      Even here I will put off my hope, and keep it
      No longer for my flatterer. He is drowned
      Whom thus we stray to find; and the sea mocks

---

¹¹⁴*tabor:* small drum worn at the side.   ¹¹⁷*Nobody:* alluding to the picture of No-body —
a man all head, legs, and arms, but without trunk — on the title page of the anonymous
comedy *No-body and Some-body.*   ¹³⁹*Wilt come:* Caliban lingers because the other two are being
distracted from his purpose by the music.   III.iii. ¹*By'r Lakin:* by our Lady.   ³*forthrights and
meanders:* straight and winding paths.   ⁵*attached:* seized.

Our frustrate search on land. Well, let him go.   10
Antonio [*Aside to Sebastian.*]: I am right glad that he's so out of hope.
Do not for one repulse forgo the purpose
That you resolved t' effect.
Sebastian [*Aside to Antonio.*]:   The next advantage
Will we take throughly°.
Antonio [*Aside to Sebastian.*]:   Let it be tonight;
For, now they are oppressed with travel, they   15
Will not nor cannot use such vigilance
As when they are fresh.
Sebastian [*Aside to Antonio.*]:   I say tonight. No more.

> *Solemn and strange music; and Prospero on the top° (invisible). Enter several
> strange shapes, bringing in a banquet; and dance about it with gentle actions
> of salutations; and, inviting the king [Alonso] &c. to eat, they depart.*

Alonso: What harmony is this? My good friends, hark!
Gonzalo: Marvelous sweet music!
Alonso: Give us kind keepers°, heavens! What were these?   20
Sebastian: A living drollery°. Now I will believe
That there are unicorns; that in Arabia
There is one tree, the phoenix' throne; one phoenix
At this hour reigning there.
Antonio: I'll believe both;
And what does else want credit°, come to me,   25
And I'll be sworn 'tis true. Travelers ne'er did lie,
Though fools at home condemn 'em.
Gonzalo: If in Naples
I should report this now, would they believe me
If I should say I saw such islanders?
(For certes these are people of the island)   30
Who, though they are of monstrous shape, yet note,
Their manners are more gentle, kind, than of
Our human generation you shall find
Many — nay, almost any.
Prospero [*Aside.*]:   Honest lord,
Thou hast said well; for some of you there present   35
Are worse than devils.
Alonso: I cannot too much muse°
Such shapes, such gesture, and such sound, expressing
(Although they want the use of tongue) a kind
Of excellent dumb discourse.
Prospero [*Aside.*]:   Praise in departing°.
Francisco: They vanished strangely.
Sebastian: No matter, since   40
They have left their viands behind; for we have stomachs.

---

¹⁴*throughly:* thoroughly.   ¹⁷*the top:* upper stage (or perhaps a playing area above it).   ²⁰*kind keepers:* guardian angels.   ²¹*drollery:* puppet show.   ²⁵*credit:* believing.   ³⁶*muse:* wonder at.
³⁹*Praise in departing:* Save your praise for the end.

Will't please you taste of what is here?

Alonso: Not I.

Gonzalo: Faith, sir, you need not fear. When we were boys,
          Who would believe that there were mountaineers
          Dewlapped° like bulls, whose throats had hanging at 'em   45
          Wallets of flesh? Or that there were such men
          Whose heads stood in their breasts? Which now we find
          Each putter-out of five for one° will bring us
          Good warrant of.

Alonso: I will stand to, and feed;
          Although my last, no matter, since I feel   50
          The best is past. Brother, my lord the duke,
          Stand to, and do as we.

*Thunder and lightning. Enter Ariel, like a harpy; claps his wings upon the
table; and with a quaint device° the banquet vanishes.*

Ariel: You are three men of sin, whom destiny —
         That hath to instrument° this lower world
         And what is in't — the never-surfeited sea   55
         Hath caused to belch up you and on this island,
         Where man doth not inhabit, you 'mongst men
         Being most unfit to live. I have made you mad;
         And even with suchlike valor° men hang and drown
         Their proper selves. [*Alonso, Sebastian, &c. draw their swords.*] You fools!
                 I and my fellows   60
         Are ministers of Fate. The elements,
         Of whom your swords are tempered°, may as well
         Wound the loud winds, or with bemocked-at stabs
         Kill the still-closing° waters, as diminish
         One dowle° that's in my plume°. My fellow ministers   65
         Are like invulnerable. If you could hurt°,
         Your swords are now too massy° for your strengths
         And will not be uplifted. But remember
         (For that's my business to you) that you three
         From Milan did supplant good Prospero;   70
         Exposed unto the sea, which hath requit it°,
         Him and his innocent child; for which foul deed
         The pow'rs, delaying, not forgetting, have
         Incensed the seas and shores, yea, all the creatures,
         Against your peace. Thee of thy son, Alonso,   75
         They have bereft; and do pronounce by me
         Ling'ring perdition (worse than any death

---

⁴⁵*Dewlapped:* with skin hanging from the neck (like mountaineers with goiter).   ⁴⁸*putter-out
. . . one:* traveler who insures himself by depositing a sum of money to be repaid fivefold if
he returns safely (i.e., any ordinary traveler will confirm nowadays those reports we used to
think fanciful).   ⁵²*quaint device:* ingenious device (of stage mechanism).   ⁵⁴*to instrument:* as its
instrument.   ⁵⁹*suchlike valor:* i.e., the courage that comes of madness.   ⁶²*tempered:* composed.
⁶⁴*still-closing:* ever closing again (as soon as wounded).   ⁶⁵*dowle:* bit of down; *plume:* plumage.
⁶⁶*If . . . hurt:* even if you could hurt us.   ⁶⁷*massy:* heavy.   ⁷¹*requit it:* avenged that crime.

Can be at once) shall step by step attend
You and your ways; whose wraths to guard you from,
Which here, in this most desolate isle, else falls   80
Upon your heads, is nothing but heart's sorrow°
And a clear life ensuing.

*He vanishes in thunder; then, to soft music, enter the Shapes again, and dance
with mocks and mows°, and carrying out the table.*

Prospero: Bravely the figure of this harpy hast thou
Performed, my Ariel; a grace it had, devouring°.
Of my instruction hast thou nothing bated°   85
In what thou hadst to say. So, with good life°
And observation strange°, my meaner ministers°
Their several kinds have done°. My high charms work,
And these, mine enemies, are all knit up
In their distractions. They now are in my pow'r;   90
And in these fits I leave them, while I visit
Young Ferdinand, whom they suppose is drowned,
And his and mine loved darling.   [*Exit above.*]
Gonzalo: I' th' name of something holy, sir, why stand you
In this strange stare?
Alonso: O, it is monstrous, monstrous!   95
Methought the billows spoke and told me of it;
The winds did sing it to me; and the thunder,
That deep and dreadful organ pipe, pronounced
The name of Prosper; it did bass my trespass°.
Therefore my son i' th' ooze is bedded; and   100
I'll seek him deeper than e'er plummet sounded
And with him there lie mudded.   *Exit.*
Sebastian: But one fiend at a time,
I'll fight their legions o'er°!
Antonio: I'll be thy second.

Exeunt [Sebastian and Antonio].

Gonzalo: All three of them are desperate; their great guilt,
Like poison given to work a great time after,   105
Now 'gins to bite the spirits. I do beseech you,
That are of suppler joints, follow them swiftly
And hinder them from what this ecstasy°
May now provoke them to.
Adrian: Follow, I pray you.   *Exeunt omnes°.*

---

⁸¹*nothing . . . sorrow:* only repentance (will protect you from the wrath of these powers).
⁸²*mocks and mows:* mocking gestures and grimaces. ⁸⁴*devouring:* i.e., in making the banquet
disappear. ⁸⁵*bated:* omitted. ⁸⁶*good life:* good lifelike acting. ⁸⁷*observation strange:* remarkable attention to my wishes; *meaner ministers:* i.e., inferior to Ariel. ⁸⁸*Their . . . done:* have acted
the parts their natures suited them for. ⁹⁹*bass my trespass:* i.e., made me understand my
trespass by turning it into music for which the thunder provided the bass part. ¹⁰³*o'er:* one
after another to the last. ¹⁰⁸*ecstasy:* madness. ¹⁰⁹*Exeunt omnes:* "They all go out."

ACT IV

Scene I. [*In front of Prospero's cell.*]

Enter Prospero, Ferdinand, and Miranda.

Prospero: If I have too austerely punished you,
　　　Your compensation makes amends; for I
　　　Have given you here a third of mine own life,
　　　Or that for which I live; who once again
　　　I tender to thy hand. All thy vexations　　　　　　　　5
　　　Were but my trials of thy love, and thou
　　　Hast strangely° stood the test. Here, afore heaven,
　　　I ratify this my rich gift. O Ferdinand,
　　　Do not smile at me that I boast her off°,
　　　For thou shalt find she will outstrip all praise　　　10
　　　And make it halt° behind her.
Ferdinand:　　　　　　　　　　　I do believe it
　　　Against an oracle°.
Prospero: Then, as my gift, and thine own acquisition
　　　Worthily purchased, take my daughter. But
　　　If thou dost break her virgin-knot before　　　　　15
　　　All sanctimonious° ceremonies may
　　　With full and holy rite be minist'red,
　　　No sweet aspersion° shall the heavens let fall
　　　To make this contract grow°; but barren hate,
　　　Sour-eyed disdain, and discord shall bestrew　　　20
　　　The union of your bed with weeds so loathly
　　　That you shall hate it both. Therefore take heed,
　　　As Hymen's lamps shall light you°.
Ferdinand:　　　　　　　　　　　　As I hope
　　　For quiet days, fair issue, and long life,
　　　With such love as 'tis now, the murkiest den,　　　25
　　　The most opportune° place, the strong'st suggestion
　　　Our worser genius can°, shall never melt
　　　Mine honor into lust, to take away
　　　The edge° of that day's celebration
　　　When I shall think or Phoebus' steeds are foundered°　　30
　　　Or Night kept chained below°.
Prospero:　　　　　　　　　　　Fairly spoke.
　　　Sit then and talk with her; she is thine own.
　　　What, Ariel°! My industrious servant, Ariel!

IV.i. ⁷*strangely:* wonderfully. ⁹*boast her off:* includes perhaps the idea of showing her off.
¹¹*halt:* limp. ¹²*Against an oracle:* though an oracle should declare otherwise. ¹⁶*sanctimonious:*
holy. ¹⁸*aspersion:* blessing (like rain on crops). ¹⁹*grow:* become fruitful. ²³*As Hymen's
. . . you:* i.e., as earnestly as you pray that the torch of the god of marriage shall burn without
smoke (a good omen for wedded happiness). ²⁶*opportune:* pronounced "oppórtune." ²⁷*Our
. . . can:* our evil spirit can offer. ²⁹*edge:* keen enjoyment. ³⁰*foundered:* lamed. ³⁰⁻³¹*or
Phoebus' . . . below:* i.e., that either day will never end or night will never come. ³³*What, Ariel:*
summoning Ariel.

[*Enter Ariel.*]

Ariel: What would my potent master? Here I am.

Prospero: Thou and thy meaner fellows your last service   35
   Did worthily perform; and I must use you
   In such another trick. Go bring the rabble°,
   O'er whom I give thee pow'r, here to this place.
   Incite them to quick motion; for I must
   Bestow upon the eyes of this young couple   40
   Some vanity of° mine art. It is my promise,
   And they expect it from me.

Ariel: Presently?

Prospero: Ay, with a twink.

Ariel: Before you can say "Come" and "Go,"
   And breathe twice and cry, "So, so,"   45
   Each one, tripping on his toe,
   Will be here with mop and mow°.
   Do you love me, master? No?

Prospero: Dearly, my delicate Ariel. Do not approach
   Till thou dost hear me call.

Ariel: Well; I conceive°.   *Exit.*   50

Prospero: Look thou be true°. Do not give dalliance
   Too much the rein; the strongest oaths are straw
   To th' fire i' th' blood. Be more abstemious,
   Or else good night your vow!

Ferdinand: I warrant you, sir.
   The white cold virgin snow upon my heart°   55
   Abates the ardor of my liver°.

Prospero: Well.
   Now come, my Ariel; bring a corollary°
   Rather than want a spirit. Appear, and pertly!
   No tongue! All eyes! Be silent.

Soft music. Enter Iris°.

Iris: Ceres, most bounteous lady, thy rich leas°   60
   Of wheat, rye, barley, fetches°, oats, and peas;
   Thy turfy mountains, where live nibbling sheep,
   And flat meads thatched with stover°, them to keep;
   Thy banks with pionèd and twillèd brims°,
   Which spongy April at thy hest betrims   65
   To make cold nymphs chaste crowns; and thy broom groves,

---

³⁷*rabble:* "thy meaner fellows." ⁴¹*vanity of:* illusion conjured up by. ⁴⁷*mop and mow:* gestures
and grimaces. ⁵⁰*conceive:* understand. ⁵¹*be true:* Prospero appears to have caught the lovers
in an embrace. ⁵⁵*white . . . heart:* her pure white breast on mine (?). ⁵⁶*liver:* supposed seat
of sexual passion. ⁵⁷*corollary:* surplus (of spirits). ⁵⁹*Iris:* goddess of the rainbow and Juno's
messenger. ⁶⁰*leas:* meadows. ⁶¹*fetches:* vetch (a kind of forage). ⁶³*meads . . . stover:* meadows covered with a kind of grass used for winter fodder. ⁶⁴*pionèd . . . brims:* obscure; may
refer to the trenched and ridged edges of banks that have been repaired after the erosions
of winter.

Whose shadow the dismissèd bachelor loves,
Being lasslorn; thy pole-clipt vineyard°;
And thy sea-marge, sterile and rocky-hard,
Where thou thyself dost air° — the queen o' th' sky°,   70
Whose wat'ry arch and messenger am I,
Bids thee leave these, and with her sovereign grace,

Juno descends°.

Here on this grass plot, in this very place,
To come and sport; her peacocks fly amain°.
Approach, rich Ceres, her to entertain.   75

Enter Ceres.

Ceres: Hail, many-colored messenger, that ne'er
   Dost disobey the wife of Jupiter,
   Who, with thy saffron wings, upon my flow'rs
   Diffusest honey drops, refreshing show'rs,
   And with each end of thy blue bow dost crown   80
   My bosky° acres and my unshrubbed down,
   Rich scarf to my proud earth. Why hath thy queen
   Summoned me hither to this short-grassed green?
Iris: A contract of true love to celebrate
   And some donation freely to estate°   85
   On the blessed lovers.
Ceres: Tell me, heavenly bow,
   If Venus or her son, as thou dost know,
   Do now attend the queen? Since they did plot
   The means that dusky Dis my daughter got°,
   Her and her blind boy's scandaled° company   90
   I have forsworn.
Iris: Of her society
   Be not afraid; I met her deity
   Cutting the clouds towards Paphos°, and her son
   Dove-drawn with her. Here thought they to have done
   Some wanton charm upon this man and maid,   95
   Whose vows are, that no bed-right shall be paid
   Till Hymen's torch be lighted. But in vain;
   Mars's hot minion is returned again°,
   Her waspish-headed son° has broke his arrows,
   Swears he will shoot no more, but play with sparrows   100
   And be a boy right out°.

---

⁶⁸*pole-clipt vineyard:* i.e., vineyard whose vines grow neatly around (embrace) poles (though possibly the word is "poll-clipped," i.e., pruned).   ⁷⁰*air:* take the air; *queen o' th' sky:* Juno.
⁷²This direction seems to come too soon, but the machine may have lowered her very slowly.
⁷⁴*amain:* swiftly (peacocks, sacred to Juno, drew her chariot).   ⁸¹*bosky:* shrubbed.   ⁸⁵*estate:*
bestow.   ⁸⁹*dusky . . . got:* alluding to the abduction of Proserpine by Pluto (Dis), god of the underworld.   ⁹⁰*scandaled:* scandalous.   ⁹³*Paphos:* in Cyprus, center of Venus' cult.   ⁹⁸*Mars's
. . . again:* Mars' lustful mistress (Venus) is on her way back to Paphos.   ⁹⁹*waspish-headed son:*
Cupid is irritable and stings with his arrows.   ¹⁰¹*boy right out:* an ordinary boy.

[*Juno alights.*]

Ceres: Highest queen of state,
          Great Juno, comes; I know her by her gait.
Juno: How does my bounteous sister? Go with me
          To bless this twain, that they may prosperous be
          And honored in their issue.   105

          They sing.

Juno: Honor, riches, marriage blessing,
                         Long continuance, and increasing,
                         Hourly joys be still° upon you!
                         Juno sings her blessings on you.
[*Ceres*]:   Earth's increase, foison° plenty,   110
                         Barns and garners never empty,
                         Vines with clust'ring bunches growing,
                         Plants with goodly burden bowing;
                         Spring come to you at the farthest
                         In the very end of harvest°.   115
                         Scarcity and want shall shun you,
                         Ceres' blessing so is on you.
Ferdinand: This is a most majestic vision, and
          Harmonious charmingly. May I be bold
          To think these spirits?
Prospero: Spirits, which by mine art   120
          I have from their confines called to enact
          My present fancies.
Ferdinand: Let me live here ever!
          So rare a wond'red° father and a wise
          Makes this place Paradise.

          Juno and Ceres whisper, and send Iris on employment.

Prospero: Sweet now, silence!
          Juno and Ceres whisper seriously.   125
          There's something else to do. Hush and be mute,
          Or else our spell is marred.
Iris: You nymphs, called Naiades, of the windring° brooks,
          With your sedged crowns and ever-harmless looks,
          Leave your crisp° channels, and on this green land   130
          Answer your summons; Juno does command.
          Come, temperate nymphs, and help to celebrate
          A contract of true love; be not too late.

          Enter certain Nymphs.

          You sunburned sicklemen, of August weary,
          Come hither from the furrow and be merry.   135

108*still:* ever. 110*foison:* abundance. 114–15*Spring . . . harvest:* i.e., May there be no winter in
your lives. 123*wond'red:* possessed of wonders; i.e., both wonderful and wonder-working,
and therefore to be wondered at. 128*windring:* winding and wandering (?). 130*crisp:* rippling.

Make holiday; your rye-straw hats put on,
And these fresh nymphs encounter everyone
In country footing°.

Enter certain Reapers, properly habited. They join with the Nymphs in a graceful dance; towards the end whereof Prospero starts suddenly and speaks°; after which, to a strange, hollow, and confused noise, they heavily° vanish.

Prospero [Aside.]: I had forgot that foul conspiracy
    Of the beast Caliban and his confederates   140
    Against my life. The minute of their plot
    Is almost come. [*To the Spirits.*] Well done! Avoid°! No more!
Ferdinand: This is strange. Your father's in some passion
    That works him strongly.
Miranda: Never till this day
    Saw I him touched with anger so distempered°.   145
Prospero: You do look, my son, in a movèd sort°,
    As if you were dismayed; be cheerful, sir.
    Our revels now are ended. These our actors,
    As I foretold you, were all spirits and
    Are melted into air, into thin air;   150
    And, like the baseless fabric of this vision,
    The cloud-capped towers, the gorgeous palaces,
    The solemn temples, the great globe itself,
    Yea, all which it inherit°, shall dissolve,
    And, like this insubstantial pageant faded,   155
    Leave not a rack° behind. We are such stuff
    As dreams are made on, and our little life
    Is rounded with a sleep. Sir, I am vexed.
    Bear with my weakness; my old brain is troubled.
    Be not disturbed with my infirmity.   160
    If you be pleased, retire into my cell
    And there repose. A turn or two I'll walk
    To still my beating mind.
Ferdinand, Miranda: We wish your peace.

                      Exit [Ferdinand, with Miranda].
Prospero: Come with a thought! I thank thee°, Ariel. Come.

    Enter Ariel.

Ariel: Thy thoughts I cleave to. What's thy pleasure?
Prospero: Spirit,   165
    We must prepare to meet with Caliban.
Ariel: Ay, my commander. When I presented° Ceres,
    I thought to have told thee of it, but I feared

---

[138]*footing:* dance.   [138]*speaks:* breaking the spell, which depends on silence; *heavily:* reluctantly. [142]*Avoid:* Begone!   [145]*distempered:* violent.   [146]*movèd sort:* troubled state.   [154]*it inherit:* occupy it.   [156]*rack:* wisp of cloud.   [164]*I thank thee:* i.e., for the masque (?).   [167]*presented:* acted the part of (?) introduced (?).

Lest I might anger thee.

Prospero: Say again, where didst thou leave these varlets°?   170

Ariel: I told you, sir, they were red-hot with drinking;
    So full of valor that they smote the air
    For breathing in their faces, beat the ground
    For kissing of their feet; yet always bending°
    Towards their project. Then I beat my tabor;   175
    At which like unbacked° colts they pricked their ears,
    Advanced° their eyelids, lifted up their noses
    As they smelt music. So I charmed their ears
    That calflike they my lowing followed through
    Toothed briers, sharp furzes, pricking goss°, and thorns,   180
    Which ent'red their frail shins. At last I left them
    I' th' filthy mantled° pool beyond your cell,
    There dancing up to th' chins, that the foul lake
    O'erstunk their feet.

Prospero: This was well done, my bird.
    Thy shape invisible retain thou still.   185
    The trumpery° in my house, go bring it hither
    For stale° to catch these thieves.

Ariel: I go, I go.   *Exit.*

Prospero: A devil, a born devil, on whose nature
    Nurture can never stick; on whom my pains,
    Humanely taken, all, all lost, quite lost!   190
    And as with age his body uglier grows,
    So his mind cankers. I will plague them all,
    Even to roaring.

Enter Ariel, loaden with glistering apparel, &c.

                Come, hang them on this line°.

[Prospero and Ariel remain, invisible.] Enter Caliban, Stephano, and Trinculo, all wet.

Caliban: Pray you tread softly, that the blind mole may not
    Hear a foot fall. We now are near his cell.   195

Stephano: Monster, your fairy, which you say is a harmless fairy, has done
little better than played the Jack° with us.

Trinculo: Monster, I do smell all horse piss, at which my nose is in great
indignation.

Stephano: So is mine. Do you hear, monster? If I should take a displeasure   200
against you, look you —

Trinculo: Thou wert but a lost monster.

Caliban: Good my lord, give me thy favor still.
    Be patient, for the prize I'll bring thee to

---

¹⁷⁰*varlets:* ruffians.   ¹⁷⁴*bending:* directing their steps.   ¹⁷⁶*unbacked:* unbroken.   ¹⁷⁷*Advanced:* lifted up.   ¹⁸⁰*goss:* gorse.   ¹⁸²*filthy mantled:* covered with filthy scum.   ¹⁸⁶*trumpery:* the "glistering apparel" mentioned in the next stage direction.   ¹⁸⁷*stale:* decoy.   ¹⁹³*line:* lime tree (linden).   ¹⁹⁷*Jack:* (1) knave (2) jack-o'-lantern, will-o'-the-wisp.

1038 Comedy

Shall hoodwink° this mischance. Therefore speak softly.   205
All's hushed as midnight yet.
Trinculo: Ay, but to lose our bottles in the pool —
Stephano: There is not only disgrace and dishonor in that, monster, but
an infinite loss.
Trinculo: That's more to me than my wetting. Yet this is your harmless   210
fairy, monster.
Stephano: I will fetch off my bottle, though I be o'er ears° for my labor.
Caliban: Prithee, my king, be quiet. See'st thou here?
This is the mouth o' th' cell. No noise, and enter.
Do that good mischief which may make this island   215
Thine own forever, and I, thy Caliban,
For aye thy footlicker.
Stephano: Give me thy hand. I do begin to have bloody thoughts.
Trinculo: O King Stephano! O peer°! O worthy Stephano, look what a
wardrobe here is for thee!   220
Caliban: Let it alone, thou fool! It is but trash.
Trinculo: O, ho, monster! We know what belongs to a frippery°. O King
Stephano!
Stephano: Put off that gown, Trinculo! By this hand, I'll have that gown!
Trinculo: Thy grace shall have it.   225
Caliban: The dropsy drown this fool! What do you mean
To dote thus on such luggage°? Let 't alone,
And do the murder first. If he awake,
From toe to crown he'll fill our skins with pinches,
Make us strange stuff.   230
Stephano: Be you quiet, monster. Mistress line, is not this my jerkin°?
[*Takes it down.*] Now is the jerkin under the line°. Now, jerkin, you
are like to lose your hair and prove a bald jerkin°.
Trinculo: Do, do°! We steal by line and level°, and 't like° your grace.
Stephano: I thank thee for that jest. Here's a garment for 't. Wit shall not   235
go unrewarded while I am king of this country. "Steal by line
and level" is an excellent pass of pate°. There's another garment
for 't.
Trinculo: Monster, come put some lime° upon your fingers, and away with
the rest.   240
Caliban: I will have none on 't. We shall lose our time
And all be turned to barnacles°, or to apes
With foreheads villainous low.
Stephano: Monster, lay-to your fingers; help to bear this away where my

---

²⁰⁵*hoodwink:* put out of sight.   ²¹²*o'er ears:* i.e., over my ears in water.   ²¹⁹*peer:* alluding to the
song "King Stephen was and a worthy peer; / His breeches cost him but a crown," quoted
in *Othello* II.iii.   ²²²*frippery:* old-clothes shop; i.e., we are good judges of castoff clothes.
²²⁷*luggage:* useless encumbrances.   ²³¹*jerkin:* kind of jacket.   ²³²*under the line:* pun: (1) under
the lime tree (2) under the equator.   ²³³*bald jerkin:* sailors proverbially lost their hair from
fevers contracted while crossing the equator.   ²³⁴*Do, do:* Fine, fine!   ²³⁴*by . . . level:* by plumb
line and carpenter's level; i.e., according to rule (with pun on *line*).   ²³⁴*and 't like:* if it please.
²³⁷*pass of pate:* sally of wit.   ²³⁹*lime:* bird lime (which is sticky; thieves have sticky fingers).
²⁴²*barnacles:* kind of geese supposed to have developed from shellfish.

hogshead of wine is, or I'll turn you out of my kingdom. Go to, carry   245
    this.
Trinculo: And this.
Stephano: Ay, and this.

*A noise of hunters heard. Enter divers Spirits in shape of dogs and hounds,
hunting them about; Prospero and Ariel setting them on.*

Prospero: Hey, Mountain, hey!
Ariel: Silver! There it goes, Silver!   250
Prospero: Fury, Fury! There, Tyrant, there! Hark, hark!
    [*Caliban, Stephano, and Trinculo are driven out.*]
    Go, charge my goblins that they grind their joints
    With dry convulsions°, shorten up their sinews
    With agèd° cramps, and more pinch-spotted make them
    Than pard or cat o' mountain°.
Ariel: Hark, they roar!   255
Prospero: Let them be hunted soundly. At this hour
    Lies at my mercy all mine enemies.
    Shortly shall all my labors end, and thou
    Shalt have the air at freedom. For a little,
    Follow, and do me service.   *Exeunt.*   260

ACT V

Scene I. [*In front of Prospero's cell.*]

Enter Prospero in his magic robes, and Ariel.

Prospero: Now does my project gather to a head.
    My charms crack not, my spirits obey, and Time
    Goes upright with his carriage°. How's the day?
Ariel: On the sixth hour, at which time, my lord,
    You said our work should cease.
Prospero: I did say so   5
    When first I raised the tempest. Say, my spirit,
    How fares the king and's followers?
Ariel: Confined together
    In the same fashion as you gave in charge,
    Just as you left them — all prisoners, sir,
    In the line grove which weather-fends° your cell.   10
    They cannot budge till your release°. The king,
    His brother, and yours abide all three distracted,
    And the remainder mourning over them,
    Brimful of sorrow and dismay; but chiefly

---

²⁵³*dry convulsions:* such as come when the joints are dry from old age.   ²⁵⁴*agèd:* i.e., such as old people have.   ²⁵⁵*pard . . . mountain:* leopard or catamount.   V.i. ²⁻³*Time . . . carriage:* time does not stoop under his burden (because there is so little left to do).   ¹⁰*weather-fends:* protects from the weather.   ¹¹*till your release:* until released by you.

Him that you termed, sir, the good old Lord Gonzalo.   15
His tears runs down his beard like winter's drops
From eaves of reeds°. Your charm so strongly works 'em,
That if you now beheld them, your affections
Would become tender.
Prospero: Dost thou think so, spirit?
Ariel: Mine would, sir, were I human.
Prospero: And mine shall.   20
Hast thou, which art but air, a touch, a feeling
Of their afflictions, and shall not myself
One of their kind, that relish all as sharply,
Passion° as they, be kindlier moved than thou art?
Though with their high wrongs I am struck to th' quick,   25
Yet with my nobler reason 'gainst my fury
Do I take part. The rarer action is
In virtue than in vengeance. They being penitent,
The sole drift of my purpose doth extend
Not a frown further. Go, release them, Ariel.   30
My charms I'll break, their senses I'll restore,
And they shall be themselves.
Ariel: I'll fetch them, sir.   *Exit.*
Prospero: Ye elves of hills, brooks, standing lakes, and groves,
And ye that on the sands with printless foot
Do chase the ebbing Neptune, and do fly him°   35
When he comes back; you demi-puppets that
By moonshine do the green sour ringlets° make,
Whereof the ewe not bites; and you whose pastime
Is to make midnight mushrumps°, that rejoice
To hear the solemn curfew; by whose aid   40
(Weak masters° though ye be) I have bedimmed
The noontide sun, called forth the mutinous winds,
And 'twixt the green sea and the azured vault
Set roaring war; to the dread rattling thunder
Have I given fire and rifted Jove's stout oak   45
With his own bolt; the strong-based promontory
Have I made shake and by the spurs° plucked up
The pine and cedar; graves at my command
Have waked their sleepers, oped, and let 'em forth
By my so potent art. But this rough magic   50
I here abjure; and when I have required°
Some heavenly music (which even now I do)
To work mine end upon their senses that°
This airy charm is for, I'll break my staff,
Bury it certain fathoms in the earth,   55

---

¹⁷*eaves of reeds:* i.e., a thatched roof.   ²⁴*Passion:* verb.   ³⁵*fly him:* fly with him.   ³⁷*green sour ringlets:* "fairy rings," little circles of rank grass supposed to be formed by the dancing of fairies.   ³⁹*mushrumps:* mushrooms.   ⁴¹*masters:* masters of supernatural power.   ⁴⁷*spurs:* roots. ⁵¹*required:* asked for.   ⁵³*their senses that:* the senses of those whom.

And deeper than did ever plummet sound
I'll drown my book.

Solemn music.

*Here enters Ariel before; then Alonso, with a frantic gesture, attended by
Gonzalo; Sebastian and Antonio in like manner, attended by Adrian and
Francisco. They all enter the circle which Prospero had made, and there stand
charmed; which Prospero observing, speaks.*

A solemn air, and° the best comforter
To an unsettled fancy, cure thy brains,
Now useless, boiled within thy skull! There stand,   60
For you are spell-stopped.
Holy Gonzalo, honorable man,
Mine eyes, ev'n sociable to the show of thine,
Fall fellowly drops°. The charm dissolves apace;
And as the morning steals upon the night,   65
Melting the darkness, so their rising senses
Begin to chase the ignorant fumes that mantle
Their clearer reason. O good Gonzalo,
My true preserver, and a loyal sir
To him thou follow'st, I will pay thy graces   70
Home° both in word and deed. Most cruelly
Didst thou, Alonso, use me and my daughter.
Thy brother was a furtherer in the act.
Thou art pinched for't now, Sebastian. Flesh and blood,
You, brother mine, that entertained ambition,   75
Expelled remorse° and nature°; whom, with Sebastian
(Whose inward pinches therefore are most strong),
Would here have killed your king, I do forgive thee,
Unnatural though thou art. Their understanding
Begins to swell, and the approaching tide   80
Will shortly fill the reasonable shore,
That now lies foul and muddy. Not one of them
That yet looks on me or would know me. Ariel,
Fetch me the hat and rapier in my cell.
I will discase° me, and myself present   85
As I was sometime Milan. Quickly, spirit!
Thou shalt ere long be free.   [*Exit Ariel and returns immediately.*]

Ariel sings and helps to attire him:

> Where the bee sucks, there suck I;
> In a cowslip's bell I lie;
> There I couch when owls do cry.   90
> On the bat's back I do fly
> After summer merrily.

---

⁵⁸*and:* which is.   ⁶³⁻⁶⁴*sociable . . . drops:* associating themselves with the (tearful) appearance
of your eyes, shed tears in sympathy.   ⁷⁰⁻⁷¹*pay . . . Home:* repay thy favors thoroughly.
⁷⁶*remorse:* pity.   ⁷⁶*nature:* natural feeling.   ⁸⁵*discase:* disrobe.

> Merrily, merrily shall I live now
> Under the blossom that hangs on the bough.

Prospero: Why, that's my dainty Ariel! I shall miss thee,   95
  But yet thou shalt have freedom; so, so, so.
  To the king's ship, invisible as thou art!
  There shalt thou find the mariners asleep
  Under the hatches. The master and the boatswain
  Being awake, enforce them to this place,   100
  And presently°, I prithee.
Ariel: I drink the air before me, and return
  Or ere your pulse twice beat.   *Exit.*
Gonzalo: All torment, trouble, wonder, and amazement
  Inhabits here. Some heavenly power guide us   105
  Out of this fearful country!
Prospero: Behold, sir king,
  The wronged Duke of Milan, Prospero.
  For more assurance that a living prince
  Does now speak to thee, I embrace thy body,
  And to thee and thy company I bid   110
  A hearty welcome.
Alonso: Whe'r° thou be'st he or no,
  Or some enchanted trifle° to abuse me,
  As late I have been, I not know. Thy pulse
  Beats, as of flesh and blood; and, since I saw thee,
  Th' affliction of my mind amends, with which,   115
  I fear, a madness held me. This must crave°
  (And if this be at all°) a most strange story.
  Thy dukedom I resign and do entreat
  Thou pardon me my wrongs. But how should Prospero
  Be living and be here?
Prospero: First, noble friend,   120
  Let me embrace thine age, whose honor cannot
  Be measured or confined.
Gonzalo: Whether this be
  Or be not, I'll not swear.
Prospero: You do yet taste
  Some subtleties° o' th' isle, that will not let you
  Believe things certain. Welcome, my friends all.   125

[Aside to Sebastian and Antonio.]

  But you, my brace of lords, were I so minded,
  I here could pluck his highness' frown upon you,
  And justify° you traitors. At this time
  I will tell no tales.

---

¹⁰¹*presently:* immediately.   ¹¹¹*Whe'r:* whether.   ¹¹²*trifle:* apparition.   ¹¹⁶*crave:* require (to account for it).   ¹¹⁷*And . . . all:* if this is really happening.   ¹²⁴*subtleties:* deceptions (referring to pastries made to look like something else — e.g., castles made out of sugar).   ¹²⁸*justify:* prove.

Sebastian [*Aside.*]:   The devil speaks in him.
Prospero: No.
          For you, most wicked sir, whom to call brother   130
          Would even infect my mouth, I do forgive
          Thy rankest fault — all of them; and require
          My dukedom of thee, which perforce I know
          Thou must restore.
Alonso: If thou beest Prospero,
          Give us particulars of thy preservation;   135
          How thou hast met us here, whom three hours since
          Were wracked upon this shore; where I have lost
          (How sharp the point of this remembrance is!)
          My dear son Ferdinand.
Prospero: I am woe° for't, sir.
Alonso: Irreparable is the loss, and Patience   140
          Says it is past her cure.
Prospero: I rather think
          You have not sought her help, of whose soft grace
          For the like loss I have her sovereign aid
          And rest myself content.
Alonso: You the like loss?
Prospero: As great to me, as late°, and supportable ¹⁴⁵   145
          To make the dear° loss, have I means much weaker
          Than you may call to comfort you; for I
          Have lost my daughter.
Alonso: A daughter?
          O heavens, that they were living both in Naples,
          The king and queen there! That they were, I wish   150
          Myself were mudded in that oozy bed
          Where my son lies. When did you lose your daughter?
Prospero: In this last tempest. I perceive these lords
          At this encounter do so much admire°
          That they devour their reason, and scarce think   155
          Their eyes do offices° of truth, their words
          Are natural breath. But, howsoev'r you have
          Been justled from your senses, know for certain
          That I am Prospero, and that very duke
          Which was thrust forth of Milan, who most strangely   160
          Upon this shore, where you were wracked, was landed
          To be the lord on't. No more yet of this;
          For 'tis a chronicle of day by day,
          Not a relation for a breakfast, nor
          Befitting this first meeting. Welcome, sir;   165
          This cell's my court. Here have I few attendants,
          And subjects none abroad°. Pray you look in.

---

¹³⁹*woe:* sorry.   ¹⁴⁵*As . . . late:* as great to me as your loss, and as recent; *supportable:* pronounced
"súpportable."   ¹⁴⁶*dear:* intensifies the meaning of the noun.   ¹⁵⁴*admire:* wonder.   ¹⁵⁶*do
offices:* perform services.   ¹⁶⁷*abroad:* i.e., on the island.

My dukedom since you have given me again,
I will requite you with as good a thing,
At least bring forth a wonder to content ye   170
As much as me my dukedom.

Here Prospero discovers° Ferdinand and Miranda playing at chess.

Miranda: Sweet lord, you play me false.
Ferdinand: No, my dearest love,
  I would not for the world.
Miranda: Yes, for a score of kingdoms you should wrangle,
  And I would call it fair play°.
Alonso: If this prove   175
  A vision of the island, one dear son
  Shall I twice lose.
Sebastian: A most high miracle!
Ferdinand: Though the seas threaten, they are merciful.
  I have cursed them without cause. [*Kneels.*]
Alonso: Now all the blessings
  Of a glad father compass thee about!   180
  Arise, and say how thou cam'st here.
Miranda: O, wonder!
  How many goodly creatures are there here!
  How beauteous mankind is! O brave new world
  That has such people in't!
Prospero: 'Tis new to thee.
Alonso: What is this maid with whom thou wast at play?   185
  Your eld'st° acquaintance cannot be three hours.
  Is she the goddess that hath severed us
  And brought us thus together?
Ferdinand: Sir, she is mortal;
  But by immortal providence she's mine.
  I chose her when I could not ask my father   190
  For his advice, nor thought I had one. She
  Is daughter to this famous Duke of Milan,
  Of whom so often I have heard renown
  But never saw before; of whom I have
  Received a second life; and second father   195
  This lady makes him to me.
Alonso: I am hers.
  But, O, how oddly will it sound that I
  Must ask my child forgiveness!
Prospero: There, sir, stop.
  Let us not burden our remembrance with

A heaviness that's gone.

Gonzalo: I have inly wept,   200
Or should have spoke ere this. Look down, you gods,
And on this couple drop a blessèd crown!
For it is you that have chalked forth the way
Which brought us hither.

Alonso: I say amen, Gonzalo.

Gonzalo: Was Milan thrust from Milan that his issue   205
Should become kings of Naples? O, rejoice
Beyond a common joy, and set it down
With gold on lasting pillars. In one voyage
Did Claribel her husband find at Tunis,
And Ferdinand her brother found a wife   210
Where he himself was lost; Prospero his dukedom
In a poor isle; and all of us ourselves
When no man was his own.

Alonso [*To Ferdinand and Miranda.*]: Give me your hands.
Let grief and sorrow still° embrace his heart
That doth not wish you joy.

Gonzalo: Be it so! Amen!   215

Enter Ariel, with the Master and Boatswain amazedly following.

O, look, sir; look, sir! Here is more of us!
I prophesied if a gallows were on land,
This fellow could not drown. Now, blasphemy,
That swear'st grace o'erboard°, not an oath on shore?
Hast thou no mouth by land? What is the news?   220

Boatswain: The best news is that we have safely found
Our king and company; the next, our ship,
Which, but three glasses° since, we gave out split,
Is tight and yare° and bravely rigged as when
We first put out to sea.

Ariel [*Aside to Prospero.*]:   Sir, all this service   225
Have I done since I went.

Prospero [*Aside to Ariel.*]:   My tricksy spirit!

Alonso: These are not natural events; they strengthen
From strange to stranger. Say, how came you hither?

Boatswain: If I did think, sir, I were well awake,
I'd strive to tell you. We were dead of sleep   230
And (how we know not) all clapped under hatches;
Where, but even now, with strange and several° noises
Of roaring, shrieking, howling, jingling chains,
And moe° diversity of sounds, all horrible,
We were awaked; straightway at liberty;   235
Where we, in all our trim, freshly beheld

---

²¹⁴*still:* forever.   ²¹⁹*That . . . o'erboard:* that (at sea) swearest enough to cause grace to be
withdrawn from the ship.   ²²³*glasses:* hours.   ²²⁴*yare:* shipshape.   ²³²*several:* various.
²³⁴*moe:* more.

Our royal, good, and gallant ship, our master
Cap'ring to eye° her. On a trice, so please you,
Even in a dream, were we divided from them
And were brought moping° hither.

Ariel [Aside to Prospero.]:   Was't well done?   240
Prospero [Aside to Ariel.]: Bravely, my diligence. Thou shalt be free.
Alonso: This is as strange a maze as e'er men trod,
And there is in this business more than nature
Was ever conduct° of. Some oracle
Must rectify our knowledge.
Prospero: Sir, my liege,   245
Do not infest your mind with beating on
The strangeness of this business. At picked leisure,
Which shall be shortly, single I'll resolve you
(Which to you shall seem probable) of every
These happened accidents°; till when, be cheerful   250
And think of each thing well. [*Aside to Ariel.*] Come hither, spirit.
Set Caliban and his companions free.
Untie the spell. [*Exit Ariel.*] How fares my gracious sir?
There are yet missing of your company
Some few odd lads that you remember not.   255

*Enter Ariel, driving in Caliban, Stephano, and Trinculo, in their stolen
apparel.*

Stephano: Every man shift for all the rest, and let no man take care for
himself; for all is but fortune. Coragio°, bully-monster, coragio!
Trinculo: If these be true spies which I wear in my head, here's a goodly
sight.
Caliban: O Setebos°, these be brave spirits indeed!   260
How fine my master is! I am afraid
He will chastise me.
Sebastian: Ha, ha!
What things are these, my Lord Antonio?
Will money buy 'em?
Antonio: Very like. One of them
Is a plain fish and no doubt marketable.   265
Prospero: Mark but the badges° of these men, my lords,
Then say if they be true°. This misshapen knave,
His mother was a witch, and one so strong
That could control the moon, make flows and ebbs,
And deal in her command without her power°.   270
These three have robbed me, and this demi-devil

---

²³⁸*Cap'ring to eye:* dancing to see.   ²⁴⁰*moping:* in a daze.   ²⁴⁴*conduct:* conductor.   ²⁴⁸⁻⁵⁰*single
. . . accidents:* I myself will solve the problems (and my story will make sense to you) concerning
each and every incident that has happened.   ²⁵⁷*Coragio:* courage (Italian).   ²⁶⁰*Setebos:* the god
of Caliban's mother.   ²⁶⁶*badges:* worn by servants to indicate to whose service they belong;
in this case, the stolen clothes are badges of their rascality.   ²⁶⁷*true:* honest.   ²⁷⁰*deal . . . power:*
i.e., dabble in the moon's realm without the moon's legitimate authority.

(For he's a bastard one) had plotted with them
To take my life. Two of these fellows you
Must know and own; this thing of darkness I
Acknowledge mine.
Caliban: I shall be pinched to death.   275
Alonso: Is not this Stephano, my drunken butler?
Sebastian: He is drunk now. Where had he wine?
Alonso: And Trinculo is reeling ripe. Where should they
Find this grand liquor that hath gilded 'em?
How cam'st thou in this pickle?   280
Trinculo: I have been in such a pickle, since I saw you last, that I fear me
will never out of my bones. I shall not fear flyblowing°.
Sebastian: Why, how now, Stephano?
Stephano: O, touch me not! I am not Stephano, but a cramp.
Prospero: You'd be king o' the isle, sirrah?   285
Stephano: I should have been a sore° one then.
Alonso: This is a strange thing as e'er I looked on.
Prospero: He is as disproportioned in his manners
As in his shape. Go, sirrah, to my cell;
Take with you your companions. As you look   290
To have my pardon, trim it handsomely.
Caliban: Ay, that I will; and I'll be wise hereafter,
And seek for grace. What a thrice-double ass
Was I to take this drunkard for a god
And worship this dull fool!
Prospero: Go to! Away!   295
Alonso: Hence, and bestow your luggage where you found it.
Sebastian: Or stole it rather.   *[Exeunt Caliban, Stephano, and Trinculo.]*
Prospero: Sir, I invite your highness and your train
To my poor cell, where you shall take your rest
For this one night; which, part of it, I'll waste°   300
With such discourse as, I not doubt, shall make it
Go quick away — the story of my life,
And the particular accidents° gone by
Since I came to this isle. And in the morn
I'll bring you to your ship, and so to Naples,   305
Where I have hope to see the nuptial
Of these our dear-beloved solemnizèd°;
And thence retire me to my Milan, where
Every third thought shall be my grave.
Alonso: I long
To hear the story of your life, which must   310
Take° the ear strangely.
Prospero: I'll deliver° all;

---

²⁸²*flyblowing:* pickling preserves meat from flies.   ²⁸⁶*sore:* (1) tyrannical (2) aching.   ³⁰⁰*waste:*
spend.   ³⁰³*accidents:* incidents.   ³⁰⁷*solemnizèd:* pronounced "solémnizèd."   ³¹¹*Take:* captivate;
deliver: tell.

And promise you calm seas, auspicious gales,
And sail so expeditious that shall catch°
Your royal fleet far off. [*Aside to Ariel.*] My Ariel, chick,
That is thy charge. Then to the elements   315
Be free, and fare thou well! [*To the others.*] Please you, draw near.

Exeunt omnes.

EPILOGUE

Spoken by Prospero:

Now my charms are all o'erthrown,
And what strength I have's mine own,
Which is most faint. Now 'tis true
I must be here confined by you,
Or sent to Naples. Let me not,   5
Since I have my dukedom got
And pardoned the deceiver, dwell
In this bare island by your spell;
But release me from my bands°
With the help of your good hands°.   10
Gentle breath° of yours my sails
Must fill, or else my project fails,
Which was to please. Now I want°
Spirits to enforce, art to enchant;
And my ending is despair   15
Unless I be relieved by prayer°,
Which pierces so that it assaults
Mercy itself and frees all faults.
As you from crimes would pardoned be,
Let your indulgence set me free.   *Exit.*   20

QUESTIONS

ACT I

1. In the shipwreck scene, how does the boatswain treat his noble passengers? How do they behave? What traits of character does Antonio display?
2. What does Prospero reveal to his daughter about her history? In the telling, what does he reveal about himself? To what extent are his difficulties the result of his own mistakes?
3. How does Prospero calm Miranda's sorrow over the shipwreck?
4. Who is Ariel? What does he want of Prospero? For what does he owe Prospero his gratitude?
5. How is Caliban introduced? What has soured Prospero and Miranda against him? To what extent is their disappointment in him their own fault?

---

³¹³*catch:* catch up with. Epi. ⁹*bands:* bonds. ¹⁰*hands:* i.e., applause to break the spell. ¹¹*Gentle breath:* i.e., favorable comment. ¹³*want:* lack. ¹⁶*prayer:* i.e., this petition.

6. What impression do Ferdinand and Miranda make upon each other? What magic does Prospero hope to work in regard to the two of them? Why then does he treat Ferdinand as he does?

ACT II

1. What do we learn about the reason for the voyage that ended in shipwreck for Alonso and his companions? Why does Alonso express regret for his daughter's marriage to the King of Tunis?
2. What is the nature of the commonwealth that Gonzalo imagines? How do his companions react to his description of it?
3. In what ways do Alonso's circumstances resemble Prospero's? To what extent is Alonso responsible for what has befallen him?
4. Why does Ariel, after first putting Gonzalo to sleep, awaken him? How do you explain that the sound described by Sebastian as "a hollow burst of bellowing" (line 297) struck Gonzalo only as "a humming" (line 303)?
5. Of what does Caliban complain at the start of Scene II? What do his outcry and his subsequent worship of Stephano reveal about Caliban's nature?

ACT III

1. What task has Prospero ordered Ferdinand to perform? How does the young man bear it? How does his plight affect Miranda?
2. Consider Miranda's behavior toward Ferdinand. How might her approach differ had she grown up not in isolation on a savage isle but in society?
3. What plot do Caliban, Stephano, and Trinculo agree to carry out? What effect do Ariel's interpolations have upon the scene? What distracts the plotters from immediately carrying out their plans?
4. How do we know that Antonio and Sebastian have not given up their plans affecting Alonso?
5. How does Prospero bring Alonso and his companions under his power? Describe Ariel's role in the proceedings. What seems to be Prospero's motive for allowing the King to continue believing that Ferdinand is dead?

ACT IV

1. What is Ferdinand's reward for his fidelity in carrying out Prospero's test?
2. What motivates Prospero to bring to an abrupt end the masque he has conjured up for Ferdinand and Miranda?
3. By what means does Prospero put Caliban, Stephano, and Trinculo to rout when they enter his cell?

ACT V

1. In lines 17 – 30, what possible actions does Prospero seem to consider? Does he end by changing his mind, or does he merely confirm a decision made earlier?
2. Why do you think Prospero decides to renounce his magic? (See his speech, lines 33 – 57.)
3. How do you account for Prospero's decision not to expose Sebastian and Antonio as the traitors they are (lines 126 – 29)? Do you think his silence might prove dangerous for Alonso in the future? Why, or why not?

4. To whom is Prospero speaking in lines 130 – 34? How can you tell? What do you infer from the lack of a reply to this speech?
5. To what extent is Miranda's reaction to her royal visitors (lines 181 – 84) ironic? What does this speech reveal about her?
6. Do you believe Caliban when he says, "I'll be wise hereafter, / And seek for grace" (lines 295 – 96)? Discuss.
7. How would you reply to someone who made the following criticism? — "Prospero didn't have to make such a big production of restoring Ferdinand to his father and forgiving everyone. He was just showing off"?

GENERAL QUESTIONS

1. What is a "romantic comedy" and how does *The Tempest* fit this definition? What moments of "low comedy" does the play contain?
2. In what respects does Prospero seem almost godlike? Where in the play does he reveal his human limitations?
3. What traits of Caliban seem human? In what respects is he a creature of a different kind? What aspects of "nature" might Caliban and Ariel be said to embody?
4. Consider any one of the play's many situations of dramatic irony (in which we, the spectators, know more than the ignorant or deceived characters on stage). Does this situation seem included for its own enjoyable sake, or does it in any way advance the story?
5. Some characters in *The Tempest* have been carefully and extensively educated. Who are they? What effect does their education seem to have had on each of them?
6. What are the parallels in the play between the characters of high degree and their humbler companions? What further parallels between them does Shakespeare suggest?
7. Robert Langbaum, who edited the text of *The Tempest,* calls the storm at the start of the play "an illusion created to regenerate the social order." What evidence do you find for believing that a theme in the play is that traditional social distinctions ought to be maintained? Do you think Shakespeare a snob?
8. How much importance does Shakespeare seem to find in the idea of a basic order or harmony in the natural world? Point to any scenes or passages that make this theme clear.
9. What seems to determine the play's occasional switches from poetry to prose?
10. How is music important in this play? Consider not only the songs, but any speeches in which you find music mentioned.
11. Why do you suppose people keep trying to read *The Tempest* as Shakespeare's farewell to the stage? Consider Prospero's speech beginning "Our revels now are ended" (IV, 148 – 163), his vow to break his magic wand or staff (V, 54), his freeing Ariel, his epilogue, and any other evidence you can find that might support this view. What arguments can be raised against reading the play as autobiography?

Woody Allen
DEATH KNOCKS   1971

Woody Allen, actor, author, and filmmaker, was born in New York City in 1935. He was ejected from both New York University and City College in his freshman year. In 1952 he became a writer of television comedy for Sid Caesar, Art Carney, Herb Shriner, and others, and in 1964 decided to become a comedian himself. Allen appeared in nightclubs and on television, and wrote two long-running Broadway comedies, Don't Drink the Water *and* Play It Again Sam *(in which he starred; later he made a film of it). His first film script was for* What's New Pussycat *(1964). With* Take the Money and Run *(1969) he became a star, writer, and director.* Annie Hall *(1977) he not only acted, directed, and wrote, but also produced. Allen has continued to maintain such personal control over all aspects of his films, including the recent* Hannah and Her Sisters *(1985). As a writer, he has contributed to* The New Yorker, Playboy, *and other magazines, and has published three collections of humor, including* Getting Even *(1971), in which "Death Knocks" first appeared. Allen says of himself, "His one regret in life is that he is not someone else."*

(The play takes place in the bedroom of the Nat Ackermans' two-story house, somewhere in Kew Gardens°. The carpeting is wall-to-wall. There is a big double bed and a large vanity. The room is elaborately furnished and curtained, and on the walls there are several paintings and a not really attractive barometer. Soft theme music as the curtain rises. Nat Ackerman, a bald, paunchy fifty-seven-year-old dress manufacturer is lying on the bed finishing off tomorrow's Daily News. *He wears a bathrobe and slippers, and reads by a bed light clipped to the white headboard of the bed. The time is near midnight. Suddenly we hear a noise, and Nat sits up and looks at the window.)*

Nat: What the hell is that?

(Climbing awkwardly through the window is a sombre, caped figure. The intruder wears a black hood and skintight black clothes. The hood covers his head but not his face, which is middle-aged and stark white. He is something like Nat in appearance. He huffs audibly and then trips over the windowsill and falls into the room.)

Death (for it is no one else): Jesus Christ. I nearly broke my neck.
Nat (watching with bewilderment): Who are you?
Death: Death.
Nat: Who?
Death: Death. Listen — can I sit down? I nearly broke my neck. I'm shaking like a leaf.
Nat: Who *are* you?
Death: Death. You got a glass of water?

Kew Gardens: residential section in Queens, a borough of New York City.

Nat: Death? What do you mean, Death?

Death: What is wrong with you? You see the black costume and the whitened face?

Nat: Yeah.

Death: Is it Halloween?

Nat: No.

Death: Then I'm Death. Now can I get a glass of water — or a Fresca?

Nat: If this is some joke —

Death: What kind of joke? You're fifty-seven? Nat Ackerman? One eighteen Pacific Street? Unless I blew it — where's that call sheet? *(He fumbles through pocket, finally producing a card with an address on it. It seems to check.)*

Nat: What do you want with me?

Death: What do I want? What do you think I want?

Nat: You must be kidding. I'm in perfect health.

Death (unimpressed): Uh-huh. *(Looking around)* This is a nice place. You do it yourself?

Nat: We had a decorator, but we worked with her.

Death (looking at picture on the wall): I love those kids with the big eyes.

Nat: I don't want to go yet.

Death: You don't want to go? Please don't start in. As it is, I'm nauseous from the climb.

Nat: What climb?

Death: I climbed up the drainpipe. I was trying to make a dramatic entrance. I see the big windows and you're awake reading. I figure it's worth a shot. I'll climb up and enter with a little — you know . . . *(Snaps fingers)* Meanwhile, I get my heel caught on some vines, the drainpipe breaks, and I'm hanging by a thread. Then my cape begins to tear. Look, let's just go. It's been a rough night.

Nat: You broke my drainpipe?

Death: Broke. It didn't break. It's a little bent. Didn't you hear anything? I slammed into the ground.

Nat: I was reading.

Death: You must have really been engrossed. *(Lifting newspaper Nat was reading)* "NAB COEDS IN POT ORGY." Can I borrow this?

Nat: I'm not finished.

Death: Er — I don't know how to put this to you, pal . . .

Nat: Why didn't you just ring downstairs?

Death: I'm telling you, I could have, but how does it look? This way I get a little drama going. Something. Did you read *Faust*°?

Nat: What?

Death: And what if you had company? You're sitting there with important people. I'm Death — I should ring the bell and traipse right in the front? Where's your thinking?

Nat: Listen, Mister, it's very late.

Faust: dramatic poem by Johann Wolfgang von Goethe (1749 – 1832), based on the legend of the sixteenth-century scholar who sells his soul to the devil in exchange for youth, knowledge, and magical power.

Death: Yeah. Well, you want to go?

Nat: Go where?

Death: Death. It. The Thing. The Happy Hunting Grounds. *(Looking at his own knee)* Y'know, that's a pretty bad cut. My first job, I'm liable to get gangrene yet.

Nat: Now, wait a minute. I need time. I'm not ready to go.

Death: I'm sorry. I can't help you. I'd like to, but it's the moment.

Nat: How can it be the moment? I just merged with Modiste Originals.

Death: What's the difference, a couple of bucks more or less.

Nat: Sure, what do you care? You guys probably have all your expenses paid.

Death: You want to come along now?

Nat (studying him): I'm sorry, but I cannot believe you're Death.

Death: Why? What'd you expect — Rock Hudson?

Nat: No, it's not that.

Death: I'm sorry if I disappointed you.

Nat: Don't get upset. I don't know, I always thought you'd be . . . uh . . . taller.

Death: I'm five seven. It's average for my weight.

Nat: You look a little like me.

Death: Who should I look like? I'm your death.

Nat: Give me some time. Another day.

Death: I can't. What do you want me to say?

Nat: One more day. Twenty-four hours.

Death: What do you need it for? The radio said rain tomorrow.

Nat: Can't we work out something?

Death: Like what?

Nat: You play chess?

Death: No, I don't.

Nat: I once saw a picture of you playing chess°.

Death: Couldn't be me, because I don't play chess. Gin rummy, maybe.

Nat: You play gin rummy?

Death: Do I play gin rummy? Is Paris a city?

Nat: You're good, huh?

Death: Very good.

Nat: I'll tell you what I'll do —

Death: Don't make any deals with me.

Nat: I'll play you gin rummy. If you win, I'll go immediately. If I win, give me some more time. A little bit — one more day.

Death: Who's got time to play gin rummy?

Nat: Come on. If you're so good.

Death: Although I feel like a game . . .

Nat: Come on. Be a sport. We'll shoot for a half hour.

Death: I really shouldn't.

Nat: I got the cards right here. Don't make a production.

Death: All right, come on. We'll play a little. It'll relax me.

---

a picture of you playing chess: In Swedish director Ingmar Bergman's film *The Seventh Seal* (1956), set in the Middle Ages, a knight plays a game of chess for his life with whitefaced, skeletal Death.

Nat (getting cards, pad, and pencil): You won't regret this.

Death: Don't give me a sales talk. Get the cards and give me a Fresca and put out something. For God's sake, a stranger drops in, you don't have potato chips or pretzels.

Nat: There's M&M's downstairs in a dish.

Death: M&M's. What if the President came? He'd get M&M's too?

Nat: You're not the President.

Death: Deal.

(Nat deals, turns up a five.)

Nat: You want to play a tenth of a cent a point to make it interesting?

Death: It's not interesting enough for you?

Nat: I play better when money's at stake.

Death: Whatever you say, Newt.

Nat: Nat. Nat Ackerman. You don't know my name?

Death: Newt, Nat — I got such a headache.

Nat: You want that five?

Death: No.

Nat: So pick.

Death (surveying his hand as he picks): Jesus, I got nothing here.

Nat: What's it like?

Death: What's what like?

(Throughout the following, they pick and discard.)

Nat: Death.

Death: What should it be like? You lay there.

Nat: Is there anything after?

Death: Aha, you're saving twos.

Nat: I'm asking. Is there anything after?

Death (absently): You'll see.

Nat: Oh, then I will actually see something?

Death: Well, maybe I shouldn't have put it that way. Throw.

Nat: To get an answer from you is a big deal.

Death: I'm playing cards.

Nat: All right, play, play.

Death: Meanwhile, I'm giving you one card after another.

Nat: Don't look through the discards.

Death: I'm not looking. I'm straightening them up. What was the knock card°?

Nat: Four. You ready to knock already?

Death: Who said I'm ready to knock? All I asked was what was the knock card.

Nat: And all I asked was is there anything for me to look forward to.

Death: Play.

Nat: Can't you tell me anything? Where do we go?

---

knock card: an unmatched card. In gin rummy, according to *Hoyle's Rules of Games,* "Cards in hand that are not formed in matched sets are called *deadwood.* A player may legally *knock* whenever the total of his deadwood is 10 points or less. To knock is to end the play with a showdown."

Death: We? To tell you the truth, *you* fall in a crumpled heap on the floor.

Nat: Oh, I can't wait for that! Is it going to hurt?

Death: Be over in a second.

Nat: Terrific. *(Sighs)* I needed this. A man merges with Modiste Originals . . .

Death: How's four points?

Nat: You're knocking?

Death: Four points is good?

Nat: No, I got two.

Death: You're kidding.

Nat: No, you lose.

Death: Holy Christ, and I thought you were saving sixes.

Nat: No. Your deal. Twenty points and two boxes. Shoot. *(Death deals.)* I must fall on the floor, eh? I can't be standing over the sofa when it happens?

Death: No. Play.

Nat: Why not?

Death: Because you fall on the floor! Leave me alone. I'm trying to concentrate.

Nat: Why must it be on the floor? That's all I'm saying! Why can't the whole thing happen and I'll stand next to the sofa?

Death: I'll try my best. Now can we play?

Nat: That's all I'm saying. You remind me of Moe Lefkowitz. He's also stubborn.

Death: I remind him of Moe Lefkowitz. I'm one of the most terrifying figures you could possibly imagine, and him I remind of Moe Lefkowitz. What is he, a furrier?

Nat: You should be such a furrier. He's good for eighty thousand a year. Passementeries°. He's got his own factory. Two points.

Death: What?

Nat: Two points. I'm knocking. What have you got?

Death: My hand is like a basketball score.

Nat: And it's spades.

Death: If you didn't talk so much.

(They redeal and play on.)

Nat: What'd you mean before when you said this was your first job?

Death: What does it sound like?

Nat: What are you telling me — that nobody ever went before?

Death: Sure they went. But I didn't take them.

Nat: So who did?

Death: Others.

Nat: There's others?

Death: Sure. Each one has his own personal way of going.

Nat: I never knew that.

Death: Why should you know? Who are you?

Nat: What do you mean who am I? Why — I'm nothing?

Death: Not nothing. You're a dress manufacturer. Where do you come to knowledge of the eternal mysteries?

Passementeries: fancy trimmings for clothes, made of cord, beads, or gold or silver thread.

Nat: What are you talking about? I make a beautiful dollar. I sent two kids through college. One is in advertising, the other's married. I got my own home. I drive a Chrysler. My wife has whatever she wants. Maids, mink coat, vacations. Right now she's at the Eden Roc°. Fifty dollars a day because she wants to be near her sister. I'm supposed to join her next week, so what do you think I am — some guy off the street?

Death: All right. Don't be so touchy.

Nat: Who's touchy?

Death: How would you like it if I got insulted quickly?

Nat: Did I insult you?

Death: You didn't say you were disappointed in me?

Nat: What do you expect? You want me to throw you a block party?

Death: I'm not talking about that. I mean me personally. I'm too short, I'm this, I'm that.

Nat: I said you looked like me. It's like a reflection.

Death: All right, deal, deal.

> *(They continue to play as music steals in and the lights dim until all is in total darkness. The lights slowly come up again, and now it is later and their game is over. Nat tallies.)*

Nat: Sixty-eight . . . one-fifty . . . Well, you lose.

Death (dejectedly looking through the deck): I knew I shouldn't have thrown that nine. Damn it.

Nat: So I'll see you tomorrow.

Death: What do you mean you'll see me tomorrow?

Nat: I won the extra day. Leave me alone.

Death: You were serious?

Nat: We made a deal.

Death: Yeah, but —

Nat: Don't "but" me. I won twenty-four hours. Come back tomorrow.

Death: I didn't know we were actually playing for time.

Nat: That's too bad about you. You should pay attention.

Death: Where am I going to go for twenty-four hours?

Nat: What's the difference? The main thing is I won an extra day.

Death: What do you want me to do — walk the streets?

Nat: Check into a hotel and go to a movie. Take a *schvitz*°. Don't make a federal case.

Death: Add the score again.

Nat: Plus you owe me twenty-eight dollars.

Death: What?

Nat: That's right, Buster. Here it is — read it.

Death (going through pockets): I have a few singles — not twenty-eight dollars.

Nat: I'll take a check.

Death: From what account?

Nat: Look who I'm dealing with.

Death: Sue me. Where do I keep my checking account?

Eden Roc: a luxury hotel in Miami Beach.

take a schvitz: go soak in a steam room in a bathhouse.

Nat: All right, gimme what you got and we'll call it square.

Death: Listen, I need that money.

Nat: Why should you need money?

Death: What are you talking about? You're going to the Beyond.

Nat: So?

Death: So — you know how far that is?

Nat: So?

Death: So where's gas? Where's tolls?

Nat: We're going by car!

Death: You'll find out. *(Agitatedly)* Look — I'll be back tomorrow, and you'll give me a chance to win the money back. Otherwise I'm in definite trouble.

Nat: Anything you want. Double or nothing we'll play. I'm liable to win an extra week or a month. The way you play, maybe years.

Death: Meantime I'm stranded.

Nat: See you tomorrow.

Death (being edged to the doorway): Where's a good hotel? What am I talking about hotel, I got no money. I'll go sit in Bickford's°. *(He picks up the* News.)

Nat: Out. Out. That's my paper. *(He takes it back.)*

Death (exiting): I couldn't just take him and go. I had to get involved in rummy.

Nat (calling after him): And be careful going downstairs. On one of the steps the rug is loose.

(And, on cue, we hear a terrific crash. Nat sighs, then crosses to the bedside table and makes a phone call.)

Nat: Hello, Moe? Me. Listen, I don't know if somebody's playing a joke, or what, but Death was just here. We played a little gin . . . No, *Death.* In person. Or somebody who claims to be Death. But, Moe, he's such a *schlep*°!

CURTAIN

Questions

1. Explain the pun in the play's title. (If you aren't a gin rummy player, see the note on page 1055.) From what other incongruities does *Death Knocks* derive its humor? (There are several of these; just indicate any that strike you in particular.)
2. What kind of person is Nat? What does he value? How does he feel about himself?
3. In what ways does Allen make Death seem human — almost like someone you know?
4. Point to lines in the play in which Nat's words, uttered with perfect seriousness, make us laugh. Do we laugh with Nat or at him?
5. What trait of Nat's saves him, at least temporarily, from being carted off by Death?
6. What is Death's attitude toward Nat? What clues in the play seem to indicate that Nat's feelings toward Death are similar?

Bickford's: one of a chain of cafeterias.
schlep: Yiddish, "dull idiot."

7. Do you at all identify with Nat? Why, or why not?
8. How do you think an audience in 1971 would have reacted to the reference to Rock Hudson? How might an audience respond today?
9. What would it take to convert *Death Knocks* from a comedy into a tragedy? Admittedly, this change would be a terrible idea, but entertain it for a moment and you will realize a few things about comedy and tragedy. To begin with, what major alterations would you need to make in the characters of Nat and Death?

THE THEATER OF MOLIÈRE

Still ringed by walls built in the Middle Ages to defend the city against attack, Paris in the mid-seventeenth century could barely hold its large and swelling populace. Streets at night were ill-lit and dangerous. To encourage theater-goers, plays had to be performed by day. Beside the river Seine stood the Louvre, residence of King Louis XIV — who was seldom there. He much preferred his magnificent new palace in the country at Versailles, where he had ordered his nobles to reside, that he might keep a suspicious eye on them. France was an absolute monarchy, and Louis ruled with a fist of iron. As he himself had declared, he *was* the government, "The State: it is I." Yet Louis was a generous patron of the arts, and under his patronage French drama experienced a golden age. In comedy from this era, the supreme name is that of Molière, the favorite comic playwright of Louis and his glittering court.

A typical playhouse of Molière's time would probably remind you of a commercial theater in a large city today. Modeled after the playhouses of sixteenth-century Italy, it featured a **picture-frame stage:** one that holds the action within a **proscenium arch,** or a gateway standing (as the word *proscenium* indicates) "in front of the scenery." This manner of constructing a playhouse in effect divided the actors from their audience. Spectators sat in one room (its fourth wall cut away) and watched actors perform in another. Painted in realistic detail, scenery was made to look like city streets, Greek temples, or royal palaces. Stage and auditorium were artificially lighted (by blazing chandeliers), and a curtain rose and fell, slicing the drama into acts. Further, in a liberalization of traditional codes, women were permitted to be actresses — although sometimes a comic female role would still be taken by a man in drag. Costumes could be so heavy and elaborate that their wearers could hardly walk. Formal gowns dragged their trains across the stage, and actors often wore armor, hats burdened with ostrich plumes, and stiff hip boots laced from ankle to thigh. It was a theater in which language was generally far livelier than physical action, and the usual leaps were those of wit.

This, then, was the French **neoclassical theater** (*neo* meaning "new"), so called because its plays were inspired by classical literature, especially Latin, and by the theories of Aristotle in his *Poetics* (at least as sixteenth-century Italian literary critics interpreted them, making them into strict doctrine). In this neoclassical theater, the **unities** were law. According to the critics, a play must be coherent in its span of time, in its locale, and in the nature of its action. Its events must take place within twenty-four hours, and at just one location. It must be entirely tragic or entirely comic, not a mingling. Contrary to the theorists, of course, many great plays defy such arbitrary rules: *Othello* defies all three. In his formal verse plays, Molière generally observes these unities; in his farces, he freely violates them.

Today, in a high school French class, students usually read one of Molière's strictly unified plays in witty verse. Among the enduring favorites are *The School for Wives* (1662), a satire on the narrow schooling given to girls; *Tartuffe* (1664), a satire on a religious hypocrite; *The Misanthrope* (1666), a satire on an antisocial man; and *The Bourgeois Gentleman* (1670), a satire on a middle-class man's aspirations to culture. Brilliant as they are, these glossily polished, slightly cerebral plays are not all there is to Molière. In his own time, he was beloved in all his variety, for he also wrote song-and-dance shows, comic ballets, and — especially popular — broad farces such as *The Physician in Spite of Himself.*

Such farces were patterned after the Italian **commedia dell' arte** ("artistic comedy"), a kind of theater developed by professional comedians who traveled from town to town. In Italy during the late Renaissance, while neoclassical theaters revived the tragedies of the Roman playwright Seneca, the commedia regaled crowds at country fairs and in outdoor marketplaces. This popular art was known for sight gags and for familiar stock characters in masks or whiteface — such as Harlequin, a clown; Columbine, his peppery sweetheart; and Pantaloon, a doddering duffer. Skilled in improvisation, its players often would begin a show with nothing but a familiar situation to work with, making up lines and stage business right in front of an audience. As a young man Molière himself may have acted in one of these traveling companies.

In its time, *The Physician in Spite of Himself* was one of Molière's most popular comedies, and of all his plays it runs second only to *Tartuffe* in number of recorded performances over three centuries. In the original production Molière, who loved nothing better than a huge show-stopping laugh, played the title role of the supposed physician, Sganarelle. The farce was first staged only two months after Molière's *The Misanthrope.* Thus "the most serious of Molière's plays," Morris Bishop points out, "was succeeded by the loudest and funniest."

Molière
THE PHYSICIAN IN SPITE OF HIMSELF 1666

Translated by Morris Bishop

Molière — the stage name of Jean Baptiste Poquelin (1622 – 73) — is the great French comic dramatist. Like Shakespeare, he was both playwright and actor, earning a living both from the commercial stage and from performances at court. Born and raised in Paris, young Poquelin turned his back on his father's upholstery business. Smitten with the stage, he founded his own company of players, went bankrupt, and served time in prison for debt. At last free, undiscouraged, he spent twelve years touring the country, acting and directing before tough rural crowds, deepening his skills. When he returned to Paris in 1658, it was as a master. Invited to entertain young Louis XIV at court, Molière and his troupe performed a comedy he had written, and the delighted king rewarded him with a theater of his own in Paris. As an actor, Molière was called phenomenal. Acrobat and quick-change artist, he once acted two roles at once, holding a debate with himself on stage, quickly switching costumes, leaping in and out of view. He died a trouper. While starring in his play The Imaginary Invalid, *he was stricken by a hemorrhage of the lungs, collapsed after taking his bows, and in a few hours expired. After his death, his troupe merged into a new company, today the Comédie-Française in Paris, which still performs his great plays.*

Characters

Sganarelle, a woodcutter
Martine, his wife
Monsieur Robert, his neighbor
Géronte, a wealthy gentleman
Lucinde, his daughter
Léandre, suitor of Lucinde
Valère, steward of Géronte
Lucas, a peasant
Jacqueline, his wife
Thibaut, a peasant
Perrin, his son

ACT I

The scene is the exterior of Sganarelle's tumbledown house. Enter Sganarelle and Martine, quarreling.

Sganarelle: I won't. I tell you I won't. And when I say something around here, it's an order.

Martine: And I tell you that I'll tell you how to behave. I didn't marry you in order to put up with your tricks and dodges.

Sganarelle: Oh, what a burden is a wife, is it not indeed! How right was Aristotle, when he said that a wife is worse than a demon°!

Martine: What a smart fellow it is, with his half-wit Aristotle!

Sganarelle: Yes, a smart fellow. You won't find another woodcutter who knows how to argue like me, and who worked for a famous doctor for six years, and who knew his First Latin Book by heart when he was a boy.

Martine: A plague on the champion fool!

Sganarelle: A plague on the slut!

Martine: Cursed be the day and the hour when I took it into my head to say "I do!"

Sganarelle: Cursed be the cuckold of a notary who made me sign my own destruction!

Martine: It's a nice thing for you to complain of that affair! Should you let a single minute go by without thanking heaven for having me for your wife? Did you deserve to marry a person like me?

Sganarelle: Certainly you did me too much honor; and I had good reason to congratulate myself on our wedding night! Damnation! Don't get me going on that topic; I could say a few things —

Martine: And what could you say?

Sganarelle: That's enough. We'll drop the subject. Just remember that we know what we know, and you were very lucky to find me.

Martine: What do you mean, lucky to find you? A man who is bringing me to the poorhouse, a drunkard, a good-for-nothing, who eats up everything I've got —

Sganarelle: That's a lie. I drink part of it.

Martine: — who is selling off, bit by bit, everything in the house —

Sganarelle: We mustn't let our possessions possess us.

Martine: — who has even got rid of my own bed —

Sganarelle: You won't sleep so late.

Martine: — who won't leave a single stick of furniture in the house —

Sganarelle: That makes moving easier.

Martine: — and who spends the whole day, from morning till night, drinking and gambling.

Sganarelle: Well, I hate to be bored.

Martine: And while that goes on, what do you expect me to do with my family?

Sganarelle: Anything you like.

Martine: I have four poor little children on my hands.

Sganarelle: Put them on the floor.

Martine: And they keep forever crying out for bread.

Sganarelle: Give them a good whipping. When I have had plenty to eat and drink, I like everyone in the house to have his bellyful.

Martine: And you expect, you drunken lout, that things are going to go on forever this way?

Sganarelle: My dear wife, calm down.

Martine: And I'm to put up with your drink and debauchery to the end of time?

Sganarelle: Now, let's not get excited, darling.

Aristotle, when he said . . . demon!: Aristotle, of course, said no such thing.

Martine: And I won't find some way to make you behave?

Sganarelle: Sweetie, you know I'm not very patient, and I have a strong right arm.

Martine: I'm not afraid of your threats.

Sganarelle: My little lollipop, you're itching for something, as usual.

Martine: I'll show you I'm not afraid of you.

Sganarelle: My dainty pet, there's something you want me to give you.

Martine: You think you frighten me with your talk?

Sganarelle: Fair object of my eternal vows, I'll knock your ears in.

Martine: Boozer!

Sganarelle: I shall flog and flail you.

Martine: Souse!

Sganarelle: I shall pummel and buffet.

Martine: Dirty no-good!

Sganarelle: I shall administer the lash.

Martine: Rascal! Puppy! Deceiver! Coward! Scoundrel! Gallows-bird! Beggar! Waster! Rogue! Villain! Thief!

Sganarelle (takes a stick and beats her): Well, you asked for it.

Martine: Oh, oh, oh, oh!

Sganarelle: That's the best way to calm you down.

(Enter Monsieur Robert.)

M. Robert: Hello! Here, here, here! What's all this! This is an outrage! Confound the fellow, for beating his wife that way!

Martine (her arms akimbo, forces Monsieur Robert backward step by step during the following dialogue): And supposing I want to have him beat me?

M. Robert: Oh, well, then, I consent heartily.

Martine: What are you meddling for?

M. Robert: I was quite wrong.

Martine: Is it any business of yours?

M. Robert: No; no indeed.

Martine: Will you take a look at this butter-in, who wants to prevent husbands from beating their wives?

M. Robert: I take it all back.

Martine: Do you have some interest in the matter?

M. Robert: None at all.

Martine: Then why do you stick your nose in?

M. Robert: I'm sorry.

Martine: Mind your own business.

M. Robert: I will indeed.

Martine: I like to be beaten.

M. Robert: Excellent.

Martine: It doesn't hurt you any.

M. Robert: Quite right.

Martine: And you're a fool to come meddling in things which are no affair of yours.

(Martine slaps Monsieur Robert's face. Monsieur Robert escapes her, runs to center, and is confronted by Sganarelle.)

M. Robert: Comrade, with all my heart I ask your pardon. Go ahead, beat and drub your wife properly. I will help you, if you like.

(During the following dialogue, Sganarelle forces Monsieur Robert backward, threateningly, paralleling the previous business with Martine.)

Sganarelle: But I don't like.

M. Robert: Oh, well, that's different.

Sganarelle: I want to beat her if I want to; and I don't want to beat her if I don't want to.

M. Robert: Splendid!

Sganarelle: She's my wife; she isn't your wife.

M. Robert: That's right.

Sganarelle: You can't give me any orders.

M. Robert: I agree; I agree.

Sganarelle: I don't need any help from you.

M. Robert: Absolutely not.

Sganarelle: And you're an insolent meddler, to come and interfere in other people's affairs. Learn that Cicero says: "Put not the bark between thy finger and the tree."° *(Sganarelle beats Monsieur Robert, and drives him off the stage. He returns to Martine.)* Well now, let's make peace. Shake hands.

Martine: Yes, indeed! After beating me that way!

Sganarelle: That's nothing. Shake hands.

Martine: I don't want to.

Sganarelle: Eh?

Martine: No.

Sganarelle: My sweet little wife!

Martine: I won't.

Sganarelle: Oh, come on!

Martine: Nothing of the sort.

Sganarelle: Come on, come on!

Martine: No. I'd rather be angry.

Sganarelle: What, for just a trifle? Come on!

Martine: Let me alone.

Sganarelle: Shake hands, I tell you.

Martine: You hurt me too much.

Sganarelle: All right then, I ask your pardon. Give me your hand.

Martine: Oh, very well. I pardon you. *(Aside)* But you'll pay for it!

Sganarelle: You're silly to take the matter seriously. Those little flare-ups are sometimes necessary to true friendship; and five or six good wallops, between lovers, merely stimulate affection. Now I'm off to the woods. I promise to bring in today more than a hundred bundles of kindling wood.   *(Exit Sganarelle.)*

Martine: Well, no matter how I pretend, I can't forget how you hurt me. I'd like to find a good way to punish you for that beating. I know that a

---

Cicero says, "Put not the bark . . . tree": Sganarelle misquotes the popular proverb, "Don't put your finger between the tree and the bark," meaning, "Don't stick your nose into things that are none of your business." It is doubtful that this proverb can be found in the works of Cicero, Roman philosopher and orator.

woman always has a way to take revenge on her husband. But that's too dainty a punishment for that scalawag; it wouldn't be satisfaction enough for the way he's treated me. I want a revenge he'll feel down to his bones.

(Enter Valère and Lucas. They do not immediately perceive Martine.)

Lucas: By gosh and by gum! Ain't that a queer job we took on! I be switched if I know how she's going to turn out.

Valère: Well, Uncle Lucas, what can we do? We have to obey our master. And besides, we both have an interest in the recovery of his daughter, the young mistress. No doubt we'll get some good presents at her marriage, which is postponed by her illness. Horace is quite likely to be accepted as a suitor, and he's free with his money. And although she has shown her preference for a certain Léandre, you know very well that her father has always refused to accept him as a son-in-law.

Martine (who has been absorbedly meditating, without noticing Valère and Lucas): I wonder if I can't cook up some scheme to get my revenge.

Lucas: But what kind of fool idea has the master took into his noodle, now the doctors say they're all up a tree?

Valère: Well, sometimes, by just hunting, one finds unexpected help; and often among simple people in out-of-the-way places . . .

Martine: Yes, I'm going to get my revenge, at any price. Those cudgel blows still smart; I won't stand for them. *(In her distraction, she bumps into the newcomers)* Oh, gentlemen, I ask your pardon. I didn't see you; I was trying to think out an answer to some troubles of mine.

Valère: Everyone has his troubles in this world. In fact, we were trying to find an answer to some troubles of our own.

Martine: Would it be anything I could help you in?

Valère: Possibly. We are trying to find a gifted man, a special sort of doctor, who might bring some relief to our master's daughter. She has been attacked by a disease which suddenly deprived her of all power of speech. Several physicians have already exhausted all their science on her. But sometimes one runs across people who possess some wonderful secrets of nature, certain special remedies, which accomplish what the regular doctors can't do. That's what we're looking for.

Martine (aside): Heaven inspires me with a great idea for getting revenge on my rapscallion husband! *(Aloud)* You couldn't land on a better person to give you a tip. There's a fellow around here who is just wonderful for desperate cases.

Valère: Do tell me, where could we find him?

Martine: You can find him now in that little wood over yonder. He's amusing himself by cutting wood.

Lucas: A doctor cutting wood!

Valère: Amusing himself by gathering herbs, you mean?

Martine: No; he's a very peculiar man who enjoys doing that. He's queer, fantastic, crotchety; you'd never take him for what he is. He goes around dressed in funny old clothes, and sometimes he pretends to be ignorant; he keeps all his knowledge hidden, and he always hates to exercise the marvelous talents for medicine which heaven has given him.

Valère: It's a remarkable thing that great men always have some fantasticality, some little touch of folly mingled with their knowledge.

Martine: This man's folly is greater than you'd believe. Sometimes it goes so far that he has to be beaten before he'll admit his abilities; and I warn you that if he's in that mood you'll never make him admit he's a doctor, unless you both take sticks and pound him well until he finally confesses what he'll hide from you at first. That's what we do around here when we need his services.

Valère: What a strange folly!

Martine: True enough; but afterwards, you'll see that he can do real marvels.

Valère: What's his name?

Martine: His name is Sganarelle. It's easy to recognize him. He has a big black beard, and he wears a ruff, and a green and yellow coat.

Lucas: Green and yaller! He's a doctor for parrots, then?°

Valère: But is it really true that he's so clever as all that?

Martine: Why, he's a man who works miracles! Six months ago there was a woman here given up by all the other doctors. They thought she was dead, and were getting ready to lay her out. And six hours afterwards the man I'm telling about was dragged in by main strength. He looked her over and put a little drop of something or other in her mouth, and right away she got up off her bed and started walking around the room as if nothing had happened.

Lucas: Aha!

Valère: It must have been a drop of potable gold°.

Martine: You may be right. And only three weeks ago a twelve-year-old boy fell down from the top of the belfry, and he landed on the pavement and broke his arms, his legs, and his head. Well, as soon as they brought in this fellow, he rubbed the boy all over with a certain ointment he knows how to make. And immediately the boy stood right up, and ran off to shoot marbles.

Lucas: Aha!

Valère: That man must have the universal panacea.

Martine: No doubt about it.

Lucas: By gee and by golly! That's just the man we're alookin' for. Let's go git him.

Valère: We are much obliged to you for your useful suggestion.

Martine: But anyhow, remember the warning I gave you.

Lucas: Dad-burn and dad-blast! Trust us! If all he needs is a beating up, we've got the pig in the poke.   *(Exit Martine.)*

Valère: We were very lucky to run into that good woman. She really gives me some high hopes.

(Enter Sganarelle, *brandishing a bottle and singing.)*

Sganarelle: La, la, la.

Valère: I heard someone cutting wood; and now he's singing.

---

a doctor for parrots, then? Sganarelle's garb seems unlike that of doctors, who traditionally dressed in black.

potable gold: Gold dust suspended in a liquid, taken by the spoonful, was long prescribed as medicine.

Sganarelle: La, la, la . . . That's enough work for a while. Let's take a little breather. *(He drinks)* Nothing like woodcutting to dry a man out. *(He sings)*

> Oh, how pretty
> Is my little brown jug!
> Oh, how pretty
> Is your glug-glug-glug!
> But everybody else would be jealous of me
> If you were always as full as can be;
> So little brown jug, let me give you a hug,
> Turn your pretty bottom up, little brown jug!

God's truth, we must defend ourselves against morbid melancholia.

Valère: That's the man himself.

Lucas: I reckon you're right; we've landed smack onto him.

Valère: Let's get closer.

Sganarelle: Naughty little bottle! How I love my little cutie! *(Perceives Lucas and Valère; watches them, turning alternately toward one and the other; lets his voice die away)* Everybody else . . . would be . . . jealous of me . . . What the devil! Have those fellows got it in for somebody?

Valère: That's the man, certainly.

Lucas: It's his spit and image, like they told us.

Sganarelle: They are whispering to each other. What's the idea?

(He puts his bottle on the ground. As Valère makes him a deep bow, Sganarelle suspects him of designs on the bottle, whisks it to the other side. When Lucas makes a similar bow, Sganarelle seizes the bottle and holds it against his stomach.)

Valère: I beg your pardon, sir. Aren't you the gentleman named Sganarelle?

Sganarelle: What's all this?

Valère: I am asking you if your name isn't Sganarelle.

Sganarelle (after making a close inspection of Valère, and then of Lucas): Well, yes and no. Depends on what you want.

Valère: All we want is to pay him our warmest respects.

Sganarelle: In that case, my name is Sganarelle.

Valère: Sir, we are delighted to meet you. We have been referred to you for our present purposes; so we have come to implore your assistance in our present need.

Sganarelle: If it is something, gentlemen, which pertains to my little business, I am prepared to render you every service.

Valère: Sir, you are all too kind. But, sir, put on your hat, I beg you; you might find the sunshine too strong.

Lucas: Yes, kindly put your lid on.

Sganarelle (aside): Polite, anyhow.

Valère: Sir, you must not find it strange that we have recourse to you. Men of ability are always sought out; and we have been informed of your exceptional capacities.

Sganarelle: It is true, gentlemen, that I am probably the first man in the world in the kindling-wood line.

Valère: Ah, sir —

Sganarelle: I spare no pains or trouble. I go so far as to say that no criticism of my kindling wood is possible.

Valère: Sir, that matter is not in question.

Sganarelle: But observe that I sell it at a hundred and ten sous for a hundred sticks.

Valère: We needn't discuss that.

Sganarelle: I assure you that I can't give it to you for less.

Valère: Sir, we have been informed —

Sganarelle: If you have been informed, you know that that is the price.

Valère: Sir, please don't be ridiculous.

Sganarelle: Nothing ridiculous about it. I can't take off a penny.

Valère: Let's take another approach —

Sganarelle: Of course you can get it cheaper elsewhere. There is kindling wood and kindling wood. But as for my kindling wood —

Valère: Sir, let's drop this subject —

Sganarelle: I swear to you that you can't have it for a farthing less.

Valère: Damn!

Sganarelle: No, on my conscience, that's the price you'll have to pay. I am speaking with all sincerity, and I'm not the kind of man who would overcharge.

Valère: Why, sir, should a person like you indulge in these clumsy pretenses? Why degrade yourself to talk in such a way? Why should a learned man, a physician like you, try to disguise himself before the public, and keep his great talents hidden?

Sganarelle (aside): He's crazy.

Valère: Sir, kindly do not dissimulate with us.

Sganarelle: What?

Lucas: No use fiddlin' around with us; we know what's what.

Sganarelle: What! What are you trying to give me? What do you take me for?

Valère: We take you for what you are: a great physician.

Sganarelle: Physician yourself. I'm no physician, and I never have been.

Valère (to Lucas): There's his mania. *(To Sganarelle)* Sir, kindly make no further denials. Do not force us to extreme and painful measures.

Sganarelle: What do you mean?

Valère: To expedients which would be distressing to us.

Sganarelle: 'Struth! Use any expedients you like. I'm not a physician, and I don't know what you're talking about.

Valère (to Lucas): I can see that we'll have to employ the usual system. *(To Sganarelle)* Once more, sir, I beg you to admit you are what you are.

Lucas: Gol-ding and gol-darn! No more messin' around! Come clean and spit it out and say you're a doctor!

Sganarelle (aside): They give me a pain!

Valère: Why deny what everyone knows?

Lucas: What's the use of all this flimflam? What good does it do you?

Sganarelle: Gentlemen, I tell you simply and flatly: I am not a doctor.

Valère: You are not a doctor?

Sganarelle: No.

Lucas: You ain't no doctor?

Sganarelle: No, I tell you.

Valère: Since you insist, we'll have to go through with it.

(Valère and Lucas pick up sticks and beat Sganarelle.)

Sganarelle: Oh, oh, oh! Gentlemen, I am anything you like!

Valère: Why, sir, do you oblige us to resort to this violence?

Lucas: Why do you bullyrag us into beating you up?

Valère: Let me assure you of my profoundest regrets.

Lucas: B'jeez, I'm sorry, Doc.

Sganarelle: What the devil is all this, anyway? Is it a joke? Or are you both crazy, to insist I'm a doctor?

Valère: What? You still won't surrender? You won't admit you're a doctor?

Sganarelle: Like the devil I'm a doctor!

Lucas: It ain't true you're a doc, hey?

Sganarelle: No, plague take me! *(Valère and Lucas beat Sganarelle)* Oh, oh! All right, gentlemen, all right! I'm a doctor, if that's what you want! I'm a physician, and an apothecary too, if you like. I'll consent to everything rather than be beaten to death.

Valère: Why, that's excellent, sir. I am delighted to see you in a reasonable mood.

Lucas: I sure am tickled to hear you talk thataway.

Valère: I ask your most sincere pardon.

Lucas: Please excuse me for takin' the liberty.

Sganarelle (aside): Hey, hey! Maybe I'm the one who was mistaken! Maybe I've become a doctor without knowing it.

Valère: Sir, you will have no reason to regret revealing your true self. I am sure you will have every reason for satisfaction.

Sganarelle: But, gentlemen, tell me, couldn't you be mistaken yourselves? Is it quite certain that I'm a physician?

Lucas: Yes, by ding and by dog!

Sganarelle: Honestly?

Valère: Unquestionably.

Sganarelle: The devil take me if I knew it!

Valère: What do you mean? You're the cleverest doctor on earth!

Sganarelle: Aha!

Lucas: A doc who's cured I don't know how many ails and complaints.

Sganarelle: Bless my soul!

Valère: A woman was considered dead for six hours; they were ready to lay her out, when you gave her a drop of something and she came to and began walking around the room.

Sganarelle: I'll be hanged!

Lucas: A twelve-year-old boy fell down off the top of a belfry, and he got his arms and legs and head busted; and you put some kind of salve onto him, and he stood right up on his feet and went off and shot marbles!

Sganarelle: Marbles!

Valère: In short, sir, you will be well satisfied with our treatment; and you will earn whatever you like, if you let us take you to a certain place.

Sganarelle: I will earn whatever I like?

Valère: Yes.

Sganarelle: Oho! I'm a physician! No question about it. It had slipped my mind; but now I remember. What is the trouble? Where do we have to go?

Valère: We'll take you there. We are to see a girl who has lost her speech.

Sganarelle: Faith, I haven't found it.

Valère: He likes his little joke. Come on, sir.

Sganarelle: Without a doctor's gown?

Valère: We'll get one.

Sganarelle (solemnly presents his bottle to Valère): Take that. That's what I keep my potions in. *(Turns to Lucas; spits on the ground)* Now, you walk in front. Doctor's orders.

Lucas: By gosh and by golly! There's the kind of doctor I like! I think he'll do all right, because he's funny°.

ACT II

A room in Géronte's house. Géronte, Valère, Lucas, and Jacqueline are discovered.

Valère: Yes, sir, I think you will be satisfied. We have brought you the greatest physician on earth.

Lucas: Yes, by dad and by dang; he's a feller who can't be beat. All the others ain't knee-high to him.

Valère: He's a man who has made some marvelous cures.

Lucas: He even cured some who was dead.

Valère: He's a little eccentric, as I told you. And sometimes he has spells when his wits wander and he doesn't seem quite himself.

Lucas: Yes, he likes to be funny; and sometimes, pardon the liberty, you might say he'd been hit on the head with an ax.

Valère: But under it all, he's a man of profound knowledge. Sometimes he says some very remarkable things.

Lucas: When he puts his mind to it, he spits it out as if he was reading right off a book.

Valère: His reputation has spread about the region, and everyone goes to consult him.

Géronte: I am dying to see him. Bring him to me right away.

Valère: I'll go and fetch him. *(Exit Valère.)*

Jacqueline: Land's sake, sir, this man won't do no more than the others. It'll be six of one and half a dozen of the other. The best medicine you could give your daughter, if you'll heed me, would be a fine likely husband she'd be sweet on.

Géronte: Well, well, my good nurse! You have a lot of opinions to express!

Lucas: Shut up, old girl! You got no call to stick your nose in.

Jacqueline: I vow and declare that all these doctors won't do no more good than so much plain water; and your daughter needs something else than rhubarb and senna; and a husband is a poultice who cures all a young girl's troubles.

Géronte: Is she in any state now to be saddled with a husband, with her present

---

because he's funny: Some critics see in this phrase a reference to Molière's pique at the relative ill success of *The Misanthrope* [Translator's note].

affliction? And when I proposed to marry her off, didn't she oppose my wishes?

Jacqueline: Sure and certain she did. You wanted to rig her out with a husband she couldn't abide. Why didn't you pick that Monsieur Léandre she was crazy about? She would have been fine and obedient; and I bet you he'd take her right now, the way she is, if you wanted to give her to him.

Géronte: That Léandre is not the right person. He is much poorer than the other man.

Jacqueline: He's got a rich uncle, and he's the heir.

Géronte: All these great expectations seem to me very chancy. There's nothing like having your own money in your own hands. It's very risky to count on property which someone else intends for you. Death doesn't always listen to the prayers and pleas of the heirs; and a man has time to starve, while he is waiting for someone else to die so that he may live his own life.

Jacqueline: Well, I've always heard folks tell that in marriage, like in everything else, it's better to be happy than rich. Fathers and mothers have that confounded habit of always asking "How much has he got?" and "How much has she got?" Old Uncle Pierre married his daughter Simonette to big Thomas because he had a quarter of a vineyard more than young Robin, who she'd set her heart on. And now the poor critter has turned as yellow as a lemon, and she ain't been hearty and chipper since. There's a fine example for you, sir. All we've got in this world is our pleasure; and I'd rather give my daughter to a good husband she'd cotton to than have all the farms of La Beauce°.

Géronte: Pest and plague! My good nurse, how your tongue runs away with you! Silence, please! You take too much interest in my affairs; and you'll curdle your milk.

Lucas (to Jacqueline): By heck and by hang! Shut up! You're too fresh and uppity! *(Tapping smartly on Géronte's breast)* Master here ain't got no call for your advice; he knows what he's got to do. You stick to giving the baby a good suck, and don't go in for argufyin'. Master here is the father of his own daughter, and he's got sense enough to see what's good for her.

Géronte: Easy there! Take it easy!

Lucas: Master, sir, I want to mortify her a little and teach her fittin' respect.

Géronte: Yes, but you don't need such vivid demonstrations.

  (Enter Valère.)

Valère: Sir, prepare yourself. Here is our doctor coming in.

  (Enter Sganarelle, in a doctor's gown, with a tall pointed hat.)

Géronte: Sir, I am delighted to see you in my house. We are in great need of your services.

Sganarelle: Hippocrates says . . . that we should both put on our hats.

Géronte: Hippocrates says that?

Sganarelle: Yes.

Géronte: In what chapter, if you please?

La Beauce: region around Chartres, one of the richest agricultural districts in France.

Sganarelle: In his chapter on hats.

Géronte: Since Hippocrates says to, we must do it.

Sganarelle: Doctor, having learned of the marvelous things —

Géronte: Whom are you addressing, if you please?

Sganarelle: You.

Géronte: I'm not a doctor.

Sganarelle: You aren't a doctor?

Géronte: No, really.

Sganarelle (takes a stick and beats him): Positively?

Géronte: Positively! Oh, oh, oh!

Sganarelle: You're a doctor now. That's the only diploma I ever had.

Géronte (to Valère): What kind of madman have you brought me?

Valère: Well, I told you he was a rather whimsical doctor.

Géronte: Yes; but deuce take his whimsicalities.

Lucas: Don't pay it no mind, sir; it's just his fun.

Géronte: I don't like that kind of fun.

Sganarelle: Sir, I ask your pardon for the liberty I took.

Géronte: I am at your service, sir.

Sganarelle: I am sorry.

Géronte: Not at all, not at all.

Sganarelle: The little beating up —

Géronte: No harm was done.

Sganarelle: — which I had the honor to bestow upon you —

Géronte: Let's drop the subject. Sir, I have a daughter who has fallen into a strange illness.

Sganarelle: I am overjoyed, sir, that your daughter has some need of me. I could go farther, and wish with all my heart that you also needed me, you and your entire family, so that I might give evidence of my eagerness to be of use to you.

Géronte: I am much obliged to you for your kind attentions.

Sganarelle: I assure you that I speak with the utmost sincerity.

Géronte: You do me too much honor.

Sganarelle: What is your daughter's name?

Géronte: Lucinde.

Sganarelle: Lucinde! There is an excellent name for medication! Lucinde!

Géronte: I'll go and see what she is up to.

Sganarelle: Who is that fine big woman?

Géronte: She is the wet nurse of my small boy.   *(Exit Géronte.)*

Sganarelle: Pest and pox! What a handsome article! Ah, wet nurse, charming wet nurse, all my medicine is the very humble slave of your wet-nursery! How I should like to be the fortunate little babe who is imbibing the milk of your good graces! *(He pats her breast)* All my remedies, all my knowledge, all my capacities are at your service, and —

Lucas: With your kind permission, Doctor, sir, leave my wife be, if you please.

Sganarelle: What! She's your wife?

Lucas: Yes.

Sganarelle (opens his arms, preparatory to embracing Lucas, but turns and enclasps Jacqueline): Oh, really, I didn't know that, but I'm delighted, for the love of you both.

Lucas (pulling at Sganarelle): Take it easy, if you please.

Sganarelle: I assure you that I rejoice that we are thus bound together. *(He starts to embrace Lucas, dodges, throws his arms about Jacqueline)* I felicitate her for having such a husband as you; and I felicitate you for having such a beautiful and modest wife, and so well built.

Lucas (pulling at Sganarelle): By gum and by gravy! No more compliments, I pray and plead.

Sganarelle: Don't you want me to rejoice with you about your happy marriage?

Lucas: With me, all you like; but with my wife, you needn't be so dum polite.

Sganarelle: But I am equally concerned with the happiness of both of you. *(Same business)* And if I embrace you to demonstrate my joy, I must, in all fairness, make the same demonstration to her.

Lucas (pulling him again): By jeez and by jingo! Doctor, what a lot of blather!

(Enter Géronte.)

Géronte: Doctor, my daughter will be here in a moment.

Sganarelle: I await her, sir, with all my medicines at hand.

Géronte: Where are they?

Sganarelle (tapping his forehead): Here.

Géronte: Very good.

Sganarelle (trying to feel Jacqueline's breast): But as I take a deep interest in the entire family, I must test your nurse's milk, and I must therefore examine her breast.

Lucas (pulling Sganarelle away and making him spin around): Not on your life; we won't have no truck with that.

Sganarelle: It is a physician's business to inspect the nurses' breasts.

Lucas: None of that business here, thanking you kindly.

Sganarelle: Are you so brazen as to oppose a medical man? Out! Away!

Lucas: I don't care a hoot.

Sganarelle (menacingly): I shall give you a case of fever!

Jacqueline (takes Lucas by the arm, and spins him around): Get out! Ain't I big enough to stand up for myself, if he tries to do something that ain't right?

Lucas: I don't want him to go pawing you.

Sganarelle: Shame on the jealous rascal!

Géronte: Here comes my daughter.

(Enter Lucinde.)

Sganarelle: Is this the patient?

Géronte: Yes. She is my only daughter, and I should be heartbroken if she should die.

Sganarelle: She'd better not; she can't die without a doctor's prescription.

Géronte: Come, bring a chair for the doctor.

Sganarelle: There is a patient who is by no means repulsive. I think that a sound man could put up with her very nicely.

(Lucinde laughs.)

Géronte: You made her laugh, sir.

Sganarelle: Excellent. When the doctor makes the patient laugh at him, that's a very good sign. *(To Lucinde)* Well now, what's the trouble? What's the matter with you? Do you feel any pains?

Lucinde (pointing to her mouth, head, and throat): Ank, eek, onk, ank.

Sganarelle: What did you say?

Lucinde (gesturing): Ank, eek, onk, ank, ank, eek, onk.

Sganarelle: How's that?

Lucinde: Ank, eek, onk.

Sganarelle (imitating her): Ank, eek, onk, ank, ank. I don't get you. What the devil kind of language is that?

Géronte: Monsieur, that is just her trouble. She has become dumb, and so far no one has been able to discover the cause. Her misfortune has caused the postponement of her marriage.

Sganarelle: What for?

Géronte: The man she is to marry wants to wait for her to be cured before concluding the affair.

Sganarelle: And who is the fool who doesn't want his wife to be dumb? I wish to God mine had that disease! I'd take good care not to cure her.

Géronte: Anyway, sir, we beg you to make all your best efforts to relieve her of her malady.

Sganarelle: Don't worry. Tell me, does this illness distress her very much?

Géronte: Yes, sir.

Sganarelle: Good. Does she feel much pain?

Géronte: Very much.

Sganarelle: Splendid! Does she go — you know where?

Géronte: Yes.

Sganarelle: Copiously?

Géronte: As to that, I am unable to say.

Sganarelle: The results are . . . salubrious?

Géronte: I am unfamiliar with such matters.

Sganarelle (to Lucinde): Give me your arm . . . There is a pulse which indicates . . . that your daughter is dumb.

Géronte: Why yes, sir, that is exactly her trouble. You discovered it immediately.

Sganarelle: Aha!

Jacqueline: Look how quick he guessed it!

Sganarelle: A really good doctor knows things right away. An ignoramus would have been confused; he would have said, "Maybe it's this, maybe it's that." But I go right to the heart of the matter, and I tell you that your daughter is dumb.

Géronte: Yes; but I wish you could tell me how that comes about.

Sganarelle: Nothing is easier. That comes from the fact that she has lost her power of speech.

Géronte: Very good. But what, if you please, is the cause of her losing her power of speech?

Sganarelle: All the best authors will tell you . . . that it is an obstruction to the tongue's action.

Géronte: But further, what is your opinion about this obstruction to the tongue's action?

Sganarelle: Aristotle, on that head, says . . . some very fine things.

Géronte: I can well believe it.

Sganarelle: Oh, he was a big man!

Géronte: Assuredly.

Sganarelle (raising his arm): A really big man! Bigger than me — by so much. To return to our diagnosis, then, I maintain that this obstruction to the tongue's action is caused by certain humors, which we scientists call peccant humors°. Peccant, that is to say . . . peccant humors. Since the vapors caused by the exhalation of the influences which arise in the diseased area, arriving . . . you might say . . . at . . . Do you understand Latin?

Géronte: Not a word.

Sganarelle (jumping up): You don't understand Latin?

Géronte: No.

Sganarelle (gesturing): Cabricias arci thuram, catalamus, singulariter, nominativo haec Musa — or "the Muse" — bonus, bona, bonum, Deus sanctus, estne oratio latinas? Etiam, yes. Quare — why? Quia substantivo et adjectivum concordat in generi, numerum, et casus°.

Géronte: Oh, why did I never study?

Jacqueline: There's a smart man for you!

Lucas: Yes, that's so grand I don't catch on to a single word.

Sganarelle: Now these vapors I refer to, making a passage from the left side, where the liver is, to the right side, where the heart is, it comes about that the lungs, which we call in Latin *armyan,* having a communication with the brain, which we term in Greek *nasmus,* by means of the vena cava, which we denominate in Hebrew *cubile,* encounter on their path the aforesaid vapors, which fill the ventricles of the scapula; and because the aforesaid vapors — give close heed to this argument, please — because the aforesaid vapors have a certain malignity — I beg you to pay the closest attention.

Géronte: Yes.

Sganarelle: Because they have a certain malignity, which is caused — I must ask you to be attentive —

Géronte: Oh, I am.

Sganarelle: — which is caused by the acridity of the humors engendered in the concavity of the diaphragm, it then happens that the vapors — ossabundus, nequeys, nequer, potarinum, quipsa milus. And that is exactly how it comes about that your daughter is dumb.

Jacqueline: Oh, wasn't that lovely, husband!

Lucas: Why ain't I got that gift of gab!

Géronte: I am sure that no one could argue the case better. There is just one thing that bothers me: the position of the liver and the heart. It seems to me that you place them wrongly; and the heart is on the left side, and the liver on the right.

Sganarelle: Yes, that is the way it used to be. But we have changed all that; now we use an entirely new method in medicine.

---

peccant humors: In ancient medicine, the humors are four elemental fluids that make up the body, determining by their balance or imbalance one's state of health. *Peccant* means "sinning." Sganarelle, of course, is making up his own jargon.

Cabricias . . . casus: The first four words belong to no language; the rest is garbled Latin. The last word, *casus,* means both "case" and "fall." In the original production, Molière, playing Sganarelle, in giving this speech worked himself up to a frenzy and on the last word flung himself into a chair, which fell over backward.

Géronte: Oh, I didn't know that. I ask your pardon for my ignorance.

Sganarelle: No harm done. You aren't obliged to be as well informed as we are.

Géronte: Assuredly. But, sir, what do you think we ought to do for this disease?

Sganarelle: What I think we ought to do?

Géronte: Yes.

Sganarelle: My opinion is that we should put her back to bed, and give her as treatment a quantity of bread soaked in wine.

Géronte: Why is that, sir?

Sganarelle: Because in wine and bread united there is a sympathetic virtue which makes people talk. Don't you know that that is what they give parrots, and thus they learn to speak?

Géronte: That's true. Oh, the great man! Quick! Get some bread and wine!

Sganarelle: I will come back this evening and see how she's doing. *(Exit Lucinde and Lucas. Jacqueline starts to go; Sganarelle stops her)* Wait a minute, you. *(To Géronte)* Sir, there is a wet nurse who needs some of my little remedies.

Jacqueline: Who, me? I'm feeling fine.

Sganarelle: That's bad, nurse, very bad. Such good health is alarming. It wouldn't be a bad idea to give you a nice little bloodletting, or a nice little emollient enema.

Géronte: But, sir, that is something I don't understand. Why should you be bled when you aren't sick?

Sganarelle: Never mind; it's a very salutary system. As we drink for fear of being thirsty, we should be bled for the illness which hasn't yet arrived°. That's preventive medicine.

Jacqueline: Land's sakes, I won't have none of that. I don't want to turn my body into no drug store.

Sganarelle: You are rebellious toward medicine; but we'll get you down in the end. *(Exit Jacqueline)* I bid you good day, sir.

Géronte: Wait a minute, please.

Sganarelle: What do you want to do?

Géronte: Give you some money, sir.

Sganarelle (hoisting his gown and thrusting his hand backward, as Géronte opens his purse): I won't take money, sir.

Géronte: But, sir —

Sganarelle: Not at all.

Géronte: But just a moment!

Sganarelle: By no means.

Géronte: But please!

Sganarelle: Don't be absurd.

Géronte: There you are.

Sganarelle: I'll do nothing of the sort.

Géronte: Oh!

Sganarelle: Money is not my motive.

Géronte: I believe you.

Sganarelle (weighing the coins): They aren't short weight?

Géronte: No, sir.

---

bled . . . arrived: To induce bleeding was thought to promote health.

Sganarelle: I am not a mercenary physician.

Géronte: I am well aware of it.

Sganarelle: I don't seek personal advantage.

Géronte: I never had such an idea.

(Exit Géronte. Sganarelle brings his hand forward and looks at the money.)

Sganarelle: Well, not so bad, not so bad! If only —

(Enter Léandre.)

Léandre: Sir, I have been watching my chance to see you for a long time. I have come to implore your assistance.

Sganarelle (seizing Léandre's wrist): The pulse is very bad.

Léandre: I am not sick, sir; that is not my reason for coming to see you.

Sganarelle: If you aren't sick, why the devil didn't you say so?

Léandre: Please! To put it briefly, my name is Léandre, and I'm in love with Lucinde, whom you've just examined. And since I have no access to her, because of her father's animosity, I have ventured to ask you to aid my love, and to play a little trick, to give me the chance of saying to her a couple of words, on which my happiness and my life absolutely depend.

Sganarelle (angrily): What do you take me for? How do you dare address yourself to me to help you in a love affair, and to degrade the dignity of a physician to such base employments!

Léandre: Sir, please don't make so much noise!

Sganarelle (thrusting him backward): I'll make all the noise I like! You are an impertinent puppy!

Léandre: Calm down, sir.

Sganarelle: A blundering fool!

Léandre: Please, sir —

Sganarelle: I'll show you that I'm not that kind of a man, and it is the height of insolence —

Léandre (pulling out a purse and handing it to Sganarelle): But, sir —

Sganarelle: — to make such a proposition . . . I'm not referring to you personally, for you're a good fellow, and I should be delighted to do you a service. But there are some impertinent puppies around who misjudge people entirely; and I freely grant that that sort of thing makes me angry.

Léandre: I ask your pardon, sir, for the liberty —

Sganarelle: Not at all, not at all. What is the story?

Léandre: You must know then, sir, that this illness you are trying to cure is only pretended. The doctors have argued about it in due form. They have given their opinions; some say it comes from the brain; others, from the intestines, or from the spleen, or from the liver. But the fact is that love is the real cause, and that Lucinde has invented this affliction only to escape from a threatening marriage. But I am afraid we may be overseen together; let's leave this spot, and I'll tell you as we go what I want from you.

Sganarelle: Let's be on our way, sir. You have given me an almost inconceivable sympathy for your love. The patient will either die, or she'll be yours — or I'm no doctor.

ACT III

The scene is a sylvan° setting, near Géronte's house. (In modern stage productions the scene commonly remains the same as in Act II.) Léandre, disguised as an apothecary, and Sganarelle are discovered.

Léandre: It seems to me I'm rather good as an apothecary; and as the father never saw much of me, I think this gown and wig will be a sufficient disguise.

Sganarelle: By all means.

Léandre: The only thing is, I'd like to know a few big medical terms, to decorate my speech and make me sound professional.

Sganarelle: Go on, that's not necessary. All you need is the costume. In fact, I don't know any more than you do.

Léandre: What?

Sganarelle: I'm damned if I know anything about medicine! You're a good fellow, and I'm willing to confide in you, as you have confided in me.

Léandre: What! You aren't in fact —

Sganarelle: No, I tell you. I was kicked into the medical profession. I never had any idea of being a scholar; I didn't get beyond the third grade. I don't know how they got this maggot in their heads; but when I saw they were bound and determined that I was a physician, I decided to be one, no matter who got hurt. Still, you wouldn't believe how the idea has got around, and how pigheaded everybody is in taking me for a great healer. People come from all over to consult me. If things go on this way, maybe I'll stick to medicine for the rest of my life. I think it's the best trade there is, for whether you do well or badly, you get paid just the same. We never get blamed for doing a bad job; and we cut the cloth we work on to please ourselves. A cobbler making shoes can't spoil a piece of leather without paying for the damage; but in this job we can spoil a man without its costing us a penny. The blunders aren't our fault; they're always the fault of the man who dies. In short, the nice thing about this profession is that dead men have a most marvelous decency and discretion; you never hear a dead man complain of the doctor who killed him.

Léandre: It is true that the dead are uncommonly polite on this subject.

(Enter Thibaut and Perrin.)

Sganarelle: Here are some fellows who look as though they are coming for a consultation. You go and wait for me near your lady's house.

(Exit Léandre.)

Thibaut: Doctor, sir, me and my son, we've come to see you.

Sganarelle: What's the matter?

Thibaut: His poor mother, her name is Perrette, she's been sick abed going on now six months.

Sganarelle (thrusting out his hand): And what do you expect me to do about it?

Thibaut: We'd like for you to give us some little dohickus for to cure her.

Sganarelle: I'd have to know the kind of illness she has.

sylvan: wooded.

Thibaut: She's sick with hypocrisy, sir.

Sganarelle: Hypocrisy?

Thibaut: Yes; I mean to say she's all swole up; and they do tell it's a lot of seriosities she's got inside, and her liver, her stomach, her spleen, or what you may call it, is just amakin' water instead of blood. Every two days she gits the fever and shakes, with lastitudes and miseries in the leg mussicles. You can hear in her throat phlegm like to choke her, and now and then she has syncopations and compulsions, so I'm afeared she's goin' to pass away. We've got in our village a pothecary, pardon the expression, who has give her a lot of messes, and I've paid out more than a dozen good crowns in enemies, begging your pardon, and setatives to make her set better, and infections and cordialities. But all that, as the feller says, has just been water down the train. He wanted to give her a kind o' physic called a medic wine, but to tell you the honest truth, I was scared it would finish her. I hear tell the big doctors have killed off a terrible lot of folks with that invention°.

Sganarelle (irritably wiggling his thrust-out hand): Come to the point, my friend, come to the point.

Thibaut: The point is, sir, that we've come to ask you what we ought for to do.

Sganarelle: I don't understand you at all.

Perrin: Sir, my mother is ailing; and here's two crowns we've brung you to give us a cure.

Sganarelle: Ah, I understand you perfectly! There is a young man who speaks clearly, and knows how to express himself. You say your mother is ill with dropsy, that her whole body is swollen up, that she has fever, and pains in the legs, that she has syncopes and convulsions, or, that is, fainting fits?

Perrin: Oh, yes, sir, that's it perzackly.

Sganarelle: I understood you immediately. Your father doesn't know what he's talking about. And now you want a remedy?

Perrin: Yes, sir.

Sganarelle: A remedy to cure her?

Perrin: That's the way we kind o' look at it.

Sganarelle: Look, here's a piece of cheese you must make her swallow.

Perrin: Cheese, sir?

Sganarelle: Yes, it's a specially prepared cheese, with gold, coral, pearls, and other precious substances ground up in it.

Perrin: Sir, we are much beholden to you; we'll make her swaller it straight off.

Sganarelle: That's right. And if she dies, don't fail to give her the best possible burial.

(Exit Perrin and Thibaut. The scene changes to a room in Géronte's house, as in Act II. Enter Sganarelle and Jacqueline.)

Sganarelle: Ah, here is the lovely wet nurse! Ah, wet nurse of my heart, I am delighted to see you again! The vision of you is the rhubarb, cassia, and senna which purge all the melancholy of my soul!

I hear tell . . . that invention: The efficacy of emetic wine, containing antimony, was then a subject of fierce medical controversy [Translator's note].

Jacqueline: My stars alive! Doctor, sir, that's too fine talk for me, and I don't understand any of your Latin.

Sganarelle: Fall ill, nurse, I pray you. Fall ill, for love of me. I would be only too delighted to cure you.

(Enter Lucas. He approaches the speakers stealthily and unobserved.)

Jacqueline: Much obliged. I'd liefer not take none of your cures.

Sganarelle: How I pity you, fair wet nurse, for having such a jealous, troublesome husband!

Jacqueline: Ah, well, sir, it's penance for my sins. Where the goat is tied, there she has to graze.

Sganarelle: What, such a bumpkin, a hick! A man who watches you every minute, and won't let anyone even speak to you!

Jacqueline: Oh, dear, you ain't seen nothing yet. That's just a sample of his jealous turn of mind.

Sganarelle: Is it possible! That a man should have so base a character as to mistreat a person like you! Ah, lovely wet nurse, I know some people, not very far from here, who would think themselves happy even to kiss the sweet utensils of your trade! How could it happen that a beautiful creature like you should fall into such hands as his! That such a coarse lout, brutal, stupid, a fool — pardon me, nurse, if I speak in this way of your husband —

Jacqueline: Ah, sir, I know very well he deserves all them names.

Sganarelle: Yes, certainly, nurse, he deserves them. He would further deserve that you plant a certain adornment on his brow°, to punish him for his suspicions.

Jacqueline: It's true that if I only thought about what's good for him, he might drive me to some pretty goings-on.

Sganarelle: On my word, you wouldn't do badly to revenge yourself on him, with someone's help. He's the kind of man, I tell you, who deserves exactly that. And if, fair nurse, I were fortunate enough to be chosen as the instrument —

(Both become aware of Lucas's presence behind them. Both escape to opposite sides of the stage, and exit. Enter Géronte.)

Géronte: Hello, Lucas. You haven't seen our doctor around?

Lucas: Yes, by gee and by jiminy! I seen him, and my wife too!

Géronte: I wonder where he can be.

Lucas: I don't know; but I wisht he was in hell's fire.

Géronte: Go and find out what my daughter is doing.

(Exit Lucas. Enter Sganarelle and Léandre)

Ah, monsieur, I was just asking where you were.

Sganarelle: I was dallying in the courtyard. *(Aside)* Expelling the superfluity of my potations. *(Aloud)* And how is our patient doing?

Géronte: A little worse, since she took your medicine.

Sganarelle: Good; good! That's a sign it's working.

Géronte: Yes; but while it's working, I'm afraid it will undo her completely.

---

adornment on his brow: A deceived husband was said to wear horns.

Sganarelle: Don't worry. I have remedies which are proof against everything. I am waiting for her to come to her death agony.

Géronte: Who is that man with you?

Sganarelle (imitating an apothecary administering an enema): He's —

Géronte: What?

Sganarelle: He's the man —

Géronte: Eh?

Sganarelle: The man who —

Géronte: Oh, I understand.

Sganarelle: Your daughter will need him.

(Enter Lucinde and Jacqueline.)

Jacqueline (to Géronte): Sir, here's your daughter. She wants to walk around a bit.

Sganarelle: That will do her good. Apothecary, feel her pulse, while I discuss her illness with you, sir. *(Exit Jacqueline. Léandre draws Lucinde to one side of the stage. Sganarelle pulls Géronte to the other side, puts his arm over Géronte's shoulders, his hand under Géronte's chin. As Géronte tries to see what his daughter and Léandre are doing, Sganarelle turns Géronte's face toward his own. In current productions, Sganarelle resorts to every burlesque device to block Géronte's view, even standing on a chair and spreading his gown wide as a screen)* Sir, it is a great and subtle question among the learned, whether women are easier to cure than men. I beg you to listen attentively to this. Some say yes; others say no; and I say yes and no. Inasmuch as the incongruity of the opaque humors which are to be found in the natural temperament of women are the reason that the grosser nature forever attempts to overmaster the sensitive nature, we see that the variation of their opinions depends upon the oblique movement of the moon's circle; and as the sun, which casts its rays upon the concavity of the earth, finds —

Lucinde: No, I am entirely incapable of ever changing my feelings.

Géronte: My daughter is speaking! Oh, what power was in the remedy! Oh, what a wonderful doctor! How indebted I am to you, sir, for this marvelous cure! How can I reward you for your services!

Sganarelle (walking to and fro, and wiping his brow): There is a case which caused me a lot of trouble.

Lucinde: Yes, Father, I have recovered my power of speech; but I have recovered it in order to tell you that I will never have any other husband than Léandre, and there's no use in your trying to give me to Horace.

Géronte: But —

Lucinde: Nothing can shake my resolution.

Géronte: What —

Lucinde: You can argue all you please.

Géronte: If —

Lucinde: All your talk will do no good.

Géronte: I —

Lucinde: I have made up my mind about it.

Géronte: But —

Lucinde: There is no parental authority which can force me to marry in spite of myself.

Géronte: I have —

Lucinde: Do whatever you like; it's no good.

Géronte: He —

Lucinde: My heart can never submit to such tyranny.

Géronte: There —

Lucinde: And I will take refuge in a convent rather than marry a man I don't love.

Géronte: But —

Lucinde (in a deafening shout): No! By no manner of means! Absolutely not! You're wasting your time! I won't do it! It's all settled!

Géronte: What a flood of talk! I can't stand up against it. Doctor, I beg you to make her dumb again.

Sganarelle: That, I fear, is impossible. All I can do, to serve you, is to make you deaf, if you like.

Géronte: No, thanks. *(To Lucinde)* So you think —

Lucinde: No. All your arguments will do no good.

Géronte: You will marry Horace, and you will do it this very day.

Lucinde: I'll die first.

Sganarelle: Good Lord, stop! Let me medicate the affair. The woman is still sick, and I know the remedy we must employ.

Géronte: Is it possible, sir, that you can also cure this malady of the mind?

Sganarelle: Yes. Let me handle it. I have remedies for everything, and our apothecary will help in this cure. *(To Léandre)* A word with you. You perceive that her infatuation with Léandre is entirely contrary to her father's wishes, and that there is no time to lose; her humors are much inflamed, and it is necessary to find very promptly a remedy for this disease, which might easily get worse with delay. Personally, I see only one cure, which is a dose of purgative getawayum, which you will combine properly with two drachms of matrimonium in pill form. She may make some difficulty about taking this medicine, but as you're a clever man at your trade, you will have to persuade her, and make her swallow the dose the best way you can. Now you two go and take a turn around the garden, in order to prepare her humors, while I have a talk with her father. But above all don't lose time. The remedy, quickly, the panacea! *(Exit Léandre and Lucinde.)*

Géronte: Doctor, what are those drugs you just mentioned? I don't think I have ever heard of them.

Sganarelle: They are drugs one uses only in critical cases.

Géronte: Did you ever hear of such insolence as hers?

Sganarelle: Girls are sometimes a little headstrong.

Géronte: You can't imagine how mad she is about that Léandre.

Sganarelle: The heat of the blood has that effect on young minds.

Géronte: Ever since I discovered the violence of my daughter's attachment, I've kept her locked up.

Sganarelle: Very wise.

Géronte: And I've kept them from having any communication with each other.

Sganarelle: Excellent.

Géronte: If I'd allowed them to see each other, some folly would have resulted.

Sganarelle: No doubt.

Géronte: I think she'd have been capable of running away with him.

Sganarelle: Sensibly argued.

Géronte: I've been warned that he's been making all sorts of efforts to speak to her.

Sganarelle: The scoundrel!

Géronte: But he's wasting his time.

Sganarelle: Ha, ha!

Géronte: I'll keep him from seeing her, all right.

Sganarelle: He's not dealing with a simpleton. You know more tricks than he does. Anyone will have to get up early to catch you napping.

(*Enter Lucas.*)

Lucas: By cripes and by crikey, sir, hell's apoppin'! Your daughter has gone and run off with her Léandre! The pothecary, it was him; and that there doctor was the one who done the trick!

Géronte: What! I'm ruined! Call the police! Don't let him escape! Traitor! I'll have you punished by the law! 				(*Exit Géronte.*)

Lucas: Dad-burn, dad-blame, and dad-rot! Doctor, sir, you're going to git hung; so don't move.

(*Enter Martine.*)

Martine: Oh, dear, what a lot of trouble I had finding this house! (*To Lucas*) Why, how do you do? Tell me, what happened to the doctor I recommended to you?

Lucas: There he is, there. He's going to git hung.

Martine: What! My husband is going to get hung? Oh, dear! What did he do, then?

Lucas: He got our master's daughter kidnapped.

Martine: Alas, my dear husband, is it true they're going to hang you?

Sganarelle: Well, you see. Oh!

Martine: Are you going to let yourself die in front of everybody?

Sganarelle: And what can I do about it?

Martine: If you'd even finished cutting our wood, it would be some consolation.

Sganarelle: Get out of here; you're breaking my heart.

Martine: No, I'm going to stay in order to cheer you up. I won't leave until I've seen you hung.

Sganarelle: Ah!

(*Enter Géronte.*)

Géronte (to Sganarelle): The police chief will be here soon; they'll put you in a place where you'll be good and secure.

Sganarelle (kneeling, hat in hand): Alas! You couldn't change it to a little flogging?

Géronte: No, no; the law must take its course. But what's this?

(*Enter Léandre, Lucinde, and Jacqueline.*)

Léandre (to Géronte): Sir, I am Léandre, come to present myself to you, and to entrust Lucinde to your power. We had proposed to flee together, and to get married; but we have given up this purpose in favor of more honorable behavior. I do not wish to steal your daughter from you; I desire to receive her only from your own hands. I have further news for you, sir; I have just received letters informing me that my uncle is dead, and I inherit all his property.

Géronte (who has been threatening Léandre with a stick, now throws it away): Sir, your merits are most worthy of consideration; and I give you my daughter with the utmost joy.

Sganarelle: The art of medicine had a narrow escape.

Martine (to Sganarelle): Since you aren't going to be hung, do me the favor of being a doctor; I am the one who gained this honor for you.

Sganarelle: Yes, you are the one who gained me some fine beatings.

Léandre: The result is so happy that you shouldn't bear her any ill will.

Sganarelle: All right. I pardon you the beatings in consideration of the dignity to which you have elevated me. But prepare yourself from now on to treat with great respect a man of my importance; and remember that a doctor's anger is terrible!

Questions

ACT I

1. What sort of person is Sganarelle? How would you characterize his wife?
2. Describe the relationship between Sganarelle and Martine. How would you explain their negative reactions to Monsieur Robert, the neighbor who tries to intercede first for Martine and then for Sganarelle?
3. What motivates Martine to tell Valère and Lucas that her woodcutter husband is really a physician?

ACT II

1. How would you explain the high praise Valère and Lucas bestow upon Sganarelle when describing him to Géronte?
2. What opposing views do Géronte and Jacqueline express about marriage? What does their exchange suggest about the causes of Lucinde's malady? Are they right or wrong?
3. What, besides the money Léandre offers, motivates Sganarelle to hear the young man out?
4. What if anything does the byplay between Sganarelle and the wet nurse contribute to the story?

ACT III

1. The scene in which Thibault and Perrin appear is often omitted from modern productions of the play. What justification can you see for such an omission? What might any producer gain by leaving the scene in?
2. Do you think the play's pat ending a cop-out, or can it be justified?

General Questions

1. What two distinct stories are told in *The Physician in Spite of Himself*?
2. How does translator Morris Bishop make clear the difference in rank between the peasants and the higher-caste characters? In your opinion, how well does he succeed in making these differences funny?
3. To what extent does the play depend on verbal jokes? On slapstick and other visual humor?
4. Point to passages in which Molière satirizes physicians. Which of their alleged traits are targets for his sharpest barbs?

5. Bishop translates the play into American. The Irish playwright Lady Gregory translated it into rural Irish. If interested, see her *Collected Plays* IV, ed. Ann Saddlemyer (Gerrards Cross: Colin Smythe, 1971). In general, do you approve of this tendency to make Molière's characters citizens of the translator's country? Would Bishop have improved his version if he had omitted all touches of dialect and slang?
6. What in Molière's farce seems true to life? What seems improbable?
7. Do you think these improbabilities hurt the play? Why, or why not?

Suggestions for Writing

1. Write a critical appreciation of your favorite comedian, your favorite comedy film, or your favorite comedy show on television. Try to account for your admiration, and (if possible) for what makes your subject so risible.
2. "Comedy on Campus," or "Comedy in Everyday Life." This paper might depend on what you have observed lately. Give examples.
3. If you were cast in the role of Sganarelle or of Lucinde (the mute daughter) in *The Physician in Spite of Himself,* how would you prepare yourself to act the part? (You can vary this suggestion if you like, casting yourself as a different Molière character or as a character in a different comedy.)
4. Write a short word portrait of Prospero, Miranda, Caliban, or another character in *The Tempest,* summing up all that makes the character distinctive and memorable.
5. Compare and contrast Ariel, that strange supernatural character in *The Tempest,* with that strange supernatural character Death in *Death Knocks.* (For this writing task, a tone of grave seriousness is not essential.)
6. "Moments of Farce in *The Tempest.*" What do they contribute to the play?
7. Write a brief second act for *Death Knocks,* in which Death returns to Nat's place for another try — or perhaps attempts to corner Nat in a different setting. With a friend, give a reading of your script before the class. Invite audience reactions.

35 The Modern Theater

REALISM AND NONREALISM

As the twentieth century began, realism in the theaters of Western Europe, England, and America appeared to have won a resounding victory. (**Realism** in drama, like realism in fiction, may be broadly defined as an attempt to reproduce faithfully the surface appearance of life, especially that of ordinary people in everyday situations.) The theater had been slow to admit controversial or unpleasant themes, and slow to shed its trappings of Victorian romanticism. But now actors less often declaimed their passions in oratorical style in front of backdrops painted with waterfalls and volcanoes, while stationed exactly at the center of the stage as if to sing "duets meant to bring forth applause" (as Swedish playwright August Strindberg complained). By 1891 even Victorian London had witnessed a production of a play that frankly portrayed a man dying of venereal disease — Henrik Ibsen's *Ghosts.*

In the theater of realism, a room was represented by a **box set** — three walls that joined in two corners and a ceiling that tilted as if seen in perspective — replacing drapery walls that had billowed and doors that had flapped, not slammed. Instead of posing at stage-center to deliver key speeches, actors were instructed to speak from wherever the dramatic situation placed them, and now and then turn their backs upon the audience. They were to behave as if they lived in a room with the fourth wall sliced away, unaware that they had an audience.

This realistic convention is familiar to us today, not only from realistic plays but from the typical television soap opera or situation comedy that takes place in such a three-walled room, with every cup and spoon revealed by the camera. But such realism went against a long tradition. Watching a play by Sophocles, the spectators, we may safely assume, had to exert their imagination. We do not expect an ancient Greek tragedy literally to represent the lives of ordinary people in everyday situations. On the contrary a tragedy, according to Aristotle, its leading ancient theorist, represents an "action of supreme importance," an extraordinary moment in the life of a king or queen or other person of high estate. An open-air stage, though Sophocles adorned it with painted scenery, could hardly change day into night as lighting technicians commonly do today, nor aspire to reproduce in detail a whole palace. Such limitations prevail upon the theater of Shakespeare as well, encouraging the Bard to flesh out his scene with vivid language, making the spectator willing to imagine that the simple stage — the "wooden O" — is a forest, a stormswept landscape, or a battlefield. In the classic No theater of Japan, spectators recognize conventional props: a simple framework is a boat, four posts and a roof are a palace, an actor's fan may be any useful object — a paintbrush, say, or a knife. In such a nonrealistic theater, the playwright, unhampered by stage sets, can shift scenes as rapidly as the audience can imagine.

In the realistic three-walled room, actors could hardly rant (or, Hamlet said, "tear a passion to tatters") without seeming foolish. Another effect of more lifelike direction was to discourage use of such devices as the soliloquy and the **aside** (villain to audience: "Heh! heh! Now she's in me power!"). To encourage actors even further in imitating reality, the influential director Constantin Stanislavsky of the Moscow Art Theater developed his famous system to help actors feel at home inside a playwright's characters. One of Stanislavsky's exercises was to have actors search their memories for personal experiences like those of the characters in the play; another was to have the actors act out things a character did *not* do in the play but might do in life. The system enabled Stanislavsky to bring authenticity to his productions of Chekhov's plays and of Maxim Gorky's *The Lower Depths* (1902), a play that showed the tenants in a sordid lodging house drinking themselves to death (and hanging themselves) in surroundings of realistic squalor.

Gorky's play is a masterpiece of **naturalism**, a kind of realism in fiction and drama dealing with the more brutal or unpleasant aspects of reality. As codified by French novelist and playwright Émile Zola, who influenced Ibsen, naturalism viewed a person as a creature whose acts are determined by heredity and environment; and Zola urged writers to study their characters' behavior with the detachment of zoologists studying animals.

No sooner had realism and naturalism won the day than a reaction arose. One opposing force was the **Symbolist movement** in the French theater, most influentially expressed by Belgian playwright Maurice Maeterlinck. Like French Symbolist poets Charles Baudelaire and Stéphane Mallarmé, Maeterlinck assumes that the visible world reflects a spirit world we cannot directly perceive. Accordingly, his plays are filled with hints and portents: suggestive objects (jeweled rings, veils, distant candles), mysterious locales (crumbling castles, dim grottoes), vague sounds from afar, dialogue rich in silences and unfinished sentences. In *The Intruder*, (1890), a blind man sees the approach of Death. In *Pelléas and Mélisande* (1892) occurs a typical bit of Symbolist stage business: a small boy stands on his grandfather's shoulders to peer through a high window and speak of wonders invisible to an audience. (For more about symbolism and Symbolists, see Chapters Eight and Twenty-four.)

Elsewhere, others were working along similar lines. In Russia, Anton Chekhov, whose plays on the surface appeared realistic, built some of his best around a symbol *(The Seagull, The Cherry Orchard).* In Ireland, poet William Butler Yeats, who in 1899 had helped found the Irish Dramatic Movement, was himself of a different mind from the realistic playwrights whose work he had helped produce in Dublin's Abbey Theater. Drawing on Irish lore and legend, Yeats wrote (among other plays) "plays for dancers" to be performed in drawing rooms, often in friends' homes, with simple costumes and props, a few masked actors, and a very few musicians. In Sweden, August Strindberg, who earlier had won fame as a naturalist, reversed direction and in *The Dream Play* (1902) and *The Ghost Sonata* (1907) introduced characters who change their identities and, ignoring space and time, move across dreamlike landscapes. In these plays, Strindberg anticipated the movement called **expressionism** in German theater after World War I. Delighting in bizarre sets and exaggerated makeup and costuming, expressionist playwrights and producers sought to reflect intense states of emotion and, sometimes, to depict the world through lunatic eyes. A classic example (on film) is *The Cabinet of Dr. Caligari,* made in Berlin in 1919 – 1920, in which a hypnotist sends forth a subject to murder people. Garbed in jet black, the killer sleepwalks through a town of lopsided houses, twisted streets, and railings that tilt at gravity-defying angles. In expressionist movies and plays, madness is objectified, and dreams become realities.

In 1893 Strindberg had complained of producers who represented a kitchen by a drapery painted with pictures of kettles; but by 1900, realistic play production had gone to opposite extremes. In the 1920s the curtain rose upon a Broadway play with a detailed replica of a Schrafft's restaurant, complete to the last fork and folded napkin. (Still, critic George Jean Nathan remarked, no matter how elaborate a stage dinner, the table never seemed to have any butter.) Theaters housed increasingly complicated machines, making it all the easier to present scenes full of realistic detail. Elevators lifted heavy sets swiftly and quietly into place; other sets, at the touch of a button, revolved on giant turntables. Theaters became warehouses for huge ready-made scenery.

Some playwrights fought domination by the painstakingly realistic set. Bertolt Brecht in Germany and Luigi Pirandello in Italy conceived plays to be performed on bare stages — gas pipes and plaster in full view — to remind spectators that they beheld events in a theater, not in the world. In reaction against the traditional picture-frame stage (see p. 1059), theaters were designed, such as the **arena theater** or **theater in the round**, in which the audience sits on all four sides of the performing area; and the **flexible theater**, in which the seats are movable. Such theaters usually are not commercial (most of which maintain their traditional picture-frame stages, built decades ago). Rather, the alternative theaters are found in college and civic playhouses, in large cities, in storefronts, and in converted lofts. Proponents of arena staging claim that it brings actors and audience into greater intimacy; opponents, that it keeps the actors artificially circulating like goldfish in a bowl. Perhaps it is safe to say only that some plays lend themselves to being seen head-on in a picture frame; others, to being surrounded.

In recent years, some theater companies in America have questioned not only the value of the picture-frame stage, but the value of any stage at all. Such experimental groups follow in the footsteps of Antonin Artaud, French poet and playwright, whose collected manifestos, *The Theater and Its Double* (1938), argue for a theater without a stage, in which the spectacle takes place all around (and in the midst of) the spectators.[1] In the 1960s, according to one historian, "everything came into question: the place of the performer in the theater; the place of the audience; the function of the playwright and the usefulness of a written script; the structure of the playhouse, and later the need for any kind of playhouse; and finally, the continued existence of theater as a relevant force in a changing culture."[2] Young actors and playwrights joined **ensembles** (companies of amateurs or semiprofessionals working together to create new plays, sometimes living together in a commune). Some ensembles offered plays anywhere they could: in streets, in parks, on rooftops, in parking lots, even in laundromats. Unlike traditional plays, such works obviously sought to shatter the boundary between actors and audience, and to attain such realism that the play can hardly be distinguished from the stream of passing life. At one performance of the Firehouse Theater, the audience was invited to take part:

> "Would you like to see Faust or be Faust?" Those who chose to "see" Faust kept their roles as spectators. Those who chose to "be" Faust were enclosed in a vast communal bedsheet, given a powdered soap with which to perform a ritual hand-washing of one another, and then brought into close physical contact for up to thirty minutes as they swayed back and forth to an om-like chant.[3]

Ensembles, though some have been pretentious, at least have recalled that drama can be a kind of ritual, with living participants. Yet such experiments raise vexing questions. Can a play break down the distinction between art and "real life" without losing any life that, in a conventional play, the playwright's art holds fast?

In the theater of today, realistic glimpses of ordinary lives have vied with the absurd and fantastic. (The theater of the absurd, a school of nonrealist playwrights, is dealt with later in this chapter.) Some of the most influential recent American plays have been realistic — like Marsha Nor-

[1]See especially "The Theater of Cruelty (First Manifesto)" in *The Theater and Its Double,* translated by Mary Caroline Richards (New York: Grove, 1958).
[2]Arthur Sainer, *The Radical Theatre Notebook* (New York: Avon, 1975) 15.
[3]Sainer, 72.

man's Pulitzer Prize-winning " 'Night, Mother" (1983) in which, trapped in an unchanging three-walled living room in a modest house, a mother tries to argue her daughter out of suicide. It seems safe to guess that the stage will long need both the life that playwrights can observe and the lives that they can imagine.

Henrik Ibsen
A Doll House   1879

Translated by Rolf Fjelde

> *Henrik Ibsen (1828 – 1906) was born in Skien, a seaport in Norway.
> When he was six, his father's business losses suddenly reduced his wealthy
> family to poverty. After a brief attempt to study medicine, young Ibsen worked
> as stage manager in provincial Bergen; then, becoming known as a play-
> wright, moved to Oslo as artistic director of the National Theater — practi-
> cal experiences that gained him firm grounding in his craft. Discouraged
> when his theater failed and the king turned down his plea for a grant to
> enable him to write, Ibsen left Norway and for twenty-seven years lived in
> Italy and Germany. There, in his middle years (1879 – 91), he wrote most
> of his famed plays about small-town life, among them* A Doll House,
> Ghosts, An Enemy of the People, The Wild Duck, *and* Hedda Gabler.
> *Introducing social problems to the stage, these plays aroused storms of contro-
> versy. Although best known as a realist, Ibsen early in his career wrote poetic
> dramas based on Norwegian history and folklore: the tragedy* Brand *(1866)
> and the powerful, wildly fantastic* Peer Gynt *(1867). He ended as a
> symbolist in* John Gabriel Borkman *(1896) and* When We Dead
> Awaken *(1899), both encompassing huge mountains that heaven-assault-
> ing heroes try to climb. Late in life Ibsen returned to Oslo, honored at last
> both at home and abroad.*

Characters

Torvald Helmer, a lawyer
Nora, his wife
Dr. Rank
Mrs. Linde
Nils Krogstad, a bank clerk
The Helmers' three small children
Anne-Marie, their nurse
Helene, a maid
A Delivery Boy

The action takes place in Helmer's residence.

ACT I

A comfortable room, tastefully but not expensively furnished. A door to the right in the back wall leads to the entryway; another to the left leads to Helmer's study. Between these doors, a piano. Midway in the left-hand wall a door, and further back a window. Near the window a round table with an armchair and a small sofa. In the right-hand wall, toward the rear, a door, and nearer the foreground a porcelain stove with two armchairs and a rocking chair beside it. Between the stove and the side door, a small table. Engravings on the walls. An étagère with china figures and other small art objects; a small bookcase with richly bound books; the floor carpeted; a fire burning in the stove. It is a winter day.

A bell rings in the entryway; shortly after we hear the door being unlocked. Nora comes into the room, humming happily to herself; she is wearing street clothes and carries an armload of packages, which she puts down on the table to the right. She has left the hall door open; and through it a Delivery Boy is seen, holding a Christmas tree and a basket, which he gives to the Maid who let them in.

Nora: Hide the tree well, Helene. The children mustn't get a glimpse of it till this evening, after it's trimmed. *(To the Delivery Boy, taking out her purse.)* How much?

Delivery Boy: Fifty, ma'am.

Nora: There's a crown. No, keep the change. *(The Boy thanks her and leaves. Nora shuts the door. She laughs softly to herself while taking off her street things. Drawing a bag of macaroons from her pocket, she eats a couple, then steals over and listens at her husband's study door.)* Yes, he's home. *(Hums again as she moves to the table right.)*

Helmer (from the study): Is that my little lark twittering out there?

Nora (busy opening some packages): Yes, it is.

Helmer: Is that my squirrel rummaging around?

Nora: Yes!

Helmer: When did my squirrel get in?

Nora: Just now. *(Putting the macaroon bag in her pocket and wiping her mouth.)* Do come in, Torvald, and see what I've bought.

Helmer: Can't be disturbed. *(After a moment he opens the door and peers in, pen in hand.)* Bought, you say? All that there? Has the little spendthrift been out throwing money around again?

Nora: Oh, but Torvald, this year we really should let ourselves go a bit. It's the first Christmas we haven't had to economize.

Helmer: But you know we can't go squandering.

Nora: Oh yes, Torvald, we can squander a little now. Can't we? Just a tiny, wee bit. Now that you've got a big salary and are going to make piles and piles of money.

Helmer: Yes — starting New Year's. But then it's a full three months till the raise comes through.

Nora: Pooh! We can borrow that long.

Helmer: Nora! *(Goes over and playfully takes her by the ear.)* Are your scatterbrains off again? What if today I borrowed a thousand crowns, and you squandered them over Christmas week, and then on New Year's Eve a roof tile fell on my head, and I lay there —

Nora (putting her hand on his mouth): Oh! Don't say such things!

Helmer: Yes, but what if it happened — then what?

Nora: If anything so awful happened, then it just wouldn't matter if I had debts or not.

Helmer: Well, but the people I'd borrowed from?

Nora: Them? Who cares about them! They're strangers.

Helmer: Nora, Nora, how like a woman! No, but seriously, Nora, you know what I think about that. No debts! Never borrow! Something of freedom's lost — and something of beauty, too — from a home that's founded on borrowing and debt. We've made a brave stand up to now, the two of us; and we'll go right on like that the little while we have to.

Nora (going toward the stove): Yes, whatever you say, Torvald.

Helmer (following her): Now, now, the little lark's wings mustn't droop. Come on, don't be a sulky squirrel. *(Taking out his wallet.)* Nora, guess what I have here.

Nora (turning quickly): Money!

Helmer: There, see. *(Hands her some notes.)* Good grief, I know how costs go up in a house at Christmastime.

Nora: Ten — twenty — thirty — forty. Oh, thank you, Torvald; I can manage no end on this.

Helmer: You really will have to.

Nora: Oh yes, I promise I will! But come here so I can show you everything I bought. And so cheap! Look, new clothes for Ivar here — and a sword. Here a horse and a trumpet for Bob. And a doll and a doll's bed here for Emmy; they're nothing much, but she'll tear them to bits in no time anyway. And here I have dress material and handkerchiefs for the maids. Old Anne-Marie really deserves something more.

Helmer: And what's in that package there?

Nora (with a cry): Torvald, no! You can't see that till tonight!

Helmer: I see. But tell me now, you little prodigal, what have you thought of for yourself?

Nora: For myself? Oh, I don't want anything at all.

Helmer: Of course you do. Tell me just what — within reason — you'd most like to have.

Nora: I honestly don't know. Oh, listen, Torvald —

Helmer: Well?

Nora (fumbling at his coat buttons, without looking at him): If you want to give me something, then maybe you could — you could —

Helmer: Come on, out with it.

Nora (hurriedly): You could give me money, Torvald. No more than you think you can spare; then one of these days I'll buy something with it.

Helmer: But Nora —

Nora: Oh, please, Torvald darling, do that! I beg you, please. Then I could hang the bills in pretty gilt paper on the Christmas tree. Wouldn't that be fun?

Helmer: What are those little birds called that always fly through their fortunes?

Nora: Oh yes, spendthrifts; I know all that. But let's do as I say, Torvald; then I'll have time to decide what I really need most. That's very sensible, isn't it?

Helmer (smiling): Yes, very — that is, if you actually hung onto the money I give you, and you actually used it to buy yourself something. But it goes for the house and for all sorts of foolish things, and then I only have to lay out some more.

Nora: Oh, but Torvald —

Helmer: Don't deny it, my dear little Nora. *(Putting his arm around her waist.)* Spendthrifts are sweet, but they use up a frightful amount of money. It's incredible what it costs a man to feed such birds.

Nora: Oh, how can you say that! Really, I save everything I can.

Helmer (laughing): Yes, that's the truth. Everything you can. But that's nothing at all.

Nora (humming, with a smile of quiet satisfaction): Hm, if you only knew what expenses we larks and squirrels have, Torvald.

Helmer: You're an odd little one. Exactly the way your father was. You're never at a loss for scaring up money; but the moment you have it, it runs right out through your fingers; you never know what you've done with it. Well, one takes you as you are. It's deep in your blood. Yes, these things are hereditary, Nora.

Nora: Ah, I could wish I'd inherited many of Papa's qualities.

Helmer: And I couldn't wish you anything but just what you are, my sweet little lark. But wait; it seems to me you have a very — what should I call it? — a very suspicious look today —

Nora: I do?

Helmer: You certainly do. Look me straight in the eye.

Nora (looking at him): Well?

Helmer (shaking an admonitory finger): Surely my sweet tooth hasn't been running riot in town today, has she?

Nora: No. Why do you imagine that?

Helmer: My sweet tooth really didn't make a little detour through the confectioner's?

Nora: No, I assure you, Torvald —

Helmer: Hasn't nibbled some pastry?

Nora: No, not at all.

Helmer: Nor even munched a macaroon or two?

Nora: No, Torvald, I assure you, really —

Helmer: There, there now. Of course I'm only joking.

Nora (going to the table, right): You know I could never think of going against you.

Helmer: No, I understand that; and you *have* given me your word. *(Going over to her.)* Well, you keep your little Christmas secrets to yourself, Nora darling. I expect they'll come to light this evening, when the tree is lit.

Nora: Did you remember to ask Dr. Rank?

Helmer: No. But there's no need for that; it's assumed he'll be dining with us. All the same, I'll ask him when he stops by here this morning. I've ordered some fine wine. Nora, you can't imagine how I'm looking forward to this evening.

Nora: So am I. And what fun for the children, Torvald!

Helmer: Ah, it's so gratifying to know that one's gotten a safe, secure job, and with a comfortable salary. It's a great satisfaction, isn't it?

Nora: Oh, it's wonderful!

Helmer: Remember last Christmas? Three whole weeks before, you shut yourself in every evening till long after midnight, making flowers for the

Christmas tree, and all the other decorations to surprise us. Ugh, that was the dullest time I've ever lived through.

Nora: It wasn't at all dull for me.

Helmer (smiling): But the outcome *was* pretty sorry, Nora.

Nora: Oh, don't tease me with that again. How could I help it that the cat came in and tore everything to shreds.

Helmer: No, poor thing, you certainly couldn't. You wanted so much to please us all, and that's what counts. But it's just as well that the hard times are past.

Nora: Yes, it's really wonderful.

Helmer: Now I don't have to sit here alone, boring myself, and you don't have to tire your precious eyes and your fair little delicate hands —

Nora (clapping her hands): No, is it really true, Torvald, I don't have to? Oh, how wonderfully lovely to hear! *(Taking his arm.)* Now I'll tell you just how I've thought we should plan things. Right after Christmas — *(The doorbell rings.)* Oh, the bell. *(Straightening the room up a bit.)* Somebody would have to come. What a bore!

Helmer: I'm not at home to visitors, don't forget.

Maid (from the hall doorway): Ma'am, a lady to see you —

Nora: All right, let her come in.

Maid (to Helmer): And the doctor's just come too.

Helmer: Did he go right to my study?

Maid: Yes, he did.

> *Helmer goes into his room. The Maid shows in Mrs. Linde, dressed in traveling clothes, and shuts the door after her.*

Mrs. Linde (in a dispirited and somewhat hesitant voice): Hello, Nora.

Nora (uncertain): Hello —

Mrs. Linde: You don't recognize me.

Nora: No, I don't know — but wait, I think — *(Exclaiming.)* What! Kristine! Is it really you?

Mrs. Linde: Yes, it's me.

Nora: Kristine! To think I didn't recognize you. But then, how could I? *(More quietly.)* How you've changed, Kristine!

Mrs. Linde: Yes, no doubt I have. In nine — ten long years.

Nora: Is it so long since we met! Yes, it's all of that. Oh, these last eight years have been a happy time, believe me. And so now you've come in to town, too. Made the long trip in the winter. That took courage.

Mrs. Linde: I just got here by ship this morning.

Nora: To enjoy yourself over Christmas, of course. Oh, how lovely! Yes, enjoy ourselves, we'll do that. But take your coat off. You're not still cold? *(Helping her.)* There now, let's get cozy here by the stove. No, the easy chair there! I'll take the rocker here. *(Seizing her hands.)* Yes, now you have your old look again; it was only in that first moment. You're a bit more pale, Kristine — and maybe a bit thinner.

Mrs. Linde: And much, much older, Nora.

Nora: Yes, perhaps a bit older; a tiny, tiny bit; not much at all. *(Stopping short; suddenly serious.)* Oh, but thoughtless me, to sit here, chattering away. Sweet, good Kristine, can you forgive me?

Mrs. Linde: What do you mean, Nora?

Nora (softly): Poor Kristine, you've become a widow.

Mrs. Linde: Yes, three years ago.

Nora: Oh, I knew it, of course: I read it in the papers. Oh, Kristine, you must believe me; I often thought of writing you then, but I kept postponing it, and something always interfered.

Mrs. Linde: Nora dear, I understand completely.

Nora: No, it was awful of me, Kristine. You poor thing, how much you must have gone through. And he left you nothing?

Mrs. Linde: No.

Nora: And no children?

Mrs. Linde: No.

Nora: Nothing at all, then?

Mrs. Linde: Not even a sense of loss to feed on.

Nora (looking incredulously at her): But Kristine, how could that be?

Mrs. Linde (smiling wearily and smoothing her hair): Oh, sometimes it happens, Nora.

Nora: So completely alone. How terribly hard that must be for you. I have three lovely children. You can't see them now; they're out with the maid. But now you must tell me everything —

Mrs. Linde: No, no, no, tell me about yourself.

Nora: No, you begin. Today I don't want to be selfish. I want to think only of you today. But there *is* something I must tell you. Did you hear of the wonderful luck we had recently?

Mrs. Linde: No, what's that?

Nora: My husband's been made manager in the bank, just think!

Mrs. Linde: Your husband? How marvelous!

Nora: Isn't it? Being a lawyer is such an uncertain living, you know, especially if one won't touch any cases that aren't clean and decent. And of course Torvald would never do that, and I'm with him completely there. Oh, we're simply delighted, believe me! He'll join the bank right after New Year's and start getting a huge salary and lots of commissions. From now on we can live quite differently — just as we want. Oh, Kristine, I feel so light and happy! Won't it be lovely to have stacks of money and not a care in the world?

Mrs. Linde: Well, anyway, it would be lovely to have enough for necessities.

Nora: No, not just for necessities, but stacks and stacks of money!

Mrs. Linde (smiling): Nora, Nora, aren't you sensible yet? Back in school you were such a free spender.

Nora (with a quiet laugh): Yes, that's what Torvald still says. *(Shaking her finger.)* But "Nora, Nora" isn't as silly as you all think. Really, we've been in no position for me to go squandering. We've had to work, both of us.

Mrs. Linde: You too?

Nora: Yes, at odd jobs — needlework, crocheting, embroidery, and such — *(casually)* and other things too. You remember that Torvald left the department when we were married? There was no chance of promotion in his office, and of course he needed to earn more money. But that first year he drove himself terribly. He took on all kinds of extra work that kept him going morning and night. It wore him down, and then he fell deathly ill. The doctors said it was essential for him to travel south.

Mrs. Linde: Yes, didn't you spend a whole year in Italy?

Nora: That's right. It wasn't easy to get away, you know. Ivar had just been born. But of course we had to go. Oh, that was a beautiful trip, and it saved Torvald's life. But it cost a frightful sum, Kristine.

Mrs. Linde: I can well imagine.

Nora: Four thousand, eight hundred crowns it cost. That's really a lot of money.

Mrs. Linde: But it's lucky you had it when you needed it.

Nora: Well, as it was, we got it from Papa.

Mrs. Linde: I see. It was just about the time your father died.

Nora: Yes, just about then. And, you know, I couldn't make that trip out to nurse him. I had to stay here, expecting Ivar any moment, and with my poor sick Torvald to care for. Dearest Papa, I never saw him again, Kristine. Oh, that was the worst time I've known in all my marriage.

Mrs. Linde: I know how you loved him. And then you went off to Italy?

Nora: Yes. We had the means now, and the doctors urged us. So we left a month after.

Mrs. Linde: And your husband came back completely cured?

Nora: Sound as a drum!

Mrs. Linde: But — the doctor?

Nora: Who?

Mrs. Linde: I thought the maid said he was a doctor, the man who came in with me.

Nora: Yes, that was Dr. Rank — but he's not making a sick call. He's our closest friend, and he stops by at least once a day. No, Torvald hasn't had a sick moment since, and the children are fit and strong, and I am, too. *(Jumping up and clapping her hands.)* Oh, dear God, Kristine, what a lovely thing to live and be happy! But how disgusting of me — I'm talking of nothing but my own affairs. *(Sits on a stool close by Kristine, arms resting across her knees.)* Oh, don't be angry with me! Tell me, is it really true that you weren't in love with your husband? Why did you marry him, then?

Mrs. Linde: My mother was still alive, but bedridden and helpless — and I had my two younger brothers to look after. In all conscience, I didn't think I could turn him down.

Nora: No, you were right there. But was he rich at the time?

Mrs. Linde: He was very well off, I'd say. But the business was shaky, Nora. When he died, it all fell apart, and nothing was left.

Nora: And then — ?

Mrs. Linde: Yes, so I had to scrape up a living with a little shop and a little teaching and whatever else I could find. The last three years have been like one endless workday without a rest for me. Now it's over, Nora. My poor mother doesn't need me, for she's passed on. Nor the boys, either; they're working now and can take care of themselves.

Nora: How free you must feel —

Mrs. Linde: No — only unspeakably empty. Nothing to live for now. *(Standing up anxiously.)* That's why I couldn't take it any longer out in that desolate hole. Maybe here it'll be easier to find something to do and keep my mind occupied. If I could only be lucky enough to get a steady job, some office work —

Nora: Oh, but Kristine, that's so dreadfully tiring, and you already look so tired. It would be much better for you if you could go off to a bathing resort.

Mrs. Linde (going toward the window): I have no father to give me travel money, Nora.

Nora (rising): Oh, don't be angry with me.

Mrs. Linde (going to her): Nora dear, don't you be angry with me. The worst of my kind of situation is all the bitterness that's stored away. No one to work for, and yet you're always having to snap up your opportunities. You have to live; and so you grow selfish. When you told me the happy change in your lot, do you know I was delighted less for your sakes than for mine?

Nora: How so? Oh, I see. You think maybe Torvald could do something for you.

Mrs. Linde: Yes, that's what I thought.

Nora: And he will, Kristine! Just leave it to me; I'll bring it up so delicately — find something attractive to humor him with. Oh, I'm so eager to help you.

Mrs. Linde: How very kind of you, Nora, to be so concerned over me — doubly kind, considering you really know so little of life's burdens yourself.

Nora: I — ? I know so little — ?

Mrs. Linde (smiling): Well, my heavens — a little needlework and such — Nora, you're just a child.

Nora (tossing her head and pacing the floor): You don't have to act so superior.

Mrs. Linde: Oh?

Nora: You're just like the others. You all think I'm incapable of anything serious —

Mrs. Linde: Come now —

Nora: That I've never had to face the raw world.

Mrs. Linde: Nora dear, you've just been telling me all your troubles.

Nora: Hm! Trivia! *(Quietly.)* I haven't told you the big thing.

Mrs. Linde: Big thing? What do you mean?

Nora: You look down on me so, Kristine, but you shouldn't. You're proud that you worked so long and hard for your mother.

Mrs. Linde: I don't look down on a soul. But it *is* true: I'm proud — and happy, too — to think it was given to me to make my mother's last days almost free of care.

Nora: And you're also proud thinking of what you've done for your brothers.

Mrs. Linde: I feel I've a right to be.

Nora: I agree. But listen to this, Kristine — I've also got something to be proud and happy for.

Mrs. Linde: I don't doubt it. But whatever do you mean?

Nora: Not so loud. What if Torvald heard! He mustn't, not for anything in the world. Nobody must know, Kristine. No one but you.

Mrs. Linde: But what is it, then?

Nora: Come here. *(Drawing her down beside her on the sofa.)* It's true — I've also got something to be proud and happy for. I'm the one who saved Torvald's life.

Mrs. Linde: Saved — ? Saved how?

Nora: I told you about the trip to Italy. Torvald never would have lived if he hadn't gone south —

Mrs. Linde: Of course; your father gave you the means —

Nora (smiling): That's what Torvald and all the rest think, but —

Mrs. Linde: But — ?

Nora: Papa didn't give us a pin. I was the one who raised the money.

Mrs. Linde: You? That whole amount?

Nora: Four thousand, eight hundred crowns. What do you say to that?

Mrs. Linde: But Nora, how was it possible? Did you win the lottery?

Nora (disdainfully): The lottery? Pooh! No art to that.

Mrs. Linde: But where did you get it from then?

Nora (humming, with a mysterious smile): Hmm, tra-la-la-la.

Mrs. Linde: Because you couldn't have borrowed it.

Nora: No? Why not?

Mrs. Linde: A wife can't borrow without her husband's consent.

Nora (tossing her head): Oh, but a wife with a little business sense, a wife who knows how to manage —

Mrs. Linde: Nora, I simply don't understand —

Nora: You don't have to. Whoever said I *borrowed* the money? I could have gotten it other ways. *(Throwing herself back on the sofa.)* I could have gotten it from some admirer or other. After all, a girl with my ravishing appeal —

Mrs. Linde: You lunatic.

Nora: I'll bet you're eaten up with curiosity, Kristine.

Mrs. Linde: Now listen here, Nora — you haven't done something indiscreet?

Nora (sitting up again): Is it indiscreet to save your husband's life?

Mrs. Linde: I think it's indiscreet that without his knowledge you —

Nora: But that's the point: he mustn't know! My Lord, can't you understand? He mustn't ever know the close call he had. It was to *me* the doctors came to say his life was in danger — that nothing could save him but a stay in the south. Didn't I try strategy then! I began talking about how lovely it would be for me to travel abroad like other young wives; I begged and I cried; I told him please to remember my condition, to be kind and indulge me; and then I dropped a hint that he could easily take out a loan. But at that, Kristine, he nearly exploded. He said I was frivolous, and it was his duty as man of the house not to indulge me in whims and fancies — as I think he called them. Aha, I thought, now you'll just have to be saved — and that's when I saw my chance.

Mrs. Linde: And your father never told Torvald the money wasn't from him?

Nora: No, never. Papa died right about then. I'd considered bringing him into my secret and begging him never to tell. But he was too sick at the time — and then, sadly, it didn't matter.

Mrs. Linde: And you've never confided in your husband since?

Nora: For heaven's sake, no! Are you serious? He's so strict on that subject. Besides — Torvald, with all his masculine pride — how painfully humiliating for him if he ever found out he was in debt to me. That would just ruin our relationship. Our beautiful, happy home would never be the same.

Mrs. Linde: Won't you ever tell him?

Nora (thoughtfully, half smiling): Yes — maybe sometime, years from now, when I'm no longer so attractive. Don't laugh! I only mean when Torvald loves me less than now, when he stops enjoying my dancing and dressing up and reciting for him. Then it might be wise to have something in reserve — *(Breaking off.)* How ridiculous! That'll never happen — Well, Kristine, what do you think of my big secret? I'm capable of something too, hm? You can imagine, of course, how this thing hangs over me. It really hasn't been easy meeting the payments on time. In the business world there's what they call quarterly interest and what they call amortization, and these are always so terribly hard to manage. I've had to skimp a little here and there, wherever I could, you know. I could hardly spare anything from my house allowance, because Torvald has to live well. I couldn't let the children go poorly dressed; whatever I got for them, I felt I had to use up completely — the darlings!

Mrs. Linde: Poor Nora, so it had to come out of your own budget, then?

Nora: Yes, of course. But I was the one most responsible, too. Every time Torvald gave me money for new clothes and such, I never used more than half; always bought the simplest, cheapest outfits. It was a godsend that everything looks so well on me that Torvald never noticed. But it did weigh me down at times, Kristine. It *is* such a joy to wear fine things. You understand.

Mrs. Linde: Oh, of course.

Nora: And then I found other ways of making money. Last winter I was lucky enough to get a lot of copying to do. I locked myself in and sat writing every evening till late in the night. Ah, I was tired so often, dead tired. But still it was wonderful fun, sitting and working like that, earning money. It was almost like being a man.

Mrs. Linde: But how much have you paid off this way so far?

Nora: That's hard to say, exactly. These accounts, you know, aren't easy to figure. I only know that I've paid out all I could scrape together. Time and again I haven't known where to turn. *(Smiling.)* Then I'd sit here dreaming of a rich old gentleman who had fallen in love with me —

Mrs. Linde: What! Who is he?

Nora: Oh, really! And that he'd died, and when his will was opened, there in big letters it said, "All my fortune shall be paid over in cash, immediately, to that enchanting Mrs. Nora Helmer."

Mrs. Linde: But Nora dear — who *was* this gentleman?

Nora: Good grief, can't you understand? The old man never existed; that was only something I'd dream up time and again whenever I was at my wits' end for money. But it makes no difference now; the old fossil can go where he pleases for all I care; I don't need him or his will — because now I'm free. *(Jumping up.)* Oh, how lovely to think of that, Kristine! Carefree! To know you're carefree, utterly carefree; to be able to romp and play with the children, and to keep up a beautiful, charming home — everything just the way Torvald likes it! And think, spring is coming, with big blue skies. Maybe we can travel a little then. Maybe I'll see the ocean again. Oh yes, it *is* so marvelous to live and be happy!

The front doorbell rings.

Mrs. Linde (rising): There's the bell. It's probably best that I go.

Nora: No, stay. No one's expected. It must be for Torvald.

Maid (from the hall doorway): Excuse me, ma'am — there's a gentleman here to see Mr. Helmer, but I didn't know — since the doctor's with him —

Nora: Who is the gentleman?

Krogstad (from the doorway): It's me, Mrs. Helmer.

Mrs. Linde starts and turns away toward the window.

Nora (stepping toward him, tense, her voice a whisper): You? What is it? Why do you want to speak to my husband?

Krogstad: Bank business — after a fashion. I have a small job in the investment bank, and I hear now your husband is going to be our chief —

Nora: In other words, it's —

Krogstad: Just dry business, Mrs. Helmer. Nothing but that.

Nora: Yes, then please be good enough to step into the study. *(She nods indifferently as she sees him out by the hall door, then returns and begins stirring up the stove.)*

Mrs. Linde: Nora — who was that man?

Nora: That was a Mr. Krogstad — a lawyer.

Mrs. Linde: Then it really was him.

Nora: Do you know that person?

Mrs. Linde: I did once — many years ago. For a time he was a law clerk in our town.

Nora: Yes, he's been that.

Mrs. Linde: How he's changed.

Nora: I understand he had a very unhappy marriage.

Mrs. Linde: He's a widower now.

Nora: With a number of children. There now, it's burning. *(She closes the stove door and moves the rocker a bit to one side.)*

Mrs. Linde: They say he has a hand in all kinds of business.

Nora: Oh? That may be true: I wouldn't know. But let's not think about business. It's so dull.

Dr. Rank enters from Helmer's study.

Rank (still in the doorway): No, no, really — I don't want to intrude, I'd just as soon talk a little while with your wife. *(Shuts the door, then notices Mrs. Linde.)* Oh, beg pardon. I'm intruding here too.

Nora: No, not at all. *(Introducing him.)* Dr. Rank, Mrs. Linde.

Rank: Well now, that's a name much heard in this house. I believe I passed the lady on the stairs as I came.

Mrs. Linde: Yes, I take the stairs very slowly. They're rather hard on me.

Rank: Uh-hm, some touch of internal weakness?

Mrs. Linde: More overexertion, I'd say.

Rank: Nothing else? Then you're probably here in town to rest up in a round of parties?

Mrs. Linde: I'm here to look for work.

Rank: Is that the best cure for overexertion?

Mrs. Linde: One has to live, Doctor.

Rank: Yes, there's a common prejudice to that effect.

Nora: Oh, come on, Dr. Rank — you really do want to live yourself.

Rank: Yes, I really do. Wretched as I am, I'll gladly prolong my torment indefinitely. All my patients feel like that. And it's quite the same, too, with the morally sick. Right at this moment there's one of those moral invalids in there with Helmer —

Mrs. Linde (softly): Ah!

Nora: Who do you mean?

Rank: Oh, it's a lawyer, Krogstad, a type you wouldn't know. His character is rotten to the root — but even he began chattering all-importantly about how he had to *live.*

Nora: Oh? What did he want to talk to Torvald about?

Rank: I really don't know. I only heard something about the bank.

Nora: I didn't know that Krog — that this man Krogstad had anything to do with the bank.

Rank: Yes, he's gotten some kind of berth down there. *(To Mrs. Linde.)* I don't know if you also have, in your neck of the woods, a type of person who scuttles about breathlessly, sniffing out hints of moral corruption, and then maneuvers his victim into some sort of key position where he can keep an eye on him. It's the healthy these days that are out in the cold.

Mrs. Linde: All the same, it's the sick who most need to be taken in.

Rank (with a shrug): Yes, there we have it. That's the concept that's turning society into a sanatorium.

Nora, lost in her thoughts, breaks out into quiet laughter and claps her hands.

Rank: Why do you laugh at that? Do you have any real idea of what society is?

Nora: What do I care about dreary old society? I was laughing at something quite different — something terribly funny. Tell me, Doctor — is everyone who works in the bank dependent now on Torvald?

Rank: Is that what you find so terribly funny?

Nora (smiling and humming): Never mind, never mind! *(Pacing the floor.)* Yes, that's really immensely amusing: that we — that Torvald has so much power now over all those people. *(Taking the bag out of her pocket.)* Dr. Rank, a little macaroon on that?

Rank: See here, macaroons! I thought they were contraband here.

Nora: Yes, but these are some that Kristine gave me.

Mrs. Linde: What? I — ?

Nora: Now, now, don't be afraid. You couldn't possibly know that Torvald had forbidden them. You see, he's worried they'll ruin my teeth. But hmp! Just this once! Isn't that so, Dr. Rank? Help yourself! *(Puts a macaroon in his mouth.)* And you too, Kristine. And I'll also have one, only a little one — or two, at the most. *(Walking about again.)* Now I'm really tremendously happy. Now there's just one last thing in the world that I have an enormous desire to do.

Rank: Well! And what's that?

Nora: It's something I have such a consuming desire to say so Torvald could hear.

Rank: And why can't you say it?

Nora: I don't dare. It's quite shocking.

Mrs. Linde: Shocking?

Rank: Well, then it isn't advisable. But in front of us you certainly can. What do you have such a desire to say so Torvald could hear?

Nora: I have such a huge desire to say — to hell and be damned!

Rank: Are you crazy?

Mrs. Linde: My goodness, Nora!

Rank: Go on, say it. Here he is.

Nora (hiding the macaroon bag): Shh, shh, shh!

Helmer comes in from his study, hat in hand, overcoat over his arm.

Nora (going toward him): Well, Torvald dear, are you through with him?

Helmer: Yes, he just left.

Nora: Let me introduce you — this is Kristine, who's arrived here in town.

Helmer: Kristine — ? I'm sorry, but I don't know —

Nora: Mrs. Linde, Torvald dear. Mrs. Kristine Linde.

Helmer: Of course. A childhood friend of my wife's, no doubt?

Mrs. Linde: Yes, we knew each other in those days.

Nora: And just think, she made the long trip down here in order to talk with you.

Helmer: What's this?

Mrs. Linde: Well, not exactly —

Nora: You see, Kristine is remarkably clever in office work, and so she's terribly eager to come under a capable man's supervision and add more to what she already knows —

Helmer: Very wise, Mrs. Linde.

Nora: And then when she heard that you'd become a bank manager — the story was wired out to the papers — then she came in as fast as she could and — Really, Torvald, for my sake you can do a little something for Kristine, can't you?

Helmer: Yes, it's not at all impossible. Mrs. Linde, I suppose you're a widow?

Mrs. Linde: Yes.

Helmer: Any experience in office work?

Mrs. Linde: Yes, a good deal.

Helmer: Well, it's quite likely that I can make an opening for you —

Nora (clapping her hands): You see, you see!

Helmer: You've come at a lucky moment, Mrs. Linde.

Mrs. Linde: Oh, how can I thank you?

Helmer: Not necessary. *(Putting his overcoat on.)* But today you'll have to excuse me —

Rank: Wait, I'll go with you. *(He fetches his coat from the hall and warms it at the stove.)*

Nora: Don't stay out long, dear.

Helmer: An hour; no more.

Nora: Are you going too, Kristine?

Mrs. Linde (putting on her winter garments): Yes, I have to see about a room now.

Helmer: Then perhaps we can all walk together.

Nora (helping her): What a shame we're so cramped here, but it's quite impossible for us to —

Mrs. Linde: Oh, don't even think of it! Good-bye, Nora dear, and thanks for everything.

Nora: Good-bye for now. Of course you'll be back this evening. And you too, Dr. Rank. What? If you're well enough? Oh, you've got to be! Wrap up tight now.

In a ripple of small talk the company moves out into the hall; children's voices are heard outside on the steps.

Nora: There they are! There they are! *(She runs to open the door. The children come in with their nurse, Anne-Marie.)* Come in, come in! *(Bends down and kisses them.)* Oh, you darlings — ! Look at them, Kristine. Aren't they lovely!

Rank: No loitering in the draft here.

Helmer: Come, Mrs. Linde — this place is unbearable now for anyone but mothers.

Dr. Rank, Helmer, and Mrs. Linde go down the stairs. Anne-Marie goes into the living room with the children. Nora follows, after closing the hall door.

Nora: How fresh and strong you look. Oh, such red cheeks you have! Like apples and roses. *(The children interrupt her throughout the following.)* And it was so much fun? That's wonderful. Really? You pulled both Emmy and Bob on the sled? Imagine, all together! Yes, you're a clever boy, Ivar. Oh, let me hold her a bit, Anne-Marie. My sweet little doll baby! *(Takes the smallest from the nurse and dances with her.)* Yes, yes, Mama will dance with Bob as well. What? Did you throw snowballs? Oh, if I'd only been there! No, don't bother, Anne-Marie — I'll undress them myself. Oh yes, let me. It's such fun. Go in and rest; you look half frozen. There's hot coffee waiting for you on the stove. *(The nurse goes into the room to the left. Nora takes the children's winter things off, throwing them about, while the children talk to her all at once.)* Is that so? A big dog chased you? But it didn't bite? No, dogs never bite little, lovely doll babies. Don't peek in the packages, Ivar! What is it? Yes, wouldn't you like to know. No, no, it's an ugly something. Well? Shall we play? What shall we play? Hide-and-seek? Yes, let's play hide-and-seek. Bob must hide first. I must? Yes, let me hide first. *(Laughing and shouting, she and the children play in and out of the living room and the adjoining room to the right. At last Nora hides under the table. The children come storming in, search, but cannot find her, then hear her muffled laughter, dash over to the table, lift the cloth up and find her. Wild shouting. She creeps forward as if to scare them. More shouts. Meanwhile, a knock at the hall door; no one has noticed it. Now the door half opens, and Krogstad appears. He waits a moment; the game goes on.)*

Krogstad: Beg pardon, Mrs. Helmer —

Nora (with a strangled cry, turning and scrambling to her knees): Oh! What do you want?

Krogstad: Excuse me. The outer door was ajar; it must be someone forgot to shut it —

Nora (rising): My husband isn't home, Mr. Krogstad.

Krogstad: I know that.

Nora: Yes — then what do you want here?

Krogstad: A word with you.

Nora: With — ? *(To the children, quietly.)* Go in to Anne-Marie. What? No, the strange man won't hurt Mama. When he's gone, we'll play some more. *(She leads the children into the room to the left and shuts the door after them. Then, tense and nervous):* You want to speak to me?

Krogstad: Yes, I want to.

Nora: Today? But it's not yet the first of the month —

Krogstad: No, it's Christmas Eve. It's going to be up to you how merry a Christmas you have.

Nora: What is it you want? Today I absolutely can't —

Krogstad: We won't talk about that till later. This is something else. You do have a moment to spare, I suppose?

Nora: Oh yes, of course — I do, except —

Krogstad: Good. I was sitting over at Olsen's Restaurant when I saw your husband go down the street —

Nora: Yes?

Krogstad: With a lady.

Nora: Yes. So?

Krogstad: If you'll pardon my asking: wasn't that lady a Mrs. Linde?

Nora: Yes.

Krogstad: Just now come into town?

Nora: Yes, today.

Krogstad: She's a good friend of yours?

Nora: Yes, she is. But I don't see —

Krogstad: I also knew her once.

Nora: I'm aware of that.

Krogstad: Oh? You know all about it. I thought so. Well, then let me ask you short and sweet: is Mrs. Linde getting a job in the bank?

Nora: What makes you think you can cross-examine me, Mr. Krogstad — you, one of my husband's employees? But since you ask, you might as well know — yes, Mrs. Linde's going to be taken on at the bank. And I'm the one who spoke for her, Mr. Krogstad. Now you know.

Krogstad: So I guessed right.

Nora (pacing up and down): Oh, one does have a tiny bit of influence, I should hope. Just because I am a woman, don't think it means that — When one has a subordinate position, Mr. Krogstad, one really ought to be careful about pushing somebody who — hm —

Krogstad: Who has influence?

Nora: That's right.

Krogstad (in a different tone): Mrs. Helmer, would you be good enough to use your influence on my behalf?

Nora: What? What do you mean?

Krogstad: Would you please make sure that I keep my subordinate position in the bank?

Nora: What does that mean? Who's thinking of taking away your position?

Krogstad: Oh, don't play the innocent with me. I'm quite aware that your friend would hardly relish the chance of running into me again; and I'm also aware now whom I can thank for being turned out.

Nora: But I promise you —

Krogstad: Yes, yes, yes, to the point: there's still time, and I'm advising you to use your influence to prevent it.

Nora: But Mr. Krogstad, I have absolutely no influence.

Krogstad: You haven't? I thought you were just saying —

Nora: You shouldn't take me so literally. I! How can you believe that I have any such influence over my husband?

Krogstad: Oh, I've known your husband from our student days. I don't think the great bank manager's more steadfast than any other married man.

Nora: You speak insolently about my husband, and I'll show you the door.

Krogstad: The lady has spirit.

Nora: I'm not afraid of you any longer. After New Year's, I'll soon be done with the whole business.

Krogstad (restraining himself): Now listen to me, Mrs. Helmer. If necessary, I'll fight for my little job in the bank as if it were life itself.

Nora: Yes, so it seems.

Krogstad: It's not just a matter of income; that's the least of it. It's something else — All right, out with it! Look, this is the thing. You know, just like all the others, of course, that once, a good many years ago, I did something rather rash.

Nora: I've heard rumors to that effect.

Krogstad: The case never got into court; but all the same, every door was closed in my face from then on. So I took up those various activities you know about. I had to grab hold somewhere; and I dare say I haven't been among the worst. But now I want to drop all that. My boys are growing up. For their sakes, I'll have to win back as much respect as possible here in town. That job in the bank was like the first rung in my ladder. And now your husband wants to kick me right back down in the mud again.

Nora: But for heaven's sake, Mr. Krogstad, it's simply not in my power to help you.

Krogstad: That's because you haven't the will to — but I have the means to make you.

Nora: You certainly won't tell my husband that I owe you money?

Krogstad: Hm — what if I told him that?

Nora: That would be shameful of you. *(Nearly in tears.)* This secret — my joy and my pride — that he should learn it in such a crude and disgusting way — learn it from you. You'd expose me to the most horrible unpleasantness —

Krogstad: Only unpleasantness?

Nora (vehemently): But go on and try. It'll turn out the worse for you, because then my husband will really see what a crook you are, and then you'll *never* be able to hold your job.

Krogstad: I asked if it was just domestic unpleasantness you were afraid of?

Nora: If my husband finds out, then of course he'll pay what I owe at once, and then we'd be through with you for good.

Krogstad (a step closer): Listen, Mrs. Helmer — you've either got a very bad memory, or else no head at all for business. I'd better put you a little more in touch with the facts.

Nora: What do you mean?

Krogstad: When your husband was sick, you came to me for a loan of four thousand, eight hundred crowns.

Nora: Where else could I go?

Krogstad: I promised to get you that sum —

Nora: And you got it.

Krogstad: I promised to get you that sum, on certain conditions. You were so involved in your husband's illness, and so eager to finance your trip, that I guess you didn't think out all the details. It might just be a good idea to remind you. I promised you the money on the strength of a note I drew up.

Nora: Yes, and that I signed.

Krogstad: Right. But at the bottom I added some lines for your father to guarantee the loan. He was supposed to sign down there.

Nora: Supposed to? He did sign.

Krogstad: I left the date blank. In other words, your father would have dated his signature himself. Do you remember that?

Nora: Yes, I think —

Krogstad: Then I gave you the note for you to mail to your father. Isn't that so?

Nora: Yes.

Krogstad: And naturally you sent it at once — because only some five, six days later you brought me the note, properly signed. And with that, the money was yours.

Nora: Well, then; I've made my payments regularly, haven't I?

Krogstad: More or less. But — getting back to the point — those were hard times for you then, Mrs. Helmer.

Nora: Yes, they were.

Krogstad: Your father was very ill, I believe.

Nora: He was near the end.

Krogstad: He died soon after?

Nora: Yes.

Krogstad: Tell me, Mrs. Helmer, do you happen to recall the date of your father's death? The day of the month, I mean.

Nora: Papa died the twenty-ninth of September.

Krogstad: That's quite correct; I've already looked into that. And now we come to a curious thing — *(taking out a paper)* which I simply cannot comprehend.

Nora: Curious thing? I don't know —

Krogstad: This is the curious thing: that your father co-signed the note for your loan three days after his death.

Nora: How — ? I don't understand.

Krogstad: Your father died the twenty-ninth of September. But look. Here your father dated his signature October second. Isn't that curious, Mrs. Helmer? *(Nora is silent.)* Can you explain it to me? *(Nora remains silent.)* It's also remarkable that the words "October second" and the year aren't written in your father's hand, but rather in one that I think I know. Well, it's easy to understand. Your father forgot perhaps to date his signature, and then someone or other added it, a bit sloppily, before anyone knew of his death. There's nothing wrong in that. It all comes down to the signature. And there's no question about *that*, Mrs. Helmer. It really *was* your father who signed his own name here, wasn't it?

Nora (after a short silence, throwing her head back and looking squarely at him): No, it wasn't. *I* signed Papa's name.

Krogstad: Wait, now — are you fully aware that this is a dangerous confession?

Nora: Why? You'll soon get your money.

Krogstad: Let me ask you a question — why didn't you send the paper to your father?

Nora: That was impossible. Papa was so sick. If I'd asked him for his signature, I also would have had to tell him what the money was for. But I couldn't tell him, sick as he was, that my husband's life was in danger. That was just impossible.

Krogstad: Then it would have been better if you'd given up the trip abroad.

Nora: I couldn't possibly. The trip was to save my husband's life. I couldn't give that up.

Krogstad: But didn't you ever consider that this was a fraud against me?

Nora: I couldn't let myself be bothered by that. You weren't any concern of mine. I couldn't stand you, with all those cold complications you made, even though you knew how badly off my husband was.

Krogstad: Mrs. Helmer, obviously you haven't the vaguest idea of what you've involved yourself in. But I can tell you this: it was nothing more and nothing worse than I once did — and it wrecked my whole reputation.

Nora: You? Do you expect me to believe that you ever acted bravely to save your wife's life?

Krogstad: Laws don't inquire into motives.

Nora: Then they must be very poor laws.

Krogstad: Poor or not — if I introduce this paper in court, you'll be judged according to law.

Nora: This I refuse to believe. A daughter hasn't a right to protect her dying father from anxiety and care? A wife hasn't a right to save her husband's life? I don't know much about laws, but I'm sure that somewhere in the books these things are allowed. And you don't know anything about it — you who practice the law? You must be an awful lawyer, Mr. Krogstad.

Krogstad: Could be. But business — the kind of business we two are mixed up in — don't you think I know about that? All right. Do what you want now. But I'm telling you *this:* if I get shoved down a second time, you're going to keep me company. *(He bows and goes out through the hall.)*

Nora (pensive for a moment, then tossing her head): Oh, really! Trying to frighten me! I'm not so silly as all that. *(Begins gathering up the children's clothes, but soon stops.)* But — ? No, but that's impossible! I did it out of love.

The Children (in the doorway, left): Mama, that strange man's gone out the door.

Nora: Yes, yes, I know it. But don't tell anyone about the strange man. Do you hear? Not even Papa!

The Children: No, Mama. But now will you play again?

Nora: No, not now.

The Children: Oh, but Mama, you promised.

Nora: Yes, but I can't now. Go inside; I have too much to do. Go in, go in, my sweet darlings. *(She herds them gently back in the room and shuts the door after them. Settling on the sofa, she takes up a piece of embroidery and makes some stitches, but soon stops abruptly.)* No! *(Throws the work aside, rises, goes to the hall door and calls out.)* Helene! Let me have the tree in here. *(Goes to the table, left, opens the table drawer, and stops again.)* No, but that's utterly impossible!

Maid (with the Christmas tree): Where should I put it, ma'am?

Nora: There. The middle of the floor.

Maid: Should I bring anything else?

Nora: No, thanks. I have what I need.

The Maid, who has set the tree down, goes out.

Nora (absorbed in trimming the tree): Candles here — and flowers here. That terrible creature! Talk, talk, talk! There's nothing to it at all. The tree's going to be lovely. I'll do anything to please you, Torvald. I'll sing for you, dance for you —

Helmer comes in from the hall, with a sheaf of papers under his arm.

Nora: Oh! You're back so soon?

Helmer: Yes. Has anyone been here?

Nora: Here? No.

Helmer: That's odd. I saw Krogstad leaving the front door.

Nora: So? Oh yes, that's true. Krogstad was here a moment.

Helmer: Nora, I can see by your face that he's been here, begging you to put in a good word for him.

Nora: Yes.

Helmer: And it was supposed to seem like your own idea? You were to hide it from me that he'd been here. He asked you that, too, didn't he?

Nora: Yes, Torvald, but —

Helmer: Nora, Nora, and you could fall for that? Talk with that sort of person and promise him anything? And then in the bargain, tell me an untruth.

Nora: An untruth — ?

Helmer: Didn't you say that no one had been here? *(Wagging his finger.)* My little songbird must never do that again. A songbird needs a clean beak to warble with. No false notes. *(Putting his arm about her waist.)* That's the way it should be, isn't it? Yes, I'm sure of it. *(Releasing her.)* And so, enough of that. *(Sitting by the stove.)* Ah, how snug and cozy it is here. *(Leafing among his papers.)*

Nora (busy with the tree, after a short pause): Torvald!

Helmer: Yes.

Nora: I'm so much looking forward to the Stenborgs' costume party, day after tomorrow.

Helmer: And I can't wait to see what you'll surprise me with.

Nora: Oh, that stupid business!

Helmer: What?

Nora: I can't find anything that's right. Everything seems so ridiculous, so inane.

Helmer: So my little Nora's come to *that* recognition?

Nora (going behind his chair, her arms resting on its back): Are you very busy, Torvald?

Helmer: Oh —

Nora: What papers are those?

Helmer: Bank matters.

Nora: Already?

Helmer: I've gotten full authority from the retiring management to make all necessary changes in personnel and procedure. I'll need Christmas week for that. I want to have everything in order by New Year's.

Nora: So that was the reason this poor Krogstad —

Helmer: Hm.

Nora (still leaning on the chair and slowly stroking the nape of his neck): If you weren't so very busy, I would have asked you an enormous favor, Torvald.

Helmer: Let's hear. What is it?

Nora: You know, there isn't anyone who has your good taste — and I want so much to look well at the costume party. Torvald, couldn't you take over and decide what I should be and plan my costume?

Helmer: Ah, is my stubborn little creature calling for a lifeguard?

Nora: Yes, Torvald, I can't get anywhere without your help.

Helmer: All right — I'll think it over. We'll hit on something.

Nora: Oh, how sweet of you. *(Goes to the tree again. Pause.)* Aren't the red flowers pretty — ? But tell me, was it really such a crime that this Krogstad committed?

Helmer: Forgery. Do you have any idea what that means?

Nora: Couldn't he have done it out of need?

Helmer: Yes, or thoughtlessness, like so many others. I'm not so heartless that I'd condemn a man categorically for just one mistake.

Nora: No, of course not, Torvald!

Helmer: Plenty of men have redeemed themselves by openly confessing their crimes and taking their punishment.

Nora: Punishment — ?

Helmer: But now Krogstad didn't go that way. He got himself out by sharp practices, and that's the real cause of his moral breakdown.

Nora: Do you really think that would — ?

Helmer: Just imagine how a man with that sort of guilt in him has to lie and cheat and deceive on all sides, has to wear a mask even with the nearest and dearest he has, even with his own wife and children. And with the children, Nora — that's where it's most horrible.

Nora: Why?

Helmer: Because that kind of atmosphere of lies infects the whole life of a home. Every breath the children take in is filled with the germs of something degenerate.

Nora (coming closer behind him): Are you sure of that?

Helmer: Oh, I've seen it often enough as a lawyer. Almost everyone who goes bad early in life has a mother who's a chronic liar.

Nora: Why just — the mother?

Helmer: It's usually the mother's influence that's dominant, but the father's works in the same way, of course. Every lawyer is quite familiar with it. And still this Krogstad's been going home year in, year out, poisoning his own children with lies and pretense; that's why I call him morally lost. *(Reaching his hands out toward her.)* So my sweet little Nora must promise me never to plead his cause. Your hand on it. Come, come, what's this? Give me your hand. There, now. All settled. I can tell you it'd be impossible for me to work alongside of him. I literally feel physically revolted when I'm anywhere near such a person.

Nora (withdraws her hand and goes to the other side of the Christmas tree): How hot it is here! And I've got so much to do.

Helmer (getting up and gathering his papers): Yes, and I have to think about getting some of these read through before dinner. I'll think about your costume, too. And something to hang on the tree in gilt paper, I may even see about that. *(Putting his hand on her head.)* Oh you, my darling little songbird. *(He goes into his study and closes the door after him.)*

Nora (softly, after a silence): Oh, really! It isn't so. It's impossible. It must be impossible.

Anne-Marie (in the doorway, left): The children are begging so hard to come in to Mama.

Nora: No, no, no, don't let them in to me! You stay with them, Anne-Marie.

Anne-Marie: Of course, ma'am. *(Closes the door.)*

Nora (pale with terror): Hurt my children — ! Poison my home? *(A moment's pause; then she tosses her head.)* That's not true. Never. Never in all the world.

ACT II

Same room. Beside the piano the Christmas tree now stands stripped of ornaments, burned-down candle stubs on its ragged branches. Nora's street clothes lie on the sofa. Nora, alone in the room, moves restlessly about; at last she stops at the sofa and picks up her coat.

Nora (dropping the coat again): Someone's coming! *(Goes toward the door, listens.)* No — there's no one. Of course — nobody's coming today, Christmas Day — or tomorrow, either. But maybe — *(Opens the door and looks out.)* No, nothing in the mailbox. Quite empty. *(Coming forward.)* What nonsense! He won't do anything serious. Nothing terrible could happen. It's impossible. Why, I have three small children.

Anne-Marie, with a large carton, comes in from the room to the left.

Anne-Marie: Well, at last I found the box with the masquerade clothes.

Nora: Thanks. Put it on the table.

Anne-Marie (does so): But they're all pretty much of a mess.

Nora: Ahh! I'd love to rip them in a million pieces!

Anne-Marie: Oh, mercy, they can be fixed right up. Just a little patience.

Nora: Yes, I'll go get Mrs. Linde to help me.

Anne-Marie: Out again now? In this nasty weather? Miss Nora will catch cold — get sick.

Nora: Oh, worse things could happen — How are the children?

Anne-Marie: The poor mites are playing with their Christmas presents, but —

Nora: Do they ask for me much?

Anne-Marie: They're so used to having Mama around, you know.

Nora: Yes. But Anne-Marie, I *can't* be together with them as much as I was.

Anne-Marie: Well, small children get used to anything.

Nora: You think so? Do you think they'd forget their mother if she was gone for good?

Anne-Marie: Oh, mercy — gone for good!

Nora: Wait, tell me, Anne-Marie — I've wondered so often — how could you ever have the heart to give your child over to strangers?

Anne-Marie: But I had to, you know, to become little Nora's nurse.

Nora: Yes, but how could you *do* it?

Anne-Marie: When I could get such a good place? A girl who's poor and who's gotten in trouble is glad enough for that. Because that slippery fish, he didn't do a thing for me, you know.

Nora: But your daughter's surely forgotten you.

Anne-Marie: Oh, she certainly has not. She's written to me, both when she was confirmed and when she was married.

Nora (clasping her about the neck): You old Anne-Marie, you were a good mother for me when I was little.

Anne-Marie: Poor little Nora, with no other mother but me.

Nora: And if the babies didn't have one, then I know that you'd — What silly talk! *(Opening the carton.)* Go in to them. Now I'll have to — Tomorrow you can see how lovely I'll look.

Anne-Marie: Oh, there won't be anyone at the party as lovely as Miss Nora. *(She goes off into the room, left.)*

Nora (begins unpacking the box, but soon throws it aside): Oh, if I dared to go out. If only nobody would come. If only nothing would happen here while I'm out. What craziness — nobody's coming. Just don't think. This muff — needs a brushing. Beautiful gloves, beautiful gloves. Let it go. Let it go! One, two, three, four, five, six — *(With a cry.)* Oh, there they are! *(Poises to move toward the door, but remains irresolutely standing. Mrs. Linde enters from the hall, where she has removed her street clothes.)*

Nora: Oh, it's you, Kristine. There's no one else out there? How good that you've come.

Mrs. Linde: I hear you were up asking for me.

Nora: Yes, I just stopped by. There's something you really can help me with. Let's get settled on the sofa. Look, there's going to be a costume party tomorrow evening at the Stenborgs' right above us, and now Torvald wants me to go as a Neapolitan peasant girl and dance the tarantella that I learned in Capri.

Mrs. Linde: Really, are you giving a whole performance?

Nora: Torvald says yes, I should. See, here's the dress. Torvald had it made for me down there; but now it's all so tattered that I just don't know —

Mrs. Linde: Oh, we'll fix that up in no time. It's nothing more than the trimmings — they're a bit loose here and there. Needle and thread? Good, now we have what we need.

Nora: Oh, how sweet of you!

Mrs. Linde (sewing): So you'll be in disguise tomorrow, Nora. You know what? I'll stop by then for a moment and have a look at you all dressed up. But listen, I've absolutely forgotten to thank you for that pleasant evening yesterday.

Nora (getting up and walking about): I don't think it was as pleasant as usual yesterday. You should have come to town a bit sooner, Kristine — Yes, Torvald really knows how to give a home elegance and charm.

Mrs. Linde: And you do, too, if you ask me. You're not your father's daughter for nothing. But tell me, is Dr. Rank always so down in the mouth as yesterday?

Nora: No, that was quite an exception. But he goes around critically ill all the time — tuberculosis of the spine, poor man. You know, his father was a disgusting thing who kept mistresses and so on — and that's why the son's been sickly from birth.

Mrs. Linde (lets her sewing fall to her lap): But my dearest Nora, how do you know about such things?

Nora (walking more jauntily): Hmp! When you've had three children, then you've had a few visits from — from women who know something of medicine, and they tell you this and that.

Mrs. Linde (resumes sewing; a short pause): Does Dr. Rank come here every day?

Nora: Every blessed day. He's Torvald's best friend from childhood, and *my* good friend, too. Dr. Rank almost belongs to this house.

Mrs. Linde: But tell me — is he quite sincere? I mean, doesn't he rather enjoy flattering people?

Nora: Just the opposite. Why do you think that?

Mrs. Linde: When you introduced us yesterday, he was proclaiming that he'd often heard my name in this house; but later I noticed that your husband hadn't the slightest idea who I really was. So how could Dr. Rank — ?

Nora: But it's all true, Kristine. You see, Torvald loves me beyond words, and, as he puts it, he'd like to keep me all to himself. For a long time he'd almost be jealous if I even mentioned any of my old friends back home. So of course I dropped that. But with Dr. Rank I talk a lot about such things, because he likes hearing about them.

Mrs. Linde: Now listen, Nora; in many ways you're still like a child. I'm a good deal older than you, with a little more experience. I'll tell you something: you ought to put an end to all this with Dr. Rank.

Nora: What should I put an end to?

Mrs. Linde: Both parts of it, I think. Yesterday you said something about a rich admirer who'd provide you with money —

Nora: Yes, one who doesn't exist — worse luck. So?

Mrs. Linde: Is Dr. Rank well off?

Nora: Yes, he is.

Mrs. Linde: With no dependents?

Nora: No, no one. But —

Mrs. Linde: And he's over here every day?

Nora: Yes, I told you that.

Mrs. Linde: How can a man of such refinement be so grasping?

Nora: I don't follow you at all.

Mrs. Linde: Now don't try to hide it, Nora. You think I can't guess who loaned you the forty-eight hundred crowns?

Nora: Are you out of your mind? How could you think such a thing! A friend of ours, who comes here every single day. What an intolerable situation that would have been!

Mrs. Linde: Then it really wasn't him.

Nora: No, absolutely not. It never even crossed my mind for a moment — And he had nothing to lend in those days; his inheritance came later.

Mrs. Linde: Well, I think that was a stroke of luck for you, Nora dear.

Nora: No, it never would have occurred to me to ask Dr. Rank — Still, I'm quite sure that if I had asked him —

Mrs. Linde: Which you won't, of course.

Nora: No, of course not. I can't see that I'd ever need to. But I'm quite positive that if I talked to Dr. Rank —

Mrs. Linde: Behind your husband's back?

Nora: I've got to clear up this other thing; *that's* also behind his back. I've *got* to clear it all up.

Mrs. Linde: Yes, I was saying that yesterday, but —

Nora (pacing up and down): A man handles these problems so much better than a woman —

Mrs. Linde: One's husband does, yes.

Nora: Nonsense. *(Stopping.)* When you pay everything you owe, then you get your note back, right?

Mrs. Linde: Yes, naturally.

Nora: And can rip it into a million pieces and burn it up — that filthy scrap of paper!

Mrs. Linde (looking hard at her, laying her sewing aside, and rising slowly): Nora, you're hiding something from me.

Nora: You can see it in my face?

Mrs. Linde: Something's happened to you since yesterday morning. Nora, what is it?

Nora (hurrying toward her): Kristine! *(Listening.)* Shh! Torvald's home. Look, go in with the children a while. Torvald can't bear all this snipping and stitching. Let Anne-Marie help you.

Mrs. Linde (gathering up some of the things): All right, but I'm not leaving here until we've talked this out. *(She disappears into the room, left, as Torvald enters from the hall.)*

Nora: Oh, how I've been waiting for you, Torvald dear.

Helmer: Was that the dressmaker?

Nora: No, that was Kristine. She's helping me fix up my costume. You know, it's going to be quite attractive.

Helmer: Yes, wasn't that a bright idea I had?

Nora: Brilliant! But then wasn't I good as well to give in to you?

Helmer: Good — because you give in to your husband's judgment? All right, you little goose, I know you didn't mean it like that. But I won't disturb you. You'll want to have a fitting, I suppose.

Nora: And you'll be working?

Helmer: Yes. *(Indicating a bundle of papers.)* See. I've been down to the bank. *(Starts toward his study.)*

Nora: Torvald.

Helmer (stops): Yes.

Nora: If your little squirrel begged you, with all her heart and soul, for something — ?

Helmer: What's that?

Nora: Then would you do it?

Helmer: First, naturally, I'd have to know what it was.

Nora: Your squirrel would scamper about and do tricks, if you'd only be sweet and give in.

Helmer: Out with it.

Nora: Your lark would be singing high and low in every room —

Helmer: Come on, she does that anyway.

Nora: I'd be a wood nymph and dance for you in the moonlight.

Helmer: Nora — don't tell me it's that same business from this morning?

Nora (coming closer): Yes, Torvald, I beg you, please!

Helmer: And you actually have the nerve to drag that up again?

Nora: Yes, yes, you've got to give in to me; you *have* to let Krogstad keep his job in the bank.

Helmer: My dear Nora, I've slated his job for Mrs. Linde.

Nora: That's awfully kind of you. But you could just fire another clerk instead of Krogstad.

Helmer: This is the most incredible stubbornness! Because you go and give an impulsive promise to speak up for him, I'm expected to —

Nora: That's not the reason, Torvald. It's for your own sake. That man does writing for the worst papers; you said it yourself. He could do you any amount of harm. I'm scared to death of him —

Helmer: Ah, I understand. It's the old memories haunting you.

Nora: What do you mean by that?

Helmer: Of course, you're thinking about your father.

Nora: Yes, all right. Just remember how those nasty gossips wrote in the papers about Papa and slandered him so cruelly. I think they'd have had him dismissed if the department hadn't sent you up to investigate, and if you hadn't been so kind and open-minded toward him.

Helmer: My dear Nora, there's a notable difference between your father and me. Your father's official career was hardly above reproach. But mine is; and I hope it'll stay that way as long as I hold my position.

Nora: Oh, who can ever tell what vicious minds can invent? We could be so snug and happy now in our quiet, carefree home — you and I and the children, Torvald! That's why I'm pleading with you so —

Helmer: And just by pleading for him you make it impossible for me to keep him on. It's already known at the bank that I'm firing Krogstad. What if it's rumored around now that the new bank manager was vetoed by his wife —

Nora: Yes, what then — ?

Helmer: Oh yes — as long as our little bundle of stubbornness gets her way — ! I should go and make myself ridiculous in front of the whole office — give people the idea I can be swayed by all kinds of outside pressure. Oh, you can bet I'd feel the effects of that soon enough! Besides — there's something that rules Krogstad right out at the bank as long as I'm the manager.

Nora: What's that?

Helmer: His moral failings I could maybe overlook if I had to —

Nora: Yes, Torvald, why not?

Helmer: And I hear he's quite efficient on the job. But he was a crony of mine back in my teens — one of those rash friendships that crop up again and again to embarrass you later in life. Well, I might as well say it straight out: we're on a first-name basis. And that tactless fool makes no effort at all to hide it in front of others. Quite the contrary — he thinks that entitles him to take a familiar air around me, and so every other second he comes booming out with his "Yes, Torvald!" and "Sure thing, Torvald!" I tell you, it's been excruciating for me. He's out to make my place in the bank unbearable.

Nora: Torvald, you can't be serious about all this.

Helmer: Oh no? Why not?

Nora: Because these are such petty considerations.

Helmer: What are you saying? Petty? You think I'm petty!

Nora: No, just the opposite, Torvald dear. That's exactly why —

Helmer: Never mind. You call my motives petty; then I might as well be just that. Petty! All right! We'll put a stop to this for good. *(Goes to the hall door and calls.)* Helene!

Nora: What do you want?

Helmer (searching among his papers): A decision. *(The Maid comes in.)* Look here; take this letter; go out with it at once. Get hold of a messenger and have him deliver it. Quick now. It's already addressed. Wait, here's some money.

Maid: Yes, sir. *(She leaves with the letter.)*

Helmer (straightening his papers): There, now, little Miss Willful.

Nora (breathlessly): Torvald, what was that letter?

Helmer: Krogstad's notice.

Nora: Call it back, Torvald! There's still time. Oh, Torvald, call it back! Do it for my sake — for your sake, for the children's sake! Do you hear, Torvald; do it! You don't know how this can harm us.

Helmer: Too late.

Nora: Yes, too late.

Helmer: Nora dear, I can forgive you this panic, even though basically you're insulting me. Yes, you are! Or isn't it an insult to think that *I* should be afraid of a courtroom hack's revenge? But I forgive you anyway, because this shows so beautifully how much you love me. *(Takes her in his arms.)* This is the way it should be, my darling Nora. Whatever comes, you'll see: when it really counts, I have strength and courage enough as a man to take on the whole weight myself.

Nora (terrified): What do you mean by that?

Helmer: The whole weight, I said.

Nora (resolutely): No, never in all the world.

Helmer: Good. So we'll share it, Nora, as man and wife. That's as it should be. *(Fondling her.)* Are you happy now? There, there, there — not these frightened dove's eyes. It's nothing at all but empty fantasies — Now you should run through your tarantella and practice your tambourine. I'll go to the inner office and shut both doors, so I won't hear a thing; you can make all the noise you like. *(Turning in the doorway.)* And when Rank comes, just tell him where he can find me. *(He nods to her and goes with his papers into the study, closing the door.)*

Nora (standing as though rooted, dazed with fright, in a whisper): He really could do it. He will do it. He'll do it in spite of everything. No, not that, never, never! Anything but that! Escape! A way out — *(The doorbell rings.)* Dr. Rank! Anything but that! *Anything,* whatever it is! *(Her hands pass over her face, smoothing it; she pulls herself together, goes over and opens the hall door. Dr. Rank stands outside, hanging his fur coat up. During the following scene, it begins getting dark.)*

Nora: Hello, Dr. Rank. I recognized your ring. But you mustn't go in to Torvald yet; I believe he's working.

Rank: And you?

Nora: For you, I always have an hour to spare — you know that. *(He has entered, and she shuts the door after him.)*

Rank: Many thanks. I'll make use of these hours while I can.

Nora: What do you mean by that? While you can?

Rank: Does that disturb you?

Nora: Well, it's such an odd phrase. Is anything going to happen?

Rank: What's going to happen is what I've been expecting so long — but I honestly didn't think it would come so soon.

Nora (gripping his arm): What is it you've found out? Dr. Rank, you have to tell me!

Rank (sitting by the stove): It's all over with me. There's nothing to be done about it.

Nora (breathing easier): Is it you — then — ?

Rank: Who else? There's no point in lying to one's self. I'm the most miserable of all my patients, Mrs. Helmer. These past few days I've been auditing my internal accounts. Bankrupt! Within a month I'll probably be laid out and rotting in the churchyard.

Nora: Oh, what a horrible thing to say.

Rank: The thing itself is horrible. But the worst of it is all the other horror before it's over. There's only one final examination left; when I'm finished with that, I'll know about when my disintegration will begin. There's something I want to say. Helmer with his sensitivity has such a sharp distaste for anything ugly. I don't want him near my sickroom.

Nora: Oh, but Dr. Rank —

Rank: I won't have him in there. Under no condition. I'll lock my door to him — As soon as I'm completely sure of the worst, I'll send you my calling card marked with a black cross, and you'll know then the wreck has started to come apart.

Nora: No, today you're completely unreasonable. And I wanted you so much to be in a really good humor.

Rank: With death up my sleeve? And then to suffer this way for somebody else's sins. Is there any justice in that? And in every single family, in some way or another, this inevitable retribution of nature goes on —

Nora (her hands pressed over her ears): Oh, stuff! Cheer up! Please — be gay!

Rank: Yes, I'd just as soon laugh at it all. My poor, innocent spine, serving time for my father's gay army days.

Nora (by the table, left): He was so infatuated with asparagus tips and *pâté de foie gras,* wasn't that it?

Rank: Yes — and with truffles.

Nora: Truffles, yes. And then with oysters, I suppose?

Rank: Yes, tons of oysters, naturally.

Nora: And then the port and champagne to go with it. It's so sad that all these delectable things have to strike at our bones.

Rank: Especially when they strike at the unhappy bones that never shared in the fun.

Nora: Ah, that's the saddest of all.

Rank (looks searchingly at her): Hm.

Nora (after a moment): Why did you smile?

Rank: No, it was you who laughed.

Nora: No, it was you who smiled, Dr. Rank!

Rank (getting up): You're even a bigger tease than I'd thought.

Nora: I'm full of wild ideas today.

Rank: That's obvious.

Nora (putting both hands on his shoulders): Dear, dear Dr. Rank, you'll never die for Torvald and me.

Rank: Oh, that loss you'll easily get over. Those who go away are soon forgotten.

Nora (looks fearfully at him): You believe that?

Rank: One makes new connections, and then —

Nora: Who makes new connections?

Rank: Both you and Torvald will when I'm gone. I'd say you're well under way already. What was that Mrs. Linde doing here last evening?

Nora: Oh, come — you can't be jealous of poor Kristine?

Rank: Oh yes, I am. She'll be my successor here in the house. When I'm down under, that woman will probably —

Nora: Shh! Not so loud. She's right in there.

Rank: Today as well. So you see.

Nora: Only to sew on my dress. Good gracious, how unreasonable you are. *(Sitting on the sofa.)* Be nice now, Dr. Rank. Tomorrow you'll see how beautifully I'll dance; and you can imagine then that I'm dancing only for you — yes, and of course for Torvald, too — that's understood. *(Takes various items out of the carton.)* Dr. Rank, sit over here and I'll show you something.

Rank (sitting): What's that?

Nora: Look here. Look.

Rank: Silk stockings.

Nora: Flesh-colored. Aren't they lovely? Now it's so dark here, but tomorrow — No, no, no, just look at the feet. Oh well, you might as well look at the rest.

Rank: Hm —

Nora: Why do you look so critical? Don't you believe they'll fit?

Rank: I've never had any chance to form an opinion on that.

Nora (glancing at him a moment): Shame on you. *(Hits him lightly on the ear with the stockings.)* That's for you. *(Puts them away again.)*

Rank: And what other splendors am I going to see now?

Nora: Not the least bit more, because you've been naughty. *(She hums a little and rummages among her things.)*

Rank (after a short silence): When I sit here together with you like this, completely easy and open, then I don't know — I simply can't imagine — whatever would have become of me if I'd never come into this house.

Nora (smiling): Yes, I really think you feel completely at ease with us.

Rank (more quietly, staring straight ahead): And then to have to go away from it all —

Nora: Nonsense, you're not going away.

Rank (his voice unchanged): — and not even be able to leave some poor show of gratitude behind, scarcely a fleeting regret — no more than a vacant place that anyone can fill.

Nora: And if I asked you now for — ? No —

Rank: For what?

Nora: For a great proof of your friendship —

Rank: Yes, yes?

Nora: No, I mean — for an exceptionally big favor —

Rank: Would you really, for once, make me so happy?

Nora: Oh, you haven't the vaguest idea what it is.

Rank: All right, then tell me.

Nora: No, but I can't, Dr. Rank — it's all out of reason. It's advice and help, too — and a favor —

Rank: So much the better. I can't fathom what you're hinting at. Just speak out. Don't you trust me?

Nora: Of course. More than anyone else. You're my best and truest friend, I'm sure. That's why I want to talk to you. All right, then, Dr. Rank: there's something you can help me prevent. You know how deeply, how inexpressibly dearly Torvald loves me; he'd never hesitate a second to give up his life for me.

Rank (leaning close to her): Nora — do you think he's the only one —

Nora (with a slight start): Who — ?

Rank: Who'd gladly give up his life for you.

Nora (heavily): I see.

Rank: I swore to myself you should know this before I'm gone. I'll never find a better chance. Yes, Nora, now you know. And also you know now that you can trust me beyond anyone else.

Nora (rising, natural and calm): Let me by.

Rank (making room for her, but still sitting): Nora —

Nora (in the hall doorway): Helene, bring the lamp in. *(Goes over to the stove.)* Ah, dear Dr. Rank, that was really mean of you.

Rank (getting up): That I've loved you just as deeply as somebody else? Was *that* mean?

Nora: No, but that you came out and told me. That was quite unnecessary —

Rank: What do you mean? Have you known — ?

The Maid comes in with the lamp, sets it on the table, and goes out again.

Rank: Nora — Mrs. Helmer — I'm asking you: have you known about it?

Nora: Oh, how can I tell what I know or don't know? Really, I don't know what to say — Why did you have to be so clumsy, Dr. Rank! Everything was so good.

Rank: Well, in any case, you now have the knowledge that my body and soul are at your command. So won't you speak out?

Nora (looking at him): After that?

Rank: Please, just let me know what it is.

Nora: You can't know anything now.

Rank: I have to. You mustn't punish me like this. Give me the chance to do whatever is humanly possible for you.

Nora: Now there's nothing you can do for me. Besides, actually, I don't need any help. You'll see — it's only my fantasies. That's what it is. Of course!

(Sits in the rocker, looks at him, and smiles.) What a nice one you are, Dr. Rank. Aren't you a little bit ashamed, now that the lamp is here?

Rank: No, not exactly. But perhaps I'd better go — for good?

Nora: No, you certainly can't do that. You must come here just as you always have. You know Torvald can't do without you.

Rank: Yes, but *you?*

Nora: You know how much I enjoy it when you're here.

Rank: That's precisely what threw me off. You're a mystery to me. So many times I've felt you'd almost rather be with me than with Helmer.

Nora: Yes — you see, there are some people that one loves most and other people that one would almost prefer being with.

Rank: Yes, there's something to that.

Nora: When I was back home, of course I loved Papa most. But I always thought it was so much fun when I could sneak down to the maids' quarters, because they never tried to improve me, and it was always so amusing, the way they talked to each other.

Rank: Aha, so it's *their* place that I've filled.

Nora (jumping up and going to him): Oh, dear, sweet Dr. Rank, that's not what I mean at all. But you can understand that with Torvald it's just the same as with Papa —

The Maid enters from the hall.

Maid: Ma'am — please! *(She whispers to Nora and hands her a calling card.)*

Nora (glancing at the card): Ah! *(Slips it into her pocket.)*

Rank: Anything wrong?

Nora: No, no, not at all. It's only some — it's my new dress —

Rank: Really? But — there's your dress.

Nora: Oh, that. But this is another one — I ordered it — Torvald mustn't know —

Rank: Ah, now we have the big secret.

Nora: That's right. Just go in with him — he's back in the inner study. Keep him there as long as —

Rank: Don't worry. He won't get away. *(Goes into the study.)*

Nora (to the Maid): And he's standing waiting in the kitchen?

Maid: Yes, he came up by the back stairs.

Nora: But didn't you tell him somebody was here?

Maid: Yes, but that didn't do any good.

Nora: He won't leave?

Maid: No, he won't go till he's talked with you, ma'am.

Nora: Let him come in, then — but quietly. Helene, don't breathe a word about this. It's a surprise for my husband.

Maid: Yes, yes, I understand — *(Goes out.)*

Nora: This horror — it's going to happen. No, no, no, it can't happen, it mustn't. *(She goes and bolts Helmer's door. The Maid opens the hall door for Krogstad and shuts it behind him. He is dressed for travel in a fur coat, boots, and a fur cap.)*

Nora (going toward him): Talk softly. My husband's home.

Krogstad: Well, good for him.

Nora: What do you want?

Krogstad: Some information.

Nora: Hurry up, then. What is it?

Krogstad: You know, of course, that I got my notice.

Nora: I couldn't prevent it, Mr. Krogstad. I fought for you to the bitter end, but nothing worked.

Krogstad: Does your husband's love for you run so thin? He knows everything I can expose you to, and all the same he dares to —

Nora: How can you imagine he knows anything about this?

Krogstad: Ah, no — I can't imagine it either, now. It's not at all like my fine Torvald Helmer to have so much guts —

Nora: Mr. Krogstad, I demand respect for my husband!

Krogstad: Why, of course — all due respect. But since the lady's keeping it so carefully hidden, may I presume to ask if you're also a bit better informed than yesterday about what you've actually done?

Nora: More than you ever could teach me.

Krogstad: Yes, I *am* such an awful lawyer.

Nora: What is it you want from me?

Krogstad: Just a glimpse of how you are, Mrs. Helmer. I've been thinking about you all day long. A cashier, a night-court scribbler, a — well, a type like me also has a little of what they call a heart, you know.

Nora: Then show it. Think of my children.

Krogstad: Did you or your husband ever think of mine? But never mind. I simply wanted to tell you that you don't need to take this thing too seriously. For the present, I'm not proceeding with any action.

Nora: Oh no, really! Well — I knew that.

Krogstad: Everything can be settled in a friendly spirit. It doesn't have to get around town at all; it can stay just among us three.

Nora: My husband must never know anything of this.

Krogstad: How can you manage that? Perhaps you can pay me the balance?

Nora: No, not right now.

Krogstad: Or you know some way of raising the money in a day or two?

Nora: No way that I'm willing to use.

Krogstad: Well, it wouldn't have done you any good, anyway. If you stood in front of me with a fistful of bills, you still couldn't buy your signature back.

Nora: Then tell me what you're going to do with it.

Krogstad: I'll just hold onto it — keep it on file. There's no outsider who'll even get wind of it. So if you've been thinking of taking some desperate step —

Nora: I have.

Krogstad: Been thinking of running away from home —

Nora: I have!

Krogstad: Or even of something worse —

Nora: How could you guess that?

Krogstad: You can drop those thoughts.

Nora: How could you guess I was thinking of *that?*

Krogstad: Most of us think about *that* at first. I thought about it too, but I discovered I hadn't the courage —

Nora (lifelessly): I don't either.

Krogstad (relieved): That's true, you haven't the courage? You too?

Nora: I don't have it — I don't have it.

Krogstad: It would be terribly stupid, anyway. After that first storm at home blows out, why, then — I have here in my pocket a letter for your husband —

Nora: Telling everything?

Krogstad: As charitably as possible.

Nora (quickly): He mustn't ever get that letter. Tear it up. I'll find some way to get money.

Krogstad: Beg pardon, Mrs. Helmer, but I think I just told you —

Nora: Oh, I don't mean the money I owe you. Let me know how much you want from my husband, and I'll manage it.

Krogstad: I don't want any money from your husband.

Nora: What do you want, then?

Krogstad: I'll tell you what. I want to recoup, Mrs. Helmer; I want to get on in the world — and there's where your husband can help me. For a year and a half I've kept myself clean of anything disreputable — all that time struggling with the worst conditions; but I was satisfied, working my way up step by step. Now I've been written right off, and I'm just not in the mood to come crawling back. I tell you, I want to move on. I want to get back in the bank — in a better position. Your husband can set up a job for me —

Nora: He'll never do that!

Krogstad: He'll do it. I know him. He won't dare breathe a word of protest. And once I'm in there together with him, you just wait and see! Inside of a year, I'll be the manager's right-hand man. It'll be Nils Krogstad, not Torvald Helmer, who runs the bank.

Nora: You'll never see the day!

Krogstad: Maybe you think you can —

Nora: I have the courage now — for *that.*

Krogstad: Oh, you don't scare me. A smart, spoiled lady like you —

Nora: You'll see; you'll see!

Krogstad: Under the ice, maybe? Down in the freezing, coal-black water? There, till you float up in the spring, ugly, unrecognizable, with your hair falling out —

Nora: You don't frighten me.

Krogstad: Nor do you frighten me. One doesn't do these things, Mrs. Helmer. Besides, what good would it be? I'd still have him safe in my pocket.

Nora: Afterwards? When I'm no longer — ?

Krogstad: Are you forgetting that *I'll* be in control then over your final reputation? *(Nora stands speechless, staring at him.)* Good; now I've warned you. Don't do anything stupid. When Helmer's read my letter, I'll be waiting for his reply. And bear in mind that it's your husband himself who's forced me back to my old ways. I'll never forgive him for that. Good-bye, Mrs. Helmer. *(He goes out through the hall.)*

Nora (goes to the hall door, opens it a crack, and listens): He's gone. Didn't leave the letter. Oh no, no, that's impossible too! *(Opening the door more and more.)* What's that? He's standing outside — not going downstairs. He's thinking it over? Maybe he'll — ? *(A letter falls in the mailbox; then Krogstad's footsteps are heard, dying away down a flight of stairs. Nora gives a muffled cry and runs over toward the sofa table. A short pause.)* In the mailbox. *(Slips warily over to the hall door.)* It's lying there. Torvald, Torvald — now we're lost!

Mrs. Linde (entering with the costume from the room, left): There now, I can't see anything else to mend. Perhaps you'd like to try —

Nora (in a hoarse whisper): Kristine, come here.

Mrs. Linde (tossing the dress on the sofa): What's wrong? You look upset.

Nora: Come here. See that letter? *There!* Look — through the glass in the mailbox.

Mrs. Linde: Yes, yes, I see it.

Nora: That letter's from Krogstad —

Mrs. Linde: Nora — it's Krogstad who loaned you the money!

Nora: Yes, and now Torvald will find out everything.

Mrs. Linde: Believe me, Nora, it's best for both of you.

Nora: There's more you don't know. I forged a name.

Mrs. Linde: But for heaven's sake — ?

Nora: I only want to tell you that, Kristine, so that you can be my witness.

Mrs. Linde: Witness? Why should I — ?

Nora: If I should go out of my mind — it could easily happen —

Mrs. Linde: Nora!

Nora: Or anything else occurred — so I couldn't be present here —

Mrs. Linde: Nora, Nora, you aren't yourself at all!

Nora: And someone should try to take on the whole weight, all of the guilt, you follow me —

Mrs. Linde: Yes, of course, but why do you think — ?

Nora: Then you're the witness that it isn't true, Kristine. I'm very much myself; my mind right now is perfectly clear; and I'm telling you: nobody else has known about this; I alone did everything. Remember that.

Mrs. Linde: I will. But I don't understand all this.

Nora: Oh, how could you ever understand it? It's the miracle now that's going to take place.

Mrs. Linde: The miracle?

Nora: Yes, the miracle. But it's so awful, Kristine. It mustn't take place, not for anything in the world.

Mrs. Linde: I'm going right over and talk with Krogstad.

Nora: Don't go near him; he'll do you some terrible harm!

Mrs. Linde: There was a time once when he'd gladly have done anything for me.

Nora: He?

Mrs. Linde: Where does he live?

Nora: Oh, how do I know? Yes. *(Searches in her pocket.)* Here's his card. But the letter, the letter — !

Helmer (from the study, knocking on the door): Nora!

Nora (with a cry of fear): Oh! What is it? What do you want?

Helmer: Now, now, don't be so frightened. We're not coming in. You locked the door — are you trying on the dress?

Nora: Yes, I'm trying it. I'll look just beautiful, Torvald.

Mrs. Linde (who has read the card): He's living right around the corner.

Nora: Yes, but what's the use? We're lost. The letter's in the box.

Mrs. Linde: And your husband has the key?

Nora: Yes, always.

Mrs. Linde: Krogstad can ask for his letter back unread; he can find some excuse —

Nora: But it's just this time that Torvald usually —

Mrs. Linde: Stall him. Keep him in there. I'll be back as quick as I can. *(She hurries out through the hall entrance.)*

Nora (goes to Helmer's door, opens it, and peers in): Torvald!

Helmer (from the inner study): Well — does one dare set foot in one's own living room at last? Come on, Rank, now we'll get a look — *(In the doorway.)* But what's this?

Nora: What, Torvald dear?

Helmer: Rank had me expecting some grand masquerade.

Rank (in the doorway): That was my impression, but I must have been wrong.

Nora: No one can admire me in my splendor — not till tomorrow.

Helmer: But Nora dear, you look so exhausted. Have you practiced too hard?

Nora: No, I haven't practiced at all yet.

Helmer: You know, it's necessary —

Nora: Oh, it's absolutely necessary, Torvald. But I can't get anywhere without your help. I've forgotten the whole thing completely.

Helmer: Ah, we'll soon take care of that.

Nora: Yes, take care of me, Torvald, please! Promise me that? Oh, I'm so nervous. That big party — You must give up everything this evening for me. No business — don't even touch your pen. Yes? Dear Torvald, promise?

Helmer: It's a promise. Tonight I'm totally at your service — you little helpless thing. Hm — but first there's one thing I want to — *(Goes toward the hall door.)*

Nora: What are you looking for?

Helmer: Just to see if there's any mail.

Nora: No, no, don't do that, Torvald!

Helmer: Now what?

Nora: Torvald, please. There isn't any.

Helmer: Let me look, though. *(Starts out. Nora, at the piano, strikes the first notes of the tarantella. Helmer, at the door, stops.)* Aha!

Nora: I can't dance tomorrow if I don't practice with you.

Helmer (going over to her): Nora dear, are you really so frightened?

Nora: Yes, so terribly frightened. Let me practice right now; there's still time before dinner. Oh, sit down and play for me, Torvald. Direct me. Teach me, the way you always have.

Helmer: Gladly, if it's what you want. *(Sits at the piano.)*

Nora (snatches the tambourine up from the box, then a long, varicolored shawl, which she throws around herself, whereupon she springs forward and cries out): Play for me now! Now I'll dance!

Helmer plays and Nora dances. Rank stands behind Helmer at the piano and looks on.

Helmer (as he plays): Slower. Slow down.

Nora: Can't change it.

Helmer: Not so violent, Nora!

Nora: Has to be just like this.

Helmer (stopping): No, no, that won't do at all.

Nora (laughing and swinging her tambourine): Isn't that what I told you?

Rank: Let me play for her.

Helmer (getting up): Yes, go on. I can teach her more easily then.

> *Rank sits at the piano and plays; Nora dances more and more wildly. Helmer has stationed himself by the stove and repeatedly gives her directions; she seems not to hear them; her hair loosens and falls over her shoulders; she does not notice, but goes on dancing. Mrs. Linde enters.*

Mrs. Linde (standing dumbfounded at the door): Ah — !

Nora (still dancing): See what fun, Kristine!

Helmer: But Nora darling, you dance as if your life were at stake.

Nora: And it is.

Helmer: Rank, stop! This is pure madness. Stop it, I say!

> *Rank breaks off playing, and Nora halts abruptly.*

Helmer (going over to her): I never would have believed it. You've forgotten everything I taught you.

Nora (throwing away the tambourine): You see for yourself.

Helmer: Well, there's certainly room for instruction here.

Nora: Yes, you see how important it is. You've got to teach me to the very last minute. Promise me that, Torvald?

Helmer: You can bet on it.

Nora: You mustn't, either today or tomorrow, think about anything else but me; you mustn't open any letters — or the mailbox —

Helmer: Ah, it's still the fear of that man —

Nora: Oh yes, yes, that too.

Helmer: Nora, it's written all over you — there's already a letter from him out there.

Nora: I don't know. I guess so. But you mustn't read such things now; there mustn't be anything ugly between us before it's all over.

Rank (quietly to Helmer): You shouldn't deny her.

Helmer (putting his arm around her): The child can have her way. But tomorrow night, after you've danced —

Nora: Then you'll be free.

Maid (in the doorway, right): Ma'am, dinner is served.

Nora: We'll be wanting champagne, Helene.

Maid: Very good, ma'am. *(Goes out.)*

Helmer: So — a regular banquet, hm?

Nora: Yes, a banquet — champagne till daybreak! *(Calling out.)* And some maca-roons, Helene. Heaps of them — just this once.

Helmer (taking her hands): Now, now, now — no hysterics. Be my own little lark again.

Nora: Oh, I will soon enough. But go on in — and you, Dr. Rank. Kristine, help me put up my hair.

Rank (whispering, as they go): There's nothing wrong — really wrong, is there?

Helmer: Oh, of course not. It's nothing more than this childish anxiety I was telling you about. *(They go out, right.)*

Nora: Well?

Mrs. Linde: Left town.

Nora: I could see by your face.

Mrs. Linde: He'll be home tomorrow evening. I wrote him a note.

Nora: You shouldn't have. Don't try to stop anything now. After all, it's a wonderful joy, this waiting here for the miracle.

Mrs. Linde: What is it you're waiting for?

Nora: Oh, you can't understand that. Go in to them: I'll be along in a moment.

Mrs. Linde goes into the dining room. Nora stands a short while as if composing herself; then she looks at her watch.

Nora: Five. Seven hours to midnight. Twenty-four hours to the midnight after, and then the tarantella's done. Seven and twenty-four? Thirty-one hours to live.

Helmer (in the doorway, right): What's become of the little lark?

Nora (going toward him with open arms): Here's your lark!

ACT III

Same scene. The table, with chairs around it, has been moved to the center of the room. A lamp on the table is lit. The hall door stands open. Dance music drifts down from the floor above. Mrs. Linde sits at the table, absently paging through a book, trying to read, but apparently unable to focus her thoughts. Once or twice she pauses, tensely listening for a sound at the outer entrance.

Mrs. Linde (glancing at her watch): Not yet — and there's hardly any time left. If only he's not — (*Listening again.*) Ah, there he is. (*She goes out in the hall and cautiously opens the outer door. Quiet footsteps are heard on the stairs. She whispers:*) Come in. Nobody's here.

Krogstad (in the doorway): I found a note from you at home. What's back of all this?

Mrs. Linde: I just *had* to talk to you.

Krogstad: Oh? And it just *had* to be here in this house?

Mrs. Linde: At my place it was impossible; my room hasn't a private entrance. Come in; we're all alone. The maid's asleep, and the Helmers are at the dance upstairs.

Krogstad (entering the room): Well, well, the Helmers are dancing tonight? Really?

Mrs. Linde: Yes, why not?

Krogstad: How true — why not?

Mrs. Linde: All right, Krogstad, let's talk.

Krogstad: Do we two have anything more to talk about?

Mrs. Linde: We have a great deal to talk about.

Krogstad: I wouldn't have thought so.

Mrs. Linde: No, because you've never understood me, really.

Krogstad: Was there anything more to understand — except what's all too common in life? A calculating woman throws over a man the moment a better catch comes by.

Mrs. Linde: You think I'm so thoroughly calculating? You think I broke it off lightly?

Krogstad: Didn't you?

Mrs. Linde: Nils — is that what you really thought?

Krogstad: If you cared, then why did you write me the way you did?

Mrs. Linde: What else could I do? If I had to break off with you, then it was my job as well to root out everything you felt for me.

Krogstad (wringing his hands): So that was it. And this — all this, simply for money!

Mrs. Linde: Don't forget I had a helpless mother and two small brothers. We couldn't wait for you, Nils; you had such a long road ahead of you then.

Krogstad: That may be; but you still hadn't the right to abandon me for somebody else's sake.

Mrs. Linde: Yes — I don't know. So many, many times I've asked myself if I did have that right.

Krogstad (more softly): When I lost you, it was as if all the solid ground dissolved from under my feet. Look at me; I'm a half-drowned man now, hanging onto a wreck.

Mrs. Linde: Help may be near.

Krogstad: It was near — but then you came and blocked it off.

Mrs. Linde: Without my knowing it, Nils. Today for the first time I learned that it's you I'm replacing at the bank.

Krogstad: All right — I believe you. But now that you know, will you step aside?

Mrs. Linde: No, because that wouldn't benefit you in the slightest.

Krogstad: Not "benefit" me, hm! I'd step aside anyway.

Mrs. Linde: I've learned to be realistic. Life and hard, bitter necessity have taught me that.

Krogstad: And life's taught me never to trust fine phrases.

Mrs. Linde: Then life's taught you a very sound thing. But you do have to trust in actions, don't you?

Krogstad: What does that mean?

Mrs. Linde: You said you were hanging on like a half-drowned man to a wreck.

Krogstad: I've good reason to say that.

Mrs. Linde: I'm also like a half-drowned woman on a wreck. No one to suffer with; no one to care for.

Krogstad: You made your choice.

Mrs. Linde: There wasn't any choice then.

Krogstad: So — what of it?

Mrs. Linde: Nils, if only we two shipwrecked people could reach across to each other.

Krogstad: What are you saying?

Mrs. Linde: Two on one wreck are at least better off than each on his own.

Krogstad: Kristine!

Mrs. Linde: Why do you think I came into town?

Krogstad: Did you really have some thought of me?

Mrs. Linde: I have to work to go on living. All my born days, as long as I can remember, I've worked, and it's been my best and my only joy. But now I'm completely alone in the world; it frightens me to be so empty and lost. To work for yourself — there's no joy in that. Nils, give me something — someone to work for.

Krogstad: I don't believe all this. It's just some hysterical feminine urge to go out and make a noble sacrifice.

Mrs. Linde: Have you ever found me to be hysterical?

Krogstad: Can you honestly mean this? Tell me — do you know everything about my past?

Mrs. Linde: Yes.

Krogstad: And you know what they think I'm worth around here.

Mrs. Linde: From what you were saying before, it would seem that with me you could have been another person.

Krogstad: I'm positive of that.

Mrs. Linde: Couldn't it happen still?

Krogstad: Kristine — you're saying this in all seriousness? Yes, you are! I can see it in you. And do you really have the courage, then — ?

Mrs. Linde: I need to have someone to care for; and your children need a mother. We both need each other. Nils, I have faith that you're good at heart — I'll risk everything together with you.

Krogstad (gripping her hands): Kristine, thank you, thank you — Now I know I can win back a place in their eyes. Yes — but I forgot —

Mrs. Linde (listening): Shh! The tarantella. Go now! Go on!

Krogstad: Why? What is it?

Mrs. Linde: Hear the dance up there? When that's over, they'll be coming down.

Krogstad: Oh, then I'll go. But — it's all pointless. Of course, you don't know the move I made against the Helmers.

Mrs. Linde: Yes, Nils, I know.

Krogstad: And all the same, you have the courage to — ?

Mrs. Linde: I know how far despair can drive a man like you.

Krogstad: Oh, if I only could take it all back.

Mrs. Linde: You easily could — your letter's still lying in the mailbox.

Krogstad: Are you sure of that?

Mrs. Linde: Positive. But —

Krogstad (looks at her searchingly): Is that the meaning of it, then? You'll save your friend at any price. Tell me straight out. Is that it?

Mrs. Linde: Nils — anyone who's sold herself for somebody else once isn't going to do it again.

Krogstad: I'll demand my letter back.

Mrs. Linde: No, no.

Krogstad: Yes, of course. I'll stay here till Helmer comes down; I'll tell him to give me my letter again — that it only involves my dismissal — that he shouldn't read it —

Mrs. Linde: No, Nils, don't call the letter back.

Krogstad: But wasn't that exactly why you wrote me to come here?

Mrs. Linde: Yes, in that first panic. But it's been a whole day and night since then, and in that time I've seen such incredible things in this house. Helmer's got to learn everything; this dreadful secret has to be aired; those two have to come to a full understanding; all these lies and evasions can't go on.

Krogstad: Well, then, if you want to chance it. But at least there's one thing I can do, and do right away —

Mrs. Linde (listening): Go now, go, quick! The dance is over. We're not safe another second.

Krogstad: I'll wait for you downstairs.

Mrs. Linde: Yes, please do; take me home.

Krogstad: I can't believe it; I've never been so happy. *(He leaves by way of the outer door; the door between the room and the hall stays open.)*

Mrs. Linde (straightening up a bit and getting together her street clothes): How different now! How different! Someone to work for, to live for — a home to build. Well, it is worth the try! Oh, if they'd only come! *(Listening.)* Ah, there they are. Bundle up. *(She picks up her hat and coat. Nora's and Helmer's voices can be heard outside; a key turns in the lock, and Helmer brings Nora into the hall almost by force. She is wearing the Italian costume with a large black shawl about her; he has on evening dress, with a black domino open over it.)*

Nora (struggling in the doorway): No, no, no, not inside! I'm going up again. I don't want to leave so soon.

Helmer: But Nora dear —

Nora: Oh, I beg you, please, Torvald. From the bottom of my heart, *please* — only an hour more!

Helmer: Not a single minute, Nora darling. You know our agreement. Come on, in we go; you'll catch cold out here. *(In spite of her resistance, he gently draws her into the room.)*

Mrs. Linde: Good evening.

Nora: Kristine!

Helmer: Why, Mrs. Linde — are you here so late?

Mrs. Linde: Yes, I'm sorry, but I did want to see Nora in costume.

Nora: Have you been sitting here, waiting for me?

Mrs. Linde: Yes. I didn't come early enough; you were all upstairs; and then I thought I really couldn't leave without seeing you.

Helmer (removing Nora's shawl): Yes, take a good look. She's worth looking at, I can tell you that, Mrs. Linde. Isn't she lovely?

Mrs. Linde: Yes, I should say —

Helmer: A dream of loveliness, isn't she? That's what everyone thought at the party, too. But she's horribly stubborn — this sweet little thing. What's to be done with her? Can you imagine, I almost had to use force to pry her away.

Nora: Oh, Torvald, you're going to regret you didn't indulge me, even for just a half hour more.

Helmer: There, you see. She danced her tarantella and got a tumultuous hand — which was well earned, although the performance may have been a bit too naturalistic — I mean it rather overstepped the proprieties of art. But never mind — what's important is, she made a success, an overwhelming success. You think I could let her stay on after that and spoil the effect? Oh no; I took my lovely little Capri girl — my capricious little Capri girl, I should say — took her under my arm; one quick tour of the ballroom, a curtsy to every side, and then — as they say in novels — the beautiful vision disappeared. An exit should always be effective, Mrs. Linde, but that's what I can't get Nora to grasp. Phew, it's hot in here. *(Flings the domino on a chair and opens the door to his room.)* Why's it dark in here? Oh yes, of course. Excuse me. *(He goes in and lights a couple of candles.)*

Nora (in a sharp, breathless whisper): So?

Mrs. Linde (quietly): I talked with him.

Nora: And — ?

Mrs. Linde: Nora — you must tell your husband everything.

Nora (dully): I knew it.

Mrs. Linde: You've got nothing to fear from Krogstad, but you have to speak out.

Nora: I won't tell.

Mrs. Linde: Then the letter will.

Nora: Thanks, Kristine. I know now what's to be done. Shh!

Helmer (reentering): Well, then, Mrs. Linde — have you admired her?

Mrs. Linde: Yes, and now I'll say good night.

Helmer: Oh, come, so soon? Is this yours, this knitting?

Mrs. Linde: Yes, thanks. I nearly forgot it.

Helmer: Do you knit, then?

Mrs. Linde: Oh yes.

Helmer: You know what? You should embroider instead.

Mrs. Linde: Really? Why?

Helmer: Yes, because it's a lot prettier. See here, one holds the embroidery so, in the left hand, and then one guides the needle with the right — so — in an easy, sweeping curve — right?

Mrs. Linde: Yes, I guess that's —

Helmer: But, on the other hand, knitting — it can never be anything but ugly. Look, see here, the arms tucked in, the knitting needles going up and down — there's something Chinese about it. Ah, that was really a glorious champagne they served.

Mrs. Linde: Yes, good night, Nora, and don't be stubborn any more.

Helmer: Well put, Mrs. Linde!

Mrs. Linde: Good night, Mr. Helmer.

Helmer (accompanying her to the door): Good night, good night. I hope you get home all right. I'd be very happy to — but you don't have far to go. Good night, good night. *(She leaves. He shuts the door after her and returns.)* There, now, at last we got her out the door. She's a deadly bore, that creature.

Nora: Aren't you pretty tired, Torvald?

Helmer: No, not a bit.

Nora: You're not sleepy?

Helmer: Not at all. On the contrary, I'm feeling quite exhilarated. But you? Yes, you really look tired and sleepy.

Nora: Yes, I'm very tired. Soon now I'll sleep.

Helmer: See! You see! I was right all along that we shouldn't stay longer.

Nora: Whatever you do is always right.

Helmer (kissing her brow): Now my little lark talks sense. Say, did you notice what a time Rank was having tonight?

Nora: Oh, was he? I didn't get to speak with him.

Helmer: I scarcely did either, but it's a long time since I've seen him in such high spirits. *(Gazes at her a moment, then comes nearer her.)* Hm — it's marvelous, though, to be back home again — to be completely alone with you. Oh, you bewitchingly lovely young woman!

Nora: Torvald, don't look at me like that!

Helmer: Can't I look at my richest treasure? At all that beauty that's mine, mine alone — completely and utterly.

Nora (moving around to the other side of the table): You mustn't talk to me that way tonight.

Helmer (following her): The tarantella is still in your blood, I can see — and it makes you even more enticing. Listen. The guests are beginning to go. *(Dropping his voice.)* Nora — it'll soon be quiet through this whole house.

Nora: Yes, I hope so.

Helmer: You do, don't you, my love? Do you realize — when I'm out at a party like this with you — do you know why I talk to you so little, and keep such a distance away; just send you a stolen look now and then — you know why I do it? It's because I'm imagining then that you're my secret darling, my secret young bride-to-be, and that no one suspects there's anything between us.

Nora: Yes, yes; oh, yes, I know you're always thinking of me.

Helmer: And then when we leave and I place the shawl over those fine young rounded shoulders — over that wonderful curving neck — then I pretend that you're my young bride, that we're just coming from the wedding, that for the first time I'm bringing you into my house — that for the first time I'm alone with you — completely alone with you, your trembling young beauty! All this evening I've longed for nothing but you. When I saw you turn and sway in the tarantella — my blood was pounding till I couldn't stand it — that's why I brought you down here so early —

Nora: Go away, Torvald! Leave me alone. I don't want all this.

Helmer: What do you mean? Nora, you're teasing me. You will, won't you? Aren't I your husband — ?

A knock at the outside door.

Nora (startled): What's that?

Helmer (going toward the hall): Who is it?

Rank (outside): It's me. May I come in a moment?

Helmer (with quiet irritation): Oh, what does he want now? *(Aloud.)* Hold on. *(Goes and opens the door.)* Oh, how nice that you didn't just pass us by!

Rank: I thought I heard your voice, and then I wanted so badly to have a look in. *(Lightly glancing about.)* Ah, me, these old familiar haunts. You have it snug and cozy in here, you two.

Helmer: You seemed to be having it pretty cozy upstairs, too.

Rank: Absolutely. Why shouldn't I? Why not take in everything in life? As much as you can, anyway, and as long as you can. The wine was superb —

Helmer: The champagne especially.

Rank: You noticed that too? It's amazing how much I could guzzle down.

Nora: Torvald also drank a lot of champagne this evening.

Rank: Oh?

Nora: Yes, and that always makes him so entertaining.

Rank: Well, why shouldn't one have a pleasant evening after a well-spent day?

Helmer: Well spent? I'm afraid I can't claim that.

Rank (slapping him on the back): But I can, you see!

Nora: Dr. Rank, you must have done some scientific research today.

Rank: Quite so.

Helmer: Come now — little Nora talking about scientific research!

Nora: And can I congratulate you on the results?

Rank: Indeed you may.

Nora: Then they were good?

Rank: The best possible for both doctor and patient — certainty.

Nora (quickly and searchingly): Certainty?

Rank: Complete certainty. So don't I owe myself a gay evening afterwards?

Nora: Yes, you're right, Dr. Rank.

Helmer: I'm with you — just so long as you don't have to suffer for it in the morning.

Rank: Well, one never gets something for nothing in life.

Nora: Dr. Rank — are you very fond of masquerade parties?

Rank: Yes, if there's a good array of odd disguises —

Nora: Tell me, what should we two go as at the next masquerade?

Helmer: You little featherhead — already thinking of the next!

Rank: We two? I'll tell you what: you must go as Charmed Life —

Helmer: Yes, but find a costume for *that!*

Rank: Your wife can appear just as she looks every day.

Helmer: That was nicely put. But don't you know what you're going to be?

Rank: Yes, Helmer, I've made up my mind.

Helmer: Well?

Rank: At the next masquerade I'm going to be invisible.

Helmer: That's a funny idea.

Rank: They say there's a hat — black, huge — have you never heard of the hat that makes you invisible? You put it on, and then no one on earth can see you.

Helmer (suppressing a smile): Ah, of course.

Rank: But I'm quite forgetting what I came for. Helmer, give me a cigar, one of the dark Havanas.

Helmer: With the greatest pleasure. *(Holds out his case.)*

Rank: Thanks. *(Takes one and cuts off the tip.)*

Nora (striking a match): Let me give you a light.

Rank: Thank you. *(She holds the match for him; he lights the cigar.)* And now good-bye.

Helmer: Good-bye, good-bye, old friend.

Nora: Sleep well, Doctor.

Rank: Thanks for that wish.

Nora: Wish me the same.

Rank: You? All right, if you like — Sleep well. And thanks for the light. *(He nods to them both and leaves.)*

Helmer (his voice subdued): He's been drinking heavily.

Nora (absently): Could be. *(Helmer takes his keys from his pocket and goes out in the hall.)* Torvald — what are you after?

Helmer: Got to empty the mailbox; it's nearly full. There won't be room for the morning papers.

Nora: Are you working tonight?

Helmer: You know I'm not. Why — what's this? Someone's been at the lock.

Nora: At the lock — ?

Helmer: Yes, I'm positive. What do you suppose — ? I can't imagine one of the maids — ? Here's a broken hairpin. Nora, it's yours —

Nora (quickly): Then it must be the children —

Helmer: You'd better break them of that. Hm, hm — well, opened it after all. *(Takes the contents out and calls into the kitchen.)* Helene! Helene, would you put out the lamp in the hall. *(He returns to the room, shutting the hall door, then displays the handful of mail.)* Look how it's piled up. *(Sorting through them.)* Now what's this?

Nora (at the window): The letter! Oh, Torvald, no!

Helmer: Two calling cards — from Rank.

Nora: From Dr. Rank?

Helmer (examining them): "Dr. Rank, Consulting Physician." They were on top. He must have dropped them in as he left.

Nora: Is there anything on them?

Helmer: There's a black cross over the name. See? That's a gruesome notion. He could almost be announcing his own death.

Nora: That's just what he's doing.

Helmer: What! You've heard something? Something he's told you?

Nora: Yes. That when those cards came, he'd be taking his leave of us. He'll shut himself in now and die.

Helmer: Ah, my poor friend! Of course I knew he wouldn't be here much longer. But so soon — And then to hide himself away like a wounded animal.

Nora: If it has to happen, then it's best it happens in silence — don't you think so, Torvald?

Helmer (pacing up and down): He'd grown right into our lives. I simply can't imagine him gone. He with his suffering and loneliness — like a dark cloud setting off our sunlit happiness. Well, maybe it's best this way. For him, at least. *(Standing still.)* And maybe for us too, Nora. Now we're thrown back on each other, completely. *(Embracing her.)* Oh you, my darling wife, how can I hold you close enough? You know what, Nora — time and again I've wished you were in some terrible danger, just so I could stake my life and soul and everything, for your sake.

Nora (tearing herself away, her voice firm and decisive): Now you must read your mail, Torvald.

Helmer: No, no, not tonight. I want to stay with you, dearest.

Nora: With a dying friend on your mind?

Helmer: You're right. We've both had a shock. There's ugliness between us — these thoughts of death and corruption. We'll have to get free of them first. Until then — we'll stay apart.

Nora (clinging about his neck): Torvald — good night! Good night!

Helmer (kissing her on the cheek): Good night, little songbird. Sleep well, Nora. I'll be reading my mail now. *(He takes the letters into his room and shuts the door after him.)*

Nora (with bewildered glances, groping about, seizing Helmer's domino, throwing it around her, and speaking in short, hoarse, broken whispers): Never see him again. Never, never. *(Putting her shawl over her head.)* Never see the children either — them, too. Never, never. Oh, the freezing black water! The depths — down — Oh, I wish it were over — He has it now; he's reading it — now. Oh no, no, not yet. Torvald, good-bye, you and the children — *(She starts for the hall; as she does, Helmer throws open his door and stands with an open letter in his hand.)*

Helmer: Nora!

Nora (screams): Oh — !

Helmer: What is this? You know what's in this letter?

Nora: Yes, I know. Let me go! Let me out!

Helmer (holding her back): Where are you going?

Nora (struggling to break loose): You can't save me, Torvald!

Helmer (slumping back): True! Then it's true what he writes? How horrible! No, no, it's impossible — it can't be true.

Nora: It *is* true. I've loved you more than all this world.

Helmer: Ah, none of your slippery tricks.

Nora (taking one step toward him): Torvald — !

Helmer: What *is* this you've blundered into!

Nora: Just let me loose. You're not going to suffer for my sake. You're not going to take on my guilt.

Helmer: No more playacting. *(Locks the hall door.)* You stay right here and give me a reckoning. You understand what you've done? Answer! You understand?

Nora (looking squarely at him, her face hardening): Yes. I'm beginning to understand everything now.

Helmer (striding about): Oh, what an awful awakening! In all these eight years — she who was my pride and joy — a hypocrite, a liar — worse, worse — a criminal! How infinitely disgusting it all is! The shame! *(Nora says nothing and goes on looking straight at him. He stops in front of her.)* I should have suspected something of the kind. I should have known. All your father's flimsy values — Be still! All your father's flimsy values have come out in you. No religion, no morals, no sense of duty — Oh, how I'm punished for letting him off! I did it for your sake, and you repay me like this.

Nora: Yes, like this.

Helmer: Now you've wrecked all my happiness — ruined my whole future. Oh, it's awful to think of. I'm in a cheap little grafter's hands; he can do anything he wants with me, ask for anything, play with me like a puppet — and I can't breathe a word. I'll be swept down miserably into the depths on account of a featherbrained woman.

Nora: When I'm gone from this world, you'll be free.

Helmer: Oh, quit posing. Your father had a mess of those speeches too. What good would that ever do me if you were gone from this world, as you say? Not the slightest. He can still make the whole thing known; and if he does, I could be falsely suspected as your accomplice. They might even think that I was behind it — that I put you up to it. And all that I can thank you for — you that I've coddled the whole of our marriage. Can you see now what you've done to me?

Nora (icily calm): Yes.

Helmer: It's so incredible, I just can't grasp it. But we'll have to patch up whatever we can. Take off the shawl. I said, take it off! I've got to appease him somehow or other. The thing has to be hushed up at any cost. And as for you and me, it's got to seem like everything between us is just as it was — to the outside world, that is. You'll go right on living in this house, of course. But you can't be allowed to bring up the children; I don't dare trust you with them — Oh, to have to say this to someone I've loved so much! Well, that's done with. From now on happiness doesn't matter; all that matters is saving the bits and pieces, the appearance — *(The doorbell rings. Helmer starts.)* What's that? And so late. Maybe the worst — ? You think he'd — ? Hide, Nora! Say you're sick. *(Nora remains standing motionless. Helmer goes and opens the door.)*

Maid *(half dressed, in the hall):* A letter for Mrs. Helmer.

Helmer: I'll take it. *(Snatches the letter and shuts the door.)* Yes, it's from him. You don't get it; I'm reading it myself.

Nora: Then read it.

Helmer *(by the lamp):* I hardly dare. We may be ruined, you and I. But — I've got to know. *(Rips open the letter, skims through a few lines, glances at an enclosure, then cries out joyfully.)* Nora! *(Nora looks inquiringly at him.)* Nora! Wait — better check it again — Yes, yes, it's true. I'm saved. Nora, I'm saved!

Nora: And I?

Helmer: You too, of course. We're both saved, both of us. Look. He's sent back your note. He says he's sorry and ashamed — that a happy development in his life — oh, who cares what he says! Nora, we're saved! No one can hurt you. Oh, Nora, Nora — but first, this ugliness all has to go. Let me see — *(Takes a look at the note.)* No, I don't want to see it; I want the whole thing to fade like a dream. *(Tears the note and both letters to pieces, throws them into the stove and watches them burn.)* There — now there's nothing left — He wrote that since Christmas Eve you — Oh, they must have been three terrible days for you, Nora.

Nora: I fought a hard fight.

Helmer: And suffered pain and saw no escape but — No, we're not going to dwell on anything unpleasant. We'll just be grateful and keep on repeating: it's over now, it's over! You hear me, Nora? You don't seem to realize — it's over. What's it mean — that frozen look? Oh, poor little Nora, I understand. You can't believe I've forgiven you. But I have, Nora; I swear I have. I know that what you did, you did out of love for me.

Nora: That's true.

Helmer: You loved me the way a wife ought to love her husband. It's simply the means that you couldn't judge. But you think I love you any the less for not knowing how to handle your affairs? No, no — just lean on me; I'll guide you and teach you. I wouldn't be a man if this feminine help-lessness didn't make you twice as attractive to me. You mustn't mind those sharp words I said — that was all in the first confusion of thinking my world had collapsed. I've forgiven you, Nora; I swear I've forgiven you.

Nora: My thanks for your forgiveness. *(She goes out through the door, right.)*

Helmer: No, wait — *(Peers in.)* What are you doing in there?

Nora *(inside):* Getting out of my costume.

Helmer *(by the open door):* Yes, do that. Try to calm yourself and collect your thoughts again, my frightened little songbird. You can rest easy now; I've got wide wings to shelter you with. *(Walking about close by the door.)* How snug and nice our home is, Nora. You're safe here; I'll keep you like a hunted dove I've rescued out of a hawk's claws. I'll bring peace to your poor, shuddering heart. Gradually it'll happen, Nora; you'll see. Tomorrow all this will look different to you; then everything will be as it was. I won't have to go on repeating I forgive you; you'll feel it for yourself. How can you imagine I'd ever conceivably want to disown you — or even blame you in any way? Ah, you don't know a man's heart, Nora. For a man there's something indescribably sweet and satisfying in knowing he's forgiven his wife — and forgiven her out of a full and open heart. It's as if she belongs to him in two ways now: in a sense he's given her fresh into the world again, and she's become his wife and his child as well. From now on that's what you'll be to me — you little, bewildered, helpless thing. Don't be afraid of anything, Nora; just open your heart to me, and I'll be conscience and will to you both — *(Nora enters in her regular clothes.)* What's this? Not in bed? You've changed your dress?

Nora: Yes, Torvald, I've changed my dress.

Helmer: But why now, so late?

Nora: Tonight I'm not sleeping.

Helmer: But Nora dear —

Nora (looking at her watch): It's still not so very late. Sit down, Torvald; we have a lot to talk over. *(She sits at one side of the table.)*

Helmer: Nora — what is this? That hard expression —

Nora: Sit down. This'll take some time. I have a lot to say.

Helmer (sitting at the table directly opposite her): You worry me, Nora. And I don't understand you.

Nora: No, that's exactly it. You don't understand me. And I've never understood you either — until tonight. No, don't interrupt. You can just listen to what I say. We're closing out accounts, Torvald.

Helmer: How do you mean that?

Nora (after a short pause): Doesn't anything strike you about our sitting here like this?

Helmer: What's that?

Nora: We've been married now eight years. Doesn't it occur to you that this is the first time we two, you and I, man and wife, have ever talked seriously together?

Helmer: What do you mean — seriously?

Nora: In eight whole years — longer even — right from our first acquaintance, we've never exchanged a serious word on any serious thing.

Helmer: You mean I should constantly go and involve you in problems you couldn't possibly help me with?

Nora: I'm not talking of problems. I'm saying that we've never sat down seriously together and tried to get to the bottom of anything.

Helmer: But dearest, what good would that ever do you?

Nora: That's the point right there: you've never understood me. I've been wronged greatly, Torvald — first by Papa, and then by you.

Helmer: What! By us — the two people who've loved you more than anyone else?

Nora (shaking her head): You never loved me. You've thought it fun to be in love with me, that's all.

Helmer: Nora, what a thing to say!

Nora: Yes, it's true now, Torvald. When I lived at home with Papa, he told me all his opinions, so I had the same ones too; or if they were different I hid them, since he wouldn't have cared for that. He used to call me his doll-child, and he played with me the way I played with my dolls. Then I came into your house —

Helmer: How can you speak of our marriage like that?

Nora (unperturbed): I mean, then I went from Papa's hands into yours. You arranged everything to your own taste, and so I got the same taste as you — or I pretended to; I can't remember. I guess a little of both, first one, then the other. Now when I look back, it seems as if I'd lived here like a beggar — just from hand to mouth. I've lived by doing tricks for you, Torvald. But that's the way you wanted it. It's a great sin what you and Papa did to me. You're to blame that nothing's become of me.

Helmer: Nora, how unfair and ungrateful you are! Haven't you been happy here?

Nora: No, never. I thought so — but I never have.

Helmer: Not — not happy!

Nora: No, only lighthearted. And you've always been so kind to me. But our home's been nothing but a playpen. I've been your doll-wife here, just as at home I was Papa's doll-child. And in turn the children have been my dolls. I thought it was fun when you played with me, just as they thought it fun when I played with them. That's been our marriage, Torvald.

Helmer: There's some truth in what you're saying — under all the raving exaggeration. But it'll all be different after this. Playtime's over; now for the schooling.

Nora: Whose schooling — mine or the children's?

Helmer: Both yours and the children's, dearest.

Nora: Oh, Torvald, you're not the man to teach me to be a good wife to you.

Helmer: And you can say that?

Nora: And I — how am I equipped to bring up children?

Helmer: Nora!

Nora: Didn't you say a moment ago that that was no job to trust me with?

Helmer: In a flare of temper! Why fasten on that?

Nora: Yes, but you were so very right. I'm not up to the job. There's another job I have to do first. I have to try to educate myself. You can't help me with that. I've got to do it alone. And that's why I'm leaving you now.

Helmer (jumping up): What's that?

Nora: I have to stand completely alone, if I'm ever going to discover myself and the world out there. So I can't go on living with you.

Helmer: Nora, Nora!

Nora: I want to leave right away. Kristine should put me up for the night —

Helmer: You're insane! You've no right! I forbid you!

Nora: From here on, there's no use forbidding me anything. I'll take with me whatever is mine. I don't want a thing from you, either now or later.

Helmer: What kind of madness is this!

Nora: Tomorrow I'm going home — I mean, home where I came from. It'll be easier up there to find something to do.

Helmer: Oh, you blind, incompetent child!

Nora: I must learn to be competent, Torvald.

Helmer: Abandon your home, your husband, your children! And you're not even thinking what people will say.

Nora: I can't be concerned about that. I only know how essential this is.

Helmer: Oh, it's outrageous. So you'll run out like this on your most sacred vows.

Nora: What do you think are my most sacred vows?

Helmer: And I have to tell you that! Aren't they your duties to your husband and children?

Nora: I have other duties equally sacred.

Helmer: That isn't true. What duties are they?

Nora: Duties to myself.

Helmer: Before all else, you're a wife and a mother.

Nora: I don't believe in that any more. I believe that, before all else, I'm a human being, no less than you — or anyway, I ought to try to become one. I know the majority thinks you're right, Torvald, and plenty of books agree with you, too. But I can't go on believing what the majority says, or what's written in books. I have to think over these things myself and try to understand them.

Helmer: Why can't you understand your place in your own home? On a point like that, isn't there one everlasting guide you can turn to? Where's your religion?

Nora: Oh, Torvald, I'm really not sure what religion is.

Helmer: What — ?

Nora: I only know what the minister said when I was confirmed. He told me religion was this thing and that. When I get clear and away by myself, I'll go into that problem too. I'll see if what the minister said was right, or, in any case, if it's right for me.

Helmer: A young woman your age shouldn't talk like that. If religion can't move you, I can try to rouse your conscience. You do have some moral feeling? Or, tell me — has that gone too?

Nora: It's not easy to answer that, Torvald. I simply don't know. I'm all confused about these things. I just know I see them so differently from you. I find out, for one thing, that the law's not at all what I'd thought — but I can't get it through my head that the law is fair. A woman hasn't a right to protect her dying father or save her husband's life! I can't believe that.

Helmer: You talk like a child. You don't know anything of the world you live in.

Nora: No, I don't. But now I'll begin to learn for myself. I'll try to discover who's right, the world or I.

Helmer: Nora, you're sick; you've got a fever. I almost think you're out of your head.

Nora: I've never felt more clearheaded and sure in my life.

Helmer: And — clearheaded and sure — you're leaving your husband and children?

Nora: Yes.

Helmer: Then there's only one possible reason.

Nora: What?

Helmer: You no longer love me.

Nora: No. That's exactly it.

Helmer: Nora! You can't be serious!

Nora: Oh, this is so hard, Torvald — you've been so kind to me always. But I can't help it. I don't love you any more.

Helmer (struggling for composure): Are you also clearheaded and sure about that?

Nora: Yes, completely. That's why I can't go on staying here.

Helmer: Can you tell me what I did to lose your love?

Nora: Yes, I can tell you. It was this evening when the miraculous thing didn't come — then I knew you weren't the man I'd imagined.

Helmer: Be more explicit; I don't follow you.

Nora: I've waited now so patiently eight long years — for, my Lord, I know miracles don't come every day. Then this crisis broke over me, and such a certainty filled me: *now* the miraculous event would occur. While Krogstad's letter was lying out there, I never for an instant dreamed that you could give in to his terms. I was so utterly sure you'd say to him: go on, tell your tale to the whole wide world. And when he'd done that —

Helmer: Yes, what then? When I'd delivered my own wife into shame and disgrace — !

Nora: When he'd done that, I was so utterly sure that you'd step forward, take the blame on yourself and say: I am the guilty one.

Helmer: Nora — !

Nora: You're thinking I'd never accept such a sacrifice from you? No, of course not. But what good would my protests be against you? That was the miracle I was waiting for, in terror and hope. And to stave that off, I would have taken my life.

Helmer: I'd gladly work for you day and night, Nora — and take on pain and deprivation. But there's no one who gives up honor for love.

Nora: Millions of women have done just that.

Helmer: Oh, you think and talk like a silly child.

Nora: Perhaps. But you neither think nor talk like the man I could join myself to. When your big fright was over — and it wasn't from any threat against me, only for what might damage you — when all the danger was past, for you it was just as if nothing had happened. I was exactly the same, your little lark, your doll, that you'd have to handle with double care now that I'd turned out so brittle and frail. *(Gets up.)* Torvald — in that instant it dawned on me that for eight years I've been living here with a stranger, and that I'd even conceived three children — oh, I can't stand the thought of it! I could tear myself to bits.

Helmer (heavily): I see. There's a gulf that's opened between us — that's clear. Oh, but Nora, can't we bridge it somehow?

Nora: The way I am now, I'm no wife for you.

Helmer: I have the strength to make myself over.

Nora: Maybe — if your doll gets taken away.

Helmer: But to part! To part from you! No, Nora, no — I can't imagine it.

Nora (going out, right): All the more reason why it has to be. *(She reenters with her coat and a small overnight bag, which she puts on a chair by the table.)*

Helmer: Nora, Nora, not now! Wait till tomorrow.

Nora: I can't spend the night in a strange man's room.

Helmer: But couldn't we live here like brother and sister —

Nora: You know very well how long that would last. *(Throws her shawl about her.)* Good-bye, Torvald. I won't look in on the children. I know they're in better hands than mine. The way I am now, I'm no use to them.

Helmer: But someday, Nora — someday — ?

Nora: How can I tell? I haven't the least idea what'll become of me.

Helmer: But you're my wife, now and wherever you go.

Nora: Listen, Torvald — I've heard that when a wife deserts her husband's house just as I'm doing, then the law frees him from all responsibility. In any case, I'm freeing you from being responsible. Don't feel yourself bound, any more than I will. There has to be absolute freedom for us both. Here, take your ring back. Give me mine.

Helmer: That too?

Nora: That too.

Helmer: There it is.

Nora: Good. Well, now it's all over. I'm putting the keys here. The maids know all about keeping up the house — better than I do. Tomorrow, after I've left town, Kristine will stop by to pack up everything that's mine from home. I'd like those things shipped up to me.

Helmer: Over! All over! Nora, won't you ever think about me?

Nora: I'm sure I'll think of you often, and about the children and the house here.

Helmer: May I write you?

Nora: No — never. You're not to do that.

Helmer: Oh, but let me send you —

Nora: Nothing. Nothing.

Helmer: Or help you if you need it.

Nora: No. I accept nothing from strangers.

Helmer: Nora — can I never be more than a stranger to you?

Nora (picking up the overnight bag): Ah, Torvald — it would take the greatest miracle of all —

Helmer: Tell me the greatest miracle!

Nora: You and I both would have to transform ourselves to the point that — Oh, Torvald, I've stopped believing in miracles.

Helmer: But I'll believe. Tell me! Transform ourselves to the point that — ?

Nora: That our living together could be a true marriage. *(She goes out down the hall.)*

Helmer (sinks down on a chair by the door, face buried in his hands): Nora! Nora! *(Looking about and rising.)* Empty. She's gone. *(A sudden hope leaps in him.)* The greatest miracle — ?

From below, the sound of a door slamming shut.

QUESTIONS

ACT I

1. From the opening conversation between Helmer and Nora, what are your impressions of him? Of her? Of their marriage?
2. At what moment in the play do you understand why it is called *A Doll House?*

3. In what ways does Mrs. Linde provide a contrast with Nora?
4. What in Krogstad's first appearance on stage, and in Dr. Rank's remarks about him, indicates that the bank clerk is a menace?
5. Of what illegal deed is Nora guilty? How does she justify it?
6. When the curtain falls on Act I, what problems now confront Nora?

ACT II

1. As Act II opens, what are your feelings on seeing the stripped, ragged Christmas tree? How is it suggestive?
2. What events that soon occur make Nora's situation even more difficult?
3. How does she try to save herself?
4. Why does Nora fling herself into the wild tarantella?

ACT III

1. For what possible reasons does Mrs. Linde pledge herself to Krogstad?
2. How does Dr. Rank's announcement of his impending death affect Nora and Helmer?
3. What is Helmer's reaction to learning the truth about Nora's misdeed? Why does he blame Nora's father? What is revealing (of Helmer's own character) in his remark, "From now on happiness doesn't matter; all that matters is saving the bits and pieces, the appearance. . . ."?
4. When Helmer finds that Krogstad has sent back the note, what is his response? How do you feel toward him?
5. How does the character of Nora develop in this act?
6. How do you interpret her final slamming of the door?

GENERAL QUESTIONS

1. In what ways do you find Nora a victim? In what ways at fault?
2. Try to state the theme of the play. Does it involve women's rights? Self-fulfillment?
3. What dramatic question does the play embody? At what moment can this question first be stated?
4. What is the crisis? In what way is this moment or event a "turning point"? (In what new direction does the action turn?)
5. Eric Bentley, in an essay titled "Ibsen, Pro and Con" (*In Search of Theater,* New York: Knopf, 1953), criticizes the character of Krogstad, calling him "a mere pawn of the plot." "When convenient to Ibsen, he is a blackmailer. When inconvenient, he is converted." Do you agree or disagree?
6. Why is the play considered a work of realism? Is there anything in it that does not seem realistic?
7. In what respects does *A Doll House* seem to apply to life today? Is it in any way dated? Could there be a Nora in North America in the 1980s?

William Butler Yeats

PURGATORY 1939

William Butler Yeats (1865 – 1939), Irish poet and playwright, is the subject of a biography on page 816. Purgatory, his next-to-last play, reflects Yeats's admiration for the stark simplicity and poetic intensity he had discovered in the classic Nō plays of Japan — in which two or three actors appear on a stage with a few props, such as one lone twisted tree.

Persons in the Play

A Boy
An Old Man

Scene. *A ruined house and a bare tree in the background.*

Boy: Half-door, hall door,
    Hither and thither day and night,
    Hill or hollow, shouldering this pack,
    Hearing you talk.
Old Man: Study that house.
    I think about its jokes and stories;   5
    I try to remember what the butler
    Said to a drunken gamekeeper
    In mid-October, but I cannot.
    If I cannot, none living can.
    Where are the jokes and stories of a house,   10
    Its threshold gone to patch a pig-sty?
Boy: So you have come this path before?
Old Man: The moonlight falls upon the path,
    The shadow of a cloud upon the house,
    And that's symbolical; study that tree,   15
    What is it like?
Boy: A silly old man.
Old Man: It's like — no matter what it's like.
    I saw it a year ago stripped bare as now,
    So I chose a better trade.
    I saw it fifty years ago   20
    Before the thunderbolt had riven it,
    Green leaves, ripe leaves, leaves thick as butter,
    Fat, greasy life. Stand there and look,
    Because there is somebody in that house.

(The Boy puts down pack and stands in the doorway.)

Boy: There's nobody here.
Old Man: There's somebody there.   25

Boy: The floor is gone, the windows gone,
　　　And where there should be roof there's sky,
　　　And here's a bit of an egg-shell thrown
　　　Out of a jackdaw's nest.
Old Man:　　　　　　　　But there are some
　　　That do not care what's gone, what's left:　　　　　　30
　　　The souls in Purgatory that come back
　　　To habitations and familiar spots.
Boy: Your wits are out again.
Old Man:　　　　　　　　Re-live
　　　Their transgressions, and that not once
　　　But many times; they know at last　　　　　　35
　　　The consequence of those transgressions
　　　Whether upon others or upon themselves;
　　　Upon others, others may bring help,
　　　For when the consequence is at an end
　　　The dream must end; if upon themselves,　　　　　　40
　　　There is no help but in themselves
　　　And in the mercy of God.
Boy:　　　　　　　　I have had enough!
　　　Talk to the jackdaws, if talk you must.
Old Man: Stop! Sit there upon that stone.
　　　That is the house where I was born.　　　　　　45
Boy: The big old house that was burnt down?
Old Man: My mother that was your grand-dam owned it,
　　　This scenery and this countryside,
　　　Kennel and stable, horse and hound —
　　　She had a horse at the Curragh°, and there met　　　　　　50
　　　My father, a groom in a training stable,
　　　Looked at him and married him.
　　　Her mother never spoke to her again,
　　　And she did right.
Boy:　　　　　　　　What's right and wrong?
　　　My grand-dad got the girl and the money.　　　　　　55
Old Man: Looked at him and married him,
　　　And he squandered everything she had.
　　　She never knew the worst, because
　　　She died in giving birth to me,
　　　But now she knows it all, being dead.　　　　　　60
　　　Great people lived and died in this house;
　　　Magistrates, colonels, members of Parliament,
　　　Captains and Governors, and long ago
　　　Men that had fought at Aughrim and the Boyne°.

---

⁵⁰*the Curragh:* flatlands in County Sligo, Ireland. The name is synonymous with horse racing.
⁶⁴*Aughrim and the Boyne:* in Ireland, scenes of two battles (1691), in which William of Orange, Protestant king of England, defeated his exiled rival James II, a Roman Catholic. This outcome confirmed British rule over Ireland for the next two centuries. Yeats, by the way, believed that some of his own ancestors had fought on the winning side in the Battle of the Boyne.

Some that had gone on Government work   65
To London or to India came home to die,
Or came from London every spring
To look at the may-blossom in the park.
They had loved the trees that he cut down
To pay what he had lost at cards   70
Or spent on horses, drink and women;
Had loved the house, had loved all
The intricate passages of the house,
But he killed the house; to kill a house
Where great men grew up, married, died,   75
I here declare a capital offense.

Boy: My God, but you had luck! Grand clothes,
And maybe a grand horse to ride.

Old Man: That he might keep me upon his level
He never sent me to school, but some   80
Half-loved me for my half of her:
A gamekeeper's wife taught me to read,
A Catholic curate taught me Latin.
There were old books and books made fine
By eighteenth-century French binding, books   85
Modern and ancient, books by the ton.

Boy: What education have you given me?

Old Man: I gave the education that befits
A bastard that a peddler got
Upon a tinker's daughter° in a ditch.   90
When I had come to sixteen years old
My father burned down the house when drunk.

Boy: But that is my age, sixteen years old,
At the Puck Fair.

Old Man: And everything was burnt;
Books, library, all were burnt.   95

Boy: Is what I have heard upon the road the truth,
That you killed him in the burning house?

Old Man: There's nobody here but our two selves?

Boy: Nobody, Father.

Old Man: I stuck him with a knife,
That knife that cuts my dinner now,   100
And after that I left him in the fire.
They dragged him out, somebody saw
The knife-wound but could not be certain
Because the body was all black and charred.
Then some that were his drunken friends   105
Swore they would put me upon trial,
Spoke of quarrels, a threat I had made.
The gamekeeper gave me some old clothes,

---

⁹⁰*tinker's daughter:* In Ireland, tinkers are Gypsies: wandering tinsmiths, menders of pots and
pans.

I ran away, worked here and there
Till I became a peddler on the roads,   110
No good trade, but good enough
Because I am my father's son,
Because of what I did or may do.
Listen to the hoof-beats! Listen, listen!
Boy: I cannot hear a sound.
Old Man: Beat! Beat!   115
This night is the anniversary
Of my mother's wedding night,
Or of the night wherein I was begotten.
My father is riding from the public-house,
A whiskey-bottle under his arm.   120

(A window is lit showing a young girl.)

Look at the window; she stands there
Listening, the servants are all in bed,
She is alone, he has stayed late
Bragging and drinking in the public-house.
Boy: There's nothing but an empty gap in the wall.   125
You have made it up. No, you are mad!
You are getting madder every day.
Old Man: It's louder now because he rides
Upon a gravelled avenue
All grass today. The hoof-beat stops,   130
He has gone to the other side of the house,
Gone to the stable, put the horse up.
She has gone down to open the door.
This night she is no better than her man
And does not mind that he is half drunk,   135
She is mad about him. They mount the stairs.
She brings him into her own chamber.
And that is the marriage-chamber now.
The window is dimly lit again.

Do not let him touch you! It is not true   140
That drunken men cannot beget,
And if he touch he must beget
And you must bear his murderer.
Deaf! Both deaf! If I should throw
A stick or a stone they would not hear;   145
And that's a proof my wits are out.
But there's a problem: she must live
Through everything in exact detail,
Driven to it by remorse, and yet
Can she renew the sexual act   150
And find no pleasure in it, and if not,
If pleasure and remorse must both be there,

Which is the greater?
                    I lack schooling.
Go fetch Tertullian; he and I
Will ravel all that problem out   155
Whilst those two lie upon the mattress
Begetting me.
                    Come back! Come back!
And so you thought to slip away,
My bag of money between your fingers,
And that I could not talk and see!   160
You have been rummaging in the pack.

(The light in the window has faded out.)

Boy: You never gave me my right share.
Old Man: And had I given it, young as you are,
    You would have spent it upon drink.
Boy: What if I did? I had a right   165
    To get it and spend it as I chose.
Old Man: Give me that bag and no more words.
Boy: I will not.
Old Man: I will break your fingers.

(They struggle for the bag. In the struggle it drops, scattering the money. The Old Man staggers but does not fall. They stand looking at each other. The window is lit up. A man is seen pouring whiskey into a glass.)

Boy: What if I killed you? You killed my grand-dad,
    Because you were young and he was old.   170
    Now I am young and you are old.
Old Man (staring at window): Better-looking, those sixteen years —
Boy: What are you muttering?
Old Man: Younger — and yet
    She should have known he was not her kind.
Boy: What are you saying? Out with it!   175

(Old Man points to window.)

My God! The window is lit up
And somebody stands there, although
The floorboards are all burnt away.
Old Man: The window is lit up because my father
    Has come to find a glass for his whiskey.   180
    He leans there like some tired beast.
Boy: A dead, living, murdered man!
Old Man: "Then the bride-sleep fell upon Adam":
    Where did I read those words?
                    And yet
There's nothing leaning in the window   185
But the impression upon my mother's mind;
Being dead she is alone in her remorse.

Boy: A body that was a bundle of old bones
Before I was born. Horrible! Horrible!

(He covers his eyes.)

Old Man: That beast there would know nothing, being nothing,   190
If I should kill a man under the window
He would not even turn his head.

(He stabs the Boy.)

My father and my son on the same jack-knife!
That finishes — there — there — there —

(He stabs again and again. The window grows dark.)

'Hush-a-bye baby, thy father's a knight,   195
Thy mother a lady, lovely and bright.'
No, that is something that I read in a book,
And if I sing it must be to my mother,
And I lack rhyme.

(The stage has grown dark except where the tree stands in white light.)

                    Study that tree.
It stands there like a purified soul,   200
All cold, sweet, glistening light.
Dear mother, the window is dark again,
But you are in the light because
I finished all that consequence.
I killed that lad because had he grown up   205
He would have struck a woman's fancy,
Begot, and passed pollution on.
I am a wretched foul old man
And therefore harmless. When I have stuck
This old jack-knife into a sod   210
And pulled it out all bright again,
And picked up all the money that he dropped,
I'll to a distant place, and there
Tell my old jokes among new men.

(He cleans the knife and begins to pick up money.)

Hoof-beats! Dear God,   215
How quickly it returns — beat — beat — !

Her mind cannot hold up that dream.
Twice a murderer and all for nothing,
And she must animate that dead night
Not once but many times!
                    O God,   220
Release my mother's soul from its dream!
Mankind can do no more. Appease
The misery of the living and the remorse of the dead.

1. What obsessions drive the Old Man to return with the Boy to the ruined house?
2. For what reasons does the Old Man hate his father? Explain the Old Man's feelings toward his mother.
3. What does the Old Man hear and see that the Boy does not? Why do you think the Boy fails to perceive these things?
4. What motivates the Old Man to shout "Do not let him touch you!"? What motivates the Boy to try to make off with the money?
5. What does the Old Man hope to accomplish by murdering the Boy? (Look carefully at lines 31 – 42.) What bitterly ironic situation results instead?
6. Explain the rules of this Purgatory, insofar as you can. What torment must the mother's soul endure?
7. Which of these themes do you find important in Yeats's play? Justify your answer.

   a. Spirits, who live on after their deaths, exert power over the living.

   b. Everything that happens is God's will.

   c. Alcohol causes much unhappiness.

   d. We all must pass some time in Purgatory to atone for our sins.

   e. Kill your son before he kills you.

   f. Bad blood will out.

   g. History repeats itself.

8. In this story of the Old Man and his family, events are arranged out of chronological order. Suppose Yeats had arranged them in a chronology, starting with the mother's first meeting the father and falling in love with him. How would *Purgatory* have been a much different play? What would have been lost?
9. Imagine the play on stage. How might its scene — ruined house, bare tree — contribute to its effectiveness?
10. How does this play remind you of the Fitts and Fitzgerald version of *Oedipus Rex*? Consider any resemblances in plot, theme, staging, and use of language and poetry.
11. Scholar and critic Douglas Archibald suggests that *Purgatory* is, among other things, "a parable about the decline of the Anglo-Irish gentry." What do you know about Anglo-Irish gentry? If not enough, read a short history of modern Ireland in an encyclopedia. What evidence do you find in the play to support Archibald's view?

TRAGICOMEDY AND THE ABSURD

Fresh attitudes toward play production and theater design reflect fresh conceptions of drama. One of the more prominent developments in mid-twentieth-century drama has been the rise of **tragicomedy,** found in plays that not only stir us to pity and fear (echoing Aristotle's description of the effect of tragedy), but to laughter as well. Although tragicomedy is a kind of drama we think modern, it is by no means a new invention. The term was used (although jokingly) by the Roman writer of comedy Plautus in about 185 B.C., and later critics have applied it to plays of the classical

Greek dramatist Euripides — notably *Alcestis,* in which apparently tragic events jostle with snappy repartee and end happily.

Since ancient times, playwrights have mingled laughter and tears, defying the neoclassical doctrine requiring adherence to the unities (discussed on page 1060). Shakespeare is fond of tragicomic minglings: in *Hamlet,* the prince jokes with a gravedigger; in *Antony and Cleopatra,* the queen commits suicide with a poisonous asp brought to her by a wise-cracking clown. In the tragedies of Shakespeare and others, passages of clownish humor are sometimes called **comic relief,** meaning that the comedy introduces a sharp contrast. But such passages can do more than provide relief. In *Othello* (III, iv, 1 – 16), the clown's banter with Desdemona for a moment makes the surrounding tragedy seem, by comparison, more poignant and intense.

No one doubts that *Othello* is a tragedy, but some twentieth-century plays leave us bemused: should we laugh or cry? One of the most talked-about plays since World War II, Samuel Beckett's *Waiting for Godot,* portrays two clownish tramps who mark time in a wasteland, wistfully looking for a savior who never arrives. (Contemporary drama, by the way, has often featured such **antiheroes:** ordinary people, inglorious and inarticulate, who carry on not from bravery but from inertia.)[4] We cannot help laughing at the tramps' painful situation; or, turning the idea around, we feel deeply moved by their ridiculous plight. Surely, a modern tragicomedy like *Godot* does not show us great souls suffering greatly — as Edith Hamilton said we are shown in a classical tragedy.

But perhaps the effect of such a play takes time to sink in. Contemporary playwright Edward Albee suggests that sometimes the spectator's sense of relief after experiencing pity and fear (Aristotle calls it *katharsis*) may be a delayed reaction: "I don't feel that catharsis in a play necessarily takes place during the course of a play. Often it should take place afterwards."[5] If Albee is right, we may be amused while watching a tragicomedy, then go home and feel deeply stirred by it.

Straddling the fence between tragedy and comedy, Beckett portrays people whose suffering seems ridiculous. His play belongs to the **theater of the absurd:** a general name for a constellation of plays first staged in Paris in the 1950s. "For the modern critical spirit, nothing can be taken entirely seriously, nor entirely lightly," according to Eugène Ionesco, one of the movement's leading playwrights and chief voices. A human being, such playwrights assume, is a helpless waif alone in a universe that confronts him with ridiculous obstacles. In Ionesco's *Amédée* (1953), a couple share an apartment with a gigantic corpse that keeps swelling relentlessly; in his *Rhinoceros* (1958), the human race starts turning into rhinos, except for one man, who remains human and isolated. A favorite theme in the theater of the absurd is that communication between people is impossible.

[4]The rise of the antihero in recent fiction is discussed briefly on page 75. These remarks apply to drama as well.
[5]"The Art of the Theater," interview in *The Paris Review,* No. 39, Fall 1966.

Language is therefore futile: Ionesco's *The Bald Soprano* (1948) accordingly pokes fun at polite social conversation in a scene with dialogue consisting entirely of illogical strings of catchphrases. In *Endgame* (1957), Samuel Beckett also burlesques small talk, and dramatizes his sense of the present condition of mankind: the main character is blind and paralyzed and his legless parents live inside two garbage cans. Oddly, the effect of the play isn't total gloom: we leave the theater both amused and bemused by it.[6]

Fashions in drama change along with playwrights' convictions, and today the theater of the absurd seems no longer the dominant influence on new drama in America. Along with other protests of the 1960s, guerrilla street theater seems to have spent its force. Of late, some loudly applauded new plays have been neither absurd nor revolutionary. David Mamet's *American Buffalo* (1975) realistically portrays three petty thieves in a junk shop as they plot to steal a coin collection. Albert Innaurato's *Gemini* (1977) takes a realistic (and comic) view of life in a Philadelphia neighborhood only a little less depressed than the rundown lodging house in Gorky's *The Lower Depths*. In both plays, the dialogue shows high fidelity to ordinary speech (a lowbrow woman to her common-law spouse in *Gemini:* "I'll just pick out of your plate"). The American theater may have entered an era of "new naturalism," suggests critic Richard Gilman.[7] At least it appears that, in many recent plays, fantasy and absurdity are out, straightforward realism is in, communication between human beings is still possible, and events on stage follow in logical (and chronological) order. Still, many of our finest contemporary playwrights have learned from the theater of the absurd. Edward Albee is one of them.

Edward Albee
THE ZOO STORY 1959

Edward Albee, born in 1928, was adopted by millionaire foster parents who gave him his name. As a boy, he was dismissed from Lawrenceville, a preparatory school, and Valley Forge, a military academy, before settling in at Choate School, where he began to write. He started college at Trinity in Hartford, Connecticut, but soon dropped out to become a writer of radio scripts. Living in Greenwich Village for ten years beginning in 1948, he held jobs as an office boy, a record salesman, a bartender, and a Western Union messenger. In 1958, in a three-week burst of energy, he wrote The Zoo Story, *first performed in 1959 in West Berlin and in the following year (to critical acclaim) at the Provincetown Playhouse in New York. Other plays followed, among them* The Death of Bessie Smith, The Sandbox

---

[6]For an excellent study of the theater of the absurd, see Martin Esslin, *The Theatre of the Absurd,* revised edition (New York: Overlook, 1973).
[7]"Out Goes Absurdism — In comes the New Naturalism," *The New York Times Book Review,* 19 March 1978.

(both in 1960), The American Dream (1961), Who's Afraid of Virginia Woolf? (1962; later a successful film); Tiny Alice (1964), Malcolm (which failed on Broadway after a five-day run), and A Delicate Balance (which received a Pulitzer prize; both in 1966); Seascape (1975), Listening (1977), and The Man Who Had Three Arms (1983).

The Players

Peter: A man in his early forties, neither fat nor gaunt, neither handsome nor homely. He wears tweeds, smokes a pipe, carries horn-rimmed glasses. Although he is moving into middle age, his dress and his manner would suggest a man younger.

Jerry: A man in his late thirties, not poorly dressed, but carelessly. What was once a trim and lightly muscled body has begun to go to fat; and while he is no longer handsome, it is evident that he once was. His fall from physical grace should not suggest debauchery; he has, to come closest to it, a great weariness.

The Scene: It is Central Park; a Sunday afternoon in summer; the present. There are two park benches, one toward either side of the stage; they both face the audience. Behind them: foliage, trees, sky. At the beginning, Peter is seated on one of the benches.

As the curtain rises, Peter is seated on the bench stage-right. He is reading a book. He stops reading, cleans his glasses, goes back to reading. Jerry enters.

Jerry: I've been to the zoo. *(Peter doesn't notice.)* I said, I've been to the zoo. MISTER, I'VE BEEN TO THE ZOO!
Peter: Hm? . . . What? . . . I'm sorry, were you talking to me?
Jerry: I went to the zoo, and then I walked until I came here. Have I been walking north?
Peter (puzzled): North? Why . . . I . . . I think so. Let me see.
Jerry (pointing past the audience): Is that Fifth Avenue?
Peter: Why yes; yes, it is.
Jerry: And what is that cross street there; that one, to the right?
Peter: That? Oh, that's Seventy-fourth Street.
Jerry: And the zoo is around Sixty-fifth Street; so, I've been walking north.
Peter (anxious to get back to his reading): Yes, it would seem so.
Jerry: Good old north.
Peter (lightly, by reflex): Ha, ha.
Jerry (after a slight pause): But not due north.
Peter: I . . . well, no, not due north; but, we . . . call it north. It's northerly.
Jerry (watches as Peter, anxious to dismiss him, prepares his pipe): Well, boy; you're not going to get lung cancer, are you?
Peter (looks up a little annoyed, then smiles): No, sir. Not from this.
Jerry: No, sir. What you'll probably get is cancer of the mouth, and then you'll have to wear one of those things Freud wore after they took one whole side of his jaw away. What do they call those things?

Peter (uncomfortable): A prosthesis?

Jerry: The very thing! A prosthesis. You're an educated man, aren't you? Are you a doctor?

Peter: Oh, no; no. I read about it somewhere; *Time* magazine, I think. *(He turns to his book.)*

Jerry: Well, *Time* magazine isn't for blockheads.

Peter: No, I suppose not.

Jerry (after a pause): Boy, I'm glad that's Fifth Avenue there.

Peter (vaguely): Yes.

Jerry: I don't like the west side of the park much.

Peter: Oh? *(Then, slightly wary, but interested.)* Why?

Jerry (offhand): I don't know.

Peter: Oh. *(He returns to his book.)*

Jerry (he stands for a few seconds, looking at Peter, who finally looks up again, puzzled): Do you mind if we talk?

Peter (obviously minding): Why . . . no, no.

Jerry: Yes you do; you do.

Peter (puts his book down, his pipe out and away, smiling): No, really; I don't mind.

Jerry: Yes you do.

Peter (finally decided): No; I don't mind at all, really.

Jerry: It's . . . it's a nice day.

Peter (stares unnecessarily at the sky): Yes. Yes, it is; lovely.

Jerry: I've been to the zoo.

Peter: Yes, I think you said so . . . didn't you?

Jerry: You'll read about it in the papers tomorrow, if you don't see it on your TV tonight. You have TV, haven't you?

Peter: Why yes, we have two; one for the children.

Jerry: You're married!

Peter (with pleased emphasis): Why, certainly.

Jerry: It isn't a law, for God's sake.

Peter: No . . . no, of course not.

Jerry: And you have a wife.

Peter (bewildered by the seeming lack of communication): Yes!

Jerry: And you have children.

Peter: Yes; two.

Jerry: Boys?

Peter: No, girls . . . both girls.

Jerry: But you wanted boys.

Peter: Well . . . naturally, every man wants a son, but . . .

Jerry (lightly mocking): But that's the way the cookie crumbles?

Peter (annoyed): I wasn't going to say that.

Jerry: And you're not going to have any more kids, are you?

Peter (a bit distantly): No. No more. *(Then back, and irksome.)* Why did you say that? How would you know about that?

Jerry: The way you cross your legs, perhaps; something in the voice. Or maybe I'm just guessing. Is it your wife?

Peter (furious): That's none of your business! *(A silence.)* Do you understand? *(Jerry nods. Peter is quiet now.)* Well, you're right. We'll have no more children.

Jerry (softly): That *is* the way the cookie crumbles.

Peter (forgiving): Yes . . . I guess so.

Jerry: Well, now; what else?

Peter: What were you saying about the zoo . . . that I'd read about it, or see . . .?

Jerry: I'll tell you about it, soon. Do you mind if I ask you questions?

Peter: Oh, not really.

Jerry: I'll tell you why I do it; I don't talk to many people — except to say like: give me a beer, or where's the john, or what time does the feature go on, or keep your hands to yourself, buddy. You know — things like that.

Peter: I must say I don't . . .

Jerry: But every once in a while I like to talk to somebody, really *talk;* like to get to know somebody, know all about him.

Peter (lightly laughing, still a little uncomfortable): And am I the guinea pig for today?

Jerry: On a sun-drenched Sunday afternoon like this? Who better than a nice married man with two daughters and . . . uh . . . a dog? *(Peter shakes his head.)* No? Two dogs. *(Peter shakes his head again.)* Hm. No dogs? *(Peter shakes his head, sadly.)* Oh, that's a shame. But you look like an animal man. CATS? *(Peter nods his head, ruefully.)* Cats! But, that can't be your idea. No, sir. Your wife and daughters? *(Peter nods his head.)* Is there anything else I should know?

Peter (he has to clear his throat): There are . . . there are two parakeets. One . . . uh . . . one for each of my daughters.

Jerry: Birds.

Peter: My daughters keep them in a cage in their bedroom.

Jerry: Do they carry disease? The birds.

Peter: I don't believe so.

Jerry: That's too bad. If they did you could set them loose in the house and the cats could eat them and die, maybe. *(Peter looks blank for a moment, then laughs.)* And what else? What do you do to support your enormous household?

Peter: I . . . uh . . . I have an executive position with a . . . a small publishing house. We . . . uh . . . we publish textbooks.

Jerry: That sounds nice; very nice. What do you make?

Peter (still cheerful): Now look here!

Jerry: Oh, come on.

Peter: Well, I make around eighteen thousand a year, but I don't carry more than forty dollars at any one time . . . in case you're a . . . a holdup man . . . ha, ha, ha.

Jerry (ignoring the above): Where do you live? *(Peter is reluctant.)* Oh, look; I'm not going to rob you, and I'm not going to kidnap your parakeets, your cats, or your daughters.

Peter (too loud): I live between Lexington and Third Avenue, on Seventy-fourth Street.

Jerry: That wasn't so hard, was it?

Peter: I didn't mean to seem . . . ah . . . it's that you don't really carry on a conversation; you just ask questions, and I'm . . . I'm normally . . . uh . . . reticent. Why do you just stand there?

Jerry: I'll start walking around in a little while, and eventually I'll sit down. *(Recalling.)* Wait until you see the expression on his face.

Peter: What? Whose face? Look here; is this something about the zoo?

Jerry (distantly): The what?

Peter: The zoo; the zoo. Something about the zoo.

Jerry: The zoo?

Peter: You've mentioned it several times.

Jerry (still distant, but returning abruptly): The zoo? Oh, yes; the zoo. I was there before I came here. I told you that. Say, what's the dividing line between upper-middle-middle-class and lower-upper-middle-class?

Peter: My dear fellow, I . . .

Jerry: Don't my dear fellow me.

Peter (unhappily): Was I patronizing? I believe I was; I'm sorry. But, you see, your question about the classes bewildered me.

Jerry: And when you're bewildered you become patronizing?

Peter: I . . . I don't express myself too well, sometimes. *(He attempts a joke on himself.)* I'm in publishing, not writing.

Jerry (amused, but not at the humor): So be it. The truth *is: I* was being patronizing.

Peter: Oh, now; you needn't say that.

It is at this point that Jerry may begin to move about the stage with slowly increasing determination and authority, but pacing himself, so that the long speech about the dog comes at the high point of the arc.

Jerry: All right. Who are your favorite writers? Baudelaire and J. P. Marquand?

Peter (wary): Well, I like a great many writers; I have a considerable . . . catholicity of taste, if I may say so. Those two men are fine, each in his way. *(Warming up.)* Baudelaire, of course . . . uh . . . is by far the finer of the two, but Marquand has a place . . . in our . . . uh . . . national . . .

Jerry: Skip it.

Peter: I . . . sorry.

Jerry: Do you know what I did before I went to the zoo today? I walked all the way up Fifth Avenue from Washington Square; all the way.

Peter: Oh; you live in the Village! *(This seems to enlighten Peter.)*

Jerry: No, I don't. I took the subway down to the Village so I could walk all the way up Fifth Avenue to the zoo. It's one of those things a person has to do; sometimes a person has to go a very long distance out of his way to come back a short distance correctly.

Peter (almost pouting): Oh, I thought you lived in the Village.

Jerry: What were you trying to do? Make sense out of things? Bring order? The old pigeonhole bit? Well, that's easy; I'll tell you. I live in a four-story brownstone roominghouse on the upper West Side between Columbus Avenue and Central Park West. I live on the top floor; rear; west. It's a laughably small room, and one of my walls is made of beaverboard; this beaverboard separates my room from another laughably small room, so I assume that the two rooms were once one room, a small room, but not necessarily laughable. The room beyond my beaverboard wall is occupied by a colored queen who always keeps his door open; well, not always, but *always* when he's plucking his eyebrows, which he does with Buddhist concentration. This colored queen has rotten teeth, which is rare, and he has a Japanese kimono, which is also pretty rare; and he wears this kimono to and from the john in the hall, which is pretty frequent. I mean, he goes to the john a lot. He never bothers me, and he never brings anyone up to his room. All he does is pluck his eyebrows, wear his kimono and go to the john. Now, the two front rooms on my floor are a little larger, I guess; but they're pretty small, too. There's a Puerto Rican family in one of them, a husband, a wife, and some kids; I don't know how many. These people entertain a lot. And in the other front room, there's somebody living there, but I don't know who it is. I've never seen who it is. Never. Never ever.

Peter (embarrassed): Why . . . why do you live there?

Jerry (from a distance again): I don't know.

Peter: It doesn't sound like a very nice place . . . where you live.

Jerry: Well, no; it isn't an apartment in the East Seventies. But, then again, I don't have one wife, two daughters, two cats and two parakeets. What I do have, I have toilet articles, a few clothes, a hot plate that I'm not supposed to have, a can opener, one that works with a key, you know; a knife, two forks, and two spoons, one small, one large; three plates, a cup, a saucer, a drinking glass, two picture frames, both empty, eight or nine books, a pack of pornographic playing cards, regular deck, an old Western Union typewriter that prints nothing but capital letters, and a small strongbox without a lock which has in it . . . what? Rocks! Some rocks . . . sea-rounded rocks I picked up on the beach when I was a kid. Under which . . . weighed down . . . are some letters . . . please letters . . . please why don't you do this, and please when will you do that letters. And when letters, too. When will you write? When will you come? When? These letters are from more recent years.

Peter (stares glumly at his shoes, then): About those two empty picture frames . . . ?

Jerry: I don't see why they need any explanation at all. Isn't it clear? I don't have pictures of anyone to put in them.

Peter: Your parents . . . perhaps . . . a girl friend . . .

Jerry: You're a very sweet man, and you're possessed of a truly enviable innocence. But good old Mom and good old Pop are dead . . . you know? . . . I'm broken up about it, too . . . I mean really. BUT. That particular vaudeville act is playing the cloud circuit now, so I don't see how I can look at them, all neat and framed. Besides, or, rather, to be pointed about it, good old Mom walked out on good old Pop when I was ten and a half years old; she embarked on an adulterous turn of our southern states . . . a journey of a year's duration . . . and her most constant companion . . . among others, among many others . . . was a Mr. Barleycorn. At least, that's what good old Pop told me after he went down . . . came back . . . brought her body north. We'd received the news between Christmas and New Year's, you see, that good old Mom had parted with the ghost in some dump in Alabama. And, without the ghost . . . she was less welcome. I mean, what was she? A stiff . . . a northern stiff. At any rate, good old Pop celebrated the New Year for an even two weeks and then slapped into the front of a somewhat moving city omnibus, which sort of cleaned things out family-wise. Well no; then there was Mom's sister, who was given neither to sin nor the consolations of the bottle. I moved in on her, and my memory of her is slight excepting I remember still that she did all things dourly: sleeping, eating, working, praying. She dropped dead on the stairs to her apartment, my apartment then, too, on the afternoon of my high school graduation. A terribly middle-European joke, if you ask me.

Peter: Oh, my; oh, my.

Jerry: Oh, your what? But that was a long time ago, and I have no feeling about any of it that I care to admit to myself. Perhaps you can see, though, why good old Mom and good old Pop are frameless. What's your name? Your first name?

Peter: I'm Peter.

Jerry: I'd forgotten to ask you. I'm Jerry.

Peter (with a slight, nervous laugh): Hello, Jerry.

Jerry (nods his hello): And let's see now; what's the point of having a girl's picture, especially in two frames? I have two picture frames, you remember. I never see the pretty little ladies more than once, and most of them wouldn't be caught in the same room with a camera. It's odd, and I wonder if it's sad.

Peter: The girls?

Jerry: No. I wonder if it's sad that I never see the little ladies more than once. I've never been able to have sex with, or, how is it put? . . . make love to anybody more than once. Once; that's it . . . Oh, wait; for a week and a half, when I was fifteen . . . and I hang my head in shame that puberty was late . . . I was a h-o-m-o-s-e-x-u-a-l. I mean, I was queer . . . *(very fast)* . . . queer, queer, queer . . . with bells ringing, banners snapping in the wind. And for those eleven days, I met at least twice a day with the park superintendent's son . . . a Greek boy, whose birthday was the same as mine, except he was a year older. I think I was very much in love . . . maybe just with sex. But that was the jazz of a very special hotel, wasn't it? And now; oh, do I love the little ladies; really, I love them. For about an hour.

Peter: Well, it seems perfectly simple to me. . . .

Jerry (angry): Look! Are you going to tell me to get married and have parakeets?

Peter (angry himself): Forget the parakeets! And stay single if you want to. It's no business of mine. I didn't start this conversation in the . . .

Jerry: All right, all right. I'm sorry. All right? You're not angry?

Peter (laughing): No, I'm not angry.

Jerry (relieved): Good. *(Now back to his previous tone.)* Interesting that you asked me about the picture frames. I would have thought that you would have asked me about the pornographic playing cards.

Peter (with a knowing smile): Oh, I've seen those cards.

Jerry: That's not the point. *(Laughs.)* I suppose when you were a kid you and your pals passed them around, or you had a pack of your own.

Peter: Well, I guess a lot of us did.

Jerry: And you threw them away just before you got married.

Peter: Oh, now; look here. I didn't *need* anything like that when I got older.

Jerry: No?

Peter (embarrassed): I'd rather not talk about these things.

Jerry: So? Don't. Besides, I wasn't trying to plumb your postadolescent sexual life and hard times; what I wanted to get at is the value difference between pornographic playing cards when you're a kid, and pornographic playing cards when you're older. It's that when you're a kid you use the cards as a substitute for a real experience, and when you're older you use real experience as a substitute for the fantasy. But I imagine you'd rather hear about what happened at the zoo.

Peter (enthusiastic): Oh, yes; the zoo. *(Then, awkward.)* That is . . . if you. . . .

Jerry: Let me tell you about why I went . . . well, let me tell you some things. I've told you about the fourth floor of the roominghouse where I live. I think the rooms are better as you go down, floor by floor. I guess they are; I don't know. I don't know any of the people on the third and second floors. Oh, wait! I do know that there's a lady living on the third floor, in the front. I know because she cries all the time. Whenever I go out or come back in, whenever I pass her door, I always hear her crying, muffled, but . . . very determined. Very determined indeed. But the one I'm getting to, and all about the dog, is the landlady. I don't like to use words that are too harsh in describing people. I don't like to. But the landlady is a fat, ugly, mean, stupid, unwashed, misanthropic, cheap, drunken bag of garbage. And you may have noticed that I very seldom use profanity, so I can't describe her as well as I might.

Peter: You describe her . . . vividly.

Jerry: Well, thanks. Anyway, she has a dog, and I will tell you about the dog, and she and her dog are the gatekeepers of my dwelling. The woman is bad enough; she leans around in the entrance hall, spying to see that I don't bring in things or people, and when she's had her midafternoon pint of lemon-flavored gin she always stops me in the hall, and grabs ahold of my coat or my arm, and she presses her disgusting body up against me to keep me in a corner so she can talk to me. The smell of her body and her breath . . . you can't imagine it . . . and somewhere, somewhere in the back of that pea-sized brain of hers, an organ developed just enough to let her eat, drink, and emit, she has some foul parody of sexual desire. And I, Peter, I am the object of her sweaty lust.

Peter: That's disgusting. That's . . . horrible.

Jerry: But I have found a way to keep her off. When she talks to me, when she presses herself to my body and mumbles about her room and how I should come there, I merely say: but, Love; wasn't yesterday enough for you, and the day before? Then she puzzles, she makes slits of her tiny eyes, she sways a little, and then, Peter . . . and it is at this moment that I think I might be doing some good in that tormented house . . . a simple-minded smile begins to form on her unthinkable face, and she giggles and groans as she thinks about yesterday and the day before; as she believes and relives what never happened. Then, she motions to that black monster of a dog she has, and she goes back to her room. And I am safe until our next meeting.

Peter: It's so . . . unthinkable. I find it hard to believe that people such as that really *are.*

Jerry (lightly mocking): It's for reading about, isn't it?

Peter (seriously): Yes.

Jerry: And fact is better left to fiction. You're right, Peter. Well, what I have been meaning to tell you about is the dog; I shall, now.

Peter (nervously): Oh, yes; the dog.

Jerry: Don't go. You're not thinking of going, are you?

Peter: Well . . . no, I don't think so.

Jerry (as if to a child): Because after I tell you about the dog, do you know what then? Then . . . then I'll tell you about what happened at the zoo.

Peter (laughing faintly): You're . . . you're full of stories, aren't you?

Jerry: You don't *have* to listen. Nobody is holding you here; remember that. Keep that in your mind.

Peter (irritably): I know that.

Jerry: You do? Good.

The following long speech, it seems to me, should be done with a great deal of action, to achieve a hypnotic effect on Peter, and on the audience, too. Some specific actions have been suggested, but the director and the actor playing Jerry might best work it out for themselves.

ALL RIGHT. *(As if reading from a huge billboard.)* THE STORY OF JERRY AND THE DOG! *(Natural again.)* What I am going to tell you has something to do with how sometimes it's necessary to go a long distance out of the way in order to come back a short distance correctly; or, maybe I only think that it has something to do with that. But, it's why I went to the zoo today, and why I walked north . . . northerly, rather . . . until I came here. All right. The dog, I think I told you, is a black monster of a beast: an oversized head, tiny, tiny ears, and eyes . . . bloodshot, infected, maybe; and a body you can see the ribs through the skin. The dog is black, all black; all black except for the bloodshot eyes, and . . . yes . . . and an open sore on its . . . *right* forepaw; that is red, too. And, oh yes; the poor monster, and I do believe it's an old dog . . . it's certainly a misused one . . . almost always has an erection . . . of sorts. That's red, too. And . . . what else? . . . oh, yes; there's a gray-yellow-white color, too, when he bares his fangs. Like this: Grrrrrrr! Which is what he did when he saw me for the first time . . . the day I moved in. I worried about that animal the very first minute I met him. Now, animals don't take to me like Saint Francis had birds hanging off him all the time. What I mean is: animals are indifferent to me . . . like people *(he smiles slightly)* . . . most of the time. But this dog wasn't indifferent. From the very beginning he'd snarl and then go for me, to get one of my legs. Not like he was rabid, you know; he was sort of a stumbly dog, but he wasn't half-assed, either. It was a good, stumbly run; but I always got away. He got a piece of my trouser leg, look, you can see right here, where it's mended; he got that the second day I lived there; but, I kicked free and got upstairs fast, so that was that. *(Puzzles.)* I still don't know to this day how the other roomers manage it, but you know what I *think:* I think it had to do only with me. Cozy. So. Anyway, this went on for over a week, whenever I came in; but never when I went out. That's funny. Or, it *was* funny. I could pack up and live in the street for all the dog cared. Well, I thought about it up in my room one day, one of the times after I'd bolted upstairs, and I made up my mind. I decided: First, I'll kill the dog with kindness, and if that doesn't work . . . I'll just kill him. *(Peter winces.)* Don't react, Peter; just listen. So, the next day I went out and bought a bag of hamburgers, medium rare, no catsup, no onion; and on the way home I threw away all the rolls and kept just the meat.

Action for the following, perhaps.

When I got back to the roominghouse the dog was waiting for me. I half opened the door that led into the entrance hall, and there he was; waiting for me. It figured. I went in, very cautiously, and I had the hamburgers, you remember; I opened the bag, and I set the meat down about twelve feet from where the dog was snarling at me. Like so! He snarled; stopped snarling; sniffed; moved slowly; then faster; then faster toward the meat. Well, when he got to it he stopped, and he looked at me. I smiled; but tentatively, you understand. He turned his face back to the hamburgers, smelled, sniffed some more, and then . . . RRRAAAAGGGGGHHHH, like that . . . he tore into them. It was as if he had never eaten anything in his life before, except like garbage. Which might very well have been the truth. I don't think the landlady ever eats anything but garbage. But. He ate all the hamburgers, almost all at once, making sounds in his throat like a woman. *Then,* when he'd finished the meat, the hamburger, and tried to eat the paper, too, he sat down and smiled. I think he smiled; I know cats do. It was a very gratifying few moments. Then, BAM, he snarled and made for me again. He didn't get me this time, either. So, I got upstairs, and I lay down on my bed and started to think about the dog again. To be truthful, I was offended, and I was damn mad, too. It was six perfectly good hamburgers with not enough pork in them to make it disgusting. I was offended. But, after a while, I decided to try it for a few more days. If you think about it, this dog had what amounted to an antipathy toward me; really. And, I wondered if I mightn't overcome this antipathy. So, I tried it for five more days, but it was always the same: snarl, sniff; move; faster; stare; gobble; RAAGGGHHH; smile; snarl; BAM. Well, now; by this time Columbus Avenue was strewn with hamburger rolls and I was less offended than disgusted. So, I decided to kill the dog.

Peter raises a hand in protest.

Oh, don't be so alarmed, Peter; I didn't succeed. The day I tried to kill the dog I bought only one hamburger and what I thought was a murderous portion of rat poison. When I bought the hamburger I asked the man not to bother with the roll, all I wanted was the meat. I expected some reaction from him, like: we don't sell no hamburgers without rolls; or, wha' d'ya wanna do, eat it out'a ya han's? But no; he smiled benignly, wrapped up the hamburger in waxed paper, and said: A bite for ya pussy-cat? I wanted to say: No, not really; it's part of a plan to poison a dog I know. But, you can't say "a dog I know" without sounding funny; so I said, a little too loud, I'm afraid, and too formally: YES, A BITE FOR MY PUSSY-CAT. People looked up. It always happens when I try to simplify things; people look up. But that's neither hither nor thither. So. On my way back to the roominghouse, I kneaded the hamburger and the rat poison together between my hands, at that point feeling as much sadness as disgust. I opened the door to the entrance hall, and there the monster was, waiting to take the offering and then jump me. Poor bastard; he never learned that the moment he took to smile before he went for me gave me time enough to get out of range. BUT, there he was; malevolence with an erection, waiting. I put the poison patty down, moved toward the stairs and watched. The poor animal gobbled the food down as usual, smiled, which made me almost sick, and then BAM. But, I sprinted up the stairs, as usual, and the dog didn't get me, as usual. AND IT CAME TO PASS THAT THE BEAST WAS DEATHLY ILL. I knew this because he no longer attended me, and because the landlady sobered up. She stopped me in the hall the same evening of the attempted murder and confided the information that God had struck her puppy-dog a surely fatal blow. She had forgotten her bewildered lust, and her eyes were wide open for the first time. They looked like the dog's eyes. She sniveled and implored me to pray for the animal. I wanted to say to her: Madam, I have myself to pray for, the colored queen, the Puerto Rican family, the person in the front room whom I've never seen, the woman who cries deliberately behind her closed door, and the rest of the people in all roominghouses, everywhere; besides, Madam, I don't understand how to pray. But . . . to simplify things . . . I told her I would pray. She looked up. She said that I was a liar, and that I probably wanted the dog to die. I told her, and there was so much truth here, that I didn't want the dog to die. I didn't, and not just because I'd poisoned him. I'm afraid that I must tell you I wanted the dog to live so that I could see what our new relationship might come to.

Peter indicates his increasing displeasure and slowly growing antagonism.

Please understand, Peter; that sort of thing is important. You must believe me; it *is* important. We have to know the effect of our actions. *(Another deep sigh.)* Well, anyway; the dog recovered. I have no idea why, unless he was a descendant of the puppy that guarded the gates of hell or some such resort. I'm not up on my mythology. *(He pronounces the word myth-o-* logy.) Are you?

Peter sets to thinking, but Jerry goes on.

At any rate, and you've missed the eight-thousand-dollar question, Peter; at any rate, the dog recovered his health and the landlady recovered her thirst, in no way altered by the bow-wow's deliverance. When I came home from a movie that was playing on Forty-second Street, a movie I'd seen, or one that was very much like one or several I'd seen, after the landlady told me puppykins was better, I was so hoping for the dog to be waiting for me. I was . . . well, how would you put it . . . enticed? . . . fascinated? . . . no, I don't think so . . . heart-shatteringly anxious, that's it; I was heart-shatteringly anxious to confront my friend again.

Peter reacts scoffingly.

Yes, Peter; friend. That's the only word for it. I was heart-shatteringly et cetera to confront my doggy friend again. I came in the door and advanced, unafraid, to the center of the entrance hall. The beast was there . . . looking at me. And, you know, he looked better for his scrape with the nevermind. I stopped; I looked at him; he looked at me. I think . . . I think we stayed a long time that way . . . still, stone-statue . . . just looking at one another. I looked more into his face than he looked into mine. I mean, I can concentrate longer at looking into a dog's face than a dog can concentrate at looking into mine, or into anybody else's face, for that matter. But during that twenty seconds or two hours that we looked into each other's face, we made contact. Now, here is what I had wanted to happen: I loved the dog now, and I wanted him to love me. I had tried to love, and I had tried to kill, and both had been unsuccessful by themselves. I hoped . . . and I don't really know why I expected the dog to understand anything, much less my motivations . . . I hoped that the dog would understand.

Peter seems to be hypnotized.

It's just . . . it's just that . . . *(Jerry is abnormally tense, now)* . . . it's just that if you can't deal with people, you have to make a start somewhere. WITH ANIMALS! *(Much faster now, and like a conspirator.)* Don't you see? A person has to have some way of dealing with SOMETHING. If not with people . . . if not with people . . . SOMETHING. With a bed, with a cockroach, with a mirror . . . no, that's too hard, that's one of the last steps. With a cockroach, with a . . . with a carpet, a roll of toilet paper . . . no, not that, either . . . that's a mirror, too; always check bleeding. You see how hard it is to find things? With a street corner, and too many lights, all colors reflecting on the oily-wet streets . . . with a wisp of smoke, a wisp . . . of smoke . . . with . . . with pornographic playing cards, with a strongbox . . . WITHOUT A LOCK . . . with love, with vomiting, with crying, with fury because the pretty little ladies aren't pretty little ladies, with making money with your body which is an act of love and I could prove it, with howling because you're alive; with God. How about that? WITH GOD WHO IS A COLORED QUEEN WHO WEARS A KIMONO AND PLUCKS HIS EYEBROWS, WHO IS A WOMAN WHO CRIES WITH DETERMINATION BEHIND HER CLOSED DOOR . . . with God who, I'm told, turned his back on the whole thing some time ago . . . with . . . some day, with people. *(Jerry sighs the next word heavily.)* People. With an idea; a concept. And where better, where ever better in this humiliating excuse for a jail, where better to communicate one single, simpleminded idea than in an entrance hall? Where? It would be A START! Where better to make a beginning . . . to understand and just possibly be understood . . . a beginning of an understanding, than with . . .

Here Jerry seems to fall into almost grotesque fatigue.

. . . than with A DOG. Just that; a dog.

Here there is a silence that might be prolonged for a moment or so; then Jerry wearily finishes his story.

A dog. It seemed like a perfectly sensible idea. Man is a dog's best friend, remember. So: the dog and I looked at each other. I longer than the dog. And what I saw then has been the same ever since. Whenever the dog and I see each other we both stop where we are. We regard each other with a mixture of sadness and suspicion, and then we feign indifference. We walk past each other safely; we have an understanding. It's very sad, but you'll have to admit that it is an understanding. We had made many attempts at contact, and we had failed. The dog has returned to garbage, and I to solitary but free passage. I have not returned. I mean to say, I have *gained* solitary free passage, if that much further loss can be said to be gain. I have learned that neither kindness nor cruelty by themselves, independent of each other, creates any effect beyond themselves; and I have learned that the two combined, together, at the same time, are the teaching emotion. And what is gained is loss. And what has been the result: the dog and I have attained a compromise; more of a bargain, really. We neither love nor hurt because we do not try to reach each other. And, *was* trying to feed the dog an act of love? And, perhaps, was the dog's attempt to bite me *not* an act of love? If we can so misunderstand, well then, why have we invented the word love in the first place?

There is silence. Jerry moves to Peter's bench and sits down beside him. This is the first time Jerry has sat down during the play.

The Story of Jerry and the Dog: the end.

Peter is silent.

Well, Peter? *(Jerry is suddenly cheerful.)* Well, Peter? Do you think I could sell that story to the *Reader's Digest* and make a couple of hundred bucks for *The Most Unforgettable Character I've Ever Met?* Huh?

Jerry is animated, but Peter is disturbed.

Oh, come on now, Peter; tell me what you think.

Peter (numb): I . . . I don't understand what . . . I don't think I . . . *(Now, almost tearfully.)* Why did you tell me all of this?

Jerry: Why not?

Peter: I DON'T UNDERSTAND!

Jerry (furious, but whispering): That's a lie.

Peter: No. No, it's not.

Jerry (quietly): I tried to explain it to you as I went along. I went slowly; it all has to do with . . .

Peter: I DON'T WANT TO HEAR ANY MORE. I don't understand you, or your landlady, or her dog. . . .

Jerry: Her dog! I thought it was my . . . No. No, you're right. It *is* her dog. *(Looks at Peter intently, shaking his head.)* I don't know what I was thinking about; of course you don't understand. *(In a monotone, wearily.)* I don't live in your block; I'm not married to two parakeets, or whatever your setup is. I am a *permanent transient,* and my home is the sickening roominghouses on the West Side of New York City, which is the greatest city in the world. Amen.

Peter: I'm . . . I'm sorry; I didn't mean to . . .

Jerry: Forget it. I suppose you don't quite know what to make of me, eh?

Peter (a joke): We get all kinds in publishing. *(Chuckles.)*

Jerry: You're a funny man. *(He forces a laugh.)* You know that? You're a very . . . a richly comic person.

Peter (modestly, but amused): Oh, now, not really. *(Still chuckling.)*

Jerry: Peter, do I annoy you, or confuse you?

Peter (lightly): Well, I must confess that this wasn't the kind of afternoon I'd anticipated.

Jerry: You mean, I'm not the gentleman you were expecting.

Peter: I wasn't expecting anybody.

Jerry: No, I don't imagine you were. But I'm here, and I'm not leaving.

Peter (consulting his watch): Well, you may not be, but I must be getting home soon.

Jerry: Oh, come on; stay a while longer.

Peter: I really should get home; you see . . .

Jerry (tickles Peter's ribs with his fingers): Oh, come on.

Peter (he is very ticklish; as Jerry continues to tickle him his voice becomes falsetto): No, I . . . OHHHHH! Don't do that. Stop, stop. Ohhh, no, no.

Jerry: Oh, come on.

Peter (as Jerry tickles): Oh, hee, hee, hee. I must go. I . . . hee, hee, hee. After all, stop, stop, hee, hee, hee, after all, the parakeets will be getting dinner ready soon. Hee, hee. And the cats are setting the table. Stop, stop, and, and . . . *(Peter is beside himself now)* . . . and we're having . . . hee, hee . . . uh . . . ho, ho, ho.

Jerry stops tickling Peter, but the combination of the tickling and his own mad whimsy has Peter laughing almost hysterically. As his laughter continues, then subsides, Jerry watches him, with a curious fixed smile.

Jerry: Peter?

Peter: Oh, ha, ha, ha, ha, ha. What? What?

Jerry: Listen, now.

Peter: Oh, ho, ho. What . . . what is it, Jerry? Oh, my.

Jerry (mysteriously): Peter, do you want to know what happened at the zoo?

Peter: Ah, ha, ha. The what? Oh, yes; the zoo. Oh, ho, ho. Well, I had my own zoo there for a moment with . . . hee, hee, the parakeets getting dinner ready, and the . . . ha, ha, whatever it was, the . . .

Jerry (calmly): Yes, that was very funny, Peter. I wouldn't have expected it. But do you want to hear about what happened at the zoo, or not?

Peter: Yes. Yes, by all means; tell me what happened at the zoo. Oh, my. I don't know what happened to me.

Jerry: Now I'll let you in on what happened at the zoo; but first, I should tell you why I went to the zoo. I went to the zoo to find out more about the way people exist with animals, and the way animals exist with each other, and with people too. It probably wasn't a fair test, what with everyone separated by bars from everyone else, the animals for the most part from each other, and always the people from the animals. But, if it's a zoo, that's the way it is. *(He pokes Peter on the arm.)* Move over.

Peter (friendly): I'm sorry, haven't you enough room? *(He shifts a little.)*

Jerry (smiling slightly): Well, all the animals are there, and all the people are there, and it's Sunday and all the children are there. *(He pokes Peter again.)* Move over.

Peter (patiently, still friendly): All right.

He moves some more, and Jerry has all the room he might need.

Jerry: And it's a hot day, so all the stench is there, too, and all the balloon sellers, and all the ice cream sellers, and all the seals are barking, and all the birds are screaming. *(Pokes Peter harder.)* Move over!

Peter (beginning to be annoyed): Look here, you have more than enough room! *(But he moves more, and is now fairly cramped at one end of the bench.)*

Jerry: And I am there, and it's feeding time at the lions' house, and the lion keeper comes into the lion cage, one of the lion cages, to feed one of the lions. *(Punches Peter on the arm, hard.)* MOVE OVER!

Peter (very annoyed): I can't move over any more, and stop hitting me. What's the matter with you?

Jerry: Do you want to hear the story? *(Punches Peter's arm again.)*

Peter (flabbergasted): I'm not so sure! I certainly don't want to be punched in the arm.

Jerry (punches Peter's arm again): Like that?

Peter: Stop it! What's the matter with you?

Jerry: I'm crazy, you bastard.

Peter: That isn't funny.

Jerry: Listen to me, Peter. I want this bench. You go sit on the bench over there, and if you're good I'll tell you the rest of the story.

Peter (flustered): But . . . whatever for? What *is* the matter with you? Besides, I see no reason why I should give up this bench. I sit on this bench almost every Sunday afternoon, in good weather. It's secluded here; there's never anyone sitting here, so I have it all to myself.

Jerry (softly): Get off this bench, Peter; I want it.

Peter (almost whining): No.

Jerry: I said I want this bench, and I'm going to have it. Now get over there.

Peter: People can't have everything they want. You should know that; it's a rule; people can have some of the things they want, but they can't have everything.

Jerry (laughs): Imbecile! You're slow-witted!

Peter: Stop that!

Jerry: You're a vegetable! Go lie down on the ground.

Peter (intense): Now *you* listen to me. I've put up with you all afternoon.

Jerry: Not really.

Peter: LONG ENOUGH. I've put up with you long enough. I've listened to you because you seemed . . . well, because I thought you wanted to talk to somebody.

Jerry: You put things well; economically, and, yet . . . oh, what is the word I want to put justice to your . . . JESUS, you make me sick . . . get off here and give me my bench.

Peter: MY BENCH!

Jerry (pushes Peter almost, but not quite, off the bench): Get out of my sight.

Peter (regaining his position): God da . . . mn you. That's enough! I've had enough of you. I will not give up this bench; you can't have it, and that's that. Now, go away.

Jerry snorts but does not move.

Go away, I said.

Jerry does not move.

Get away from here. If you don't move on . . . you're a bum . . . that's what you are. . . . If you don't move on, I'll get a policeman here and make you go.

Jerry laughs, stays.

I warn you, I'll call a policeman.

Jerry (softly): You won't find a policeman around here; they're all over on the west side of the park chasing fairies down from trees or out of the bushes. That's all they do. That's their function. So scream your head off; it won't do you any good.

Peter: POLICE! I warn you, I'll have you arrested. POLICE! *(Pause.)* I said POLICE! *(Pause.)* I feel ridiculous.

Jerry: You look ridiculous: a grown man screaming for the police on a bright Sunday afternoon in the park with nobody harming you. If a policeman *did* fill his quota and come sludging over this way he'd probably take you in as a nut.

Peter (with disgust and impotence): Great God, I just came here to read, and now you want me to give up the bench. You're mad.

Jerry: Hey, I got news for you, as they say. I'm on your precious bench, and you're never going to have it for yourself again.

Peter (furious): Look, you; get off my bench. I don't care if it makes any sense or not. I want this bench to myself; I want you OFF IT!

Jerry (mocking): Aw . . . look who's mad.

Peter: GET OUT!

Jerry: No.

Peter: I WARN YOU!

Jerry: Do you know how ridiculous you look *now?*

Peter (his fury and self-consciousness have possessed him): It doesn't matter. *(He is almost crying.)* GET AWAY FROM MY BENCH!

Jerry: Why? You have everything in the world you want; you've told me about your home, and your family, and *your own* little zoo. You have everything, and now you want this bench. Are these the things men fight for? Tell me, Peter, is this bench, this iron and this wood, is this your honor? Is this the thing in the world you'd fight for? Can you think of anything more absurd?

Peter: Absurd? Look, I'm not going to talk to you about honor, or even try to explain it to you. Besides, it isn't a question of honor; but even if it were, you wouldn't understand.

Jerry (contemptuously): You don't even know what you're saying, do you? This is probably the first time in your life you've had anything more trying to face than changing your cats' toilet box. Stupid! Don't you have any idea, not even the slightest, what other people *need?*

Peter: Oh, boy, listen to you; well, you don't need this bench. That's for sure.

Jerry: Yes; yes, I do.

Peter (quivering): I've come here for years; I have hours of great pleasure, great satisfaction, right here. And that's important to a man. I'm a responsible person, and I'm GROWNUP. This is my bench, and you have no right to take it away from me.

Jerry: Fight for it, then. Defend yourself; defend your bench.

Peter: You've *pushed* me to it. Get up and fight.

Jerry: Like a man?

Peter (still angry): Yes, like a man, if you insist on mocking me even further.

Jerry: I'll have to give you credit for one thing: you *are* a vegetable, and a slightly nearsighted one, I think . . .

Peter: THAT'S ENOUGH. . . .

Jerry: . . . but, you know, as they say on TV all the time — you know — and I mean this, Peter, you have a certain dignity; it surprises me. . . .

Peter: STOP!

Jerry (rises lazily): Very well, Peter, we'll battle for the bench, but we're not evenly matched.

He takes out and clicks open an ugly-looking knife.

Peter (suddenly awakening to the reality of the situation): You are mad! You're stark raving mad! YOU'RE GOING TO KILL ME!

But before Peter has time to think what to do, Jerry tosses the knife at Peter's feet.

Jerry: There you go. Pick it up. You have the knife and we'll be more evenly matched.

Peter (horrified): No!

Jerry (rushes over to Peter, grabs him by the collar; Peter rises; their faces almost touch): Now you pick up that knife and you fight with me. You fight for your self-respect; you fight for that goddamned bench.

Peter (struggling): No! Let . . . let go of me! He . . . Help!

Jerry (slaps Peter on each "fight"): You fight, you miserable bastard; fight for that bench; fight for your parakeets; fight for your cats, fight for your two daughters; fight for your wife; fight for your manhood, you pathetic little vegetable. *(Spits in Peter's face.)* You couldn't even get your wife with a male child.

Peter (breaks away, enraged): It's a matter of genetics, not manhood, you . . . you monster.

He darts down, picks up the knife and backs off a little; he is breathing heavily.

I'll give you one last chance; get out of here and leave me alone!

He holds the knife with a firm arm, but far in front of him, not to attack, but to defend.

Jerry (sighs heavily): So be it!

With a rush he charges Peter and impales himself on the knife. Tableau: For just a moment, complete silence, Jerry impaled on the knife at the end of Peter's still firm arm. Then Peter screams, pulls away, leaving the knife in Jerry. Jerry is motionless, on point. Then he, too, screams, and it must be the sound of an infuriated and fatally wounded animal. With the knife in him, he stumbles back to the bench that Peter had vacated. He crumbles there, sitting, facing Peter, his eyes wide in agony, his mouth open.

Peter (whispering): Oh my God, oh my God, oh my God. . . . *(He repeats these words many times, very rapidly.)*

Jerry (Jerry is dying; but now his expression seems to change. His features relax, and while his voice varies, sometimes wrenched with pain, for the most part he seems removed from his dying. He smiles): Thank you, Peter. I mean that, now; thank you very much.

Edward Albee 1165

Peter's mouth drops open. He cannot move; he is transfixed.

Oh, Peter, I was so afraid I'd drive you away. *(He laughs as best he can.)* You don't know how afraid I was you'd go away and leave me. And now I'll tell you what happened at the zoo. I think . . . I think this is what happened at the zoo . . . I think. I think that while I was at the zoo I decided that I would walk north . . . northerly, rather . . . until I found you . . . or somebody . . . and I decided that I would talk to you . . . I would tell you things . . . and things that I would tell you would . . . Well, here we are. You see? Here we are. But . . . I don't know . . . could I have planned all this? No . . . no, I couldn't have. But I think I did. And now I've told you what you wanted to know, haven't I? And now you know all about what happened at the zoo. And now you know what you'll see in your TV, and the face I told you about . . . you remember . . . the face I told you about . . . my face, the face you see right now. Peter . . . Peter? . . . Peter . . . thank you. I came unto you *(he laughs, so faintly)* and you have comforted me. Dear Peter.

Peter (almost fainting): Oh my God!

Jerry: You'd better go now. Somebody might come by, and you don't want to be here when anyone comes.

Peter (does not move, but begins to weep): Oh my God, oh my God.

Jerry (most faintly, now; he is very near death): You won't be coming back here any more, Peter; you've been dispossessed. You've lost your bench, but you've defended your honor. And Peter, I'll tell you something now; you're not really a vegetable; it's all right, you're an animal. You're an animal, too. But you'd better hurry now, Peter. Hurry, you'd better go . . . see?

Jerry takes a handkerchief and with great effort and pain wipes the knife handle clean of fingerprints.

Hurry away, Peter.

Peter begins to stagger away.

Wait . . . wait, Peter. Take your book . . . book. Right here . . . beside me . . . on your bench . . . my bench, rather. Come . . . take your book.

Peter starts for the book, but retreats.

Hurry . . . Peter.

Peter rushes to the bench, grabs the book, retreats.

Very good, Peter . . . very good. Now . . . hurry away.

Peter hesitates for a moment, then flees, stage-left.

Hurry away. . . . *(His eyes are closed now.)* Hurry away, your parakeets are making the dinner . . . the cats . . . are setting the table . . .

Peter (off stage; a pitiful howl): OH MY GOD!

Jerry (his eyes still closed, he shakes his head and speaks; a combination of scornful mimicry and supplication): Oh . . . my . . . God.

He is dead.

CURTAIN

QUESTIONS

1. Point out some of the ways in which Jerry likens people to animals. Consider in particular Jerry's story of the dog. What is the point of this story? What does it have to do with the play's overall story about Jerry and Peter? At the end, what is suggested by having both characters scream or howl?
2. How is a zoo ("with everyone separated by bars from everyone else," as Jerry says) a fitting metaphor for modern urban society? By what acts or gestures does Jerry try to break down the "bars" between Peter and himself?
3. What suggestions do you find in Jerry's picture frames that lack pictures? In the park bench, which Peter thinks he owns?
4. Does the play contain any elements of plot structure that seem traditional? Point out any apparent crisis or climax.
5. What is the major dramatic question in *The Zoo Story*? Where in the play does this question first arise?
6. What is meaningful in Jerry's repeated statement, "Sometimes a person has to go a very long distance out of his way in order to come back a short distance correctly"?
7. What events and what attitudes in the play mark it as belonging to the theater of the absurd?
8. Is there anything in *The Zoo Story* that seems realistic — recognizably faithful to ordinary life?

SUGGESTIONS FOR WRITING

1. In a paragraph or two, demonstrate how Nora in *A Doll House* resembles or differs from a feminist of today.
2. Put yourself in the character of Torvald Helmer in *A Doll House,* and write a defense of him as he himself might write it.
3. Compare and contrast *Purgatory* and *Oedipus Rex,* looking for any element or elements that the two plays have in common.
4. Choose the play in this chapter that you think might best lend itself to television. Then tell your reader how you would go about adapting it. What changes or deletions, if any, would you make in the play? What problems would you expect to meet in transferring it to a television screen?
5. Write an imaginary conversation in dialogue form between either Jerry or Peter of *The Zoo Story* and Nat Ackerman of Woody Allen's *Death Knocks* (in Chapter Thirty-four). First decide what common interests they might have to talk about.
6. Read the eleven poems by Yeats in this book. Then in your own words explain how the poems and *Purgatory* throw light on each other. Do you find any similar characters, themes, symbols, or imagery?
7. Make up casting lists for all three plays in this chapter, selecting well-known actors of movies and television whom you think well suited to portray all the characters. Then write a justification for each of your choices, referring not only to the well-known actors but also to the plays.
8. How do Ibsen and Yeats give us starkly different views of what is "real"? In a few paragraphs, compare and contrast *A Doll House* with *Purgatory.* To keep your paper manageable, you might care to deal with just one of these elements: the main characters (true to life? larger than life? simpler than in life?), stage directions (faithful or unfaithful to the world we know?), language (poetic or prosaic? — can you give examples?).

36 Evaluating a Play

To **evaluate** a play is to decide whether the play is any good or not; and if it is good, how good it is in relation to other plays of its kind. In the theater, evaluation is usually thought to be the task of the play reviewer (or, with nobler connotations, "drama critic"), ordinarily a person who sees a new play on its first night and who then tells us, in print or over the air, what the play is about, how well it is done, and whether or not we ought to go to see it. Enthroned in an excellent free seat, the drama critic apparently plies a glamorous trade. What fun it must be to whittle a nasty epigram: to be able to observe, as did a critic of a faltering production of *Uncle Tom's Cabin,* that "The Siberian wolf hound was weakly supported."

Unless you find a job on a large city newspaper or radio station, however, or write for a college paper, or broadcast on a campus FM station, the opportunities to be a drama critic today are probably few and strictly limited. Much more significant, for most of us, is the task of evaluation we undertake for our own satisfaction. We see a play, or a film or a drama on television, and then we make up our minds about it; and we often have to decide whether to recommend it to anyone else.

To evaluate new drama isn't easy. (And in this discussion, let us define *drama* broadly as including not only plays, but anything that actors perform in the movies or on television, for most of us see more movies and television programs than plays.) But at least a part of the process of evaluation has already been accomplished for us. To produce a new play, even in an amateur theater, or to produce a new drama for the movies or for television, is complicated and involves large sums of money and the efforts of many people. Sifted from a mountain of submitted playscripts, already subjected to long scrutiny and evaluation, a new play or film, whether or not it is of deep interest, arrives with a built-in air of professional competence. It is probably seldom that a dull play written by the producer's relative or friend finds enough financial backers to reach the stage; only on the fictitious Broadway of Mel Brooks's film *The Producers* could there be a musical comedy as awful as *Springtime for Hitler.* Nor do most college and civic theaters afford us much opportunity to see thoroughly inept plays;

usually they give us new productions of *Oedipus Rex* or *Pygmalion;* or else (if they are less adventurous) new versions of whatever succeeded on Broadway in the recent past.

And so new plays — the few that we do see — are usually, like television drama, somebody's safe investment. More often than not, our powers of evaluation confront only slick, pleasant, and efficient mediocrity. We owe it to ourselves to discriminate; and here are a few suggestions designed to help you tell the difference between an ordinary, run-of-the-reel product, and a work of drama that may offer high reward.

1. Discard any inexorable rules you may have collected that affirm what a drama ought to be. (One such rule states that a tragedy is innately superior to a comedy, no matter how deep a truth a comedy may strike.) Never mind the misinterpreters of Aristotle who insist that a play must "observe the unities" — that is, must unfold its events in one day and in one place, and must keep tragedy and comedy strictly apart. (Shakespeare ignores such rules.) There is no sense in damning a play for lacking "realism" (what if it's an expressionist play, or a fantasy?), or in belaboring the failure of its plot to fit into a pyramid structure.

2. Instead, watch the play (or read it) alertly, with your mind and your senses open wide. Recall that theaters, such as the classic Greek theater of Sophocles, impose conventions. Do not condemn *Oedipus Rex* for the reason one spectator gave: "That damned chorus keeps sticking their noses in!" Do not complain that Hamlet utters soliloquies; nor that, in the same play, some speeches (when the speakers exit) rime unnaturally.

3. Ask yourself if the characters are fully realized. Do their actions follow from the kinds of persons they are, or does the action seem to impose itself upon them, making the play seem falsely contrived? Does the resolution arrive (as in a satisfying play) because of the nature of the characters; or are the characters saved (or destroyed) merely by some *deus ex machina,* or nick-of-time arrival of the Marines?

4. Recognize drama that belongs to a family: a *farce,* say, or a *comedy of manners,* or a **melodrama** — a play in which suspense and physical action are the prime ingredients. Recognizing such a familiar type of drama may help make some things clear to you, and may save you from attacking a play for being what it is, in fact, supposed to be. After all, there can be satisfying melodramas, and excellent plays may have melodramatic elements. What is wrong with thrillers is not that they have suspense, but that suspense is all they have. Awhirl with furious action, they employ stick-figure characters.

5. If there are symbols, ask how well they belong to their surrounding worlds. Do they help to reveal meaning, or merely decorate? In Tennessee Williams's *The Glass Menagerie,* Laura's collection of figurines is much more than simply ornamental.

6. Test the play or film for **sentimentality,** the failure of a dramatist, actor, or director caused by expecting from us a greater emotional response than we are given reason to feel. (For further discussion of sentimentality, see page 654.)

7. Decide what it is that you admire or dislike, and, for a play, whether it is the play that you admire or dislike, or the production. (It is useful to draw this distinction if you are evaluating the play and not the production.)

8. Ask yourself what the theme is. What does the drama reveal? How far and how deeply does its statement go; how readily can we apply it beyond the play to the human world outside? Be slow, of course, to attribute to the playwright the opinions of the characters.

Follow all these steps and you may find that evaluating plays, movies, and television plays is a richly meaningful activity. It may reveal wisdom and pleasure that had previously bypassed you. It may even help you decide what to watch in the future, how to choose those works of drama which help you to fulfill — not merely to spend — your waking life.

SUGGESTIONS FOR WRITING

1. Read the printed text of a contemporary play not included in this book. If you can see the play on stage, so much the better. Then, in an essay of 500 to 750 words, state your considered opinion of it.

   Among interesting plays to consider are *Master Harold and the Boys* by Athol Fugard, *American Buffalo* by David Mamet, *'Night, Mother* by Marsha Norman, *The Birthday Party* or *The Caretaker* by Harold Pinter, *Equus* or *Amadeus* by Peter Shaffer, *for colored girls who have considered suicide / when the rainbow is enuf* by Ntozake Shange, *Buried Child* by Sam Shepherd, *Dogg's Hamlet, Cahoot's Macbeth* by Tom Stoppard, *Sweeney Todd, the Demon Barber of Fleet Street,* a musical by Hugh Wheeler and Steven Sondheim, and *The Effect of Gamma Rays on Man-in-the-Moon Marigolds* by Paul Zindel.

2. Attend a performance of a play and write a critical review. Consider both the play itself and the production. (For advice on reviewing, and a sample review, see page 1412.)

3. In Chapter Thirty-seven, "Plays for Further Reading," read *The Glass Menagerie* and *Death of a Salesman.* Then, in an essay of 700 words or more, decide which play deserves the larger palm, so to speak. Support your opinion with evidence.

37 Plays for Further Reading

All the world's a stage,
And all the men and women merely players:
They have their exits and their entrances,
And one man in his time plays many parts,
His acts being seven ages. At first, the infant
Mewling° and puking in the nurse's arms.   *bawling*
Then the whining schoolboy with his satchel
And shining morning face, creeping like snail
Unwillingly to school. And then the lover,
Sighing like furnace, with a woeful ballad
Made to his mistress' eyebrow. Then a soldier
Full of strange oaths and bearded like the pard°,   *leopard*
Jealous in honor, sudden and quick in quarrel,
Seeking the bubble reputation
Even in the cannon's mouth. And then the justice,
In fair round belly with good capon lined,
With eyes severe and beard of formal cut,
Full of wise saws° and modern instances°;   *sayings; examples*
And so he plays his part. The sixth age shifts
Into the lean and slippered pantaloon°,   *old man (from*
With spectacles on nose and pouch on side;   *Pantalone in*
His youthful hose well saved, a world too wide   *the commedia*
For his shrunk shank, and his big manly voice   *dell' arte)*
Turning again toward childish treble, pipes
And whistles in his sound. Last scene of all
That ends this strange eventful history
Is second childishness and mere oblivion,
Sans teeth, sans eyes, sans taste, sans everything.
— William Shakespeare, *As You Like It,* II, vii

Sophocles

ANTIGONÊ

441 B.C.

An English Version by Dudley Fitts and Robert Fitzgerald

> *Sophocles (496? – 406 B.C.), Athenian dramatist, is the subject of a bio-graphical note on page 859, preceding his play* Oedipus Rex. *Antigonê was produced in 441 B.C.; the* Oedipus Rex, *not until fourteen or fifteen years later. Although written earlier than its companion play,* Antigonê *relates events supposed to have followed long after.*

Characters

Antigonê
Ismenê
Eurydicê
Creon
Haimon
Teiresias
A Sentry
A Messenger
Chorus

Scene. *Before the palace of Creon, King of Thebes. A central double door, and two lateral doors. A platform extends the length of the façade, and from this platform three steps lead down into the "orchestra," or chorus-ground.*

Time. *Dawn of the day after the repulse of the Argive army from the assault on Thebes.*

PROLOGUE°

> *Antigonê and Ismenê enter from the central door of the palace.*

Antigonê: Ismenê, dear sister,
   You would think that we had already suffered enough
   For the curse on Oedipus°.
   I cannot imagine any grief

Prologue: Portion of the play containing the exposition, or explanation of what has gone before and what is now happening.

[3] *the curse on Oedipus:* As Sophocles tells in *Oedipus Rex,* the King of Thebes discovered that he had lived his life under a curse. Unknowingly, he had slain his father and married his mother. On realizing this terrible truth, Oedipus put out his own eyes and departed into exile. Now, years later, as *Antigonê* opens, Antigonê and Ismenê, daughters of Oedipus, are recalling how their two brothers died. After the abdication of their father, the brothers had ruled Thebes together. But they fell to quarreling. When Eteoclês expelled Polyneicês, the latter returned with an army and attacked the city. The two brothers killed each other in combat, leaving the throne to Creon. The new king of Thebes has buried Eteoclês with full honors, but, calling Polyneicês a traitor, has decreed that his body shall be left to the crows — an especially terrible decree, for a rotting corpse might offend Zeus, bring down plague, blight, and barrenness upon Thebes, and prevent the soul of a dead hero from entering the Elysian Fields, abode of those favored by the gods.

That you and I have not gone through. And now — 5
Have they told you of the new decree of our King Creon?

Ismenê: I have heard nothing: I know
That two sisters lost two brothers, a double death
In a single hour; and I know that the Argive army
Fled in the night; but beyond this, nothing. 10

Antigonê: I thought so. And that is why I wanted you
To come out here with me. There is something we must do.

Ismenê: Why do you speak so strangely?

Antigonê: Listen, Ismenê:
Creon buried our brother Eteoclês 15
With military honors, gave him a soldier's funeral,
And it was right that he should; but Polyneicês,
Who fought as bravely and died as miserably, —
They say that Creon has sworn
No one shall bury him, no one mourn for him, 20
But his body must lie in the fields, a sweet treasure
For carrion birds to find as they search for food.
That is what they say, and our good Creon is coming here
To announce it publicly; and the penalty —
Stoning to death in the public square!

There it is, 25
And now you can prove what you are:
A true sister, or a traitor to your family.

Ismenê: Antigonê, you are mad! What could I possibly do?

Antigonê: You must decide whether you will help me or not.

Ismenê: I do not understand you. Help you in what? 30

Antigonê: Ismenê, I am going to bury him. Will you come?

Ismenê: Bury him! You have just said the new law forbids it.

Antigonê: He is my brother. And he is your brother, too.

Ismenê: But think of the danger! Think what Creon will do!

Antigonê: Creon is not strong enough to stand in my way. 35

Ismenê: Ah sister!
Oedipus died, everyone hating him
For what his own search brought to light, his eyes
Ripped out by his own hand; and Iocastê died,
His mother and wife at once: she twisted the cords 40
That strangled her life; and our two brothers died,
Each killed by the other's sword. And we are left:
But oh, Antigonê,
Think how much more terrible than these
Our own death would be if we should go against Creon 45
And do what he has forbidden! We are only women,
We cannot fight with men, Antigonê!
The law is strong, we must give in to the law
In this thing, and in worse. I beg the Dead
To forgive me, but I am helpless: I must yield 50
To those in authority. And I think it is dangerous business
To be always meddling.

Antigonê: If that is what you think,

I should not want you, even if you asked to come.
You have made your choice, you can be what you want to be.
But I will bury him; and if I must die,   55
I say that this crime is holy: I shall lie down
With him in death, and I shall be as dear
To him as he to me.
                    It is the dead,
Not the living, who make the longest demands:
We die for ever . . .
                    You may do as you like,   60
Since apparently the laws of the gods mean nothing to you.
Ismenê: They mean a great deal to me; but I have no strength
    To break laws that were made for the public good.
Antigonê: That must be your excuse, I suppose. But as for me,
    I will bury the brother I love.
Ismenê: Antigonê,   65
    I am so afraid for you!
Antigonê: You need not be:
    You have yourself to consider, after all.
Ismenê: But no one must hear of this, you must tell no one!
    I will keep it a secret, I promise!
Antigonê: O tell it! Tell everyone!
    Think how they'll hate you when it all comes out   70
    If they learn that you knew about it all the time!
Ismenê: So fiery! You should be cold with fear.
Antigonê: Perhaps. But I am doing only what I must.
Ismenê: But can you do it? I say that you cannot.
Antigonê: Very well: when my strength gives out,   75
    I shall do no more.
Ismenê: Impossible things should not be tried at all.
Antigonê: Go away, Ismenê:
    I shall be hating you soon, and the dead will too,
    For your words are hateful. Leave me my foolish plan: 80
    I am not afraid of the danger; if it means death,
    It will not be the worst of deaths — death without honor.
Ismenê: Go then, if you feel that you must.
    You are unwise,
    But a loyal friend indeed to those who love you.   85

Exit into the palace. Antigonê goes off, left. Enter the Chorus.

PARODOS°

                                                        Strophe 1

Chorus: Now the long blade of the sun, lying
    Level east to west, touches with glory

Parodos: a song sung by the chorus on first entering. Its *strophe* (according to scholarly theory) was sung while the chorus danced from stage right to stage left; its *antistrophe,* while they danced back again. Another parodos follows the prologue of *Oedipus Rex.*

Thebes of the Seven Gates. Open, unlidded
Eye of golden day! O marching light
Across the eddy and rush of Dircê's stream°,
Striking the white shields of the enemy
Thrown headlong backward from the blaze of morning!
Choragos°: Polyneicês their commander
Roused them with windy phrases,
He the wild eagle screaming
Insults above our land,
His wings their shields of snow,
His crest their marshalled helms.

Antistrophe 1

Chorus: Against our seven gates in a yawning ring
The famished spears came onward in the night;
But before his jaws were sated with our blood,
Or pinefire took the garland of our towers,
He was thrown back; and as he turned, great Thebes —
No tender victim for his noisy power —
Rose like a dragon behind him, shouting war.
Choragos: For God hates utterly
The bray of bragging tongues;
And when he beheld their smiling,
Their swagger of golden helms,
The frown of his thunder blasted
Their first man from our walls.

Strophe 2

Chorus: We heard his shout of triumph high in the air
Turn to a scream; far out in a flaming arc
He fell with his windy torch, and the earth struck him.
And others storming in fury no less than his
Found shock of death in the dusty joy of battle.
Choragos: Seven captains at seven gates
Yielded their clanging arms to the god
That bends the battle-line and breaks it.
These two only, brothers in blood,
Face to face in matchless rage,
Mirroring each the other's death,
Clashed in long combat.

Antistrophe 2

Chorus: But now in the beautiful morning of victory
Let Thebes of the many chariots sing for joy!
With hearts for dancing we'll take leave of war:
Our temples shall be sweet with hymns of praise,
And the long nights shall echo with our chorus.

5

10

15

20

25

30

35

40

---

[5] *Dirce's stream:* river near Thebes. [8] *Choragos:* leader of the Chorus and principal commentator on the play's action.

SCENE I

Choragos: But now at last our new King is coming:
   Creon of Thebes, Menoikeus' son.
   In this auspicious dawn of his reign
   What are the new complexities
   That shifting Fate has woven for him?   5
   What is his counsel? Why has he summoned
   The old men to hear him?

   *Enter Creon from the palace, center. He addresses the Chorus from the top
   step.*

Creon: Gentlemen: I have the honor to inform you that our Ship of State,
   which recent storms have threatened to destroy, has come safely to
   harbor at last, guided by the merciful wisdom of Heaven. I have   10
   summoned you here this morning because I know that I can depend
   upon you: your devotion to King Laïos was absolute; you never
   hesitated in your duty to our late ruler Oedipus; and when Oedipus
   died, your loyalty was transferred to his children. Unfortunately, as
   you know, his two sons, the princes Eteoclês and Polyneicês, have   15
   killed each other in battle; and I, as the next in blood, have succeeded
   to the full power of the throne.

   I am aware, of course, that no Ruler can expect complete loyalty from his subjects until he has been tested in office. Nevertheless,
   I say to you at the very outset that I have nothing but contempt for   20
   the kind of Governor who is afraid, for whatever reason, to follow
   the course that he knows is best for the State; and as for the man
   who sets private friendship above the public welfare, — I have no
   use for him, either. I call God to witness that if I saw my country
   headed for ruin, I should not be afraid to speak out plainly; and I   25
   need hardly remind you that I would never have any dealings with
   an enemy of the people. No one values friendship more highly than
   I; but we must remember that friends made at the risk of wrecking
   our Ship are not real friends at all.

   These are my principles, at any rate, and that is why I have   30
   made the following decision concerning the sons of Oedipus: Eteoclês, who died as a man should die, fighting for his country, is to be
   buried with full military honors, with all the ceremony that is usual
   when the greatest heroes die; but his brother Polyneicês, who broke
   his exile to come back with fire and sword against his native city and   35
   the shrines of his fathers' gods, whose one idea was to spill the blood
   of his blood and sell his own people into slavery — Polyneicês, I say,
   is to have no burial: no man is to touch him or say the least prayer
   for him; he shall lie on the plain, unburied; and the birds and the
   scavenging dogs can do with him whatever they like.   40

   This is my command, and you can see the wisdom behind it.
   As long as I am King, no traitor is going to be honored with the loyal
   man. But whoever shows by word and deed that he is on the side
   of the State, — he shall have my respect while he is living and my
   reverence when he is dead.   45

Choragos: If that is your will, Creon son of Menoikeus,
　　You have the right to enforce it: we are yours.
Creon: That is my will. Take care that you do your part.
Choragos: We are old men: let the younger ones carry it out.
Creon: I do not mean that: the sentries have been appointed.　　　50
Choragos: Then what is it that you would have us do?
Creon: You will give no support to whoever breaks this law.
Choragos: Only a crazy man is in love with death!
Creon: And death it is; yet money talks, and the wisest
　　Have sometimes been known to count a few coins too many.　　55

　　Enter Sentry from left.

Sentry: I'll not say that I'm out of breath from running, King, because
　　every time I stopped to think about what I have to tell you, I felt
　　like going back. And all the time a voice kept saying, "You fool,
　　don't you know you're walking straight into trouble?"; and then
　　another voice: "Yes, but if you let somebody else get the news to　　60
　　Creon first, it will be even worse than that for you!" But good sense
　　won out, at least I hope it was good sense, and here I am with a story
　　that makes no sense at all; but I'll tell it anyhow, because, as they
　　say, what's going to happen's going to happen and —
Creon: Come to the point. What have you to say?　　　65
Sentry: I did not do it. I did not see who did it. You must not punish me
　　for what someone else has done.
Creon: A comprehensive defense! More effective, perhaps,
　　If I knew its purpose. Come: what is it?
Sentry: A dreadful thing . . . I don't know how to put it —　　70
Creon: Out with it!
Sentry:　　　　　　Well, then;
　　The dead man —
　　　　　　　Polyneicês —

Pause. The Sentry is overcome, fumbles for words. Creon waits impassively.

　　　　　　　　out there —
　　　　　　　　　　someone, —
New dust on the slimy flesh!

Pause. No sign from Creon.

Someone has given it burial that way, and
Gone . . .　　　75

Long pause. Creon finally speaks with deadly control.

Creon: And the man who dared do this?
Sentry:　　　　　　　　　I swear I
　　Do not know! You must believe me!
　　　　　　　　Listen:
　　The ground was dry, not a sign of digging, no,
　　Not a wheeltrack in the dust, no trace of anyone.
　　It was when they relieved us this morning: and one of them,　　80

The corporal, pointed to it.
                              There it was,
The strangest —
                    Look:
The body, just mounded over with light dust: you see?
Not buried really, but as if they'd covered it
Just enough for the ghost's peace. And no sign   85
Of dogs or any wild animal that had been there.

And then what a scene there was! Every man of us
Accusing the other: we all proved the other man did it,
We all had proof that we could not have done it.
We were ready to take hot iron in our hands,   90
Walk through fire, swear by all the gods,
It was not I!
I do not know who it was, but it was not I!

Creon's rage has been mounting steadily, but the Sentry is too intent upon his
story to notice it.

And then, when this came to nothing, someone said
A thing that silenced us and made us stare   95
Down at the ground: you had to be told the news,
And one of us had to do it! We threw the dice,
And the bad luck fell to me. So here I am,
No happier to be here than you are to have me:
Nobody likes the man who brings bad news.   100

Choragos: I have been wondering, King: can it be that the gods have done
    this?
Creon (furiously): Stop!
    Must you doddering wrecks
    Go out of your heads entirely? "The gods"!   105
    Intolerable!
    The gods favor this corpse? Why? How had he served them?
    Tried to loot their temples, burn their images,
    Yes, and the whole State, and its laws with it!
    Is it your senile opinion that the gods love to honor bad men?   110
    A pious thought! —
                        No, from the very beginning
    There have been those who have whispered together,
    Stiff-necked anarchists, putting their heads together,
    Scheming against me in alleys. These are the men,
    And they have bribed my own guard to do this thing.   115
    (Sententiously.) Money!
    There's nothing in the world so demoralizing as money.
    Down go your cities,
    Homes gone, men gone, honest hearts corrupted,
    Crookedness of all kinds, and all for money!
    (To Sentry.)   But you —   120
    I swear by God and by the throne of God,
    The man who has done this thing shall pay for it!

Find that man, bring him here to me, or your death
Will be the least of your problems: I'll string you up
Alive, and there will be certain ways to make you   125
Discover your employer before you die;
And the process may teach you a lesson you seem to have missed:
The dearest profit is sometimes all too dear:
That depends on the source. Do you understand me?
A fortune won is often misfortune.   130
Sentry: King, may I speak?
Creon: Your very voice distresses me.
Sentry: Are you sure that it is my voice, and not your conscience?
Creon: By God, he wants to analyze me now!
Sentry: It is not what I say, but what has been done, that hurts you.
Creon: You talk too much.
Sentry: Maybe; but I've done nothing.   135
Creon: Sold your soul for some silver: that's all you've done.
Sentry: How dreadful it is when the right judge judges wrong!
Creon: Your figures of speech
May entertain you now; but unless you bring me the man,
You will get little profit from them in the end.   140

Exit Creon into the palace.

Sentry: "Bring me the man" — !
I'd like nothing better than bringing him the man!
But bring him or not, you have seen the last of me here.
At any rate, I am safe!   *(Exit Sentry.)*

ODE I°

Strophe 1

Chorus: Numberless are the world's wonders, but none
More wonderful than man; the stormgray sea
Yields to his prows, the huge crests bear him high;
Earth, holy and inexhaustible, is graven
With shining furrows where his plows have gone   5
Year after year, the timeless labor of stallions.

Antistrophe 1

The lightboned birds and beasts that cling to cover,
The lithe fish lighting their reaches of dim water,
All are taken, tamed in the net of his mind;
The lion on the hill, the wild horse windy-maned,   10
Resign to him; and his blunt yoke has broken
The sultry shoulders of the mountain bull.

Ode I: first song sung by the Chorus, who at the same time danced. Here again, as in the parodos, *strophe* and *antistrophe* probably divide the song into two movements of the dance: right-to-left, then left-to-right.

Words also, and thought as rapid as air,
He fashions to his good use; statecraft is his,
And his the skill that deflects the arrows of snow,   15
The spears of winter rain: from every wind
He has made himself secure — from all but one:
In the late wind of death he cannot stand.

O clear intelligence, force beyond all measure!
O fate of man, working both good and evil!   20
When the laws are kept, how proudly his city stands!
When the laws are broken, what of his city then?
Never may the anárchic man find rest at my hearth,
Never be it said that my thoughts are his thoughts.

SCENE II

Reenter Sentry leading Antigonê.

Choragos: What does this mean? Surely this captive woman
    Is the Princess, Antigonê. Why should she be taken?
Sentry: Here is the one who did it! We caught her
    In the very act of burying him. — Where is Creon?
Choragos: Just coming from the house.

Enter Creon, center.

Creon: What has happened?   5
    Why have you come back so soon?
Sentry (expansively):   O King,
    A man should never be too sure of anything:
    I would have sworn
    That you'd not see me here again: your anger
    Frightened me so, and the things you threatened me with;   10
    But how could I tell then
    That I'd be able to solve the case so soon?
    No dice-throwing this time: I was only too glad to come!
    Here is this woman. She is the guilty one:
    We found her trying to bury him.   15
    Take her, then; question her; judge her as you will.
    I am through with the whole thing now, and glad of it.
Creon: But this is Antigonê! Why have you brought her here?
Sentry: She was burying him, I tell you!
Creon (severely):   Is this the truth?
Sentry: I saw her with my own eyes. Can I say more?   20
Creon: The details: come, tell me quickly!
Sentry: It was like this:
    After those terrible threats of yours, King,
    We went back and brushed the dust away from the body.

The flesh was soft by now, and stinking,
So we sat on a hill to windward and kept guard.   25
No napping this time! We kept each other awake.
But nothing happened until the white round sun
Whirled in the center of the round sky over us:
Then, suddenly,
A storm of dust roared up from the earth, and the sky   30
Went out, the plain vanished with all its trees
In the stinging dark. We closed our eyes and endured it.
The whirlwind lasted a long time, but it passed;
And then we looked, and there was Antigonê!
I have seen   35
A mother bird come back to a stripped nest, heard
Her crying bitterly a broken note or two
For the young ones stolen. Just so, when this girl
Found the bare corpse, and all her love's work wasted,
She wept, and cried on heaven to damn the hands   40
That had done this thing.
                And then she brought more dust
And sprinkled wine three times for her brother's ghost.

We ran and took her at once. She was not afraid,
Not even when we charged her with what she had done.
She denied nothing.
            And this was a comfort to me,   45
And some uneasiness: for it is a good thing
To escape from death, but it is no great pleasure
To bring death to a friend.
               Yet I always say
There is nothing so comfortable as your own safe skin!
Creon (slowly, dangerously): And you, Antigonê,   50
    You with your head hanging, — do you confess this thing?
Antigonê: I do. I deny nothing.
Creon (to Sentry):   You may go.   *(Exit Sentry.)*
    (To Antigonê.) Tell me, tell me briefly:
    Had you heard my proclamation touching this matter?
Antigonê: It was public. Could I help hearing it?   55
Creon: And yet you dared defy the law.
Antigonê: I dared.
    It was not God's proclamation. That final Justice
    That rules the world below makes no such laws.

    Your edict, King, was strong,
    But all your strength is weakness itself against   60
    The immortal unrecorded laws of God.
    They are not merely now: they were, and shall be,
    Operative for ever, beyond man utterly.

    I knew I must die, even without your decree:
    I am only mortal. And if I must die   65

Now, before it is my time to die,
Surely this is no hardship: can anyone
Living, as I live, with evil all about me,
Think Death less than a friend? This death of mine
Is of no importance; but if I had left my brother   70
Lying in death unburied, I should have suffered.
Now I do not.
            You smile at me. Ah Creon,
Think me a fool, if you like; but it may well be
That a fool convicts me of folly.

Choragos: Like father, like daughter: both headstrong, deaf to reason!   75
She has never learned to yield:
Creon: She has much to learn.
The inflexible heart breaks first, the toughest iron
Cracks first, and the wildest horses bend their necks
At the pull of the smallest curb.
                         Pride? In a slave?
This girl is guilty of a double insolence,   80
Breaking the given laws and boasting of it.
Who is the man here,
She or I, if this crime goes unpunished?
Sister's child, or more than sister's child,
Or closer yet in blood — she and her sister   85
Win bitter death for this!
(To Servants.)   Go, some of you,
Arrest Ismenê. I accuse her equally.
Bring her: you will find her sniffling in the house there.

Her mind's a traitor: crimes kept in the dark
Cry for light, and the guardian brain shudders;   90
But how much worse than this
Is brazen boasting of barefaced anarchy!
Antigonê: Creon, what more do you want than my death?
Creon: Nothing.
That gives me everything.
Antigonê: Then I beg you: kill me.
This talking is a great weariness: your words   95
Are distasteful to me, and I am sure that mine
Seem so to you. And yet they should not seem so:
I should have praise and honor for what I have done.
All these men here would praise me
Were their lips not frozen shut with fear of you.   100
(Bitterly.) Ah the good fortune of kings,
Licensed to say and do whatever they please!
Creon: You are alone here in that opinion.
Antigonê: No, they are with me. But they keep their tongues in leash.
Creon: Maybe. But you are guilty, and they are not.   105
Antigonê: There is no guilt in reverence for the dead.
Creon: But Eteoclês — was he not your brother too?
Antigonê: My brother too.

Creon: And you insult his memory?

Antigonê (softly): The dead man would not say that I insult it.

Creon: He would: for you honor a traitor as much as him.   110

Antigonê: His own brother, traitor or not, and equal in blood.

Creon: He made war on his country. Eteoclês defended it.

Antigonê: Nevertheless, there are honors due all the dead.

Creon: But not the same for the wicked as for the just.

Antigonê: Ah Creon, Creon,   115
> Which of us can say what the gods hold wicked?

Creon: An enemy is an enemy, even dead.

Antigonê: It is my nature to join in love, not hate.

Creon (finally losing patience): Go join them then; if you must have your love,
> Find it in hell!   120

Choragos: But see, Ismenê comes:

> *Enter Ismenê, guarded.*

> Those tears are sisterly, the cloud
> That shadows her eyes rains down gentle sorrow.

Creon: You too, Ismenê,
> Snake in my ordered house, sucking my blood   125
> Stealthily — and all the time I never knew
> That these two sisters were aiming at my throne!
>
>   Ismenê,
> Do you confess your share in this crime, or deny it?
> Answer me.

Ismenê: Yes, if she will let me say so. I am guilty.   130

Antigonê (coldly): No, Ismenê. You have no right to say so.
> You would not help me, and I will not have you help me.

Ismenê: But now I know what you meant; and I am here
> To join you, to take my share of punishment.

Antigonê: The dead man and the gods who rule the dead   135
> Know whose act this was. Words are not friends.

Ismenê: Do you refuse me, Antigonê? I want to die with you:
> I too have a duty that I must discharge to the dead.

Antigonê: You shall not lessen my death by sharing it.

Ismenê: What do I care for life when you are dead?   140

Antigonê: Ask Creon. You're always hanging on his opinions.

Ismenê: You are laughing at me. Why, Antigonê?

Antigonê: It's a joyless laughter, Ismenê.

Ismenê: But can I do nothing?

Antigonê: Yes. Save yourself. I shall not envy you.
> There are those who will praise you; I shall have honor, too.   145

Ismenê: But we are equally guilty!

Antigonê: No more, Ismenê.
> You are alive, but I belong to Death.

Creon (to the Chorus): Gentlemen, I beg you to observe these girls:
> One has just now lost her mind; the other,
> It seems, has never had a mind at all.   150

Ismenê: Grief teaches the steadiest minds to waver, King.

Creon: Yours certainly did, when you assumed guilt with the guilty!

Ismenê: But how could I go on living without her?
Creon: You are.
　　She is already dead.
Ismenê: But your own son's bride!
Creon: There are places enough for him to push his plow.　　155
　　I want no wicked women for my sons!
Ismenê: O dearest Haimon, how your father wrongs you!
Creon: I've had enough of your childish talk of marriage!
Choragos: Do you really intend to steal this girl from your son?
Creon: No; Death will do that for me.
Choragos: Then she must die?　　160
Creon (ironically): You dazzle me.
　　　　　　　　　— But enough of this talk!
　　(To Guards.) You, there, take them away and guard them well:
　　For they are but women, and even brave men run
　　When they see Death coming. *Exeunt Ismenê, Antigonê, and Guards.*

ODE II

　　　　　　　　　　　　　　　　　　　　　　　Strophe 1
Chorus: Fortunate is the man who has never tasted God's vengeance!
　　Where once the anger of heaven has struck, that house is shaken
　　For ever: damnation rises behind each child
　　Like a wave cresting out of the black northeast,
　　When the long darkness under sea roars up　　　　　　　　5
　　And bursts drumming death upon the windwhipped sand.

　　　　　　　　　　　　　　　　　　　　　Antistrophe 1
　　I have seen this gathering sorrow from time long past
　　Loom upon Oedipus' children: generation from generation
　　Takes the compulsive rage of the enemy god.
　　So lately this last flower of Oedipus' line　　　　　　10
　　Drank the sunlight! but now a passionate word
　　And a handful of dust have closed up all its beauty.

　　　　　　　　　　　　　　　　　　　　　　　Strophe 2
　　　　What mortal arrogance
　　　　Transcends the wrath of Zeus?
　　Sleep cannot lull him nor the effortless long months　　15
　　Of the timeless gods: but he is young for ever,
　　And his house is the shining day of high Olympos.
　　　　All that is and shall be,
　　　　And all the past, is his.
　　No pride on earth is free of the curse of heaven.　　　20

　　　　　　　　　　　　　　　　　　　　　Antistrophe 2
　　The straying dreams of men
　　　　May bring them ghosts of joy:

1184 Plays for Further Reading

But as they drowse, the waking embers burn them;
Or they walk with fixed eyes, as blind men walk.
But the ancient wisdom speaks for our own time: 25
    Fate works most for woe
    With Folly's fairest show.
Man's little pleasure is the spring of sorrow.

SCENE III

Choragos: But here is Haimon, King, the last of all your sons.
    Is it grief for Antigonê that brings him here,
    And bitterness at being robbed of his bride?

    Enter Haimon.

Creon: We shall soon see, and no need of diviners.
                             — Son,
    You have heard my final judgment on that girl: 5
    Have you come here hating me, or have you come
    With deference and with love, whatever I do?
Haimon: I am your son, father. You are my guide.
    You make things clear for me, and I obey you.
    No marriage means more to me than your continuing wisdom.   10
Creon: Good. That is the way to behave: subordinate
    Everything else, my son, to your father's will.
    This is what a man prays for, that he may get
    Sons attentive and dutiful in his house,
    Each one hating his father's enemies,   15
    Honoring his father's friends. But if his sons
    Fail him, if they turn out unprofitably,
    What has he fathered but trouble for himself
    And amusement for the malicious?
                       So you are right
    Not to lose your head over this woman.   20
    Your pleasure with her would soon grow cold, Haimon,
    And then you'd have a hellcat in bed and elsewhere.
    Let her find her husband in Hell!
    Of all the people in this city, only she
    Has had contempt for my law and broken it.   25

    Do you want me to show myself weak before the people?
    Or to break my sworn word? No, and I will not.
    The woman dies.
    I suppose she'll plead "family ties." Well, let her.
    If I permit my own family to rebel,   30
    How shall I earn the world's obedience?
    Show me the man who keeps his house in hand,
    He's fit for public authority.
                    I'll have no dealings

With lawbreakers, critics of the government:
Whoever is chosen to govern should be obeyed —   35
Must be obeyed, in all things, great and small,
Just and unjust! O Haimon,
The man who knows how to obey, and that man only,
Knows how to give commands when the time comes.
You can depend on him, no matter how fast   40
The spears come: he's a good soldier, he'll stick it out.

Anarchy, anarchy! Show me a greater evil!
This is why cities tumble and the great houses rain down,
This is what scatters armies!
No, no: good lives are made so by discipline.   45
We keep the laws then, and the lawmakers,
And no woman shall seduce us. If we must lose,
Let's lose to a man, at least! Is a woman stronger than we?
Choragos: Unless time has rusted my wits,
    What you say, King, is said with point and dignity.   50
Haimon (boyishly earnest): Father:
Reason is God's crowning gift to man, and you are right
To warn me against losing mine. I cannot say —
I hope that I shall never want to say! — that you
Have reasoned badly. Yet there are other men   55
Who can reason, too; and their opinions might be helpful.
You are not in a position to know everything
That people say or do, or what they feel:
Your temper terrifies — everyone
Will tell you only what you like to hear.   60
But I, at any rate, can listen; and I have heard them
Muttering and whispering in the dark about this girl.
They say no woman has ever, so unreasonably,
Died so shameful a death for a generous act:
"She covered her brother's body. Is this indecent?   65
She kept him from dogs and vultures. Is this a crime?
Death? — She should have all the honor that we can give her!"

This is the way they talk out there in the city.

You must believe me:
Nothing is closer to me than your happiness.   70
What could be closer? Must not any son
Value his father's fortune as his father does his?
I beg you, do not be unchangeable:
Do not believe that you alone can be right.
The man who thinks that,   75
The man who maintains that only he has the power
To reason correctly, the gift to speak, the soul —
A man like that, when you know him, turns out empty.

It is not reason never to yield to reason!

In flood time you can see how some trees bend,   80
And because they bend, even their twigs are safe,
While stubborn trees are torn up, roots and all.
And the same thing happens in sailing:
Make your sheet fast, never slacken, — and over you go,
Head over heels and under: and there's your voyage.   85
Forget you are angry! Let yourself be moved!
I know I am young; but please let me say this:
The ideal condition
Would be, I admit, that men should be right by instinct;
But since we are all too likely to go astray,   90
The reasonable thing is to learn from those who can teach.
Choragos: You will do well to listen to him, King,
If what he says is sensible. And you, Haimon,
Must listen to your father. — Both speak well.
Creon: You consider it right for a man of my years and experience   95
To go to school to a boy?
Haimon: It is not right
If I am wrong. But if I am young, and right,
What does my age matter?
Creon: You think it right to stand up for an anarchist?
Haimon: Not at all. I pay no respect to criminals.   100
Creon: Then she is not a criminal?
Haimon: The City would deny it, to a man.
Creon: And the City proposes to teach me how to rule?
Haimon: Ah. Who is it that's talking like a boy now?
Creon: My voice is the one voice giving orders in this City!   105
Haimon: It is no City if it takes orders from one voice.
Creon: The State is the King!
Haimon: Yes, if the State is a desert.

    Pause.

Creon: This boy, it seems, has sold out to a woman.
Haimon: If you are a woman: my concern is only for you.
Creon: So? Your "concern"! In a public brawl with your father!   110
Haimon: How about you, in a public brawl with justice?
Creon: With justice, when all that I do is within my rights?
Haimon: You have no right to trample on God's right.
Creon (completely out of control): Fool, adolescent fool! Taken in by a woman!
Haimon: You'll never see me taken in by anything vile.   115
Creon: Every word you say is for her!
Haimon (quietly, darkly):   And for you.
And for me. And for the gods under the earth.
Creon: You'll never marry her while she lives.
Haimon: Then she must die. — But her death will cause another.
Creon: Another?   120

Have you lost your senses? Is this an open threat?
Haimon: There is no threat in speaking to emptiness.
Creon: I swear you'll regret this superior tone of yours!
     You are the empty one!
Haimon: If you were not my father,
     I'd say you were perverse.   125
Creon: You girl-struck fool, don't play at words with me!
Haimon: I am sorry. You prefer silence.
Creon: Now, by God —
     I swear, by all the gods in heaven above us,
     You'll watch it, I swear you shall!
     (To the Servants.)   Bring her out!
     Bring the woman out! Let her die before his eyes!   130
     Here, this instant, with her bridegroom beside her!
Haimon: Not here, no; she will not die here, King.
     And you will never see my face again.
     Go on raving as long as you've a friend to endure you.

                                                       (Exit Haimon.)

Choragos: Gone, gone.   135
     Creon, a young man in a rage is dangerous!
Creon: Let him do, or dream to do, more than a man can.
     He shall not save these girls from death.
Choragos: These girls?
     You have sentenced them both?
Creon: No, you are right.
     I wil not kill the one whose hands are clean.   140
Choragos: But Antigonê?
Creon (somberly):   I will carry her far away
     Out there in the wilderness, and lock her
     Living in a vault of stone. She shall have food,
     As the custom is, to absolve the State of her death.
     And there let her pray to the gods of hell: 145
     They are her only gods:
     Perhaps they will show her an escape from death,
     Or she may learn,
                    though late,
     That piety shown the dead is pity in vain.   *(Exit Creon.)*

ODE III

                                                                Strophe

Chorus: Love, unconquerable
     Waster of rich men, keeper
     Of warm lights and all-night vigil
     In the soft face of a girl:
     Sea-wanderer, forest-visitor!   5
     Even the pure Immortals cannot escape you,

And mortal man, in his one day's dusk,
Trembles before your glory.

Antistrophe

Surely you swerve upon ruin
The just man's consenting heart,   10
As here you have made bright anger
Strike between father and son —
And none has conquered but Love!
A girl's glánce wórking the will of heaven:
Pleasure to her alone who mocks us,   15
Merciless Aphroditê°.

SCENE IV

Choragos (as Antigonê enters guarded): But I can no longer stand in awe of this,
Nor, seeing what I see, keep back my tears.
Here is Antigonê, passing to that chamber
Where all find sleep at last.

Strophe 1

Antigonê: Look upon me, friends, and pity me   5
Turning back at the night's edge to say
Good-by to the sun that shines for me no longer;
Now sleepy Death
Summons me down to Acheron°, that cold shore:
There is no bridesong there, nor any music.   10
Chorus: Yet not unpraised, not without a kind of honor,
You walk at last into the underworld;
Untouched by sickness, broken by no sword.
What woman has ever found your way to death?

Antistrophe 1

Antigonê: How often I have heard the story of Niobê°,   15
Tantalos' wretched daughter, how the stone
Clung fast about her, ivy-close: and they say
The rain falls endlessly
And sifting soft snow; her tears are never done.
I feel the loneliness of her death in mine.   20
Chorus: But she was born of heaven, and you
Are woman, woman-born. If her death is yours,
A mortal woman's, is this not for you
Glory in our world and in the world beyond?

---

[16]*Aphroditê:* Goddess of love and beauty. [9]*Acheron:* river in Hades, domain of the dead.
[15]*story of Niobê:* in which this mother, when her fourteen children were slain, wept so copiously
that she was transformed to a stone on Mount Sipylus. Her tears became the mountain's
streams.

Sophocles: Scene IV 1189

Antigonê: You laugh at me. Ah, friends, friends,   25
    Can you not wait until I am dead? O Thebes,
    O men many-charioted, in love with Fortune,
    Dear springs of Dircê, sacred Theban grove,
    Be witnesses for me, denied all pity,
    Unjustly judged! and think a word of love   30
    For her whose path turns
    Under dark earth, where there are no more tears.
Chorus: You have passed beyond human daring and come at last
    Into a place of stone where Justice sits.
    I cannot tell   35
    What shape of your father's guilt appears in this.

Antigonê: You have touched it at last: that bridal bed
    Unspeakable, horror of son and mother mingling:
    Their crime, infection of all our family!
    O Oedipus, father and brother!   40
    Your marriage strikes from the grave to murder mine.
    I have been a stranger here in my own land:
    All my life
    The blasphemy of my birth has followed me.
Chorus: Reverence is a virtue, but strength   45
    Lives in established law: that must prevail.
    You have made your choice,
    Your death is the doing of your conscious hand.

Antigonê: Then let me go, since all your words are bitter,
    And the very light of the sun is cold to me.   50
    Lead me to my vigil, where I must have
    Neither love nor lamentation; no song, but silence.

    Creon interrupts impatiently.

Creon: If dirges and planned lamentations could put off death,
    Men would be singing for ever.
    (To the Servants.)   Take her, go!
    You know your orders: take her to the vault   55
    And leave her alone there. And if she lives or dies,
    That's her affair, not ours: our hands are clean.
Antigonê: O tomb, vaulted bride-bed in eternal rock,
    Soon I shall be with my own again
    Where Persephonê° welcomes the thin ghosts underground: 60
    And I shall see my father again, and you, mother,
    And dearest Polyneicês —

---

⁶⁰*Persephonê:* whom Pluto, god of the underworld, abducted to be his queen. (See D. H. Lawrence's poem "Bavarian Gentians," page 625.)

dearest indeed

To me, since it was my hand
That washed him clean and poured the ritual wine:
And my reward is death before my time!   65

And yet, as men's hearts know, I have done no wrong,
I have not sinned before God. Or if I have,
I shall know the truth in death. But if the guilt
Lies upon Creon who judged me, then, I pray,
May his punishment equal my own.
Choragos: O passionate heart,   70
Unyielding, tormented still by the same winds!
Creon: Her guards shall have good cause to regret their delaying.
Antigonê: Ah! That voice is like the voice of death!
Creon: I can give you no reason to think you are mistaken.
Antigonê: Thebes, and you my fathers' gods,   75
And rulers of Thebes, you see me now, the last
Unhappy daughter of a line of kings,
Your kings, led away to death. You will remember
What things I suffer, and at what men's hands,
Because I would not transgress the laws of heaven.   80
(To the Guards, simply.) Come: let us wait no longer.

(Exit Antigonê, left, guarded.)

ODE IV

Strophe 1

Chorus: All Danaê's beauty was locked away
In a brazen cell where the sunlight could not come:
A small room still as any grave, enclosed her.
Yet she was a princess too,
And Zeus in a rain of gold poured love upon her°.   5
O child, child,
No power in wealth or war
Or tough sea-blackened ships
Can prevail against untiring Destiny!

Antistrophe 1

And Dryas' son° also, that furious king,   10
Bore the god's prisoning anger for his pride:

[1-5] *All Danaê's beauty . . . poured love upon her:* In legend, when an oracle told Acrisius, king of Argos, that his daughter Danaê would bear a son who would grow up to slay him, he locked the princess into a chamber made of bronze, lest any man impregnate her. But Zeus, father of the gods, entered Danaê's prison in a shower of gold. The resultant child, the hero Perseus, was accidentally to fulfill the prophecy by killing Acrisius with an ill-aimed discus throw.
[10] *Dryas' son:* King Lycurgus of Thrace, whom Dionysos, god of wine, caused to be stricken with madness.

Sealed up by Dionysos in deaf stone,
His madness died among echoes.
So at the last he learned what dreadful power
His tongue had mocked: 15
For he had profaned the revels,
And fired the wrath of the nine
Implacable Sisters° that love the sound of the flute.

Strophe 2

And old men tell a half-remembered tale
Of horror° where a dark ledge splits the sea   20
And a double surf beats on the gráy shóres:
How a king's new woman, sick
With hatred for the queen he had imprisoned,
Ripped out his two sons' eyes with her bloody hands
While grinning Arês watched the shuttle plunge   25
Four times: four blind wounds crying for revenge,

Antistrophe 2

Crying, tears and blood mingled. — Piteously born,
Those sons whose mother was of heavenly birth!
Her father was the god of the North Wind
And she was cradled by gales,   30
She raced with young colts on the glittering hills
And walked untrammeled in the open light:
But in her marriage deathless Fate found means
To build a tomb like yours for all her joy.

SCENE V

Enter blind Teiresias, led by a boy. The opening speeches of Teiresias should be in singsong contrast to the realistic lines of Creon.

Teiresias: This is the way the blind man comes, Princes, Princes,
    Lockstep, two heads lit by the eyes of one.
Creon: What new thing have you to tell us, old Teiresias?
Teiresias: I have much to tell you: listen to the prophet, Creon.
Creon: I am not aware that I have ever failed to listen.   5
Teiresias: Then you have done wisely, King, and ruled well.
Creon: I admit my debt to you. But what have you to say?
Teiresias: This, Creon: you stand once more on the edge of fate.

---

¹⁸*Sisters:* the Muses, nine sister goddesses who presided over poetry and music, arts and sciences.   ^{19 – 20}*a half-remembered tale of horror:* As the Chorus recalls in the rest of this song, the point of this tale is that being nobly born will not save one from disaster. King Phineas cast off his first wife Cleopatra (not the later Egyptian queen, but the daughter of Boreas, god of the north wind) and imprisoned her in a cave. Out of hatred for Cleopatra, the cruel Eidothea, second wife of the king, blinded her stepsons. Arês, god of war, was said to gloat over bloodshed.

Creon: What do you mean? Your words are a kind of dread.
Teiresias: Listen, Creon: 10
    I was sitting in my chair of augury, at the place
    Where the birds gather about me. They were all a-chatter,
    As is their habit, when suddenly I heard
    A strange note in their jangling, a scream, a
    Whirring fury; I knew that they were fighting,   15
    Tearing each other, dying
    In a whirlwind of wings clashing. And I was afraid.
    I began the rites of burnt-offering at the altar,
    But Hephaistos° failed me: instead of bright flame,
    There was only the sputtering slime of the fat thigh-flesh   20
    Melting: the entrails dissolved in gray smoke,
    The bare bone burst from the welter. And no blaze!

    This was a sign from heaven. My boy described it,
    Seeing for me as I see for others.

    I tell you, Creon, you yourself have brought   25
    This new calamity upon us. Our hearths and altars
    Are stained with the corruption of dogs and carrion birds
    That glut themselves on the corpse of Oedipus' son.
    The gods are deaf when we pray to them, their fire
    Recoils from our offering, their birds of omen   30
    Have no cry of comfort, for they are gorged
    With the thick blood of the dead.
                       O my son,
    These are no trifles! Think: all men make mistakes,
    But a good man yields when he knows his course is wrong,
    And repairs the evil. The only crime is pride.   35

    Give in to the dead man, then: do not fight with a corpse —
    What glory is it to kill a man who is dead?
    Think, I beg you:
    It is for your own good that I speak as I do.
    You should be able to yield for your own good.   40
Creon: It seems that prophets have made me their especial province.
    All my life long
    I have been a kind of butt for the dull arrows
    Of doddering fortune-tellers!
                    No, Teiresias:
    If your birds — if the great eagles of God himself   45
    Should carry him stinking bit by bit to heaven,
    I would not yield. I am not afraid of pollution:
    No man can defile the gods.
                 Do what you will,
    Go into business, make money, speculate

---

[19]*Hephaistos:* god of fire.

In India gold or that synthetic gold from Sardis,   50
Get rich otherwise than by my consent to bury him.
Teiresias, it is a sorry thing when a wise man
Sells his wisdom, lets out his words for hire!
Teiresias: Ah Creon! Is there no man left in the world —
Creon: To do what? — Come, let's have the aphorism!   55
Teiresias: No man who knows that wisdom outweighs any wealth?
Creon: As surely as bribes are baser than any baseness.
Teiresias: You are sick, Creon! You are deathly sick!
Creon: As you say: it is not my place to challenge a prophet.
Teiresias: Yet you have said my prophecy is for sale.   60
Creon: The generation of prophets has always loved gold.
Teiresias: The generation of kings has always loved brass.
Creon: You forget yourself! You are speaking to your King.
Teiresias: I know it. You are a king because of me.
Creon: You have a certain skill; but you have sold out.   65
Teiresias: King, you will drive me to words that —
Creon: Say them, say them!
    Only remember: I will not pay you for them.
Teiresias: No, you will find them too costly.
Creon: No doubt. Speak:
    Whatever you say, you will not change my will.
Teiresias: Then take this, and take it to heart!   70
    The time is not far off when you shall pay back
    Corpse for corpse, flesh of your own flesh.
    You have thrust the child of this world into living night,
    You have kept from the gods below the child that is theirs:
    The one in a grave before her death, the other,   75
    Dead, denied the grave. This is your crime:
    And the Furies and the dark gods of Hell
    Are swift with terrible punishment for you.

    Do you want to buy me now, Creon?

                                      Not many days,
    And your house will be full of men and women weeping,   80
    And curses will be hurled at you from far
    Cities grieving for sons unburied, left to rot
    Before the walls of Thebes.

    These are my arrows, Creon: they are all for you.

    (To Boy.) But come, child: lead me home.   85
    Let him waste his fine anger upon younger men.
    Maybe he will learn at last
    To control a wiser tongue in a better head.   *(Exit Teiresias.)*
Choragos: The old man has gone, King, but his words
    Remain to plague us. I am old, too,   90

But I cannot remember that he was ever false.
Creon: That is true. . . . It troubles me.
   Oh it is hard to give in! but it is worse
   To risk everything for stubborn pride.
Choragos: Creon: take my advice.
Creon: What shall I do?   95
Choragos: Go quickly: free Antigonê from her vault
   And build a tomb for the body of Polyneicês.
Creon: You would have me do this!
Choragos: Creon, yes!
   And it must be done at once: God moves
   Swiftly to cancel the folly of stubborn men.   100
Creon: It is hard to deny the heart! But I
   Will do it: I will not fight with destiny.
Choragos: You must go yourself, you cannot leave it to others.
Creon: I will go.
            — Bring axes, servants:
   Come with me to the tomb. I buried her, I   105
   Will set her free.
               Oh quickly!
   My mind misgives —
   The laws of the gods are mighty, and a man must serve them
   To the last day of his life!   *(Exit Creon.)*

PAEAN°

                                                Strophe 1

Choragos: God of many names
Chorus: O Iacchos
                      son
   of Kadmeian Sémelê
              O born of the Thunder!
   Guardian of the West
            Regent
   of Eleusis' plain
         O Prince of maenad Thebes
   and the Dragon Field by rippling Ismenós°:   5

Paean: a song of praise or prayer, here to Dionysos, god of wine.
[1-5] *God of many names . . . Dragon Field by rippling Ismenós:* Dionysos was also called Iacchos (or, by the Romans, Bacchus). He was the son of Zeus ("the Thunderer") and of Sémelê, daughter of Kadmos (or Cadmus), legendary founder of Thebes. "Regent of Eleusis' plain" is another name for Dionysos, honored in secret rites at Eleusis, a town northwest of Athens. "Prince of maenad Thebes" is yet another: the Maenads were women of Thebes said to worship Dionysos with wild orgiastic rites. Kadmos, so the story goes, sowed dragon's teeth in a field beside the river Ismenós. Up sprang a crop of fierce warriors who fought among themselves until only five remained. These victors became the first Thebans.

Choragos: God of many names
Chorus: the flame of torches
   flares on our hills
          the nymphs of Iacchos
   dance at the spring of Castalia°:
   from the vine-close mountain
              come ah come in ivy:
   Evohé evohé!° sings through the streets of Thebes   10

Choragos: God of many names
Chorus: Iacchos of Thebes
   heavenly Child
         of Sémelê bride of the Thunderer!
   The shadow of plague is upon us:
             come
   with clement feet
         oh come from Parnasos
   down the long slopes
         across the lamenting water   15

Choragos: Iô° Fire! Chorister of the throbbing stars!
   O purest among the voices of the night!
   Thou son of God, blaze for us!
Chorus: Come with choric rapture of circling Maenads
   Who cry *Iô Iacche!*
         God of many names!   20

EXODOS°

Enter Messenger from left.

Messenger: Men of the line of Kadmos, you who live
   Near Amphion's citadel°,
         I cannot say
   Of any condition of human life "This is fixed,
   This is clearly good, or bad." Fate raises up,
   And Fate casts down the happy and unhappy alike: 5
   No man can foretell his Fate.

---

[8]*Castalia:* a spring on Mount Parnassus, named for a maiden who drowned herself in it to avoid rape by the god Apollo. She became a nymph, or nature spirit, dwelling in its waters. In the temple of Delphi, at the mountain's foot, priestesses of Dionysos (the "nymphs of Iacchos") used the spring's waters in rites of purification.   [10]*Evohé evohé!:* cry of the Maenads in supplicating Dionysos: "Come forth, come forth!"   [16]*Iô:* "Hail" or "Praise be to. . . ."

Exodos: the final scene, containing the play's resolution.

[2]*Amphion's citadel:* a name for Thebes. Amphion, son of Zeus, had built a wall around the city by playing so beautifully on his lyre that the charmed stones leaped into their slots.

Take the case of Creon:

Creon was happy once, as I count happiness:
Victorious in battle, sole governor of the land,
Fortunate father of children nobly born.
And now it has all gone from him! Who can say   10
That a man is still alive when his life's joy fails?
He is a walking dead man. Grant him rich,
Let him live like a king in his great house:
If his pleasure is gone, I would not give
So much as the shadow of smoke for all he owns.   15
Choragos: Your words hint at sorrow: what is your news for us?
Messenger: They are dead. The living are guilty of their death.
Choragos: Who is guilty? Who is dead? Speak!
Messenger: Haimon.
Haimon is dead; and the hand that killed him
Is his own hand.
Choragos: His father's? or his own?   20
Messenger: His own, driven mad by the murder his father had done.
Choragos: Teiresias, Teiresias, how clearly you saw it all!
Messenger: This is my news: you must draw what conclusions you can
         from it.
Choragos: But look: Eurydicê, our Queen:
Has she overheard us?   25

Enter Eurydicê from the palace, center.

Eurydicê: I have heard something, friends:
As I was unlocking the gate of Pallas'° shrine,
For I needed her help today, I heard a voice
Telling of some new sorrow. And I fainted
There at the temple with all my maidens about me.   30
But speak again: whatever it is, I can bear it:
Grief and I are no strangers.
Messenger: Dearest Lady,
I will tell you plainly all that I have seen.
I shall not try to comfort you: what is the use,
Since comfort could lie only in what is not true?   35
The truth is always best.
I went with Creon

To the outer plain where Polyneicês was lying,
No friend to pity him, his body shredded by dogs.
We made our prayers in that place to Hecatê
And Pluto°, that they would be merciful. And we bathed   40
The corpse with holy water, and we brought
Fresh-broken branches to burn what was left of it,
And upon the urn we heaped up a towering barrow

---

[27] *Pallas:* Pallas Athene, goddess of wisdom, and hence an excellent source of advice. [39–40] *Hecatê and Pluto:* two fearful divinities — the goddess of witchcraft and sorcery and the king of Hades, underworld of the dead.

Of the earth of his own land.
                            When we were done, we ran
To the vault where Antigonê lay on her couch of stone.   45
One of the servants had gone ahead,
And while he was yet far off he heard a voice
Grieving within the chamber, and he came back
And told Creon. And as the King went closer,
The air was full of wailing, the words lost,   50
And he begged us to make all haste. "Am I a prophet?"
He said, weeping, "And must I walk this road,
The saddest of all that I have gone before?
My son's voice calls me on. Oh quickly, quickly!
Look through the crevice there, and tell me   55
If it is Haimon, or some deception of the gods!"

We obeyed; and in the cavern's farthest corner
We saw her lying:
She had made a noose of her fine linen veil
And hanged herself. Haimon lay beside her,   60
His arms about her waist, lamenting her,
His love lost under ground, crying out
That his father had stolen her away from him.

When Creon saw him the tears rushed to his eyes
And he called to him: "What have you done, child? Speak to me. 65
What are you thinking that makes your eyes so strange?
O my son, my son, I come to you on my knees!"
But Haimon spat in his face. He said not a word,
Staring —
            And suddenly drew his sword
And lunged. Creon shrank back, the blade missed; and the boy,   70
Desperate against himself, drove it half its length
Into his own side, and fell. And as he died
He gathered Antigonê close in his arms again,
Choking, his blood bright red on her white cheek.
And now he lies dead with the dead, and she is his   75
At last, his bride in the house of the dead.

                                    Exit Eurydicê into the palace.

Choragos: She has left us without a word. What can this mean?
Messenger: It troubles me, too; yet she knows what is best,
     Her grief is too great for public lamentation,
     And doubtless she has gone to her chamber to weep   80
     For her dead son, leading her maidens in his dirge.

     Pause.

Choragos: It may be so: but I fear this deep silence.
Messenger: I will see what she is doing. I will go in.

                                    Exit Messenger into the palace.

Enter Creon with attendants, bearing Haimon's body.

Choragos: But here is the king himself: oh look at him,
　　Bearing his own damnation in his arms.　　　　　　　　　　　85
Creon: Nothing you say can touch me any more.
　　My own blind heart has brought me
　　From darkness to final darkness. Here you see
　　The father murdering, the murdered son —
　　And all my civic wisdom!　　　　　　　　　　　　　　　　90

　　Haimon my son, so young, so young to die,
　　I was the fool, not you; and you died for me.
Choragos: That is the truth; but you were late in learning it.
Creon: This truth is hard to bear. Surely a god
　　Has crushed me beneath the hugest weight of heaven,　　　　95
　　And driven me headlong a barbaric way
　　To trample out the thing I held most dear.

　　The pains that men will take to come to pain!

Enter Messenger from the palace.

Messenger: The burden you carry in your hands is heavy,
　　But it is not all: you will find more in your house.　　　　100
Creon: What burden worse than this shall I find there?
Messenger: The Queen is dead.
Creon: O port of death, deaf world,
　　Is there no pity for me? And you, Angel of evil,`
　　I was dead, and your words are death again.　　　　　　　105
　　Is it true, boy? Can it be true?
　　Is my wife dead? Has death bred death?
Messenger: You can see for yourself.

The doors are opened and the body of Eurydicê is disclosed within.

Creon: Oh pity!
　　All true, all true, and more than I can bear!　　　　　　　110
　　O my wife, my son!
Messenger: She stood before the altar, and her heart
　　Welcomed the knife her own hand guided,
　　And a great cry burst from her lips for Megareus° dead,
　　And for Haimon dead, her sons; and her last breath　　　　115
　　Was a curse for their father, the murderer of her sons.
　　And she fell, and the dark flowed in through her closing eyes.
Creon: O God, I am sick with fear.
　　Are there no swords here? Has no one a blow for me?
Messenger: Her curse is upon you for the deaths of both.　　120
Creon: It is right that it should be. I alone am guilty.
　　I know it, and I say it. Lead me in,

---

[114] *Megareus:* Son of Creon and brother of Haimon, Megareus was slain in the unsuccessful
attack upon Thebes.

Quickly, friends.
I have neither life nor substance. Lead me in.
Choragos: You are right, if there can be right in so much wrong.   125
The briefest way is best in a world of sorrow.
Creon: Let it come,
Let death come quickly, and be kind to me.
I would not ever see the sun again.
Choragos: All that will come when it will; but we, meanwhile,   130
Have much to do. Leave the future to itself.
Creon: All my heart was in that prayer!
Choragos: Then do not pray any more: the sky is deaf.
Creon: Lead me away. I have been rash and foolish.
I have killed my son and my wife.   135
I look for comfort; my comfort lies here dead.
Whatever my hands have touched has come to nothing.
Fate has brought all my pride to a thought of dust.

*As Creon is being led into the house, the Choragos advances and speaks directly
to the audience.*

Choragos: There is no happiness where there is no wisdom;
No wisdom but in submission to the gods.   140
Big words are always punished,
And proud men in old age learn to be wise.

Tennessee Williams

THE GLASS MENAGERIE   1945

*Tennessee Williams (1914 – 1983) was born Thomas Lanier Williams in
Columbus, Mississippi, went to high school in St. Louis, and was graduated
from the University of Iowa. As an undergraduate, he saw a performance
of Ibsen's* Ghosts *and determined to be a playwright himself. His family
bore a close resemblance to the Wingfields in* The Glass Menagerie: *his
mother came from a line of Southern bluebloods (Tennessee pioneers); his
sister Rose suffered from incapacitating shyness; and as a young man Williams himself, like Tom, worked at a job he disliked (in a shoe factory where
his father worked), wrote poetry, sought refuge in moviegoing, and finally left
home to wander and hold odd jobs. He worked as a bellhop in a New Orleans
hotel, a teletype operator in Jacksonville, Florida, an usher and a waiter in
New York. In 1945* The Glass Menagerie *scored success on Broadway,
winning a Drama Critics Circle award. Two years later Williams received
a Pulitzer prize for* A Streetcar Named Desire, *a grim, powerful study of
a woman's illusions and frustrations, set in New Orleans. In 1955, another
Pulitzer prize went to* Cat on a Hot Tin Roof. *Besides other plays, including* Summer and Smoke *(1948),* Sweet Bird of Youth *(1959),* The
Night of the Iguana *(1961),* Small Craft Warnings *(1973),* Clothes

for a Summer Hotel *(1980), and* A House Not Meant to Stand *(1981), Williams wrote two novels, poetry, essays, short stories, and* Memoirs *(1975).*

Nobody, not even the rain, has such small hands.
E. E. Cummings

Characters

Amanda Wingfield, the mother. A little woman of great but confused vitality clinging frantically to another time and place. Her characterization must be carefully created, not copied from type. She is not paranoiac, but her life is paranoia. There is much to admire in Amanda, and as much to love and pity as there is to laugh at. Certainly she has endurance and a kind of heroism, and though her foolishness makes her unwittingly cruel at times, there is tenderness in her slight person.

Laura Wingfield, her daughter. Amanda, having failed to establish contact with reality, continues to live vitally in her illusions, but Laura's situation is even graver. A childhood illness has left her crippled, one leg slightly shorter than the other, and held in a brace. This defect need not be more than suggested on the stage. Stemming from this, Laura's separation increases till she is like a piece of her own glass collection, too exquisitely fragile to move from the shelf.

Tom Wingfield, her son. And the narrator of the play. A poet with a job in a warehouse. His nature is not remorseless, but to escape from a trap he has to act without pity.

Jim O'Connor, the gentleman caller. A nice, ordinary, young man.

Scene. *An alley in St. Louis.*

Part I. *Preparation for a Gentleman Caller.*
Part II. *The Gentleman Calls.*

Time. *Now and the Past.*

SCENE I

The Wingfield apartment is in the rear of the building, one of those vast hive-like conglomerations of cellular living-units that flower as warty growths in overcrowded urban centers of lower middle-class population and are symptomatic of the impulse of this largest and fundamentally enslaved section of American society to avoid fluidity and differentiation and to exist and function as one interfused mass of automatism.

    The apartment faces an alley and is entered by a fire-escape, a structure whose name is a touch of accidental poetic truth, for all of these huge buildings are always burning with the slow and implacable fires of human desperation. The fire-escape is included in the set — that is, the landing of it and steps descending from it.

    The scene is memory and is therefore nonrealistic. Memory takes a lot of poetic license. It omits some details; others are exaggerated, according to the emotional value of the articles it touches, for memory is seated predominantly in the heart. The interior is therefore rather dim and poetic.

At the rise of the curtain, the audience is faced with the dark, grim rear wall of the Wingfield tenement. This building, which runs parallel to the footlights, is flanked on both sides by dark, narrow alleys which run into murky canyons of tangled clotheslines, garbage cans and the sinister latticework of neighboring fire-escapes. It is up and down these side alleys that exterior entrances and exits are made, during the play. At the end of Tom's opening commentary, the dark tenement wall slowly reveals (by means of a transparency) the interior of the ground floor Wingfield apartment.

Downstage is the living room, which also serves as a sleeping room for Laura, the sofa unfolding to make her bed. Upstage, center, and divided by a wide arch or second proscenium with transparent faded portieres (or second curtain), is the dining room. In an old-fashioned what-not in the living room are seen scores of transparent glass animals. A blown-up photograph of the father hangs on the wall of the living room, facing the audience, to the left of the archway. It is the face of a very handsome young man in a doughboy's First World War cap. He is gallantly smiling, ineluctably smiling, as if to say, "I will be smiling forever."

The audience hears and sees the opening scene in the dining room through both the transparent fourth wall of the building and the transparent gauze portieres of the dining-room arch. It is during this revealing scene that the fourth wall slowly ascends, out of sight. This transparent exterior wall is not brought down again until the very end of the play, during Tom's final speech.

The narrator is an undisguised convention of the play. He takes whatever license with dramatic convention as is convenient to his purposes.

Tom enters dressed as a merchant sailor from the alley, stage left, and strolls across the front of the stage to the fire-escape. There he stops and lights a cigarette. He addresses the audience.

Tom: Yes, I have tricks in my pocket, I have things up my sleeve. But I am the opposite of a stage magician. He gives you illusion that has the appearance of truth. I give you truth in the pleasant disguise of illusion. To begin with, I turn back time. I reverse it to that quaint period, the thirties, when the huge middle class of America was matriculating in a school for the blind. Their eyes had failed them, or they had failed their eyes, and so they were having their fingers pressed forcibly down on the fiery Braille alphabet of a dissolving economy. In Spain there was revolution. Here there was only shouting and confusion. In Spain there was Guernica. Here there were disturbances of labor, sometimes pretty violent, in otherwise peaceful cities such as Chicago, Cleveland, Saint Louis. . . . This is the social background of the play.

(Music.)

The play is memory. Being a memory play, it is dimly lighted, it is sentimental, it is not realistic. In memory everything seems to happen to music. That explains the fiddle in the wings. I am the narrator of the play, and also a character in it. The other characters are my mother, Amanda, my sister, Laura, and a gentleman caller who appears in the final scenes. He is the most realistic character in the play, being an emissary from a world of reality that we were somehow set apart from. But since I have a poet's weakness for symbols, I am using this character also as a symbol; he is the long delayed but always expected something that we live for. There is a fifth character in the play who doesn't appear except in this larger-than-life photograph over the mantel. This is our father who left us a long time ago. He was a telephone man who fell in love with long distances; he gave up his job with the telephone company and skipped the light fantastic out of town . . . The last we heard of him was a picture post-card from Mazatlan, on the Pacific coast of Mexico, containing a message of two words — "Hello — Good-bye!" and an address. I think the rest of the play will explain itself. . . .

Amanda's voice becomes audible through the portieres.

(Legend On Screen: "Où Sont Les Neiges.")°

He divides the portieres and enters the upstage area.
     Amanda and Laura are seated at a drop-leaf table. Eating is indicated by gestures without food or utensils. Amanda faces the audience. Tom and Laura are seated in profile.
     The interior has lit up softly and through the scrim we see Amanda and Laura seated at the table in the upstage area.

Amanda (calling): Tom?
Tom: Yes, Mother.
Amanda: We can't say grace until you come to the table!
Tom: Coming, Mother. *(He bows slightly and withdraws, reappearing a few moments later in his place at the table.)*
Amanda (to her son): Honey, don't *push* with your *fingers.* If you have to push with something, the thing to push with is a crust of bread. And chew — chew! Animals have sections in their stomachs which enable them to digest food without mastication, but human beings are supposed to chew their food before they swallow it down. Eat food leisurely, son, and really enjoy it. A well-cooked meal has lots of delicate flavors that have to be held in the mouth for appreciation. So chew your food and give your salivary glands a chance to function!

Tom deliberately lays his imaginary fork down and pushes his chair back from the table.

Tom: I haven't enjoyed one bite of this dinner because of your constant directions on how to eat it. It's you that makes me rush through meals with your hawk-like attention to every bite I take. Sickening — spoils my appetite — all this discussion of animals' secretion — salivary glands — mastication!
Amanda (lightly): Temperament like a Metropolitan star! *(He rises and crosses downstage.)* You're not excused from the table.

(Legend . . . Neiges.''): "Where are the snows (of yesteryear)?" A slide bearing this line by the French poet François Villon is to be projected on a stage wall.

Tom: I am getting a cigarette.
Amanda: You smoke too much.

   Laura rises.

Laura: I'll bring in the blanc mange.

   He remains standing with his cigarette by the portieres during the following.

Amanda (rising): No, sister, no, sister — you be the lady this time and I'll be the
   darky.
Laura: I'm already up.
Amanda: Resume your seat, little sister — I want you to stay fresh and pretty
   — for gentlemen callers!
Laura: I'm not expecting any gentlemen callers.
Amanda (crossing out to kitchenette. Airily): Sometimes they come when they are
   least expected! Why, I remember one Sunday afternoon in Blue Moun-
   tain — *(Enters kitchenette.)*
Tom: I know what's coming!
Laura: Yes. But let her tell it.
Tom: Again?
Laura: She loves to tell it.

   Amanda returns with bowl of dessert.

Amanda: One Sunday afternoon in Blue Mountain — your mother re-
   ceived — *seventeen!* — gentlemen callers! Why, sometimes there weren't
   chairs enough to accommodate them all. We had to send the nigger over
   to bring in folding chairs from the parish house.
Tom (remaining at portieres): How did you entertain those gentlemen callers?
Amanda: I understood the art of conversation!
Tom: I bet you could talk.
Amanda: Girls in those days *knew* how to talk, I can tell you.
Tom: Yes?

(Image: Amanda As A Girl On A Porch Greeting Callers.)

Amanda: They knew how to entertain their gentlemen callers. It wasn't enough
   for a girl to be possessed of a pretty face and a graceful figure — although
   I wasn't slighted in either respect. She also needed to have a nimble wit
   and a tongue to meet all occasions.
Tom: What did you talk about?
Amanda: Things of importance going on in the world! Never anything coarse
   or common or vulgar. *(She addresses Tom as though he were seated in the vacant chair
   at the table though he remains by portieres. He plays this scene as though he held the book.)*
   My callers were gentlemen — all! Among my callers were some of the
   most prominent young planters of the Mississippi Delta — planters and
   sons of planters!

   *Tom motions for music and a spot of light on Amanda. Her eyes lift, her face glows,
   her voice becomes rich and elegiac.*

(Screen Legend: "Où Sont Les Neiges.")

There was young Champ Laughlin who later became vice-president of the Delta Planters Bank. Hadley Stevenson who was drowned in Moon Lake and left his widow one hundred and fifty thousand in Government bonds. There were the Cutrere brothers, Wesley and Bates. Bates was one of my bright particular beaux! He got in a quarrel with that wild Wainright boy. They shot it out on the floor of Moon Lake Casino. Bates was shot through the stomach. Died in the ambulance on his way to Memphis. His widow was also well-provided for, came into eight or ten thousand acres, that's all. She married him on the rebound — never loved her — carried my picture on him the night he died! And there was that boy that every girl in the Delta had set her cap for! That beautiful, brilliant young Fitzhugh boy from Green County!

Tom: What did he leave his widow?

Amanda: He never married! Gracious, you talk as though all of my old admirers had turned up their toes to the daisies!

Tom: Isn't this the first you mentioned that still survives?

Amanda: That Fitzhugh boy went North and made a fortune — came to be known as the Wolf of Wall Street! He had the Midas touch, whatever he touched turned to gold! And I could have been Mrs. Duncan J. Fitzhugh, mind you! But — I picked your *father!*

Laura (rising): Mother, let me clear the table.

Amanda: No dear, you go in front and study your typewriter chart. Or practice your shorthand a little. Stay fresh and pretty! — It's almost time for our gentlemen callers to start arriving. *(She flounces girlishly toward the kitchenette.)* How many do you suppose we're going to entertain this afternoon?

Tom throws down the paper and jumps up with a groan.

Laura (alone in the dining room): I don't believe we're going to receive any, Mother.

Amanda (reappearing, airily): What? No one — not one? You must be joking! *(Laura nervously echoes her laugh. She slips in a fugitive manner through the half-open portieres and draws them gently behind her. A shaft of very clear light is thrown on her face against the faded tapestry of the curtains.)* **(Music: "The Glass Menagerie" Under Faintly.)** *(Lightly.)* Not one gentleman caller? It can't be true! There must be a flood, there must have been a tornado!

Laura: It isn't a flood, it's not a tornado, Mother. I'm just not popular like you were in Blue Mountain. . . . *(Tom utters another groan. Laura glances at him with a faint, apologetic smile. Her voice catching a little.)* Mother's afraid I'm going to be an old maid.

(The Scene Dims Out With "Glass Menagerie" Music.)

SCENE II

"Laura, Haven't You Ever Liked Some Boy?"

On the dark stage the screen is lighted with the image of blue roses.
    Gradually Laura's figure becomes apparent and the screen goes out.
    The music subsides.
    Laura is seated in the delicate ivory chair at the small clawfoot table.

She wears a dress of soft violet material for a kimono — her hair tied back from her forehead with a ribbon.

She is washing and polishing her collection of glass.

Amanda appears on the fire-escape steps. At the sound of her ascent, Laura catches her breath, thrusts the bowl of ornaments away and seats herself stiffly before the diagram of the typewriter keyboard as though it held her spellbound. Something has happened to Amanda. It is written in her face as she climbs to the landing: a look that is grim and hopeless and a little absurd.

She has on one of those cheap or imitation velvety-looking cloth coats with imitation fur collar. Her hat is five or six years old, one of those dreadful cloche hats that were worn in the late twenties, and she is clasping an enormous black patent-leather pocketbook with nickel clasp and initials. This is her fulldress outfit, the one she usually wears to the D.A.R.

Before entering she looks through the door.

She purses her lips, opens her eyes wide, rolls them upward and shakes her head.

Then she slowly lets herself in the door. Seeing her mother's expression Laura touches her lips with a nervous gesture.

Laura: Hello, Mother, I was — *(She makes a nervous gesture toward the chart on the wall. Amanda leans against the shut door and stares at Laura with a martyred look.)*

Amanda: Deception? Deception? *(She slowly removes her hat and gloves, continuing the swift suffering stare. She lets the hat and gloves fall on the floor — a bit of acting.)*

Laura (shakily): How was the D.A.R. meeting? *(Amanda slowly opens her purse and removes a dainty white handkerchief which she shakes out delicately and delicately touches to her lips and nostrils.)* Didn't you go the D.A.R. meeting, Mother?

Amanda (faintly, almost inaudibly): — No. — No. *(Then more forcibly.)* I did not have the strength — to go the D.A.R. In fact, I did not have the courage! I wanted to find a hole in the ground and hide myself in it forever! *(She crosses slowly to the wall and removes the diagram of the typewriter keyboard. She holds it in front of her for a second, staring at it sweetly and sorrowfully — then bites her lips and tears it in two pieces.)*

Laura (faintly): Why did you do that, Mother? *(Amanda repeats the same procedure with the chart of the Gregg Alphabet.)* Why are you —

Amanda: Why? Why? How old are you, Laura?

Laura: Mother, you know my age.

Amanda: I thought that you were an adult; it seems that I was mistaken. *(She crosses slowly to the sofa and sinks down and stares at Laura.)*

Laura: Please don't stare at me, Mother.

Amanda closes her eyes and lowers her head. Count ten.

Amanda: What are we going to do, what is going to become of us, what is the future?

Count ten.

Laura: Has something happened, Mother? *(Amanda draws a long breath and takes out the handkerchief again. Dabbing process.)* Mother, has — something happened?

Amanda: I'll be all right in a minute. I'm just bewildered — *(count five)* — by life. . . .

Laura: Mother, I wish that you would tell me what's happened.

Amanda: As you know, I was supposed to be inducted into my office at the D.A.R. this afternoon. **(Image: A Swarm of Typewriters.)** But I stopped off at Rubicam's Business College to speak to your teachers about your having a cold and ask them what progress they thought you were making down there.

Laura: Oh. . . .

Amanda: I went to the typing instructor and introduced myself as your mother. She didn't know who you were. Wingfield, she said. We don't have any such student enrolled at the school! I assured her she did, that you had been going to classes since early in January. "I wonder," she said, "if you could be talking about that terribly shy little girl who dropped out of school after only a few days' attendance?" "No," I said, "Laura, my daughter, has been going to school every day for the past six weeks!" "Excuse me," she said. She took the attendance book out and there was your name, unmistakably printed, and all the dates you were absent until they decided that you had dropped out of school. I still said, "No, there must have been some mistake! There must have been some mix-up in the records!" And she said, "No — I remember her perfectly now. Her hand shook so that she couldn't hit the right keys! The first time we gave a speed-test, she broke down completely — was sick at the stomach and almost had to be carried into the wash-room! After that morning she never showed up any more. We phoned the house but never got any answer" — while I was working at Famous and Barr, I suppose, demonstrating those — Oh! I felt so weak I could barely keep on my feet. I had to sit down while they got me a glass of water! Fifty dollars' tuition, all of our plans — my hopes and ambitions for you — just gone up the spout, just gone up the spout like that. *(Laura draws a long breath and gets awkwardly to her feet. She crosses to the victrola and winds it up.)* What are you doing?

Laura: Oh! *(She releases the handle and returns to her seat.)*

Amanda: Laura, where have you been going when you've gone out pretending that you were going to business college?

Laura: I've just been going out walking.

Amanda: That's not true.

Laura: It is. I just went walking.

Amanda: Walking? Walking? In winter? Deliberately courting pneumonia in that light coat? Where did you walk to, Laura?

Laura: It was the lesser of two evils, Mother. **(Image: Winter Scene In Park.)** I couldn't go back up. I — threw up — on the floor!

Amanda: From half past seven till after five every day you mean to tell me you walked around in the park, because you wanted to make me think that you were still going to Rubicam's Business College?

Laura: It wasn't as bad as it sounds. I went inside places to get warmed up.

Amanda: Inside where?

Laura: I went in the art museum and the bird-houses at the Zoo. I visited the penguins every day! Sometimes I did without lunch and went to the movies. Lately I've been spending most of my afternoons in the Jewel-box, that big glass house where they raise the tropical flowers.

Amanda: You did all this to deceive me, just for the deception? *(Laura looks down.)* Why?

Laura: Mother, when you're disappointed, you get that awful suffering look on your face, like the picture of Jesus' mother in the museum!

Amanda: Hush!

Laura: I couldn't face it.

Pause. A whisper of strings.

(Legend: "The Crust Of Humility.")

Amanda (hopelessly fingering the huge pocketbook): So what are we going to do the rest of our lives? Stay home and watch the parades go by? Amuse ourselves with the glass menagerie, darling? Eternally play those worn-out phonograph records your father left as a painful reminder of him? We won't have a business career — we've given that up because it gave us nervous indigestion! *(Laughs wearily.)* What is there left but dependency all our lives? I know so well what becomes of unmarried women who aren't prepared to occupy a position. I've seen such pitiful cases in the South — barely tolerated spinsters living upon the grudging patronage of sister's husband or brother's wife! — stuck away in some little mouse-trap of a room — encouraged by one in-law to visit another — little birdlike women without any nest — eating the crust of humility all their life! Is that the future that we've mapped out for ourselves? I swear it's the only alternative I can think of! It isn't a very pleasant alternative, is it? Of course — some girls *do* marry. *(Laura twists her hands nervously.)* Haven't you ever liked some boy?

Laura: Yes I liked one once. *(Rises.)* I came across his picture a while ago.

Amanda (with some interest): He gave you his picture?

Laura: No, it's in the year-book.

Amanda (disappointed): Oh — a high-school boy.

(Screen Image: Jim As A High-School Hero Bearing A Silver Cup.)

Laura: Yes. His name was Jim. *(Laura lifts the heavy annual from the clawfoot table.)* Here he is in *The Pirates of Penzance.*

Amanda (absently): The what?

Laura: The operetta the senior class put on. He had a wonderful voice and we sat across the aisle from each other Mondays, Wednesdays and Fridays in the Aud. Here he is with the silver cup for debating! See his grin?

Amanda (absently): He must have had a jolly disposition.

Laura: He used to call me — Blue Roses.

(Image: Blue Roses.)

Amanda: Why did he call you such a name as that?

Laura: When I had that attack of pleurosis — he asked me what was the matter when I came back. I said pleurosis — he thought that I said Blue Roses! So that's what he always called me after that. Whenever he saw me, he'd holler, "Hello, Blue Roses!" I didn't care for the girl that he went out with. Emily Meisenbach. Emily was the best-dressed girl at Soldan. She never struck me, though, as being sincere . . . It says in the Personal Section — they're engaged. That's — six years ago! They must be married by now.

Amanda: Girls that aren't cut out for business careers usually wind up married to some nice man. *(Gets up with a spark of revival.)* Sister, that's what you'll do!

Laura utters a startled, doubtful laugh. She reaches quickly for a piece of glass.

Laura: But, Mother —
Amanda: Yes? *(Crossing to photograph.)*
Laura (in a tone of frightened apology): I'm — crippled!

(Image: Screen.)

Amanda: Nonsense! Laura, I've told you never, never to use that word. Why, you're not crippled, you just have a little defect — hardly noticeable, even! When people have some slight disadvantage like that, they cultivate other things to make up for it — develop charm — and vivacity — and — *charm!* That's all you have to do! *(She turns again to the photograph.)* One thing your father had *plenty of* — was *charm!*

Tom motions to the fiddle in the wings.

(The Scene Fades Out With Music.)

SCENE III

(Legend On The Screen: "After The Fiasco — ")

Tom speaks from the fire-escape landing.

Tom: After the fiasco at Rubicam's Business College, the idea of getting a gentleman caller for Laura began to play a more important part in Mother's calculations. It became an obsession. Like some archetype of the universal unconscious, the image of the gentleman caller haunted our small apartment. . . . **(Image: Young Man At Door With Flowers.)** An evening at home rarely passed without some allusion to this image, this spectre, this hope. . . . Even when he wasn't mentioned, his presence hung in Mother's preoccupied look and in my sister's frightened, apologetic manner — hung like a sentence passed upon the Wingfields! Mother was a woman of action as well as words. She began to take logical steps in the planned direction. Late that winter and in the early spring — realizing that extra money would be needed to properly feather the nest and plume the bird — she conducted a vigorous campaign on the telephone, roping in subscribers to one of those magazines for matrons called *The Home-maker's Companion,* the type of journal that features the serialized sublimations of ladies of letters who think in terms of delicate cup-like breasts, slim, tapering waists, rich, creamy thighs, eyes like wood-smoke in autumn, fingers that soothe and caress like strains of music, bodies as powerful as Etruscan sculpture.

(Screen Image: Glamor Magazine Cover.)

Amanda enters with phone on long extension cord. She is spotted in the dim stage.

Amanda: Ida Scott? This is Amanda Wingfield! We *missed* you at the D.A.R. last Monday! I said to myself: She's probably suffering with that sinus condition! How is that sinus condition? Horrors! Heaven have mercy! — You're a Christian martyr, yes, that's what you are, a Christian martyr! Well, I just now happened to notice that your subscription to the *Companion's* about to expire! Yes, it expires with the next issue, honey! — just when that wonderful new serial by Bessie Mae Hopper is getting off to such an exciting start. Oh, honey, it's something that you can't miss! You remember how *Gone With the Wind* took everybody by storm? You simply couldn't go out if you hadn't read it. All everybody *talked* was Scarlett O'Hara. Well, this is a book that critics already compare to *Gone With the Wind.* It's the *Gone With the Wind* of the post-World War generation! — What? — Burning? — Oh, honey, don't let them burn, go take a look in the oven and I'll hold the wire! Heavens — I think she's hung up!

(Dim Out.)

(Legend On Screen: "You Think I'm In Love With Continental Shoemakers?")

Before the stage is lighted, the violent voices of Tom and Amanda are heard. They are quarreling behind the portieres. In front of them stands Laura with clenched hands and panicky expression.
   A clear pool of light on her figure throughout this scene.

Tom: What in Christ's name am I —
Amanda *(shrilly):* Don't you use that —
Tom: Supposed to do!
Amanda: Expression! Not in my —
Tom: Ohhh!
Amanda: Presence! Have you gone out of your senses?
Tom: I have, that's true, *driven* out!
Amanda: What is the matter with you, you — big — big — IDIOT!
Tom: Look — I've got *no thing,* no single thing —
Amanda: Lower your voice!
Tom: In my life here that I can call my OWN! Everything is —
Amanda: Stop that shouting!
Tom: Yesterday you confiscated my books! You had the nerve to —
Amanda: I took that horrible novel back to the library — yes! That hideous book by that insane Mr. Lawrence. *(Tom laughs wildly.)* I cannot control the output of diseased minds or people who cater to them — *(Tom laughs still more wildly.)* BUT I WON'T ALLOW SUCH FILTH BROUGHT INTO MY HOUSE! No, no, no, no, no!
Tom: House, house! Who pays rent on it, who makes a slave of himself to —

Amanda (fairly screeching): Don't you DARE to —

Tom: No, no, *I* mustn't say things! *I've* got to just —

Amanda: Let me tell you —

Tom: I don't want to hear any more! *(He tears the portieres open. The upstage area is lit with a turgid smoky red glow.)*

Amanda's hair is in metal curlers and she wears a very old bathrobe, much too large for her slight figure, a relic of the faithless Mr. Wingfield.

  An upright typewriter and a wild disarray of manuscripts are on the drop-leaf table. The quarrel was probably precipitated by Amanda's interruption of his creative labor. A chair lying overthrown on the floor.

  Their gesticulating shadows are cast on the ceiling by the fiery glow.

Amanda: You *will* hear more, you —

Tom: No, I won't hear more, I'm going out!

Amanda: You come right back in —

Tom: Out, out out! Because I'm —

Amanda: Come back here, Tom Wingfield! I'm not through talking to you!

Tom: Oh, go —

Laura (desperately): Tom!

Amanda: You're going to listen, and no more insolence from you! I'm at the end of my patience! *(He comes back toward her.)*

Tom: What do you think I'm at? Aren't I supposed to have any patience to reach the end of, Mother? I know, I know. It seems unimportant to you, what I'm *doing* — what I *want* to do — having a little *difference* between them! You don't think that —

Amanda: I think you've been doing things that you're ashamed of. That's why you act like this. I don't believe that you go every night to the movies. Nobody goes to the movies night after night. Nobody in their right minds goes to the movies as often as you pretend to. People don't go to the movies at nearly midnight, and movies don't let out at two A.M. Come in stumbling. Muttering to yourself like a maniac! You get three hours' sleep and then go to work. Oh, I can picture the way you're doing down there. Moping, doping, because you're in no condition.

Tom (wildly): No, I'm in no condition!

Amanda: What right have you got to jeopardize your job? Jeopardize the security of us all? How do you think we'd manage if you were —

Tom: Listen! You think I'm crazy *about* the *warehouse?* *(He bends fiercely toward her slight figure.)* You think I'm in love with the Continental Shoemakers? You think I want to spend fifty-five *years* down there in that — *celotex interior!* with — *fluorescent — tubes!* Look! I'd rather somebody picked up a crowbar and battered out my brains — than go back mornings! I *go!* Every time you come in yelling that God damn *"Rise and Shine!" "Rise and Shine!"* I say to myself *"How lucky dead people are!"* But I get up. I *go!* For sixty-five dollars a month I give up all that I dream of doing and being *ever!* And you say self — *self's* all I ever think of. Why, listen, if self is what I thought of, Mother, I'd be where he is — GONE! *(Pointing to father's picture.)* As far as the system of transportation reaches! *(He starts past her. She grabs his arm.)* Don't grab at me, Mother!

Amanda: Where are you going?

Tom: I'm going to the *movies!*

Amanda: I don't believe that lie!

Tom (crouching toward her, overtowering her tiny figure. She backs away, gasping): I'm going to opium dens! Yes, opium dens, dens of vice and criminals' hang-outs, Mother. I've joined the Hogan gang, I'm a hired assassin, I carry a tommy-gun in a violin case! I run a string of cat-houses in the Valley! They call me Killer, Killer Wingfield, I'm leading a double-life, a simple, honest warehouse worker by day, by night a dynamic *czar* of the *underworld, Mother.* I go to gambling casinos, I spin away fortunes on the roulette table! I wear a patch over one eye and a false mustache, sometimes I put on green whiskers. On those occasions they call me — *El Diablo!* Oh, I could tell you things to make you sleepless! My enemies plan to dynamite this place. They're going to blow us all sky-high some night! I'll be glad, very happy, and so will you! You'll go up, up on a broomstick, over Blue Mountain with seventeen gentlemen callers! You ugly — babbling old — witch. . . . *(He goes through a series of violent, clumsy movements, seizing his overcoat, lunging to the door, pulling it fiercely open. The women watch him, aghast. His arm catches in the sleeve of the coat as he struggles to pull it on. For a moment he is pinioned by the bulky garment. With an outraged groan he tears the coat off again, splitting the shoulders of it, and hurls it across the room. It strikes against the shelf of Laura's glass collection, there is a tinkle of shattering glass. Laura cries out as if wounded.)*

(Music Legend: "The Glass Menagerie.")

Laura (shrilly): My glass! — menagerie. . . . *(She covers her face and turns away.)*

But Amanda is still stunned and stupefied by the "ugly witch" so that she barely notices this occurrence. Now she recovers her speech.

Amanda (in an awful voice): I won't speak to you — until you apologize! *(She crosses through portieres and draws them together behind her. Tom is left with Laura. Laura clings weakly to the mantel with her face averted. Tom stares at her stupidly for a moment. Then he crosses to shelf. Drops awkwardly to his knees to collect the fallen glass, glancing at Laura as if he would speak but couldn't.)*

"The Glass Menagerie" steals in as

(The Scene Dims Out.)

SCENE IV

The interior is dark. Faint in the alley.

A deep-voiced bell in a church is tolling the hour of five as the scene commences.

Tom appears at the top of the alley. After each solemn boom of the bell in the tower, he shakes a little noise-maker or rattle as if to express the tiny spasm of man in contrast to the sustained power and dignity of the Almighty. This and the unsteadiness of his advance make it evident that he has been drinking.

As he climbs the few steps to the fire-escape landing light steals up inside. Laura appears in night-dress, observing Tom's empty bed in the front room.

Tom fishes in his pockets for the door-key, removing a motley assortment of articles in the search, including a perfect shower of movie-ticket stubs and an empty bottle. At last he finds the key, but just as he is about to insert it, it slips from his fingers. He strikes a match and crouches below the door.

Tom (bitterly): One crack — and it falls through!

Laura opens the door.

Laura: Tom! Tom, what are you doing?
Tom: Looking for a door-key.
Laura: Where have you been all this time?
Tom: I have been to the movies.
Laura: All this time at the movies?
Tom: There was a very long program. There was a Garbo picture and a Mickey Mouse and a travelogue and a newsreel and a preview of coming attractions. And there was an organ solo and a collection for the milk-fund — simultaneously — which ended up in a terrible fight between a fat lady and an usher!
Laura (innocently): Did you have to stay through everything?
Tom: Of course! And, oh, I forgot! There was a big stage show! The headliner on this stage show was Malvolio the Magician. He performed wonderful tricks, many of them, such as pouring water back and forth between pitchers. First it turned to wine and then it turned to beer and then it turned to whiskey. I know it was whiskey it finally turned into because he needed somebody to come up out of the audience to help him, and I came up — both shows! It was Kentucky Straight Bourbon. A very generous fellow, he gave souvenirs. *(He pulls from his back pocket a shimmering rainbow-colored scarf.)* He gave me this. This is his magic scarf. You can have it, Laura. You wave it over a canary cage and you get a bowl of gold-fish. You wave it over the gold-fish bowl and they fly away canaries. . . . But the wonderfullest trick of all was the coffin trick. We nailed him into a coffin and he got out of the coffin without removing one nail. *(He has come inside.)* There is a trick that would come in handy for me — get me out of this 2 by 4 situation! *(Flops onto bed and starts removing shoes.)*
Laura: Tom — Shhh!
Tom: What you shushing me for?
Laura: You'll wake up Mother.
Tom: Goody, goody! Pay 'er back for all those "Rise an' Shines." *(Lies down, groaning.)* You know it don't take much intelligence to get yourself into a nailed-up coffin, Laura. But who in hell ever got himself out of one without removing one nail?

As if in answer, the father's grinning photograph lights up.

(Scene Dims Out.)

Immediately following: The church bell is heard striking six. At the sixth stroke the alarm clock goes off in Amanda's room, and after a few moments we hear her calling: "Rise and Shine! Rise and Shine! Laura, go tell your brother to rise and shine!"

Tom (sitting up slowly): I'll rise — but I won't shine.

The light increases.

Amanda: Laura, tell your brother his coffee is ready.

Laura slips into front room.

Laura: Tom! it's nearly seven. Don't make Mother nervous. *(He stares at her stupidly. Beseechingly.)* Tom, speak to Mother this morning. Make up with her, apologize, speak to her!
Tom: She won't to me. It's her that started not speaking.
Laura: If you just say you're sorry she'll start speaking.
Tom: Her not speaking — is that such a tragedy?
Laura: Please — please!
Amanda (calling from kitchenette): Laura, are you going to do what I asked you to do, or do I have to get dressed and go out myself?
Laura: Going, going — soon as I get on my coat! *(She pulls on a shapeless felt hat with nervous, jerky movement, pleadingly glancing at Tom. Rushes awkwardly for coat. The coat is one of Amanda's inaccurately made-over, the sleeves too short for Laura.)* Butter and what else?
Amanda (entering upstage): Just butter. Tell them to charge it.
Laura: Mother, they make such faces when I do that.
Amanda: Sticks and stones may break my bones, but the expression on Mr. Garfinkel's face won't harm us! Tell your brother his coffee is getting cold.
Laura (at door): Do what I asked you, will you, will you, Tom?

He looks sullenly away.

Amanda: Laura, go now or just don't go at all!
Laura (rushing out): Going — going! *(A second later she cries out. Tom springs up and crosses to the door. Amanda rushes anxiously in. Tom opens the door.)*
Tom: Laura?
Laura: I'm all right. I slipped, but I'm all right.
Amanda (peering anxiously after her): If anyone breaks a leg on those fire-escape steps, the landlord ought to be sued for every cent he possesses! *(She shuts door. Remembers she isn't speaking and returns to other room.)*

As Tom enters listlessly for his coffee, she turns her back to him and stands rigidly facing the window on the gloomy gray vault of the areaway. Its light on her face with its aged but childish features is cruelly sharp, satirical as a Daumier print.

(Music Under: "Ave Maria.")

Tom glances sheepishly but sullenly at her averted figure and slumps at the table. The coffee is scalding hot; he sips it and gasps and spits it back in the cup. At his gasp, Amanda catches her breath and half turns. Then catches herself and turns back to window.

> *Tom blows on his coffee, glancing sidewise at his mother. She clears her throat. Tom clears his. He starts to rise. Sinks back down again, scratches his head, clears his throat again. Amanda coughs. Tom raises his cup in both hands to blow on it, his eyes staring over the rim of it at his mother for several moments. Then he slowly sets the cup down and awkwardly and hesitantly rises from the chair.*

Tom (hoarsely): Mother. I — I apologize. Mother. *(Amanda draws a quick, shuddering breath. Her face works grotesquely. She breaks into childlike tears.)* I'm sorry for what I said, for everything that I said, I didn't mean it.

Amanda (sobbingly): My devotion has made me a witch and so I make myself hateful to my children!

Tom: No, you *don't.*

Amanda: I worry so much, don't sleep, it makes me nervous!

Tom (gently): I understand that.

Amanda: I've had to put up a solitary battle all these years. But you're my right-hand bower! Don't fall down, don't fail!

Tom (gently): I try, Mother.

Amanda (with great enthusiasm): Try and you will SUCCEED! *(The notion makes her breathless.)* Why, you — you're just *full* of natural endowments! Both of my children — they're *unusual* children! Don't you think I know it? I'm so — *proud!* Happy and — feel I've — so much to be thankful for but — Promise me one thing, son!

Tom: What, Mother?

Amanda: Promise, son, you'll — never be a drunkard!

Tom (turns to her grinning): I will never be a drunkard, Mother.

Amanda: That's what frightened me so, that you'd be drinking! Eat a bowl of Purina!

Tom: Just coffee, Mother.

Amanda: Shredded wheat biscuit?

Tom: No. No, Mother, just coffee.

Amanda: You can't put in a day's work on an empty stomach. You've got ten minutes — don't gulp! Drinking too-hot liquids makes cancer of the stom-ach. . . . Put cream in.

Tom: No, thank you.

Amanda: To cool it.

Tom: No! No, thank you, I want it black.

Amanda: I know, but it's not good for you. We have to do all that we can to build ourselves up. In these trying times we live in, all that we have to cling to is — each other. . . . That's why it's so important to — Tom, I — I sent out your sister so I could discuss something with you. If you hadn't spoken I would have spoken to you. *(Sits down.)*

Tom (gently): What is it, Mother, that you want to discuss?

Amanda: Laura!

Tom puts his cup down slowly.

(Legend On Screen: "Laura.")

(Music: "The Glass Menagerie.")

Tom: — Oh. — Laura . . .

Amanda (touching his sleeve): You know how Laura is. So quiet but — still water runs deep! She notices things and I think she — broods about them. *(Tom looks up.)* A few days ago I came in and she was crying.

Tom: What about?

Amanda: You.

Tom: Me?

Amanda: She has an idea that you're not happy here.

Tom: What gave her that idea?

Amanda: What gives her any idea? However, you do act strangely. I — I'm not criticizing, understand *that!* I know your ambitions do not lie in the warehouse, that like everybody in the whole wide world — you've had to — make sacrifices, but — Tom — Tom — life's not easy, it calls for — Spartan endurance! There's so many things in my heart that I cannot describe to you! I've never told you but I — *loved* your father. . . .

Tom (gently): I know that, Mother.

Amanda: And you — when I see you taking after his ways! Staying out late — and — well, you *had* been drinking the night you were in that — terrifying condition! Laura says that you hate the apartment and that you go out nights to get away from it! Is that true, Tom?

Tom: No. You say there's so much in your heart that you can't describe to me. That's true of me, too. There's so much in my heart that I can't describe to *you!* So let's respect each other's —

Amanda: But, why — *why,* Tom — are you always so *restless?* Where do you go to, nights?

Tom: I — go to the movies.

Amanda: Why do you go to the movies so much, Tom?

Tom: I go to the movies because — I like adventure. Adventure is something I don't have much of at work, so I go to the movies.

Amanda: But, Tom, you go to the movies *entirely* too *much!*

Tom: I like a lot of adventure.

> *Amanda looks baffled, then hurt. As the familiar inquisition resumes he becomes hard and impatient again. Amanda slips back into her querulous attitude toward him.*

(Image On Screen: Sailing Vessel With Jolly Roger.)

Amanda: Most young men find adventure in their careers.

Tom: Then most young men are not employed in a warehouse.

Amanda: The world is full of young men employed in warehouses and offices and factories.

Tom: Do all of them find adventure in their careers?

Amanda: They do or they do without it! Not everybody has a craze for adventure.

Tom: Man is by instinct a lover, a hunter, a fighter, and none of those instincts are given much play at the warehouse!

Amanda: Man is by instinct! Don't quote instinct to me! Instinct is something that people have got away from! It belongs to animals! Christian adults don't want it!

Tom: What do Christian adults want, then, Mother?

Amanda: Superior things! Things of the mind and the spirit! Only animals have to satisfy instincts! Surely your aims are somewhat higher than theirs! Than monkeys — pigs —

Tom: I reckon they're not.

Amanda: You're joking. However, that isn't what I wanted to discuss.

Tom (rising): I haven't much time.

Amanda (pushing his shoulders): Sit down.

Tom: You want me to punch in red at the warehouse, Mother?

Amanda: You have five minutes. I want to talk about Laura.

(Legend: "Plans And Provisions.")

Tom: All right! What about Laura?

Amanda: We have to be making plans and provisions for her. She's older than you, two years, and nothing has happened. She just drifts along doing nothing. It frightens me terribly how she just drifts along.

Tom: I guess she's the type that people call home girls.

Amanda: There's no such type, and if there is, it's a pity! That is unless the home is hers, with a husband!

Tom: What?

Amanda: Oh, I can see the handwriting on the wall as plain as I see the nose in front of my face! It's terrifying! More and more you remind me of your father! He was out all hours without explanation — Then *left! Goodbye!* And me with the bag to hold. I saw that letter you got from the Merchant Marine. I know what you're dreaming of. I'm not standing here blindfolded. Very well, then. Then *do* it! But not till there's somebody to take your place.

Tom: What do you mean?

Amanda: I mean that as soon as Laura has got somebody to take care of her, married, a home of her own, independent — why, then you'll be free to go wherever you please, on land, on sea, whichever way the wind blows! But until that time you've got to look out for your sister. I don't say me because I'm old and don't matter! I say for your sister because she's young and dependent. I put her in business college — a dismal failure! Frightened her so it made her sick to her stomach. I took her over to the Young People's League at the church. Another fiasco. She spoke to nobody, nobody spoke to her. Now all she does is fool with those pieces of glass and play those worn-out records. What kind of a life is that for a girl to lead!

Tom: What can I do about it?

Amanda: Overcome selfishness! Self, self, self is all that you ever think of! *(Tom springs up and crosses to get his coat. It is ugly and bulky. He pulls on a cap with earmuffs.)* Where is your muffler? Put your wool muffler on! *(He snatches it angrily from the closet and tosses it around his neck and pulls both ends tight.)* Tom! I haven't said what I had in mind to ask you.

Tom: I'm too late to —

Amanda (catching his arms — very importunately. Then shyly): Down at the warehouse, aren't there some — nice young men?

Tom: No!

Amanda: There *must* be — *some* . . .

Tom: Mother —

Gesture.

Amanda: Find out one that's clean-living — doesn't drink and — ask him out for sister!

Tom: What?

Amanda: For *sister!* To *meet!* Get *acquainted!*

Tom (stamping to door): Oh, my go-osh!

Amanda: Will you? *(He opens door. Imploringly.)* Will you? *(He starts down.)* Will you? *Will* you, dear?

Tom (calling back): YES!

Amanda closes the door hesitantly and with a troubled but faintly hopeful expression.

(Screen Image: Glamor Magazine Cover.)

Spot Amanda at phone.

Amanda: Ella Cartwright? This is Amanda Wingfield! How are you, honey? How is that kidney condition? *(Count five.)* Horrors! *(Count five.)* You're a Christian martyr, yes, honey, that's what you are, a Christian martyr! Well, I just happened to notice in my little red book that your subscription to the *Companion* has just run out! I knew that you wouldn't want to miss out on the wonderful serial starting in this new issue. It's by Bessie Mae Hopper, the first thing she's written since *Honeymoon for Three.* Wasn't that a strange and interesting story? Well, this one is even lovelier, I believe. It has a sophisticated society background. It's all about the horsey set on Long Island!

(Fade Out.)

SCENE V

(Legend On Screen: "Annunciation.") *Fade with music.*

It is early dusk of a spring evening. Supper has just been finished in the Wingfield apartment. Amanda and Laura in light colored dresses are removing dishes from the table, in the upstage area, which is shadowy, their movements formalized almost as a dance or ritual, their moving forms as pale and silent as moths.

 Tom, in white shirt and trousers, rises from the table and crosses toward the fire-escape.

Amanda (as he passes her): Son, will you do me a favor?

Tom: What?

Amanda: Comb your hair! You look so pretty when your hair is combed! *(Tom slouches on sofa with evening paper. Enormous caption "Franco Triumphs.")* There is only one respect in which I would like you to emulate your father.

Tom: What respect is that?

Amanda: The care he always took of his appearance. He never allowed himself to look untidy. *(He throws down the paper and crosses to fire-escape.)* Where are you going?

Tom: I'm going out to smoke.

Amanda: You smoke too much. A pack a day at fifteen cents a pack. How much would that amount to in a month? Thirty times fifteen is how much, Tom? Figure it out and you will be astounded at what you could save. Enough to give you a night-school course in accounting at Washington U! Just think what a wonderful thing that would be for you, son!

Tom is unmoved by the thought.

Tom: I'd rather smoke. *(He steps out on landing, letting the screen door slam.)*

Amanda (sharply): I know! That's the tragedy of it. . . . *(Alone, she turns to look at her husband's picture.)*

(Dance Music: "All The World Is Waiting For The Sunrise!")

Tom (to the audience): Across the alley from us was the Paradise Dance Hall. On evenings in spring the windows and doors were open and the music came outdoors. Sometimes the lights were turned out except for a large glass sphere that hung from the ceiling. It would turn slowly about and filter the dusk with delicate rainbow colors. Then the orchestra played a waltz or a tango, something that had a slow and sensuous rhythm. Couples would come outside, to the relative privacy of the alley. You could see them kissing behind ash-pits and telephone poles. This was the compensation for lives that passed like mine, without any change or adventure. Adventure and change were imminent in this year. They were waiting around the corner for all these kids. Suspended in the mist over Berchtesgaden, caught in the folds of Chamberlain's umbrella — In Spain there was Guernica! But here there was only hot swing music and liquor, dance halls, bars, and movies, and sex that hung in the gloom like a chandelier and flooded the world with brief, deceptive rainbows. . . . All the world was waiting for bombardments!

Amanda turns from the picture and comes outside.

Amanda (sighing): A fire-escape landing's a poor excuse for a porch. *(She spreads a newspaper on a step and sits down, gracefully and demurely as if she were settling into a swing on a Mississippi veranda.)* What are you looking at?

Tom: The moon.

Amanda: Is there a moon this evening?

Tom: It's rising over Garfinkel's Delicatessen.

Amanda: So it is! A little silver slipper of a moon. Have you made a wish on it yet?

Tom: Um-hum.

Amanda: What did you wish for?

Tom: That's a secret.

Amanda: A secret, huh? Well, I won't tell mine either. I will be just as mysterious as you.

Tom: I bet I can guess what yours is.

Amanda: Is my head so transparent?

Tom: You're not a sphinx.

Amanda: No, I don't have secrets. I'll tell you what I wished for on the moon.

Success and happiness for my precious children! I wish for that whenever there's a moon, and when there isn't a moon, I wish for it, too.

Tom: I thought perhaps you wished for a gentleman caller.

Amanda: Why do you say that?

Tom: Don't you remember asking me to fetch one?

Amanda: I remember suggesting that it would be nice for your sister if you brought home some nice young man from the warehouse. I think I've made that suggestion more than once.

Tom: Yes, you have made it repeatedly.

Amanda: Well?

Tom: We are going to have one.

Amanda: What?

Tom: A gentleman caller!

(The Annunciation Is Celebrated With Music.)

Amanda rises.

(Image On Screen: Caller With Bouquet.)

Amanda: You mean you have asked some nice young man to come over?

Tom: Yep. I've asked him to dinner.

Amanda: You really did?

Tom: I did!

Amanda: You did, and did he — *accept?*

Tom: He did!

Amanda: Well, well — well, well! That's — lovely!

Tom: I thought that you would be pleased.

Amanda: It's definite, then?

Tom: Very definite.

Amanda: Soon?

Tom: Very soon.

Amanda: For heaven's sake, stop putting on and tell me some things, will you?

Tom: What things do you want me to tell you?

Amanda: Naturally I would like to know when he's *coming!*

Tom: He's coming tomorrow.

Amanda: Tomorrow?

Tom: Yep. Tomorrow.

Amanda: But, Tom!

Tom: Yes, Mother?

Amanda: Tomorrow gives me no time!

Tom: Time for what?

Amanda: Preparations! Why didn't you phone me at once, as soon as you asked him, the minute that he accepted? Then, don't you see, I could have been getting ready!

Tom: You don't have to make any fuss.

Amanda: Oh, Tom, Tom, Tom, of course I have to make a fuss! I want things nice, not sloppy! Not thrown together. I'll certainly have to do some fast thinking, won't I?

Tom: I don't see why you have to think at all.

Amanda: You just don't know. We can't have a gentleman caller in a pig-sty! All my wedding silver has to be polished, the monogrammed table linen ought to be laundered! The windows have to be washed and fresh curtains put up. And how about clothes? We have to *wear* something, don't we?

Tom: Mother, this boy is no one to make a fuss over!

Amanda: Do you realize he's the first young man we've introduced to your sister? It's terrible, dreadful, disgraceful that poor little sister has never received a single gentleman caller! Tom, come inside! *(She opens the screen door.)*

Tom: What for?

Amanda: I want to ask you some things.

Tom: If you're going to make such a fuss, I'll call it off, I'll tell him not to come.

Amanda: You certainly won't do anything of the kind. Nothing offends people worse than broken engagements. It simply means I'll have to work like a Turk! We won't be brilliant, but we'll pass inspection. Come on inside. *(Tom follows, groaning.)* Sit down.

Tom: Any particular place you would like me to sit?

Amanda: Thank heavens I've got that new sofa! I'm also making payments on a floor lamp I'll have sent out! And put the chintz covers on, they'll brighten things up! Of course I'd hoped to have these walls re-papered. . . . What is the young man's name?

Tom: His name is O'Connor.

Amanda: That, of course, means fish — tomorrow is Friday! I'll have that salmon loaf — with Durkee's dressing! What does he do? He works at the warehouse?

Tom: Of course! How else would I —

Amanda: Tom, he — doesn't drink?

Tom: Why do you ask me that?

Amanda: Your father *did!*

Tom: Don't get started on that!

Amanda: He *does* drink, then?

Tom: Not that I know of!

Amanda: Make sure, be certain! The last thing I want for my daughter's a boy who drinks!

Tom: Aren't you being a little premature? Mr. O'Connor has not yet appeared on the scene!

Amanda: But will tomorrow. To meet your sister, and what do I know about his character? Nothing! Old maids are better off than wives of drunkards!

Tom: Oh, my God!

Amanda: Be still!

Tom (leaning forward to whisper): Lots of fellows meet girls whom they don't marry!

Amanda: Oh, talk sensibly, Tom — and don't be sarcastic! *(She has gotten a hairbrush.)*

Tom: What are you doing?

Amanda: I'm brushing that cow-lick down! What is this young man's position at the warehouse?

Tom (submitting grimly to the brush and the interrogation): This young man's position is that of a shipping clerk, Mother.

Amanda: Sounds to me like a fairly responsible job, the sort of a job *you* would be in if you just had more *get-up*. What is his salary? Have you got any idea?

Tom: I would judge it to be approximately eighty-five dollars a month.

Amanda: Well — not princely, but —

Tom: Twenty more than I make.

Amanda: Yes, how well I know! But for a family man, eighty-five dollars a month is not much more than you can just get by on. . . .

Tom: Yes, but Mr. O'Connor is not a family man.

Amanda: He might be, mightn't he? Some time in the future?

Tom: I see. Plans and provisions.

Amanda: You are the only young man that I know of who ignores the fact that the future becomes the present, the present the past, and the past turns into everlasting regret if you don't plan for it!

Tom: I will think that over and see what I can make of it.

Amanda: Don't be supercilious with your mother! Tell me some more about this — what do you call him?

Tom: James D. O'Connor. The D. is for Delaney.

Amanda: Irish on *both* sides! *Gracious!* And doesn't drink?

Tom: Shall I call him up and ask him right this minute?

Amanda: The only way to find out about those things is to make discreet inquiries at the proper moment. When I was a girl in Blue Mountain and it was suspected that a young man drank, the girl whose attentions he had been receiving, if any girl *was,* would sometimes speak to the minister of his church, or rather her father would if her father was living, and sort of feel him out on the young man's character. That is the way such things are discreetly handled to keep a young woman from making a tragic mistake!

Tom: Then how did you happen to make a tragic mistake?

Amanda: That innocent look of your father's had everyone fooled! He *smiled* — the world was *enchanted!* No girl can do worse than put herself at the mercy of a handsome appearance! I hope that Mr. O'Connor is not too good-looking.

Tom: No, he's not too good-looking. He's covered with freckles and hasn't too much of a nose.

Amanda: He's not right-down homely, though?

Tom: Not right-down homely. Just medium homely, I'd say.

Amanda: Character's what to look for in a man.

Tom: That's what I've always said, Mother.

Amanda: You've never said anything of the kind and I suspect you would never give it a thought.

Tom: Don't be suspicious of me.

Amanda: At least I hope he's the type that's up and coming.

Tom: I think he really goes in for self-improvement.

Amanda: What reason have you to think so?

Tom: He goes to night school.

Amanda (beaming): Splendid! What does he do, I mean study?

Tom: Radio engineering and public speaking!

Amanda: Then he has visions of being advanced in the world! Any young man who studies public speaking is aiming to have an executive job some day! And radio engineering? A thing for the future! Both of these facts are very illuminating. Those are the sort of things that a mother should know concerning any young man who comes to call on her daughter. Seriously or — not.

Tom: One little warning. He doesn't know about Laura. I didn't let on that we had dark ulterior motives. I just said, why don't you come have dinner with us? He said okay and that was the whole conversation.

Amanda: I bet it was! You're eloquent as an oyster. However, he'll know about Laura when he gets here. When he sees how lovely and sweet and pretty she is, he'll thank his lucky stars he was asked to dinner.

Tom: Mother, you mustn't expect too much of Laura.

Amanda: What do you mean?

Tom: Laura seems all those things to you and me because she's ours and we love her. We don't even notice she's crippled any more.

Amanda: Don't say crippled! You know that I never allow that word to be used!

Tom: But face facts, Mother. She is and — that's not all —

Amanda: What do you mean "not all"?

Tom: Laura is very different from other girls.

Amanda: I think the difference is all to her advantage.

Tom: Not quite all — in the eyes of others — strangers — she's terribly shy and lives in a world of her own and those things make her seem a little peculiar to people outside the house.

Amanda: Don't say peculiar.

Tom: Face the facts. She is.

(The Dance-hall Music Changes To A Tango That Has A Minor And Somewhat Ominous Tone.)

Amanda: In what way is she peculiar — may I ask?

Tom (gently): She lives in a world of her own — a world of — little glass ornaments, Mother. . . . *(Gets up. Amanda remains holding brush, looking at him, troubled.)* She plays old phonograph records and — that's about all — *(He glances at himself in the mirror and crosses to door.)*

Amanda (sharply): Where are you going?

Tom: I'm going to the movies. *(Out screen door.)*

Amanda: Not to the movies, every night to the movies! *(Follows quickly to screen door.)* I don't believe you always go to the movies! *(He is gone. Amanda looks worriedly after him for a moment. Then vitality and optimism return and she turns from the door. Crossing to portieres.)* Laura! Laura! *(Laura answers from kitchenette.)*

Laura: Yes, Mother.

Amanda: Let those dishes go and come in front! *(Laura appears with dish towel. Gaily.)* Laura, come here and make a wish on the moon!

Laura (entering): Moon — moon?

Amanda: A little silver slipper of a moon. Look over your left shoulder, Laura, and make a wish! *(Laura looks faintly puzzled as if called out of sleep. Amanda seizes her shoulders and turns her at an angle by the door.)* Now! Now, darling, *wish!*

Laura: What shall I wish for, Mother?

Amanda (her voice trembling and her eyes suddenly filling with tears): Happiness! Good Fortune!

The violin rises and the stage dims out.

SCENE VI

(Image: High-School Hero.)

Tom: And so the following evening I brought Jim home to dinner. I had known Jim slightly in high school. In high school Jim was a hero. He had tremendous Irish good nature and vitality with the scrubbed and polished look of white chinaware. He seemed to move in a continual spotlight. He was a star in basketball, captain of the debating club, president of the senior class and the glee club and he sang the male lead in the annual light operas. He was always running or bounding, never just walking. He seemed always at the point of defeating the law of gravity. He was shooting with such velocity through his adolescence that you would logically expect him to arrive at nothing short of the White House by the time he was thirty. But Jim apparently ran into more interference after his graduation from Soldan. His speed had definitely slowed. Six years after he left high school he was holding a job that wasn't much better than mine.

(Image: Clerk.)

He was the only one at the warehouse with whom I was on friendly terms. I was valuable to him as someone who could remember his former glory, who had seen him win basketball games and the silver cup in debating. He knew of my secret practice of retiring to a cabinet of the washroom to work on poems when business was slack in the warehouse. He called me Shakespeare. And while the other boys in the warehouse regarded me with suspicious hostility, Jim took a humorous attitude toward me. Gradually his attitude affected the others, their hostility wore off and they also began to smile at me as people smile at an oddly fashioned dog who trots across their path at some distance.

I knew that Jim and Laura had known each other at Soldan, and I had heard Laura speak admiringly of his voice. I didn't know if Jim remembered her or not. In high school Laura had been as unobtrusive as Jim had been astonishing. If he did remember Laura, it was not as my sister, for when I asked him to dinner, he grinned and said, "You know, Shakespeare, I never thought of you as having folks!"

He was about to discover that I did. . . .

(Light Up Stage.)

(Legend On Screen: "The Accent Of A Coming Foot.")

Friday evening. It is about five o'clock of a late spring evening which comes "scattering poems in the sky."

A delicate lemony light is in the Wingfield apartment.

Amanda has worked like a Turk in preparation for the gentleman caller. The results are astonishing. The new floor lamp with its rose-silk shade is in place, a colored paper lantern conceals the broken light fixture in the ceiling, new billowing white curtains are at the windows, chintz covers are on chairs and sofa, a pair of new sofa pillows make their initial appearance.

Open boxes and tissue paper are scattered on the floor.

Laura stands in the middle with lifted arms while Amanda crouches before her, adjusting the hem of the new dress, devout and ritualistic. The dress is colored and designed by memory. The arrangement of Laura's hair is changed; it is softer and more becoming. A fragile, unearthly prettiness has come out in Laura: she is like a piece of translucent glass touched by light, given a momentary radiance, not actual, not lasting.

Amanda (impatiently): Why are you trembling?

Laura: Mother, you've made me so nervous!

Amanda: How have I made you nervous?

Laura: By all this fuss! You make it seem so important!

Amanda: I don't understand you, Laura. You couldn't be satisfied with just sitting home, and yet whenever I try to arrange something for you, you seem to resist it. *(She gets up.)* Now take a look at yourself. No, wait! Wait just a moment — I have an idea!

Laura: What is it now?

Amanda produces two powder puffs which she wraps in handkerchiefs and stuffs in Laura's bosom.

Laura: Mother, what are you doing?

Amanda: They call them "Gay Deceivers"!

Laura: I won't wear them!

Amanda: You will!

Laura: Why should I?

Amanda: Because, to be painfully honest, your chest is flat.

Laura: You make it seem like we were setting a trap.

Amanda: All pretty girls are a trap, a pretty trap, and men expect them to be.
(Legend: "A Pretty Trap.") Now look at yourself, young lady. This is the prettiest you will ever be! I've got to fix myself now! You're going to be surprised by your mother's appearance! *(She crosses through portieres, humming gaily.)*

Laura moves slowly to the long mirror and stares solemnly at herself.

A wind blows the white curtains inward in a slow, graceful motion and with a faint, sorrowful sighing.

Amanda (offstage): It isn't dark enough yet. *(She turns slowly before the mirror with a troubled look.)*

(Legend On Screen: "This Is My Sister: Celebrate Her With Strings!" Music.)

Amanda (laughing, off): I'm going to show you something. I'm going to make a spectacular appearance!

Laura: What is it, Mother?

Amanda: Possess your soul in patience — you will see! Something I've resurrected from that old trunk! Styles haven't changed so terribly much after all. . . . *(She parts the portieres.)* Now just look at your mother! *(She wears a girlish frock of yellowed voile with a blue silk sash. She carries a bunch of jonquils — the legend of her youth is nearly revived. Feverishly.)* This is the dress in which I led the cotillion. Won the cakewalk twice at Sunset Hill, wore one spring to the Governor's ball in Jackson! See how I sashayed around the ballroom, Laura? *(She raises her skirt and does a mincing step around the room.)* I wore it on Sundays for my gentlemen callers! I had it on the day I met your father — I had malaria fever all that spring. The change of climate from East Tennessee to the Delta — weakened resistance — I had a little temperature all the time — not enough to be serious — just enough to make me restless and giddy! Invitations poured in — parties all over the Delta! — "Stay in bed," said Mother, "you have fever!" — but I just wouldn't. — I took quinine but kept on going, going! — Evenings, dances! — Afternoons, long, long rides! Picnics — lovely! — So lovely, that country in May. — All lacy with dogwood, literally flooded with jonquils! — That was the spring I had the craze for jonquils. Jonquils became an absolute obsession. Mother said, "Honey, there's no more room for jonquils." And still I kept bringing in more jonquils. Whenever, wherever I saw them, I'd say, "Stop! Stop! I see jonquils!" I made the young men help me gather the jonquils! It was a joke, Amanda and her jonquils! Finally there were no more vases to hold them, every available space was filled with jonquils. No vases to hold them? All right, I'll hold them myself! And then I — *(She stops in front of the picture.)* **(Music)** met your father! Malaria fever and jonquils and then — this — boy. . . . *(She switches on the rose-colored lamp.)* I hope they get here before it starts to rain. *(She crosses upstage and places the jonquils in bowl on table.)* I gave your brother a little extra change so he and Mr. O'Connor could take the service car home.

Laura (with altered look): What did you say his name was?
Amanda: O'Connor.
Laura: What is his first name?
Amanda: I don't remember. Oh, yes, I do. It was — Jim!

Laura sways slightly and catches hold of a chair.

(Legend On Screen: "Not Jim!")

Laura (faintly): Not — Jim!
Amanda: Yes, that was it, it was Jim! I've never known a Jim that wasn't nice!

(Music: Ominous.)

Laura: Are you sure his name is Jim O'Connor?
Amanda: Yes. Why?
Laura: Is he the one that Tom used to know in high school?
Amanda: He didn't say so. I think he just got to know him at the warehouse.
Laura: There was a Jim O'Connor we both knew in high school — *(Then, with effort.)* If that is the one that Tom is bringing to dinner — you'll have to excuse me, I won't come to the table.
Amanda: What sort of nonsense is this?
Laura: You asked me once if I'd ever liked a boy. Don't you remember I showed you this boy's picture?
Amanda: You mean the boy you showed me in the year book?

Laura: Yes, that boy.

Amanda: Laura, Laura, were you in love with that boy?

Laura: I don't know, Mother. All I know is I couldn't sit at the table if it was him!

Amanda: It won't be him! It isn't the least bit likely. But whether it is or not, you will come to the table. You will not be excused.

Laura: I'll have to be, Mother.

Amanda: I don't intend to humor your silliness, Laura. I've had too much from you and your brother, both! So just sit down and compose yourself till they come. Tom has forgotten his key so you'll have to let them in, when they arrive.

Laura (panicky): Oh, Mother — *you* answer the door!

Amanda (lightly): I'll be in the kitchen — busy!

Laura: Oh, Mother, please answer the door, don't make me do it!

Amanda (crossing into kitchenette): I've got to fix the dressing for the salmon. Fuss, fuss — silliness! — over a gentleman caller!

Door swings shut. Laura is left alone.

(Legend: "Terror!")

She utters a low moan and turns off the lamp — sits stiffly on the edge of the sofa, knotting her fingers together.

(Legend On Screen: "The Opening Of A Door!")

Tom and Jim appear on the fire-escape steps and climb to landing. Hearing their approach, Laura rises with a panicky gesture. She retreats to the portieres.

    The doorbell. Laura catches her breath and touches her throat. Low drums.

Amanda (calling): Laura, sweetheart! The door!

Laura stares at it without moving.

Jim: I think we just beat the rain.

Tom: Uh-huh. *(He rings again, nervously. Jim whistles and fishes for a cigarette.)*

Amanda (very, very gaily): Laura, that is your brother and Mr. O'Connor! Will you let them in, darling?

Laura crosses toward kitchenette door.

Laura (breathlessly): Mother — you go to the door!

Amanda steps out of kitchenette and stares furiously at Laura. She points imperiously at the door.

Laura: Please, please!

Amanda (in a fierce whisper): What is the matter with you, you silly thing?

Laura (desperately): Please, you answer it, *please!*

Amanda: I told you I wasn't going to humor you, Laura. Why have you chosen this moment to lose your mind?

Laura: Please, please, please, you go!

Amanda: You'll have to go to the door because I can't!

Laura (despairingly): I can't either!

Amanda: Why?

Laura: I'm *sick!*

Amanda: I'm sick, too — of your nonsense! Why can't you and your brother be normal people? Fantastic whims and behavior! *(Tom gives a long ring.)* Preposterous goings on! Can you give me one reason — *(Calls out lyrically.)* COMING! JUST ONE SECOND! — why should you be afraid to open a door? Now you answer it, Laura!

Laura: Oh, oh, oh . . . *(She returns through the portieres. Darts to the victrola and winds it frantically and turns it on.)*

Amanda: Laura Wingfield, you march right to that door!

Laura: Yes — yes, Mother!

> *A faraway, scratchy rendition of "Dardanella" softens the air and gives her strength to move through it. She slips to the door and draws it cautiously open. Tom enters with the caller, Jim O'Connor.*

Tom: Laura, this is Jim. Jim, this is my sister, Laura.

Jim (stepping inside): I didn't know that Shakespeare had a sister!

Laura (retreating stiff and trembling from the door): How — how do you do?

Jim (heartily extending his hand): Okay!

> *Laura touches it hesitantly with hers.*

Jim: Your hand's *cold*, Laura!

Laura: Yes, well — I've been playing the victrola. . . .

Jim: Must have been playing classical music on it! You ought to play a little hot swing music to warm you up!

Laura: Excuse me — I haven't finished playing the victrola. . . .

> *She turns awkwardly and hurries into the front room. She pauses a second by the victrola. Then catches her breath and darts through the portieres like a frightened deer.*

Jim (grinning): What was the matter?

Tom: Oh — with Laura? Laura is — terribly shy.

Jim: Shy, huh? It's unusual to meet a shy girl nowadays. I don't believe you ever mentioned you had a sister.

Tom: Well, now you know. I have one. Here is the *Post Dispatch.* You want a piece of it?

Jim: Uh-huh.

Tom: What piece? The comics?

Jim: Sports! *(Glances at it.)* Ole Dizzy Dean is on his bad behavior.

Tom (disinterest): Yeah? *(Lights cigarette and crosses back to fire-escape door.)*

Jim: Where are *you* going?

Tom: I'm going out on the terrace.

Jim (goes after him): You know, Shakespeare — I'm going to sell you a bill of goods!

Tom: What goods?

Jim: A course I'm taking.

Tom: Huh?

Jim: In public speaking! You and me, we're not the warehouse type.

Tom: Thanks — that's good news. But what has public speaking got to do with it?

Jim: It fits you for — executive positions!

Tom: Awww.

Jim: I tell you it's done a helluva lot for me.

(Image: Executive At Desk.)

Tom: In what respect?

Jim: In every! Ask yourself what is the difference between you an' me and men in the office down front? Brains? — No! — Ability? — No! Then what? Just one little thing —

Tom: What is that one little thing?

Jim: Primarily it amounts to — social poise! Being able to square up to people and hold your own on any social level!

Amanda (offstage): Tom?

Tom: Yes, Mother?

Amanda: Is that you and Mr. O'Connor?

Tom: Yes, Mother.

Amanda: Well, you just make yourselves comfortable in there.

Tom: Yes, Mother.

Amanda: Ask Mr. O'Connor if he would like to wash his hands.

Jim: Aw — no — thank you — I took care of that at the warehouse. Tom —

Tom: Yes?

Jim: Mr. Mendoza was speaking to me about you.

Tom: Favorably?

Jim: What do you think?

Tom: Well —

Jim: You're going to be out of a job if you don't wake up.

Tom: I am waking up —

Jim: You show no signs.

Tom: The signs are interior.

(Image On Screen: The Sailing Vessel With Jolly Roger Again.)

Tom: I'm planning to change. *(He leans over the rail speaking with quiet exhilaration. The incandescent marquees and signs of the first-run movie houses light his face from across the alley. He looks like a voyager.)* I'm right at the point of committing myself to a future that doesn't include the warehouse and Mr. Mendoza or even a night-school course in public speaking.

Jim: What are you gassing about?

Tom: I'm tired of the movies.

Jim: Movies!

Tom: Yes, movies! Look at them — *(A wave toward the marvels of Grand Avenue.)* All of those glamorous people — having adventures — hogging it all, gobbling the whole thing up! You know what happens? People go to the *movies* instead of *moving!* Hollywood characters are supposed to have all the adventures for everybody in America, while everybody in America sits in a dark room and watches them have them! Yes, until there's a war. That's when adventure becomes available to the masses! *Everyone's* dish, not only Gable's! Then the people in the dark room come out of the dark room to have some adventures themselves — Goody, goody — It's our turn now, to go to the South Sea Island — to make a safari — to be exotic, far-off — But I'm not patient. I don't want to wait till then. I'm tired of the *movies* and I am *about* to *move!*

Jim (incredulously): Move?

Tom: Yes.

Jim: When?

Tom: Soon!

Jim: Where? Where?

Theme three music seems to answer the question, while Tom thinks it over. He searches among his pockets.

Tom: I'm starting to boil inside. I know I seem dreamy, but inside — well, I'm boiling! Whenever I pick up a shoe, I shudder a little thinking how short life is and what I am doing! — Whatever that means. I know it doesn't mean shoes — except as something to wear on a traveler's feet! *(Finds paper.)* Look —

Jim: What?

Tom: I'm a member.

Jim (reading): The Union of Merchant Seamen.

Tom: I paid my dues this month, instead of the light bill.

Jim: You will regret it when they turn the lights off.

Tom: I won't be here.

Jim: How about your mother?

Tom: I'm like my father. The bastard son of a bastard! See how he grins? And he's been absent going on sixteen years!

Jim: You're just talking, you drip. How does your mother feel about it?

Tom: Shhh — Here comes Mother! Mother is not acquainted with my plans!

Amanda (enters portieres): Where are you all?

Tom: On the terrace, Mother.

They start inside. She advances to them. Tom is distinctly shocked at her appearance. Even Jim blinks a little. He is making his first contact with girlish Southern vivacity and in spite of the night-school course in public speaking is somewhat thrown off the beam by the unexpected outlay of social charm.

Certain responses are attempted by Jim but are swept aside by Amanda's gay laughter and chatter. Tom is embarrassed but after the first shock Jim reacts very warmly. Grins and chuckles, is altogether won over.

(Image: Amanda As A Girl.)

Amanda (coyly smiling, shaking her girlish ringlets): Well, well, well, so this is Mr. O'Connor. Introductions entirely unnecessary. I've heard so much about you from my boy. I finally said to him, Tom — good gracious! — why don't you bring this paragon to supper? I'd like to meet this nice young man at the warehouse! — Instead of just hearing him sing your praises so much! I don't know why my son is so stand-offish — that's not Southern behavior! Let's sit down and — I think we could stand a little more air in here! Tom, leave the door open. I felt a nice fresh breeze a moment ago. Where has it gone? Mmm, so warm already! And not quite summer, even. We're going to burn up when summer really gets started. However, we're having — we're having a very light supper. I think light things are better fo' this time of year. The same as light clothes are. Light clothes an' light food are what warm weather calls fo'. You know our blood gets so thick during th' winter — it takes a while fo' us to *adjust* ou'selves! — when the season changes . . . It's come so quick this year. I wasn't prepared. All of a sudden — heavens! Already summer! — I ran to the trunk an' pulled out this light dress — Terribly old! Historical almost! But feels so good — so good an' co-ol, y'know. . . .

Tom: Mother —

Amanda: Yes, honey?

Tom: How about — supper?

Amanda: Honey, you go ask Sister if supper is ready! You know that Sister is in full charge of supper! Tell her you hungry boys are waiting for it. *(To Jim.)* Have you met Laura?

Jim: She —

Amanda: Let you in? Oh, good, you've met already! It's rare for a girl as sweet an' pretty as Laura to be domestic! But Laura is, thank heavens, not only pretty but also very domestic. I'm not at all. I never was a bit. I never could make a thing but angel-food cake. Well, in the South we had so many servants. Gone, gone, gone. All vestiges of gracious living! Gone completely! I wasn't prepared for what the future brought me. All of my gentlemen callers were sons of planters and so of course I assumed that I would be married to one and raise my family on a large piece of land with plenty of servants. But man proposes — and woman accepts the proposal! — To vary that old, old saying a little bit — I married no planter! I married a man who worked for the telephone company! — that gallantly smiling gentleman over there! *(Points to the picture.)* A telephone man who — fell in love with long-distance! — Now he travels and I don't even know where! — But what am I going on for about my — tribulations? Tell me yours — I hope you don't have any! Tom?

Tom (returning): Yes, Mother?

Amanda: Is supper nearly ready?

Tom: It looks to me like supper is on the table.

Amanda: Let me look — *(She rises prettily and looks through portieres.)* Oh, lovely — But where is Sister?

Tom: Laura is not feeling well and she says that she thinks she'd better not come to the table.

Amanda: What? — Nonsense! — Laura? Oh, Laura!

Laura (offstage, faintly): Yes, Mother.

Amanda: You really must come to the table. We won't be seated until you come to the table! Come in, Mr. O'Connor. You sit over there and I'll — Laura? Laura Wingfield! You're keeping us waiting, honey! We can't say grace until you come to the table!

The back door is pushed weakly open and Laura comes in. She is obviously quite faint, her lips trembling, her eyes wide and staring. She moves unsteadily toward the table.

(Legend: "Terror!")

Outside a summer storm is coming abruptly. The white curtains billow inward at the windows and there is a sorrowful murmur and deep blue dusk.
Laura suddenly stumbles — She catches at a chair with a faint moan.

Tom: Laura!
Amanda: Laura! *(There is a clap of thunder.)* **(Legend: "Ah!")** *(Despairingly.)* Why, Laura, you *are* sick, darling! Tom, help your sister into the living room, dear! Sit in the living room, Laura — rest on the sofa. Well! *(To the gentleman caller.)* Standing over the hot stove made her ill! — I told her that it was just too warm this evening, but — *(Tom comes back in. Laura is on the sofa.)* Is Laura all right now?
Tom: Yes.
Amanda: What *is* that? Rain? A nice cool rain has come up! *(She gives the gentleman caller a frightened look.)* I think we may — have grace — now . . . *(Tom looks at her stupidly.)* Tom, honey — you say grace!
Tom: Oh . . . "For these and all thy mercies —" *(They bow their heads, Amanda stealing a nervous glance at Jim. In the living room Laura, stretched on the sofa, clenches her hand to her lips, to hold back a shuddering sob.)* God's Holy Name be praised —

(The Scene Dims Out.)

SCENE VII

(A Souvenir.)

Half an hour later. Dinner is just being finished in the upstage area which is concealed by the drawn portieres.
As the curtain rises Laura is still huddled upon the sofa, her feet drawn under her, her head resting on a pale blue pillow, her eyes wide and mysteriously watchful. The new floor lamp with its shade of rose-colored silk gives a soft, becoming light to her face, bringing out the fragile, unearthly prettiness which usually escapes attention. There is a steady murmur of rain, but it is slackening and stops soon after the scene begins; the air outside becomes pale and luminous as the moon breaks out.
A moment after the curtain rises, the lights in both rooms flicker and go out.

Jim: Hey, there, Mr. Light Bulb!

Amanda laughs nervously.

(Legend: "Suspension Of A Public Service.")

Amanda: Where was Moses when the lights went out? Ha-ha. Do you know the answer to that one, Mr. O'Connor?

Jim: No, Ma'am, what's the answer?

Amanda: In the dark! *(Jim laughs appreciatively.)* Everybody sit still. I'll light the candles. Isn't it lucky we have them on the table? Where's a match? Which of you gentlemen can provide a match?

Jim: Here.

Amanda: Thank you, sir.

Jim: Not at all, Ma'am!

Amanda: I guess the fuse has burnt out. Mr. O'Connor, can you tell a burnt-out fuse? I know I can't and Tom is a total loss when it comes to mechanics. **(Sound: Getting Up: Voices Recede A Little To Kitchenette.)** Oh, be careful you don't bump into something. We don't want our gentleman caller to break his neck. Now wouldn't that be a fine howdy-do?

Jim: Ha-ha! Where is the fuse-box?

Amanda: Right here next to the stove. Can you see anything?

Jim: Just a minute.

Amanda: Isn't electricity a mysterious thing? Wasn't it Benjamin Franklin who tied a key to a kite? We live in such a mysterious universe, don't we? Some people say that science clears up all the mysteries for us. In my opinion it only creates more! Have you found it yet?

Jim: No, Ma'am. All these fuses look okay to me.

Amanda: Tom!

Tom: Yes, Mother?

Amanda: That light bill I gave you several days ago. The one I told you we got the notices about?

Tom: Oh. — Yeah.

(Legend: "Ha!")

Amanda: You didn't neglect to pay it by any chance?

Tom: Why, I —

Amanda: Didn't! I might have known it!

Jim: Shakespeare probably wrote a poem on that light bill, Mrs. Wingfield.

Amanda: I might have known better than to trust him with it! There's such a high price for negligence in this world!

Jim: Maybe the poem will win a ten-dollar prize.

Amanda: We'll just have to spend the remainder of the evening in the nineteenth century, before Mr. Edison made the Mazda lamp!

Jim: Candlelight is my favorite kind of light.

Amanda: That shows you're romantic! But that's no excuse for Tom. Well, we got through dinner. Very considerate of them to let us get through dinner before they plunged us into everlasting darkness, wasn't it, Mr. O'Connor?

Jim: Ha-ha!

Amanda: Tom, as a penalty for your carelessness you can help me with the dishes.

Jim: Let me give you a hand.

Amanda: Indeed you will not!

Jim: I ought to be good for something.

Amanda: Good for something? *(Her tone is rhapsodic.)* You? Why, Mr. O'Connor, nobody, *nobody's* given me this much entertainment in years — as you have!

Jim: Aw, now, Mrs. Wingfield!

Amanda: I'm not exaggerating, not one bit! But Sister is all by her lonesome. You go keep her company in the parlor! I'll give you this lovely old candelabrum that used to be on the altar at the church of the Heavenly Rest. It was melted a little out of shape when the church burnt down. Lightning struck it one spring. Gypsy Jones was holding a revival at the time and he intimated that the church was destroyed because the Episcopalians gave card parties.

Jim: Ha-ha.

Amanda: And how about coaxing Sister to drink a little wine? I think it would be good for her! Can you carry both at once?

Jim: Sure. I'm Superman!

Amanda: Now, Thomas, get into this apron!

> *The door of kitchenette swings closed on Amanda's gay laughter; the flickering light approaches the portieres.*
>
> *Laura sits up nervously as he enters. Her speech at first is low and breathless from the almost intolerable strain of being alone with a stranger.*

(The Legend: "I Don't Suppose You Remember Me At All!")

> *In her first speeches in this scene, before Jim's warmth overcomes her paralyzing shyness, Laura's voice is thin and breathless as though she has run up a steep flight of stairs.*
>
> *Jim's attitude is gently humorous. In playing this scene it should be stressed that while the incident is apparently unimportant, it is to Laura the climax of her secret life.*

Jim: Hello, there, Laura.

Laura (faintly): Hello. *(She clears her throat.)*

Jim: How are you feeling now? Better?

Laura: Yes. Yes, thank you.

Jim: This is for you. A little dandelion wine. *(He extends it toward her with extravagant gallantry.)*

Laura: Thank you.

Jim: Drink it — but don't get drunk! *(He laughs heartily. Laura takes the glass uncertainly; laughs shyly.)* Where shall I set the candles?

Laura: Oh — oh, anywhere . . .

Jim: How about here on the floor? Any objections?

Laura: No.

Jim: I'll spread a newspaper under to catch the drippings. I like to sit on the floor. Mind if I do?

Laura: Oh, no.

Jim: Give me a pillow?

Laura: What?

Jim: A pillow!

Laura: Oh . . . *(Hands him one quickly.)*

Jim: How about you? Don't you like to sit on the floor?

Laura: Oh — yes.

Jim: Why don't you, then?

Laura: I — will.

Jim: Take a pillow! *(Laura does. Sits on the other side of the candelabrum. Jim crosses his legs and smiles engagingly at her.)* I can't hardly see you sitting way over there.

Laura: I can — see you.

Jim: I know, but that's not fair, I'm in the limelight. *(Laura moves her pillow closer.)* Good! Now I can see you! Comfortable?

Laura: Yes.

Jim: So am I. Comfortable as a cow. Will you have some gum?

Laura: No, thank you.

Jim: I think that I will indulge, with your permission. *(Musingly unwraps it and holds it up.)* Think of the fortune made by the guy that invented the first piece of chewing gum. Amazing, huh? The Wrigley Building is one of the sights of Chicago. — I saw it summer before last when I went up to the Century of Progress. Did you take in the Century of Progress?

Laura: No, I didn't.

Jim: Well, it was quite a wonderful exposition. What impressed me most was the Hall of Science. Gives you an idea of what the future will be in America, even more wonderful than the present time is! *(Pause. Smiling at her.)* Your brother tells me you're shy. Is that right, Laura?

Laura: I — don't know.

Jim: I judge you to be an old-fashioned type of girl. Well, I think that's a pretty good type to be. Hope you don't think I'm being too personal — do you?

Laura (hastily, out of embarrassment): I believe I *will* take a piece of gum, if you — don't mind. *(Clearing her throat.)* Mr. O'Connor, have you — kept up with your singing?

Jim: Singing? Me?

Laura: Yes. I remember what a beautiful voice you had.

Jim: When did you hear me sing?

(Voice Offstage In The Pause.)

Voice (offstage):
> O blow, ye winds, heigh-ho,
> A-roving I will go!
> I'm off to my love
> With a boxing glove —
> Ten thousand miles away!

Jim: You say you've heard me sing?

Laura: Oh, yes! Yes, very often . . . I — don't suppose you remember me — at all?

Jim (smiling doubtfully): You know I have an idea I've seen you before. I had that idea soon as you opened the door. It seemed almost like I was about to remember your name. But the name that I started to call you — wasn't a name! And so I stopped myself before I said it.

Laura: Wasn't it — Blue Roses?

Jim (springs up, grinning): Blue Roses! My gosh, yes — Blue Roses! That's what

I had on my tongue when you opened the door! Isn't it funny what tricks your memory plays? I didn't connect you with the high school somehow or other. But that's where it was; it was high school. I didn't even know you were Shakespeare's sister! Gosh, I'm sorry.

Laura: I didn't expect you to. You — barely knew me!

Jim: But we did have a speaking acquaintance, huh?

Laura: Yes, we — spoke to each other.

Jim: When did you recognize me?

Laura: Oh, right away!

Jim: Soon as I came in the door?

Laura: When I heard your name I thought it was probably you. I knew that Tom used to know you a little in high school. So when you came in the door — Well, then I was — sure.

Jim: Why didn't you *say* something, then?

Laura (breathlessly): I didn't know what to say, I was — too surprised!

Jim: For goodness' sakes! You know, this sure is funny!

Laura: Yes! Yes, isn't it, though . . .

Jim: Didn't we have a class in something together?

Laura: Yes, we did.

Jim: What class was that?

Laura: It was — singing — Chorus!

Jim: Aw!

Laura: I sat across the aisle from you in the Aud.

Jim: Aw.

Laura: Mondays, Wednesdays and Fridays.

Jim: Now I remember — you always came in late.

Laura: Yes, it was so hard for me, getting upstairs. I had that brace on my leg — it clumped so loud!

Jim: I never heard any clumping.

Laura (wincing at the recollection): To me it sounded like — thunder!

Jim: Well, well, well. I never even noticed.

Laura: And everybody was seated before I came in. I had to walk in front of all those people. My seat was in the back row. I had to go clumping all the way up the aisle with everyone watching!

Jim: You shouldn't have been self-conscious.

Laura: I know, but I was. It was always such a relief when the singing started.

Jim: Aw, yes, I've placed you now! I used to call you Blue Roses. How was it that I got started calling you that?

Laura: I was out of school a little while with pleurosis. When I came back you asked me what was the matter. I said I had pleurosis — you thought I said Blue Roses. That's what you always called me after that!

Jim: I hope you didn't mind.

Laura: Oh, no — I liked it. You see, I wasn't acquainted with many — people. . . .

Jim: As I remember you sort of stuck by yourself.

Laura: I — I — never had much luck at — making friends.

Jim: I don't see why you wouldn't.

Laura: Well, I — started out badly.

Jim: You mean being —

Laura: Yes, it sort of — stood between me —

Jim: You shouldn't have let it!

Laura: I know, but it did, and —

Jim: You were shy with people!

Laura: I tried not to be but never could —

Jim: Overcome it?

Laura: No, I — I never could!

Jim: I guess being shy is something you have to work out of kind of gradually.

Laura (sorrowfully): Yes — I guess it —

Jim: Takes time!

Laura: Yes —

Jim: People are not so dreadful when you know them. That's what you have to remember! And everybody has problems, not just you, but practically everybody has got some problems. You think of yourself as having the only problems, as being the only one who is disappointed. But just look around you and you will see lots of people as disappointed as you are. For instance, I hoped when I was going to high school that I would be further along at this time, six years later, than I am now — You remember that wonderful write-up I had in *The Torch?*

Laura: Yes! *(She rises and crosses to table.)*

Jim: It said I was bound to succeed in anything I went into! *(Laura returns with the annual.)* Holy Jeez! *The Torch! (He accepts it reverently. They smile across it with mutual wonder. Laura crouches beside him and they begin to turn through it. Laura's shyness is dissolving in his warmth.)*

Laura: Here you are in *Pirates of Penzance!*

Jim (wistfully): I sang the baritone lead in that operetta.

Laura (rapidly): So — *beautifully!*

Jim (protesting): Aw —

Laura: Yes, yes — beautifully — beautifully!

Jim: You heard me?

Laura: All three times!

Jim: No!

Laura: Yes!

Jim: All three performances?

Laura (looking down): Yes.

Jim: Why?

Laura: I — wanted to ask you to — autograph my program.

Jim: Why didn't you ask me to?

Laura: You were always surrounded by your own friends so much that I never had a chance to.

Jim: You should have just —

Laura: Well, I — thought you might think I was —

Jim: Thought I might think you was — what?

Laura: Oh —

Jim (with reflective relish): I was beleaguered by females in those days.

Laura: You were terribly popular!

Jim: Yeah —

Laura: You had such a — friendly way —

Jim: I was spoiled in high school.

Laura: Everybody — liked you!

Jim: Including you?

Laura: I — yes, I — I did, too — *(She gently closes the book in her lap.)*

Jim: Well, well, well! — Give me that program, Laura. *(She hands it to him. He signs it with a flourish.)* There you are — better late than never!

Laura: Oh, I — what a — surprise!

Jim: My signature isn't worth very much right now. But some day — maybe — it will increase in value! Being disappointed is one thing and being discouraged is something else. I am disappointed but I'm not discouraged. I'm twenty-three years old. How old are you?

Laura: I'll be twenty-four in June.

Jim: That's not old age!

Laura: No, but —

Jim: You finished high school?

Laura (with difficulty): I didn't go back.

Jim: You mean you dropped out?

Laura: I made bad grades in my final examinations. *(She rises and replaces the book and the program. Her voice strained.)* How is — Emily Meisenbach getting along?

Jim: Oh, that kraut-head!

Laura: Why do you call her that?

Jim: That's what she was.

Laura: You're not still — going with her?

Jim: I never see her.

Laura: It said in the Personal Section that you were — engaged!

Jim: I know, but I wasn't impressed by that — propaganda!

Laura: It wasn't — the truth?

Jim: Only in Emily's optimistic opinion!

Laura: Oh —

(Legend: "What Have You Done Since High School?")

Jim lights a cigarette and leans indolently back on his elbows smiling at Laura with a warmth and charm which light her inwardly with altar candles. She remains by the table and turns in her hands a piece of glass to cover her tumult.

Jim (after several reflective puffs on a cigarette): What have you done since high school? *(She seems not to hear him.)* Huh? *(Laura looks up.)* I said what have you done since high school, Laura?

Laura: Nothing much.

Jim: You must have been doing something these six long years.

Laura: Yes.

Jim: Well, then, such as what?

Laura: I took a business course at business college —

Jim: How did that work out?

Laura: Well, not very — well — I had to drop out, it gave me — indigestion —

Jim laughs gently.

Jim: What are you doing now?

Laura: I don't do anything — much. Oh, please don't think I sit around doing nothing! My glass collection takes up a good deal of my time. Glass is something you have to take good care of.

Jim: What did you say — about glass?

Laura: Collection I said — I have one — *(She clears her throat and turns away again, acutely shy).*

Jim (abruptly): You know what I judge to be the trouble with you? Inferiority complex! Know what that is? That's what they call it when someone low-rates himself! I understand it because I had it, too. Although my case was not so aggravated as yours seems to be. I had it until I took up public speaking, developed my voice, and learned that I had an aptitude for science. Before that time I never thought of myself as being outstanding in any way whatsoever! Now I've never made a regular study of it, but I have a friend who says I can analyze people better than doctors that make a profession of it. I don't claim that to be necessarily true, but I can sure guess a person's psychology, Laura! *(Takes out his gum.)* Excuse me, Laura. I always take it out when the flavor is gone. I'll use this scrap of paper to wrap it in. I know how it is to get it stuck on a shoe. Yep — that's what I judge to be your principal trouble. A lack of confidence in yourself as a person. You don't have the proper amount of faith in yourself. I'm basing that fact on a number of your remarks and also on certain observations I've made. For instance that clumping you thought was so awful in high school. You say that you even dreaded to walk into class. You see what you did? You dropped out of school, you gave up an education because of a clump, which as far as I know was practically non-existent! A little physical defect is what you have. Hardly noticeable even! Magnified thousands of times by imagination! You know what my strong advice to you is? Think of yourself as *superior* in some way!

Laura: In what way would I think?

Jim: Why, man alive, Laura! Just look about you a little. What do you see? A world full of common people! All of 'em born and all of 'em going to die! Which of them has one-tenth of your good points! Or mine! Or anyone else's, as far as that goes — Gosh! Everybody excels in some one thing. Some in many! *(Unconsciously glances at himself in the mirror.)* All you've got to do is discover in *what!* Take me, for instance. *(He adjusts his tie at the mirror.)* My interest happens to lie in electro-dynamics. I'm taking a course in radio engineering at night school, Laura, on top of a fairly responsible job at the warehouse. I'm taking that course and studying public speaking.

Laura: Ohhhh.

Jim: Because I believe in the future of television! *(Turning back to her.)* I wish to be ready to go up right along with it. Therefore I'm planning to get in on the ground floor. In fact, I've already made the right connections and all that remains is for the industry itself to get under way! Full steam — *(His eyes are starry.)* Knowledge — Zzzzzp! *Money* — Zzzzzzp! — *Power!* That's the cycle democracy is built on! *(His attitude is convincingly dynamic. Laura stares at him, even her shyness eclipsed in her absolute wonder. He suddenly grins.)* I guess you think I think a lot of myself!

Laura: No — o-o-o, I —

Jim: Now how about you? Isn't there something you take more interest in than anything else?

Laura: Well, I do — as I said — have my — glass collection —

A peal of girlish laughter from the kitchen.

Jim: I'm not right sure I know what you're talking about. What kind of glass is it?

Laura: Little articles of it, they're ornaments mostly! Most of them are little animals made out of glass, the tiniest little animals in the world. Mother calls them a glass menagerie! Here's an example of one, if you'd like to see it! This one is one of the oldest. It's nearly thirteen. *(He stretches out his hand.)* **(Music: "The Glass Menagerie.")** Oh, be careful — if you breathe, it breaks!

Jim: I'd better not take it. I'm pretty clumsy with things.

Laura: Go on, I trust you with him! *(Places it in his palm.)* There now — you're holding him gently! Hold him over the light, he loves the light! You see how the light shines through him?

Jim: It sure does shine!

Laura: I shouldn't be partial, but he is my favorite one.

Jim: What kind of a thing is this one supposed to be?

Laura: Haven't you noticed the single horn on his forehead?

Jim: A unicorn, huh?

Laura: Mmm-hmmm!

Jim: Unicorns, aren't they extinct in the modern world?

Laura: I know!

Jim: Poor little fellow, he must feel sort of lonesome.

Laura (smiling): Well, if he does he doesn't complain about it. He stays on a shelf with some horses that don't have horns and all of them seem to get along nicely together.

Jim: How do you know?

Laura (lightly): I haven't heard any arguments among them!

Jim (grinning): No arguments, huh? Well, that's a pretty good sign! Where shall I set him?

Laura: Put him on the table. They all like a change of scenery once in a while!

Jim (stretching): Well, well, well, well — Look how big my shadow is when I stretch!

Laura: Oh, oh, yes — it stretches across the ceiling!

Jim (crossing to door): I think it's stopped raining. *(Opens fire-escape door.)* Where does the music come from?

Laura: From the Paradise Dance Hall across the alley.

Jim: How about cutting the rug a little, Miss Wingfield?

Laura: Oh, I —

Jim: Or is your program filled up? Let me have a look at it. *(Grasps imaginary card.)* Why, every dance is taken! I'll just have to scratch some out. **(Waltz Music: "La Golondrina.")** Ahhh, a waltz! *(He executes some sweeping turns by himself, then holds his arms toward Laura.)*

Laura (breathlessly): I — can't dance!

Jim: There you go, that inferiority stuff!

Laura: I've never danced in my life!

Jim: Come on, try!

Laura: Oh, but I'd step on you!

Jim: I'm not made out of glass.

Laura: How — how — how do we start?

Jim: Just leave it to me. You hold your arms out a little.

Laura: Like this?

Jim: A little bit higher. Right. Now don't tighten up, that's the main thing about it — relax.

Laura (laughing breathlessly): It's hard not to.

Jim: Okay.

Laura: I'm afraid you can't budge me.

Jim: What do you bet I can't? *(He swings her into motion.)*

Laura: Goodness, yes, you can!

Jim: Let yourself go, now, Laura, just let yourself go.

Laura: I'm —

Jim: Come on!

Laura: Trying!

Jim: Not so stiff — Easy does it!

Laura: I know but I'm —

Jim: Loosen th' backbone! There now, that's a lot better.

Laura: Am I?

Jim: Lots, lots better! *(He moves her about the room in a clumsy waltz.)*

Laura: Oh, my!

Jim: Ha-ha!

Laura: Goodness, yes you can!

Jim: Ha-ha-ha! *(They suddenly bump into the table, Jim stops.)* What did we hit on?

Laura: Table.

Jim: Did something fall off it? I think —

Laura: Yes.

Jim: I hope that it wasn't the little glass horse with the horn!

Laura: Yes.

Jim: Aw, aw, aw. Is it broken?

Laura: Now it is just like all the other horses.

Jim: It's lost its —

Laura: Horn! It doesn't matter. Maybe it's a blessing in disguise.

Jim: You'll never forgive me. I bet that that was your favorite piece of glass.

Laura: I don't have favorites much. It's no tragedy, Freckles. Glass breaks so easily. No matter how careful you are. The traffic jars the shelves and things fall off them.

Jim: Still I'm awfully sorry that I was the cause.

Laura (smiling): I'll just imagine he had an operation. The horn was removed to make him feel less — freakish! *(They both laugh.)* Now he will feel more at home with the other horses, the ones that don't have horns . . .

Jim: Ha-ha, that's very funny! *(Suddenly serious.)* I'm glad to see that you have a sense of humor. You know — you're — well — very different! Surprisingly different from anyone else I know! *(His voice becomes soft and hesitant with a genuine feeling.)* Do you mind me telling you that? *(Laura is abashed beyond speech.)* You make me feel sort of — I don't know how to put it! I'm usually pretty good at expressing things, but — This is something that I don't know how to say! *(Laura touches her throat and clears it — turns the broken unicorn in her hands.)* *(Even softer.)* Has anyone ever told you that you were pretty? **(Pause: Music.)** *(Laura looks up slowly, with wonder, and shakes her head.)* Well, you are! In a very different way from anyone else. And all the nicer because of the difference, too. *(His voice becomes low and husky. Laura turns away, nearly faint with the novelty of her emotions.)* I wish you were my sister. I'd teach you to have some confidence in yourself. The different people are not like other people, but being different is nothing to be ashamed of. Because other people are not such wonderful people. They're one hundred times one thousand. You're one times one! They walk all over the earth. You just stay here. They're common as — weeds, but — you — well, you're — *Blue Roses!*

(Image On Screen: Blue Roses.)

(Music Changes.)

Laura: But blue is wrong for — roses . . .
Jim: It's right for you — You're — pretty!
Laura: In what respect am I pretty?
Jim: In all respects — believe me! Your eyes — your hair — are pretty! Your hands are pretty! *(He catches hold of her hand.)* You think I'm making this up because I'm invited to dinner and have to be nice. Oh, I could do that! I could put on an act for you, Laura, and say lots of things without being very sincere. But this time I am. I'm talking to you sincerely. I happened to notice you had this inferiority complex that keeps you from feeling comfortable with people. Somebody needs to build your confidence up and make you proud instead of shy and turning away and — blushing — Somebody ought to — ought to — *kiss* you, Laura! *(His hand slips slowly up her arm to her shoulder.)* **(Music Swells Tumultuously.)** *(He suddenly turns her about and kisses her on the lips. When he releases her Laura sinks on the sofa with a bright, dazed look. Jim backs away and fishes in his pocket for a cigarette.)* **(Legend On Screen: "Souvenir.")** Stumble-john! *(He lights the cigarette, avoiding her look. There is a peal of girlish laughter from Amanda in the kitchen. Laura slowly raises and opens her hand. It still contains the little broken glass animal. She looks at it with a tender, bewildered expression.)* Stumble-john! I shouldn't have done that — That was way off the beam. You don't smoke, do you? *(She looks up, smiling, not hearing the question. He sits beside her a little gingerly. She looks at him speechlessly — waiting. He coughs decorously and moves a little farther aside as he considers the situation and senses her feelings, dimly, with perturbation. Gently.)* Would you — care for a — mint? *(She doesn't seem to hear him but her look grows brighter even.)* Peppermint — Life Saver? My pocket's a regular drug store — wherever I go . . . *(He pops a mint in his mouth. Then gulps and decides to make a clean breast of it. He speaks slowly and gingerly.)* Laura, you know, if I had a sister like you, I'd do the same thing as Tom, I'd bring out fellows — introduce her to them. The right type of boys of a type to — appreciate her. Only — well — he made a mistake about me. Maybe I've got no call to be saying this. That may not have been the idea in having me over. But what if it was? There's nothing wrong about that. The only trouble is that in my case — I'm not in a situation to — do the right thing. I can't take down your number and say I'll phone. I can't call up next week and — ask for a date. I thought I had better explain the situation in case you misunderstood it and — hurt your feel-

ings. . . . *(Pause. Slowly, very slowly, Laura's look changes, her eyes returning slowly from his to the ornament in her palm.)*

Amanda utters another gay laugh in the kitchen.

Laura *(faintly):* You — won't — call again?
Jim: No, Laura, I can't. *(He rises from the sofa.)* As I was just explaining, I've — got strings on me, Laura, I've — been going steady! I go out all the time with a girl named Betty. She's a home-girl like you, and Catholic, and Irish, and in a great many ways we — get along fine. I met her last summer on a moonlight boat trip up the river to Alton, on the *Majestic.* Well — right away from the start it was — love! **(Legend: Love!)** *(Laura sways slightly forward and grips the arm of the sofa. He fails to notice, now enrapt in his own comfortable being.)* Being in love has made a new man of me! *(Leaning stiffly forward, clutching the arm of the sofa, Laura struggles visibly with her storm. But Jim is oblivious, she is a long way off.)* The power of love is really pretty tremendous! Love is something that — changes the whole world, Laura! *(The storm abates a little and Laura leans back. He notices her again.)* It happened that Betty's aunt took sick, she got a wire and had to go to Centralia. So Tom — when he asked me to dinner — I naturally just accepted the invitation, not knowing that you — that he — that I — *(He stops awkwardly.)* Huh — I'm a stumble-john! *(He flops back on the sofa. The holy candles in the altar of Laura's face have been snuffed out! There is a look of almost infinite desolation. Jim glances at her uneasily.)* I wish that you would — say something. *(She bites her lip which was trembling and then bravely smiles. She opens her hand again on the broken glass ornament. Then she gently takes his hand and raises it level with her own. She carefully places the unicorn in the palm of his hand, then pushes his fingers closed upon it.)* What are you — doing that for? You want me to have him? — Laura? *(She nods.)* What for?
Laura: A — souvenir . . .

She rises unsteadily and crouches beside the victrola to wind it up.

(Legend On Screen: "Things Have A Way Of Turning Out So Badly.")

(Or Image: "Gentleman Caller Waving Good-bye! — Gaily.")

At this moment Amanda rushes brightly back in the front room. She bears a pitcher of fruit punch in an old-fashioned cut-glass pitcher and a plate of macaroons. The plate has a gold border and poppies painted on it.

Amanda: Well, well, well! Isn't the air delightful after the shower? I've made you children a little liquid refreshment. *(Turns gaily to the gentleman caller.)* Jim, do you know that song about lemonade?

> "Lemonade, lemonade
> Made in the shade and stirred with a spade —
> Good enough for any old maid!"

Jim *(uneasily):* Ha-ha! No — I never heard it.
Amanda: Why, Laura! You look so serious!
Jim: We were having a serious conversation.

Amanda: Good! Now you're better acquainted!

Jim (uncertainly): Ha-ha! Yes.

Amanda: You modern young people are much more serious-minded than my generation. I was so gay as a girl!

Jim: You haven't changed, Mrs. Wingfield.

Amanda: Tonight I'm rejuvenated! The gaiety of the occasion, Mr. O'Connor! *(She tosses her head with a peal of laughter. Spills lemonade.)* Oooo! I'm baptizing myself!

Jim: Here — let me —

Amanda (setting the pitcher down): There now. I discovered we had some maraschino cherries. I dumped them in, juice and all!

Jim: You shouldn't have gone to that trouble. Mrs. Wingfield.

Amanda: Trouble, trouble? Why it was loads of fun! Didn't you hear me cutting up in the kitchen? I bet your ears were burning! I told Tom how outdone with him I was for keeping you to himself so long a time! He should have brought you over much, much sooner! Well, now that you've found your way, I want you to be a very frequent caller! Not just occasional but all the time. Oh, we're going to have a lot of gay times together! I see them coming! Mmm, just breathe that air! So fresh, and the moon's so pretty! I'll skip back out — I know where my place is when young folks are having a — serious conversation!

Jim: Oh, don't go out, Mrs. Wingfield. The fact of the matter is I've got to be going.

Amanda: Going, now? You're joking! Why, it's only the shank of the evening, Mr. O'Connor!

Jim: Well, you know how it is.

Amanda: You mean you're a young workingman and have to keep working-men's hours. We'll let you off early tonight. But only on the condition that next time you stay later. What's the best night for you? Isn't Saturday night the best night for you workingmen?

Jim: I have a couple of time-clocks to punch, Mrs. Wingfield. One at morning, another one at night!

Amanda: My, but you *are* ambitious! You work at night, too?

Jim: No, Ma'am, not work but — Betty! *(He crosses deliberately to pick up his hat. The band at the Paradise Dance Hall goes into a tender waltz.)*

Amanda: Betty? Betty? Who's — Betty! *(There is an ominous cracking sound in the sky.)*

Jim: Oh, just a girl. The girl I go steady with! *(He smiles charmingly. The sky falls.)*

(Legend: "The Sky Falls.")

Amanda (a long-drawn exhalation): Ohhhh . . . Is it a serious romance, Mr. O'Connor?

Jim: We're going to be married the second Sunday in June.

Amanda: Ohhhh — how nice! Tom didn't mention that you were engaged to be married.

Jim: The cat's not out of the bag at the warehouse yet. You know how they are. They call you Romeo and stuff like that. *(He stops at the oval mirror to put on his hat. He carefully shapes the brim and the crown to give a discreetly dashing effect.)* It's been a wonderful evening, Mrs. Wingfield. I guess this is what they mean by Southern hospitality.

Amanda: It really wasn't anything at all.

Jim: I hope it don't seem like I'm rushing off. But I promised Betty I'd pick her up at the Wabash depot, an' by the time I get my jalopy down there her train'll be in. Some women are pretty upset if you keep 'em waiting.

Amanda: Yes, I know — The tyranny of women! *(Extends her hand.)* Goodbye, Mr. O'Connor. I wish you luck — and happiness — and success! All three of them, and so does Laura! — Don't you, Laura?

Laura: Yes!

Jim (taking her hand): Goodbye, Laura. I'm certainly going to treasure that souvenir. And don't you forget the good advice I gave you. *(Raises his voice to a cheery shout.)* So long, Shakespeare! Thanks again, ladies — Good night!

He grins and ducks jauntily out.

> *Still bravely grimacing, Amanda closes the door on the gentleman caller. Then she turns back to the room with a puzzled expression. She and Laura don't dare to face each other. Laura crouches beside the victrola to wind it.*

Amanda (faintly): Things have a way of turning out so badly. I don't believe that I would play the victrola. Well, well — well — Our gentleman caller was engaged to be married! Tom!

Tom (from back): Yes, Mother?

Amanda: Come in here a minute. I want to tell you something awfully funny.

Tom (enters with macaroon and a glass of the lemonade): Has the gentleman caller gotten away already?

Amanda: The gentleman caller has made an early departure. What a wonderful joke you played on us!

Tom: How do you mean?

Amanda: You didn't mention that he was engaged to be married.

Tom: Jim? Engaged?

Amanda: That's what he just informed us.

Tom: I'll be jiggered! I didn't know about that.

Amanda: That seems very peculiar.

Tom: What's peculiar about it?

Amanda: Didn't you call him your best friend down at the warehouse?

Tom: He is, but how did I know?

Amanda: It seems extremely peculiar that you wouldn't know your best friend was going to be married!

Tom: The warehouse is where I work, not where I know things about people!

Amanda: You don't know things anywhere! You live in a dream; you manufacture illusions! *(He crosses to door.)* Where are you going?

Tom: I'm going to the movies.

Amanda: That's right, now that you've had us make such fools of ourselves. The effort, the preparations, all the expense! The new floor lamp, the rug, the clothes for Laura! All for what? To entertain some other girl's fiancé! Go to the movies, go! Don't think about us, a mother deserted, an unmarried sister who's crippled and has no job! Don't let anything interfere with your selfish pleasure! Just go, go, go — to the movies!

Tom: All right, I will! The more you shout about my selfishness to me the quicker I'll go, and I won't go to the movies!

Amanda: Go, then! Then go to the moon — you selfish dreamer!

Tom smashes his glass on the floor. He plunges out on the fire-escape, slamming the door. Laura screams — cut by door.

Dance-hall music up. Tom goes to the rail and grips it desperately, lifting his face in the chill white moonlight penetrating the narrow abyss of the alley.

(Legend On Screen: "And So Good-bye . . .")

Tom's closing speech is timed with the interior pantomime. The interior scene is played as though viewed through sound-proof glass. Amanda appears to be making a comforting speech to Laura who is huddled upon the sofa. Now that we cannot hear the mother's speech, her silliness is gone and she has dignity and tragic beauty. Laura's dark hair hides her face until at the end of the speech she lifts it to smile at her mother. Amanda's gestures are slow and graceful, almost dancelike, as she comforts the daughter. At the end of her speech she glances a moment at the father's picture — then withdraws through the portieres. At close of Tom's speech, Laura blows out the candles, ending the play.

Tom: I didn't go to the moon, I went much further — for time is the longest distance between two places — Not long after that I was fired for writing a poem on the lid of a shoe-box. I left Saint Louis. I descended the steps of this fire-escape for a last time and followed, from then on, in my father's footsteps, attempting to find in motion what was lost in space — I traveled around a great deal. The cities swept about me like dead leaves, leaves that were brightly colored but torn away from the branches. I would have stopped, but was pursued by something. It always came upon me unawares, taking me altogether by surprise. Perhaps it was a familiar bit of music. Perhaps it was only a piece of transparent glass. Perhaps I am walking along a street at night, in some strange city, before I have found companions. I pass the lighted window of a shop where perfume is sold. The window is filled with pieces of colored glass, tiny transparent bottles in delicate colors, like bits of a shattered rainbow. Then all at once my sister touches my shoulder. I turn around and look into her eyes . . . Oh, Laura, Laura, I tried to leave you behind me, but I am more faithful than I intended to be! I reach for a cigarette, I cross the street, I run into the movies or a bar, I buy a drink, I speak to the nearest stranger — anything that can blow your candles out! *(Laura bends over the candles.)* — for nowadays the world is lit by lightning! Blow out your candles, Laura — and so goodbye . . .

She blows the candles out.

(The Scene Dissolves.)

COMPARE:

The Glass Menagerie and Tennessee Williams's "How to Stage *The Glass Menagerie*," (page 1326).

Arthur Miller

DEATH OF A SALESMAN

1949

Certain Private Conversations in Two Acts and a Requiem

> *Arthur Miller, born in 1915 into a lower-income Jewish family in New York's Harlem, grew up in Brooklyn. He studied playwriting at the University of Michigan (class of '38), later wrote radio scripts, and in World War II worked as a steamfitter. When the New York Drama Critics named his* All My Sons *best play of 1947, Miller told an interviewer, "I don't see how you can write anything decent without using as your basis the question of right and wrong." (The play is about a guilty manufacturer of defective aircraft parts.)* Death of a Salesman *(1949) made Miller famous.* The Crucible *(1953), a dramatic indictment of the Salem witch trials, gained him further attention at a time when Senator Joseph McCarthy was conducting loyalty investigations. For a while (1956 – 61) Miller was the husband of actress Marilyn Monroe, whom the main character of his* All That Fall *(1964) resembles. Among Miller's other plays are* A View from the Bridge *(1955),* The Price *(1968),* The Creation of the World and Other Businesses *(1972), and* Playing for Time *(1980), a play for television. He has written two novels,* Focus *(1945), a study of antisemitism, and* The Misfits *(1960), which he made into a screenplay featuring Monroe. Recently, Miller has professed himself disenchanted with Broadway theater. In 1983 he directed an all-Chinese cast in a production of* Death of a Salesman *in Peking. The play was successfully revived in New York in 1983, and later on television, with Dustin Hoffman playing Willy Loman.*

The action takes place in Willy Loman's house and yard and in various places he visits in the New York and Boston of today.

Throughout the play, in the stage directions, left and right mean stage left and stage right.

ACT I

A melody is heard, played upon a flute. It is small and fine, telling of grass and trees and the horizon. The curtain rises.

Before us is the Salesman's house. We are aware of towering, angular shapes behind it, surrounding it on all sides. Only the blue light of the sky falls upon the house and forestage; the surrounding area shows an angry glow of orange. As more light appears, we see a solid vault of apartment houses around the small, fragile-seeming home. An air of the dream clings to the place, a dream rising out of reality. The kitchen at center seems actual enough, for there is a kitchen table with three chairs, and a refrigerator. But no other fixtures are seen. At the back of the kitchen there is a draped entrance, which leads to the livingroom. To the right of the kitchen, on a level raised two feet, is a bedroom furnished only with a brass bedstead and a straight chair. On a shelf over the bed a silver athletic trophy stands. A window opens onto the apartment house at the side.

Behind the kitchen, on a level raised six and a half feet, is the boys' bedroom, at present barely visible. Two beds are dimly seen, and at the back of the room a dormer window. (This bedroom is above the unseen livingroom.) At the left a stairway curves up to it from the kitchen.

The entire setting is wholly or, in some places, partially transparent. The roof-line of the house is one-dimensional; under and over it we see the apartment buildings. Before the house lies an apron, curving beyond the forestage into the orchestra. This forward area serves as the back yard as well as the locale of all Willy's imaginings and of his city scenes. Whenever the action is in the present the actors observe the imaginary wall-lines, entering the house only through the door at the left. But in the scenes of the past these boundaries are broken, and characters enter or leave a room by stepping "through" a wall onto the forestage.

From the right, Willy Loman, the Salesman, enters, carrying two large sample cases. The flute plays on. He hears but is not aware of it. He is past sixty years of age, dressed quietly. Even as he crosses the stage to the doorway of the house, his exhaustion is apparent. He unlocks the door, comes into the kitchen, and thankfully lets his burden down, feeling the soreness of his palms. A word-sigh escapes his lips — it might be "Oh, boy, oh, boy." He closes the door, then carries his cases out into the livingroom, through the draped kitchen doorway.

Linda, his wife, has stirred in her bed at the right. She gets out and puts on a robe, listening. Most often jovial, she has developed an iron repression of her exceptions to Willy's behavior — she more than loves him, she admires him, as though his mercurial nature, his temper, his massive dreams and little cruelties, served her only as sharp reminders of the turbulent longings within him, longings which she shares but lacks the temperament to utter and follow to their end.

Linda (hearing Willy outside the bedroom, calls with some trepidation): Willy!
Willy: It's all right. I came back.
Linda: Why? What happened? *(Slight pause.)* Did something happen, Willy?
Willy: No, nothing happened.
Linda: You didn't smash the car, did you?
Willy (with casual irritation): I said nothing happened. Didn't you hear me?
Linda: Don't you feel well?
Willy: I am tired to the death. *(The flute has faded away. He sits on the bed beside her, a little numb.)* I couldn't make it. I just couldn't make it, Linda.
Linda (very carefully, delicately): Where were you all day? You look terrible.
Willy: I got as far as a little above Yonkers. I stopped for a cup of coffee. Maybe it was the coffee.
Linda: What?
Willy (after a pause): I suddenly couldn't drive any more. The car kept going onto the shoulder, y'know?
Linda (helpfully): Oh. Maybe it was the steering again. I don't think Angelo knows the Studebaker.
Willy: No, it's me, it's me. Suddenly I realize I'm goin' sixty miles an hour and I don't remember the last five minutes. I'm — I can't seem to — keep my mind to it.
Linda: Maybe it's your glasses. You never went for your new glasses.

Willy: No, I see everything. I came back ten miles an hour. It took me nearly four hours from Yonkers.

Linda (resigned): Well, you'll just have to take a rest, Willy, you can't continue this way.

Willy: I just got back from Florida.

Linda: But you didn't rest your mind. Your mind is overactive, and the mind is what counts, dear.

Willy: I'll start out in the morning. Maybe I'll feel better in the morning. *(She is taking off his shoes.)* These goddam arch supports are killing me.

Linda: Take an aspirin. Should I get you an aspirin? It'll soothe you.

Willy (with wonder): I was driving along, you understand? And I was fine. I was even observing the scenery. You can imagine, me looking at scenery, on the road every week of my life. But it's so beautiful up there, Linda, the trees are so thick, and the sun is warm. I opened the windshield and just let the warm air bathe over me. And then all of a sudden I'm goin' off the road! I'm tellin' ya, I absolutely forgot I was driving. If I'd've gone the other way over the white line I might've killed somebody. So I went on again — and five minutes later I'm dreamin' again, and I nearly — *(He presses two fingers against his eyes.)* I have such thoughts, I have such strange thoughts.

Linda: Willy, dear. Talk to them again. There's no reason why you can't work in New York.

Willy: They don't need me in New York. I'm the New England man. I'm vital in New England.

Linda: But you're sixty years old. They can't expect you to keep traveling every week.

Willy: I'll have to send a wire to Portland. I'm supposed to see Brown and Morrison tomorrow morning at ten o'clock to show the line. Goddammit, I could sell them! *(He starts putting on his jacket.)*

Linda (taking the jacket from him): Why don't you go down to the place tomorrow and tell Howard you've simply got to work in New York? You're too accommodating, dear.

Willy: If old man Wagner was alive I'd a been in charge of New York now! That man was a prince, he was a masterful man. But that boy of his, that Howard, he don't appreciate. When I went north the first time, the Wagner Company didn't know where New England was!

Linda: Why don't you tell those things to Howard, dear?

Willy (encouraged): I will, I definitely will. Is there any cheese?

Linda: I'll make you a sandwich.

Willy: No, go to sleep. I'll take some milk. I'll be up right away. The boys in?

Linda: They're sleeping. Happy took Biff on a date tonight.

Willy (interested): That so?

Linda: It was so nice to see them shaving together, one behind the other, in the bathroom. And going out together. You notice? The whole house smells of shaving lotion.

Willy: Figure it out. Work a lifetime to pay off a house. You finally own it, and there's nobody to live in it.

Linda: Well, dear, life is a casting off. It's always that way.

Willy: No, no, some people — some people accomplish something. Did Biff say anything after I went this morning?

Linda: You shouldn't have criticized him, Willy, especially after he just got off the train. You mustn't lose your temper with him.

Willy: When the hell did I lose my temper? I simply asked him if he was making any money. Is that a criticism?

Linda: But, dear, how could he make any money?

Willy (worried and angered): There's such an undercurrent in him. He became a moody man. Did he apologize when I left this morning?

Linda: He was crestfallen, Willy. You know how he admires you. I think if he finds himself, then you'll both be happier and not fight any more.

Willy: How can he find himself on a farm? Is that a life? A farmhand? In the beginning, when he was young, I thought, well, a young man, it's good for him to tramp around, take a lot of different jobs. But it's more than ten years now and he has yet to make thirty-five dollars a week!

Linda: He's finding himself, Willy.

Willy: Not finding yourself at the age of thirty-four is a disgrace!

Linda: Shh!

Willy: The trouble is he's lazy, goddammit!

Linda: Willy, please!

Willy: Biff is a lazy bum!

Linda: They're sleeping. Get something to eat. Go on down.

Willy: Why did he come home? I would like to know what brought him home.

Linda: I don't know. I think he's still lost, Willy. I think he's very lost.

Willy: Biff Loman is lost. In the greatest country in the world a young man with such — personal attractiveness, gets lost. And such a hard worker. There's one thing about Biff — he's not lazy.

Linda: Never.

Willy (with pity and resolve): I'll see him in the morning; I'll have a nice talk with him. I'll get him a job selling. He could be big in no time. My God! Remember how they used to follow him around in high school? When he smiled at one of them their faces lit up. When he walked down the street . . . *(He loses himself in reminiscences.)*

Linda (trying to bring him out of it): Willy, dear, I got a new kind of American-type cheese today. It's whipped.

Willy: Why do you get American when I like Swiss?

Linda: I just thought you'd like a change —

Willy: I don't want a change! I want Swiss cheese. Why am I always being contradicted?

Linda (with a covering laugh): I thought it would be a surprise.

Willy: Why don't you open a window in here, for God's sake?

Linda (with infinite patience): They're all open, dear.

Willy: The way they boxed us in here. Bricks and windows, windows and bricks.

Linda: We should've bought the land next door.

Willy: The street is lined with cars. There's not a breath of fresh air in the neighborhood. The grass don't grow any more, you can't raise a carrot in the back yard. They should've had a law against apartment houses. Remember those two beautiful elm trees out there? When I and Biff hung the swing between them?

Linda: Yeah, like being a million miles from the city.

Willy: They should've arrested the builder for cutting those down. They massacred the neighborhood. *(Lost.)* More and more I think of those days, Linda. This time of year it was lilac and wisteria. And then the peonies would come out, and the daffodils. What fragrance in this room!

Linda: Well, after all, people had to move somewhere.

Willy: No, there's more people now.

Linda: I don't think there's more people. I think —

Willy: There's more people! That's what's ruining this country! Population is getting out of control. The competition is maddening! Smell the stink from that apartment house! And another on the other side . . . How can they whip cheese?

On Willy's last line, Biff and Happy raise themselves up in their beds, listening.

Linda: Go down, try it. And be quiet.

Willy (turning to Linda, guiltily): You're not worried about me, are you, sweetheart?

Biff: What's the matter?

Happy: Listen!

Linda: You've got too much on the ball to worry about.

Willy: You're my foundation and my support, Linda.

Linda: Just try to relax, dear. You make mountains out of molehills.

Willy: I won't fight with him any more. If he wants to go back to Texas, let him go.

Linda: He'll find his way.

Willy: Sure. Certain men just don't get started till later in life. Like Thomas Edison, I think. Or B. F. Goodrich. One of them was deaf. *(He starts for the bedroom doorway.)* I'll put my money on Biff.

Linda: And Willy — if it's warm Sunday we'll drive in the country. And we'll open the windshield, and take lunch.

Willy: No, the windshields don't open on the new cars.

Linda: But you opened it today.

Willy: Me? I didn't. *(He stops.)* Now isn't that peculiar! Isn't that a remarkable — *(He breaks off in amazement and fright as the flute is heard distantly.)*

Linda: What, darling?

Willy: That is the most remarkable thing.

Linda: What, dear?

Willy: I was thinking of the Chevvy. *(Slight pause.)* Nineteen twenty-eight . . . when I had that red Chevvy — *(Breaks off.)* That funny? I coulda sworn I was driving that Chevvy today.

Linda: Well, that's nothing. Something must've reminded you.

Willy: Remarkable. Ts. Remember those days? The way Biff used to simonize that car? The dealer refused to believe there was eighty thousand miles on it. *(He shakes his head.)* Heh! *(To Linda.)* Close your eyes, I'll be right up. *(He walks out of the bedroom.)*

Happy (to Biff): Jesus, maybe he smashed up the car again!

Linda (calling after Willy): Be careful on the stairs, dear! The cheese is on the middle shelf! *(She turns, goes over to the bed, takes his jacket, and goes out of the bedroom.)*

Light has risen on the boys' room. Unseen, Willy is heard talking to himself, "Eighty thousand miles," and a little laugh. Biff gets out of bed, comes downstage a bit, and stands attentively. Biff is two years older than his brother Happy, well built, but in these days bears a worn air and seems less self-assured. He has succeeded less, and his dreams are stronger and less acceptable than Happy's. Happy is tall, powerfully made. Sexuality is like a visible color on him, or a scent that many women have discovered. He, like his brother, is lost, but in a different way, for he has never allowed himself to turn his face toward defeat and is thus more confused and hard-skinned, although seemingly more content.

Happy (getting out of bed): He's going to get his license taken away if he keeps that up. I'm getting nervous about him, y'know, Biff?

Biff: His eyes are going.

Happy: No, I've driven with him. He sees all right. He just doesn't keep his mind on it. I drove into the city with him last week. He stops at a green light and then it turns red and he goes. *(He laughs.)*

Biff: Maybe he's color-blind.

Happy: Pop? Why he's got the finest eye for color in the business. You know that.

Biff (sitting down on his bed): I'm going to sleep.

Happy: You're not still sour on Dad, are you, Biff?

Biff: He's all right, I guess.

Willy (underneath them, in the livingroom): Yes, sir, eighty thousand miles — eighty-two thousand!

Biff: You smoking?

Happy (holding out a pack of cigarettes): Want one?

Biff (taking a cigarette): I can never sleep when I smell it.

Willy: What a simonizing job, heh!

Happy (with deep sentiment): Funny, Biff, y'know? Us sleeping in here again? The old beds. *(He pats his bed affectionately.)* All the talk that went across those two beds, huh? Our whole lives.

Biff: Yeah. Lotta dreams and plans.

Happy (with a deep and masculine laugh): About five hundred women would like to know what was said in this room.

They share a soft laugh.

Biff: Remember that big Betsy something — what the hell was her name — over on Bushwick Avenue?

Happy (combing his hair): With the collie dog!

Biff: That's the one. I got you in there, remember?

Happy: Yeah, that was my first time — I think. Boy, there was a pig! *(They laugh, almost crudely.)* You taught me everything I know about women. Don't forget that.

Biff: I bet you forgot how bashful you used to be. Especially with girls.

Happy: Oh, I still am, Biff.

Biff: Oh, go on.

Happy: I just control it, that's all. I think I got less bashful and you got more so. What happened, Biff? Where's the old humor, the old confidence? *(He shakes Biff's knee. Biff gets up and moves restlessly about the room.)* What's the matter?

Biff: Why does Dad mock me all the time?

Happy: He's not mocking you, he —

Biff: Everything I say there's a twist of mockery on his face. I can't get near him.

Happy: He just wants you to make good, that's all. I wanted to talk to you about Dad for a long time, Biff. Something's — happening to him. He — talks to himself.

Biff: I noticed that this morning. But he always mumbled.

Happy: But not so noticeable. It got so embarrassing I sent him to Florida. And you know something? Most of the time he's talking to you.

Biff: What's he say about me?

Happy: I can't make it out.

Biff: What's he say about me?

Happy: I think the fact that you're not settled, that you're still kind of up in the air . . .

Biff: There's one or two other things depressing him, Happy.

Happy: What do you mean?

Biff: Never mind. Just don't lay it all to me.

Happy: But I think if you just got started — I mean — is there any future for you out there?

Biff: I tell ya, Hap, I don't know what the future is. I don't know — what I'm supposed to want.

Happy: What do you mean?

Biff: Well, I spent six or seven years after high school trying to work myself up. Shipping clerk, salesman, business of one kind or another. And it's a measly manner of existence. To get on that subway on the hot mornings in summer. To devote your whole life to keeping stock, or making phone calls, or selling or buying. To suffer fifty weeks of the year for the sake of a two-week vacation, when all you really desire is to be outdoors, with your shirt off. And always to have to get ahead of the next fella. And still — that's how you build a future.

Happy: Well, you really enjoy it on a farm? Are you content out there?

Biff (with rising agitation): Hap, I've had twenty or thirty different kinds of jobs since I left home before the war, and it always turns out the same. I just realized it lately. In Nebraska when I herded cattle, and the Dakotas, and Arizona, and now in Texas. It's why I came home now, I guess, because I realized it. This farm I work on, it's spring there now, see? And they've got about fifteen new colts. There's nothing more inspiring or — beautiful than the sight of a mare and a new colt. And it's cool there now, see? Texas is cool now, and it's spring. And whenever spring comes to where I am, I suddenly get the feeling, my God, I'm not gettin' anywhere! What the hell am I doing, playing around with horses, twenty-eight dollars a week! I'm thirty-four years old, I oughta be makin' my future. That's when I come running home. And now, I get here, and I don't know what to do with myself. *(After a pause.)* I've always made a point of not wasting my life, and everytime I come back here I know that all I've done is to waste my life.

Happy: You're a poet, you know that, Biff? You're a — you're an idealist!

Biff: No, I'm mixed up very bad. Maybe I oughta get married. Maybe I oughta get stuck into something. Maybe that's my trouble. I'm like a boy. I'm not married, I'm not in business, I just — I'm like a boy. Are you content, Hap? You're a success, aren't you? Are you content?

Happy: Hell, no!

Biff: Why? You're making money, aren't you?

Happy (moving about with energy, expressiveness): All I can do now is wait for the merchandise manager to die. And suppose I get to be merchandise manager? He's a good friend of mine, and he just built a terrific estate on Long Island. And he lived there about two months and sold it, and now he's building another one. He can't enjoy it once it's finished. And I know that's just what I would do. I don't know what the hell I'm workin' for. Sometimes I sit in my apartment — all alone. And I think of the rent I'm paying. And it's crazy. But then, it's what I always wanted. My own apartment, a car, and plenty of women. And still, goddammit, I'm lonely.

Biff (with enthusiasm): Listen, why don't you come out West with me?

Happy: You and I, heh?

Biff: Sure, maybe we could buy a ranch. Raise cattle, use our muscles. Men built like we are should be working out in the open.

Happy (avidly): The Loman Brothers, heh?

Biff (with vast affection): Sure, we'd be known all over the counties!

Happy (enthralled): That's what I dream about, Biff. Sometimes I want to just rip my clothes off in the middle of the store and outbox that goddam merchandise manager. I mean I can outbox, outrun, and outlift anybody in that store, and I have to take orders from those common, petty sons-of-bitches till I can't stand it any more.

Biff: I'm tellin' you, kid, if you were with me I'd be happy out there.

Happy (enthused): See, Biff, everybody around me is so false that I'm constantly lowering my ideals . . .

Biff: Baby, together we'd stand up for one another, we'd have someone to trust.

Happy: If I were around you —

Biff: Hap, the trouble is we weren't brought up to grub for money. I don't know how to do it.

Happy: Neither can I!

Biff: Then let's go!

Happy: The only thing is — what can you make out there?

Biff: But look at your friend. Builds an estate and then hasn't the peace of mind to live in it.

Happy: Yeah, but when he walks into the store the waves part in front of him. That's fifty-two thousand dollars a year coming through the revolving door, and I got more in my pinky finger than he's got in his head.

Biff: Yeah, but you just said —

Happy: I gotta show some of those pompous, self-important executives over there that Hap Loman can make the grade. I want to walk into the store the way he walks in. Then I'll go with you, Biff. We'll be together yet, I swear. But take those two we had tonight. Now weren't they gorgeous creatures?

Biff: Yeah, yeah, most gorgeous I've had in years.

Happy: I get that any time I want, Biff. Whenever I feel disgusted. The only trouble is, it gets like bowling or something. I just keep knockin' them over and it doesn't mean anything. You still run around a lot?

Biff: Naa. I'd like to find a girl — steady, somebody with substance.

Happy: That's what I long for.

Biff: Go on! You'd never come home.

Happy: I would! Somebody with character, with resistance! Like Mom, y'know? You're gonna call me a bastard when I tell you this. That girl Charlotte I was with tonight is engaged to be married in five weeks. *(He tries on his new hat.)*

Biff: No kiddin'!

Happy: Sure, the guy's in line for the vice-presidency of the store. I don't know what gets into me, maybe I just have an overdeveloped sense of competition or something, but I went and ruined her, and furthermore I can't get rid of her. And he's the third executive I've done that to. Isn't that a crummy characteristic? And to top it all, I go to their weddings! *(Indignantly, but laughing.)* Like I'm not supposed to take bribes. Manufacturers offer me a hundred-dollar bill now and then to throw an order their way. You know how honest I am, but it's like this girl, see. I hate myself for it. Because I don't want the girl, and, still, I take it and — I love it!

Biff: Let's go to sleep.

Happy: I guess we didn't settle anything, heh?

Biff: I just got one idea that I think I'm going to try.

Happy: What's that?

Biff: Remember Bill Oliver?

Happy: Sure, Oliver is very big now. You want to work for him again?

Biff: No, but when I quit he said something to me. He put his arm on my shoulder, and he said, "Biff, if you ever need anything, come to me."

Happy: I remember that. That sounds good.

Biff: I think I'll go to see him. If I could get ten thousand or even seven or eight thousand dollars I could buy a beautiful ranch.

Happy: I bet he'd back you. 'Cause he thought highly of you, Biff, I mean, they all do. You're well liked, Biff. That's why I say to come back here, and we both have the apartment. And I'm tellin' you, Biff, any babe you want . . .

Biff: No, with a ranch I could do the work I like and still be something. I just wonder though. I wonder if Oliver still thinks I stole that carton of basketballs.

Happy: Oh, he probably forgot that long ago. It's almost ten years. You're too sensitive. Anyway, he didn't really fire you.

Biff: Well, I think he was going to. I think that's why I quit. I was never sure whether he knew or not. I know he thought the world of me, though. I was the only one he'd let lock up the place.

Willy (below): You gonna wash the engine, Biff?

Happy: Shh!

Biff looks at Happy, who is gazing down, listening. Willy is mumbling in the parlor.

Happy: You hear that?

They listen. Willy laughs warmly.

Biff (growing angry): Doesn't he know Mom can hear that?

Willy: Don't get your sweater dirty, Biff!

A look of pain crosses Biff's face.

Happy: Isn't that terrible? Don't leave again, will you? You'll find a job here. You gotta stick around. I don't know what to do about him, it's getting embarrassing.

Willy: What a simonizing job!

Biff: Mom's hearing that!

Willy: No kiddin', Biff, you got a date? Wonderful!

Happy: Go on to sleep. But talk to him in the morning, will you?

Biff (reluctantly getting into bed): With her in the house. Brother!

Happy (getting into bed): I wish you'd have a good talk with him.

The light on their room begins to fade.

Biff (to himself in bed): That selfish, stupid . . .

Happy: Sh . . . Sleep, Biff.

Their light is out. Well before they have finished speaking, Willy's form is dimly seen below in the darkened kitchen. He opens the refrigerator, searches in there, and takes out a bottle of milk. The apartment houses are fading out, and the entire house and surroundings become covered with leaves. Music insinuates itself as the leaves appear.

Willy: Just wanna be careful with those girls, Biff, that's all. Don't make any promises. No promises of any kind. Because a girl, y'know, they always believe what you tell 'em, and you're very young, Biff, you're too young to be talking seriously to girls.

Light rises on the kitchen. Willy, talking, shuts the refrigerator door and comes downstage to the kitchen table. He pours milk into a glass. He is totally immersed in himself, smiling faintly.

Willy: Too young entirely, Biff. You want to watch your schooling first. Then when you're all set, there'll be plenty of girls for a boy like you. *(He smiles broadly at a kitchen chair.)* That so? The girls pay for you? *(He laughs.)* Boy, you must really be makin' a hit.

Willy is gradually addressing — physically — a point offstage, speaking through the wall of the kitchen, and his voice has been rising in volume to that of a normal conversation.

Willy: I been wondering why you polish the car so careful. Ha! Don't leave the hubcaps, boys. Get the chamois to the hubcaps. Happy, use newspaper on the windows, it's the easiest thing. Show him how to do it, Biff! You see, Happy? Pad it up, use it like a pad. That's it, that's it, good work. You're doin' all right, Hap. *(He pauses, then nods in approbation for a few seconds, then looks upward.)* Biff, first thing we gotta do when we get time is clip that big branch over the house. Afraid it's gonna fall in a storm and hit the roof. Tell you what. We get a rope and sling her around, and then we climb up there with a couple of saws and take her down. Soon as you finish the car, boys, I wanna see ya. I got a surprise for you, boys.

Biff (offstage): Whatta ya got, Dad?

Willy: No, you finish first. Never leave a job till you're finished — remember that. *(Looking toward the "big trees.")* Biff, up in Albany I saw a beautiful hammock. I think I'll buy it next trip, and we'll hang it right between those two elms. Wouldn't that be something? Just swingin' there under those branches. Boy, that would be . . .

Young Biff and Young Happy appear from the direction Willy was addressing. Happy carries rags and a pail of water. Biff, wearing a sweater with a block "S," carries a football.

Biff (pointing in the direction of the car offstage): How's that, Pop, professional?
Willy: Terrific. Terrific job, boys. Good work, Biff.
Happy: Where's the surprise, Pop?
Willy: In the back seat of the car.
Happy: Boy! *(He runs off.)*
Biff: What is it, Dad? Tell me, what'd you buy?
Willy (laughing, cuffs him): Never mind, something I want you to have.
Biff (turns and starts off): What is it, Hap?
Happy (offstage): It's a punching bag!
Biff: Oh, Pop!
Willy: It's got Gene Tunney's signature on it!

Happy runs onstage with a punching bag.

Biff: Gee, how'd you know we wanted a punching bag?
Willy: Well, it's the finest thing for the timing.
Happy (lies down on his back and pedals with his feet): I'm losing weight, you notice, Pop?
Willy (to Happy): Jumping rope is good too.
Biff: Did you see the new football I got?
Willy (examining the ball): Where'd you get a new ball?
Biff: The coach told me to practice my passing.
Willy: That so? And he gave you the ball, heh?
Biff: Well, I borrowed it from the locker room. *(He laughs confidentially.)*
Willy (laughing with him at the theft): I want you to return that.
Happy: I told you he wouldn't like it!
Biff (angrily): Well, I'm bringing it back!
Willy (stopping the incipient argument, to Happy): Sure, he's gotta practice with a regulation ball, doesn't he? *(To Biff.)* Coach'll probably congratulate you on your initiative!
Biff: Oh, he keeps congratulating my initiative all the time, Pop.
Willy: That's because he likes you. If somebody else took that ball there'd be an uproar. So what's the report, boys, what's the report?
Biff: Where'd you go this time, Dad? Gee we were lonesome for you.
Willy (pleased, puts an arm around each boy and they come down to the apron): Lonesome, heh?
Biff: Missed you every minute.
Willy: Don't say? Tell you a secret, boys. Don't breathe it to a soul. Someday I'll have my own business, and I'll never have to leave home any more.
Happy: Like Uncle Charley, heh?
Willy: Bigger than Uncle Charley! Because Charley is not — liked. He's liked, but he's not — well liked.

Biff: Where'd you go this time, Dad?

Willy: Well, I got on the road, and I went north to Providence. Met the Mayor.

Biff: The Mayor of Providence!

Willy: He was sitting in the hotel lobby.

Biff: What'd he say?

Willy: He said, "Morning!" And I said, "You've got a fine city here, Mayor." And then he had coffee with me. And then I went to Waterbury. Waterbury is a fine city. Big clock city, the famous Waterbury clock. Sold a nice bill there. And then Boston — Boston is the cradle of the Revolution. A fine city. And a couple of other towns in Mass., and on to Portland and Bangor and straight home!

Biff: Gee, I'd love to go with you sometime, Dad.

Willy: Soon as summer comes.

Happy: Promise?

Willy: You and Hap and I, and I'll show you all the towns. America is full of beautiful towns and fine, upstanding people. And they know me, boys, they know me up and down New England. The finest people. And when I bring you fellas up, there'll be open sesame for all of us, 'cause one thing, boys: I have friends. I can park my car in any street in New England, and the cops protect it like their own. This summer, heh?

Biff and Happy (together): Yeah! You bet!

Willy: We'll take our bathing suits.

Happy: We'll carry your bags, Pop!

Willy: Oh, won't that be something! Me comin' into the Boston stores with you boys carryin' my bags. What a sensation!

Biff is prancing around, practicing passing the ball.

Willy: You nervous, Biff, about the game?

Biff: Not if you're gonna be there.

Willy: What do they say about you in school, now that they made you captain?

Happy: There's a crowd of girls behind him everytime the classes change.

Biff (taking Willy's hand): This Saturday, Pop, this Saturday — just for you, I'm going to break through for a touchdown.

Happy: You're supposed to pass.

Biff: I'm takin' one play for Pop. You watch me, Pop, and when I take off my helmet, that means I'm breakin' out. Then you watch me crash through that line!

Willy (kisses Biff): Oh, wait'll I tell this in Boston!

Bernard enters in knickers. He is younger than Biff, earnest and loyal, a worried boy.

Bernard: Biff, where are you? You're supposed to study with me today.

Willy: Hey, looka Bernard. What're you lookin' so anemic about, Bernard?

Bernard: He's gotta study, Uncle Willy. He's got Regents next week.

Happy (tauntingly, spinning Bernard around): Let's box, Bernard!

Bernard: Biff! (He gets away from Happy.) Listen, Biff, I heard Mr. Birnbaum say that if you don't start studyin' math he's gonna flunk you, and you won't graduate. I heard him!

Willy: You better study with him, Biff. Go ahead now.

Bernard: I heard him!

Biff: Oh, Pop, you didn't see my sneakers! *(He holds up a foot for Willy to look at.)*

Willy: Hey, that's a beautiful job of printing!

Bernard (wiping his glasses): Just because he printed University of Virginia on his sneakers doesn't mean they've got to graduate him, Uncle Willy!

Willy (angrily): What're you talking about? With scholarships to three universities they're gonna flunk him?

Bernard: But I heard Mr. Birnbaum say —

Willy: Don't be a pest, Bernard! *(To his boys.)* What an anemic!

Bernard: Okay, I'm waiting for you in my house, Biff.

> *Bernard goes off. The Lomans laugh.*

Willy: Bernard is not well liked, is he?

Biff: He's liked, but he's not well liked.

Happy: That's right, Pop.

Willy: That's just what I mean. Bernard can get the best marks in school, y'understand, but when he gets out in the business world, y'understand, you are going to be five times ahead of him. That's why I thank Almighty God you're both built like Adonises. Because the man who makes an appearance in the business world, the man who creates personal interest, is the man who gets ahead. Be liked and you will never want. You take me, for instance. I never have to wait in line to see a buyer. "Willy Loman is here!" That's all they have to know, and I go right through.

Biff: Did you knock them dead, Pop?

Willy: Knocked 'em cold in Providence, slaughtered 'em in Boston.

Happy (on his back, pedaling again): I'm losing weight, you notice, Pop?

> *Linda enters, as of old, a ribbon in her hair, carrying a basket of washing.*

Linda (with youthful energy): Hello, dear!

Willy: Sweetheart!

Linda: How'd the Chevvy run?

Willy: Chevrolet, Linda, is the greatest car ever built. *(To the boys.)* Since when do you let your mother carry wash up the stairs?

Biff: Grab hold there, boy!

Happy: Where to, Mom?

Linda: Hang them up on the line. And you better go down to your friends, Biff. The cellar is full of boys. They don't know what to do with themselves.

Biff: Ah, when Pop comes home they can wait!

Willy (laughs appreciatively): You better go down and tell them what to do, Biff.

Biff: I think I'll have them sweep out the furnace room.

Willy: Good work, Biff.

Biff (goes through wall-line of kitchen to doorway at back and calls down): Fellas! Everybody sweep out the furnace room! I'll be right down!

Voices: All right! Okay, Biff.

Biff: George and Sam and Frank, come out back! We're hangin' up the wash! Come on, Hap, on the double! *(He and Happy carry out the basket.)*

Linda: The way they obey him!

Willy: Well, that's training, the training. I'm tellin' you, I was sellin' thousands and thousands, but I had to come home.

Linda: Oh, the whole block'll be at that game. Did you sell anything?

Willy: I did five hundred gross in Providence and seven hundred gross in Boston.

Linda: No! Wait a minute, I've got a pencil. *(She pulls pencil and paper out of her apron pocket.)* That makes your commission . . . Two hundred — my God! Two hundred and twelve dollars!

Willy: Well, I didn't figure it yet, but . . .

Linda: How much did you do?

Willy: Well, I — I did — about a hundred and eighty gross in Providence. Well, no — it came to — roughly two hundred gross on the whole trip.

Linda (without hesitation): Two hundred gross. That's . . . *(She figures.)*

Willy: The trouble was that three of the stores were half closed for inventory in Boston. Otherwise I woulda broke records.

Linda: Well, it makes seventy dollars and some pennies. That's very good.

Willy: What do we owe?

Linda: Well, on the first there's sixteen dollars on the refrigerator —

Willy: Why sixteen?

Linda: Well, the fan belt broke, so it was a dollar eighty.

Willy: But it's brand new.

Linda: Well, the man said that's the way it is. Till they work themselves in, y'know.

They move through the wall-line into the kitchen.

Willy: I hope we didn't get stuck on that machine.

Linda: They got the biggest ads of any of them!

Willy: I know, it's a fine machine. What else?

Linda: Well, there's nine-sixty for the washing machine. And for the vacuum cleaner there's three and a half due on the fifteenth. Then the roof, you got twenty-one dollars remaining.

Willy: It don't leak, does it?

Linda: No, they did a wonderful job. Then you owe Frank for the carburetor.

Willy: I'm not going to pay that man! That goddam Chevrolet, they ought to prohibit the manufacture of that car!

Linda: Well, you owe him three and a half. And odds and ends, comes to around a hundred and twenty dollars by the fifteenth.

Willy: A hundred and twenty dollars! My God, if business don't pick up I don't know what I'm gonna do!

Linda: Well, next week you'll do better.

Willy: Oh, I'll knock them dead next week. I'll go to Hartford. I'm very well liked in Hartford. You know, the trouble is, Linda, people don't seem to take to me.

They move onto the forestage.

Linda: Oh, don't be foolish.

Willy: I know it when I walk in. They seem to laugh at me.

Linda: Why? Why would they laugh at you? Don't talk that way, Willy.

Willy moves to the edge of the stage. Linda goes into the kitchen and starts to darn stockings.

Willy: I don't know the reason for it, but they just pass me by. I'm not noticed.

Linda: But you're doing wonderful, dear. You're making seventy to a hundred dollars a week.

Willy: But I gotta be at it ten, twelve hours a day. Other men — I don't know — they do it easier. I don't know why — I can't stop myself — I talk too much. A man oughta come in with a few words. One thing about Charley. He's a man of few words, and they respect him.

Linda: You don't talk too much, you're just lively.

Willy (smiling): Well, I figure, what the hell, life is short, a couple of jokes. *(To himself.)* I joke too much! *(The smile goes.)*

Linda: Why? You're —

Willy: I'm fat. I'm very — foolish to look at, Linda. I didn't tell you, but Christmas time I happened to be calling on F. H. Stewarts, and a salesman I know, as I was going in to see the buyer I heard him say something about — walrus. And I — I cracked him right across the face. I won't take that. I simply will not take that. But they do laugh at me. I know that.

Linda: Darling . . .

Willy: I gotta overcome it. I know I gotta overcome it. I'm not dressing to advantage, maybe.

Linda: Willy, darling, you're the handsomest man in the world —

Willy: Oh, no, Linda.

Linda: To me you are. *(Slight pause.)* The handsomest.

From the darkness is heard the laughter of a woman. Willy doesn't turn to it, but it continues through Linda's lines.

Linda: And the boys, Willy. Few men are idolized by their children the way you are.

Music is heard as behind a scrim, to the left of the house, The Woman, dimly seen, is dressing.

Willy (with great feeling): You're the best there is, Linda, you're a pal, you know that? On the road — on the road I want to grab you sometimes and just kiss the life outa you.

The laughter is loud now, and he moves into a brightening area at the left, where The Woman has come from behind the scrim and is standing, putting on her hat, looking into a "mirror" and laughing.

Willy: 'Cause I get so lonely — especially when business is bad and there's nobody to talk to. I get the feeling that I'll never sell anything again, that I won't make a living for you, or a business, a business for the boys. *(He talks through The Woman's subsiding laughter; The Woman primps at the "mirror.")* There's so much I want to make for —

The Woman: Me? You didn't make me, Willy. I picked you.

Willy (pleased): You picked me?

The Woman (who is quite proper-looking, Willy's age): I did. I've been sitting at that desk watching all the salesmen go by, day in, day out. But you've got such a sense of humor, and we do have such a good time together, don't we?

Willy: Sure, sure. *(He takes her in his arms.)* Why do you have to go now?

The Woman: It's two o'clock . . .

Willy: No, come on in! *(He pulls her.)*

The Woman: . . . my sisters'll be scandalized. When'll you be back?

Willy: Oh, two weeks about. Will you come up again?

The Woman: Sure thing. You do make me laugh. It's good for me. *(She squeezes his arm, kisses him.)* And I think you're a wonderful man.

Willy: You picked me, heh?

The Woman: Sure. Because you're so sweet. And such a kidder.

Willy: Well, I'll see you next time I'm in Boston.

The Woman: I'll put you right through to the buyers.

Willy (slapping her bottom): Right. Well, bottoms up!

The Woman (slaps him gently and laughs): You just kill me, Willy. *(He suddenly grabs her and kisses her roughly.)* You kill me. And thanks for the stockings. I love a lot of stockings. Well, good night.

Willy: Good night. And keep your pores open!

The Woman: Oh, Willy!

> *The Woman bursts out laughing, and Linda's laughter blends in. The Woman disappears into the dark. Now the area at the kitchen table brightens. Linda is sitting where she was at the kitchen table, but now is mending a pair of silk stockings.*

Linda: You are, Willy. The handsomest man. You've got no reason to feel that —

Willy (coming out of The Woman's dimming area and going over to Linda): I'll make it all up to you, Linda, I'll —

Linda: There's nothing to make up, dear. You're doing fine, better than —

Willy (noticing her mending): What's that?

Linda: Just mending my stockings. They're so expensive —

Willy (angrily, taking them from her): I won't have you mending stockings in this house! Now throw them out!

> *Linda puts the stockings in her pocket.*

Bernard (entering on the run): Where is he? If he doesn't study!

Willy (moving to the forestage, with great agitation): You'll give him the answers!

Bernard: I do, but I can't on a Regents! That's a state exam! They're liable to arrest me!

Willy: Where is he? I'll whip him, I'll whip him!

Linda: And he'd better give back that football, Willy, it's not nice.

Willy: Biff! Where is he? Why is he taking everything?

Linda: He's too tough with the girls, Willy. All the mothers are afraid of him!

Willy: I'll whip him!

Bernard: He's driving the car without a license!

> *The Woman's laugh is heard.*

Willy: Shut up!

Linda: All the mothers —

Willy: Shut up!

Bernard (backing quietly away and out): Mr. Birnbaum says he's stuck up.

Willy: Get outa here!

Bernard: If he doesn't buckle down he'll flunk math! *(He goes off.)*

Linda: He's right, Willy, you've gotta —

Willy (exploding at her): There's nothing the matter with him! You want him to be a worm like Bernard? He's got spirit, personality . . .

As he speaks, Linda, almost in tears, exits into the livingroom. Willy is alone in the kitchen, wilting and staring. The leaves are gone. It is night again, and the apartment houses look down from behind.

Willy: Loaded with it. Loaded! What is he stealing? He's giving it back, isn't he? Why is he stealing? What did I tell him? I never in my life told him anything but decent things.

Happy in pajamas has come down the stairs; Willy suddenly becomes aware of Happy's presence.

Happy: Let's go now, come on.

Willy (sitting down at the kitchen table): Huh! Why did she have to wax the floors herself? Everytime she waxes the floors she keels over. She knows that!

Happy: Shh! Take it easy. What brought you back tonight?

Willy: I got an awful scare. Nearly hit a kid in Yonkers. God! Why didn't I go to Alaska with my brother Ben that time! Ben! That man was a genius, that man was success incarnate! What a mistake! He begged me to go.

Happy: Well, there's no use in —

Willy: You guys! There was a man started with the clothes on his back and ended up with diamond mines!

Happy: Boy, someday I'd like to know how he did it.

Willy: What's the mystery? The man knew what he wanted and went out and got it! Walked into a jungle, and comes out, the age of twenty-one, and he's rich! The world is an oyster, but you don't crack it open on a mattress!

Happy: Pop, I told you I'm gonna retire you for life.

Willy: You'll retire me for life on seventy goddam dollars a week? And your women and your car and your apartment, and you'll retire me for life! Christ's sake, I couldn't get past Yonkers today! Where are you guys, where are you? The woods are burning! I can't drive a car!

Charley has appeared in the doorway. He is a large man, slow of speech, laconic, immovable. In all he says, despite what he says, there is pity, and, now, trepidation. He has a robe over his pajamas, slippers on his feet. He enters the kitchen.

Charley: Everything all right?

Happy: Yeah, Charley, everything's . . .

Willy: What's the matter?

Charley: I heard some noise. I thought something happened. Can't we do something about the walls? You sneeze in here, and in my house hats blow off.

Happy: Let's go to bed, Dad. Come on.

Charley signals to Happy to go.

Willy: You go ahead, I'm not tired at the moment.

Happy (to Willy): Take it easy, huh? *(He exits.)*

Willy: What're you doin' up?

Charley (sitting down at the kitchen table opposite Willy): Couldn't sleep good. I had a heartburn.

Willy: Well, you don't know how to eat.

Charley: I eat with my mouth.

Willy: No, you're ignorant. You gotta know about vitamins and things like that.

Charley: Come on, let's shoot. Tire you out a little.

Willy (hesitantly): All right. You got cards?

Charley (taking a deck from his pocket): Yeah, I got them. Someplace. What is it with those vitamins?

Willy (dealing): They build up your bones. Chemistry.

Charley: Yeah, but there's no bones in a heartburn.

Willy: What are you talkin' about? Do you know the first thing about it?

Charley: Don't get insulted.

Willy: Don't talk about something you don't know anything about.

> *They are playing. Pause.*

Charley: What're you doin' home?

Willy: A little trouble with the car.

Charley: Oh. *(Pause.)* I'd like to take a trip to California.

Willy: Don't say.

Charley: You want a job?

Willy: I got a job, I told you that. *(After a slight pause.)* What the hell are you offering me a job for?

Charley: Don't get insulted.

Willy: Don't insult me.

Charley: I don't see no sense in it. You don't have to go on this way.

Willy: I got a good job. *(Slight pause.)* What do you keep comin' in here for?

Charley: You want me to go?

Willy (after a pause, withering): I can't understand it. He's going back to Texas again. What the hell is that?

Charley: Let him go.

Willy: I got nothin' to give him, Charley, I'm clean, I'm clean.

Charley: He won't starve. None a them starve. Forget about him.

Willy: Then what have I got to remember?

Charley: You take it too hard. To hell with it. When a deposit bottle is broken you don't get your nickel back.

Willy: That's easy enough for you to say.

Charley: That ain't easy for me to say.

Willy: Did you see the ceiling I put up in the livingroom?

Charley: Yeah, that's a piece of work. To put up a ceiling is a mystery to me. How do you do it?

Willy: What's the difference?

Charley: Well, talk about it.

Willy: You gonna put up a ceiling?

Charley: How could I put up a ceiling?

Willy: Then what the hell are you bothering me for?

Charley: You're insulted again.

Willy: A man who can't handle tools is not a man. You're disgusting.

Charley: Don't call me disgusting, Willy.

Uncle Ben, carrying a valise and an umbrella, enters the forestage from around the right corner of the house. He is a stolid man, in his sixties, with a mustache and an authoritative air. He is utterly certain of his destiny, and there is an aura of far places about him. He enters exactly as Willy speaks.

Willy: I'm getting awfully tired, Ben.

Ben's music is heard. Ben looks around at everything.

Charley: Good, keep playing; you'll sleep better. Did you call me Ben?

Ben looks at his watch.

Willy: That's funny. For a second there you reminded me of my brother Ben.

Ben: I have only a few minutes. *(He strolls, inspecting the place. Willy and Charley continue playing.)*

Charley: You never heard from him again, heh? Since that time?

Willy: Didn't Linda tell you? Couple of weeks ago we got a letter from his wife in Africa. He died.

Charley: That so.

Ben (chuckling): So this is Brooklyn, eh?

Charley: Maybe you're in for some of his money.

Willy: Naa, he had seven sons. There's just one opportunity I had with that man . . .

Ben: I must make a train, William. There are several properties I'm looking at in Alaska.

Willy: Sure, sure! If I'd gone with him to Alaska that time, everything would've been totally different.

Charley: Go on, you'd froze to death up there.

Willy: What're you talking about?

Ben: Opportunity is tremendous in Alaska, William. Surprised you're not up there.

Willy: Sure, tremendous.

Charley: Heh?

Willy: There was the only man I ever met who knew the answers.

Charley: Who?

Ben: How are you all?

Willy (taking a pot, smiling): Fine, fine.

Charley: Pretty sharp tonight.

Ben: Is Mother living with you?

Willy: No, she died a long time ago.

Charley: Who?

Ben: That's too bad. Fine specimen of a lady, Mother.

Willy (to Charley): Heh?

Ben: I'd hoped to see the old girl.

Charley: Who died?

Ben: Heard anything from Father, have you?

Willy (unnerved): What do you mean, who died?

Charley (taking a pot): What're you talkin' about?

Ben (looking at his watch): William, it's half-past eight!

Willy (as though to dispel his confusion he angrily stops Charley's hand): That's my build!

Charley: I put the ace —

Willy: If you don't know how to play the game I'm not gonna throw my money away on you!

Charley (rising): It was my ace, for God's sake!

Willy: I'm through, I'm through!

Ben: When did Mother die?

Willy: Long ago. Since the beginning you never knew how to play cards.

Charley (picks up the cards and goes to the door): All right! Next time I'll bring a deck with five aces.

Willy: I don't play that kind of game!

Charley (turning to him): You should be ashamed of yourself!

Willy: Yeah?

Charley: Yeah! *(He goes out.)*

Willy (slamming the door after him): Ignoramus!

Ben (as Willy comes toward him through the wall-line of the kitchen): So you're William.

Willy (shaking Ben's hand): Ben! I've been waiting for you so long! What's the answer? How did you do it?

Ben: Oh, there's a story in that.

> *Linda enters the forestage, as of old, carrying the wash basket.*

Linda: Is this Ben?

Ben (gallantly): How do you do, my dear.

Linda: Where've you been all these years? Willy's always wondered why you —

Willy (pulling Ben away from her impatiently): Where is Dad? Didn't you follow him? How did you get started?

Ben: Well, I don't know how much you remember.

Willy: Well, I was just a baby, of course, only three or four years old —

Ben: Three years and eleven months.

Willy: What a memory, Ben!

Ben: I have many enterprises, William, and I have never kept books.

Willy: I remember I was sitting under the wagon in — was it Nebraska?

Ben: It was South Dakota, and I gave you a bunch of wild flowers.

Willy: I remember you walking away down some open road.

Ben (laughing): I was going to find Father in Alaska.

Willy: Where is he?

Ben: At that age I had a very faulty view of geography, William. I discovered after a few days that I was heading due south, so instead of Alaska, I ended up in Africa.

Linda: Africa!

Willy: The Gold Coast!

Ben: Principally, diamond mines.

Linda: Diamond mines!

Ben: Yes, my dear. But I've only a few minutes —

Willy: No! Boys! Boys! *(Young Biff and Happy appear.)* Listen to this. This is your Uncle Ben, a great man! Tell my boys, Ben!

Ben: Why, boys, when I was seventeen I walked into the jungle, and when I was twenty-one I walked out. *(He laughs.)* And by God I was rich.

Willy (to the boys): You see what I been talking about? The greatest things can happen!

Ben (glancing at his watch): I have an appointment in Ketchikan Tuesday week.

Willy: No, Ben! Please tell about Dad. I want my boys to hear. I want them to know the kind of stock they spring from. All I remember is a man with a big beard, and I was in Mamma's lap, sitting around a fire, and some kind of high music.

Ben: His flute. He played the flute.

Willy: Sure, the flute, that's right!

New music is heard, a high, rollicking tune.

Ben: Father was a very great and a very wild-hearted man. We would start in Boston, and he'd toss the whole family into the wagon, and then he'd drive the team right across the country; through Ohio, and Indiana, Michigan, Illinois, and all the Western states. And we'd stop in the towns and sell the flutes that he'd made on the way. Great inventor, Father. With one gadget he made more in a week than a man like you could make in a lifetime.

Willy: That's just the way I'm bringing them up, Ben — rugged, well liked, all-around.

Ben: Yeah? *(To Biff.)* Hit that, boy — hard as you can. *(He pounds his stomach.)*

Biff: Oh, no, sir!

Ben (taking boxing stance): Come on, get to me! *(He laughs.)*

Willy: Go to it, Biff! Go ahead, show him!

Biff: Okay! *(He cocks his fist and starts in.)*

Linda (to Willy): Why must he fight, dear?

Ben (sparring with Biff): Good boy! Good boy!

Willy: How's that, Ben, heh?

Happy: Give him the left, Biff!

Linda: Why are you fighting?

Ben: Good boy! *(Suddenly comes in, trips Biff, and stands over him, the point of his umbrella poised over Biff's eye.)*

Linda: Look out, Biff!

Biff: Gee!

Ben (patting Biff's knee): Never fight fair with a stranger, boy. You'll never get out of the jungle that way. *(Taking Linda's hand and bowing.)* It was an honor and a pleasure to meet you, Linda.

Linda (withdrawing her hand coldly, frightened): Have a nice — trip.

Ben (to Willy): And good luck with your — what do you do?

Willy: Selling.

Ben: Yes. Well . . . *(He raises his hand in farewell to all.)*

Willy: No, Ben, I don't want you to think . . . *(He takes Ben's arm to show him.)* It's Brooklyn, I know, but we hunt too.

Ben: Really, now.

Willy: Oh, sure, there's snakes and rabbits and — that's why I moved out here. Why, Biff can fell any one of these trees in no time! Boys! Go right over to where they're building the apartment house and get some sand. We're gonna rebuild the entire front stoop right now! Watch this, Ben!

Biff: Yes, sir! On the double, Hap!

Happy (as he and Biff run off): I lost weight, Pop, you notice?

Charley enters in knickers, even before the boys are gone.

Charley: Listen, if they steal any more from that building the watchman'll put the cops on them!

Linda (to Willy): Don't let Biff . . .

Ben laughs lustily.

Willy: You shoulda seen the lumber they brought home last week. At least a dozen six-by-tens worth all kinds of money.

Charley: Listen, if that watchman —

Willy: I gave them hell, understand. But I got a couple of fearless characters there.

Charley: Willy, the jails are full of fearless characters.

Ben (clapping Willy on the back, with a laugh at Charley): And the stock exchange, friend!

Willy (joining in Ben's laughter): Where are the rest of your pants?

Charley: My wife bought them.

Willy: Now all you need is a golf club and you can go upstairs and go to sleep. *(To Ben.)* Great athlete! Between him and his son Bernard they can't hammer a nail!

Bernard (rushing in): The watchman's chasing Biff!

Willy (angrily): Shut up! He's not stealing anything!

Linda (alarmed, hurrying off left): Where is he? Biff, dear! *(She exits.)*

Willy (moving toward the left, away from Ben): There's nothing wrong. What's the matter with you?

Ben: Nervy boy. Good!

Willy (laughing): Oh, nerves of iron, that Biff!

Charley: Don't know what it is. My New England man comes back and he's bleedin', they murdered him up there.

Willy: It's contacts, Charley, I got important contacts!

Charley (sarcastically): Glad to hear it, Willy. Come in later, we'll shoot a little casino. I'll take some of your Portland money. *(He laughs at Willy and exits.)*

Willy (turning to Ben): Business is bad, it's murderous. But not for me, of course.

Ben: I'll stop by on my way back to Africa.

Willy (longingly): Can't you stay a few days? You're just what I need, Ben, because I — I have a fine position here, but I — well, Dad left when I was such a baby and I never had a chance to talk to him and I still feel — kind of temporary about myself.

Ben: I'll be late for my train.

They are at opposite ends of the stage.

Willy: Ben, my boys — can't we talk? They'd go into the jaws of hell for me, see, but I —

Ben: William, you're being first-rate with your boys. Outstanding, manly chaps!

Willy (hanging on to his words): Oh, Ben, that's good to hear! Because sometimes I'm afraid that I'm not teaching them the right kind of — Ben, how should I teach them?

Ben (giving great weight to each word, and with a certain vicious audacity): William, when I walked into the jungle, I was seventeen. When I walked out I was twenty-one. And, by God, I was rich! *(He goes off into darkness around the right corner of the house.)*

Willy: . . . was rich! That's just the spirit I want to imbue them with! To walk into a jungle! I was right! I was right! I was right!

Ben is gone, but Willy is still speaking to him as Linda, in nightgown and robe, enters the kitchen, glances around for Willy, then goes to the door of the house, looks out and sees him. Comes down to his left. He looks at her.

Linda: Willy, dear? Willy?

Willy: I was right!

Linda: Did you have some cheese? *(He can't answer.)* It's very late, darling. Come to bed, heh?

Willy (looking straight up): Gotta break your neck to see a star in this yard.

Linda: You coming in?

Willy: What ever happened to that diamond watch fob? Remember? When Ben came from Africa that time? Didn't he give me a watch fob with a diamond in it?

Linda: You pawned it, dear. Twelve, thirteen years ago. For Biff's radio correspondence course.

Willy: Gee, that was a beautiful thing. I'll take a walk.

Linda: But you're in your slippers.

Willy (starting to go around the house at the left): I was right! I was! *(Half to Linda, as he goes, shaking his head.)* What a man! There was a man worth talking to. I was right!

Linda (calling after Willy): But in your slippers, Willy!

Willy is almost gone when Biff, in his pajamas, comes down the stairs and enters the kitchen.

Biff: What is he doing out there?

Linda: Sh!

Biff: God Almighty, Mom, how long has he been doing this?

Linda: Don't, he'll hear you.

Biff: What the hell is the matter with him?

Linda: It'll pass by morning.

Biff: Shouldn't we do anything?

Linda: Oh, my dear, you should do a lot of things, but there's nothing to do, so go to sleep.

Happy comes down the stairs and sits on the steps.

Happy: I never heard him so loud, Mom.

Linda: Well, come around more often; you'll hear him. *(She sits down at the table and mends the lining of Willy's jacket.)*

Biff: Why didn't you ever write me about this, Mom?

Linda: How would I write to you? For over three months you had no address.

Biff: I was on the move. But you know I thought of you all the time. You know that, don't you, pal?

Linda: I know, dear, I know. But he likes to have a letter. Just to know that there's still a possibility for better things.

Biff: He's not like this all the time, is he?

Linda: It's when you come home he's always the worst.

Biff: When I come home?

Linda: When you write you're coming, he's all smiles, and talks about the future, and — he's just wonderful. And then the closer you seem to come, the more shaky he gets, and then, by the time you get here, he's arguing, and he seems angry at you. I think it's just that maybe he can't bring himself to — to open up to you. Why are you so hateful to each other? Why is that?

Biff (evasively): I'm not hateful, Mom.

Linda: But you no sooner come in the door than you're fighting!

Biff: I don't know why. I mean to change. I'm tryin', Mom, you understand?

Linda: Are you home to stay now?

Biff: I don't know. I want to look around, see what's doin'.

Linda: Biff, you can't look around all your life, can you?

Biff: I just can't take hold, Mom. I can't take hold of some kind of a life.

Linda: Biff, a man is not a bird, to come and go with the springtime.

Biff: Your hair . . . *(He touches her hair.)* Your hair got so gray.

Linda: Oh, it's been gray since you were in high school. I just stopped dyeing it, that's all.

Biff: Dye it again, will ya? I don't want my pal looking old. *(He smiles.)*

Linda: You're such a boy! You think you can go away for a year and . . . You've got to get it into your head now that one day you'll knock on this door and there'll be strange people here —

Biff: What are you talking about? You're not even sixty, Mom.

Linda: But what about your father?

Biff (lamely): Well, I meant him too.

Happy: He admires Pop.

Linda: Biff, dear, if you don't have any feeling for him, then you can't have any feeling for me.

Biff: Sure I can, Mom.

Linda: No. You can't just come to see me, because I love him. *(With a threat, but only a threat, of tears.)* He's the dearest man in the world to me, and I won't have anyone making him feel unwanted and low and blue. You've got to make up your mind now, darling, there's no leeway any more. Either he's your father and you pay him that respect, or else you're not to come here. I know he's not easy to get along with — nobody knows that better than me — but . . .

Willy (from the left, with a laugh): Hey, hey, Biffo!

Biff (starting to go out after Willy): What the hell is the matter with him? *(Happy stops him.)*

Linda: Don't — don't go near him!

Biff: Stop making excuses for him! He always, always wiped the floor with you. Never had an ounce of respect for you.

Happy: He's always had respect for —

Biff: What the hell do you know about it?

Happy (surlily): Just don't call him crazy!

Biff: He's got no character — Charley wouldn't do this. Not in his own house — spewing out that vomit from his mind.

Happy: Charley never had to cope with what he's got to.

Biff: People are worse off than Willy Loman. Believe me, I've seen them!

Linda: Then make Charley your father, Biff. You can't do that, can you? I don't say he's a great man. Willy Loman never made a lot of money. His name was never in the paper. He's not the finest character that ever lived. But he's a human being, and a terrible thing is happening to him. So attention must be paid. He's not to be allowed to fall into his grave like an old dog. Attention, attention must be finally paid to such a person. You called him crazy —

Biff: I didn't mean —

Linda: No, a lot of people think he's lost his — balance. But you don't have to be very smart to know what his trouble is. The man is exhausted.

Happy: Sure!

Linda: A small man can be just as exhausted as a great man. He works for a company thirty-six years this March, opens up unheard-of territories to their trademark, and now in his old age they take his salary away.

Happy (indignantly): I didn't know that, Mom.

Linda: You never asked, my dear! Now that you get your spending money someplace else you don't trouble your mind with him.

Happy: But I gave you money last —

Linda: Christmas time, fifty dollars! To fix the hot water it cost ninety-seven fifty! For five weeks he's been on straight commission, like a beginner, an unknown!

Biff: Those ungrateful bastards!

Linda: Are they any worse than his sons? When he brought them business, when he was young, they were glad to see him. But now his old friends, the old buyers that loved him so and always found some order to hand him in a pinch — they're all dead, retired. He used to be able to make six, seven calls a day in Boston. Now he takes his valises out of the car and puts them back and takes them out again and he's exhausted. Instead of walking he talks now. He drives seven hundred miles, and when he gets there no one knows him any more, no one welcomes him. And what goes through a man's mind, driving seven hundred miles home without having earned a cent? Why shouldn't he talk to himself? Why? When he has to go to Charley and borrow fifty dollars a week and pretend to me that it's his pay? How long can that go on? How long? You see what I'm sitting here and waiting for? And you tell me he has no character? The man who never worked a day but for your benefit? When does he get the medal for that? Is this his reward — to turn around at the age of sixty-three and find his sons, who he loved better than his life, one a philandering bum —

Happy: Mom!

Linda: That's all you are, my baby! *(To Biff.)* And you! What happened to the love you had for him? You were such pals! How you used to talk to him on the phone every night! How lonely he was till he could come home to you!

Biff: All right, Mom. I'll live here in my room, and I'll get a job. I'll keep away from him, that's all.

Linda: No, Biff. You can't stay here and fight all the time.

Biff: He threw me out of this house, remember that.

Linda: Why did he do that? I never knew why.

Biff: Because I know he's a fake and he doesn't like anybody around who knows!

Linda: Why a fake? In what way? What do you mean?

Biff: Just don't lay it all at my feet. It's between me and him — that's all I have to say. I'll chip in from now on. He'll settle for half my pay check. He'll be all right. I'm going to bed. *(He starts for the stairs.)*

Linda: He won't be all right.

Biff (turning on the stairs, furiously): I hate this city and I'll stay here. Now what do you want?

Linda: He's dying, Biff.

Happy turns quickly to her, shocked.

Biff (after a pause): Why is he dying?

Linda: He's been trying to kill himself.

Biff (with great horror): How?

Linda: I live from day to day.

Biff: What're you talking about?

Linda: Remember I wrote you that he smashed up the car again? In February?

Biff: Well?

Linda: The insurance inspector came. He said that they have evidence. That all these accidents in the last year — weren't — weren't — accidents.

Happy: How can they tell that? That's a lie.

Linda: It seems there's a woman . . . *(She takes a breath as —)*

Biff (sharply but contained): ⎤ What woman?

Linda (simultaneously): ⎦ . . . and this woman . . .

Linda: What?

Biff: Nothing. Go ahead.

Linda: What did you say?

Biff: Nothing. I just said what woman?

Happy: What about her?

Linda: Well, it seems she was walking down the road and saw his car. She says that he wasn't driving fast at all, and that he didn't skid. She says he came to that little bridge, and then deliberately smashed into the railing, and it was only the shallowness of the water that saved him.

Biff: Oh, no, he probably just fell asleep again.

Linda: I don't think he fell asleep.

Biff: Why not?

Linda: Last month . . . *(With great difficulty.)* Oh, boys, it's so hard to say a thing like this! He's just a big stupid man to you, but I tell you there's more good in him than in many other people. *(She chokes, wipes her eyes.)* I was looking for a fuse. The lights blew out, and I went down the cellar. And behind the fuse box — it happened to fall out — was a length of rubber pipe — just short.

Happy: No kidding?

Linda: There's a little attachment on the end of it. I knew right away. And sure enough, on the bottom of the water heater there's a new little nipple on the gas pipe.

Happy (angrily): That — jerk.

Biff: Did you have it taken off?

Linda: I'm — I'm ashamed to. How can I mention it to him? Every day I go down and take away that little rubber pipe. But, when he comes home, I put it back where it was. How can I insult him that way? I don't know what to do. I live from day to day, boys. I tell you, I know every thought in his mind. It sounds so old-fashioned and silly, but I tell you he put his whole life into you and you've turned your backs on him. *(She is bent over in the chair, weeping, her face in her hands.)* Biff, I swear to God! Biff, his life is in your hands!

Happy (to Biff): How do you like that damned fool!

Biff (kissing her): All right, pal, all right. It's all settled now. I've been remiss. I know that, Mom. But now I'll stay, and I swear to you, I'll apply myself. *(Kneeling in front of her, in a fever of self-reproach.)* It's just — you see, Mom, I don't fit in business. Not that I won't try. I'll try, and I'll make good.

Happy: Sure you will. The trouble with you in business was you never tried to please people.

Biff: I know, I —

Happy: Like when you worked for Harrison's. Bob Harrison said you were tops, and then you go and do some damn fool thing like whistling whole songs in the elevator like a comedian.

Biff (against Happy): So what? I like to whistle sometimes.

Happy: You don't raise a guy to a responsible job who whistles in the elevator!

Linda: Well, don't argue about it now.

Happy: Like when you'd go off and swim in the middle of the day instead of taking the line around.

Biff (his resentment rising): Well, don't you run off? You take off sometimes, don't you? On a nice summer day?

Happy: Yeah, but I cover myself!

Linda: Boys!

Happy: If I'm going to take a fade the boss can call any number where I'm supposed to be and they'll swear to him that I just left. I'll tell you something that I hate to say, Biff, but in the business world some of them think you're crazy.

Biff (angered): Screw the business world!

Happy: All right, screw it! Great, but cover yourself!

Linda: Hap, Hap!

Biff: I don't care what they think! They've laughed at Dad for years, and you know why? Because we don't belong in this nut-house of a city! We should be mixing cement on some open plain, or — or carpenters. A carpenter is allowed to whistle!

Willy walks in from the entrance of the house, at left.

Willy: Even your grandfather was better than a carpenter. *(Pause. They watch him.)* You never grew up. Bernard does not whistle in the elevator, I assure you.

Biff (as though to laugh Willy out of it): Yeah, but you do, Pop.

Willy: I never in my life whistled in an elevator! And who in the business world thinks I'm crazy?

Biff: I didn't mean it like that, Pop. Now don't make a whole thing out of it, will ya?

Willy: Go back to the West! Be a carpenter, a cowboy, enjoy yourself!

Linda: Willy, he was just saying —

Willy: I heard what he said!

Happy (trying to quiet Willy): Hey, Pop, come on now . . .

Willy (continuing over Happy's line): They laugh at me, heh? Go to Filene's, go to the Hub, go to Slattery's, Boston. Call out the name Willy Loman and see what happens! Big shot!

Biff: All right, Pop.

Willy: Big!

Biff: All right!

Willy: Why do you always insult me?

Biff: I didn't say a word. *(To Linda.)* Did I say a word?

Linda: He didn't say anything, Willy.

Willy (going to the doorway of the livingroom): All right, good night, good night.

Linda: Willy, dear, he just decided . . .

Willy (to Biff): If you get tired hanging around tomorrow, paint the ceiling I put up in the livingroom.

Biff: I'm leaving early tomorrow.

Happy: He's going to see Bill Oliver, Pop.

Willy (interestedly): Oliver? For what?

Biff (with reserve, but trying, trying): He always said he'd stake me. I'd like to go into business, so maybe I can take him up on it.

Linda: Isn't that wonderful?

Willy: Don't interrupt. What's wonderful about it? There's fifty men in the City of New York who'd stake him. *(To Biff.)* Sporting goods?

Biff: I guess so. I know something about it and —

Willy: He knows something about it! You know sporting goods better than Spalding, for God's sake! How much is he giving you?

Biff: I don't know, I didn't even see him yet, but —

Willy: Then what're you talkin' about?

Biff (getting angry): Well, all I said was I'm gonna see him, that's all!

Willy (turning away): Ah, you're counting your chickens again.

Biff (starting left for the stairs): Oh, Jesus, I'm going to sleep!

Willy (calling after him): Don't curse in this house!

Biff (turning): Since when did you get so clean!

Happy (trying to stop them): Wait a . . .

Willy: Don't use that language to me! I won't have it!

Happy (grabbing Biff, shouts): Wait a minute! I got an idea. I got a feasible idea. Come here, Biff, let's talk this over now, let's talk some sense here. When I was down in Florida last time, I thought of a great idea to sell sporting goods. It just came back to me. You and I, Biff — we have a line, the Loman Line. We train a couple of weeks, and put on a couple of exhibitions, see?

Willy: That's an idea!

Happy: Wait! We form two basketball teams, see? Two water-polo teams. We play each other. It's a million dollars' worth of publicity. Two brothers, see? The Loman Brothers. Displays in the Royal Palms — all the hotels.

And banners over the ring and the basketball court: "Loman Brothers."
Baby, we could sell sporting goods!

Willy: That is a one-million-dollar idea.

Linda: Marvelous!

Biff: I'm in great shape as far as that's concerned.

Happy: And the beauty of it is, Biff, it wouldn't be like a business. We'd be
out playin' ball again . . .

Biff (enthused): Yeah, that's . . .

Willy: Million-dollar . . .

Happy: And you wouldn't get fed up with it, Biff. It'd be the family again.
There'd be the old honor, and comradeship, and if you wanted to go off
for a swim or somethin' — well, you'd do it! Without some smart cooky
gettin' up ahead of you!

Willy: Lick the world! You guys together could absolutely lick the civilized
world.

Biff: I'll see Oliver tomorrow. Hap, if we could work that out . . .

Linda: Maybe things are beginning to —

Willy (wildly enthused, to Linda): Stop interrupting! *(To Biff.)* But don't wear sport
jacket and slacks when you see Oliver.

Biff: No, I'll —

Willy: A business suit, and talk as little as possible, and don't crack any jokes.

Biff: He did like me. Always liked me.

Linda: He loved you!

Willy (to Linda): Will you stop! *(To Biff.)* Walk in very serious. You are not
applying for a boy's job. Money is to pass. Be quiet, fine, and serious.
Everybody likes a kidder, but nobody lends him money.

Happy: I'll try to get some myself, Biff. I'm sure I can.

Willy: I can see great things for you, kids, I think your troubles are over. But
remember, start big and you'll end big. Ask for fifteen. How much you
gonna ask for?

Biff: Gee, I don't know —

Willy: And don't say "Gee." "Gee" is a boy's word. A man walking in for
fifteen thousand dollars does not say "Gee!"

Biff: Ten, I think, would be top though.

Willy: Don't be so modest. You always started too low. Walk in with a big
laugh. Don't look worried. Start off with a couple of your good stories to
lighten things up. It's not what you say, it's how you say it — because
personality always wins the day.

Linda: Oliver always thought the highest of him —

Willy: Will you let me talk?

Biff: Don't yell at her, Pop, will ya?

Willy (angrily): I was talking, wasn't I!

Biff: I don't like you yelling at her all the time, and I'm tellin' you, that's all.

Willy: What're you, takin' over this house?

Linda: Willy —

Willy (turning on her): Don't take his side all the time, goddammit!

Biff (furiously): Stop yelling at her!

Willy (suddenly pulling on his cheek, beaten down, guilt ridden): Give my best to Bill
Oliver — he may remember me. *(He exits through the livingroom doorway.)*

Linda (her voice subdued): What'd you have to start that for? *(Biff turns away.)* You see how sweet he was as soon as you talked hopefully? *(She goes over to Biff.)* Come up and say good night to him. Don't let him go to bed that way.

Happy: Come on, Biff, let's buck him up.

Linda: Please, dear. Just say good night. It takes so little to make him happy. Come. *(She goes through the livingroom doorway, calling upstairs from within the livingroom.)* Your pajamas are hanging in the bathroom, Willy!

Happy (looking toward where Linda went out): What a woman! They broke the mold when they made her. You know that, Biff?

Biff: He's off salary. My God, working on commission!

Happy: Well, let's face it: he's no hot-shot selling man. Except that sometimes, you have to admit, he's a sweet personality.

Biff (deciding): Lend me ten bucks, will ya? I want to buy some new ties.

Happy: I'll take you to a place I know. Beautiful stuff. Wear one of my striped shirts tomorrow.

Biff: She got gray. Mom got awful old. Gee, I'm gonna go in to Oliver tomorrow and knock him for a —

Happy: Come on up. Tell that to Dad. Let's give him a whirl. Come on.

Biff (steamed up): You know, with ten thousand bucks, boy!

Happy (as they go into the livingroom): That's the talk, Biff, that's the first time I've heard the old confidence out of you! *(From within the livingroom, fading off.)* You're gonna live with me, kid, and any babe you want you just say the word . . . *(The last lines are hardly heard. They are mounting the stairs to their parents' bedroom.)*

Linda (entering her bedroom and addressing Willy, who is in the bathroom. She is straightening the bed for him): Can you do anything about the shower? It drips.

Willy (from the bathroom): All of a sudden everything falls to pieces! Goddam plumbing, oughta be sued, those people. I hardly finished putting it in and the thing . . . *(His words rumble off.)*

Linda: I'm just wondering if Oliver will remember him. You think he might?

Willy (coming out of the bathroom in his pajamas): Remember him? What's the matter with you, you crazy? If he'd've stayed with Oliver he'd be on top by now! Wait'll Oliver gets a look at him. You don't know the average caliber any more. The average young man today — *(he is getting into bed)* — is got a caliber of zero. Greatest thing in the world for him was to bum around.

Biff and Happy enter the bedroom. Slight pause.

Willy (stops short, looking at Biff): Glad to hear it, boy.

Happy: He wanted to say good night to you, sport.

Willy (to Biff): Yeah. Knock him dead, boy. What'd you want to tell me?

Biff: Just take it easy, Pop. Good night. *(He turns to go.)*

Willy (unable to resist): And if anything falls off the desk while you're talking to him — like a package or something — don't you pick it up. They have office boys for that.

Linda: I'll make a big breakfast —

Willy: Will you let me finish? *(To Biff.)* Tell him you were in the business in the West. Not farm work.

Biff: All right, Dad.

Linda: I think everything —

Willy (going right through her speech): And don't undersell yourself. No less than fifteen thousand dollars.

Biff (unable to bear him): Okay. Good night, Mom. *(He starts moving.)*

Willy: Because you got a greatness in you, Biff, remember that. You got all kinds a greatness . . . *(He lies back, exhausted. Biff walks out.)*

Linda (calling after Biff): Sleep well, darling!

Happy: I'm gonna get married, Mom. I wanted to tell you.

Linda: Go to sleep, dear.

Happy (going): I just wanted to tell you.

Willy: Keep up the good work. *(Happy exits.)* God . . . remember that Ebbets Field game? The championship of the city?

Linda: Just rest. Should I sing to you?

Willy: Yeah. Sing to me. *(Linda hums a soft lullaby.)* When that team came out — he was the tallest, remember?

Linda: Oh, yes. And in gold.

> *Biff enters the darkened kitchen, takes a cigarette, and leaves the house. He comes downstage into a golden pool of light. He smokes, staring at the night.*

Willy: Like a young god. Hercules — something like that. And the sun, the sun all around him. Remember how he waved to me? Right up from the field, with the representatives of three colleges standing by? And the buyers I brought, and the cheers when he came out — Loman, Loman, Loman! God Almighty, he'll be great yet. A star like that, magnificent, can never really fade away!

> *The light on Willy is fading. The gas heater begins to glow through the kitchen wall, near the stairs, a blue flame beneath red coils.*

Linda (timidly): Willy, dear, what has he got against you?

Willy: I'm so tired. Don't talk any more.

> *Biff slowly returns to the kitchen. He stops, stares toward the heater.*

Linda: Will you ask Howard to let you work in New York?

Willy: First thing in the morning. Everything'll be all right.

> *Biff reaches behind the heater and draws out a length of rubber tubing. He is horrified and turns his head toward Willy's room, still dimly lit, from which the strains of Linda's desperate but monotonous humming rise.*

Willy (staring through the window into the moonlight): Gee, look at the moon moving between the buildings!

> *Biff wraps the tubing around his hand and quickly goes up the stairs. Curtain.*

ACT II

> *Music is heard, gay and bright. The curtain rises as the music fades away. Willy, in shirt sleeves, is sitting at the kitchen table, sipping coffee, his hat in his lap. Linda is filling his cup when she can.*

Willy: Wonderful coffee. Meal in itself.

Linda: Can I make you some eggs?

Willy: No. Take a breath.

Linda: You look so rested, dear.

Willy: I slept like a dead one. First time in months. Imagine, sleeping till ten on a Tuesday morning. Boys left nice and early, heh?

Linda: They were out of here by eight o'clock.

Willy: Good work!

Linda: It was so thrilling to see them leaving together. I can't get over the shaving lotion in this house.

Willy (smiling): Mmm —

Linda: Biff was very changed this morning. His whole attitude seemed to be hopeful. He couldn't wait to get downtown to see Oliver.

Willy: He's heading for a change. There's no question, there simply are certain men that take longer to get — solidified. How did he dress?

Linda: His blue suit. He's so handsome in that suit. He could be a — anything in that suit!

Willy gets up from the table. Linda holds his jacket for him.

Willy: There's no question, no question at all. Gee, on the way home tonight I'd like to buy some seeds.

Linda (laughing): That'd be wonderful. But not enough sun gets back there. Nothing'll grow any more.

Willy: You wait, kid, before it's all over we're gonna get a little place out in the country, and I'll raise some vegetables, a couple of chickens . . .

Linda: You'll do it yet, dear.

Willy walks out of his jacket. Linda follows him.

Willy: And they'll get married, and come for a weekend. I'd build a little guest house. 'Cause I got so many fine tools, all I'd need would be a little lumber and some peace of mind.

Linda (joyfully): I sewed the lining . . .

Willy: I could build two guest houses, so they'd both come. Did he decide how much he's going to ask Oliver for?

Linda (getting him into the jacket): He didn't mention it, but I imagine ten or fifteen thousand. You going to talk to Howard today?

Willy: Yeah. I'll put it to him straight and simple. He'll just have to take me off the road.

Linda: And Willy, don't forget to ask for a little advance, because we've got the insurance premium. It's the grace period now.

Willy: That's a hundred . . . ?

Linda: A hundred and eight, sixty-eight. Because we're a little short again.

Willy: Why are we short?

Linda: Well, you had the motor job on the car . . .

Willy: That goddam Studebaker!

Linda: And you got one more payment on the refrigerator . . .

Willy: But it just broke again!

Linda: Well, it's old, dear.

Willy: I told you we should've bought a well-advertised machine. Charley bought a General Electric and it's twenty years old and it's still good, that son-of-a-bitch.

Linda: But, Willy —

Willy: Whoever heard of a Hastings refrigerator? Once in my life I would like to own something outright before it's broken! I'm always in a race with the junkyard! I just finished paying for the car and it's on its last legs. The refrigerator consumes belts like a goddam maniac. They time those things. They time them so when you finally paid for them, they're used up.

Linda (buttoning up his jacket as he unbuttons it): All told, about two hundred dollars would carry us, dear. But that includes the last payment on the mortgage. After this payment, Willy, the house belongs to us.

Willy: It's twenty-five years!

Linda: Biff was nine years old when we bought it.

Willy: Well, that's a great thing. To weather a twenty-five year mortgage is —

Linda: It's an accomplishment.

Willy: All the cement, the lumber, the reconstruction I put in this house! There ain't a crack to be found in it any more.

Linda: Well, it served its purpose.

Willy: What purpose? Some stranger'll come along, move in, and that's that. If only Biff would take this house, and raise a family . . . *(He starts to go.)* Good-by, I'm late.

Linda (suddenly remembering): Oh, I forgot! You're supposed to meet them for dinner.

Willy: Me?

Linda: At Frank's Chop House on Forty-eighth near Sixth Avenue.

Willy: Is that so! How about you?

Linda: No, just the three of you. They're gonna blow you to a big meal!

Willy: Don't say! Who thought of that?

Linda: Biff came to me this morning, Willy, and he said, "Tell Dad, we want to blow him to a big meal." Be there six o'clock. You and your two boys are going to have dinner.

Willy: Gee whiz! That's really somethin'. I'm gonna knock Howard for a loop, kid. I'll get an advance, and I'll come home with a New York job. Goddammit, now I'm gonna do it!

Linda: Oh, that's the spirit, Willy!

Willy: I will never get behind a wheel the rest of my life!

Linda: It's changing, Willy, I can feel it changing!

Willy: Beyond a question. G'by, I'm late. *(He starts to go again.)*

Linda (calling after him as she runs to the kitchen table for a handkerchief): You got your glasses?

Willy (feels for them, then comes back in): Yeah, yeah, got my glasses.

Linda (giving him the handkerchief): And a handkerchief.

Willy: Yeah, handkerchief.

Linda: And your saccharine?

Willy: Yeah, my saccharine.

Linda: Be careful on the subway stairs.

She kisses him, and a silk stocking is seen hanging from her hand. Willy notices it.

Willy: Will you stop mending stockings? At least while I'm in the house. It gets me nervous. I can't tell you. Please.

Linda hides the stocking in her hand as she follows Willy across the forestage in front of the house.

Linda: Remember, Frank's Chop House.

Willy (passing the apron): Maybe beets would grow out there.

Linda (laughing): But you tried so many times.

Willy: Yeah. Well, don't work hard today. *(He disappears around the right corner of the house.)*

Linda: Be careful!

As Willy vanishes, Linda waves to him. Suddenly the phone rings. She runs across the stage and into the kitchen and lifts it.

Linda: Hello? Oh, Biff! I'm so glad you called, I just . . . Yes, sure, I just told him. Yes, he'll be there for dinner at six o'clock, I didn't forget. Listen, I was just dying to tell you. You know that little rubber pipe I told you about? That he connected to the gas heater? I finally decided to go down the cellar this morning and take it away and destroy it. But it's gone! Imagine? He took it away himself, it isn't there! *(She listens.)* When? Oh, then you took it. Oh — nothing, it's just that I'd hoped he'd taken it away himself. Oh, I'm not worried, darling, because this morning he left in such high spirits, it was like the old days! I'm not afraid any more. Did Mr. Oliver see you? . . . Well, you wait there then. And make a nice impression on him, darling. Just don't perspire too much before you see him. And have a nice time with Dad. He may have big news too! . . . That's right, a New York job. And be sweet to him tonight, dear. Be loving to him. Because he's only a little boat looking for a harbor. *(She is trembling with sorrow and joy.)* Oh, that's wonderful, Biff, you'll save his life. Thanks, darling. Just put your arm around him when he comes into the restaurant. Give him a smile. That's the boy . . . Good-by, dear. . . . You got your comb? . . . That's fine. Good-by, Biff dear.

In the middle of her speech, Howard Wagner, thirty-six, wheels on a small typewriter table on which is a wire-recording machine and proceeds to plug it in. This is on the left forestage. Light slowly fades on Linda as it rises on Howard. Howard is intent on threading the machine and only glances over his shoulder as Willy appears.

Willy: Pst! Pst!

Howard: Hello, Willy, come in.

Willy: Like to have a little talk with you, Howard.

Howard: Sorry to keep you waiting. I'll be with you in a minute.

Willy: What's that, Howard?

Howard: Didn't you ever see one of these? Wire recorder.

Willy: Oh. Can we talk a minute?

Howard: Records things. Just got delivery yesterday. Been driving me crazy, the most terrific machine I ever saw in my life. I was up all night with it.

Willy: What do you do with it?

Howard: I bought it for dictation, but you can do anything with it. Listen to this. I had it home last night. Listen to what I picked up. The first one is my daughter. Get this. *(He flicks the switch and "Roll out the Barrel" is heard being whistled.)* Listen to that kid whistle.

Willy: That is lifelike, isn't it?

Howard: Seven years old. Get that tone.

Willy: Ts, ts. Like to ask a little favor if you . . .

The whistling breaks off, and the voice of Howard's Daughter is heard.

His Daughter: "Now you, Daddy."

Howard: She's crazy for me! *(Again the same song is whistled.)* That's me! Ha! *(He winks.)*

Willy: You're very good!

The whistling breaks off again. The machine runs silent for a moment.

Howard: Sh! Get this now, this is my son.

His Son: "The capital of Alabama is Montgomery; the capital of Arizona is Phoenix; the capital of Arkansas is Little Rock; the capital of California is Sacramento . . ." *(And on, and on.)*

Howard (holding up five fingers): Five years old, Willy!

Willy: He'll make an announcer some day!

His Son (continuing): "The capital . . ."

Howard: Get that — alphabetical order! *(The machine breaks off suddenly.)* Wait a minute. The maid kicked the plug out.

Willy: It certainly is a —

Howard: Sh, for God's sake!

His Son: "It's nine o'clock, Bulova watch time. So I have to go to sleep."

Willy: That really is —

Howard: Wait a minute! The next is my wife.

They wait.

Howard's Voice: "Go on, say something." *(Pause.)* "Well, you gonna talk?"

His Wife: "I can't think of anything."

Howard's Voice: "Well, talk — it's turning."

His Wife (shyly, beaten): "Hello." *(Silence.)* "Oh, Howard, I can't talk into this . . ."

Howard (snapping the machine off): That was my wife.

Willy: That is a wonderful machine. Can we —

Howard: I tell you, Willy, I'm gonna take my camera, and my bandsaw, and all my hobbies, and out they go. This is the most fascinating relaxation I ever found.

Willy: I think I'll get one myself.

Howard: Sure, they're only a hundred and a half. You can't do without it. Supposing you wanna hear Jack Benny, see? But you can't be at home at that hour. So you tell the maid to turn the radio on when Jack Benny comes on, and this automatically goes on with the radio . . .

Willy: And when you come home you . . .

Howard: You can come home twelve o'clock, one o'clock, any time you like, and you get yourself a Coke and sit yourself down, throw the switch, and there's Jack Benny's program in the middle of the night!

Willy: I'm definitely going to get one. Because lots of time I'm on the road, and I think to myself, what I must be missing on the radio!

Howard: Don't you have a radio in the car?

Willy: Well, yeah, but who ever thinks of turning it on?

Howard: Say, aren't you supposed to be in Boston?

Willy: That's what I want to talk to you about, Howard. You got a minute?

(He draws a chair in from the wing.)

Howard: What happened? What're you doing here?

Willy: Well . . .

Howard: You didn't crack up again, did you?

Willy: Oh, no. No . . .

Howard: Geez, you had me worried there for a minute. What's the trouble?

Willy: Well, to tell you the truth, Howard, I've come to the decision that I'd rather not travel any more.

Howard: Not travel! Well, what'll you do?

Willy: Remember, Christmas time, when you had the party here? You said you'd try to think of some spot for me here in town.

Howard: With us?

Willy: Well, sure.

Howard: Oh, yeah, yeah. I remember. Well, I couldn't think of anything for you, Willy.

Willy: I tell ya, Howard. The kids are all grown up, y'know. I don't need much any more. If I could take home — well, sixty-five dollars a week, I could swing it.

Howard: Yeah, but Willy, see I —

Willy: I tell ya why, Howard. Speaking frankly and between the two of us, y'know — I'm just a little tired.

Howard: Oh, I could understand that, Willy. But you're a road man, Willy, and we do a road business. We've only got a half-dozen salesmen on the floor here.

Willy: God knows, Howard, I never asked a favor of any man. But I was with the firm when your father used to carry you in here in his arms.

Howard: I know that, Willy, but —

Willy: Your father came to me the day you were born and asked me what I thought of the name of Howard, may he rest in peace.

Howard: I appreciate that, Willy, but there just is no spot here for you. If I had a spot I'd slam you right in, but I just don't have a single, solitary spot.

He looks for his lighter. Willy has picked it up and gives it to him. Pause.

Willy (with increasing anger): Howard, all I need to set my table is fifty dollars a week.

Howard: But where am I going to put you, kid?

Willy: Look, it isn't a question of whether I can sell merchandise, is it?

Howard: No, but it's a business, kid, and everybody's gotta pull his own weight.

Willy (desperately): Just let me tell you a story, Howard —

Howard: 'Cause you gotta admit, business is business.

Willy (angrily): Business is definitely business, but just listen for a minute. You don't understand this. When I was a boy — eighteen, nineteen — I was already on the road. And there was a question in my mind as to whether selling had a future for me. Because in those days I had a yearning to go to Alaska. See, there were three gold strikes in one month in Alaska, and I felt like going out. Just for the ride, you might say.

Howard (barely interested): Don't say.

Willy: Oh, yeah, my father lived many years in Alaska. He was an adventurous man. We've got quite a little streak of self-reliance in our family. I thought I'd go out with my older brother and try to locate him, and maybe settle in the North with the old man. And I was almost decided to go, when I met a salesman in the Parker House. His name was Dave Singleman. And he was eighty-four years old, and he'd drummed merchandise in thirty-one states. And old Dave, he'd go up to his room, y'understand, put on his green velvet slippers — I'll never forget — and pick up his phone and call the buyers, and without ever leaving his room, at the age of eighty-four, he made his living. And when I saw that, I realized that selling was the greatest career a man could want. 'Cause what could be more satisfying than to be able to go, at the age of eighty-four, into twenty or thirty different cities, and pick up a phone, and be remembered and loved and helped by so many different people? Do you know? when he died — and by the way he died the death of a salesman, in his green velvet slippers in the smoker of the New York, New Haven and Hartford, going into Boston — when he died, hundreds of salesmen and buyers were at his funeral. Things were sad on a lotta trains for months after that. *(He stands up. Howard has not looked at him.)* In those days there was personality in it, Howard. There was respect, and comradeship, and gratitude in it. Today, it's all cut and dried, and there's no chance for bringing friendship to bear — or personality. You see what I mean? They don't know me any more.

Howard (moving away, to the right): That's just the thing, Willy.

Willy: If I had forty dollars a week — that's all I'd need. Forty dollars, Howard.

Howard: Kid, I can't take blood from a stone, I —

Willy (desperation is on him now): Howard, the year Al Smith was nominated, your father came to me and —

Howard (starting to go off): I've got to see some people, kid.

Willy (stopping him): I'm talking about your father! There were promises made across this desk! You mustn't tell me you've got people to see — I put thirty-four years into this firm, Howard, and now I can't pay my insurance! You can't eat the orange and throw the peel away — a man is not a piece of fruit! *(After a pause.)* Now pay attention. Your father — in 1928 I had a big year. I averaged a hundred and seventy dollars a week in commissions.

Howard (impatiently): Now, Willy, you never averaged —

Willy (banging his hand on the desk): I averaged a hundred and seventy dollars a week in the year of 1928! And your father came to me — or rather, I was in the office here — it was right over this desk — and he put his hand on my shoulder —

Howard (getting up): You'll have to excuse me, Willy, I gotta see some people. Pull yourself together. *(Going out.)* I'll be back in a little while.

On Howard's exit, the light on his chair grows very bright and strange.

Willy: Pull myself together! What the hell did I say to him? My God, I was yelling at him! How could I! *(Willy breaks off, staring at the light, which occupies the chair, animating it. He approaches this chair, standing across the desk from it.)* Frank, Frank, don't you remember what you told me that time? How you put your hand on my shoulder, and Frank . . . *(He leans on the desk and as he speaks the dead man's name he accidentally switches on the recorder, and instantly —)*

Howard's Son: ". . . of New York is Albany. The capital of Ohio is Cincinnati, the capital of Rhode Island is . . ." *(The recitation continues.)*

Willy (leaping away with fright, shouting): Ha! Howard! Howard! Howard!

Howard (rushing in): What happened?

Willy (pointing at the machine, which continues nasally, childishly, with the capital cities): Shut it off! Shut it off!

Howard (pulling the plug out): Look, Willy . . .

Willy (pressing his hands to his eyes): I gotta get myself some coffee. I'll get some coffee . . .

Willy starts to walk out. Howard stops him.

Howard (rolling up the cord): Willy, look . . .

Willy: I'll go to Boston.

Howard: Willy, you can't go to Boston for us.

Willy: Why can't I go?

Howard: I don't want you to represent us. I've been meaning to tell you for a long time now.

Willy: Howard, are you firing me?

Howard: I think you need a good long rest, Willy.

Willy: Howard —

Howard: And when you feel better, come back, and we'll see if we can work something out.

Willy: But I gotta earn money, Howard. I'm in no position —

Howard: Where are your sons? Why don't your sons give you a hand?

Willy: They're working on a very big deal.

Howard: This is no time for false pride, Willy. You go to your sons and tell them that you're tired. You've got two great boys, haven't you?

Willy: Oh, no question, no question, but in the meantime . . .

Howard: Then that's that, heh?

Willy: All right, I'll go to Boston tomorrow.

Howard: No, no.

Willy: I can't throw myself on my sons. I'm not a cripple!

Howard: Look, kid, I'm busy this morning.

Willy (grasping Howard's arm): Howard, you've got to let me go to Boston!

Howard (hard, keeping himself under control): I've got a line of people to see this morning. Sit down, take five minutes, and pull yourself together, and then go home, will ya? I need the office, Willy. *(He starts to go, turns, remembering the recorder, starts to push off the table holding the recorder.)* Oh, yeah. Whenever you can this week, stop by and drop off the samples. You'll feel better, Willy, and then come back and we'll talk. Pull yourself together, kid, there's people outside.

Howard exits, pushing the table off left. Willy stares into space, exhausted. Now the music is heard — Ben's music — first distantly, then closer, closer. As Willy speaks, Ben enters from the right. He carries valise and umbrella.

Willy: Oh, Ben, how did you do it? What is the answer? Did you wind up the Alaska deal already?

Ben: Doesn't take much time if you know what you're doing. Just a short business trip. Boarding ship in an hour. Wanted to say good-by.

Willy: Ben, I've got to talk to you.

Ben (glancing at his watch): Haven't the time, William.

Willy (crossing the apron to Ben): Ben, nothing's working out. I don't know what to do.

Ben: Now, look here, William. I've bought timberland in Alaska and I need a man to look after things for me.

Willy: God, timberland! Me and my boys in those grand outdoors!

Ben: You've a new continent at your doorstep, William. Get out of these cities, they're full of talk and time payments and courts of law. Screw on your fists and you can fight for a fortune up there.

Willy: Yes, yes! Linda! Linda!

Linda enters as of old, with the wash.

Linda: Oh, you're back?

Ben: I haven't much time.

Willy: No, wait! Linda, he's got a proposition for me in Alaska.

Linda: But you've got — *(To Ben.)* He's got a beautiful job here.

Willy: But in Alaska, kid, I could —

Linda: You're doing well enough, Willy!

Ben (to Linda): Enough for what, my dear?

Linda (frightened of Ben and angry at him): Don't say those things to him! Enough to be happy right here, right now. *(To Willy, while Ben laughs.)* Why must everybody conquer the world? You're well liked, and the boys love you, and someday — *(to Ben)* — why, old man Wagner told him just the other day that if he keeps it up he'll be a member of the firm, didn't he, Willy?

Willy: Sure, sure. I am building something with this firm, Ben, and if a man is building something he must be on the right track, mustn't he?

Ben: What are you building? Lay your hand on it. Where is it?

Willy (hesitantly): That's true, Linda, there's nothing.

Linda: Why? *(To Ben.)* There's a man eighty-four years old —

Willy: That's right, Ben, that's right. When I look at that man I say, what is there to worry about?

Ben: Bah!

Willy: It's true, Ben. All he has to do is go into any city, pick up the phone, and he's making his living and you know why?

Ben (picking up his valise): I've got to go.

Willy (holding Ben back): Look at this boy!

Biff, in his high school sweater, enters carrying suitcase. Happy carries Biff's shoulder guards, gold helmet, and football pants.

Willy: Without a penny to his name, three great universities are begging for him, and from there the sky's the limit, because it's not what you do, Ben. It's who you know and the smile on your face! It's contacts, Ben, contacts! The whole wealth of Alaska passes over the lunch table at the Commodore Hotel, and that's the wonder, the wonder of this country, that a man can end with diamonds here on the basis of being liked! *(He turns to Biff.)* And that's why when you get out on that field today it's important. Because thousands of people will be rooting for you and loving you. *(To Ben, who has again begun to leave.)* And Ben! when he walks into a business office his name will sound out like a bell and all the doors will open to him! I've seen it, Ben, I've seen it a thousand times! You can't feel it with your hand like timber, but it's there!

Ben: Good-by, William.

Willy: Ben, am I right? Don't you think I'm right? I value your advice.

Ben: There's a new continent at your doorstep, William. You could walk out rich. Rich. *(He is gone.)*

Willy: We'll do it here, Ben! You hear me? We're gonna do it here!

Young Bernard rushes in. The gay music of the boys is heard.

Bernard: Oh, gee, I was afraid you left already!

Willy: Why? What time is it?

Bernard: It's half-past one!

Willy: Well, come on, everybody! Ebbets Field next stop! Where's the pennants? *(He rushes through the wall-line of the kitchen and out into the livingroom.)*

Linda (to Biff): Did you pack fresh underwear?

Biff (who has been limbering up): I want to go!

Bernard: Biff, I'm carrying your helmet, ain't I?

Happy: No, I'm carrying the helmet.

Bernard: Oh, Biff, you promised me.

Happy: I'm carrying the helmet.

Bernard: How am I going to get in the locker room?

Linda: Let him carry the shoulder guards. *(She puts her coat and hat on in the kitchen.)*

Bernard: Can I, Biff? 'Cause I told everybody I'm going to be in the locker room.

Happy: In Ebbets Field it's the clubhouse.

Bernard: I meant the clubhouse. Biff!

Happy: Biff!

Biff (grandly, after a slight pause): Let him carry the shoulder guards.

Happy (as he gives Bernard the shoulder guards): Stay close to us now.

Willy rushes in with the pennants.

Willy (handing them out): Everybody wave when Biff comes out on the field. *(Happy and Bernard run off.)* You set now, boy?

The music has died away.

Biff: Ready to go, Pop. Every muscle is ready.

Willy (at the edge of the apron): You realize what this means?

Biff: That's right, Pop.

Willy (feeling Biff's muscles): You're comin' home this afternoon captain of the All-Scholastic Championship Team of the City of New York.

Biff: I got it, Pop. And remember, pal, when I take off my helmet, that touchdown is for you.

Willy: Let's go! *(He is starting out, with his arm around Biff, when Charley enters, as of old, in knickers.)* I got no room for you, Charley.

Charley: Room? For what?

Willy: In the car.

Charley: You goin' for a ride? I wanted to shoot some casino.

Willy (furiously): Casino! *(Incredulously.)* Don't you realize what today is?

Linda: Oh, he knows, Willy. He's just kidding you.

Willy: That's nothing to kid about!

Charley: No, Linda, what's goin' on?

Linda: He's playing in Ebbets Field.

Charley: Baseball in this weather?

Willy: Don't talk to him. Come on, come on! *(He is pushing them out.)*

Charley: Wait a minute, didn't you hear the news?

Willy: What?

Charley: Don't you listen to the radio? Ebbets Field just blew up.

Willy: You go to hell! *(Charley laughs. Pushing them out.)* Come on, come on! We're late.

Charley (as they go): Knock a homer, Biff, knock a homer!

Willy (the last to leave, turning to Charley): I don't think that was funny, Charley. This is the greatest day of his life.

Charley: Willy, when are you going to grow up?

Willy: Yeah, heh? When this game is over, Charley, you'll be laughing out of the other side of your face. They'll be calling him another Red Grange. Twenty-five thousand a year.

Charley (kidding): Is that so?

Willy: Yeah, that's so.

Charley: Well, then, I'm sorry, Willy. But tell me something.

Willy: What?

Charley: Who is Red Grange?

Willy: Put up your hands. Goddam you, put up your hands!

Charley, chuckling, shakes his head and walks away, around the left corner of the stage. Willy follows him. The music rises to a mocking frenzy.

Willy: Who the hell do you think you are, better than everybody else? You don't know everything, you big, ignorant, stupid . . . Put up your hands!

Light rises, on the right side of the forestage, on a small table in the reception room of Charley's office. Traffic sounds are heard. Bernard, now mature, sits whistling to himself. A pair of tennis rackets and an overnight bag are on the floor beside him.

Willy (offstage): What are you walking away for? Don't walk away! If you're going to say something say it to my face! I know you laugh at me behind my back. You'll laugh out of the other side of your goddam face after this game. Touchdown! Touchdown! Eighty thousand people! Touchdown! Right between the goal posts.

Bernard is a quiet, earnest, but self-assured young man. Willy's voice is coming from right upstage now. Bernard lowers his feet off the table and listens. Jenny, his father's secretary, enters.

Jenny (distressed): Say, Bernard, will you go out in the hall?

Bernard: What is that noise? Who is it?

Jenny: Mr. Loman. He just got off the elevator.

Bernard (getting up): Who's he arguing with?

Jenny: Nobody. There's nobody with him. I can't deal with him any more, and your father gets all upset everytime he comes. I've got a lot of typing to do, and your father's waiting to sign it. Will you see him?

Willy (entering): Touchdown! Touch — *(He sees Jenny.)* Jenny, Jenny, good to see you. How're ya? Workin'? Or still honest?

Jenny: Fine. How've you been feeling?

Willy: Not much any more, Jenny. Ha, ha! *(He is surprised to see the rackets.)*

Bernard: Hello, Uncle Willy.

Willy (almost shocked): Bernard! Well, look who's here! *(He comes quickly, guiltily, to Bernard and warmly shakes his hand.)*

Bernard: How are you? Good to see you.

Willy: What are you doing here?

Bernard: Oh, just stopped by to see Pop. Get off my feet till my train leaves. I'm going to Washington in a few minutes.

Willy: Is he in?

Bernard: Yes, he's in his office with the accountant. Sit down.

Willy (sitting down): What're you going to do in Washington?

Bernard: Oh, just a case I've got there, Willy.

Willy: That so? *(indicating the rackets.)* You going to play tennis there?

Bernard: I'm staying with a friend who's got a court.

Willy: Don't say. His own tennis court. Must be fine people, I bet.

Bernard: They are, very nice. Dad tells me Biff's in town.

Willy (with a big smile): Yeah, Biff's in. Working on a very big deal, Bernard.

Bernard: What's Biff doing?

Willy: Well, he's been doing very big things in the West. But he decided to establish himself here. Very big. We're having dinner. Did I hear your wife had a boy?

Bernard: That's right. Our second.

Willy: Two boys! What do you know!

Bernard: What kind of a deal has Biff got?

Willy: Well, Bill Oliver — very big sporting-goods man — he wants Biff very badly. Called him in from the West. Long distance, carte blanche, special deliveries. Your friends have their own private tennis court?

Bernard: You still with the old firm, Willy?

Willy (after a pause): I'm — I'm overjoyed to see how you made the grade, Bernard, overjoyed. It's an encouraging thing to see a young man really — really — Looks very good for Biff — very — *(He breaks off, then.)* Bernard — *(He is so full of emotion, he breaks off again.)*

Bernard: What is it, Willy?

Willy (small and alone): What — what's the secret?

Bernard: What secret?

Willy: How — how did you? Why didn't he ever catch on?

Bernard: I wouldn't know that, Willy.

Willy (confidentially, desperately): You were his friend, his boyhood friend. There's something I don't understand about it. His life ended after that Ebbets Field game. From the age of seventeen nothing good ever happened to him.

Bernard: He never trained himself for anything.

Willy: But he did, he did. After high school he took so many correspondence courses. Radio mechanics; television; God knows what, and never made the slightest mark.

Bernard (taking off his glasses): Willy, do you want to talk candidly?

Willy (rising, faces Bernard): I regard you as a very brilliant man, Bernard. I value your advice.

Bernard: Oh, the hell with the advice, Willy. I couldn't advise you. There's just one thing I've always wanted to ask you. When he was supposed to graduate, and the math teacher flunked him —

Willy: Oh, that son-of-a-bitch ruined his life.

Bernard: Yeah, but, Willy, all he had to do was go to summer school and make up that subject.

Willy: That's right, that's right.

Bernard: Did you tell him not to go to summer school?

Willy: Me? I begged him to go. I ordered him to go!

Bernard: Then why wouldn't he go?

Willy: Why? Why! Bernard, that question has been trailing me like a ghost for the last fifteen years. He flunked the subject, and laid down and died like a hammer hit him!

Bernard: Take it easy, kid.

Willy: Let me talk to you — I got nobody to talk to. Bernard, Bernard, was it my fault? Y'see? It keeps going around in my mind, maybe I did something to him. I got nothing to give him.

Bernard: Don't take it so hard.

Willy: Why did he lay down? What is the story there? You were his friend!

Bernard: Willy, I remember, it was June, and our grades came out. And he'd flunked math.

Willy: That son-of-a-bitch!

Bernard: No, it wasn't right then. Biff just got very angry, I remember, and he was ready to enroll in summer school.

Willy (surprised): He was?

Bernard: He wasn't beaten by it at all. But then, Willy, he disappeared from the block for almost a month. And I got the idea that he'd gone up to New England to see you. Did he have a talk with you then?

Willy stares in silence.

Bernard: Willy?

Willy (with a strong edge of resentment in his voice): Yeah, he came to Boston. What about it?

Bernard: Well, just that when he came back — I'll never forget this, it always mystifies me. Because I'd thought so well of Biff, even though he'd always taken advantage of me. I loved him, Willy, y'know? And he came back after that month and took his sneakers — remember those sneakers with "University of Virginia" printed on them? He was so proud of those, wore them every day. And he took them down in the cellar, and burned them up in the furnace. We had a fist fight. It lasted at least half an hour. Just the two of us, punching each other down the cellar, and crying right through it. I've often thought of how strange it was that I knew he'd given up his life. What happened in Boston, Willy?

Willy looks at him as at an intruder.

Bernard: I just bring it up because you asked me.

Willy (angrily): Nothing. What do you mean, "What happened?" What's that got to do with anything?

Bernard: Well, don't get sore.

Willy: What are you trying to do, blame it on me? If a boy lays down is that my fault?

Bernard: Now, Willy, don't get —

Willy: Well, don't — don't talk to me that way! What does that mean, "What happened?"

Charley enters. He is in his vest, and he carries a bottle of bourbon.

Charley: Hey, you're going to miss that train. *(He waves the bottle.)*

Bernard: Yeah, I'm going. *(He takes the bottle.)* Thanks, Pop. *(He picks up his rackets and bag.)* Good-by, Willy, and don't worry about it. You know, "If at first you don't succeed . . ."

Willy: Yes, I believe in that.

Bernard: But sometimes, Willy, it's better for a man just to walk away.

Willy: Walk away?

Bernard: That's right.

Willy: But if you can't walk away?

Bernard (after a slight pause): I guess that's when it's tough. *(Extending his hand.)* Good-by, Willy.

Willy (shaking Bernard's hand): Good-by, boy.

Charley (an arm on Bernard's shoulder): How do you like this kid? Gonna argue a case in front of the Supreme Court.

Bernard (protesting): Pop!

Willy (genuinely shocked, pained, and happy): No! The Supreme Court!

Bernard: I gotta run. 'By, Dad!

Charley: Knock 'em dead, Bernard!

Bernard goes off.

Willy (as Charley takes out his wallet): The Supreme Court! And he didn't even mention it!

Charley (counting out money on the desk): He don't have to — he's gonna do it.

Willy: And you never told him what to do, did you? You never took any interest in him.

Charley: My salvation is that I never took any interest in anything. There's some money — fifty dollars. I got an accountant inside.

Willy: Charley, look . . . *(With difficulty.)* I got my insurance to pay. If you can manage it — I need a hundred and ten dollars.

Charley doesn't reply for a moment; merely stops moving.

Willy: I'd draw it from my bank but Linda would know, and I . . .

Charley: Sit down, Willy.

Willy (moving toward the chair): I'm keeping an account of everything, remember. I'll pay every penny back. *(He sits.)*

Charley: Now listen to me, Willy.

Willy: I want you to know I appreciate . . .

Charley (sitting down on the table): Willy, what're you doin'? What the hell is goin' on in your head?

Willy: Why? I'm simply . . .

Charley: I offered you a job. You can make fifty dollars a week. And I won't send you on the road.

Willy: I've got a job.

Charley: Without pay? What kind of a job is a job without pay? *(He rises.)* Now, look, kid, enough is enough. I'm no genius but I know when I'm being insulted.

Willy: Insulted!

Charley: Why don't you want to work for me?

Willy: What's the matter with you? I've got a job.

Charley: Then what're you walkin' in here every week for?

Willy (getting up): Well, if you don't want me to walk in here —

Charley: I am offering you a job.

Willy: I don't want your goddam job!

Charley: When the hell are you going to grow up?

Willy (furiously): You big ignoramus, if you say that to me again I'll rap you one! I don't care how big you are! *(He's ready to fight.)*

> Pause.

Charley (kindly, going to him): How much do you need, Willy?

Willy: Charley, I'm strapped. I'm strapped. I don't know what to do. I was just fired.

Charley: Howard fired you?

Willy: That snotnose. Imagine that? I named him. I named him Howard.

Charley: Willy, when're you gonna realize that them things don't mean anything? You named him Howard, but you can't sell that. The only thing you got in this world is what you can sell. And the funny thing is that you're a salesman, and you don't know that.

Willy: I've always tried to think otherwise, I guess. I always felt that if a man was impressive, and well liked, that nothing —

Charley: Why must everybody like you? Who liked J. P. Morgan? Was he impressive? In a Turkish bath he'd look like a butcher. But with his pockets on he was very well liked. Now listen, Willy, I know you don't like me, and nobody can say I'm in love with you, but I'll give you a job because — just for the hell of it, put it that way. Now what do you say?

Willy: I — I just can't work for you, Charley.

Charley: What're you, jealous of me?

Willy: I can't work for you, that's all, don't ask me why.

Charley (angered, takes out more bills): You been jealous of me all your life, you damned fool! Here, pay your insurance. *(He puts the money in Willy's hand.)*

Willy: I'm keeping strict accounts.

Charley: I've got some work to do. Take care of yourself. And pay your insurance.

Willy (moving to the right): Funny, y'know? After all the highways, and the trains, and the appointments, and the years, you end up worth more dead than alive.

Charley: Willy, nobody's worth nothin' dead. *(After a slight pause.)* Did you hear what I said?

Willy stands still, dreaming.

Charley: Willy!

Willy: Apologize to Bernard for me when you see him. I didn't mean to argue with him. He's a fine boy. They're all fine boys, and they'll end up big — all of them. Someday they'll all play tennis together. Wish me luck, Charley. He saw Bill Oliver today.

Charley: Good luck.

Willy (on the verge of tears): Charley, you're the only friend I got. Isn't that a remarkable thing? *(He goes out.)*

Charley: Jesus!

Charley stares after him a moment and follows. All light blacks out. Suddenly raucous music is heard, and a red glow rises behind the screen at right. Stanley, a young waiter, appears, carrying a table, followed by Happy, who is carrying two chairs.

Stanley (putting the table down): That's all right, Mr. Loman, I can handle it myself. *(He turns and takes the chairs from Happy and places them at the table.)*

Happy (glancing around): Oh, this is better.

Stanley: Sure, in the front there you're in the middle of all kinds a noise. Whenever you got a party, Mr. Loman, you just tell me and I'll put you back here. Y'know, there's a lotta people they don't like it private, because when they go out they like to see a lotta action around them because they're sick and tired to stay in the house by theirself. But I know you, you ain't from Hackensack. You know what I mean?

Happy (sitting down): So how's it coming, Stanley?

Stanley: Ah, it's a dog's life. I only wish during the war they'd a took me in the Army. I coulda been dead by now.

Happy: My brother's back, Stanley.

Stanley: Oh, he come back, heh? From the Far West.

Happy: Yeah, big cattle man, my brother, so treat him right. And my father's coming too.

Stanley: Oh, your father too!

Happy: You got a couple of nice lobsters?

Stanley: Hundred per cent, big.

Happy: I want them with the claws.

Stanley: Don't worry, I don't give you no mice. *(Happy laughs.)* How about some wine? It'll put a head on the meal.

Happy: No. You remember, Stanley, that recipe I brought you from overseas? With the champagne in it?

Stanley: Oh, yeah, sure. I still got it tacked up yet in the kitchen. But that'll have to cost a buck apiece anyways.

Happy: That's all right.

Stanley: What'd you, hit a number or somethin'?

Happy: No, it's a little celebration. My brother is — I think he pulled off a big deal today. I think we're going into business together.

Stanley: Great! That's the best for you. Because a family business, you know what I mean? — that's the best.

Happy: That's what I think.

Stanley: 'Cause what's the difference? Somebody steals? It's in the family. Know what I mean? *(Sotto voce.)* Like this bartender here. The boss is goin' crazy what kinda leak he's got in the cash register. You put it in but it don't come out.

Happy (raising his head): Sh!

Stanley: What?

Happy: You notice I wasn't lookin' right or left, was I?

Stanley: No.

Happy: And my eyes are closed.

Stanley: So what's the — ?

Happy: Strudel's comin'.

Stanley (catching on, looks around): Ah, no, there's no —

He breaks off as a furred, lavishly dressed Girl enters and sits at the next table. Both follow her with their eyes.

Stanley: Geez, how'd ya know?

Happy: I got radar or something. *(Staring directly at her profile.)* Oooooooo . . . Stanley.

Stanley: I think that's for you, Mr. Loman.

Happy: Look at that mouth. Oh, God. And the binoculars.

Stanley: Geez, you got a life, Mr. Loman.

Happy: Wait on her.

Stanley (going to The Girl's table): Would you like a menu, ma'am?

Girl: I'm expecting someone, but I'd like a —

Happy: Why don't you bring her — excuse me, miss, do you mind? I sell champagne, and I'd like you to try my brand. Bring her a champagne, Stanley.

Girl: That's awfully nice of you.

Happy: Don't mention it. It's all company money. *(He laughs.)*

Girl: That's a charming product to be selling, isn't it?

Happy: Oh, gets to be like everything else. Selling is selling, y'know.

Girl: I suppose.

Happy: You don't happen to sell, do you?

Girl: No, I don't sell.

Happy: Would you object to a compliment from a stranger? You ought to be on a magazine cover.

Girl (looking at him a little archly): I have been.

Stanley comes in with a glass of champagne.

Happy: What'd I say before, Stanley? You see? She's a cover girl.

Stanley: Oh, I could see, I could see.

Happy (to The Girl): What magazine?

Girl: Oh, a lot of them. *(She takes the drink.)* Thank you.

Happy: You know what they say in France, don't you? "Champagne is the drink of the complexion" — Hya, Biff!

Biff has entered and sits with Happy.

Biff: Hello, kid. Sorry I'm late.

Happy: I just got here. Uh, Miss — ?

Girl: Forsythe.

Happy: Miss Forsythe, this is my brother.

Biff: Is Dad here?

Happy: His name is Biff. You might've heard of him. Great football player.

Girl: Really? What team?

Happy: Are you familiar with football?

Girl: No, I'm afraid I'm not.

Happy: Biff is quarterback with the New York Giants.

Girl: Well, that is nice, isn't it? *(She drinks.)*

Happy: Good health.

Girl: I'm happy to meet you.

Happy: That's my name. Hap. It's really Harold, but at West Point they called me Happy.

Girl (now really impressed): Oh, I see. How do you do? *(She turns her profile.)*

Biff: Isn't Dad coming?

Happy: You want her?

Biff: Oh, I could never make that.

Happy: I remember the time that idea would never come into your head. Where's the old confidence, Biff?

Biff: I just saw Oliver —

Happy: Wait a minute. I've got to see that old confidence again. Do you want her? She's on call.

Biff: Oh, no. *(He turns to look at The Girl.)*

Happy: I'm telling you. Watch this. *(Turning to The Girl.)* Honey? *(She turns to him.)* Are you busy?

Girl: Well, I am . . . but I could make a phone call.

Happy: Do that, will you, honey? And see if you can get a friend. We'll be here for a while. Biff is one of the greatest football players in the country.

Girl (standing up): Well, I'm certainly happy to meet you.

Happy: Come back soon.

Girl: I'll try.

Happy: Don't try, honey, try hard.

The Girl exits. Stanley follows, shaking his head in bewildered admiration.

Happy: Isn't that a shame now? A beautiful girl like that? That's why I can't get married. There's not a good woman in a thousand. New York is loaded with them, kid!

Biff: Hap, look —

Happy: I told you she was on call!

Biff (strangely unnerved): Cut it out, will ya? I want to say something to you.

Happy: Did you see Oliver?

Biff: I saw him all right. Now look, I want to tell Dad a couple of things and I want you to help me.

Happy: What? Is he going to back you?

Biff: Are you crazy? You're out of your goddam head, you know that?

Happy: Why? What happened?

Biff (breathlessly): I did a terrible thing today, Hap. It's been the strangest day I ever went through. I'm all numb, I swear.

Happy: You mean he wouldn't see you?

Biff: Well, I waited six hours for him, see? All day. Kept sending my name in. Even tried to date his secretary so she'd get me to him, but no soap.

Happy: Because you're not showin' the old confidence, Biff. He remembered you, didn't he?

Biff (stopping Happy with a gesture): Finally, about five o'clock, he comes out. Didn't remember who I was or anything. I felt like such an idiot, Hap.

Happy: Did you tell him my Florida idea?

Biff: He walked away. I saw him for one minute. I got so mad I could've torn the walls down! How the hell did I ever get the idea I was a salesman there? I even believed myself that I'd been a salesman for him! And then he gave me one look and — I realized what a ridiculous lie my whole life has been! We've been talking in a dream for fifteen years. I was a shipping clerk.

Happy: What'd you do?

Biff (with great tension and wonder): Well, he left, see. And the secretary went out. I was all alone in the waiting-room. I don't know what came over me, Hap. The next thing I know I'm in his office — paneled walls, everything. I can't explain it. I — Hap, I took his fountain pen.

Happy: Geez, did he catch you?

Biff: I ran out. I ran down all eleven flights. I ran and ran and ran.

Happy: That was an awful dumb — what'd you do that for?

Biff (agonized): I don't know, I just — wanted to take something, I don't know. You gotta help me, Hap. I'm gonna tell Pop.

Happy: You crazy? What for?

Biff: Hap, he's got to understand that I'm not the man somebody lends that kind of money to. He thinks I've been spiting him all these years and it's eating him up.

Happy: That's just it. You tell him something nice.

Biff: I can't.

Happy: Say you got a lunch date with Oliver tomorrow.

Biff: So what do I do tomorrow?

Happy: You leave the house tomorrow and come back at night and say Oliver is thinking it over. And he thinks it over for a couple of weeks, and gradually it fades away and nobody's the worse.

Biff: But it'll go on forever!

Happy: Dad is never so happy as when he's looking forward to something!

Willy enters.

Happy: Hello, scout!

Willy: Gee, I haven't been here in years!

Stanley has followed Willy in and sets a chair for him. Stanley starts off but Happy stops him.

Happy: Stanley!

Stanley stands by, waiting for an order.

Biff (going to Willy with guilt, as to an invalid): Sit down, Pop. You want a drink?

Willy: Sure, I don't mind.

Biff: Let's get a load on.

Willy: You look worried.

Biff: N-no. (*To Stanley.*) Scotch all around. Make it doubles.

Stanley: Doubles, right. (*He goes.*)

Willy: You had a couple already, didn't you?

Biff: Just a couple, yeah.

Willy: Well, what happened, boy? *(Nodding affirmatively, with a smile.)* Everything go all right?

Biff (takes a breath, then reaches out and grasps Willy's hand): Pal . . . *(He is smiling bravely, and Willy is smiling too.)* I had an experience today.

Happy: Terrific, Pop.

Willy: That so? What happened?

Biff (high, slightly alcoholic, above the earth): I'm going to tell you everything from first to last. It's been a strange day. *(Silence. He looks around, composes himself as best he can, but his breath keeps breaking the rhythm of his voice.)* I had to wait quite a while for him, and —

Willy: Oliver?

Biff: Yeah, Oliver. All day, as a matter of cold fact. And a lot of — instances — facts, Pop, facts about my life came back to me. Who was it, Pop? Who ever said I was a salesman with Oliver?

Willy: Well, you were.

Biff: No, Dad, I was a shipping clerk.

Willy: But you were practically —

Biff (with determination): Dad, I don't know who said it first, but I was never a salesman for Bill Oliver.

Willy: What're you talking about?

Biff: Let's hold on to the facts tonight, Pop. We're not going to get anywhere bullin' around. I was a shipping clerk.

Willy (angrily): All right, now listen to me —

Biff: Why don't you let me finish?

Willy: I'm not interested in stories about the past or any crap of that kind because the woods are burning, boys, you understand? There's a big blaze going on all around. I was fired today.

Biff (shocked): How could you be?

Willy: I was fired, and I'm looking for a little good news to tell your mother, because the woman has waited and the woman has suffered. The gist of it is that I haven't got a story left in my head, Biff. So don't give me a lecture about facts and aspects. I am not interested. Now what've you got to say to me?

Stanley enters with three drinks. They wait until he leaves.

Willy: Did you see Oliver?

Biff: Jesus, Dad!

Willy: You mean you didn't go up there?

Happy: Sure he went up there.

Biff: I did. I — saw him. How could they fire you?

Willy (on the edge of his chair): What kind of a welcome did he give you?

Biff: He won't even let you work on commission?

Willy: I'm out! *(Driving.)* So tell me, he gave you a warm welcome?

Happy: Sure, Pop, sure!

Biff (driven): Well, it was kind of —

Willy: I was wondering if he'd remember you. *(To Happy.)* Imagine, man doesn't see him for ten, twelve years and gives him that kind of a welcome!

Happy: Damn right!

Biff (trying to return to the offensive): Pop, look —

Willy: You know why he remembered you, don't you? Because you impressed him in those days.

Biff: Let's talk quietly and get this down to the facts, huh?

Willy (as though Biff had been interrupting): Well, what happened? It's great news, Biff. Did he take you into his office or'd you talk in the waiting-room?

Biff: Well, he came in, see, and —

Willy (with a big smile): What'd he say? Betcha he threw his arm around you.

Biff: Well, he kinda —

Willy: He's a fine man. *(To Happy.)* Very hard man to see, y'know.

Happy (agreeing): Oh, I know.

Willy (to Biff): Is that where you had the drinks?

Biff: Yeah, he gave me a couple of — no, no!

Happy (cutting in): He told him my Florida idea.

Willy: Don't interrupt. *(To Biff.)* How'd he react to the Florida idea?

Biff: Dad, will you give me a minute to explain?

Willy: I've been waiting for you to explain since I sat down here! What happened? He took you into his office and what?

Biff: Well — I talked. And — and he listened, see.

Willy: Famous for the way he listens, y'know. What was his answer?

Biff: His answer was — *(He breaks off, suddenly angry.)* Dad, you're not letting me tell you what I want to tell you!

Willy (accusing, angered): You didn't see him, did you?

Biff: I did see him!

Willy: What'd you insult him or something? You insulted him, didn't you?

Biff: Listen, will you let me out of it, will you just let me out of it!

Happy: What the hell!

Willy: Tell me what happened!

Biff (to Happy): I can't talk to him!

A single trumpet note jars the ear. The light of green leaves stains the house, which holds the air of night and a dream. Young Bernard enters and knocks on the door of the house.

Young Bernard (frantically): Mrs. Loman, Mrs. Loman!

Happy: Tell him what happened!

Biff (to Happy): Shut up and leave me alone!

Willy: No, no! You had to go and flunk math!

Biff: What math? What're you talking about?

Young Bernard: Mrs. Loman, Mrs. Loman!

Linda appears in the house, as of old.

Willy (wildly): Math, math, math!

Biff: Take it easy, Pop!

Young Bernard: Mrs. Loman!

Willy (furiously): If you hadn't flunked you'd've been set by now!

Biff: Now, look, I'm gonna tell you what happened, and you're going to listen to me.

Young Bernard: Mrs. Loman!

Biff: I waited six hours —

Happy: What the hell are you saying?

Biff: I kept sending in my name but he wouldn't see me. So finally he . . . *(He continues unheard as light fades low on the restaurant.)*

Young Bernard: Biff flunked math!

Linda: No!

Young Bernard: Birnbaum flunked him! They won't graduate him!

Linda: But they have to. He's gotta go to the university. Where is he? Biff! Biff!

Young Bernard: No, he left. He went to Grand Central.

Linda: Grand — You mean he went to Boston!

Young Bernard: Is Uncle Willy in Boston?

Linda: Oh, maybe Willy can talk to the teacher. Oh, the poor, poor boy!

Light on house area snaps out.

Biff (at the table, now audible, holding up a gold fountain pen): . . . so I'm washed up with Oliver, you understand? Are you listening to me?

Willy (at a loss): Yeah, sure. If you hadn't flunked —

Biff: Flunked what? What're you talking about?

Willy: Don't blame everything on me! I didn't flunk math — you did! What pen?

Happy: That was awful dumb, Biff, a pen like that is worth —

Willy (seeing the pen for the first time): You took Oliver's pen?

Biff (weakening): Dad, I just explained it to you.

Willy: You stole Bill Oliver's fountain pen!

Biff: I didn't exactly steal it! That's just what I've been explaining to you!

Happy: He had it in his hand and just then Oliver walked in, so he got nervous and stuck it in his pocket!

Willy: My God, Biff!

Biff: I never intended to do it, Dad!

Operator's voice: Standish Arms, good evening!

Willy (shouting): I'm not in my room!

Biff (frightened): Dad, what's the matter? *(He and Happy stand up.)*

Operator: Ringing Mr. Loman for you!

Willy: I'm not there, stop it!

Biff (horrified, gets down on one knee before Willy): Dad, I'll make good, I'll make good. *(Willy tries to get to his feet. Biff holds him down.)* Sit down now.

Willy: No, you're no good, you're no good for anything.

Biff: I am, Dad, I'll find something else, you understand? Now don't worry about anything. *(He holds up Willy's face.)* Talk to me, Dad.

Operator: Mr. Loman does not answer. Shall I page him?

Willy (attempting to stand, as though to rush and silence the Operator): No, no, no!

Happy: He'll strike something, Pop.

Willy: No, no . . .

Biff (desperately, standing over Willy): Pop, listen! Listen to me! I'm telling you something good. Oliver talked to his partner about the Florida idea. You listening? He — he talked to his partner, and he came to me . . . I'm going to be all right, you hear? Dad, listen to me, he said it was just a question of the amount!

Willy: Then you . . . got it?

Happy: He's gonna be terrific, Pop!

Willy (trying to stand): Then you got it, haven't you? You got it! You got it!

Biff (agonized, holds Willy down): No, no. Look, Pop. I'm supposed to have lunch with them tomorrow. I'm just telling you this so you'll know that I can still make an impression, Pop. And I'll make good somewhere, but I can't go tomorrow, see?

Willy: Why not? You simply —

Biff: But the pen, Pop!

Willy: You give it to him and tell him it was an oversight!

Happy: Sure, have lunch tomorrow!

Biff: I can't say that —

Willy: You were doing a crossword puzzle and accidentally used his pen!

Biff: Listen, kid, I took those balls years ago, now I walk in with his fountain pen? That clinches it, don't you see? I can't face him like that! I'll try elsewhere.

Page's voice: Paging Mr. Loman!

Willy: Don't you want to be anything?

Biff: Pop, how can I go back?

Willy: You don't want to be anything, is that what's behind it?

Biff (now angry at Willy for not crediting his sympathy): Don't take it that way! You think it was easy walking into that office after what I'd done to him? A team of horses couldn't have dragged me back to Bill Oliver!

Willy: Then why'd you go?

Biff: Why did I go? Why did I go? Look at you! Look at what's become of you!

> *Off left, The Woman laughs.*

Willy: Biff, you're going to go to that lunch tomorrow, or —

Biff: I can't go. I've got no appointment!

Happy: Biff, for . . . !

Willy: Are you spiting me?

Biff: Don't take it that way! Goddammit!

Willy (strikes Biff and falters away from the table): You rotten little louse! Are you spiting me?

The Woman: Someone's at the door, Willy!

Biff: I'm no good, can't you see what I am?

Happy (separating them): Hey, you're in a restaurant! Now cut it out, both of you! *(The Girls enter.)* Hello, girls, sit down.

> *The Woman laughs, off left.*

Miss Forsythe: I guess we might as well. This is Letta.

The Woman: Willy, are you going to wake up?

Biff (ignoring Willy): How're ya, miss, sit down. What do you drink?

Miss Forsythe: Letta might not be able to stay long.

Letta: I gotta get up very early tomorrow. I got jury duty. I'm so excited! Were you fellows ever on a jury?

Biff: No, but I been in front of them! *(The Girls laugh.)* This is my father.

Letta: Isn't he cute? Sit down with us, Pop.

Happy: Sit him down, Biff!

Biff (going to him): Come on, slugger, drink us under the table. To hell with it! Come on, sit down, pal.

On Biff's last insistence, Willy is about to sit.

The Woman *(now urgently):* Willy, are you going to answer the door!

The Woman's call pulls Willy back. He starts right, befuddled.

Biff: Hey, where are you going?
Willy: Open the door.
Biff: The door?
Willy: The washroom . . . the door . . . where's the door?
Biff *(leading Willy to the left):* Just go straight down.

Willy moves left.

The Woman: Willy, Willy, are you going to get up, get up, get up, get up?

Willy exits left.

Letta: I think it's sweet you bring your daddy along.
Miss Forsythe: Oh, he isn't really your father!
Biff *(at left, turning to her resentfully):* Miss Forsythe, you've just seen a prince walk by. A fine, troubled prince. A hard-working, unappreciated prince. A pal, you understand? A good companion. Always for his boys.
Letta: That's so sweet.
Happy: Well, girls, what's the program? We're wasting time. Come on, Biff. Gather round. Where would you like to go?
Biff: Why don't you do something for him?
Happy: Me!
Biff: Don't you give a damn for him, Hap?
Happy: What're you talking about? I'm the one who —
Biff: I sense it, you don't give a good goddam about him. *(He takes the rolled-up hose from his pocket and puts it on the table in front of Happy.)* Look what I found in the cellar, for Christ's sake. How can you bear to let it go on?
Happy: Me? Who goes away? Who runs off and —
Biff: Yeah, but he doesn't mean anything to you. You could help him — I can't! Don't you understand what I'm talking about? He's going to kill himself, don't you know that?
Happy: Don't I know it! Me!
Biff: Hap, help him! Jesus . . . help him . . . Help me, help me, I can't bear to look at his face! *(Ready to weep, he hurries out, up right.)*
Happy *(starting after him):* Where are you going?
Miss Forsythe: What's he so mad about?
Happy: Come on, girls, we'll catch up with him.
Miss Forsythe *(as Happy pushes her out):* Say, I don't like that temper of his!
Happy: He's just a little overstrung, he'll be all right!
Willy *(off left, as The Woman laughs):* Don't answer! Don't answer!
Letta: Don't you want to tell your father —
Happy: No, that's not my father. He's just a guy. Come on, we'll catch Biff, and, honey, we're going to paint this town! Stanley, where's the check! Hey, Stanley!

They exit. Stanley looks toward left.

Stanley (calling to Happy indignantly): Mr. Loman! Mr. Loman!

> *Stanley picks up a chair and follows them off. Knocking is heard off left. The Woman enters, laughing. Willy follows her. She is in a black slip; he is buttoning his shirt. Raw, sensuous music accompanies their speech.*

Willy: Will you stop laughing? Will you stop?

The Woman: Aren't you going to answer the door? He'll wake the whole hotel.

Willy: I'm not expecting anybody.

The Woman: Whyn't you have another drink, honey, and stop being so damn self-centered?

Willy: I'm so lonely.

The Woman: You know you ruined me, Willy? From now on, whenever you come to the office, I'll see that you go right through to the buyers. No waiting at my desk any more, Willy. You ruined me.

Willy: That's nice of you to say that.

The Woman: Gee, you are self-centered! Why so sad? You are the saddest self-centeredest soul I ever did see-saw. *(She laughs. He kisses her.)* Come on inside, drummer boy. It's silly to be dressing in the middle of the night. *(As knocking is heard.)* Aren't you going to answer the door?

Willy: They're knocking on the wrong door.

The Woman: But I felt the knocking. And he heard us talking in here. Maybe the hotel's on fire!

Willy (his terror rising): It's a mistake.

The Woman: Then tell him to go away!

Willy: There's nobody there.

The Woman: It's getting on my nerves, Willy. There's somebody standing out there and it's getting on my nerves!

Willy (pushing her away from him): All right, stay in the bathroom here, and don't come out. I think there's a law in Massachusetts about it, so don't come out. It may be that new room clerk. He looked very mean. So don't come out. It's a mistake, there's no fire.

> *The knocking is heard again. He takes a few steps away from her, and she vanishes into the wing. The light follows him, and now he is facing Young Biff, who carries a suitcase. Biff steps toward him. The music is gone.*

Biff: Why didn't you answer?

Willy: Biff! What are you doing in Boston?

Biff: Why didn't you answer? I've been knocking for five minutes, I called you on the phone —

Willy: I just heard you. I was in the bathroom and had the door shut. Did anything happen home?

Biff: Dad — I let you down.

Willy: What do you mean?

Biff: Dad . . .

Willy: Biffo, what's this about? *(Putting his arm around Biff.)* Come on, let's go downstairs and get you a malted.

Biff: Dad, I flunked math.

Willy: Not for the term?

Biff: The term. I haven't got enough credits to graduate.

Willy: You mean to say Bernard wouldn't give you the answers?

Biff: He did, he tried, but I only got a sixty-one.

Willy: And they wouldn't give you four points?

Biff: Birnbaum refused absolutely. I begged him, Pop, but he won't give me those points. You gotta talk to him before they close the school. Because if he saw the kind of man you are, and you just talked to him in your way, I'm sure he'd come through for me. The class came right before practice, see, and I didn't go enough. Would you talk to him? He'd like you, Pop. You know the way you could talk.

Willy: You're on. We'll drive right back.

Biff: Oh, Dad, good work! I'm sure he'll change it for you!

Willy: Go downstairs and tell the clerk I'm checkin' out. Go right down.

Biff: Yes, Sir! See, the reason he hates me, Pop — one day he was late for class so I got up at the blackboard and imitated him. I crossed my eyes and talked with a lithp.

Willy (laughing): You did? The kids like it?

Biff: They nearly died laughing!

Willy: Yeah? What'd you do?

Biff: The thquare root of thixty twee is . . . *(Willy bursts out laughing; Biff joins him.)* And in the middle of it he walked in!

Willy laughs and The Woman joins in offstage.

Willy (without hesitating): Hurry downstairs and —

Biff: Somebody in there?

Willy: No, that was next door.

The Woman laughs offstage.

Biff: Somebody got in your bathroom!

Willy: No, it's the next room, there's a party —

The Woman (enters, laughing. She lisps this): Can I come in? There's something in the bathtub, Willy, and it's moving!

Willy looks at Biff, who is staring open-mouthed and horrified at The Woman.

Willy: Ah — you better go back to your room. They must be finished painting by now. They're painting her room so I let her take a shower here. Go back, go back . . . *(He pushes her.)*

The Woman (resisting): But I've got to get dressed, Willy, I can't —

Willy: Get out of here! Go back, go back . . . *(Suddenly striving for the ordinary.)* This is Miss Francis, Biff, she's a buyer. They're painting her room. Go back, Miss Francis, go back . . .

The Woman: But my clothes, I can't go out naked in the hall!

Willy (pushing her offstage): Get outa here! Go back, go back!

Biff slowly sits down on his suitcase as the argument continues offstage.

The Woman: Where's my stockings? You promised me stockings, Willy!

Willy: I have no stockings here!

The Woman: You had two boxes of size nine sheers for me, and I want them!

Willy: Here, for God's sake, will you get outa here!

The Woman (enters holding a box of stockings): I just hope there's nobody in the hall. That's all I hope. *(To Biff.)* Are you football or baseball?

Biff: Football.

The Woman (angry, humiliated): That's me too. G'night. *(She snatches her clothes from Willy, and walks out.)*

Willy (after a pause): Well, better get going. I want to get to the school first thing in the morning. Get my suits out of the closet. I'll get my valise. *(Biff doesn't move.)* What's the matter? *(Biff remains motionless, tears falling.)* She's a buyer. Buys for J. H. Simmons. She lives down the hall — they're painting. You don't imagine — *(He breaks off. After a pause.)* Now listen, pal, she's just a buyer. She sees merchandise in her room and they have to keep it looking just so . . . *(Pause. Assuming command.)* All right, get my suits. *(Biff doesn't move.)* Now stop crying and do as I say. I gave you an order. Biff, I gave you an order! Is that what you do when I give you an order? How dare you cry! *(Putting his arm around Biff.)* Now look, Biff, when you grow up you'll understand about these things. You mustn't — you mustn't overemphasize a thing like this. I'll see Birnbaum first thing in the morning.

Biff: Never mind.

Willy (getting down beside Biff): Never mind! He's going to give you those points. I'll see to it.

Biff: He wouldn't listen to you.

Willy: He certainly will listen to me. You need those points for the U. of Virginia.

Biff: I'm not going there.

Willy: Heh? If I can't get him to change that mark you'll make it up in summer school. You've got all summer to —

Biff (his weeping breaking from him): Dad . . .

Willy (infected by it): Oh, my boy . . .

Biff: Dad . . .

Willy: She's nothing to me, Biff. I was lonely, I was terribly lonely.

Biff: You — you gave her Mama's stockings! *(His tears break through and he rises to go.)*

Willy (grabbing for Biff): I gave you an order!

Biff: Don't touch me, you — liar!

Willy: Apologize for that!

Biff: You fake! You phony little fake! You fake! *(Overcome, he turns quickly and weeping fully goes out with his suitcase. Willy is left on the floor on his knees.)*

Willy: I gave you an order! Biff, come back here or I'll beat you! Come back here! I'll whip you!

Stanley comes quickly in from the right and stands in front of Willy.

Willy (shouts at Stanley): I gave you an order . . .

Stanley: Hey, let's pick it up, pick it up, Mr. Loman. *(He helps Willy to his feet.)* Your boys left with the chippies. They said they'll see you home.

A second waiter watches some distance away.

Willy: But we were supposed to have dinner together.

Music is heard, Willy's theme.

Stanley: Can you make it?

Willy: I'll — sure, I can make it. *(Suddenly concerned about his clothes.)* Do I — I look all right?

Stanley: Sure, you look all right. *(He flicks a speck off Willy's lapel.)*

Willy: Here — here's a dollar.

Stanley: Oh, your son paid me. It's all right.

Willy (putting it in Stanley's hand): No, take it. You're a good boy.

Stanley: Oh, no, you don't have to . . .

Willy: Here — here's some more, I don't need it any more. *(After a slight pause.)* Tell me — is there a seed store in the neighborhood?

Stanley: Seeds? You mean like to plant?

As Willy turns, Stanley slips the money back into his jacket pocket.

Willy: Yes. Carrots, peas . . .

Stanley: Well, there's hardware stores on Sixth Avenue, but it may be too late now.

Willy (anxiously): Oh, I'd better hurry. I've got to get some seeds. *(He starts off to the right.)* I've got to get some seeds, right away. Nothing's planted. I don't have a thing in the ground.

Willy hurries out as the light goes down. Stanley moves over to the right after him, watches him off. The other waiter has been staring at Willy.

Stanley (to the waiter): Well, whatta you looking at?

The waiter picks up the chairs and moves off right. Stanley takes the table and follows him. The light fades on this area. There is a long pause, the sound of the flute coming over. The light gradually rises on the kitchen, which is empty. Happy appears at the door of the house, followed by Biff. Happy is carrying a large bunch of long-stemmed roses. He enters the kitchen, looks around for Linda. Not seeing her, he turns to Biff, who is just outside the house door, and makes a gesture with his hands, indicating "Not here, I guess." He looks into the livingroom and freezes. Inside, Linda, unseen, is seated, Willy's coat on her lap. She rises ominously and quietly and moves toward Happy, who backs up into the kitchen, afraid.

Happy: Hey, what're you doing up? *(Linda says nothing but moves toward him implacably.)* Where's Pop? *(He keeps backing to the right, and now Linda is in full view in the doorway to the livingroom.)* Is he sleeping?

Linda: Where were you?

Happy (trying to laugh it off): We met two girls, Mom, very fine types. Here, we brought you some flowers. *(Offering them to her.)* Put them in your room, Ma.

She knocks them to the floor at Biff's feet. He has now come inside and closed the door behind him. She stares at Biff, silent.

Happy: Now what'd you do that for? Mom, I want you to have some flowers —

Linda (cutting Happy off, violently to Biff): Don't you care whether he lives or dies?

Happy (going to the stairs): Come upstairs, Biff.

Biff (with a flare of disgust, to Happy): Go away from me! *(To Linda.)* What do you mean, lives or dies? Nobody's dying around here, pal.

Linda: Get out of my sight! Get out of here!

Biff: I wanna see the boss.

Linda: You're not going near him!

Biff: Where is he? *(He moves into the livingroom and Linda follows.)*

Linda (shouting after Biff): You invite him for dinner. He looks forward to it all day — *(Biff appears in his parents' bedroom, looks around, and exits)* — and then you desert him there. There's no stranger you'd do that to!

Happy: Why? He had a swell time with us. Listen, when I — *(Linda comes back into the kitchen)* — desert him I hope I don't outlive the day!

Linda: Get out of here!

Happy: Now look, Mom . . .

Linda: Did you have to go to women tonight? You and your lousy rotten whores!

Biff re-enters the kitchen.

Happy: Mom, all we did was follow Biff around trying to cheer him up! *(To Biff.)* Boy, what a night you gave me!

Linda: Get out of here, both of you, and don't come back! I don't want you tormenting him any more. Go on now, get your things together! *(To Biff.)* You can sleep in his apartment. *(She starts to pick up the flowers and stops herself.)* Pick up this stuff, I'm not your maid any more. Pick it up, you bum, you!

Happy turns his back to her in refusal. Biff slowly moves over and gets down on his knees, picking up the flowers.

Linda: You're a pair of animals! Not one, not another living soul would have had the cruelty to walk out on that man in a restaurant!

Biff (not looking at her): Is that what he said?

Linda: He didn't have to say anything. He was so humiliated he nearly limped when he came in.

Happy: But, Mom he had a great time with us —

Biff (cutting him off violently): Shut up!

Without another word, Happy goes upstairs.

Linda: You! You didn't even go in to see if he was all right!

Biff (still on the floor in front of Linda, the flowers in his hand; with self-loathing): No. Didn't. Didn't do a damned thing. How do you like that, heh? Left him babbling in a toilet.

Linda: You louse. You . . .

Biff: Now you hit it on the nose! *(He gets up, throws the flowers in the wastebasket.)* The scum of the earth, and you're looking at him!

Linda: Get out of here!

Biff: I gotta talk to the boss, Mom. Where is he?

Linda: You're not going near him. Get out of this house!

Biff (with absolute assurance, determination): No. We're gonna have an abrupt conversation, him and me.

Linda: You're not talking to him!

Hammering is heard from outside the house, off right. Biff turns toward the noise.

Linda (suddenly pleading): Will you please leave him alone?

Biff: What's he doing out there?

Linda: He's planting the garden!
Biff (quietly): Now? Oh, my God!

> *Biff moves outside, Linda following. The light dies down on them and comes up on the center of the apron as Willy walks into it. He is carrying a flashlight, a hoe and a handful of seed packets. He raps the top of the hoe sharply to fix it firmly, and then moves to the left, measuring off the distance with his foot. He holds the flashlight to look at the seed packets, reading off the instructions. He is in the blue of night.*

Willy: Carrots . . . quarter-inch apart. Rows . . . one-foot rows. *(He measures it off.)* One foot. *(He puts down a package and measures off.)* Beets. *(He puts down another package and measures again.)* Lettuce. *(He reads the package, puts it down.)* One foot — *(He breaks off as Ben appears at the right and moves slowly down to him.)* What a proposition, ts, ts. Terrific, terrific. 'Cause she's suffered, Ben, the woman has suffered. You understand me? A man can't go out the way he came in, Ben, a man has got to add up to something. You can't, you can't — *(Ben moves toward him as though to interrupt.)* You gotta consider, now. Don't answer so quick. Remember, it's a guaranteed twenty-thousand-dollar proposition. Now look, Ben, I want you to go through the ins and outs of this thing with me. I've got nobody to talk to, Ben, and the woman has suffered, you hear me?
Ben (standing still, considering): What's the proposition?
Willy: It's twenty thousand dollars on the barrelhead. Guaranteed, gilt-edged, you understand?
Ben: You don't want to make a fool of yourself. They might not honor the policy.
Willy: How can they dare refuse? Didn't I work like a coolie to meet every premium on the nose? And now they don't pay off? Impossible!
Ben: It's called a cowardly thing, William.
Willy: Why? Does it take more guts to stand here the rest of my life ringing up a zero?
Ben (yielding): That's a point, William. *(He moves, thinking, turns.)* And twenty thousand — that *is* something one can feel with the hand, it is there.
Willy (now assured, with rising power): Oh, Ben, that's the whole beauty of it! I see it like a diamond, shining in the dark, hard and rough, that I can pick up and touch in my hand. Not like — like an appointment! This would not be another damned-fool appointment, Ben, and it changes all the aspects. Because he thinks I'm nothing, see, and so he spites me. But the funeral — *(Straightening up.)* Ben, that funeral will be massive! They'll come from Maine, Massachusetts, Vermont, New Hampshire! All the old-timers with the strange license plates — that boy will be thunder-struck, Ben, because he never realized — I am known! Rhode Island, New York, New Jersey — I am known, Ben, and he'll see it with his eyes once and for all. He'll see what I am, Ben! He's in for a shock, that boy!
Ben (coming down to the edge of the garden): He'll call you a coward.
Willy (suddenly fearful): No, that would be terrible.
Ben: Yes. And a damned fool.
Willy: No, no, he mustn't, I won't have that! *(He is broken and desperate.)*
Ben: He'll hate you, William.

> *The gay music of the boys is heard.*

Willy: Oh, Ben, how do we get back to all the great times? Used to be so full of light, and comradeship, the sleigh-riding in winter, and the ruddiness on his cheeks. And always some kind of good news coming up, always something nice coming up ahead. And never even let me carry the valises in the house, and simonizing, simonizing that little red car! Why, why can't I give him something and not have him hate me?

Ben: Let me think about it. *(He glances at his watch.)* I still have a little time. Remarkable proposition, but you've got to be sure you're not making a fool of yourself.

Ben drifts off upstage and goes out of sight. Biff comes down from the left.

Willy (suddenly conscious of Biff, turns and looks up at him, then begins picking up the packages of seeds in confusion): Where the hell is that seed? *(Indignantly.)* You can't see nothing out here! They boxed in the whole goddam neighborhood!

Biff: There are people all around here. Don't you realize that?

Willy: I'm busy. Don't bother me.

Biff (taking the hoe from Willy): I'm saying good-by to you, Pop. *(Willy looks at him, silent, unable to move.)* I'm not coming back any more.

Willy: You're not going to see Oliver tomorrow?

Biff: I've got no appointment, Dad.

Willy: He put his arm around you, and you've got no appointment?

Biff: Pop, get this now, will you? Everytime I've left it's been a fight that sent me out of here. Today I realized something about myself and I tried to explain it to you and I — I think I'm just not smart enough to make any sense out of it for you. To hell with whose fault it is or anything like that. *(He takes Willy's arm.)* Let's just wrap it up, heh? Come on in, we'll tell Mom. *(He gently tries to pull Willy to the left.)*

Willy (frozen, immobile, with guilt in his voice): No, I don't want to see her.

Biff: Come on! *(He pulls again, and Willy tries to pull away.)*

Willy (highly nervous): No, no, I don't want to see her.

Biff (tries to look into Willy's face, as if to find the answer there): Why don't you want to see her?

Willy (more harshly now): Don't bother me, will you?

Biff: What do you mean, you don't want to see her? You don't want them calling you yellow, do you? This isn't your fault; it's me, I'm a bum. Now come inside! *(Willy strains to get away.)* Did you hear what I said to you?

Willy pulls away and quickly goes by himself into the house. Biff follows.

Linda (to Willy): Did you plant, dear?

Biff (at the door, to Linda): All right, we had it out. I'm going and I'm not writing any more.

Linda (going to Willy in the kitchen): I think that's the best way, dear. 'Cause there's no use drawing it out, you'll just never get along.

Willy doesn't respond.

Biff: People ask where I am and what I'm doing, you don't know, and you don't care. That way it'll be off your mind and you can start brightening up again. All right? That clears it, doesn't it? *(Willy is silent, and Biff goes to him.)* You gonna wish me luck, scout? *(He extends his hand.)* What do you say?

Linda: Shake his hand, Willy.

Willy (turning to her, seething with hurt): There's no necessity to mention the pen at all, y'know.

Biff (gently): I've got no appointment, Dad.

Willy (erupting fiercely): He put his arm around . . . ?

Biff: Dad, you're never going to see what I am, so what's the use of arguing? If I strike oil I'll send you a check. Meantime forget I'm alive.

Willy (to Linda): Spite, see?

Biff: Shake hands, Dad.

Willy: Not my hand.

Biff: I was hoping not to go this way.

Willy: Well, this is the way you're going. Good-by.

Biff looks at him a moment, then turns sharply and goes to the stairs.

Willy (stops him with): May you rot in hell if you leave this house!

Biff (turning): Exactly what is it that you want from me?

Willy: I want you to know, on the train, in the mountains, in the valleys, wherever you go, that you cut down your life for spite!

Biff: No, no.

Willy: Spite, spite, is the word of your undoing! And when you're down and out, remember what did it. When you're rotting somewhere beside the railroad tracks, remember, and don't you dare blame it on me!

Biff: I'm not blaming it on you!

Willy: I won't take the rap for this, you hear?

Happy comes down the stairs and stands on the bottom step, watching.

Biff: That's just what I'm telling you!

Willy (sinking into a chair at the table, with full accusation): You're trying to put a knife in me — don't think I don't know what you're doing!

Biff: All right, phony! Then let's lay it on the line. *(He whips the rubber tube out of his pocket and puts it on the table.)*

Happy: You crazy —

Linda: Biff! *(She moves to grab the hose, but Biff holds it down with his hand.)*

Biff: Leave it there! Don't move it!

Willy (not looking at it): What is that?

Biff: You know goddam well what that is.

Willy (caged, wanting to escape): I never saw that.

Biff: You saw it. The mice didn't bring it into the cellar! What is this supposed to do, make a hero out of you? This supposed to make me sorry for you?

Willy: Never heard of it.

Biff: There'll be no pity for you, you hear it? No pity!

Willy (to Linda): You hear the spite!

Biff: No, you're going to hear the truth — what you are and what I am!

Linda: Stop it!

Willy: Spite!

Happy (coming down toward Biff): You cut it now!

Biff (to Happy): The man don't know who we are! The man is gonna know! *(To Willy.)* We never told the truth for ten minutes in this house!

Happy: We always told the truth!

Biff (turning on him): You big blow, are you the assistant buyer? You're one of the two assistants to the assistant, aren't you?

Happy: Well, I'm practically —

Biff: You're practically full of it! We all are! And I'm through with it. *(To Willy.)* Now hear this, Willy, this is me.

Willy: I know you!

Biff: You know why I had no address for three months? I stole a suit in Kansas City and I was in jail. *(To Linda, who is sobbing.)* Stop crying. I'm through with it.

Linda turns away from them, her hands covering her face.

Willy: I suppose that's my fault!

Biff: I stole myself out of every good job since high school!

Willy: And whose fault is that?

Biff: And I never got anywhere because you blew me so full of hot air I could never stand taking orders from anybody! That's whose fault it is!

Willy: I hear that!

Linda: Don't, Biff!

Biff: It's goddam time you heard that! I had to be boss big shot in two weeks, and I'm through with it!

Willy: Then hang yourself! For spite, hang yourself!

Biff: No! Nobody's hanging himself, Willy! I ran down eleven flights with a pen in my hand today. And suddenly I stopped, you hear me? And in the middle of that office building, do you hear this? I stopped in the middle of that building and I saw — the sky. I saw the things that I love in this world. The work and the food and time to sit and smoke. And I looked at the pen and said to myself, what the hell am I grabbing this for? Why am I trying to become what I don't want to be? What am I doing in an office, making a contemptuous, begging fool of myself, when all I want is out there, waiting for me the minute I say I know who I am! Why can't I say that, Willy? *(He tries to make Willy face him, but Willy pulls away and moves to the left.)*

Willy (with hatred, threateningly): The door of your life is wide open!

Biff: Pop! I'm a dime a dozen, and so are you!

Willy (turning on him now in an uncontrolled outburst): I am not a dime a dozen! I am Willy Loman, and you are Biff Loman!

Biff starts for Willy, but is blocked by Happy. In his fury, Biff seems on the verge of attacking his father.

Biff: I am not a leader of men, Willy, and neither are you. You were never anything but a hard-working drummer who landed in the ash can like all the rest of them! I'm one dollar an hour, Willy! I tried seven states and couldn't raise it. A buck an hour! Do you gather my meaning? I'm not bringing home any prizes any more, and you're going to stop waiting for me to bring them home!

Willy (directly to Biff): You vengeful, spiteful mut!

Biff breaks from Happy. Willy, in fright, starts up the stairs. Biff grabs him.

Biff (at the peak of his fury): Pop, I'm nothing! I'm nothing, Pop. Can't you understand that? There's no spite in it any more. I'm just what I am, that's all.

Biff's fury has spent itself, and he breaks down, sobbing, holding on to Willy, who dumbly fumbles for Biff's face.

Willy (astonished): What're you doing? What're you doing? *(To Linda.)* Why is he crying?

Biff (crying, broken): Will you let me go, for Christ's sake? Will you take that phony dream and burn it before something happens? *(Struggling to contain himself, he pulls away and moves to the stairs.)* I'll go in the morning. Put him — put him to bed. *(Exhausted, Biff moves up the stairs to his room.)*

Willy (after a long pause, astonished, elevated): Isn't that remarkable? Biff — he likes me!

Linda: He loves you, Willy!

Happy (deeply moved): Always did, Pop.

Willy: Oh, Biff! *(Staring wildly.)* He cried! Cried to me. *(He is choking with his love, and now cries out his promise.)* That boy — that boy is going to be magnificent!

Ben appears in the light just outside the kitchen.

Ben: Yes, outstanding, with twenty thousand behind him.

Linda (sensing the racing of his mind, fearfully, carefully): Now come to bed, Willy. It's all settled now.

Willy (finding it difficult not to rush out of the house): Yes, we'll sleep. Come on. Go to sleep, Hap.

Ben: And it does take a great kind of man to crack the jungle.

In accents of dread, Ben's idyllic music starts up.

Happy (his arm around Linda): I'm getting married, Pop, don't forget it. I'm changing everything. I'm gonna run that department before the year is up. You'll see, Mom. *(He kisses her.)*

Ben: The jungle is dark but full of diamonds, Willy.

Willy turns, moves, listening to Ben.

Linda: Be good. You're both good boys, just act that way, that's all.

Happy: 'Night, Pop. *(He goes upstairs.)*

Linda (to Willy): Come, dear.

Ben (with greater force): One must go in to fetch a diamond out.

Willy (to Linda, as he moves slowly along the edge of the kitchen, toward the door): I just want to get settled down, Linda. Let me sit alone for a little.

Linda (almost uttering her fear): I want you upstairs.

Willy (taking her in his arms): In a few minutes, Linda. I couldn't sleep right now. Go on, you look awful tired. *(He kisses her.)*

Ben: Not like an appointment at all. A diamond is rough and hard to the touch.

Willy: Go on now. I'll be right up.

Linda: I think this is the only way, Willy.

Willy: Sure, it's the best thing.

Ben: Best thing!

Willy: The only way. Everything is gonna be — go on, kid, get to bed. You look so tired.

Linda: Come right up.

Willy: Two minutes.

> *Linda goes into the livingroom, then reappears in her bedroom. Willy moves just outside the kitchen door.*

Willy: Loves me. *(Wonderingly.)* Always loved me. Isn't that a remarkable thing? Ben, he'll worship me for it!

Ben (with promise): It's dark there, but full of diamonds.

Willy: Can you imagine that magnificence with twenty thousand dollars in his pocket?

Linda: (calling from her room): Willy! Come up!

Willy (calling from the kitchen): Yes! Yes! Coming! It's very smart, you realize that, don't you, sweetheart? Even Ben sees it. I gotta go, baby. 'By! By! *(Going over to Ben, almost dancing.)* Imagine? When the mail comes he'll be ahead of Bernard again!

Ben: A perfect proposition all around.

Willy: Did you see how he cried to me? Oh, if I could kiss him, Ben!

Ben: Time, William, time!

Willy: Oh, Ben, I always knew one way or another we were gonna make it, Biff and I!

Ben (looking at his watch): The boat. We'll be late. *(He moves slowly off into the darkness.)*

Willy (elegiacally, turning to the house): Now when you kick off, boy, I want a seventy-yard boot, and get right down the field under the ball, and when you hit, hit low and hit hard, because it's important, boy. *(He swings around and faces the audience.)* There's all kinds of important people in the stands, and the first thing you know . . . *(Suddenly realizing he is alone.)* Ben! Ben, where do I . . . ? *(He makes a sudden movement of search.)* Ben, how do I . . . ?

Linda (calling): Willy, you coming up?

Willy (uttering a gasp of fear, whirling about as if to quiet her): Sh! *(He turns around as if to find his way; sounds, faces, voices, seem to be swarming in upon him and he flicks at them, crying.)* Sh! Sh! *(Suddenly music, faint and high, stops him. It rises in intensity, almost to an unbearable scream. He goes up and down on his toes, and rushes off around the house.)* Shhh!

Linda: Willy?

> *There is no answer. Linda waits. Biff gets up off his bed. He is still in his clothes. Happy sits up. Biff stands listening.*

Linda (with real fear): Willy, answer me! Willy!

> *There is the sound of a car starting and moving away at full speed.*

Linda: No!

Biff (rushing down the stairs): Pop!

> *As the car speeds off, the music crashes down in a frenzy of sound, which becomes the soft pulsation of a single cello string. Biff slowly returns to his bedroom. He and Happy gravely don their jackets. Linda slowly walks out of her room. The music has developed into a dead march. The leaves of day are appearing over everything. Charley and Bernard, somberly dressed, appear and knock on the kitchen door. Biff and Happy slowly descend the stairs to the kitchen as Charley and Bernard enter. All stop a moment when Linda, in clothes of mourning, bearing a little bunch of roses, comes*

through the draped doorway into the kitchen. She goes to Charley and takes his arm. Now all move toward the audience, through the wall-line of the kitchen. At the limit of the apron, Linda lays down the flowers, kneels, and sits back on her heels. All stare down at the grave.

REQUIEM

Charley: It's getting dark, Linda.

> *Linda doesn't react. She stares at the grave.*

Biff: How about it, Mom? Better get some rest, heh? They'll be closing the gate soon.

> *Linda makes no move. Pause.*

Happy (deeply angered): He had no right to do that! There was no necessity for it. We would've helped him.

Charley (grunting): Hmmm.

Biff: Come along, Mom.

Linda: Why didn't anybody come?

Charley: It was a very nice funeral.

Linda: But where are all the people he knew? Maybe they blame him.

Charley: Naa. It's a rough world, Linda. They wouldn't blame him.

Linda: I can't understand it. At this time especially. First time in thirty-five years we were just about free and clear. He only needed a little salary. He was even finished with the dentist.

Charley: No man only needs a little salary.

Linda: I can't understand it.

Biff: There were a lot of nice days. When he'd come home from a trip; or on Sundays, making the stoop; finishing the cellar; putting on the new porch; when he built the extra bathroom; and put up the garage. You know something, Charley, there's more of him in that front stoop than in all the sales he ever made.

Charley: Yeah. He was a happy man with a batch of cement.

Linda: He was so wonderful with his hands.

Biff: He had the wrong dreams. All, all, wrong.

Happy (almost ready to fight Biff): Don't say that!

Biff: He never knew who he was.

Charley (stopping Happy's movement and reply. To Biff.) Nobody dast blame this man. You don't understand: Willy was a salesman. And for a salesman, there is no rock bottom to the life. He don't put a bolt to a nut, he don't tell you the law or give you medicine. He's a man out there in the blue, riding on a smile and a shoeshine. And when they start not smiling back — that's an earthquake. And then you get yourself a couple of spots on your hat, and you're finished. Nobody dast blame this man. A salesman is got to dream, boy. It comes with the territory.

Biff: Charley, the man didn't know who he was.

Happy (infuriated): Don't say that!

Biff: Why don't you come with me, Happy?

Happy: I'm not licked that easily. I'm staying right in this city, and I'm gonna beat this racket! *(He looks at Biff, his chin set.)* The Loman Brothers!

Biff: I know who I am, kid.

Happy: All right, boy. I'm gonna show you and everybody else that Willy Loman did not die in vain. He had a good dream. It's the only dream you can have — to come out number-one man. He fought it out here, and this is where I'm gonna win it for him.

Biff (with a hopeless glance at Happy, bends toward his mother): Let's go, Mom.

Linda: I'll be with you in a minute. Go on, Charley. *(He hesitates.)* I want to, just for a minute. I never had a chance to say good-by.

Charley moves away, followed by Happy. Biff remains a slight distance up and left of Linda. She sits there, summoning herself. The flute begins, not far away, playing behind her speech.

Linda: Forgive me, dear. I can't cry. I don't know what it is, but I can't cry. I don't understand it. Why did you ever do that? Help me, Willy, I can't cry. It seems to me that you're just on another trip. I keep expecting you. Willy, dear, I can't cry. Why did you do it? I search and search and I search, and I can't understand it, Willy. I made the last payment on the house today. Today, dear. And there'll be nobody home. *(A sob rises in her throat.)* We're free and clear. *(Sobbing more fully, released.)* We're free. *(Biff comes slowly toward her.)* We're free . . . We're free . . .

Biff lifts her to her feet and moves out up right with her in his arms. Linda sobs quietly. Bernard and Charley come together and follow them, followed by Happy. Only the music of the flute is left on the darkening stage as over the house the hard towers of the apartment buildings rise into sharp focus, and —

THE CURTAIN FALLS

COMPARE:

Death of a Salesman and Arthur Miller's essay "Tragedy and the Common Man" (page 1328).

38 Criticism: On Drama

From A Proposed Agreement between the Playwright and the Spectator

It is also agreed that every man here exercise his own judgment and not censure by contagion, or upon trust, from another's voice or face that sits by him . . . that he be fixed and settled in his censure, that what he approves or not approves today he will do the same tomorrow; and, if tomorrow, the next day; and so the next week, if need be; and not be brought about by any that sits on the bench with him, though they indict and arraign plays daily.

          — The Scrivener, in Ben Jonson's *Bartholomew Fair* (1614)

Aristotle (384 – 322 B.C.)
TRAGEDY [1]

(about 330 B.C.)

Tragedy is an imitation of an action of high importance, complete and of some amplitude; in language enhanced by distinct and varying beauties; acted not narrated; by means of pity and fear effecting its purgation of these emotions. By the beauties enhancing the language I mean rhythm and melody; by "distinct and varying" I mean that some are produced by meter alone, and others at another time by melody. . . .

What will produce the tragic effect? Since, then, tragedy, to be at its finest, requires a complex, not a simple, structure, and its structure should also imitate fearful and pitiful events (for that is the peculiarity of this sort of imitation), it is clear: first, that decent people must not be shown passing from good fortune to misfortune (for that is not fearful or pitiful but disgusting); again, vicious people must not be shown passing from misfortune to good fortune (for that is the most untragic situation possible — it has none of the requisites, it is neither humane, not pitiful, nor fearful); nor again should an utterly evil man fall from good fortune into misfortune (for though a plot of that kind would be humane, it would not induce pity or fear — pity is induced by undeserved misfortune, and fear by the misfortunes of normal people, so that this situation will be neither pitiful nor fearful). So we are left with the man between these extremes: that is to say, the kind of man who neither is distinguished for excellence and virtue, nor comes to grief on account of baseness and vice, but on account of some error; a man of great reputation and prosperity, like Oedipus and Thyestes and conspicuous people of such families as theirs. So, to be well formed, a fable must be single rather than (as some say) double — there must be no change from misfortune to good fortune, but only the opposite, from good fortune to misfortune; the cause must not be vice, but a great error; and the man must be either of the type specified or better, rather than worse. This is borne out by the practice of poets; at first they picked a fable at random and made an inventory of its contents, but now the finest tragedies are plotted, and concern a few families — for example, the tragedies about Alcmeon, Oedipus, Orestes, Meleager, Thyestes, Telephus, and any others whose lives were attended by terrible experiences or doings.

This is the plot that will produce the technically finest tragedy. Those critics are therefore wrong who censure Euripides on this very ground — because he does this in his tragedies, and many of them end in misfortune; for it is, as I have said, the right thing to do. This is clearly demonstrated on the stage in the competitions, where such plays, if they succeed, are the most tragic, and Euripides, even if he is inefficient in every other respect, still shows himself the most tragic of our poets. The next best plot, which is said by some people to be the best, is the tragedy with a double plot, like the *Odyssey,* ending in one way for the better people and in the opposite way for the worse. But it is the weakness of theatrical performances that gives priority to this kind; when poets write what the audience would like to happen, they are in leading strings.° This is not the pleasure proper to tragedy, but rather to comedy, where

[1] Translated by L. J. Potts.
TRAGEDY. *in leading strings:* each is led, as by a string, wherever the audience wills.

the greatest enemies in the fable, say Orestes and Aegisthus, make friends and go off at the end, and nobody is killed by anybody.

The pity and fear can be brought about by the *Mise en scène*°; but they can also come from the mere plotting of the incidents, which is preferable, and better poetry. For, without seeing anything, the fable ought to have been so plotted that if one heard the bare facts, the chain of circumstances would make one shudder and pity. That would happen to any one who heard the fable of the *Oedipus*. To produce this effect by the *Mise en scène* is less artistic and puts one at the mercy of the technician; and those who use it not to frighten but merely to startle have lost touch with tragedy altogether. We should not try to get all sorts of pleasure from tragedy, but the particular tragic pleasure. And clearly, since this pleasure coming from pity and fear has to be produced by imitation, it is by his handling of the incidents that the poet must create it.

Let us, then, take next the kind of circumstances that seem terrible or lamentable. Now, doings of that kind must be between friends, or enemies, or neither. If an enemy injures an enemy, there is no pity either beforehand or at the time, except on account of the bare fact; nor is there if they are neutral; but when sufferings are engendered among the affections — for example, if murder is done or planned, or some similar outrage is committed, by brother on brother, or son on father, or mother on son, or son on mother — that is the thing to aim at. . . .

In Character there are four things to aim at. First and foremost, that it should be good of its kind: a speech or action will be moral if (as I have said) it shows a preference, and the morality will be good if the preference is good of its kind. This is possible in every class. There are good women and good slaves; yet the former class is no doubt inferior, and the latter altogether low. — Secondly, that it should be appropriate: for instance, any one can have a brave character, but there are kinds of courage, as well as kinds of sagacity, that may be inappropriate to a woman. — Thirdly, that it should be lifelike; this is distinct from making the character good and appropriate as defined above. — And fourthly, that it should be consistent; even if the person who is the original of the imitation is inconsistent, and inconsistency is the basis of his character, it is none the less necessary to make him consistently inconsistent. An example of an unnecessarily low character is Menelaus in the *Orestes;* of the unseemly and inappropriate, the lament of Odysseus in the *Scylla,* and the speech of Melanippe; of the inconsistent, Iphigeneia at Aulis — her character as a suppliant is quite unlike her later self.

And in the characterization, as in the plotting of the incidents, the aim should always be either necessity or probability: so that they say or do such things as it is necessary or probable that they would, being what they are; and that for this to follow that is either necessary or probable. (Thus it is clear that the untying of the fable should follow on the circumstances of the fable itself, and not be done *ex machina,* as it is in the *Medea,* or in Book Two of the *Iliad.* But the *deus ex machina*° should be used for matters outside the drama — either things that happened before and that man could not know, or future events that need to be announced prophetically; for we allow the gods to see everything. As for extravagant incidents, there should be none in the story, or if

---

Mise en scène: arrangement of actors and scenery. *Deus ex machina:* "god out of the machine," or an arbitrary way of concluding a play. For a discussion of this term see page 858.

there are they should be kept outside the tragedy, as is the one in the *Oedipus* of Sophocles.)

Since tragedy is an imitation of people above the normal, we must be like good portrait-painters, who follow the original model closely, but refine on it; in the same way the poet, in imitating people whose character is choleric or phlegmatic, and so forth, must keep them as they are and at the same time make them attractive. So Homer made Achilles noble, as well as a pattern of obstinacy.

— *Poetics*, VI, XIII – XV

Sigmund Freud (1856 – 1939)

THE DESTINY OF OEDIPUS [2]

1900

If *Oedipus Rex* moves a modern audience no less than it did the contemporary Greek one, the explanation can only be that its effect does not lie in the contrast between destiny and human will, but is to be looked for in the particular nature of the material on which that contrast is exemplified. There must be something which makes a voice within us ready to recognize the compelling force of destiny in the *Oedipus,* while we can dismiss as merely arbitrary such dispositions as are laid down in *Die Ahnfrau°* or other modern tragedies of destiny. And a factor of this kind is in fact involved in the story of King Oedipus. His destiny moves us only because it might have been ours — because the oracle laid the same curse upon us before our birth as upon him. It is the fate of all of us, perhaps, to direct our first sexual impulse towards our mother and our first hatred and our first murderous wish against our father. Our dreams convince us that that is so. King Oedipus, who slew his father Laïos and married his mother Iocastê, merely shows us the fulfillment of our own childhood wishes. But, more fortunate than he, we have meanwhile succeeded, insofar as we have not become psychoneurotics, in detaching our sexual impulses from our mothers and in forgetting our jealousy of our fathers. Here is one in whom these primeval wishes of our childhood have been fulfilled, and we shrink back from him with the whole force of the repression by which those wishes have since that time been held down within us. While the poet, as he unravels the past, brings to light the guilt of Oedipus, he is at the same time compelling us to recognize our own inner minds, in which those same impulses, though suppressed, are still to be found. The contrast with which the closing Chorus leaves us confronted —

> This is the king who solved the famous riddle
> And towered up, most powerful of men.
> No mortal eyes but looked on him with envy,
> Yet in the end ruin swept over him.

— strikes as a warning at ourselves and our pride, at us who since our childhood have grown so wise and so mighty in our own eyes. Like Oedipus, we

---

[2]Translated by James Strachey. The lines from *Oedipus Rex* are given in the version of Dudley Fitts and Robert Fitzgerald.
THE DESTINY OF OEDIPUS. *Die Ahnfrau:* "The Foremother," a verse play by Franz Grillparzer (1791 – 1872), Austrian dramatist and poet.

live in ignorance of these wishes, repugnant to morality, which have been forced upon us by Nature, and after their revelation we may all of us well seek to close our eyes to the scenes of our childhood.

— *The Interpretation of Dreams*

E. R. Dodds (1893 – 1979)
Sophocles and Divine Justice   1966

I take it, then, as reasonably certain that while Sophocles did not pretend that the gods are in any human sense just he nevertheless held that they are entitled to our worship. Are those two opinions incompatible? Here once more we cannot hope to understand Greek literature if we persist in looking at it through Christian spectacles. To the Christian it is a necessary part of piety to believe that God is just. And so it was to Plato and to the Stoics. But the older world saw no such necessity. If you doubt this, take down the *Iliad* and read Achilles' opinion of what divine justice amounts to (xxiv. 525 – 33); or take down the Bible and read the Book of Job. Disbelief in divine justice as measured by human yardsticks can perfectly well be associated with deep religious feeling. "Men," said Heraclitus, "find some things unjust, other things just; but in the eyes of God all things are beautiful and good and just." I think that Sophocles would have agreed.

— On Misunderstanding the *Oedipus Rex*

Charles Paul Segal
Antigonê's womanly nature   1964

It is again among the tragic paradoxes of Antigonê's position that she who accepts the absolutes of death has a far fuller sense of the complexities of life. Creon, who lacks a true "reverence" for the gods, the powers beyond human life, also lacks a deep awareness of the complexities within the human realm. Hence he tends to see the world in terms of harshly opposed categories, right and wrong, reason and folly, youth and age, male and female. He scornfully joins old age with foolishness in speaking to the chorus (I, 103 – 4) and refuses to listen to his son's advice because he is younger (III, 90ff., esp. 95 – 98). Yet his opposition of old and young is later to be turned against him by Teiresias (see V, 23ff.), and he is, in the end, to be "taught" by the young son (see III, 95 – 96) who dies, Creon laments, "young with a young fate" (Exodos, 92 – 93).

All these categories imply the relation of superior and inferior, stronger and weaker. This highly structured and aggressive view of the world Creon expresses perhaps most strikingly in repeatedly formulating the conflict between Antigonê and himself in terms of the woman trying to conquer the man. He sees in Antigonê a challenge to his whole way of living and his basic attitudes toward the world. And of course he is right, for Antigonê's full acceptance of her womanly nature, her absolute valuation of the bonds of blood and affection, is a total denial of Creon's obsessively masculine rationality.

Antigonê's acceptance of this womanly obligation stands out the more by contrast with Ismenê's rejection of it: "We must consider," Ismenê says, "that we were born as women with women's nature, and are not such as to fight with men" (Prologue 46 – 47). Ismenê feels her womanhood as something negative, as a weakness. Antigonê finds in it a source of strength. Ismenê capitulates to Creon's view; Antigonê resists and finds in her "nature" a potent heroism which cuts across Creon's dichotomizing of things and has its echoes even after her death in the equally womanly, though less significant, death of Eurydice.

It is Antigonê's very "nature," even more than her actions, which stands in such challenging opposition to Creon. Thus she concludes her first, and most important, clash with Creon with the pointed line: "It is my nature not to share in hating *(synechthein),* but to share in loving *(symphilein)*" (II, 118). Her words not only answer Creon's charge that Polyneices is an enemy and hence deserving of hate, not love (II, 117), but also expose more of the fundamental differences between the two protagonists. In the conflict over basic terms like "law," "piety," "profit," lies much of the movement of the play. The words for "love" and "hate" used by Creon and Antigonê in II, 117 – 18 (and throughout the play) have a certain ambiguity. *Echthros,* "enemy," means also personally "hated"; *philos,* "friend," means also an intimately "loved one." Creon simply identifies the two meanings; that is, he identifies "love" as personal and emotional *(philein)* with political agreement (I, 12ff.) and "hate" with political enmity. But Antigonê's being and her action place into dramatic conflict the question of who deserves "love" and who "hate." Hence at the end of their first encounter Creon answers Antigonê's "It is my nature not to share in hating but to share in loving" with one of his characteristic dichotomies of man-woman, superior-inferior: "Go below then and love them, if love them you must; but no woman will rule me while I live" (II, 119 – 20).

Creon's definition of man by his civic or political relations alone extends to areas other than "love." He can conceive of "honor" only for benefactors of the state (I, 31 – 34) and angrily rejects any idea that the gods could "honor" a traitor (I, 103ff.). He again presumes that human and divine — or political and religious — values exactly coincide. Antigonê, on the other hand, looks at "honor" in terms of what is due to the gods.

— "Sophocles' Praise of Man and the Conflicts of the *Antigonê*"

Thomas Rymer (1643? – 1713)
THE FAULTS OF OTHELLO   1692

Nothing is more odious in Nature than an improbable lie; and, certainly, never was any play fraught, like this of *Othello,* with improbabilities. . . . Othello is made a Venetian general. We see nothing done by him, nor related concerning him, that comports with the condition of a general, or indeed of a man, unless the killing himself, to avoid a death the law was about to inflict upon him. When his jealousy had wrought him up to a resolution of his taking revenge for the supposed injury, he sets Iago to the fighting part, to kill Cassio, and chooses himself to murder the silly woman his wife, that was like to make no resistance.

His love and his jealousy are no part of a soldier's character, unless for comedy. . . .

So much ado, so much stress, so much passion and repetition about an handkerchief! Why was this not called *The Tragedy of the Handkerchief?* Had it been Desdemona's garter, the sagacious Moor might have smelt a rat, but the handkerchief is so remote a trifle, no booby . . . could make any consequence from it.

We may learn here that a woman never loses her tongue, even though after she is stifled:

> *Desdemona:* O, falsely, falsely murdered!
> *Emilia:* O Lord! What cry is that?
> *Othello:* That? What?
> *Emilia:* Out and alas! that was my lady's voice.
> Help! Help, ho! Help! O lady, speak again!
> Sweet Desdemona! O sweet mistress, speak!
> *Desdemona:* A guiltless death I die.
> *Emilia:* O, who hath done this deed?
> *Desdemona:* Nobody — I myself. Farewell.
> Commend me to my kind lord. O, farewell!   (V, ii, 121 – 124)

But from this scene to the end of the play we meet with nothing but blood and butchery, described much-what° to the style of the last speeches and confessions of the persons executed at Tyburn,° with this difference: that there we have the fact, and the due course of justice, whereas our poet against all justice and reason, against all law, humanity, and Nature, in a barbarous arbitrary way, executes and makes havoc of his subjects, hab-nab, as they come to hand. Desdemona dropped her handkerchief; therefore, she must be stifled. Othello, by law to be broken on the wheel, by the poet's cunning escapes with cutting his own throat. Cassio, for I know not what, comes off with a broken shin. Iago murders his benefactor Roderigo, as this were poetical gratitude. Iago is not yet killed, because there never yet was such a villain alive.

— *A Short View of Tragedy*

Samuel Johnson (1709 – 1784)

"SHAKESPEARE HAS NO HEROES"   1765

Other dramatists can only gain attention by hyperbolical or aggravated characters, by fabulous and unexampled excellence or depravity, as the writers of barbarous romances invigorated the reader by a giant and a dwarf; and he that should form his expectations of human affairs from the play or from the tale would be equally deceived. Shakespeare has no heroes; his scenes are occupied only by men, who act and speak as the reader thinks that he should himself have spoken or acted on the same occasion; even where the agency is supernatural, the dialogue is level with life. Other writers disguise the most natural passions and most frequent incidents so that he who contemplates

THE FAULTS OF OTHELLO. *much-what:* nearly or "pretty much."   *Tyburn:* In London, site of a gallows where criminals were publicly hanged.

them in the book will not know them in the world: Shakespeare approximates the remote, and familiarizes the wonderful; the event which he represents will not happen, but, if it were possible, its effects would probably be such as he has assigned; and it may be said that he has not only shown human nature as it acts in real exigencies, but as it would be found in trials to which it cannot be exposed. . . .

Shakespeare's plays are not in the rigorous and critical sense either tragedies or comedies, but compositions of a distinct kind; exhibiting the real state of sublunary nature, which partakes of good and evil, joy and sorrow, mingled with endless variety of proportion and innumerable modes of combination; and expressing the course of the world, in which the loss of one is the gain of another; in which, at the same time, the reveler is hasting to his wine, and the mourner burying his friend; in which the malignity of one is sometimes defeated by the frolic of another; and many mischiefs and many benefits are done and hindered without design.

Out of this chaos of mingled purposes and casualties the ancient poets, according to the laws which custom had prescribed, selected some of the crimes of men, and some their absurdities; some the momentous vicissitudes of life, and some the lighter occurrences; some the terrors of distress, and some the gaities of prosperity. Thus rose the two modes of imitation, known by the names of *tragedy* and *comedy,* compositions intended to promote different ends by contrary means, and considered as so little allied that I do not recollect among the Greeks or Romans a single writer who attempted both.

Shakespeare has united the powers of exciting laughter and sorrow not only in one mind, but in one composition. Almost all his plays are divided between serious and ludicrous characters, and, in the successive evolutions of the design, sometimes produce seriousness and sorrow, and sometimes levity and laughter.

That this is a practice contrary to the rules of criticism will be readily allowed; but there is always an appeal open from criticism to nature. The end of writing is to instruct; the end of poetry is to instruct by pleasing. That the mingled drama may convey all the instruction of tragedy or comedy cannot be denied, because it includes both in its alternations of exhibition, and approaches nearer than either to the appearance of life, by showing how great machinations and slender designs may promote or obviate one another, and the high and the low co-operate in the general system by unavoidable concatenation.

— Preface to Shakespeare

Sylvan Barnet

THE TEMPEST: OLD CONVENTIONS, NEW MEANINGS   1974

Like some of the early comedies, which are ultimately indebted in varying degrees to late Greek and Roman comedy, *The Tempest* has a shipwreck (compare *The Comedy of Errors* and *Twelfth Night*), an irritable father (compare Egeus in *A Midsummer Night's Dream*), and a character who more or less manipulates the plot (compare Rosalind in *As You Like It*). Like *The Comedy of Errors,* possibly Shakespeare's earliest comedy, it obeys the ancient traditions of unity of time and place: the play spans only a few hours and occurs in one locale. But despite these and other resemblances, the unusual amount of spectacle in *The Tempest* — and, more important, the serious tone — ties the play to Shakespeare's other last plays. The old conventions are here, but with new meanings: *The Tempest* is concerned with guilt and forgiveness, royal children, wonderful quasi-resurrections, and finally reunions. "These are not natural events, they strengthen / From strange, to stranger" (V.i.227 – 28). The pastoral setting, implying the freshness and vitality of nature, prominent in parts of *Cymbeline* under the thin disguise of the Welsh countryside and in *The Winter's Tale* in the Bohemian shepherds' feast, is presented in *The Tempest* in the mysterious island — though this island means different things to different people: to one observer the grass looks "lush and lusty," but to another the grass is "indeed tawny." Pastoralism appears too in the masque of Ceres and Juno and the dance of nymphs and harvesters. Again there is a shipwreck, and again the results prove beneficent. Those who are cast upon the island find, strangely, that their "garments, being, as they were, drenched in the sea, hold, notwithstanding, their freshness and glosses, being rather new-dyed than stained with salt water" (II.i.64 – 67). This note of renewal or regeneration is variously sounded throughout the play. Suffering brings renewal: "Some kinds of baseness / Are nobly undergone, and most poor matters / Point to rich ends" (III.i.2 – 4). Even Caliban, more a beast than a man, though acknowledged by Prospero as Prospero's educational failure, at last resolves to "seek for grace," thus suggesting that the most rudimentary kind of human being can make some moral progress. Not Caliban but Antonio, Prospero's brother, is the real failure, for Antonio's silence in the reconciliation scene suggests the limits of Prospero's power: the shipwreck manufactured by Prospero can only provide the opportunity for repentance, but it cannot force repentance, for a man has the freedom to remain recalcitrant if he wishes. Still, much goodness has been found:

> In one voyage
> Did Claribel her husband find at Tunis,
> And Ferdinand her brother found a wife
> Where he himself was lost; Prospero his dukedom
> In a poor isle; and all of us ourselves
> When no man was his own.   (V.i.208 – 13)

The sense of providence, strong in the last plays, is embodied in *The Tempest* chiefly by the magician Prospero, who raises and allays the storm that helps to regenerate and reconcile. (But Prospero, though in some ways godlike, is not God; before the play began he was so enraptured by "secret studies" that he shirked the cares of the state, and during the play he learns to pity and, apparently, to forego vengeance and to forgive — somewhat grudgingly — the wrongdoer.)

Because *The Tempest* is probably the last play that is entirely Shakespeare's (he seems to have had a collaborator for *Henry VIII* and *The Two Noble Kinsmen*), there is a tendency to see in Prospero, the magician who can call up visions but who at the end breaks his staff and abjures his "potent art," a picture of Shakespeare putting down his pen and contemplating retirement to

Stratford. There is no great harm in such a reading as long as it does not reduce the play to an autobiographical scrap. It would be a pity to see in *The Tempest* only a farewell to the theater and to fail to notice that Prospero goes not to retirement but to the active role of ruling in Milan as the duke.

— A Short Guide to Shakespeare

Bernard Shaw (1856 – 1950)

Ibsen and the Familiar Situation 1913

Up to a certain point in the last act, *A Doll's House* is a play that might be turned into a very ordinary French drama by the excision of a few lines, and the substitution of a sentimental happy ending for the famous last scene: indeed the very first thing the theatrical wiseacres did with it was to effect exactly this transformation, with the result that the play thus pithed had no success and attracted no notice worth mentioning. But at just that point in the last act, the heroine very unexpectedly (by the wiseacres) stops her emotional acting and says: 'We must sit down and discuss all this that has been happening between us.' And it was by this new technical feature: this addition of a new movement, as musicians would say, to the dramatic form, that *A Doll's House* conquered Europe and founded a new school of dramatic art. . . .

The drama was born of old from the union of two desires: the desire to have a dance and the desire to hear a story. The dance became a rant: the story became a situation. When Ibsen began to make plays, the art of the dramatist had shrunk into the art of contriving a situation. And it was held that the stranger the situation, the better the play. Ibsen saw that, on the contrary, the more familiar the situation, the more interesting the play. Shakespeare had put ourselves on the stage but not our situations. Our uncles seldom murder our fathers, and cannot legally marry our mothers; we do not meet witches; our kings are not as a rule stabbed and succeeded by their stabbers; and when we raise money by bills we do not promise to pay pounds of our flesh. Ibsen supplies the want left by Shakespeare. He gives us not only ourselves, but ourselves in our own situations. The things that happen to his stage figures are things that happen to us. One consequence is that his plays are much more important to us than Shakespeare's. Another is that they are capable both of hurting us cruelly and of filling us with excited hopes of escape from idealistic tyrannies, and with visions of intenser life in the future.

— The Quintessence of Ibsenism (second edition)

Edward Albee (b. 1928)

The Theater of the Absurd 1962

What of this theater in which, for example, a legless old couple live out their lives in twin ashcans, surfacing occasionally for food or conversation (Samuel Beckett's *Endgame*); in which a man is seduced, and rather easily, by a girl with three well-formed and functioning noses (Eugène Ionesco's *Jack, or The Sub-*

mission); in which, on the same stage, one group of Negro actors is playing at pretending to be Negro (Jean Genêt's *The Blacks*)?

What of this theater? Is it, as it has been accused of being, obscure, sordid, destructive, anti-theater, perverse, and absurd (in the sense of foolish)? Or is it merely, as I have so often heard it put, that, "This sort of stuff is too depressing, too . . . too mixed up; I go to the theater to relax and have a good time"?

I would submit that it is this latter attitude — that the theater is a place to relax and have a good time — in conflict with the purpose of The Theater of the Absurd — which is to make a man face up to the human condition as it really is — that has produced all the brouhaha and the dissent. I would submit that The Theater of the Absurd, in the sense that it is truly the contemporary theater, facing as it does man's condition as it is, is the Realistic theater of our time; and that the supposed Realistic theater — the term used here to mean most of what is done on Broadway — in the sense that it panders to the public need for self-congratulation and reassurance and presents a false picture of ourselves to ourselves, is, with an occasional very lovely exception, really and truly The Theater of the Absurd.

— *Which Theater Is the Absurd One?*

Tennessee Williams (1914 – 1983)
How to stage The Glass Menagerie   1945

Being a "memory play," *The Glass Menagerie* can be presented with unusual freedom of convention. Because of its considerably delicate or tenuous material, atmospheric touches and subtleties of direction play a particularly important part. Expressionism and all other unconventional techniques in drama have only one valid aim, and that is a closer approach to truth. When a play employs unconventional techniques, it is not, or certainly shouldn't be, trying to escape its responsibility of dealing with reality, or interpreting experience, but is actually or should be attempting to find a closer approach, a more penetrating and vivid expression of things as they are. The straight realistic play with its genuine Frigidaire and authentic ice-cubes, its characters that speak exactly as its audience speaks, corresponds to the academic landscape and has the same virtue of a photographic likeness. Everyone should know nowadays the unimportance of the photographic in art: that truth, life, or reality is an organic thing which the poetic imagination can represent or suggest, in essence, only through transformation, through changing into other forms than those which were merely present in appearance.

These remarks are not meant as a preface only to this particular play. They have to do with a conception of a new, plastic theater which must take the place of the exhausted theater of realistic conventions if the theater is to resume vitality as a part of our culture.

THE SCREEN DEVICE. There is *only one important difference between the original and acting version of the play* and that is the *omission* in the latter of the device which I tentatively included in my *original* script. This device was the use of a screen on which were projected magic-lantern slides bearing images or titles. I do not regret the omission of this device from the present Broadway production. The extraordinary power of Miss Taylor's performance° made it suitable to have the utmost simplicity in the physical production. But I think it may be interesting to some readers to see how this device was conceived. So I am putting it into the published manuscript. These images and legends, projected from behind, were cast on a section of wall between the front-room and dining-room areas, which should be indistinguishable from the rest when not in use.

The purpose of this will probably be apparent. It is to give accent to certain values in each scene. Each scene contains a particular point (or several) which is structurally the most important. In an episodic play, such as this, the basic structure or narrative line may be obscured from the audience; the effect may seem fragmentary rather than architectural. This may not be the fault of the play so much as a lack of attention in the audience. The legend or image upon the screen will strengthen the effect of what is merely allusion in the writing and allow the primary point to be made more simply and lightly than if the entire responsibility were on the spoken lines. Aside from this structural value, I think the screen will have a definite emotional appeal, less definable but just as important. An imaginative producer or director may invent many other uses for this device than those indicated in the present script. In fact the possibilities of the device seem much larger to me than the instance of this play can possibly utilize.

THE MUSIC. Another extra-literary accent in this play is provided by the use of music. A single recurring tune, "The Glass Menagerie," is used to give emotional emphasis to suitable passages. This tune is like circus music, not when you are on the grounds or in the immediate vicinity of the parade, but when you are at some distance and very likely thinking of something else. It seems under those circumstances to continue almost interminably and it weaves in and out of your preoccupied consciousness; then it is the lightest, most delicate music in the world and perhaps the saddest. It expresses the surface vivacity of life with the underlying strain of immutable and inexpressible sorrow. When you look at a piece of delicately spun glass you think of two things: how beautiful it is and how easily it can be broken. Both of those ideas should be woven into the recurring tune, which dips in and out of the play as if it were carried on a wind that changes. It serves as a thread of connection and allusion between the narrator with his separate point in time and space and the subject of his story. Between each episode it returns as reference to the emotion, nostalgia, which is the first condition of the play. It is primarily Laura's music and therefore comes out most clearly when the play focuses upon her and the lovely fragility of glass which is her image.

THE LIGHTING. The lighting in the play is not realistic. In keeping with the atmosphere of memory, the stage is dim. Shafts of light are focused on selected

How to stage *The Glass Menagerie. Miss Taylor's performance:* In the original Broadway production of the play in 1945, the role of Amanda Wingfield, the mother, was played by veteran actress Laurette Taylor.

areas or actors, sometimes in contradistinction to what is the apparent center. For instance, in the quarrel scene between Tom and Amanda, in which Laura has no active part, the clearest pool of light is on her figure. This is also true of the supper scene, when her silent figure on the sofa should remain the visual center. The light upon Laura should be distinct from the others, having a peculiar pristine clarity such as light used in early religious portraits of female saints or madonnas. A certain correspondence to light in religious paintings, such as El Greco's, where the figures are radiant in atmosphere that is relatively dusky, could be effectively used throughout the play. (It will also permit a more effective use of the screen.) A free, imaginative use of light can be of enormous value in giving a mobile, plastic quality to plays of a more or less static nature.

— The Author's Production Notes to *The Glass Menagerie*

Arthur Miller (b. 1915)
Tragedy and the Common Man[3]   1949

In this age few tragedies are written. It has often been held that the lack is due to a paucity of heroes among us, or else that modern man has had the blood drawn out of his organs of belief by the skepticism of science, and the heroic attack on life cannot feed on an attitude of reserve and circumspection. For one reason or another, we are often held to be below tragedy — or tragedy above us. The inevitable conclusion is, of course, that the tragic mode is archaic, fit only for the very highly placed, the kings or the kingly, and where this admission is not made in so many words it is most often implied.

I believe that the common man is as apt a subject for tragedy in its highest sense as kings were. On the face of it this ought to be obvious in the light of modern psychiatry, which bases its analysis upon classific formulations, such as the Oedipus and Orestes complexes, for instance, which were enacted by royal beings, but which apply to everyone in similar emotional situations.

More simply, when the question of tragedy in art is not at issue, we never hesitate to attribute to the well-placed and the exalted the very same mental processes as the lowly. And finally, if the exaltation of tragic action were truly a property of the high-bred character alone, it is inconceivable that the mass of mankind should cherish tragedy above all other forms, let alone be capable of understanding it.

As a general rule, to which there may be exceptions unknown to me, I think the tragic feeling is evoked in us when we are in the presence of a character who is ready to lay down his life, if need be, to secure one thing — his sense of personal dignity. From Orestes to Hamlet, Medea to Macbeth, the underlying struggle is that of the individual attempting to gain his "rightful" position in his society.

Sometimes he is one who has been displaced from it, sometimes one who seeks to attain it for the first time, but the fateful wound from which the inevitable events spiral is the wound of indignity, and its dominant force is

[3]A complete essay, originally published in *The New York Times*.

indignation. Tragedy, then, is the consequence of a man's total compulsion to evaluate himself justly.

In the sense of having been initiated by the hero himself, the tale always reveals what has been called his "tragic flaw," a failing that is not peculiar to grand or elevated characters. Nor is it necessarily a weakness. The flaw, or crack in the character, is really nothing — and need be nothing — but his inherent unwillingness to remain passive in the face of what he conceives to be a challenge to his dignity, his image of his rightful status. Only the passive, only those who accept their lot without active retaliation, are "flawless." Most of us are in that category.

But there are among us today, as there always have been, those who act against the scheme of things that degrades them, and in the process of action, everything we have accepted out of fear or insensitivity or ignorance is shaken before us and examined, and from this total onslaught by an individual against the seemingly stable cosmos surrounding us — from this total examination of the "unchangeable" environment — comes the terror and the fear that is classically associated with tragedy.

More important, from this total questioning of what has been previously unquestioned, we learn. And such a process is not beyond the common man. In revolutions around the world, these past thirty years, he has demonstrated again and again this inner dynamic of all tragedy.

Insistence upon the rank of the tragic hero, or the so-called nobility of his character, is really but a clinging to the outward forms of tragedy. If rank or nobility of character was indispensable, then it would follow that the problems of those with rank were the particular problems of tragedy. But surely the right of one monarch to capture the domain from another no longer raises our passions, nor are our concepts of justice what they were to the mind of an Elizabethan king.

The quality in such plays that does shake us, however, derives from the underlying fear of being displaced, the disaster inherent in being torn away from our chosen image of what and who we are in this world. Among us today this fear is as strong, and perhaps stronger, than it ever was. In fact, it is the common man who knows this fear best.

Now, if it is true that tragedy is the consequence of a man's total compulsion to evaluate himself justly, his destruction in the attempt posits a wrong or an evil in his environment. And this is precisely the morality of tragedy and its lesson. The discovery of the moral law, which is what the enlightenment of tragedy consists of, is not the discovery of some abstract or metaphysical quantity.

The tragic right is a condition of life, a condition in which the human personality is able to flower and realize itself. The wrong is the condition which suppresses man, perverts the flowing out of his love and creative instinct. Tragedy enlightens — and it must, in that it points the heroic finger at the enemy of man's freedom. The thrust for freedom is the quality in tragedy which exalts. The revolutionary questioning of the stable environment is what terrifies. In no way is the common man debarred from such thoughts or such actions.

Seen in this light, our lack of tragedy may be partially accounted for by the turn which modern literature has taken toward the purely psychiatric view of life, or the purely sociological. If all our miseries, our indignities, are born and bred within our minds, then all action, let alone the heroic action, is obviously impossible.

And if society alone is responsible for the cramping of our lives, then the protagonist must needs be so pure and faultless as to force us to deny his validity as a character. From neither of these views can tragedy derive, simply because neither represents a balanced concept of life. Above all else, tragedy requires the finest appreciation by the writer of cause and effect.

No tragedy can therefore come about when its author fears to question absolutely everything, when he regards any institution, habit or custom as being either everlasting, immutable or inevitable. In the tragic view the need of man to wholly realize himself is the only fixed star, and whatever it is that hedges his nature and lowers it is ripe for attack and examination. Which is not to say that tragedy must preach revolution.

The Greeks could probe the very heavenly origin of their ways and return to confirm the rightness of laws. And Job could face God in anger, demanding his right, and end in submission. But for a moment everything is in suspension, nothing is accepted, and in this stretching and tearing apart of the cosmos, in the very action of so doing, the character gains "size," the tragic stature which is spuriously attached to the royal or the high born in our minds. The commonest of men may take on that stature to the extent of his willingness to throw all he has into the contest, the battle to secure his rightful place in his world.

There is a misconception of tragedy with which I have been struck in review after review, and in many conversations with writers and readers alike. It is the idea that tragedy is of necessity allied to pessimism. Even the dictionary says nothing more about the word than that it means a story with a sad or unhappy ending. This impression is so firmly fixed that I almost hesitate to claim that in truth tragedy implies more optimism in its author than does comedy, and that its final result ought to be the reinforcement of the onlooker's brightest opinions of the human animal.

For, if it is true to say that in essence the tragic hero is intent upon claiming his whole due as a personality, and if this struggle must be total and without reservation, then it automatically demonstrates the indestructible will of man to achieve his humanity.

The possibility of victory must be there in tragedy. Where pathos rules, where pathos is finally derived, a character has fought a battle he could not possibly have won. The pathetic is achieved when the protagonist is, by virtue of his witlessness, his insensitivity, or the very air he gives off, incapable of grappling with a much superior force.

Pathos truly is the mode for the pessimist. But tragedy requires a nicer balance between what is possible and what is impossible. And it is curious, although edifying, that the plays we revere, century after century, are the tragedies. In them, and in them alone, lies the belief — optimistic, if you will — in the perfectibility of man.

It is time, I think, that we who are without kings, took up this bright thread of our history and followed it to the only place it can possibly lead in our time — the heart and spirit of the average man.

SUPPLEMENT: WRITING

Writing about Literature

All of us have some powers of reasoning and perception. And when we come to a story, a poem, or a play, we can do little other than to trust whatever powers we have, like one who enters a shadowy room, clutching a decent candle.

After all, in the study of literature, common sense (poet Gerard Manley Hopkins said) is never out of place. For most of a class hour, a renowned English professor rhapsodized about the arrangement of the contents of W. H. Auden's *Collected Poems.* Auden, he claimed, was a master of thematic continuity, who had brilliantly placed the poems in the best possible order, in which (to the ingenious mind) they complemented each other. Near the end of the hour, his theories were punctured — with a great inaudible pop — when a student, timidly raising a hand, pointed out that Auden had arranged the poems in the book not according to theme but in alphabetical order according to the first word of each poem. The professor's jaw dropped: "Why didn't you say that sooner?" The student was apologetic: "I — I was afraid I'd sound too *ordinary.*"

Emerson makes a similar point in his essay, "The American Scholar": "Meek young men grow up in libraries, believing it their duty to accept the views which Cicero, which Locke, which Bacon have given; forgetful that Cicero, Locke, and Bacon were only young men in libraries when they wrote these books." Don't be afraid to state a conviction, though it seems obvious. Does it matter that you may be repeating something that, once upon a time or even just the other day, has been said before? There are excellent old ideas as well as new.

SOME APPROACHES TO LITERATURE

Most writers of critical essays follow a few familiar approaches to stories, poems, and plays. Underlying each of these four approaches is a specific way of regarding the nature of a work of literature.

1. *The Work by Itself.* This view assumes a story, poem, or play to be an individual entity, existing on its page, which we can read and understand in its own right, without necessarily studying the life of its author,

or the age in which it was written, or its possible effect on its readers. This is the approach in most papers written in response to college assignments; to study just the work (and not its backgrounds or its influence) does not require the student to spend prolonged time doing research in a library. The three common ways of writing a paper discussed in this book — explication, analysis, and comparison and contrast — deal mainly with the work of literature in itself.

2. *The Work as Imitation of Life.* Aristotle called the art of writing a tragedy *mimesis:* the imitation or re-creation of an action that is serious and complete in itself. From this classic theory in the *Poetics* comes the view that a work of literature in some ways imitates the world or the civilization in which it was produced. We can say that Ibsen's play *A Doll House* places before our eyes actors whose lifelike speeches and movements represent members of an upper-middle-class society in provincial Norway in the late nineteenth century and that the play reflects their beliefs and attitudes. Not only the subject and theme of a work imitate life in this view: John Ciardi remarked that the heroic couplet, dominant stanza form in poetry read by educated people in eighteenth-century England, reflects, in its exact form and its use of antitheses, the rhythms of the minuet — another contemporary form, fashionable also among the well-to-do: "now on this hand, now on that." The writer considering literature as imitation usually studies the world that the literary work imitates. He or she goes into the ideas underlying the writer's society, showing how the themes, assumptions, and conventions of the writer's work arose out of that time and that place. Obviously, this analysis takes more research than one can do for a weekly paper; it is usually the approach taken for a book or a dissertation, or perhaps an honors thesis or a term paper. (The other two approaches we will mention also take research.) Reasonably short studies of the relation between the work and its world are, however, sometimes possible: "World War II as Seen in Henry Reed's 'Naming of Parts' "; "Faulkner's 'Barn Burning': A Mirror of Mississippi?"

3. *The Work as Expression.* In this view, a work of literature expresses the feelings of the person who wrote it; therefore, to study it, one studies the author's life. Typical paper topics: *"A Glass Menagerie* and the Early Life of Tennessee Williams"; "Sylvia Plath's Lost Father and Her View of Him in 'Daddy.' " To write any truly deep-reaching biographical criticism takes research, clearly, but one could write a term paper on topics such as these by reading a biography.

Biographical criticism fell into temporary disrepute around 1920, when T. S. Eliot questioned the assumption that a poem has to be a personal statement of the poet's thoughts and emotions.[1] Eliot and other critics did much to clear the air of speculation that the "Ode on a Grecian Urn" may

---

[1]See Eliot's essay "Tradition and the Individual Talent," in *Selected Essays* (New York: Harcourt, 1932).

have been shaped by what Keats had had for breakfast. Evidently, in any search for what went on in an author's mind, and for the influence of life upon work, absolute certainty is unattainable. Besides, such an approach can be grossly reductive — holding, for example, that Shakespeare was sad when he wrote his tragedies and especially happy when he wrote *A Midsummer Night's Dream.* Still, some works do gain in meaning from even a slight knowledge of the author's biography. In reading *Moby-Dick,* it helps to know that Herman Melville served aboard a whaling vessel.

4. *The Work as Influence.* From this perspective, a literary work is a force that affects people. It stirs responses in them, rouses their emotions, perhaps argues for ideas that change their minds. The artist, said Tolstoi in a famous pronouncement *(What Is Art?),* "hands on to others those feelings he himself has felt, that they too may be moved, and experience them." Part of the function of art, Tolstoi continued, is to enlighten and to lead its audience into an acceptance of better moral attitudes (religious faith, or a sense of social justice). The critic who takes this approach generally deals with the ideas that a literary work imparts and the reception of those ideas by a particular audience: "Did *Uncle Tom's Cabin* Cause the Civil War?"; "The Early Reception of Allen Ginsberg's *Howl*"; "Ed Bullins's Plays and Their Newly Proud Black Audience." As you can see, this whole approach is closely related to viewing a literary work as an imitation of life. Still another way of discussing a work's influence is to trace its effect upon other writers: "Robert Frost's Debt to Emily Dickinson"; *"Moby-Dick* and William Faulkner's *The Bear:* Two Threatened Wildernesses."

BEGINNING

Offered a choice of literary works to write about, you probably will do best if, instead of choosing what you think will impress your instructor, you choose what appeals to you. And how to find out what appeals? Whether you plan to write a short paper that requires no research beyond the story or poem or play itself, or a long term paper that will take you to the library, the first stage of your project is reading — and note taking. To concentrate your attention, one time-honored method is to read with a pencil, marking (if the book is yours) passages that stand out in importance, jotting brief notes in a margin (*"Key symbol — this foreshadows the ending"; "Dramatic irony"; "IDIOT!!!";* or other possibly useful remarks). In a long story or poem or play, some students asterisk passages that cry for comparison; for instance, all the places in which they find the same theme or symbol. Later, at a glance, they can review the highlights of a work and, when writing a paper about it, quickly refer to evidence. This method shoots holes in a book's resale value, but many find the sacrifice worthwhile. Patient souls who dislike butchering a book prefer to take notes on looseleaf notebook paper, holding one sheet beside a page in the book and giving it the book's page number. Later, in writing a paper, they can place book page and companion note page together again. This method has the advantage of affording a lot of room for note taking; it is a good one for short poems closely packed with complexities.

But by far the most popular method of taking notes (besides writing on the pages of books) is to write on index cards — the 3 × 5 kind, for brief notes and titles; 5 × 8 cards for longer notes. Write on one side only; notes on the back of the card usually get overlooked later. Cards are easy to shuffle and, in organizing your material, to deal. To save work, instead of copying out on a card the title and author of a book you're taking a note from, just keep a numbered list of the books you're using. Then, when making a note, you need write only the book's identifying number on the card in order to identify your source. (Later, when writing footnotes, you can translate the number into title, author, and other information.)

Now that coin-operated photocopy machines are to be found in many libraries, you no longer need to spend hours copying by hand whole poems and longer passages. If accuracy is essential (surely it is) and if a poem or passage is long enough to be worth the investment of a few cents, you can lay photocopied material into place in your paper with transparent tape or rubber cement. The latest copyright law permits students and scholars to reproduce books and periodicals in this fashion; it does not, however, permit making a dozen or more copies for public sale.

Certain literary works, because they offer intriguing difficulties, have attracted professional critics by the score. On library shelves, great phalanxes of critical books now stand at the side of James Joyce's complex novels *Ulysses* and *Finnegans Wake,* and T. S. Eliot's allusive poem *The Waste Land.* The student who undertakes to study such works seriously is well advised to profit from the critics' labors. Chances are, too, that even in discussing a relatively uncomplicated work you will want to seek the aid of the finest critics. If you quote them, quote them exactly, in quotation marks, and give them credit. When employed in any but the most superlative student paper, a brilliant phrase (or even a not-so-brilliant sentence) from a renowned critic is likely to stand out like a golf ball in a garter snake's midriff, and most English instructors are likely to recognize it. If you rip off the critic's words, then go ahead and steal the whole essay, for good critics write in seamless unities. Then, when apprehended, you can exclaim — like the student whose term paper was found to be the work of a well-known scholar — "I've been robbed! That paper cost me twenty dollars!" But of course the worst rip-off is the one the student inflicted on himself, having got nothing for his money out of a college course but a little practice in touch typing.

Taking notes on your readings, you will want to jot down the title of every book you might refer to in your paper, and the page number of any passage you might wish to quote. Even if you summarize a critic's idea in your own words, rather than quote, you have to give credit to your source. Nothing is cheaper to give than proper credit. Certainly it's easier to take notes while you read than to have to run back to the library during the final typing.

Choose a topic appropriate to the assigned length of your paper. How do you know the probable length of your discussion until you write it? When in doubt, you are better off to define your topic narrowly. Your paper will be stronger if you go deeper into your subject than if you choose some gigantic subject and then find yourself able to touch on it only superficially. A thorough explication of a short story is hardly possible in a paper of 250 words. There are, in truth, four-line poems whose surface 250 words might only begin to scratch. A profound topic ("The Character of Shakespeare's Hamlet") might overflow a book; but a topic more narrowly defined ("Hamlet's Views of Acting"; "Hamlet's Puns") might result in a more nearly manageable term paper. You can narrow and focus a large topic while you work your way into it. A general interest in "Hemingway's Heroes" might lead you, in reading, taking notes, and thinking further, to the narrower topic, "Jake Barnes: Spokesman for Hemingway's Views of War."

Many student writers find it helpful, in defining a topic, to state an emerging idea for a paper in a provisional **thesis sentence:** a summing-up of the one main idea or argument that the paper will embody. (A thesis sentence is for your own use; you don't have to implant it in your paper unless your instructor asks for it.) A good statement of a thesis is not just a disembodied subject; it comes with both subject and verb. ("The Downfall of Oedipus Rex" is not yet a complete idea for a paper; "What Caused the Downfall of Oedipus Rex?" is.) A thesis sentence may help you see for yourself what the author is *saying about* a subject. Not a full thesis, and not a sentence, "The Isolation of City-dwellers in Edward Albee's *A Zoo Story* " might be a decent title for a paper. But it isn't a useful thesis because it doesn't indicate what one might say about that isolation (nor what Albee is saying about it). It may be obvious that isolation isn't desirable, but a clearer and more workable thesis sentence might be, "In *A Zoo Story* Albee shows how city-dwellers' isolation from one another prompts one city dweller to action"; the writer might well go on to demonstrate just what that action is.

DISCOVERING AND PLANNING

Writing is not likely to proceed in a straight line. Like thought, it often goes by fits and starts, by charges and retreats and mopping-up operations. All the while you take notes, you discover material to write about; all the while you tool over your topic in your mind, you plan. It is the nature of ideas, those headstrong things, to happen in any order they desire. While you continue to plan, while you write a draft, and while you revise, expect to keep discovering new thoughts — perhaps the best thoughts of all. If you do, be sure to let them in.

Topic in hand (which may get drastically changed as you continue), you begin to sort out your miscellaneous notes, thoughts, and impressions. If you can see that you haven't had enough ideas, you may wish to

brainstorm — to set yourself, say, fifteen minutes in which to write down as fast as you can all the ideas on your topic that come into your head, without worrying whether they are going to be useful. (You can look over the results and decide that later.) Another method of discovery is to **freewrite:** to write rapidly and uncritically, letting your thoughts tumble onto paper as fast as your pen, typewriter, or word processor can capture them. Sometimes these methods will goad the unconscious into coming up with unexpectedly good ideas; at least, you will generate more potentially useful raw material.

To outline or not to outline? Unless your topic, by its nature, suggests some obvious way to organize your paper ("An Explication of a Wordsworth Sonnet" might mean simply working through the poem line by line), then some kind of outline will probably help. In high school or other prehistoric times, you perhaps learned how to construct a beautiful outline, laid out with Roman numerals, capital letters, Arabic numerals, and lower-case letters. It was a thing of beauty and symmetry, and possibly even had something to do with paper writing. But if now you are skeptical of the value of outlining, reflect: not every outline needs to be detailed and elaborate. Some students, of course, find it helpful to outline in detail — particularly if they are planning a long term paper involving several literary works, comparing and contrasting several aspects of them. For a 500-word analysis of a short story's figures of speech, though, all you might need is a simple list of points to make, scribbled down in the order in which you will make them. This order is probably not, of course, the order in which the points first occurred to you. Thoughts, when they first come to mind, can be a confused rabble.

While granting the need for order in a piece of writing, the present writer confesses that he is a reluctant outliner. His tendency (or curse) is to want to keep whatever random thoughts occur to him; to polish his prose right then and there; and finally to try to juggle his disconnected paragraphs into something like logical order. The usual result is that he has large blocks of illogical thought left over. This process is wasteful, and if you can learn to live with an outline, then you belong to the legion of the blessed, and will never know the pain of scrapping pages that cost you hours. On the other hand, you will never know the joy of meandering — of bursting into words and surprising yourself. As novelist E. M. Forster remarked, "How do I know what I think until I see what I say?"

An outline, if you use one, is not meant to stand as an achievement in itself. It should — as Ezra Pound said literary criticism ought to do — consume itself and disappear. Here is a once-valuable outline not worth keeping — a very informal one that enabled a student to organize the paper that appears on page 1354, "The Hearer of 'The Tell-Tale Heart.'" Before he wrote, the student jotted down the ideas that had occurred to him. Looking them over, he could see that certain ones predominated. Since the aim of his paper was to analyze Poe's story for its point of view, he began with some notes about the narrator of the story. His other leading ideas had emerged as questions: is the story supposed to be a ghost story or an account of a delusion? Can we read the whole thing as a nightmare, having no reality outside the narrator's mind? Having seen that his thoughts weren't a totally disconnected jumble, he drew connections. Going down his list, he numbered with the same numbers those ideas that belonged together.

```
Point     1  Killer is mad -- can listen in on Hell.
  of
 view     2  He is obsessed with the Evil Eye.

          1  He thinks he is sane, we know he's mad.

             Old man rich -- a miser?

             Is this a ghost story?  NO!  Natural explanations

                for the heartbeat:

          4  His mind is playing tricks.

             Hears his own heart (Hoffman's idea).

          3  Maybe the whole story is only his dream?

             Poe must have been crazy too.
```

The numbers now showed him the order in which he planned to take up each of his four chief ideas. Labeling with the number "1" his remarks about the narrator, he decided to open his paper with them, and to declare at once that they indicated the story's point of view. As you can tell from his finished paper, he discarded two notions that didn't seem to relate to his purpose: the point about the old man's wealth, and the speculation (which he realized he couldn't prove) that Poe himself was probably mad. Having completed this rough outline, he felt encouraged to return to Poe's story, and on rereading it, noticed a few additional points, which you will find in his paper. His outline didn't tell him exactly what to say at every moment, but it was clear and easy to follow.

DRAFTING AND REVISING

Seated at last, or striking some other businesslike stance,[2] you prepare to write, only to find yourself besieged with petty distractions. All of a sudden you remember a friend you had promised to call, some dry cleaning you were supposed to pick up, a neglected Coke (in another room)

[2]R. H. Super of the University of Michigan wrote a definitive biography of Walter Savage Landor while standing up, typing on a machine atop a filing cabinet.

growing warmer and flatter by the minute. If your paper is to be written, you have one course of action: to collar these thoughts and for the moment banish them.

When first you draft your paper — that is, when you write it out in the rough — you will probably do best to write rapidly. At this early stage, you don't need to be fussy about spelling, grammar, and punctuation. To be sure, those picayune details matter, but you can worry about them later on, when you are **editing** (combing through your draft repairing grammar, cutting excess words, making small verbal improvements) and **proofreading** (going over your finished paper line by line, checking it for typographical or other mistakes). Right now, it is more important to get your thoughts down on paper in a steady flow than to keep taking time out to check spellings in the dictionary. Forge ahead, and don't be too nastily self-critical. Perhaps when you write your draft you won't even want to look at all those notes on your reading that you collected so industriously. When you come to a place where a note will fit, you might just insert a reminder to yourself, such as SEE CARD 19, or SEE ARISTOTLE ON COMEDY.

Let us admit that writing about literature is a fussier kind of writing than turning out a narrative essay called, "My Most Exciting Experience." You may need to draft some of your paper slowly and painstakingly. You'll find yourself coping with all sorts of small problems, many of them simple and mechanical. What, for instance, will you call the author whose work you are dealing with? Decide at the outset. Most critics favor the author's last name alone: "Dickinson implies . . ." ("Miss Dickinson" or "Ms. Dickinson" may sound fussily polite; "Emily," too chummy.) Will you include footnotes in your paper and, if so, do you know how they work? (Some pointers on handling the pesky things will come in a few pages.)

You will want to give credit to any critics who helped you out, and properly to do so is to be painstaking. To paraphrase a critic, you do more than just rearrange the critic's words and phrases; you translate them into language of your own. Say you wish to refer to an insight of Randall Jarrell, who comments on the images of spider, flower, and moth in Robert Frost's poem "Design":

> Notice how the *heal-all,* because of its name, is the one flower in all the world picked to be the altar for this Devil's Mass; notice how holding up the moth brings something ritual and hieratic, a ghostly, ghastly formality to this priest and its sacrificial victim. . . .

It would be incorrect to say, without quotation marks:

```
Frost picks the heal-all as the one flower in all the world to be

the altar for this Devil's Mass.  There is a ghostly, ghastly
```

formality to the spider holding up the moth, like a priest holding

a sacrificial victim.

That rewording, although not exactly in Jarrell's language, manages to steal his memorable phrases without giving him credit. Nor is it sufficient just to list Jarrell's essay in a bibliography at the end of your paper. If you do, you are still a crook; you merely point to the scene of your crime. What is needed, clearly, is to think through Jarrell's words to the point he is making; and if you want to keep any of his striking phrases (and why not?), put them in quotation marks:

As Randall Jarrell points out, Frost portrays the spider as a kind

of priest in a Mass, or Black Mass, elevating the moth like an

object for sacrifice, with "a ghostly, ghastly formality."

To be scrupulous in your acknowledgment, tell where you found your quotation from Jarrell, citing the book and the page. (See "Documenting Your Sources," page 1343.) But unless your instructor expects you to write such a formal, documented paper, the passage as it now stands would make sufficiently clear your source, and your obligation.

One more word of Dutch-uncle warning. In this book you are offered a vocabulary with which to discuss literature: a flurry of terms such as *irony*, *symbol*, and *image*, printed in **boldface** when first introduced. In your writing you may decide to enlist a few of them. And yet, critical terminology — especially if unfamiliar — can tempt a beginning critic to sling it about. Nothing can be less sophisticated, or more misleading, than a technical term grandly misapplied: "The *myth-symbolism* of this *rime scheme* leaves one aghast." Far better to choose plain words you're already at ease with. Your instructor, no doubt, has met many a critical term and is not likely to be impressed by the mere sight of another one. Knowingly selected and placed, a critical term can help sharpen a thought and make it easier to handle. Clearly it is less cumbersome to refer to the *tone* of a story than to have to say, "the way the author makes you feel that she feels about what she is talking about." But the paper-writer who declares, "The tone of this poem is full of ironic imagery," fries words to a hash — mixed up and indigestible.

When you write your first draft, by the way, leave plenty of space between lines and enormous margins. Then, when later thoughts come to you, you can easily squeeze them in.

Does any writer write with perfection on first try, and drop ideas with a single shot? Some writers have claimed to do so — among them the English novelist Anthony Trollope, who thought it "unmanly" not to write a thought right the first time. Jack Kerouac, leading novelist of the beat generation of the 1950s, believed in spontaneous prose. He used to write entire novels on uncut ribbons of teletype paper, thus saving himself the interruption of stopping at the bottom of each page. His specialty, though, was fiction of ecstasy and hallucination, not essays in explication, or comparison and contrast. For most of us, however, good writing is largely a matter of revising — of going back over our first thoughts word by word. Painstaking revision is more than a matter of tidying grammar and spelling: in the process of reconsidering our words, we sometimes discover fresher and sharper ideas. "Writing and rewriting," says John Updike, "are a constant search for what one is saying."

To achieve effective writing, you have to have the courage to be wild. Aware that no reader need see your rough drafts, you can treat them mercilessly — scissor them apart, rearrange their pieces, reassemble them into a stronger order, using staples or tape or glue. The art of revising calls for a textbook in itself, but here are a few simple suggestions:

1. Insofar as your deadline allows, be willing to revise as many times as need be.

2. Don't think of revision as the simple chore of fixing up spelling mistakes. That's proofreading, and it comes last. When you revise, be willing to cut and slash, to discover new insights, to move blocks of words around so that they follow in a stronger order. Stand ready to question your whole approach to a work of literature, to entertain the notion of throwing everything you have written into the wastebasket and starting over again.

3. At this stage, you may find it helpful to enlist outside advice — from your instructor, from your roommate or your mate, from any friend who will read your rough draft and give you a reaction. If you can enlist such a willing reader, ask: What isn't clear to you?

4. If you (or your willing reader) should find any places that aren't readily understandable, single them out for rewriting. After all, you don't need to revise a whole draft if only parts of it need work. Try rewriting any especially troublesome passage or paragraph.

5. Short, skimpy paragraphs of one or two sentences may indicate places that call for more thought, or more material. Can you supply them with more evidence, more explanation, more example and illustration?

6. A time-tested method of revising is to lay aside your manuscript for a while, forget about it, and then after a long interval (the Roman poet Horace recommended nine years, but obviously that won't do), go back to it for a fresh look. If you have time, take a nap or a walk, or at least a yawn and a stretch before you take yet another look.

7. When your paper is in a *last* draft — that's the time to edit it. Once you have your ideas in firm shape, you can check those uncertain spellings, look up the agreement of verbs in a grammar book or handbook, make your pronouns and numbers agree, cut needless words, pull out a weak

word and send in a stronger one. Back when you were drafting, to get prematurely fussy about such small things might have frozen you up. But once you feel satisfied that you have made yourself clear, you can be as fussy as you like.

If you type your papers, it is a great help to become a reasonably expert typist — one whose method is other than the Christopher Columbus method (to discover a key and land on it). Then you can revise while you retype. All to what end? "Each clear sentence," according to Robert Russell, "is that much ground stripped clean of the undergrowth of one's own confusion. Sometimes it's thrilling to feel you have written even a single paragraph that makes sense."[3]

THE FORM OF YOUR FINISHED PAPER

Now that you have smoothed your final draft as fleck-free as you can, your instructor may have specific advice for the form of your finished paper. If none is forthcoming, it is only reasonable

1. to choose standard letter-size (8½ × 11) paper;
2. to give your name at the top of your title page;
3. to leave an inch or more of margin on all four sides of each page, and a few inches of blank paper or an additional sheet after your conclusion, so that your instructor can offer comment;
4. to doublespace, or (if you handwrite) to use paper with widely spaced lines.

And what of titles of works discussed: when to put them in quotation marks, when to underline them? One rule of thumb is that titles of works shorter than book length rate quotation marks (poems, short stories, articles); but titles of books (including book-length poems: *The Odyssey*), plays, and periodicals take underlining. (In a manuscript to be set in type, an underline is a signal to the compositor to use *italics*.)

DOCUMENTING YOUR SOURCES

When you quote from other writers, when you lift their information, when you summarize or paraphrase their ideas, make sure you give them their due. Document everything you take. Identify the writer by name; cite the very book, magazine, newspaper, pamphlet, letter, or other source you are using, and the page or pages you are indebted to.

By so doing, you invite your readers to go to your original source and check up on you. Most readers won't bother, of course, but at least your

[3] *To Catch an Angel* (New York: Vanguard, 1962) 301.

invitation enlists their confidence. Besides, the duty to document keeps you carefully looking at your sources — and so helps keep your writing accurate and responsible.

The latest and most efficient way for writers to document their sources is that recommended in the *MLA Handbook for Writers of Research Papers,* 2nd ed. (New York: Modern Language Association of America, 1984). In the long run, whether you write an immense term paper citing a hundred sources or a short paper citing only three or four, the MLA's advice will save you and your reader time and trouble.

These pointers cannot take the place of the *MLA Handbook* itself; but the gist of the method is this. Begin by listing your sources: all the works from which you're going to quote, summarize, paraphrase, or take information. Later on, when you type up your paper in finished form, you're going to *end* it with a neat copy of this list (once called a *bibliography,* now entitled *Works Cited*). But right now, in writing your paper, every time you refer to one of these works, you need give only enough information to help a reader locate it in your Works Cited. Usually, you can just give (in parentheses) an author's last name and a page citation. You incorporate this information right in the text of your paper, most often at the end of a sentence:

> One recent investigation has suggested that few people who submit poems to small literary magazines bother to read those magazines; or indeed, bother to read poems by anybody else (Horton 108-09).

Say you will want to cite *two* books or magazine articles by Horton — how to tell them apart? In your text, condense the title of each article into a word or two.

> One recent investigation has shown that few people who submit poems to small literary magazines bother to read those magazines (Horton, "Magazines" 108-09).

If you have mentioned the name of the author in the body of your paper, you need give only the page number:

> As a recent investigator, Louise Horton, has suggested, few people who submit poems to small literary magazines bother to read those magazines (108-09).

The beauty of this method is that you don't have to stop every two minutes to write a footnote identifying your source in full detail. At the end of your paper, in your list of works cited, your reader can find a fuller description of your source — in this case, a magazine article:

Horton, Louise. "Who Reads Small Literary Magazines and What Good Do They Do?" Texas Review Spring/Summer 1984: 108-13.

It's imperative to keep citations in your text brief and snappy, lest they hinder the flow of your prose. You may wish to append a note supplying a passage of less important (yet possibly valuable) information or making careful qualifying statements ("On the other hand, not every expert agrees. John Binks finds that poets are often a little magazine's only cash customers; while Molly MacGuire maintains that . . ."). If you want to put in some such aside, and suspect that you couldn't give it in your text without interrupting your paper awkwardly, then cast it into a **footnote** (a note placed at the bottom of a page) or an **endnote** (a note placed at the end of a paper). Given a choice, most writers prefer endnotes. Far easier to collect all the notes at the end of a paper than to use footnotes — as any writer knows who has had to retype pages and pages again and again, to make the footnotes fit.[4]

How do you drop in such notes? The number of each consecutive note comes (following any punctuation) after the last word of a sentence. So that the number will stand out, you roll your typewriter carriage up a click (or order your word-processor to do a superscript), thus lifting the number slightly above the usual level of your prose.

as other observers have claimed.[1]

When you come to type the footnote or endnote itself, skip five spaces, elevate the number again, skip a space, and proceed.

[1] John Binks, to name only one such observer, finds . . .

Although now useful mainly for such slightly longwinded asides, footnotes and endnotes are time-honored ways to document *all* sources in a research paper. Indeed, some instructors still prefer them to the new MLA guidelines, and urge students to use such notes to indicate every writer cited. Though such notes take more work, they have the advantage

[4] Nowadays, some word-processing programs make life easier for footnoters by helping to format each footnote and by automatically dropping it in at the bottom of its page.

of hiding dull data away from your reader's eyes, enabling you to end sentences with powerful bangs and inconspicuous note numbers instead of whimpering parentheses (Glutz-Finnegan, *Lesser Corollary* 1029 – 30). Besides, in a brief paper containing only one citation or two, to use footnotes or endnotes may be simpler and less showy than to compile a Works Cited list that has only two entries. (For an example of a student paper with a single footnote, see page 1354.)

Large-mindedly, the *MLA Handbook* tolerates the continued use of footnotes and endnotes for documentation — indeed, offers advice for their preparation, which we will follow here. If you do use footnotes or endnotes to document all your sources, here is how to format them. A note identifying a magazine article looks like this:

> 16 Louise Horton, "Who Reads Small Literary Magazines and What Good Do They Do?" <u>Texas Review</u> Spring/Summer 1984: 108–09.

Notice that, in notes, the author's first name comes first. (In a list of Works Cited, you work differently: you put last name first, so that you can readily arrange your list of authors in easy-to-consult alphabetical order.) A footnote or endnote for a reference to a book (and not a magazine article) looks like this:

> 17 Elizabeth Frank, <u>Louise Bogan: A Portrait</u> (New York: Knopf, 1985) 59–60.

Should you return later to cite another place in Frank's book, you need not repeat all its information. Just write:

> 18 Frank 192.

If in your paper you refer to *two* books by Elizabeth Frank, give the full title of each in the first note citing it. Then, if you cite it again, use a shortened form of its title:

> 19 Frank, <u>Bogan</u> 192.

Your readers should not have to interrupt their reading of your essay to glance down at a note simply to find out whom you are quoting. It is poor form to write:

> Dylan Thomas's poem "Fern Hill" is a memory of the poet's
>
> childhood: of his Aunt Ann Jones's farm, where he spent his
>
> holidays. "Time, which has an art to throw dust on all things,

broods over the poem."[1] The farm, indeed, is a lost paradise -- a

personal garden of Eden.

----

[1] William York Tindall, A Reader's Guide to Dylan Thomas
(New York: Noonday, 1962) 268.

That is annoying, because the reader has to stop reading and look at the footnote to find out who made that resonant statement about Time brooding over the poem. A better way:

"Time," as William York Tindall has observed, "which has an art

to throw dust on all things, broods over the poem."[1]

----

[1] A Reader's Guide to Dylan Thomas (New York: Noonday,
1962) 268.

What to do now but hand in your paper? "And good riddance," you may feel, after such an expenditure of thinking, time, and energy. But a good paper is not only worth submitting, it is worth keeping. If you return to it, after a while, you may find to your surprise that it will preserve and even renew what you have learned.

KEEPING A JOURNAL

The essay is not, of course, the only medium in which you can write your responses to literature. Many instructors ask students to keep a **journal:** a day-to-day account of what they read and how they react to it. A great advantage in keeping a journal is that you can express your thoughts and feelings immediately, before they grow cold. You can set down all your miscellaneous reactions to what you read, whether or not they fit into a paper topic. (If you have to write a paper later on, your journal just might suggest topics galore.) Depending on what your instructor thinks essential, your journal may take in all your reading for the course; or you may concentrate on the work of some writer or writers, or on one kind of story. As you read (or afterward), you can jot down anything you notice that you wish to remember. Does a theme in a story, or a line of dialogue, strike you forcefully? Make a note of it. Does something in the story not make sense? Record your bewilderment. Your journal is personal: a place for you to sound off, to express your feelings. Don't just copy your class notes into it; don't simply quote the stories. Mere length of your entries will not impress your instructor, either: try for insights. A paragraph or two will probably suffice to set down your main reactions to most stories. In keeping a journal (a kind of writing primarily for yourself), you don't rewrite; and so you need not feel obliged to polish your prose. Your aim is to store information without delay: to wrap words around your reactions and observations.

Keeping a journal will be satisfying only if you keep it up to date. Record your feelings and insights while you still have a story freshly in mind. Get weeks behind and have to grind out a journal from scratch, the night before it is due, and the whole project will decay into meaningless drudgery. But faithfully do a little reading and a little writing every day or so, and you will find yourself keeping track of the life of your mind. When your journal is closed, you will have a lively record not only of the literature you have read, but also of your involvement with it.

Robert Wallace (b. 1932)
THE GIRL WRITING HER ENGLISH PAPER   1979

lies on one hip by the fire,
blond, in jeans.

The wreckage of her labor, elegant as Eden
or petals from a tree,
surrounds her —   5

a little farm, smoke rising from the ashtray,
book, notebooks, papers, fields;
a poem's furrows.

If the lights were to go out suddenly,
stars would be overhead,   10
their light come in.

Writing about a Story

Like any coherent, forceful essay, a good discussion of fiction doesn't just toss forth a random lot of impressions. It makes some point about which the writer feels strongly. In order to write a meaningful paper, then, you need something you *want* to say — a meaningful topic. For suggestions on finding such a topic (also some pointers on organizing, writing, revising, and finishing your paper), please see "Writing about Literature," which begins on page 1333. The advice there may be applied to papers on fiction, poetry, and drama. Some methods especially useful for writing about stories are gathered in the present chapter.

Unlike a brief poem, or a painting you can take in with one long glance, a work of fiction — even a short story — may be too complicated to hold all at once in the mind's eye. Before you can write about it, you may need to give it two or more careful readings, and even then, as you begin to think further about it, you will probably have to thumb through it to reread passages. The first time through, perhaps it is best just to read attentively, open to whatever pleasure and wisdom the story may afford. On second look, you may find it useful to read with pencil in hand, either to mark your personal copy or to take notes to jog your memory. To see the design and meaning of a story need not be a boring chore — any more than it is to land a fighting fish and to study it with admiration.

In this chapter, all the discussions and examples refer to Edgar Allan Poe's short story "The Tell-Tale Heart" (page 38). If you haven't already read it, you can do so in only a few minutes, so that the rest of the chapter will make more sense to you.

EXPLICATING

Explication is the patient unfolding of meanings in a work of literature. An explication — that is, an essay that follows this method — proceeds carefully through a story, poem, or play, usually interpreting it line by line — perhaps even word by word. A good explication dwells on details, as well as on larger things. It brings them to the attention of a reader who might have missed them (the reader probably hasn't read so closely as the writer of the explication). Alert and willing to take pains, the writer of such an essay notices anything meaningful that isn't obvious, whether it is a colossal theme suggested by a symbol, or a little hint contained in a single word.

To write an honest explication of a story takes time and space, probably too much time and space to devote to a long and complex story unless you are writing a huge term paper, an honors thesis, or a dissertation. A thorough explication of Nathaniel Hawthorne's "The Birthmark" would be likely to run much longer than the rich and intriguing short story itself. Ordinarily, the method of explication is best suited to a paper that deals only with a short passage or section of a story: a key scene, a crucial conversation, a statement of theme, an opening or closing paragraph. Storytellers who are especially fond of language invite closer attention to their words than others do. Edgar Allan Poe, for one, is a poet sensitive to the rhythms of his sentences, and a symbolist whose stories abound in suggestions. Here is an explication, by a student, of a short but essential passage in "The Tell-Tale Heart." The passage occurs in the third paragraph of the story, and (to help us follow the explication) the student quotes it in full at the beginning of her paper.

By Lantern Light: An Explication of a Passage
in "The Tell-Tale Heart"

And every night, about midnight, I turned the latch of his door and opened it -- oh, so gently! And then, when I had made an opening sufficient for my head, I put in a dark lantern, all closed, closed, so that no light shone out, and then I thrust in my head. Oh, you would have laughed to see how cunningly I thrust it in! I moved it slowly -- very, very slowly, so that I might not disturb the old man's sleep. It took me an hour to place my whole head within the opening so far that I could see him as he lay upon his bed. Ha! -- would a madman have been so wise as this? And then, when my head was well in the room, I undid the lantern cautiously -- oh, so cautiously -- cautiously (for the hinges creaked) -- I undid it just so much that a single thin ray fell upon the vulture eye. And this I did for seven long nights -- every night just at midnight -- but I found the eye always closed; and so it was impossible to do the work; for it was not the old man who vexed me, but his Evil Eye.

Although Poe has indicated in the first lines of his story that the

person who addresses us is insane, it is only when we come to the

speaker's account of his preparations for murdering the old man that we

imagine him in action, and so find his madness fully revealed. Even more convincingly than his earlier words (for we might _possibly_ think that someone

who claims to hear things in heaven and hell is a religious mystic),

these preparations reveal him to be mad. What strikes us is that they

are so elaborate and meticulous. A significant detail is the exactness

of his schedule for spying: "every night just at midnight." The words

with which he describes his motions also convey the most extreme care

(and I will indicate them with italics): "how wisely I proceeded -- with

what caution," "I turned the latch of his door and opened it -- oh, so

gently!" "how cunningly I thrust [my head] in! I moved it slowly, very

slowly," "I undid the lantern cautiously -- oh, so cautiously --

cautiously." Taking a whole hour to intrude his head into the room, he

asks, "Ha! would a madman be as wise as this?" But of course the word

wise is unconsciously ironic, for clearly it is not wisdom the speaker

displays, but an absurd degree of care, an almost fiendish ingenuity.

Such behavior, I understand, is typical of certain mental illnesses.

All his careful preparations that he thinks prove him sane only convince

us instead that he is mad.

Obviously his behavior is self-defeating. He wants to catch the

"vulture eye" open, and yet he takes all these pains not to disturb

the old man's sleep. If he behaved logically, he might go barging into

the bedroom with his lantern ablaze, shouting at the top of his voice.

And yet, if we can see things his way, there is a strange logic to his

reasoning. He regards the eye as a creature in itself, quite apart from

its possessor. "It was not," he says, "the old man who vexed me, but

his Evil Eye." Apparently, to be inspired to do his deed, the madman

needs to behold the eye -- at least, this is my understanding of his

remark, "I found the eye always closed; and so it was impossible to do

the work." Poe's choice of the word work, by the way, is also revealing.

Murder is made to seem a duty or a job; and anyone who so regards murder

is either extremely cold-blooded, like a hired killer for a gangland assassination, or else deranged. Besides, the word suggests again the curious sense of detachment that the speaker feels toward the owner of the eye.

   In still another of his assumptions, the speaker shows that he is madly logical, or operating on the logic of a dream. There seems a dreamlike relationship between his dark lantern "all closed, closed, so that no light shone out," and the sleeping victim. When the madman opens his lantern so that it emits a single ray, he is hoping that the eye in the old man's head will be open too, letting out its corresponding gleam. The latch that he turns so gently, too, seems like the eye, whose lid needs to be opened in order for the murderer to go ahead. It is as though the speaker is <u>trying</u> to get the eyelid to lift. By taking such great pains and by going through all this nightly ritual, he is practicing some kind of magic, whose rules are laid down not by our logic, but by the logic of dreams.

An unusually well-written paper, "By Lantern Light" cost the student two or three careful revisions. Rather than attempting to say something about *everything* in the passage from Poe, she selects only the details that strike her as most meaningful. In her very first sentence, she briefly shows us how the passage functions in the context of Poe's story: how it clinches our suspicions that the narrator is mad. In writing her paper, the student went by the following rough, simple outline — nothing more than a list of the points she wanted to express:

1. Speaker's extreme care and exactness -- typical of some mental illnesses.

2. Speaker doesn't act by usual logic but by a crazy logic.

3. Dreamlike connection between latch & lantern and old man's eye.

As she wrote, she followed her brief list, setting forth her ideas one at a time, one idea to a paragraph. There is a different (and still easier) way to organize an explication: just work through the original passage line by line or sentence by sentence. The danger of this procedure is that you may find yourself falling into a boring singsong: "In the first sentence I noticed . . . ," "In the next sentence . . . ," "Now in the third sentence . . . ," "Finally, in the last paragraph. . . ." (If you choose to organize an explication in such a way, then boldly vary your transitions.) Notice that the student who wrote "By Lantern Light" doesn't inch through the passage sentence by sentence, but freely takes up its details in whatever order she likes. Less fussy than Poe's madman, she neatly writes in three corrections, saving herself retyping. And why, in her first paragraph, does she change Poe's word *it* to *my head*? Coming upon a piece of a sentence quoted out of context, the reader might forget what *it* refers to — and so the writer places the alteration in brackets, to indicate that the changed words are her own.

In a long critical essay in which we don't adhere to one method all the way through, the method of explication may appear from time to time — as when the critic, in discussing a story, stops to unravel a particularly knotty passage. But useful as it may be to know how to write an explication of fiction, it is probably still more useful (in most literature courses) to know how to write an analysis.

ANALYZING

Assignment: "Write an **analysis** of a story or novel." What do you do? Following the method of analysis (from the Greek: "breaking up"), you separate a story or novel into its components, then (usually) select one part for close study. One likely topic for an analysis might be "The Character of James Thurber's Mr. Martin" (referring to "The Catbird Seat"), in which the writer would concentrate on showing us Martin's highly individual features and traits of personality. Other typical analyses might be written about, say, "Folk Humor in Mark Twain's *Huckleberry Finn*," or "Gothic Elements in a Story by Joyce Carol Oates" (referring to "Where Are You Going, Where Have You Been?"), or "The Unidentified Narrator in 'A Rose for Emily.' " To be sure, no element of a story dwells in isolation from the story's other elements. In "The Tell-Tale Heart," the madness of the leading character apparently makes it necessary to tell the story from a special point of view and probably helps determine the author's choice of theme, setting, symbolism, tone, style, and ironies. But it would be mind-boggling to try to study all those elements simultaneously. For this reason, when we write an analysis we generally study just one element, though we may suggest — probably at the start of the essay — its relation to the whole story. Indeed, analysis is the method used in this book, in which, chapter by chapter, we have separated fiction into its components of plot, point of view, character, tone and style, and so on. If you have read the discussion on the plot of "Godfather Death" (page 6), or the attempt to state the theme of Hemingway's "A Clean, Well-Lighted Place" (page 122), then you have already read some brief essays in analysis. Here is a student-written analysis of "The Tell-Tale Heart," dealing with just one element — the story's point of view.

The Hearer of the Tell-Tale Heart

Although there are many things we do not know about the narrator of Edgar Allan Poe's story "The Tell-Tale Heart" -- is he a son? a servant? a companion? -- there is one thing we are sure of from the start. He is mad. In the opening paragraph, Poe makes the narrator's condition unmistakeable, not only from his excited and worked-up speech (full of dashes and exclamation points), but also from his wild claims. He says it is merely some disease which has sharpened his senses that has made people call him crazy. Who but a madman, however, would say, "I heard all things in the heaven and in the earth," and brag how his ear is a kind of CB radio, listening in on Hell? Such a statement leaves no doubt that the point of view in the story is an ironic one.

Because the participating narrator is telling his story in the first person, some details in the story stand out more than others. When the narrator goes on to tell how he watches the old man sleeping, he rivets his attention on the old man's "vulture eye." When a ray from his lantern finds the Evil Eye open, he says, "I could see nothing else of the old man's face or person." Actually, the reader can see almost nothing else about the old man anywhere in the rest of the story. All we are told is that the old man treated the younger man well, and we gather that the old man was rich, because his house is full of treasures. We do not have a clear idea of what the old man looks like, though, nor do we know how he talks, for we are not given any of his words. Our knowledge of him is mainly confined to his eye and its effect on the narrator. This confinement gives that symbolic eye a lot of importance in the story. The narrator tells us all we know and directs our attention to parts of it.

This point of view raises an interesting question. Since we are
on the narrator
dependent/for all our information, how do we know the whole story isn't just a nightmare in his demented mind? We have really no way to

be sure it isn't, as far as I can see. I assume, however, that there really is a dark shuttered house and an old man and real policemen who start snooping around when screams are heard in the neighborhood, because it is a more memorable story if it is a crazy man's view of reality than if it is all just a terrible dream. But we can't take stock in the madman's interpretation of what happens. Poe keeps putting distances between what the narrator says and what we are supposed to think, apparently. For instance: the narrator has boasted that he is calm and clear in the head, but as soon as he starts (in the second paragraph) trying to explain why he killed the old man, we gather that he is confused, to say the least. "I think it was his eye!" the narrator exclaims, as if not quite sure. As he goes on to explain how he conducted the murder, we realize that he is a man with a fixed idea working with a patience that is certainly mad, almost diabolical.

Some readers might wonder if "The Tell-Tale Heart" is a story of the supernatural. Is the heartbeat that the narrator hears a ghost come back to haunt him? Here, I think, the point of view is our best guide to what to believe. The simple explanation for the heartbeat is this: it is all in the madman's mind. Perhaps he feels such guilt that he starts hearing things. Another explanation is possible, one suggested by Daniel Hoffman, a critic who has discussed the story: the killer hears the sound of his own heart.[1] Hoffman's explanation (which I don't like as well as mine) also is a natural one, and it fits the story as a whole. Back when the narrator first entered the old man's bedroom to kill him, the heartbeat sounded so loud to him that he was afraid the neighbors would hear it too. Evidently they didn't, and so Hoffman may be right in thinking that the sound was only that of his own heart pounding in his ears. Whichever explanation you take, it is a more down-to-earth and reasonable explanation than that (as the narrator believes) the heart is still alive, even though its owner has been cut to pieces. Then, too, the police keep chatting. If they heard the heartbeat too, wouldn't they leap to their feet, draw their guns, and look all around the room? As the author has kept showing us in the rest of the story, the narrator's view of things is ~~always~~ untrustworthy. You don't kill someone just because you dislike the look in his eye. You don't think that such a murder is funny. For all its Gothic atmosphere of the old dark house with a secret hidden inside, "The Tell-Tale Heart" is not a ghost story. We have only to see its point of view to know that it is a study in abnormal psychology.

---

[1]Poe Poe Poe Poe Poe Poe Poe (New York: Anchor, 1973), 227.

A temptation in writing an analysis is to want to include all sorts of insights that the writer proudly wishes to display, even though they aren't related to the main idea. In the preceding essay, the student resists this temptation admirably. In fairly plump and ample paragraphs, he works out his ideas, and he supports his contentions with specific references to Poe's story. Although his paper is not brilliantly written and contains no insight so fresh as the suggestion (by the writer of the first paper) that the madman's lantern is like the old man's head, still, it is a good brief analysis. By sticking faithfully to his purpose and by confronting the problems he raises ("how do we know the whole story isn't just a nightmare?"), the writer persuades us that he understands not only the story's point of view, but the story in its entirety.

Our analysis so far deals with one element in Poe's story: point of view. In another familiar writing assignment, the **card report,** one is asked to analyze a story into its *several* elements. Usually confined to the front and back of one 5 × 8-inch index card, such a report is just as challenging to write as an essay, if not more so. To do the job well, you have to see the story in its elements, then specify them succinctly and accurately. Here (on the following pages) is a typical card report listing and detailing the essentials of "The Tell-Tale Heart." In this assignment, the student was asked to include:

1. The title of the story and the date of its original publication.
2. The author's name and dates.
3. The name (if any) of the main character, together with a description of that character's dominant traits or features.
4. Other characters in the story, dealt with in the same fashion.
5. A short description of the setting.
6. The narrator of the story. (To identify him or her is, of course, to define the point of view from which the story is told.)

```
(Student's name)                              (Course and section)

Story:  "The Tell-Tale Heart," 1850
Author:  Edgar Allan Poe (1809-1849)

     Central character:  An unnamed younger man whom people call mad,
who claims that a nervous disease has greatly sharpened his sense
perceptions.  He is proud of his own cleverness.  Other characters:
The old man, whose leading feature is one pale blue, filmed eye; said
to be rich, kind, and lovable.  Also three policemen, not individually
described.
     Setting:  A shuttered house full of wind, mice, and treasures;
pitch dark even in the afternoon.
     Narrator:  The madman himself.
     Events in summary:  (1) Dreading one vulturelike eye of the old
man he shares a house with, a madman determines to kill its owner.
(2) Each night he spies on the sleeping old man, but finding the eye
shut, he stays his hand.  (3) On the eighth night, finding the eye open,
he suffocates its owner beneath the mattress and conceals the dismem-
bered body under the floor of the bedchamber.  (4) Entertaining some
inquiring police officers in the very room where the body lies hidden,
the killer again hears (or thinks he hears) the beat of his victim's
heart.  (5) Terrified, convinced that the police also hear the heart-
beat growing louder, the killer confesses his crime.
     Tone:  Horror at the events described, skepticism toward the
narrator's claims to be sane, revulsion (or at least detachment) from
his gaiety and laughter.
```

Front of Card

7. A terse summary of the main events of the story, given in chronological order.

8. A description of the general tone of the story, as well as it can be sensed: the author's apparent feelings toward the central character or the main events.

9. Some comments on the style in which the story is written. (Brief illustrative quotations are helpful, insofar as space permits.)

10. Whatever kinds of irony the story contains, and what they contribute to the story.

11. In a sentence, the story's main theme.

12. Leading symbols (if the story has any), with an educated guess at whatever each symbol suggests.

13. Finally, an evaluation of the story as a whole, concisely setting forth the student's opinion of it. (Some instructors regard this as the most important part of the report, and most students find that, by the time they have so painstakingly separated the ingredients of the story, they have arrived at a definite opinion of it.)

To fit so much on one card is, admittedly, somewhat like trying to engrave the Declaration of Independence on the head of a pin. The student who wrote this succinct report had to spoil a few trial cards before he was able to do it. Every word has to count, and making them count is a

Back of Card

discipline worthwhile in almost any sort of expository writing. Some students enjoy the challenge. In doing such a report, though you may feel severely limited, you'll probably be surprised at how thoroughly you come to understand a story. Besides, if you care to keep the card for future reference, it won't take much storage room. A longer story, even a novel, may be analyzed in the same way; but insist on taking a second card if you are asked to analyze some especially hefty and complicated novel — say, Leo Tolstoi's panoramic, thousand-page *War and Peace.*

COMPARING AND CONTRASTING

If you were to write on "The Humor of Frank O'Connor's 'First Confession' and Alice Walker's 'Everyday Use,' " you would probably employ one or two other methods. You might use **comparison,** placing the two stories side by side and pointing out their similarities; or you might use **contrast,** pointing out their differences. Most of the time, in dealing with a pair of stories, you will find them similar in some ways and different in others; and so you will be using both methods in writing your paper. No law requires you to devote equal space to each method. You might have to do more contrasting than comparing, or the other way around. If the stories are obviously similar but subtly different, you will probably compare them briefly, listing the similarities, and then, at greater length, contrast them by calling attention to their important differences. If, however, the stories at first glance seem as different as peas from polecats, and yet they are in fact closely related, you'll probably spend most of your time comparing them rather than contrasting them. (You might not just compare and contrast, but also analyze, in that you might select one element of the stories for your investigation.) Other topics for papers involving two stories might be "The Experience of Coming of Age in James Joyce's 'Araby' and William Faulkner's 'Barn Burning' "; and "The Fascinated Prey: A Comparison of the Situations of Connie in Joyce Carol Oates's 'Where Are You Going, Where Have You Been?' and Rose in Alice Munro's 'Wild Swans.' "

Your paper, of course, will hang together better if you choose a pair of stories that apparently have much in common than if you choose two as unlike as cow and canteloupe. Before you start writing, think: Do the two stories you've selected throw some light on each other? An essay that likened W. Somerset Maugham's terse, ironic fable "The Appointment in Samarra" with William Faulkner's rich, complex "Barn Burning" just might reveal unexpected similarities. More likely, it would seem strained and pointless.

You can also write an essay in comparison and contrast that deals with just one story. You might consider, say, the attitudes of the younger waiter and the older waiter in Hemingway's "A Clean, Well-Lighted Place." In Flannery O'Connor's "Revelation," you might contrast Mrs. Turpin's smug view of herself with young Mary Grace's merciless view of her.

If your topic calls for both comparison and contrast, and you are dealing with two stories, don't write the first half of your paper all about one story, then pivot and write the second half about the other, never permitting the two to mingle. The result probably would not be a unified essay in contrast and comparison, but two separate commentaries yoked together. One workable way to organize such a paper is to make (before you begin) a brief list of points to look for in each story, then, as you write, to consider each point — first in one story and then in the other. Here is a simple outline for an essay bringing together William Faulkner's "A Rose for Emily" and Flannery O'Connor's "Revelation." The topic is "Two Would-be Aristocrats: The Characters of Emily Grierson and Mrs. Turpin."

1. Character's view of her own innate superiority

    a. Emily

    b. Mrs. Turpin

2. Author's evaluation of character's moral worth

   a. Emily

   b. Mrs. Turpin

3. Character's ability to change

   a. Emily

   b. Mrs. Turpin

It is best, however, not to follow such an outline in plodding, mechanical fashion ("Well, now it's time to whip over to Mrs. Turpin again"), lest your readers feel they are watching a back-and-forth tennis match. Some points are bound to interest you more than others, and, when they do, you will want to give them greater emphasis.

SUGGESTIONS FOR WRITING

What kinds of topics are likely to result in papers that will reveal something about works of fiction? Here is a list of typical topics, suitable to papers of various lengths, offered in the hope of stimulating your own ideas. For other topics, see Suggestions for Writing at the end of every chapter. For specific advice on finding a topic of your own, see Writing about Literature, page 1335.

TOPICS FOR BRIEF PAPERS (250 – 500 words)

1. Consider a short story in which the central character has to make a decision or must take some decisive step that will alter the rest of his or her life. Faulkner's "Barn Burning" is one such story; another is Updike's "A & P." As concisely and as thoroughly as you can, explain the nature of the character's decision, the reasons for it, and its probable consequences (as suggested by what the author tells us).

2. Write an informal (rather than a complete) explication of the opening paragraph or first few lines of a story. Show us how it prepares us for what will happen. (An alternate topic: take instead a *closing* paragraph and sum up whatever insight it leaves us with.) Don't feel obliged to deal with everything in the passage, as you would do in writing a more nearly complete explication. Within this suggested word length, limit your discussion to whatever strikes you as most essential.

3. Make a card report (see page 1356) on a short story in the Stories for Further Reading or one suggested by your instructor. Include all the elements in the report illustrated in this chapter (unless your instructor wishes you to emphasize some element or offers other advice).

4. Show how reading a specific short story caused you to change or modify an attitude or opinion you once had.

5. Just for fun, try writing a different ending to one of the short stories in this anthology. What does this exercise suggest about the wisdom of the author in ending things as done in the original? (Try to keep a sense of the author's style.)

6. Another wild idea: Write a *sequel* to one of your favorite short stories — or at least the beginning of a sequel, enough to give your reader a sense of it.

7. Argue from your own experience that a character in any story behaves (or doesn't behave) as people behave in life.

Topics for More Extended Papers (600 – 1,000 words)

1. Choose a short passage (one of, say, three or four sentences) in a story, a passage that interests you. Perhaps it will contain a decisive moment in a plot, a revealing comment on a character, or a statement of the story's major theme. Then write a reasonably thorough explication. Like the writer of the paper "By Lantern Light" (page 1350), go through the passage in some detail, noticing words that especially convey the author's meanings.

2. Write an analysis of a short story, singling out an element such as the author's voice (tone, style, irony), point of view, character, theme, symbolism, or Gothic elements (if the story has any). Try to show how this element functions in the story as a whole. For a typical paper in response to this assignment, see "The Hearer of 'The Tell-Tale Heart'" (page 1354).

3. Analyze a story in which a character experiences some realization or revelation. How does the writer prepare us for the moment of enlightenment? What is the nature of each realization or revelation? How does it affect the character? Stories to consider might include "Araby," "Greasy Lake," "Gimpel the Fool," "Revelation," "The Chrysanthemums," "The Death of Ivan Ilych," "The Garden-Party," and "Roman Fever."

4. Explore how humor functions in a story. What is funny? How is humor implied by the story's tone or style? Does humor help set forth a theme, or reveal character? Any of the following stories deserves exploration: "A & P," "First Confession," "Greasy Lake," "The Catbird Seat," "Gimpel the Fool," "Everyday Use," "Revelation," "A Hunger Artist," "Brief Encounter," "The Conversion of the Jews," and "My Man Bovanne."

5. For anyone interested in a career in teaching: Explain how you would teach a story, either to an imaginary class or to the class you belong to now. Perhaps you might arrange with your instructor to write about a story your class hasn't read yet; and then, after writing your paper, actually to teach the story in class.

6. See if you can discover a new Stephen Crane — another journalist who brings literary skill to reporting (as Crane does in "The Open Boat"). In an essay, examine some news story, interview, or feature that you think reads like excellent fiction. Point out whatever elements of good storytelling you find in it. (Is there a plot? Lively dialogue? Suspense? Vivid style? Thought-provoking theme? Rounded characters, or at least memorable ones? Shrewd choice of a point of view?) For such a story, consult your daily newspaper or a weekly news magazine. Supply a clipping or copy of your discovery along with your finished paper.

7. If your daily newspaper lacks literary quality but you'd like to try that last topic, see any of the following books. Each contains some reporting that will show you storytelling art:

    Nora Ephron, *Crazy Salad: Some Things About Women* (New York: Knopf, 1975). Includes a portrait of the first woman umpire and a cutthroat national baking competition.

    John Hersey, *Hiroshima* (New York: Knopf, 1946). The first atomic holocaust as seen by six survivors.

    Garrison Keillor, *Lake Wobegon Days* (New York: Viking, 1985). Gentle comic reports of a practically vanished small-town way of life.

    Larry L. King, *Of Outlaws, Con-men, Whores, Politicians, and Other Artists* (New York: Viking, 1978). Includes a memoir of a gambling contest, "Shoot-out with Amarillo Slim."

    Lillian Ross, *Reporting* (New York: Dodd, 1981). Seven classic essays in journalism, among them a profile of Ernest Hemingway.

Hunter S. Thompson, *The Great Shark Hunt* (New York: Summit Books, 1979). Reports of politics, sports, and pleasure-seeking in the 1960s and 1970s.

Tom Wolfe, *The Right Stuff* (New York: Farrar, 1979). The story of America's first astronauts.

TOPICS FOR LONG PAPERS (1,500 WORDS OR MORE)

1. Selecting a short story from the anthology in this book, or taking one suggested by your instructor, write an informal essay setting forth (as thoroughly as you can) your understanding of it. Point out any difficulties you encountered in first reading the story, for the benefit of other students who might meet the same difficulties. If you find particularly complicated passages, briefly explicate them. An ample statement of the meaning of the story probably will not deal only with plot or only with theme, but will also consider how the story is written and structured.

2. Dealing with a single element of fiction, write an analysis of Tolstoi's *The Death of Ivan Ilych*, or of some other long story that your instructor suggests.

3. Take a short story in which most of the events take place in the physical world (rather than inside some character's mind), and translate it into a one-act play, complete with stage directions. After you have done so, you might present a reading of it with the aid of other members of the class and then perhaps discuss what you had to do to the story to make a play of it.

4. Taking an author in this book whose work appeals to you, read at least three or four of his or her other stories. Then write an analysis of them, concentrating on an element of fiction that you find present in all.

5. Again going beyond this book to read other stories, compare and contrast two writers' handling of a similar theme. Let your essay build to a conclusion in which you state your opinion: which author's expression of theme is deeper, or more memorable?

Writing a Story

FINDING A STORY

Whether or not you aspire to be a new Doris Lessing or D. H. Lawrence, writing a story may reveal to you much firsthand knowledge. At the very least, you may learn some of the ways in which a good story is crafted, and you may acquire a keener sense of the art it requires. Then, when you read stories in the future, you will enjoy them as an insider does.

Not everyone, of course, is a born storyteller. If someone tells you of something that happened the other day and practically puts you to sleep, you realize that it takes both talent and skill to recognize a story worth telling and to narrate it effectively. Yet most people who can write expository prose clearly and vigorously can, with enough effort, write at least a brief story that will satisfy themselves, and perhaps others. Generally, the skilled writer of fiction is a skilled reader of fiction, too. Among famed storytellers, Erskine Caldwell, author of *Tobacco Road,* may be the only one to claim that reading never did him any good. Before you attempt a story of your own, you would do well to read the works of master storytellers — as many as possible. In this book, you'll find a fair sampling; but if you are serious about wanting to write stories, you will want to read whole collections by authors you admire. Read not only for entertainment, read critically. Notice how a story is woven together. For what possible purpose does the writer tell it from one point of view, instead of from another? What do the actions of the characters show us about the kinds of people they are? Are events given in chronological order? If not, what does the writer achieve by so departing from chronology? Such questions may seem dry, but if you apply them to living stories, they may help give you a few insights into the storyteller's art.

Some beginning writers, remarked Flannery O'Connor, think they know what a short story is until they try to write one — "Then they find themselves writing a sketch with an essay woven through it, or an editorial with a character in it, or a case history with a moral, or some other mongrel thing."[1] But what, exactly, is a story? According to O'Connor, it is a form of writing in which characters and events influence each other. "If you start with a real personality, a real character," she explained to an audience of aspiring writers, "then something is bound to happen."[2] This would seem another way of saying, "Character is action" — the words of a master storyteller, Henry James.[3]

For an event to be charged with meaning in fiction, it has to produce an effect on someone. E. M. Forster has explained, "Consider the death of a queen. If it is in a story we say, 'and then?' "[4] In such a story a writer might tell how the queen's death in some way altered the life of an obscure commoner. Read outstanding short stories of the past century and, in most, you will find a character led to act — or left, as a result of some dramatic event, deeply illumined and fundamentally changed. Most stories in this book exhibit the tradition that James defined: stories in which characters think, feel, and react, causing things to happen. Recently, however, many fiction writers have experimented with radically different concepts of character (discussed briefly in Chapter Four). As a result, in many contemporary stories, character seems hardly to matter and events sometimes occur without apparent human control. If recent fiction intrigues you, then closely read the stories of Franz Kafka, Gabriel García Márquez, T. Coraghessan Boyle, Joyce Carol Oates, and Alice Walker (all represented in this book), as well as those of John Barth, Donald Barthelme, Russell Edson, Samuel Beckett, and others. You will meet a few stories in which writers appear to devise new rules for storytelling. If you are a novice at writing fiction, however, you might do well, before trying to change the rules, first to watch a fair number of games.

Let us assume that you have a working sense of the nature of a short story. Where do you find a story to tell? Evidently, if you take Flannery O'Connor's advice and start with a "real character," then to unfold a story you have only to imagine that character in some dramatic situation or confrontation. Then you imagine how he or she will respond to it. In O'Connor's own story "Revelation," we see her procedure. First she establishes the nature of Mrs. Turpin, a racist prig full of smug self-congratulation. Then, after a flung textbook strikes Mrs. Turpin in the brow, O'Connor shows us her main character going through anguished change. Of course, there is no one approved and infallible method of story-finding. Writers begin with anything that sparks them into motion. Henry James could find the germ for a story — even for a whole novel — in an anecdote

[1] "The Nature and Aim of Fiction" in *Mystery and Manners,* ed. Sally and Robert Fitzgerald (New York: Farrar, 1961), 66.
[2] "Writing Short Stories," *Mystery* 106.
[3] "Anthony Trollope" (1883), reprinted in part in *Theory of Fiction: Henry James,* ed. James E. Miller, Jr. (Lincoln: U of Nebraska P, 1972), 200.
[4] *Aspects of the Novel,* quoted by Eric S. Rabkin in the epigraph for his study *Narrative Suspense* (Ann Arbor: U of Michigan P, 1973).

told him at a dinner party. Another source of seedling stories, for novelist and short story writer J. F. Powers, is small human-interest items in a daily newspaper. Robert Ludlum, author of popular spy novels, says, "I start with an idea, with something that outrages, amuses, or interests me. Then I try to find the story line that will support the basic idea."[5] (Ludlum, no Flannery O'Connor-like prober of souls, writes a kind of fiction in which ingenious plot, not character, counts most.)

Endless stories surround you, if only you can recognize them. Your daily life may prove your most fruitful source. You need not live a story in order to write it, though: you can overhear it, or observe it in the lives of others. As an aid to memory, many distinguished fiction writers have kept notebooks. There, in rough form, they record whatever sticks in their minds as grist for stories. F. Scott Fitzgerald filled his notebook with "Things Overheard," "Nonsense and Stray Phrases," "Scenes," "Situations," and "Descriptions of Girls." Nathaniel Hawthorne jotted down hundreds of ideas for stories he meant to write. (One that didn't materialize: "A stove possessed by a Devil.") In his own profound notebooks, Henry James not only saved bits and scraps (such as names he thought up for possible characters), he analyzed his stories as he worked on them, listing problems and solutions. Some writers, whether or not they ever turn their notebooks into finished stories, find that notebook-keeping sharpens their powers of observation. Keep such a notebook, after your own fashion, and you may well find yourself opening your eyes wide to the stories that surround you, and also fine-tuning your ears.

THE PROCESS OF STORYTELLING

In the heyday of pulp magazines (so called for their cheap paper) many professional writers of fiction relied on a mechanical gadget called Plotto — a sort of writer's Ouija board. Constructing a story for *Dime Western* or *Spicy Detective,* a writer would spin a little tin arrow to a number, then look up the number in an accompanying book. A few spins would indicate all the necessary ingredients: type of hero, type of villain, setting, kind of conflict, complication ("an earthquake"), crisis, climax, and conclusion. When the writer cooked the ingredients into a story, the result brought a penny a word.

Some more highly literate storytellers, though they don't own a Plotto board, lay out the elements of a story before they write. One believer in thorough planning was P. G. Wodehouse, author of ingeniously plotted novels of screwball dwellers in posh mansions in rural England. Everything in a story, declared Wodehouse, should be carefully figured out

[5]Reply to a questioner, quoted by Robert Charm, "From Pen to Podium," Boston *Globe,* 11 May 1982: 15.

ahead of time: "Once you go saying to yourself, 'This is a pretty weak plot as it stands, but I'm such a hell of a writer that my magic touch will make it OK,' you're sunk."[6] Other writers, less insistent on firm scaffolding, begin writing with only a character or a situation in mind, letting themselves be surprised (along with the reader) as the story unfolds. Flannery O'Connor, it would seem, was such a writer. In her short story "Good Country People," a Bible salesman steals a woman's artificial leg. O'Connor has recalled that she didn't know he was going to do so until ten or twelve lines before she came to describe the theft. Yet, she later realized, the salesman's astonishing act followed from the kind of man he was and from the nature of his victim.[7]

Whether they lay plans carefully or casually, writers often will meet a surprise in the act of telling a story. At times a character will behave unpredictably, especially a lifelike character who grows larger under the pen. Tolstoi, who began writing *Anna Karenina* determined to condemn an unfaithful woman, found himself, as he wrote his immense novel, coming to view his adulterous main character with greater compassion. He had imagined Anna as physically unattractive and boorish in her manners, but his descriptions of her became kinder and more sympathetic as he wrote on.

Like runners who first limber up their muscles before hitting the track, some writers warm up before they write. George Fox, author of popular novels (*Amok, Without Music*) and filmscripts, starts out by writing "a lot of drivel about the hero's childhood, about the setting, about a certain car." Perhaps none of this "drivel" will appear in his finished story. As he writes a description of a character, perhaps things start to happen, and the story begins to move. Then Fox drops ten or twenty pages of warm-up exercise into his trashbasket. Hero and setting, he finds, have become vivid in his imagination.

Early in writing a story, you have to make crucial decisions. One is your choice of the person to narrate the story — the point of view. Tolstoi, in writing *The Death of Ivan Ilych,* at first cast his story into the form of a diary kept by Ivan during his last days. Later, as Tolstoi reviewed what he had written, he decided against this device. He then completely rewrote the story in the third person. No doubt he had realized that the story required a narrator able to see Ivan both from without and from within. Such a narrator, besides, could survive Ivan's death and portray his mourners. In effective storytelling, perhaps a writer's most important decision is to select the most appropriate point of view. How to decide which point of view is best? Try telling the story to yourself in different ways, as if through the eyes of different narrators.

[6]Interview with Gerald Clarke, *Paris Review* 64 (1975): 155.
[7]"Writing Short Stories," *Mystery and Manners* 100.

Still another decision that greatly matters is how thoroughly each part of your story needs to be told. Which events will you set forth in brief summaries, which in full scenes? Drawing a scene, you visualize it in detail. You thus enable your readers to see it in their minds' eye as if they beheld it on a stage or a screen. In John Updike's "A & P," most of the story takes place in one extended scene in a supermarket, including a few interior thoughts of Sammy, the narrator. That we may visualize the action, Updike includes plenty of physical details: the story takes place "under the fluorescent lights, against all those stacked packages," and the girls who trigger Sammy's big decision are described with loving care. For another vivid scene, see Faulkner's "Barn Burning," in which the boy's father marches into Major de Spain's mansion, streaking the rug with filth. In a well-told story, we usually find the most highly dramatic moments set forth in scenes. For as long as a scene transpires, the reader lives it.

In employing the method of **summary,** you tell what happens in fewer words. You boil down events to their essentials and set them forth in a more general way. In the Grimm brothers' "Godfather Death," we find summary in the statement, "It wasn't long before the young man had become the most famous doctor in the world." In this one sentence, the taleteller covers events that, if told in scenes, might have required many chapters. Summary is the method of narration most of us employ in conversation: "I was in a little car crash last night. A truck slammed me in the tailgate and stove in my rear end." In fiction, a story containing scenes may also employ summary — for the less dramatic events, perhaps, or for getting over a long expanse of time that doesn't need to be chronicled in detail. In Singer's "Gimpel the Fool" the narrator summarizes: "I wandered over the land and good people did not neglect me. After many years I became old and white. . . ." Here, Singer's apparent purpose isn't to give us a complete history of Gimpel's later life. Instead, it is to show that, during his years of wandering, the supposed fool becomes a wiser man. Summary may also be valuable to supply background information that the reader needs. With wonderful economy, D. H. Lawrence begins "The Rocking-Horse Winner" with a summary: "There was a woman who was beautiful, who started with all the advantages, yet she had no luck. She married for love, and the love turned to dust." In a few words, summary can convey all the information we need more effectively than many scenes.

To decide which events to summarize and which to depict in scenes is a challenge to many storytellers. Beginning writers sometimes tell too large a part of their story in sketchy summary form, neglecting to set forth the dramatic moments in detailed scenes — and therefore, failing to milk these moments for all they are worth. Still, good storytellers know that, although vivid scenes are what readers best remember, summary at times is indispensable. With a short passage of summary, the writer can move along quickly to a scene. Divide your story into scenes, P. G. Wodehouse advised, "and have as little stuff in between as possible."[8]

Some writers, when shifting scenes, don't even use summary. To waft a character from one place to another, they will end a scene, leave some white space, and open the next scene with the character already arrived at a destination. Perhaps they will use a **time-marker,** or a brief phrase of transition, to indicate that some while has gone by: *"An hour later"* — that's the time-marker — "Cassidy was shoving open the bleary glass door of the Tenth Precinct Station."

A word of warning: Don't pretend to feelings you don't feel, or attitudes you can't call your own. In later life, Eudora Welty recalled with amusement the opening line of a story she had written as a girl trying to maintain a sophistication she hadn't really had: "Monsieur Boule inserted a delicate dagger into Mademoiselle's left side and departed with a poised immediacy."[9]

Some storytellers work slowly, taking pains to find the right words on their first try. Others, like Frank O'Connor, dash off a rough draft of a story, saving the pains for later. O'Connor would start writing "any sort of rubbish which will cover the main outlines of the story," just to get it down in writing and be able to look at it. "When I draft a story I never think of writing nice sentences," he explained. "It's the design of the story which to me is most important, the thing that tells you there's a bad gap in the narrative here and you really ought to fill that up in some way or another."[10] Satisfied with his design, O'Connor would then work on the story's texture, rewriting a story as many as fifty times. " 'First Confession,' " he said, "has appeared in three quite different forms from the first day when *Lovat Dickson's Magazine* printed it, so I may now hope its ghost has ceased to haunt me."[11]

Not every writer of fiction believes in profound revision. "You know," Ann Beattie told a writers' conference, "I'm not capable of major revision at all. That's why I throw things out a lot."[12] D. H. Lawrence was another believer in letting first thoughts stand. If dissatisfied with a story, he would write the whole thing over from scratch. This strenuous custom accounts for there being at least three complete and separate versions of his novel *Lady Chatterley's Lover.*

At the opposite extreme is the "bleeder," the writer who lets go of each word as reluctantly as though it were a drop of blood. Perhaps the

[8]Interview with Clarke, 152.
[9]*One Writer's Beginnings* (Cambridge: Harvard UP, 1984), 85 – 6.
[10]Interview with Anthony Whittier, *Writers at Work: The* Paris Review *Interviews* (New York: Viking, 1959) 167 – 8.
[11]Foreword to the *Stories of Frank O'Connor* (New York: Knopf, 1952).
[12]Quoted by Gelarch Asayesh, news story on the New England Writers' Conference, Boston *Globe,* 8 July 1982.

most celebrated bleeder in literary history was Gustave Flaubert, who rewrote his work with masochistic devotion, seeking to reflect in his style the clarity and precision of classical music. "May I die like a dog," he wrote to a friend, "rather than hasten the ripening of a sentence by a single second!"[13] (See other remarks by Flaubert upon his labors, page 398; and for a conflicting view of style, the comment by Thomas Hardy, page 399.)

Most professional writers of fiction probably reside somewhere between perfectionism and "Oh, let it all hang out." If, in looking over what they have written they spy a passage they can improve, they improve it. Because it is usually easier to delete than to amplify, some write at great length, putting in everything they can think of, and then, in revising the story, shorten it. Georges Simenon, French writer of mystery novels, sometimes reduced his first versions by as much as half. Simenon declared that he hated "show-off writing," and so would strike out any word or sentence that called attention to its own cleverness. So stern was Simenon in his deletions that he rendered his prose almost totally colorless. In his way, James Thurber also distrusted too-obvious delight in one's own words. In writing a humorous story, he observed, "you're likely to be very gleeful with what you've first put down." But careful rewriting can transfer the glee from writer to reader. "You go over and over it . . . to make the piece sound less as if you were having a lot of fun with it yourself."[14]

If we can generalize at all, it may be safe to say that most professional writers first write a much rougher version of a story than they finish with. Although in some of his working habits Truman Capote may have been unique (he wrote *second* drafts on a peculiar kind of yellow paper), he was like most writers in bringing a story to completion stage by stage. After writing a first draft in longhand, Capote would type another draft, which he then retired for a week or a month. "When I take it out again," he said, "I read it as coldly as possible, then read it aloud to a friend or two, and decide what changes I want to make and whether or not I want to publish it." (Capote threw away hundreds of thousands of words that didn't seem publishable.) "But if all goes well, I type the final version on white paper."[15]

As you can see, professional writers of fiction tend to be patient and demanding self-critics. They cultivate an ability to step out of themselves and to inspect a story as though with a reader's eyes. To be sure, problems will appear, problems deeper than whether to delete an adjective. A major character may prove useless and a minor character may assume swaggering proportions. A plot that had rolled along smoothly may run into a pothole and fall apart. Mark Twain, in writing *Huckleberry Finn,* called his masterpiece "that damned book" as he struggled with it. For seven years he kept

[13]Letter to Maxim du Camp, June 19, 1852, *Selected Letters,* tr. Francis Steegmuller (New York: Vintage, 1957) 132.
[14]Interview with George Plimpton and Max Steele, *Writers* 88.
[15]Interview with Pati Hill, *Writers* 296 – 7.

casting aside his manuscript and returning to it. Something in him seemed unwilling to finish the book, and in the midst of his labors on it he took time out to produce his autobiographical *Life on the Mississippi* and an inferior but more tractable novel, *The Prince and the Pauper.* In spinning forth a story, every veteran writer of fiction perhaps has encountered knots. Fortunately, in trying to undo them, the writer has a powerful ally: the unconscious. Joyce Carol Oates has suggested a remedy for writer's block caused by running into deep problems. When the mind halts before a problem it can't solve, the writer had best put aside the story for a while, and sleep on it, until the trustworthy unconscious comes up with a solution.[16]

To write a novel that will soar to the top of bestseller lists and set every reviewer to babbling praise — this is a cherished American dream. In actuality, your chances of achieving great rewards from fiction are somewhat like your chances of winning a million dollars by playing blackjack at Las Vegas. Although a few professional writers make a living by regularly churning out paperback novels in some popular genre such as romance, Gothic, or science fiction, few serious first novelists meet much favor these days with readers or publishers. If you write short stories, you will find it even harder to reach a wide audience. Little magazines, with circulations of a few hundred dedicated readers, are today the principal medium for short fiction. Lately, however, hope for the short story has blossomed. Collections of stories by distinguished old hands (Eudora Welty, John Cheever) have proved bestsellers; and more and more publishers, including some university presses, have been welcoming volumes of stories.

Like poets, most short-story writers nowadays practice their demanding art for reasons other than the prospects of money and renown. What satisfactions reside in writing short stories? May you discover them, by writing a story that pleases you, your instructor, and your friends.

Suggestions for Writing

1. Reviewing the illustrations of fable and tale in Chapter One (those by W. Somerset Maugham and the brothers Grimm), write a brief supernatural or fantastic tale, or a fable with a point to it.
2. In three separate paragraphs, try beginning a story in three distinctly different ways. You might try, for instance, relating an incident from three points of view; or try beginning a story with a summary, the opening of a scene, and a descriptive passage introducing a person or a setting.
3. Recount a dream you vividly remember, in which something exciting or astonishing occurred. (This is an exercise; the result does not have to be a complete story. You may find, though, that a longer story will suggest itself.)
4. Here is a writing exercise suggested by novelist R. V. Cassill. Take the first three paragraphs of a story you admire, and with the text open beside you, write three parallel paragraphs of careful imitation. Keep the same number of

[16]Cited by Rust Hills, *Writing in General and the Short Story in Particular* (Boston: Houghton, 1977) 191.

sentences, of the same general length and complexity. Imitate any proper names, characteristic detail, "emotional state of the characters." Reproduce the point of view. "In a word," says Cassill, "you cannot do this sort of imitation without thinking pretty nimbly about what you are doing. You are performing one of the kinds of thought that is part of original composition." (From *Writing Fiction,* New York: Pocket Books, 1962.)

5. Following George Fox's method of warming up, write ten or more pages of carefree exercise material, portraying in detail some strong and colorful character, or a weak and appealing one. If the character you envision interests you, try to imagine such a person confronted with some challenge. Then go on to write the story that ensues.

6. Recall some dramatic event in your life, or some event that you know from vivid secondhand reports. Bring it alive in the form of a scene, including dialogue and description if they seem necessary.

7. Write a skeletal novel in summary form, taking three or four pages to encompass all the main events in it. Then select one dramatic moment from your summary and present it in the form of a scene of about 1,000 to 2,000 words.

8. Invent names for ten or twelve imaginary characters, wildly assorted in age, walk of life, and personality. Then describe in two or three sentences the person each name suggests to you. (Here are three memorable fictional names from the novels of Henry James, for instance: Lambert Strether, Fleda Vetch, and Mrs. Bread.)

9. Following the procedure of J. F. Powers, scan a newspaper for some two-inch-long comic or touching story of relatively small news value but of much human interest. Write the tale or short story it suggests to you.

10. Choose a place you know well and write a story that might have happened there twenty-five, fifty, or a hundred years ago. An alternative idea might be to set your story in the future. (For inspiration, see "The Portable Phonograph" or a current science-fiction magazine.)

11. In a short story, show how a brief moment alters the course of a character's life. For illustrations of such stories, see "A & P," "Greasy Lake," "Revelation," and "The Jilting of Granny Weatherall."

Writing about a Poem

Assignment: a paper about a poem. You can approach it as a grim duty, of course: any activity can so be regarded. For Don Juan, in Spanish legend, even the act of love became a chore. But the act of writing, like the act of love, is much easier if your feelings take part in it. Write about anything you dislike and don't understand, and you not only set yourself the labors of Hercules, but you guarantee your reader discouragingly hard labor, too.

To write about a poem informatively, you need first to experience it. It helps to live with the poem for as long as possible: there is little point in trying to encompass the poem in a ten-minute tour of inspection on the night before the paper falls due. However challenging, writing about poetry has immediate rewards, and to mention just one, the poem you spend time with and write about is going to mean much more to you than poems skimmed ever do.

Most of the problems you will meet in writing about a poem will be the same ones you meet in writing about a play or a story: finding a topic, organizing your thoughts, writing, revising. For general advice on writing papers about any kind of literature, see "Writing about Literature" on page 1333. In a few ways, however, a poem requires a different approach. In this chapter we will deal briefly with some of them, and will offer a few illustrations of papers that students have written. These papers may not be works of inimitable genius, but they are pretty good papers, the likes of which most students can write with a modest investment of time and care.

Briefer than most stories and most plays, lyric poems *look* easier to write about. They call, however, for your keenest attention. You may find that, before you can discuss a short poem, you will have to read it slowly and painstakingly, with your mind (like your pencil) sharp and ready. Unlike a play or a short story, a lyric poem tends to have very little plot, and perhaps you will find little to say about what happens in it. In order to understand a poem, you'll need to notice elements other than narrative: the connotations or suggestions of its words, surely, and the rhythm of phrases and lines. The subtleties of language, almost apart from story, are so essential to a poem (and so elusive) that Robert Frost was moved to say, "Poetry is what gets lost in translation." Once in a while, of course, you'll read a story whose prose abounds in sounds, rhythms, figures of speech, imagery, and other elements you expect of poetry. Certain novels of Herman Melville and William Faulkner contain paragraphs that, if extracted, seem in themselves prose poems — so lively are they in their word-play, so rich in metaphor. But such writing is exceptional, and the main business of most fiction is to get a story told. An extreme case of a fiction writer who didn't want his prose to sound poetic is Georges Simenon, best known for his mystery novels, who said that whenever he noticed in his manuscript any word or phrase that called attention to itself, he struck it out. That method of writing would never do for a poet, who revels in words and phrases that fix themselves in memory. It is safe to say that, in order to write well about a poem, you have to read it carefully enough to remember at least part of it word for word.

Let's consider three commonly useful approaches to writing about poetry.

EXPLICATING

In an **explication** (literally, "an unfolding") of a poem, a writer explains the entire poem in detail, unraveling any complexities to be found in it. This method is a valuable one in approaching a lyric poem, especially if the poem is rich in complexities (or in suggestions worth rendering explicit). Most poems that you'll ever be asked to explicate are short enough to discuss thoroughly within a limited time; fully to explicate a long and involved work, such as John Milton's epic *Paradise Lost*, might require a lifetime. (To explicate a short passage of Milton's long poem would be a more usual course assignment.)

All the details or suggestions in a poem that a sensitive and intelligent reader might consider, the writer of an explication considers and tries to unfold. These might include allusions, the denotations or connotations of words, the possible meanings of symbols, the effects of certain sounds and rhythms and formal elements (rime schemes, for instance), the sense of any statements that contain irony, and other particulars. Not intent on ripping a poem to pieces, the author of a useful explication instead tries to show how each part contributes to the whole.

An explication is easy to organize. You can start with the first line of the poem and keep working straight on through. An explication should not be confused with a paraphrase. A paraphrase simply puts the words of the poem into other words; it is a sort of translation, useful in getting at the plain prose sense and therefore especially helpful in clarifying a poem's main theme. Perhaps in writing an explication you will wish to do some paraphrasing; but an explication (unlike a paraphrase) does not simply restate: it explains a poem, in great detail.

Here, for example, is a famous poem by Robert Frost, followed by a student's concise explication. (The assignment was to explain whatever in "Design" seemed most essential, in not more than 750 words.)

ROBERT FROST (1874 – 1963)*
DESIGN   1936

I found a dimpled spider, fat and white,
On a white heal-all, holding up a moth
Like a white piece of rigid satin cloth —
Assorted characters of death and blight
Mixed ready to begin the morning right,   5
Like the ingredients of a witches' broth —
A snow-drop spider, a flower like a froth,
And dead wings carried like a paper kite.

What had that flower to do with being white,
The wayside blue and innocent heal-all?   10
What brought the kindred spider to that height,
Then steered the white moth thither in the night?
What but design of darkness to appall? —
If design govern in a thing so small.

An Unfolding of Robert Frost's "Design"

"I always wanted to be very observing," Robert Frost once said, after reading his poem "Design" to an audience. Then he added, "But I have always been afraid of my own observations" (Cook 126-27). What could he have observed that could scare him? Let's observe the poem close up.

Starting with the title, "Design," any reader of this poem will find it full of meaning. As Webster's New World Dictionary defines design, the word can denote among other things a plan, or "purpose; intention; aim." Some arguments for the existence of God (I remember from Sunday School) are based on the "argument from design": that because the world shows a systematic order, there must be a Designer who made it. But the word design can also mean "a secret or sinister scheme" -- such as we attribute to a "designing person." As we shall see, Frost's poem incorporates all of these meanings. His poem raises the old philosophic question of whether there is a Designer, an evil Designer, or no Designer at all. Frost probably read William James on this question, as a critic has shown convincingly (Poirier 245-50).

Like many other sonnets, the poem is divided into two parts. The first eight lines draw a picture centering on the spider, who at first seems almost jolly. It is dimpled and fat like a baby, or Santa Claus. It stands on a wild flower whose name, heal-all, seems an irony: a heal-all is supposed to cure any disease, but it certainly has no power to restore life to the dead moth. (Later, in line ten, we learn that the heal-all used to be blue. Presumably it has died and become bleached-looking.) In this second line we discover, too, that the spider has hold of another creature. Right away we might feel sorry for the moth, were it not for the simile applied to it in line three: "Like a white piece of rigid satin cloth." Suddenly the moth becomes not a creature but a piece of fabric -- lifeless and dead -- and yet satin has connotations also beautiful. For me satin, used in rich ceremonial costumes such as coronation gowns and brides' dresses, has a formality and luxury about it. Besides, there is great accuracy in the word: the smooth and slightly plush surface of satin is like the powder-smooth surface of moths' wings. But this "cloth," rigid and white, could be the lining to Dracula's coffin.

In the fifth line an invisible hand enters. The characters are "mixed" like ingredients in an evil potion. Some force doing the mixing is behind the scene. The characters in themselves are innocent enough, but when brought together and concocted, their whiteness and look of rigor mortis are overwhelming. There is something diabolical in the spider's feast. The "morning right" echoes the word rite, a

ritual -- in this case apparently a Black Mass or a Witches' Sabbath.
The simile in line seven ("a flower like a froth") is more ambiguous
and harder to describe. A froth is white, foamy, and delicate --
something found on a brook in the woods or on a beach after a wave
recedes. However, in the natural world, froth also can be ugly: the
foam on a dead dog's mouth. The dualism in nature -- its beauty and its
horror -- is there in that one simile.

So far, the poem has portrayed a small, frozen scene, with the
dimpled killer holding its victim as innocently as a boy holds a kite.
Already, Frost has hinted that Nature may be, as Radcliffe Squires
suggests, "nothing but an ash-white plain without love or faith or hope,
where ignorant appetites cross by chance" (87). Now, in the last six
lines of the sonnet, Frost comes out and directly states his theme.
What else could bring these deathly pale, stiff things together "but
design of darkness to appall?" The question is clearly rhetorical,
meant to be answered, "Why, nothing but that, of course!" I take the
next-to-last line to mean, "What except a design so dark and sinister
that we're appalled by it?" "Appall," by the way, is the second pun in
the poem: it sounds like a pall or shroud. Steered carries the suggestion of a steering-wheel or rudder that some pilot had to control.
Like the word brought, it implies that some Captain charted the paths
of spider, heal-all, and moth, so that they arrived together.

Having suggested that the universe is in the hands of that sinister
Captain (Fate? the Devil?), Frost adds a final note of doubt. The Bible tells
us that "His eye is on the sparrow," but at the moment the poet doesn't
seem sure. Maybe, he hints, when things in the universe drop below a
certain size, they pass completely out of the Designer's notice. When
creatures are that little, maybe He doesn't bother to govern them, but
just lets them run wild. And possibly the same ~~idiotic~~ mindless chance is all

that governs human lives. Maybe we're not even sinners in the hands of

an angry God, but ~~amazingly~~ are nothing but little dic/e being slung.

And that -- because it is even more senseless -- is the worst suspicion

of all.

Works Cited

Cook, Reginald. <u>Robert Frost: A Living Voice</u>. Amherst: U of Massa-
    chusetts P, 1974.

Poirier, Richard. <u>Robert Frost: The Work of Knowing</u>. New York: Ox-
    ford UP, 1977.

Squires, Radcliffe. <u>The Major Themes of Robert Frost</u>. Ann Arbor: U
    of Michigan P, 1963.

This excellent paper, while finding something worth unfolding in
every line in Frost's poem, does so without seeming mechanical. Notice
that, although the student proceeds through the poem from the title to the
last line, she takes up points when necessary, in any sequence. In paragraph two, the writer looks ahead to the end of the poem and briefly states
its main theme. (She does so in order to relate this theme to the poem's
title.) In the third paragraph, she deals with the poem's *later* image of the
heal-all, relating it to the first image. Along the way, she comments on the
form of the poem ("Like many other sonnets"), on its similes and puns,
its denotations and connotations.

Incidentally, this paper demonstrates good use of manuscript form,
following the *MLA Handbook,* 2nd ed. Brief references (in parentheses) tell
us where the writer found Frost's remarks before an audience, name the
critic (Poirier) who showed that Frost had read the philosopher William
James, and give page numbers for these sources and for another, a book
by Radcliffe Squires. At the end of the paper, a list of these works cited
uses abbreviations for *University* and *Press* that the *MLA Handbook* recommends (but doesn't insist upon). This paper demonstrates, too, how to
make final corrections without retyping. In the last paragraph, notice how
the student legibly added a word and neatly changed another word by
crossing it out and writing a substitute above it. In her next-to-last sentence, the writer clearly transposes two letters with a handy mark ( ),
deletes a word, and strikes out a superfluous letter.

It might seem that to work through a poem line by line is a lockstep
task; and yet there can be high excitement in it. Randall Jarrell once wrote
an explication of "Design" in which he managed to convey such excitement. In the following passage taken from it, see if you can sense the

writer's joy in his work. (Don't, incidentally, feel obliged to compare the quality of your own insights with Jarrell's, nor the quality of your own prose. Be fair to yourself: unlike most students, Jarrell had the advantage of being an excellent poet and a gifted critic; besides, he had read and pondered Frost for years before he wrote his essay, and as a teacher he probably had taught "Design" many times.)

> Frost's details are so diabolically good that it seems criminal to leave some unremarked; but notice how *dimpled, fat,* and *white* (all but one; all but one) come from our regular description of any baby; notice how the *heal-all,* because of its name, is the one flower in all the world picked to be the altar for this Devil's Mass; notice how *holding up* the moth brings something ritual and hieratic, a ghostly, ghastly formality, to this priest and its sacrificial victim; notice how terrible to the fingers, how full of the stilling rigor of death, that *white piece of rigid satin cloth* is. And *assorted characters of death and blight* is, like so many things in this poem, sharply ambiguous: *a mixed bunch of actors* or *diverse representative signs.* The tone of the phrase *assorted characters of death and blight* is beautifully developed in the ironic Breakfast-Club-calisthenics, Radio-Kitchen heartiness of *mixed ready to begin the morning right* (which assures us, so unreassuringly, that this isn't any sort of Strindberg *Spook Sonata,* but hard fact), and concludes in the *ingredients* of the witches' broth, giving the soup a sort of cuddly shimmer that the cauldron in *Macbeth* never had; the *broth,* even, is brought to life — we realize that witches' broth *is* broth, to be supped with a long spoon.[1]

Evidently, Jarrell's cultural interests are broad: ranging from August Strindberg's ground-breaking modern classic down to the Breakfast Club (a once-popular radio program that cheerfully exhorted its listeners to march around their tables). And yet breadth of knowledge, however much it deepens and enriches Jarrell's writing, isn't all that he brings to the reading of poetry. For him, an explication isn't a dull plod, but a voyage of discovery. His prose — full of figures of speech (*diabolically good, cuddly shimmer*) — conveys the apparent delight he takes in showing off his findings. Such a joy, of course, can't be acquired deliberately. But it can grow, the more you read and study poetry.

ANALYZING

An **analysis** of a poem, like a news commentator's analysis of a crisis in the Middle East or a chemist's analysis of an unknown fluid, separates its subject into elements, as a means to understanding that subject — to see what composes it. Usually, the writer of such an essay singles out one of those elements for attention: "Imagery of Light and Darkness in Frost's 'Design'"; "The Character of Satan in *Paradise Lost.*"

[1]From *Poetry and the Age* (New York: Knopf, 1953).

Like explication, analysis can be particularly useful in dealing with a short poem. Unlike explication (which inches through a poem line by line), analysis often suits a long poem too, because it allows the writer to discuss just one manageable element in the poem. A good analysis casts intense light upon a poem from one direction. If you care enough about a poem, and about some perspective on it — its theme, say, or its symbolism, or its singability — writing an analysis can enlighten and give pleasure.

In this book you probably have met a few brief analyses: the discussion of connotations in John Masefield's "Cargoes" (page 471), for instance, or the examination of symbols in T. S. Eliot's "The *Boston Evening Transcript*" (page 612). In fact, most of the discussions in this book are analytic. Temporarily, we have separated the whole art of poetry into elements such as tone, irony, literal meaning, suggestions, imagery, figures of speech, sound, rhythm, and so on. No element of a poem, of course, exists apart from all the other elements. Still, by taking a closer look at particular elements, one at a time, we see them more clearly and more easily study them.

Long analyses of metrical feet, rime schemes, and indentations tend to make ponderous reading: such formal and technical elements are perhaps the hardest to discuss engagingly. And yet formal analysis (at least a little of it) can be interesting and illuminating: it can measure the very pulse beat of lines. If you do care about the technical side of poetry, then write about it, by all means. You will probably find it helpful to learn the terms for the various meters, stanzas, fixed forms, and other devices, so that you can summon them to your aid with confidence. Here is a short formal analysis of "Design" by a student who evidently cares for technicalities yet who manages not to be a bore in talking about them. Concentrating on the sonnet form of Frost's poem, the student actually casts light upon the poem in its entirety.

The Design of "Design"

For "Design," the sonnet form has at least two advantages. First, as in most strict ~Italian~ sonnets, the argument of the poem falls into two parts. In the octave Frost draws his pale still-life of spider, flower, and moth; then in the sestet he contemplates the meaning of it. The sestet deals with a more general idea: the possible existence of a vindictive deity who causes the spider to catch the moth, and no doubt also causes other suffering. Frost weaves his own little web. The unwary reader is led into the poem by its opening story, and pretty soon is struggling with more than he expected. Even the rime scheme, by the way, has something to do with the poem's meaning. The word white ends the first line of the sestet. The same sound is echoed in the rimes that follow. All in all, half the lines in the poem end in an "ite." It seems as if Frost places great weight on the whiteness of his little scene, for the riming words both introduce the term white and keep reminding us of it.

A sonnet has a familiar design, and that is its second big advantage to this particular poem. In a way, writing "Design" as a sonnet almost seems a foxy joke. (I can just imagine Frost chuckling to himself, wondering if anyone will get it.) A sonnet, being a classical form, is an orderly world with certain laws in it. There is ready-made irony in its containing a meditation on whether there is any order in the universe at large. Obviously there's design in back of the poem, but is there any design to insect life, or human life? Whether or not the poet can answer this question (and it seems he can't), at least he discovers an order while writing the poem. Actually, that is just what Frost said a poet achieves: "a momentary stay against confusion."[1]

Although design clearly governs in this poem -- in "this thing so small" -- the design isn't entirely predictable. The poem starts out as an Italian sonnet, with just two riming sounds; then (unlike an Italian sonnet) it keeps the "ite" rimes going. It ends in a couplet, like a Shakespearean sonnet. From these unexpected departures from the pattern of the Italian sonnet announced in the opening lines, I get the impression that Frost's poem is somewhat like the larger universe. It looks perfectly orderly, until you notice the small details in it.

[1] Robert Frost, "The Figure a Poem Makes," preface, Complete Poems of Robert Frost (New York: Holt, 1949) vi.

Unlike the student paper on pages 1374–1377, that documented its references (inside parentheses), "The Design of 'Design' " uses an endnote to cite its one outside source. (In so doing, it follows the form for such notes suggested in the *MLA Handbook, 2nd ed.*) To do so seems sensible here. This writer doesn't need a list of works cited, for such a list might have looked skimpy, like a one-car funeral. (In the endnote, by the way, *Holt* is a short, MLA-recommended contraction for the full name of the publisher: Holt, Rinehart, and Winston, Inc.)

COMPARING AND CONTRASTING

To write a **comparison** of two poems, you place them side by side and point out their likenesses; to write a **contrast,** you point out their differences. If you wish, you can combine the two methods in the same paper. For example, even though you may emphasize similarities you may also call attention to differences, or vice versa.

Such a paper makes most sense if you pair two poems that have much in common. It would be possible to compare Eliza Cook's sentimentalized elegy "The Old Arm-Chair" with John Milton's profound "Lycidas," but comparison would be difficult, perhaps futile. Though both poems are in English, the two seem hopelessly remote from each other in diction, in tone, in complexity, and in worth.

Having found, however, a couple of poems that throw light on each other, you then go on in your paper to show further, unsuspected resemblances — not just the ones that are obvious (" 'Design' and 'Wing-Spread' are both about bugs"). The interesting resemblances are ones that take thinking to discover. Similarly, you may want to show noteworthy differences — besides those your reader will see without any help.

In comparing two poems, you may be tempted to discuss one of them and be done with it, then spend the latter half of your paper discussing the other. This simple way of organizing an essay can be dangerous if it leads you to keep the two poems in total isolation from each other. The whole idea of such an assignment, of course, is to get you to do some comparing. There is nothing wrong in discussing all of poem A first, then discussing poem B — *if* in discussing B you keep looking back at A. Another procedure is to keep comparing the two poems all the way through your paper — dealing first, let's say, with their themes; then with their metaphors; and finally, with their respective merits.

More often than not, a comparison is an analysis: a study of a theme common to two poems, for instance; or of two poets' similar fondness for the myth of Eden. But you also can evaluate poems by comparing and contrasting them: placing them side by side in order to decide which poet deserves the brighter laurels. Here, for example, is a paper that considers "Design" and "Wing-Spread," a poem of Abbie Huston Evans (first printed in 1938, two years later than Frost's poem). By comparing and contrasting the two poems for (1) their language and (2) their themes, this student shows us reasons for his evaluation.

"Wing-Spread" Does a Dip

The midge spins out to safety

Through the spider's rope;

But the moth, less lucky,

Has to grope.

Mired in glue-like cable   5

See him foundered swing

By the gap he opened

With his wing,

Dusty web enlacing

All that blue and beryl.   10

In a netted universe

Wing-spread is peril.

-- Abbie Huston Evans

"Wing-Spread," quoted above, is a good poem, but it is not in the

same class with "Design." Both poets show us a murderous spider and an

unlucky moth, but there are two reasons for Robert Frost's superiority.

One is his more suggestive use of language, the other is his more

memorable theme.

Let's start with language. "Design" is full of words and phrases

rich in suggestions. "Wing-Spread," by comparison, contains few. To

take just one example, Frost's "dimpled spider, fat and white" is

certainly a more suggestive description. Actually, Evans doesn't describe her spider; she just says, "the spider's rope." (I have to hand Evans the palm for showing us the spider and moth in action. In Frost's view, they are dead and petrified -- but I guess that is the impression he is after.) In "Design," the spider's dimples show that it is like a chubby little kid, who further turns out to be a kite-flier. This seems an odd, almost freaky way to look at a spider. I find it more refreshing than Evans's view (although I like her word <u>cable</u>, suggesting that the spider's web is a kind of suspension bridge). Frost's word-choice -- his harping on <u>white</u> -- paints a more striking scene than Evans's slightly vague "All that blue and beryl." Except for her personification of the moth in her second stanza, Evans doesn't go in for any figures of speech, and even that one isn't a clear personification -- she simply gives the moth a sex by referring to it as "him." Frost's striking metaphors, similes, and even puns (<u>right</u>, <u>appall</u>) show him, as usual, to be a master of figures of speech. He calls the moth's wings "satin cloth" and "a paper kite"; Evans just refers in line 8 to a moth's wing. As far as the language of the two poems goes, you might as well compare a vase brimming with flowers and a single flower stuck in a vase. (That is a poor metaphor, since Frost's poem contains only one flower, but I hope you will know what I mean.)

In fairness to Evans, I would say that she picks a pretty good solitary flower. And her poem has powerful sounds: short lines with the riming words coming at us again and again very frequently. In theme, however, "Wing-Spread" seems much more narrow than "Design." The first time I read Evans's poem all I felt was: Ho hum, the moth too was wide and got stuck. The second time I read it, I figured that she is saying something with a universal application. This message comes out in line 11, in "a netted universe." That is the most interesting phrase in her poem, one that you can think about. <u>Netted</u> makes me imagine the universe as being full of nets rigged by someone who is fishing for us. Maybe, like Frost, Evans sees an evil plan operating. She does not, though,

investigate it. She says that the midge escapes because it is tiny.

On the other hand, things with wide wing-spreads get stuck. Her theme

as I read it is, "Be small and inconspicuous if you want to survive," or

maybe, "Isn't it too bad that in this world the big beautiful types

crack up and die, while the miserable little puny punks keep sailing?"

Now, that is a valuable idea. I have often thought that very same

thing myself. But Frost's closing note ("If design govern in a thing

so small") is really devastating, because it raises a huge uncertainty.

"Wing-Spread" leaves us with not much besides a moth stuck in a web, and

a moral. In both language and theme, "Design" climbs to a higher

altitude.

HOW TO QUOTE A POEM

Preparing to discuss a short poem, it is a good idea to emulate the student who wrote on "Wing-Spread" and to quote the whole text of the poem at the beginning of your paper, with its lines numbered. Then you can refer to it with ease, and your instructor, without having to juggle a book, can follow you.

Quoted to illustrate some point, memorable lines can add interest to your paper, and good commentators on poetry tend to be apt quoters, helping their readers to experience a word, a phrase, a line, or a passage that otherwise might be neglected. However, to quote from poetry is slightly more awkward than to quote from prose. There are lines to think about — important and meaningful units whose shape you will need to preserve. If you are quoting more than a couple of lines, it is good policy to arrange your quotation just as its lines occur in the poem, white space and all:

At the outset, the poet tells us of his discovery of

          a dimpled spider, fat and white,
     On a white heal-all, holding up a moth
     Like a white piece of rigid satin cloth --

and implies that the small killer is both childlike and sinister.

But if you are quoting less than two lines of verse, it would seem wasteful of paper to write:

```
The color white preoccupies Frost.  The spider is

                        fat and white,
          On a white heal-all

and even the victim moth is pale, too.
```

In such a case, it saves space to transform Frost's line arrangement into prose:

```
The color white preoccupies Frost.  The spider is "fat and white, /

On a white heal-all" -- and even the victim moth is pale, too.
```

Here, a diagonal (/) indicates the writer's respect for where the poet's lines begin and end. Some writers prefer to note line-breaks without diagonals, just by keeping the initial capital letter of a line (if there is any): "fat and white, On a white heal-all. . . ." Incidentally, the ellipsis (. . .) in that last remark indicates that words are omitted from the end of Frost's sentence; the fourth dot is a period. Some writers — meticulous souls — also stick in an ellipsis at the *beginning* of a quotation, if they're leaving out words from the beginning of a sentence in the original:

```
The color white preoccupies Frost in his description of the spider

". . .fat and white, / On a white heal-all. . . ."
```

Surely there's no need for an initial ellipsis, though, if you begin quoting at the beginning of a sentence. No need for a final ellipsis, either, if your quotation goes right to the end of a sentence in the original. If it is obvious that only a phrase is being quoted, no need for an ellipsis in any case:

```
The speaker says he "found a dimpled spider" and he goes on to

portray it as a kite-flying boy.
```

If you leave out whole lines, indicate the omission by an ellipsis all by itself on a line:

```
The midge spins out to safety
Through the spider's rope;
          . . .
In a netted universe
Wing-spread is peril.
```

BEFORE YOU BEGIN

Ready at last to write, you will have spent considerable time in reading, thinking, and feeling. After having chosen your topic, you probably will have taken a further look at the poem or poems you have picked, letting further thoughts and feelings come to you. The quality of your paper will depend, above all, upon the quality of your readiness to write.

Exploring a poem, a sensitive writer handles it with care and affection as though it were a living animal, and, done with it, leaves it still alive. The unfeeling writer, on the other hand, disassembles the poem in a dull, mechanical way, like someone with a blunt ax filling an order for one horse-skeleton. Again, to write well is a matter of engaging your feelings. Writing to a deadline, on an assigned topic, you easily can sink into a drab, workaday style, especially if you regard the poet as some uninspired builder of chicken-coops who hammers themes and images into place, and then slaps the whole thing with a coat of words. Certain expressions, if you lean on them habitually, may tempt you to think of the poet in that way. Here, for instance, is a discussion — by a plodding writer — of Robert Frost's poem.

> The symbols Frost uses in "Design" are very successful. Frost
>
> makes the spider stand for Nature. He wants us to see Nature as
>
> blind and cruel. He also employs good sounds. He uses a lot of
>
> i's because he is trying to make you think of falling rain.

(Underscored words are worth questioning.) What's wrong with that comment? While understandable, the words *uses* and *employs* seem to lead the writer to see Frost only as a conscious tool-manipulator. To be sure, Frost in a sense "uses" symbols, but did he grab hold of them and lay them into his poem? For all we know, perhaps the symbols arrived quite unbidden, and used the poet. To write a good poem, Frost maintained, a poet himself has to be surprised. (How, by the way, can we hope to know what a poet *wants* to do? And there isn't much point in saying that the poet is *trying to* do something. He has already done it, if he has written a good poem.) At least, it is likely that Frost didn't plan to fulfill a certain quota of *i*-sounds. Writing his poem, not by following a blueprint but probably by bringing it slowly to the surface of his mind (like Elizabeth Bishop's hooked fish), Frost no doubt had enough to do without trying to engineer the reactions of his possible audience. Like all true symbols, Frost's spider doesn't *stand for* anything. The writer would be closer to the truth to say that the spider *suggests* or *reminds us* of Nature, or of certain forces in the natural world. (Symbols just hint, they don't indicate.)

After the student discussed the paper in a conference, he rewrote the first two sentences like this:

```
The symbols in Frost's "Design" are highly effective. The

spider, for instance, suggests the blindness and cruelty of Nature.

Frost's word-sounds, too, are part of the meaning of his poem, for

the i's remind the reader of falling rain.
```

Not every reader of "Design" will hear rain falling, but the student's revision probably comes closer to describing the experience of the poem most of us know.

In writing about poetry, an occasional note of self-doubt can be useful: now and then a *perhaps* or a *possibly,* an *it seems* or a modest *I suppose.* Such expressions may seem timid shilly-shallying, but at least they keep the writer from thinking, "I know all there is to know about this poem."

Facing the showdown with your empty sheaf of paper, however, you can't worry forever about your critical vocabulary. To do so is to risk the fate of the centipede in a bit of comic verse, who was running along efficiently until someone asked, "Pray, which leg comes after which?," whereupon "He lay distracted in a ditch/Considering how to run." It is a safe bet that your instructor is human. Your main task as a writer is to communicate to another human being your sensitive reading of a poem.

Suggestions for Writing

Topics for Brief Papers (250 – 500 words)

1. Write a concise *explication* of a short poem of your choice, or one suggested by your instructor. In a paper this brief, probably you won't have room to explain everything in the poem; explain what you think most needs explaining. (An illustration of one such explication appears on page 1374.)
2. Write an *analysis* of a short poem, first deciding which one of its elements to deal with. (An illustration of such an analysis appears on page 1379.) For examples, here are a few specific topics:

   "Kinds of Irony in Hardy's 'The Workbox' "

   "The Attitude of the Speaker in Marvell's 'To His Coy Mistress' "

   "Folk Ballad Traits in Randall's 'Ballad of Birmingham' "

   "An Extended Metaphor in Rich's 'Diving into the Wreck.' " (Explain the one main comparison that the poem makes and show how the whole poem makes it. Other likely possibilities for a paper on extended metaphor: Dickinson's "Because I could not stop for Death," Levertov's "The Ache of Marriage," Nemerov's "Storm Windows," Frost's "The Silken Tent.")

"What the Skunks Mean in Lowell's 'Skunk Hour' "

"The Rhythms of Plath's 'Daddy' "

(To locate any of these poems, see the Index to Authors, Titles, and Quotations at the back of this book.)

3. Select a poem in which the main speaker is a character who for any reason interests you. You might consider, for instance, Betjeman's "In Westminster Abbey," Browning's "My Last Duchess" or "Soliloquy of the Spanish Cloister," or Eliot's "Love Song of J. Alfred Prufrock." Then write a brief profile of this character, drawing only on what the poem tells you (or reveals). What is the character's approximate age? Situation in life? Attitude toward self? Attitude toward others? General personality? Do you find this character admirable?

4. Although each of these poems tells a story, what happens in the poem isn't necessarily obvious: Cummings's "anyone lived in a pretty how town," Eliot's "Love Song of J. Alfred Prufrock," Lawrence's "A Youth Mowing," Stafford's "At the Klamath Berry Festival," Winters's "At the San Francisco Airport," James Wright's "A Blessing." Choose one of these poems and in a paragraph sum up what you think happens in it. Then in a second paragraph ask yourself: what, *besides* the element of story, did you consider in order to understand the poem?

5. Think of someone you know (or someone you can imagine) whose attitude toward poetry in general is dislike. Suggest a poem for that person to read — a poem that you like — and, addressing your skeptical reader, point out whatever you find to enjoy in it, that you think the skeptic just might enjoy too.

6. Keeping in mind what Coleridge and Jarrell have to say about "obscurity" in poetry (see their statements in Chapter 31), write a brief defense of some poem you like against the possible charge that it is obscure.

TOPICS FOR MORE EXTENSIVE PAPERS (600 – 1,000 WORDS)

1. Write an explication of a poem short enough for you to work through line by line — for instance, Emily Dickinson's "My Life had stood – a loaded Gun" or MacLeish's "The End of the World." As if offering your reading experience to a friend who hadn't read the poem before, try to point out all the leading difficulties you encountered, and set forth in detail your understanding of any lines that contain such difficulties.

2. Write an explication of a longer poem — for instance, Eliot's "Love Song of J. Alfred Prufrock," Hardy's "Convergence of the Twain," Rich's "Diving into the Wreck," or Wagoner's "Staying Alive." Although you will not be able to go through every line of the poem, explain what you think most needs explaining.

3. In this book, you will find from five to eleven poems by each of these poets: Blake, Dickinson, Donne, Frost, Hardy, Hopkins, Housman, Keats, Roethke, Shakespeare, Stevens, Tennyson, Whitman, William Carlos Williams, Wordsworth, and Yeats; and multiple selections for many more. (See Index to Authors, Titles, and Quotations.) After you read a few poems by a poet who interests you, write an analysis of *more than one* of the poet's poems. To do this, you will need to select just one characteristic theme (or other element) to deal with — something typical of the poet's work, not found only in a single poem. Here are a few specific topics for such an analysis:

"What Angers William Blake? A Look at Three Poems of Protest"

"How Emily Dickinson's Lyrics Resemble Hymns"

"The Humor of Robert Frost"

"John Keats's Sensuous Imagery"

"The Vocabulary of Music in Poems of Wallace Stevens"

"Non-free Verse: Patterns of Sound in Three Poems of William Carlos Williams"

"Yeats as a Poet of Love"

4. Compare and contrast two poems in order to evaluate them: which is more satisfying and effective poetry? To make a meaningful comparison, be sure to choose two poems that genuinely have much in common: perhaps a similar theme or subject. (For an illustration of such a paper, see the one given in this chapter. For suggestions of poems to compare, see the Anthology.)
5. Evaluate by the method of comparison two versions of a poem: early and late drafts, perhaps, or two translations from another language. For parallel versions to work on, see Chapter Fourteen, "Alternatives."
6. If the previous topic appeals to you, consider this. In 1912, twenty-four years before he printed "Design," Robert Frost sent a correspondent this early version:

IN WHITE

A dented spider like a snow drop white
On a white Heal-all, holding up a moth
Like a white piece of lifeless satin cloth —
Saw ever curious eye so strange a sight? —
Portent in little, assorted death and blight   5
Like ingredients of a witches' broth? —
The beady spider, the flower like a froth,
And the moth carried like a paper kite.

What had that flower to do with being white,
The blue prunella every child's delight.   10
What brought the kindred spider to that height?
(Make we no thesis of the miller's plight.)
What but design of darkness and of night?
Design, design! Do I use the word aright?

Compare "In White" with "Design." In what respects is the finished poem superior?

TOPICS FOR LONG PAPERS (1,500 WORDS OR MORE)

1. Write a line-by-line explication of a poem rich in matters to explain, or a longer poem that offers ample difficulty. While relatively short, Donne's "A Valediction: Forbidding Mourning" or Hopkins's "The Windhover" are poems that will take a good bit of time to explicate; but even a short, apparently simple poem such as Frost's "Stopping by Woods on a Snowy Evening" can provide more than enough to explicate thoughtfully in a longer paper.
2. Write an analysis of the work of one poet (as suggested above, in the third topic for more extensive papers) in which you go beyond this book to read an entire collection of that poet's work.
3. Write an analysis of a certain theme (or other element) that you find in the work of two or more poets. It is probable that in your conclusion you will want to set the poets' work side by side, comparing or contrasting it, and perhaps making some evaluation. Sample topics:

"Langston Hughes, Etheridge Knight, and Dudley Randall as Prophets of Social Change."

"What It Is to Be a Woman: The Special Knowledge of Sylvia Plath, Anne Sexton, Adrienne Rich, and Olga Broumas."

"Language of Science in Some Poems of Eberhart, Merrill, and Ammons"
4. Taking from Chapter 31 a passage of criticism, see what light it will cast on a poem that interests you. You might test Gray's "Elegy" by Poe's dictum that there is no such thing as a long poem. (Does the "Elegy" flag in intensity?) Or try reading several poems of Robert Frost, looking for the "sound of sense" (which Frost explains in his letter to John Bartlett).

Writing a Poem

HOW DOES A POEM BEGIN?

After you have read much poetry and (as Keats said) "traveled in the realms of gold," it is natural to want to write a poem. And why shouldn't you? Whether or not you aspire ever to publish your work, the attempt itself offers profound satisfactions; and it offers, too, a way to become a finer reader of poetry. To learn how to carry a football may not equip you to play for the Oilers, but it may help you appreciate the timing and skill of an Earl Campbell. In a roughly similar way, you may find yourself better able to perceive the artistry of an excellent sonnet from having written a sonnet of your own — even a merely acceptable one.

Poems, like new comets, tend to arrive mysteriously. Sometimes they go burning right past a serious, hard-working poet only to dawn, as though by accident, upon a madman, an idler, or a child. This may be why no one has ever devised a formula for synthesizing memorable poems. "A good poet," said Randall Jarrell, "is someone who manages, in a lifetime of standing out in thunderstorms, to be struck by lightning five or six times." In this view, poetic inspiration, like grace, is something beyond human control. Still, most of the best lightning bolts tend to strike those poets who keep waiting patiently, writing and rewriting and discarding, keeping their lightning rods lifted as they work. As Louis Pasteur said — speaking of scientists — "Chance favors the prepared mind."

Teachers of creative writing do not promise to create poets. All they can try to create is an atmosphere in which good poems may be written, given a hearing, and perhaps rendered stronger and more concise. As a member of a class or writing workshop, you have certain advantages. At least, you have companions in your struggles and chagrins. You may even find a sympathetic audience.

Even though the writing of poetry cannot be taught with great efficiency, some knowledge useful to poets can be imparted. What does a poet need to know? Half-jokingly, W. H. Auden once proposed a College for Bards with this curriculum:

1. In addition to English, at least one ancient language, probably Greek or Hebrew, and two modern languages would be required.

2. Thousands of lines of poetry in these languages would be learned by heart.

3. The library would contain no books of literary criticism, and the only critical exercise required of students would be the writing of parodies.

4. Courses in prosody, rhetoric, and comparative philology would be required of all students, and every student would have to select three courses out of courses in mathematics, natural history, geology, meteorology, archeology, mythology, liturgics, and cooking.

5. Every student would be required to look after a domestic animal and cultivate a garden plot.[1]

Auden, though he pokes fun at the notion of systematically training poets, makes constructive suggestions. He would have the aspiring poet study languages and something besides literature, and store up some poetry in memory. William Butler Yeats, too, thought that poets learn mainly by reading the work of other poets. There can be no "singing school" except the study of great poems — monuments, Yeats calls them, of the human soul's magnificence. (See "Sailing to Byzantium," page 660.)

Begin by reading. Don't limit yourself to poems assigned for college credit. Until you explore poetry more widely and roam around in it, how will you know what kind you most care to write? Pick up current poetry magazines, read your contemporaries. Browse in anthologies: recent paperbacks, surveys of older literature. Browse in bookshops. Lift some dust from library stacks. Read methodically or read by whim. Whatever poetry you come to love may nourish a poem you will write.

As you read, make your own personal, selective anthology. Don't let in a poem of Tennyson just because your instructor thinks it is great stuff, let it in only because you cherish it. Instead of just banging out Xerox copies of the poems you admire, you would do well to copy them by hand into a book with blank pages, or to type them on looseleaf notebook paper. By doing so, you'll pay close attention to them, and you'll grow accustomed to seeing excellent poetry (no matter whose) flow from your fingertips. If you would please the ghost of W. H. Auden, you'll say aloud the poems from your personal anthology until you can say them by heart. The suggestion that you memorize poetry may strike you as boring, but its benefits may be surprising. You just might transfer some poetry from your head down to your viscera and into your bones. Then, the music of words, especially their rhythms, will become part of you. Your own work may well prove richer for knowing poetry on a deeper level than that of the mind and eye.

It would save time, of course, not to read anything, but simply to look into your heart and write. And yet, because poetry is (among other things)

[1]"The Poet and the City" in *The Dyer's Hand* (New York: Random, 1962).

an art of choosing words and arranging them, the usual result of just looking into one's heart and writing is a lot of words hastily chosen and stodgily arranged. "But," the novice might protest, "why should I read Keats and Yeats and the Beats? I don't want to be influenced by all those old birds — I want to be myself!" Excellent poets, though they may be bundles of influences, are still themselves. In truth, when you are starting out, you can learn a great deal by deliberately imitating the work of any excellent poets you deeply love. Spenser studied Chaucer; Keats studied Spenser; Tennyson and Stevens studied Keats. (Auden said he began by imitating Thomas Hardy, because Hardy's work looked imitable.) If you borrow any mannerisms from your models, they will probably disappear as soon as you gain in confidence. Although the novice poet is sometimes urged, "Discover your own voice!" such advice can lead to a painful self-consciousness. Your own voice is probably the last thing to concern yourself about. Certainly it would be a mistake to settle on any one particular voice or style before you have practiced singing in many registers. Imitate whomever you choose, and see what you can do best. Try a Levertovian lyric or a Miltonic meditation. Let out a Whitmanic yawp. Express what you feel in the strongest words you can find, and your voice will take care of itself. It will be your own, in the end, though Donne or Emily Dickinson went into the training of it.

From your reading, you will probably notice that long-lasting poems — those that remain in print after a century or more — tend to express powerful feelings. "In poetry," as Ezra Pound observed, "only emotion endures." Certainly, to name only one instance, the ballad of "Edward" remains vital after hundreds of years, still brimming with sorrow and hate. Asked by a student, "What shall I write about?" Karl Shapiro replied, "Praise something — anything!" — and that is good advice. Although it is possible to write a memorable poem out of piddling, nugatory feelings (or a poem about being unable to feel anything, like Eliot's "The *Boston Evening Transcript*"), a poem written out of love, or loathing, is more likely to radiate energy. (One of John Donne's most energetic poems begins with the impassioned outburst, "For God's sake hold your tongue, and let me love.")

Very often, beginning to write a poem is a process of discovering, and opening, some deep resource of feeling. You have to search within yourself; no map can lead you to such a discovery. Whatever quickens your imagination is your resource. It may be a dream or a nightmare. It may be the memory of some moving experience. At times, your resource may lie in some unexpected place. You might want to write — as Whitman, Keats, and Elizabeth Bishop did — a deeply felt poem about a spider, a piece of ancient pottery, or a filling station.

This is not to say that you can mechanically cram your past life into your poetry-mill and grind it into poems. Although poems may rise from your experience, sometimes in becoming a poem the experience will "suffer a sea change / Into something rich and strange" (like the drowned man's bones in the song in Shakespeare's *Tempest*). You have to leave room for your imagination freely to operate, to transform the raw matter of experience however it will. You will probably limit and constrict your poetry if you regard it as a diary to be kept — as a complete and faithful transcript of what happens to you. Your imagination may yearn to improve upon the literal truth for the sake of the truth of art. Inevitably, a successful poem (even one that sticks to the facts) will be more than journalism. It will be, as Robert Frost memorably described it, "a performance in words."

If it takes feelings to write a memorable poem, yet in poetry the hardest thing to do is to talk about those feelings directly. Readers grow weary of poets who bleat, "Woe is me! I'm so lonely! How miserably sterile I feel!" But probably no reader has ever failed to sympathize with the poet who begins, "Western wind, when wilt thou blow, / The small rain down can rain?" Such a poem does not *discuss* the poet's feelings. It utters them, and it points to objects in the world that invite the reader to feel similarly. Notice that in a modern example, Philip Dow's "Drunk Last Night With Friends, I Go to Work Anyway" (page 620), the speaker omits any description of his inner condition. Instead of expounding on the horrors of a hangover, he reports what the boss said, and what he finds out in the weed patch. Rather than telling us what we should feel, the poet gives us occasion to feel a complex blend of helplessness, misery, and happiness.

Drink or drugs, by the way, seem of little aid to poets in search of inspiration. The trouble with trying to write while stoned (according to one contemporary) is that poetry may seem too far below you to be worth noticing. Coleridge's visionary "Kubla Khan," though possibly inspired by an opium dream, was written by daylight, after the poet for years had stored his mind with descriptions of exotic landscapes in accounts of travel and exploration. In this regard, the poet Robert Wallace has made an excellent suggestion: "Get high on what you write." Some poets try to prod the unconscious by natural means. Donald Hall has testified to the advantages of rising before dawn and writing poetry when thoughts seem fruitful, being close to dream. (However, some writers who try Hall's method find themselves staring sleepily at blank paper.)

Novice poets sometimes begin a poem in a language clouded not with dream, but with gaseous abstraction:

> Indifferent cosmos!
> O ye cryptic force!
> Don't you notice our pitiful human
> Agonies and sufferings?
> Are we mere tools of careless, crushing Fate?

Far better for a poet to open his eyes and begin with whatever small object he sees:

> I found a dimpled spider, fat and white,
> On a white heal-all, holding up a moth . . .

Unlike the novice's complaint about the indifference of the universe, Robert Frost's lines on a similar theme are many times more inviting — more striking, more definite.

Poetry, then, tends to inhere not in abstract editorial stands, but in particulars. William Carlos Williams's brief poem about eating the plums in the ice box (page 445) may not be great, but it is human, and hard to forget. Sources for poems may lurk in front of your eyes. The advice of W. Somerset Maugham to budding novelists may be useful to poets, too: Keep a notebook of any memorable details you observe, and any revealing bits of conversation you overhear. Jot them down for the sole purpose of gaining skill in noticing and recording them. Feel no duty to incorporate this material into anything you write. Perhaps none of it will ever be of any use to you.

All right, then, how is your poem to begin? Some poets begin with something to say, then strive for the best way of saying it. Others start with nothing much in mind. In the grip of strong but perhaps woolly and indefinite feelings, they play around with words until they discover to their surprise that they have said something. Evidently, a poem can arise from any adequate provocation. T. S. Eliot, speaking of the habits of poets in general, but probably referring to his own, said that at times a rhythm will begin to course through a poet's mind even before there are words to embody it. Some poets begin from a memorable image; Ezra Pound said he began writing "In a Station of the Metro" from being haunted by a glimpse of a woman's face. Following still another procedure, Dylan Thomas and many other poets have taken some promising line or phrase that swam to mind, and without knowing where it might lead, have trustingly gone on with it. Clearly, what matters isn't whether you begin with an idea or an emotion, a rhythm or an image, a phrase or a line. What matters is that, somehow, you begin.

Plunge in and blunder about. Why be afraid of a blank sheet of paper? You're writing only a first draft. No one is judging you. True poets, as they start to write a poem, don't worry whether a reader will find it admirable. They are too busy finding the words for an idea (or emotion, or rhythm) before it can get away. If you begin to write in a state of high excitement, by all means keep going until you simmer down. Let the words flow. Are some of them not the right ones? Have you misspelled something? No matter, you can make repairs later. Go on with your task and, whatever you do, don't stop to congratulate yourself on your splendid workmanship, or to contemplate the poetic process. The point may be expressed in this "Ars Poetica," or poem about how poetry is written:

> The goose that laid the golden egg
> Died looking up its crotch
> To find out how its sphincter worked.
> Would you lay well? Don't watch.

Later on, of course, you will want to examine your first draft critically; but for now, write as though you were divinely inspired and sustained. When you revise and try to amend your faults, you can view yourself as the lowest sinner. When you write a first draft, you are (with any luck) bringing something out of obscure depths, raising it to the surface. It may mean more than you consciously know. If you are going ahead blindly — that is, if you have begun to write without any burning idea in mind — let the poem choose its own direction. See where it wants to go. Be reluctant to bark orders to it.

A quite different method of composition, which some poets find fruitful, is to compose a poem entirely in the mind, revolving it around and around, saying it over to oneself and trying to perfect it before setting it down on paper. The result tends to have a certain seamless consistency. This method, though, will probably work only for poets who write short poems in rime and meter — devices that help to hold a poem in the mind — or for those with excellent memories.

In a first draft, it is usually a good idea to write everything out in great detail, even at the risk of driveling. If, when you revise, you discover that changes are necessary, it is generally easier to delete than to amplify. A common reason for failure — for the poem that nobody knows what to make of, or feels any positive reaction toward — is mistakenly to assume that the reader is as thoroughly grounded in the facts behind the poem as the poet is. Sometimes, however, a reader will fail to grasp a poem because some vital bit of knowledge still lies within the poet's mind, folded like a green bud. In your first draft, spell out the background of the poem. Define its setting, flesh out any people in it. Show us how they relate to one another, and why they behave the way they do. Perhaps you will only set down a lot of unnecessary explanation, but when you revise, you will then have all the matter arrayed before you, and you can easily see what to cut, or to retain.

Special challenges face anyone who writes a poem in meter and rime. Most students who attempt a traditionally formal poem, such as a ballad or a sonnet, quickly discover that to write skillfully in meter and rime is difficult. Thwarted by the requirements of strict form, they feel hindered from saying things. "This straitjacket isn't for me," they hastily conclude, adding that, anyhow, contemporary poets don't use such moldy-fig devices. It is true that most don't. Formally, poetry these days is wide open — or, some would say, the quest for form in poetry has moved away from meter and rime and has proceeded in other directions. Auden, although an oldfangled formalist himself, said he could understand why. Many poets, he believed, now distrust meter and rime because such forms imply repetition and discipline — "all that is most boring and lifeless in modern life: road drills, time-clock punching, bureaucratic regulations."[2]

[2]"The Virgin and the Dynamo," *The Dyer's Hand.*

There are still poets, however, for whom meter and rime do not denote lockstep routine, but rather, meaningful music. Continuing to work mainly in traditional form, Helen Adam, Anthony Hecht, Geoffrey Hill, Philip Larkin, W. D. Snodgrass, Richard Wilbur, and others are not merely affirming their loyalty to an outworn fashion. In their work, meter and rime help to impress a poem powerfully upon the reader's inner ear. As Stanley Kunitz, not arguing for a return to meter and rime but observing the current state of poetry, has shrewdly remarked, the flight from these traditional elements "has made poetry easier to write, but harder to remember."

Writing a poem in rime is like walking blindfolded down a dark road with your hand in the hand of an inexorable guide. With the conscious, lighted portion of your mind, you may want to express some idea. But a line that ends in *year* must be followed by another ending in *atmosphere, beer, bier, bombardier, cashier, deer, friction-gear, frontier,* or some other word that probably would not have occurred if the rime scheme had not suggested it. As Rolfe Humphries once pointed out, rime sometimes "makes you think of better things than you would all by yourself." Far from being a coldly rational process of filling a form with wordage, to write a riming poem is to pit yourself against (or to enter into a playful relationship with) some of the wildest and most chaotic forces of the unconscious.

Learn to write a decent poem in rimed stanzas, and you will have at your fingertips certain skills useful in writing poems of any kind. You will know, for instance, how to condense a thought to its gist, from having wrestled with metrical lines that allow you only so many syllables. In revising and finishing your poem, you will become an old hand at replacing stumbling words and phrases with rhythmic ones, at choosing words for their sounds as well as their senses. But this won't be easy. Although the iambic rhythm is native to English, learning to speak in it with ease and grace is almost like learning a foreign language. Alexander Pope's observation remains accurate:

True ease in writing comes from art, not chance,
As those move easiest who have learned to dance.

With practice, the day will come when a rime or a metrical line will spring to your lips almost thoughtlessly. And then, even if you decide to write poetry in *open* forms, you will do so from choice, not from inability to do otherwise. At the moment, it is commonly assumed that open form is intrinsically superior to closed form in poetry; but in truth, the form of an excellent poem, whether open or closed, is whatever the poem requires. The poet's task is to discover it.

Whatever your formal preference, it is probably a mistake to try to plan out the direction of your poetic career, and then grimly oblige yourself to go in it. Better to write a hundred poems and place them in a row, and see where they have taken you. Your life will shape what you write, and the words you write in. Richard Hugo, speaking hyperbolically, has argued that the study of poetry writing fulfills a unique function: "Creative writing is the last class you can go where your life as an individual is important."[3] Professors of mathematics, natural history, and geology might well argue that individual lives matter in their disciplines, too; but Hugo is surely right in at least one regard. Writing a poem calls for a kind of knowledge that only a poet can provide.

By the way, if a poem doesn't come to you all in one sitting, don't despair. Forget about it for a while. It may need more time to gather its forces. Many poets carefully save their fragments: lines and passages that arrive easily, but which do not immediately want to go anywhere. In dry seasons, when inspiration is scarce, they can look back over their notebooks, and sometimes a fragment will spring to life at last, and grow into an entire poem. Try this and see if you have any luck with it. For many, being a poet is like being a beggar: like standing with outstretched bowl by the side of a road, hoping for charity. Thankful poets keep whatever a passing Muse may throw, whether it is a Brasher doubloon or only a bent bottlecap.

ON BLOTTING OUT LINES

Your first draft is done, and the excitement of writing it has cooled. Your next step is to take a step back from it.

A hard but necessary part of being a poet is to try to see your work through a reader's eyes. How to reread it with detachment? The advice of the Roman poet Horace — to put aside a poem for nine years — may seem too discouraging. At least, you can put your poem aside for a week, or even overnight. You may then take a more nearly objective look at it. To help distance yourself from it, try reading it aloud — at least to yourself. Friends may be asked for their criticism, but it is a rare friend who is also a competent critic of poetry. Probably it is best to try to cultivate your own faculties for tough and demanding self-criticism.

Told that his friend Shakespeare in writing his plays never blotted out a line, Ben Jonson wished he had blotted a thousand. (Scholars, by the way, think that even Shakespeare blotted many lines.[4]) Although there is a school of thought that holds for total spontaneity in writing, and for leaving words just the way they land on a page, most poets probably feel that second thoughts, too, can be spontaneous, and often more memorable. If you regard your first draft as holy writ, and refuse to make any changes in it, you may be preserving a work of genius, but more probably you will be passing up your chance to write a good poem. Poets usually don't mind

---

[3]Quoted by Harriet Heyman, "Eleven American Poets," *Life* (Apr. 1981), 89.
[4]In Shakespeare's plays, at least a few passages exist in what seem to be both earlier and revised versions, thanks to the printer who, apparently by mistake, included both. A celebrated instance of such a passage occurs in *Romeo and Juliet* II, ii, 187 – 190.

revision; in fact, they find the task fascinating. "What happiness!" exclaimed Yeats, in a letter to a friend, on facing months of demanding rewriting. (It was Yeats, incidentally, who pointed out that, no less than the original act of writing a poem, the act of revision may be inspired.) A contemporary poet, James Dickey, says he writes a poem over and over in many ways. "After I've tried every possible way I can think of," he explains, "I finally get maybe not absolutely the right poem, but the poem that is less wrong than the others."[5]

Is there not a danger that much revision will drain the life out of a poem — or cause it to become ornate and needlessly complicated? Perhaps; but more often, the poem that seems beautifully simple, as if casually dropped from the lips, is the result of hard work; while the poem that the poet didn't retouch makes difficult reading. As you can tell from the two versions Yeats made of his "Old Pensioner," the one written a half-century later, far from lacking in life, seems the more youthful and spontaneous. (For these and other illustrations of poets' revisions, see pages 635 – 639.)

Working on your second draft, you have the leisure to look up spellings and to verify information. For the poet who is struck for a rime, a riming dictionary will suggest some likely — and some outlandish — possibilities. When in such a fix, you will probably do better to proceed down the alphabet (air, bear, bare, care, dare . . .) and discover a rime among common words you know already. Rimes will strike your reader as reached-for and strange if you enlist them from far beyond your vocabulary.

Some poets make a typewritten first draft, then revise in longhand. When additions, deletions, and substitutions accumulate and the page becomes too crosshatched to decipher, they type a fresh version (keeping the old version just in case they botch the revision and want to go back to the original and start over). Some poets — Richard Wilbur is one — prefer to keep working on a single poem till it is done; others simultaneously revise many poems, going around and making fresh moves like a chess master playing all comers.

In your first draft, when you were trying to include everything essential, you could allow yourself a multitude of words. But in revising and striving for concision, you have to select what is essential and decide what to leave out. Ask yourself whether every line — every word — deserves the room it occupies. Does it *do* anything? To decide, imagine your poem without the word or line. Begin your inspection with your opening lines. Are they valuable, or do they only delay the reader's entry into something more essential? What if, instead, the poem began with some line that now comes later? Opening lines, of course, don't have to be sensational, but there is much to be said for a beginning that stops the reader in his tracks and hangs on to him:

[5] *Self-Interviews,* edited by Barbara and James Reiss (New York: Doubleday, 1970) 64.

You do not do, you do not do
Any more, black shoe
In which I have lived like a foot . . .

(To quote Sylvia Plath's brilliant opening to "Daddy.") Samuel Johnson, that down-to-earth critic, insisted that a writer's first duty is to excite the reader of his work "to *read it through,*" and to that purpose, it helps to be interesting. Don't be afraid to be obvious. Go ahead and say, if necessary, "I started Early – Took my Dog – /And visited the Sea," or whatever will begin a story, or clearly set forth a situation. Excellent poems may be clear and yet be profound — like bodies of water.

Here are some other questions to ask yourself while you revise:

1. Does this poem express what I feel? Does it claim to feel more than I do — that is, is it sentimental? Or does it hang back, afraid to declare itself? (If it does, see if you can persuade the feelings out into the open.) The advice of W. D. Snodgrass is worth remembering:

> Our only hope as artists is to continually ask ourselves, "Am I writing what I *really* think? Not what is acceptable; not what my favorite intellectual would think in this situation; not what I wish I felt. Only what I cannot help thinking."[6]

2. Somewhere in its first half-dozen lines, does the poem offer the reader any temptation to go on reading? If so, something will have been begun: perhaps a story, dramatic situation, metaphor, or intriguing perplexity. To recognize it, you will need to put yourself into the reader's seat. One veteran teacher of poetry-writing, John Ciardi, placed great weight on engaging a reader early. Ciardi sometimes penciled a line underneath the line in the poem at which, out of boredom or disgust, he quit reading.

3. Is there anything in my poem that doesn't make sense to me? *(Careful! Such a difficulty may not be a fault!)* Does the difficulty come in stating something I feel to be valuable, or is it just an unsuccessful attempt to say something unimportant or needlessly explanatory? If it is the latter, away with it.

Here is some further advice, from Ezra Pound:

> Use no superfluous word, no adjective which does not reveal something.
>
> Don't use such an expression as 'dim lands *of peace.*' It dulls the image. It mixes an abstraction with the concrete. It comes from the writer's not realizing that the natural object is always the *adequate* symbol.
>
> Go in fear of abstractions. Do not retell in mediocre verse what has already been done in good prose. Don't think any intelligent person is going to be deceived when you try to shirk all the difficulties of the unspeakably difficult art of good prose by chopping your composition into line lengths. . . .

[6]"Finding a Poem," *In Radical Pursuit* (New York: Harper, 1974) 32.

Don't be 'viewy' — leave that to the writers of pretty little philosophic essays. Don't be descriptive; remember that the painter can describe a landscape much better than you can, and that he has to know a deal more about it.

When Shakespeare talks of the 'Dawn in russet mantle clad' he presents something which the painter does not present. There is in this line of his nothing that one can call description; he presents. . . .

If you are using a symmetrical form, don't put in what you want to say and then fill up the remaining vacuums with slush.[7]

In Pound's view, a poet ought to pay attention to vivid detail, and usually that is good advice. But like all general advice to poets, it is not to be followed absolutely. Some details may point us nowhere. They distract us from what matters, and they will need to be cut. Philip Dow probably wouldn't have improved "Drunk Last Night with Friends, I go to Work Anyway," by naming the brand of beer the speaker preferred, nor by describing the picture on its label.

Evidently, the details to render vividly are the ones that mean the most. Unless you agree with Edgar Allan Poe that a short intense poem is the only true poem (see page 828), revision isn't a matter of polishing an entire poem to a level of high intensity. Long poems, said T. S. Eliot in "The Music of Poetry," naturally contain prosaic passages as well as intensely "poetic" ones. See the advice of Yeats (page 637) on the need for deliberately putting in a bit of dullness now and again.

Of all the skills a poet has, one of the most valuable is to know where to end lines. If your poem happens to be written in meter and rime, where to end lines is clearly suggested for you: lines end on riming words, or they end when their metrical expectation has been fulfilled. (An iambic pentameter line stops on its tenth syllable, give or take a syllable or two.) But in "free verse" or formally open poetry, you do not have any guidance other than your mind and eye and ear. To place your line breaks effectively calls for much care during revision, and at all times, a certain sensibility. Because the ending of a line compels your readers to make a slight pause — at least a moment for their eyes to relocate at the beginning of the next line — the placement of these pauses is a great resource to you. If most of your lines end on strong words (such as verbs and nouns), the effect is different from that of slicing your lines after weak words (such as articles — a, the — or prepositions). To see this truth for yourself, study the ways in which lines end in William Carlos Williams's "The Dance" (page 588).

Early in life, William Carlos Williams decided that it seemed pretentious to begin each line with a capital. Such avoidance of convention is neither right nor wrong, and your choice depends on the effect you are

[7]Excerpts from "A Retrospect," *Literary Essays of Ezra Pound,* ed. T. S. Eliot (New York: New Directions, 1954) 4 – 6.

after. Any evident attempt to defy convention calls attention to itself. Say "i think, therefore i am," and you aren't necessarily being modest. The effect is as though you were to print the letter *I* in red. E. E. Cummings, who favored the small letter *i*, was, according to many who knew him, an egotist.

When should you declare your poem done? Never, according to the French poet Paul Valéry, who said that a poem is never finished, only abandoned in despair. Other poets feel a definite sense of completion — as did Yeats, to whom a poem came shut with a click. But if you hear no such click, just stop when you see no more verbiage to prune, no more weak words to tighten.

If by now a title for your poem hasn't occurred to you, you may want to consider one. Some poets, to be sure, dispense with any title — as was the usual practice of Cummings and Emily Dickinson. To a reader, however, a title may be a help. If a poem is difficult, its title can show the reader how to take hold of it. An explicit title can supply needed background, tell us who is speaking, or explain a dramatic situation. By calling his poem "Soliloquy of the Spanish Cloister," Robert Browning indicates that we listen in on the thoughts of a single character, a monk in a religious order. Even a flatly indicative title ("Stopping by a Market in Pismo Beach to Buy Wine for a Wedding Present") may be more helpful to a reader than a merely decorative title ("Subterfuge with Sea-green Raisins").

REACHING AN AUDIENCE

Few contemporary poets seem to follow the custom of Emily Dickinson and store their poems in the family attic. Most poets want to share their work with the world, and some, as soon as they have written a first poem, rush to send it to a magazine. Hopes of instant acclaim, of course, often meet with disappointment. "Don't imagine," Ezra Pound warned, "that you can please the expert before you have spent at least as much effort on the art of verse as the average piano teacher spends on the art of music." Nevertheless, if you master your art, it is reasonable to expect that sooner or later people will listen to it.

In a writing class, you already have an audience: your fellow students, your instructor. Still, some beginning poets feel reluctant to display their work even to friendly eyes. They have an uncomfortable sense, at first, that they are being asked to parade their inmost emotions in public, while at the same time they risk being ridiculed for their weak artistry. That is why a writing class needs to agree that the poems its members share are to be regarded as works of the imagination, not as personal diaries. As for the risk of ridicule, nobody expects the beginner to be T. S. Eliot. Probably you will find your fellow students reading your poems as considerately and sympathetically as (they trust) you'll read theirs. As for your instructor, don't worry. He or she has seen worse poems.

If you *enjoy* reading your poems aloud, live audiences may be yours for the asking. Does your campus have a coffeehouse or other room in which to hold readings? Audience responses, while sometimes misleading, can encourage you. Be aware, however, that audiences like to laugh together, and often prefer funny, outrageous, immediately understandable poems to more difficult, subtle ones that require more than one hearing. If any of your fellow student poets are interested, it may be even more valuable to form a small group for mutual criticism and support.

Some novice poets crave early publication, and some who hurry into print are later sorry. Should the day arrive, however, when, tired of staring at a tall stack of beautiful finished poems, you just have to break into print, why not begin near home? Submit poems to your campus literary magazine, if there is any. If there isn't, can you see about starting one? Another alternative is to bring out your own magazine of limited circulation, with the aid of a mimeograph or a copier. Eventually, you may decide that your work belongs in magazines of wider readership — but first, make sure it is ready. Unlike your fellow students and your instructor, who know you personally and are likely to sympathize with your creative labors, the editor of a national magazine, to whom you are only a licked stamp, cares for nothing but what you can show on cold white paper. A writing class may deal patiently with a faulted poem, taking time to rummage it for meaning, but the glance of an overworked editor will be more cursory. A bungled opening, a cliché, a line of bombast or sentiment, and back goes the manuscript with a rejection slip. Not that this threat should discourage you. Just realize that, in trying to print your poems, you'll be venturing forth into a crowded marketplace.

At the moment, American poetry seems in the throes of an inflation: Karl Shapiro, somewhat grimly, has called it a "poetry glut." For a number of reasons (including, no doubt, the popularity of creative writing programs), thousands of people today are trying to throng into print. Perhaps, in a world of social-security numbers sorted out into zip-code areas, they feel nameless, and so hope to make a lasting name — however small — by writing poetry. Whatever the explanation, in the latest *Directory of American Poets and Fiction Writers,* 4,341 published poets are listed — an incomplete listing at that.[8] Although the ranks of poets are thick, recent years have seen a dwindling in the number of paying markets for a poem. Few magazines currently sold on newsstands regularly print poetry: *The Atlantic, The New Yorker* — the list expires.

Still, poets need not consign their work to their attics. Lately, in noncommercial publishing, there has been a tremendous explosion of en-

[8] 1985 – 86 edition (New York: Poets & Writers, 1985).

ergy. As the latest *International Directory of Little Magazines and Small Presses* will indicate,[9] literary publishers now number in the thousands. **Little magazines,** periodicals edited and published as labors of love, exist not to turn a profit but to turn up new writing. A few such magazines, thick and printed handsomely, appear on more or less regular schedules. The majority, less expensively produced, usually lag behind their declared frequencies. Most little magazines, if well established, reach an audience of perhaps 500 to 5,000.[10]

Read a magazine before sending it your work; if need be, write off (and pay) for a sample copy. There is no sense in offering, say, a pastoral elegy in heroic couplets to the radically experimental *Hanging Loose,* or a pornographic punk rock song to *The American Scholar.* Decent respect for editors requires that along with your poems you enclose a stamped, self-addressed envelope; send original copies, not carbons or Xeroxes; and submit a poem to one magazine at a time.

Delmore Schwartz once made a brilliant observation: a poet is wise to write as much and to publish as little as possible. With so many non-commercial publishers, it is a safe bet that any halfway competent poet who persists in licking stamps will break into print sooner or later. Yet the difficulty for poets today is not merely to be printed, but to be read. Ours seems a time of more good voices than good listeners. It is, besides, an age of disagreement and diversity. Ask any published poets what they think of poetry, and they will probably tell you that most poetry now being printed, other than their own, is bad or mediocre. But ask any six poets (selected at random) which other poets among their contemporaries they admire, and you will receive six lists of names with little duplication. To add to the confusion about what is excellent (or, some might say, to add to the merriment), most literary critics, as if discouraged by the vastness of the task of keeping up with contemporary poetry, have folded their practices. (To be sure, a very few brave and overworked critics of contemporary poetry are still operating.) Some poets feel that, since criticism isn't a help to them anyhow, who needs it? Still, without critics, who used to be poets' most devoted readers, it is more difficult for excellence to be recognized. Two truths seem evident. It is hard for a new poet today to gain an audience and a reputation. And yet, in the last few years, despite all odds, several excellent new poets have succeeded in doing so.

If you are a dedicated poet, and your work truly deserves your

[9]Edited by Len Fulton and Ellen Ferber, and published annually by Dustbooks, Box 100, Paradise, CA 95969. It may be in the reference department of your library.

[10]Among the heftier and more faithfully appearing little magazines are *Antaeus, Grand Street, Hudson Review, Paris Review, Ploughshares,* and *Threepenny Review;* also those reviews subsidized by universities (*Georgia Review, Indiana Review, Massachusetts Review, Tri-Quarterly, Sewanee Review,* and others). *Poetry,* which printed the early poems of Eliot, Frost, Marianne Moore, and Stevens, still issues monthly from Chicago, as essential as ever. The influential *American Poetry Review,* a bimonthly in tabloid newspaper format, claims the largest circulation of any little magazine: according to one report, more than 20,000.

dedication, you'll keep faith that you will eventually find your audience. You'll listen to the voice of your Muse, not to the siren warblings of the marketplace. (In John Ciardi's view, it is hardly possible to prostitute your talent for poetry, anyway, there being so few paying customers.) You will become a severer critic of your own work than your fellow students or your instructor. Although when you send out your poems to the handsome magazines you'll have to elbow through a crowd, you can be sure that, among contenders for immortality, there can no more be any rivalry than there is among gold prospectors. That is, when poets strike paydirt and achieve renown, it is usually because they have stalwart backs, eyes for a gleam, and likely claims, not because they know someone at the assay office.

Apparently, poets are not paid in bullion. In fact, nowhere in the English-speaking world at the moment is the writing of poems a full-time paying occupation. Most poets survive by other honest trades (such as teaching), receiving nothing or almost nothing for their poems, making a spare dollar from an occasional reading. Still, most derive ample compensation. No one has better summed up the payment of being a poet than John Keats, in a letter to a friend: "I should write for the mere yearning and fondness I have for the beautiful, even if my night's labors should be burnt every morning and no eye shine upon them." For any poet so intently dedicated, writing a poem is today — as it always has been — its own considerable, immediate reward.

SUGGESTIONS FOR WRITING

Doing finger exercises is generally less fruitful to a poet than trying to write poems. Here are a few suggestions that might result in poems, if they arouse any responses in you.

1. Try to recall, and recapture in a poem, some experience that deeply moved you. The experience does not have to be anything world-shaking or traumatic; it might be as small as a memory from early childhood, a chance meeting with someone, a visit to a beach, the realization that some ordinary object is beautiful.

2. Try writing a poem in a voice *remote* from your own — speaking, say, as a character in history or fiction or film; an ordinary citizen in a different place or time; a child; an octogenarian. (For one famous illustration of a poet's speaking through a mask or persona, see Robert Browning's "Soliloquy of the Spanish Cloister," page 698. Presumably Browning set himself a problem: What would a hate-filled, envious monk think and mutter about a devout brother? Then, having imagined such a character, the poet found the character some artful and appropriate words.)

3. Attempt a poem in which you convey the joy of performing some simple, familiar, routine act: running, driving a car, peeling an orange, stroking a cat, changing a baby — or whatever you like to do.

4. Here is an experiment suggested by Ezra Pound: Write words to a well-known tune "in such a way that the words will not be distorted when one sings them."

5. Find, in a current magazine, a poem that strikes you as silly, pretentious, or simple-minded. Write a take-off on it.

6. Taking the same weak poem, try to revise it, freely cutting it or adding to it. See if you can make of it something worth reading.
7. The aim of the following experiment is to lead you to wrestle with arbitrary difficulties. Observe some limitation that may seem to you pointless, but which might set up a certain tension within your poem — provide a bottle (to echo Richard Wilbur) for your genie to try to burst out of. For instance, write a poem entirely in simple declarative subject-plus-verb sentences. Write a poem that is all one metaphor (like, for example, Emily Dickinson's "Because I could not stop for Death" or Whitman's "A Noiseless Patient Spider." Write a poem in blank verse (the form of Tennyson's "Ulysses"). Or, as Theodore Roethke was fond of asking his students to do, write a poem without adjectives.
8. Write a poem in praise of someone you admire, allowing yourself no general terms (*beautiful, wonderful,* etc.); try to describe the person in language so specific that a reader, too, will find your subject admirable.
9. Write a curse in verse: a damnation of someone or something you can't abide.
10. From an opening line (or lines) supplied by your instructor, try to develop a poem. Then compare the result with poems developed by others from the same beginning.
11. In verse (whether rimed or open), write a letter to a friend. For neoclassical examples, see the works of Swift and Pope (the latter's "Epistle to Dr. Arbuthnot" and other epistles in particular); for less formal contemporary examples, see Richard Hugo's collection *31 Letters and 13 Dreams* (New York: Norton, 1977) — mostly verse-letters to fellow poets.
12. Write a poem in the form of a dialogue between two people. (Christina Rossetti's "Uphill" may help illustrate such an exchange of speeches.)
13. Intently observe something for twenty or thirty minutes, then write a poem full of images through which your reader, too, can apprehend it. An excellent object for scrutiny would be any small living thing that will stand still long enough: an animal, bird, tropical fish, insect, or plant.
14. In a bookstore or library, select a book of poems that appeal to you. Take it home and read it thoroughly. If you have chosen well, the book may quicken your feelings and encourage you, too, to devote yourself to words. See if you can write a poem suggested or inspired by it — not necessarily an imitation.

Writing about a Play

METHODS

How is writing about a play any different from writing about a short story or a poem? Differences will quickly appear if you are writing about a play you have actually seen performed. Although, like a story or a poem, a play in print is usually the work of one person (and it is relatively fixed and changeless), a play on stage may be the joint effort of seventy or eighty people — actors, director, costumers, set designers, and technicians — and in its many details it may change from season to season, or even from night to night. Later on in this chapter, you will find some advice on reviewing a performance of a play, as you might do for a class assignment or for publication in, say, a campus newspaper. But in a literature course, for the most part, you will probably write about the plays you quietly read, and behold only in the theater of your mind. At least one advantage in writing about a printed play is that you can always go back and reread it, unlike the reviewer who, unless provided with a script, has nothing but memory to rely on.

Before you begin to write, it makes sense to read the *whole* play — not just the dialogue, but also everything in italics: descriptions of scenes, instructions to the actors, and other stage directions. This point may seem obvious, but the meaning of a scene, or even of an entire play, may depend on the tone of voice in which an actor is supposed to deliver a line. At the end of *A Doll House,* we need to pay attention to what Ibsen tells the actor playing Helmer — *"A sudden hope leaps in him"* — if we are to understand that, when Nora departs, she ignores Helmer's last desperate hope for a reconciliation, and she slams the door emphatically. And of course there is a resounding meaning in the final stage direction, in "the sound of a door slamming shut."

Taking notes on passages you will want to quote or refer to in your paper, you can use a concise method for keeping track of them. Jot down the numbers of act, scene, and line — for instance: I, ii, 42. Later, when you write, this handy shorthand will save space, and you can use it both in footnotes and in the body of your essay. Even if you do without footnotes, you can still indicate the exact lines you are quoting, or referring to:

Iago's hypocrisy, apparent in his famous defense of his good name

(III, iii, 157–161), is aptly summed up by Roderigo, who accuses

him: "Your words and performances are no kin together" (IV, ii,

180–181).

Any of the methods frequently applied in writing about fiction and poetry — explication, analysis, comparison and contrast — can serve in writing about a play. All three methods are discussed in "Writing about a Story," and again in "Writing about a Poem." (For student papers that illustrate explication, see pages 1349 and 1373; analysis, pages 1353 and 1378; comparison and contrast, pages 1358 and 1381.) For using these methods to write about plays in particular, here are a few suggestions.

A whole play is too much to cover in an ordinary **explication** — a detailed, line-by-line unfolding of meaning. An explication of *Othello* could take years; a more reasonable class assignment would be to explicate a single key speech or passage from a play: Iago's description of a "deserving woman" (*Othello,* II, i, 145 – 57); or the first song of the chorus in *Oedipus Rex.*

If you decide to write an essay by the method of **comparison and contrast** (two methods, actually, but they usually work together), you might set two plays side by side and point out their similarities and differences. Again, watch out: do not bite off more than you can chew. A profound topic — "The Self-deceptions of Othello and Oedipus" — might do for a three-hundred-page dissertation, but an essay of a mere thousand words could treat it only sketchily. Probably the dual methods of comparison and contrast are most useful for a long term paper on a large but finite topic: "Attitudes Toward Marriage in *A Doll House* and *Trifles,*" "Sinister Humor in *Death Knocks* and *The Zoo Story.*" In a shorter paper, you might confine your comparing and contrasting to the same play: "Willy's Illusions and Biff's in *Death of a Salesman.*"

For writing about drama, **analysis** (a separation into elements) is an especially useful method. You can consider just one element in a play, and so your topic tends to be humanly manageable — "Animal Imagery in Some Speeches from *Othello,*" or "The Theme of Fragility in *The Glass Menagerie.*" Not all plays, however, contain every element you might find in fiction and poetry. Unlike a short story or a novel, a play does not ordinarily have a narrator. In most plays, the point of view is that of the audience, who see the events not through some narrator's eyes, but through their own. [1] And though it is usual for a short story to be written in an all-pervading style, some plays seem written in as many styles as there are speaking characters. (But you might well argue that in the Fitts and Fitzgerald version of *Oedipus Rex*, a consistently elevated style informs all the speeches, or that in Susan Glaspell's *Trifles* both main characters speak the same language.) Rime schemes and metrical patterns, elements familiar in traditional poetry, are seldom found in contemporary plays, which tend to sound like ordinary conversation. To be sure, some plays *are* written in poetic forms: the blank verse of the greater portion of *Othello, The Tempest*, and *Purgatory*. (If, by the way, you wish any advice to heed in quoting passages from a play in blank verse or in rime, see "How To Quote a Poem," on page 1384.) Despite whatever some plays may lack, most plays have more than enough elements for analysis, including characters, themes, tone, irony, imagery, figures of speech, symbols, myths, and conventions.

Ready to begin writing an analysis of a play, you might think at first that one element — the plot — ought to be particularly easy to detach from the rest, and write about. But beware. In a good play (as in a good novel or short story), plot and character and theme are likely to be one, not perfectly simple to tell apart. Besides, if in your essay you were to summarize the events in the play, and then stop, you wouldn't tell your readers much that they couldn't observe for themselves just by reading the play, or by seeing it. In a meaningful, informative analysis, the writer does not merely isolate an element, but also shows how it functions within its play and why it is necessary to the whole.

WRITING A CARD REPORT

Instead of an essay, some instructors like to assign a **card report.** If asked to write a card report on a play, you will find yourself writing a kind of analysis. To do so, you first single out elements of a play, then you list them on 5 × 8-inch index cards as concisely as possible. Such an exercise is often assigned in a class studying fiction; and one student's card report on the Edgar Allan Poe story, "The Tell-Tale Heart," appears on page 38. When you deal with a play, however, you will need to include some elements different from those in a short story. And because a full-length play may take more room to summarize than a short story, your instructor may suggest that, if necessary, you take two cards (four sides) for your

---

[1]Point of view in drama is a study in itself; this mere mention grossly simplifies the matter. Some playwrights attempt to govern what the spectator sees, trying to make the stage become the mind of a character. An obvious example is the classic German film *The Cabinet of Dr. Caligari,* in which the scenery is distorted as though perceived by a lunatic. Some plays contain characters who act as narrators, directly addressing the audience in much the way that first-person narrators in fiction often address the reader. In Tennessee Williams's *The Glass Menagerie,* Tom Wingfield behaves like such a narrator, introducing scenes, commenting on the action. So does the psychiatrist Martin Dysart in Peter Shaffer's *Equus* (1974). But such a character in a play does not alter our angle of vision, our physical point of view.

report. Still, in order to write a good card report, you have to be both brief and specific. Before you start, sort out your impressions of the play, and try to decide which characters, scenes, and lines of dialogue are the most important and memorable. Reducing your scattered impressions to essentials, you will have to reexamine what you have read; and when you get done, you will know the play much more thoroughly. It is not easy to write readable comments within so small a space; and you may find such a report taking as much thought and effort as any analysis you have ever written in essay form.

Here is an example: a card report on Susan Glaspell's one-act play, *Trifles*. (For the play itself, see page 839.) By including only the elements that seemed most important, the writer managed to analyze the brief play on the front and back of one card. Still, he managed to work in a few pertinent quotations to give a sense of the play's remarkable language, and to make a few observations of his own. Although the report does not say everything about Glaspell's little masterpiece, an adequate criticism of the play could hardly be much briefer. For this report, the writer was assigned to include:

1. The playwright's name, nationality, and dates.
2. The title of the play and the date of its first performance.

Front of Card

```
(Student's name)                    (Course and section)

Susan Glaspell, American, 1882-1948        Trifles, 1916

    Central characters: Mrs. Peters, the sheriff's nervous wife,
dutiful but capable of independent thought, not "married to the law" --
whose past sorrows make her able to sympathize with a woman accused of
murder. Mrs. Hale, native of the region, who personally knows the
accused; a more decisive person.
    Other characters: The County Attorney, self-important but short-
sighted young male supremacist. The Sheriff, a man of only middling
intelligence, another sexist pig. Hale, a farmer, a cautious man.
Not seen on stage but much discussed, two others are central to the
story: Minnie Foster (Wright), the accused, a once-happy music lover
reduced to near despair by years of grim marriage and isolation; and
John Wright, the victim, who had a reputation for hard, tightfisted
cruelty.
    Scene: The kitchen of a gloomy farmhouse in Nebraska after the
arrest of a wife on suspicion of murder; little things left in disarray.
    Major dramatic question: Why did Minnie Wright kill her husband?
When this question is answered, a new major dramatic question is raised:
Will Mrs. Peters and Mrs. Hale cover up incriminating evidence?
    Events: In the exposition, Sheriff and C.A., investigating the
death of Wright, hear Hale tell how he found the body and a distracted
Mrs. Wright. Then (1) C.A. starts looking for a motive. (2) His
jeering at Mrs. Wright (and all women) for their concern with "trifles,"
his criticizing Mrs. Wright's housekeeping, cause Mrs. Peters and Mrs.
Hale to rally to the woman's defense. [continued on back of card]
```

3. The central character or characters, with a brief description that includes leading traits.

4. Other characters, also described.

5. The scene or scenes and, if the play does not take place in the present, the time of its action.

6. The dramatic question. This question is whatever the play leads us to ask ourselves: some conflict whose outcome we wonder about, some uncertainty to the resolution of which we look forward. (For a more detailed discussion of dramatic questions, see page 852.)

7. A brief summary of the play's principal events, in the order in which the playwright presents them. If you are reporting on a play longer than *Trifles,* you may find it simplest to take each act, perhaps each scene, and sum up what happens in it.

8. The tone of the play, as best you can detect it. Try to describe the playwright's apparent feelings toward the characters or what happens to them.

9. The language spoken in the play: try to describe it. Does any character speak with a choice of words or with figures of speech that strike you as unusual, distinctive, poetic — or maybe dull and drab? Does language indicate a character's background or place of birth? Brief quotations, in what space you have, will be valuable.

Back of Card

```
[Events, continued]     (3) When the two women find evidence that Mrs.
Wright had a moment of panic (a patch of wild sewing in an otherwise
calm quilt), Mrs. Hale destroys it.  (4) Mrs. Peters finds more evi-
dence: a wrecked birdcage.  (5) The women find a canary with its neck
wrung and realize that Minnie killed her husband in a similar way.
(6) The women more firmly align themselves with Minnie when Mrs.
Peters recalls her own sorrows, and Mrs. Hale decides her own failure
to visit Minnie was "a crime."  (7) The C.A. unwittingly provides Mrs.
Peters with a means to smuggle out the canary.  (8) The two women
unite to seize the evidence.
    Tone:  Made clear in the women's dialogue:  mingled horror and
sadness at what has happened, compassion for a fellow woman, smoldering
resentment toward men who crush women.
    Language:  The plain speech of farm people, with a dash of rural
Midwestern slang (red-up for tidy; Hale's remark that the accused woman
was "kind of done up").  Unschooled speech:  Mrs. Hale says ain't --
and yet her speech rises at moments to simple poetry:  "She used to
sing.  He killed that too."  Glaspell hints the self-importance of the
County Attorney by his heavy reliance on the first person ("I think I'd
rather . . .", his prefacing statements with "I guess . . .").
    Central theme:  Women, in their supposed concern for trifles, see
more deeply than men do.
    Symbols:  The broken birdcage and the dead canary, both suggesting
the music and the joy that John Wright stifled in Minnie and the
terrible quiet that his deed left.
    Evaluation:  A powerful, successful realistic play that conveys
its theme with great economy.  As feminist literature, it seems still
fresh; in the points it makes, more than seventy years ahead of its time.
```

10. In a sentence, try to sum up the play's central theme. If you find none, say so. But plays often contain more themes than one — which of them seems most clearly borne out by the main events?

11. Any symbols you notice, and believe to matter. Try to state in a few words what each suggests.

12. A concise evaluation of the play: what did you think of it? (For more suggestions on being a drama critic, see Chapter Thirty-six, "Evaluating a Play.")

REVIEWING A PLAY

Writing a **play review,** a brief critical account of an actual performance, involves making an evaluation. To do so, you first have to decide what to evaluate: the work of the playwright; the work of the actors, director, and production staff; or the work of both. If the play is some classic of Shakespeare or Ibsen, evidently the more urgent task for a reviewer is not to evaluate the playwright's work, but to evaluate the success of the actors, director, and production staff in interpreting it. To be sure, a reviewer's personal feelings toward a play (even a towering classic) may deserve mention. Writing of an Ibsen masterpiece, the critic H. L. Mencken made a memorable comment remarking that, next to being struck down by a taxicab and having his hat smashed, he could think of no worse punishment than going to another production of *Rosmersholm.* But a newer, less well-known play is probably more in need of evaluation.

To judge a live performance is, in many ways, more of a challenge than to judge a play read in a book. Obviously there is much to consider besides the playwright's script: acting, direction, costumes, sets, lighting, perhaps music, anything else that contributes to one's total experience in the theater. Still, many students find that to write a play review is more stimulating — and even more fun — than most writing assignments. And although the student with experience in acting or in stagecraft may be a more knowing reviewer than the student without such experience, the latter may prove just as capable in responding to a play and in judging it fairly and perceptively.

In the chapter "Evaluating a Play," we assumed that in order to judge a play one has to understand it, and be aware of its conventions. (For a list of things to consider in judging a play, whether staged or printed, see pages 1169 – 1170.) Some plays will evoke a strong positive or negative response in the reviewer, either at once or by the time the final curtain tumbles; others will need to be pondered. Incidentally, harsh evaluations sometimes tempt a reviewer to flashes of wit. One celebrated flash is Eugene Field's observation of an actor in a production of *Hamlet,* that "he played the king as though he were in constant fear that somebody else was going to play the ace." The comment isn't merely nasty; it implies that Field had closely watched the actor's performance and had discerned what was wrong with it. Readers, of course, have a right to expect that reviewers do not just sneer (or gush praise), but clearly set forth reasons for their feelings.

Reviewing plays seems an art with few fixed rules, but in general, an adequate play review usually gives us a small summary of the play — for the reader unacquainted with it — and perhaps also indicates what the play is about: its theme. If the play is familiar and often performed, some comment on the director's whole approach to it may be useful. Is the production exactly what you'd expect, or are there any fresh and apparently original innovations? And if the production is fresh, does it achieve its freshness by violating the play? (The director of one college production of *Othello* — a fresh, but not entirely successful, innovation — emphasized the play's being partly set in Venice by staging it in the campus swimming pool, with actors floating about on barges and a homemade gondola.) Does the play seem firmly directed, so that the actors neither lag nor hurry, and so that they speak and gesture not in an awkward, stylized manner, but naturally? Are they well cast? Usually, also, a reviewer pays attention to the performances of the leading actors, or principals; and to the costumes, sets, and lighting, if these are noteworthy. The theater itself may deserve mention. Is it distractingly uncomfortable? For this play, is it strikingly suitable or unsuitable? (*Othello* afloat might seem awkward and artificial. We may be so nervous about the gondola tipping over that we can't pay attention to the lines.) And if, all along, the reviewer has not been making clear an opinion of the play and its production, an opinion will probably come in the concluding paragraph.

For further pointers, read a few professional play reviews in magazines such as *The New Yorker, Time, Newsweek, The New Criterion, Hudson Review,* and others; or on the entertainment pages of a metropolitan newspaper. Here is a good, concise review of an amateur production of *Trifles* as it might be written for a college newspaper, but similar to what your instructor might ask you to write for a course assignment.

<u>Trifles</u> Scores Mixed Success
in Monday Players' Production

Women have come a long way since 1916. At least, that impression was

conveyed yesterday when the Monday Players presented Susan Glaspell's

classic play <u>Trifles</u> in Alpaugh Theater.
     one-act

At first, in Glaspell's taut story of two subjugated farm women who

figure out why a fellow farm woman strangled her husband, Lloyd Fox and

Cal Federicci get to strut around. As a small-town sheriff and a county attorney, they lord it over the womenfolk, making sexist-pig remarks about women in general. Fox and Boyd obviously enjoy themselves as the pompous types that Glaspell means them to be.

But of course it is the women with their keen eyes for small details who prove the superior detectives. In the demanding roles of the two Nebraska Miss Marples, Kathy Betts and Ruth Fine cope as best they can with what is asked of them. Fine is especially convincing. As Mrs. Hale, a friend of the wife accused of the murder, she projects a growing sense of independence. Visibly smarting under the verbal lashes of the menfolk, she seems to straighten her spine inch by inch as the play goes on.

Unluckily for Betts, director Alvin Klein seems determined to view Mrs. Peters as a comedian. Though Glaspell's stage directions call the woman "nervous," I doubt she is supposed to be quite so fidgety as Betts makes her. Betts vibrates like a tuning fork every time a new clue turns up, and when obliged to smell a dead canary bird (another clue), you would think she was whiffing a dead hippopotamus. Mrs. Peters, whose sad past includes a lost baby and a kitten some maniac chopped up with a hatchet, is no figure of fun to my mind. Played for laughs, her character fails to grow visibly on stage, as Fine makes Mrs. Hale grow.

Klein, be it said in his favor, makes the quiet action proceed at a brisk pace. Feminists in the audience must have been a little embarrassed, though, by his having Betts and Fine deliver every speech defending women in an extra-loud voice. After all, Glaspell makes her points clear enough just by showing us what she shows. Not everything is overstated, however. As a farmer who found the murder victim, Cal Valdez acts his part with quiet authority.

Despite flaws in its direction, this powerful play still spell-binds an audience. Anna Winterbright's set, seen last week as a background for <u>Dracula</u> and just slightly touched up, provides appro-priate gloom.

Suggestions for Writing

Finding a topic you care to write about is, of course, your most important step toward writing a valuable paper. (For some general advice on topic-finding, see pages 1335-1337.) The following list of suggestions is not meant to replace your own ideas but to stimulate them.

Topics for Brief Papers (250 – 500 words)

1. When the curtain comes down on the conclusion of some plays, the audience is left to decide exactly what finally happened. In a short informal essay, state your interpretation of the conclusion of one of these plays: *The Tempest, A Doll House, The Zoo Story, The Glass Menagerie.* Don't just give a plot summary; tell what you think the conclusion means.

2. Sum up the main suggestions you find in one of these meaningful objects (or actions): the handkerchief in *Othello*; the Christmas tree in *A Doll House* (or Nora's doing a wild tarantella); the park bench in *The Zoo Story*; Laura's collection of figurines in *The Glass Menagerie*.

3. Here is an exercise in being terse. Write a card report on a short, one-scene play (other than *Trifles*) and confine your remarks to both sides of one 5 × 8-inch card. (For further instructions see page 1409.) A possible subject: Woody Allen's *Death Knocks*.

4. Review a play you have seen within recent memory and have felt strongly about (or against). Give your opinion of *either* the performance or the playwright's writing, with reasons for your evaluation.

5. Write an essay entitled, "Why I Prefer Plays to Films" (or vice versa). Cite some plays and films to support your argument. (If you have never seen any professional plays, pick some other topic.)

Topics for More Extended Papers (600 – 1,000 words)

1. From a play you have enjoyed, choose a passage that strikes you as difficult, worth reading closely. Try to pick a passage not longer than about 200 words, or twenty lines. Explicate it, working through it sentence by sentence or line by line. For instance, any of these passages might be considered memorable (and essential to their plays):

   Oedipus to Teiresias, speech beginning, "Wealth, power, craft or statesmanship!" (*Oedipus Rex*, Scene I, 163 – 186).

   Iago's soliloquy, "Thus do I ever make my fool my purse" (*Othello*, I, iii, 356 – 377).

   Jerry's passage beginning "It's just…it's just that…it's just that if you can't deal with people, you have to make a start somewhere. WITH ANIMALS!" (*The Zoo Story*, paragraph near the end of Jerry's dog story monologue).

   Tom Wingfield's opening speech, "Yes, I have tricks in my pocket," through "I think the rest of the play will explain itself. . . ." (*The Glass Menagerie*, Scene I).

2. Take just a single line or sentence from a play — one that stands out for some reason as greatly important. Perhaps it states a theme, reveals a character, or serves as a crisis (or turning point). Write an essay demonstrating its importance: how it functions, why it is necessary. Some possible lines:

   Iago to Roderigo: "I am not what I am" (*Othello*, I, i, 62).

   Amanda to Tom: "You live in a dream; you manufacture illusions!" (*The Glass Menagerie*, VII).

Charley to Biff: "A salesman is got to dream, boy. It comes with the territory" (*Death of a Salesman,* the closing Requiem).

3. Write an essay in analysis, in which you single out an element of a play for examination — character, plot, setting, theme, dramatic irony, tone, language, symbolism, conventions, or any other element. Try to relate this element to the play as a whole. Sample topics: "The Function of Teiresias in *Oedipus Rex*," "Imagery of Poison in *Othello* (or *A Doll House*)," "The Character of Caliban in *The Tempest*," "Molière's Use of Slapstick in *The Physician in Spite of Himself*," "The Setting of *Purgatory*," "Irony in *Antigonê*," "Williams's Use of Magic-Lantern Slides in *The Glass Menagerie*," "The Theme of Success in *Death of a Salesman*."

4. Compare a character, situation, or theme in a play with a similar element in a short story. For instance: women's role in society as seen in *Trifles* and in Tillie Olsen's "I Stand Here Ironing"; pretending to be what one isn't in *The Physician in Spite of Himself* and in James Thurber's "The Catbird Seat"; supernatural power in *The Tempest* and in Nathaniel Hawthorne's "The Birthmark"; the character of Death in *Death Knocks* and in the Grimm folk tale "Godfather Death."

5. Imagine a completely different ending for a play you have read, one that especially interests you. Briefly summarize the new resolution you have in mind. Then, looking back over the play's earlier scenes, tell what would happen to the rest of the play if it were to acquire this new ending. What else would need to be changed? What, if anything, does this exercise reveal?

6. In an essay, consider how you would go about staging a play of Shakespeare, Molière, or some other classic, in modern dress, with sets representing the world of today. What problems would you face? Can such an attempt ever succeed?

TOPICS FOR LONG PAPERS (1,500 WORDS OR MORE)

1. Choosing any of the three works in Chapter Thirty-seven, "Plays for Further Reading," or taking some other modern or contemporary play your instructor suggests, report any difficulties you encountered in reading and responding to it. Explicate any troublesome passages for the benefit of other readers.

2. Compare and contrast two plays — a play in this book and another play by the same author — with attention to one element. For instance: "The Theme of Woman's Independence in Ibsen's *A Doll House* and *Hedda Gabler*"; "Antirealism in the Stagecraft of Tennessee Williams: *The Glass Menagerie* and *Camino Real*"; or "Christian Symbols and Allusions in Williams's *Menagerie* and *Night of the Iguana*."

3. Compare and contrast in *The Glass Menagerie* and *Death of a Salesman* the elements of dream-life and fantasy.

4. For at least a month, keep a journal of your experience in watching drama on stage, movie screen, or television. Make use of any skills you have learned from your reading and study of plays, and try to demonstrate how you have become a more critical and perceptive member of the viewing audience.

5. If you have ever acted or taken part in staging plays, consult with your instructor and see whether you both find that your experience could enable you to write a substantial paper. With the aid of specific recollections, perhaps, you might sum up what you have learned about the nature of drama or about what makes a play effective.

6. Watch a film version of a play, then read the original as produced on stage. What differences do you find, and how do you account for them? You might, for instance, compare the film *Amadeus* with Peter Shaffer's stage play of the same name.

Writing a Play

"Playwriting," declares one novice playwright, "is a cinch. You have a bunch of actors standing or sitting around, and all you have to do is give them lines." Yet there is more to the writing of a play than that, if we are to believe some of our leading playwrights' testimony.

Unless a play is a closet drama, to be read but not performed, it is both a literary work and — when it comes alive in a theater — a team effort involving actors, director, producer, and many other specialists. For this reason, it is no accident that some of the finest playwrights have themselves been actors: Shakespeare, Molière, Harold Pinter. Writing a play calls for a sense of what will "go" on stage: what will keep an audience intently listening and watching. This sort of knowledge isn't acquired only from reading in a library. To write a good play, it may help to read masterpieces; but it is also essential to see plays performed, and if possible, to take part in them. Edward Albee, although not an actor himself, has remarked: "I've read and seen hundreds of plays, starting with Sophocles right up to the present day. As a playwright I imagine that in one fashion or another I've been influenced by every single play I've ever experienced."[1]

The effective playwright writes with a glowing stage in mind, not merely setting down words but visualizing their end result. What particular arrangement of people on stage, what physical objects or properties, what sets and costumes, what "stage business" (or visible activity that interests the spectator) will help make the play watchable? In *The Glass Menagerie*, an audience finds it fascinating to behold Laura arranging her collection of glass figurines with loving care, as the light glitters on them. Playwrights who make good use of the stage often lead us to focus upon something: even if (as in *The Zoo Story*) it is an object as ordinary as a park bench. The drama critic George Jean Nathan remarked, somewhat sarcastically, that he had never seen an American play fail if its set featured the headlight of a train that slowly moved across the rear of the stage, or if its set contained a large crystal chandelier. Why is it, he wondered, that

---

[1]Interview with William Flanagan, *The Paris Review* 39 (Fall 1966) 106.

"no actor, however incompetent, who has put a putty mole on his cheek and adorned himself with a seedy frock coat and stovepipe hat has failed completely in impressing the critics that he was a pretty good Lincoln?"[2] The answer may be that, at the very least, the audience is given something to watch — will Honest Abe's putty mole fall off?

Such matters may seem trivial, but a play, to be effective on the boards, has to engage not only our minds and our emotions, but also our senses. Of course, the mere entrance of an actor can interest an audience tremendously — as does, in *The Glass Menagerie,* the long-awaited arrival of Jim, the gentleman caller. In all dramatic literature, it would be hard to find a more entertaining departure from a stage than that of Shakespeare's Antigonus in *A Winter's Tale:* "Exit, pursued by a bear."

How does the composition of a play begin? The playwright first needs a dramatic situation to present and some characters for whom an audience will care. Personal history may supply inspiration, as it seems to have done in *The Glass Menagerie,* a play apparently full of memories drawn from the playwright's early life. Although the painfully shy Laura is not an exact portrait of his sister Rose (Laura "was like Miss Rose only in her inescapable 'difference,' " Williams has written), the name of Rose suggests Laura's nickname "Blue Roses." A young woman with "lovely, heartbreaking eyes," Rose felt acute anxiety in male company. She was pressed by her mother to make a painful social début at the Knoxville Country Club. For a time she was courted by a junior executive, an ambitious young man who soon suspended his attentions. After the break-up, Rose suffered from mysterious illnesses, showed symptoms of withdrawal, and eventually was committed to the Missouri State Asylum. (Williams tells her story in his *Memoirs.*[3]) Like Tom Wingfield, apparently Williams as a young man was a restless dreamer and aspiring writer who left home to wander the country.

Not all plays, of course, begin in autobiography. As a playwright Shakespeare, a refurbisher of old plays and tales and a cribber from history, seems more interested in others' lives than in his own. In fact, he seldom invented his own stories. Only two of his thirty-six plays *(The Tempest* and *Love's Labor's Lost)* are based on plots that, as far as we know, he originated. Edward Albee urges novice playwrights in search of inspiration to read plays by other people: "Know what everyone has written. But don't always read masterpieces, read some failures too. If anything, it's encouraging."[4]

Some playwrights carefully plan their plots before they write; others are more willing to let their characters hand them a surprise. Recalling a

[2]"Marginalia," *The World of George Jean Nathan,* ed. Charles Angoff (New York: Knopf, 1952) 470.
[3](New York: Doubleday, 1975) 116 – 28.
[4]Talk to students at Johns Hopkins University quoted by Dick Carpenter, "Names and Faces," *Boston Globe* 13 Apr. 1983.

time when he and Elliott Nugent were collaborating on a comedy, *The Male Animal,* James Thurber recalled that Nugent was a believer in thorough plotting, who searched for the most effective possible moment at which to ring down the curtain on an act.

> Nugent would say, "Well, Thurber, we've got our problem, we've got all these people in the living room. Now what are we going to do with them?" I'd say that I didn't know and couldn't tell him until I'd sat down at the typewriter and found out.[5]

For Albee, writing a play is a matter of finishing it in the unconscious mind, then sitting down to write and finding out what it is. Spending from six months to a year and a half in reflecting on what to write, Albee begins setting words on paper only when he "more or less" knows what is going to happen (although not exactly how the characters will move from one situation to another).

> I write a first draft quite rapidly. Read it over. Make a few pencil corrections, where I think I've got the rhythms wrong in the speeches, for example, and then retype the whole thing. And in the retyping I discover that maybe one or two more speeches will come in. One or two more things will happen, but not much. Usually what I put down first is what we go into rehearsal with.[6]

Whether a believer in strict, thorough advance plotting or in letting a play take shape in the typewriter, a playwright cannot tell an actor *everything* to do on stage. Plays that stay alive for centuries provide roles that actors enjoy taking. A great character leaves an actor room for interpretation: how to play Hamlet or Othello is a challenge that fine actors welcome. An incompetent playwright, according to Frank O'Connor, will "pull an actor because he'll tell him what to do, but a really good playwright will give you a part that you can do what you like with."[7] A good playwright, too, has an ear for dialogue that sounds human. Harold Pinter, the English playwright whose characters usually speak the most ordinary, unpoetic sort of speech, says that as he writes each line he reads it aloud to himself. Silences, and their placement, are equally important. In French, a famous play by Jean-Jacques Bernard, *Martine,* centers on a simple peasant girl who loses the great love of her life — and her one chance for happiness. Because she is inarticulate, she falls silent at moments when it is clear to the audience that her emotions are intense.

Once a play is finished, the playwright stands to learn from seeing it performed. Broadway plays, when they go into rehearsal, often involve the playwright who watches, prepared to change, add, or delete passages

---

[5]Interview with George Plimpton and Max Steele, *Writers at Work:* The Paris Review *Interviews* (New York: Viking 1959) 87.
[6]Flanagan, 116.
[7]Interview with Anthony Whittier, *Writers at Work* 169.

that do not seem to work when actually staged. Even if the performance of a play is just a reading of the script by a playwright's friends or by fellow students in a class, the novice playwright will find the experience valuable. Do certain lines give the actors unnecessary difficulty? Does the stage seem cluttered with people who have nothing to do but stand around? These are the sorts of discoveries that sometimes only a production will afford. Besides, the prime pleasure in writing a play may be to see it brought to life.

Suggestions for Writing

1. In collaboration with another student (or others), write a one-act play from five to ten minutes in playing time, for two or three actors. Cast it, rehearse it, revise it if necessary, and then perform it in front of your class.
2. Write a scene (or perhaps just a page-long passage) that might be inserted without violence into one of the plays in this book. A play with a relatively free and episodic structure (such as *The Zoo Story*) might better admit such an addition than a tightly constructed one (such as *A Doll House*). As best you can, imitate the playwright's language and stage directions. Keep the characters consistent with their natures in the rest of the play. Then read aloud to the class that portion containing your addition (together with some of the original text), and see if anyone can detect where the playwright's words stop and yours begin.
3. Transform a short story you admire into a script for a play in one act. Include a description of sets, lighting, and costumes; stage directions; and advice for the actors wherever necessary. Some likely stories to consider are "Godfather Death," "A & P," "First Confession," "The Tell-Tale Heart," "Everyday Use," "Roman Fever," and "The Portable Phonograph."

Acknowledgments (continued)

James Joyce. "Araby" from *Dubliners* by James Joyce. Originally published by B. W. Huebsch, Inc. in 1916. Definitive text Copyright © 1967 by the Estate of James Joyce. Reprinted by permission of Viking Penguin Inc. Excerpt from *Stephen Hero* reprinted by permission of The Society of Authors as the literary representative of the Estate of James Joyce, Jonathan Cape Ltd., and the Executors of the James Joyce Estate.

Franz Kafka. "A Hunger Artist." Reprinted by permission of Schocken Books Inc. from *The Penal Colony* by Franz Kafka, translated by Willa and Edwin Muir. Copyright © 1948, 1975 by Schocken Books Inc.

D. H. Lawrence. "The Rocking-Horse Winner" from *The Complete Short Stories of D. H. Lawrence*, Volume Three. Copyright 1933 by the Estate of D. H. Lawrence. Copyright renewed 1961 by Angelo Ravagli and C. M. Weekley, as Executors of the Estate of Frieda Lawrence Ravagli. Copyright © 1974 The Estate of Frieda Lawrence Ravagli. Reprinted by permission of Viking Penguin Inc., Laurence Pollinger Ltd., and the Estate of Frieda Lawrence Ravagli.

Ursula K. LeGuin. "The Wife's Story" from *The Compass Rose: Short Stories by Ursula K. LeGuin*. Copyright © 1982 by Ursula LeGuin. Reprinted by permission of Harper & Row, Publishers, Inc.

Doris Lessing. "A Woman on a Roof" from *A Man and Two Women* by Doris Lessing. Copyright © 1958, 1962, 1963 by Doris Lessing. Reprinted by permission of Simon & Schuster, Inc., and Jonathan Clowes, Ltd., London, on behalf of Doris Lessing.

Katherine Mansfield. "The Garden-Party." Copyright 1922 by Alfred A. Knopf, Inc. and renewed 1950 by John Middleton Murry. Reprinted from *The Short Stories of Katherine Mansfield*, by permission of the publisher.

Gabriel García Márquez. "The Night of the Curlews" from *Innocent Erendira and Other Stories by Gabriel Garcia Márquez*, translated by Gregory Rabassa. English translation copyright © 1978 by Harper and Row, Publishers, Inc. Reprinted by permission of Harper & Row, Publishers, Inc.

W. Somerset Maugham. "Appointment in Samarra" from *Sheppey* by W. Somerset Maugham. Copyright 1933 by W. Somerset Maugham. Reprinted by permission of Doubleday Company and A. P. Watt on behalf of The Executors of the Estate of Somerset Maugham.

Alice Munro. "Wild Swans" from *The Beggar Maid* and *Who Do You Think You Are?* Copyright © 1977, 1978 by Alice Munro. Reprinted by permission of Alfred A. Knopf, Inc. and Macmillan of Canada, a division of Canada Publishing Corporation.

Joyce Carol Oates. "Where Are You Going? Where Have You Been?" Reprinted from *The Wheel of Love* by Joyce Carol Oates by permission of the publisher, The Vanguard Press, Inc. Copyright © 1970, 1969, 1968, 1967, 1965 by The Vanguard Press Inc.

Flann O'Brien (pseud., Brian O'Nolan). "Two in One" from *A Flann O'Brien Reader*, edited by Stephen Jones (New York: The Viking Press, 1978, pp. 321–326). First printed in the *Journal of Irish Literature*. Copyright 1978 by the Estate of Flann O'Brien and copyright 1978 by Viking Penguin, Inc. Reprinted by permission of Brandt & Brandt Literary Agency.

Flannery O'Connor. "Revelation" from *Everything That Rises Must Converge* by Flannery O'Connor. Copyright © 1964, 1965 by the Estate of Mary Flannery O'Connor. Reprinted with the permission of Farrar, Straus & Giroux, Inc.

Frank O'Connor. "First Confession." Copyright 1951 by Frank O'Connor. Reprinted from *Collected Stories*, by Frank O'Connor, by permission of Alfred A. Knopf, Inc. and Joan Daves. Excerpt from interview with Frank O'Connor from *Writers at Work: The Paris Review Interviews*, First Series. Edited by Malcolm Cowley. Copyright © 1957, 1958 by The Paris Review, Inc. Reprinted by permission of Viking Penguin, Inc.

Tillie Olsen. "I Stand Here Ironing" excerpted from the book *Tell Me a Riddle* by Tillie Olsen. Copyright © 1956 by Tillie Olsen. Reprinted by permission of Delacorte Press/Seymour Lawrence.

Katharine Anne Porter. "The Jilting of Granny Weatherall." Copyright 1930, 1958 by Katherine Anne Porter. Reprinted from her volume *Flowering Judas and Other Stories* by permission of Harcourt Brace Jovanovich, Inc.

Philip Roth. "Conversion of the Jews" from *Goodbye, Columbus* by Philip Roth. Copyright © 1959 by Philip Roth. Reprinted by permission of Houghton Mifflin Company.

Isaac Bashevis Singer. "Gimpel the Fool" by Isaac Bashevis Singer, translated by Saul Bellow from *A Treasury of Yiddish Stories*, edited by Irving Howe and Eliezer Greenberg. Copyright 1953, renewed © 1981 by Isaac Bashevis Singer. Reprinted by permission of Viking Penguin Inc.

John Steinbeck. "The Chrysanthemums" from *The Long Valley* by John Steinbeck. Copyright 1937, © 1965 by John Steinbeck. Reprinted by permission of Viking Penguin Inc.

Nagai Tatsuo. "Brief Encounter," translated by Edward Seidensticker. From *Japan Quarterly* VII, 2 (1960). Copyright © 1960 by Nagai Tatsuo. Reprinted by permission of Nagai Tatsuo, Edward Seidensticker and *Japan Quarterly*.

James Thurber. "The Catbird Seat." Copyright © 1945 James Thurber. Copyright © 1973 Helen W. Thurber and Rosemary T. Sauers. From *The Thurber Carnival*, published by Harper & Row. Reprinted by permission.

Leo Tolstoy. "The Death of Ivan Ilych" from *The Death of Ivan Ilych and Other Stories* by Leo Tolstoy translated by Louise and Aylmer Maude. Reprinted by permission of Oxford University Press.

John Updike. "A & P." Copyright © 1962 by John Updike. Reprinted from *Pigeon Feathers and Other Stories*, by John Updike, by permission of Alfred A. Knopf, Inc. Originally appeared in *The New Yorker*.

Alice Walker. "Everyday Use" from *In Love & Trouble*, copyright © 1973 by Alice Walker. Reprinted by permission of Harcourt Brace Jovanovich, Inc.

Eudora Welty. "A Worn Path" from *A Curtain of Green and Other Stories*, copyright © 1941, 1969 by Eudora Welty. Reprinted by permission of Harcourt Brace Jovanovich, Inc.

Edith Wharton. "Roman Fever," (Copyright 1934 Liberty Magazine; copyright renewed 1962 William R. Tyler) in *Roman Fever and Other Stories*. Copyright © 1964 Charles Scribner's Sons. Reprinted with the permission of Charles Scribner's Sons. Excerpt from "Telling a Short Story," in *The Writing of Fiction*. Copyright 1925 by Charles Scribner's Sons, copyright renewed 1953 Frederick R. King. Reprinted with the permission of Charles Scribner's Sons.

E. B. White. "The Door" from *Poems and Sketches of E. B. White*. Copyright 1939, 1967 by E. B. White. Reprinted by permission of Harper and Row, Publishers, Inc.

Virginia Woolf. Excerpt from "Modern Fiction" from *The Common Reader*, First Series by Virginia Woolf. Copyright 1925 by Harcourt Brace Jovanovich, Inc., renewed 1953 by Leonard Woolf. Reprinted by permission of Harcourt Brace Jovanovich, Inc., the Author's Estate and The Hogarth Press. Virginia Woolf, "A Haunted House" from *A Haunted House and Other Stories* by Virginia Woolf. Copyright 1944, 1972 by Harcourt Brace Jovanovich, Inc. Reprinted by permission of Harcourt Brace Jovanovich, Inc., the Author's Estate and The Hogarth Press.

POETRY

The paintings by Pieter Breughel on page 588 (*The Kermess*, collection of Kunsthistoriches Museum, Vienna) and page 679 (*Landscape with Fall of Icarus*, collection of Museum der Schöne Kunste, Brussels) are reproduced courtesy of Marburg Art Reference Bureau.

A. R. Ammons. "Spring Coming" from *Collected Poems 1951–1971* by A. R. Ammons. Reprinted with permission of W. W. Norton & Company, Inc. Copyright © 1972 by A. R. Ammons.

Anonymous. Lines from "Carnation Milk is the best in the land . . ." quoted in *Confessions of an Advertising Man* by David Ogilvy. Copyright © 1963 by David Ogilvy. Reprinted with the permission of Atheneum Publishers.

John Ashbery. "City Afternoon" from *Self Portrait in a Convex Mirror*, by John Ashbery, Copyright © 1972, 1973, 1974, 1975 by John Ashbery. Originally published in *The New Yorker*. "The Cathedral Is" from *As We Know*, by John Ashbery. Copyright © 1979 by John Ashbery. Reprinted by permission of Viking Penguin Inc.

Margaret Atwood. "You fit into me" from *Selected Poems* by Margaret Atwood. Copyright © 1976 by Margaret Atwood. Reprinted by permission of Simon & Schuster, Inc. and the author.

W. H. Auden. "As I Walked Out One Evening," "Musée des Beaux Arts," and "The Unknown Citizen." Copyright 1940 and renewed 1968 by W. H. Auden. Reprinted from *W. H. Auden: Collected Poems*, by W. H. Auden, edited by Edward Mendelson, by permission of Random House, Inc., and Faber and Faber Ltd. "James Watt" from *Academic Graffiti*, by W. H. Auden. Copyright © 1960 by W. H. Auden. Reprinted by permission of Random House, Inc. and Faber and Faber Ltd.

David B. Axelrod. "Once in a While a Protest Poem" from *A Dream of Feet* by David B. Axelrod. Reprinted by permission of the poet and Cross Cultural Communications.

R. L. Barth. "The Insert" from *Forced-Marching to the Styx: Vietnam War Poems* by R. L. Barth (1983). Reprinted by permission of Perivale Press.

Max Beerbohm. "On the imprint of the first English edition of *The Works of Max Beerbohm*" from *Max in Verse*. Reprinted by permission of Sir Geoffrey Keynes.

Hilaire Belloc. "The Hippopotamus" from *Cautionary Verses* by Hilaire Belloc. Published 1940 by Gerald Duckworth & Co. Ltd., 1941 by Alfred A. Knopf, Inc. Reprinted by permission of the publishers.

Bruce Bennett. "Leader," © 1984 by Bruce Bennett. Used by permission.

Edmund Clerihew Bentley. "Sir Christopher Wren" from *Clerihews Complete* by E. C. Bentley. Reprinted by permission of Curtis Brown, London.

John Betjeman. "In Westminster Abbey" from *Collected Poems* by John Betjeman (Houghton Mifflin Company, 1959). Reprinted by permission of John Murray Publishers Ltd.

Elizabeth Bishop. "The Fish," "Filling Station," "Sestina," and lines from "Little Exercise" from *The Complete Poems* by Elizabeth Bishop. Copyright 1940, 1946, 1949, 1952, 1953, © 1955, 1956, 1959, 1960, 1961, 1962, 1964, 1965 by Elizabeth Bishop. Reprinted by permission of Farrar, Straus & Giroux, Inc.

Robert Bly. "Driving to Town Late to Mail a Letter" from *Silence in the Snowy Field* by Robert Bly (Wesleyan University Press, 1962) and "Inward Conversation." Reprinted by permission of the poet.

Louise Bogan. "The Dream" from *The Blue Estuaries* by Louise Bogan. Copyright 1938, © 1968 by Louise Bogan. Reprinted by permission of Farrar, Straus & Giroux, Inc.

David Bottoms. "Smoking in an Open Grave" from *Shooting Rats at the Bibb County Dump* by David Bottoms. Copyright © 1980 by David Bottoms. Reprinted by permission of William Morrow & Company.

Richard Brautigan. "Haiku Ambulance," excerpted from the book *The Pill Versus the Springhill Mine Disaster* by Richard Brautigan. Copyright © 1968 by Richard Brautigan. Reprinted by permission of Delacorte Press/Seymour Lawrence.

John Malcolm Brinnin. "The Ascension: 1925" excerpted from the book *Skin Diving in the Virgins and Other Poems* by John Malcolm Brinnin. Copyright © 1943, 1944, 1949, 1950, 1951, 1952, 1953, 1956, 1958, 1960, 1962, 1963, 1970 by John Malcolm Brinnin. Reprinted by permission of Delacorte Press/Seymour Lawrence.

Van K. Brock. Quotation of three lines from "Driving at Dawn" from *The Hard Essential Landscape* by Van K. Brock (University Presses of Florida, 1979). Copyright © 1979 by Van K. Brock. Reprinted by permission.

Gwendolyn Brooks. "We Real Cool. The Pool Players. Seven at the Golden Shovel." Copyright © 1959 by Gwendolyn Brooks. "The Rites for Cousin Vit." Copyright 1949 by Gwendolyn Brooks Blakely. "Sadie and Maud." Copyright 1944, renewed 1972 by Gwendolyn Brooks Blakely. From *The World of Gwendolyn Brooks*. Reprinted by permission of Harper and Row, Publishers, Inc.

Olga Broumas. "Cinderella" from *Beginning With O* by Olga Broumas, Vol. 72 of the Yale Series of Younger Poets. Copyright © 1977 by Olga Broumas. Reprinted by permission of Yale University Press.

Christopher Bursk. "First Aid at 4 A.M." from *Place of Residence* by Christopher Bursk, copyright 1983 by Christopher Bursk, Sparrow Poverty Pamphlet, Sparrow Press. Reprinted by permission.

Taniguchi Buson. "The Sudden Chilliness" from *An Introduction to Haiku* by Harold G. Henderson. Copyright © 1958 by Harold G. Henderson. Reprinted by permission of Doubleday & Company, Inc.

Roy Campbell. "On Some South African Novelists" from *Adamastor* by Roy Campbell. Reprinted by permission of Francisco Campbell Custodio and Ad. Donker (Pty) Ltd.

Bliss Carman. Quotation of two lines from "A Vagabond Song" from *Bliss Carman's Poems*. Reprinted by permission of Dodd, Mead & Company and McClelland & Stewart Ltd.

Fred Chappell. "Skin Flick." Reprinted by permission of Louisiana State University Press from *The World Between the Eyes* by Fred Chappell, copyright 1971.

Geoffrey Chaucer. Lines from Part I. "Merciles Beaute" from *The Works of Geoffrey Chaucer*, Second Edition, edited by F. N. Robinson (1957). Reprinted by permission of Houghton Mifflin Company.

G. K. Chesterton. "The Donkey" from *The Wild Knight and Other Poems* by G. K. Chesterton. Reprinted by permission of J. M. Dent & Sons Ltd.

Amy Clampitt. "The Cormorant in His Element" from *The Kingfisher: Poems by Amy Clampitt*. Copyright © 1983 by Amy Clampitt. Reprinted by permission of Alfred A. Knopf, Inc.

Louise Clifton. "to the unborn and waiting children" reprinted by permission from *Two-Headed Woman*, by Lucille Clifton (Amherst: University of Massachusetts Press, 1980). Copyright © 1980 by the University of Massachusetts Press.

Leonard Cohen. "All There Is to Know about Adolph Eichmann" from *Selected Poems 1956–1968* by Leonard Cohen. Copyright © 1964 by Leonard Cohen. Reprinted by permission of Viking Penguin Inc.

Cid Corman. "The Tortoise" from *Words for Each Other* by Cid Corman. First appeared in *In Good Time*. Reprinted by permission of André Deutsch Ltd. Translation of the haiku by Issa from *One Man's Moon: Fifth Haiku* used with permission of Gnomon Press and the author.

Frances Cornford. "The Watch" from *Collected Poems* by Frances Cornford (Cresset Press). Reprinted by permission of Barrie & Jenkins Ltd.

Hart Crane. "My Grandmother's Love Letters" is reprinted from *The Complete Poems and Selected Letters and Prose of Hart Crane*, edited by Brom Weber, with the permission of Liveright Publishing Corporation. Copyright 1933, © 1958, 1966 by Liveright Publishing Corporation.

Robert Crawford. "My Iambic Pentameter Lines." Copyright © 1986 by Robert J. Crawford. Used by permission of the poet.

Robert Creeley. "Oh No" and "The Lover" from Robert Creeley, *For Love: Poems 1950–1960*. Copyright © 1962 by Robert Creeley (New York: Charles Scribner's Sons, 1962). Reprinted with the permission of Charles Scribner's Sons.

Countee Cullen. "For a Lady I Know" from *On These I Stand* by Countee Cullen. Copyright 1925 by Harper & Row, Publishers, Inc., renewed 1953 by Ida M. Cullen. Reprinted by permission of Harper & Row, Publishers, Inc.

E. E. Cummings. "anyone lived in a pretty how town" from "anyone lived . . . ." (copyright 1940 by E. E. Cummings, renewed 1968 by Marion Morehouse Cummings) and "a politician is an arse upon" (copyright 1944 by E. E. Cummings, renewed 1972 by Nancy T. Andrews). Reprinted from *Complete Poems 1913–1962* by E. E. Cummings by permission of Harcourt Brace Jovanovich, Inc. "Buffalo Bill's" and "in Just-" are reprinted with the permission of Liveright Publishing Corporation from *Tulips and Chimneys* by E. E. Cummings. Copyright 1923, 1925 and renewed 1951, 1953 by E. E. Cummings. Copyright © 1973, 1976 by the Trustees for the E. E. Cummings Trust. Copyright © 1973, 1976 by George James Firmage.

J. V. Cunningham. "Friend, on this scaffold," "You serve the best wines . . . ," and "This Humanist whom . . ." from *The Exclusions of a Rhyme* by J. V. Cunningham. Copyright © 1971 by J. V. Cunningham. Reprinted by permission of The Ohio University Press, Athens.

Peter Davison. "The Last Word" (Part IV of "Four Love Poems") from *Pretending to Be Asleep* by Peter Davison. Copyright © 1970 by Peter Davison. Reprinted by permission of Atheneum Publishers.

Walter de la Mare. "The Listeners" from *The Complete Poems* by Walter de la Mare, © 1969 by The Literary Trustees of Walter de la Mare. Reprinted by permission of The Literary Trustees of Walter de la Mare and The Society of Authors as their representative.

Emily Dickinson. "Because I could not stop for Death," "I heard a Fly buzz – when I died," "I like to see it lap the Miles," "I started Early – Took my Dog," "The Lightning is a yellow Fork," "The Soul selects her own Society," "Victory comes late," "It dropped so low – in my regard," "A Dying Tiger – moaned for drink," "My Life had stood – a Loaded Gun," and lines from "Hope is the thing with feathers" reprinted by permission of the publishers and Trustees of Amherst College from *The Poems of Emily Dickinson,* edited by Thomas H. Johnson, Cambridge, Mass., The Belknap Press of Harvard University Press, copyright 1951, © 1955, 1979, 1983 by the President and Fellows of Harvard College. Twenty-two lines from "My Life had stood – a Loaded Gun," from *The Complete Poems of Emily Dickinson,* edited by Thomas H. Johnson. Copyright 1929 by Martha Dickinson Bianchi; Copyright © renewed 1957 by Mary L. Hampson. By permission of Little, Brown and Company in association with the Atlantic Monthly Press.

Emanuel diPasquale. "Rain" reprinted by permission of the poet.

Philip Dow. "Drunk Last Night with Friends, I Go to Work Anyway" from *Paying Back the Sea* by Philip Dow (1979). Reprinted by permission of Carnegie-Mellon University Press.

Norman Dubie. "The Funeral" is reprinted from *The Springhouse: Poems by Norman Dubie* with the permission of the author and W. W. Norton & Company, Inc. Copyright © 1986 by Norman Dubie.

Alan Dugan. "Love Song: I and Thou" from *Poems* by Alan Dugan. Copyright © 1961 by Alan Dugan. First published by Yale University Press. Reprinted by permission.

Richard Eberhart. "The Fury of Aerial Bombardment" from *Collected Poems 1930–1976* by Richard Eberhart. Copyright © 1960, 1976 by Richard Eberhart. Reprinted by permission of Oxford University Press, Inc.

T. S. Eliot. "Journey of the Magi," "Virginia" (from "Landscapes"), "The Love Song of J. Alfred Prufrock," and "*The Boston Evening Transcript*" from *Collected Poems 1909–1962* by T. S. Eliot. Copyright 1936 by Harcourt Brace Jovanovich, Inc., copyright © 1963, 1964 by T. S. Eliot. Excerpt from "Tradition and the Individual Talent" from *Selected Essays* by T. S. Eliot. Reprinted by permission of the publishers, Harcourt Brace Jovanovich, Inc. and Faber and Faber Ltd.

James Emanuel. "The Negro." Copyright © 1968 by James Emanuel. Reprinted by permission of Broadside Press.

Abbie Huston Evans. "Wing Spread," reprinted from *Collected Poems* by Abbie Huston Evans by permission of the University of Pittsburgh Press. © 1950 by Abbie Huston Evans.

Donald Finkel. "Gesture" from *The Garbage Wars.* Copyright © 1970 by Donald Finkel. Reprinted with the permission of Atheneum Publishers, Inc.

Robert Francis. "Catch" from *The Orb Weaver* by Robert Francis. Copyright © 1960 by Robert Francis. Reprinted by permission of Wesleyan University Press.

Robert Frost. "Desert Places," "Stopping by Woods on a Snowy Evening," "Never Again Would Birds' Song Be the Same," "Design," "The Secret Sits," "Fire and Ice," "The Silken Tent," and "The Woodpile" from *The Poetry of Robert Frost* edited by Edward Connery Lathem. Copyright © 1969 by Holt, Rinehart and Winston, Publishers. Copyright 1923, 1936, 1942, 1951, © 1958 by Robert Frost. Copyright © 1964, 1967, 1970 by Lesley Frost Ballantine. "In White" from *The Dimensions of Robert Frost* by Reginald L. Cook. Copyright © 1958 by Reginald L. Cook. Letter to John Bartlett (letter No. 53) from *Selected Letters of Robert Frost* edited by Lawrence Thompson. Copyright © 1964 by Lawrence Thompson and Holt, Rinehart and Winston. Reprinted by permission of Holt, Rinehart and Winston, Publishers.

Tess Gallagher. "Under Stars" (copyright 1978 Tess Gallagher) is from *Under Stars* by Tess Gallagher, published by Graywolf Press. Reprinted by permission.

Gary Gildner. "First Practice" reprinted from *First Practice* by Gary Gildner. By permission of the University of Pittsburgh Press. © 1969 by Gary Gildner.

Allen Ginsberg. "A Supermarket in California" from *Collected Poems 1947–1980* by Allen Ginsberg. Copyright © 1955 by Allen Ginsberg. Reprinted by permission of Harper & Row, Publishers, Inc.

Dana Gioia. "California Hills in August." Reprinted by permission, © 1982 Dana Gioia. Originally in *The New Yorker.*

Paul Goodman. Three lines from "Hokku" from *Collected Poems,* by Paul Goodman, edited by Taylor Stoehr. Copyright © 1973 by The Estate of Paul Goodman. Reprinted by permission of Random House, Inc.

Robert Graves. "Down, Wanton, Down" from *Collected Poems* by Robert Graves. Copyright 1939, © 1955, 1958, 1961, 1965 by Robert Graves. Reprinted by permission of Robert Graves.

Ronald Gross. "Yield" from *Pop Poems* by Ronald Gross. Copyright © 1967 by Ronald Gross. Reprinted by permission of Simon & Schuster, Inc.

Bruce Guernsey. "Louis B. Russell," *Xanadu,* Vol. 1, No. 1, Summer 1975. Copyright 1975 by Long Island Poetry Collective, Inc. Reprinted by permission of the Long Island Poetry Collective, Inc., and the poet.

Arthur Guiterman. "On the Vanity of Earthly Greatness" from *Gaily the Troubadour* by Arthur Guiterman. Copyright 1936 by E. P. Dutton & Co., Inc.; renewed 1954 by Mrs. Vita Lindo Guiterman. Reprinted by permission of Louise H. Sclove.

R. S. Gwynn. Lines from *The Narcissiad* by R. S. Gwynn (Cedar Rock Press, 1981). Reprinted by permission of the publisher and the poet.

H. D. (Hilda Doolittle). "Heat" from *Selected Poems* by Hilda Doolittle. Copyright © 1957 by Norman Holmes Pearson. Reprinted by permission of New Directions Publishing Corporation.

Donald Hall. "Names of Horses" from *Kicking the Leaves* (Harper & Row). Reprinted by permission. © 1977 The New Yorker Magazine, Inc.

William Harmon. The first selection from "Ms. D.'s College Diary—Aetat. 150" ("The Soul selects her own sorority . . .") by William Harmon. Copyright © 1981 by William Harmon. Reprinted by permission of the poet.

Robert Hayden. "Those Winter Sundays" is reprinted from *Collected Poems of Robert Hayden,* edited by Frederick Glaysher, with the permission of Liveright Publishing Corporation. Copyright © 1985 by Erma Hayden.

James Hayford. "Mason's Trick" from *At Large on the Land* by James Hayford (Oriole Books, 1983). Reprinted by permission.

Seamus Heaney. "Sunlight" (first poem from "Mossbawn: Two Poems in Dedication for Mary Heaney") from *North* by Seamus Heaney. Copyright © 1975 by Seamus Heaney. Reprinted by permission of Faber and Faber Ltd.

Anthony Hecht. "The Vow" from *The Hard Hours.* Copyright © 1967 Anthony Hecht. Reprinted with the permission of Atheneum Publishers, Inc.

Geoffrey Hill. "Merlin" from *Somewhere Is Such a Kingdom: Poems 1952–1971* by Geoffrey Hill. Copyright © 1975 by Geoffrey Hill. Reprinted by permission of Houghton Mifflin Company and André Deutsch Ltd.

Michael Hogan. "Spring," copyright © 1975, 1976 by Michael Hogan, from *Soon It Will Be Morning* (Austin: Cold Mountain Press, 1976). Permission from the author is gratefully acknowledged.

John Hollander. "Swan and Shadow" from John Hollander, *Types of Shape.* Copyright © 1969 by John Hollander (New York: Atheneum, 1969). Reprinted with the permission of Atheneum Publishers.

Garrett Kaoru Hongo. "The Hongo Store." Copyright © 1977 by Garrett Kaoru Hongo. Reprinted from *Yellow Light* by permission of Wesleyan University Press.

A. E. Housman. "Loveliest of trees, the cherry now," "Terence, this is stupid stuff," "To an Athlete Dying Young," "When I was one-and-twenty," "With rue my heart is laden," "Eight O'Clock," and "Epitaph on an Army of Mercenaries." From "A Shropshire Lad"—authorized edition—and from "Last Poems" in *The Collected Poems of A. E. Housman.* Copyright 1922, 1939, 1940, © 1965 by Holt, Rinehart and Winston. Copyright © 1967, 1968 by Robert E. Symons. Copyright 1950 by Barclays Bank Ltd. Reprinted by permission of Holt, Rinehart and Winston, Publishers, and The Society of Authors as the literary representative of the Estate of A. E. Housman, and Jonathan Cape Ltd., publishers of A. E. Housman's *Collected Poems.*

Richard Howard. "Meditation" from *Les Fleurs du Mal* by Charles Baudelaire, translated by Richard Howard. Translation copyright © 1982 by Richard Howard. Reprinted by permission of David R. Godine, Publisher, Boston.

Acknowledgments 1423

Langston Hughes. "Dream Deferred." Copyright 1951 by Langston Hughes. Reprinted from *The Panther and the Lash: Poems of Our Times*, by Langston Hughes, by permission of Alfred A. Knopf, Inc. "Subway Rush Hour" from *Montage of a Dream Deferred*. Reprinted by permission of Harold Ober Associates Incorporated. Copyright 1951 by Langston Hughes. Copyright renewed 1979 by George Houston Bass.

Richard Hugo. "In Your Young Dream" is reprinted from *13 Letters and 13 Dreams: Poems by Richard Hugo*, by permission of W. W. Norton & Company, Inc. Copyright © 1977 by W. W. Norton & Company, Inc.

T. E. Hulme. "Image" from *The Life and Opinions of T. E. Hulme* by Alun R. Jones. Copyright 1960 by Alun R. Jones. Reprinted by permission of Beacon Press.

Virgil Hutton. Two haiku, "Dusk over the lake" and "The moving shadows," first appeared in *Modern Haiku*, 1978, and *Modern Haiku*, 1984. By permission of the poet and the publisher.

David Ignatow. "Get the Gasworks." Copyright © 1948 by David Ignatow. Reprinted from *Figures of the Human* by permission of Wesleyan University Press.

Randall Jarrell. "A Sick Child" (Copyright 1949 by Randall Jarrell, renewed © 1976 by Mary von Schrader Jarrell), "The Death of the Ball Turret Gunner" (Copyright 1945, renewed © 1973 by Mary von Schrader Jarrell). Reprinted from *The Complete Poems* by Randall Jarrell by permission of Farrar, Straus & Giroux, Inc. Two excerpts from *Poetry and the Age* by Randall Jarrell. Copyright 1952, 1953 by Randall Jarrell. Reprinted by permission of Mary von Schrader Jarrell. "Well Water" reprinted with permission of Macmillan Publishing Company from *The Lost World* by Randall Jarrell. Copyright © 1965 by Randall Jarrell.

Donald Justice. "On the Death of Friends in Childhood" from *Selected Poems* by Donald Justice. Copyright © 1979 by Donald Justice. Reprinted with the permission of Atheneum Publishers, Inc.

Greg Keeler. Lines from "There Ain't No Such Thing as a Montana Cowboy," *The Limberlost Review*, 1979. Reprinted by permission of the poet.

Jane Kenyon. "The Suitor" from *From Room to Room*, © 1978 by Jane Kenyon. Reprinted courtesy of Alice James Books, 138 Mt. Auburn St., Cambridge, MA 02138.

James C. Kilgore. "The White Man Pressed the Locks" from *Poets on the Platform*. Copyright © 1970 by James C. Kilgore. Reprinted by permission of the poet.

Hugh Kingsmill. "What, still alive at twenty-two" from *The Best of Hugh Kingsmill*. Reprinted by permission of Victor Gollancz Ltd.

Galway Kinnell. "Blackberry Eating" and "St. Francis and the Sow" from *Mortal Acts, Mortal Words* by Galway Kinnell. Copyright © 1980 by Galway Kinnell. Reprinted by permission of Houghton Mifflin Company.

Carolyn Kizer. "The Intruder" from *Mermaid in the Basement: Poems for Women* by Carolyn Kizer (Copper Canyon Press, 1984). Reprinted by permission of the publisher.

Etheridge Knight. "For Black Poets Who Think of Suicide" from *Poems from Prison* by Etheridge Knight. Copyright © 1968 by Etheridge Knight. Reprinted by permission of Broadside Press.

William Knott (Saint Geraud). "Poem" from *The Naomi Poems: Corpse and Beans* by Saint Geraud. Copyright © 1968 by William Knott. Used by permission of Allyn and Bacon, Inc.

Kenneth Koch. "Mending Sump" from *The New American Poetry*, edited by Donald M. Allen. Copyright © 1960 by Kenneth Koch. Reprinted by permission of International Creative Management.

Ted Kooser. "Flying at Night." Reprinted from *One World at a Time* by Ted Kooser by permission of the University of Pittsburgh Press. © 1985 by Ted Kooser.

Richard Kostelanetz. "Disintegration" from *Visual Language* (Assembling Press, 1970). Reprinted by permission of the poet.

M. Krishnamurti. "The Spirit's Odyssey" from *The Cloth of Gold* by M. Krishnamurti. Reprinted by permission of Charles E. Tuttle Co., Inc., Tokyo.

Philip Larkin. "Home is so Sad" and "A Study of Reading Habits." Reprinted by permission of Faber and Faber Ltd. from *The Whitsun Weddings* by Philip Larkin.

D. H. Lawrence. "A Youth Mowing," "Piano," and "Bavarian Gentians." From *The Complete Poems of D. H. Lawrence*, ed. by Vivian de Sola Pinto and F. Warren Roberts. Copyright © 1964, 1971 by Angelo Ravagli and C. M. Weekleu, Executors of The Estate of Frieda Lawrence Ravagli. Reprinted by permission of Viking Penguin Inc.

Irving Layton. "The Bull Calf" from *A Red Carpet for the Sun*. Reprinted by permission of the poet.

Brad Leithauser. "Trauma" from *Hundreds of Fireflies*, by Brad Leithauser. Copyright © 1981 by Brad Leithauser. Reprinted by permission of Alfred A. Knopf, Inc.

Denise Levertov. "Six Variations, iii" from *The Jacob's Ladder* by Denise Levertov. Copyright © 1958, 1969 by Denise Levertov Goodman. "Leaving Forever" (Copyright © 1963 by Denise Levertov) and "The Ache of Marriage" (Copyright © 1964 by Denise Levertov Goodman) from *Poems 1960–1967* by Denise Levertov. Reprinted by permission of New Directions Publishing Corporation.

Philip Levine. "To a Child Trapped in a Barber Shop." Reprinted from *Not This Pig* by permission of Wesleyan University Press. Copyright © 1968 by Philip Levine.

Janet Lewis. "Girl Help" from *Poems 1924–1944* by Janet Lewis. Copyright 1950 by Janet Lewis. Reprinted with the permission of The Ohio University Press, Athens.

J. A. Lindon. "My Garden," reprinted by permission of Hazel J. Lindon.

Federico Garcia Lorca. "La Guitarra" (translated by Keith Waldrop) from *Obras Completas*. Copyright © Aguilar S. A. de Ediciónes 1954. All rights reserved. Reprinted by permission of New Directions Publishing Corporation.

Robert Lowell. "Meditation" from *Imitations* by Robert Lowell. Copyright © 1958, 1959, 1960, 1961 by Robert Lowell. "Skunk Hour" from *Life Studies* by Robert Lowell. Copyright © 1956, 1959 by Robert Lowell. Reprinted by permission of Farrar, Straus & Giroux, Inc.

Hugh MacDiarmid. "Wheesht, Wheesht" and "Another Epitaph on an Army of Mercenaries," reprinted with permission of Macmillan Publishing Company from *Collected Poems* by Hugh MacDiarmid. © 1948, 1962 Christopher Murray Grieve.

Archibald MacLeish. "Ars Poetica" and "The End of the World" from *New and Collected Poems 1917–1976* by Archibald MacLeish. Copyright © 1976 by Archibald MacLeish. Reprinted by permission of Houghton Mifflin Company.

John Masefield. "Cargoes," reprinted with permission of Macmillan Publishing Company from *Poems* by John Masefield (New York: Macmillan, 1953).

Rod McKuen. "Thoughts on Capital Punishment" from *Stanyan Street and Other Sorrows*, by Rod McKuen. Copyright 1954, © 1960, 1961, 1962, 1963, 1964, 1965, 1966 by Rod McKuen. Reprinted by permission of Random House, Inc.

James Merrill. "Laboratory Poem" from *The Country of a Thousand Years of Peace*. Copyright © 1951, 1952, 1953, 1954, 1957, 1958, 1970 James Merrill; copyrights renewed © 1979, 1980, 1981, 1982 James Merrill. Reprinted with the permission of Atheneum Publishers, Inc.

W. S. Merwin. "Song of Man Chipping an Arrowhead" from *Writings to an Unfinished Accompaniment*. Copyright © 1973 W. S. Merwin. Reprinted with the permission of Atheneum Publishers, Inc.

Charlotte Mew. "Fame" from *Charlotte Mew, Collected Poems and Prose*, edited by Val Wagner (Manchester, England: Carcanet Press, 1981). Copyright © 1981 The Estate of Charlotte Mew. Reprinted by permission of the publisher.

Josephine Miles. "Reason" from *Poems 1930–1960* by Josephine Miles. Copyright © 1960 by Indiana University Press. Reprinted by permission of the publisher, Indiana University Press.

Edna St. Vincent Millay. "Counting-out Rhyme" from *Collected Poems* by Edna St. Vincent Millay, published by Harper & Row. Copyright 1928, © 1956 by Edna St. Vincent Millay and Norma Millay Ellis. Reprinted by permission of Norma Millay Ellis.

N. Scott Momaday. "The Delight Song of Tsoai-talee" from *The Gourd Dancer* by N. Scott Momaday. Copyright © 1975 by N. Scott Momaday. Reprinted by permission of Harper & Row, Publishers, Inc.

Marianne Moore. "The Mind Is an Enchanting Thing," reprinted with permission of Macmillan Publishing Company from *Collected Poems* by Marianne Moore. Copyright 1944, and renewed 1972 by Marianne Moore.

Edwin Morgan. "Siesta of a Hungarian Snake" from *The Second Life* by Edwin Morgan. Copyright © 1968 by Edwin Morgan and Edinburgh University Press. Reprinted by permission of Edinburgh University Press.

Howard Moss. "Shall I Compare Thee to a Summer's Day?" from Modified Sonnets in *A Swim Off the Rocks*. Copyright © 1976 by Howard Moss. Reprinted with the permission of Atheneum Publishers, Inc.

Ogden Nash. "Very Like a Whale" from *Verses from 1929 On* by Ogden Nash. Copyright 1934 by The Curtis Publishing Company. First appeared in *The Saturday Evening Post*. By permission of Little, Brown and Company.

Willie Nelson. "Heaven and Hell" from the album *Phases and Stages* by Willie Nelson. © 1974 Willie Nelson Music. Used by permission.

Howard Nemerov. "Storm Windows" from *The Collected Poems of Howard Nemerov* (University of Chicago Press). Copyright © 1977 by Howard Nemerov. Reprinted by permission of the poet.

John Frederick Nims. "Love Poem" from *The Iron Pastoral*. Copyright, 1947, by John Frederick Nims. "Contemplation" from *Of Flesh and Bone*. Copyright © 1967 by Rutgers University. Reprinted by permission of the poet.

Sharon Olds. "The One Girl at the Boys Party" from *The Dead and the Living*, by Sharon Olds. Copyright © 1983 by Sharon Olds. Reprinted by permission of Alfred A. Knopf, Inc.

Mary Oliver. "Rain in Ohio" from *American Primitive: Poems* by Mary Oliver. Copyright © 1981 by Mary Oliver. First appeared in *The Atlantic Monthly*. By permission of Little, Brown and Company in association with the Atlantic Monthly Press.

Charles Olson. "La Chute," copyright by Charles Olson. Reprinted by permission of the Estate of Charles Olson.

Wilfred Owen. "Dulce et Decorum Est" and "Anthem for Doomed Youth" from *The Collected Poems of Wilfred Owen* edited by C. Day Lewis. Copyright Chatto & Windus Ltd. 1946, © 1963. Reprinted by permission of New Directions Publishing Corporation, the Owen Estate, and Chatto & Windus Ltd.

Dorothy Parker. "Résumé" from *The Portable Dorothy Parker*. Copyright © 1926, 1954 by Dorothy Parker. Reprinted by permission of Viking Penguin Inc.

Linda Pastan. "Ethics" is reprinted from *Waiting for My Life*, Poems by Linda Pastan, with the permission of the author and W. W. Norton & Company, Inc. Copyright © 1981 by Linda Pastan. First appeared in *Poetry*, December 1979. "Jump Cabling" from *Light Year '85* (Bits Press). Reprinted by permission of the poet.

Laurence Perrine. "Janus," *Poetry*, June 1984. Copyright © 1984 by Laurence Perrine. Reprinted by permission of the poet.

Robert Phillips. "Running on Empty" from *Running on Empty: New Poems* by Robert Phillips. Copyright 1984, Robert Phillips. Reprinted by permission of the poet.

Sylvia Plath. "Daddy" (Copyright © 1963 by Ted Hughes) and "Morning Song" (Copyright © 1961 by Ted Hughes) from *Ariel* by Sylvia Plath. Published by Harper & Row, Publishers, Inc. and Faber and Faber, London. Copyright Ted Hughes, 1965. "Metaphors" from *Crossing the Water* by Sylvia Plath. Copyright © 1960 by Ted Hughes. Published by Harper & Row, Publishers, Inc. and Faber and Faber, London. Copyright Ted Hughes, 1971. Reprinted by permission of Harper & Row, Publishers, Inc. and Olwyn Hughes, representing the estate of Sylvia Plath.

Cole Porter. Lines from "You're the Top" by Cole Porter. Copyright © 1934 (renewed) Warner Bros. Inc. All Rights Reserved. Used by permission.

Ezra Pound. "In a Station of the Metro" and "The River Merchant's Wife" from *Personae* by Ezra Pound. Copyright 1926 by Ezra Pound. Reprinted by permission of New Directions Publishing Corporation. Excerpt from "A Retrospect" from *Literary Essays of Ezra Pound* edited by T. S. Eliot, copyright 1935 by Ezra Pound, and excerpt from *ABC of Reading*, copyright 1934 by Ezra Pound. Reprinted by permission of New Directions Publishing Corporation and Faber and Faber Ltd. First six lines from "III Hiang Niao" reprinted by permission of the publishers from Ezra Pound, *Shih-Ching: The Classic Anthology Defined by Confucius;* Cambridge, Mass.: Harvard University Press. Copyright 1954 by the President and Fellows of Harvard College. Renewed © 1982 by Mary DeRachewiltz and Omar Pound.

James Preston. "Sunfish Races." Copyright © 1986 by James Preston. Used by permission of the poet.

Paul Ramsey. "A Poet Defended" from *Light Year '85* (Bits Press). Reprinted by permission of the poet.

Dudley Randall. "Ballad of Birmingham" from *Poem Counterpoem* by Margaret Danner and Dudley Randall. Copyright © 1966 by Dudley Randall. Reprinted by permission of the poet.

John Crowe Ransom. "Bells for John Whiteside's Daughter," copyright 1924 by Alfred A. Knopf, Inc. and renewed 1952 by John Crowe Ransom. Reprinted from *Selected Poems Third Edition, Revised and Enlarged*, by John Crowe Ransom, by permission of Alfred A. Knopf, Inc.

Henry Reed. "Naming of Parts" from *A Map of Verona* by Henry Reed (1946). Reprinted by permission of Jonathan Cape Ltd.

Kenneth Rexroth. "A dawn in a tree of birds . . ." from *New Poems* by Kenneth Rexroth. Copyright © 1974 by Kenneth Rexroth. Reprinted by permission of New Directions Publishing Corporation.

Adrienne Rich. "Diving into the Wreck" and "Aunt Jennifer's Tigers" from *Poems: Selected and New, 1950–1954* by Adrienne Rich. "Song" from *Diving in the the Wreck* by Adrienne Rich. Copyright © 1975, 1973, 1971, 1969, 1966 by W. W. Norton & Company, Inc. Copyright © 1967, 1963, 1962, 1961, 1960, 1959, 1958, 1957, 1956, 1955, 1954, 1953, 1952, 1951 by Adrienne Rich. Reprinted with the permission of W. W. Norton & Company.

Theodore Roethke. "I Knew a Woman" (Copyright 1954 by Theodore Roethke), "The Waking" (Copyright 1953 by Theodore Roethke), "My Papa's Waltz" (Copyright 1942 by Hearst Magazines, Inc.), "Root Cellar" (Copyright 1943 by Modern Poetry Association, Inc.), "Night Crow" (Copyright 1944 by Saturday Review Association, Inc.), and "Elegy for Jane" (Copyright 1950 by Theodore Roethke). Reprinted from *The Collected Poems of Theodore Roethke* by permission of Doubleday & Company, Inc.

Raymond Roseliep. "campfire extinguished" from *Listen to Light: Haiku* by Raymond Roseliep. Copyright © 1980 by Raymond Roseliep (Alembic Press, Ithaca, N.Y.). Reprinted by permission of the poet.

Gibbons Ruark. "The rose growing into the house" from *Reeds* by Gibbons Ruark (Lubbock: Texas Tech Press, 1978). Reprinted by permission of the publisher.

Paul Ruffin. "Hotel Fire: New Orleans" from *Lighting the Furnace Pilot* (Spoon River Poetry Press, 1980). Reprinted by permission of the poet.

Carl Sandburg. "Fog" from *Chicago Poems* by Carl Sandburg. Copyright 1916 by Holt, Rinehart and Winston, Inc.; renewed 1944 by Carl Sandburg. Reprinted by permission of Harcourt Brace Jovanovich, Inc.

Aram Saroyan. Lines from "crickets" from *Works* by Aram Saroyan. Copyright © 1966 by Aram Saroyan. Reprinted by permission of the poet.

Gjertrud Schnackenberg. "Signs" from *The Lamplit Answer* by Gjertrud Schnackenberg. Copyright © 1982, 1985 by Gjertrud Schnackenberg. Reprinted by permission of Farrar, Straus & Giroux, Inc.

Winfield Townley Scott. "Mrs. Severin," reprinted with permission of Macmillan Publishing Company from *Collected Poems, 1937–1962* by Winfield Townley Scott. Copyright 1951 by Winfield Townley Scott, renewed 1979 by Lindsay B. Scott.

Bettie Sellers. "In the Counselor's Waiting Room" from *Morning of the Red-Tailed Hawk* by Bettie Sellers (University Center, MI: Green River Press, 1981). Reprinted by permission.

Anne Sexton. "To a Friend Whose Work Has Come to Triumph" from *All My Pretty Ones* by Anne Sexton. Copyright © 1962 by Anne Sexton. Lines from "Eighteen Days Without You" from *Love Poems* by Anne Sexton. Copyright © 1967, 1968, 1969 by Anne Sexton. Reprinted by permission of Houghton Mifflin Company.

Karl Shapiro. "The Dirty Word." Copyright 1947 by Karl Shapiro. Reprinted from *Selected Poems*, by Karl Shapiro, by permission of Random House, Inc.

Stephen Shu-ning Liu. "My Father's Martial Art." Copyright © 1981 by The Antioch Review, Inc. First appeared in *The Antioch Review*, Vol. 39, No. 3 (Summer, 1981). Reprinted by permission of the Editors.

Charles Simic. "The Butcher Shop" from *Dismantling the Silence* by Charles Simic. Copyright © 1971 by Charles Simic. Reprinted by permission of the publisher, George Braziller, Inc.

Paul Simon. "Richard Cory" from the album *Sounds of Silence*. © 1966 by Paul Simon. Reprinted by permission.

Louis Simpson. "The Boarder." Copyright © 1959 by Louis Simpson. Reprinted from *A Dream of Governors* by permission of Wesleyan University Press.

L. E. Sissman. Lines from "In and Out: A Home Away from Home" from *Dying: An Introduction* by E. L. Sissman. Copyright © 1967 by E. L. Sissman. By permission of Little, Brown and Company in association with the Atlantic Monthly Press.

Knute Skinner. "The Cold Irish Earth" from *A Close Sky Over Killas-Puglonane* (The Dolman Press Ltd., 1968). Reprinted by permission of the poet and the publisher.

Barbara Herrnstein Smith. Excerpt from *Poetic Disclosure: A Study of How Poems End* by Barbara Herrnstein Smith. Copyright © 1968 by The University of Chicago Press. All rights reserved. Reprinted by permission of The University of Chicago Press.

Stevie Smith. "I Remember" from *Selected Poems* by Stevie Smith. Copyright © 1962, 1964 by Stevie Smith. Reprinted by permission of New Directions Publishing Corporation.

William Jay Smith. "American Primitive" from *The Traveler's Tree* by William Jay Smith. Copyright © 1980 by William Jay Smith. Reprinted by permission of Persea Books, Inc.

W. D. Snodgrass. "The Operation." Copyright © 1959 by W. D. Snodgrass. Reprinted from *Heart's Needle*, by W. D. Snodgrass, by permission of Alfred A. Knopf, Inc.

Gary Snyder. "Hitch Haiku" from *The Back Country* by Gary Snyder. Copyright © 1968 by Gary Snyder. Reprinted by permission of New Directions Publishing Corporation. "Mid-August at Sourdough Mountain Lookout" from *Riprap* by Gary Snyder (Kyoto: Origin Press, 1959). Reprinted by permission of the poet.

Richard Snyder. "A Mongoloid Child Handling Shells on the Beach" from *Keeping in Touch* (The Ashland Poetry Press, 1971). Reprinted by permission.

Gary Soto. "Black Hair." Reprinted from *Black Hair* by Gary Soto by permission of the University of Pittsburgh Press. © 1985 by Gary Soto.

Bruce Springsteen. "Born to Run." Copyright © 1975 Bruce Springsteen. Reprinted by permission of Bruce Springsteen. All rights reserved.

William Stafford. "Traveling Through the Dark" (Copyright © 1960 by William Stafford) and "At the Klamath Berry Festival (Copyright © 1961 by William Stafford) from *Stories That Could Be True* by William Stafford. Reprinted by permission of Harper & Row, Publishers, Inc.

George Starbuck. "Margaret Are You Drug" from "Translations from the English" in *White Paper: Poems* by George Starbuck. Copyright © 1965 by George Starbuck. First appeared in *The Atlantic*. By permission of Little, Brown and Company in association with the Atlantic Monthly Press.

Timothy Steele. "Here Lies Sir Tact." Reprinted by permission of Louisiana State University Press from *Uncertainties and Rest* by Timothy Steele, copyright © 1979. "Timothy" from *Nine Poems* by Timothy Steele, © 1984 by Timothy Steele. Reprinted by permission of the publisher, R. L. Barth.

James Stephens. "The Wind" and "A Glass of Beer." Reprinted with permission of Macmillan Publishing Company and The Society of Authors on behalf of the copyright holder, Mrs. Iris Wise, from *Collected Poems* by James Stephens. "The Wind" copyright 1915 by Macmillan Publishing Company, renewed 1943 by James Stephens. "A Glass of Beer" copyright 1918 by Macmillan Publishing Company, renewed 1946 by James Stephens.

Wallace Stevens. "The Emperor of Ice Cream," "Disillusionment of Ten O'Clock," "Peter Quince at the Clavier," "Thirteen Ways of Looking at a Blackbird," "Anecdote of the Jar," and lines from "Sunday Morning" and "Bantam in Pine-Woods" (Copyright 1923 and renewed 1951 by Wallace Stevens) from *The Collected Poems of Wallace Stevens*, by Wallace Stevens. Nine Proverbs from "Adagia" from *Opus Posthumous* by Wallace Stevens, edited by Samuel French Morse. Copyright © 1957 by Elsie Stevens and Holly Stevens. Reprinted by permission of Alfred A. Knopf, Inc.

Michael Stillman. "In Memoriam John Coltrane" from *Memories of Grace Street* by Michael Stillman, reprinted from *Occident* (Berkeley, Fall 1971). Reprinted by permission of the poet.

May Swenson. "Question" from *New and Selected Things Taking Place* by May Swenson. Copyright © 1954 by May Swenson. By permission of Little, Brown and Company in association with the Atlantic Monthly Press.

John Tagliabue. "Maine vastly covered with much snow" from *The Great Day: Poems 1962–1983* by John Tagliabue (The Alembic Press, 1984). Reprinted by permission of the publisher.

Henry Taylor. "Riding a One-Eyed Horse" from *An Afternoon of Pocket Billiards* by Henry Taylor (Salt Lake City: University of Utah Press Poetry Series, 1975). Copyright © 1975 by Henry Taylor. Reprinted by permission of the University of Utah Press.

Cornelius J. Ter Maat. "Etienne de Silhouette" reprinted by permission of the poet.

Dylan Thomas. "Fern Hill" and "Do not go gentle into that good night" from *The Poems of Dylan Thomas*. Copyright 1952 by Dylan Thomas, copyright 1939, 1946 by New Directions Publishing Corporation. Line from *Under Milk Wood* by Dylan Thomas. Copyright 1954 by New Directions Publishing Corporation. All Rights Reserved. Reprinted by permission of New Directions Publishing Corporation and David Higham Associates Limited.

Jean Toomer. "Reapers" is reprinted from *Cane* by Jean Toomer, with the permission of Liveright Publishing Corporation. Copyright 1923 by Boni & Liveright. Copyright renewed 1951 by Jean Toomer.

John Updike. "Ex-Basketball Player," copyright © 1957, 1982 by John Updike. Reprinted from *The Carpentered Hen and Other Tame Creatures*, by John Updike, by permission of Alfred A. Knopf, Inc. "Winter Ocean" from *Telephone Poles and Other Poems*, by John Updike. Copyright © 1960 by John Updike. Reprinted by permission of Alfred A. Knopf, Inc.

Nicholas Virgilio. "Into the blinding sun . . ." first appeared in *American Haiku* Magazine, Vol. II, No. 1, 1964, Plattesville, Wisconsin. Reprinted by permission of the poet.

David Wagoner. "Staying Alive" from *Collected Poems 1956–1976* by David Wagoner. Copyright © 1976 by Indiana University Press. Reprinted by permission of the publisher, Indiana University Press.

Keith Waldrop. "Proposition II" from *The Garden of Effort* (Burning Deck Publishers, 1975). Reprinted by permission.

Rosmarie Waldrop. "The Relaxed Abalone" from *The Relaxed Abalone: Or What-You-May-Find* by Rosmarie Waldrop (Burning Deck Publishers, 1970). Reprinted by permission.

Robert Wallace. "The Girl Writing Her English Paper" from *Swimmer in the Rain* by Robert Wallace (Carnegie-Mellon University Press, 1979). Reprinted by permission of the publisher.

Wang Wei. "Bird-Singing Stream," translated by Wai-lim Yip. Reprinted by permission of Wai-lim Yip.

Ruth Whitman. "Castoff Skin" from *The Passion of Lizzie Borden*. Copyright © 1973 by Ruth Whitman. Reprinted by permission of October House.

Richard Wilbur. "In the Elegy Season," "A Simile for Her Smile," and "Museum Piece" from *Ceremony and Other Poems*, copyright 1950, 1978 by Richard Wilbur. "Sleepless on Crown Point" from *The Mind Reader*, copyright © 1973 by Richard Wilbur. Reprinted by permission of Harcourt Brace Jovanovich, Inc.

Miller Williams. "On the Symbolic Consideration of Hands and the Significance of Death" from *Halfway from Hoxie: New and Selected Poems* by Miller Williams. Copyright © 1964, 1968, 1971, 1973 by Miller Williams. Reprinted by permission of the publisher, Louisiana State University Press.

Peter Williams. "When she was here, Li Bo, she was like cold summer lager." Copyright © 1978 by Peter Williams. First appeared in *Taxi*, a publication of the William Carlos Williams Poetry Center of the Paterson (NJ) Public Library. Reprinted by permission of the poet.

William Carlos Williams. "The Great Figure," "Spring and All," "Poem," "This Is Just to Say," "The Red Wheelbarrow," "To Waken an Old Lady," "The Descent of Winter" and lines from "The Waitress" from *Collected Earlier Poems* by William Carlos Williams. Copyright 1938 by New Directions Publishing Corporation. "The Dance" from *Collected Later Poems* by William Carlos Williams. Copyright 1954 by William Carlos Williams. Two excerpts from *Interviews with William Carlos*

Williams: *"Speaking Straight Ahead,"* edited by Linda Wagner. Copyright © 1966 by the Estate of William Carlos Williams. Reprinted by permission of New Directions Publishing Corporation.

Yvor Winters. "At the San Francisco Airport" from *Collected Poems* by Yvor Winters. Copyright 1952, © 1960 by Yvor Winters. Reprinted with the permission of the Ohio University Press, Athens.

James Wright. "A Blessing" and "Autumn Begins in Martins Ferry, Ohio" from *The Branch Will Not Break* by James Wright. Copyright © 1961, 1962 by James Wright. Reprinted by permission of Wesleyan University Press. "Saying Dante Aloud" from *Moments of an Italian Summer.* Copyright © 1976 by James Wright. Reprinted by permission of The Dryad Press.

Richard Wright. One stanza from "Haiku" in *Richard Wright Reader,* edited by Ellen Wright and Michel Fabre. Copyright © 1978 by Ellen Wright and Richard Fabre. Reprinted by permission of Harper & Row, Publishers, Inc.

William Butler Yeats. "The Magi," "To a Friend Whose Work Has Come to Nothing" (Copyright 1916 by Macmillan Publishing Company, renewed 1944 by Bertha Georgie Yeats), "The Second Coming" (Copyright 1924 by Macmillan Publishing Company, renewed 1952 by Bertha Georgie Yeats), "Sailing to Byzantium," "Leda and the Swan," and lines from "Among School Children" (Copyright 1928 by Macmillan Publishing Company, renewed 1956 by Bertha Georgie Yeats), "Crazy Jane Talks to the Bishop," lines from "For Anne Gregory" (Copyright 1933 by Macmillan Publishing Company, renewed 1962 by Bertha Georgie Yeats). Reprinted with permission of Macmillan Publishing Company, Michael Yeats, and Macmillan (London) Ltd. from *The Poems of W. B. Yeats,* edited by Richard J. Finneran. "The Lake Isle of Innisfree," "Who Goes with Fergus?" and "The Lamentation of the Old Pensioner" from *The Poems of W. B. Yeats,* edited by Richard J. Finneran, and "The Old Pensioner" from *The Variorum Edition of the Poems of W. B. Yeats,* edited by Peter Allt and Russell K. Alspach, reprinted by permission of Michael Yeats and Macmillan (London) Ltd.

Paul Zimmer. "The Day Zimmer Lost Religion" from *The Zimmer Poems* by Paul Zimmer. Copyright © 1976 by Paul Zimmer. Reprinted by permission of The Dryad Press.

DRAMA

Edward Albee. *The Zoo Story.* Copyright © 1960 by Edward Albee. Reprinted by permission of Coward, McCann & Geoghegan, Inc. *The Zoo Story* is the sole property of the author and is fully protected by copyright. It may not be acted either by professionals or amateurs without written consent. Public readings, and radio and television broadcasts are likewise forbidden. All enquiries concerning these rights should be addressed to the William Morris Agency, 1350 Avenue of the Americas, New York, NY 10019. Excerpt from "Which Theatre Is the Absurd One?" by Edward Albee (*The New York Times Magazine,* February 25, 1962) reprinted by permission of the William Morris Agency on behalf of the author. Copyright © 1962 by Edward Albee.

Woody Allen. *Death Knocks.* Copyright © 1968 by Woody Allen. Reprinted from *Getting Even,* by Woody Allen, by permission of Random House, Inc.

Aristotle. Excerpts from Aristotle's *Poetics* (Chapters 6, 13, 14, and 15) as translated by L. J. Potts in *Aristotle on the Art of Fiction,* 1959, published by Cambridge University Press. Copyright by Cambridge University Press. Reproduced by permission of Cambridge University Press.

Sylvan Barnet. Excerpts from *A Short Guide to Shakespeare* by Sylvan Barnet, copyright © 1984 by Harcourt Brace Jovanovich, Inc. Reprinted by permission of the publisher.

E. R. Dodds. Excerpt from "On Misunderstanding the *Oedipus Rex"* by E. R. Dodds from *Greece and Rome,* vol. XIII (1966). Reprinted by permission of Oxford University Press.

R. C. Flickinger. Drawing on page 857. "The Lycurgos Theatre of Dionysus at Athens" from *Greek Theatre and Its Drama,* p. 64. Reprinted by permission of The University of Chicago Press.

Sigmund Freud. Excerpt from *The Interpretation of Dreams,* by Sigmund Freud, translated by James Strachey, published in the United States by Basic Books, Inc., New York, by arrangement with George Allen Unwin Ltd. and The Hogarth Press, Ltd., London.

Susan Glaspell. "Trifles". Reprinted by permission of DODD, MEAD & COMPANY, INC. from *Plays* by Susan Glaspell. Copyright 1920 by Dodd, Mead & Company, Inc. Copyright renewed 1948 by Susan Glaspell.

Henrik Ibsen. *A Doll House* from *Henrik Ibsen: The Complete Major Prose Plays,* translated by Rolf Fjelde. Copyright © 1965, 1970, 1978 by Rolf Fjelde. Reprinted by arrangement with The New American Library, Inc., New York, N.Y.

Robert Langbaum. Footnotes from *The Tempest* by Robert Langbaum, as reprinted in *The Complete Signet Classic Shakespeare* by Sylvan Barnet are reprinted by permission of Harcourt Brace Jovanovich, Inc.

Arthur Miller. *Death of a Salesman* by Arthur Miller. Copyright 1949 by Arthur Miller. Copyright renewed 1977 by Arthur Miller. Reprinted by permission of Viking Penguin, Inc. This play in its printed form is designed for the reading public only. All dramatic rights in it are fully protected by copyright, and no public performance—professional or amateur—may be given without the written permission of the author and payment of royalty. As the courts have also ruled that the public reading of a play constitutes a public performance, no such reading may be given except under the conditions stated above. Communication should be addressed to the author's representative. International Creative Management, Inc., 40 West 57th Street, New York, New York 10019. "Tragedy and the Common Man" by Arthur Miller from *Theater Essays of Arthur Miller,* edited by Robert A. Martin. Copyright 1949 by Arthur Miller. Copyright renewed 1977 by Arthur Miller. Originally published in *The New York Times.* Reprinted by permission of Viking Penguin, Inc.

Molière. *The Physician in Spite of Himself.* From *Eight Plays by Molière,* translated by Morris Bishop. Copyright © 1957 by Morris Bishop. Reprinted by permission of Random House, Inc.

Charles Paul Segal. Excerpt from "Sophocles' Praise of Man and the Conflicts of the *Antigone"* as printed in *Sophocles: A Collection of Critical Essays* (Twentieth Century Views Series; Prentice-Hall, 1966). Reprinted by permission of the author.

William Shakespeare, *The Tragedy of Othello,* edited by Alvin Kernan. Copyright © 1963 by Alvin Kernan. Copyright © 1963 by Sylvan Barnet. Reprinted by arrangement with The New American Library, New York, N.Y.

Bernard Shaw. Excerpt from *The Quintessence of Ibsenism* by George Bernard Shaw reprinted by permission of The Society of Authors on behalf of the Bernard Shaw Estate.

Sophocles, *The Antigone of Sophocles: An English Version* by Dudley Fitts and Robert Fitzgerald, copyright 1939 by Harcourt Brace Jovanovich, Inc.; renewed 1967 by Dudley Fitts and Robert Fitzgerald. Reprinted by permission of the publisher. *CAUTION:* All rights, including professional, amateur, motion picture, recitation, lecturing, performance, public reading, radio broadcasting, and television are strictly reserved. Inquiries on all rights should be addressed to Harcourt Brace Jovanovich, Inc., Copyrights and Permissions Department, Orlando, Florida 32887.

Sophocles, *The Oedipus Rex of Sophocles: An English Version* by Dudley Fitts and Robert Fitzgerald, copyright 1949 by Harcourt Brace Jovanovich, Inc.; renewed 1977 by Cornelia Fitts and Robert Fitzgerald. Reprinted by permission of the publishers. *CAUTION:* All rights, including professional, amateur, motion picture, recitation, lecturing, public reading, radio broadcasting and television are strictly reserved. Inquiries on all rights should be addressed to Harcourt Brace Jovanovich, Inc., Copyrights and Permissions Department, Orlando, Florida 32887.

Tennessee Williams. *The Glass Menagerie* and accompanying Production Notes. From *The Glass Menagerie,* by Tennessee Williams. Copyright 1945 by Tennessee Williams and Edwina D. Williams and renewed 1973 by Tennessee Williams. Reprinted by permission of Random House, Inc.

William Butler Yeats. *Purgatory.* Reprinted with permission of Macmillan Publishing Company from *Collected Plays of W. B. Yeats* by W. B. Yeats. Copyright 1934, 1952 by Macmillan Publishing Company, renewed 1962 by Bertha Georgie Yeats, and 1980 by Anne Yeats. Reprinted by permission also of A. P. Watt Ltd. on behalf of Michael B. Yeats and Macmillan London, Ltd.

INDEX TO FIRST LINES OF POETRY

I saw in Louisiana a live-oak growing, 785
I shoot the Hippopotamus, 541
I shudder thinking, 447
I sing of a maiden, 685
I started Early–Took my Dog, 706
"Is there anybody there?" said the Traveller, 478
It dropped so low–in my Regard, 498
I tell you, hopeless grief is passionless, 576
It felt like the zero in brook ice, 711
It is a cold and snowy night. The main street is deserted, 490
It is a God-damned lie to say that these, 440
It little profits that an idle king, 777
It was in and about the Martinmas time, 520
It was my bridal night I remember, 597
I wakened on my hot, hard bed, 533
I wake to sleep, and take my waking slow, 762
I wandered lonely as a cloud, 428
I wander through each chartered street, 472
I was angry at my friend, 606
I went into my mother as, 702
I will arise and go now, and go to Innisfree, 791
I will consider the outnumbering dead, 476

James Watt, 581
Janus writes books for women's liberation, 455
Jenny kissed me when we met, 596
John Anderson my jo, John, 655
Julius Caesar, 538
Just as my fingers on these keys, 774
Just off the highway to Rochester, Minnesota, 788

Lately I think of my love for you and the rose, 512
Let me take this other glove off, 434
Let us go then, you and I, 713
lies on one hip by the fire, 1348
Life is like a jagged tooth, 651
Like a drummer's brush, 534
Listen to the coal, 547
Little children you will all go, 511
"London: JOHN LANE, *The Bodley Head,* 557
Long-expected one and twenty, 475
Look at him there in his stovepipe hat, 771
Lord, who created man in wealth and store, 603
Love bade me welcome; yet my soul drew back, 726
Love is like the wild rose-briar, 693
Loveliest of trees, the cherry now, 413
Love set you going like a fat gold watch, 755

Many-maned scud-thumper, tub, 533
Margaret, are you grieving, 729
Mark but this flea, and mark in this, 708

Maud went to college, 694
Mild and slow and young, 536
Mingled, 734
"Mother dear, may I go downtown, 757
Mrs. Severin came home from the Methodist Encampment, 763
Much have I traveled in the realms of gold, 737
My arm sweeps down, 601
My clumsiest dear, whose hands shipwreck vases, 750
my drum, hollowed out thru the thin slit, 602
My heart leaps up when I behold, 467
My life had stood–a Loaded Gun, 706
My mistress' eyes are nothing like the sun, 664
My mother—preferring the strange to the tame, 739
My parents felt those rumblings, 728
My prime of youth is but a frost of cares, 503
My wife is like my shirt, 651

Nautilus Island's hermit, 744
Nay, nay, my boy—'tis not for me, 642
Never saw him, 465
"Never shall a young man, 790
No, no, go not to Lethe, neither twist, 736
Not every man has gentians in his house, 625
Nothing is plumb, level or square, 711
Nothing would sleep in that cellar, dank as a ditch, 482
Now all the truth is out, 791
Now as at all times I can see in the mind's eye, 793
Now as I was young and easy under the apple boughs, 779
Now hardly here and there an hackney-coach, 776

O Captain! my Captain! our fearful trip is done, 666
O God, in the dream the terrible horse began, 692
Oh, but it is dirty! 690
Oh, my love is like a red, red rose, 511
Old age is, 787
Old houses were scaffolding once, 489
"O 'Melia, my dear, this does everything crown! 462
O Moon, when I gaze on thy beautiful face, 650
On a flat road runs the well-train'd runner, 489
On a starred night Prince Lucifer uprose, 746
One side of his world is always missing, 447
One thing that literature would be greatly the better for, 508
Only one guy and, 487
On the one-ton temple bell, 486
O Rose, thou art sick! 691

There is a garden in her face, 664
There ought to be capital punishment for cars, 656
There was an old man of Khartoum, 580
There was a sunlit absence, 724
There was such speed in her little body, 758
There were three ravens sat on a tree, 683
The robin cries: *rain!* 81
These, in the day when heaven was falling, 440
The sea is calm tonight, 686
The selfsame surface that billowed once with, 700
The sleep of this night deepens, 718
The Soul, reaching, throwing out for love, 639
The Soul selects her own Society, 544
The splendor falls on castle walls, 537
The terra cotta girl, 441
The thing could barely stand. Yet taken, 742
The time is after dinner, Cigarettes, 619
The time you won your town the race, 733
The tusks that clashed in mighty brawls, 663
The war chief danced the old way, 773
The whiskey on your breath, 420
The wind stood up and gave a shout, 501
The world is charged with the grandeur of God, 542
The world is too much with us; late and soon, 627
They called it Annandale—and I was there, 429
They flee from me that sometime did me seke, 789
They say that Richard Cory owns, 518
This *Humanist* whom no beliefs constrained, 579
This is the terminal: the light, 787
This living hand, now warm and capable, 569
Thou art indeed just, Lord, if I contend, 730
Thou ill-formed offspring of my feeble brain, 422
Threading the palm, a web of little lines, 619
Three drunks, a leg on one quite gone, bereft, 580
Three poets, in three distant ages born, 455
Today we have naming of parts. Yesterday, 758
To freight cars in the air, 565
To see a world in a grain of sand, 497
Traveling through the dark I found a deer, 656
Treason doth never prosper; what's the reason? 579
True Ease in Writing comes from Art, not Chance, 530
Turning and turning in the widening gyre, 627

'Twas brillig, and the slithy toves, 456
Two boys uncoached are tossing a poem together, 417
Tyger! Tyger! burning bright! 692

Victory comes late, 587

Watch people stop by bodies in funeral homes, 450
We bury ourselves to get high, 671
We dance round in a ring and suppose, 510
We lie back to back. Curtains, 497
Well, sometimes it's Heaven, and sometimes it's Hell, 526
We real cool. We, 554
We shall not ever meet them bearded in heaven, 736
Western wind, when wilt thou blow, 686
We stood by a pond that winter day, 615
What a girl called "the dailiness of life," 735
What happens to a dream deferred? 733
What passing-bells for these who die as cattle? 751
What, still alive at twenty-two? 645
What thoughts I have of you tonight, Walt Whitman, for I walked, 719
Wheesht, wheesht, my foolish hert, 461
When daisies pied and violets blue, 766
Whenever Richard Cory went down town, 518
When fishes flew and forests walked, 701
When getting my nose in a book, 741
When he came home Mother said he looked, 767
When icicles hang by the wall, 766
When I consider how my light is spent, 747
When, in disgrace with Fortune and men's eyes, 765
When I saw that clumsy crow, 621
When I saw your head bow, I knew I had beaten you, 449
When I take my girl to the swimming party, 751
When I was one-and-twenty, 564
When my mother died I was very young, 441
When our cars touched, 601
When she was here, Li Bo, she was like cold summer lager, 499
While my hair was still cut straight across my forehead, 755
Whose woods these are I think I know, 717
Who will go drive with Fergus now, 532
"Why dois your brand sae drap wi' bluid, 681
With rue my heart is laden, 556

Yet once more, O ye laurels, and once more, 629

INDEX TO AUTHORS AND TITLES

(Each page number immediately following a poet's name indicates a line or passage from a poem quoted in the text.)

To the Student

Part of our job as publishers is to try to improve our textbooks. In revising them, we pay close attention to the experience of both instructors and students who have used the previous edition. At some time your instructor will be asked to comment on *Literature: An Introduction to Fiction, Poetry, and Drama*, 4th Edition, but right now we would like to hear from you. After all, though your instructor assigned this book, you are the one who paid for it.

Please help us by completing this questionnaire and returning it to College English, Little, Brown and Company, 34 Beacon Street, Boston, MA 02108.

School _____

Instructor's name _____

Title of course _____

1. How did you like *Literature?* _____

_____

2. Did you find it too easy? _____ Too difficult? _____ About right? _____

3. Which statement comes closest to expressing your feelings about reading and studying literature? Please check one, or supply your own statement.

_____ Love to read literature. It's my favorite subject.

_____ Usually enjoy reading most literature.

_____ Can take it or leave it.

_____ Don't usually find much of interest in most literature.

_____ Literature just is not for me.

4. In general, which form of literature do you most enjoy reading and find most rewarding? Please rate in 1, 2, 3 order:

_____ Fiction _____ Poetry _____ Drama

5. Which chapters of the book did you find most interesting? _____

_____

6. Which chapters did you like least? _____

_____

7. Which stories were your favorites? _____

_____

Were there any you disliked? _____

_____

8. Which poems were your favorites? _____

_____

Were there any you disliked? _____

_____

9. Which plays were your favorites? _____

_____

Were there any you disliked? _____

_____

10. Are any writers not included whom you would have liked to study? _____

_____

11. Did you find the supplement on writing very helpful?____ Somewhat

helpful?____ Of no help?____ How could we make it more useful to

you? _____

_____

12. Any other suggestions or reactions: _____

_____

May we quote you in our advertising efforts? Yes____ No____

Signature _____ Date _____

Mailing address _____

Thank you!

INDEX TO TERMS